Information Research

Second Edition

Carla List
Plattsburgh State University

KENDALL/HUNT PUBLISHING COMPANY
4050 Westmark Drive Dubuque, Iowa 52002

Book Team

Chairman and Chief Executive Officer Mark C. Falb
Vice President, Director of National Book Program Alfred C. Grisanti
Editorial Development Supervisor Georgia Botsford
Developmental Editor Liz Recker
Prepress Project Coordinator Sheri Hosek
Prepress Editor Shelly Ansel
Permissions Editor Colleen Zelinsky
Design Manager Jodi Splinter
Designer Deb Howes
Senior Vice President, College Division Thomas W. Gantz
Vice President and National Field Manager Brian Johnson
Managing Editor, College Field Paul Gormley
Associate Editor, College Field Joe Sabella

Previously titled *An Introduction to Information Research*

ISBN 0-7872-9057-2

Printed in the United States of America
10 9 8 7 6 5 4 3 2 1

Thank you to my colleague, Nancy J. Hoshlyk,
for her invaluable assistance with this edition.

CONTENTS

PREFACE

- What were the contributions of African Americans during the period of the American Civil War?
- What time is it?
- Does this drug have any adverse side effects?
- How cold is it outside this morning?
- Explain kleptomania, its causes and treatment.
- How much is left in my checking account?
- What did reviewers say about Margaret Atwood's novel, *Alias Grace*?
- When is the next hockey game at the home rink?
- How has the United States dealt with the Japanese-Americans who were interned in American concentration camps during World War II?
- Am I eligible for this program/contest/loan/etc.?
- Is the "greenhouse effect" serious or is it an over-dramatized issue?
- Does bilingual education limit its recipients in their adult lives?
- Who took the remote control for the TV?

Do any of these questions sound like something you've asked and answered already? Probably so. All these questions require information to answer them, and often getting that information will require you to do some "research." Research is investigation, detective work, exploration of something unknown. If you've answered any of these questions, you've been doing information research even though you may not have realized it and you'll continue doing it all your life, both on the job and off.

This book is about the more formal type of information research, the type that you do in an academic setting to fulfill a research assignment. Such an assignment can require you to write a paper, prepare a report, or present a speech in which you support whatever you say with information found through research. How you perform your research will affect your final product. This book explains the concepts behind information, its organization, tools used to find information, and how to identify useful tools and appropriate information; it relates these concepts to the steps in the research process. Understanding what information is and the way it is organized, and seeing clearly the individual components of the research process should make your research more efficient.

Remember that the real end-product of information research is increasing your store of knowledge about the research topic. Increasing your knowledge is a task that will be required of you not only in college but also "on the job." Electronic information technology may make that task seem far more complex than it was in the past, but the technology hasn't changed the fundamental organizational principles of information systems; it has changed the speed with which they can be used. When you learn the basics of information systems—how they're organized, how they work—you'll be able to do information research more easily and keep up with changes in information technology for the rest of your life.

Electronic information tools and technologies have changed everything, or so it seems in this new millennium. Some remote controls have the feature of being sound sensitive so that you can clap and they'll beep to let you know they fell between the cushions of the couch. There are now many electronic-only journals available on the World Wide Web, and even the Web is now just "the Web" because we're all so familiar with it. Style manuals have expanded to include examples of citation formats for numerous electronically formatted information sources: Web pages, online versions of print periodical articles, information gleaned from chat rooms. You can have an all-electronic bank account in some parts of the globe so balancing your checkbook may be done completely online.

The introduction to the first edition of this book remains accurate. Information research is still research regardless of the tools used. And information tools and resources are still just that whether they're electronic or "old-fashioned" print versions. The process has changed insofar as it incorporates electronic means much more often than in the past, but some topics may still be researched entirely OFF-line. And teachers can only repeat the same warning they've given for years: Just *because* you find something electronically it's not *always* better than something you find using a print tool or source.

Electronic access to information has made pre-thinking a search ever more important. Computers can search faster now although **they still don't think.** And they are still the scanners of previous years . . . with upgraded scanning procedures and much, much more information that they can scan. That makes it imperative that your commands to them be as clear as you can make them. When you understand how information research tools and sources are organized and arranged, you'll be well prepared to get what you need.

This preparation is becoming more important on college campuses as they incorporate "information literacy" into their requirements for graduation. Information literacy can be defined briefly as the abilities to know when you need information, to know where and how to find information to fill that need, and to use the found information ethically and effectively. These are capabilities that you'll need throughout your life, not just while you're in college. This book addresses information literacy because it continues to be a book of concepts and not of tools, of how tools work and not just how to work them. It will help you learn how to find where your needed information is stored and how to make the storage systems work to retrieve that information. In other words, it will help you learn how to do information research.

From a reference librarian's viewpoint, the fun of information research continues to be enhanced by technology. And while it may never become "fun" for you, the book should help to make your research more efficient and more successful.

Carla List
May 2002

About the Author

Carla List has been teaching information research to undergraduates at Plattsburgh State University of New York (SUNY) since 1981. She received her Master of Arts in Library Science from the University of Iowa. She received the State University of New York Chancellor's Award for Excellence in Librarianship in 1995, and was named the Librarian of the Year 1997 by the Eastern New York Chapter of the Association of College and Research Libraries.

Chapter 1

The Organization of Information

In This Chapter, You Will Learn . . .

- Why organizing information is important
- Different ways to organize information
- The various classification systems used in libraries including the Library of Congress Classification System and the US Superintendent of Documents Classification System
- The differences among analytical, factual, subjective, objective, primary, and secondary information

What Is Information?

"Data becomes information only when it's put into a context."

National Public Radio reporter John McChesney

If you were asked this question, you might answer with a description of some printed information, the written knowledge found in books and magazines and newspapers. You would be right, but that is only a fraction of what "information" includes. One pretty complete definition of the word comes from the American Library Association, a group of information experts: "all ideas, facts, and imaginative works of the mind which have been communicated, recorded, published and/or distributed formally or informally in any format." This means that information can be a fact that was recorded by a person using a stylus to etch it on a stone tablet, a folk tale that was handed down orally for many generations, a comic book that was printed and distributed to thousands of readers, or an idea that was communicated electronically through computers or television.

Information is everywhere and in great quantity. How can you deal with the vast amounts you encounter? Organization of information makes it manageable and helps you handle it rather than being overwhelmed by it.

What Is Organization?

How organized are you? Does it make any difference in your life? Can you be organized without keeping lists or straightening stacks of things? What is organization, anyway?

You organize things all the time, that is, you arrange things into a system so that the arrangement makes the parts "interdependent."

◆ Examples

Your class schedule. Your classes aren't all held at the same time; you registered for one course that meets on Mondays, Wednesdays, and Fridays at 11:00 a.m., but not all your courses meet then. "Of course not," you say, "I'd never be able to go to all of them if they all met at the same time." So you registered for another course that meets at 1:00 p.m. Mondays, Wednesdays, and Fridays, even though that course had a section that meets at 11:00 on those days. The scheduling of the second course depended on the timing of the first course. And this interdependence is evident throughout your schedule.

To organize is "to form . . . into a whole consisting of interdependent parts."

Webster's Collegiate Dictionary

◆ ◆ ◆

Your collection of sound recordings, whether this is MP3 recordings, compact disks, cassette tapes, or even vinyl albums. You've made organizational decisions in this collection that indicate that you understand how the items in the collection relate to each other and to the whole. If all you do when you buy a new recording is drop it into the front of the box, crate, stand, or drawer with the rest of your collection, you've demonstrated a type of "organization by accession," in other words, the most recent item goes in front. This works well if you don't have too many recordings. But if your collection continues to grow you'll lose track of your moldy oldies and eventually you'll have trouble finding the recording you want to include in your new MP3 file. Sure, that CD is somewhere in the back, but how do you search for it? As your collection grows you move to a more sophisticated level of organization: you "organize by content," that is, you use what's on the recording, the contents of the CD, to help you decide where to put it. You'll use the information you find there to group your recordings by artist, or by type of music. You relate the parts to each other and to the whole collection; in other words, you create a system. You organize the information in your world in this and many other ways.

Why Is It Necessary to Organize Information?

Now that you know what information is, you can see that the value of any item of information will be enhanced if that item can be used more than once, heard by more than one person, viewed by more than one viewer, or communicated to more than one receiver. Re-use of information won't be possible if it cannot be found after its first use. If there were no access to the vast amount of information that is available, there might as well be no information.

Organization provides access to information.

How does organization provide access? Organization is the arrangement of items into a system. A system establishes rules, or reasons for arranging items in certain ways, and then applies them consistently to the materials it organizes. In a good system the reasons that form the basis for the system remain the same throughout and are readily apparent or easily learned. Thus you, as a user of a system, can be confident that the way you learned how to find items one time in a particular system will work a second time, and a third time. Some systems you're familiar with include telephone books, libraries, and grocery stores. A type of system you'll meet soon, if you do not already know it, is a *directory* of resources on the Internet. According to Greg R. Notess at "Search Engine Showdown" online, "Subject directories include human-selected Internet resources and are arranged and classified in hierarchical topics. Most search engines and portals have a subject directory component or partner." *Yahoo!*, which is a directory with a search engine, illustrates this last statement in Figure 1-1.

What Are Some Ways to Organize Information?

Information is often organized by using several criteria. One basic question can be asked about many information systems: Is the information in the system arranged by **content** or by **format**?

If you want more than one piece of information about a subject, you'll have to have some way of finding many items grouped together because they all have the same content. Content is the major approach to arranging information.

Format refers to the *medium* used to present or store information. Information comes in many configurations:

- It's audible (You heard it on the grapevine).
- Visual (You can read the writing on the wall).
- Audio-visual (Did you hear/see Sting's new music video?).
- Digital (You know those numbers mean something).

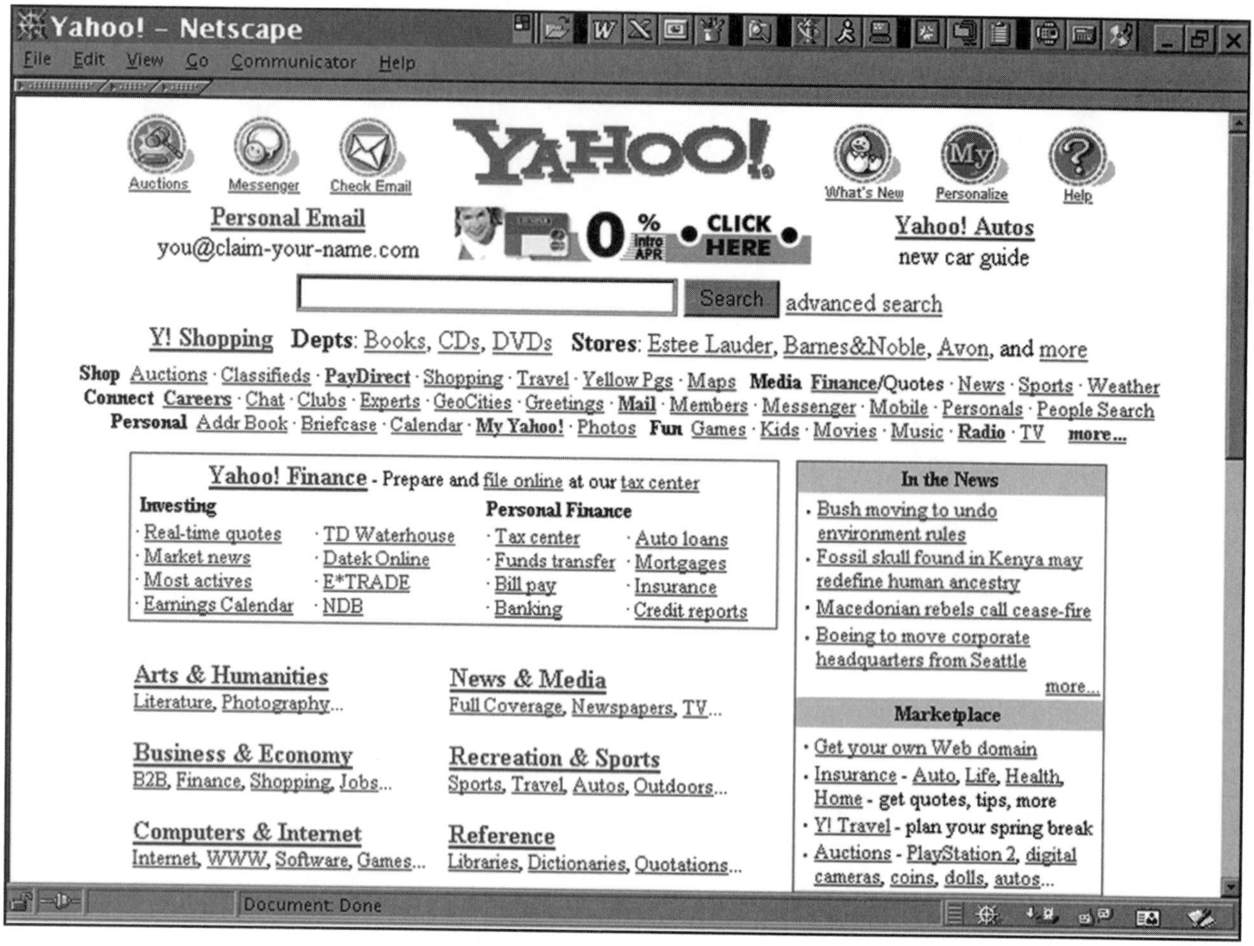

Figure 1-1: An Example of Organization on the World Wide Web: Yahoo!, a Web Directory

Each of these configurations is a format, and within each there are variations like microfilm or paper, color or black-and-white, slide-tape programs or videocassettes, and DVDs—compact discs that hold music or software or video. Electronic resources, those found on the Internet, provide information in yet another format. Formats affect the ease of access to information, and can be used as another way to organize it. A brief discussion of organization by format can be found near the end of this chapter.

Content and Organization of Information

Content has two meanings:

1. The *subject* of the information in an item.
2. The *characteristic* of information in an item which is
   - Factual or analytical,
   - Subjective or objective,
   - Primary or secondary.

Most information systems use the first meaning of content here, that is, subject, as the first criterion for their organization of materials. Examples of this include the phone book, split into residential and business sections;

libraries, with materials arranged by subject; and grocery stores, with produce in one area and dairy products in another.

You often seek information by subject:

- What's the phone number of a pizza delivery service? You look up "pizza" in the *Yellow Pages* of the phone book.
- What movies are playing in town? You look on the pages of the newspaper that advertise entertainment.

These are examples of searching for information by subject. Many businesses use subject-based organization systems for storage because it simplifies access to their goods. Information systems are no different. In libraries, and now on the Internet also, materials are grouped by subject because it simplifies your search for more than one item about your topic. Once you learn how a particular system arranges its subjects, you're able to search efficiently for your information needs, from pizza delivery to articles for a research paper assignment.

Most information is organized by subject.

There are variations among subject-based organization systems. Some systems differ because the items being organized are very different. For example, the *Yellow Pages* organizes a set of materials that are quite different from those in a library, so those two systems are similar but different. But sometimes the differences are to be found among systems of the same kind, that is, two libraries may use different systems even though both systems are based on the subject of the materials organized. How can you move from one system to another without getting confused? A good way to learn about a new system is to compare it to one you already know.

A call number is the label used to keep books on the same subject together on the shelves.

One subject-based information system that many people are familiar with is the Dewey Decimal Classification System. This system organizes information by looking at the subject content of books and assigning numbers to those subjects. A library that uses the Dewey system looks at every information item, determines its subject and puts it with other items that deal with similar subjects by giving it the Dewey Decimal "call number" assigned to that subject, and then shelving like numbers together. You know how to use this system: you get the call number for a book and you search for that number in the "stacks" (library-ese for the rows of bookshelves). Do you need to know any more about it? Not really. And that's how any subject-based information system works.

Classification Systems

The Library of Congress (LC) Classification System

The subject-based system used in most college and university libraries and in some large public libraries is the Library of Congress Classification System, or "LC" system. LC differs from the Dewey Decimal System in that it uses letters and numbers as the labels for its subject classes. This *alphanumeric* system results in the capability to expand far beyond a system that uses only numbers. Figure 1-2 shows you both the Dewey Decimal and the LC call numbers for the same books.

An important thing to remember about a classification system is that it allows the assignment of only one subject-number to each item in the system. This means that a book that is about several different subjects will

Library of Congress	Title	Dewey Decimal
GR 105 .B688	Curses! Broiled Again! The Hottest Urban Legends Going	398.2 B
GR 110 .M77 P57	Pissing in the Snow & Other Ozark Folktales	398.2097 P
GR 105 .B7	The Study of American Folklore	398.307 B
GR 113.5 .C36 M35	Tales Until Dawn; The World of a Cape Breton Gaelic Story-Teller	398.21 Mac

Figure 1-2: LC and Dewey Decimal Call Numbers

have only one of its subjects represented by the call number assigned to it. For example, if you find a book on traditional medicine and Mexican-American folklore, it will have a call number that groups it with only one of those subjects, in this case, with the GR111's, for "Folklore." Figure 1-3 shows you an example of this.

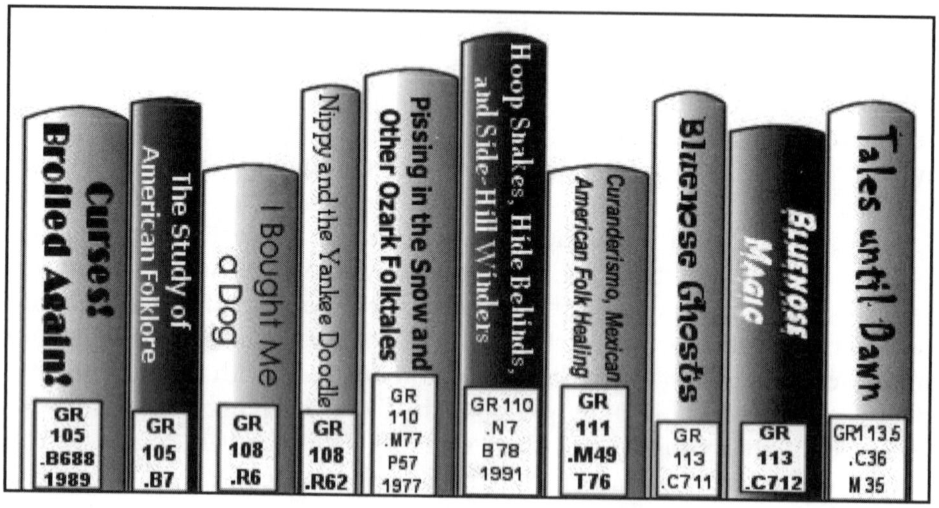

Figure 1-3: A Typical Shelf of Books Arranged by LC Call Number

When you discover the call number for a particular subject, all the materials that share that call number are about the same subject.

The U.S. Superintendent of Documents (SuDocs) Classification System

There is another classification system used in many libraries that is almost but not quite a subject-based system. It is the U.S. Superintendent of Documents (SuDocs) Classification System. SuDocs numbers perform the same task that LC call numbers do: they group documents together on the shelves, but they do it by cabinet-level agency rather than by subject. Education, Labor, Environment, and Treasury are a few agencies represented in the system.

The agencies work almost as a subject system because many of the documents produced by an agency will be about the subject that the agency is named. For example, most of the documents from the Department of Education are clearly about educational issues. Those that don't appear to be directly related to education are usually about a subject that does relate to the department in a less apparent way. It is reasonable for educators to be concerned with issues of child abuse, for example, so this may be a subject covered in a Department of Education document.

Figure 1-4 provides the SuDocs numbers, issuing agencies and titles for several government documents.

SuDocs Number *(Agency in parentheses)*	***Document Title***
C 3.186: P-70/2/NO.30 (Dept. of Commerce, Economics and Statistics Administration, Bureau of the Census)	Who's Minding the Kids? : Child Care Arrangements, Fall 1988
HE 20.3702: C44/10 (Dept. of Health and Human Services)	Comparative Study of Traditional and Modern Medicine in Chinese Societies
PE 1.10/8: H34 (Peace Corps)	Health, Population, and Nutrition Systems in LDC's: A Handbook
SBA 1.32/2: MP 29 (Small Business Administration)	How to Start a Quality Child Care Business
Y 3.Ed 8/9: 2 P 92 (Intergovernmental Advisory Council on Education, United States Dept. of Education)	A report to the President of the United States: national networking conference topic: the absent parent: Washington, D.C., May 9-10, 1988
Y 4.J 89/2: S.hrg.102-649 (U.S. Congress. Senate. Committee on the Judiciary)	Protecting children in day care: building a national background check system: hearing before the Committee on the Judiciary, United States Senate, One Hundred Second Congress, first session, on the National Child Protection Act of 1991, November 12, 1991

Figure 1-4: Examples of Documents Numbered Using the Superintendent of Documents (SuDocs) Classification System

Once you've learned the location of your library's government documents, you've discovered another avenue that may well lead to extremely helpful information when explored.

The LC system, and to a lesser extent, the Superintendent of Documents system, rely on content to arrange information materials by subject. *Content* can also refer to the information characteristics that vary among information materials.

Information Characteristics

Do you need:

- **Analytical** information or **factual** information?
- **Subjective** information or **objective**?
- **Primary** or **secondary** information?

You may never have asked yourself these questions in exactly these words but the answers to them affect your information research. You already unconsciously know the difference between objective and subjective, and analytical or factual information. You demonstrate this knowledge by asking a friend for her review of the local pizza places and not taking out a book on pizza; by looking in the Reference Collection of a library when you need only a definition or a statistic, rather than checking out whole books; or by looking for a few recent and specific periodical articles when you have to do a persuasive speech and provide evidence to support your view of your topic, rather than just asking your roommate's opinion on your topic. But if you *consciously* make a decision about what you need, you go to the right place first. You *begin* by looking for the information characteristic(s) you need.

Factual or Analytical

"Just the facts, ma'am," as Detective Joe Friday of* Dragnet *would say.

Factual information is made up of facts, and a fact is "the statement of a thing done or existing," according to the *American Heritage Dictionary*. Factual information can provide answers to questions such as:

- "What's today's date?"
- "Who won the Pulitzer Prize for Fiction in 1997?"
- "What were the main characters' names in that play by Wendy Wasserstein?"

Who's Who in American Art *and the* Dictionary of Economics *are examples of factual sources.*

A purely factual information source provides no explanation of its statements, just as a purely factual question often requires only a short, nonexplanatory answer from a friend or a quick look-up in a fact source. The federal government publishes many documents that fall into this category, as do numerous other publishers.

When you decide that you need factual information only, you're most likely to seek short-answer sources. These sources include dictionaries, atlases, handbooks, and directories, and usually will be found in a library's Reference Room or Reference Collection. The Reference Collection can be both a "print collection," meaning not computerized, or a collection of online sources. Many college libraries have clearly labeled online Reference Collections. The collections often include electronic versions of titles such as the CIA's *World Factbook, WWWebster Dictionary and Thesaurus*, and the *Handbook of International Financial Statistics*.

Reference sources are kept separate from the other books in a library and clearly labeled on many library Web sites because their content makes them most useful in a quick-look-up way.

◆ EXAMPLES

You wouldn't read the *Dictionary of Concepts in General Psychology* from cover to cover to discover Freud's place in psychology. Rather you'll use the book briefly in the Reference Room to get that information.

◆ ◆ ◆

You won't have to check out a book such as *International Marketing Data and Statistics* for four weeks when you can open it to one page and see the table that lists the number of cinema screens and cinema revenue per country. You'll find this book in a Reference Room or in an online version of a Reference Collection.

Background sources, such as encyclopedias, provide factual information* within a context, *and are excellent places to begin research on a topic that's new to you.

Some reference sources include factual information that has been put into a broader context. Encyclopedias and some handbooks comprise this type of source. An example is the *Oxford Companion to the Mind.* Such background sources are designed to provide fairly short answers to questions and to give you a general overview of a subject. They are still not the type of in-depth analysis that you need to take home for an extended loan so they are grouped (organized) with other similar sources, most often in a Reference Room or an online Reference Collection. If you know nothing about a topic that you have to research for a class, does it make sense to start your search by looking in a computer index for periodical articles? Not usually, because periodical articles are often narrowly focused on one aspect of a topic and you do not yet know what all the aspects are. You need an overview of your topic, the kind of basic explanation that's found in an encyclopedia. Try using *Britannica Online* or Microsoft's *Encarta* to find an aspect of the topic "poverty" that you might explore for a paper in your Introduction to Sociology class.

However, when you know that you need to do your own analysis of a topic, you seldom look only in the Reference Room for your information sources. You look in a different place for in-depth, analytical information to help you.

Analytical information is found in books and periodical articles, and on Web sites provided by experts in various fields.

Analytical information is an *interpretation* of facts. It's the information provided by your professor when she explains the meaning of a paragraph in your philosophy text, or the discussion you find in several periodical articles that examine the implications of the genocide committed in Rwanda on the Hutu by the Tutsi peoples. Analytical information includes interpretations and analyses of facts, usually by experts.

A search for analytical information may begin but cannot be completed in the Reference Collection of a library. Such a search requires information from periodical articles and books and Web sites and perhaps government documents that discusses the interrelations among, implications of, and reasons behind actions, ideas, works of art, and events. Usually it takes more than one source to provide a thorough analysis of a topic, so you as a researcher will have to find a system that groups items of the same subject together. Your familiarity with the LC system will help you find books grouped together on a topic. If you know of a government agency that is interested in your topic, you know that you'll find that agency's documents grouped together in the SuDocs system. A good Internet directory will group links on different topics so your searching is simplified.

Not all information materials are physically grouped together by subject, but the content of those materials is organized through indexing systems. The chapters in this text entitled "Making the Systems Work" and "The Research Process" will help you learn to search by subject for books or periodical articles or government documents or Internet sources.

Objective or Subjective

An editorial provides subjective information.

Another characteristic of information is its subjectivity or objectivity. Opinions or personal viewpoints and usually some facts comprise subjective information, while nonjudgmental and balanced reporting should be found in objective information.

◆ **EXAMPLE**

The difference between subjective and objective information sources might be your friend's opinion of the Baha'i faith (subjective source) and a list of the tenets of that religion found in the *Encyclopedia of Religion* (objective source). When do you need one and when should you seek the other?

Often subjective information and objective information appear in the same source.

Objective information should present all sides of a topic. It usually includes basic facts within a clear context that provides you with a sense of the whole topic. Objective information often enables you to choose a single aspect of a topic that will be manageable for your research. Many encyclopedias strive to provide just this type of help.

Subjective information is helpful once you know what you're looking for. This property of information refers to the opinions expressed on a topic. These opinions can include:

- A classmate's evaluation of your professor
- A reviewer's column about a recent book
- A scientist's comments about a colleague's research findings
- An editorial in a newspaper or journal.

Subjective information often provides assistance when your job is to evaluate a subject. Most subjective information is found in (nonreference) books and periodical articles. Many Web sites provide subjective information. For example, a site found at *www.globalwarming.org* is sponsored by the Cooler Heads Coalition, a subgroup of the National Consumer Coalition. Such a group will provide information on its Web site that supports *its* view of the topic.

Primary or Secondary

Sometimes you're assigned to find and analyze raw data in a research project, or to locate and use the first report of a scientific breakthrough. Other times you have a personal wish to see an on-the-scene account of an incident. These are instances of needs for primary information sources.

- What is primary information and how does it differ from secondary?
- How does this affect its place in an information system, and therefore affect your information research?

Primary information is information in its original form. A primary source provides information that has not been published anywhere else, or put into a context or interpreted or translated by anyone else. Examples of primary sources are:

- People, such as the professor who tells you about what happened in the class you missed because you were ill
- Accounts of events written by a reporters on the scene, such as the Web site and newspaper articles about the Iditarod sled-dog race in Alaska
- A first report of a scientific study, such as the medical journal article that first reported the research that discovered the causative virus in AIDS
- An original artwork
- A handwritten manuscript, such as the example in Figure 1-5 A
- The diary of a Danish writer published on the World Wide Web, as illustrated in Figure 1-5 B.

Primary information is a first appearance of information and much of its value as a source derives from this fact. Some primary sources are original manuscripts and letters that require special preservation techniques. These sources are very often fragile or rare and may be kept in a library's Special

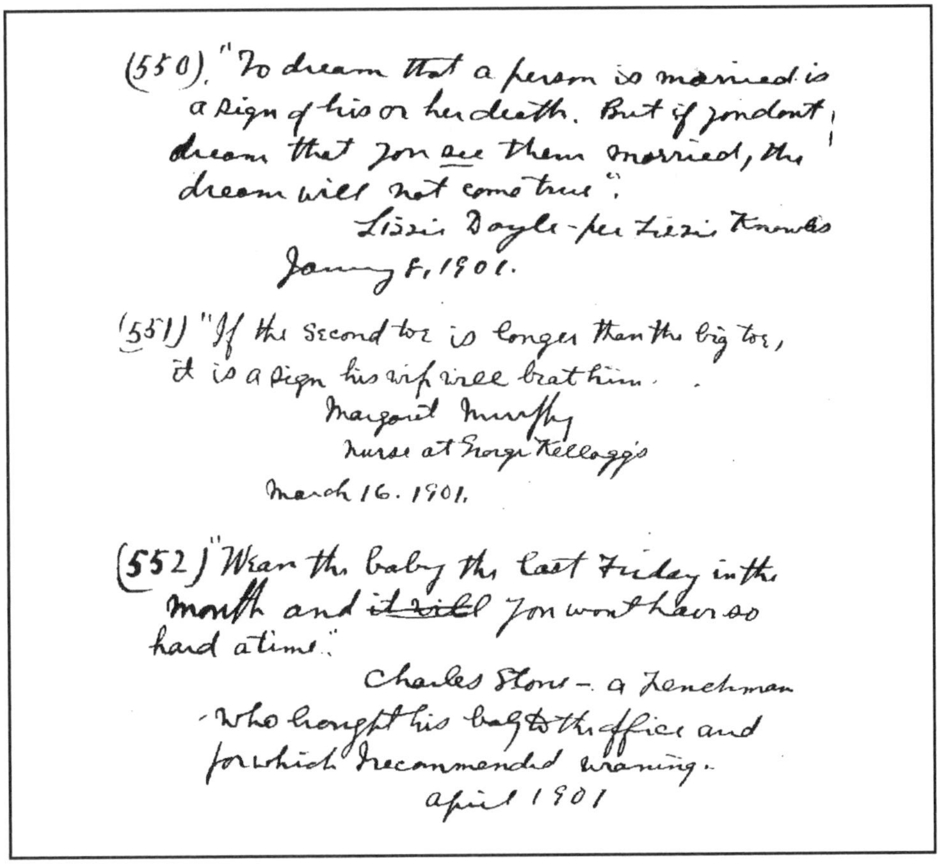
(550). "To dream that a person is married is a sign of his or her death. But if you don't dream that you see them married, the dream will not come true."
Lizzie Doyle - per Lizzie Knowles
Jany 8, 1901.

(551) "If the second toe is longer than the big toe, it is a sign his wife will beat him."
Margaret Murphy
nurse at George Kellogg's
March 16. 1901.

(552) "Wean the baby the last Friday in the month and ~~it will~~ you won't have so hard a time."
Charles Stone - a Frenchman
who brought his bag to the office and
for which I recommended weaning.
April 1901

Figure 1-5A: Primary Source: Handwritten Notebook of Folk Wisdom

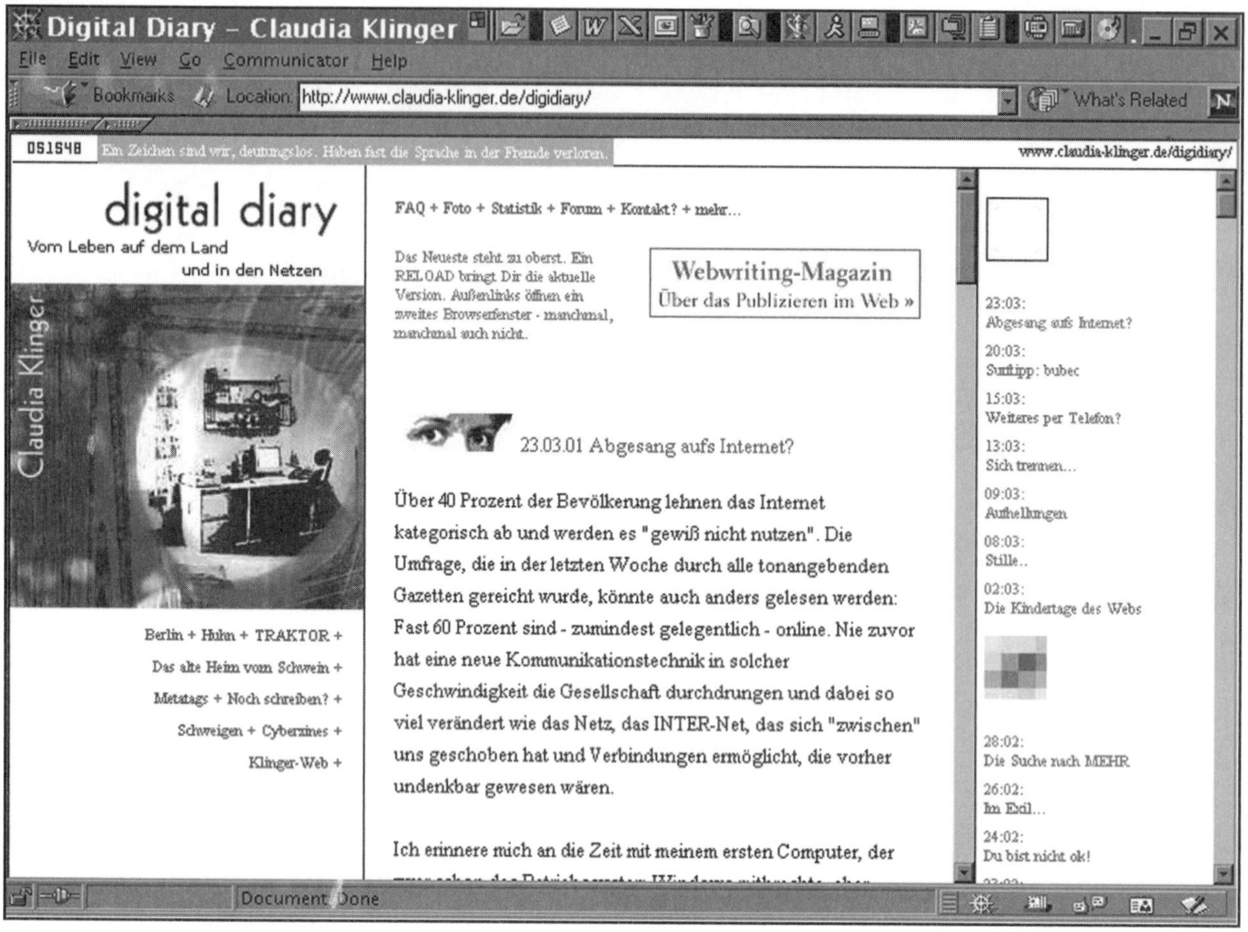

Figure 1-5 B: Primary Source: An Excerpt from a Diary from the World Wide Web (<http://www.astro.unibas.ch/!matthias/diary1.html>)

Collections, or in a library that is itself a special collection. Many of these fragile sources are now appearing on the Web, digitized so that they can be used by many and yet not be damaged by handling. While the digitized image itself is a reprocessing of the original, you, as an undergraduate student, might be allowed to cite it as a primary source if your professor knows the format in which you used it.

Primary information sometimes can be secondary information also.

Secondary information has been removed in some way from its original (primary) source and repackaged. It is information that is a restatement, examination, or interpretation of information from one or more primary sources. Examples of secondary sources include:

- A friend who provides his notes to you from the class you missed (he interpreted what the professor said and passed that interpretation on to you)
- A television documentary that follows the Iditarod and explores how it's won relatively often by women mushers
- A newspaper report telling about the journal article on the AIDS virus discovery
- An article that critiques a painting or novel
- An article discussing the literary merit of diaries

Secondary sources also include information tools that lead you to primary information, such as periodical indexes or bibliographies that cite primary works. For example:

- A bibliography of diaries is a secondary source because it's a list of diaries, not the diaries themselves, and it provides you with enough information to allow you to find the primary sources, the diaries.
- A newspaper index is a secondary source in that it helps you locate the issues of the *New York Times* that would have articles about the Iditarod by giving you citations to exact dates and pages.

Books are often considered secondary sources because they are analyzing and synthesizing information taken from other sources. See Figure 1-6. But be aware that some books are also primary sources because they are the first publication of that particular synthesis.

Figure 1-6: Secondary Source: A Book About Folklore

Tertiary information is even further removed than secondary information from a primary source. A tertiary information source is one that leads you to secondary information, such as the bibliography (tertiary source) that accompanies an encyclopedia article, which is, in turn, a secondary source that has repackaged many primary sources; or an index to periodical literature (tertiary source) that leads you to an article, which is a secondary source because it discusses an event using primary sources in its analysis. See Figure 1-7.

You use tertiary and secondary information sources for information that is secondary or primary.

Primary sources are "fundamental, authoritative documents relating to a subject, used in the preparation of a later work, e.g., original records, contemporary documents, etc., synonymous with original sources and source material." Secondary sources are "any material other than primary sources used in the preparation of a written work." (Young 176, 201) Primary sources are often important in fields such as history, where contemporary accounts of events and ideas may differ from present-day accounts of the

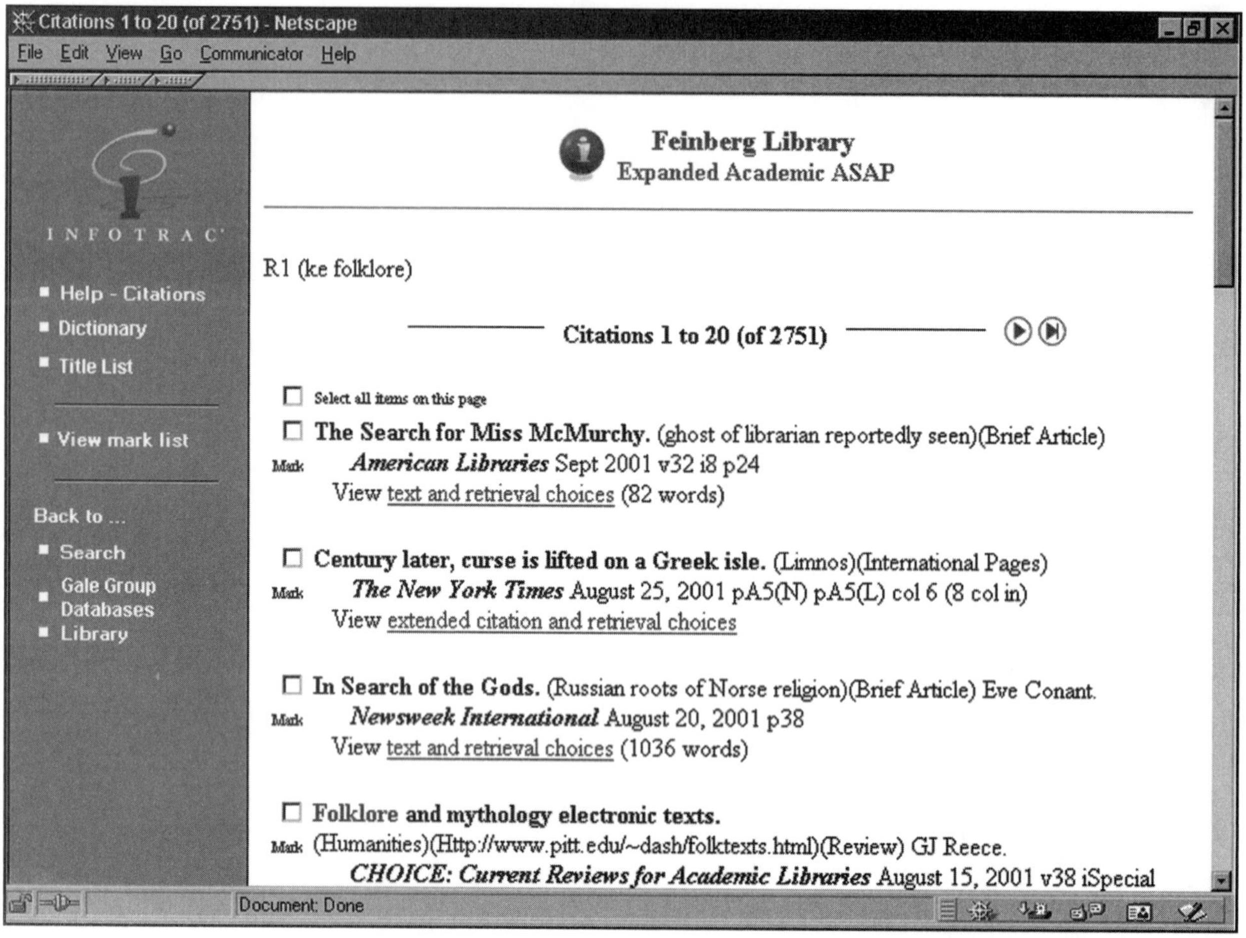

Figure 1-7: A Tertiary Source: Excerpt from a Periodicals Index (used via the World Wide Web)

same events and ideas, and in science, where primary reports provide research that is then built upon by later research. Raw data such as statistics that have been collected but not analyzed, first reports of research studies, original artworks, electronic news reports available on the Internet, newspaper, magazine, and journal accounts of a subject comprise primary information and are frequently found by using secondary sources.

The characteristics of information that are discussed above can be used to organize information materials, even when those materials are assigned LC subject classifications. Characteristics such as primary and secondary, or factual and analytical can create subgroups that also use LC subject classes. This means that you'll find areas in libraries, usually Reference Collections, that include only indexes and abstracting services (secondary/tertiary sources), or encyclopedias and statistical sources and handbooks (factual sources that are secondary). A library's rare and fragile books (often primary sources) may be kept in a Special Collections area. The books in each of these areas are still most often arranged by LC call number, even though their characteristics are quite different.

You can greatly improve the efficiency of your research process if you know what type of information you're seeking because you'll then go to the right area first, and once you're in that area you'll see that the materials are most often arranged by subject. Figure 1-8 summarizes the various characteristics of information.

Type	Definition	Examples
Factual	• Made up of facts	• Today's date • Winner of a Pulitzer prize • Historical events
Analytical	• Interpretation of facts	• Professor explaining a paragraph in your philosophy text • Periodicals examining the implication of genocide
Subjective	• Opinions or personal viewpoints and some facts	• Classmate's evaluation of your professor • Reviewer's column about a recent book • Editorial in a newspaper
Objective	• Nonjudgmental & balanced reporting • Presenting all sides of a topic	• Lists of a religion's tenets found in an encyclopedia
Primary	• Information in its original form • Information that has not been published anywhere else	• People's accounts of events at which they were present • First report of a scientific study • Original artwork • Handwritten manuscripts
Secondary	• Removed in some way from its original source and repackaged	• Friend providing you notes from a class you missed • Newspaper report telling about a journal article • An article that critiques a novel

Figure 1-8: The Various Characteristics of Information

Format and Organization of Information

Another very common way to organize information materials is by **format**. The basic concept behind a format-based information system is this: The physical attributes of items determine where they go.

◆ EXAMPLE

You do not store your recordings on your heater or on your drafty windowsill; the formats of your sound recordings helped you make the organizational decision to keep them in a place with a more stable temperature.

Format refers to the physical form of an information source. Major formats are:

- **Books** that are mainly bound volumes, with perhaps a few microform volumes in some libraries.
- **Periodicals** that can be divided into:
  - Unbound loose issues
  - Microformats (microfilm or microfiche)
  - Bound paper volumes

- **Nonprint media** includes many of the newer technologies in information storage and retrieval, such as electronic systems, cassettes (audio and video), and compact disks.

Periodicals and Nonprint Media, and Government Documents

What an information source is "made of"—its format—may dictate where it's stored.

In many places, not just libraries, *periodicals* are kept separate from books. A bookstore uses racks to display the magazines it sells and often keeps them near a cashier's station, while it keeps its books on shelves throughout the store. In your home you handle any magazines you buy or subscribe to differently from the way you handle your books. In the same way, libraries usually have a Periodicals Collection that consists of magazines, journals, and newspapers, and that is separate from the book stacks. Periodicals in microformats frequently are with or near the paper periodicals in a library. Microfilm and microfiche make up the microformats that are used commonly to preserve older volumes of periodicals. Microformats may be shelved near their paper counterparts, but some libraries keep their microformat collections separate from all paper materials.

Nonprint materials comprise another category that is handled differently from books and periodicals. You usually keep the nonprint materials that you have in your home near the equipment needed to use them, such as videocassettes near your VCR and computer software near your computer. Most libraries do the same and have separate sections where nonprint materials are shelved near their related equipment.

A *government documents* collection could be considered a collection that is almost organized by format, just as previously you learned that it could be considered to be almost arranged by subject. Documents are frequently separated from a library's main book collection because of the way the issuing government dictates that they must be handled by the library. In addition to nonbook handling and storage requirements, there may be several unique classification systems for documents. These numbering schemes, especially the SuDocs system for federal documents, make the separation easier for a library because the library can use the systems to shelve documents; it then doesn't have to create new numbers for them. A government documents collection may include materials from the U.S. (federal) government and perhaps from the state, city or county governments, and maybe even from foreign governments or international governmental groups such as UNESCO.

If you know the format of the information you're looking for, you'll look in different places for different formats. Remember that organization based on physical differences is not necessarily related to the subject content of the materials. You may find that the microfilm and microfiche volumes of periodicals are organized the same way that the unbound and bound paper volumes are, that is, neither is grouped by subject but rather they're arranged alphabetically, usually by title.

Finding Information Sources in Different Organization Systems

Libraries ("physical" ones, as distinct from "virtual," or all-electronic, ones) provide access to information that is in "paper" form—meaning that it is nonelectronic. In your institution's library you need to know which organization systems are used in order to get into your hands the particular book or periodical article or videotape that you want. This means that you must know:

Give yourself a tour of your library to get acquainted with all its systems!

- Does your library use Dewey Decimal or LC call numbers in its main book collection?
- Does your library keep its periodicals in an area separate from the main book collection?
- Are the periodicals organized alphabetically or by call number?
- Are nonprint materials such as sound- and video-recordings shelved with books or in a different location?
- Are government documents given LC call numbers and shelved with books, or do they follow the documents' unique numbering systems so that they are shelved in their own space?
- Are there smaller areas that repeat the major system, such as the Reference Room using LC call numbers?

A tour, either a formal guided tour or a self-guided, map-in-hand tour, is one of the best approaches to learning how things are organized and where they are in your library. You should answer the following questions to your satisfaction when you take your tour:

- Can you find a book in the stacks after you've learned how to get its call number from the library's catalog?
- If you need a quick fact, are there "quick-answer" sources in the Reference Room? Does the Reference Collection use LC call numbers?
- Where can you use the index(es) that will help you find periodical articles on your topic?
- How can you tell if the library has the latest issue of a periodical you need?
- Can you check out the videotapes in the library's collection?
- What services does the library offer that you can use—photocopying, interlibrary loans, access to your e-mail?
- And . . . be sure to find the Reference Desk so that you know where to come when you have any questions!

Your understanding of the concepts that are used to organize information will contribute to your ease in doing information research. It will make your work in the library and with electronic information materials efficient and productive.

Chapter Concepts

- *Ideas that have been communicated* is an apt definition of the word "information."
- Organization provides access to information; to organize anything is to arrange it so that there are relationships among the items organized, and between the parts and the whole.
- A major criterion for organizing information is its subject matter, as used by the Library of Congress (LC) Classification System.
- LC uses letter-and-number (alphanumeric) combinations to identify its subject categories; the Superintendent of Documents (SuDocs) system links issuing agencies to its alphanumeric scheme.
- The content of information material can be analyzed for its characteristics: factual or analytical, subjective or objective, or primary or secondary.
- Primary information is a first presentation or publication, and secondary information is a repackaging of primary information through indexing, analysis, or discussion. The distinction between primary information and secondary information can be important, especially in some subject areas such as history and science.
- Being aware of the information characteristic(s) you're seeking will make your research more efficient.
- It is common to organize information by format, meaning the physical configuration of the information, such as a library grouping together books, separate from periodicals, and separate from nonprint media.
- Libraries often use combinations of systems to organize information, frequently separating different physical formats or information characteristics, while using LC call numbers to arrange materials together within each group.

Name: ______________________________ **Date:** ______________

REVIEW QUESTIONS

1. The LC Classification system groups materials by subject. Why?

____
____
____
____
____

2. Is the information available on the World Wide Web organized? Explain your answer. (If you have no experience on the Web at this point, return to this question after you've used the Web!)

____
____
____
____
____

3. Your research on the Battle of Plattsburgh in the American War of 1812 would change if your professor required primary rather than secondary information. Explain why this factor would change it.

____
____
____
____
____

4. Describe an organization system that you have established and used in your own life. Name each criterion for arrangement and explain why you used it.

5. You learn the call number for books about witchcraft. Describe how you can use this information to "read the shelves" to see what your college's library has on this subject without physically going there.

6. Find two different systems used to organize information in your library. Explain why you think the library finds it necessary to use both of them rather than just one.

Chapter 2

INFORMATION TECHNOLOGY

IN THIS CHAPTER, YOU WILL LEARN . . .

- The basic non-technical concepts of computers and their function
- Common terms or jargon in the field of information technology
- Differences between the Internet and the World Wide Web
- What's "on the Net"
- About searching for information on the World Wide Web
- About E-mail usage

An Unpredictable Future

Richard Saul Wurman said in his 1989 book, *Information Anxiety,* "More new information has been produced in the last 30 years than in the previous 5,000. About 1,000 books are published internationally every day, and the total of all printed knowledge doubles every eight years." It's hard to predict the number of books that will be published every day in the future; in 2000 it was up to approximately 1,276 titles being published around the world per day. Many writers have warned of the death of the printed word for some time. Our era, the beginning of the 21st century, is one of transition for methods of information provision and access. Electronic information is growing explosively in myriad directions simultaneously. No one knows how soon most information will be available only through electronic means. Forecasts about the future of information are almost impossible.

News about information technology is everywhere today. *Newsweek* has its front matter, "Cyberscope." *U.S. News and World Report* has its section entitled "Business and Technology." The *New York Times* devotes a segment to your "Personal Computer" in its weekly *Science Times* section. These and many other "paper" (meaning printed on paper) sources are making visible efforts to provide information about information technology. There is already a common abbreviation for it: I. T.

Information technology is contributing to bringing information to you faster and more readily than ever before. You may be overwhelmed by the flood of information available to you today on almost any subject, but you can easily learn some techniques to help you manage the flood. This chapter will get you started. First it will provide you with a very general and nontechnical understanding of computers. Though the chapter is meant for a novice computer user, or "newbie," the experienced computer user also will learn about the concepts that underlie the machines. The chapter will discuss the Internet and the World Wide Web, what they are and what they do, and how you can make them a useful resource for your information needs.

The examples given in the chapter were current at the time that it was last updated (early through mid-2001). However, the information on the Internet and the Web changes very, very rapidly, so that you may not be able to duplicate exactly what you see in the examples.

Computers: A Brief, Nontechnical Introduction

Computers are machines. They are built by humans to perform many tasks that humans used to do themselves. In the information world, they store and manipulate information. The following is a rudimentary explanation of the basic workings of a computer. It is a first introduction for a new computer user and is not comprehensive or detailed; for in-depth descriptions and discussions you may want to take a course on computers. This short description is merely a beginning, an introduction intended only to acquaint you with a fundamental idea of the way computers work. It's followed by a short glossary that will provide some definitions for terms related to the Internet and the World Wide Web as well as to computers in general.

When people hear the word "computer," they frequently think first of a screen that's similar to a television screen.

- The true computer is the central processing unit, or *CPU,* inside the computer case or tower; in personal computers (PCs) it is microprocessors or chips. This is the piece of hardware that does the real computing, the electronic work.
- The screen that people think is a computer is actually its *monitor;* it allows the user to see the computer's work.
- Another standard component of a computer is its *keyboard,* the typewriter-like set of keys you use to send commands to the CPU.
- The keyboard is often accompanied by a *mouse,* a handheld tool that is used to guide and point the *cursor,* a movable onscreen icon that indicates where action will take place on the computer screen.
- Almost all computers now include a *modem,* which connects the computer to a communication line. It converts computer-readable data into a form that can be communicated over telephone lines. Frequently the modem is internal but it may be an added component.
- There may or may not be a printer connected to a computer.

The standard components of a computer are its CPU (central processing unit), monitor (screen), keyboard, mouse, and modem.

A computer does not and cannot think. A computer is a machine that follows commands, and it does this better than almost anything else can. *You* think, because you're a human being, and you give commands to the computer through its keyboard. There are very complex sets of commands that are pre-written (programmed); these comprise the various *programs* or *software* or *applications* that the CPU follows. You use the software installed on a computer by typing additional commands that enable the CPU to perform tasks such as word processing or creating numerical tables and graphs on spreadsheets.

Computer programs are sets of commands that are followed precisely by the CPU as it performs tasks.

A computer program requires you to use particular keystrokes to command the computer to perform particular functions; this may be referred to as a *protocol.* Different computers may require you to use different keystrokes to perform the same task. The keystrokes are unlike for particular reasons, for example, two operating systems (e.g., Macintosh and Windows) may have different keyboards. Or several types of programs may perform the same function. For example, both drawing programs and spreadsheet programs can produce a printed page, but because the programs are different, the protocols that command the CPU to send the information to the printer may not be the same. You will want to understand a few of these basic concepts that all computers use so that you can easily adapt when you're asked for a different keystroke when using a computer that you haven't used before.

You're already a computer user. So many devices use computers internally that you unknowingly send commands many times daily. You may already be a knowledgeable computer user, but if not, you soon will be experienced at employing electronic wizardry to get information that you need. Please be assured that **it is virtually impossible for a user to break a computer**. Keys may stick when you press them, or you might use an incorrect key combination and get an unexpected result, but in neither of these cases have you "broken the computer." Remember to ask for help if you get stuck, confused or lost in your computer work. Don't let your frustration with the technology get in the way of your quest for information!

It is virtually impossible for a user to break a computer.

An Introductory I.T. Glossary

Nearly all subject areas and disciplines, professions and crafts have their own languages or jargon. The field of information technology is no exception; it has its own words and phrases that are used frequently in the field. Below is a glossary of some of these terms. The definitions are intentionally nonscientific and are addressed to you as a novice user. The words and initialisms are used by people with experience in doing information research. Soon you'll be using them, too, and "talking the talk" of I.T.

Note: The terms in the following glossary are arranged to relate to one another, beginning with some computer basics and moving into I. T. terms. All terms also appear alphabetically in the "Glossary" section of this textbook.

computer: "A device that computes, esp. an electronic machine that performs high-speed mathematical or logical calculations or that assembles, stores, correlates, or otherwise processes and prints information derived from coded data in accordance with a predetermined program." *(American Heritage Dictionary)* Please note that the definition does NOT include the word "think" anywhere!

operating system (OS): the basic computer programming used by a computer to work with various programs or software. The *American Heritage Dictionary* definition is: "Computer software designed to complement the hardware of a specific data processing system." Examples of operating systems are DOS, which was the IBM standard OS for years, and Windows OS and Windows95, -98 and -2000 that have replaced DOS. Apple computers have used their own operating systems, including MacOS. Also part of the field is Linux, a Unix-type OS that is available for free download from the Web at www.linux.org (as of May 2001).

hardware: the physical components of a computer, i.e., the keyboard, CPU, monitor, modem, and any other equipment that make up a computer

peripheral(s): "...devices, such as disk drives, printers, modems ... that are connected to a computer. ... Although *peripheral* often implies 'additional but not essential,' many peripheral devices are critical elements of a fully functioning and useful computer system." *(Microsoft Press Computer Dictionary)*

modem: communications device that converts the digital data from a computer into analog format that can be transmitted over telephone lines; short for **mo**dulator/**dem**odulator.

software: written computer programs that are used by the operating system of a computer. Examples of software include games, such as *Myst;* word processing programs, such as *WordPerfect;* and budgeting applications, such as *Quicken.* Software can also be called programs or applications.

protocol: "common set of rules and 'language' agreed upon by networked computers to allow communication. With so many different types of computers and operating systems on the Internet, agreed upon protocols are a must," according to the "Internet Glossary" at the *MacintoshOS* Web site. You may be told, "the protocols for the program are different on different computers;" this means that you'll have to use different keystrokes to perform the same function on two different computers.

icon: a picture on a computer that represents a category or file of information, and may be clicked on to connect to that information. Examples of icons include graphics such as a telephone for an online address book, a pencil for a drawing program, or a music note for an application that plays compact audio disks. See Figure 2-1.

Figure 2-1: Examples of Icons

The **cursor** is also an icon. It is usually a flashing rectangle, a vertical line, or an arrow, plain or somewhat stylized that indicates where action will take place on the computer screen. The mouse or the arrow keys manipulate the cursor.

click on: the action you take to activate a link or a button on the screen of a computer. You may use a mouse to move the cursor to the item (a button is usually an icon and a link may be both an icon and a colored and underlined word, phrase, or URL) and then press the mouse button (click).

database: "a structured collection of data: information that has been organized in such a form that it is retrievable through a computer system." So says *The Cyberspace Lexicon*. **Librarians often refer to any computerized index as a database; usually they mean those bibliographic databases that they can access because they pay subscription fees.** Most bibliographic databases provide periodical literature, or references to the articles in periodicals, as well as materials other than periodicals such as book chapters, or references to them.

Internet: a **net**work of computer networks throughout the world, i.e., **inter**national. The Internet is often referred to as "the Net." The phrase "surfing the Net" means exploring sites, i.e., viewing the information available on computers connected through this network.

World Wide Web: a way to use the Internet. It's a protocol that links information in hypertext format. It's also called "the Web," and you may see it shortened to WWW or sometimes to W3 in print. "Surfing the Web" is a very common phrase meaning to look for information or for anything of interest using the Web.

client-server: an interaction between a user and a computer that works this way, according to the "Internet Glossary" at the *MacintoshOS* Web site: "When you and your computer are searching for or accessing information on another computer, you are the client. The other computer is the server, and together you are using client/server technology. The server stores the info and makes it available to all authorized clients." Your client to use the Web may be the *Netscape Navigator* browser; the Web is the protocol it uses.

browser: another word for client. The most frequently used Web browsers are *Netscape Navigator,* and *Internet Explorer.* Both *Netscape Navigator* and *Internet Explorer* are graphical browsers that are able to capture all the graphics for which the Web is rightfully famous.

Web site: any resource available on the World Wide Web. A Web site may simply refer you to information, or it may provide the full text of an article or research paper, a short video, or an excerpt from—or even a complete—sound recording. It may also be a short block of information about a person, an institution or a business , or a catalog from which you may order materials directly using a credit card. An exciting aspect of the Web is the diversity found in Web sites.

Home Page: the beginning or "Home" screens of a Web resource. A Home Page is somewhat like the title page of a book in that it is the starting point for that resource, even though you may use the resource without ever going to its Home Page.

link(s): connection(s) to other Web resources provided at a Web site. Links are usually underlined and of a color different from the rest of the text on a screen. They may also be icons. When you use a mouse, you will see the cursor's arrow change to a pointing finger when the mouse positions the cursor over a link.

◆ EXAMPLE

The link to "The Catacombs of Paris" that is found on the Home Page for the WebMuseum, Paris; Paris: Tours. This means that when you click on the phrase, *"Visit Paris,"* and then on the word *Catacombs,* you "jump" to that Web site. In reality you download the information from that site so that you can use it; you don't really "go" anywhere! (As of spring 2002 you could "take" this tour by going to http://www.oir.ucf.edu/wm/ and clicking as stated above.)

---

download: to bring to your computer or to a floppy disk information that is on another computer. Opening a Web resource is actually a temporary download of the information from the resource. Many Web sites allow you to permanently download information that you find there, such as text, images, or software, and to print it or store it or to use it on your own computer.

ftp: *f*ile *t*ransfer *p*rotocol, which is a method for downloading information from an Internet resource to your own computer.

http: *h*yper*t*ext *t*ransfer *p*rotocol, which is what is used to display the information that is written in HTML. A URL, or address on the Web, most commonly begins <http://> to let the computer know that the information at the Web site is in hypertext format.

HTML: *H*yper*T*ext *M*arkup *L*anguage, the computer language used to make information readable at many Web sites. Other languages also are currently in use.

hypertext: a term coined by Ted Nelson in 1964 that refers to text that includes links to other information sources. Hypertext allows a user to move in a nonlinear fashion through information sources; by contrast, regular text requires a user to read from the beginning of a line (or page or chapter or book) to the end of it, in a linear fashion.

URL: *U*niversal *R*esource *L*ocator, an address on the World Wide Web. A URL is often put in between < > brackets to set it off from text. You do *not* type the brackets when you use the URL. The URL for the National Museum of the American Indian of the Smithsonian (as of spring 2002) is:

http://www.nmai.si.edu/

Currently you're able to type in a Web address without even typing the "www" part. Most browsers will type that for you. For example, if you type *alltheweb.com* into your browser's location bar, it will complete the URL *and* download the Web site to your computer.

If you wish to know what each of the segments in any URL mean, see one of the various detailed discussions of URLs, such as that in *The World Wide Web Unleashed 1997* or in the online version of that book. See also the discussion about URLs in Chapter 7 of this book.

search engine: software used to search through the myriad sites on the World Wide Web. A search engine works much like an electronic index does, searching through sites on the Internet for matches to the strings of letters (words) you type in. Items retrieved include the URL for each Web site. Examples of search engines (as of June 2001) are AltaVista and FAST Search. There are numerous sites that compare features of search engines. One is available at

http://faculty.plattsburgh.edu/dennis.kimmage/HyperResearch.htm

directory (a.k.a. Internet subject directory or Web directory): good beginning point for Web research. A Web directory is constructed by a person who has reviewed Web sites and chosen those he or she considers worth exploring, then organizes the selections by subject, or by another defined scheme. An example of a Web directory is John December's "The Top of the Web," pictured in Figure 2-2.

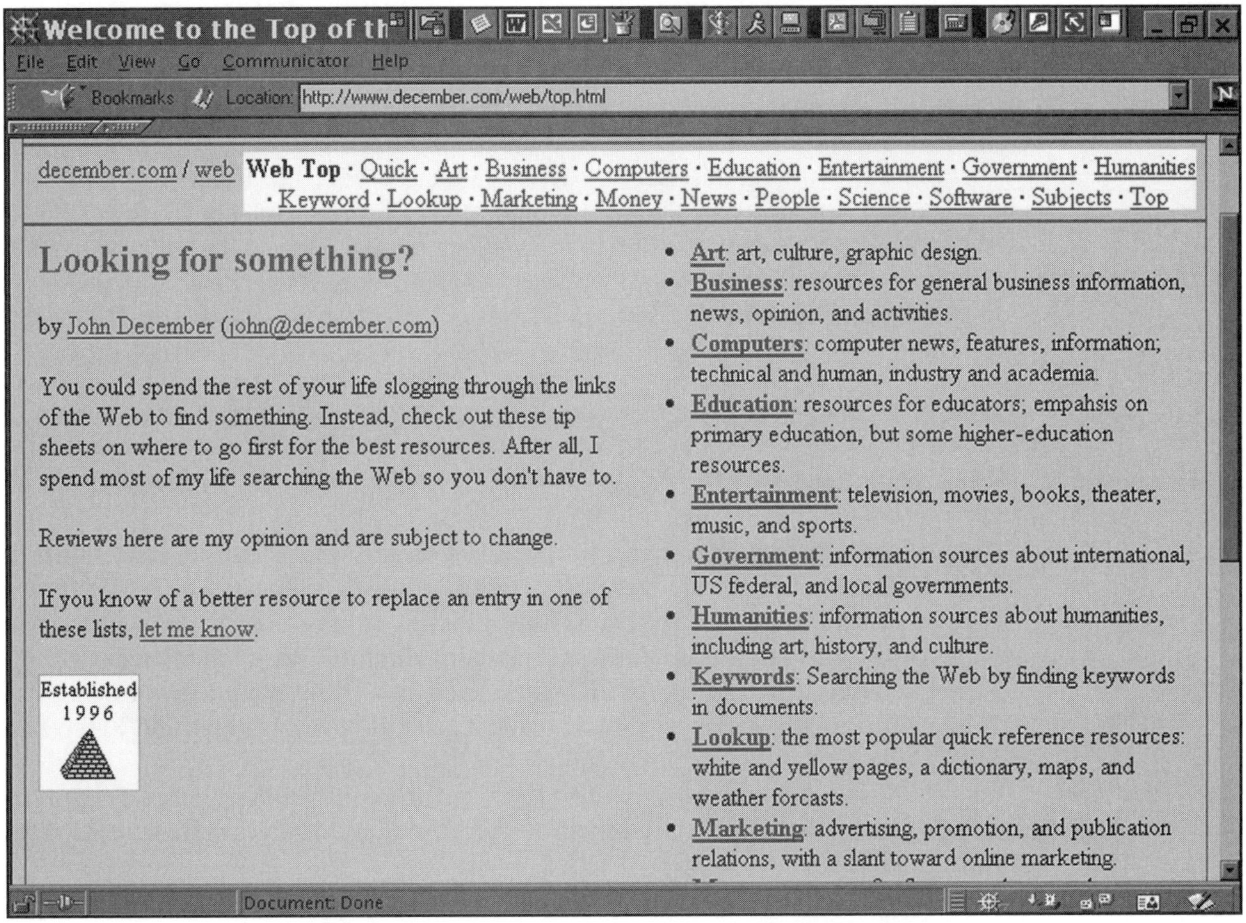

Figure 2-2: Example of a Web Directory (Reprinted with the permission of the author)

portal: "a main guide that includes a search engine, plus additional content (such as current news, entertainment info, etc.), designed to keep you at the portal for as long as possible. A good example would be *Yahoo*, Netscape's *Netcenter, CNN, AOL,* etc." This is according to the Web site, mainportals.com. There are different types of portals. Many colleges and universities create Internet portals that are meant to be gateways to their own services and to the Internet/Web, without the marketing goals of commercial Web portals.

e-mail: electronic mail. E-mail is a means of communicating with another person using the Internet. An e-mail message is a written letter or memo or note that is transmitted electronically, almost a written phone call.

usercode, username: the "name" used for one's computer account. An example of a username (the terms usercode and username are usually interchangeable) is smit5096. This sample usercode was created from the first four letters of a person's last name and four digits that were randomly assigned by the user's institutional computer center. An approach used by many commercial Internet-access providers is to allow the user to select his/her own usercode. You may become YankeeFan#1 or a similar name under such an approach! Think of the vanity license plates you've seen if you need ideas for your username.

A complete Internet address consists of the usercode and the name and location of the computer she/he is using. For example, the author's Internet address (spring 2002) is: <carla.list@plattsburgh.edu> An e-mail user at one site will address a message to a friend at another site by using the friend's usercode and Internet address.

While the terms usercode and username often may be used interchangeably, this is not always the case. Read carefully any instructions for creating and using your username or usercode.

listserv: an electronic mailing list used for communication purposes. A listserv is set up such that a subscriber sends a message to a central point and the message is then distributed to all other subscribers who read and react to it. The best listservs are moderated, that is, a designated person screens all messages sent "to the list" and distributes only those that relate to the subject matter to which the list is dedicated. There are listservs for virtually any subject or profession. There are also myriad electronic bulletin boards and discussion lists.

For a more comprehensive glossary of additional computer and Internet terms that have understandable definitions, go to *Glossary of Internet Terms* at <http://www.matisse.net/files/glossary.html> (as of mid-2001). Or see any of the numerous paper versions of dictionaries in the computer science field; they have QA76.5 as the first line of their Library of Congress call numbers and you should be able to find at least one in the Reference Collection of your library.

Now that you have some of the terminology under your belt, you're ready to learn how to use those words and the tools and actions they describe.

The Internet and the World Wide Web

Is there a difference between "the Net" and "the Web"? Most people now refer only to the Web. "The Web" and "the Net" have been used seemingly interchangeably, but there is a difference.

The Internet began about 30 years ago as a new communication tool among scientists, most of whom were doing research for the U.S. government. They connected their computers through telephone lines so that they could communicate with each other and with some international colleagues about the subjects of their shared research. Soon it became obvious that scholars in all fields could use this communication network to improve their research and the National Science Foundation assumed funding of the Net. Today the NSF is no longer funding it and it is self-sufficient. It's not clear that this self-sufficiency can be sustained long-term, and many experts believe, along with Bennett Falk, author of *The Internet Roadmap*, that the Internet "will be the next public utility."

An "ISP" such as AOL is a service; it is NOT the World Wide Web or the Internet.

The Internet is a network of networks. It is not a service such as EarthLink or America Online. They and other similar commercial ventures, called

ISPs, or Internet Service Providers, are services that are sold to customers, services that allow customers to use the Internet by giving them access to the companies' computers (servers). They offer the use of Web browsers as one of the services their subscribers receive with their access.

The hypertext format of the Web allows nonlinear thinking and research.

In the earlier days of the Internet, communicating over it was rather cumbersome and required at least a basic level of computer knowledge. Then a few technological advances resulted in the World Wide Web, which was created as a graphical interface to the Internet. This meant that information available on the Net could include graphic images as well as text; this capability soon expanded to include animation and sound. The Web is a *protocol* that is used by a browser. *FOLDOC, Free On-Line Dictionary of Computing,* says that a browser "gives some means of viewing the contents of nodes (or 'pages') and of navigating from one node to another." Information available on the Internet was reformatted using HyperText Markup Language and other programming languages that make connections to other Internet resources by embedding their computer addresses within the text as **links.** Not all Internet resources have been reformatted using HTML; some sites are doing retrospective conversions, others have no such plans but allow the information to be downloaded in other computer languages; still others are already moving into newer formatting protocols.

Information that's available on the Web introduces you to a slightly different manner of thinking. The information isn't necessarily linear, or something that needs to be read from beginning to end. Instead, a Web site usually provides that type of information, but it also provides the links described above that allow you to break the line of thought in the text and follow an idea that occurred within the line.

◆ Example

The 1996 Web site on which the Chicago Historical Society and Northwestern University collaborated about the great fire of Chicago. The site is entitled "The Chicago Fire and the Web of Memory." In the Web of Memory you find links in "The O'Leary Legend" screens that enable you to go to the official report of the origin of the fire (was it really Mrs. O'Leary's cow?) and then return to the essay, or go to a gallery with images from the time of the fire (1871) and then return to the essay . . . or not. (This site, by the way, is a good example of the availability of primary information on the Web; the copies of the original reports and artwork might be very acceptable to a professor who requires you to use primary sources in her history course.)

Links make the Web a new step in information use, transmission, and storage.

The distinction, therefore, between the World Wide Web and the Internet is that the Web allows you to use the Net in a way that includes graphics (pictures) and other enhancements. The Web and the Net are not one and the same. Many libraries and college computer labs have computers available that constantly have a Web browser running, and you can simply start using the Web to get information from the Net when you touch the keyboard and use the mouse. Be aware that the Net can be used without using the Web. This is becoming increasingly rare, but if you hear terms such as "Archie" and "gopher," they refer to using it this way. For more information about the Net before and without the Web, see your librarian.

What's "On the Net" and How to Look for It

It will be a very long time, if ever, before "everything is on the Web."

Resources available on the Net were initially data used by high-level researchers and were relatively difficult to access. Now the Web makes accessible resources that run the gamut from complete computer programs available for downloading, to entire books, both new and old. There is much free information available but the Web is becoming more and more commercial; many sites now require a subscription to allow access to more than a surface look. In the continuum you find such things as:

- Health information—including bibliographies, referrals, and self-exam directions
- Subscription bibliographic databases that provide references to periodical articles and books
- Personal "chat lines" on which users converse electronically
- Listservs for discussion of almost any topic you can think of
- Samples of new cartoons and music videos

The joy of the Net is in its diversity.

William Gibson, who coined the term *cyberspace* in 1981, said in 1996 that the joy of the Net is in its diversity. Your first exploration will convince you that diversity is the name of the game. That makes exploration both frustrating and fun.

How do you explore, or "surf" the Net? It has been described rather aptly as a library with thousands, perhaps millions of books—all thrown on the floor. The Net developed so rapidly that initially there was little effort to organize the information available. More people are attempting now to impose some organization, and currently there are several methods of Net exploration. Using the Net without the Web is becoming less frequent so this discussion will now focus on the Web and the resources it makes available, keeping in mind that the information is on the Net and the Web is what makes it easily accessible.

Browsing the Web

You can explore the Web with no desired goal other than to find odd and amusing tidbits.

One approach to information accessible via the Web is pure adventure: use a Web directory such as *Yahoo!* and find the "What's New" link on the screen. Then begin clicking on links you find interesting. Often one link leads to another in unforeseen ways and it's fun to follow their convoluted paths. This method is a perfect demonstration of the nonlinear hypertext approach to information. You may "get lost" in the information you find, but you can always back up or go Home or quit; look for instructions on your screen about how to do this.

Searching for Information on the Web

A more systematic means to retrieving information from the Net is to use a **search engine.** There is a growing number of these engines, software that allows you to search through information on the Net as you would in an electronic bibliographic database. (*InfoTrac* and *ProQuest* are examples of electronic bibliographic databases.) Remember that the Web is not a database. When you use a search engine to look for information on the Web, you'll get a low percentage of the type of sources that databases lead you to, that is, you'll probably get few periodical articles or book chapters. You will get a variety of types of information sources, and you'll have to screen them carefully because no one has done that for you the way most bibliographic databases do since they cover only published periodicals and perhaps books.

You can explore the Web with a goal of finding in-depth information on a particular topic.

A search engine works much the same as does an electronic index (bibliographic database) such as *ProQuest.* Some search engines examine the "full text," or all words on all pages of every Web site they cover. Others index more sites but don't cover every word. To use a search engine, you type a word or phrase that you're researching into its text box and the search engine looks for a match for that word or phrase in all the sites it indexes. Figure 2-3 gives an example of the beginning of a search on the topic *illegal immigrants* using one such search engine, *AllTheWeb.*

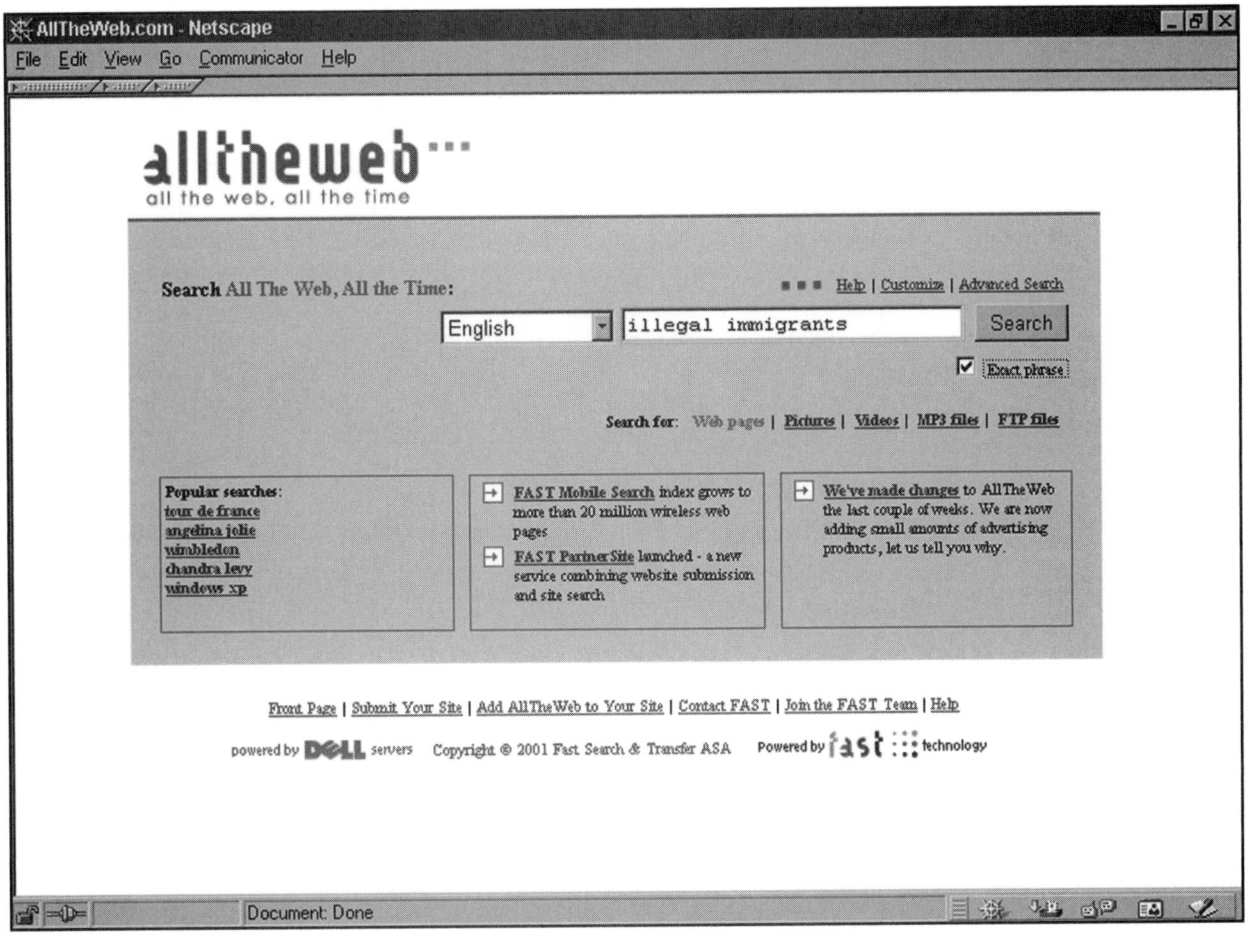

Figure 2-3: The Opening Screen of the Search Engine AllTheWeb (www.alltheweb.com) with a Search for "illegal immigrants" in the Text Box

Once you've submitted your search, the software takes your "search string," in our example it's the phrase "illegal immigrants," and matches it against all the Web sites it covers. (Go to Chapters 5 and 6 in this book for a thorough discussion of how a computer performs a search and how you can make it most efficient.) The computer then displays a list of pages to choose from; each page in the list includes the phrase somewhere in the part of the site that the search engine scanned. Figure 2-4 shows the first screen of hits. A "hit" is a match found, usually in the text, in a search of a database by a computer or in a Web search by a search engine.

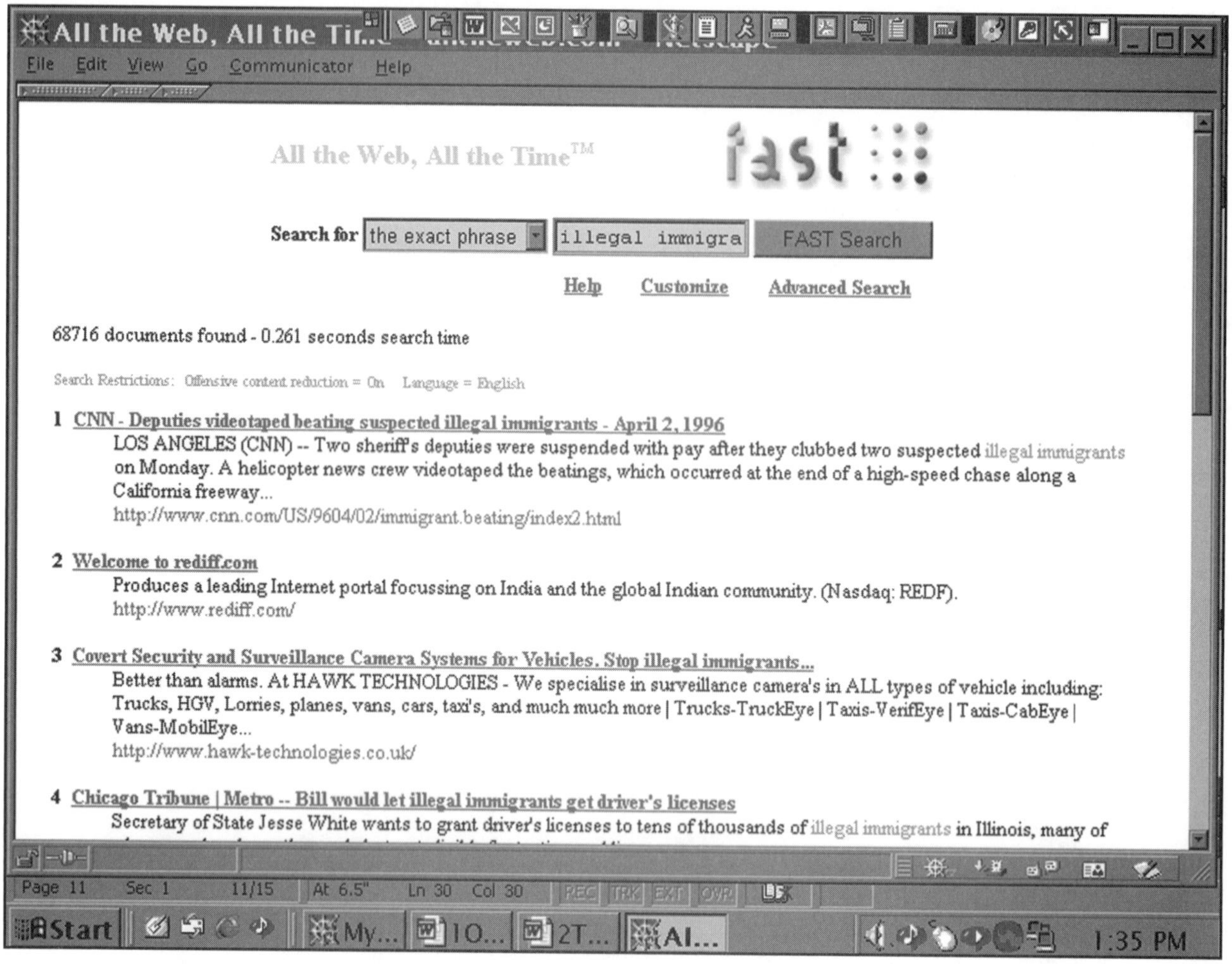

Figure 2-4: First Page of Hits from a Web Search for "illegal immigrants"

The first line, just below the text box, indicates how many Web pages included your search terms and how long the search took. Then comes the first group of links to Web pages that include your terms.

The title of the page is a link, that is, you may click on it and go to the page. (Remember that you don't really "go" anywhere, but rather your computer downloads information from the page so you can use it on your computer.) Most search engines also provide in the list of matches brief descriptions of the pages, usually taken from the first lines of the pages' texts. The last line of the entry is the page's URL, or Web address.

After you select a page you think may be relevant, you may click on its link and get the information from the page. Figure 2-5 shows the first screen of the first link shown in Figure 2-4. (Remember that the information here was downloaded in mid-2002; it may not have the same URL today, or may no longer even be available on the Web!)

CNN - Deputies videot...

File Edit View Go Communicator Help

CNN Interactive U.S. News

CONTENTS CNN HOME PAGE

SEARCH MAIN U.S. NEWS PAGE

Deputies suspended after caught beating suspected illegal immigrants

April 2, 1996
Web posted at: 11:05 a.m. EST

LOS ANGELES (CNN) -- Two sheriff's deputies were suspended with pay after they clubbed two suspected illegal immigrants on Monday. A helicopter news crew videotaped the beatings, which occurred at the end of a high-speed chase along a California freeway. (700K QuickTime movie)

The Los Angeles County Sheriff's Department has launched a criminal investigation into the incident, said Sgt. Mark Lohman of the Riverside County Sheriff's Department.

The videotape shows a Riverside County sheriff's deputy swing his baton at one suspect six times. He can also be seen aiming another three blows at a

Document: Done

Figure 2-5: The First Screen of the First Site That Included the Phrase "illegal immigrants"

It's possible to do far more focused searches using Web search engines. You note that in Figure 2-4 there were 68,716 hits that include "illegal immigrants" as a phrase. It would take you quite awhile to peruse all those pages, but you might be able to refine your search using the same techniques you would use in an electronic periodicals index. See the search engine's "Help" link and Chapters 5 and 6 in this textbook for help in devising more focused search strategies for your forays onto the Web.

You must cite Web resources that you use in your research, just as you must cite other information sources.

Much of the information that you get from the Web can be used in scholarly research but you must be careful about it. You should learn how to do quick evaluations of Web pages so that you know if one is a waste of time for your research assignments (but maybe fun to explore!). The Web resource also should meet the same standards that you use to evaluate other information resources. See Chapter 7 in this textbook for help in setting up your evaluation criteria. You will also get information there about how to cite your Web resources in the bibliographies of your research projects.

Connecting to Your Local Electronic Network

Not all computers at your institution will be running a Web browser at all times. Nor will you always want to use only the Web; there are other information technology functions and providers that you may want to access. Your college, your public library, and your local government all may have their own computer networks with information and tools that are

Every time you initiate activity on your chosen network, you must open your computer account by typing in your username and password.

helpful to you, most of them accessible through the Web, some not. How do you get to them?

In order to have access to non-Web resources, you first must connect to a "host" computer that serves as your link to the Internet, your "server." For this you need an active computer account. Most college students are allowed to use their campus computers as the hosts for their accounts and homes to their electronic mailboxes. Many portals now also offer this service, e.g., *America Online*, *Yahoo!*, and *Hotmail*. You must activate your computer account every time you use electronic mail (see below) or access the information available on and through your server. You need two things for this very basic step that is repeated every time you use the host.

First, you must have a **username** or **usercode.** Your institution is likely to assign it to you for your account on its server, but you may have the opportunity to create it yourself, as is the case with many ISPs, such as *AOL*. If you are able to devise your own username, remember that you may want to preserve some privacy so that your complete real name isn't broadcast to the world on the Net. Use a pseudonym!

YOU are responsible for your computer account. Do NOT give your password to anyone.

Next you must have a **password** that will allow only you to use your account and your electronic mailbox. Your password is something you create yourself and most host computer systems require that it be a certain size, such as six to nine characters. A password usually may contain both letters and numbers, and to strengthen security, most computers do not allow any word that can be found in a dictionary to be used as a password. You might use a person's or pet's name with a number in it, e.g., Fluffy3; you may use a number combination that you can remember easily—but NOT your birth date or Social Security number; you could use an abbreviation that is meaningful to you, for example, oscysbtdel—the first letters of the words in the first line of the "Star Spangled Banner." Whatever you devise, make your password something you'll remember!

You are **NOT** to provide your password to *anyone*. Another person who has access to your password can use your account for offensive or illegal purposes and **you** will be held responsible.

◆ EXAMPLE

A threatening letter sent to the president of your institution using your account. Imagine the consequences you could face if you let a friend use your account, even just once for a compelling reason, and he did this as a prank! Also, your institution may rescind all your computer access privileges if you give someone else access to your account.

E-Mail

Long-distance communication with colleagues, friends, and family members has been part of the Internet since its inception. It is known as **electronic mail,** or **e-mail.** This communication method is easy and can be fun because of the connections you can initiate or reestablish with others. There are several e-mail utilities that educational institutions may use. They include programs with names such as *Pine* and *Eudora*. Whatever is in use at your institution, it will follow the same basic principles used by all such e-mail software.

With your usercode established and a password that is uniquely yours, you now have to learn the steps and shortcuts of your particular e-mail program. Remember that different computers may use different keystrokes for the same function.

E-mail programs may use slightly different wording or keystrokes but all share similar fundamentals.

◆ EXAMPLE

A computer with one operating system may use the F4 function key to display a screen of data, and a computer with a different OS might use the ALT and D keys together for the same function.

You need to know how your institution's e-mail utility works on the various computers and keyboards that you might use. Or find out if you can use the e-mail account you use at home to get your institution's mail.

In order to communicate electronically you should learn the basics:

- How to send messages.
- How to "view," or see, the list of messages that are waiting in your mailbox and then how to read them.
- How to save messages and other information you receive.
- How to reply to messages.
- How to "forward" a message to another e-mail user.
- How to delete messages.

These procedures may be taught in workshops on using e-mail, or in an information literacy or information research course. If your institution offers such training sessions or courses, you would be wise to attend one.

You'll discover that the more you use the computer for information and communication needs, the more comfortable you become with it, and the better you get at using it. While it will be some time before electronic information completely replaces all the other forms now available, you're already part of that transition, incorporating it into your daily life more and more.

Chapter Concepts

- Computers are machines that cannot think but can very ably follow the commands that you give them.
- The Internet is a network of computer networks, and the World Wide Web is a protocol that gives you access to the information available on the Internet.
- The Web is a graphical browser, software that allows you to see and hear the information on the Net. Examples of browsers are *Netscape Navigator* and *Internet Explorer*.
- Information that is accessible on the Web provides links to related information at other Web sites and pages; links are the computer addresses of other resources.
- Links allow you to follow information in a nonlinear way, to explore information related to one resource by going to other resources at any time.
- Not all information available through the Web is free. Many sites require you or your institution to pay a subscription fee for complete access.
- Search engines allow you to search for particular information on the Web. They scan Web sites to find matches to your search string(s) in a manner very similar to the way electronic periodicals indexes work.
- Focused research pays off because it results in information sources that are clearly related to the topic you consciously selected.
- Electronic mail (e-mail) is a way of communicating with others using the Internet.

Name: ______________________________ **Date:** ______________

Review Questions

1. What must you do in order to use the World Wide Web at your institution? Please explain all steps, including location(s), on or off campus, where you have access to the Web.

____

____

____

____

____

2. Use the search engine at *Yahoo!* to find the home page of a college/university in which you're interested. Describe the steps—all of them—that you took to get to the site.

____

____

____

____

____

3. Is there any way you can use the Internet without using the Web? Explain your answer.

____

____

____

____

____

4. Describe how you would search to discover if one of your professors has material on the Web.

5. You're in the middle of a Web session when the computer stops functioning completely. Have you broken it? What do you do?

Chapter 3

How Information Is Presented

In This Chapter, You Will Learn . . .

- What an access tool is, and what it does
- The different types of access tools
- What an access point is
- How to use access points to look up information within an access tool
- About searching with computerized access tools and paper access tools
- How to use access tools to evaluate sources

Information Access and Presentation

The first chapter of this book states that information must be accessible so that it can be used again. Information must be organized in order to be accessible; without organization it's a meaningless jumble. Organization provides access. Access is affected by the way in which information is presented. This chapter will introduce you to some of the ways in which it's presented in information research tools. You'll become acquainted with several different types of "access tools," the "access points" they provide, and the "search terms" you use. You'll learn how to evaluate information sources by using access tools, before you get the actual sources in hand.

Access Tools

"Access tool" is another name for a secondary or tertiary information source that leads you to information about your topic. Many access tools now also provide the complete information source in their "full-text" databases.

A tool is something you use to help you accomplish a task. In the case of information research, an access tool is an information source that helps you by leading you to information. It may provide the actual material that you'll read or view, or it may only give you enough information to find that material. Think of a gardening shovel: it doesn't put in your plants itself but rather it provides a way for you to do that. Access tools work for you in a similar manner. **The tools for information research are catalogs and bibliographies, and indexes and abstracting services.** Computers have advanced indexes and abstracting services significantly from their paper origins, but they are still access tools . . . with added features.

NOTE: The terms "computerized" and "electronic" and "online" are used interchangeably in this book in most discussions of computerized information sources.

A **catalog** is a file of records for the information sources in a library's collections, the majority of which are books. The records in any catalog describe the contents of the collection(s) covered by the catalog.

A catalog is an access tool that is used to find books, not periodical articles.

- A small library may have only a *card catalog,* a catalog on 3x5 cards.
- Another library may have an *online catalog* (a catalog on computer, sometimes called an *opac*) for its main book collection and may also have a card catalog for a smaller collection within itself, such as a Local History Collection Catalog.
- At the other end of the spectrum is a mega-catalog that is really numerous catalogs for many institutions that are searched simultaneously on the Internet using a particular computer program or database.

A **bibliography** is a list of materials on a given subject or by a given author. It may be the list of references found at the end of a book or at the end of a chapter in a book, or at the end of a research paper or an article in a periodical. A bibliography also can be a book-length list of materials on one subject, for example, *American Indian Studies, A Bibliographic Guide;* or materials by and about one author, for example, *Margaret Atwood, A Reference Guide.* Most bibliographies currently are available only in paper but some are beginning to appear electronically. The lists of resources in electronic-only bibliographies frequently are limited to the Internet resources available on various subjects, for example, "Internet Resources on

Disabilities," on the University of Kansas Department of Special Education Web site.

An **index** and an **abstracting service** provide similar help: they make available the contents of periodicals, often by analyzing and organizing the contents by subject. An index provides just the information—a bibliographic citation—needed to find the article, while an abstracting service provides the same type of citation as well as an "abstract," a short summary describing the content of the article. Many indexes and abstracting services are electronic in format—on compact disks or accessible through the Internet, and they also may be available in paper. Computers are making these types of tools into virtual information sources because more and more of the tools are "full-text," that is, they provide the entire text of the information source they have led you to. It's important to remember, however, that not all full-text databases contain the complete text of *every* article for which they have a citation. And you also need to be aware that many full-text tools don't provide the same graphics you would see in the print version of the information source.

Computers are stretching the concept of access "tool" because they're making possible the inclusion of the full text of an information source along with the citation. Use of many "tools" today results in finding the whole source, not just a reference to it.

See Figure 3-1 for an example of the references found in an electronic index. This type of tool is what's often meant when information researchers refer to a "database." (Not all databases are electronic indexes, however. See Chapter 2 for the real definition of that word.)

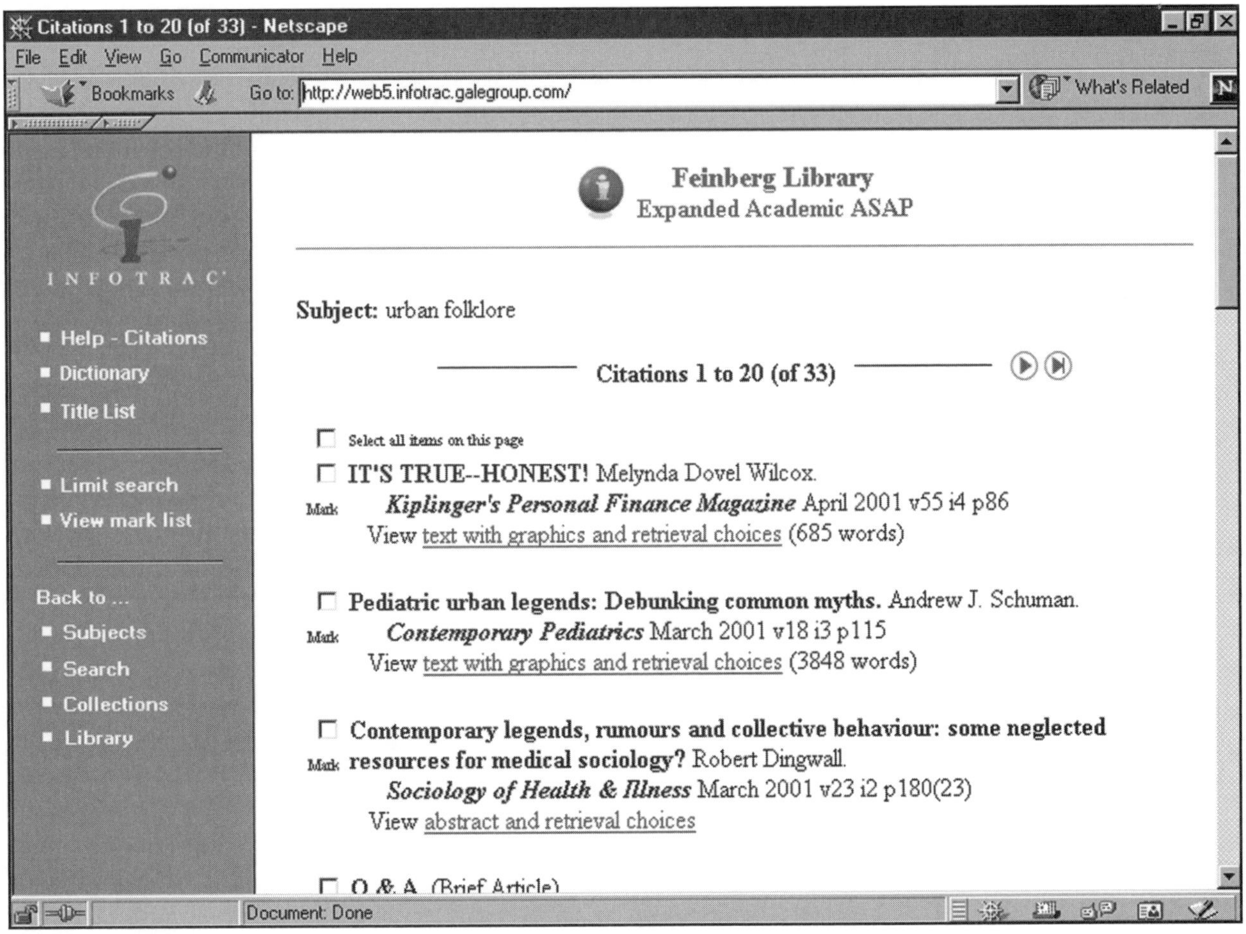

Figure 3-1: References (Records) in a Database (Computerized Periodicals Index)

Is a Search Engine an Access Tool?

Many students go first to the Web when trying to find information on any topic. One of the most popular first stops is *Yahoo!* Students use the site as a search engine (it's actually a portal—see the glossary in Chapter 2).

- Does it provide the same service a true database provides? Not really, but close. *Yahoo!*'s software searches the sites in its purview for the term entered by the searcher and returns all pages that include the term.
- Will the student get information from the Web on her topic? The answer is almost always yes.
- Are all "hits" relevant? The answer is almost always no. The percentage of relevant hits is often quite low, especially when hundreds of thousands of sites are found. When a searcher uses a database that is a periodicals index, on the other hand, a far greater percentage of hits is relevant.

See "How a Computer Does a Search" in Chapter 5 for a more complete explanation of how both searches are performed. There are numerous sites available that explain search engines and compare their work. A good example is "HyperResearch: Using Web Subject Directories and Search Engines"

<http://faculty.plattsburgh.edu/dennis.kimmage/HyperResearch.htm>.

A search engine, then, is not really an access tool . . . but you could say that it functions like one.

What's in Access Tools

What's in access tools? **Access tools contain *references* to information sources.** The *American Heritage Dictionary*'s definition of reference is a "note in a publication referring the reader to another publication." That's how an access tool provides access: it *refers* you to the source that has the information. An access tool consists of many references to many sources and each of the references is a *record* that includes enough information to find each source. Full-text tools go one step further and provide the entire text of the source.

Records in Access Tools

Access tools organize information by arranging systematically the records they contain. **A record is the description of an information source in an access tool,** the "source" being the book, periodical article, or sound recording. Records in access tools can be called *references, entries, citations,* and of course, *records*. These names are interchangeable because they all mean basically the same thing and include the same elements.

Each record contains all the information necessary to enable you to find the item it describes:

- The author(s),
- The title,
- The publishing information. (This description, of course, refers to records in databases that are not full-text.)

Each of these elements is contained in its own area in the record. In electronic tools these areas are called **fields** and usually the fields are clearly labeled so that you can identify the elements immediately, that is, you can recognize in a record an author as separate from the title of the periodical in which her article was published. The same elements are present in the records in paper access tools but they are not usually labeled as fields. Figure 3-2 shows two records for the same book, illustrating the difference between records from an online catalog and a paper version catalog (or card catalog).

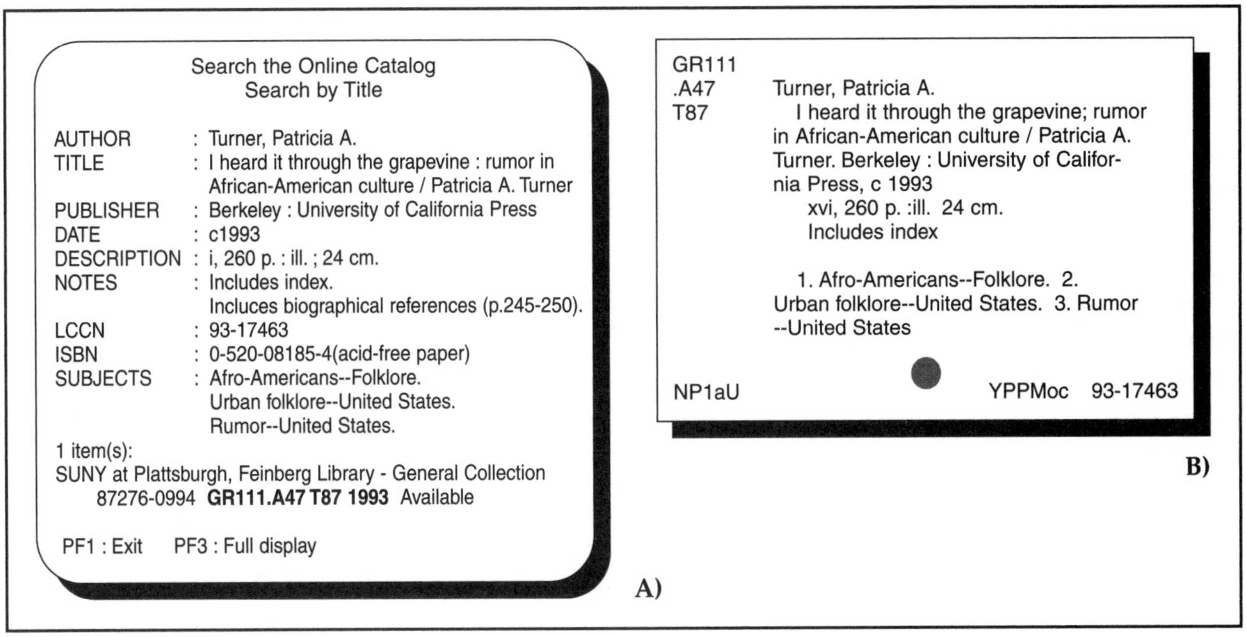
Search the Online Catalog
Search by Title

AUTHOR : Turner, Patricia A.
TITLE : I heard it through the grapevine : rumor in African-American culture / Patricia A. Turner
PUBLISHER : Berkeley : University of California Press
DATE : c1993
DESCRIPTION : i, 260 p. : ill. ; 24 cm.
NOTES : Includes index.
Incluces biographical references (p.245-250).
LCCN : 93-17463
ISBN : 0-520-08185-4(acid-free paper)
SUBJECTS : Afro-Americans--Folklore.
Urban folklore--United States.
Rumor--United States.

1 item(s):
SUNY at Plattsburgh, Feinberg Library - General Collection
87276-0994 **GR111.A47 T87 1993** Available

PF1 : Exit PF3 : Full display

A)

GR111
.A47
T87
Turner, Patricia A.
I heard it through the grapevine; rumor in African-American culture / Patricia A. Turner. Berkeley : University of California Press, c 1993
xvi, 260 p. :ill. 24 cm.
Includes index

1. Afro-Americans--Folklore. 2. Urban folklore--United States. 3. Rumor --United States

NP1aU YPPMoc 93-17463

B)

Figure 3-2: Records for a Book: A) Online Catalog Record with Fields; B) Card (Paper) Catalog Record

The online catalog record shows all its fields with their labels, or *field tags*, on the left. The catalog card (paper version) doesn't have the fields labeled, meaning that you have to know where to look for what, that is, you have to know how the fields are most commonly arranged in order to cite the author as author and not mistake the publisher for the author!

◆ EXAMPLES

SO: meaning source—the source of the article, which equals the title of the periodical

◆◆◆

JN: meaning journal name—refers to the periodical title

◆◆◆

TI: meaning title. But does the TI refer to the title of the article or the title of the periodical? This varies from tool to tool and you MUST know which it means before you go looking for the information source in the library!

◆◆◆

PY: meaning publication year—the year that the book or article was published

◆◆◆

AU: meaning author. Other information that might be included here, such as the name of a translator, often must be included in your citation of the source.

Field names and their field tags may change from tool to tool. For example, one database labels the periodical-title field JN for Journal Name while another calls the same field SO for Source. You must become familiar with common field tags. If you don't know what some of the field tags in your database mean, especially if you can't find an element that you think is necessary for your citation, use the tool's Help screens or ask a librarian for help in deciphering the tags.

Citations

An access tool provides enough information for the reader to find each information source, just as you do when you "cite your sources." This is true whether the tool is full-text or not.

The word citation comes from the word cite, which means, "to quote as an authority or example; to mention as support, illustration or proof," according to the *American Heritage Dictionary.* You've probably provided citations (typed a bibliography) for research projects you've done because your instructor required you to "cite your sources" that you used for information on your topic. So you know one place where citations can be found: at the end of your research reports and papers. These are not the only places that lists of citations occur; they are found with nearly all scholarly research. There are bibliographies after journal articles and at the ends of books, and there are also book-length bibliographies, as described earlier in this chapter. You can even consider a library's catalog a bibliography. It's a (greatly expanded!) list of citations, citing all the materials in a library.

The elements you find in any access tool's record are the same as those in a bibliography citation that you create: author, title, and publishing information. These three components may be arranged differently depending on the type of bibliography you're using. Most often the sequence is:

1. author(s),
2. title,
3. publishing information.

Some examples of citations, similar to those that you would include in a bibliography for a research report, are given in Figure 3-3. The last cita-

Jason, H. "'Contemporary Legend'—To Be or Not to Be?" *Folklore* 102.1 (1991): 106-107.

Matsumoto, Craig. "Internet Group Surfaces as Prime Slayer of Urban Legends." *Business Journal Serving San Jose & Silicon Valley* 18 (Sept., 1995): 7.

Turner, Patricia A. *I Heard It on the Grapevine; Rumor in African American Folklore.* Berkeley: U of Cal. P., 1993.

Mikkelson, Barbara; and David P. Mikkelson. "Urban Legends Reference Pages: Toxin du jour." 1995-2001. <http://www.snopes.com/toxins> 31 July 2001.

Figure 3-3: Examples of Citations from a Bibliography in a Student's Research Paper

tion illustrates how to cite a World Wide Web site. There's a more thorough discussion of different citation styles in Chapter 7 of this book.

There are other citation examples in Figure 3-4. These are records from various access tools. While their style, typefaces, and the order of the elements differ, notice how they all include the same information:

Take apart a citation in any access tool and you find the same elements you use in your citations.

- Author (when the author is named),
- Title (including a subtitle if there is one),
- Publishing information.

In the case of periodicals, the publishing information is:

- The name of the periodical and its volume/issue number(s),
- Its date, and the page(s) on which the article was published.

The publishing information for books is:

- The place of publication (city, and sometimes state or country),
- Publisher,
- Year.

All the standard components of a citation are present in all the examples, except for the city in the Web example. **The elements in a citation correspond to the main fields in a record.**

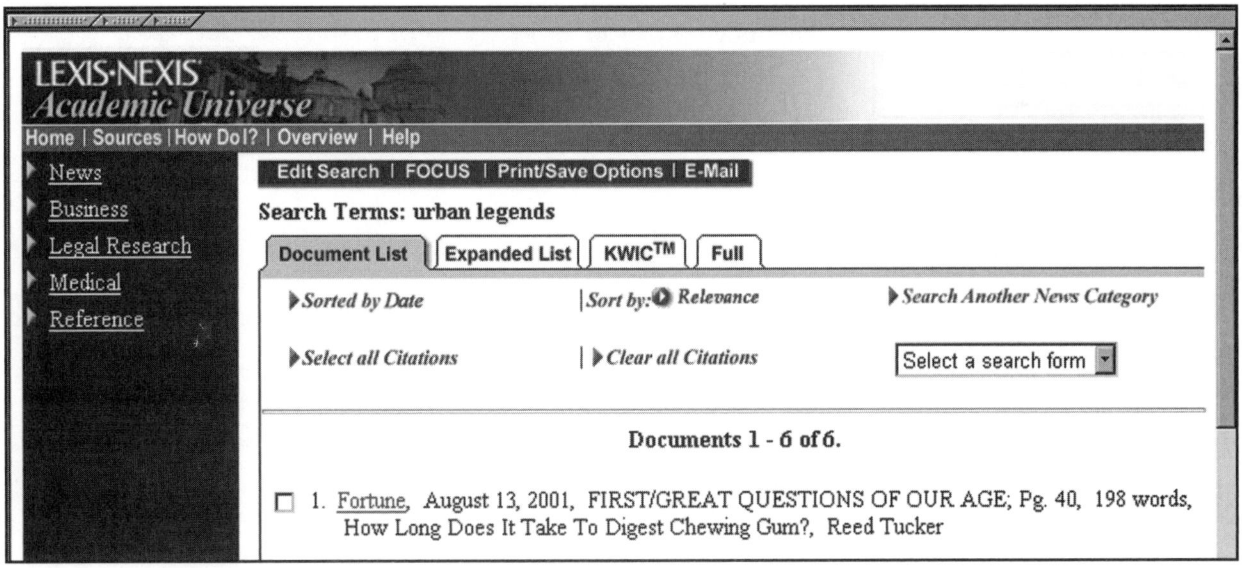

Figure 3-4A: (A) Citation from *Lexis/Nexis Academic Universe*

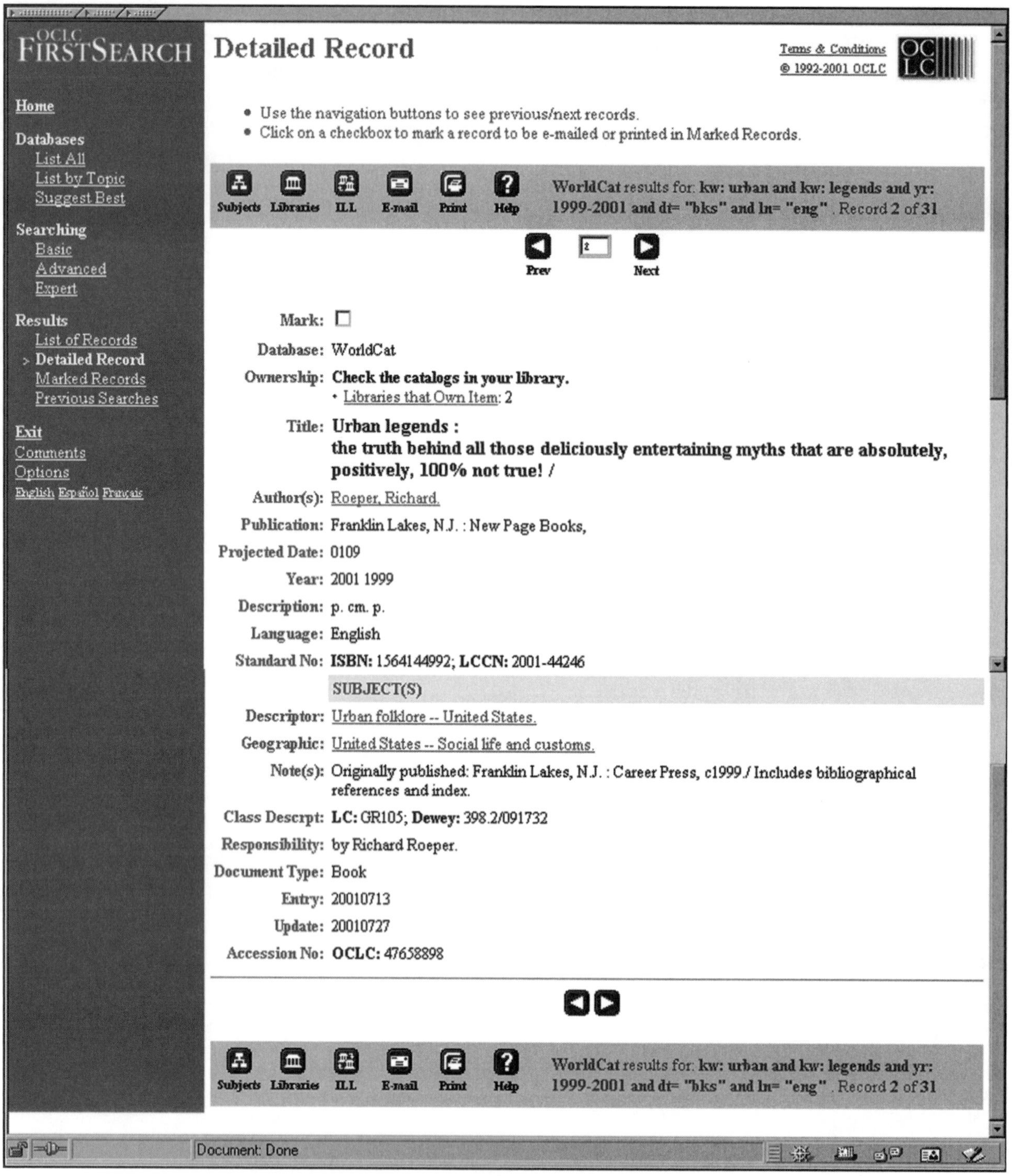

Figure 3-4B: (B) Citation from an Online Catalog (*WorldCat* from *OCLC FirstSearch*)

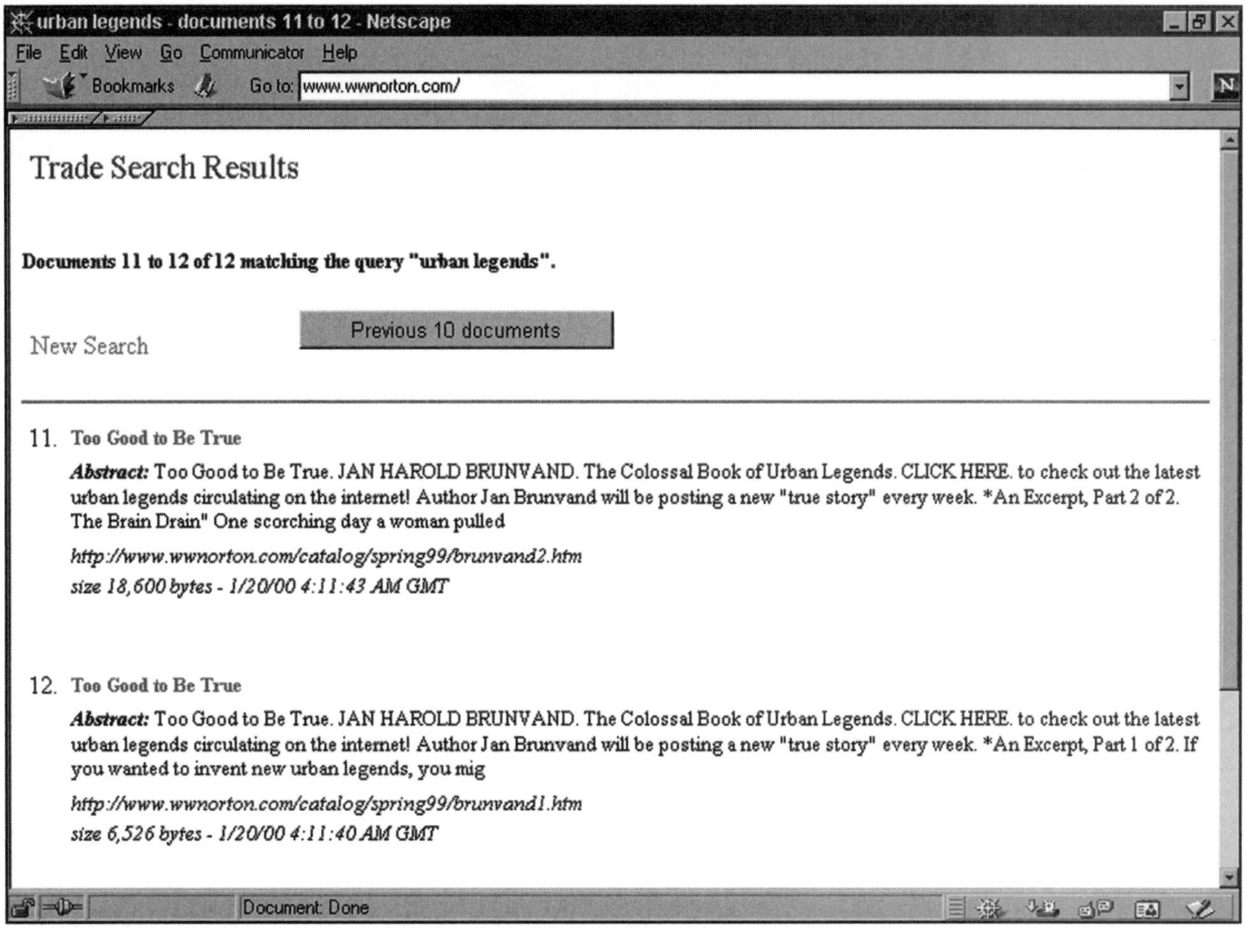

Figure 3-4C: (C) Citations from a Publisher's Site on the World Wide Web

What Access Tools Do

Access tools provide access. In reality all of them index something, that is, **an access tool provides systematic access to the content of an information source.**

An access tool is a tool because it helps you find sources.

◆ EXAMPLE

You have often used an index in a book. Think of what you did. You looked under a person's name or an event or an idea in the "Index" in the back of the book. In this alphabetical list of names and subjects you found reference to the page(s) on which your person or event or idea was mentioned. You would then look on the page(s) listed in the index because you knew there was information there on your person, event, or idea.

A **single book's** index is just a small index; it's a guide only to the contents of that book. A **library's catalog** is a much larger index in that it is a "systematic guide" to a group of materials, providing access (guiding you) to the books it includes. A **periodicals** index is a guide to the contents of many separate magazines and journals. A **bibliography,** especially a book-length bibliography, performs the same way an index does through its arrangement of citations of materials that are on one subject or by one author.

After you've searched in an access tool you use the reference you found there to retrieve the actual information source—the book or article about your topic. Figure 3-1 shows an example of information provided by a periodicals index database when your search term is "urban folklore." Your next step after using the index would be to determine if your library has the materials that you identified as worthwhile when using the index. If the library subscribes to the periodical, you can go get the article. If your library doesn't have the periodical, you can make use of the Interlibrary Loan service that the library offers. Ask your librarian for information about this valuable, and often low-cost or free service. Of course, if the database is a full-text database, you simply have to click on the appropriate link to see the entire article. You can then print the article or read it on the computer. Full-text databases take the "go get it" step out of the process. See Figure 3-5 for an example of the first screen of an article that is completely included in a full-text periodicals index.

Your library's catalog serves as an index to the books in the library by giving you not the whole books on the screen but rather enough information for you to find the books. That is, the catalog provides their call numbers and perhaps some information about where in the building(s) those call numbers are shelved.

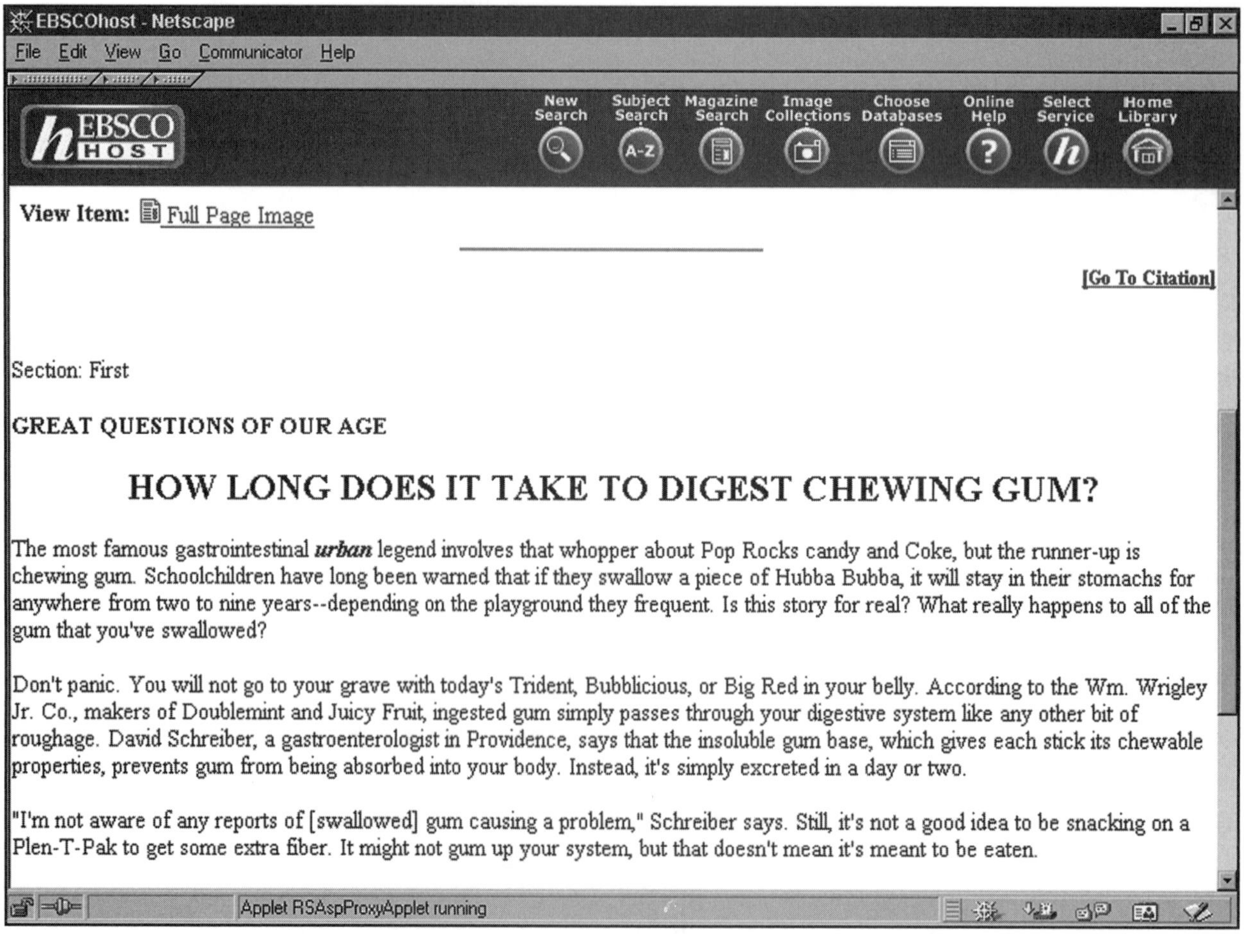

Figure 3-5: The First Screen of a Periodical Article That Is Available on a "Full-Text" Index
Tucker Reed, *Fortune*, 8/13/2001.

Formats of Access Tools

Most access tools are available both online (on computer) and in paper. The different formats may include different parts, e.g., the paper version may be an index that provides only citations while the online version provides the full text of the articles it indexes. There is an increasing number of tools that are only online. You're probably familiar with some access tools in both of these formats. Examples of familiar access tools include:

- Any library's catalog, online or card
- Periodicals indexes such as *Reader's Guide to Periodical Literature*, online or in paper
- *InfoTrac Magazine Index*, an online-only tool

Some are general in scope, some subject field-oriented.

◆ EXAMPLE

Education majors soon learn about *ERIC*, the online combined version of a periodicals index *(Current Index to Journals in Education [CIJE])* and an abstracting service *(Resources in Education [RIE])*.

See Chapter 4 for more information about subject fields and their tools.

There are numerous book-length bibliographies on various subjects that are in paper format only, such as *Monsters, A Guide to Information on Unaccounted for Creatures, including Bigfoot, Many Water Monsters, and Other Irregular Animals.*

How Access Tools Work

Many online tools were created from their paper predecessors. The records within a paper access tool are organized by grouping together those on a particular subject, or by putting all records into an alphabetical list by their authors' names, or by listing all records alphabetically by title. Some paper tools use two or more organization schemes combined, e.g., subject and author, or author and title. The organization schemes provide the "access points" you use in the tools. Different paper tools may provide different access points—and computerized access tools provide them all. Once you learn the standard access points, you'll be able to recognize them in most access tools. So what are "access points"?

Access Points and Search Terms

An access point is one way that you use an access tool, that is, it's one way that you can look up something in a particular tool. Each access point is a way to search in that tool, a part of a record that provides access to the whole record. Access points are:

- The titles of sources you're trying to find in a catalog
- The authors in a bibliography
- The subject that you type into a database or into a search engine's textbox

Access points are the ways you're able to search in an access tool; your search term depends on the access point you choose.

These are the most common access points used by information systems: title, author, and subject. Others may be report numbers, types of documents, or language of the information source. Some information systems allow you to search by any of the three most common, some by only one or two, some by anything at all in the record.

A **search term** is the actual word(s) or number(s) you look up in an access tool. It's the access point. It may be only one word, it may be a phrase of several words, or it may be a report or document number. Databases allow you to use almost anything as your access point/search term. It's often helpful to know which access points are available in the tool you choose so that you can decide what your search term(s) will be.

Authors and Titles as Access Points and Search Terms

Each of the elements in a citation or record is a potential access point. You're familiar with some access points if you ever searched in a library's catalog to see if the library has any books by your favorite author, or if you used the catalog to find out if the library has a copy of a book for which your professor gave you only the title. You were using the access points of author in the first instance and title in the second. Author and title access points often make research easy because they are yes/no searches: Are there any works in this library by Ursula LeGuin? Does the library have *The Cider House Rules*?

Computerized access tools allow easy searching by author and title; you should keep these access points in mind as you use these tools. If you use title as your access point, most computerized tools allow you to enter any word from a title and simply specify that you are looking for it as a word in the title. You may have to be more precise when using author as an access point. Some electronic tools require that you invert the author's name (put the last name first) when you use it as a search term. In other words, the access point of author may be usable only with a specified format for search terms; check each tool to find out if this is the case in each.

How Access Tools Differ

In the past, the main difference among access tools was due mostly to their formats: paper tools may not provide author and title access points while computerized tools usually do. Computerized access tools frequently offer more access points than paper indexes do.

Because most tools are now electronic, either online or on CD-ROMs, the main difference among them is the amount of information provided in the records. Library catalogs generally furnish citations that include the title of a book, its author(s), and the publishing information. Periodicals databases provide this information for the articles they list. A database citation also names the periodical, its volume, and date—information you need to find the article. In some databases all information is full-text, in others only some of the entries include the entire text. Most databases also supply a summary of the cited item. The summary is called an "abstract." If the database is not completely full-text, the abstract enables you to evaluate a source before you ever see it "in the flesh." It helps you decide at an early point in your research if the source is relevant to your topic and therefore worth tracking down. Figure 3-6 shows a periodicals database entry for a periodical article and a record with an abstract from paper version of a tool.

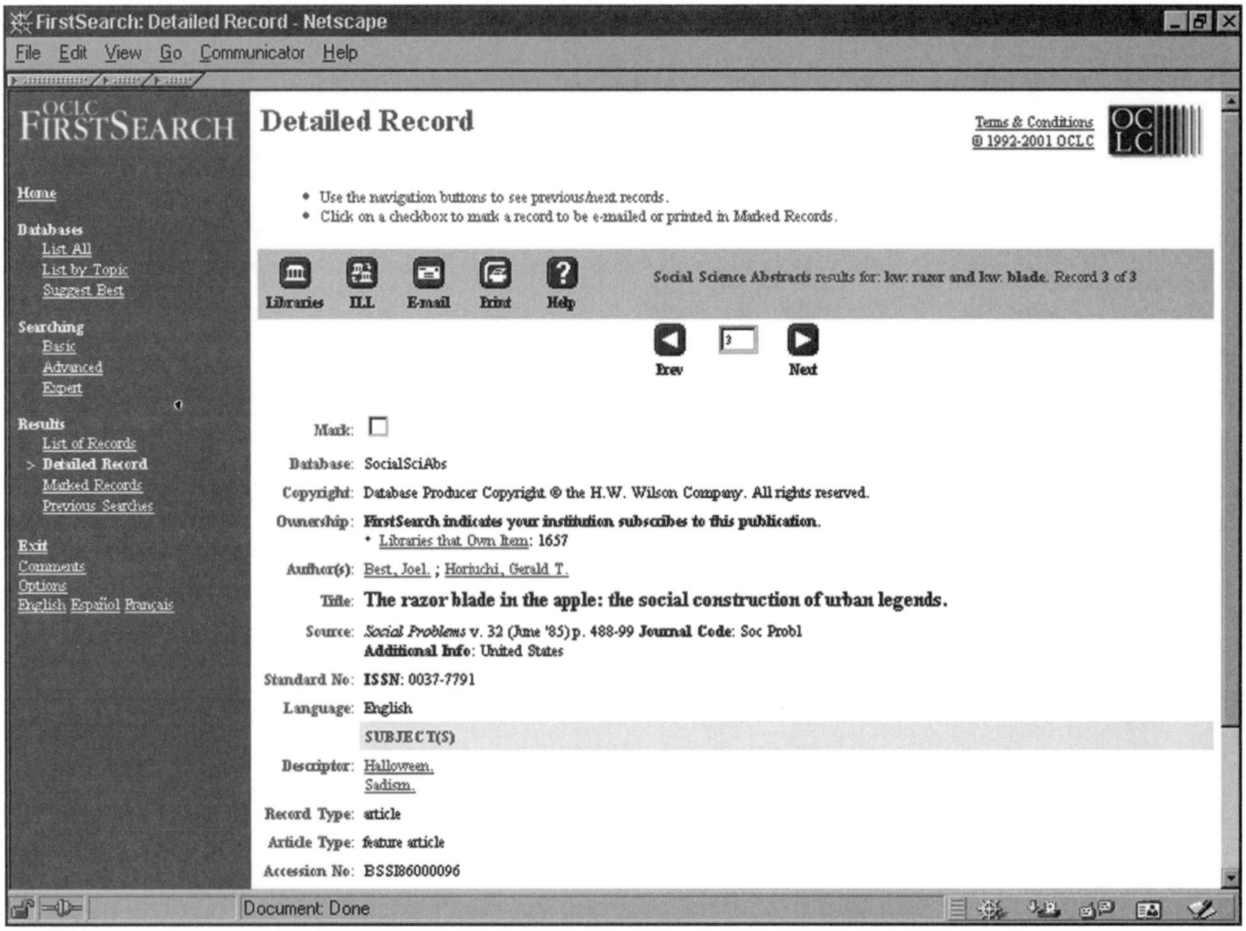

Figure 3-6A: (A) Entry from an Online Periodicals Database

24A:1851. 1958-83

Best, Joel and Horiuchi, Gerald T. THE RAZOR BLADE IN THE APPLE: THE SOCIAL CONSTRUCTION OF URBAN LEGENDS. *Social Problems 1985 32(5): 488-499.* Examines the widespread belief that anonymous sadists give children dangerous treats on Halloween. A review of news stories about Halloween sadism during 1958-83 suggests that the threat has been greatly exaggerated. Halloween Sadism can be viewed as an urban legend that emerged during the early 1970's to give expression to growing fears about the safety of children, the danger of crime, and other sources of social strain.

Figure 3-6B: (B) Entry from a Paper Version of an Abstracting Service

Search engines usually do not provide abstracts of the Web pages they retrieve on their searches. If the list of pages is "annotated," it usually includes the first words in the text of the page. While not a summary of the page's content, this information can serve the same purpose that an abstract does, that is, it allows you to decide if you want to look at the page or to move on to the next in the list.

How You Work with Access Tools

Searching Computerized Access Tools

A good search using the computer usually is one that uses more than one word as a search term.

A computerized access tool allows you to use almost any element in the record as an access point. The steps that you follow can be minimal:

1. You type your search term(s) and the computer retrieves the relevant record(s).
2. You then scan the list of records and command the computer to print those you deem acceptable. (This is an improved version of many student searches that are described as, "You go to the computer and type something in and print all the stuff that comes up.")

The process that actually occurs when you search electronic tools is this:

1. You command the computer via the search term you typed.
2. That term is actually part of a command that tells the computer to scan all the data in all the records in the tool until an exact match is found between what you typed and what is scanned.
3. Anything that has your string of letters is included in the set. **The computer does not evaluate the materials retrieved**.

You can command the computer to scan for almost any access point in one field or in all fields.

◆ **EXAMPLE**

Let's say you want to search for George Orwell's novel, *1984*. You can command the computer to scan all fields to find a match for that title, or to scan only the title field for it. This latter strategy eliminates the possibility of finding unwanted matches that have that year in their publication-year fields.

Usually there are on-screen directions that guide you in doing such "field-specific" searches. The directions will change from computer to computer, and even among several tools that are accessible on the same computer. You may have already experienced the differences among search engines and their protocols! Learn what the correct field tags and command formats are for the tool you wish to use. Use the "Help" or "Search Tips" screens, or ask a librarian for help.

Searching Paper Access Tools

The steps in using paper indexes may be familiar to you.

1. You look up your search term alphabetically.
2. When you find it, you also find listed under it the references to information sources relevant to it.
3. You copy down the references and go to retrieve the sources.

A search in a paper abstracting service requires you to take one more step in addition to those just described. You still look up your access point alphabetically but you usually find only an "entry number" or "abstract number" rather than the information in a citation. See Figure 3-7.

SUBJECT INDEX

—. Quebec. 16c-20c. *24A:3177 24C:1581*

Folklore. *See also* Folk Medicine: Folk Songs: Legends; Myths and Symbols Occult Sciences.

—. *Aisling* (genre). Ireland. Western genre. ca 1600–1890. *24A:656 24C:2924*

—. Alamo (battle). Art, Literature. Revolution. Texas. 1836–95. 1986. *24A:2316 24C:10156*

—. Children. Crime and Criminals. Halloween. 1958–83. *24A:1851 24C:8012*

—. Children. Indians. Navajo Indians. Skinwalkers. 190–83. *24B:2226 24C:478*

—. Chinook Indians. Indians. Myths and Symbols. ca 1909. *24A:108 24C:526*

—. Chippewa Indians (review article). Indians. North Central States. 20c. *24A:100 24C:538*

—. Christmas. Europe. Myths and Symbols. Santa Claus. 3c-20c. *24A:3294 24C:2103*

—. Collections. Indexes. Oral history. 1977-85. *24A:5556 24C:11616*

—. Colorado, Southern. New Mexico. Northern. Spaniards. 1902–32. *24B:2558 24C:10683*

—. Copyright. Indians. Law. ca 1983. *24C:555*

—. Death and Dying. Monsters. Pennsylvania (Penns Valley). 1880–1976. *24A:2119 24C:9079*

America: History & Life v.24D, p. 150

Figure 3-7: Excerpt from the Subject Index Section of an Abstracting Service (Paper Version)

You then have to go to the portion of the abstracting service that contains the abstracts and look for the entry numbers you found. Once you find the abstracts, you will also find the complete citation that enables you to find the sources themselves. Remember that most print versions of abstracting services have separate sections for their access points, that is, many have a separate author index, a subject index, an institution index, and perhaps other indexes as well. You begin your search in one of these indexes and always move then to the abstracts to get the citations.

Using Access Tools to Evaluate Sources

You should evaluate, *during your research,* the information that you're finding. This is a process that can save you time later because it means you won't retrieve sources that you can't really use. It may also save you money, or at least paper, when you decide *what* to print from a full-text database or from the Web. How can you evaluate *while* you're researching? You can use the information in access tools themselves to evaluate the sources they cite—before you ever print, or find and copy the references.

Use clues in access tools to evaluate sources for their value in your research.

You want each of your information sources to be relevant to your topic and authoritative in its subject field. You can best determine this by examining the source itself. But to avoid going to the stacks for books that are of little relevance or downloading Web sites that aren't authoritative or waiting to photocopy articles that are too technical for your needs, you can look at the entries in an access tool for clues to help cull out sources you don't want to pursue. Author and title fields can help you evaluate potential information sources.

Using the Title Field to Evaluate a Source

Take the title first. A title often has a word or a phrase in it that can help you determine the relevance of the source to your topic. Usually scholarly sources have subtitles with their titles to explain further what the source is about. You can often decide whether or not a source fits the scope of your topic if you read carefully its whole title in an access tool. The titles below are similar titles for different books; notice how the subtitle, or lack of one, affects your ability to estimate each book's focus.

African Folk Medicine: Practices and Beliefs of the Bambara and Other Peoples

American Folk Medicine

Folk Medicine

Folk Medicine: A Chapter in the History of Culture

Folk Medicine: The Art & the Science

Using the Author Field to Evaluate a Source

An author whose name appears often in your research is probably an authority.

An author can also be indicative of a source's applicability to your research. The status of an author is not often determined easily at the beginning of your research, especially if the whole subject field is new to you. But as you continue to search for information on your topic, you may see one author's name occurring again and again in different access tools. Or you may find her mentioned in an encyclopedia article as an authority in the field, and then cited in the bibliography of that article. Sometimes you'll encounter an author's name as the second or third author of one article and the first author of another. In this case you may have found work by a whole research team and all of the team's authors can now be searched as authorities.

Print only the citations that are worth tracking down or articles and Web sites that are worth reading and citing!

Read through a number of the records that you retrieve in your research before you print *any*. Be selective! Use access tools to do a preliminary evaluation of an information source when you find the first references to it and you'll save yourself a lot of time when you go to the book stacks or to the periodicals collection, or when you consider whether to request the material from a different library through interlibrary loan. Be just as selective when using a full-text database or the Web: not everything retrieved is always relevant and it might be a waste of your time and paper to "print all."

Don't be a passive researcher! Use the information provided by the access tool to *select* information that is truly relevant to your research.

Access to "Invisible" Information

The "invisible college" was formed when communicating scholarly information was dangerous or illegal.

Direct communication among scientists and scholars has been part of the information cycle for a very long time. It was called by many the "invisible college" because it wasn't a formally organized system. These "colleges" were groups of people who were working in the same subject field and who communicated with each other through meetings, correspondence, and telephone calls, all informal means of communication that weren't recorded anywhere. Today that communication is referred to as "networking." Networking includes e-mail, and even the conversations that occur between colleagues at meetings. People go to conferences not only to hear the presentations of the speakers but also to network with their counterparts from other institutions, whether those institutions are banks, colleges, or laboratories.

A recent addition to the communication of "invisible" information is electronic technology. Many students, scholars, and scientists now belong to electronic networks that have services such as listservs and bulletin boards that allow direct communication with colleagues around the world. No longer do researchers have to wait for the publication of reports in paper journals, a process that can take months or years, because much of that information is now published first or solely electronically.

◆ EXAMPLE

In the recent past the immediacy of information available only electronically was dramatically demonstrated by news that came out of the newly formed nations in eastern Europe; conflicts in some countries kept standard news sources unavailable to the public, but individuals were able to send out reports on their personal computers via the Internet.

Since the invisible college is informal, usually unpublished information, how do you as a researcher have access to it? You may gain access through another person, for example, your professor, who got information from an electronic service. Your professor may be a good source to try whether or not he's connected to electronic networks because he almost certainly is connected to the invisible network of direct communication among colleagues in his subject field.

Another access route to unpublished material is through access tools that include prepublication information and announcements. These are periodicals databases that note that there is an article on your topic that will be published in a journal although the issue of the journal is not yet available. Electronic information is available to anyone who has a computer with a modem for connecting to various computer networks, or with a direct connection to the Internet.

Chapter Concepts

- Access tools provide access to information because they consist of references to information sources such as books and periodical articles.
- Access tools include bibliographies, catalogs, and periodicals databases The last type here includes indexing and abstracting services, both electronic and in paper.
- Information in access tools is organized into records, also called citations, entries, and references.
- A record in an access tool is made up of fields that together contain enough information to enable you to find the actual source: author, title, and publishing information, each in its own field(s) in the record. Many records in full-text databases also include the "full text" of the information source itself.
- An access point is a searchable field in a record; a search term is the word or phrase or number you look up.
- All elements in the records of access tools are potentially usable as access points, and computerized tools provide the greatest number of access points.
- Author and title are used easily as search terms in electronic tools because a computer can be commanded to scan those fields to find matches for an author's name or word(s) in a title. Author and title searches are "field specific" searches.
- Information sources should be evaluated before they're retrieved by using the clues contained in the references in access tools.
- Clues in access tools' entries include words or phrases in the title (and subtitle) of an article or book, and an author's name appearing often in one or more tools.
- Electronic technology is opening up another source for information that has been less accessible in the past, the "invisible college" that is the network of communication among scholars and scientists.

Name: ______________________________ **Date:** ______________

Review Questions

1. You go to a library at a college you're visiting and it has a computer catalog whose records look different from those in your own college's library catalog. What similarities would you expect to find in both catalogs' records?

____

____

____

____

____

2. Explain what an index does. You may use any kind of index as an example: one in the back of a book, one with a multivolume encyclopedia, a library's catalog, a periodicals database, a search engine on the Web.

____

____

____

____

____

3. You need to write abstracts of three periodical articles for an assignment due tomorrow. The periodicals databases in your library are not working for the day, but the library's online catalog is working. Where can you get references for some *articles* to look at?

____

____

____

____

____

4. Could any part a complete information source, i.e., part of a book or periodical article, ever be used as an access tool? Explain your answer.

5. Describe any network of "invisible" communication that you're a part of. (This does not have to be a network associated with your college studies.) How would anyone else gain access to the information that's communicated in this network?

Chapter 4

Analyzing a Research Topic

In This Chapter, You Will Learn . . .

- How to refine a topic to make it fit the available information tools and to stay within the guidelines of the assignment
- The difference between a "topic" and a "subject"
- How to use information sources to find out what aspects there are to a topic
- The three major divisions of knowledge in the information research world
- How to use subject field-oriented, discipline-oriented, or general sources and tools, alone or in combination when doing research

The Parts of Information Research

You do information research every day and many times each day. Look at the questions in the Introduction to this textbook. Have you asked any one of those in the last 24 hours? (The whereabouts of the TV remote control is usually the one!) You can easily identify which questions in that list are those that you regard as more formal "information research" questions. How do you go about such scholarly investigation?

There are several parts to information research.

Frequently the most difficult part of beginning information research is figuring out just what needs to be researched!

1. You must refine your topic to make it fit the information tools you'll use and to stay within the guidelines of your research assignment. In order to do this you have to understand the relationship of your topic to both broader and narrower areas of knowledge.
2. You must devise a **search strategy**. This means that you'll have to make a series of decisions about where to look for information on your topic.
3. You must select appropriate information tools.

You know that many resources are accessible through electronic means; you'll have to choose which of these online tools will have the most information about your particular topic. But the fact that there are many computerized tools does not mean that you should think of the computer as the only place to do all your research. Your topic must be your guide in the tools that you use, whether those tools are electronic or in paper versions.

Refining a Topic

Frequently a research project begins as a vague or broad search on a topic that's totally new to you. For a student just learning about the topic, this can be an overwhelming task. You may take a common but misguided approach to beginning research for such an assignment: You go to the nearest computer and type in the topic in hopes that the computer will provide some suggestions of how to handle the assignment. (Many researchers today rely on *Yahoo!* to do this.) You learn instead that there is a staggering amount of information on the topic, seemingly none of it sorted into manageable groups. You panic. Or it may appear that there is no information at all. You panic. A quick analysis of the topic may save you from despair—and from changing your topic!

Facets of a Topic

What facet or angle or aspect of the topic do you want to examine? Very often a topic doesn't seem broad until you start to research it, when you discover that many topics have various aspects that can be researched. Your decision about this is a crucial one.

Take a topic like "drugs" that's assigned to you in one of your courses. That topic can be examined from a surprising number of angles, and your choice of the angle will determine which information sources will be best for your research. See Figure 4-1 for examples of how the broad topic of "drugs" could be handled.

DRUGS — Some possible topics

A. Education about drugs
  1. Dangers of addictive drugs
  2. Peer pressure and drugs
  3. Use of prescriptions (e.g., insulin)

B. Society and drugs
  1. Drug abuse
     a. Societal causes of abuse
     b. Legal vs. illegal drugs
     c. Effects of drug use/abuse on society
     d. Government programs
  2. Athletics and drugs
     a. Professional athletics
     b. College athletics
     c. High school athletics
  3. Business and drugs
     a. Drug testing of employees
     b. High stress jobs and drug use
     c. Drug trafficking as a profession

C. Laws on drugs
  1. Use of prisoners in product testing
  2. Federal drug interdiction programs
  3. Mandatory sentences for drug trafficking crimes
  4. International relations and drug trafficking
  5. Federal regulations involving prescription drugs

D. Pharmacology of drugs
  1. Interactions
  2. Side effects
  3. Testing
  4. Chemical action

E. Psychology of drugs
  1. Adverse psychological effects vs. physiological efficacy of drugs
  2. Hallucinogens; etc.

F. Etc., etc.

Figure 4-1: Some Possible Facets of One Topic

Even topics that seem more focused than this obviously broad example have aspects that narrow your focus and make your research more manageable. A clue that you may be working with a topic that's too broad is the retrieval of a very large number of information sources in your first search. Often you can reduce this number easily by selecting one aspect of the many that appear in the records you scan.

A clue that you may be working with a topic that's too broad is the retrieval of a very large number of information sources in your first search.

Topics and Subject Fields

What's the difference between a topic and a subject? The words are often used interchangeably; their shared definition is that they are the "theme" of something, e.g., a book, a paper, or a sermon. When you do information research, it may be better for you to distinguish a topic from a subject. A **topic** is the idea you're researching and its **subject field** is the field of knowledge or study into which your idea (topic) fits.

You investigate a subject field for information on your topic.

The first question to ask when analyzing a topic is, What is the subject field you're researching? You may think the answer to this is easy and sometimes it is. If you're looking in the *Yellow Pages* for pizza delivery, obviously the subject field of your search is pizza. If your research paper assignment is the topic "archaeology," that may be your subject field also. But what is your subject field if your topic is the need to increase government funding for drug abuse programs? If you look up "drug abuse" in any information tool, will you always find materials that deal with government funding of rehabilitation programs? No. "Drug abuse" all by itself isn't at all indicative of the true subject field you're investigating. Your topic really is government funding of social programs with drug abuse being just one aspect of this larger topic. Government funding of social programs becomes the area in which you're likely to find information about your particular aspect, drug abuse programs. Your subject field, in this case, isn't exactly the same as your topic.

When you know the subject field of your topic, you can more easily use information resources and tools appropriate to that field.

So how do you figure out your subject field if you're not sure about it? Probably the easiest way for a college student to ascertain the subject field of any topic is to determine which college department might teach a course on it. The departments correspond to subject fields in many information systems. These fields are related in turn to information tools and sources. The topic on research funding, above, might be assigned in a sociology course because of the "social programs" aspect, or in a course in political science because the topic deals with government policy. The subject field of this topic, then, could be either sociology or political science. Figure 4-2 contains some topics and related subject fields.

Relating your topic to a subject field is not always easy. Once you learn how to discover such a relationship, you can move more quickly to the resources that are particular to the field. Using Figure 4-2 means that for the "drugs" topic, you would now know to look for information about educating patients about drugs in a nursing book rather than looking for a book on prescription drugs. You can see how much it helps to know which angle you want to follow early in your research.

Some topics fit into several subject fields at once.

There are topics that are never going to fit neatly into only one subject field. Rather, they fall into several subject fields at once.

◆ EXAMPLES

Many in the subject field of anthropology, where a study of a native people is both an examination of a society and an historical investigation of a country or geographical region

◆ ◆ ◆

Those in the subject field of women's studies, where many topics are examined from a feminine/ist viewpoint

◆ ◆ ◆

Even an apparently single-focused topic such as advertising can fit into several subject fields because it may use psychological studies as a part of marketing strategy, for example, thus combining psychology and business. Working with this type of topic is almost the reverse of examining one facet of a one-subject topic because you may need to do research in several subject fields, rather than identifying one field and limiting your research to it.

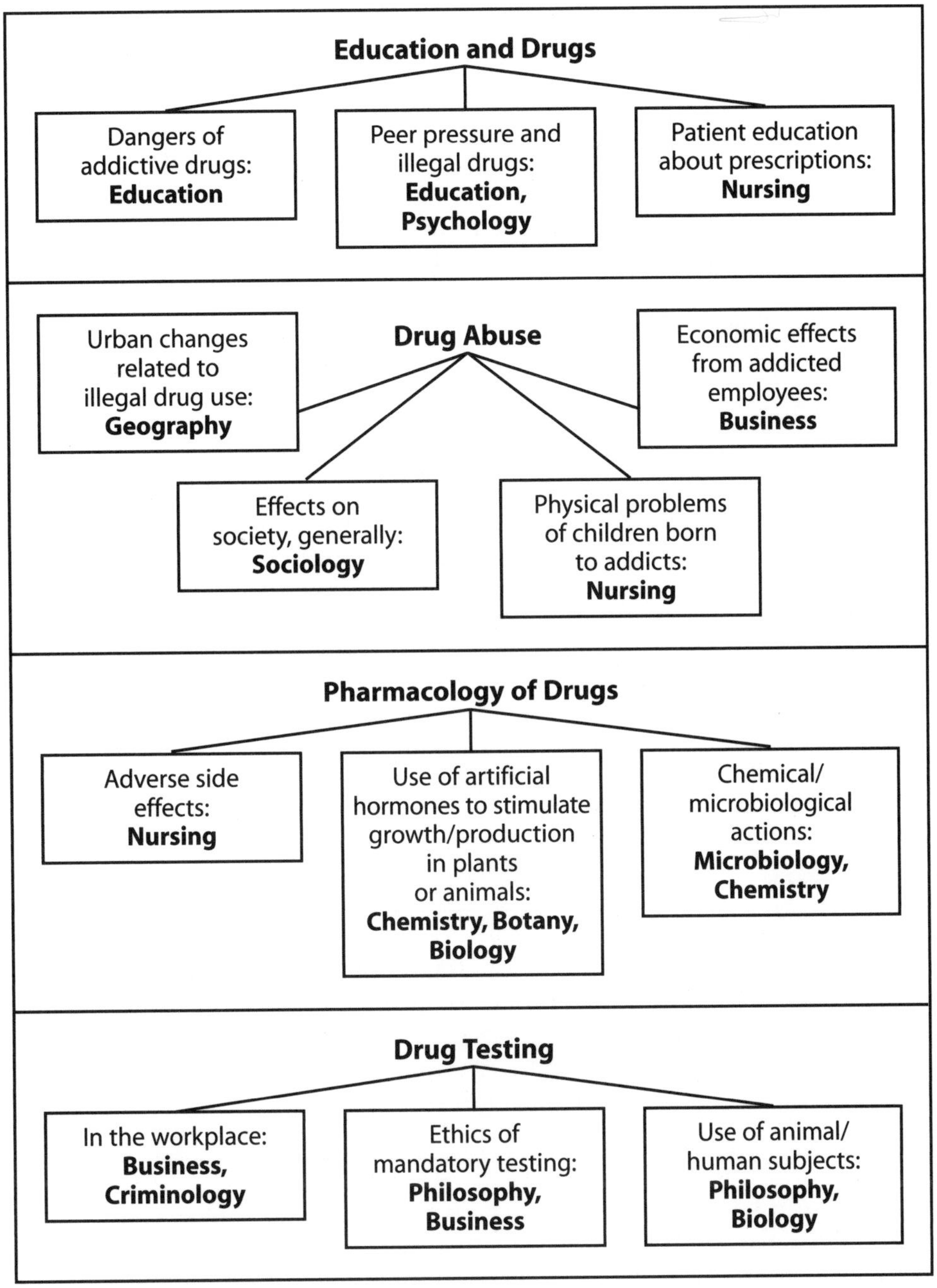

Figure 4-2: Facets of Some Topics and Possible Related Subject Fields (College Departments)

Getting Help in Analyzing Your Topic: Information Sources for Research

How can you find out what aspects there are to a topic, or if your topic fits in several subject fields? You can use information sources that give you an objective overview of the whole subject field that is the foundation for your topic. NOTE: A "source" here is distinguished from a "tool" because a source will give you information about your topic that you can use immediately, while a tool will only *refer* you to sources.

Encyclopedias and the "Introduction" sections in general books provide overviews of subject areas.

Information sources such as encyclopedias give you overviews of topics. Not only do encyclopedias provide the various facets of a subject field but most often they also use the terminology that is common to the field. Thus they introduce you to the right words to use as search terms when you continue your information research. For example, when researching some of the topics in Figure 4-2, you would learn to use the term "drug interactions" instead of looking under "effects of mixing drugs," or to use "peer groups" instead of "classmates" when investigating student-to-student drug education programs. Another information source in this category is the "Introduction" section in a general book on your subject field.

Encyclopedias, by presenting the known viewpoints in a subject field, can help you focus your research on one aspect of your original topic.

A topic will be included in an encyclopedia that covers your subject field; there will not be a whole encyclopedia about every topic.

◆ **EXAMPLE**

A student looking for a source of information on the broad topic, "African history." Looking in general sources on Africa, she comes upon information about apartheid and discovers how recently that political system was created and then abolished. The next information she seeks will deal more specifically with apartheid, and soon she knows that she really prefers her topic to focus even more narrowly on the history of apartheid.

For topics that fall into several subject fields, objective overviews will usually point them out.

◆ **EXAMPLE**

Photography, where the article in an encyclopedia of art deals as much with the technological development of photography as it does with famous artists in this medium. Thus a researcher would learn to look for information on photography both in art and technology sources, or decide to focus on just one or the other aspect of the topic.

If you're unable to find specifics on your original topic in its subject field, or if what you find is too specific, what alternatives do you have? You can go to the "discipline" in which your subject field fits and look for information there.

The Subject Field/Discipline Relationship

In information research the word discipline refers to one of three major divisions of knowledge: the disciplines are:

- **The *Sciences***
- **The *Social Sciences***
- **The *Humanities***

Each discipline includes many subject fields. (Your professor, an expert in a particular subject field, may refer to his field as a discipline, for example, "the discipline of chemistry." In order to keep our discussion clear, "discipline" will not be used that way in this book.)

Knowing the relationship of your topic to its subject field and discipline enables you to choose a research tool appropriate to your topic.

The **Sciences** discipline includes the "hard" science subject fields, such as physics, computer science, and medicine. "Soft" sciences, such as demographics and political science, are parts of the **Social Sciences** discipline. The **Humanities** include all the arts—visual, literary, and performing, and subject fields such as religion and philosophy. It's pretty easy to put some subject fields into their appropriate disciplines: mathematics and biology are obviously parts of the Sciences; sociology and education fit into the Social Sciences; literature, theater, and languages, including English, are considered Humanities.

It's harder to relate some other subject fields to just one discipline, for example, where should psychology go? Think of all those experiments with rats and monkeys; it could be a "hard" science with that empirical testing. But what about counseling, which is an important aspect of the same subject field? Does psychology fit into the Sciences or into the Social Sciences? The answer is yes . . . to both. Psychology is an *interdisciplinary* subject field that is most often considered a Social Science. Another interdisciplinary subject field may be anthropology because part of the field deals with social and cultural studies (Social Sciences) and another part deals with archaeology, considered part of history (Humanities). The subject field of history, in turn, can be included in either the Social Sciences or the Humanities. Figure 4-3 presents commonly accepted subject field/discipline relationships and the letters that represent their Library of Congress classifications—the letters that begin their LC call number(s).

The relationship between a subject field and its discipline is important to you in information research. It means that there is a broader area of knowledge in which to look for information if you're having a hard time finding it in a narrower subject field. This relationship is similar to that between a subject field and its topic.

◆ EXAMPLES

You would not find a complete encyclopedia on the Kentucky rifle, but you would find information about that particular rifle in an encyclopedia on firearms. Your topic is the rifle and the subject field is firearms.

◆ ◆ ◆

You would look for information about government funding of drug abuse programs in encyclopedias and indexes in sociology or political science, or even more broadly, in an encyclopedia or index in the social sciences, because there is no encyclopedia devoted only to government funding. (There is at least one index devoted to government publications, but not only to funding issues.)

The topic/subject field/discipline relationship provides flexibility for you to broaden or narrow your search to a manageable area.

SCIENCES
General Q

Agriculture	S	Environmental Science	TD-TJ
Astronomy	QB	Food and Nutrition	TX
Biology	QH-QR	Geology	QE
Biochemistry	QH, QD, QP	Hearing and Speech	QP, RC, RF
Biophysics	QH	Mathematics	QA
Microbiology	QR	Medicine	R
Chemistry	QD	Medical Technology	RB
Computer Science	QA76, TK	Nursing	RT
Ecology	QH	Physics	QC
Engineering	TA-TN		

SOCIAL SCIENCES
General H

Anthropology	GF-GT	Geography	G-GF
Business	HF-HJ	Law	K
Accounting	HF	Political Science	J-JX
Finance	HG	Psychology	BF, RC
Hotel & Restaurant Management	TX	Behavioral	BF
Management	HD	Clinical	RC
Marketing	HF	Sociology	HM-HX
Canadian Studies	F	Child-Family Studies	HQ
Economics	HB-HC	Criminology/Criminal Justice	HV
Education	L-LJ	Human Services	HV
Counseling	LB, BF	Social Work	HV
Elementary Education	LB	Sports	GV
Secondary Education	LB	Women's Studies	HQ
Special Education	LC		
Health Education	LB		

HUMANITIES
(No General Area for ALL Humanities)

Art	N	English Literature	PR
Graphic Arts	NC	French Language	PQ
Photography	TR	French Literature	PQ
Communications/Mass Media	P, PN	German Language	PF
History	C-F	German Literature	PT
Latin America, Canada	F	Spanish Language	PC
Non-American	D	Spanish Literature	PQ
United States	E, F	Music	M
Literature/Languages	P-PT	Philosophy	B-BD, BH-BJ
American Literature	PS	Religion	BI-BX
English Literature	PE	Theater	PN

MISCELLANEOUS

Biographies	CT	Library Science	Z
Bibliographies	Z	Military & Naval Sciences	U-V
Encyclopedias	AE		

Figure 4-3: Subject Fields by Discipline, with Library of Congress Classification Letters

Topics, Subject Fields, Disciplines, and Scope

An information source or tool may cover a wide range of topics or a narrow range of topics. The range of a source or tool is called its *scope*. The scope of a source can:

- Cover one subject field or a cluster of subject fields within a discipline.
- It can cover an entire discipline.
- It can have a general scope that encompasses subject fields from several or all the disciplines.

Depending on your topic, you might use *subject field-oriented*, *discipline-oriented*, or *general* sources and tools, alone or in combination, in your information research.

A source that covers an entire discipline is very likely to have something about the subject field in which your topic fits.

In the LC system:

- Sources and tools that cover all the Social Sciences have call numbers beginning with H.
- Tools and sources that cover all the Sciences have call numbers beginning with Q.
- The Humanities do not have one classification letter that covers all.

This means that you, as a researcher, can go to the H's (not the HA's or HV's) to find an information source such as the *International Encyclopedia of the Social Sciences,* whose scope covers the entire discipline; or to the Q's (not the QA's or QH's) for a source such as the *McGraw-Hill Encyclopedia of Science and Technology* for information about most of the subject fields included in the Sciences. This is especially good to remember when you're in a Reference Collection where the Q or H sections are relatively small and good for "browsing"—just looking at the bookshelves in a section to find information. That's where you'll find sources such as science dictionaries or social sciences encyclopedias, and where you'll be able to answer questions such as, What is the chemical formula of aspirin? or, What is the "Optimum Population Theory"?

Sources with a general scope have a little bit on everything; the more focused the source, the more detailed the information it provides.

If you follow the subject field/discipline relationship to its broadest end, you encounter sources that are general in scope, that is, they organize information from all subject fields. Examples of general sources include the *Encyclopaedia Britannica* (online and in paper), and general tools such as InfoTrac's *Expanded Academic ASAP™* online.

You may think of subject field-oriented sources as only books, because you're familiar with a whole book on a topic, for example, *Psychotropic Drugs: A Manual for Emergency Management of Overdosage.* But another subject field-oriented source would be the *Encyclopedia of Drug Abuse,* found in the HV's in your library's Reference Collection. It could be contrasted to a discipline-oriented source such as the *International Encyclopedia of the Social Sciences,* from the H's, or a general source—any encyclopedia shelved in the AE's. Subject field- and discipline-oriented tools are available in many areas. For a "drugs" topic from a medicine/sciences angle, you could use *Medline,* an index to medical periodicals, or *General Science Abstracts,* which covers periodicals from many scientific areas, including medicine.

Does a book in the Reference Room deal only with philosophy? If so, it's an example of a source that has a subject field-oriented scope.

Making the Topic/Subject Field/Discipline Relationship Work

If you're unsure about which aspect you'll investigate or about what the aspects of your topic are, or if you're unfamiliar with terminology in the field, where do you start? You can use a general source to get a description or definition of your topic's subject field, or you can use a discipline-oriented source to give a broad overview of the subject field and see what aspects can be examined. A subject field-oriented source can also give you an overview, as shown in the earlier example of the student researching apartheid.

◆ EXAMPLE

This process might be the research done by a student who looks up "drugs" in a psychology encyclopedia because the topic was assigned in his psychology class, and through this research he discovers that he'll focus on either the addictive process or on the counseling of drug users.

Use your topic's subject field and discipline to help you find reference books with relevant statistics, tables, or biographies.

You need to know about the relationship of your topic to its subject field and its discipline because the success of your information research may depend on it. If you can't find anything in a general source on the particular subject field you're researching, you have to make a decision about where to go next. You can try looking either in the broad area of the whole discipline or in a subject field-oriented source. While the general source can provide information on your topic (or almost anything), the subject field-oriented source is often a better choice because it will be more tightly focused on its field. It will use subject field-specific terminology and include a more detailed breakdown of the field than general sources.

◆ EXAMPLE

Is there little of interest in the general database *ArticleFirst* on your topic of a specific drug interaction between two prescription drugs? If you understand the topic/subject field/discipline relationship, you can now decide to use either *Medline* (subject field tool) or *General Science Abstracts* (discipline tool). When you use a subject field- or discipline-oriented source, you know you'll get more specific information immediately.

You can see how it's possible to narrow or broaden your topic as you begin to react to the information you find (or don't find). You may have in your head the perfect title for your paper or presentation. Often you find yourself looking for this exact title as you do your research! It's highly unlikely that you'll find it in information sources. What you really must do in your research is fit your topic to the information sources and systems that are available to you and gather enough information to *create* the paper with your perfect title.

Analyzing Your Topic and Using the Web

Web-surfing is not the easiest way to focus your research on a topic about which you know little!

The technology of the Internet and the World Wide Web have not changed the way you should approach your topic, especially when you're just beginning your research. There are an increasing number of search engines (see Chapters 2, 5, and 6) that you may use to search the Web. This may lead you to believe that you don't need to know your topic's subject field or its discipline to use them: you just type your topic into the search engine's text box and let it "find stuff" for you. The problem with this approach is that it is highly likely that your hard-working search engine will deliver an overwhelming amount of information to you, *not sorted* in any way that's useful to you. Many new researchers go no further than the first list of Web sites retrieved.

You can improve your research on the Web by using the same process that's described above, which sharpens the focus of your research in any information tools and sources you decide to use. You may want to use the Web to give you an idea of what's available on your topic or what some of its subfields are; in that case you're using it as you would any other general source—to begin your research. But because there is so much information accessible through the Web, this approach will take some time. If you do find an interesting angle through this approach, you will probably want to re-search the topic, looking for only the aspect that you chose for your assignment. Be sure to evaluate very carefully the information about your topic that you find on the Web!

Where to Start . . . Really

This chapter includes a lot of information that many student researchers may see as unnecessarily complicated. Their approach will continue to be to go to the computer and to type their topic in, to select the needed number of references from the first screen or two that appear, and to go on their merry way. They won't run into trouble with this approach until they reach the *end* of their work—the writing of the paper or presentation. Then there's a good chance they'll have to work hard to tie together the disparate ideas from the materials they've collected.

◆ EXAMPLE

A student needed to write a 10-page paper on "poverty" and use at least five sources. When she collected information, it was from a full-text database and a couple of neat-looking Web sites. It was her job to connect, then, (1) the article on single mothers and poverty to (2) the Web site from the Southern Poverty Law Center to (3) the article on homelessness to (4) the article on the connection between low income and drug use to (5) the Web site about trends in teen pregnancy. That would be a tough job, especially in 10 pages! It would have been far easier if she had *selected* all five sources on the same single aspect of her topic.

Many computerized resources provide information that covers a small aspect of a topic very deeply. The majority of periodical articles do this—you don't find many "overview" articles on poverty in magazines and journals. You do find articles about the many aspects of poverty. But if you don't know what all the aspects of the topic are, or which one you want to research, these narrowly focused sources can be more confusing than helpful.

Thinking about a topic at the beginning of your research takes time. But it'll pay off at the end, when you discover that you focused your *research* enough to collect materials that you can *easily* relate to each other . . . and write a good paper.

Chapter Concepts

- Topic analysis involves determining what subject field you're really investigating early in your research on the topic.
- Often the topic you're researching is one aspect of a larger subject field.
- Some topics are "interdisciplinary," meaning that they fit into more than one discipline at the same time.
- Subject fields can be grouped into three major categories or *disciplines;* they are the Sciences, the Social Sciences, and the Humanities.
- The subject field/discipline relationship in information systems allows you to broaden or narrow your research by using less or more focused sources to get information on your topic.
- The scope of an information source or tool can be subject field-oriented, discipline-oriented, or general.
- If you're unsure about what aspects there are to your topic, you can begin your research in a source that provides an overview of a field, such as a subject field or discipline encyclopedia.
- You should go through the same process of determining your topic's subject field before you use the Web for research, to help you avoid retrieving less than relevant information.
- Focused research pays off because it results in information sources that are clearly related to the topic you consciously selected.

Name: ______________________________ **Date:** ______________

Review Questions

1. As you proceed with your research you find that your topic changed and that you'll pursue a perspective of the topic different from the one you began with. For example, your paper for your Mass Media class started out with "media ethics" as its topic and now you're researching pornography. How and why did this happen? Be specific in your explanation.

____

____

____

____

____

2. Give an example of:
   - ◆ a topic that could fit into three different subject fields and name them

     ____

   - ◆ a single topic that has three different aspects that could be researched

     ____

   - ◆ a topic that would require interdisciplinary research

     ____

3. Select one topic below. Relate it to its subject field(s) and discipline (s). Explain your reasoning.

   - The right of a terminally ill person to determine what methods should or should not be used to save her/his own life
   - The Russian space travel program
   - The use of non-union workers, foreign or domestic, by U.S. companies
   - The use of national achievement tests for all students to measure the effectiveness of each school as a basis for its federal funding
   - Gay rights

   ____

   ____

   ____

   ____

   ____

4. Which topic from Question 3 above, if any, would be best served by use of primary information sources? Explain your reasoning.

   ____

   ____

   ____

   ____

   ____

5. Knowing the subject field of your research topic and the scopes of several information sources in a library's Reference Collection can make your research much more efficient. Use a specific topic as an example and explain how. (You may use one of the topics above and actual titles from the Reference Collection in your answer, but it is not required that you do so.)

   ____

   ____

   ____

   ____

   ____

Chapter 5

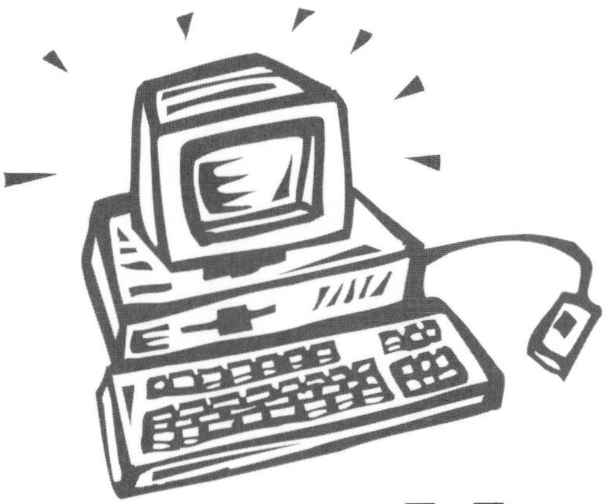

Making the Systems Work

In This Chapter, You Will Learn . . .

- About information searching using electronic tools
- How to use a subject as an access point when searching
- How a computer performs a search
- About vocabularies used in access tools
- Where to find descriptors or subject headings to use as search terms when using different access tools
- About various types of computer searching

Subject-Author Access Point

Chapter 3 on the presentation of information introduced you to access points, different ways of looking for information in an access tool. Two of these access points are author and title. Subject is another access point. It may be familiar to you because you've used an index in a book or a catalog in a library: you wanted to find information about something so you looked up the subject you were researching. This chapter will first discuss searching in electronic tools and then will focus on using subject as an access point.

How a Computer Does a Search

What you recognize as a word or phrase the computer's program perceives as a data pattern.

When you do a search in a computerized access tool:

1. You type a search term, press <Enter> and wait until the computer screen shows the records that were retrieved. What really happens in this search is that you command the computer to scan *every one* of the gazillion entries in that database to find a match for the search term you typed. The computer is a scanner; what you think of as a *word* or a *term* is nothing more than data patterns to its program.
2. After you type a search term, the computer scans through the entire text of every one of the records in its memory to find a match for that data pattern you entered.
3. It then compiles into a **set** every record in which there's a match and it shows you the results.
4. From your review of records in the set *you* select those that are appropriate to your needs.

(The word "you" is stressed to remind you that **the computer makes no decisions for you**, rather it makes data matches and *you* choose those that are relevant.)

This same type of "mechanical" scanning process is used when you look for information on the Web. Search engines work much like computerized indexes in that they scan the Web pages that they cover, looking for a match to the search term you typed, and creating sets of matching items. One important difference between a search done in a database and one done on the Web is that no Web search engine scans *all* Web pages while a database search program does scan all its content. You may use several different search engines to do your search. This will probably increase the number of hits, but there is a good deal of overlap among search engines.

A computer isn't really searching; it's scanning for a match.

The search term you use is very often a term that you think describes your research topic. Yet the computer often retrieves records that seem to be completely unrelated to the topic. You need to understand how indexes, especially computerized periodicals indexes and library catalogs, provide subject access. This understanding will help you get "cleaner" results in all your searches.

Subject as Access Point

The most common way for you to do information research, an approach that is pretty efficient, is to look in one place for references to numerous information sources that are on the same subject as your topic. Rather than looking for a source by one particular author or one book with a certain title, you search by subject. You look up a subject in an access tool to see what records on your topic are grouped there.

Not all access tools use the same word or phrase to describe your subject. You often have to look under different terms in different tools. A typical subject search in three access tools might proceed like this:

1. You type "DATE RAPE" into InfoTrac's *Expanded Academic ASAP*™ on the computer to get periodical articles on the topic. The computer screen reads,

   DATE RAPE

   See Acquaintance rape

2. You move to the term "acquaintance rape." You've analyzed your topic and you know that you want only the records on one aspect of this topic, dating situations, so you scan all that were retrieved under "acquaintance rape" and print only those that deal with dating.
3. You then go to the library's catalog and look for information under "acquaintance rape" because you just learned from your periodicals index search that it might be better to use this term in the catalog as a subject heading. It is. You find a few entries in the catalog and write down their call numbers.
4. You decide to check one more access tool, *Women's Studies Abstracts.* When you look in this tool you discover that the term to use here is "date rape" because "acquaintance rape" is used to describe a slightly different phenomenon from what you're interested in.
5. After reading the abstracts of articles in this tool you print the citations of those most relevant to your research, and collecting all your newfound references, you go off in search of the articles, books, and videocassettes you've discovered.

You've just done a "subject search." What went on in that process?

Subject Headings and Descriptors

Information is very often organized by subject matter. What does this mean? It means that a person working for a particular library or for the publisher of a periodicals index looks at the contents of an information source (a book, periodical or newspaper article, or a videotape) and decides what that source is about, what its subject is. In a library, a catalog librarian assigns the source, most often a book, a small number of **subject headings** that describe the source's subjects, and puts a call number on the source so that it will be put on a shelf with other items that have similar subject content. At a periodicals indexing company, the process is very similar, only the person is usually indexing periodical articles. The indexer assigns several terms to **describe the subject of the information source.** These terms may be called **descriptors** or subject headings.

The librarian or indexer then puts an entry for the source into the access tool. In a library catalog the entry is a catalog record. The complete record includes author, title, publishing information, subject headings, and call number. In a periodicals database the entry may be just the bibliographic citation for an article—author, article title and page numbers, periodical title, volume, and date. It may be the citation with descriptors and an abstract. An increasing number of online databases include the citation and the entire text of the article—sometimes with an abstract, too!

Subject headings and descriptors are assigned by humans who look at the content of information sources.

The work of the catalogers and indexers make it possible for you to use a subject as an access point; descriptors/subject headings are access points in almost all access tools. All records for a particular subject are listed under the appropriate heading. In paper tools the subject headings are listed alphabetically, but alphabetical order isn't important to you in a computerized tool. See Figure 5-1 for examples from several access tools of subject headings/descriptors.

```
                          SUNY Plattsburgh Library
                          Search by Subject Heading
                                               (Approx. 175 headings)
Search request: RAPE
                                               Help key for assistance
  1:*    3 rec.  Acquaintance rape
  2:*    4 rec.     RT Dating violence
  3:*    1 rec.  Acquaintance rape--Georgia--Atlanta--Fiction
  4:*    7 rec.  Acquaintance rape--United States
  5:*    2 rec.  Acquaintance rape--United States--Case studies
  6:*    1 rec.  Acquaintance rape--United States--Prevention
  7:     1 rec.  Acquaintance rape--United States--Prevention--Handbooks,
                 manuals, etc.
  8:*    1 rec.  Gang rape--California
  9:     1 rec.  Gang rape--New Jersey--Glen Ridge
 10:     1 rec.  Gang rape--United States--Case studies
 11:     1 rec.  Male rape--Great Britain--Psychological aspects
 12:     1 rec.  Male rape victims--Great Britain--Psychology
 13:     1 rec.  Pope, Alexander, 1688-1714. Rape of the lock
 14:*    2 rec.  Pope, Alexander, 1688-1744. Rape of the lock

PF1: Cancel                                                  <Next Scrn>
Select one or more headings: _

Connected 0:00:50   VT100   TCP/IP   SCROLL   CAPS   NUM   Capture   Print echo
```

Figure 5-1A: (A) Subject Headings in a Library's Online Catalog

Rape

See also

Acquaintance rape

Attitudes toward rape

Rape victims

Statutory rape

Trials (Rape)

Heterosexual and homosexual coercion, sexual orientation and sexual roles in medical students, N. McConaghy and R. Zamir. Bibl *Arch Sex Behav* v24 p489–402 O '95

In search of gender justice: sexual assault and the criminal justice system. J. Gregory and S. Lees. bibl *Fem Rev* no48 p80–93 Aut '94

"It's hard to change what we want to change: rape crisis

Figure 5-1B: (B) A Paper Periodicals Index

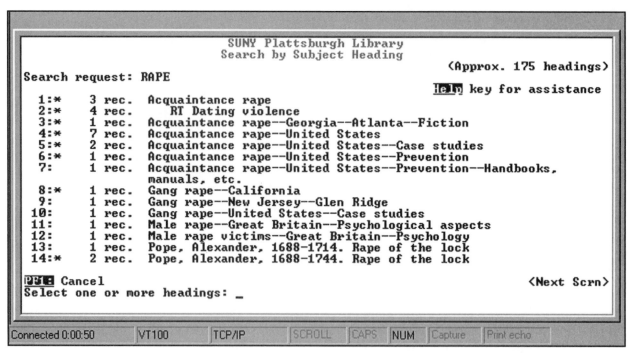

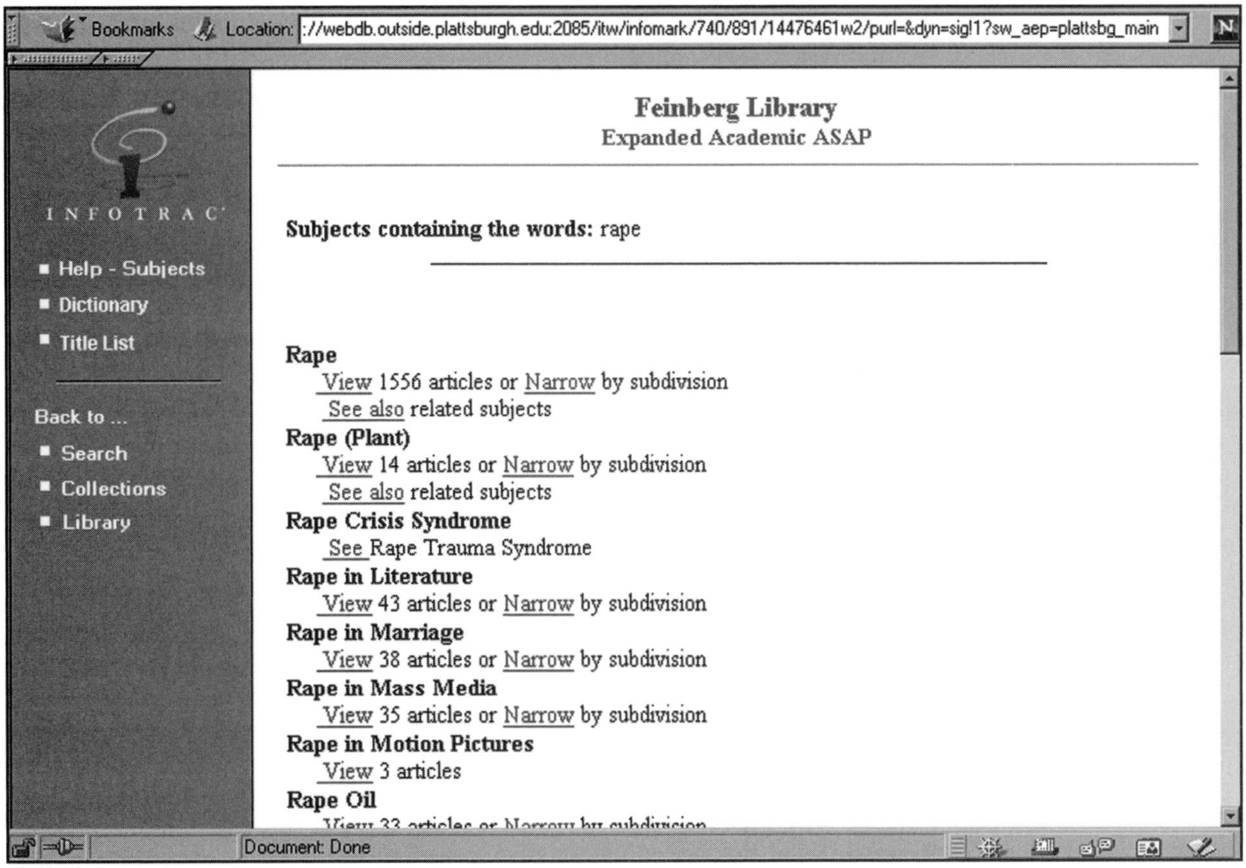

Figure 5-1C: (C) "Subjects" List in a Periodicals Database—InfoTrac Expanded Academic ASAP™

"Subject Headings" or "Descriptors"

Throughout the discussion above the terms descriptor and subject heading are used interchangeably. Are they really the same thing? In most tools they are. Both are names for the subject access point in access tools. But some tools distinguish between subject headings and descriptors. The surest way to use these terms correctly and efficiently in any tool is to find that tool's explanation of each. Use the Help screens in a computerized tool and the introductory pages in a paper tool to find out whether it uses "subject heading" or "descriptor" as its subject access point. You also must discover the field tag for the one used so that you can search the tool successfully.

Vocabularies in Access Tools

Controlled Vocabulary Systems

In the above search on date rape you discovered the vocabularies of the access tools you used. Some of the tools required you to use *acquaintance rape* as a subject heading or descriptor, although you had started with the search term *date rape* in mind. When an access tool requires you to use its terminology, it's an illustration of how the tool is controlling your search vocabulary. A tool that forces you to use its terms—saying "See . . ." or "Use . . ." rather than performing the search immediately—operates under a **controlled vocabulary** system. This type of system is one in which an indexer, in assigning subject headings/descriptors to information sources, is limited to a specified list of terms that you as a searcher are also limited to.

◆ Example

An indexer cannot decide on one day to put sources about date rape under *date rape* and on another day to put them under *acquaintance rape* and on yet another day to put them under *violence in dating situations* and on still another day to put them under *sexual assault by known person(s)*, and so on.

A controlled vocabulary limits the terms an indexer can use; in this case, the one term used to describe sources about date rape is *acquaintance rape*. You also could be limited to the approved list of subject headings/descriptors, although this is not the case with most databases.

Uncontrolled Vocabularies

Figure 5-2 is an illustration of a person/situation, which can be described in various ways. Below the illustration is a list of terms that were suggested by students to describe the illustration.

How many of these terms would you actually use in an access tool to look for information on this condition? Not too many? You're right. The list with the illustration is an example of an *uncontrolled* vocabulary, one that uses any number of words and terms for the same concept. Your "unofficial" list, the one that includes slang and everyday terminology, has

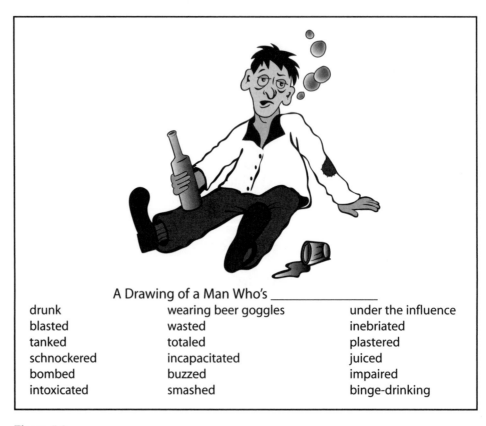

A Drawing of a Man Who's ________

drunk	wearing beer goggles	under the influence
blasted	wasted	inebriated
tanked	totaled	plastered
schnockered	incapacitated	juiced
bombed	buzzed	impaired
intoxicated	smashed	binge-drinking

Figure 5-2

significantly more terms than the list of "official" terms, those you would use in research. Why is there such a difference? It's likely that you believe (correctly) that you can't look in most information sources under slang terms or terms that change frequently the way some "buzzwords" do. Why not?

The shorter list of terms you think of as "official" includes terms that are more formal than those in your own vocabulary list. These formal terms are ones that are used in serious discussions of a subject, or in information sources of a nature more scholarly than everyday conversation. There's a standardization of terminology that you're aware of intuitively: you would be much more likely to look for information on the condition of the fellow above under the terms *alcoholic impairment* or *drunkenness* than under *blasted* or *wearing beer goggles*.

You instinctively know not to use slang to look for scholarly information.

There are several reasons that standardized terminology is used in access tools. Two of these include:

- Buzzwords that become outdated quickly aren't used because they change too rapidly. Many slang words fall into this category. Examples abound: the bee's knees, square, hip, groovy, far out, gnarly.
- Overly technical terms will be unknown to a large segment of the researchers using some tools.

But specialized terms, or jargon, are commonly used in access tools that are subject-oriented and they may be used in general access tools when more common terms are less accurate. Examples of such terms are ozone layer, DNA, and aerobic.

Slang or highly technical terms are not what you would use in research, or at least you wouldn't try them first when you look up a subject in an access tool. You do try terms that could be considered standard English. You're often successful when you take this approach, finding that "adolescent pregnancy" is more successful than "unwed teen mothers," for example, or that the term "acquaintance rape" is used in an access tool but "forced sex" isn't. The standardized terms that you use in most access tools are part of the controlled vocabulary that's used by each tool.

Descriptors/subject headings are usually standard English words and phrases.

What does a controlled vocabulary indexing system mean to you, the researcher? It means that once you discover the term used by an access tool to describe your topic, you can find all records to sources about that topic under that term in that tool. As you discovered in the search process described above, use of the same or similar terms often overlaps among several tools. Frequently there are also closely related terms that are used to describe subjects similar to that of the one term. For example, there are two LC subject headings, ACQUAINTANCE RAPE and DATING VIOLENCE, that describe subjects that are obviously closely related but not quite the same phenomenon. A well-controlled vocabulary allows for fine distinctions such as this, making your research very efficient once you've discovered the most appropriate subject heading for your topic. This approach works especially well if you've had a chance to see which descriptors/subject headings the tool considers to be related. You can see these relationships in the *thesaurus* that the tool may provide.

A thesaurus provides you with controlled vocabulary terms and their relationships.

Thesauri (or Thesauruses)

Some access tools supply the list of their controlled vocabulary terms in a **thesaurus.** You may have used a thesaurus in the past to find synonyms when writing a paper. In the case of an access tool, the thesaurus isn't a list of synonyms but rather **is a list of descriptors/subject headings that shows you relationships** that the tool establishes among its controlled terms. These relationships usually include a *main term* with its *broader and narrower terms* (BTs and NTs) and other *related terms* (RTs) that can't be put easily into a hierarchical arrangement with the main term. See the section below, "Free-Text Searches to Find Your Topic's Descriptor(s)."

A thesaurus usually labels its terms clearly so that you can easily select those most relevant to your research. Examples of thesaurus entries are given in Figure 5-3. They are taken from a thesaurus that is used and available in many libraries, the *Thesaurus of Psychological Index Terms.* It details the controlled vocabulary for the *PsycINFO* database and its paper counterpart, *Psychological Abstracts.* The thesaurus is often included on the com-

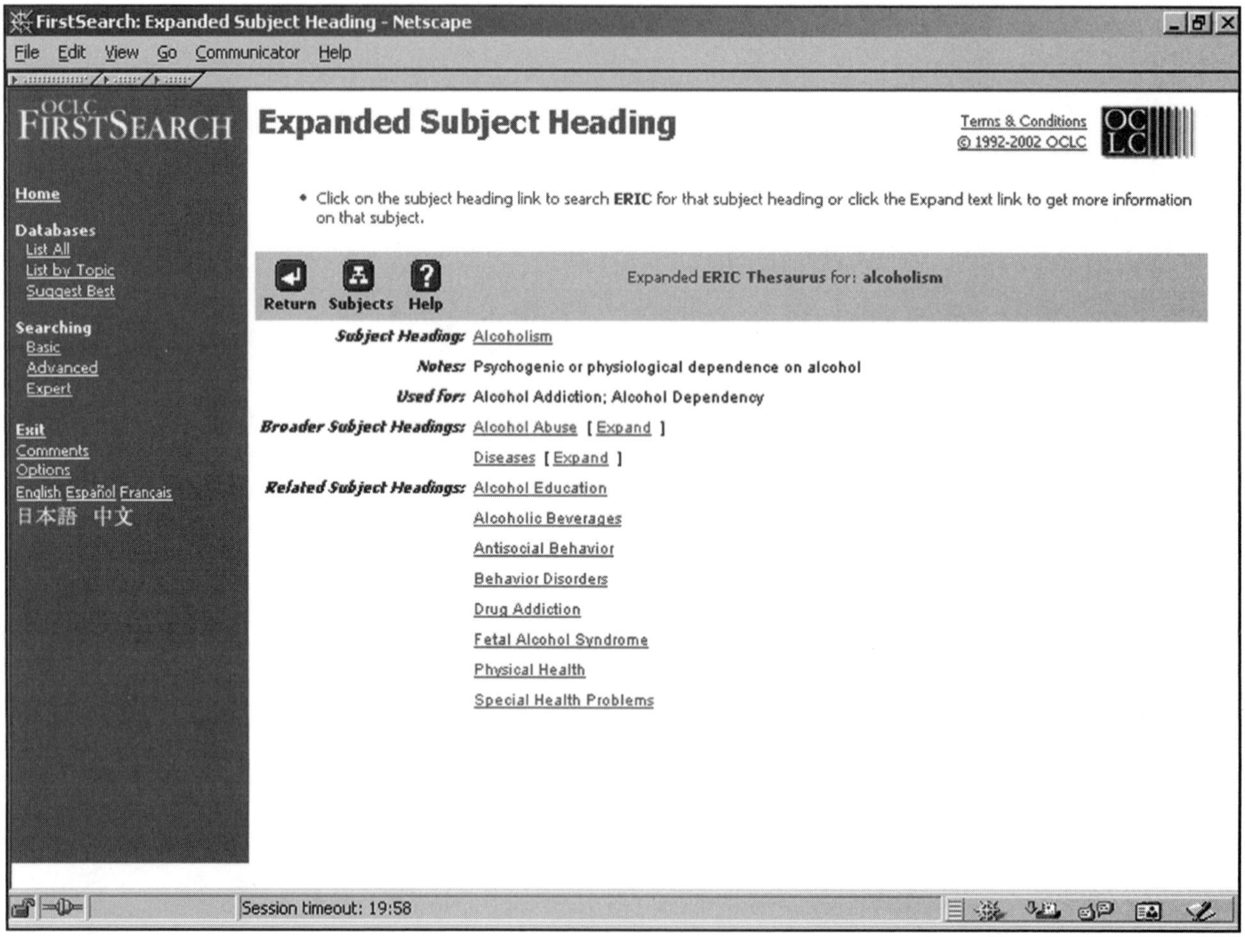

Figure 5-3: Examples of Thesaurus Entries

puter with *PsycINFO.* If the entire thesaurus isn't available online with a database, you may use other ways to discover the authorized terms for your topic.

You also can use a thesaurus to help you analyze a topic. You can get an idea of the facets of a broad topic in the narrower terms, or you can use the broader terms to look for information on your topic if your focus appears to be too narrow. Related terms can help you understand how a term is defined in a tool, and may suggest a more precise or more appropriate descriptor to use.

Subject Searching by Computer

Now you know where to find descriptors or subject headings to use as search terms when you use different access tools. Do you always have to use a controlled vocabulary when you want to do a computer search? That's a good question.

The type of computer search described above, that is, typing *date rape* and pressing <Enter>, is a **free-text search.** This could also be called an uncontrolled vocabulary search of sorts. In a free-text search the computer finds all matches for your search term wherever they appear, in any field of any record regardless of the context in which that term occurs. When you use *alcohol abuse* as a search term in the *PsycINFO* database, the computer actually performs the search illustrated in Figure 5-4.

No.	*Records*	*Request*
#1:	38400	alcohol
#2:	50993	abuse
#3:	14266	alcohol abuse

Figure 5-4: A Free-Text Search in *PsycINFO*

Figure 5-4 shows that there are thousands of records in a psychology tool that use the word *alcohol* and even more that use the word *abuse.* The computer had to scan through all 89,393 records that included each word to sort for only those that included both . . . and then the words are not necessarily adjacent to one another (forming the phrase *alcohol abuse*) and therefore not carrying the meaning you want. See Figure 5-5 for one of the records found in this search; the words in the search term are circled.

This search would be much more efficient if the searcher would find the controlled vocabulary term for the concept and search for articles on it. In other words, now would be a good time to use the thesaurus and find a descriptor.

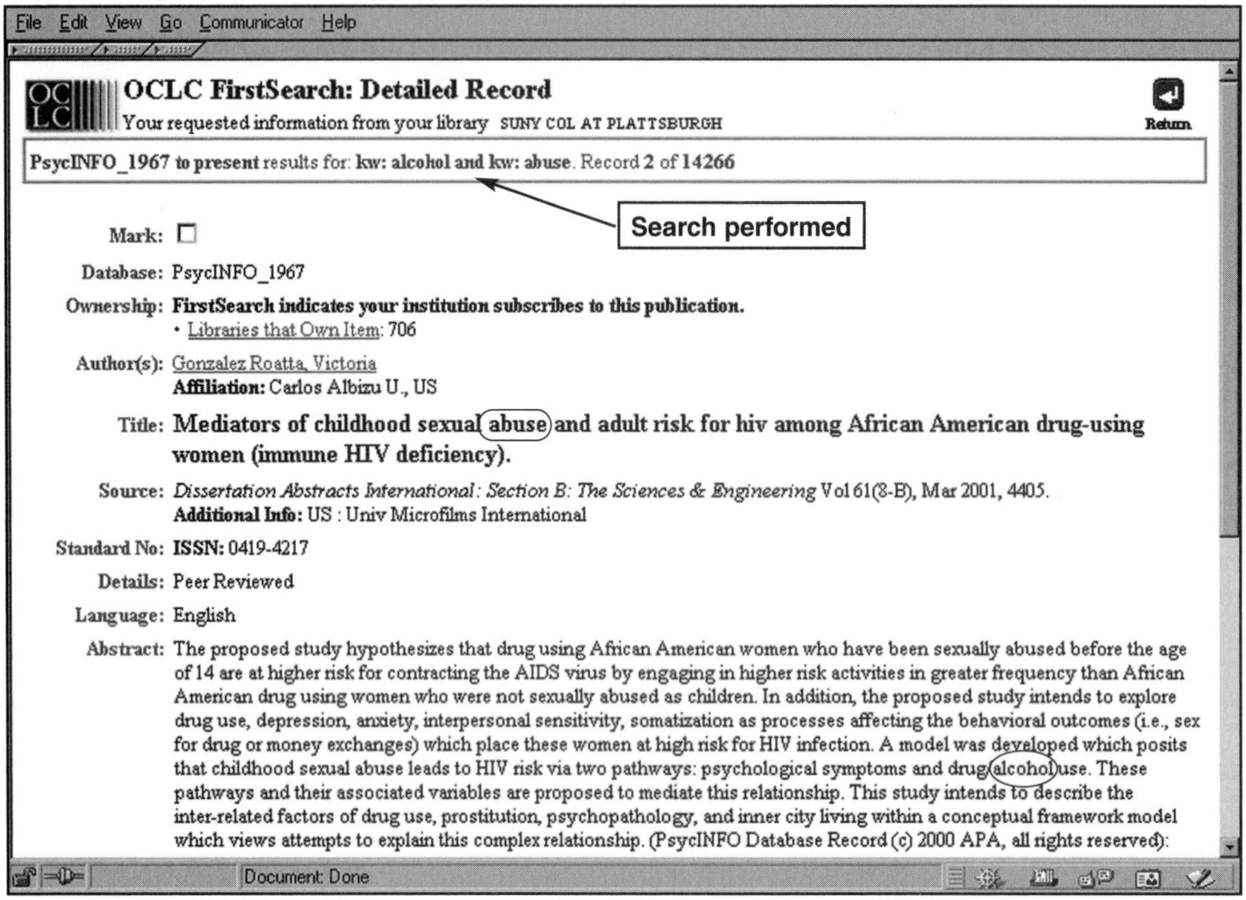

Figure 5-5: A Record Retrieved in the Free-Text Search from Figure 5-4 (PsycINFO Database)

Searching by Descriptor

A descriptor is a term that describes the content of a source.

How will searching by descriptor change your search? When you select a term from a tool's thesaurus and use it as a search term it affects your search in two ways:

- First, it limits the number of fields that the computer scans to only one field, the descriptor/subject heading field. Obviously this reduces the search time significantly.
- Second, the fact that you're using a descriptor as a search term means that the records retrieved will actually be **about** the term used; they won't be records that just happen to have the term anywhere in them. Remember that a descriptor was assigned to that source by someone who has examined it and therefore the descriptor *describes* the subject of the source. An illustration of the difference between a free-text search of the concept *alcohol abuse* and a search for materials on the same concept using the descriptor *alcohol abuse* can be seen by comparing Figure 5-4 to Figure 5-6.

The search statement in Figure 5-6 reads "su = 'alcohol abuse'." The phrase *su* = tells the computer to search only in the "subject" (descriptor)

No.	Records	Request
#1:	5264	su = "alcohol abuse"

Figure 5-6: Descriptor Search in *PsycINFO*

field. Therefore the search results won't include false hits such as the record from the free-text search (Figure 5-5) and the number of records retrieved will be significantly lower. This is clearly a case where less is better!

Using a thesaurus can help you avoid the lengthy wait of a free-text search in which the computer scans hundreds of thousands of records for one term that is present in many records, and can instead make a search faster and more focused from the beginning. Some researchers ask if a computer search, because it is a scan of complete records, is always more thorough than one done by hand. You can see that scanning entire records may be thorough, but it may actually make the search far less efficient than one restricted to a particular field through your use of an approved descriptor.

When to Do Free-Text Searches

Does all the discussion above mean that you can't ever use free-text searching and get what you need? Not at all. Sometimes the controlled vocabulary terms in a tool simply don't capture the idea you're seeking. Certain topics use extremely specific terms that are your easiest access points.

Free-text searches can be used most efficiently in particular instances.

◆ Examples

If you need information about a particular psychological test, the most efficient search strategy is to use the title of the test as a free-text search term.

◆ ◆ ◆

If the concept you're researching is very new and there's not yet a controlled vocabulary term for it, you should try the term that's being used in the field as a free-text search term.

◆ ◆ ◆

Information about an approach to classroom discipline that's called "assertive discipline" isn't found easily in education tools using the controlled vocabulary terms for discipline, but is found very quickly using the phrase "assertive discipline" as a free-text search term.

These are instances in which free-text searching is your best approach.

Some tools use only a free-text approach and don't give you the opportunity to command the computer where to scan. There currently are no controlled vocabulary approaches to the information available on the Web. Some search engines allow you to limit the scan to specified fields, e.g., the title of the site, its URL (address), or its summary; many also permit you to use multi-term search strategies (see the discussion of Boolean searching below), but there is not yet a search engine that allows you to use descriptors, search terms used by human site-reviewers that truly describe the contents of Web sites. After a few forays into this vast plain of information

Searches of the Web are most often free-text searches.

There currently are no controlled vocabulary approaches to the information available on the Web.

you'll discover that since you cannot limit your searches by using descriptors, you must do it by using sophisticated search strategies.

Free-Text Searches to Find Your Topic's Descriptor(s)

Many periodicals databases include a feature that provides you with the opportunity to perform a controlled vocabulary search even though the databases' thesauri aren't available to you. These databases include "live links" from some fields included in the records. This means that you can use a free-text search to find records that **might** be relevant, and from those retrieved, go to the descriptor (subject) field and use the descriptor links to focus your search.

◆ **EXAMPLE**

The topic *"reading difficulties."* When a researcher uses that phrase as a beginning search term the computer retrieves 5,143 records. From a record that included the phrase in the title of the information source—so that the researcher is confident that the source is relevant—the researcher clicked on the **descriptor** *READING DIFFICULTIES* and found 3,402 sources on the topic. All 3,402 use that term to describe their contents so they are bound to be more relevant than at least 1,741 of those originally retrieved. If you remember that links are almost always underlined and in a color different from plain text, you'll know immediately if a database offers the "live link" feature.

◆

A successful search frequently requires you to use several search terms. The terms may be descriptors only, free-text terms only, or a combination of the two. For example, you may start a search with a free-text approach, find at least one appropriate descriptor, and continue the search using both. This often works well when you want to limit your focus to a particular age group or gender.

◆ **EXAMPLE**

A search on the use of assertive discipline . . . but only at the high school level. You could search using *assertive discipline* and then find the appropriate descriptor for your desired age group, in this case, HIGH SCHOOL STUDENTS.

◆

The main thing to remember is to choose a technique that will work well with the topic being researched and the tool being used. Be prepared to try several methods in various tools. Flexibility is a characteristic of good research.

Searches Using More Than One Search Term

Boolean Searching in Computerized Tools

When you're doing research on a focused topic in an organized database such as a periodicals index or a library catalog, you often have to look under only one search term to get relevant records. For example, *Buddhism* is a particular name referring to a particular religion, and using it alone will result in many records you can review and select from. But even though *Buddhism* sounds very focused and easily researched, it can be too broad; in other words, it can result in far too many records being retrieved to make your review easy. In a paper tool you have the luxury of scanning a whole page and your eyes often adjust quickly to searching for subheadings or other visual clues that narrow the focus of your search. In a computer you don't always have this luxury, and it's sometimes hard to remember that the computer makes no decisions for you. You may have to narrow your search by entering at least one additional search term. You're now moving into **Boolean searching.**

Boolean searching in an electronic tool or on the Web allows you to manipulate sets of records that have terms matching your search terms. It requires that you use more than one search term and that you connect the terms with a **Boolean operator** (read further). The three steps in Boolean searching are:

1. The computer scans for one search term and compiles all the records with that term into a set, Set 1.
2. Then it scans for the second search term you type and it groups all those records into a separate set, Set 2.
3. Next it searches through the two sets for records that appear in both, related according to the meaning of the Boolean operator you used. This action results in a new set, Set 3.

If you remember "set theory" from your math education, you're already familiar with what happens in a Boolean search.

◆ EXAMPLE

You could use the term *Buddhism* as your first term and the descriptor *afterlife* as your second. A Boolean search connecting these terms with the operator AND would retrieve only the records that somehow include both *Buddhism and afterlife.*

Boolean Operators

You have to use a Boolean operator to manipulate sets in a search that uses Boolean logic. **Boolean operators are AND, OR, NOT.** These operators may look like regular words, but they aren't. They are powerful *commands* that tell the computer to re-scan the sets it has compiled and to separate out only those records that each command allows. Figures 5-7, 5-9, and 5-11, called Venn diagrams, illustrate how the sets of records are scanned using different operators and then compiled.

The operator **AND** requires that the records include all search terms that were connected by the operator. You would type the search statement *Buddhism AND afterlife* so that you get only those articles that include BOTH your search terms. Those articles are in Set 3, represented by the overlapping shaded area in the Venn diagram (Figure 5-7).

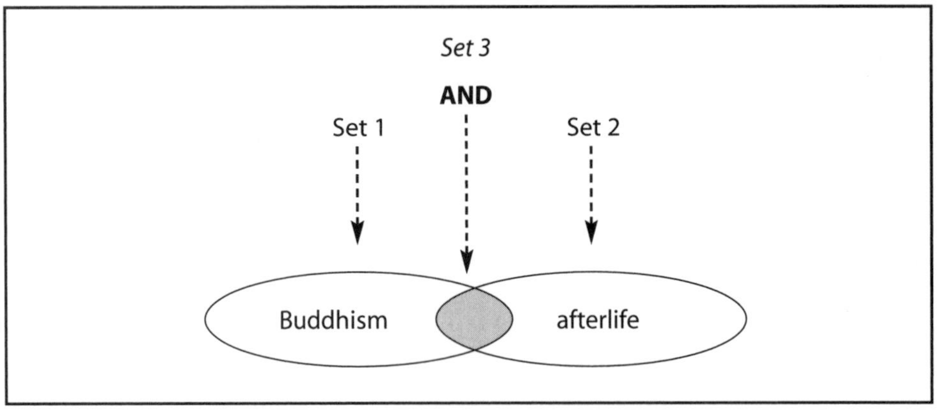

Figure 5.7

Figure 5-8 shows the steps that occur in a search using the Boolean operator AND. All records in this set "R3" must have BOTH search terms.

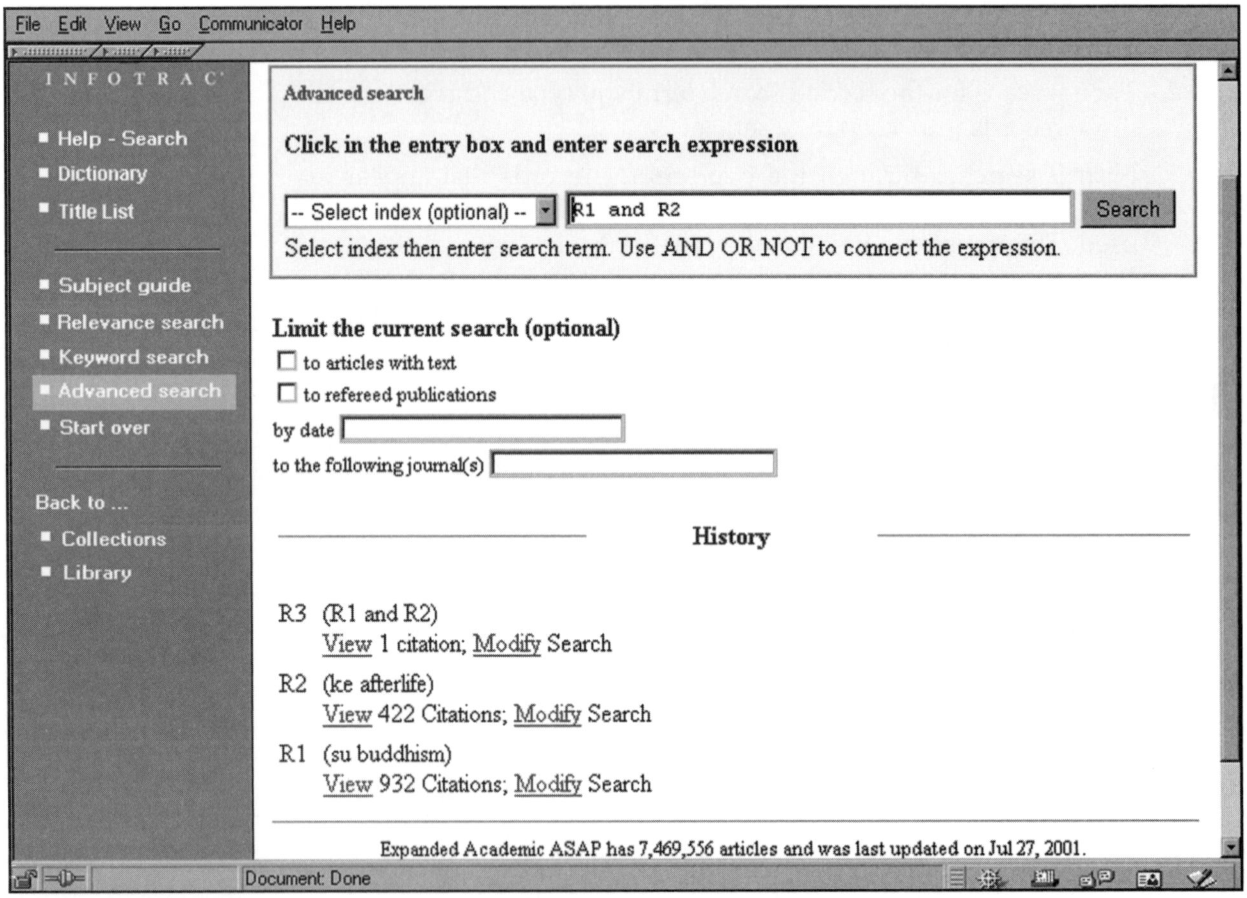

Figure 5-8: A Sample Search in InfoTrac's *Expanded Academic ASAP*™ Using the Boolean Operator *AND*

The operator **OR** commands the computer to compile a set of records that includes any *one or more* of the search terms connected by the operator. **OR** is used with synonyms or closely related terms; an example of this is *afterlife* OR *reincarnation*. Those areas are represented by the shaded area in Figure 5-9.

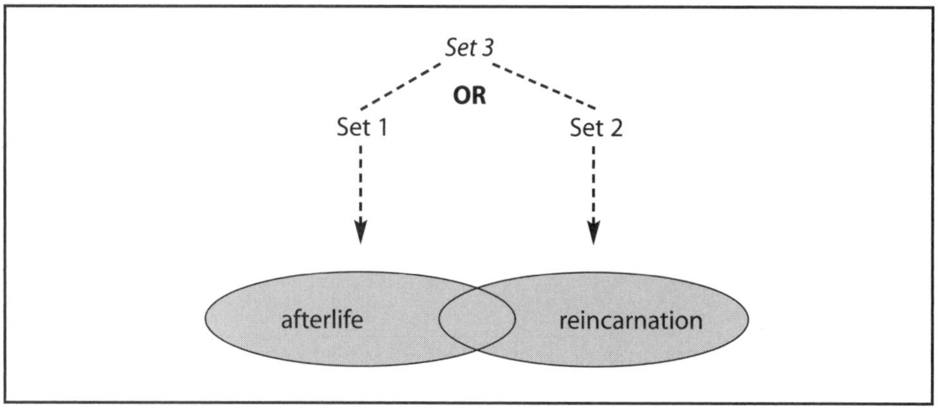

Figure 5-9

It's possible for you to use more than one operator at a time. Figure 5-10 shows a search using both AND *and* OR in the same search. The search statement for such a strategy would include parentheses, much as you must enclose mathematical operations within parentheses in equations: *Buddhism* AND (*afterlife* OR *reincarnation*). The search terms within the parentheses are described as "nested." See the bottom of the screen in Figure 5-10 to see the search statement with nested terms.

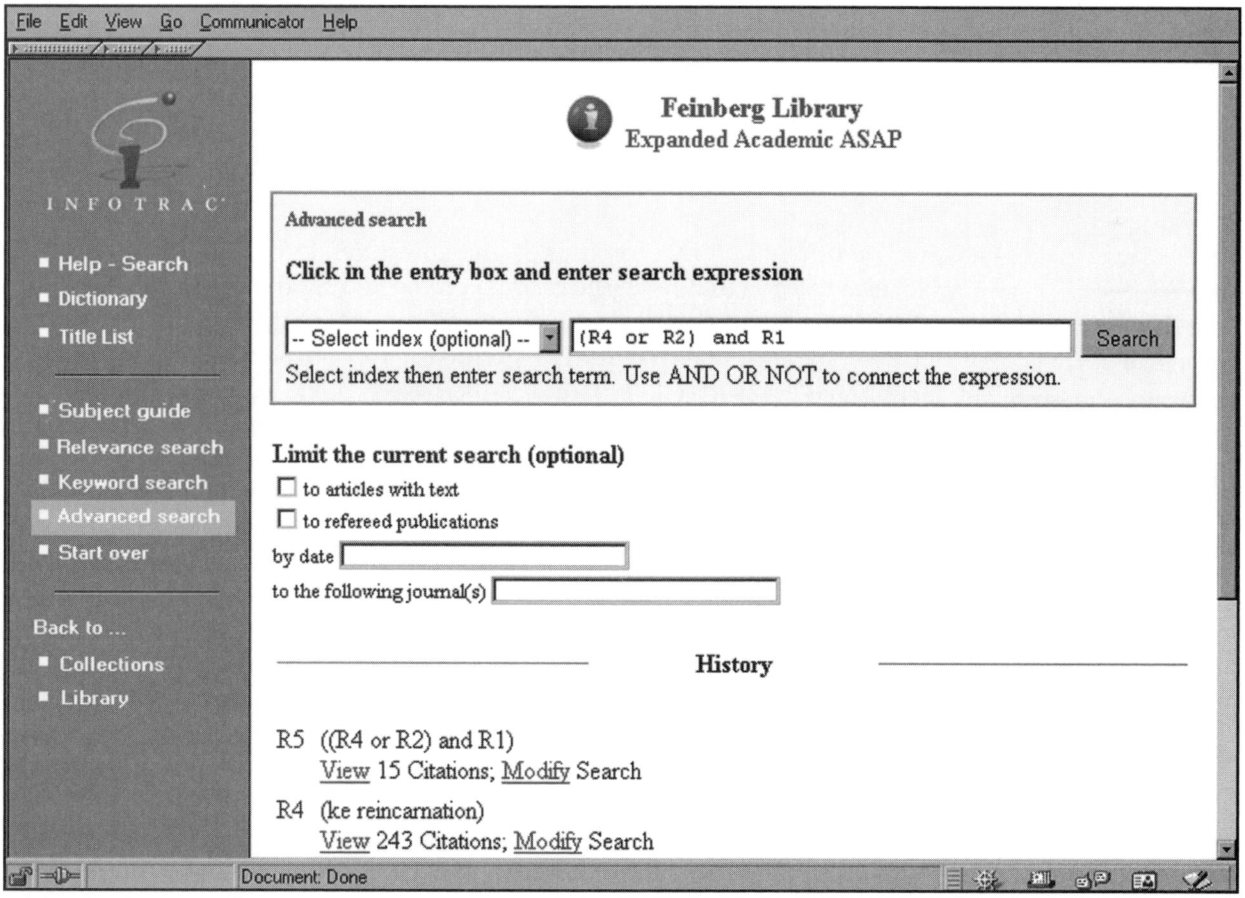

Figure 5-10: A Search in InfoTrac's *Expanded Academic ASAP*[a] Using Two Boolean Operators

Figure 5-11 shows a Venn diagram of the search in Figure 5-10. The shaded area represents all articles in the database that include the terms *Buddhism* AND *afterlife* OR *Buddhism* AND *reincarnation.*

If you were to require the articles to be about Buddhism and afterlife *and* reincarnation, articles that would possibly compare the notions of reincarnation with life after death and then deal with them *both* from a Buddhist perspective, your resulting set would be the darkly shaded area in Figure 5-11.

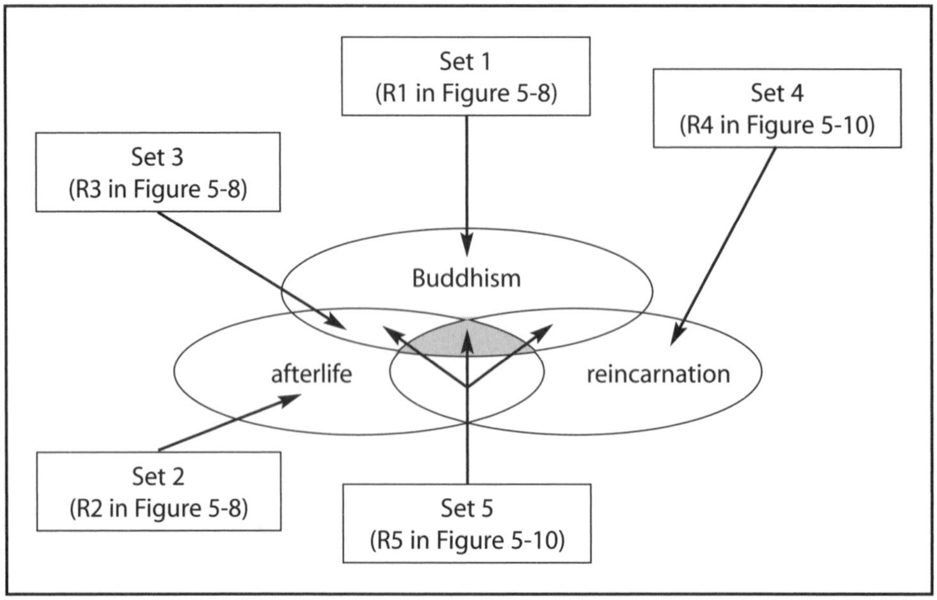

Figure 5-11: A Venn Diagram of a Search Using Two Boolean Operators

The Boolean operator AND narrows a search; OR broadens it.

The operator **NOT** commands the computer to exclude from the final set any records that have the term(s) connected by the operator. For example, if you typed *Buddhism NOT Zen,* all records that included *Zen* for any reason, in any context, would be excluded. You can see that the use of NOT could have results you hadn't anticipated; very possibly some of the records about Buddhism would only mention the word *Zen* and actually would be records that were relevant to your research on *Buddhism* and *reincarnation,* but the use of the operator NOT eliminated them from the set you could review. Using a common search engine on the Web, for example, a search using the word *Buddhism* resulted in 338,640 pages retrieved (as of July 2001—up from 2,130 in 1997!). "NOT-ing" out *Zen* dropped that number to 288,470. It's impossible to guess how many of those 100,170 sites that were eliminated might have been relevant. The best advice is to use this operator with extreme caution, or not at all without help from a librarian.

Boolean operators are powerful commands and they can make your research in a computerized tool very clean and efficient.

- **AND** narrows a search because it requires that all records have more than one search item. It can reduce very quickly the number of retrieved records.

- **OR** broadens a search because it retrieves records that include your original search term or any synonym you enter. This is a very helpful technique when you are finding too few records on a topic.

  NOTE: The biggest difficulty with **AND** and **OR** is that they look so much like regular words, but they function the opposite way.

- **NOT** is one that must be used with extreme care because it can exclude records you actually could use. **NOT** is used very carefully even by experienced searchers.

Search engines have allowed Boolean searching from their beginnings. They perform invisible Boolean searches when you enter a multi-word phrase, just as many periodicals databases do. It's for this reason that many search engines encourage you to put quotation marks around search terms that are multi-word phrases. Without the quotation marks the search engine does a scan for each term separately, then "ANDs" them together. This often results in an overwhelming number of hits, many of which aren't relevant at all. Protocols for intentional Boolean searches may vary from search engine to search engine, just as they vary among databases. For example, some search engines ask you to put a plus-sign (+) in front of words you require in the sites retrieved while *AllTheWeb,* among others, offers an "Advanced Search" page to allow you to select Boolean operators—but they're written as "must contain" rather than AND.

You can do a Boolean search on a computer in an amazingly short time either in a database or on the Web, and your search can be very successful, depending on the terms that you type. This is a good way to use descriptors or subject headings. Even Web searches go better with those (usually) more precise search terms. It also works well to combine free-text terms with descriptors, or with other free-text terms. "Performing a Boolean search" sounds a little scary but you already do it frequently . . . and painlessly!

Analyzing a Topic for Boolean Searching

Boolean searching requires that you break down your research topic into its component concepts. The components must be separated in order to command the computer to make sets using Boolean operators.

Almost all topics have at least two concepts in them that can be identified, and then combined using Boolean operators.

◆ EXAMPLE

Many librarians have watched a novice researcher type a statement such as *women as stereotypes in advertising* and leave the computer frustrated because the student kept getting "0 records" as her response. Why did this happen? The researcher didn't understand that the computer could not separate out the components of her topic statement; it scanned for the data-pattern *[women as stereotypes in advertising]* and found no exact matches. There may have been records in the scanned database that had phrases such as "women are portrayed stereotypically in many ads," or "the woman's role in this advertisement demonstrates stereotyping," but these were not *identical* to the phrase the computer was trying to match. Computer programs are improving in this area and make attempts to search for phrases when they are somewhat common. But with the above topic the researcher needed to break out the separate parts that made up the whole. She was really looking for information about women, information about stereotypes, and information about advertising. She then would have commanded to scan for women AND stereotypes AND advertising. If the computer had received that command, it probably would have retrieved a usable number of usable records.

This breakdown of a topic into its conceptual components is something that you would do intuitively when glancing through a column of records in a paper tool: you would select only those that have the components you want. You probably would not copy down all the citations you find, not only because you want to shorten the number you have to hand copy but also because you want to copy only those you consider relevant, those that have all your concepts. If an experienced information researcher, such as a librarian, examined the list of records you copied from a paper tool, he would probably see a common thread running through them, one that you may not even have been aware of. For example, if you had looked in the paper index, *Business Periodicals Index,* under the descriptor *women in advertising,* you would have selected only those citations that seemed to you to deal with *stereotyping.* You would have made intuitive decisions about the aspects of your topic that you thought were present in the citations you copied.

Breaking your topic into its actual components helps you control the amount of information you retrieve.

An easy way to identify the concepts is to write down your topic and then break it apart, putting separate concepts into separate columns. The topic of "classroom discipline" is easily separated because not all discussions of discipline, even in education sources, deal with classrooms. And if you're really looking for discipline techniques to use in the classroom, "techniques" becomes a third concept. Your search statement would go from *classroom discipline* to *classroom* AND discipline AND technique**. (See Chapter 6 for information about the asterisks in this search statement.) The concepts-in-columns approach also allows you to write down synonyms that you think might be used. Figure 5-12 shows how this is done.

Columns are "AND-ed" **across,** in the search statement that you type into the computer, while terms that go **down** in a single column (synonyms) are "OR-ed." The above search could be typed: *discipline AND classroom AND (techniques or methods or approaches).* The nesting (parentheses) is necessary to command the computer to perform the Boolean functions in the correct order.

	AND		AND	
discipline	|	classroom	|	techniques OR methods OR approaches

Figure 5-12: Breaking a Topic into Searchable Component Concepts

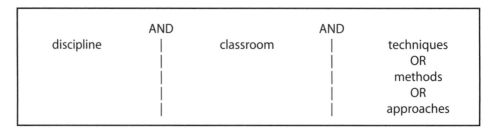

An advantage to writing down your search this way is that you know what the components are, and therefore can add or subtract them as you encounter too much or too little information. For example, if using the entire search statement retrieved too few records, you could drop one concept, *classroom,* for example, and just look for records about different discipline techniques. After you've written out your searches in this way several times, you start separating concepts in your head. At this point, you're starting to "think like a researcher." And *that* is the key to successful information research!

A computer does nothing intuitively. You have to tell the computer explicitly about the concepts you need and you do this by typing the search terms for them. The computer does NOT know what you're looking for; the computer doesn't "know" anything. If you expect it to intuit things for you, it will disappoint you. If you command it correctly, it will retrieve correctly.

Chapter Concepts

- A computerized access tool works like an electronic scanner, scanning records in its database to find matches for exactly what you typed in. The computer then compiles sets of the records in which it perceives matches.
- Subject access points in access tools can be called *subject headings* or *descriptors*. They describe the contents of information sources.
- Subject headings/descriptors are often part of a controlled vocabulary system by which an access tool limits the number of terms used to describe a topic.
- Many access tools provide researchers with a list of their authorized search terms in a thesaurus and label their terms to show relationships. Common labels include BT for broader terms, NT for narrower terms, and RT for related terms.
- A search technique known as free-text searching commands the computer to scan all fields in all records to try to find matches for the search term entered.
- Descriptor searching commands the computer to scan only the descriptor field of records for a match of the controlled vocabulary term, or descriptor, that you typed.
- Many searches benefit from both free-text and descriptor searching.
- Boolean searching allows you to use the Boolean operators AND or OR or NOT to manipulate the sets of records retrieved.
- AND narrows a search because it requires that all records in the final set include *all* search terms that were connected with AND. OR broadens a search because it creates sets of records that include *any* of the synonymous or closely related search terms that are connected with OR. NOT excludes records from a search.

Name: ____________________ Date: __________

Review Questions

1. Use a topic of your choice to illustrate a controlled vocabulary system. Create a list of your own unauthorized terms to describe the topic, then create a separate list of authorized terms you would expect to find in the controlled vocabulary of an index.

2. Suggest a topic that would be better researched using a free-text approach rather than a descriptor search in an electronic tool. Explain your reasoning.

3. Select one topic below. Using columns, list the concepts in the topic and how you would manipulate them using Boolean operators. Provide terms you think would be related or synonymous when possible. (You do not have to use any tool's thesaurus to do this.)

   - "Facilitated communication" as a technique used with autistic persons
   - The role of pesticides in environmental changes
   - Long-term effects of Microsoft and NBC collaboration
   - Slavery in the Caribbean
   - Standard of living in the U.S. compared with ______ (select another country)

4. You search for information on interpretive dance in the Balinese culture by using the search statement *interpretive dance in Balinese culture* and find no resources. How could you improve the search statement?

5. Search engines on the Web do not used controlled vocabulary. How would you avoid retrieving 60,000 hits on the topic *cigarette smoking*?

Chapter 6

THE RESEARCH PROCESS

IN THIS CHAPTER, YOU WILL LEARN . . .

- The steps in the information research process
- How to analyze the final project to determine the correct research steps
- About choosing appropriate access tools
- When to search the World Wide Web for information
- Tips on information search techniques
- Various protocols of access points
- How to use search engines, the access tools for the World Wide Web

Performing Research Requires Steps to be Followed

The research process is the series of steps that you perform to retrieve relevant information. Every topic about which you need information requires that you take at least two or more separate steps to get that information. Yet there's no single set of steps that can be applied to every information research question. That's why going to the Web first for every information need doesn't guarantee success. Your search process may include one, several or all of various steps such as:

- Deciding what your topic's subject field is.
- Fitting that subject field to a discipline.
- Selecting appropriate research tools.
- Focusing and refocusing your topic so that it fits the information systems that are available to you—broadening your topic if you're not finding enough information or narrowing it if you're finding too much and can't decide what to choose.

In addition to these steps there's the process of evaluating your topic in relation to the desired product of your research—paper, report, speech—because this affects where you do your research just as knowing your subject field does. When you put these operations together, you come up with a complete picture of the research process.

What are the steps in the research process and which step comes first? The answers to these questions vary. As stated above, there is no single plan or scheme that is "THE research process" that will answer every individual information need. Discovering the steps that could exist in any research process is similar to analyzing any process you're familiar with. Think about the process you go through to use an ATM (automated teller machine) by doing a quick run-through of a typical ATM transaction (at a machine that doesn't offer a "fast money" type of one-button service!):

1. Go to the "money machine."
2. Insert your card.
3. Type your code.
4. Type how much money you want.
5. Get the money.
6. Leave.

Right? Ah, but there are a few minor steps overlooked in this description. The ATM process actually looks more like this:

1. Discover where an ATM is located—one that is authorized by your bank to be used with your card.
2. Go to the ATM.
3. Insert your card.
4. Key in your personal identification number.

5. Select the type of transaction you want: Withdrawal? Deposit? Balance Report?
6. Select your account type: Checking? Savings? Credit Card?
7. Key in the amount of cash you want.
8. Check your typing; make any necessary corrections and press the appropriate "Enter" key.
9. Wait for the money drawer to open and remove the cash when it does.
10. Decide if you want another transaction: Yes? No? Assuming No,
11. Remove your card when it's returned and remove your paper receipt.
12. Go spend your cash.

This is a bit more complicated than you thought, isn't it? You perform all these steps without usually thinking of them as separate entities, but each is a distinct component of a whole process. Some of the early steps, such as deciding which ATM to use, you really only think about the very first time you need to find a machine in a new city or neighborhood. Others are substeps of the larger ones and it's only the bigger steps you remember. But the less visible steps are important because they often are the real movers of the process, especially when they involve decision making. This is also true when you're doing information research.

Planning Your Research Process

Many of the steps in the research process are intuitive decisions that you've been doing unconsciously in every research project you've done in the past. Making those decisions *consciously* now means that you've planned your research, anticipating outcomes and preparing to handle them in various ways. With a strategy for your research you give yourself the most important attribute of successful research: **flexibility.** A conscious search strategy, or plan for your research, means you'll use a minimal amount of time to retrieve references to information sources that will satisfy your information need. You'll be able to plan your research strategy if you're familiar with the steps in the process.

Steps in the Information Research Process

Once you become aware of the steps involved in the research process, especially those you now do intuitively, you can backtrack to any step and make different choices if your first decisions prove unworkable. So what are the steps in information research? These are listed in Figure 6-1.

The number and variety of steps in this process make it obvious that a plan of the process can minimize your search time. The construction of this plan doesn't have to be a time-consuming chore. It should instead be an organization of your ideas so that you provide yourself with alternatives should one step in the process be less successful than you had hoped.

In order for you to make a plan, you have to know what you need. Analyze your information needs based on the requirements of your assignment.

- ✓ Ascertain the subject field of your topic.
- ✓ Determine the discipline into which your subject field fits.
- ✓ Decide what type(s) of information you need:
  - ✓ Factual or analytical?
  - ✓ Objective or subjective?
  - ✓ Primary or secondary?
- ✓ Determine the quantity of information you need:
  - ✓ Enough for a 15-page paper?
  - ✓ Support materials for a 3-minute speech?
  - ✓ One or two sources required by your instructor?
- ✓ Decide how current your information must be:
  - ✓ Only very recent?
  - ✓ Only historical?
  - ✓ Some historical and some current?
- ✓ Decide how scholarly or how technical your information must be:
  - ✓ Materials that can be used by experts in your subject field?
  - ✓ Materials that can be used by the "general public"?
- ✓ Choose appropriate access tool(s)—and don't overlook paper ones!
- ✓ Determine which access points can be used in the access tool(s) you selected.
- ✓ Use the access points available:
  - ✓ Use the most specific search terms possible.
  - ✓ Use free-text searching and searching by descriptor as appropriate.
- ✓ Evaluate the references you find using clues in their records.
- ✓ Locate the sources you selected after evaluating their records in the access tool(s).
- ✓ Evaluate the sources you find after locating them.
- ✓ Use the sources—read them, don't just photocopy or print them!
- ✓ Cite the sources you used.

Figure 6-1

The Product of Information Research

Notice that the steps in the research process above aren't numbered. That's because there are information questions that don't require that you use all the steps, and questions that require that some of the steps be repeated during the research process. Some of the steps are more thoroughly discussed in other chapters of this book. Part of this chapter deals with the steps that use your final product to help you make decisions *before* you start your research. These are steps such as deciding:

How are you going to use the information you find? Let the answer to this question help shape your research.

- How much information you need
- How current your information has to be
- How technical the information should be

All of these parts of your need-analysis depend on the end-use of the information you retrieve in your research. Look at that final product carefully.

Most college students think of "doing research" only in a laboratory, or maybe online or in a library. These aren't the only places research is conducted. Much scientific research involves "outdoor laboratories" and much information research is conducted from homes, offices, and dorm rooms over electronic networks. **Research is simply the exploration of a topic.** The real product of your information research is your increased understanding of the research topic.

A common motive for information research is an assignment in a college course, and it's this model that's used for the analysis to follow. The reason a professor assigns a research project is to enable a student to learn about the various ways the topic is viewed, and then to synthesize these views. The paper or report or speech that is turned in by the student is the mode of communicating this ability to synthesize new information and to demonstrate increased understanding of the topic.

Type of Assignment and How Much Information You Need

Analyze your assigned final product and use it to make decisions about your research process. How much information do you need? This depends on the type of assignment you were given. If it's a fifteen-page "research paper," obviously the professor wants you to understand the topic fairly well by the end of your research. You'll usually need more than one information source to arrive at that level of understanding. Most often this type of assignment includes a requirement for a bibliography of ___ number of sources; in other words, your professor knows that you'll need at least that number to get a good view of your topic. On the other hand, an instructor who assigns a three-minute speech may not require a bibliography at all. But if that speech has to persuade someone to your point of view, can you do that with little or no authoritative information? Probably not. You'll need some reliable sources to back up your opinion. Another type of assignment, a group project, often asks that each member only report about only one facet of the topic, but it's difficult to present information on one aspect without knowing how that aspect fits into the whole, so your research may need to be broader than you thought originally. These are examples of how the type of project affects your research.

A 15–20 page analysis paper will require a greater number of information sources than a 2–3 page factual report.

How much do you know about the topic already? This will influence how much more information you need. If you already know something about the topic, you can use that knowledge as a jumping-off point and add information. Sometimes all you need is information to support the knowledge you already have, authorities to affirm what you already know. Other times you may know something about the topic but it's not enough to produce a report of the depth required by the assignment. If your research topic is completely new to you, that is, you know nothing about it, you'll have to begin somewhere that can give you a clue about how much information on the topic is out there.

Adjust the number of your sources to the requirements of your assignment or to your information need. If the requirements aren't spelled out, for example, if your professor doesn't require eight sources, or two books and two journal articles, or five scholarly sources, *you'll* have to decide how much research is necessary to support the assignment. Think about your audience and your topic to make this decision.

Intended Audience

Who will hear your presentation or read your paper? This influences your search strategy.

When you convey your synthesis of your newly acquired knowledge in the required paper or speech or report, you have to tailor it to the intended audience. This means that the level of expertise you should attain and then demonstrate must also take into account the level of knowledge of the reader or listener.

◆ **EXAMPLE**

There may be two very different levels of understanding in the audiences for two assignments on the same topic. A speech on apartheid in a first-year communications course calls for a level of understanding of apartheid (that you attain through your research) that is fairly rudimentary. A discussion of apartheid in a thesis written for a fourth-year honors course in political science requires that level to be far more sophisticated.

Each assignment carries with it a different level of complexity about its subject that you're expected to reach through your research and to demonstrate in your final synthesis.

The following sections present some criteria you should consider when beginning your research. As with the criteria discussed in Chapter 3—authority of the author and relevance of the title to your topic—these can be judged by using clues in the records in access tools.

Current or Historical Information

Your topic might clearly dictate the need for very recent or older information, or both.

Take another look at the topic you're researching. How recent do your information sources have to be? Do you need only current information, or only historical sources about your topic, or will a combination of older and recent information be the best? The topic itself often indicates an answer to this part of your information question.

You can use the topic/subject field/discipline analysis that is discussed in Chapter 4 to help you here:

- Many topics that fall into the discipline of the Sciences most often require only current sources to provide the latest and best information, e.g., the role of vitamins in nutrition.
- Numerous topics in the Humanities can use older sources because the topics are often timeless and classical or pertain to a certain era in history or literature, .e.g., the influence of Aristotle on drama.
- Topics in the Social Sciences frequently benefit most from a combination of older with recent sources to provide views over time supplemented with current thinking on the topics, e.g., the efficacy of the juvenile justice system in the United States.

Many topics need combinations of older and newer information.

You may not be able to use the topic/subject field/discipline relationship as the deciding factor in this step, however, because it doesn't always apply so neatly.

◆ EXAMPLE

You could be assigned to report on the discovery of mathematician Fermat's last theorem (a historical Sciences question), or to speak about the minimalist music of Philip Glass (a relatively recent Humanities investigation), or to present current views of various police policies in light of the anti-globalization protests (a very recent Social Sciences topic).

Basically **your topic determines the timeliness criterion for your research** and this influences which access tools and information sources you'll use. This is an easy check during your research: just look at the dates of every tool you use and every source you find.

All this is not to say that you can overlook very recent articles on historical or classic topics. Every year sees the publication of new articles on the works of Shakespeare or new analyses of historical events and eras. Such topics undoubtedly benefit from the latest research, but they are also well served by analyses done years ago.

Keep in mind that the need for current information, either alone or in combination with older sources, does not mean that the Web should be your *only* access tool. There are many Web sites that haven't been updated since they were opened in the late 1990s and some are devoted to topics that need constant updating. Your library's databases can provide information sources that span several decades—and they're easily searchable by subject. A "mixed search" of both the Web *and* your library's databases is often the best approach—for all topics.

A "mixed search" of both the Web* and *your library's databases is often the best approach—for all topics.

General or Technical Information

The decision about whether to use technical information sources or to rely on general materials depends on your own level of knowledge about your topic, as well as that of your intended audience. Assignments made in a course where all students are new to the subject will rarely ask for expert-level research. As you progress through your college career and get into the more focused courses in your major field of study, the expected level of technicality and scholarship in research assignments will increase until you're asked to demonstrate an advanced understanding of the subject. There's additional discussion of this criterion in Chapter 7.

Information that is a little above your present level of knowledge often provides the best learning experience.

Choosing Appropriate Access Tools

Each of the steps you take in your research process is an individual decision. Each is a separate part of the process and dependent on your knowledge of your information need. **The tool(s) you use are determined by what you need.** A student who heads immediately to a periodicals database at the beginning of every research project may be overlooking the fact that periodical articles don't always provide broad and basic information on a topic. Rather, periodical articles frequently focus on narrower aspects of topics—and a beginning researcher doesn't know what other aspects there might be. Research for lower division course assignments may best begin in an encyclopedia or a general book, even if it's only to get an idea of which aspect you'll research in periodicals indexes.

◆ Examples

Where would you go *first* to research the topic, *minority demographics since 1945*, for a 100-level Sociology course? As a student in such a beginning-level course you probably know nothing about the topic. You need to get some background information, perhaps the type of overview that an encyclopedia article could provide. Which encyclopedia should you use—a general one? a subject field- or discipline-oriented one? And if the latter, which subject field? which discipline? The strategy for this research project should really include thought about these questions. Once you determine the subject field and discipline in which this topic fits, you could find the corresponding LC areas in a Reference Collection and browse in the stacks there. This research takes only a few minutes and can be very rewarding. After you've given yourself some background on the topic, you can then move to periodical databases with a better idea of what to look for—and probably with some good search terms.

◆ ◆ ◆

The more sophisticated your information needs become, the more sophisticated research strategy you'll use.

If you have even a slight idea of the meaning of the topic, you could begin your research by trying to see if someone has already compiled a bibliography that covers it. In this case you could start your research in a library's catalog, using the subject as your access point and looking to see if there is a book whose subject field includes the terms BIBLIOGRAPHY as well as DEMOGRAPHICS and MINORITIES.

◆ ◆ ◆

If you receive this assignment in an upper division course, you might begin your research knowing enough about the topic to realize that you can focus on the demographics and the time period, or you can focus on minorities and the time period. Your decision about which of these concepts to address first may send you to different access tools—even if you choose the Web as your main (not ONLY!) access tool. You'll search under different terms depending on your approach.

After you've gained some experience in information research, you'll know where to start looking for various topics. For example, you'll know that the topic above requires historical information on population trends, and that statistical sources, periodical literature, and government documents all used together will provide the best information on population trends. Therefore, you'll do some of your research in a government documents database or Web site, possibly using some of the CD-ROMs from the government that provide census figures and analyses. Web sites may give you statistics and periodicals databases could yield references to articles about the aspect of the topic you'll address. Advanced research makes use of the many tools and resources available—both online and off.

Fit the tool to the topic.

Different projects and topics need different types of information, so choosing appropriate access tools is elementary to good research. When you know that you need only recent information, you'll go to a periodicals database or to the Web early in your research. When you know that you need a thorough analysis of a complex topic and that the currency of the information is not a crucial factor, you'll go to a library's catalog first to search for books. Consider also which tool will be more suited to the level of scholarship and technicality that you require; searching in a periodicals index could actually be counterproductive when you don't need anything more than an encyclopedia article or a statistic you could find on the Web.

When to Use the Web

Resources on the Web are increasing daily. Some students believe that the Web has **replaced** "older" access tools such as periodicals databases. This is not the reality. The Web is a terrific tool for many college research topics. It can provide extremely current information on some topics, but not all the information found there can be considered reliable. You may want to try using several search engines to see whether your topic is covered somewhere on the Web. The biggest danger for researchers who rely solely on the Web is that information found there may be less reliable than that found through periodicals databases.

You have to be so careful about the reliability of information from the Web that you may not want to use it first for all your research.

A point that researchers often are not aware of is that many Web sites are beginning to charge users for their information. Some newspapers, for example, provide an abbreviated version of their print counterparts so that you can get some, but not all of their news free online. They also may limit access to their online archives unless you are a paid subscriber. Other Web services are appearing that will provide a search engine along with a large library of online materials that you can use . . . for a monthly or annual fee. Cost may be a factor in your research. Be sure you know what's free—and what's not!—when you're online.

Many libraries subscribe to online databases for their users who can then explore them free of charge. The databases can be very expensive but provide excellent access to information. Remember the adage, "You get what you pay for." It isn't always true, but you might keep it in mind when deciding to use a search engine or a database. The databases are accessible through the Web but they aren't "the Web" *per se*. So if your professor said you cannot "use the Web" for your information sources, you most likely are able to use these online databases. Ask your professor or your librarian if you're not sure.

Understanding your information need helps you

- Decide when to begin on the Web.
- Decide when to start with a periodicals database.
- Determine when you should try the library's catalog or Reference Collection first.
- To be aware that you can't afford to overlook government documents for certain topics.
- To evaluate potential sources before you track them down physically only to discover they're not really useful.

Tips on Search Techniques

So you've analyzed your topic from every way imaginable. You used background sources if you needed them and you've armed yourself with suitable terms to use as subject headings or descriptors. When you sat down in front of a computer, you looked at the menu of tools available and *selected* the access tool(s) that you think best fit your research needs. Now

Flexibility and common sense are keys to good information research.

you could use a few search tips to make your use of these tools most efficient. What follows are general words of advice, NOT iron-clad rules of procedure. Use the techniques with a good dollop of common sense! Not every information need requires the use of all the steps in the research process that's detailed above, nor all the techniques that are discussed below, nor all the tools that are available. Remember that **good research is flexible research.**

When to Use Which Access Point

Almost any word or digit in the record of an information source can be used as an access point in electronic access tools. **Think about** which access point will be the most productive. If you know the name of an author who has written on your topic, you can use author as your access point. Then look at the records you find listed under that author: Which subject headings/descriptors are used by various access tools to describe the author's topic? Use those descriptors as new search terms for further research using a subject access point. The same technique can be used if you have the title of a book on your topic: The subject headings/descriptors that describe this book can be used to search for more sources. The tip here is to *learn to use access points to find other access points.*

When to Use Controlled Vocabulary Terms (and When not to)

Often you can move to very focused research by using the descriptors that are included in a record that you found through free-text searching.

All paper access tools require that you use their vocabulary terms. If you begin with a term that's not approved by a particular tool, either you'll find a cross-reference, such as "Inner city schools SEE Urban schools," or you'll find nothing at all, which is a strong suggestion to try another term. When you begin with a free-text search in a computerized access tool, you'll most likely get *something* for your effort. But you'll have to choose carefully from what was retrieved because the set probably includes many records that aren't relevant as well as some that are. This situation is very often magnified when doing simple searches of the Web.

Try to use one access point to learn other access points so that you can use more specific search terms.

A good rule of thumb when searching by subject is to determine the tool's descriptor/subject heading for your topic before you get too involved in your research. The proper descriptor can save you a lot of time by retrieving sets that have a high percentage of relevant records. Again, try to use one access point to learn other access points so that you can use more specific search terms. Your free-text searching enables you to do this: Look at the descriptor fields of the records you retrieve because you'll see which controlled vocabulary terms are used by the tool, and you can continue to focus your research by using them. See also the section in Chapter 5 captioned, "Free-Text Searches to Find Your Topic's Descriptor(s)."

Remember that:

- Many searches work very well using only descriptor searching.
- Some topics are well researched by doing free-text searching only.
- Others yield the best results when both free-text and descriptor searches are combined.

The tip here is to *use descriptors/subject headings whenever possible but don't limit your research to this approach only.*

When to Use Boolean Searching

Many searches in electronic access tools, including the Web, benefit from the use of Boolean logic to sift through the sets of records retrieved. Most electronic tools allow you to perform Boolean searches and many do it by default; that is, they do a Boolean search whenever you enter a multiword search term. Boolean searching is appropriate only when your topic has two or more concepts; most topics fit this description. You must be able to identify the concepts in your topic and then Boolean searching can narrow or broaden your search.

◆ **EXAMPLE**

If you begin searching for information on *wetlands* (free-text or descriptor) in an access tool about environmental subjects, you'll quickly discover that there are so many records on this topic that you *must* be more specific. At this point you should use the Boolean operator AND to add in a second concept, for example, *aquatic life*, so that the number of records drops and becomes more manageable. Now your research project has a better focus: it's *aquatic life in wetlands* and not just a general idea of wetlands. A focused topic is also easier to write about.

Know the concepts contained within your topic before you use a Boolean search statement.

The Boolean operator OR can broaden a search so that you retrieve all records that are relevant. It allows you to use numerous terms to describe the same thing (synonyms).

◆ **EXAMPLE**

The need for the operator OR in a search for articles that deal with *middle school OR junior high school*. In order to use synonyms, you must know all the separate concepts in your topic, and it helps to be ready with some synonyms for each. You also must know if the access tool you're using has a tightly controlled vocabulary that provides you with a descriptor so well-focused that you don't need to use synonyms, or if it has a looser vocabulary that will require you to provide all the different terms you can think of.

The tip here is that *Boolean searching can narrow or broaden a search when you search for the separate component concepts of your topic.*

Truncation and When to Use It

The technique of truncation can get you past many spelling questions.

Truncation is a search technique that's available in many electronic access tools. It enables you to search for a term when you're not sure of its exact spelling or whether it should be singular or plural. It **commands the computer to search for a root word**, which means that the computer scans for matches with that word regardless of its ending.

◆ **EXAMPLE**

A command to the computer to find all records with the word *latin**. The asterisk (*) is the symbol that tells the computer that all preceding letters form your root word. A search using this truncated term will result in a set of records that include any of the following words: *Latina, Latinas, Latino, Latinos, Latins, Latinate, Latin* (no additional ending), and *latin* with any other ending.

◆

(A word of advice: Don't use truncation in a Web search. Imagine the number of hits you would get searching under *teach**!) *Use truncation when you're unsure of spelling or of the need for the singular or plural form of your search term.*

The Protocols of the Access Tools

You need to be aware of any special protocols necessary to use the access points in various electronic tools. A protocol is a code that's made up of the keystrokes required by a computer program to implement a certain command.

One example of a protocol is the technique used in title searches. Often a computerized tool will require you to label your access point, for example, you must type *"(curses broiled again) in TI"* to search in one computerized catalog for the book with the title (TI) *Curses! Broiled Again!* Other catalogs will allow you to type the search statement without parentheses. Or you can select a title search as an option in some online tools, in which case your search will appear on the screen as *"TI = curses broiled again"* even if you only typed the title itself (the computer supplies the "TI=" part).

The technique used in author searches is also an example of protocol. A common protocol in some tools, both paper and electronic, is that you search for the author's name in inverse order, that is, last name first, for example *"Brunvand, Jan Harold."* Other electronic tools use a protocol of separators such as hyphens between last and first names, e.g., *Brunvand-Jan-Harold.* You also must use common sense when using author as an access point. If the author's last name is one shared by many people, e.g., Miller or Jones or Smith, you should enter as much of the first name as you know to limit the number of names scanned by the computer, e.g., *Miller, J** or *Jones, Sara** or *Smith, Nadim.*

Another example of protocol that changes from database to database is the truncation symbol. Each database requires that you learn its proper keystroke to indicate where you've cut the root word; some tools use *, some use ?, others may use a different symbol. The particular keystroke may be referred to as a "wild card" by some databases.

Many online tools offer tutorials, or at the very least, "Help" keys and screens to inform you of the protocols specific to the tools.

Many online tools offer tutorials, or at the very least, "Help" keys and screens to inform you of the protocols specific to the tools. Many libraries also offer printed guides on using their resources. "Help" sessions, such as workshops on the use of various databases, are often available as well through your library. Discover the protocols for the tool you're using and then follow them. Also discover any "Help" resources that your library provides—paper, electronic . . . and human!

Making the Web Work

Search engines are the access tools for the World Wide Web. Each works somewhat differently so it's essential that you look at any "Help" or "Information" pages they provide. In Chapter 2 there are illustrations of a search on the Web using *AllTheWeb* to search for information on *illegal immigrants.* The discussion that follows looks more closely at that search, and improves upon it.

Notice in Figure 6-2 the check-box below the Search button. This particular search engine uses this to allow you to search for this "Exact phrase." If you select this option, you greatly affect what the computer tries to match. An "exact phrase" appears as a single unbroken string of letters and spaces to the computer because the search engine's software was written that way. Therefore, the computer will scan for matches to the complete phrase. This search engine uses the check-box for this option; some search engines may require you to put a phrase within quotation marks in order to have it searched as a phrase. Others have no such choices or protocols. The default in most search engines is a simple word search that uses the Boolean operator AND and commands the computer to match individual words whenever possible. That is, the search will result in matches that merely have the words on the same Web page, and not necessarily

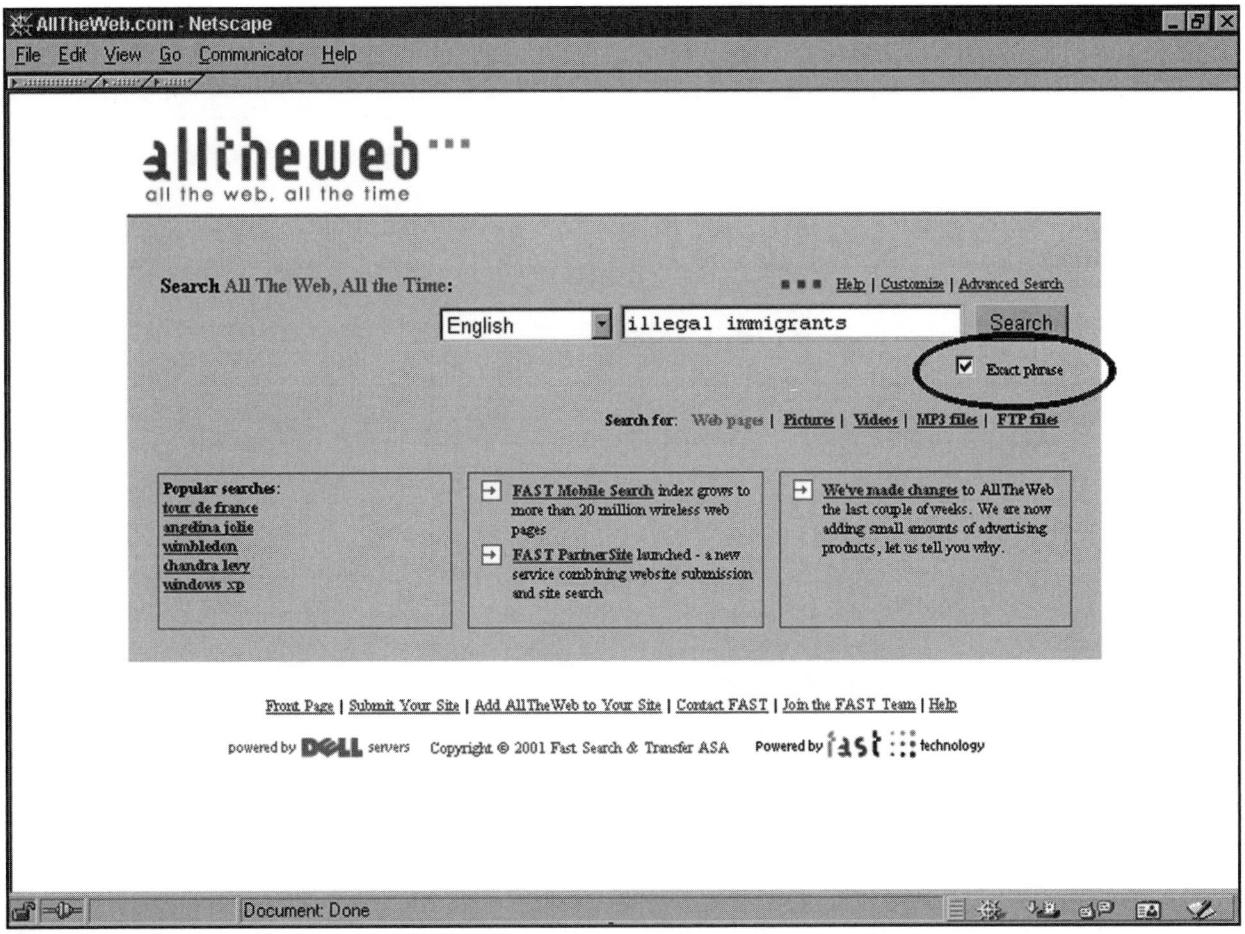

Figure 6-2: The First Screen of a Search Engine on the World Wide Web
Note the option (circled) to search by phrase rather than by individual words.

Strings of letters are just that to the computer; there is no meaning to them, either singly or in a phrase.

next to each other with the meaning you seek. In a word search, using any search engine, the words that you want to occur next to one another are received as separate strings of letters by the search engine and they are sought separately; you therefore get a "dirty" search with many false hits—hits that aren't relevant. **Remember the computer's inability to think.** Strings of letters are just that to the computer; there is no meaning to them, either singly or in a phrase.

Figure 6-3 illustrates a more complex search of the Web, this time using the *AltaVista* search engine. The menu that is open indicates that you may limit your search by language—usually a good idea on the Web!

Notice how you can command the computer to scan for similar word groups—the "nested" parenthetical statement *(illegal (immigrants OR aliens))* is a search statement for either the phrase *illegal immigrants* or the phrase *illegal aliens*. Since there is no controlled vocabulary in use on the Web, you must use search techniques such as this to control the scanning power of the search engines.

The records retrieved by a search of the Web are the names, often with descriptions, of Web pages. Figure 6-4 presents the first screen of hits from your search. Notice that your entire search statement is printed at the top of the screen. Whereas there were 124,197 hits under the broad term *illegal immigrants* in the *AllTheWeb* search, the number went to 8,563 by changing the strategy in the *AltaVista* search.

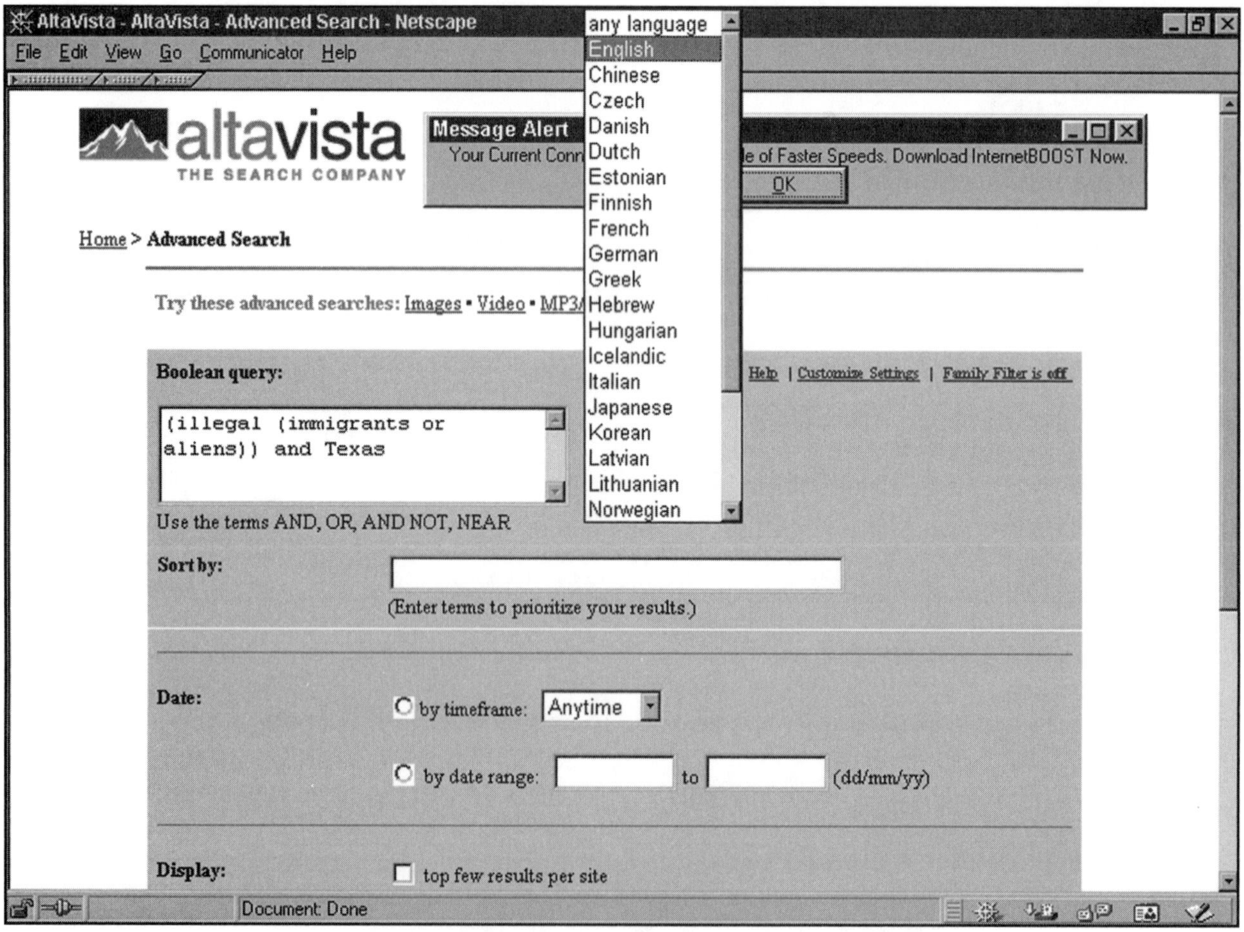

Figure 6-3: A Complex Search Using a Search Engine on the World Wide Web ("Advanced Search" in *AltaVista*)

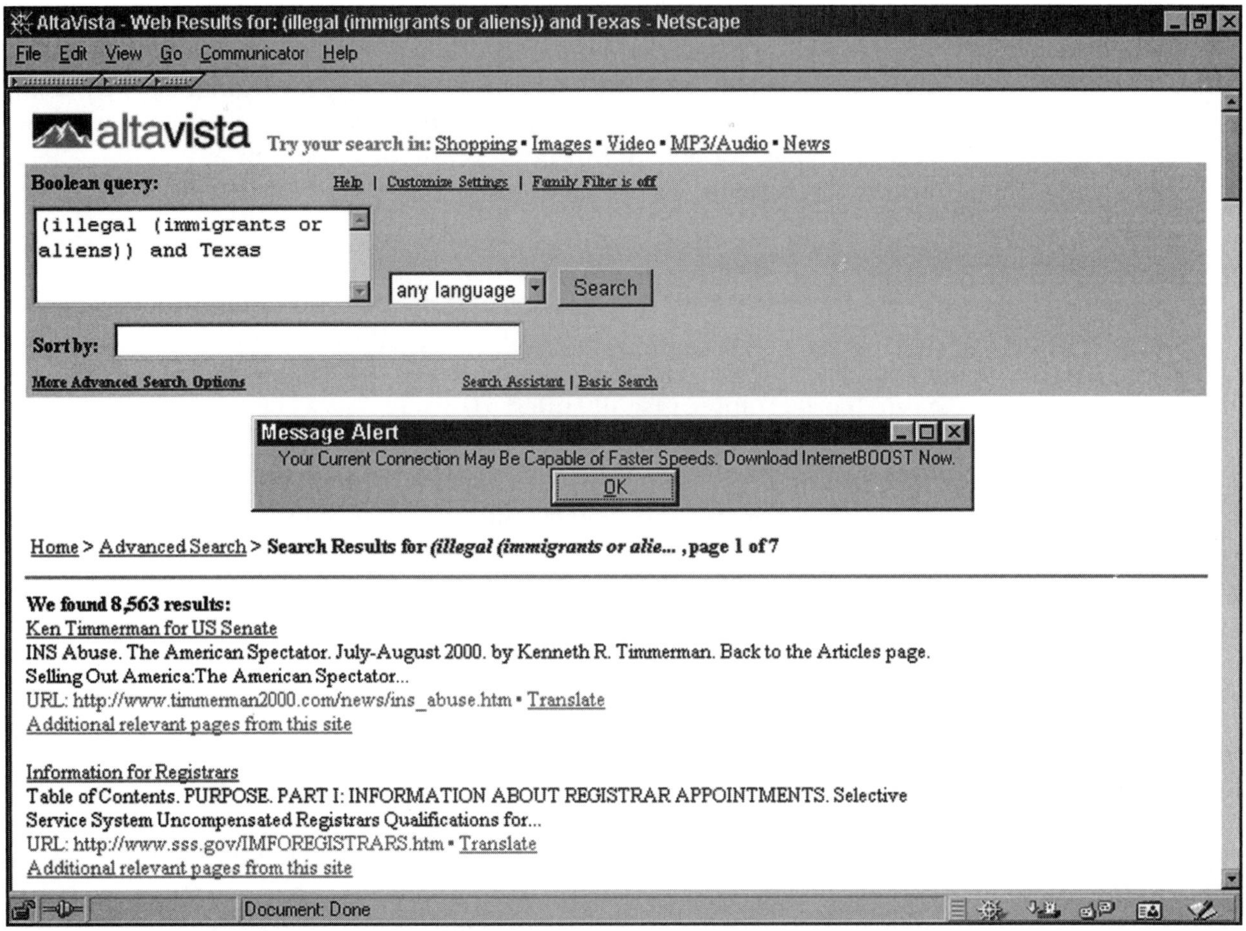

Figure 6-4: First Page of Search Result from Complex Boolean Search

Remember that search engines all do the same job, that is, they *scan* thousands of sites for matches to your search terms, and they all share some basic principles. Learn the protocols for any search engine you use and you'll be able to make your search much more efficient.

Dead Ends in Research

Sometimes as you evaluate the references you're finding, you realize that there is absolutely nothing on your topic in any access tool you've tried. What can you do when you hit a dead end?

Finding nothing relevant to your topic on your first try at research does not automatically mean that there is no information available.

There may be several reasons that you're unsuccessful in information research. The most common reason is that your information needs aren't clear to you and you started off in an inappropriate access tool or used irrelevant access points. These problems are easily corrected.

Take a minute to analyze your topic. Is the Web the *best* place to start this research project? Not necessarily. Have you looked to see what other access tools are appropriate and available? You can do this rather easily by browsing in the Reference Room/Index Area of your library or by looking through the menu of electronic tools and sources that are available on a computer network, such as the databases that your library offers. Chances are good that you'll discover a tool that covers your subject field better than a general index does.

And what term are you using in any access tool? Is it the only one that fits your topic, or is it the only one you can think of? If you answer yes to the latter question, you can change your success rate dramatically by using other information sources to help you get terminology that fits your topic. Another source of help at this point is the Reference librarian. Often the librarian can provide guidance to get you started in the best place.

Not Enough Information

But there are times that background research and help from the librarian still don't result in better information retrieval. Your topic may simply be too narrow, for example, *anorexia among ballet dancers in the Midwest*. If your "perfect" topic is so ill-suited to the access tools available that you retrieve almost no relevant information, don't change your topic. Simply broaden its scope. Drop the most restrictive part, in this case, the Midwestern locale. You can then seek information that presents an extended view of your topic, enabling you to discuss it more expansively. The resulting topic, *anorexia among ballet dancers,* is researchable, although you might even broaden it a bit more to any kind of dancer, depending on the information you could or couldn't find.

React to what you find (or don't find). Try broadening your topic if you don't find much.

You can also use synonyms to broaden your search, and employ them using Boolean logic to formulate your search statement. For example, if there were still not enough information about anorexic dancers, you might use synonyms or related terms to broaden your scope. Try *(dancers OR performers) AND (anorexia OR bulimia OR eating disorders)*. The articles you retrieve in this search are still very related to your original idea. (You'll have to supply the specifics about the location you had in mind by using sources that aren't found through periodicals indexes, such as a dancer you know who can give you information about her local company.)

Perhaps you have a topic on which very little has been published in paper or electronically, and therefore not much can be found through any access tools.

◆ EXAMPLE

A topic that might be difficult to research is *women philosophers in ancient Greece*. You can find information on *women in philosophy* and you wouldn't have too much difficulty with *philosophers in ancient Greece*, but neither would necessarily relate to the other. You could use the broadening technique suggested earlier in this chapter. That is, you could search for *women in philosophy*—dropping the most restrictive aspect of the topic. But it would change the whole topic. (Can you see the difference between this and the original topic?)

A difficult research topic requires that you reconsider your research options. You can decide to cease your efforts on this topic, in other words, to change your topic completely. Or you can pursue original research on the same topic. Original research involves sophisticated information-gathering techniques that require you to be familiar with advanced-level access tools and techniques, and often to have access to unpublished information, through electronic sources or contact with experts in the field. This type of research is done by doctoral candidates who are working on their dissertations, by masters degree candidates who are working on their theses, and sometimes by advanced undergraduates. If you're at an earlier stage in your college career and you have been advised by a librarian or other expert that this type of research will be necessary to get any information on your topic, it may be time to change your topic.

Too Much Information

If you start out with a topic that you think is about right for you to research and then present in a fifteen-page paper, and you discover that there are so many interesting articles that you can't decide which to select, don't change your topic. Simply narrow its focus. Use more specific search terms.

◆ EXAMPLE

There are thousands of books about the topic *family* listed in one library's online catalog. There are fewer than 200 books listed under *family relationships,* a more specific term you used as a search term after you discovered it by scanning a few of those *family* records.

Also remember that Boolean searching can help narrow your focus. If you use the search *aged AND family relationships,* you narrow the results in one library's catalog to less than 50 records. Both these techniques retrieve sets of more relevant records from which you could select an appropriate number without burying yourself in information.

Narrow your focus if there are too many sources to choose from.

These broadening and narrowing techniques should be options you use throughout your research process so that you can take advantage of the many access tools that exist. This includes your use of search engines on the Web. You'll discover, if you haven't already, that there is so much information available on the Web that you really need focus when you search there! Research must be flexible. Learn to react to the information you come upon and alter your research accordingly.

Evaluating as a Part of the Research Process

The flexibility that's characteristic of a good research process assumes that you're evaluating information as you go along. Evaluation is not a step to be "saved" for the end of your research. It's a continuous process that means that you don't just "print" whenever you find *anything* under a search term in a computerized index. It means that you READ THE RECORDS you find in that index BEFORE YOU PRINT *any,* and that you *select* those that are truly relevant to your topic. It cannot be overemphasized that **computers do not make research decisions, you do.** Evaluation techniques are discussed in several chapters in this book because *evaluation is a process that should be ongoing throughout your research process.*

Evaluation is not a step to be "saved" for the end of your research.

An important distinction needs to be made here: There is a clear difference between *satisfaction* and *success* in information research. This difference is widening, especially with computerized sources that retrieve sets of records for virtually any term that's typed. The mere fact that a record has your term in it does not guarantee that the record refers to a source that's relevant to your need. Many novice researchers are *satisfied* with whatever the computer retrieves and they print all records. Yet when they track down the references, they discover that many of the sources have no information relevant to their research; their searches are not *successful.* An experienced researcher makes an effort early in the search to find fitting terminology to use in appropriate access tools so that he won't waste time tracking down many irrelevant sources. He *chooses* to print only records that he judges profitable by using clues in their records. He evaluates as he goes along. He knows that evaluation makes his research successful as well as satisfying.

Chapter Concepts

- Information research is a process made of numerous individual steps, but there is no single set of steps that applies to every information need.
- Planning a research strategy is the most efficient way to conduct research.
- Analyze your information needs using the intended result—a paper, a presentation, or a group report—and its audience—less or more sophisticated—to determine the quantity and scholarship of the information needed.
- Use the topic itself to help assess the need for current or historical information.
- Finding too much or too little information should result in a careful analysis of your research process. Changing your topic should be a last resort.
- Search engines on the Web use different protocols to perform the same basic function: a scan for matches to your search term(s). Learn the protocols of any search engine you use.
- There are several methods that can refocus your research should you find too much or too little information. You may change your topic, but this is seldom the best or even the easiest solution to a research problem.
    - Broaden a topic whose search has yielded too little information:
        - Use synonyms for each concept
        - Drop one or more facets/concepts
        - Extend the time period
        - Widen the geographical focus
    - Narrow your topic when you find too much information:
        - Use specific terminology
        - Select a more focused aspect
        - Cover only a limited time period
        - Select a defined geographical area
        - Examine only one age group
- React to the information you find and use it to change your approach if necessary.

Name: ______________________________ **Date:** ______________

Review Questions

1. If you can find some books on your topic and check them out of the library, you don't have to do research to find periodical articles on the topic. Describe your reaction to this statement.

2. If you get 128,447 hits when you use your search term in a search engine on the Web, you've found the mother lode of information on your topic and you don't have to look anywhere else. Describe your reaction to this statement.

3. Select a topic below. Use the steps in information research that are listed in this chapter and arrange them to plan a search on that topic. You may omit steps or repeat steps. Explain your reasoning.

   - The trials of the man convicted of and executed for the Oklahoma City bombing (for a 3-minute informative speech)
   - Women in the military (for a 400-level Women's Studies course)
   - The use of anti-rejection drugs by liver-transplant recipients (for a 200-level Nursing course)

4. You searched for materials with the search statement *women in law enforcement* and came up with nothing. Improve your results using Boolean logic and truncation.

5. You got 30,000 Web sites as the results of a search under *Hale-Bopp comet,* using the search engine *AltaVista.* Improve the results, that is, reduce the number of false (irrelevant) hits. You may give specific directions, that is, you may use this search engine and explain what to do, or you may give more general directions without actually doing the search.

Chapter 7

Evaluating and Citing Information Sources

In This Chapter, You Will Learn . . .

- The importance of evaluating information sources based on their scholarship, authority of the authors, and timeliness
- The difference between scholarly and general information
- How to evaluate information found on the World Wide Web
- About citing research sources

Information Sources Need to be Evaluated

"It must be true, I saw it on the Web." "Someone said it on television so I know it's accurate." "But I heard it on the radio." To many people these statements indicate that an item of information is authoritative or factual. Perhaps the best example of this is the famous radio broadcast made on Halloween in 1938 by Orson Welles reading the story, "The War of the Worlds," by H. G. Wells. Thousands of people believed that *because* they heard it on the radio, Martians really were landing and humans were in mortal danger. More recently, Internet users could get information about a supposed UFO that was hiding in the wake of the Hale-Bopp comet, and some used that "reliable" information with tragic consequences. Those radio listeners and Web users accepted the *medium*, the radio or the Internet, as an indicator of validity or accuracy. In reality the medium that's used to communicate information doesn't guarantee its correctness or its truth; you evaluate information just as you command a computer. *You* must make decisions about the worth of information sources.

Worthwhile sources are those that provide information that adds to your knowledge of a topic; worthless sources are those that don't. How do you decide which ones are worthwhile? Some decisions can be made only with an information source in your hands. You can examine a book or a periodical article to see if it's at or just above your present ability to understand its subject, or if it fills a gap in your knowledge of a topic. But much evaluation can be done before you ever track down the actual source. You can use the information generated during your research to make value judgments. You can develop evaluation criteria that you can apply while you use various access tools, criteria that will help you select only those references worth pursuing.

Evaluation Criteria

Your **evaluation criteria are the standards against which you measure a source** that you encounter in your research. The source can be a print one, an audiovisual one, or an electronic one, including information found on the Web. Some standards that you can establish before you get an information source in hand include:

- Its level of scholarship
- The authority of its author(s)
- Its timeliness.

See Chapters 3 and 6 for additional discussion of these and other criteria.

Scholarly and General Sources

You must be able to recognize information that's scholarly, information by experts that's been reviewed by experts before it becomes available to you. **Scholarly sources** are aimed at an audience of practitioners or researchers or experts in various subject fields. The sources usually provide information that has met standards of quality in those fields. Scholarly information contrasts with general information. Which sources are "general" and which are "scholarly"?

General sources are intended for the nonexpert public and may present information that hasn't been reviewed by experts. They provide information that can be understood by virtually all readers, viewers, or users. Figure 7-1A shows an example of a general source. Will an article on older first-time mothers in *Newsweek* provide the kind of information you need to present an analytical report on the topic? It might be better to learn about the risks of delayed pregnancy from *The Western Journal of Medicine*, a scholarly source. But why might the latter source be better?

You're often required to use "scholarly sources only" in college research projects.

Scholarly sources are those written by experts. Figure 7-1B shows an example of a scholarly source. A *journal* article on the peace negotiations in Ireland is likely to delve more deeply into and provide a more scholarly analysis of the causes of the long-lived "troubles" than is an article in a popular general *magazine* that may provide a chronology of the crisis with a very brief analysis. This is because **a magazine has a different audience than a scholarly journal does.** The magazine aims to provide its readers with brief factual reporting that may be fleshed out with some analysis of factors involved, while the journal intends to present its audience with the latest research and scholarship carefully analyzing the causes and effects of an event or idea.

Think of a general source as similar to a "survey" course in college.

Figure 7-1A: Example of a General Source

The risks of having children in later life

Social advantage may make up for biologic disadvantage

When is the best time in life to be a mother? Or a father? These questions have been raised in the past, but the answers have left uncertainties. To address some of these issues, Nybo Andersen et al, in a study looking at maternal age and fetal loss, used a large set of data from three linked Danish health registries.[1] A digest of their original paper appears on p 331 of this month's *wjm*. Their findings are largely confirmatory of what is known or has been suspected: older age strongly increases a woman's chances of at least three untoward outcomes, namely stillbirth, miscarriage, and ectopic pregnancy. However, prospective parents concerned about their age may hope for answers to other questions as well.

Over the past 50 years or so, options for controlling or enhancing fertility have grown. These changes began with the introduction of oral contraception and have continued with the legalization of induced abortion and the development of ever more sophisticated techniques of in vitro fertilization and advances in obstetrics that ensure safe deliveries. Older women especially benefit from all of these for each has increased the age at which women bear children.

For instance, the Danish tables show trends in the rates of induced abortions over the period 1978-1992. On one side of the reproductive age span, these occur proportionately most frequently during the teens, when the greatest social disadvantage is associated with childbearing. On the other side, the greatest number, proportionately, of induced abortions occur at the latest ages, when the greatest biologic disadvantage is associated with childbearing.

The collection of such large bodies of data often limits the social and biologic variables that can be recorded. Still, the data reported by Nybo Andersen et al could have been stretched further. For example, they provide a mean length of gestation for miscarriages rather than a distribution over the range of specific gestational ages. Such an analysis obscures the relation between miscarriages at different stages of gestation and maternal age.[2] The greatest concentration of chromosomal anomalies and by far the highest rate of pregnancy loss is found early in gestation. At least 90% of such losses occur during the first trimester. At the same time, those anomalies that are trisomic and those fetuses that are less viable are strongly related to increased maternal age.

It may also not be asking too much of routine data on stillbirths to differentiate between antepartum and intrapartum losses. In recent years in developed countries most losses occur before labor, and only in these is the effect of maternal age observed.[3] Hypotheses about the causes of antepartum stillbirths occurring at advanced maternal age have included chromosomal anomalies, pre-eclampsia (especially in nulliparous women), and diabetes. None of these factors, however, contributed to the age effect observed in a large data set on stillbirths in Canada collected from 1961 to 1993.[4] Unlike the Danish series, the data in this perspective, obtained over a longer time, did show a considerable decline in the overall rate of stillbirths. It is also notable that older mothers shared in this general long-term decline in the rate. Thus, among women aged 35 years or older, the rate of stillbirths per 1000 births decreased from 16.5 in 1960-1969 to 5.8 in 1990-1993. Though the higher relative risk for older women persists, the absolute risk has been greatly reduced.

Maternal age has an impact on other aspects of reproduction for which information may not have been available in the Danish register. Among the data that are usu-

Zena Stein
Mervyn Susser
Joseph L. Mailman School of Public Health
Columbia University
600 W 168th St, PH18
New York, NY 10032

Correspondence to:
Dr Stein
zas2@columbia.edu

Competing Interests:
None declared

West J Med
2000;173:295-296

Figure 7-1B: Example of a Scholarly Source, an Article from the *Western Journal of Medicine*

◆ EXAMPLE

In art history a course such as "Art of the Western World" presents you with some information about each of a broad array of artistic periods and styles. A more advanced course, such as "Baroque and Rococo Art in Italy," would then be comparable to a scholarly source, limited to a narrower subject and providing a deeper analysis of that subject.

Each type of information fills a different need. If you as a researcher need broad, not deeply analytical information, you can find it in general sources, that is, in magazines. If you need in-depth analysis, you require a scholarly source, a journal. Figure 7-2 outlines the major differences between general and scholarly information.

The bibliographies present in most scholarly sources can serve as access tools.

Another reason that you can rely on a scholarly source for reliable information is that its author documents his or her sources by providing a bibliography. This bibliography enables you to find the information sources used by the author. Not only does citing one's sources authenticate the information presented, but it also allows you to expand your research with minimum effort: you can find the sources that are listed in a book's or article's bibliography without doing another search yourself. *An information source that includes a bibliography is most often considered a scholarly source.*

You may need to know if the scholarly sources you use are "refereed." **A refereed source is one in which information is published only after it has been reviewed by several experts** in that subject field. This may also be called a "peer-reviewed" source. Many scholarly journals follow this procedure; only a small percentage of Web sites and pages are peer reviewed. The review process is especially important when the information involves empirical research because most subject fields require that reported research be replicable, that is, that other researchers can obtain the same results using the same procedures. In recent years there have been several publicized cases involving claims of falsification of research data. Rigorous review of published research minimizes these situations and assures you of acceptable and scholarly information.

General Information	Scholarly Information
• Intended for non-expert public	• Intended for practitioners, researchers, or experts in the subject area
• May have information that has not been reviewed by experts	• Contains information that has been written and often reviewed by experts
• Provides brief factual reporting that may be fleshed out with some analyses of factors involved	• Provides information on latest research and scholarship
• Useful when a researcher needs broad information on a topic • Found in magazines and other sources	• Useful when a researcher needs in-depth analysis of a topic • Found in journals and other sources

Figure 7-2: General vs. Scholarly Information

Use your common sense when your professor doesn't require scholarly sources!

Your professor may not require "scholarly sources." This doesn't automatically mean that you can use only general sources. Think about what kind of information you're looking for: Do you need to analyze your topic closely or will you present an overview to a nonexpert audience? Do you know anything about your topic? Your answers to these questions can help you determine whether you may use sources written for nonexperts or if you have to search for scholarly sources. How can you tell whether the record in your chosen access tool is referring you to a scholarly source or a general source? Look for clues!

One way to determine the level of scholarship of a source is by its title. Few sources will have the exact title you have in mind (because often that title is the title you plan to give your own research paper!) but you can use the words in a source's title as clues to its suitability to your topic. A good rule of thumb is that if you can understand the title, you may well be able to understand the information presented in that source. This means that **you have to read through the references** that you find **and choose** only those that you think are appropriate to your needs.

You also want to know whether or not a source includes the particular angle of your topic that you've selected to research. Sometimes the title of a source alone doesn't indicate this. But if you combine clues from the title with the fact that the source was listed under a certain subject heading, the record is easier to evaluate. Let's say that you have to research the topic *math anxiety in female students.* You do a "keyword" search in a library's online catalog under *mathematics and women* and you get the record shown in Figure 7-3. Put together clues from both the TITLE and SUBJECTS fields to see if this particular source may be relevant.

AUTHOR	: Hyman Blumberg Symposium on Research in Early Childhood Education, Johns Hopkins University, 1976. 8th,. Fox, Lynn H., 1944–. Brody, Linda. Tobin, Dianne. American Association for the Advancement of Science.
TITLE	: Women and the mathematical mystique : proceedings of the eighth annual Hyman Blumberg Symposium on Research in Early Childhood Education / edited by Lynn H. Fox, Linda Brody, and Dianne Tobin
PUBLISHER	: Baltimore : Johns Hopkins University Press
DATE	: c1980
PHYS. FEAT	: viii, 211 p. : ill. ; 24 cm.
SERIES	: Studies of intellectual precocity ; 8
NOTES	"Expanded version of a symposium of the American Association for the Advancement of Science entitled 'Women and mathematics.'" Includes bibliographies and index.
LCCN	: 9-3655
ISBN	: 0-8018-2341-2 0-8018-2361-7 (pbk.)
SUBJECTS:	: Women in mathematics—Congresses. Women mathematicians—Congresses. Sex differences in education—Congresses. Mathematics—Study and teaching—Congresses.
1 item(s)	: SUNY at Plattsburgh, Feinberg Library—General Collection 87108-2663 OA27.5.H95 1976 Available

Figure 7-3: Record of a Book from a Library's Online Catalog

You can see that one of the subject headings in this record is SEX DIFFERENCES IN EDUCATION, and the book's title is *Women and the Mathematical Mystique.* Neither the subject heading nor the title explicitly says "math anxiety in female students." But words in the title combined with the subject heading indicate that the book may well be relevant to your topic. The subtitle of this work, *Proceedings of the Eighth Annual Hyman Blumberg Symposium on Research in Early Childhood Education,* notes that it deals with a particular age group. You now could surmise that you'll not only learn about girls and mathematics education, but also very probably about this relationship in preschool. If you want to work with this aspect of the topic, this source would definitely be worth examining. On the other hand, you might use the same reasoning to conclude that this source probably has too narrow a view of your topic about math anxiety so you'd opt not to use it as a source, and you wouldn't bother to print the record.

Authority

Another criterion for evaluation is the authority of the creator of an information source. This is especially true of information found on the Web. An example of an easy comparison using this standard is the difference between a professor's presentation of a concept in economics and a classmate's description of that same concept. The former is speaking with authority, that is, with expertise in the field, while the latter is speaking as a fledgling in that field. Frequently in information research the contrast isn't that dramatic or as easily determined. If you're trying to decide the worth of two different published sources, how can you tell if either or both are authoritative?

Think about your topic. Was it discussed in class? If and when it was, were the names of any experts on the subject mentioned or recommended? Often class discussions introduce the names of people who are experts in their fields, names you can then use as your access points in your research.

- In anthropology, the name Margaret Mead is still seen as authoritative in certain areas.
- In economics John Kenneth Galbraith has published well-known books.
- Akiro Kurosawa is respected as a master in film; etc.

You could look for information by these people and be certain that you've found authoritative sources. But these are examples of world-renowned authorities. Most often the names of experts in a subject field aren't that famous but they are well known to other scholars in their field. Your professor may mention her field's experts in class or require you to read material by them for her course. You can search for these "celebrities" as authors and know that you're dealing with authoritative information. And if you don't get any names from class discussions, check your textbooks; they usually have bibliographies that can lead you to numerous authorities. Sometimes your research process reveals an expert because his name appears as an author repeatedly in different access tools or Reference works; use this as a clue to expand your research. Remember to **react to the information you find and use it to find more**.

Timeliness of Information

How old is the source whose record you're looking at? Does this make a difference to you? Should it? Yes. It should help you decide if you want to track down that source because the currency of information can be vitally important to your topic. (This criterion is also discussed in Chapter 6.)

Societal values are explored in many college research topics. Novice researchers often investigate issues such as abortion, euthanasia, divorce, capital punishment, alcohol and drug use and abuse. The value of information about these topics varies depending on the age of the source: old books and articles are frequently less serviceable than current sources. An example of this in Social Sciences is the difference in the information presented in a book on abortion published prior to the 1960s and one published after the famous 1972 Supreme Court decision, *Roe* vs. *Wade.* See Figure 7-4.

Scientific topics usually require time-sensitive information. Because scientific research is *incremental,* that is, it builds on earlier research, the most current information is usually the most valuable; it's based on work that was performed and published previously. A research paper on *the role of calcium in the health of aging women,* for example, would be far less informative and possibly even incorrect if it were based on information from the 1970s rather than that published in the 1990s and 2000s. Even some topics in Humanities are better analyzed by including the latest information along with earlier work. For example, a discussion of Shakespeare's 16th century play *Romeo and Juliet* might benefit by reference to analyses of *West Side Story,* the musical that has been called the 20th-century version of the play.

CONTENTS

from *The Sanctity of Life and the Criminal Law* (1957)

Figure 7-4A: (A) A Book Published in 1957

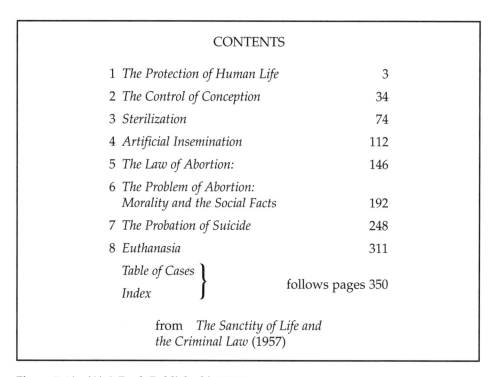

Contents

iv

from *Abortion, Medicine, and the Law.* (4th ed., completely revised, 1992)

Figure 7-4B: (B) A Book Published in 1992

Timeliness of information is an evaluation criterion that's easy to establish. Analyze your topic to determine whether you **must** use the most current information possible, or if you can use any information on the topic regardless of date.

Evaluating Information Found on the World Wide Web

The criteria—scholarly level, timeliness, and authority—are all used when evaluating information whether you find it on a bookshelf or on your computer screen. Information found via computer on the Web, however, has some unique features that require you to *evaluate it even more carefully* than your other finds.

As stated in Chapter 2, much of the excitement of the Web derives from its diversity. It's an uncensored source; at this time voluntary censorship is available to Web users through the purchase of screening software or subscriptions to ISPs that exercise control over sites to which you have access. Most search engines also currently allow you to place "filters" on their search results. But these attempts at censorship most frequently target pornographic, "X-rated," or "adult content" sites. They do not screen out unverifiable or questionable information or propaganda. You must do that.

Most Web sites are not reviewed or refereed. Anyone can put information on anything onto their Web sites. This makes for some very interesting sites, but many don't provide the level of information that you can use in a college research project. Ruth Guthrie, a professor a the University of Redlands, stated in her e-article, "Six Things I Hate about the Internet:"

Anyone can put information on anything onto their Web sites.

> Yes, if a student is writing a paper on beer, she may find 30,000 references using a simple Internet search tool. Over half of them will be advertisements, a quarter of them will have nothing to do with beer, and the remaining quarter will be Joe Schmo's Home Brew Page. The 100 references that may be high quality will take forever to find. . . .

Your skill with sophisticated search techniques (see Chapter 5) will help you over that last statement. But what about the previous one? **The biggest concerns about information on the Web are authority and validity.** Just as you seek a recognizable author when you search library catalogs, or scholarly sources when you use periodicals databases, so you must seek verification of the information on a Web page. And just as you can use clues in the access tools for paper resources, you can do the same on Web sites.

Clues on Web Pages

Look first at the top and bottom of the Web page that has the information you're interested in. Is there information about the author—whether that's a person or an organization? If not on that page, is there a link to a Home page where you can learn more about the author? Not all organizations are legitimate in the sense that their memberships are limited to experts in their subjects. The reverse of this might be that a person who is an expert in one field may have designed and published a Web page on a topic that he's particularly interested in that's out of his field; he may be in the process of becoming an expert and will provide information that can be documented—he'll include where he got the information. A good rule of thumb is to be very wary of any information that's undocumented (electronic or paper), and to think about using another source to verify it before using it. You might want to use it and note clearly that it wasn't verifiable; sometimes that fact can be an evaluative statement in itself. As an example, try a search of the Web under the term *militia* and examine the results.

Look for information on a Web author or publisher just as you would for a book or article.

Clues in the URL

A "quick and dirty" method for evaluation (similar to a "quick and dirty" computer search in which many records are retrieved but the percentage of relevant hits is low) is to use a Web site's URL for help in verifying the site's authority. The major locator in a URL is the "Domain Name," which tells the computer where your desired information is. It might be likened to the city and state in a postal address. In the first URL below, <plattsburgh.edu> is the Domain Name: <plattsburgh> says "who" the computer is and <edu> says "what" it is.

http://www.plattsburgh.**edu**	http://www.msnbc.**com**
http://www.ala.**org**	http://www.nasa.**gov**

The boldfaced segment of each of these Domain Names is called the Top Level Domain (TDL). There is a limited number of TDLs in use—that number is expanding—and their inclusion in a URL can indicate, **broadly,** what type of institution or agency or business is supporting the Web site. Those that serve as possible indicators of reliability include *edu, gov, mil,* and to a lesser extent, *org*. These TDLs tell you that the site you're visiting is on a server provided by an educational institution, a government agency, a military branch, or an organization (such as the American Library Association—ala.org, above), respectively. Remember that this is a relatively crude evaluation tool.

Some professors require verification of information found on the Web. Be sure to check with the person who assigned your research project so that you provide sufficient documentation with your newly found Web resources. For excellent help in evaluating Web resources, ask your librarian or look for Web-mounted guides, such as "Five criteria for evaluating Web pages" at <http://www.library.cornell.edu/okuref/research/webcrit.html> (as of spring 2002).

Citing Your Sources

Now you're at the end of your information research. You evaluated many records and selected some of them, located those sources and read or watched or listened to them to learn something about your topic. When you write your paper, you'll synthesize the information you found. Along with this you'll have to "cite your sources" as required by your professor. Why is this necessary? Why can't you simply hand in your paper without a bibliography?

Reasons to Cite Sources

The most important reason that you cite your sources is to give credit to those other creators, the authors of the information you used . . . and learned from. Even when you don't use direct quotes, you need to report the sources you used because you took the ideas from those sources and incorporated them with your own. You inform your audience that those creators helped you learn what you just reported in your paper.

If you don't cite the sources on which your work is based, you're guilty of **plagiarism.** To plagiarize is **"to steal and use (the ideas or writings of another) as one's own,"** according to the *American Heritage Dictionary.* **Plagiarism is a crime.** It's a theft because you imply, through your lack of documentation, that all the ideas you present in your research paper or report or speech are yours and yours alone, that they sprang full-grown from your mind with no help from anyone else, when in reality they were shaped or came from others. Plagiarism is a falsification that is punished in most college courses by a failing grade, in many colleges and universities by severe penalties including dismissal from the school, in professional circles by ostracism from one's circle of colleagues and civil suits. It's also easily avoided: Cite your sources.

Professionals list "Works Cited" or "References" or "Sources Consulted" in order to document their research. All scholarly work includes citation of sources so that researchers in that subject field can develop a picture of the research done by the author of a work. When one is familiar with a subject field, a colleague's bibliography helps to illustrate the thought process of that colleague. And in many subject fields where research is incremental, an author demonstrates the progression of her research topic through her bibliography: each citation indicates information that was used in her current research, and each in turn was built upon still earlier information. Documented research also allows a current researcher to avoid repeating earlier research; that researcher won't have to "reinvent the wheel." Documentation allows you to find the exact source cited and use its information rather than creating your own through costly or time-consuming experiments.

The Makeup of Citations

The goal of every citation is to allow the reader or viewer of that citation **to find the source used.** Citations therefore must include enough information to accomplish this. **The components of citations are universal:**

- **author(s),**
- **title,**
- **publishing information.**

The arrangement of these components will differ somewhat depending on the item being cited, especially if the citation refers to information from the Web.

The elements of every citation in a particular access tool are always put in the same order.

◆ EXAMPLES

All periodical indexes published in paper by the H. W. Wilson Company arrange the elements in this order: title of the article, name(s) of author if given, abbreviated title of the periodical, its volume, pages, and date. Never will a researcher find these elements in any other order in such print indexes as *Reader's Guide, Business Periodicals Index, Education Index, Art Index*, or any other Wilson index.

◆ ◆ ◆

Wilson OmniFile Full Text arranges fields in the citations retrieved in the order of title, personal author (if one is named), and source. That last field includes the title of the periodical, its volume, issue and date, and the page number(s) of the article. And this order is maintained in every citation in the database.

Citation Formats

Your job as a researcher is to arrange the elements into your chosen format in your bibliography. Illustrated in Figure 7-5 are a book citation, a periodical article citation, and a citation of a World Wide Web site. If you **read what those citations actually say,** they describe their own formats.

Formats are precise and consistent standards (arrangements of elements) for citations. Various professional organizations and firms have created standards that are widely accepted in academic and professional circles. They're made available to researchers through numerous **style**

Elements Necessary in Any Citation

	Books	Periodical articles	Web sites and Internet
Author:	All authors named; editor(s) usually considered author	All authors named	All authors named, personal or corporate
Title:	Complete title and complete subtitle	Complete title of article and complete title of periodical	Title of Web page /site
Publishing Information:	City, publisher, year of publication	Volume and date of periodical; page numbers of article	URL, date posted or created or updated; and date retrieved (used)

Generic Book Citation*

Lastname-Author, Firstname. The Title of the Book Is Capitalized and Underlined or Put in Italics; The Subtitle Is Also Included. City: Publisher, Year.

Generic Periodical Article Citation (with two authors)*

Lastname-Author, Firstname, & Firstname Author-Lastname. "The Title of the Article Is Capitalized and Put in Quotations Marks with a Period at the End." Journal Title Is Not Abbreviated and Is Underlined vol (Year): page-page.

Generic Web Site Citation*

Lastname, Author (if provided) or Corporate Name. "Title of the Web Page Used." Title of the Web Site Underlined. Date of creation or latest update. Name of Any Sponsor for the Site. Date you used the page <http://www.url.tdl/complete/URL/here>

*All three citations follow MLA format (see below). The periodical article shows the format for a journal article, not a magazine article. The Web citation is for a page that is part of a larger Web site.

Figure 7-5: Generic Citations

manuals. Some professional organizations that have produced style manuals include:

- The Modern Language Association (MLA)
- The American Psychological Association (APA)
- The American Chemical Society (ACS)
- The Council of Biology Editors (CBE)
- The *New York Times* newspaper

Each of these manuals provides guidelines for citation format and serves as a style guide for the layout of articles, research reports, and theses. The different style manuals are available in most libraries; there are many Web sites—often provided by libraries—that provide the segments of these manuals that cover citation formats.

If no particular citation format is specified by your professor, choose a standard format and then be consistent.

Manuals provide consistency in citation format. They require that certain elements always appear in a certain order in citations so that the user of a bibliography can understand the information in the citations and use it to locate the exact sources cited there. This means that you, as the creator of the bibliography, have to maintain the consistency established by the style manual's guidelines.

The style manual for any subject field states and usually gives examples to show exactly how the citations must be formatted in publications in that field. The following bibliographies are examples of different citation formats. Every source in each bibliography is cited according to the format specifications that are presented in each pertinent style manual.

The bibliographies include citations for:

- A book (Beard)
- An item from an edited book (Blesh)
- A magazine article (Fields-Meyer)
- A journal article from an online full text database (Foek)
- A document available from ERIC, the government's education resource clearinghouse (Francois)
- A videocassette (Lord)
- A Web site (Maloney)
- A sound recording (Orff)
- A letter to the editor in a newspaper from a full-text database (Romano).

An Eclectic Bibliography—Examples of Different Formats

MLA Format

Works Cited

Beard, Henry, and John Boswell. French for Cats: All the French Your Cat Will Ever Need. New York: Villard, 1991.

Blesh, Rudi. "Scott Joplin: Black-American Classicist." Scott Joplin Complete Piano Works. Ed. Vera Brodsky Lawrence. New York: NY Public Library, 1981. xiii-xl.

Chicken Run. Dir. Peter Lord and Nick Park. Prod. Peter Lord, David Sproxton, and Nick Park. Perf. Mel Gibson. Videocassette. DreamWorks Home Entertainment, 2000.

Fields-Meyer, Thomas, Richard Jerome, and Susan Schindehette. "Brandie Eckensviller: She Rescued Her Sister from a Vicious Attack." People Weekly 20 Nov. 2000: 136.

Foek, Anton. "Sweatshop Barbie: Exploitation of Third World Labor." The Humanist 57.1 (1997): 9-13. InfoTrac Expanded Academic ASAP. Gale Group. Feinberg Library, Plattsburgh State U. 16 Aug. 2001.

Francois, Robert, Gary Harlacher, and Bruce Smith. Improving Student Behavior in the Classroom by Using Assertive Discipline Strategies. 1999. (ERIC Document Reproduction Service No. ED431550).

Maloney, Catherine, Sara J. Lichtblau, Nadya Karpook, Carolyn Chou, and Anthony Arena-DeRosa. "Feline Reactions to Bearded Men." Annals of Improbable Research presents Hot A.I.R. Ed. Marc Abrahams. 16 August 2001. <http://www.improb.com/airchives/classical/cat/cat.html>

Orff, Carl. Carmina Burana. Perf. Prague Festival Orchestra & Chorus. Cond. Pavel Urbanek. Delta Music, 1991.

Romano, David. "Elite Fear Real Alternatives." Letter. Montreal Gazette. 27 July 2001, final ed., sec. B: 2.

*APA Format**

Italics, rather than underlining, are used for titles in this sample.

References

Beard, H., & Boswell, J. (1991). *French for cats: All the French your cat will ever need.* New York: Villard.

Blesh, R. (1981). Scott Joplin: Black-American classicist. In V. B. Lawrence (Ed.), *Scott Joplin complete piano works* (pp. xiii-xl). New York: NY Public Library.

Fields-Meyer, T., Jerome, R., & Schindehette, S. (2000, November 20). Brandie Eckensviller: She rescued her sister from a vicious attack. *People Weekly, 54,* 136.

Foek, A. (1997). Sweatshop Barbie: Exploitation of Third World labor. *The Humanist 57,* 9-13. Retrieved August 16, 2001, from InfoTrac Expanded Academic ASAP database.

Francois, R., Harlacher, G., & Smith, B. (1999). *Improving student behavior in the classroom by using assertive discipline strategies.* (ERIC Document Reproduction Service No. ED431550).

Lord, P. (Director/Producer), Sproxton, D. (Producer), & Park, N. (Director/Producer). (2000). *Chicken Run* [Motion picture]. United States: DreamWorks Home Entertainment.

Maloney, C., Lichtblau, S. J., Karpook, N., Chou, C., & Arena-DeRosa, A. (n.d.). Feline reactions to bearded men. In *Annals of Improbable Research presents Hot A.I.R.* Retrieved 16 August, 2001, from http://www.improb.com/airchives/classical/cat/cat.html

Orff, C. (1937). Carmina Burana. [Recorded by the Prague Festival Orchestra & Chorus, conducted by Pavel Urbanek]. [CD]. Los Angeles: Delta Music. (1991).

Romano, D. (2001, July 27). Elite fear real alternatives [Letter to the editor]. *Montreal Gazette,* p. B2.

---

*The 4th edition of the *Publication Manual of the American Psychological Association* shows examples of citations arranged in a paragraph format, that is, the first line is indented five spaces. However, they should be done with a hanging indention as shown above. The 5th edition of the *Manual* (2001) shows the hanging format.

*CBE Format**

The citations in this sample bibliography are numbered according to the order in which they were cited in the text of the imaginary paper, as per CBE style. This is known as the *citation-sequence system.* You may arrange them alphabetically if you use a different method of citing works in the text, that known as *name-year.* Your professor should indicate which format you should use.

1. Francois R, Harlacher G, Smith B. Improving student behavior in the classroom by using assertive discipline strategies. [Microfiche]. Rockville (MD): ERIC; 1999. 1 fiche; 24x reduction ratio. Available from ERIC, Rockville, MD; ED 431 550.
2. Blesh R. Scott Joplin: Black-American classicist. In: Lawrence VB, editor. Scott Joplin complete piano works. New York: NY Pub Lib; 1981. p xiii-xl.
3. Foek A. Sweatshop Barbie: exploitation of Third World labor. Humanist 1997;57:9-13.
4. Beard H, Boswell J. French for cats: all the French your cat will ever need. New York: Villard; 1991. 96 p.
5. Chicken run [videocassette]. Lord P, Park N, directors. Lord P, Sproxton D, Park N, producers. [Universal City, CA]: DreamWorks Home Entertainment; 2000. 84 min., sound, color, $^1/_2$ in.
6. Fields-Meyer T, Jerome R, Schindehette S. Brandie Eckensviller: she rescued her sister from a vicious attack. People Weekly 2000 November 20;54:136.
7. Elite fear real alternatives. To the editor. Romano D. Montreal Gazette 2001 July 27; Sect B:2.
8. Orff C. Carmina Burana. 1937. [Recorded by the Prague Festival Orchestra & Chorus, conducted by Pavel Urbanek]. [compact disk]. Los Angeles: Delta Music; 1991.

You can see that the differences among the various formats are slight but they're important. Use the appropriate style manual and look at *all* the examples it provides for your type of source (e.g., all the book citation examples or all the periodical article citation examples) so that you can see which example(s) match your source most closely. Note also that **you may have to combine examples from a style manual** to a get clear citation for a source you used. **Read the text** in addition to looking at the examples. The text most often includes the information applicable to sources that differ from the examples in the manual. The most important part of creating a list of citations is to include all the basic elements and to **be consistent** in your format.

---

*The citation for the compact disk (Orff) is based on the example for an audiocassette in the *CBE Manual.* The Web site is not cited here because definitive information for the format of such a citation was not available at press time. Ask your instructor if you need to cite a Web site (not a periodical article you found using a database through the Web).

Chapter Concepts

- Evaluation is the determination of the worth of an information source; it puts *you* in control of selecting relevant information sources.
- You can determine the level of scholarship, the authority of an author, and the timeliness of an information source from a reference to it in an access tool.
- Scholarship is often indicated by the type of source in which the item appears—scholarly journal or general magazine. A key sign of scholarship is the presence of a bibliography with an article; this usually indicates a "scholarly source."
- Authority of an author may be ascertained by the frequent appearance of that author's name throughout your research.
- Examine your topic to determine the need for current or historical information.
- The crime of plagiarism is the failure to cite your sources—even if you didn't use a direct quote.
- Citations all contain the same basic elements: author(s), title, and publishing information.
- The goal of any citation is to enable a reader of that citation to find the exact source that's cited there.
- Consistency in your citation format enables your readers to find the sources you used.

Name: ______________________ Date: ____________

Review Questions

1. Explain plagiarism in your own words and provide an example.

2. What do you think is the most accurate way to judge the relevance of an information source? Use a topic of your choice to show your reasoning.

3. You find 47 references in one access tool. Describe how you go about selecting the best five references on your topic from those 47. In other words, how do you decide on a few sources when confronted with many to choose from?

4. A search on the Web always retrieves only sites that are relevant to your topic. Describe your reaction to this statement.

5. You discover a Web page entitled "Hooked on Ebonics" <http://www.english.uiuc.edu/baron/essays/ebonics.htm> when you search for information on ebonics—Black English—in schools. Should you use this site as a source for your research paper? Explain how you make this decision.

References

American Heritage Dictionary of the English Language. 3d ed. Boston: Houghton, 1992.

Cotton, Bob, and Richard Oliver. *The Cyberspace Lexicon.* London: Phaidon, 1994.

Council of Biology Editors, Style Manual Committee. *Scientific Style and Format: The CBE Manual for Authors, Editors, and Publishers.* Sixth Edition. Cambridge, England: Cambridge U Pr., 1994.

Danuloff, Craig, and Deke McClelland. *Encyclopedia Macintosh.* San Francisco: SYBEX, 1990.

December, John, and Neil Randall. *The World Wide Web Unleashed 1996.* 3d ed. Indianapolis: Sams.net Publishing, 1995.

Falk, Bennett. *The Internet Roadmap.* 2d ed. San Francisco: SYBEX, 1994.

FOLDOC: Free On-Line Dictionary of Computing. May 1996. 28 September 2001 <http://foldoc.doc.ic.ac.uk/foldoc/>.

Gibson, William. "The Net Is a Waste of Time and That's Exactly What's Right about It." *The New York Times Magazine* (1996, July 14): 30–31.

Glossary of Web Terminology. Webs Etc. 1996–2000. 28 September 2001 <http://www.webs-etc.com/glossary.htm#M>

Green, Jonathon. *Dictionary of Jargon.* London: Routledge, 1987.

Guthrie, Ruth. "Six Six Things I Hate About the Internet" December 1996. 29 May 1997 <http://newton.uor.edu/FacultyFolder/RGuthrie/hinet.html>.

"Internet Resources on Disabilities." 18 May 1999. University of Kansas Department of Special Education. 19 July 2001 <http://busboy.sped.ukans.edu/disabilities/>

MacintoshOS.com; An Online Destination for Macintosh Users. "Internet Glossary." 1996. 28 September 2001 <http://www.MacintoshOS.com/internet.connectivity/internet.glossary.html>.

Microsoft Press Computer Dictionary; the Comprehensive Standard for Business, School, Library, and Home. 2d ed. Redmond, WA: Microsoft P, 1994.

Notess, Greg R. "Internet Subject Directories. Search Engine Showdown; The Users' Guide to Web Searching. 1 Nov. 2000. 21 March 2001 <http://searchengineshowdown.com/dir>

Publication Manual of the American Psychological Association. 5th ed. Washington, DC: A.P.A., 2001.

Stout, Rick. *The World Wide Web Complete Reference.* Berkeley, CA: Osborne McGraw-Hill, 1996.

Wurman, Richard Saul. *Information Anxiety Is Produced by the Ever-Widening Gap between What We Understand and What We Think We Should Understand.* New York: Doubleday, 1989.

Young, Heartsill, ed. *The ALA Glossary of Library and Information Science.* Chicago: American Library Association, 1983.

Glossary

abstracting service: an access tool that is published regularly that provides subject access to information by means of abstracts and indexes; abstracting services provide abstracts, which are "abbreviated, accurate representations of works, usually without added interpretation or criticism" (Young 1).

bibliographic record: information about an information source (e.g., a book, a recording, etc.) that completely identifies the source—its title, author(s), and publishing information—provided in a standardized form, such as a record in an index (computer or paper) for a book or a periodical article.

bibliography: "a list of works, documents, and/or bibliographic items, usually with some relationship among them, e.g., by a given author [or] on a given subject" (Young 22).

Boolean searching: use of logical operators to conduct a search. Boolean searching allows the user to search for several concepts at once by specifying that all, some, or none of the concepts be represented in every item retrieved. An example of a Boolean search topic is the risk of AIDS related to getting a tattoo. The search statement used to retrieve information on these concepts is *tattoo and AIDS.* The word "and" is the Boolean operator used to require that all materials retrieved include BOTH the concepts. Other Boolean operators are "or" and "not."

bound periodical: issues comprising volumes of a periodical that have been put together and given a hard cover; for example, the issues of volume 18, 1996, of *Women's Sports and Fitness* are bound into one physical volume. Bound volumes of periodicals are kept separate from unbound issues and microform volumes of periodicals in many libraries.

browser: another word for client. The most frequently used Web browsers are *Netscape Navigator* and *Internet Explorer.* Both *Netscape Navigator* and *Internet Explorer* are graphical browsers that are able to capture all the graphics for which the Web is rightfully famous.

browsing: reading titles in the book stacks of a library, or scanning the entries in an index or the list of sites retrieved by a Web search engine in a general, rather than specific, search for information of interest.

call number: the number assigned to an item in an information collection to indicate its location, most often based on the subject content of the item. A call number might be likened to a house number as part of an address.

catalog: "a file of bibliographic records, created according to specific and uniform principles of construction . . . which describes the materials contained in a collection [or] library." (Young 37)

CD-ROM: an initialism for Compact Disk-Read Only Memory that is one format for electronic information. Data is stored and searched digitally on a compact disk using a personal computer with compatible software. Many access tools are now available in CD-ROM format.

cite: "to quote as an authority or example; to mention as support, illustration or proof." *(American Heritage)*

click on: the action you take to activate a link or a button on the screen of a computer. You may use a mouse to move the cursor to the item (a button is usually an icon and a link may be both an icon and a colored and underlined word, phrase, or URL) and then press the mouse button (click).

client-server: an interaction between a user and a computer that works this way, according to the "Internet Glossary" at the *MacintoshOS* Web site: "When you and your computer are searching for or accessing information on another computer, you are the client. The other computer is the server, and together you are using client/server technology. The server stores the info and makes it available to all authorized clients." Your client to use the Web may be the *Netscape Navigator* browser; the Web is the protocol it uses.

collections (in a library): a group of materials kept together. Examples of collections that are common to many libraries include:

General Collection: books, some of which come with CDs or other included materials, that circulate to (can be checked out by) the library's authorized users.

Media Collection: a group of materials that are for the most part nonprint, housed with or near their appropriate equipment.

Reference Collection: information sources that provide brief authoritative information and access tools that provide reference to other sources, kept together in one area of a library and usually not allowed to circulate.

Periodicals Collection: magazines, journals, and newspapers in all their formats: unbound issues, bound volumes, and issues and volumes in microfilm and microfiche, usually kept in an area of a library apart from the general collection.

Special Collections: "collections of library materials separated from the general collection because they are of a certain form, on a certain subject, of a certain period or geographical area, rare, fragile or valuable." (Young 211) Examples of special collections are a local history collection, donated papers from a local luminary, college archives, etc.

computer: "A device that computes, esp. an electronic machine that performs high-speed mathematical or logical calculations or that assembles, stores, correlates, or otherwise processes and prints information derived from coded data in accordance with a predetermined program." *(American Heritage)* Please note that the definition does NOT include the word "think" anywhere!

controlled vocabulary indexing system: "an indexing system in which the indexer, in assigning descriptors to works, is limited to a specified list of terms called the index vocabulary." (Young 59) See also "uncontrolled vocabulary indexing system."

cross-reference: a direction from one subject heading or descriptor to another.

cursor: an icon that is usually a flashing rectangle, a vertical line, or an arrow, plain or somewhat stylized, that indicates where action will take place on the computer screen. The mouse or the arrow keys manipulate the cursor.

database: "a structured collection of data: information that has been organized in such a form that it is retrievable through a computer system." So says *The Cyberspace Lexicon.* **Librarians often refer to any computerized index as a database; usually they mean those *bibliographic* databases that they can access because they pay subscription fees.** Most bibliographic databases provide periodical literature, or references to the articles in periodicals, as well as materials other than periodicals such as book chapters, or references to them.)

descriptor: a term used to describe the subject content of an information source; also called a subject heading.

directory (a.k.a. Internet subject directory or Web directory): good beginning point for Web research. A Web directory is constructed by a person who has reviewed Web sites and chosen those he or she considers worth exploring, then organizes the selections by subject, or by another defined scheme. An example of a Web directory is John December's "The Top of the Web," in Figure 2-2.

download: to bring to your computer or to a floppy disk information that is on another computer. Opening a Web resource is actually a temporary download of the information from the resource. Many Web sites allow you to permanently download information that you find there, such as text, images, or software, and to print it or store it or to use it on your own computer.

e-mail: electronic mail. E-mail is a means of communicating with another person using the Internet. An e-mail message is a written letter or memo or note that is transmitted electronically, almost a written phone call.

field: part of a record of an information source; "a defined subdivision of a record used to record only a specific category of data," (Young 92) such as data about the author(s), the author field; or the title and subtitle, the title field; etc.

field tag: the abbreviation used by an access tool, usually in electronic form, to identify a field; also called field label.

ftp: *f*ile *t*ransfer *p*rotocol, which is a method for downloading information from an Internet resource to your own computer.

hard sciences: "the natural or physical sciences such as chemistry, physics, biology, geology, astronomy, etc." (Green 273)

hardware: the physical components of a computer, i.e., the keyboard, CPU, monitor, modem, and any other equipment that make up a computer.

hits: matches made by the computer in a search. You type a word that the computer receives as a string of letters. It then scans its entire database to find every occurrence of that word and lists the locations of those occurrences. Each item on the list is a "hit." You may get "false hits" or "false drops"; they are matches that aren't meaningful to your needs, irrelevant hits that make a search result "dirty."

Home Page: the beginning or "Home" screens of a Web resource. A Home Page is somewhat like the title page of a book in that it is the starting point for that resource, even though you may use the resource without ever going to its Home Page.

HTML: *H*yper*T*ext *M*arkup *L*anguage, the computer language used to make information readable at many Web sites. Other languages also are currently in use.

http: *h*yper*t*ext *t*ransfer *p*rotocol, which is what is used to display the information that is written in HTML. A URL, or address on the Web, most commonly begins <http://> to let the computer know that the information at the Web site is in hypertext format.

hypertext: a term coined by Ted Nelson in 1964 that refers to text that includes links to other information sources. Hypertext allows a user to move in a nonlinear fashion through information sources; by contrast, regular text requires a user to read from the beginning of a line (or page or chapter or book) to the end of it, in a linear fashion.

icon: a picture on a computer that represents a category or file of information, and may be clicked on to connect to that information. Examples of icons include graphics such as a telephone for an online address book, a pencil for a drawing program, or a music note for an application that plays compact audio disks. See Figure 2-1.

index: a systematic guide to the contents of an information source. An index consists of descriptors or other words or symbols (such as report numbers) representing the contents, and references such as page numbers for accessing the contents of the source. (Young 116) Two types of indexes are those found in the backs of books, which refer readers to pages in the books for information on the subjects in the index; and periodical indexes, which refer users to specific issues of magazines and journals that have articles on the subjects listed.

information system: an organized structure of interrelated information sources, for example, a library's collections, or a library catalog.

Internet: a *net*work of computer networks throughout the world, i.e., *inter*national. The Internet is often referred to as "the Net." The phrase "surfing the Net" means exploring sites, i.e., viewing the information available on computers connected through this network.

journal: a periodical that contains scholarly information or current information on research and development whose intended audience includes scholars, practitioners, and experts in the subject field covered by the publication. A periodical does not have to include the word journal in its title to be considered a scholarly source. Compare to the definition of "magazine."

LC: abbreviation for "Library of Congress."

link(s): connection(s) to other Web resources provided at a Web site. Links are usually underlined and of a color different from the rest of the text on a screen. They may also be icons. When you use a mouse, you may will see the cursor's arrow change to a pointing finger when the mouse positions it the cursor over a link. An example of a link is the one to "The Catacombs of Paris" that is found on the Home Page for the WebMuseum, Paris; Paris: Tours. This means that when you click on the phrase, *"Visit Paris,"* and then on the word *Catacombs,* you "jump" to that Web site. In reality you download the information from that site so that you can use it; you don't really "go" anywhere! (As of mid-2002, you could "take" this tour by going to http://www.oir.ucf.edu/wm/ and clicking as stated above.)

listserv: an electronic mailing list used for communication purposes. A listserv is set up so that a subscriber sends a message to a central point and the message is then distributed to all other subscribers who read and react to it. The best listservs are moderated, that is, a designated person screens all messages sent "to the list" and distributes only those that relate to the subject matter to which the list is dedicated. There are listservs for virtually any subject or profession. There are also a myriad of electronic bulletin boards and discussion lists.

magazine: weekly, biweekly, or monthly periodical that is intended for a general readership, usually with articles on various topics by different authors. Some periodicals that include the world journal in their titles are magazines. Compare to the definition of "journal."

microfiche: flat sheets of film containing micro-images of periodicals or books arranged in a grid pattern; see also "microfilm."

microfilm: roll film containing micro-images of periodicals or books; see also "microfiche."

modem: communications device that converts the digital data from a computer into analog format that can be transmitted over telephone lines; short for *mo*dulator/*dem*odulator.

nonprint media (sometimes called audiovisual materials): materials in audio and visual formats such as film and tape that convey information primarily by sound and image rather than by text, now also incorporating digitally stored information on compact disks that includes sound and visual recordings, and electronic information sources such as computerized encyclopedias and dictionaries and access tools such as periodicals indexes.

online: accessible through a computer, such as an online database. Sometimes this term is used instead of "electronic" or "digitally stored."

operating system (OS): the basic computer programming used by a computer to work with various programs or software. The *American Heritage Dictionary* definition is: "Computer software designed to complement the hardware of a specific data processing system." Examples of operating systems are DOS, which was the IBM standard OS for years, and Windows OS and Windows95, -98, and -2000 that have replaced DOS. Apple computers have used their own operating systems, including MacOS. Also part of the field is Linux, a Unix-type OS that is available for free download from the Web at www.linux.org (as of May 2001).

periodical: a publication that is published at regular intervals of more than one day, usually referring to magazines and journals, and often newspapers.

peripheral(s): ". . . devices, such as disk drives, printers, modems . . . that are connected to a computer. . . . Although *peripheral* often implies 'additional but not essential,' many peripheral devices are critical elements of a fully functioning and useful computer system." *(Microsoft Press Computer Dictionary)*

portal: "a main guide that includes a search engine, plus additional content (such as current news, entertainment info, etc.), designed to keep you at the portal for as long as possible. A good example would be *Yahoo*, Netscape's *Netcenter*, *CNN*, *AOL*, etc." This is according to the Web site, mainportals.com. There are different types of portals. Many colleges and universities create Internet portals that are meant to be gateways to their own services and the Internet/Web, without the marketing goals of commercial Web portals.

protocol: "common set of rules and 'language' agreed upon by networked computers to allow communication. With so many different types of computers and operating systems on the Internet, agreed upon protocols are a must," according to the "Internet Glossary" at the *MacintoshOS* Web site. You may be told, "the protocols for the program are different on different computers;" this means that you'll have to use different keystrokes to perform the same function on two different computers.

quick and dirty: a phrase used to describe a search of a computerized database in which information is retrieved swiftly but much that was retrieved is not useful. In other words, one term was typed and all occurrences of the word were retrieved regardless of context; many of the records retrieved are not relevant, making a "dirty" search. See also the definition of "hits."

record: an entry in an access tool (paper or electronic) that provides enough information about an information source to completely identify the source, arranged in a standardized form. A record includes author, title, and publishing information. See also "bibliographic record."

search engine: software used to search through the myriad sites on the World Wide Web. A search engine works much like an electronic index does, searching through sites on the Internet for matches to the strings of letters (words) you type in. Items retrieved include the URL for each Web site. Examples of search engines (as of June 2001) are AltaVista and FAST Search. There are numerous sites that compare features of search engines. One is available at

http://faculty.plattsburgh.edu/dennis.kimmage/HyperResearch.htm

search statement: a series of search terms combined to describe an information need and designed to be usable in a particular access tool. For example, a search statement that could be used in a library's catalog for information about the Lake Champlain monster is: Lake Champlain AND sea monsters.

search term: a single word, multiple-word phrase, or significant number (e.g., report number or law number), used to search for information. A search term is the term you look under in an access tool.

set: in information research, a group of records in a database that share a common element, such as the same author or the same descriptor or the same year of publication. A set is created by a computer when a searcher commands the computer to scan the database to retrieve all records that have the specified search term, for example, all records that include the word "Zaire."

soft science: "any of the social or behavioural sciences: psychology, sociology, etc." (Green 510)

software: written computer programs that are used by the operating system of a computer. Examples of software include games, such as *Myst;* word processing programs such as *WordPerfect;* and budgeting applications, such as *Quicken.* Software can also be called programs or applications.

source: a single entity from which information is retrieved, for example, a person, a book, a journal article, an index. (Young v.p.)

subject heading: a search term used to describe the subject content of an information source; also called descriptor.

telnet: a program for connecting to a remote computer on the Internet.

term: word or multi-word phrase.

thesaurus: a list of terms used in a controlled vocabulary that shows relationships among them, such as broader terms, narrower terms, and related terms.

unbound periodical issue: an edition of a periodical that is part of a volume; for example, a quarterly edition of *Ms.* magazine is an unbound issue. In many libraries unbound issues of periodicals are shelved separately from their older volumes, which may be bound or kept in microformat.

uncontrolled vocabulary indexing system: a system used to index information sources by subject, in which an indexer is not limited to a specified list of descriptors; the opposite of a "controlled vocabulary system"; also called a natural-language indexing system.

URL: *U*niversal *R*esource *L*ocator, an address on the World Wide Web. A URL is often put in between < > brackets to set it off from text. You do *not* type the brackets when you use the URL. The URL for the National Museum of the American Indian of the Smithsonian (as of mid-2001) is:

http://www.nmai.si.edu/

Currently you're able to type in a Web address without even typing the "www" part. Most browsers will type that for you. For example, if you type *alltheweb.com* into your browser's location bar, it will complete the URL *and* download the Web site to your computer.

If you wish to know what each of the segments in any URL mean, see one of the various detailed discussion of URLs, such as that in *The World Wide Web Unleashed 1997* or in the online version of that book. See also the discussion about URLs in Chapter 7 of this book.

usercode, username: the "name" used for one's computer account. An example of a username (the terms usercode and username are usually interchangeable) is smit5096. This sample usercode was created from the first four letters of a person's last name and four digits that were randomly assigned by the user's institutional computer center. An approach used by many commercial Internet-access providers is to allow the user to select his/her own usercode. You may become yankeeFan#1 or a similar name under such an approach! Think of the vanity license plates you've seen if you need ideas for your username.

A complete Internet address consists of the usercode and the name and location of the computer she/he is using. For example, the author's Internet address (mid-2002) is: <carla.list@plattsburgh.edu> An e-mail user at one site will address a message to a friend at another site by using the friend's usercode and Internet address.

While the terms usercode and username often may be used interchangeably, this is not always the case. Read carefully any instructions for creating and using your username or usercode.

Web site: any resource available on the World Wide Web. A Web site may simply refer you to information, or it may provide the full text of an article or research paper, a short video, or an excerpt from—or even a complete—sound recording. It may also be a short block of information about a person, an institution or a business, or a catalog from which you may order materials directly using a credit card. An exciting aspect of the Web is the diversity found in Web sites.

World Wide Web: a way to use the Internet. It's a protocol that links information in hypertext format. It's also called "the Web," and you may see it shortened to WWW or sometimes to W3 in print. "Surfing the Web" is a very common phrase meaning to look for information or for anything of interest using the Web.

INDEX

Numerical Models of Ocean Circulation

PROCEEDINGS OF A SYMPOSIUM

Held at
Durham, New Hampshire
October 17–20, 1972

Organized by the
Ocean Science Committee
of the
Ocean Affairs Board

NATIONAL ACADEMY OF SCIENCES

WASHINGTON, D.C. 1975

NOTICE: The study reported herein was undertaken under the aegis of the *National Academy of Sciences/National Research Council* with the express approval of the *Council of the Academy/Governing Board of the NRC.* Such approval indicated that the *Council/Board* considered that the problem is of national significance; the elucidation or solution of the problem required scientific or technical competence; and that the resources of the *NAS/NRC* were particularly suitable to the conduct of the project. The institutional responsibilities of the *Academy/NRC* were then discharged in the following manner:

The members of the study committee were selected for their individual scholarly competence and judgement with due consideration for the balance and breadth of disciplines. Responsibility for all aspects of this report rests with the study committee, to whom we express our sincere appreciation.

Although the reports of our study committees are not submitted for approval to the Academy membership nor to the Council, each report is reviewed by a second group of appropriately qualified individuals according to procedures established and monitored by the Academy's Report Review Committee. Such reviews are intended to determine, inter alia, whether the major questions and relevant points of view have been addressed and whether the reported findings, conclusions, and recommendations arose from the available data and information. Distribution of the report is approved, by the President, only after satisfactory completion of this review process.

Available from
Printing and Publishing Office, National Academy of Sciences
2101 Constitution Avenue, Washington, D.C. 20418

Library of Congress Cataloging in Publication Data

Main entry under title:

Numerical models of ocean circulation.

Includes bibliographies.
1. Ocean circulation–Mathematical models–Congresses. I. National Research Council. Ocean Science Committee.
GC228.5.N85 551.4'7'00184 74-28404
ISBN 0-309-02225-8

Printed in the United States of America

PREFACE

During the past 5 to 10 years, many significant developments in the state of the art of numerical modeling ocean circulation have evolved that parallel the equally significant developments in observational techniques for advancing our understanding of ocean dynamics. In recognition of the importance of numerical techniques as applied to ocean dynamics, including their use in guiding field and laboratory studies, the Ocean Science Committee of the Ocean Affairs Board of the National Academy of Sciences, at the request of and with support from the Office of Naval Research, organized an international symposium on numerical modeling of ocean circulation. Kirk Bryan, Allan Robinson, and I were asked by the Chairperson of the Ocean Sciences Committee, John Knauss, to serve as a Steering Committee to plan and organize the symposium.

A series of meetings of the Steering Group were held to formulate the plans of the symposium. In organizing the symposium the steering committee defined several broad objectives:

(a) to appraise the present state of the art regarding numerical models and the extent to which these can simulate existing empirical knowledge of ocean circulation and associated thermal structure;

(b) to consider some of the applications of these models in studies of the large-scale interaction of the ocean and atmosphere or as a tool in studying the distribution of tracers or in studies dealing with the response of the models to variations in the parameters characterizing the system;

(c) to assess the capability of these models for studying mesoscale and/or transient features of the circulation and their potential as a guide to field or laboratory experiments; and

(d) to review through discussion of numerical methods both the accuracy of present numerical models and the possibilities for improvement of these models.

Participation in the symposium was limited to 50 invited participants. There were 36 invited papers, excluding evening sessions. Several of these papers are reviews of various facets of the general problem of ocean circulation; others were reports of recent studies. To encourage discussion of the papers, one formal reviewer of each paper was identified to prepare a written discussion prior to the meeting. The detailed discussions of the papers at the symposium were recorded. The papers, their formal reviews, and summaries of the subsequent discussions when available are presented. The organization of these papers is patterned essentially according to the objectives of the symposium above.

A potential exists for future coupling between dynamic and biological models of the ocean. This subject is discussed in the paper in Section I by J. Walsh, in which a specific example of the interaction that occurs in an area of coastal upwelling is discussed. In addition, H. Fischer presents a review of the challenging and very pressing problems involved in modeling estuaries and small bays.

Section II contains a set of basic papers that review the present knowledge of the ocean circulation. Papers included are a review of basic concepts by V. M. Kamenkovich and of the driving forces pertinent to ocean dynamics by S. Pond, a survey by A. Gordon of the ocean circulation as deduced from hydrographic observations, and a review of modern measurement techniques by N. F. Fofonoff and D. W. Moore.

The papers in Section III relate to models of the quasi-permanent circulation and commence with a review by P. Welander of analytical models as background to the discussion of numerical models of the quasi-permanent circulation. The numerical models fall in one of two distinct categories: those that employ the observed density field as input (diagnostic models), as reviewed by A. S. Sarkisyan and V. R. Keonjiyan; and those that predict the density field (fully predictive models), as summarized by K. Bryan. These differ in two very important respects: First, the fully predictive models require several orders of magnitude greater "spin-up" time to reach equilibrium than the diagnostic models; second, the fully predictive models allow for a conversion of potential energy to kinetic energy, or vice versa. As shown in both Schulman's and Holland's papers in Section IV, the conversion of kinetic energy can be very important for maintaining the barotropic part of the circulation for any bottom topography. The preliminary results of two independent studies of the worlds ocean circulation, one by M. Cox and the other by K. Takano, complete Section III. The study by Cox employs the diagnostic method for a baroclinic model.

In Section IV the papers assembled discuss special studies using numerical models. The paper by G. Veronis concerns the use of models in the interpretation of tracer studies, while the paper by E. Schulman, as well as that of W. Holland, concerns the role of topography in stratified systems. Holland examines this question in terms of the energetics of the system.

The papers in Section V relate to modeling of transient or intermediate-scale phenomena. Included in this section are several papers on special phenomena: A. Gill reviews models of equatorial currents, J. O'Brien discusses models of coastal upwelling, transient effects in western boundary currents are discussed by P. Niiler, and G. Zilitinkevich reviews the subject of modeling of planetary boundary layers. Also included are preliminary results of an interesting study by F. Bretherton on a model of a mesoscale mid-ocean phenomena. In a model of the mesoscale mid-ocean phenomena, one must deal with the difficult problem of open boundaries, which is either of no concern or of lesser importance in large-scale ocean models. Through the study of such mesoscale systems, which allow for the presence of larger-scale circulation, it is anticipated that greater insight can be gained with respect to the parameterization of the interaction of subgrid scales with larger scales. The present state of the art in respect to large-scale models of ocean circulation is such that closure with respect to the influence of subgrid scales is achieved in an admittedly *ad hoc* manner through eddy-diffusion terms.

The papers in Section VI pertain to numerical methods. Included in the section are a paper comparing numerical methods used in the atmosphere and the ocean by H.-O. Kreiss and a paper dealing with the assessment of the accuracy of conventional finite-difference methods by B. Wendroff. Part of this section addresses questions concerned with potential avenues for improvement of existing numerical schemes employed in ocean models: G. Fix reviews different numerical methods used in various fields of mechanics, S. Orszag and M. Israeli discuss modern trends in numerical methods for hydrodynamic problems, and finally

C. Leith offers some projections concerning probable future computing machine configurations and computing methods. Much of the discussion in this section concerned ways and means of coping with the difficult problem of advecting properties with a minimum of phase distortion that is a failing of many schemes that otherwise conserve total property and total property squared.

Section VII presents three additional papers that specifically deal with the numerical simulation of laboratory experiments. These include a paper by R. Beardsley on a numerical investigation of a laboratory analogy of the wind-driven ocean, a paper by D. Boyer on numerical analysis of laboratory experiments on topographically controlled flow, and a paper by J. Hirsch that applies the spline method in a numerical analysis of the Baker-Robinson model. These numerical simulation studies of laboratory experiments are very pertinent to assessing the veracity of the numerical models in view of the greater ability for control and measurement in the laboratory experiments as compared with field surveys in the real ocean.

The discussion that follows each paper provides the reader of these proceedings with an insight that could never be obtained by reading published papers. They also show the lively differences of opinion that exist among physical oceanographers with respect to both methods and the interpretation of theoretical models.

The concluding section presents the conclusions of the symposium and a summary of the panel discussion that was held on the final day of the symposium and that addressed the important question: "Where do we go from here?"

Augmenting the regular sessions of the symposium, a special evening session included a presentation by J. O'Brien of films depicting the output of numerical models simulating five quite distinct aspects of ocean circulation.

R. O. REID
Member, Steering Committee

CONTENTS

I INTRODUCTION

INTRODUCTION

R. O. REID, A. R. ROBINSON, and K. BRYAN

The study of ocean circulation remains a scientific frontier that has had a long history and has enjoyed recent rapid progress. Only a few decades ago, it was a lonely frontier like a camp of the Lewis and Clark Expedition. Now the field has more of the character of a Colorado gold camp.

Revolutions in scientific areas are usually triggered by technical developments. Those technical developments that have recently influenced the study of ocean circulation include radiochemical techniques; fixed and free-floating, direct subsurface, current-measuring devices; continuously recording instruments; advances in data storage, retrieval, and transmission; and radio and satellite navigation. Modern computers have been essential in coping with the large masses of data, often in the form of long time series, generated by these new methods. The capabilities of these computers have advanced rapidly, a new generation being spawned every 5 years. Each generation is an order-of-magnitude faster with a comparable decrease in the cost-of-a-unit arithmetic operation.

In addition to rapid data reduction, the calculating power of large computers allows a direct attack on previously intractable and inaccessible theoretical problems in continuum mechanics. To date, computer development has been more rapid than that of numerical methods needed to exploit their full potential. This situation should change as numerical methods initiated in the precomputer era are replaced by more accurate and efficient methods matched to the capabilities of modern computers. Even with present numerical methods, solutions for linear and for some nonlinear flows have been obtained, some of them verified against analytical solutions and/or laboratory experiments.

Laboratory models with their related numerical studies also play an important role in advancing our understanding of the ocean circulation. However, the transition from the successful solution of the Navier–Stokes equations for laminar flows to the essential problem of the turbulence of ocean circulation is not straightforward. In a laboratory experiment, a relatively narrow range of scales in time and space is involved. These scales are on the lower end bounded by viscosity and on the upper end bounded by the size of the container. The span of time and space scales in the ocean is so enormous that a statistical approach must be adopted. In such an approach, the equations for the conservation of heat, momentum, and salinity must be averaged so that only the large-scale, low-frequency motions are treated explicitly in the model. The coupling between large and small scales appears as Reynolds stress terms in the momentum equations and similar eddy flux terms in the conservation equations for heat and salinity.

The specification of the Reynolds stresses (closure) in an ocean circulation model is essentially an unsolved problem. It is complex because the parameterization involves small-scale physical processes that vary in kind from the smallest to the largest scales averaged. At present, measurements in the atmosphere and laboratory turbulence experiments offer only limited guidance for the smaller scales because of the ocean's stratification in heat and salt. The Reynolds stresses for the larger scales depend on unique statistics of ocean currents that are still poorly understood. The earlier pioneering numerical models of ocean circulation are based on quite naive closure schemes. They extend earlier analytical theories of ocean circulation in some areas, but the relevance of the results must be considered as tentative. Presently two major field experiments are being carried out. Their objective is to determine the primary source of the eddy flux of heat and momentum in mid-ocean areas. Examples of such experiments are the Soviet *Polygon* experiment and the British and U.S. MODE experiment. An interesting symbiotic relation between these field experiments and numerical models has become evident.

Limited domain open-ocean numerical models of the circulation are helpful in planning and interpreting these complex observational experiments that provide data for the formulation of other, more advanced, numerical models. Other special domain and regional models are now recognized as necessary for exploring smaller or special parts of the circulation that are isolatable and complicated. These models must be used for numerical experimentation on processes and in conjunction with experimental programs. Examples are the coastal upwelling areas experiment, equatorial undercurrent studies planned in conjunction with the 1974 Global Atmospheric Research Project Tropical Atlantic Experiment, and the large-scale variation of the mixed-layer North Pacific Experiment. If these new observations and theory can provide the insights required for open-ocean closure and for the successful parameterization of special regions and processes, the long-range prospects are quite good.

The relation of circulation models to the chemistry and biology of the ocean is a new area of research, especially in paleo-oceanography.The large amounts of geologic data from the seafloor provide a picture of the configuration of the continents since Mesozoic times. Thus, numerical models of ocean circulation may be able to show how the ocean circulation responded to the geomorphic changes in the ocean basins and possibly caused the very great changes in climate that are clearly present in geological records.

Less spectacular, but of a more immediate concern, are the subtle, short-term fluctuations of climate that are taking place at present. These year-to-year changes are generally considered to be associated with the large-scale interaction of the atmosphere and the oceans, but this interaction is very complex and poorly understood. Today, the world no longer has the surpluses to deal with unforeseen droughts, extremes in temperature, and attendant crop failures. Any contribution that numerical models can make in our understanding of year-to-year climate changes will have a lasting beneficial impact on society. These will richly reward the efforts of oceanographers and others who are developing and improving numerical models of ocean circulation.

A BIOLOGICAL INTERFACE FOR NUMERICAL MODELS AND THE REAL WORLD —AN ELEGY FOR E. J. FERGUSON WOOD*

J. J. WALSH

INTRODUCTION

The role of a biological oceanographer in a symposium on numerical models of predominantly physical phenomena can be interpreted as that of a terrestrial ecologist at an oceanographic congress (Hutchinson, 1961)—to provide contrast of alternative biological approaches and needs in joint problems and solutions encountered in an interdisciplinary endeavor such as oceanography. As large-scale studies of marine ecosystems continue (Walsh, 1972a), the benefits of cross-discipline fertilization become more apparent. I would like to address some of the possible spin-off values of numerical models for both physical and biological oceanography.

The marine habitat is a geophysical fluid, and any attempts to understand biological processes therein must be firmly based in a matrix of relevant physical oceanography. Understanding of phenomena usually implies some knowledge or intuition about the future behavior of the system beyond the simple description of its past states. Prediction of the future states of complex assemblages such as marine ecosystems involves a much larger number of state variables than are usually considered by physical oceanographers, however; and, until recently, marine ecologists have restricted themselves to process studies. In the last decade, an increasing number of optimistic biological oceanographers have begun to follow the lead of their physical colleagues in constructing numerical models as an index of one's understanding of marine ecosystems.

*I would like to honor the late E. J. Ferguson Wood for his stimulus to undertake some of this work.

BIOLOGICAL SPIN-OFF

Nutrients and phytoplankton are the most common state variables chosen by biological oceanographers in the construction of mathematical models (Patten, 1968; Walsh and Dugdale, 1972). This choice reflects the relative availability of data, the status of field and laboratory techniques, and the ease of model validation. Driving forces for the steady-state numerical solution of the phytoplankton–nutrient equations usually involve the physical properties of advection and diffusion and the biological properties of herbivores, carnivores, and saprovores. Dugdale (1967) has emphasized the implications of nutrient limitation, while Steele (1972) has suggested that the phytoplankton–herbivore component of the marine food web may be the most sensitive coupling and Pomeroy (1970) has highlighted the role of nutrient regeneration. In addition, Smith (1969) has stressed the importance of the number of steps or trophic levels in the food web, Wood and Corcoran (1966) have advocated consideration of diel periodicity, and Platt (1972) has demonstrated the importance of spatial variability. The choice of state variables and level of temporal and spatial resolution of these biological models is, of course, dependent on the interests and requirements of the modelers.

One common constraint, however, is the parameterization of physical inputs to these biological models (Winter and Banse, in press). In general, biological oceanographers do not deploy current meters, nor are they theoretical hydrodynamicists. Their concepts of the important parameters and frequencies of the physical driving forces are conditioned by the interpretations of their physical colleagues

(Stommel, 1970). Numerical circulation models, one index of a physical oceanographer's concept of the physical properties of the marine habitat, are thus a necessary prerequisite for proper submodel input into biological models (O'Brien and Wroblewski, 1972).

Biological oceanographers, however, are probably not interested in incorporating all of a complicated numerical circulation model as input into their own relatively complicated models. In any case, present computing facilities would not practically promote such a marriage. At the other extreme, the succinctness of classical equations such as that for a nonconservative parameter,

$$\frac{\partial c}{\partial t} = k_x \frac{\partial^2 c}{\partial x^2} + k_y \frac{\partial^2 c}{\partial y^2} + k_z \frac{\partial^2 c}{\partial z^2} - u \frac{\partial c}{\partial x} - v \frac{\partial c}{\partial y} - w \frac{\partial c}{\partial z} \pm R,$$

with all the biology stuffed into the R term, also leaves something to be desired. Furthermore, biological modelers need to condense or expand the output of their numerical circulation models to match the spatial and temporal scales of simulation models for lower trophic levels (kilometers and hours) and higher trophic levels (degrees and months) of marine ecosystems. One might be optimistic and ask not only what the physical oceanographer can do for the biologist, but perhaps what the biological oceanographer can do for the physicist.

PHYSICAL SPIN-OFF

There are at least two classes of benefits that physical oceanographers might accrue from the activities of biological oceanographers. The first consists of traditional, descriptive biological oceanography involving the distribution of organisms; indicator species can be used to relate general circulation principles to the distribution of marine communities. The second class of input involves construction and, most importantly, validation of the biological models; if the physical inputs are improperly described or parameterized, it is unlikely that any amount of model "tuning" will produce a match between biological models and the real world.

The late E. J. Ferguson Wood was a strong advocate of plankton studies embedded in descriptive physical oceanography (Wood, 1971). Formation and the distribution of Antarctic intermediate water at the Antarctic convergence (Walsh, 1972b) and of Antarctic bottom water in the Ross and Weddell seas (Walsh, unpublished data) can be traced with the distribution of planktonic diatoms, while upwelling can be detected by the distribution of benthic diatoms in the water column (Wood, 1964; Smayda, 1966). Similarly, the distribution of zooplankton species can be used to trace the movement of water in the Gulf Stream (Scheltema, 1971), in the Gulf of Maine (Redfield, 1939), in the North Sea (Russell, 1935), and in the Oyashio current (Omori, 1967).

The biological oceanographer's ability to color the water green for his physical colleagues can be extended to more dynamic consideration of the ocean's circulation in the construction of biological simulation models. Our present research on simulation models of marine ecosystems, for example, involves a two-fold approach of seagoing simulation on IBM 1130 and PDP-11 systems and of land-based simulation on a CDC 6400 system. The seagoing facility is required for our adaptive, field-sampling programs, while the land-based simulations should provide eventual communication with complex, physical numerical models. Both simulation programs involve the same philosophy of submodel coupling but differ in the level of resolution as constrained by computer memory.

Figure 1 presents the submodel structure of a single-point, upwelling systems model with the circulation (u, v, w) and abiotic submodels (light, temperature, nutrients, and inhibitors) used as input to the coupled, biological, state variable submodels (phytoplankton; herbivorous zooplankton and fish; carnivorous nekton and benthos; and the decomposer food chain of bacteria, yeasts, and protozoans) whose temporal and spatial distribution are computed through the individual process submodels (nutrient uptake, photosynthesis, sinking, metabolic losses of excretion and respiration, grazing, predation, behavior patterns, and remineralization). The fit between the real world of easily measured phytoplankton–nutrient phenomena and both the highly parameterized seagoing model and its land-based, expanded version is used as a central focus to test the reliability of single point and spatial biological models to describe and predict the dynamics of upwelling ecosystems.

The validation step of comparing the predicted nutrient and phytoplankton fields with a small segment (5,000 km^2) of the real ocean may be of value to physical oceanographers in testing their own models. Our previous IBM 1130 shipboard models (Dugdale and Whitledge, 1970; Dugdale and MacIsaac, 1971; Walsh and Dugdale, 1971; and Cruzado, in preparation) involve a gradation of complexity in assumptions about the physical circulation and are probably too simple to substantiate anything more than general hydrodynamic principles. The two-layered, one-dimensional, phytoplankton–nutrient model (Walsh and Dugdale, 1971) of an upwelling plume off the coast of Peru did nevertheless demonstrate the necessity for proper parameterization of the physical circulation. Most of the observed offshore surface distribution of nitrate, for example, could be predicted with an appropriate downplume decay of w (the upwelling velocity), a determination by continuity of u (the downplume velocity), and a 4/3 lateral diffusion term. The biological couplings were then superimposed on this sub-model with reasonable success in predicting the offshore phytoplankton distribution.

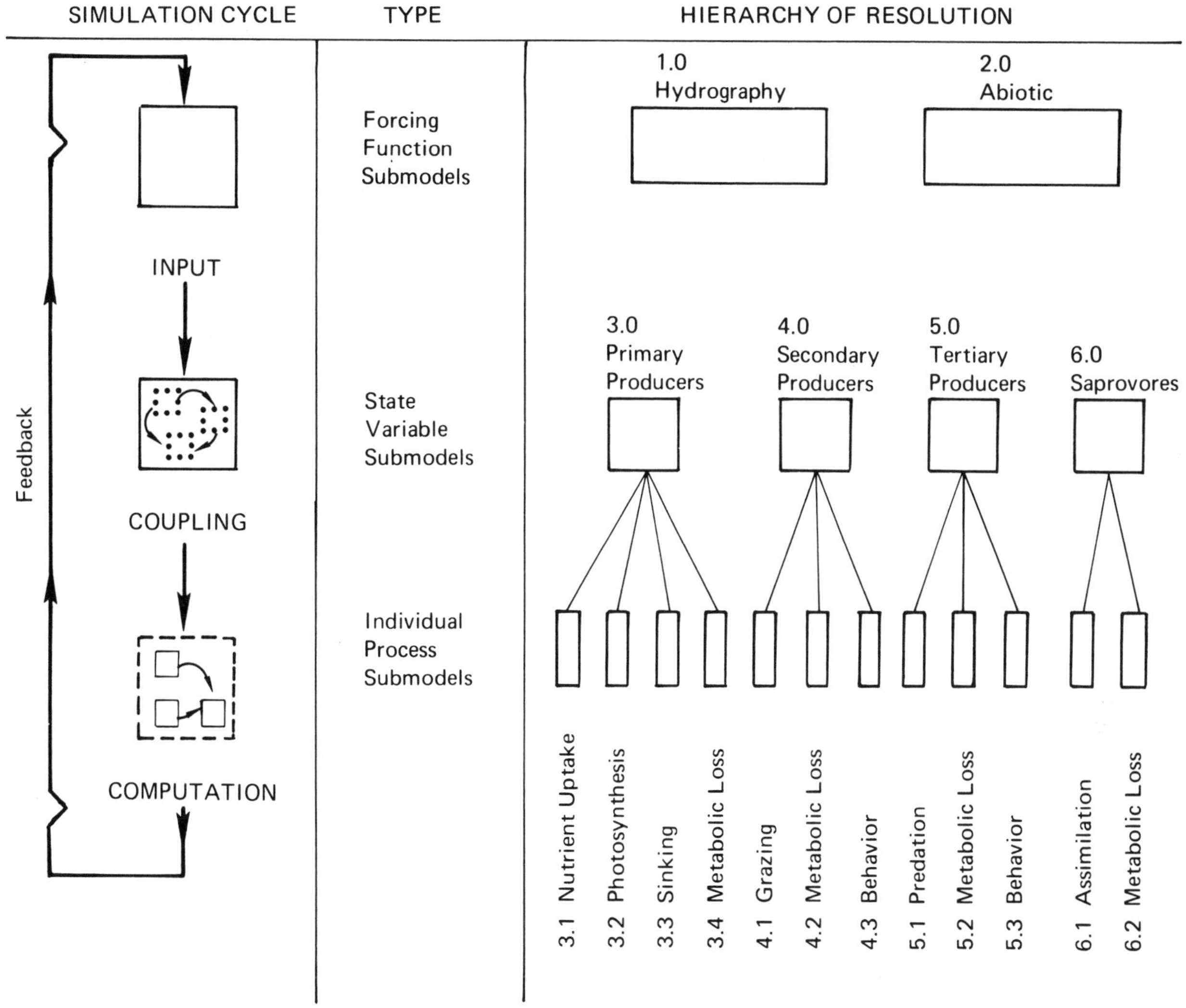

FIGURE 1 Submodel structure of an upwelling system model.

These simple models are upwards compatable with the CDC 6400 simulation program. Table 1 presents a comparison between the output, cost, and time per run of 120 iterations for the same five-state-variable, five-spatial-volume model executed with the IBM 1130 (OCEANS) and CDC 6400 (AUGUR) simulation programs. The AUGUR program (Walsh *et al.*, in preparation) is a three-dimensional simulation system capable of handling high-resolution submodels and their resultant system models with a capacity of 40 state variables at each of 30,000 grid points. The number of state variables and the geometric space are defined by the user with only seven contiguous grid points maintained in core at one time. As AUGUR scans the space for each iteration to update the state variables at every grid point, the necessary information is brought into the computer's memory, processed, and returned to the main storage device.

We are now using AUGUR to develop two- and three-dimensional models of upwelling and sewage outfall systems, as well as three-dimensional models of the Columbia River depositional patterns. The utility of these prospective models to physical oceanographers might be much greater than our previous work. Proper description of a two-dimensional plume of nutrients and phytoplankton, for example, requires a more complex and exact parameterization of the physical circulation (as suggested in Figure 2). Surface plumes of phytoplankton and nutrients could possibly be predicted by an equally poor parameterization of their physics and biology, but a match between observed and predicted biological state variables at a number of depths requires the water circulation to be properly described by the model in at least two, if not three, dimensions. Fit-of-state variables between these higher-resolution biological models and the real world could then be used to test more sophisticated circulation hypotheses.

TABLE 1 Comparison of AUGUR and OCEANS Output after 121 Iterations with a Time Step of One Hour

Offshore nitrate distribution (μg-at NO_3/liter)	OCEANS:	16.917	15.325	13.799	12.295	10.224
	AUGUR:	16.889	15.294	13.766	12.270	10.199
Offshore ammonia distribution (μg-at NH_3/liter)	OCEANS:	3.2467	3.1167	3.0046	2.9106	2.8488
	AUGUR:	3.2313	3.1013	2.9886	2.8951	2.8295
Offshore phytoplankton distribution (μg-at PN/liter)	OCEANS:	1.5482	1.5444	1.5236	1.4849	1.3342
	AUGUR:	1.5740	1.5701	1.5499	1.5114	1.3657
Offshore zooplankton distribution (μg-at PN/liter)	OCEANS:	0.0999				
	AUGUR:	0.1000				
Offshore anchoveta distribution (μg-at PN/liter)	OCEANS:	9.9999				
	AUGUR:	10.0000				
Integration scheme	OCEANS:	Euler				
	AUGUR:	Adams–Bashford				
Cost/job	OCEANS:	$15.00				
	AUGUR:	$ 8.50				
Machine time	OCEANS:	30 min				
	AUGUR:	2 min				

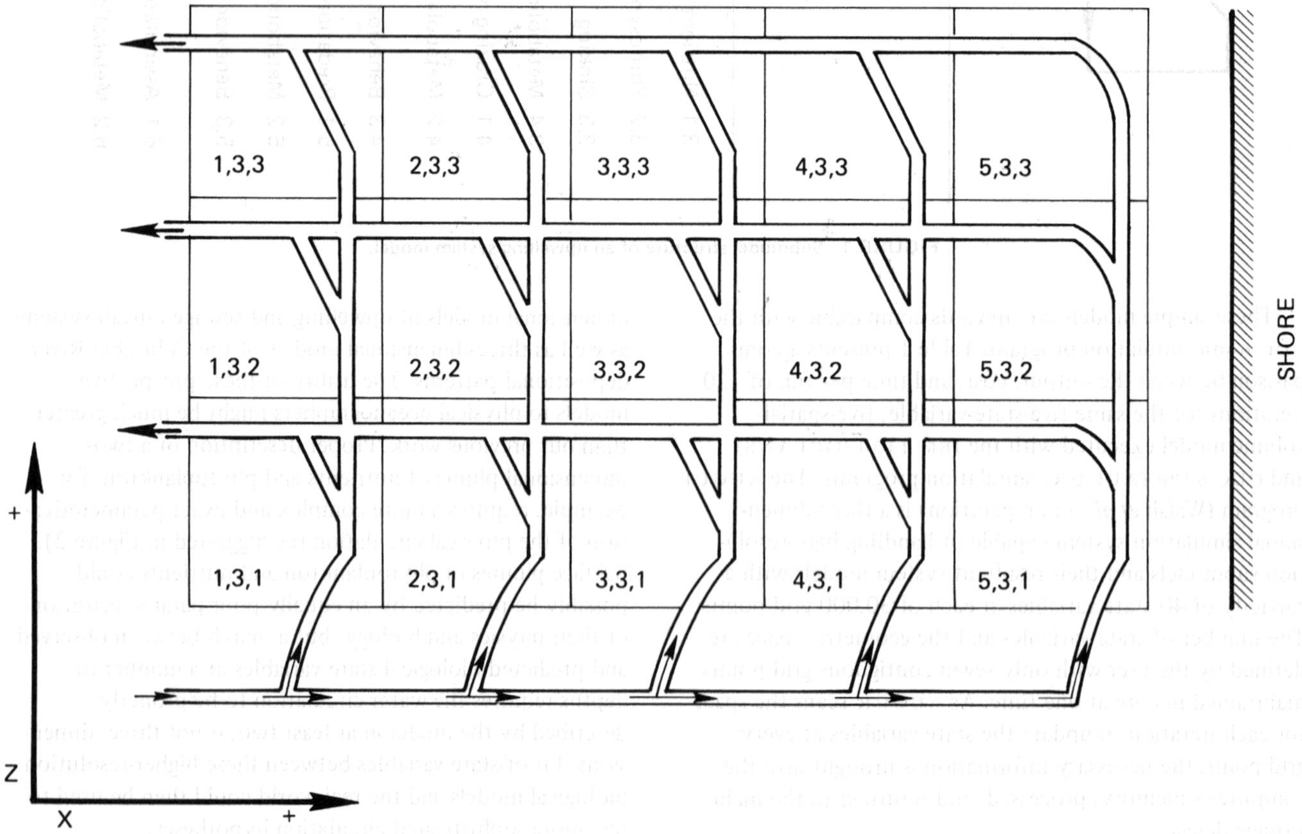

FIGURE 2 Vertical section of Peru plume model with schematic representation of the water transport.

CONCLUSION

As biological oceanographers begin to construct numerical models of marine ecosystems, the questions they ask of physical oceanographers and of themselves begin to stretch the state-of-the-art knowledge and techniques of both disciplines. Proper planning of validation studies should benefit both groups and lead to much greater information exchanges. The biological oceanographer's professional preoccupation with the complexity of living systems has led to smaller emphasis on mathematical analysis in contrast to the approaches used by physical oceanographers in studying their seemingly more tractable systems. Biologists, thus, have much to gain from a symposium replete with the latest techniques and insights into numerical models of the ocean's circulation. It is hoped that at some future date, biological simulation models and validation studies might provide feedback to physical oceanographers as well.

ACKNOWLEDGMENTS

This work was funded by Grant GB-18568 of the National Science Foundation as part of the Upwelling Biome studies within the U.S. International Biological Program.

REFERENCES

Cruzado, A. (In preparation) A computer simulation model of plant production off northwest Africa.

Dugdale, R. C. 1967. Nutrient limitation in the sea: Dynamics, identification, and significance. Limnol. Oceanogr. 12:685–95.

Dugdale, R. C., and J. J. MacIsaac. 1971. A computational model for the uptake of nitrate in the Peru upwelling region. Invest. Pesq. 35:299–308.

Dugdale, R. C., and T. E. Whitledge. 1970. Computer simulation of phytoplankton growth near a marine sewage outfall. Rev. Int. Oceanogr. Med. 17:201–10.

Hutchinson, G. E. 1961. The biologist poses some problems, pp. 85–94. *In* M. Sears, ed. Oceanography. Am. Assoc. Adv. Sci. Publ. No. 67. Washington, D.C.

O'Brien, J. J., and J. S. Wroblewski. 1972. An ecological model of the lower marine trophic levels on the continental shelf off West Florida. Geophys. Fluid Dyn. Inst. Tech. Rep. Florida State University, Tallahassee. 17 pp.

Omori, M. 1967. *Calanus cristatus* and submergence of Oyashio water. Deep-Sea Res. 14:525–32.

Patten, B. C. 1968. Mathematical models of plankton production. Int. Rev. ges. Hydrobiol. 53(3):357–408.

Platt, T. 1972. Local phytoplankton abundance and turbulence. Deep-Sea Res. 19(3):183–88.

Pomeroy, L. R. 1970. The strategy of mineral cycling. Annu. Rev. Ecol. Syst. 1:171–90.

Redfield, A. C. 1939. The history of a population of *Limacina retroversa* during its drift across the Gulf of Maine. Biol. Bull. 76:26–47.

Russell, F. S. 1935. On the value of certain plankton animals as indications of water movements in the English Channel and North Sea. J. Mar. Biol. Assoc. U. K. 20(2):309–32.

Scheltema, R. S. 1971. Dispersal of phytoplanktotrophic shipworm larvae (Bivalvia: Teredinidae) over long distances by ocean currents. Mar. Biol. 11(1):5–11.

Smayda, T. J. 1966. A quantitative analysis of the phytoplankton of the Gulf of Panama. III. General ecological conditions, and the phytoplankton dynamics at 8°45′N, 79°23′W from November 1954 to May 1957. Inter-Am. Trop. Tuna Comm. Bull. 11(5):355–612.

Smith, F. E. 1969. Effects of enrichment in mathematical models, pp. 631–45. *In* Eutrophication: Causes, Consequences, and Correctives. National Academy of Sciences, Washington, D.C.

Steele, J. H. 1972. Factors controlling marine ecosystems, pp. 209–21. *In* D. Dyrssen and D. Jagner, eds. The Changing Chemistry of the Ocean–Nobel Symposium 20. Almqvist and Wiksell, Stockholm.

Stommel, H. 1970. Future prospects for physical oceanography. Science 168(3939):1531–37.

Walsh, J. J. 1972a. Implications of a systems approach to oceanography. Science 176(4038):969–75.

Walsh, J. J. 1972b. Relative importance of habitat variables in predicting the distribution of phytoplankton at the ecotone of the Antarctic upwelling ecosystem. Ecol. Monogr. 41(4):291–309.

Walsh, J. J., P. B. Bass, and D. L. Morashima. (In preparation) AUGUR, a generalized three-dimensional CDC 6400 simulation program for analysis of aquatic ecosystems. Upwelling Biome Tech. Rep. No. 2. Department of Oceanography, University of Washington, Seattle.

Walsh, J. J., and R. C. Dugdale. 1971. A simulation model of the nitrogen flow in the Peruvian upwelling system. Invest. Pesq. 35:309–30.

Walsh, J. J., and R. C. Dugdale. 1972. Nutrient submodels and simulation models of phytoplankton production in the sea, pp. 221–25. *In* J. Kramer and H. Allen, eds. Nutrients in Natural Waters. J. Wiley and Sons, New York.

Winter, D. F., and K. Banse. (In press) A strategy for modeling primary production in stratified fjords. Proc. Second Tech. Conf. Estuaries Pac. Northwest, 16–17 March 1972. Oregon State University, Corvallis.

Wood, E. J. F. 1964. Studies in microbial ecology of the Australasian region. Nova Hedwigia 8:453–568.

Wood, E. J. F. 1971. Phytoplankton study–an appraisal. J. Cons. Int. Explor. Mer 34(1):124–27.

Wood, E. J. F., and E. F. Corcoran. 1966. Diurnal variation in phytoplankton. Bull. Mar. Sci. 16(3):383–403.

NUMERICAL MODELS OF ESTUARINE CIRCULATION AND MIXING

H. B. FISCHER

INTRODUCTION

Numerical models of estuaries are being constructed primarily to aid in studies of water quality and environmental degradation. The long-term objective is a numerical methodology capable of answering two types of questions. First, given an existing estuary, what chemical and biological changes will result from introduction of a new waste discharge? Second, what chemical and biological changes will occur if the physical character of an existing estuary is permanently changed, for instance, by dredging, diking, or a permanent change in the freshwater inflow? The first type of question is more easily answered, because, if the new discharge is dynamically passive, its distribution can be assumed to follow that of existing tracers in the estuary. The second type of question requires wholly predictive models, which first predict the distribution of currents and circulation in the estuary and then use the result to predict the distribution of pollutants. In this paper we will discuss primarily models of the second type, since they are more relevant to problems of ocean circulation.

The major problem in modeling estuaries is the degree of detail required to make the results useful. To meet the objectives required by most studies, the numerical grid size must be small enough to represent islands, embayments, headlands, etc., in sufficient detail so that the currents induced by these features are computed. Thus, although estuaries are much smaller bodies of water than oceans, the numerical modeling problems are similar. It is not possible to model a very large estuary and preserve the necessary detail without either exceeding the storage capacity of present-day computers or else simplifying the system to the extent of omitting possibly important mechanisms. Also, most estuary studies are sponsored by municipalities or sanitation districts, whose financial resources for such studies are modest. Hence, a legitimate research objective is to minimize program complexity and cost.

COMPUTATION OF TIDAL HYDRODYNAMICS

Tidal computations in rivers and coastal waters are the subject of a book by Dronkers (1964) reviewing the historical development of tidal computations and the methods available up to that time. The closing in 1932 of the Zuiderzee, in the Netherlands, necessitated practical computations of tidal hydraulics in shallow waters and stimulated development of the harmonic method described in Dronkers' book. The "Delta Project," which involved diking off large arms of the Rhine delta in the Netherlands and is still under construction, has further involved hydraulic engineers in extensive tidal computations. All of the computational methods currently in use are described by Dronkers (1969); these include the one- and two-dimensional methods of characteristics; one-dimensional, finite-difference schemes; and the two-dimensional, finite-difference scheme developed by Leendertse (1967).

Leendertse's two-dimensional model is probably of the greatest current interest, as it combines explicit and implicit computations in a useful way and has broad application. The equations to be solved are the vertically integrated equations of momentum and mass conservation:

$$\frac{\partial U}{\partial t} + U\frac{\partial U}{\partial x} + V\frac{\partial U}{\partial y} - fV + g\frac{\partial \zeta}{\partial x} + g\left[\frac{U(U^2+V^2)^{1/2}}{C^2(h+\zeta)}\right] = \tau_x, \quad (1)$$

$$\frac{\partial V}{\partial t} + U\frac{\partial V}{\partial x} + V\frac{\partial V}{\partial y} + fU + g\frac{\partial \zeta}{\partial y} + g\left[\frac{V(U^2+V^2)^{1/2}}{C^2(h+\zeta)}\right] = \tau_y, \quad (2)$$

$$\frac{\partial \zeta}{\partial t} + \frac{\partial}{\partial x}\left[(h+\zeta)U\right] + \frac{\partial}{\partial y}\left[(h+\zeta)V\right] = 0, \quad (3)$$

in which U and V are vertically averaged velocities in the x and y directions, ζ is the elevation of the water surface above a datum, h is the depth of the bottom below the datum, C is the Chezy friction coefficient, and τ_x and τ_y are wind stresses in the x and y directions. The model uses the staggered grid system shown in Figure 1; where ζ is computed at the grid point, the U and V velocities are computed at half-steps between grid points, and h is given at the center of the mesh. The computation proceeds in two half-steps. During the first, a new set of U velocities is computed along each row by an implicit finite-difference representation;

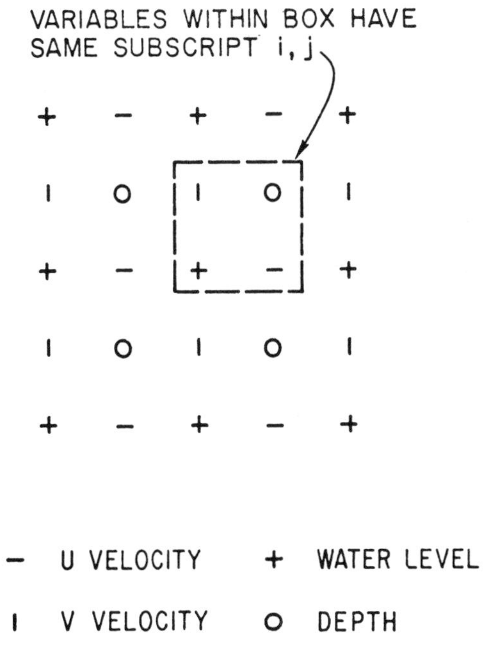

FIGURE 1 The staggered grid used in Leendertse's two-dimensional hydrodynamic model.

then a new set of V velocities is computed along each column explicitly. During the second half-step, the sequence is reversed—first V velocities are computed implicitly and then U velocities are computed explicitly.

Leendertse's method has been used in several studies of circulation in bays. Figure 2 shows one example of results obtained by this writer during a study of Botany Bay, Australia. Leendertse (1970) has extended his method to cases where a shallow area, such as a mud flat or tidal marsh, becomes exposed at lower tidal stages and has applied it to Jamaica Bay, New York (Leendertse and Gritton, 1971a,b). To date, however, results of the sort shown in Figure 2 have not been verified by any extensive field investigations. Model verification usually consists of matching observed and predicted tidal levels, because the former offer the only readily obtainable data. Matching tidal levels is much easier than matching velocities. In the Jamaica Bay study, for instance, tidal levels were matched but the comparisons available between observed and predicted velocities were not accurate. The latter may be in part because values of the Chezy friction coefficient for tidal flows are not accurately known and in part because the bathymetry may not have been accurately modeled. Both factors, however, were adjusted to improve the verification.

None of the present methods are used to compute velocities in three dimensions, nor do they include any dynamic effects of the density distribution. Hansen and Rattray (1965) have given an analytical solution for the density and velocity distributions in two dimensions in a somewhat idealized geometry, and the effect of the gravitational circulation on bottom shoaling has been recognized in an empirical way for some years in terms of the concept of "flow predominance" (Simmons, 1955; Harleman and Ippen, 1969). Progress has been made in obtaining three-dimensional solutions for circulation in lakes, as described by Liggett (1969) and Lee and Liggett (1970). In estuaries, however, important three-dimensional circulations are often induced both by the density distribution and by the bathymetry, and no computational scheme has yet been devised to model these circulations.

MASS TRANSPORT MECHANISMS IN ESTUARIES

Since no numerical mixing model is completely general and none can account for all the modes of mixing and mass transport that exist in estuaries, it is useful to discuss the mechanisms of mass transport and mixing. The numerical models can then be classified according to what mechanism is modeled.

Estuaries are often classified by degree of stratification: strongly stratified (the existence of a salt wedge or two-layer flow), partially stratified (a noticeable density difference between the surface and the bottom that is sufficient to impede vertical mixing), and well mixed (no

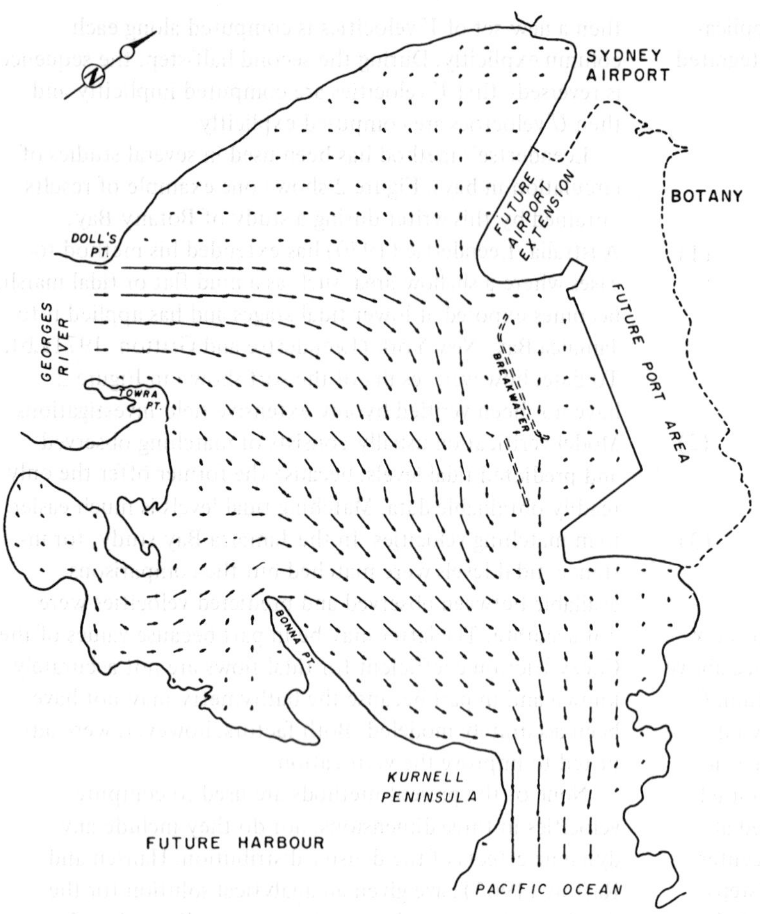

FIGURE 2 A typical two-dimensional velocity distribution in Botany Bay, Australia, that was computed with Leendertse's hydrodynamic model.

meaningful density difference between the surface and bottom). Strongly stratified estuaries require a different sort of treatment from the others; the mechanisms discussed in this section are primarily applicable to partially stratified and well-mixed estuaries. They are (a) the gravitational circulation, (b) the shear effect, (c) the phase effect, and (d) wind effects. There may, of course, be other mechanisms of lesser importance, but these are thought to be the major ones.

The gravitational circulation is the net flow induced by the longitudinal density gradient, which causes an inclination of pressure surfaces and induces a flow landward along the bottom of the estuary. This flow has been studied analytically by Hansen and Rattray (1965) and experimentally by Ippen and Harleman (1961, 1967), but in both cases only for two-dimensional cross sections corresponding to an estuary of rectangular cross section. Fischer (1972a) has suggested that the vertical circulations studied by these writers are of minor importance compared to transverse circulations generated because the cross sections of real estuaries are not rectangular. Figure 3 shows a typical distribution of the net gravitational circulation in a real estuary, in which the landward flow is concentrated in the deeper portion and the return flow is in the shallow portions. The result is a net transverse circulation, which is thought to be more important for mass transport than a vertical one.

The shear effect is the phenomenon first described by G. I. Taylor in his study of dispersion in pipes. Taylor pointed out that the velocity gradient across the cross section of a pipe would produce an apparent diffusiveness of matter along the pipe axis at a rate much greater than that of molecular diffusion. Holley *et al.* (1970) have discussed the shear effect in estuaries. Because of the oscillatory nature of the flow, the shear effect is only of minor importance in many estuaries; in others it may be important.

The phase effect is the writer's name for an effect that to date has not been widely studied. The tide in an estuary usually propagates in the form of a progressive wave, so that the times of maximum surface elevation and zero current velocity are not the same. Consider the effect of a small embayment along the side of an estuary, as shown in Figure 4. (A) A tracer cloud, distributed across the main channel, is shown approaching the embayment on a flood tide. (B) Part of the cloud has entered the embayment and part has continued up the main channel. If the water surface begins to drop, the material in the embayment will be pushed back out into the main channel. The material in the latter, however, will continue to move landward until the current re-

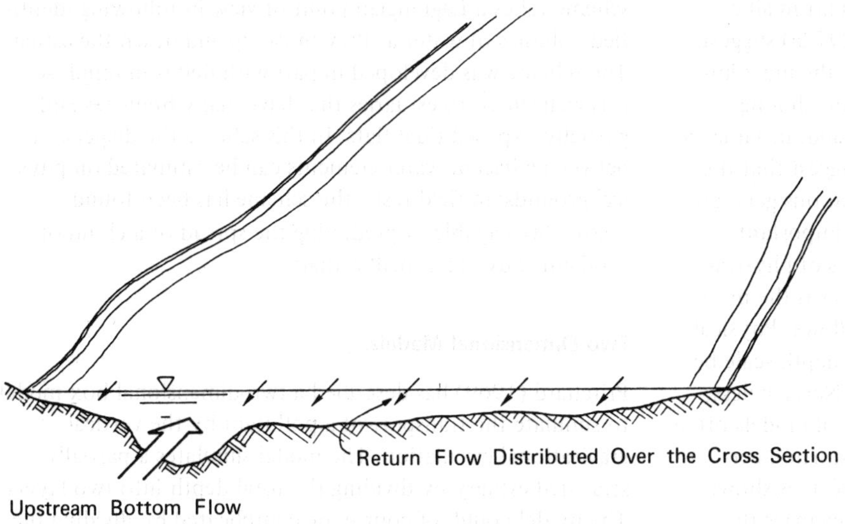

FIGURE 3 A typical landward-looking view of the distribution of the gravitational circulation over an estuary cross section.

verses. (C) The material in the embayment has reentered the main channel before the current has reversed; both groups of material are still moving landward but are separated by water that was originally seaward of the whole cloud. This mechanism adds substantially to the longitudinal dispersion of the main cloud and is entirely a result of the stage and velocity being out of phase. Incidentally, there is a superficial resemblance between Figure 4 and a drawing given by Pritchard (1969), but the latter drawing is more nearly a description of the shear effect, as he does not introduce the phase shift. Also of interest is Okubo's (1972) analysis of the effect of entrapment by embayments; this analysis, which also does not mention the phase effect, provides a basis on which it might be studied.

Wind effects can be important in wide, shallow estuaries. These estuaries are usually well mixed, so a two-dimensional analysis is often suitable. Viewed in two dimensions, a uniform wind stress acts like a body force inversely proportional to depth, resulting in a circulation in the direction of the wind in the shallows and against the wind in the deeper portions. Similar circulations have been computed in lakes.

No general statement can be made about which mass

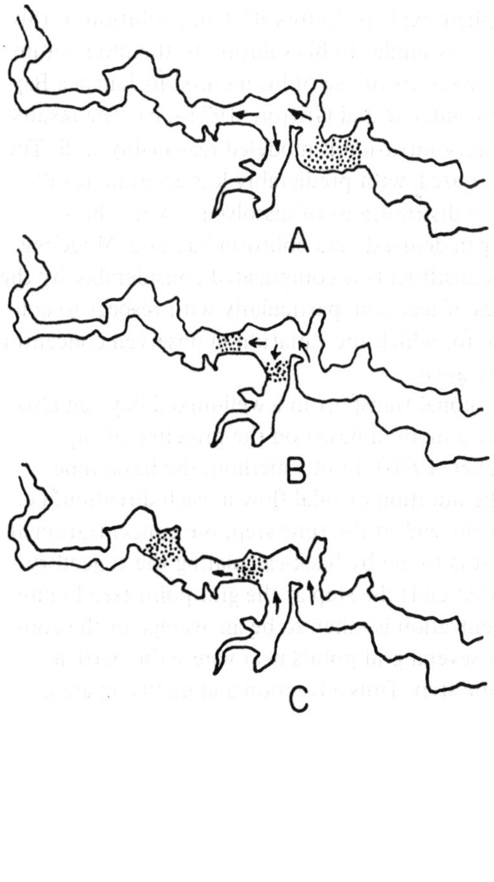

FIGURE 4 An illustration of the phase effect.

transport mechanism will be the most important in all estuaries. In the Mersey, in England, Fischer (1972a) suggests that the transverse gravitational circulation is the most important and that by itself can accomplish as much longitudinal mixing as is observed. On the other hand, in Jamaica Bay, N. Y., Leendertse's numerical studies suggest that the phase effect, broadened to include net circulations generated by the tidal wave around islands, is the most important mechanism. One may also interpret the results of physical hydraulic models to mean that the phase effect is the most important mechanism. The reasoning is as follows: Physical hydraulic models are normally distorted, the depth scale being of the order of 10 times the length scale. Nevertheless, the longitudinal salinity distribution in physical models often matches the prototype distribution. Scale distortion certainly changes the magnitude of the shear effect, as shown by Fischer and Holley (1971), and probably changes the effect of the gravitational circulation. The only effect that would be properly modeled in a distorted physical model would be the phase effect; hence it must be the most important mechanism.

MASS TRANSPORT MODELS

One-Dimensional Models.

The simplest modeling approach is to average the flow cross section and obtain an equation for conservation of mass as

$$\frac{\partial}{\partial t}(AC) + \frac{\partial}{\partial x}(UAC) = \frac{\partial}{\partial x}\left(DA\frac{\partial C}{\partial x}\right). \qquad (4)$$

In this equation, C is the concentration of a constituent, A is the cross sectional area of the estuary, U is the cross sectional average of velocity along the axis of the estuary, and D is a dispersion coefficient that includes the effect of all the mechanisms mentioned in the previous section. The magnitude of D cannot be predicted with any certainty; it is usually found empirically by observing the distribution of a tracer, such as ocean salinity. Thus models of this sort should only be used for problems of the first type mentioned in the introduction; they are not truly predictive in the sense required by the second type.

A number of solution techniques for Eq. (4) have been used. Stone and Brian (1963) showed that an optimal finite-difference representation includes a spread form of the time derivative, a centered implicit representation of the advective term, and the Crank-Nicholson approximation for the diffusive term. Thatcher and Harleman (1972) have applied this scheme in several estuaries and have described how the ocean boundary condition can be satisfied. The result is that the Stone and Brian scheme seems well suited to one-dimensional computations in estuaries.

A numerical scheme that does not use any sort of finite-difference representation is given by Fischer (1972b). The scheme takes a Lagrangian point of view in following identified volumes of water as they move up and down the estuary. The scheme was developed in part with deltas in mind, so it is well suited to estuaries that have many branches and partially exposed tidal flats. In this scheme the dispersion between adjacent water elements can be estimated on physical grounds; in field tests, the scheme has been found reasonably capable of predicting the spread of a cloud of rhodamine dye in a small estuary.

Two-Dimensional Models.

Pritchard (1969) has described a two-dimensional box model to simulate the transport of a pollutant by the vertical gravitational circulation. The model simulates a partially stratified estuary by dividing the total depth into two layers. The model could, of course, be complicated by dividing the depth into more layers and making some assumptions about transport between the layers. To the writer's knowledge, this has not been done; nor might it be useful until more is known about vertical transport in stratified flow.

In well-mixed estuaries and bays, a constituent will mix vertically rather quickly, and one can use the two-dimensional conservation of mass equation,

$$\frac{\partial}{\partial t}(HC) + \frac{\partial}{\partial x}(HUC) + \frac{\partial}{\partial y}(HVC) = \frac{\partial}{\partial x}\left(HD\frac{\partial C}{\partial x}\right) + \frac{\partial}{\partial y}\,HD\frac{\partial C}{\partial y}\;, \qquad (5)$$

where $H = h + \zeta$. Leendertse (1970) has given an alternating-direction, implicit-explicit, finite-difference solution to this equation, which is similar to his solution to the momentum equation. Some results of use of his method in Jamaica Bay are given by Leendertse and Gritton (1971a, b). The results show that salinity intrusion is modeled reasonably well. The model was also used, with predictably less accurate results, to compute the distributions of dissolved oxygen, biochemical oxygen demand, and coliform bacteria. Modeling of biological constituents is complicated considerably by the unknown rates of reaction, particularly with respect to coliform bacteria, for which the variation in observed concentrations is usually great.

Two-dimensional transport in a well-mixed bay can also be modeled by a method based on the principle of superposition (Fischer, 1970). In this method, the basic time step can be the duration of tidal flow in each direction, i.e., about 6 h. At the end of the time step, the concentration at each grid point is found by back-calculating the trajectory of a particle that ends the step at the grid point (see Figure 5). This concentration is taken to be an average of the concentrations at several grid points near where the particle started the time step. Thus advection and diffusion are in-

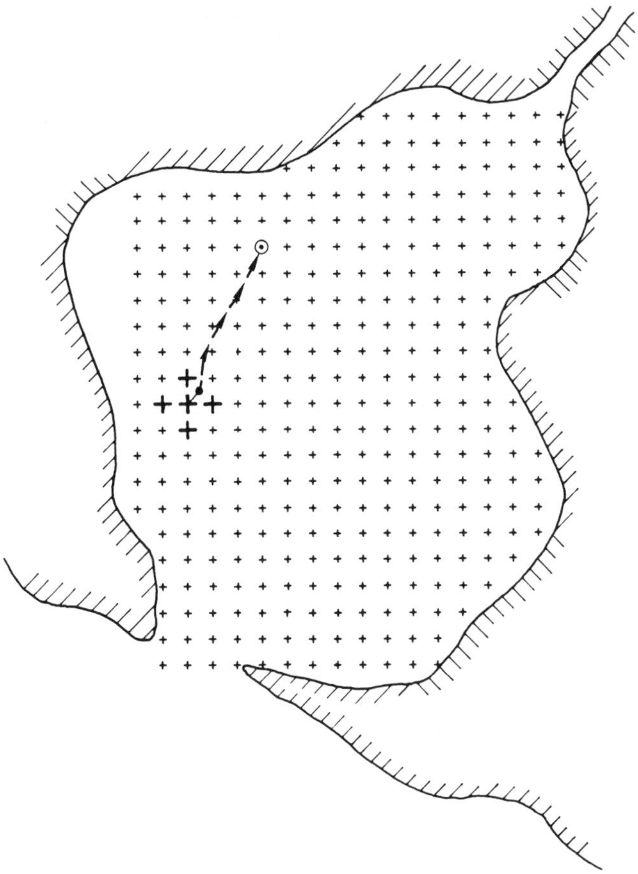

FIGURE 5 Computation of two-dimensional mass transport by a highly simplified superposition method. The line of arrows indicates the computed trajectory of a water particle during the flooding tide. The concentration at the circled dot at the end of the flood is computed by averaging the concentrations at each of the five large crosses at the beginning of the flood. The small crosses show the grid points for the computation.

cluded in the same computation. Because of the long time step, the method is much faster, although less accurate, than finite-difference methods.

Limitations and Research Needs on Mass Transport Models.

In spite of the claims of some of their makers, one-dimensional models are hardly ever predictive. Even if the one-dimensional mass transport coefficient could be predicted, the problem remains that constituents introduced at the side of most estuaries require a considerable period to become well mixed across the cross section. Ward and Fischer (1971) suggested cross sectional mixing times in the Delaware Bay estuary on the order of 4–40 days, which is longer than the decay time for many biological constituents. Until the constituent is well mixed, the one-dimensional analysis does not apply.

The primary limitation on two-dimensional models in well-mixed bays is inadequate understanding of horizontal turbulent mixing. One often finds in the literature reports of horizontal turbulent diffusion coefficients many orders of magnitude greater than the coefficients for vertical turbulent diffusion. Vertical diffusion can be explained as the result of random vertical motion; obviously, random motions of the same scale cannot cause the observed rate of horizontal diffusion. The large coefficients of so-called horizontal diffusion are caused by the spatial variability of the horizontal currents, both in magnitude and direction. If two-dimensional currents are modeled in sufficient detail, the horizontal spatial variation can be included in the numerical model; the finer the detail in the model, the smaller will be the apparent horizontal diffusions. Vertical current variations cannot be included in the model because of its two-dimensionality. Horizontal diffusion in the flow direction is caused by a vertical current shear, as described for flow down a water table by Elder (1959). Apparent horizontal diffusion is also induced transverse to the mean flow direction if there is a vertical skew in current direction; a result of this effect during a study in Lake Huron is described by Csanady (1966). Neither effect can be quantified with any degree of reliability in real estuaries.

A second major limitation is in the modeling of density-driven currents. Models that are two-dimensional in the vertical, such as Pritchard's box model, assume that constituents are well mixed and that currents are uniform in the transverse direction. Models that are two-dimensional in plan do not consider density-driven currents at all. Thus none of the present models include the transverse gravitational circulation. Methods for modeling partially stratified estuaries and gravitational currents in estuaries remain an important research need.

Finally, the problem of boundary conditions in open seas remains unsolved. Where the estuary boundary is clearly defined, one can make empirical approximations; for instance, studies have shown that of the water that passes out through the Golden Gate, approximately 75 percent returns on the following flood tide. In a numerical model, one might assume that the first hour of inflow consists of 10 percent new water and 90 percent that has just gone out; in the next hour, 20-80 percent, etc. If the boundary is one between an open bay and the ocean, an even more gross assumption would have to be made. This same problem occurs when one wants to model a partial area of a large estuary, for instance, a portion of San Francisco Bay. The assumed boundary conditions in such studies are usually highly empirical and open to question.

CONCLUSIONS

It is apparent that substantial progress has been made in numerical modeling of both the hydrodynamics and transport of constituents in estuaries. This progress is likely to continue, if only for lack of other methods for modeling the effect of waste discharges on estuaries. One alternative, use of physical hydraulic models, is extremely expensive and of doubtful accuracy; another, field studies, is even more expensive, hence the strong incentive to continue development of numerical models.

It is also apparent that we can model physical transport in estuaries better than the biology of them. We need further research on the dynamic biology of estuaries, including such subjects as the long-term effect of changes in temperature, salinity, and nutrients. Nevertheless, one must realize that numerical transport models, as they stand today, are not capable of describing many estuaries or answering many pressing questions. Cost remains an economic barrier; even with substantial funding, the studies of Jamaica Bay have spanned only a 4-day period, which may be long enough to reach an equilibrium for constituents in such a small bay but is nowhere near long enough for equilibrium in a larger system. Size of the system remains an absolute barrier; Jamaica Bay and Botany Bay are both relatively small, no more than 5 miles across, but both studies stretched the limits of the available computers. With present-day technology it has not been possible to make a realistic model, even in two dimensions, of a system, for example, as big as San Francisco Bay. When an engineer approaches a study such as the distribution of waste in San Francisco Bay, he remains an empiricist; existing numerical models may help to improve his judgment, but they do not provide final answers.

ACKNOWLEDGMENTS

Figure 2 is taken from a study of the Georges River–Botany Bay system by the firm of Brown and Caldwell, consulting engineers. The study was sponsored by the Metropolitan Water Sewerage and Drainage Board, Sydney, New South Wales, Australia. The writer is grateful for the board's permission to make use of the figure in advance of public release of the report.

REFERENCES

Csanady, G. T. 1966. Accelerated diffusion in the skewed shear flow of lake currents. J. Geophys. Res. 71:411–20.

Dronkers, J. J. 1964. Tidal Computations in Rivers and Coastal Waters. North-Holland Publishing Company, Amsterdam. 172 pp.

Dronkers, J. J. 1969. Tidal computations for rivers, coastal areas, and seas. Proc. Am. Soc. Civ. Eng. J. Hydraul. Div. 95:29–78.

Elder, J. W. 1959. The dispersion of marked fluid in turbulent shear flow. J. Fluid Mech. 5:544–60.

Fischer, H. B. 1970. A method for predicting pollutant transport in tidal waters. Water Resour. Center Contribution 132, University of California. 143 pp.

Fischer, H. B. 1972a. Mass transport mechanisms in partially stratified estuaries. J. Fluid Mech. 53:671.

Fischer, H. B. 1972b. A Lagrangian method for predicting pollutant transport in Bolinas Lagoon, Calif. USGS Prof. Pap. 582-B.

Fischer, H. B., and E. R. Holley. 1971. Analysis of the use of distorted hydraulic models for dispersion studies. Water Resour. Res. 7:46–51.

Hansen, D. V., and M. Rattray. 1965. Gravitational circulation in straits and estuaries. J. Mar. Res. 23:104–22.

Harleman, D. R. F., and A. T. Ippen. 1967. Two-dimensional aspects of salinity intrusion in estuaries: Analysis of salinity and velocity distributions. Tech. Bull. No. 13, Committee on Tidal Hydraulics, Corps of Engineers, U.S. Army. 38 pp.

Harleman, D. R. F., and A. T. Ippen. 1969. Salinity intrusion effects in estuary shoaling. Proc. Am. Soc. Civ. Eng. J. Hydraul. Div. 95:9–28.

Holley, E. R., D. R. F. Harleman, and H. B. Fischer. 1970. Dispersion in homogeneous estuary flow. Proc. Am. Soc. Civ. Eng. J. Hydraul. Div. 96:1691–1709.

Ippen, A. T., and D. R. F. Harleman. 1961. One dimensional analysis of salinity intrusion in estuaries. Tech. Bull. No. 5. Corps of Engineers, U.S. Army, Waterways Experiment Station, Vicksburg, Miss.

Lee, K. K., and J. A. Liggett. 1970. Computation for circulation in stratified lakes. Proc. Am. Soc. Civ. Eng. J. Hydraul. Div. 96: 2089–2115.

Leendertse, J. J. 1967. Aspects of a computational model for long-period water-wave propagation. Memo. RM-5294-PR. The Rand Corp., Santa Monica, Calif. 165 pp.

Leendertse, J. J. 1970. A water-quality simulation model for well-mixed estuaries and coastal seas. I. Principles of computation. Memo. RM-6230-RC. The Rand Corp., Santa Monica, Calif.

Leendertse, J. J., and E. C. Gritton. 1971a. A water-quality simulation model for well-mixed estuaries and coastal seas. II. Computational procedures. Memo. R-708-NYC. The Rand Corp., Santa Monica, Calif.

Leendertse, J. J., and E. C. Gritton. 1971b. A water-quality simulation model for well-mixed estuaries and coastal seas. III. Jamaica Bay simulation. Memo. R-709-NYC. The Rand Corp., Santa Monica, Calif.

Liggett, J. A. 1969. Unsteady circulation in shallow, homogeneous lakes. Proc. Am. Soc. Civ. Eng. J. Hydraul. Div. 95:1273–88.

Okubo, A. 1972. Effect of shoreline irregularities on streamwise dispersion in estuaries and other embayments. Manuscript submitted to the Netherlands J. Sea Res.

Pritchard, D. W. 1969. Dispersion and flushing of pollutants in estuaries. Proc. Am. Soc. Civ. Eng. J. Hydraul. Div. 95:114–24.

Simmons, H. B. 1955. Some effects of upland discharge on estuarine hydraulics. Proc. Am. Soc. Civ. Eng. 81: Sep. No. 792.

Stone, H. L., and P. T. Brian. 1963. Numerical solution of convective transport problems. Am. Inst. Chem. Eng. J. 9:681–88.

Thatcher, M. L., and D. R. F. Harleman. 1972. A mathematical model for the prediction of unsteady salinity intrusion in estuaries. MIT Parsons Lab. Rep. No. 144.

Ward, P. R. B., and H. B. Fischer. 1971. Some limitations on use of the one-dimensional dispersion equation, with comments on two papers by R. W. Paulson. Water Resour. Res. 7:215–20.

DISCUSSION

BRYAN: Figure 4 is very important for showing how important the tidal mixing is probably going to be in smaller water bodies. The models we used for ocean circulation with the rigid-lid approximation really wouldn't be appropriate to dealing with a mechanism like that unfortunately. But we could have some of the other things that you showed in Figure 3.

O'BRIEN: In the problems I've been doing I've been retaining the free-surface mode not using a rigid-lid type of approximation. And we used a semi-implicit method so that we're not bounded by the usual Courant-Friedrichs-Lewy condition. We get very large time steps, so we're modeling the physics quite well. This technique, which has been touted both by Marchuk of the Soviet Union and by Robert in the Western Hemisphere has particular advantage in these problems of the latter type, where you talk about going to three-dimensional stratified estuaries. They've been tested quite thoroughly now in the atmospheric sciences community, but there the advective speed of the motion is very close to the internal gravity wave speed, and you can't really use these methods to great advantage. But in the ocean, where there's a great disparity between the external and internal gravity wave speed and the advective speeds, one can get a very substantial speedup. I think that some of the people interested in three-dimensional estuary work may be interested in this kind of approach to the problem, because it allows you to attack the problem and still have reasonable time steps. It helps you quite a bit.

STEWART: I wonder if anybody has tried for estuaries a purely barotropic, very simple tidal model that is first just the tide going up and down, and then the baroclinic-mixing kind of model with the rigid-lid moving up and down. As far as the baroclinic motion is concerned, it's constrained.

BRETHERTON: I have a comment on this, because in the Chesapeake Bay, the only estuary area I know anything about, even in the tidal motion the frictional dissipation is very important. The tidal motions are nonlinear, not because of the advective terms that are really negligible, but because of the frictional dissipation. And one really can't take the tidal motion out of the problem in any reasonable way because of that nonlinearity.

UNIDENTIFIED: The thing that one will do, of course, and what has been done in all of these models, is to adjust the friction to suit the facts. The friction is right, because you have good data and you match it accordingly. You may have to cook up the law that relates the friction to your motion later, but you'll get the friction right. At least so far as the tidal motion is concerned.

BRETHERTON: The fact that the friction is acting on the bottom and not on the top, or in the center of the channel and not on the fringes, is critically important.

RATTRAY: I'd like to disagree with a few of the last comments. In fact, in the sort of thing that was shown here, the nonlinear advective terms in the tidal motion will become important. In fact, there are many steady circulations induced in estuaries by tidal motions due to the inertial effects. These are just the cases when the effects of horizontal mixing due to the tides will be the greatest. The other thing is, you can talk about the friction very simply in terms of giving the right tidal elevation, but it is the velocity that moves things around and that is where your more detailed frictional considerations must be included.

PHILLIPS: A brief suggestion on the comment that O'Brien made on using implicit methods. They lead to very bad phase errors in the internal gravity waves.

O'BRIEN: What Dr. Kreiss told us this morning, that when you use these schemes, high wave numbers that are in your solution have phase errors whether you use implicit or explicit methods. In one case, for high wave numbers the phases are increased; and in the other case, they're decreased. But you're still making phase errors in both cases. You still have to consider this resolution problem, which Dr. Kreiss told us about today, and make sure that you have enough points per wavelength in the important spectral part of the scheme.

II REVIEW OF PRESENT KNOWLEDGE OF THE OCEAN CIRCULATION

BASIC CONCEPTS IN MODELING THE OCEAN CIRCULATION

V. M. KAMENKOVICH

THE BASIC EQUATIONS

Under the hypothesis of local thermodynamic equilibrium, the basic equations expressing the fundamental laws of conservation, of mass, salt, momentum, are as follows:

mass conservation equation,

$$\frac{\partial \zeta}{\partial t} = -\text{div } \rho \vec{v}; \tag{1}$$

salt diffusion equation,

$$\frac{\partial \zeta s}{\partial t} = -\text{div } (\rho s v + \vec{I}); \tag{2}$$

momentum balance equation,

$$\frac{\partial \zeta v^{\alpha}}{\partial t} = -\Delta_{\beta} (\rho v^{\alpha} v^{\beta} - p^{\alpha\beta}) + \rho g^{\alpha} + 2\rho \epsilon^{\alpha\beta\gamma} v_{\beta} \Omega_{\alpha}; \tag{3}$$

and entropy balance equation,

$$\frac{\partial \zeta \eta}{\partial t} = -\text{div } (\rho \eta v + H) + \zeta, \tag{4}$$

where t is the time; ρ the density, $\rho = \rho\ (T,S,P)$; T the temperature; S the salinity; P the pressure; v the velocity; $\vec{I}$ the diffusive flux of salinity. The stress tensor, ρ, in a fluid can be written as

$$\rho^{\alpha\beta} = \rho g^{\alpha\beta} + \sigma^{\alpha\beta}, \tag{5}$$

where $g^{\alpha\beta}$ is a metric tensor (determined by the choice of the curvilinear coordinate system) and $\sigma^{\alpha\beta}$ is the viscous stress tensor; g is the gravity force; $\epsilon^{\alpha\beta\gamma}$ the unit artisymmetrical tensor; Ω the angular velocity of the earth's rotation; η the specific entropy, and H the entropy flux,

$$H = \frac{q}{T} + \left(\frac{\partial \eta}{\partial s}\right)_{T,P} S, \tag{6}$$

q is the heat flux; ζ, the entropy production due to irreversibility of the processes considered (friction, diffusion, heat conduction) is

$$\zeta = q^{\alpha} \nabla_{\alpha} \left(\frac{1}{T}\right) - \frac{1}{T} S^{\alpha} (\Delta_{\alpha} \mu)_T + \frac{1}{2T} \sigma^{\alpha\beta} e_{\alpha\beta}, \tag{7}$$

where μ is the difference of chemical potentials of salt and pure water; $e_{\alpha\beta} = \nabla_{\alpha} v_{\beta} + \nabla_{\beta} v_{\alpha}$ is the rate-of-strain tensor. The index T in $(\nabla_{\alpha} \mu)_T$ means that in calculating the gradient of $\mu\ (T,p,S)$, the temperature T is considered constant.

In Eqs. (1-7) we use tensor notation: Greek indices and only they stand for tensor characters, ∇_{α} = covariant derivative.

The second law of thermodynamics yields

$$\Theta = 0, \tag{8}$$

and the equality is possible only in the case of absence of processes of friction, heat conductivity, and diffusion.

Is it possible to relate S^{α}, q^{α}, $\sigma^{\alpha\beta}$ to basic characteristics of a fluid V^{α}, T, p, S and thereby to close the system of Eqs. (1-4)?

Formula (7) for ζ allows us to assume that each of the tensors S^{α}, q, $\sigma^{\alpha\beta}$ depends linearly and homogeneously on tensors $\nabla_{\alpha}(1/T)$, $-1/T(\nabla_{\alpha}\mu)_T$, $1/2T(e_{\alpha\beta})$. Using Onsager's principle we have for an isotropic fluid

$$\sigma_{\alpha\beta} = 2\nu'\rho\, S_{\alpha\beta} + 3\nu''\rho\, V_{\alpha\beta}', \tag{9}$$

$$S_{\alpha\beta} = \frac{1}{2} e_{\alpha\beta} - \frac{1}{3}(\operatorname{div}\vec{v})\, g_{\alpha\beta}, \tag{10}$$

$$V_{\alpha\beta} = \frac{1}{3}(\operatorname{div}\vec{v})\, g_{\alpha\beta}, \tag{11}$$

$$S_{\alpha} = -\rho D\left[\nabla_{\alpha}s + \frac{\left(\dfrac{\delta^{1}/\rho}{\delta s}\right)_{T,p}}{\left(\dfrac{\delta\mu}{\delta s}\right)_{T,p}}\nabla_{\alpha}p + \frac{\overline{\overline{K}}_T}{T}\nabla_{\alpha}T\right], \tag{12}$$

$$q_{\alpha} = -\alpha\epsilon\,\nabla_{\alpha}T + K_T\left(\frac{\delta\mu}{\delta s}\right)_{T,p} I_{\alpha}. \tag{13}$$

The coefficients $\nu'(T,p,S)$, ν'' $D,\overline{\overline{K}}_T$, $\alpha\epsilon$ are called phenomenological: ν' is the first coefficient of viscosity, ν'' is the second coefficient of viscosity. D is the coefficient of diffusion, $\overline{\overline{K}}_T$ is the parameter of thermal diffusion, and $\alpha\epsilon$ is the coefficient of heat conductivity.

From the second law of thermodynamics, Eq. (8), it follows that the coefficients ν', ν'', D, $\alpha\epsilon$ should be positive using the thermodynamic inequality $^{\alpha\epsilon}(\partial\mu/\partial s)_{T,p} > 0$.

There are some data concerning the coefficients $\alpha\epsilon$, D, ν'; but there are practically no estimates for seawater of the thermal diffusion effect (diffusive transport resulting from the existence of temperature gradient), of the barodiffusion effect (diffusive transport resulting from the existence of pressure gradient), and of heat transport resulting from the existence of diffusion. It may be that these effects will be important in some microscale phenomena. It should be noted that for an incompressible fluid ($\operatorname{div}\vec{v} = 0$) the effect of the second viscosity does not appear.

For understanding certain important approximations, used in the theory of ocean currents, it is useful to consider the problem of free eigen oscillations of small amplitude in a spherical layer of fluid of constant depth H (in considering such a problem the effects of friction, diffusion, and heat conduction are not taken into account).

The analysis of the problem (2) shows that the following types of waves can exist:

1. Gravity waves (surface and internal). The frequencies σ of surface waves can be arbitrary, but for internal waves $0 < |\sigma| < N_{max}$, where N_{max} = maximum of Vaisala frequency in the interval (O, H).
2. Planetary waves or Rossby waves (barotropic and baroclinic). The frequencies of barotropic planetary waves are in the range $0 < |\sigma| < \Omega$; for baroclinic planetary waves, $0 < |\sigma| < \min(\Omega, N_{max})$.
3. Inertial waves. These waves exist only on condition that $\Omega > N_{min}$. The frequencies of these waves are in the range $N_{min} < |\sigma| < \Omega$.
4. Acoustic waves (high-frequency oscillations).

Consider now some approximations:

1. The approximation of an incompressible nonhomogeneous fluid (i.e., sound velocity c equal to infinity). Eq. (1) is replaced by $\operatorname{div}\vec{v} = 0$, filters out acoustic waves, and causes practically no distortion of gravity, planetary, and inertial waves since $gH/c^2 \ll 1$ in the ocean.
2. The hydrostatic approximation (i.e., only the gravity force and pressure gradient are taken into account in the vertical momentum equation). This approximation distorts low-frequency gravity and planetary waves ($\sigma^2 \ll N^2_{max}$) slightly and completely filters out inertial and acoustic waves.
3. The rigid-lid approximation (i.e., kinematic condition on free surface of the ocean is replaced by the condition that vertical velocity is equal to nought at the undisturbed surface). This approximation barely distorts inertial, internal gravity, and baroclinic planetary waves, but does distort acoustic waves. Surface gravity waves are filtered out, and are replaced by Lamb waves (however at $C \to \infty$ Lamb waves disappear). Barotropic planetary waves with this approximation are transformed to nondivergent planetary waves (the distortion is very slight because usually out of the equatorial region $K^2 \gg f^2/gH$, where K = wave number, f = Coriolis parameter).
4. Geostrophic approximation (i.e., only Coriolis force and pressure gradient are taken into account in horizontal momentum equation). This approximation is valid for baroclinic planetary waves, which are propagated with practically no dispersion in middle latitudes. For barotropic planetary waves, however, only the quasi-geostrophic approximation is valid (i.e., geostrophic approximation is used for calculating separate terms in vorticity equation).

Let us go back now to the basic Eqs. (1-4) and discuss the most important approximations:

1. Boussinesq approximation: (a) Eq. (1) is replaced by $\operatorname{div}\nu = 0$ (this approximation filters out acoustic waves), (b) ρ is replaced by ρ_0 (constant average density in the ocean) in all terms except the term $\vec{g}\rho$. In principle the validity of the Boussinesq approximation is due to a small variation of density in the ocean $\vartheta\rho/\rho \ll 1$ and to the fact

that the energy of acoustic waves is negligible compared to the energy of large-scale motions.

2. Approximations to the entropy equation. Because gradients of the basic characteristics are small (squares of these gradients are negligible as compared to the gradients themselves), Eq. (4) has the form

$$\rho C_p \left\{ \frac{\delta T}{\delta t} - \frac{T}{C_p} \left(\frac{\delta(^1/\rho)}{\delta T} \right)_{p,s} \frac{\delta p}{\delta t} \right\} = -\text{div}\, q, \quad (14)$$

where C_p is the specific heat capacity at constant pressure.

This is a general form of heat conduction equation in a fluid in motion. In the adiabatic case the second term in the curly brackets is negligible.

The question concerning influence of approximations just discussed on the form of conservation or evolution laws of certain important invariants is a fundamental one. Only the simplest examples will be considered.

It is known that the equation of balance of mechanical energy may be derived from momentum equation

$$\rho \frac{\delta}{\delta t} \left(\frac{v^2}{2} + v \right) = -\nabla_\alpha \left(-p^{\alpha\beta} v_\beta\right) + p \,\text{div}\, v - \sigma_{\alpha\beta}\, e^{\alpha\beta}, \quad (15)$$

where v is the specific potential energy.

Let us take the Boussinesq approximation into account in the momentum equations. Then the analogue of (15) has the form

$$\rho_0 \frac{\delta}{\delta t} \left(\frac{v^2}{2} \right) = -\nabla_\alpha \left(-p^{\alpha\beta} v_\beta\right) + \rho g^\beta v_\beta - \sigma_{\alpha\beta}\, e^{\alpha\beta}. \quad (16)$$

For $\sigma_{\alpha\beta}\, e^{\alpha\beta} > 0$, the Boussinesq approximation does not allow conversion of internal energy into mechanical energy—only dissipation of mechanical energy is possible. Note the impossibility of representing $\rho g^\beta v_\beta$ as $\rho_0\, (\delta v/\delta t)$; therefore, Eq. (16) is written as an equation for the balance of kinetic energy.

THE EQUATIONS OF AVERAGED MOTION

Studying oceanic processes, we are dealing with a broad spectrum of motion (both temporal and spatial); and, due to the nonlinearity of the basic equations, there is an energy exchange between motions of different scales. As a rule we make the fundamental assumption that approximations listed above are valid for all energy-contained motions.

Usually large-scale motions (which are of basic interest) are singled out by the averaging of Eqs. (1–4). It should be noted that the proper concept of averaging is far from simple (it should be understood as an ensemble average defined by probability theory). Assuming the validity of the usual properties of the averaging operator, we have

$$\text{div}\, v = 0, \quad (17)$$

$$\frac{\delta}{\delta t} (\rho_0\, \bar{s}) = -\text{div} \left\{ \rho_0\, \bar{s}\, \vec{v} + \vec{I} + \rho_0\, \overline{s' \vec{v}'} \right\}, \quad (18)$$

$$\frac{\delta}{\delta t} (\rho_0\, \bar{v}^\alpha) = -\nabla_\beta \left\{ \rho_0\, \bar{v}^\alpha \bar{v}^\beta + p g^{\alpha\beta} - (\bar{\sigma}^{\alpha\beta} - \rho_0\, \overline{v'^\alpha v'^\beta}) \right\}$$
$$+ \bar{\rho} g^\alpha + 2\rho_0\, \epsilon^{\alpha\beta\gamma}\, \bar{v}_\beta\, \Omega_\gamma, \quad (19)$$

$$\frac{\delta}{\delta t} (C_p \rho_0 T) = -\text{div} \left\{ C_p \rho_0\, \bar{T}\bar{v} + \bar{q} + C_p \rho_0\, \overline{T' v'} \right\}, \quad (20)$$

where the overbar denotes the averaging and prime denotes pulsations.

The problem of closing the system of Eqs. (17-20) is a fundamental one (not solved in present time). The point is that "turbulent" fluxes $\rho_0 \overline{s'\vec{v}'}$, $-\rho_0 \overline{v'^\alpha v'^\beta}$, $C_p \rho_0\, \overline{T'\vec{v}'}$ greatly exceed average values of molecular fluxes $\bar{\vec{I}}$, $\sigma^{\alpha\beta}$, $\bar{\vec{q}}$, and naturally no general principle for averaged motions exist to give us laws similar to (9-13) for the "turbulent" fluxes.

If we assume however that turbulent motions take their energy from averaged motions, it is possible to postulate

$$F_\lambda = A_L \left(\Delta u + \frac{\cos^2 \phi}{a^2 \cos^2 \phi} u - \frac{2 \sin \phi}{a^2 \cos^2 \phi} \frac{\delta v}{\delta \lambda} \right)$$
$$+ \frac{\delta}{\delta z} A_z \frac{\delta u}{\delta z}, \quad (21)$$

$$F_\psi = A_L \left(\Delta v + \frac{\cos^2 \phi}{a^2 \cos^2 \phi} v + \frac{2 \sin \phi}{a^2 \cos^2 \phi} \frac{\delta v}{\delta \lambda} \right) + \frac{\delta}{\delta z} A_z \frac{\delta v}{\delta z}, \quad (22)$$

$$\sigma = A_{SL}\, \Delta s + \frac{\delta}{\delta z} A_{SZ} \frac{\delta s}{\delta z}, \quad (23)$$

$$Q = A_{TL}\, \Delta T + \frac{\delta}{\delta z} A_{TZ} \frac{\delta T}{\delta z}, \quad (24)$$

where F_λ, F_ψ are the horizontal components of the force of the turbulent friction (the vertical component of this force usually does not play any role); $\sigma = -\text{div}\, \rho_o\, \overline{s'\, \vec{v}\,'}$; $Q = -\text{div}\, (C_p\, \rho_o \overline{T'\, \vec{v}\,'})$; λ = longitude, δ = latitude, z = vertical distance u, z = respectively zonal and meridional components; parameters A_L, A_z are called respectively as horizontal and vertical coefficients of turbulent mixing. Numerical values of these parameters are prescribed *a priori* based on indirect arguments or are determined from additional relationships (for example, from the equation of balance of turbulent energy).

Formulas (21-24) are based essentially on analogy

with processes of molecular transport and symmetry arguments. For cases in which turbulent motion transfers its energy to the averaged motion, there are many certain arguments in favor of such a possibility, and formulas (21-24) are of course not valid.

Further, it is unlikely that complex small-scale processes in the formation of the upper well-mixed layer and seasonal thermocline (the latter effect seems to be very important in studying large-scale processes particularly in spring and summer periods) are described by formulas such as (23-24) (even assuming a vertical variation of A_z). It should be noted that in some papers efforts are undertaken to introduce a parameterization of the vertical mixing that is not based on the introduction of a mixing coefficient A_z.

The structure of Eq. (19) is similar to the corresponding unaveraged equation of motion with the Boussinesq approximation. Hence the balance equation for kinetic energy has a form

$$\rho_o \frac{\delta}{\delta t}\left(\frac{\bar{v}^2}{2}\right) = -\nabla_\alpha\left(-\bar{P}^{\alpha\beta}\,\bar{V}_\rho + \rho_o\,\overline{v'^\alpha\,v'^\beta\,\bar{v}_\beta}\right) + \bar{\rho}g^\alpha\,\bar{v} - \bar{\sigma}^{\alpha\beta}\,e_{\alpha\beta} - \rho_o\,\overline{v'^\alpha\,v'^\beta}\,\bar{e}_{\alpha\beta}, \tag{25}$$

where the term $\bar{\sigma}^{\alpha\beta}\,\bar{e}_{\alpha\beta} > 0$, but the term $\rho_o\,\overline{v'^\alpha\,v'^\beta}\,\bar{e}_{\alpha\beta}$ can in general have an arbitrary sign (the energy exchange between averaged and turbulent motions).

Let us now introduce the hydrostatic approximation. For simplicity we take momentum equations in Cartesian coordinates x, y, z. Then x, y components of friction force are as follows:

$$F_x = A_L\,\Delta u + \frac{\delta}{\delta z}A_z\frac{\delta u}{\delta z}, \tag{26}$$

$$F_y = A_L\,\Delta v + \frac{\delta}{\delta z}A_z\frac{\delta v}{\delta z}. \tag{27}$$

The balance equation for kinetic energy, integrated over a whole oceanic basin, will be

$$\rho_o \frac{\delta}{\delta t}\int_v \frac{u^2+v^2}{2}\,\delta V = \int_\Sigma (u\,\bar{L}_x + v\,\bar{L}_y)\,\delta\Sigma + \int_\Sigma g\rho\,w\,\delta V - \int_v \left\{A_L\left[\left(\frac{\delta u}{\delta x}\right)^2 + \left(\frac{\delta u}{\delta y}\right)^2 + \left(\frac{\delta v}{\delta x}\right)^2 + \left(\frac{\delta v}{\delta y}\right)^2\right] + A_z\left[\left(\frac{\delta u}{\delta z}\right)^2 + \left(\frac{\delta v}{\delta z}\right)^2\right]\right\}\delta V, \tag{28}$$

where Σ is the free surface of the ocean and $(\bar{L}_x, \bar{L}_y)$ is a wind stress. It is interesting to note, that for validity of (28) it is necessary to take a Coriolis force to be a constant.

The terms in the right-hand side of (28) are easily identified as a work (per unit time) of external and internal forces, etc. But if we take (28) in differential form such an identification will be more difficult.

Since certain approximations have been made to the basic equations, it is necessary to consider what is significant in any particular problem and to use a physically appropriate form in each case.

REVIEW: H. J. FRIEDRICH

This is an excellent report on certain basic ideas in modeling the large-scale ocean circulation. The concepts are in fact not all original, but they have not yet been established systematically in the oceanographic literature.

In the first of two sections, Kamenkovich introduces the fundamental equations of physical oceanography. These are the conservation laws for mass and momentum, an equation for salt diffusion (with the salinity concept, seawater is reduced to a two-component system), and the laws of thermodynamics supplemented by an implicit equation of state. These are also the fundamental equations of dynamical meteorology, with the only difference that in the latter the water vapor takes the place of the salinity. Thus, the equations form the backbone of geophysical fluid dynamics, a field that seems to be an aggregation of nothing but basic concepts. The concepts of potential vorticity and topographic control, scale and stability analysis, and boundary layers and turbulence are only a few prominent examples. Within the scope of his paper, a selection was obviously necessary, and Kamenkovich puts the emphasis on the concepts of filtering.

As a first step Kamenkovich outlines the phenomenological approach, which is a simple and straightforward procedure to close the fundamental system of equations. The concept makes use of Onsager's principle of a quasi-equilibrium at the molecular level in irreversible processes. This principle is used as an auxiliary to the first and second laws. However, the equations for salt diffusion and for entropy balance are immediately simplified and reduced to Fick's law for diffusion and to Fourier's law for heat conduction. The principle implies that coupling mechanisms like the Dufour effect (heat flux due to a concentration gradient) or the Soret effect (thermal diffusion; migration due to a temperature gradient) are disregarded as agents of molecular fluxes. The author points out that the reason for this conventional approximation is not experimental evidence, but rather the lack of such evidence. In view of the far more efficient turbulent fluxes in realistic models of the ocean circulation, this problem appears to be rather academic in this context.

Kamenkovich proceeds to specify the various types of normal mode waves that may exist in a stratified fluid rotating in a gravity field. In his study the waves are obtained as eigenmodes of a stratified fluid rotating in a spherical shell of constant depth. The resulting broad spectrum, reaching from high-frequency sound waves down to low-frequency planetary waves, is characteristic for the universal validity of the fundamental equations. It is precisely this general applicability, together with the nonlinear nature of the equations, which is in fact a continuous source of problems in geophysical fluid dynamics. It is, for instance, practically impossible to resolve the high frequencies and wave numbers by observations. This and related difficulties provide the background and the motivation for the important concept of filtering. The planetary rotation rate, which is equivalent to a small Rossby numer for the large-scale ocean circulation, and the characteristic magnitude of the Brunt–Vaisala frequency for stability oscillations in the stratified ocean are the critical parameters. It is also essential that the hydrosphere is extremely shallow in terms of the scale depth c^2/g and that the deviations from an isentropic reference-state remain extremely small. Under these conditions the high-frequency part of the spectrum can be filtered away without serious distortions of the low frequencies.

As far as the large-scale circulation is concerned, a time-independent, steady state is conceivable, which is coupled only at reasonably high Rossby numbers to the lowest frequencies of the spectrum. These low frequencies are primarily barotropic and baroclinic planetary waves. These waves are governed by the quasi-geostrophic balance, which explains the significance of the vorticity concept in large-scale circulation models.

The appropriate filters to obtain such a model for the ocean circulation consist of (a) the incompressibility condition, which replaces the continuity condition and filters sound waves; (b) the hydrostatic assumption, which replaces the vertical component of the momentum equation; and (c) the rigid-lid approximation, which specifies the kinematic surface condition and filters surface gravity waves.

In this sense the Boussinesq approximation is an excellent modeling concept that sufficiently accounts for buoyancy forces in the baroclinic ocean. It is noteworthy that this approximation has been employed with convincing success in numerical ocean models and it should also be mentioned that the filters involved allow certain simplifications in the phenomenological definitions of molecular fluxes. Kamenkovich further demonstrates that the Boussinesq approximation excludes the possibility of a direct energy transfer from the reservoir of internal energy into the reservoir of kinetic energy. Here would have been an opportunity to introduce the important concept of available potential energy.

It can be anticipated that the systematic exploitation of energy principles will become increasingly important as a crucial ingredient of any concept for modeling the ocean circulation. Kamenkovich uses the mechanical energy equation to illustrate the problem of consistency. In the case of such a hydrostatic circulation model it is for instance necessary to use the Coriolis force in the traditional approximation. Otherwise, a fictitious energy source would have been the consequence of the simplification. A filter has to be introduced in a consistent way into all the equations of the system, i.e., without violating fundamental physical principles. A discussion of the conservation principle for angular momentum would have served the same purpose. This procedure was followed in the well-known dispute between Phillips and Veronis.

Advanced concepts of the energy cycle and of the vorticity balance built into numerical models should provide a deeper understanding of the crucial problem of how the large-scale oceanic circulation is maintained. In the second part of his paper, Kamenkovich demonstrates that there is still a long way to go before such an ambitious goal is reached. Here the concept of the average motion is introduced, leading to the problem of closing the system. The turbulent fluxes have to be known in terms of average quantities. The conventional concept of eddy viscosities and mixing coefficients appears questionable, and it is with this parameterization of small-scale processes that new and convincing concepts are most urgently needed. In conclusion, it may confidently be expected that Vladimir Kamenkovich in particular will continue to contribute advanced concepts for modeling the large-scale ocean circulation.

BIBLIOGRAPHY

Fofonoff, N. P. 1962. The Sea, p. 3.
Gill, A. E. 1971. Philos. Trans. R. Soc. Lond. Ser. A 270:392–413.
Kamenkovich, V. M. 1967. Izv. Akad. Nauk. USSR Atmos. Oceanic Phys. 3(12).
Kamenkovich, V. M. 1969. Oceanology 9:1.
Kamenkovich, V. M., and A. B. Odulo. 1972. Izv. Akad. Nauk. USSR Atmos. Oceanic Phys. 13.
Kitaigorodsky, S. A. 1970. Physics of the air–sea interaction. Leningrad.
Kraus, E. B., and J. S. Turner. 1967. Vol. 19, p. 98.
Monin, A. S., and A. M. Yaglom. 1965. Statistical Hydromechanics, p. 1. Moscow.

THE EXCHANGES OF MOMENTUM, HEAT AND MOISTURE AT THE OCEAN–ATMOSPHERE INTERFACE

S. POND

INTRODUCTION

The ocean and atmosphere form a highly coupled, nonlinear system. Ideally, to understand and model this system, it should be treated as a single entity. Because of the very different response times (of order 1 yr for the atmosphere and some hundreds of years for the deep ocean), such a complete modeling approach is not possible, although it may ultimately be. Some interesting and revealing attempts at partially coupled numerical models have recently been made (Bryan, 1969; Manabe, 1969). However, it appears that much of the modeling will continue to be concerned with either one part of the system or the other. In either case, it is essential to take the coupling into account.

This coupling is largely effected by subgrid-scale turbulent exchanges of momentum, moisture, and sensible heat at the interface. Some other processes, which act across but are not confined to the surface, such as radiation and precipitation, are also important and must be properly incorporated.

Phillips (1972) noted that the only oceanographic parameter that is required for an atmospheric model is the surface temperature (although one might include albedo, which is affected by cloud cover and sea state). The surface temperature, however, is affected by many processes; thus, it may be necessary to model the surface layer of the ocean to obtain it. Denman (1972) has produced a model that successfully predicts the surface temperature when incoming solar radiation and wind mixing dominate (convective effects due to heat loss at the surface were not important in the cases he studied, and some extension of his model may be required to include them). This model does require a knowledge of the temperature gradient below the upper mixed layer, but this quantity is rather less subject to short-term fluctuations than the surface temperature. For model experiments rather than predictive studies, it may be possible to obtain the surface temperature from satellites (Smith *et al.*, 1970).

To produce an oceanic model, a knowledge of several transfers is required. The momentum transfer is an essential driving force for ocean circulation. Thermohaline driving, caused by surface heat exchange (net radiation; sensible and latent heat), and evaporation minus precipitation, which determines the surface salt and density balances, is also important. Nonlinear coupling between the wind-driven and thermohaline-driven circulations may not be negligible. Thus, to model and understand the ocean, all driving forces must be included simultaneously. Ultimately, the transfers will need to be known over wide regions on a synoptic basis.

In recent years, a great deal of work has been done in attempts to determine these exchanges and considerable progress has been made, although many gaps in our knowledge still exist. The remainder of this paper will be concerned with the turbulent exchanges of momentum, moisture, and sensible heat at the interface. Radiation and precipitation are important but are rather different and require separate treatment.

METHODS OF MEASURING THE EXCHANGES

The various methods that may be used for measuring the exchanges are given in many places (e.g., Lumley and Panofsky, 1964; Roll, 1965; Monin and Yaglom, 1965,

1967; Burling and Stewart, 1967; Kraus, 1972). Usually, in the first few tens of meters above the surface, the exchange rates or fluxes are nearly constant. Thus measurements can be made in this surface or "constant-flux," layer rather than right at the wave-perturbed interface. A brief review will show some of the possibilities and limitations of the various methods.

Reynolds Flux, Covariance, or Eddy Correlation Method

On the microscale, properties (other than heat transfers by radiation) must be transferred vertically and bodily with the fluid at a rate w, the vertical component of velocity, except within a few millimeters of the actual interface, where molecular diffusion may be important. Furthermore, when averaged over a reasonably large length or time (scale sizes of a few kilometers or times around one hour), w will be essentially zero in the surface layer, because for such an average, the surface is level and horizontal homogeneity is a good approximation. Thus, transfers are effected almost entirely by the fluctuating vertical velocity. The net vertical flux of any property, F, is given by $\overline{wF}$, where the overbar indicates an average (usually over time in practice). Since $\overline{w} = 0$, $\overline{wF} = \overline{wF'}$, where F' is the fluctuation in F about its average. Fluctuations of density are small in this surface layer and can be ignored in computing the Reynolds fluxes of momentum, moisture, and heat. Thus, the fluxes are:

$$\text{Momentum flux} = -\rho\,\overline{uw} = \tau,$$

$$\text{Sensible heat flux} = \rho\, C_p \overline{wT} = H_s,$$

$$\text{Moisture flux} = \overline{wq} = E,$$

$$\text{Latent heat flux} = L\,\overline{wq} = H_L, \quad (1)$$

where ρ is air density, u is the velocity fluctuation in the downstream direction (parallel to mean wind U), C_p is the specific heat at constant pressure, T is the temperature; q is the absolute humidity (mass of water vapor/unit volume), and L is the latent heat of vaporization. (In some cases specific humidity q/ρ is used, in which case the last two formulas include the factor ρ.)

Measurements of the Reynolds fluxes or covariances, $\overline{uw}$, $\overline{wT}$, and $\overline{wq}$, give the most direct estimates that can be made of the exchanges and have become more common in the last few years. The cospectra of these covariances are often obtained to verify that all scales contributing to the flux are included. When normalized, according to the Monin-Obukhov similarity theory, the cospectra are expected to be functions of stability only. However, the range of stability, typical over the ocean, is quite small; and, therefore, the normalized cospectra are nearly universal forms, except perhaps for the $\overline{wT}$ cospectra in some cases (Phelps and Pond, 1971; Pond, 1971). The range of normalized frequency required to include virtually all contributions to the fluxes is given by

$$0.001 < fz/U = z/\lambda < 10, \quad (2)$$

where f is frequency, z is height, U is mean wind speed, and λ is an "eddy size." For z/U of order one second, a record length of order 10–15 min is required to cover the whole frequency range, but three or four sequential records are needed to get reasonably good statistics at the low frequencies.

Reynolds flux measurements can be made from fixed platforms (Miyake *et al.*, 1970b; Smith, 1970), stable platforms such as *Flip* (Pond *et al.*, 1971), stabilized buoys (Hasse, 1970a), and aircraft (Kukharets and Tsvang, 1969; Bunker, 1970; Miyake *et al.*, 1970a). Such measurements would be rather difficult from a surface ship because of the large corrections necessary to remove the effect of ship motion.

Profile or Gradient Method

In the surface layer, the vertical gradients or profiles of wind speed, temperature, and humidity are expected to be universal functions when normalized according to the Monin-Obukhov similarity theory. Here only the case of near-neutral stability is given for simplicity. Paulson (1970) discusses various possible functional forms for unstable cases and Lumley and Panofsky (1964) give the currently accepted form for stable cases. In general, the gradients are increased in stable cases and decreased in unstable cases.

The near-neutral case is given by

$$\frac{dU}{dz} = \frac{u_\star}{\kappa z}, \quad (3)$$

$$\frac{d\overline{\gamma}}{dz} = \frac{\gamma_\star}{z}, \quad (4)$$

where U is mean wind speed, z is height, $u_\star = (-\overline{uw})^{1/2}$ is the friction velocity, κ (=0.4) is the Von Karman constant, γ represents a scalar variable such as temperature or humidity, and $\gamma_\star = -\overline{w\gamma}\,(\kappa u_\star)^{-1}$. Thus, it is possible to obtain estimates of the fluxes from observed profiles. Fluxes can also be estimated in nonneutral cases by using formulas incorporating effects of stability. Over the sea, in contrast to over the land, humidity is often important in determining stability. Thus, humidity, temperature, and velocity profiles are needed to determine the wind stress; lack of complete measurements may explain some of the scatter in the results from earlier wind-profile measurements at sea.

Profile methods have been fairly well tested over land, where such things as drag plates can be used to measure the stress at the surface. Over the sea, objections have been raised because of possible effects of waves on the air flow; but the effects on profiles seem to be fairly small, above one wave height or so, from the mean surface. Careful measurements of profiles over the sea show that they are well represented by the same relationships as profiles over land (Badgley *et al.*, 1972). A few comparisons have been made between profile and eddy-flux methods that show fairly consistent results (Miyake *et al.*, 1970b; Paulson *et al.*, 1972).

Profile measurements can be made from fixed towers, buoys, and perhaps from vessels such as *Flip* (although *Flip* distorts the flow, so corrections must be made). Such measurements from a ship are very difficult. Good profile measurements require great care and today are probably more difficult than Reynolds flux measurements. Measurements in the open sea at high wind speeds ($>$ 15-20 m s^{-1}) would probably be extremely difficult.

Dissipation Or Energy-Balance Method

This method is based on the idea that production of mean square fluctuations is locally balanced by molecular dissipation. For simplicity, only the case of near-neutral stability is discussed. Pond *et al.* (1971) discuss some possible approaches in unstable cases.

For mechanical energy and scalars, respectively:

$$\text{production}\left\{\begin{matrix} = -\overline{uw}\,\dfrac{dU}{dz} = \\ \\ = -\overline{w\gamma}\,\dfrac{d\bar{\gamma}}{dz} = \end{matrix}\right\}\text{dissipation}\left\{\begin{matrix} = \epsilon \\ \\ = N_\gamma . \end{matrix}\right. \quad (5)$$

Substitution of Eqs. (3-4) in Eq. (5) yields

$$-\overline{uw} = u_\star{}^2 = (\kappa\, \epsilon\, z)^{2/3}, \quad (6)$$

$$|\overline{w\gamma}| = |\kappa\, u_\star \gamma_\star| = (\kappa z)^{2/3} N_\gamma{}^{1/2}\, \epsilon^{1/6}. \quad (7)$$

The gradients are obtained from Eqs. (3-4), so this method depends on the assumptions of the Monin-Obukhov theory. Also, the hypothesis, *production = dissipation* × *function of stability*, is consistent with this theory.

To use this method, values of ϵ and N_γ are required. These values can be obtained from the high frequency or small-scale (defined by $fz/U \gtrsim 0.5$) part of the spectra of velocity and scalar fluctuations by assuming that the Kolmogoroff theory may be used, which gives

$$\phi_u = K'\, \epsilon^{2/3} k^{-5/3}, \quad (8)$$

$$\phi_\gamma = B_\gamma{}'\, N_\gamma\, \epsilon^{-1/3} k^{-5/3}, \quad (9)$$

where

$$\int_0^\infty \phi_u(k)\, dk = \overline{u^2}; \quad \epsilon = 15\nu \int_0^\infty k^2\, \phi_\gamma\, dk, \quad (10)$$

$$\int_0^\infty \phi_\gamma (k)\, dk = \overline{\gamma^2}; \quad N_\gamma = 3\eta_\gamma \int_0^\infty k^2 \phi_\gamma\, dk. \quad (11)$$

ϕ_u and ϕ_γ are one-dimensional spectra of downstream velocity and scalar fluctuations, respectively; K' and $B_\gamma{}'$ are one-dimensional Kolmogoroff constants; k is the downstream component of the radian wave number, which is obtained from the observed frequency, f, using Taylor's hypothesis ($k = 2\pi f/U$); ν is kinematic molecular viscosity; and η_γ, kinematic molecular diffusivity. Measurement of ϵ and N_γ by direct integration is rather difficult. However, the lower frequency part of the $-5/3$ range is fairly easily observed, so ϵ and N_γ can be obtained from the spectral levels in this range, although the value of $B_\gamma{}'$ is not as yet well established (Paquin and Pond, 1971).

This method has been compared with the eddy-flux method. For momentum a number of comparisons have been made (e.g., McBean *et al.*, 1971; Pond *et al.*, 1971) that show reasonable agreement at moderate wind speeds (up to about 8 m s^{-1}). For the moisture and sensible heat fluxes, only a few comparisons have been made; these are encouraging, although in some cases the dissipation method may not work for the sensible heat flux (Pond *et al.*, 1971).

The dissipation method is attractive. The measurements are easier than those used in any other technique, because a precise knowledge of the vertical direction is not required (a 5-10° tilt is acceptable, which would make a Reynolds momentum-flux measurement meaningless), and the method is insensitive to the motions of most platforms, even of surface ships. It needs further testing over a greater range of conditions by further comparisons with other techniques.

The Two-Wavelength Radiometer

A system to measure the infrared radiation in two bands has been developed for aircraft use. The effective depth beneath the surface from which infrared radiation is emitted varies with the wavelength. By observing in two narrow bands the temperatures at two depths, 0.075 and 0.025 millimeters, are obtained. Thus, estimates of both the surface temperature and the gradient in the laminar layer near the sea surface are obtained. From the gradient the total heat flow out of the surface (sensible and latent heats and back radiation) can be estimated. Initial results are encouraging (McAlister and McLeish, 1969; McAlister *et al.*, 1971);

however, the technique is difficult and estimates the total heat flow rather than the individual components.

The Ageostropic Method

This method depends on integrating the equations of motion to determine the stress as a function of height. In a horizontally uniform and stationary flow,

$$\frac{\partial \tau_{xz}}{\partial z} = \rho f(V_g - V), \qquad (12)$$

$$\frac{\partial \tau_{yz}}{\partial z} = -\rho f(U_g - U), \qquad (13)$$

where τ_{xz} and τ_{yz} are horizontal stress components, f is the Coriolis parameter, U_g and V_g are geostropic x and y wind components, and U and V are x and y observed wind components. The stress distribution can be determined if the stress is known at some level—for example, one might try to work to the top of the frictional or planetary boundary layer (~ 1-2 km), where the stress might be expected to vanish. In nonneutral stratification, thermal winds complicate the method. Hasse (1970a) and Roll (1965) discuss this method in more detail.

Budget Methods

The energy budget of the surface is used as a starting point,

$$R = H_s + H_L + G, \qquad (14)$$

where R is net radiation, G is the heat flux to the region below, and H_s and H_L, as before, are sensible and latent heat fluxes into the atmosphere. R and G must be measured. At sea, measurement of G is particularly difficult; rather careful measurements of water temperature are required and horizontal advection, often poorly known, can be very important. The method is applicable for periods of one day to the climatological scale.

To separate H_s and H_L requires either further measurements or assumptions. One possibility is to assume that H_s/H_L is proportional to $\Delta T/\Delta q$ (the Bowen ratio technique), where ΔT = average sea minus air temperature and Δq = average sea surface minus air humidity. Perhaps another possibility would be to determine E from the salt balance and observations of precipitation. Such techniques are suited more to quite large time and space scales and may not give results comparable to micro- and mesoscale methods.

Line Integral or Divergence Method

This is another type of budget method. One determines the flux of a quantity as a residual by determining the change inside a rather large volume and the fluxes through the sides and the top or bottom surfaces. The method seems feasible (Fleagle *et al.*, 1967), although it is difficult to achieve sufficient accuracy. A major observational effort with several ships and aircraft is required to get usable results.

"Wind Set-Up" Method

This method (the "historical" one) depends on estimating the stress from the observed wind "set-up," that is, the tilt of the sea surface. There are many difficulties such as those imposed by the bottom topography and wave "set-up" or "set-down" caused by nonlinear interactions of the waves (Burling and Stewart, 1967). These difficulties are probably so severe that existing measurements are not reliable. Hasse (1970a) suggests that comparison between observations and numerical calculations might allow better estimates of the stress. Waves would have to be observed and their effects reduced by careful selection of observation points so that corrections for wave set-up could be made. The method might prove useful at high wind speeds, where the effects are large, but requires thorough testing because of all the difficulties involved.

Summary of Methods

Virtually all of the methods were tried at some time or another in BOMEX (Barbados Oceanographic and Meteorological Experiment). Holland (1972) has summarized and compared the results that had been obtained to that date (see also BOMEX Bull. No. 11 for a bibliography of publications based on BOMEX data). The agreement amongst the various methods is amazingly good. Thus, useful results can be obtained in many ways, although more testing and comparing needs to be performed.

Many gaps still exist in our knowledge of the exchanges and physical processes that cause them. We still do not understand the wave-generation process (Pond, 1971; Phillips, 1972) and, therefore, do not know what effect differences in the wave field may have on the transfer mechanisms. Of most importance, we have virtually no measurements above wind speeds of 15 m s^{-1} or so. Moreover, direct measurements of sensible heat and moisture fluxes are very scanty.

However, we have learned how to measure the fluxes, even if all the details are not understood. The use of aircraft makes possible measurement over much wider areas. The dissipation technique, if it is more fully verified, may make it possible to achieve much longer time series from such places as the ocean weather stations and perhaps from ships of opportunity, thus supplying statistics of the fluxes. Some of the present techniques can be used to obtain high-wind speed observations, although such observations will not be easy. A number of groups are continuing to work on direct measurements of the fluxes, so that we should have a much larger data set over a greater range of conditions in a few years' time.

PARAMETERIZATION OF THE EXCHANGES

All of the measurements that give estimates of the fluxes are useful in increasing our understanding of the exchange processes. But most of them are rather difficult and must be made by specialists; thus, they will never be synoptically available over wide areas. For studies of larger-scale processes and their modeling, attempts must be made to parameterize the exchanges in terms of variables that are, or are likely to be, more readily available.

The bulk aerodynamic approach of parameterization uses the average wind speed, U; the average sea-minus-air temperature difference, ΔT; and the average humidity difference between the saturated air at the water surface and the air at some height, Δq. Some height in the atmospheric surface layer (commonly 10 m) is chosen as a reference level. The formulas are

$$\tau/\rho = -\overline{uw} = C_D U^2, \tag{15}$$

$$H_s/(\rho C_p) = \overline{wT} = C_T U \Delta T, \tag{16}$$

$$H_L/L = E = \overline{wq} = C_q U \Delta q, \tag{17}$$

where C_D, C_T, and C_q are nondimensional bulk aerodynamic coefficients and are sometimes referred to as the drag coefficient, Stanton number and Dalton number, respectively. Formally these coefficients may be obtained by integrating the profiles (Eqs. 3 and 4) of the Monin-Obukhov similarity theory, giving

$$U = \frac{u_\star}{\kappa}\, ln\,(z/z_o), \tag{18}$$

$$\overline{\gamma} - \overline{\gamma}_o = \gamma_\star\, ln\,(z/z_o), \tag{19}$$

where z_o, the constant of integration, is called the roughness length, and $\overline{\gamma}_o$ (temperature or humidity) is the value of $\overline{\gamma}$ at $z = z_o$. For neutral conditions, we have from Eqs. (15-19).

$$C_D = C_T = C_q = \kappa^2/[ln(z/z_o)]^2. \tag{20}$$

The coefficients are determined by the "roughness" of the surface and the reference height. For nonneutral conditions, the coefficients increase for unstable conditions and decrease for stable conditions with the scalar coefficients, C_T and C_q, showing somewhat greater rates of change than C_D, at least in unstable conditions. This point of view seems to be acceptable over land surfaces where z_o is related to the size of the surface elements (for moisture one must also correct for the degree of saturation of the soil). However, over the sea we have a wave-perturbed lower boundary and an incomplete knowledge of what is happening near it. It is better to regard the bulk aerodynamic formulas as simple, dimensionally correct, empirical parameterizations that need to be tested as directly as possible.

Momentum

A great deal more work has been done on this transfer than on the others. It appears that, although there is considerable scatter in individual values of C_D, the parameterization $\tau = \rho\, C_D U^2$ is satisfactory, at least for wind speeds up to 15 m s^{-1} C_D (10 m) $\cong 1.5 \times 10^{-3} \pm$ 10-20 percent on average in agreement with Phillip's (1972) remarks.

TABLE 1 Drag Coefficients from Various Sources

Source	Location	Method	Wind Speed Range (m/s^{-1})	10^3 C_D Mean ± Standard Deviation
Hasse (1970a)	North Sea	Eddy flux	4-11	1.21 ± 0.24
Brocks[a]	North Sea	Profile	3-12	1.29 ± 0.21
Zubkovski and Kravchenco (1967)[a]	Mediterranean Sea	Eddy flux	3-9	1.83 ± 0.84
Smith (1970)	N. Atlantic	Eddy flux	7-15	1.35 ± 0.34
Badgley *et al.* (1972)	Arabian Sea	Profile	2-8	1.4 ± ~ 0.2
Denman (1972) or Denman and Miyake (1973)	N. Pacific Stn PAPA	Dissipation	4-16	1.63 ± 0.28
Pond *et al.* (1971)	BOMEX	Eddy flux	4-7	1.52 ± 0.26[b]
		Dissipation		1.55 ± 0.40[b]
Delonibus (1971)	Argus Island	Eddy flux	4-14	1.3 ± 0.6[c]

[a] As quoted by Hasse (1970a).
[b] Determined from same data set.
[c] Only his unstable value given; his vertical velocity sensor, a propeller, may have serious response problems, particularly in stable cases when turbulence levels tend to be low.

Table 1 gives many of the more recent results obtained under more or less "open sea" conditions. The Hasse and Brocks results might be a bit low due to location (results at the University of British Columbia's somewhat sheltered coastal site seem to give lower values than those in Table 1, e.g., Miyake *et al.*, 1970b); Delonibus' instrumentation may have some deficiencies; Zubkovski and Kravchenko's results have more scatter, perhaps due to buoy motion; Pond *et al.*'s results have had to be corrected for the flow interference effects of *Flip*. In spite of all these problems, a reasonably satisfactory picture has emerged. All the results are within ±20 percent of 1.5×10^{-3} and, in view of the standard deviations, are probably not significantly different from this value.

Deacon and Webb (1962) quote many earlier results that are not inconsistent, except for the surface tilt observations, which give higher, probably anomalous, values. The formula that they suggest [$10^3\ C_D = 1.0 + 0.07\ U$ (U at 10 m in m s^{-1})] is consistent at moderate wind speeds but appears to have too strong a dependence on wind speed, so that values above 10 m s^{-1} are not consistent with the more recent results.

There is a great deal of scatter in the individual values. Much of it is probably statistical (Pond, 1971) although there are probably real variations due to sea state and stability—neither of which have been convincingly demonstrated, perhaps because the wave field is typically near saturation and dynamically similar and because the range of stability at typical observation heights (usually 10 m or less) is rather small. In view of the scatter, arguments for a trend in C_D with wind speed are hard to justify. Unfortunately, there are no reliable measurements at high wind speeds, although some indirect evidence from hurricane studies suggests that the values of C_D are similar to or slightly larger than those of Table 1, perhaps about 2×10^{-3} (Hawkins and Rubsam, 1968).

Moisture and Sensible Heat

There are only a few observations of coefficients for these exchanges, and our knowledge is not entirely satisfactory, as noted by Phillips (1972). However, I do not think the situation is quite as bleak as he does. The scatter he notes in the results of Kitaigorodski and Volkov (1965b) is rather reminiscent of the early drag coefficient results and, as he also notes, the data they had to use was not of very high quality. More recent field results (Hasse, 1970a: $10^3 C_T \sim 1$; Pond *et al.*, 1971: $10^3 C_q = 1.2 \pm 0.2$), as Phillips notes, look more promising, although the range of conditions is rather small. Hicks and Dyer (1971) obtain $10^3 C_T \sim 1.4 \pm 25$ percent from eddy-flux measurements in Bass Strait; they also point out that this value is consistent with estimates of C_q from large lakes ($\sim 1.5 \times 10^{-3}$). In addition, Wüst's extensive evaporation-pan results, as worked up by Sverdrup (1951), agree amazingly well with the Pond *et al.* results (< 5 percent difference in C_q). While one should not read too much into the numerical agreement because of pan-correction factors and the problems of working on *Flip*, this agreement suggests that the parameterization $E = C_q U \Delta q$ with $C_q \sim$ constant is reasonable, at least in the tropics, where H_L values are large and dominate over H_s values. In addition, Badgley *et al.*'s (1972) results have been examined by one of my students to evaluate C_T and C_q. The value for $10^3 C_q$ is 1.4 ± 0.4. C_T values are very scattered, in part due to uncertainties in ΔT; a reliable estimate of C_T is not possible, but the results are not in disagreement with a constant average value for C_T of the same order as the other results given here. Paulson *et al.*'s (1972) results based on profiles measured on *Flip* during BOMEX show fair agreement for E with the eddy flux and dissipation results also obtained on *Flip* by Pond *et al.* (1971). We have calculated C_q and C_T from their data and values of ΔT and Δq kindly provided by Paulson. The values are $10^3 C_q = 1.5 \pm 0.2$ and $10^3 C_T = 1.5 \pm 0.6$. Finally, several groups will be making more measurements in the near future, so considerably more data should be available soon.

There seems to be some problem with C_T in certain cases. Pond *et al.* (1971) obtain $10^3\ C_T \sim 2.5$. However, such cases may not be of practical importance, because the problem (high values of C_T) occurs in situations in which H_s/H_L is about 0.1 or less. When H_s is of importance, the parameterization $H_s = \rho C_p U \Delta T$ seems to be satisfactory. I believe this problem may be partially resolvable in terms of some computations of Coantic and Seguin (1971), which suggest that, under conditions of low winds and high average humidity, radiation-flux divergence may lead to anomalously high values of C_T when they are determined from Reynolds flux measurements. Further discussion of this problem and details of the calculations of C_T and C_q from the Badgley *et al.* (1972) and Paulson *et al.* (1972) data will be given in a note that we are preparing for submission to *Boundary-Layer Meteorology*.

The limited number of estimates of C_T and C_q are not inconsistent with the prediction of the Monin–Obukhov theory that $C_T = C_q = C_D$ for neutral stability. Most of the surface layer data, such as profiles and cospectral shapes, agree with this theory, giving some support to the prediction of equal bulk coefficients; although as noted previously, because of our lack of knowledge about the bottom part of the surface layer (below one wave height from the surface), such extrapolations may not be reliable. More data are needed. However, until they become available, for near-neutral conditions (likely to be a sufficiently good approximation in most cases, provided one uses observations in the lower part of the surface layer, $\sim$ 20 m or lower), it seems that $C_T = C_q = 1.5 \times 10^{-3}$ is a reasonable estimate to use; this suggested value should be regarded as *extremely tentative* and subject to revision as more data becomes available.

Summary of Parameterizations

On the basis of our present knowledge, it appears that, in spite of some problems, the situation looks quite hopeful. It appears that rather simple parameterizations (Eqs. 15–17) are reasonable approximations to use. More data are needed to establish the values of the coefficients, particularly at high wind speed; but it appears that they will be forthcoming in the next few years.

Alternatively, one might avoid the problem of the surface exchanges altogether in a joint model of the ocean and atmosphere by adding several levels near the interface and parameterizing the effects of the subgrid-scale turbulence sufficiently well. For example, Pandolfo (1968, 1971) in a mesoscale model, in which the eddy viscosity and diffusivity are calculated from the velocity and temperature gradients generated by the model, actually computes C_D with fair results. However, for large-scale modeling such an approach is probably not feasible, at least in the near future.

PROBLEMS AND POSSIBILITIES

Even if we had adequate parameterizations of the fluxes, there are still a number of difficulties that must be overcome in order to make use of them in models. Two types of numerical modeling may be envisioned: (a) experiments to test the importance of various processes and various ways of incorporating them, and (b) actual attempts to predict the future state of either the atmosphere, the ocean, or the whole system. For the first type, actual observations can be used as input data to determine the exchanges, and the ocean or atmosphere can be treated independently. For the second type, at least part, perhaps all, of the other fluid will have to be incorporated to obtain the necessary data to determine the exchanges. In either case, climatological data are probably not adequate as a means of determining the exchanges.

The exchange processes are very intermittent and occur in bursts when high values of U, ΔT, or Δq occur. Because of the nonlinear dynamics and differences in response time of various parts of the system, a time-varying input may produce quite different results than a constant input of the average value. Data on a more synoptic scale at each grid point, either self-generated in the model or from observations, may be required. Some numerical experiments to determine the frequency of updating of the boundary data that is required should be helpful.

Sources of the Data for Input to the Parameterizations

For predictive models, the necessary data may have to be self-generated. For experiments, observations of surface temperature and surface layer values of U, ΔT, and Δq are a minimum requirement—other parameters might be required, such as sea state. It seems that it may be possible to get satisfactory values of U from the surface pressure field (Hasse and Wagner, 1971). It may also be possible to get U from satellites (Levanon, 1971) or from radar backscatter. Surface layer values of ΔT, Δq, and the surface temperature, T_s (needed to determine the back radiation), seem to be more difficult. Perhaps the infrared sounding satellites will be able to provide the necessary data. Surface analyses of the standard observing network might be usable but the ocean areas are rather poorly observed. If some suitably instrumented moored buoys are installed, this situation would be improved.

Which value of T_s one should use is also somewhat of a problem. The actual "skin" temperature estimated from infrared radiation observations is lower than the temperature of the upper one-half meter or so—the temperature observed by a surface ship by the "bucket" method (Saunders, 1967; Hasse, 1970b). It is not clear which value is most representative. Since the exchanges are fluctuating, intermittent processes, it might be that much of the transfer occurs when the air is in contact with local "hot" spots (at the bucket temperature) that are exposed by breaking waves. This difference must be taken into account in comparing results from the two methods and in the parameterizations of H_s and H_L based on these measurements. More work needs to be done to determine the relation between the two T_s values and the best value to be used in the parameterizations.

As noted earlier, effects of stability seem to be small because existing flux observations have been obtained at small heights (10 m or less). However, if values of U, T, and q at greater heights (of order 100 m) are used to estimate the fluxes, as in some of the current models (e.g., Manabe, 1969), then stability effects will probably be significant and flux divergence may be important in some cases. Values at a lower level should be used, if possible, to avoid these problems. It should be possible to determine stability effects and include them in the parameterizations by making measurements at levels where the effects are important. Aircraft observations seem the most promising approach, but observations of the necessary bulk values, particularly T_S, which are not usually made at the same time as flux measurements, must be added to the aircraft-measurement programs.

The Importance of High Wind Speeds

Even if C_D is independent of wind speed, a significant proportion of the exchanges, particularly of momentum, occurs at high wind speeds. Strong winds are particularly important in temperate latitudes, where during any season much of the exchange occurs during cyclonic disturbances of a few days' duration. For a constant drag coefficient, 1 day at 25 m s^{-1} is equivalent to about 1 week at 10 m s^{-1} and to about 1 month at 5 m s^{-1}. If C_D increases with wind speed, the importance of high wind speeds will be even more dramatic, and the direction of the stress may be different. The effects of strong winds on the heat fluxes are not nearly so strong because, for constant aerodynamic coefficients, they are proportional to U not U^2 and the enhanced fluxes should tend to reduce ΔT and Δq.

Clearly the behavior of C_D at very high wind speeds needs to be determined. Aircraft observations have perhaps the most long-term and synoptic promise, although the measurement techniques need some verification by comparison with fixed tower observations. Careful observations from "oceanic" towers seem the most immediate way to obtain some of the necessary results.

While direct measurements of the fluxes at high wind speeds are going to be rather difficult, there are probably some simpler measurements that would allow some limits to be put on C_D at high wind speeds. Integrating over the normalized frequency band in which the exchanges occur (Eq. 2) for near and moderate winds, the observed value of neutral stability $(\overline{w^2}/\overline{u^2})^{1/2}$ is about 1/2 and that of $\overline{uw}/(\overline{u^2}\;\overline{w^2})^{1/2}$, the correlation coefficient between u and w, is about $-1/4$ (Miyake *et al.*, 1970c; Pond *et al.*, 1971). The spectral correlation coefficient, $\phi_{uw}/(\phi_u \phi_w)^{1/2}$, where ϕ_{uw} is the cospectrum $(\overline{uw} = \int_{\infty}^{-\infty} \phi_{uw} dk)$ is about $-1/2$ in the region around the peak of the cospectrum $(0.01 < fz/U < 0.1)$.

The difference between these two correlation values is caused by the difference in spectral shape at lower frequencies and by the loss of correlation due to turbulent randomization (approach towards isotropy) at higher frequencies. It seems unlikely that these values would be very different at higher wind speeds. At the most, perfect correlation near the peak could increase C_D by a factor of two, but such a dramatic effect is unlikely. Thus, to get a larger C_D, the turbulent intensity $(\overline{u^2})^{1/2}/U$ must increase. This quantity is much more easily observed than $\overline{uw}$; $\overline{u^2}$ could be determined by integrating over the bandwidth of Eq. (2) or perhaps limiting it to the region of the peak of the cospectrum $(0.01 < fz/U < 0.1)$ would give better statistical stability. Such observations could be made fairly easily from aircraft. Observations from ships might be too contaminated by ship motion, although the motion spectrum is relatively narrow and it might be possible to correct ϕ_u without actually having to measure the motion by removing the "bump" presumed to be a motion effect. A similar approach should be possible for the heat fluxes. In fact, observations of $\overline{u^2}$, $\overline{T'^2}$ and $\overline{q'^2}$ over appropriate bandwidths might provide a rather easier method of estimating the fluxes than any method currently in use. This "variance" approach ought to be tested for feasibility with currently available data and in future observational programs.

Nonlocalness of Momentum Transfer

It appears that much of the momentum transferred from the air to the water initially goes into the waves. Dobson (1971), from direct measurements of the pressure on the wave surface, which provided estimates of the momentum input to waves, estimated that about four-fifths goes into the waves. Eventually most of the momentum will pass from the waves to the currents, but this transfer may not be local. However, Phillips (1972) suggests that, since the wave field is usually near saturation, the process may be considered local, at least on the grid scale of a numerical model (grid-point separation 200 km or more). Manton (1972) has also examined this question. His results show that the transfer out of the region of input is small, except for rather small regions of rather high wind. Thus it appears that for large-scale modeling this problem may not be too serious.

Averaging or Smoothing Effects

Aerodynamic coefficients, determined by fairly direct methods, are based on measurements over time intervals of 30–60 minutes at a point or from aircraft over shorter times but equivalent space scales. Coefficients from longer duration, less direct measurements tend to be higher than 1.5×10^{-3}. The wind stress, τ, is a vector quantity. To take this fact into account, the first formula of Eq. (15) can be rewritten as $\underset{\sim}{\tau} = \rho C_D U^2 (\underset{\sim}{U}/|\underset{\sim}{U}|)$ or $\underset{\sim}{\tau} = \rho C_D \underset{\sim}{U}|\underset{\sim}{U}|$, where about 1-hour averages of U and U are appropriate. U is the mean speed and $|\underset{\sim}{U}|$ is the magnitude of the average vector wind, $\underset{\sim}{U}$. However, for a 1-hour average, the difference is usually fairly small (typically 2 percent over the sea); so either formula may be used. If one wants an average stress over several hours and longer (denoted by $\langle\;\rangle$), then one should take a proper vector average to determine $\langle\tau\rangle$, using hourly or perhaps 3-hourly values of U and $|U|$. Unfortunately, such information is not available for many places over the sea and one must use longer time-averages of U or $\underset{\sim}{U}$. But, $\langle|\underset{\sim}{U}|\rangle^2 \leqslant [\langle U\rangle\langle|\underset{\sim}{U}|\rangle] \leqslant \langle U\rangle^2 \leqslant \langle U|\underset{\sim}{U}|\rangle \leqslant \langle U^2\rangle$, so that, in general, the stress will be underestimated. Furthermore, the direction may be incorrect. Similar effects may be expected for the heat fluxes, since U may be correlated with ΔT and Δq. In practice some account is taken of this problem by using wind roses, including any available information on the frequency distribution of wind speed and direction. In general, fluxes estimated with long averages of U, ΔT, and Δq will be too low if the coefficients based on hourly averages are used. (The heat fluxes can be overestimated under some circumstances.) Alternatively, if some independent estimates of the fluxes are available, for example from budgets studies, then the coefficients derived from longer-period averages are larger than those derived from hourly averages. Some studies of this problem have been made (e.g., Malkus, 1962); but more work over a greater range of conditions, particularly in areas of cyclonic disturbances, would probably be helpful. A considerable body of data exists from the ocean weather stations that could be used for a preliminary examination of the relation between short-term and long-term coefficients.

Fortunately, the problem may not be too serious. Since more direct measurements are now possible, one need not rely on climatological data to estimate aerodynamic coefficients; indeed, one should not unless their relation to the shorter-term coefficients becomes better established. The time steps in models are now quite short, so that the coefficients from direct estimates are probably appropriate. The models do, however, have a large grid spacing and so there is some inherent spacial smoothing. Almost nothing is known of the mesoscale variability of U, ΔT, and Δq over the ocean, so it is difficult to know whether this effect is serious. Aircraft observations could fairly easily give the necessary information. Lacking any other information, a tentative approach to estimate the order of magnitude is to use our limited knowledge of time variability. A 200-km spacing may be equivalent to times of order one day for the atmosphere. It appears that there is a spectral gap in spectra of atmospheric turbulence near the surface between periods of a few minutes and one day or so (Lumley and Panofsky, 1964; Frye *et al.*, 1972). Thus, for a 1-day average, the mean square and the square of the mean may not be very different. If we can transfer this result to variability over distance, then the smoothing effects may be negligible. This question needs more thorough examination.

The parameterizations only give estimates; the actual fluxes at a particular point and time could be somewhat different. However, if the parameterization is correct on average, one might hope that the variations would be fairly small and average out as the integration proceeds.

Required Accuracy of the Parameterizations

It is not clear as yet just how accurate a parameterization is required. It seems that to some extent the models tend to compensate for errors in the parameterizations because of the integral constraints on the system. For example, if the drag coefficient is varied, the computed surface-layer wind speed varies too and the computed stress variations are not as large as the C_D variations. Bryan (1969) initially made an error in computing the wind stress for his ocean model, but comparison with a corrected run showed that most of the effects were small (except for an intensification of the wind-driven circulation in the corrected run, as might have been expected from the nature of the error). Manabe (1969) notes that over the ocean, surface-layer relative humidities computed from the model are larger than expected from observations. Perhaps this feature may be explained by his choice of C_q equivalent to 3.3×10^{-3} at 10 m. This value is probably too large and perhaps the model has compensated by lowering Δq.

In the present models the parameterizations are very simplified. Of course this simplification is necessary, as parameterization of the surface exchanges is only one of the many steps leading to a numerical model. Sometimes, the parameterizations used for surface exchanges seem rather out of date. For example, Hellerman (1967) recomputed the wind stress on the world ocean using a formulation for C_D as a function of wind speed only slightly different from the one used in a previous calculation by Hidaka (1958). Hidaka used a step function form for C_D (0.0008 for $U < 6.6$ m/s; 0.0026 for $U > 6.6$ m/s). Hellerman's C_D's were based on a 10-year-old formulation (Deacon *et al.*, 1956), which was a smoothed step function but which was not in agreement with more recent measurements, such as those reported by Deacon and Webb (1962) or Roll (1965). Hellerman did have more up-to-date climatological data, including wind-speed frequency distributions. His stress values are frequently used, but they are certainly not as good estimates as are possible. It would be instructive to recompute the stresses using both the Deacon and Webb (1962) formulation and $10^3 C_D = 1.5$ and rerunning some of the models to see how sensitive they are to such a variation in stress input. The same values for the coefficients are sometimes used over both land and sea, although it is known that they are probably different. It would be interesting to see what the effects would be if lower values over the sea were used in a model such as that of Manabe (1969) and Bryan (1969).

Some systematic experiments to find out how accurate the parameterizations need to be would be useful. There is little point in expending effort to improve a parameterization if the increased accuracy will not improve its usefulness.

CONCLUSIONS

Our ability to measure the exchanges of momentum, moisture, and sensible heat has improved a great deal in recent years. It appears that these exchanges may be estimated by fairly simple parameterizations. For winds up to 15 m s^{-1} the exchange coefficient for momentum seems adequately established. More measurements are needed of the moisture and sensible heat flux. Measurements of all three fluxes and their parameterization need to be extended to high wind speeds. Such measurements are in progress or being planned, so that adequate data should be available in the reasonably near future.

Numerical modeling is a very powerful tool in studying the large-scale dynamics of the ocean and the atmosphere. A great deal of work is in progress, so more should soon be learned of the accuracy of parameterizations needed for such models. This information will be a useful guide to those who are attempting to extend the range of, and to improve parameterizations of, the exchanges between atmosphere and ocean.

ACKNOWLEDGMENTS

I would like to thank Professor R. W. Burling and Professor R. W. Stewart for helpful discussions and comments during the preparation of this paper.

REVIEW: BY O. M. PHILLIPS

This excellent contribution by Dr. Pond leaves very little to be added. I agree with him that surface slope methods for estimating the wind stress on the water surface are unreliable, in my view, so unreliable as to be virtually useless. Besides the complications that he mentions, the effects of set-up or set-down by the wave field and the influence of bottom topography, the induced current pattern is bound to influence the mean surface slope and this is, itself, a function of the ambient stratification and the distributions of Reynolds stresses set up.

It might be profitable to consider in rather more detail the best way of obtaining measurements at wind speeds greater than 15 m s^{-1}. As Dr. Pond points out, there is a dearth of information concerning this and, at the same time, the possibility of physical processes, such as the generation of spin drift, beginning to play an important role not represented at lower wind speeds.

REFERENCES AND BIBLIOGRAPHY

Badgley, F. I., C. A. Paulson, and M. Miyake. 1972. Profiles of wind, temperature and humidity over the Arabian Sea. Int. Indian Ocean Exped. Meterol. Monogr. 6 East West Center, Honolulu, Hawaii. 66 pp.

BOMEX. 1972. Center for Experiment Design and Data Analysis, National Oceanic and Atmospheric Administration, Rockville, Md. Bull. No. 11. 83 pp.

Bowden, K. F., F. N. Frenkiel, and I. Toni, eds. 1967. Proceedings of an international symposium on boundary layers and turbulence with geophysical applications at Kyoto, Japan. Phys. Fluids Suppl. 10(9-2). American Institute of Physics, New York. 322 pp.

Bryan, K. 1969. Climate and the ocean circulation. Part 3: The ocean model. Mon. Weather Rev. 97:806-27.

Bunker, A. F. 1970. BOMEX meteorological data. Part 1: Turbulent fluxes observed from the WHOI aircraft. Part 2: Solar radiation averages. Woods Hole Oceanogr. Inst. Ref. 70-34, Woods Hole, Mass. 21 pp.

Burling, R. W., and R. W. Stewart. 1967. Ocean-atmosphere interaction (microprocesses), pp. 571-76. *In* R. Fairbridge, ed. Encyclopedia of Oceanography. Rheinholdt, New York.

Busch, N. W., and H. A. Panofsky. 1968. Recent spectra of atmospheric turbulence. Q. J. R. Meteorol. Soc. 94: 132-48.

Businger, J., M. Coantic, A. R. Mahoney, and K. Naito. 1969. Heat, moisture, and momentum fluxes in the boundary layer. C. J. Readings, ed. Radio Sci. 4(12):1381-83.

Charnock, H., and T. H. Ellison. 1967. The boundary layer in relation to large-scale motions of the atmosphere and ocean, pp. 1-11. Global Atmospheric Research Programme, Report of the Study Conference held at Stockholm, 28 June-11 July 1967, Appendix III.

Coantic, M., and B. Seguin. 1971. On the interaction of turbulent and radiative transfers in the surface layer. Boundary-Layer Meteorol. 1(3):245-63.

Cox, M. D. 1970. A mathematical model of the Indian Ocean. Deep-Sea Res. 17:47-75.

Deacon, E. L., P. A. Sheppard, and E. K. Webb. 1956. Wind profiles over the sea and the drag of the sea. Aust. J. Phys. 9:511-41.

Deacon, E. L., and E. K. Webb. 1962. Small scale interactions, pp. 43-87. *In* M. N. Hill, ed. The Sea, Vol. 1. Interscience, New York.

Deardorff, J. W. 1968. Dependence of air-sea transfer coefficients on bulk stability. J. Geophys. Res. 73:2549-57.

Delonibus, P. S. 1971. Momentum flux and wave spectra observations from an ocean tower. J. Geophys. Res. 76(27):6506-27.

Denman, K. L. 1972. The response of the upper ocean to meteorological forcing. Ph. D. Thesis. Institute of Oceanography, University of British Columbia, Vancouver. 117 pp.

Denman, K. L., and M. Miyake. 1973. The behaviour of the mean wind, the drag coefficient, and the wave field in the open ocean. J. Geophys. Res. 78:1917-31.

Dobson, F. W. 1971. Measurements of atmospheric pressure on wind-generated sea waves. J. Fluid Mech. 48(1):91-127.

Donelan, M. A. 1970. An airborne investigation of the structure of the atmospheric boundary layer over the tropical ocean. Ph. D. Thesis. University of British Columbia, Vancouver. 145 pp.

Fleagle, R. G., F. I. Badgley, and Y. Hsueh. 1967. Calculations of turbulent fluxes by integral methods. J. Atmos. Sci. 24:356-73.

Frye, D. E., S. Pond, and W. P. Elliot. 1972. A note on the kinetic energy spectrum of coastal winds. Mon. Weather Rev. 100:671-73.

Garstang, M. 1967. Sensible and latent heat exchange in low-latitude synoptic scale systems. Tellus 19:492-508.

Hasse, L. 1970a. On the determination of the vertical transports of momentum and heat in the atmospheric boundary layer at sea. Tech. Rep. No. 188, Department of Oceanography, Oregon State University, Corvallis. 55 pp. (Translation of a German article of same title in Geophys. Einzelschrift. 11. Hamburg, Verlag, 1968. 70 pp.)

Hasse, L. 1970b. The sea surface temperature deviation and the heat flow at the sea-air interface. Boundary-Layer Meteorol. 1:368-79.

Hasse, L., K. Brocks, M. Dunckel, and U. Görner. 1966. Eddy flux measurement at sea. Akademischeverlagsgessellschaft. Frankfurt am Main 39:254-57.

Hasse, L., and V. Wagner. 1971. On the relationship between geostrophic and surface wind at sea. Mon. Weather Rev. 99(4): 255-60.

Hawkins, H. F., and D. T. Rubsam. 1968. Hurricane Hilda, 1964. Part 2: Structure and budgets of the hurricane on October 1, 1964. Mon. Weather Rev. 96(9):617-36.

Hellerman, S. 1967. An updated estimate of the wind stress on the world ocean. Mon. Weather Rev. 95(9):607-26.

Hicks, B. B., and A. J. Dyer. 1971. Measurements of eddy-fluxes over the sea from an off-shore oil rig. Q. J. R. Meteorol. Soc. 96:523-28.

Hidaka, K. 1958. Computations of the wind stresses over the oceans. Rec. Oceanogr. Works Jap. 4(2):77-123.

Holland, J. Z. 1970. Preliminary report on the BOMEX sea-air interaction program. Bull. Am. Meteorol. Soc. 51(9):809-20.

Holland, J. Z. 1972. The BOMEX sea-air interaction program: Background and results to date. U.S. Department of Commerce, NOAA Tech. Mem. ERL BOMAP-9. 34 pp.

Jacob, W. J. 1967. Numerical semiprediction of monthly mean sea surface temperature. J. Geophys. Res. 72(6):1681-89.

Kitaigorodski, S. A. 1969. Small-scale atmosphere-ocean interactions. Izv. Akad. Nauk. USSR Atmos. Oceanic Phys. 5(11): 1114–31.

Kitaigorodski, S. A., and Yu. A. Volkov. 1965a. On the roughness parameter of the sea surface and the calculation of momentum flux in the near-water layer of the atmosphere. Izv. Akad. Nauk. USSR. Atmos. Oceanic Phys. 1(9):973–88.

Kitaigorodski, S. A., and Yu. A. Volkov. 1965b. Calculation of turbulent heat and humidity fluxes in an atmospheric layer near a water surface. Izv. Akad. Nauk. USSR Atmos. Oceanic Phys. 1(12):1319–36.

Kraus, E. B. 1967. Wind stress along the sea surface. *In* Adv. Geophys. 12:213–56. Academic Press, New York.

Kraus, E. B. 1972. Atmosphere-Ocean Interaction. Oxford University Press, London. 275 pp.

Kukharets, V. P., and L. R. Tsvang. 1969. Spectra of the turbulent heat flux in the atmospheric boundary layer. Izv. Akad. Nauk. USSR Atmos. Oceanic Phys. 5(11):1132–42.

Laevastu, T., and W. E. Hubert. 1970. The nature of sea surface temperature anomalies and their possible effects on weather. Fleet Numer. Weather Cent. Tech. Note 55. 13 pp.

Levanon, N. 1971. Determination of the sea surface slope distribution and wind velocity using sun glitter viewed from a synchronous satellite. J. Phys. Oceanogr. 1(3):214–20.

Lumley, J. L., and H. A. Panofsky. 1964. The Structure of Atmospheric Turbulence. Interscience, New York. 239 pp.

Malkus, J. S. 1962. Large-scale interactions, pp. 88–294. *In* M. N. Hill, ed. The Sea. Interscience, New York.

Manabe, S. 1969. Climate and the ocean circulation. Part 1: The atmospheric circulation and the hydrology of the earth's surface. Part 2: The atmospheric circulation and the effect of heat transfer by ocean currents. Mon. Weather Rev. 97:739–805.

Manton, M. J. 1972. On the wave field generated by a variable wind. Geophys. Fluid Dyn. 3:91–104.

McAllister, E. D., and W. McLeish. 1969. Heat transfer in the top millimeter of the ocean. J. Geophys. Res. 74(13):3408–14.

McAllister, E. D., W. McLeish, and E. A. Cordvan. 1971. Airborne measurements of the total heat flux from the sea during BOMEX. J. Geophys. Res. 76(8):4172–80.

McBean, G. A., R. W. Stewart, and M. Miyake. 1971. The turbulent energy budget near the surface. J. Geophys. Res. 76(27):6540–49.

Miyake, M., M. Donelan, and Y. Mitsuta. 1970a. Airborne measurement of turbulent fluxes. J. Geophys. Res. 75(24):4506–18.

Miyake, M., M. Donelan, G. McBean, C. Paulson, F. Badgley, and E. Leavitt. 1970b. Comparison of turbulent fluxes over water determined by profile and eddy correlation techniques. Q. J. R. Meteorol. Soc. 96:132–37.

Miyake, M., R. W. Stewart, and R. W. Burling. 1970c. Spectra and cospectra of turbulence over water. Q. J. R. Meteorol. Soc. 96(407):138–43.

Monin, A. S. 1969. Fundamental consequences of the interaction between atmosphere and ocean. Izv. Akad. Nauk. USSR Atmos. Oceanic Phys. 5(11):1102–13.

Monin, A. S., and A. M. Yaglom. 1965; 1967. Statistical Hydrodynamics, Vols. I and II, Nauka, Moscow. 639 pp., 720 pp. (English translation of Vol. I, updated and revised, J. L. Lumley, ed., is available from MIT Press, Cambridge, Mass., 1971, 769 pp; Vol. II, in preparation.)

O'Brien, J. J. 1970. The numerical simulation of large-scale ocean circulation, pp. 99–104. Reprinted from Proceedings of the 1970 Summer Computer Simulation Conference. Denver, Colo.

O'Brien, J. J. 1971. A two dimensional model of the wind-driven North Pacific. Invest. Pesq. 35(1):331–49.

Pandolfo, J. P. 1968. A numerical model of the atmosphere–ocean planetary boundary layer, pp. 31–40. Proceedings, WMO/IUGG Symposium on Numerical Weather Prediction. Tokyo, Japan, 26 November–4 December.

Pandolfo, J. P. 1971. Numerical experiments with alternative boundary layer formulations using BOMEX data. Boundary-Layer Meteorol. 1(3):277–89.

Paquin, J. E., and S. Pond. 1971. The determination of the Kolmogoroff constants for velocity, temperature and humidity fluctuations from second and third order structure functions. J. Fluid Mech. 50(2):257–69.

Paulson, C. A. 1970. The mathematical representation of wind speed and temperature profiles in the atmosphere surface layer. J. Appl. Meteorol. 9:857–61.

Paulson, C. A., E. Leavitt, and R. G. Fleagle. 1972. Air–sea transfer of momentum, heat and water determined from profile measurements during BOMEX. J. Phy. Oceanogr. 3:487–97.

Phelps, G. T., and S. Pond. 1971. Spectra of the temperature and humidity fluctuations and of the fluxes of moisture and sensible heat in the marine boundary layer. J. Atmos. Sci. 28(6):918–28.

Phillips, O. M. 1966. The Dynamics of the Upper Ocean. Cambridge University Press, London. 261 pp.

Phillips, O. M. 1972. Ocean coupling and response times. In parameterizations of sub-grid scale process. GARP publications series no. 8, pp. 81–91.

Pond, S. 1971. Air–sea interaction. Trans. Am. Geophys. Union (IUGG) 52(6):389–94.

Pond, S., G. T. Phelps, J. E. Paquin, G. McBean, and R. W. Stewart. 1971. Measurements of the turbulent fluxes of momentum, moisture and sensible heat over the ocean. J. Atmos. Sci. 28(6):901–17.

Priestley, C. H. B. 1959. Turbulent Transfer in the Lower Atmosphere. University of Chicago Press, Ill. 130 pp.

Priestley, C. H. B., and R. J. Taylor. 1972. On the assessment of surface heat flux and evaporation using large-scale parameters. Mon. Weather Rev. 100(2):81–92.

Roll, H. V. 1965. Physics of the Marine Atmosphere. Academic Press, New York. 426 pp.

Saunders, P. M. 1967. The aerial measurement of sea surface temperature in the infrared. J. Geophys. Res. 72(16):4109–17.

Saxton, J. A., ed. 1969. Proceedings of a colloquium on spectra of meteorological variables. Radio Sci. 4(12):1099–1398.

Smith, S. D. 1970. Thrust-anemometer measurements of wind turbulence, Reynolds stress and drag coefficient over the sea. J. Geophys. Res. 75:6758–70.

Smith, W. L., P. K. Rao, R. Koffler, and W. R. Curtis. 1970. The determination of sea-surface temperature from satellite high resolution infrared window radiation measurements. Mon. Weather Rev. 98(8):604–11.

Sverdrup, H. U. 1951. Evaporation from the oceans, pp. 1071–81. *In* Compendium of Meteorology. Am. Meteorol. Soc., Boston.

Sverdrup, H. U., M. W. Johnson, and R. H. Fleming. 1942. The Oceans. Prentice-Hall, Englewood Cliffs, New Jersey. 1087 pp.

Wyngaard, J. C., and O. R. Cote. 1971. The budgets of turbulent kinetic energy and temperature variance in the atmospheric surface layer. J. Atmos. Sci. 28(2):190–201.

Zilitinkevich, S. S. 1969. On the calculation of global phenomena of the interaction between the oceans and the atmosphere. Izv. Akad. Nauk. USSR Atmos. Oceanic Phys. 5(11):1143–59.

Zubkovski, S. L., and T. K. Kravchenko. 1967. Direct measurements of some turbulence characteristics in the surface layer of the atmopshere over water. Izv. Akad. Nauk. USSR Atmos. Oceanic Phys. 3:127–35.

DISCUSSION

KIRWAN: Steve, the boundary layer processes and parametric forms that you've shown are really pertinent to processes whose time scales are of the order of an hour, with comparable space scales. Would you comment on the relevance, if any, of these parametric studies to numerical models that require time-dependent, upper-boundary conditions for considerably larger scales.

POND: As discussed in my paper, there are problems with this difference in time scales; the measurements are based on an hour's data. If you get 1 hour's data for one estimate of the drag coefficient, it is considered fairly reasonable. Since the time steps in the model are getting shorter, the problem may not remain serious. A time step in the model on the order of 2 or 3 h is not impossible. Where you get into difficulty is when climatological values are put into this formula without adjusting the coefficients. This can and should be looked at with existing data. One of my students is working on weather-ship station P-data with this idea in mind. The spatial averaging effect is not clear. One of the saving graces is that you may get away with using standard synoptic 1- or 3-hourly values, or maybe 6- or possibly 12-hourly values. There does seem to be a spectral gap. In other words, the variance doesn't increase much until you get into longer periods of a couple of days or more; then you begin to add to the value of the square. You should be taking the mean of the square rather than the square of the mean. There is however a length-scale problem without any observations available to solve it. If at a given grid point—the actual average wind speed when the wind is varying around you—is measured, the stress estimates for the whole area near the grid points is too low. This is because nearby areas of slightly stronger wind contribute to the total variance. Now it makes a difference as to whether the variations are large or small over the time and space scale. I don't think we know what the mesoscale variability of something as simple as the wind speed is over the ocean.

RATTRAY: There's some very nice equipment for measuring windspeed. In a sailboat race, two boats go one way for about 2 miles and end up with a minute or so difference in their arrival time. But if you go from the West Coast to Honolulu, the tracks may be about 100 miles apart, and the difference in arrival may be about a day or so although they are comparable boats with comparable crews. This tells us something about the order of magnitude of variations in the wind field over large scales. Actually for differential wind speed measurements, there is no more sensitive equipment than a sailboat on a race course.

POND: I think an airplane flying around for about a year could probably answer that question.

RATTRAY: I don't think so. There is a very notable spatial variation in all scales, on the order of miles.

LEITH: I'd like to make another minor point in connection with the use of an atmospheric model that could provide the surface boundary conditions for an ocean circulation model. Probably what you would take out of an atmospheric model would be stress, heat flow, and evaporation directly rather than going through such formulas as these. It has been known for some years in atmospheric models that the same problem exists in defining the surface wind, depending on what level you take it at. But the stress is probably better defined than any such estimate of what you use of the drag coefficient C_D.

POND: In other words, let's forget about the C_D.

LEITH: Atmospheric models work reasonably well no matter what value of C_D you use, because you just adjust your internal estimate of the surface wind speed.

POND: Yes, if you do raise C_D, the surface wind drops.

LEITH: To the extent that stress is really what you want to feed into an ocean circulation model, you normally would bypass these deep detailed questions.

POND: Does the actual stress come directly out of the model?

LEITH: It could!

RATTRAY: That could be a very important consideration.

BRETHERTON: I think it is very important that we look at these formulas in this light, indeed. And in this context I think it is worth drawing people's attention to one normal method of obtaining the stress, which is currently being tried out by Professor Soumi. This is from measurement of glint from satellites looking down at the ocean. You get the direct reflection of the sun sometimes up to 30° from the zenith. The intensity of this reflection is essentially a measure of the average slope of the capillary scale. You'll find that this is well correlated with the surface stress. This is a direct measurement of the stress that we are able to do very readily with a beautiful broad coverage. Now, this is potentially so important that I think it is worthwhile concentrating some investigations and really trying to relate that stress to the capillary slope.

LARSON: Knute Agaard made a study of circulation in the North Sea based on two cases: one using 1-day-average wind speeds and the other using 5-day-average wind speeds. The difference in vigor of the circulation is about 30 percent between the 1- and 5-day average wind speed.

GALT: If you go from the atmospheric models to the ocean models with the direct stress input you have the advantage of matching up energy flux and such things quite accurately. However, because of patchiness you still end up with a verification problem. You really haven't figured out how to relate measurements to either model. You're satisfying the coupling between the atmosphere and the ocean, but you still have the problem of knowing whether you are looking at reality or not.

BRYAN: This question of the amount of momentum going into the wave field and the amount going directly into the current has concerned me for a long time. You didn't really attempt to answer that question, you just brought the matter up. For example, in a model that Pollard and Millard have of the mixed layer the stress divided by the depth is a body force acting on the water. If some of the momentum is going into the wave field, this picture may be changed seriously.

POND: The hope is that it goes out of the wave field into deeper water fairly quickly. We really don't know whether it does or not.

RATTRAY: There are some observations on continental shelves that indicate that the currents anticipate the weather systems, so maybe there is a mechanism whereby the momentum can be transferred ahead of the storm.

O'BRIEN: Is it possible that in a fully developed sea the normal stresses become as important as the tangential stress? If this is the case, then estimates of a momentum flux based on C_D would be in error.

POND: If you make measurements sufficiently high above the waves, then the stresses are tangential, and you can probably get a reasonable estimate of the momentum flux at this level. This begs the whole question, of course, of what is happening at the surface of the waves. In summary, then, you have to make measurements high above the waves and outside the spray zone to get reliable estimates of the momentum flux into the ocean.

RATTRAY: At high wind speeds, if you have to get over the waves, you're talking about a reference level considerably higher than 10 m.

POND: You can always interpolate back downwards no matter where the measurements are made. Also, at the higher wind speeds, stability is not important. Therefore, you can measure at higher levels in higher winds speeds and ignore the stability.

GILL: I am interested in the relation between C_D for a 1-h period, and the C_D for a month. Wouldn't this be a function of the velocity spectrum? Do we know very much about this?

POND: The article in *The Sea* on large-scale air–sea interaction indicates that if you take whatever C_D you have and calculate stress in a reasonable fashion, you'll get reasonable results. In these sort of calculations, however, you have to realize that the observations are biased. Ships try to stay away from regions of high wind. However, weather ships have made observations at 3-h periods for years. Something could be done with this data.

NIILER: Would somebody comment on a recent study by Christopher Welch at MIT, who calculated from synoptic data the vorticity input into the ocean? A comparison was made between these results and what one would obtain from climatological values. As I recall, the study indicated that it didn't make much difference whether you used properly averaged hourly or daily values, or the climatological values.

BRETHERTON: The errors associated with such calculations are very large. The result is that if you use climatological values in these calculations, you get a transport of 40 Sverdrups ± 50.

GENERAL OCEAN CIRCULATION

A. L. GORDON

INTRODUCTION

Ocean water is induced to move in response to the action of the wind, thermohaline alterations at the sea surface, tidal forces, and, to a lesser degree, thermal changes at the lower boundary (geothermal heat flux). The time variability of the first three of these driving mechanisms induces a time dependance on ocean circulation. The mean circulation over a period T would be considered to be the general ocean circulation if the mean varies little as T is increased. Recent measurements of ocean currents (Schwartzlose and Isaacs, 1969; Schmitz *et al.*, 1970; Rossby and Webb, 1971; Webster, 1971; Irish and Snodgrass, 1972) indicate that variability is rather large on a time scale of hours to weeks. Often major changes in current follow extended time periods of only short (order of a day) variations. Hence it is not possible to construct a picture of the general circulation based on "direct" current measurements, except in very local areas, where the average current is strong compared to the variability, or where great quantities of data are available over the long time period, as in the case of ships' drift data in reference to the immediate surface circulation (though such data may be considered as "indirect" current evidence).

Our knowledge of the general circulation is derived mainly from the distribution of seawater characteristics. The large-scale distribution of the temperature and salinity fields are analogous to a long-period, integrating, current meter. They respond to the "average" advection-diffusion condition of the ocean. Because the distributions of temperature and salinity fields are in a near-steady state, one can assume they respond to a circulation pattern nearly invariant in time and hence represent the general circulation. Comparing distributions derived from numerical models to the observed distribution of temperature and salinity fields, as well as other traces, is an important test for the models (Kuo and Veronis, 1970).

Paleo-oceanographic circulation patterns during the geological past can be studied from the sediment record (vertical and horizontal sediment distribution) obtained in piston cores. The sediment distribution can be used in much the same way as distributions of seawater parameters, since the sediment, by its terrigenous, biogenic, and isotopic composition reflects the physical oceanographic conditions at the time of deposition. Depending on the sediment thickness and rates of sedimentation, one can obtain in a few regions sediments deposited as long ago as the Cretaceous period (64 million years ago), although the paleo-oceanography of the last few million years can be studied over extensive sections of the ocean floor. The much longer drill cores obtained through the JOIDES project provide information on the sediment distribution of extensive ocean regions for earlier periods.

Recent investigations of the paleomagnetism of the seafloor have allowed reconstruction of past geography (Dietz and Holden, 1970). This information, coupled with the sediment record, gives a basis for applying to numerical models of ocean circulation realistic boundary conditions that existed in the geologic past. Numerical modeling of the paleo-ocean circulation is feasible and presents an interesting application of these methods.

The National Oceanographic Data Center (NODC) reports in their Inventory of Archived Data (1969) a total of 3.45×10^5 hydrographic stations in the world ocean. This total has increased during the last few years. Inspection of these data may very well indicate long-term drifts in the temperature and salinity fields as noted by Worthington (1954, 1956, 1966) in reference to the North Atlantic Ocean. Interesting variability in surface salinity and temperature patterns in the western, tropical Pacific Ocean are discussed by Rochford (1972). Only in recent years have we developed a long enough sequence of accurate hydrographic data to study year- or decade-long trends in the ocean. Such information is invaluable to the study of variability of the earth's weather patterns (Bjerknes, 1959; Naimas, 1970; Naimas and Born, 1970).

In order to "handle" the great amount of oceanographic data for the study of the general circulation and secular changes, an up-to-date data bank is needed in an easy-to-use format. Although the NODC efforts have aided, a more intense drive is needed to organize such a data bank and provide digitized, continuously updated hydrographic data on magnetic tapes in a standard format.

In recent years, the study of water-mass distribution with associated current meter observations has enlightened us about the abyssal circulation of the deep western boundary currents of the Pacific and Atlantic Oceans and about the magnitude of the Antarctic circumpolar current. Significant to some of these studies is the use of silicate (SiO_3) as an important indicator of circulation patterns. Silicate concentrations range from near zero in some surface waters to 130–140 μgm·at/liter, and are believed to be of greater conservation (smaller relative "decay-generation") than oxygen, which is also an often-used parameter.

ABYSSAL CIRCULATION

The major regions of formation of abyssal waters are the Norwegian-Greenland and the Weddell Seas. High-saline abyssal water is derived from the outflows of the Mediterranean and Red Seas, and a low-saline water that marks the top of the abyssal water column is formed along the polar and subpolar oceanic frontal regions of the Antarctic and northwestern Pacific and Atlantic Oceans. These regions are producers of the abyssal layer of the ocean. The slow warming of the abyssal waters by various processes allows these regions to remain source areas without a secular increase in surface density. The abyssal circulation pattern that spreads these waters is induced by a combination of thermohaline and wind influences. It is generally considered that the wind is the predominant force (Wyrtki, 1961), although the formation of these waters is a thermohaline process.

The source of abyssal waters in the Southern Hemisphere is mainly in the Weddell Sea, where the bulk of Antarctic bottom water is produced. All of this important water mass is not formed in the Weddell Sea, nor is all Antarctic bottom water of identical properties (Gordon, 1974; Gordon and Tchernia, 1972). Table 1 (Gordon, 1974) shows the basic varieties and ranges in salinity of bottom water thus far observed.

The Weddell Sea, because of its very cold bottom water, is likely the main producer of Antarctic bottom water. The most significant outward flow of bottom water is in the form of a "contour-following current" along the periphery of the Weddell basin (Hollister and Elder, 1969; Gordon, 1974). The rate of production is not known, although estimates of near 20×10^6 m^3/s to a probable upper limit of 50×10^6 m^3/s have been made (Gordon, 1971a). The bulk of Antarctic bottom water has an average potential temperature of near -1 °C. As it flows northward it mixes with warmer overlying water and is warmed from below by the geothermal flux (Olsen, 1968). Most of the bottom water enters the Atlantic and returns southward combined with the North Atlantic deep water. This combination, with additional Antarctic bottom water and circumpolar deep water, flows eastward via the Antarctic circumpolar current to enter the Indian and Pacific Oceans. Reid and Lynn (1971) trace the spreading of abyssal waters on isopycnal surfaces (the sigma value of 45.92 relative to a 4,000 decibar level is used to trace spreading of abyssal water in the world ocean). Their study and that of Lynn and Reid (1968) serve as useful guides to abyssal-water spreading.

TABLE 1 Characteristics of Observed Antarctic Bottom Water

Variety	Location	Potential Temperature (°C)	Salinity (‰)	Oxygen (ml/liter)	Silicate (ug·at/liter)
Low salinity	Western periphery of Weddell basin	−1.4	34.634–34.674	6.7	87
	Deepest parts of Weddell basin	−0.7	34.634–34.674	5.9	110
	Adelie Coast	−0.7	34.650	5.9	110
High salinity	Deep ocean adjacent to the Ross Sea	−0.5	34.738–34.754	5.6	104

The formation of North Atlantic deep water involves a transfer of warm surface water into the abyssal layers. The relatively warm, salty North Atlantic central water mass (Sverdrup *et al.*, 1942) enters the Norwegian-Greenland seas, where heat is lost to the atmosphere at the extremely large rate of 75 Kcal/cm^2 · yr (Worthington, 1970). Worthington considers the Norwegian Sea as a mediterranean basin because low-density water enters the surface layers and high density exits at depth. A water budget suggests that 9 X 10^6 m^3/s is the rate of surface-water inflow to the Norwegian Sea and 6 X 10^6 m^3/s is the rate of overflow across the Greenland-Iceland-Faroe ridge. The 6 X 10^6 m^3/s overflow combines with 4 X 10^6 m^3/s of water outside of the ridge to produce North Atlantic deep water at rate of 10 X 10^6 m^3/s, with equal amounts produced on both sides of Iceland, although Reid and Lynn (1971) consider that the principal overflow occurs between Iceland and Greenland (Denmark Strait). The overflow is found to be sporadic (Lachenbruch and Marshall, 1968; Worthington, 1969). In April 1965 Lachenbruch and Marshall found a "boluses" (after Cooper, 1955) of cold water overflowing the Denmark Strait and suggest that these are common, but of short duration and hence rarely observed. The temperature of the April 1965 "boluses" was near –0.45 °C. Worthington (1969) found temperatures near 0.0 °C during periods of maximum overflow. The sporadic overflow may be related to the highly variable water structure of the North Atlantic polar front and to the variable productivity of the fishing grounds in the Iceland region. Lee and Ellett (1967) showed that the volume of overflow and the characteristics of the overflow water may vary.

The temperature-salinity relationships of the waters of the northern North Atlantic are shown in schematic form in Figure 1. The overflow west of Iceland (Denmark Strait) varies between nearly pure Norwegian Sea water to mixtures of this water with Labrador Sea water. The resultant overflow produces the northwest Atlantic bottom water (Lee and Ellett, 1967). The potential temperature is near 1 °C with a salinity near 34.90 ‰. East of Iceland the overflow is warmer and saltier and represents a mixture of Norwegian Sea water and warm salty central North Atlantic water. Lee and Ellett call this the northeast Atlantic deep water. This latter water mass crosses the mid-ocean ridge in the vicinity of the Gibbs fracture zone at 53° N (Worthington and Volkmann, 1965) to enter the western Atlantic and mix with the Denmark Strait overflow to form North Atlantic deep water. Reid and Lynn (1971) state this as follows:

> The colder, less saline, but denser waters at 59°30′ N from the Greenland Sea have passed southward through the Denmark Strait; they pass southward west of the Ridge beneath the warmer, more saline and less dense waters from the eastern side that are now flowing northward. The vertical mixing that has taken place has cooled and freshened the Iceland–Scotland overflow water and made the Denmark Strait overflow water warmer and more saline.

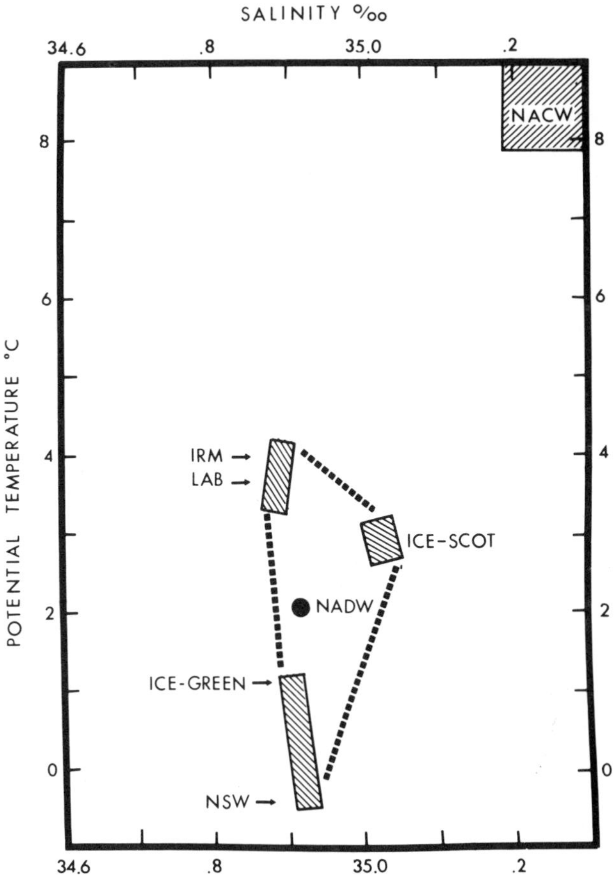

FIGURE 1 Schematic representation of potential temperature-salinity relationships of the water masses involved in North Atlantic deep water production.

The division of North Atlantic deep water into middle and lower components (the upper being the well-defined outflow from the Mediterranean Sea), as done by Wüst (1933, 1935) and mentioned by Edmond and Anderson (1971) and Reid and Lynn (1971), is a fine division. In light of the apparent time variability in the northern North Atlantic, it is not clear what these two slightly different subspecies of North Atlantic deep water signify; the two overflows may not mix entirely and the denser northwest Atlantic bottom water may become the lower North Atlantic deep water mentioned by Wüst (1935).

The North Atlantic deep water has a potential temperature of 2 °C, a salinity of approximately 34.91 ‰, and is produced (sporadically) at an average rate of 10 X 10^6 m^3/s. Because the transport of water within the deep western boundary current of the South Atlantic is roughly twice this value (Wright, 1969), additional water must be entrained, perhaps a return flow of the Antarctic bottom water (Amos, *et al.*, 1971; see Atlantic Ocean section of this chapter).

The Mediterranean outflow adds approximately 1 X 10^6

m^3/s (Ovchennikov, 1966) to the deep water. It is relatively warm and salty, initial values being 12 °C and 36.6 ‰, respectively (Wüst, 1935). The high temperatures represent a significant heat input to the abyssal waters.

In a steady-state temperature regime, the input of new cold abyssal water (Antarctic bottom water and North Atlantic deep water) must balance the input of heat by a geothermal heat flux, downward convection of relatively warm water (mainly derived from the Mediterranean Sea), and downward diffusion of heat across the thermocline.

The potential temperature-salinity-volume diagram of Montgomery (1958) shows the average potential temperature of abyssal water (defined as the water below the intermediate water masses, less than 4 °C) to be 1.70 °C for the world ocean. This would be the temperature of the waters colder than 4 °C if they were mixed. This modal temperature will be used as the reference to determine the heat input or removal by convective motion. Water masses introduced to the abyssal layer with a potential temperature above the modal temperature add calories to the abyssal waters, while addition of colder water removes calories. Of the four concentrated water masses entering the abyssal layer three add heat; these are: North Atlantic deep water, Mediterranean Sea overflow, and Red Sea overflow. The Antarctic bottom water removes the heat introduced by the three "warm" water masses, as well as the heat introduced by geothermal heat flux and downward heat diffusion.

The North Atlantic deep water is produced at a rate of 10×10^6 m^3/s and is 0.30 °C warmer than the modal temperature. Using a specific heat of 0.94 the North Atlantic deep water is found to introduce 0.28×10^{13} cal/s. The Mediterranean overflow is 10.30 °C warmer than the modal temperature and flows at a rate of 1×10^6 m^3/s, hence introduces 0.97×10^{13} cal/s. The Red Sea overflow is very warm, being near 20 °C (Düing and Schwill, 1967) with a production rate of 0.2×10^6 m^3/s (Siedler, 1968), which leads to a heat input of 0.34×10^{13} cal/s. The inflow of −1 °C Antarctic bottom water to thermally balance the convective heat input is 6.25×10^6 m^3/s (see Table 2), the largest component being the Mediterranean Sea overflow.

The heat input by geothermal heat can be calculated from the average geothermal heat flux of 1.6×10^{-6} $cal/cm^2 \cdot s$ (including the mid-ocean ridge, Bullard, 1963) and the total area of the deep-sea floor (deeper than 2,000 m) which is 3.05×10^{18} cm^2. The deep-sea geothermal heat flux is 0.5×10^{13} cal/s, which requires an inflow of 1.97×10^6 m^3/s for balance.

Additional Antarctic bottom water is needed to balance the heat input by the downward diffusion of heat. This may be approximated indirectly. Estimate of the heat loss to the atmosphere for the areas between the Antarctic polar front and Antarctica is 15,000 $cal/cm^2 \cdot yr$ (Gordon, 1971b) or 9.5×10^{13} cal/s. This difference may be made up by heat flux across the polar front and/or a greater downward diffusive heat flux in the world ocean (i.e., more Antarctic bottom water produced). If the lateral diffusion across the front is of minor importance, a total 38×10^6 m^3/s of Antarctic bottom water is needed to balance the heat budget and arrive at 15,000 $cal/cm^2 \cdot yr$ heat loss from the Antarctic waters to atmosphere (see Figure 3, and Table 2). The heat flux by diffusion across the thermocline is 7.46×10^{13} cal/s, the major heat input to abyssal waters.

TABLE 2 Heat Input Relative to the Average Abyssal Water Potential Temperature, 1.70°C

Process	Heat Input (cal/s)	Antarctic Bottom Water (−1 °C) Needed for Thermal Balance (m^3/s)
Convective		
a: North Atlantic deep water	0.28×10^{13}	1.11×10^6
b: Mediterranean overflow	0.97×10^{13}	3.81×10^6
c: Red Sea overflow	0.34×10^{13}	1.33×10^6
Geothermal heat flux	0.50×10^{13}	1.97×10^6
Diffusive heating	7.46×10^{13}	29.40×10^6
TOTAL HEAT INPUT	9.55×10^{13}	37.62×10^6

Using the abyssal waters of 3 °C or less to calculate the modal temperature (and in so doing assume the heat input from the Mediterranean and Red Sea outflow goes in total into this colder reservoir) a larger flow of Antarctic bottom water is needed for balance. The average temperature is 1.5 °C and the necessary Antarctic bottom water transport is 40.5×10^6 m^3/s. It therefore is reasonable to deduce that for thermal balance of abyssal waters an Antarctic bottom water transport of 35–40 $\times 10^6$ m^3/s is necessary.

It is clear that factors other than downward heat diffusion into abyssal waters is of significance in "driving" the abyssal circulation. The convective heating terms varied in the geological past so one would expect some variability in Antarctic bottom water production (or whatever other water mass was responsible for heat removal from abyssal waters). It is also interesting to point out that the present water masses that introduce heat to abyssal layers are mainly in the North Atlantic Ocean, where one also finds a large inflow of the Antarctic bottom water.

The total production of Antarctic bottom water of 38×10^6 m^3/s is set by the amount of sea-to-air heat exchange south of the polar front. The downward heat diffusion across the lower thermocline is introduced for balance. A higher rate of North Atlantic deep water production would add more heat to abyssal waters but it would still be small compared to the probable diffusive heat flux. Increasing the North Atlantic deep water by four times would introduce 1.12×10^{13} cal/s into abyssal waters. While this would roughly give a 1:1 ratio of Antarctic bottom water to North Atlantic deep water production rates, as suggested by Craig and Gordon (1965) on the basis of oxygen-isotope data, it requires an abyssal water renewal of 79×10^6 m^3/s. The residence time of such an ocean would be 560 years. This value is perhaps half of the expected residence time (Broecker and Li, 1970). The residence time determined using the transport values of Table 2 (a 4:1 ratio of Antarctic bottom water to North Atlantic deep water) is 890 years, closer but still below the expected value. A residence time of 1,000 years requires an input of 43.5×10^6 m^3/s.

It is possible that heat loss from sea to air south of the polar front may be partially made up by heat flux across the polar front, as mentioned above. A horizontal coefficient of turbulent mixing of 10^6 cm^2/s would introduce only 6×10^9 cal/s, far below the heat loss to the atmosphere. Thus it seems likely that most of the heat loss is balanced by a southward advection of heat by the deep water.

The 1:1 ratio arrived at by Craig and Gordon is based on an Antarctic bottom water sample in the northwestern Weddell Sea. It is probable that Antarctic bottom water is formed elsewhere around Antarctica with less intense characteristics than the variety observed flowing around the periphery of the Weddell Sea (Gordon, 1972). The less intense bottom water may have higher $\zeta\, O^{18}$ values, and so more Antarctic bottom water may be included in the world ocean abyssal waters.

The downward diffusion of heat across the thermocline may be estimated. Using a value of 1 cm^2/s for the vertical mixing coefficient and a temperature gradient of 1°/100 m for the lower part of the thermocline the downward heat flux is 0.94×10^{-4} $cal/cm^2 \cdot s$ for the ocean area between 40°N to 40°S (240×10^6 km^2 calculated from values given on page 9 of Sverdrup *et al.*, 1942) roughly. The poleward limits of the main thermocline total heat flux is found to be 22.6×10^{13} cal/s. Much of this heat is used in warming the upwelling waters. The calculations suggest that only one-third enters the abyssal waters to be returned to the surface in Antarctica.

Pacific Ocean

The abyssal circulation model of Stommel and Arons (1960a,b) shows that abyssal waters enter the Pacific Ocean from the Antarctic region, south of the Campbell Plateau, and extend into the Pacific via a narrow western boundary flow. The data of *Eltanin* cruises 28 and 29 (Scorpio Report, 1970) show that the lower section of the water column immediately east of the Campbell Plateau and the Kermadec-Tonga Ridge is of Antarctic origin. Figure 2 shows the temperature-salinity relations of stations south and east of the Campbell Plateau. The similarity of the

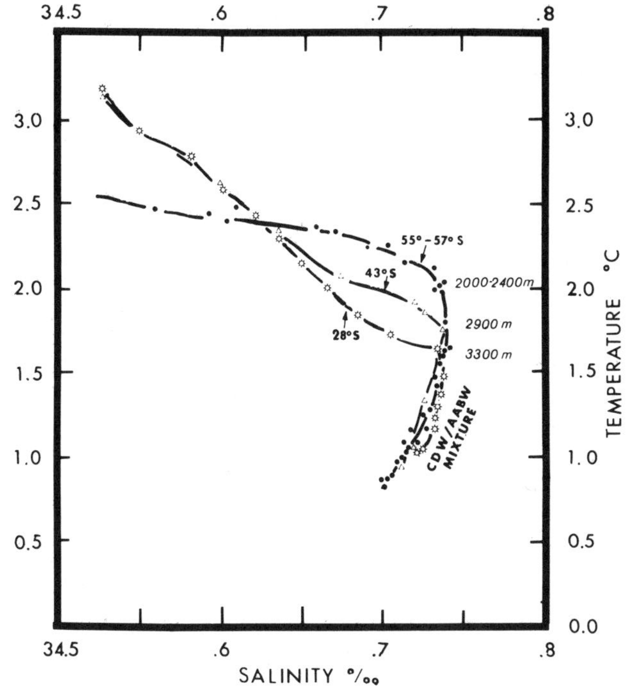

FIGURE 2 Temperature-salinity diagram of hydrographic stations of the Campbell Plateau and the deep western boundary current of the South Pacific at 43° and 28° S. *Eltanin* stations used in this figure: Cruise 28–31 43° 16′ S, 168° 30′ W; Cruise 29–151 28° 00′ S, 176° 30′ W; Cruise 50–1527 57° S, 170° E; 1529 56° S 170° E; 1531 55° S 170° E.

lower section of the water column suggests a continuous path of Antarctic water northward in the western boundary of the Pacific abyssal waters. Warren and Voorhis (1970) determine the northward transport of the deep western boundary current to be 12.9×10^6 m^3/s.

The rather sharp break in the temperature-salinity curve marks the "roof" of the undisturbed Antarctic waters in the water column. Proceeding northward, it deepens in a manner that can be considered as erosion of its upper boundary. The salinity and oxygen of the water at shallower depths than the ". . . sharp discontinuity or cusp in both potential temperature and salinity profiles . . ." (Chung, 1971) drop off rapidly with distance from the cusp, while concentration of nutrients increases. At the cusp, the salinity is at maximum, which is also associated with a silicate minimum (Figure 3) (Craig, 1972). This minimum silicate layer is carried northward with the maximum salinity from Antarctic waters by the deep western boundary current.

The increased silicate between 2,000–3,000 m (associated with a maximum in phosphate-phosphorus and nitrate-nitrogen and a minimum in oxygen) suggests that this water is not being carried northward from Antarctic waters. One would expect the general trend of decreasing nutrient concentration with decreasing depth to occur across the 2,000–

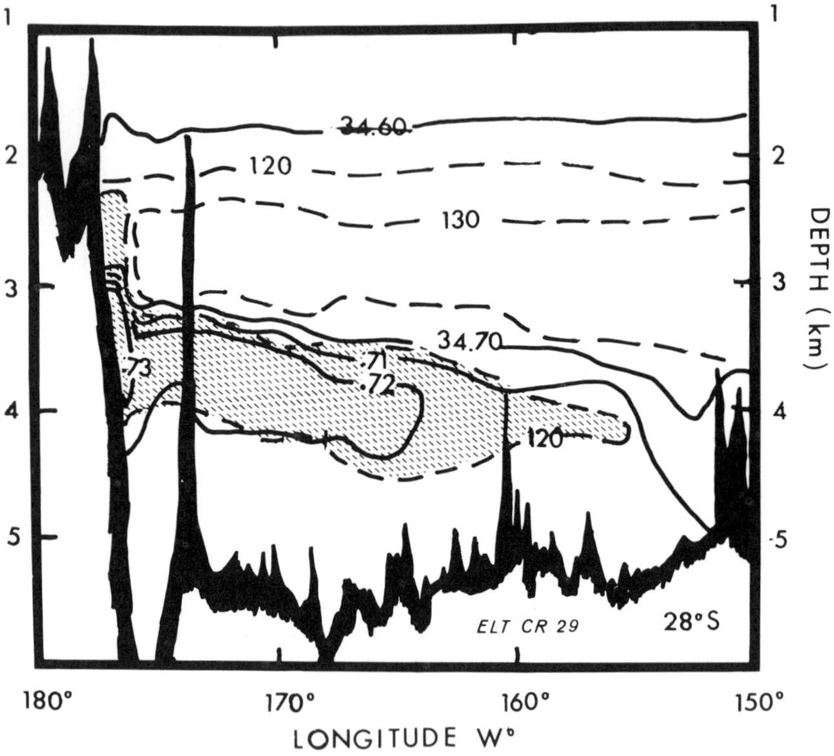

FIGURE 3 Salinity and silicate distribution in the deep western boundary current of the South Pacific at 28° S. The stippled area has silicate of less than 120 μgm·at/liter. (*Scorpio Reports*, 1970).

3,000-m interval, if that were the case. Craig (1972) points out that the maximum nutrient layer represents a southerly flow. This is supported by the direct current measurement obtained during *Eltanin* cruise 40, which indicated a zero meridional velocity "barely above the deep salinity maximum" (Warren and Voorhis, 1970), and is suggested in the Figure 5 of Reid (1965), which shows the 2,000-m maximum of inorganic phosphate-phosphorus in the Pacific along 160° W to be "connected" to the massive region of high phosphate-phosphorus water in the North Pacific.

Above the northward-flowing bottom water in the western boundary region, there is southward-flowing water, not unlike the situation found in the South Atlantic Ocean (Wüst, 1957). What about the deep western boundary flow in the Indian Ocean? The hydrographic section along 32° S given by Wyrtki (1971) shows a similar pattern in salinity, oxygen, and nutrients (the reverse in silicate gradient occurs at lower silicate values than is the case in the South Pacific, and only in the extreme western region) as shown in the South Pacific sections of *Eltanin* cruises 28 and 29. A double-layered, deep, western boundary current may be common to all the southern oceans. In the Atlantic, however, the southerly-flowing water is the North Atlantic deep water, i.e., a relatively "young" water mass rather than an oxygen-depleted, nutrient-rich water mass, as in the Pacific and Indian Oceans.

The continued flow of abyssal water northward in the Pacific Ocean has been studied in a number of recent papers (Reed, 1969; Reid, 1969; Gordon and Gerard, 1970; Chung, 1971; and Edmond *et al.*, 1971). The pattern is one of slow northern migration through the many deep passages in the western tropical Pacific, mainly via a passage immediately southeast of the Phoenix Islands, called the Tokelau trough (see Reid, 1969, and Plate 2 of Gordon and Gerard, 1970). The flow bifurcates near 15° N. One arm of the flow extends into the North Pacific in the western boundary region, and the other flows eastward through a deep passage south of the Hawaiian Islands, near 13° N and 166° W. This water then turns northward after passing the 155° W meridian. The upper boundary of the northward-flowing bottom waters in the South Pacific and parts of the North Pacific is marked by an increased temperature gradient and can be considered as a "benthic thermocline" (Chung, 1971). A benthic thermocline is also observed in the Atlantic Ocean (Amos *et al.*, 1971).

The bottom waters enter the North Pacific, north of Hawaii, from the southeast and west, where they upwell and return to the south, part of the western boundary flow. The slow warming and increasing thickness of the adiabatic temperature layer of the bottom waters (Olsen, 1968), when proceeding northward into the Alaskan basin, suggests an influence of geothermal heating. From the degree of warming of the lower kilometer (below the *in situ* temperature minimum) and a geothermal heat flux of 64 cal/cm^2·yr, it is calculated by Gordon and Gerard that a period of 750 years is necessary for flow from the western tropical Pacific to reach the upwelling zone of the North Pacific. This period is also calculated on the basis of oxygen depletion at a rate of 2×10^{-3} ml/liter·yr (Arons and Stommel, 1967).

Atlantic Ocean

The abyssal circulation of the Atlantic Ocean is more vigorous than the Pacific and Indian Oceans' abyssal circulation, the primary reason being the presence in the Atlantic of the source for both major abyssal water masses. The North Atlantic deep water flows southward along the western margins of the North Atlantic Ocean as a contour-following current (Heezen *et al.*, 1966), i.e., parallel to the isobaths, with the shallower topography to the right of the vector. A number of papers deal with the flow patterns south of the Greenland–Iceland Ridge, all confirming the contour-following model (Worthington and Volkmann, 1965; Swallow and Worthington, 1961; Jones *et al.*, 1970; Amos *et al.*, 1971).

Along the East Coast of the United States, a number of hydrographic and current-meter measurements have been obtained. These are summarized in Figure 4 (taken from Figure 12 of Amos *et al.*, 1971). The total transport of the deep western boundary current determined at each section varies from a low of $4 \times 10^6 m^3/s$ to 50×10^6 m^3/s. A recent estimation by Richardson and Knauss (1971) is 12×10^6 m^3/s, which is in agreement with Barrett (1965). The intersection of the southward-flowing deep current with the northeastward-flowing Gulf Stream in the Cape Hatteras region has been studied by Barrett (1965), Rowe and Menzies (1968), and Richardson and Knauss (1971). They observed that the southward flow is fragmented and interspersed with filaments of northward-flowing, or tranquil, water. The time variability in this region is probably large, as suggested by the time series obtained farther north (but in similar situation) by Schmitz *et al.* (1970). A sharp reversal in bottom current that perhaps was associated with a Gulf Stream meander was observed. Amos *et al.* (1971) suggest, on the basis of water-mass characteristics, a confluence of Antarctic bottom water with North Atlantic deep water in the deep western boundary current, as indicated in Figure 4. These two water sources remain distinct from one another in the Blake–Bahama region, but blend further to the south.

The southward flow of the mixture of North Atlantic deep water and Antarctic bottom water continues into the South Atlantic, incorporating more Antarctic bottom water from below, Antarctic intermediate water from above, and Mediterranean water from the side. Wright (1969) estimates a total southward flow of this combination across 32° S at 20×10^6 m^3/s, i.e., a doubling from the initial volume transport of pure North Atlantic deep water. The southward-flowing deep water eventually abuts with the less-saline circumpolar deep water that is injected into the Atlantic Ocean by the Antarctic circumpolar current via the Drake Passage. The North Atlantic deep water and the circumpolar deep water flow eastward into the Indian and Pacific Oceans (Wüst, 1933, 1935, 1936; Reid and Lynn, 1971). The Atlantic Ocean contribution to the circumpolar water remains distinct from the Drake Passage flow eastward to the Kerguelen Island area. To the east of Kerguelen, these two water masses become homogeneous (Gordon, 1971b). The Atlantic Ocean input to the circumpolar flow is small compared to the Drake Passage transport, but it introduces to Antarctic waters the salt necessary to balance the freshwater inflow into Antarctic waters (Gordon, 1971a).

Antarctic bottom water flows northward from the Weddell Sea into the Argentine basin via a gap in the Falkland fracture zone (Le Pichon *et al.*, 1971) near 50° S and 35° W. The Antarctic bottom water flows northward as a deep western boundary current over the continental rise of the Argentine coast (Wüst, 1933). It exits from the Argentine basin by way of the Rio Grande Passage and flows into the Brazil basin. It continues to spread northward and remains a distinct water mass but in decreasing degrees of concentration, as far north as 40° N in the North American basin.

The eastern Atlantic Ocean does not receive much Antarctic bottom water from the south, because of the obstruction of the mid-ocean and Walvis ridges. However, a deep passage in the mid-ocean ridge in the vicinity of the equator, the Romanche Trench, allows Antarctic bottom water to enter the eastern Atlantic Ocean (Wüst, 1933), where it spreads both north and south and may even extend in trace amounts to latitudes of the British Isles (Lee and Ellett, 1967).

The volume transport of the Antarctic bottom water is estimated by Wright (1970) to decrease from $5\text{–}6 \times 10^6$ m^3/s across 32° S to 1×10^6 m^3/s across 16° N.

The northward-flowing deep western boundary current in the South Atlantic differs from that of the South Pacific. It is composed of more concentrated Antarctic bottom water, rather than a mixture of this with circumpolar deep water. In the Indian Ocean, the deep western boundary current would most likely contain more concentrated forms of North Atlantic deep water in its upper layers and a mixture of circumpolar deep water and Antarctic bottom water in the lower layer (Ivanenkov and Gubin, 1960). Hence, the existence of the deep western boundary flow may depend on the planetary wind systems (Stommel and Arons, 1960a,b), but the actual composition would depend on the relative positions of water-mass source regions.

SURFACE CIRCULATION

The mean surface currents respond mainly to the climatic wind field. The depth to which surface circulation patterns penetrate is dependent upon the water column stratification. In tropical areas, the slope of the strong thermocline efficiently compensates for the sea-surface, dynamic-topog-

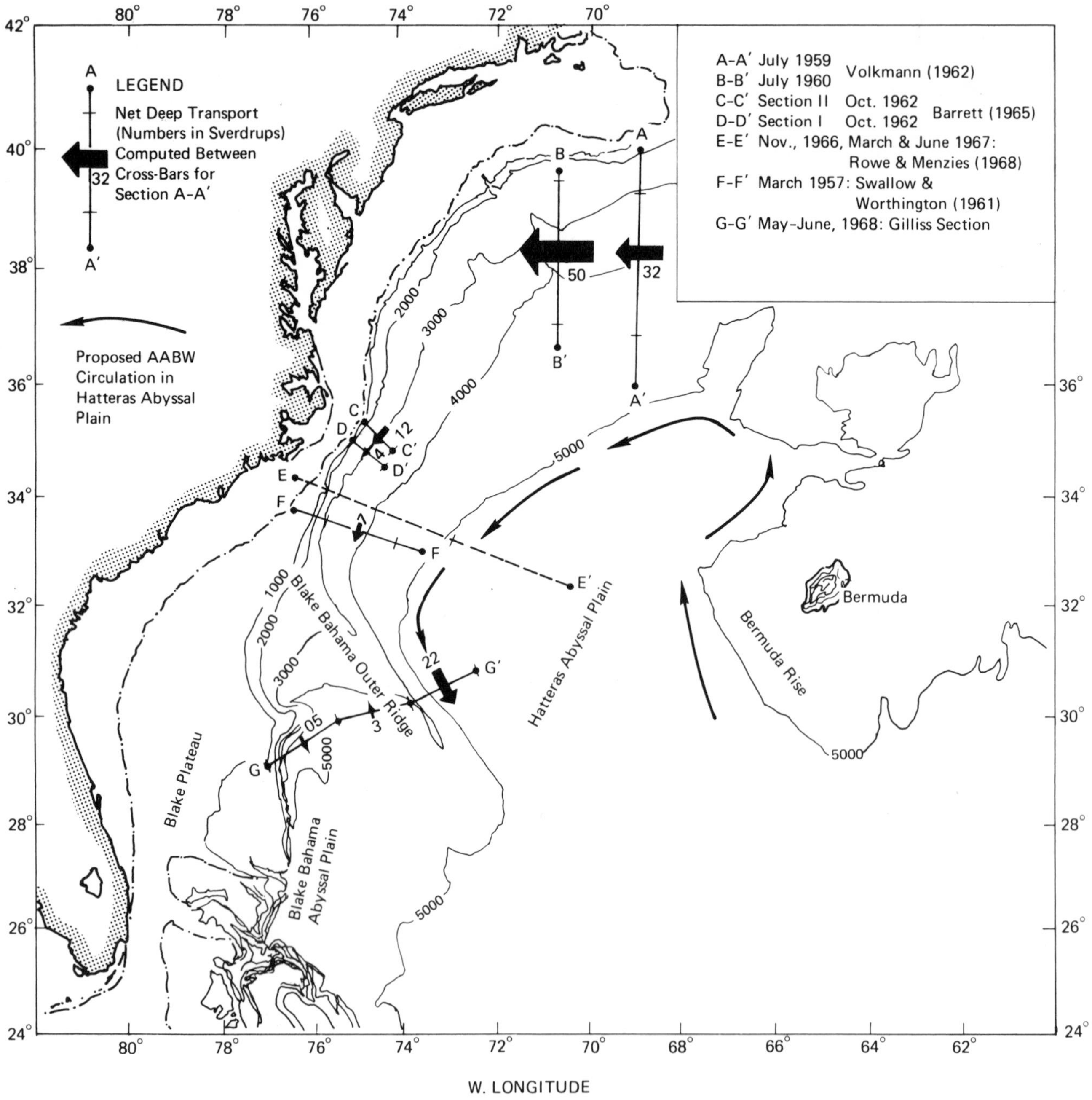

FIGURE 4 Estimate of volume transports and flow of Antarctic bottom water in the western North Atlantic (From Amos *et al.*, 1971).

raphy slope, so rapid attenuation of currents with depth occurs. Current meter data suggest that the equatorial surface circulation pattern extends to only 300-500 m. In polar regions, where waters are less stratified, the attenuation of the currents with depth is small. Maksimov and Vorob'yev (1962) suggest attenuation in Antarctic waters to the sea floor of only 40 percent. Based on water-mass characteristics, current evidence from oriented bottom photographs and the few existing near-bottom current measurements in the Arctic and Antarctic, the surface circulation pattern extends to the sea floor.

In strong pycnocline regions, a surface circulation pattern is often separated from the abyssal circulation pattern by a layer of tranquil motion. Such a zone exists in the equatorial regions and is marked by an oxygen minimum, although the latter is not necessarily a product of weak horizontal motion because the consumption rate is not constant in space (Wyrtki, 1962).

The surface circulation can conveniently be divided into three basic components: equatorial, subtropical gyre, and subpolar gyre. There is also the special case of the polar sea in the Arctic.

Equatorial Circulation

The equatorial circulation (Knauss, 1962; Metcalf *et al.*, 1962; Montgomery, 1962; Metcalf and Stalcup, 1967; Wyrtki, 1967; Tsuchiya, 1968) consists of four basic components: the north and south equatorial currents that flow westward; the surface countercurrent that occurs below the zone of minimum wind stress, generally north of the equator, although a countercurrent exists south of the equator in the western tropical Pacific; and the equatorial undercurrent, found directly on the equator below the sea surface. The equator wind system produces upwelling along the equator and along the northern fringes of the surface countercurrent.

The equatorial upwelling has a negative effect on increasing wind: As the equatorial Hadley cell increases, the upwelling also increases. This, in turn, lowers the equatorial surface temperature and has an effect of decreasing the Hadley cell (Bjerknes, 1966; Flohn, 1972). Sea-surface temperature in the equatorial Pacific Ocean shows cycles of 5–8 years in length and a strong correlation with tropical rainfall (Allison *et al.*, 1971). Such relationship of sea-surface temperature to large-scale weather patterns offers an opportunity for long-range weather prediction, if we understand the complex feedback mechanisms.

An interesting series of hydrographic and current meter observations have been made in the central and western tropical Pacific Ocean (by the group from Centre ORSTOM in Noumea, New Caledonia). Colin *et al.* (1971, 1972) discovered that along 170° E the equatorial undercurrent is divided into two cells, one at 100 m located at the bottom of the mixed layer and one at 200 m within the thermocline. A westward-flowing current, the intermediate equatorial current, is observed below the deeper undercurrent. The undercurrent extends downward to flank the intermediate equatorial current both to the north and south, at 2°30′ N and 2°30′ S.

The equatorial undercurrent at 100 m does not seem to be in geostrophic balance and reverses itself, as does the westward-flowing surface water when the trade winds are replaced by a westwind (a wind from west to east). The lower equatorial undercurrent apparently is a steady geostrophic flow composed of north equatorial countercurrent water, subtropical South Pacific water, and Coral Sea water. The geostrophically balanced intermediate equatorial current transports westward roughly the same volume of water as the deeper undercurrent. The intermediate current exists at least from 140° E to the Galapagos Islands at the depth of the isanosteric surface of 125 cl/t. There is evidence that this current exists all through the world ocean.

The double cells of the undercurrent exist from New Guinea to 150° W or 160° W. To the east, only one core near 100 m is observed.

The Pacific Ocean equatorial undercurrent (Cromwell current) has a transport in the central Pacific of 30–40 × 10^6 m^3/s (Knauss, 1962). Towards the eastern end (Galapagos Islands), the transport reduces rapidly to 2–3 × 10^6 m^3/s (Christensen, 1971), and variations in depth, width, and distance off the equator are observed. The equatorial undercurrent is also a persistent feature in the Atlantic Ocean from 38° W to 6° E, where the waters are of higher salinity than those in the Pacific but are derived from the Southern Hemisphere, in the same manner as the Cromwell current. The Indian Ocean has no steady equatorial undercurrent. It appears to occur only in the middle and late northeastern monsoon, when the east wind is acting on the tropical sea surface.

Subtropical Gyre

The subtropical anticyclonic gyre extends from northern equatorial regions to 50–60° latitude. The relief of the sea-surface topography is approximately 1 m. The density field lies in hydrostatic equilibrium, and the isothermal surfaces obtain their deepest depths below the most elevated portion of the subtropical gyre, not in the center of the gyre but strongly shifted to the western boundary near the 30th parallel (Stommel, 1965). The gyre is geneally considered to be wind-driven. However, purely wind-driven models predict volume transports of water about one-half of the geostrophically estimated transports available to Munk (1950) and perhaps one-third of current estimations. A thermohaline driving mechanism may be of some significance (Worthington, 1972; Shaw and Wyrtki, 1972).

The shape of the warm surface layer in a two-layer ocean was inspected by Shaw and Wyrtki (1972). Because we know the shape of the isothermal surfaces of the subtropical gyre better than we know parameters such as wind stress and internal viscosity of the water, they used the maximum depth of the warm-water layer to determine the frictional coefficient of 2.3 × 10^{-6} s^{-1} and a transport of 71 × 10^6 m^3/s for the subtropical gyre. The wind stress necessary to explain the shape of the subtropical gyre was 3 dyn/cm^2. The authors believe this is too large and "consequently an additional driving mechanism should be in operation, and it might be argued that this driving mechanism is given by the continuous addition of thermal energy into the warm upper layer." The northwestern and northern boundary of the subtropical gyre separate from the "wall" when the discontinuity between the warm and cold layer outcrops. This surfacing of the cold water is forced by the horizontal flow of the gyre, as the increased Coriolis parameter at higher latitudes requires increased slope of the discontinuity. Shaw and Wyrtki (1972) showed that the southernmost point of surfacing of cold water along the western boundary is critically dependent on the volume of the warm-water layer and total transport, i.e., increasing the volume shifts the separation to the north. Some warm water is possibly lost to the cold water north of the separation in a process of "overspilling," which Shaw and Wyrtki (1972) estimated to be 16×10^6 m^3/s.

Exchange of waters across the northwestern margins of the subtropical gyres occurs when the large meanders of the Gulf Stream (Stommel, 1965) become detached to produce eddies, generally in the region from 58-68° W and 35-40° S (Parker, 1971). This process is common to the south of the Gulf Stream and represents an injection of relatively cold slope water into the Sargasso Sea. These eddies or cyclonic rings (Fuglister, 1972), appear as thermal domes with cold cores, often with a surface temperature differential of 8 °C with ambient water, and have been observed to have a diameter of 110 km (after an initial elliptical shape), with a surface current around the periphery of cold water of 3 knots. The rings' lifetime apparently is near 12 months, and they slowly migrate to the southwest. At first they touch the sea floor but quickly lose contact (Barrett, 1971). Fuglister (1972) estimates a total of five to eight cyclonic rings, with an equal number of anticyclonic rings (warm Sargasso Sea water cores injected into the slope water) forming each year. This would be necessary to satisfy continuity, as the mean path of the Gulf Stream shifts seasonally, i.e., cyclonic rings are produced from April to November when the Gulf Stream shifts northward, and anticyclonic rings are produced in the period of southward movement.

The cold-water, cyclonic rings are very plentiful in the northwestern and western Sargasso Sea, although their diameter is about one-half of that observed near the area of formation. Parker (1971), on the basis of temperature, has identified 62 rings between 1932 and 1970. Barrett (1971) points out that ". . . although the effect of the ring decay is to decrease APE (available potential energy) (raise the thermocline) of the western Sargasso Sea, there must also be a renewing agency sufficient not only to balance this effect (ring decay) but also to supply in this region sufficient energy to maintain the thermocline at its maximum depth against the general upward tendency." This source is most likely the intense thermohaline activity in the western Sargasso Sea during periods of polar air mass outbreaks (Worthington, 1972).

The warm-water anticyclonic eddies have recently been discussed by Saunders (1971). These eddies are formed near 70° W and 39° N. They are slowly destroyed by heat loss to the atmosphere and by mixing. Warm-water eddies should be more common in slope waters. If this is not the case, it may indicate (and available evidence supports this) that they coalesce with the Gulf Stream.

Upstream of the large-meander and eddy-shedding region, the Gulf Stream has a higher degree of stability and shows a steady growth in transport along its route. Knauss (1969) points out that the volume transport increases from 33×10^6 m^3/s in the Florida Straits to 147×10^6 m^3/s at 64°30′ W, an increase of 7 percent per 100 km over a distance of 2,000 km downstream of the Florida Straits.

Subpolar Gyres

The subpolar gyres are best developed in the Atlantic Ocean and in the Norwegian-Greenland and Weddell Seas. In the North Atlantic, there is a transfer of warm subtropical water (or central water mass) into the Norwegian Sea. This warm, relatively high-saline water is cooled rapidly, but with only moderate freshing; and deep convection ensues to begin the process of North Atlantic deep water formation. In the North Atlantic, there is a loss of warm surface water into the abyssal layers. This must be made up elsewhere by a return of abyssal waters to the warm subtropical waters. This is accomplished by slow upwelling in the thermocline and/or a transfer of water across the oceanic polar-front zones.

In the Southern Hemisphere of the subpolar gyre, there is a separation from the subtropical gyre by the circumpolar belt of water with its strong zonal characteristics. Therefore, the Southern Hemisphere subpolar gyres are isolated from warm water and are colder than their Northern Hemisphere counterparts. The low temperature, the relatively low precipitation, the continental runoff, and the tendency of rapid mixing of melt water, causes the Antarctic surface waters to have relatively high salinity. After a reasonable amount of ice formation, deep convection is induced to form Antarctic borrom water.

In the Pacific Ocean, the northern subpolar gyre has very low surface salinity and deep convection does not occur, except in the northwestern region where some intermediate water forms (Reid, 1965). The southern subpolar gyre in the Pacific Ocean occurs in the Ross Sea region, where high-salinity (34.74°/$_{oo}$) Antarctic bottom water is formed. The Indian Ocean, of course, has no northern subpolar gyre and has only a small southern subpolar gyre in the Amery Ice Shelf region.

It is in the cyclonic gyres of the subpolar regions where deep convection takes place. Although these gyres are wind-induced, it is the thermohaline action that determines whether sinking will occur and determines the depth of convection. In these subpolar regions, the surface salinity is most important; if the salinity does not rise to levels above 34.6 °/$_{oo}$, even freezing temperatures will not allow deep convection into the abyssal layers (below the intermediate waters) of the open ocean. At higher salinities, convection will occur even at the higher temperatures, i.e., the case for the outflow of the Mediterranean Sea. In a stratified ocean, an Ekman convergence is not sufficient to induce deep convection; the thermohaline alterations resulting from sea–air–ice interaction must accompany the wind-induced convergence.

The subpolar gyre of the Weddell Sea has a very marked northern boundary. This boundary, called the Weddell-Scotia Confluence by Gordon (1967), extends from the Antarctic Peninsula into the central Scotia Sea. It has the effect of blocking the Antarctic circumpolar current transversing the Drake Passage. The strength of the Weddell Sea gyre and its northern boundary may be an important consideration in the dynamics of the Drake Passage and entire Antarctic circumpolar current.

In the northern polar sea, the high continental runoff, the confinement of the low-salinity surface water by the polar easterlies, and the surrounding land masses do not permit deep convection. The deep and bottom waters of the Arctic are formed at more southerly latitudes.

CONCLUSION

The influence of bottom topography in ocean circulation, especially in high latitudes, is well recognized. However, often the restrictions placed on flow by the primary features of the bottom topography are negated by secondary features, i.e., narrow passages. A few of these were mentioned in the above discussion: the Romanche, Gibbs, and Falkland fracture zones in the Atlantic Ocean; the Tokelau Passage and the passage south of Hawaii in the Pacific; and many secondary features in the high southern latitudes. These features play important roles in the spreading of abyssal and Antarctic waters. Yet they are not usually included in the approximation of oceanwide bottom bathymetry used in numerical modeling.

It may be desirable to model important individual features separately. This was done by Boyer (see pp. 327–339). The numerical models have yielded circulation patterns consistent with observations on a scale not previously compared.

ACKNOWLEDGMENTS

The author acknowledges the support of NSF grant GV-26230, and AEC contract AT 21-85.

REVIEW: B. A. WARREN

Arnold Gordon has given a detailed overview of recent observations of the general circulation, including some rough estimates of heat fluxes. His discussion is comprehensive, and I do not think that other oceanographers would wish to take exception to much that he has said. There are a few points, however, that might be worth emphasizing or amplifying further.

Deep Circulation

Atlantic Ocean

Twenty years ago oceanographers believed that surface water sank to great depth during winter convection in the Labrador and Irminger Seas to form the deep and bottom water of the North Atlantic. Extensive wintertime hydrographic stations, however, have shown conclusively that sinking from the surface in these areas does not reach to depths greater than about 1,500 m (Grant, 1968; Worthington and Wright, 1970). This water from the Labrador Sea does move southward between the Gulf Stream and North America, but it is *not* the North Atlantic deep water. The latter, it has been found, derives from several overflows from the Norwegian Sea (Gordon lists the pertinent references), and this discovery represents a major revision to ideas of the deep circulation in the North Atlantic.

As Gordon points out, the flow of this water away from the Norwegian Sea in a narrow boundary current has been traced through velocity measurements and water-property extrema along the northern boundary of the deep Atlantic and through velocity measurements along the East Coast of the United States. Similarly, the southward flow of North Atlantic deep water along the eastern coast of South America was recognized many years ago in contrast in water characteristics. It may be worth noting, however, that there is little direct evidence to date in the tropical North Atlantic to connect these two boundary currents, despite compelling theoretical reasons to believe that they are connected. This is not to suggest that the connection does not exist, only that the property contrasts here are too slight to show flow very clearly and that the few current measurements yet made in the area are ambiguous.

Far to the south, the manner in which surface water sinks to the bottom of the Weddell Sea to form Antarctic bottom water has been controversial and has raised some questions, including whether the sinking takes place over most of the surface of the Weddell Sea (through one mechanism or another) or is confined locally. The hydrographic sections occupied by the *Glacier* in 1968, however, show fairly convincingly that the bottom water sinks only from the edge of the continental shelf around the Weddell Sea (Seabrooke *et al.,* 1971).

Indian Ocean

Although on theoretical grounds one expects to find bottom water carried northward into the Indian Ocean from the Antarctic in a western boundary current, observations made before and during the International Indian Ocean Expedition (Wyrtki, 1971) were not adequate, because of station spacing, to show its existence. Since then, two hydrographic sections occupied to the east of Madagascar have clearly shown the current, about 400 km wide, at depths greater than 3 km with a probable volume transport of about 5 × 10^6 m^3/s (Warren, 1971). The course of this current to the north is not known. Summer observations in 1964 gave marginal evidence for a deep northward current along the Somali continental slope (Warren *et al.*, 1966), but this flow, if real, may have been a deep penetration of the seasonal Somali current, rather than a northward extension of the deep western boundary current.

It is a moot point whether, as Gordon conjectures, the deep boundary current in the South Indian Ocean is overlain by a second boundary current, flowing southward. Certainly the observations reported by Warren (1971) do not indicate this.

Pacific Ocean

The full results of the *Scorpio* Expedition (Stommel *et al.*, in press) were not available to Gordon at the time he wrote his review article. Dynamic computations, referred to zero velocity at 2 km, give a volume transport for the deep, northward-flowing boundary current near New Zealand and the Kermadec Ridge of about 19 × 10^6 m^3/s at both latitude 43° S and latitude 28° S; and nearly all the southward return flow appears to be confined to the Southwest Pacific basin, between the boundary current and the East Pacific rise, rather than being distributed fairly uniformly over the full breadth of the South Pacific (Warren, in press). On the eastern flank of the East Pacific rise there is a secondary northward-flowing current at latitude 43° S (transport about 5 × 10^6 m^3/s, estimated as above), but only a broad poorly defined net northward flow in the deep eastern Pacific at latitude 28° S.

As Gordon describes, a portion of the principal deep western boundary current has been traced northward into the tropical Pacific, where the flow evidently bifurcates (Reed, 1969), one part continuing northward into the western North Pacific, the other (probably the lesser) turning eastward south of Hawaii. The resulting deep flow pattern in the North Pacific seems unresolved to me, however. Reed (1969) clearly shows that deep water south of the Aleutians must enter the area from the west, rather than the south or east, yet deep water maps prepared by Moriyasu (1972) for the western North Pacific do not show a clear continuous northward flow from the tropics to the Aleutians. Nor is a "western boundary current" structure well-established for the deep North Pacific: Direct velocity measurements of a few days duration (Worthington and Kawai, 1972) revealed a southward current at depths of 500–3,500 m on the continental slope east of Honshu (latitude 35° N), but suggested northward flow at depth further to the east. Deep observations in the North Pacific are simply too sparse at the present time to tell a very convincing story as to how the water is moving around.

It is certainly arguable whether, as Gordon suggests, there is a southward-flowing current above the deep western boundary current of the South Pacific. Permanent ocean currents are associated with pronounced cross-stream density gradients, yet there is little to indicate such structure at these levels in the *Scorpio* sections (Stommel *et al.*, in press). Furthermore, Wyrtki's (1962) discussion of the deep layer of oxygen minimum and nutrient maxima in terms of negligible horizontal flow seems so promising to me that I have difficulty envisioning a boundary current in that layer. Indeed, there is no reason to expect the boundary current structure of the Pacific to be symmetrical to that of the Atlantic: The Atlantic has a northern source of deep water, while the Pacific does not. It might be informative to investigate through extensive numerical modeling the kinds of flow fields that are consistent in detail with the deep oxygen minima and nutrient maxima.

Surface Circulation

Gordon's discussion emphasizes the equatorial currents and the Gulf Stream. Some brief reference to work on others of the great near-surface currents may be worthwhile.

Pacific Ocean

Oceanographers will benefit greatly from a book just published, *Kuroshio* (Moriyasu, 1972), which brings together into one treatise an exhaustive and comprehensive account of virtually everything that has been learned about the Kuroshio and the general circulation of the western North Pacific. It would be futile to try to digest this wealth of material in a few sentences (or thus to say anything at all about the Kuroshio here); but it would be derelict not to hail the publication of this book as an immensely valuable research source in regional oceanography.

The analogous western boundary current of the South Pacific, the East Australian current, has been known for over a century, but it seems much less readily defined than the Kuroshio. Various geostrophic estimates of its transport, relative to 1,300 m, average 28 × 10^6 m^3/s (Hamon, 1965), but later work, revealing numerous eddy-like features and considerable time variability, raises questions concerning the continuity of the flow along the coast of Australia and its connection to the movement in the interior South Pacific (Boland and Hamon, 1970). Recalling that the Gulf Stream, at one time in the history of its exploration, also appeared filamentous and fragmentary, one wonders to what extent more detailed current-tracking will "restore" the integrity of the East Australian current.

Other features of South Pacific circulation have been reviewed recently in *Scientific Exploration of the South Pacific* (Wooster, ed.).

Indian Ocean

The major western boundary current of the Indian Ocean, the Somali current, was mapped for the first time in any detail during the International Indian Ocean Expedition (Swallow and Bruce, 1966; Bruce, 1968; Düing, 1970). Its existence as a narrow, swift current was confirmed, with surface speeds up to 350 cm/s, and directly measured volume transports in the upper 200 m of up to 62×10^6 m^3/s (although the current surely reaches deeper into the ocean than 200 m). Its subsequent flow to the east has been pictured as a large wave train, but the observations are not sufficient to assure the correctness of this interpretation. The Somali current is especially interesting, of course, because of its seasonal reversal, particularly with regard to its time of response to the southwest monsoon. Off northern Somalia, where the current achieves its greatest intensity, there are no series of observations adequate to gauge this time, but surface current measurements near latitude 2° S showed the development of intense northward flow within 10 days of the onset of strong local southerly winds (Leetmaa and Truesdale, 1972). This development occurred 3-4 weeks *before* the monsoon set in over the interior of the North Indian Ocean, however, reflecting the earlier commencement of the monsoon south of the equator and indicating greater regional heterogeneity in the formation of the Somali current than has been envisaged.

REFERENCES

Allison, L. J., J. Steranka, R. Holut, J. Hansen, F. Godshall, and G. Brabhakara. 1971. Air–sea interaction in the tropical Pacific Ocean. Publ. X651-71-191. Goddard Space Flight Center, Greenbelt, Md.

Amos, A. F., A. L. Gordon, and E. Schneider. 1971. Water masses and circulation patterns in the region of the Blake-Bahama Outer Ridge. Deep-Sea Res. 18:145–65.

Arons, A., and H. Stommel. 1967. On the abyssal circulation of the world ocean, 3. Deep-Sea Res. 14:441–57.

Barrett, J. 1965. Subsurface currents off Cape Hatteras. Deep-Sea Res. 12:173–84.

Barrett, J. 1971. Available potential energy of Gulf Stream rings. Deep-Sea Res. 18(12):1221–32.

Bjerknes, J. 1959. The recent warming of the North Atlantic, pp. 65–73. *In* B. Bolin, ed. Atmosphere and the Sea in Motion. Rockefeller Institute and Oxford University Press, New York–London.

Bjerknes, J. 1966. A possible response of the atmosphere Hadley circulation to equatorial anomalies of ocean temperature. Tellus 18:820–29.

Boland, F. M., and B. V. Hamon. 1970. The East Australian current, 1965–1968. Deep-Sea Res. 17(4):777–94.

Bruce, J. G. 1968. Comparison of near surface dynamic topography during the two monsoons in the western Indian Ocean. Deep-Sea Res. 15(6):665–77.

Bullard, E. C. 1963. The flow of heat through the floor of the ocean, pp. 218–32. *In* M. N. Hill, ed. The Sea, Vol. III. Interscience, New York.

Christensen, N. 1971. Observations of the Cromwell Current near the Galapagos Islands. Deep-Sea Res. 18(1):27–34.

Colin, C., C. Henin, P. Hisard, and C. Oudot. 1971. Le courant de Cromwell dans le Pacifique Central en Février. 1970. Cah. ORSTOM, Ser. Oceanogr. 9(2):167–86.

Colin, C., P. Hisard, and P. Rual. 1972. Currents at the equator in the western Pacific Ocean. Paper at the International Symposium on the Oceanography of the South Pacific, Wellington, N.Z., 9-15 February 1972.

Cooper, L. H. N. 1955. Deep water movements in the North Atlantic as a link between climatic changes around Iceland and biological productivity. J. Mar. Res. 14:347.

Craig, H. 1972. The analysis of a geochemical ocean section study in the western Pacific. Am. Geophys. Union Trans. 53(4):403.

Dietz, R. S., and J. C. Holden. 1970. Reconstruction of Pangasar: Breakup and dispersion of continents, Permian to present. J. Geophys. Res. 75(26):4939–56.

Düing, Walter. 1970. The Monsoon Regime of the Currents in the Indian Ocean. East-West Center Press, Honolulu. 68 pp.

Düing, W., and W. Schwill. 1967. Ausbreitung und Vermischung des salzreichen Wassers aus dem Roten Meer und aus dem Persischen Golf. "Meteor" Forschungsergeb. (Section A) 3:44–66.

Edmond, J., and G. C. Anderson. 1971. On the structure of the North Atlantic Deep Water. Deep-Sea Res. 18(1):127–33.

Edmond, J., Y. Chung, and J. G. Sclater. 1971. Pacific bottom water: Penetration east around Hawaii. J. Geophys. Res. 76(33):8089–97.

Flohn, H. 1972. Investigations of equatorial upwelling and its climatic role, pp. 93–102. *In* A. L. Gordon, ed. Studies in Physical Oceanography, Vol. I. Gordon and Breach, New York.

Fuglister, F. 1972. Cyclonic rings formed by the Gulf Stream 1965–1966, pp. 137–68. *In* A. L. Gordon, ed. Studies in Physical Oceanography, Vol. I. Gordon and Breach, New York.

Gordon, A. L. 1967. Structure of Antarctic waters between 20° W and 170° W. Antarct. Map Folio Ser., No. 6. V. Bushnell, ed. Am. Geogr. Soc., New York.

Gordon, A. L. 1971a. Oceanography of Antarctic waters. *In* J. L. Reid, ed. Antarctic Oceanology, I. Antarct. Res. Ser. 15:169–203. Am. Geophys. Union, Washington, D.C.

Gordon, A. L. 1971b. Recent physical oceanographic studies of Antarctic waters, pp. 609–30. *In* L. O. Quam, ed. Research in the Antarctic. AAAS Publ. 93.

Gordon, A. L. 1974. Varieties and variability of Antarctic bottom water. Colloques internationaux du C.N.R.S. Number 215-- Processus de Formation des Eaux Oceaniques Profondes, pp. 33–47.

Gordon, A. L., and R. D. Gerard. 1970. North Pacific bottom potential temperature, pp. 23–39. *In* J. D. Hays, ed. Geological Investigations of the North Pacific. GSA Mem. 126.

Gordon, A. L., and P. Tchernia. 1972. Waters of the continental margin off Adelie Coast, Antarctica. *In* D. E. Hayes, ed. Antarctic Oceanology II. Antarct. Res. Ser., Vol. 19. Am. Geophys. Union, Washington, D.C.

Grant, A. B. 1968. Atlas of Oceanographic Sections. Unpublished manuscript. Report A.O.L. 68-5, Atlantic Oceanographic Laboratory, Dartmouth, Nova Scotia. 80 pp.

Hamon, B. V. 1965. The East Australian current, 1960–1964. Deep-Sea Res. 12(6):899–922.

Heezen, B. C., C. L. Hollister, and W. F. Ruddiman. 1966. Shaping of the continental rise by deep geostrophic contour currents. Science 152:502–08.

Hollister, C. L., and R. Elder. 1969. Contour currents in the Weddell Sea. Deep-Sea Res. 16:99–101.

Irish, J. D., and F. E. Snodgrass. 1972. Australian–Antarctic tides. *In* D. E. Hayes, ed. Antarctic Oceanology II. Antarct. Res. Ser., Vol. 19. Am. Geophys. Union, Washington, D.C.

Ivanenkov, V. N., and F. Gubin. 1960. Water masses and hydrochemistry of the western and southern parts of the Indian Ocean. In Russian. Engl. transl. in Am. Geophys. Union Transl. 27–99 (1963).

Jones, J., M. Ewing, J. Ewing, and S. Eittreim. 1970. Influence of Norwegian Sea overflow water in sedimentation in the North Atlantic and Labrador Sea. J. Geophys. Res. 75(9):1655–80.

Knauss, J. 1962. Equatorial current systems, pp. 235–52. *In* M. N. Hill, ed. The Sea, Vol. II. Interscience, New York.

Knauss, J. 1969. A note on the transport of the Gulf Stream. Deep-Sea Res. 16(suppl.):117–24.

Kuo, H., and G. Veronis. 1970. Distribution of tracers in the deep oceans of the world. Deep-Sea Res. 17(1):29–46.

Lachenbruch, A. H., and B. V. Marshall. 1968. Heat flow and water temperature fluctuations in Denmark Strait. J. Geophys. Res. 73(18):5829–42.

Lee, A., and D. Ellett. 1965. On the contribution of overflow water from the Norwegian Sea to the hydrographic structure of the North Atlantic Ocean. Deep-Sea Res. 12(2):129–42.

Lee, A., and D. Ellett. 1967. On the water masses of the Northwest Atlantic. Deep-Sea Res. 14(2):183–90.

Leetmaa, Ants. 1972. The response of the Somali Current to the southwest monsoon of 1970. Deep-Sea Res. 19(4):319–25.

Leetmaa, Ants, and Victor Truesdale. 1972. Changes in currents in 1970 off the East African coast with the onset of the southeast monsoon. J. Geophys. Res. 77(18):3281–83.

Le Pichon, X., S. Eittreim, and W. Ludwig. 1971. Sediment transport and distribution in the Argentine basin. 1. Antarctic bottom current passage through the Falkland fracture zone, pp. 1–28. *In* L. H. Ahrens, F. Press, S. K. Runcorn, and H. C. Urey, eds. Physics and Chemistry of the Earth, Vol. 8. Pergamon Press, London.

Lynn, R. J., and J. L. Reid. 1968. Characteristics and circulation of deep and abyssal waters. Deep-Sea Res. 15:577–98.

Maksimov, I. V., and V. N. Vorob'yev. 1962. Contribution to the study of deep currents in the Antarctic Ocean. Sov. Antarct. Exp. Issue No. 1. 4(31):17–19.

Mann, C. R. 1969. Temperature and salinity characteristics of the Denmark Strait overflow. Deep-Sea Res. 16(suppl.):125–38.

Metcalf, W. G., and M. Stalcup. 1967. Origin of the Atlantic equatorial undercurrent. J. Geophys. Res. 72:4959–75.

Metcalf, W. G., A. D. Voohis, and M. C. Stalcup. 1962. The Atlantic equatorial undercurrent. J. Geophys. Res. 67:2499–2508.

Montgomery, R. 1958. Water characteristics of Atlantic Ocean and of world ocean. Deep-Sea Res. 5:134–48.

Montgomery, R. 1962. Equatorial undercurrent observations in review. J. Oceanogr. Soc. Jap. (20th Anniv. Vol.):487–98.

Moriyasu, Shigeo. 1972. Deep waters in the western North Pacific. Chap. 11 in Stommel and Yoshida, eds. Kuroshio. Univ. Tokyo Press, Tokyo. 517 pp.

Munk, W. 1950. On the wind-driven ocean circulation. J. Meteorol. 7(2):79–93.

Naimas, J. 1970. Climatic anomaly over the United States during the 1960's. Science 170(3959):741–43.

Naimas, J., and R. M. Born. 1970. Temporal coherence in the North Pacific sea surface temperature patterns. J. Geophys. Res. 75(30):5952–55.

National Oceanographic Data Center. 1969. Inventory of Archived Data. Publ. C-3. NODC, Washington, D.C.

Olsen, B. 1968. On the abyssal temperatures of the world oceans. Ph.D. Thesis. Oregon State University, Corvallis. 145 pp.

Ovchennikov, I. M. 1966. Circulation in the surface and intermediate layers of the Mediterranean. Oceanol. (Engl. transl.) 6(1):48–59.

Parker, C. E. 1971. Gulf Stream rings in the Sargasso Sea. Deep-Sea Res. 18(10):981–94.

Reed, R. K. 1969. Deep-water properties and flow in the central North Pacific. J. Mar. Res. 27:24–31.

Reid, J. L., Jr. 1965. Intermediate waters of the Pacific Ocean. Johns Hopkins Oceanogr. Stud. No. 2. Johns Hopkins Press, Baltimore.

Reid, J. L., Jr. 1969. Preliminary results of measurements of deep currents in the Pacific Ocean. Nature 221:848.

Reid, J. L., Jr., and R. J. Lynn. 1971. On the influence of the Norwegian–Greenland and Weddell Seas upon the bottom waters of the Indian and Pacific Oceans. Deep-Sea Res. 18(11):1063–88.

Richardson, P. L., and J. A. Knauss. 1971. Gulf Stream and western boundary undercurrent observations at Cape Hatteras. Deep-Sea Res. 19(11):1089–1110.

Rochford, D. 1972. Patterns of change in surface salinity and temperature in the Tasman and Coral Seas, 1966–71. Paper at the International Symposium on the Oceanography of the South Pacific, Wellington, N.Z., 9–15 February 1972.

Rossby, T., and D. Webb. 1971. The four month drift of a swallow float. Deep-Sea Res. 18(10):1035–39.

Rowe, G., and R. Menzies. 1968. Deep bottom currents off the coast of North Carolina. Deep-Sea Res. 15:711–19.

Saunders, P. M. 1971. Anticyclonic eddies formed from shoreward meander of the Gulf Stream. Deep-Sea Res. 18(12):1207–20.

Schmitz, W., A. Robinson, and F. Fuglister. 1970. Bottom velocity observations directly under the Gulf Stream. Science 170(3963): 1192–94.

Schwartzlose, R., and J. Isaacs. 1969. Transient circulation event near the deep ocean floor. Science 165 (3896):889–91.

Scorpio Report. 1970. Physical and chemical data from the Scorpio Expedition in the South Pacific Ocean–*Eltanin* cruises 28 and 29. SIO Ref. 69-15; WHOI Ref. 69-56. La Jolla, Calif. 89 pp.

Seabrooke, James D., Gary L. Hufford, and Robert B. Elder. 1971. Formation of Antarctic bottom water in the Weddell Sea. J. Geophys. Res. 76(9):2164–78.

Shaw, R., and K. Wyrtki. 1972. The shape of the warm surface layer in a subtropical gyre, pp. 179–94. *In* A. L. Gordon, ed. Studies in Physical Oceanography, Vol. 1. Gordon and Breach, New York.

Siedler, G. 1968. Schichtungs und Bewegungsverhältnisse am Südausgang des Roten Meeres. "Meteor" Forschungsergeb. (Sec-tion A) 4:1–76.

Stommel, H. 1965. The Gulf Stream, 2nd ed. University of California Press, Berkeley. 248 pp.

Stommel, H., and A. Arons. 1960a,b. On the circulation of the world ocean, 1 and 2. Deep-Sea Res. 6:140–54; 217–33.

Stommel, Henry, E. Dixon Stroup, Joseph L. Reid, and Bruce A. Warren. In press. Transpacific hydrographic sections at Lats. 43° S and 28° S. Part I: Preface. Deep-Sea Res.

Sverdrup, H., M. Johnson, and R. Fleming. 1942. The Oceans. Prentice-Hall, New Jersey. 1087 pp.

Swallow, J. C., and J. G. Bruce. 1966. Current measurements off the Somali coast during the southwest monsoon of 1964. Deep-Sea

Res. 13(5):861-88.

Swallow, J. C., and L. V. Worthington. 1961. An observation of a deep counter-current in the western North Atlantic. Deep-Sea Res. 8:1-19.

Tsuchiya, M. 1968. Upper waters of the intertropical Pacific Ocean. Johns Hopkins Oceanogr. Stud. No. 4. Johns Hopkins Press, Baltimore.

Warren, B. A. 1971. Evidence for a deep western boundary current in the South Indian Ocean. Nature Phys. Sci. 229(1):18-19.

Warren, B. A. In press. Transpacific hydrographic sections at Lats. 43°S and 28°S. Part II: Deep water. Deep-Sea Res.

Warren, B. A., and A. D. Voohis. 1970. Velocity measurements in the deep western boundary current of the South Pacific. Nature 228:849-50.

Warren, B. A., Henry Stommel, and J. C. Swallow. 1966. Water masses and patterns of flow in the Somali Basin during the southwest monsoon of 1964. Deep-Sea Res. 13(5):825-60.

Webster, F. 1971. On the intensity of horizontal ocean currents. Deep-Sea Res. 18(9):885-93.

Wooster, Warren S., ed. 1970. Scientific Exploration of the South Pacific. Natl. Acad. Sci., Washington, D.C. 257 pp.

Worthington, L. V. 1954. A preliminary note on the time scale in North Atlantic circulation. Deep-Sea Res. 3(1):234-35.

Worthington, L. V. 1956. The temperature increase in Caribbean deep water since 1933. Deep-Sea Res. 3(1):234-35.

Worthington, L. V. 1966. Recent oceanographic measurements in the Caribbean Sea. Deep-Sea Res. 13(4):731-40.

Worthington, L. V. 1969. An attempt to measure the volume transport of Norwegian Sea overflow water through the Denmark Strait. Deep-Sea Res. 16(suppl.):421-32.

Worthington, L. V. 1970. The Norwegian Sea as a mediterranean basin. Deep-Sea Res. 16(5):513-23.

Worthington, L. V. 1972. Anticyclogenesis in the oceans as a result of outbreaks of continental polar air, pp. 169-78. *In* A. L. Gordon, ed. Studies in Physical Oceanography, Vol. 1. Gordon and Breach, New York.

Worthington, L. V., and G. Volkmann. 1965. The volume transport of the Norwegian Sea overflow in the North Atlantic. Deep-Sea Res. 12:667-76.

Worthington, L. V., and W. R. Wright. 1970. North Atlantic Ocean Atlas. W.H.O.I., Woods Hole. 24 pp., 58 plates.

Worthington, L. V., and Hideo Kawai. 1972. Comparison between deep sections across the Kuroshio and Florida Current and Gulf Stream. Chap. 10 in Stommel and Yoshida, eds. Kuroshio. Univ. Tokyo Press, Tokyo. 517 pp.

Wright, R. 1969. Deep water movements in the Western Atlantic as determined by use of a box model. Deep-Sea Res. 16(suppl.): 433-46.

Wright, R. 1970. Northward transport of Antarctic bottom water in the western Atlantic Ocean. Deep-Sea Res. 17(2):367-72.

Wüst, G. A. 1933. Das Bodenwasser und die Gliederung der Atlantischen Tiefsee. Wiss. Ergeb. Dtsh. Atl. Exped. "Meteor," 1925-27, 6(1) (1) 106 pp. (Engl. transl. no. 340, by M. Slesser, U.S. Naval Oceanogr. Office, 1967).

Wüst, G. A. 1935. Schichtung und Zirkulation des Atlantischen Ozeans: Die Stratosphäre. Wiss. Ergeb. Dtsh. Atl. Exped. "Meteor," 1925-27, 6(1) (2).

Wüst, G. A. 1936. Schichtung und Zirkulation des Atlantischen Ozeans. Schnitte und Karten von Temperatur, Salzgehalt, und Dichte. Wiss. Ergeb. Dtsh. Atl. Exped. "Meteor," 1925-27, 6, Atlas, Teil A+B (Stratosphäre).

Wüst, G. A. 1957. Stromgeschwindigkeiten und Strommengen in den Tiefen des Atlantischen Ozeans. Wiss. Ergeb. Dtsh. Atl. Exped. "Meteor," 1925-27, 6(2):261-420.

Wyrtki, K. 1961. The thermohaline circulation in relation to the general circulation in the oceans. Deep-Sea Res. 8(1):39-64.

Wyrtki, K. 1962. The oxygen minima in relation to ocean circulation. Deep-Sea Res. 9:11-23.

Wyrtki, K. 1967. Circulation and water masses in the eastern equatorial Pacific Ocean. Int. J. Ocean. Limnol. 1:117-47.

Wyrtki, K. 1971. Oceanographic Atlas of the International Indian Ocean Expedition. Prepared with the assistance of E. B. Bennett and D. J. Rochford for the National Science Foundation. U.S. Government Printing Office, Washington, D.C. 531 pp.

DISCUSSION

ROBINSON: Can the diffusive character of the flow be dissociated from the dynamics of the variability?

BRETHERTON: How confident are we in the magnitude of the transport calculations of the abyssal circulation?

GORDON: The bulk of the transport probably occurs in strong currents whose width is less than 100 km. The velocity in these currents may be on the order of 10 cm/s. There could be large errors associated with geostrophic calculations for the velocity in mid-ocean regions where the velocity is on the order of mm/s.

NIILER: In warm-water circulation, direct observations of the transport indicate that the natural variability is perhaps on the order of the transport itself.

VERONIS: Thermocline theory normally requires a slow poleward flow in mid-ocean regions as a result of upwelling. On the other hand, studies of distribution of properties and Gordon's own studies suggest a flow toward the equator for these regions.

GORDON: Simple one-dimensional thermocline models cannot account for the circulation and the horizontal mixing that no doubt is taking place in the real ocean.

GATES: There's a strong possibility that transient eddies are an important mechanism in the transport of heat and salt in the ocean. Because of their transient nature, the eddy effects won't be seen in average meridional circulations. Therefore, calculations based on the average meridional circulation may be in serious error. The situation is similar to that which exists in the atmosphere where it is well known that average meridional flow cannot account for the transport of heat in the atmosphere. This is due to the presence of very vigorous mesoscale eddies.

HEAT AND SALT BALANCE WITHIN THE COLD WATERS OF THE WORLD OCEAN

A. L. GORDON and H. W. TAYLOR

THERMAL AND SALT BALANCE FOR ABYSSAL WATER

The waters below the main thermocline of the world ocean are for the most part products of polar and subpolar processes. It is possible to construct a model that satisfies both the heat and salt balance for the cold abyssal waters and is consistent with the sea-air heat and salt exchange south of the Antarctic polar front, where abyssal waters have direct access to the atmosphere. This is done by Gordon (this volume) for the heat balance of abyssal waters as follows. The average potential temperature of the waters below 4 °C is 1.7 °C (calculated from values given by Montgomery, 1958). Heat is introduced by North Atlantic deep water and Mediterranean and Red Sea outflows (all of which are warmer than the average abyssal temperature), geothermal heat flux, and downward heat diffusion across the main thermocline. The heat is eventually removed by sea-air interaction in the Antarctic region south of the polar front zone. The circuit is closed primarily by the northward flow of the cold Antarctic bottom water. Table 1 lists the heat flux and volume transport accomplished by the above mentioned processes in order to maintain thermal and volume balance.

The associated salt balance for the cold abyssal waters can be carried out in similar fashion. The average salinity of the colder than 4 °C water is 34.69°/$_{oo}$ (calculated from values given by Montgomery, 1958). Salt is added by North Atlantic deep water and Mediterranean and Red Sea outflows (which are saltier than the average abyssal water), and "removed" in the Antarctic by excess precipitation over evaporation, and continental runoff. Below the main thermocline diffusion of salt is expected to be upward since the above-lying layer of intermediate water is low in salinity. Table 2 lists the salt flux and volume transport values.

The Antarctic bottom water cannot be assumed to balance the freshwater input, since much of the freshwater input is carried northward by the low salinity Antarctic intermediate water. In the thermal budget, on the other hand, the waters of the polar front are the same or slightly warmer than the average abyssal water temperature and therefore do not effectively influence the thermal balance of abyssal waters. Including all the intermediate water masses (waters colder than 8 °C) in the abyssal water reservoir leads to an average salinity of 34.675°/$_{oo}$. In this case the diffusive salt flux across the main thermocline would be downward at a rate of 9.84×10^9 g/s.

THERMAL AND SALT BALANCE IN ANTARCTIC SURFACE WATER

A summer salt balance study of the upper 100 m of water (Antarctic surface water) from the Antarctic continental shelf to the southern extremes of the polar front zone (roughly an area of 20×10^6 km^2) indicates that a seasonal surface salinity variation of 0.1°/$_{oo}$ requires upwelling of approximately 60×10^6 m^3/s (Gordon, 1971). The estimated error of $\pm 20 \times 10^6$ m^3/s indicates this value is only a rough approximation. It is of significance, however, that the mean Ekman divergence for this region requires an upwelling of 54×10^6 m^3/s (Gordon, 1971), and the silicate budget (Edmond, 1973) also supports the 60×10^6 m^3/s upwelling rate.

The upwelling deep water is transformed to surface water

TABLE 1 Heat Balance of Waters Colder Than 4 °C (Average Potential Temperature is 1.7 °C) (After Gordon, This Volume)[a]

Source	Average Potential Temperature (°C)	Volume Flux (m^3/s)	Heat Flux (cal/s)
North Atlantic deep water	2.0	10×10^6 [b]	0.28×10^{13}
Mediterranean Sea	12.0	1×10^6 [c]	0.97×10^{13}
Red Sea	20.0	0.2×10^6 [d]	0.34×10^{13}
Geothermal heat flux	–	–	0.50×10^{13}
Diffusive heat flux	–	–	7.46×10^{13}
Antarctic bottom water (equal to sea-to-air heat transfer in Antarctic waters)	−1.0	38×10^6	9.55×10^{13}

[a] Heat flux values are given relative to the average temperature of the reservoir.
[b] Worthington, 1970
[c] Ovchennikov, 1966
[d] Siedler, 1968

on dilution by the excess precipitation over evaporation and continental runoff (1×10^{19} g/yr, Gordon, 1971), while salt is removed from the surface water reservoir by sinking of the cold saline shelfwater, which is observed at many areas of the shelf (Gordon, 1974). The low salinity water lost at the polar front removes excess surface water but not salt relative to the surface layer reservoir.

The annual salt balance of Antarctic surface water indicates cold shelf water must form from the surface water at a rate of 39×10^6 m^3/s, and outflow of surface water at the polar front must be 21×10^6 m^3/s in order to preserve a constant volume of the surface water mass (assuming no seasonal shift of the polar front zone). The annual salt flux and volume transports for Antarctic surface water are listed in Table 3.

The annual heat balance for the Antarctic surface water can also be determined. The average annual heat loss is 15 Kcal/cm^2/yr (Tolstikov, 1966, Plates 75 and 109). The heat budget is shown in Table 4. It indicates a sinking rate for shelf water of 30×10^6 m^3/s and a loss of surface water at the polar front of 30×10^6 m^3/s. While these values differ from the salt balance, they are surprisingly close. A critical number in the heat balance is the temperature of the surface water near the polar front zone. From the T/S diagrams, given by Gordon (1971), an average of 2.5 °C appears appropriate.

Naturally the Antarctic processes are strongly influenced by the seasonal advance and retreat of 2.1×10^{19} g of sea ice per year (Munk, 1966). Gordon (1971) attempted to extend his summer salt balance model into the winter months when most of the production of dense shelf water is expected. Unfortunately, a numerical error was introduced that approximately halved the rate of sinking cold shelf water. A value of 34×10^6 m^3/s was arrived at by Gordon (1971) for the rate of sinking for the six winter months, hence giving a 17×10^6 m^3/s for the yearly average. The yearly average found from the annual salt balance (Table 3) is 39×10^6 m^3/s, while that from the annual heat balance (Table 4) is 30×10^6 m^3/s, yielding a best guess of 35×10^6 m^3/s.

Gordon (1971) assumed that the mixing of the sinking cold shelf water with the deep water at a 1:1 ratio (needed

TABLE 2 Salt Balance of Water Colder Than 4 °C (Average Salinity is 34.69°/oo)[a]

Source	Average Salinity (°/oo)	Volume Flux (m^3/s)	Salt Flux (g/s)
North Atlantic deep water	34.91	10×10^6	$+2.20 \times 10^9$
Mediterranean and Red Sea outflow	36.60	1.2×10^6	$+2.29 \times 10^9$
Antarctic bottom water	34.65	38×10^6 [b]	-1.60×10^9
Diffusive salt flux for balance	–	–	-2.89×10^9 [c]

[a] Salt flux values are given relative to the average salinity of the reservoir. Positive values add salt; negative values effectively remove salt.
[b] Taken from thermal balance, Table 1.
[c] For a salt balance for waters colder than 8 °C, which would include the low salinity intermediate water masses, the diffusive salt flux across the main thermocline is downward at a rate 9.84×10^9 g/s.

TABLE 3 Annual Salt Balance of the Antarctic Surface Water (Average Salinity of 34.0°/oo)[a]

Source	Salinity (°/oo)	Volume flux (m^3/s)	Salt flux (gm/s)
Upper circum-polar deep water (upwelling)	34.60	60×10^6	$+36.0 \times 10^9$
Polar front exchange	34.00	21×10^6	0
Shelf water	34.65[b]	-39×10^6	-25.1×10^9
Runoff and pre-cipitation minus evaporation	0	0.32×10^6 [c]	-10.9×10^9

[a] Values for salt flux are given relative to the average salinity of the reservoir. Positive values add salt; negative values effectively remove salt.
[b] Taken as salinity needed for freezing point water to enable convection to the sea floor.
[c] Equals 1×10^{19} g/year.

TABLE 4 Heat Balance of the Antarctic Surface Water (Average Temperature 0 °C)[a]

Source	Temperature (°C)	Volume Flux (m^3/s)	Heat Flux (cal/s)
Upper circumpolar deep water (upwelling)	2°	+60 × 10^6	+11.3 × 10^{13}
Polar front exchange	2.5°	−30 × 10^6	− 7.1 × 10^{13}
Shelf water	−1.9°	−30 × 10^6	+ 5.4 × 10^{13}
Sea–air exchange	–	–	− 9.6 × 10^{13}

[a] Heat flux values are given relative to the average temperature of the reservoir.

to convert the characteristics of the shelf water into those of observed bottom water) would double the volume transport of Antarctic bottom water across the polar front zone. This may not be the case, since some Antarctic bottom water may remain south of the front and/or entrainment does not increase transport if momentum is conserved. The heat budget for the world ocean abyssal waters, discussed above, suggests that only 38 × 10^6 m^3/s of Antarctic bottom water are needed for balance. Hence it is possible that, though the shelf and deep waters mix in equal parts, the total volume transport remains about 35 to 40 × 10^6 m^3/s.

The above determinations are admittedly crude, but we feel that they are meaningful in that they are internally consistent and do indicate the magnitude of volume transports expected in consideration of sea-air exchange in the Antarctic region. It must be pointed out that in assuming that the effects of sea-air interaction south of the polar front are compensated entirely by outward flow of Antarctic bottom water and intermediate water, it forces rather large values for their volume transport. It is possible that some Antarctic characteristics spread northward within layers of the circumpolar deep water, which would not be included in this simple model.

ACKNOWLEDGMENT

The authors thank the Office for the International Decade of Ocean Exploration of the National Science Foundation for its support through GX41955.

REFERENCES

Edmond, J. M. 1973. The silica budget of the Antarctic circumpolar current. Nature 241(5389):391–93.

Gordon, A. L. 1971a. Oceanography of Antarctic waters. *In* J. L. Reid, ed. Antarctic Oceanology, I. Ant. Res. Serv., AGU, (15):169–203.

Gordon, A. L. 1974. Varieties and variability of Antarctic bottom water. Proceedings of the Symposium on the Formation of Bottom Water, Paris, Oct. 1972.

Gordon, A. L. General ocean circulation. This volume.

Montgomery, R. 1958. Water characteristics of Atlantic Ocean and of world ocean. Deep-Sea Res. 5:134–48.

Munk, W. H. 1966. Abyssal recipes. Deep-Sea Res. 13:707–30.

Ovchennikor, I. M. 1966. Circulation in the surface and intermediate layers of the Mediterranean. Oceanology (Eng. transl.) 6(1):48–59.

Siedler, G. 1968. Schichtungs und Bewegungsverhaltnisse am Sudausgang des Roten Meeres. "Meteor" Forsch., Section A, 4:1–77.

Tolstikov, Ye. L. 1966. Atlas of Antarctica, Vol. 1. Moscow. *In* Soviet Geography.

Worthington, L. V. 1970. The Norwegian Sea as a Mediterranean basin. Deep-Sea Res. 16(5):513–23.

MODERN MEASUREMENT TECHNIQUES

N. P. FOFONOFF and D. W. MOORE

INTRODUCTION AND GENERAL PHILOSOPHY

A basic description of the physical state of the ocean is obtained by measuring the three components of velocity—the pressure, temperature, and salinity as a function of position and time. Such a description is not achievable within the techniques and resources presently available to oceanographers. However, a rapid increase in measurement capability has been gained in recent years through the development and application of modern technology.

Perhaps the most significant advance in instrumental systems has been the development of several classes of instruments that can sample repetitively for extended periods of time. Such instruments have been designed in versions that can be fixed to the ocean boundary—surface or bottom—or suspended, allowed to drift in the interior, or be towed vertically or horizontally through the ocean. The capability of taking many samples in time (time and space if the instrument is moved) permits application of filtering techniques to separate phenomena into spectral regions of frequency and wave number. Such separation is essential to resolve the wide-band processes found in the ocean. This approach contrasts with classical methods that were based on relatively few observations in both space and time.

INSTRUMENT SYSTEMS

A brief description of some of the many types of modern instrument systems that are now in use or under development by physical oceanographers follows. This list is intended to be representative rather than comprehensive.

Fixed Instruments

By fixed instruments we mean instruments that remain approximately at their deployment position until recovery. Examples are moored current meters, moored temperature recorders, bottom-mounted pressure gauges, bottom-mounted electric and magnetic field sensors, etc.

The current meter mooring systems used at Woods Hole Oceanographic Institution (WHOI) are fairly typical. In the past, two types of mooring have been used (Fofonoff and Webster, 1971). Surface moorings use as buoyancy an 8-ft-diameter toroidal buoy at the sea surface, mooring line consisting of wire above 2,000 m in depth and nylon line below, all connected by an acoustic release to an anchor on the sea floor. Current meters are inserted at various locations along the mooring line. Subsurface moorings use buoyancy (hollow glass balls) below the sea surface to decouple the mooring line from surface wave noise. Recent experiments by WHOI have indicated that instruments on surface moorings may undergo large vertical displacements over periods of days to weeks because of high-current drag on the moorings near the surface, whereas instruments on subsurface moorings undergo much smaller excursions. Therefore subsurface moorings are now favored for measurements of deepwater currents (Gould and Sambuco, 1973).

Again, two types of recording current meters have been used on WHOI moorings. These are the Geodyne type (850) and the Vector Averaging Current Meter (VACM), manufactured by AMF. Both types use Savonius rotors as speed sensors and vanes as direction sensors, but differ fundamentally in their recording technique (Fofonoff and Webster, 1971). The 850 meters use a Savonius rotor speed sensor and a small (17 cm high by 9 cm long) vane to determine the direction of water flow. The current meter employs a "Burst" sampling scheme, i.e., a series of 22 values of rotor-revolution rate and current direction, are taken at 5-s intervals and recorded on magnetic tape. The cycle is repeated every 15 min. The 22 values are summed vectorially in the processing at Woods Hole. The vector-averaged data constitute the basic time series on which subsequent processing is performed.

The VACM employs an internal computer to do the vector summation. At every one-eighth revolution of the rotor, a direction value is measured. The internal computer then takes the sine and the cosine of the direction and adds these into two registers, one corresponding to the east velocity component and the other to the north. At the end of the 15-min recording cycle, the contents of the registers, together with the total number of rotor counts, are written on magnetic tape. During the subsequent processing, calibration constants are applied to convert the contents of the east and north registers to velocity components in cm/s. From these components the current magnitude and direction corresponding to that derived by the 850 are computed. The VACM has much better noise rejection at high frequencies because of component averaging.

Other instruments may be mounted on moorings. For example, C. Wunsch and J. Dahlen of MIT have developed a moored temperature-pressure recorder for deployment on WHOI moorings. The MIT recorders consist of a pressure housing that is an aluminum sphere, 6 in. in diameter, mounted on a steel shaft about 12 in. long. A thermistor with accuracy of .01 °C, and resolution .001 °C is mounted just inside the sphere. The existing instruments have a time constant of about 15 min, but this is adjustable. In addition, a pressure sensor is included to monitor mooring motions. The resolution of the pressure sensor (a strain gauge) is of the order of a few meters, depending upon the depth. All data is recorded on magnetic tape. Instrument lifetime can be close to a year, depending upon the variable data-sampling interval.

Another type of fixed instrumentation is bottom-mounted. An example is the fused-quartz, differential pressure gauge developed by D. J. Baker, Winfield Hill, and R. B. Wearn at Harvard University. The pressure sensor is a fused-quartz bourdon tube operated in a differential mode; the rotation of a mirror attached to the end of the tube is followed with an optical servosystem that drives a variable capacitance R-C oscillator. The outside of the tube is exposed to ambient pressure; the inside is filled with dry argon. Temperature is measured with an oscillator quartz temperature gauge placed close to the bourbon tube.

The gauge is self-contained: The frequency outputs corresponding to pressure and temperature are counted and placed on a 4-track magnetic tape together with a clock output by digital electronics. A standard AMF acoustic release and eight glass balls form the operative parts of the mooring system. The system can operate for 6 months on its two lead-acid batteries.

The gauge measures pressure with a resolution of 0.1 mm and a dynamic range of 10 m. It is designed to measure pressure signals as small as 1 cm/month; laboratory tests are consistent with this sensitivity. Temperature is measured to an accuracy of 10^{-4} °C. Each variable is sampled every 2 min. The data is recorded on a four-track magnetic tape recorder *in situ* and later transferred to computer tape with a special reader at WHOI. The data are checked for errors (bit loss, etc.) at this point and then the spectra and various correlations are computed (Baker, 1971).

Another example of bottom-mounted instrumentation is the Deep Sea Instrument Capsule developed by Frank Snodgrass at the University of California, San Diego. This device measures pressure, temperature, and current near the sea floor. In the past, a vibratron pressure sensor, a quartz-crystal temperature gauge, and a hot thermistor array as a current meter were used (Wimbush, 1972; Snodgrass, 1972). In the future, the emphasis will be on the use of resonating quartz-crystal sensors, due to their high stability and sensitivity (Irish and Snodgrass, 1972; Wimbush, 1972). The latest variation on the capsule is a version in which the capsule itself is tethered 1 km off the sea floor by a cable with a number of thermistors along it, thus providing temperature measurements at a number of depths in the deep water as well as pressure measurements at the sea floor and at the capsule location.

Electrodes can be mounted rigidly on the ocean bottom to measure the horizontal, electrical, potential gradient. The gradient is related to the total horizontal transport in the column of water above the electrodes. Instruments to measure the gradient at the ocean bottom have been developed by Sanford at WHOI and Cox at Scripps (Filloux *et al.*, 1971).

Drifting Instruments

Perhaps the most significant of the modern drifting instruments is the neutrally buoyant float. This is a device that sinks to given constant depth and drifts horizontally with the fluid at that level. The float sends out acoustic signals and is tracked from ship-borne or shore-based hydrophones. It provides a direct measurement of the Lagrangian velocity. These floats were first developed by John Swallow at NIO and were tracked from ships (Swallow, 1971). A newer version built by Vorrhis and Webb at Woods Hole Oceanographic Institution (WHOI) is capable of being tracked at long distances by means of shore-based hydrophones. Some of these floats include systems for internally recording or telemetering of other information, such as temperature and vertical motion past the instrument (Rossby and Webb, 1970; Rossby and Well, 1971).

Another drifting instrument is the autoprobe, which is similar to the neutrally buoyant float except that it can be programmed in advance to adjust its buoyancy to stay on a specified surface, such as a constant-temperature or constant-salinity surface (Burt, 1972).

Profiling Instruments

A profiler is any instrument used to make vertical profiles of some property of the water column at a given horizontal position. Profilers may be lowered from the ship on a cable to some predetermined depth or to the bottom, or they may cycle up and down a mooring line by internal buoyancy control, and they may be used in a "free-fall" mode.

The most common profiler in current use is the STD, which measures salinity and temperature versus depth (Pingree, 1970; Amos *et al.*, 1971). In the cable-lowering modes, it telemeters data up the cable for shipboard recording. In the free-fall mode, it records internally on chart paper. A new version of this, known as the CTD, is under development by Neil Brown at WHOI.

Another class of profilers give profiles of horizontal velocity. The free-fall, electromagnetic, current meter developed by T. Sanford (WHOI) measures speed and direction of horizontal ocean currents as a function of depth, utilizing electromagnetic induction. As the instrument falls through the water column, it is carried horizontally through the earth's magnetic field by the horizontal motion of the water. The induced earth's magnetic field (EMF) is measured and the horizontal velocities relative to an unknown reference velocity are inferred. That is, the vertical shear of the horizontal velocity is the inferred quantity (Drever and Sanford, 1970; Sanford, 1971).

Another type of velocity profiler employs acoustic tracking of rising or falling sound sources to infer horizontal motions of the water column. The details vary, but all of these instruments involve deployment of acoustic beacons or transponders on the sea floor before profiling can be done. The measurements do provide the actual horizontal velocity as a function of depth, rather than the vertical shear of the horizontal velocity (Pocharsky, 1961; Pocharsky and Malone, 1972).

An airdropsonde developed by W. S. Richardson at Nova University permits the determination of surface current and vertical integrals of horizontal velocity from aircraft. The relative position on the sea surface of two dye markers released from the bottom with a known time delay is a direct measure of the surface current integrated over that time interval, assuming steady conditions during the period of the experiment. The position of a dye marker that has fallen to any predetermined depth and returned to the surface relative to a marker that has remained on the surface is a direct measure of the vertical integral of the horizontal velocity from the surface to that depth, relative to the surface current (Richardson *et al.*, 1972).

The cyclosonde developed at the University of Miami is an instrument with automatic buoyancy control that cycles up and down a mooring line, measuring salinity, temperature, and horizontal velocity versus depth (Van Leer *et al.*, 1973).

Towed Instruments

These are instruments that are towed horizontally from ships to allow determination of the horizontal distribution of properties. Surface-towed instruments include the GEK for determining surface current, the thermistor chain or similar devices for determining temperature, and towed-salinity sensors.

Eli Katz from WHOI has devised a system for subsurface towing of an STD in which the depth of the instrument is adjusted periodically so that it follows a constant σ_T surface. The measured quantities are the depth of the surface as a function of position and temperature and salinity along the surface (variations of T–S) (Katz, 1973).

A "dynamic scanning" system presently being developed by E. Mollo-Christensen at MIT measures salinity, temperature, and current in the top few hundred meters of the water column while underway. Use in conjunction with an automatic navigation system enables one to deduce spatial, as well as temporal, variations. The use of such a system in conjunction and communication with a fixed buoy looks like a promising way of investigating the unsteady part of the circulation. The system presently depends on shore-based navigation equipment and therefore can only be used for near-shore work, but it will eventually be extended to open-ocean use.

REFERENCES

Amos, Gordon, and Schneider. 1971. Water masses and circulation patterns in the region of the Blake–Bahama Outer Ridge. Deep-Sea Res. 18:145–65.

Baker, D. J. 1971. The Harvard deep-sea pressure gauge, a progress report. Reports in Meteorology and Oceanography. No. 4. Harvard University, Cambridge, Mass.

Burt, K. Autoprobe, a free float mid-water observational platform for oceanographic studies of temperature and pressure. WHOI Rep. 69–42. Woods Hole, Mass.

Drever, R. G., and T. Sanford. 1970. A free-fall electromagnetic current meter instrumentation, pp. 353–70. *In* Proc. IERE Conf. Electron. Eng. Ocean Tech. IERE 8–9 Bedford Square, London.

Filloux, J., J. Larsen, and C. Cox. 1971. Chapter 17 *in* The Sea. Vol. 4, Part 1, pp. 637–93. John Wiley and Son, New York.

Fofonoff, N. P., and F. Webster. 1971. Current measurements in the western Atlantic. Philos. Trans. R. Soc. Lond. Ser. A 270:423–36.

Gould, J., and E. Sambuco. 1973. The effect of mooring type on the long term statistics of current measurements and site D. Unpublished manuscript.

Irish, J. D., and F. E. Snodgrass. 1972. Quartz crystals as multipurpose oceanographic sensors. I. Pressure. Deep-Sea Res. 19: 165–69.

Katz, E. 1973. Profile of an isopycnal surface in the main thermocline of the Sargasso Sea. Unpublished manuscript.

Pingree, R. D. 1970. In situ measurements of salinity, conductivity and temperature. Deep-Sea Res. 17:603–10.

Pocharsky, T. E. 1971. Exploring subsurface waves with neutrally buoyant floats. ISA J.

Pocharsky, T. E., and F. D. Malone. 1972. A vertical profile on deep horizontal current near Cape Lookout, North Carolina. J. Mar. Res. 30(2):163–67.

Richardson, W. S., H. White, and L. Nemeth. 1972. A technique for the direct measurement of ocean currents from aircraft. J. Mar. Res. 30(2):259–68.

Rossby, T., and D. Webb. 1970. Observing abyssal motions by tracking Swallow floats in the SOFAR channel. Deep-Sea Res. 17: 359–69.

Rossby, T., and D. Well. 1971. The four month dirft of a Swallow float. Deep-Sea Res. 18:1035–39.

Sanford, T. B. 1971. Motionally induced electric and magnetic fields in the sea. J. Geophys. Res. 76(15):3476–92.

Snodgrass, F. E. 1972. Deep-sea instrument capsule. Science 162 (3849):78–87.

Swallow, J. C. 1971. The *Aries* current measurements in the western North Atlantic. Philos. Trans. R. Soc. Lond. ser. A 270:451–60.

Van Leer, J., W. Duing, R. Erath, E. Kennelly, and A. Speidel. 1973. The cyclesonde, an unattended vertical profiler for scalar and vector quantities in the upper ocean. Technical Report. University of Miami, RSMAS 73026.

Wimbush, M. 1972. Tidal movements of the deep sea. Underwater J. 4(6):239–48.

DISCUSSION

ROBINSON: The exploitation of the new instrumentation will require simultaneously the development of new types of numerical models.

O'BRIEN: What kinds of numerical models?

ROBINSON: Numerical models of sporadic upwelling and transient mesoscale eddies that may be the important diffusers in the discussion we had on Arnold Gordon's paper. It's the parallel development of this new kind of numerical modeling and the application of these novel experimental techniques (which are now becoming scientific tools) that in my mind will lead to an understanding of the underlying physical processes that will ultimately be synthesized in a world-ocean model.

WARREN: I'd just like to mention one other development that Dennis (Moore) didn't mention that's so obviously important that everyone forgets it until he starts doing something, and that is position—latitude and longitude.

MOORE: This is supposed to be a list of what we can foresee happening in the near future. Good navigation isn't on the list.

ISRAELI: I want to ask in view of these developments if it will be possible in the future to have a large number of points, comparable to the number of mesh points in a numerical scheme, which can then be easily compared with numerical computations?

MOORE: Do you mean an actual three-dimensional map? If that is the case, I think the answer is going to be no.

CHARNEY: Except for mesoscale problems.

MOORE: To answer the question in enough detail to make sense I think would take too long, but the realistic answer even for the mesoscale problems is no, not in the timescale that you mentioned. So I think you've got to figure out what to do with a numerical model and how to compare it with sparse observations.

O'BRIEN: This is traditionally done by the meteorologists and I don't see any reason why oceanographers can't do the same thing.

III MODELS OF THE QUASI-PERMANENT CIRCULATION

ANALYTICAL MODELING OF THE OCEANIC CIRCULATION

P. WELANDER

INTRODUCTION

The present short study represents an attempt to describe the nature of the analytical theory of oceanic circulation and the results of this theory in relation to the real oceans. Some works on the problem are reviewed; however, no attempt is made to describe or even list all the relevant theoretical papers that have appeared in the hydrodynamic, meteorologic, and oceanographic literature.

Review works on the oceanic circulation have already been published, such as "Survey of Ocean Current Theory" (1957) and *The Gulf Stream* (1965) by H. Stommel, "Oceanography" (1965) and "Boundary Layers in Ocean Circulation" (1971) by A. R. Robinson, "On Theoretical Models of the Thermocline Circulation" (1969) and "Large-Scale Ocean Circulation" (1972) by G. Veronis, and "Ocean Models" (1971) by A. E. Gill. The paper "Time-Varying Currents" (1971) by M. J. Lighthill should also be mentioned, although it deals with a different class of oceanic motions. The author has profited a great deal from reading these works, which also include good bibliographies.

The following discussion will be limited to the problem of the general oceanic circulation, meaning the time-averaged, large-scale circulation. The special regime of the near-equator circulation (where the Coriolis parameter becomes small) is not included. This regime is discussed separately in a paper presented at this meeting by Gill.

Only analytical models are considered, which means that a large part of the relevant theoretical research based on numerical model work is excluded. It is, however, difficult to eliminate from one's thinking all knowledge of the oceans gained from numerical modeling, and somehow this feels unnatural. As a compromise, comments related to numerical modeling are added in footnotes.

The present review clearly is a subjective one, representing the author's own ideas on the theory of the oceanic circulation, gained from reading books and research papers, and to some extent by personal research work. Other specialists in this field may have different ideas; hopefully this study can be of help in stimulating our further discussion of the oceanic circulation problem.

THE GENERAL FORMULATION OF THE PROBLEM

The "ultimate theory" of oceanic circulation should give an answer to the following problem: Let the shape of the oceanic basins and the mass and composition of seawater be given. Apply the forcing from the overlaying atmosphere, from the sun and the moon, in the form of wind stress, air pressure, heat and water fluxes, and tidal forces. These forcings are functions of time and horizontal position. Except for the tidal forces these effects are concentrated on the oceanic surface. The bottom of the oceans can be considered as insulated; this is a sufficient approximation even for a quantitatively good theory.*

We assume that the variable forcings exhibit a statistical steady state, looking over a long time scale. These forcings acting on the closed world ocean, which posesses dissipation

* The geothermal heat is only of the order of a permill of the heat flux going through the sea surface. Still, it is not immediately obvious that it can be neglected, since this heat is delivered at around 500 atmospheres pressue, with a correspondingly increased efficiency. Estimates by the author show that the effect of the geothermal heating on the deep thermohaline circulation may be a few percent.

(viscosity, heat, and salt diffusion) is expected to produce a statistically steady motion. The large-scale part of this motion is identified as the general oceanic circulation. Associated with this circulation are, further, certain mean fields of temperature, salinity, and density. These are of special interest, since they can be readily compared with observations. The mean circulation itself cannot be measured accurately enough to allow a good comparison with the theory, except in the surface layer and in special strong currents, such as the Gulf Stream.

A complete "understanding" of the circulation does not come merely from looking at one theoretical solution that depicts the observed fields well. To obtain a real insight in the problem we also need to know how the circulation varies with the forcing functions and with different parameters of the problem.* We can achieve a further overall understanding of the problem by looking on the budget of such physical variables as mass, angular momentum, vorticity, energy, and entropy, which are associated with different conservation theorems.

Mathematically, it may not be obvious that the problem formulated above is well defined. The mathematical problem is described by a set of partial differential equations, with the velocity components—the pressure, density, temperature and salinity—as main dependent variables and time and three coordinates as independent variables. Associated with these is a set of boundary conditions that hopefully should determine a unique solution. In special cases, for example, using linearized equations and certain simple boundary conditions, it may be possible to prove that a solution, and a unique solution, exists. The general system is, however, nonlinear. The detailed time development of the system is expected to become unstable, and several solutions may exist for a given forcing and given initial conditions. Even in such a case one expects that a unique statistical steady state exists. However, mathematical experiments with some simple systems of similar nature indicate that this may not be a general result. For example, consider a circular, one-dimensional fluid loop placed in a vertical plane. If this loop is subjected to a given torque and a differential heating due to a heat flux associated with a prescribed temperature of the outside, following a Rayleigh law of conduction, it can be shown that instabilities may arise, producing growing oscillations or pulsations of the loop (Howard and Malkus, private communication; a similar system is also described by the author, 1967).

* Numerical modeling of the atmospheric and oceanic circulations commonly are aimed at producing a theoretical solution that agrees closely with the observed fields. The models are often so complex that only few numerical runs could be afforded; hence the dependence of the solution on the forcing functions and the problem parameter cannot be studied in detail.

The author studied this problem† on an analogue computer during a visit to the University of Washington last fall, with the assistance of Dr. L. Larsen. Some interesting results were obtained. In a certain parameter range the solution did not pass through the available phase-space, even after a time corresponding to many thousand "eigentimes." A good fraction of the space was left empty, but was immediately filled when the system was started from new initial conditions. This phenomena could be understood if the solution had been near-periodic, but that was not the case; in fact, the solution rather appeared ergodic and could never be seen repeating itself in time.

The real oceans represent, of course, an enormously more complex mechanical-thermodynamical system. Whether the complexity makes the probability for several quasi-steady statistical states less or more likely is not known, certainly the possibility of multisteady states must be considered.

The concept of a statistically steady circulation may fail also in another respect. It has been assumed that the forcings exhibit such a steady state. Thus, the requirement must be that the statistics of the forcings remain unchanged over a time long compared to the relevant oceanic response times. However, we may find important response times for the deep oceanic circulation of order of several hundred years. If we go to times much longer than this, main climatic variations will become evident; and possibly no statistically steady state can be defined over any length of time.

It is further assumed in the above problem that the forcings are external and prescribed. In reality, of the previously listed forcing functions only the tidal one is truly external. As one example, the heat flux at the sea surface depends critically on the state of the ocean as well as the atmosphere. For example, in a chart of the heat flux for the Atlantic, we find concentrated positive (upward) fluxes associated with the Gulf Stream. An indirect feedback link exists, obviously, through the atmospheric state. The atmosphere itself certainly is dependent on the state of the oceans. During climatic periods when the oceanic temperatures and circulation were essentially different, this feedback might well have been strongly felt. The conclusion is that only the combined oceans and atmosphere can be rigorously dealt with as an externally forced system; for this system we would, in principle, only have to specify the solar radiation

† If the angular velocity of the fluid is ω and the mass center coordinates are x and y, the governing equations are:

$$\omega' + \epsilon\omega = \alpha + \beta y,$$
$$x' - \omega y = x_o - \delta x,$$
$$y' + \omega x = y_o - \delta y,$$

where $\epsilon, \alpha, \beta, \delta, x_o, y_o$ are constants and the derivative is after time. It seems remarkable that a simple system of three ordinary differential equations can exhibit such a complicated behavior.

and the tidal forcing to determine the complete (statistical) solution.*

In our analytical studies the coupled problem obviously becomes too complicated.† The question then arises if the forced ocean circulation problem can be formulated in a meaningful way. For example, is there a meaningful way to define the thermal boundary condition in our present model?

Most models include thermal forcing in the form of a specified ocean surface temperature. It may be felt that this condition is too rigid and that heat flux would be a better specification. A further step would be to specify only an apparent air temperature T_a, and let the heat flux q be determined by a Rayleigh law, $q = -k(T_a - T)$. T_a would here be a given function of horizontal position and time. It should be noted that this law can produce both a given surface temperature (making $k \to \infty$) and a given heat flux (making $k \to 0$, $T_a \to \infty$) as special cases. From here one can go on to even more complex flux–temperature relations that can be thermodynamically derived.

Still, there are arguments for keeping the clean heat flux condition. Calculating the oceanic circulation as forced by prescribing heat flux, wind stress, etc., does not give the entire solution, but part of it is at least well solved.

The idea of treating partial problems as externally forced is often used. As a simple oceanographic example, one can look on the Ekman problem for a homogeneous water column. This can be solved completely, specifying the local wind stress and the sea surface slope as functions of time plus local bottom and initial conditions. The fact that the sea surface slope in reality is not prescribed, but is obtained by solving the complete wind stress problem over a closed basin, does not prevent us from learning something useful about the local set up of the currents by this calculation.

Engineers studying complicated servosystems theoretically and experimentally consider the different components as separate, forced systems; only in the last stage are all the subsystems coupled. The idea of looking at the oceans along such engineering lines, and thinking in terms of "black boxes," has been particularly advocated by Lighthill (1971).

To solve the partial problem of the forced oceans some generalizations of our classes of forcing functions may be needed. Not only the large-scale, semi-external forcings but also smaller scale forcings that enter in a final coupled model should be studied. For example, thermal forcings of the scale of the (climatic) Gulf Stream should be included in the forced-circulation problem.

* Numerical simulations with coupled atmospheric and oceanic models have been attempted; one interesting work along this line has been reported by Manabe and Bryan (1969).

† For understanding the problem it may be of value to look on some drastically simplified mehcanical–thermodynamical systems that can be discussed analytically. The fluid loop by Howard and Malkus mentioned earlier is an oceanic model, simplified to the extreme while retaining some important nonlinear effects. One may think of further studies of coupled loops that possibly can give us some insight in the atmosphere–ocean feedback mechanisms.

SIMPLIFIED MODELS

In order to carry out the analytical theory at all, drastic simplifications of the problem are often required. These simplifications are of different types. One type limits the problem to very small or very large parameter values. It may then be possible to linearize the problem, or to use perturbation and boundary layer techniques. The information gathered from different limiting models can often be used to construct at least a qualitative picture of the solutions in a range where the parameter values are finite, and even where they are of order one. In certain cases the information obtained from linear or weakly nonlinear models cannot, however, be extrapolated. For example, strong nonlinearities may produce instabilities, separation of boundary layers, etc., that entirely change the solution.

Another type of simplification involves drastic assumptions about the physical situation. For example, a two-layer rectangular ocean model represents such a simplification, which cannot be deduced by any obvious limiting procedure. It is assumed that the bottom topography can be neglected and that the oceans behave as two immiscible fluid layers. The task of justifying such models, if possible at all, is obviously much more difficult.

The most problematic simplification made in the oceanic circulation theory involves the turbulent effects. The problem of finding the statistical steady state of the circulation is generally replaced by a simpler, truly steady problem. It is assumed that only the steady part of the forcing has to be considered [only in a few analytical studies have the averaged effect of time-varying driving been considered, see, for example, Veronis (1966b) and Pedlosky (1967)]. Still, the time-variable part of the solution cannot be neglected. The real oceans show important time-fluctuations in the velocity, temperature, and salinity. These produce important Reynolds terms in the nonlinear time-dependent equations, that can be interpreted as turbulent friction, heat diffusion, and salt diffusion. These must necessarily be considered in the overall problem; inclusion of only molecular friction and diffusion effects leads to completely unrealistic solutions. The common assumption is that these turbulent effects can be related to the local mean fields in a way similar to that applied in a molecular case, but with much larger values for the friction and diffusion coefficients. For example, in the so-called β-plane models the form $(A_H \nabla^2 u, A_H \nabla^2 v)$ is used for the horizontal friction, where ∇^2 is the horizontal Laplacian, and similarly the forms $K_H \nabla^2 T$ and

$K_H'\nabla^2 S$ are used for the horizontal heat and salt diffusion, respectively. The values of the (kinematic) coefficients are in the range 10^6-10^9 cm^2 s^{-1}. For the vertical friction and diffusion, the corresponding terms are taken to be $(A_v u_{zz}, A_v v_{zz})$, $K_v T_{zz}$, and $K_v' S_{zz}$, respectively, with coefficients in the general range of 1-10^3 cm^2 s^{-1}. The above form for the horizontal friction is used in the classical mass transport calculation by Munk (1950), as well as in most later investigations. The validity of this friction model has, however, been questioned on logical, as well as on physical, grounds (see, for example, Kamenkovich, 1967; Bretherton and Turner, 1968; Kirwan, 1969). The strong sensitivity of the friction force to the mixing-length assumption that implicitly enters the problem has been demonstrated by the author (1972). Assuming the value $A_H = 10^8$ cm^2 s^{-1}, the friction doubles the theoretical Gulf Stream transport doubles when vorticity rather than momentum is mixed. Measurements in the Gulf Stream region actually indicate that the momentum transport does not obey the molecular-like law; rather the effective friction coefficient comes out negative (Webster, 1961; Niiler and Schmitz, 1969). In this respect the ocean behaves similarly to the atmosphere at middle latitudes. However, it may not be possible to apply the results obtained in the theory of large-scale atmospheric turbulence directly to the ocean. Apart from the difference in Rossby numbers (typically smaller in the ocean) and bottom effects (stronger topographic effects in the oceans) the existence of meridional barriers in the oceans may modify the overall turbulent field. In the atmosphere the eddies are in certain respects necessary in the absence of a net east-west pressure gradient (see Lorenz, 1967). In the oceans a net east-west pressure gradient and a corresponding net meridional geostrophic transport is, of course, possible.*

Analytical studies of the dynamics of the large-scale oceanic turbulence hardly exist. In the atmospheric case some works on the large-scale eddies based on stability theory have, however, been made. The baroclinic stability theory predicts growing disturbances in the westerlies, and their growth-rate and structure are in rough agreement with observations. The difficulty lies in closing the problem. The real eddies must become limited by nonlinear effects. Actually, they must modify the mean flow such as to make the growth-rate small. In a final statistical steady state, there should, of course, be no mean transfer from mean flow to the eddies at all, except for the part needed to balance dissipation. (For a general review of the theory of the atmospheric circulation, the large-scale eddies in the atmosphere, see Lorenz, 1967).

Another turbulent process that may be critical for the circulation theory is the vertical diffusion of heat and salt. This diffusion determines the structure of the thermocline and the associated vertical circulation. Again we expect the molecular-like model to be unrealistic. The turbulent diffusivity is not constant, but depends on the shear, the stratification, and other factors, in a way that is not well understood. The possibility of distance-generation of turbulence by traveling internal waves may have to be considered as well as the possibility of double-diffusive molecular instabilities in certain regions (salt fingers, temperature, and salinity steps).

The different circulation models used involve many approximations that cannot be well justified, but some defense for them can usually be produced. At least we understand explicitly what the approximations mean. Only in the case of the approximations for the oceanic turbulence are we completely out in the blue. For the future advancement of the oceanic circulation theory along analytical, as well as numerical, lines, a better understanding of the oceanic turbulence and the development of better models for this turbulence is probably a necessity.

WIND-DRIVEN CIRCULATION IN HOMOGENEOUS OCEANS

One class of models of the ocean circulation that has been studied in some detail deals with the wind-driven circulation in a homogeneous rectangular-shaped ocean of uniform depth. With the friction modeled by molecular-like terms as described previously, the equation governing the mass transport stream function ψ becomes

$$\frac{1}{\rho H}\left[\frac{\partial(\psi,\nabla^2\psi)}{\partial(x,y)}\right] + \beta\psi_x + \frac{1}{H}\left(\frac{A_v f}{2}\right)^{1/2}\nabla^2\psi - A_H\nabla^4\psi = \mathrm{curl}_z\tau, \qquad (1)$$

where x,y are coordinate eastward and northward; $\beta = df/dy$; H, the depth; ρ, the density; and τ, the wind stress. The equation is derived for a β-plane case with small friction (the friction however, becomes, important in boundary layers).

It should be noted that this vertical integration of the vorticity equation can be carried out both in the interior regime, where the nonlinear terms are small, and in side boundary layers where nonlinear terms may become large. In the latter case, with the pressure gradient unchanged over the depth, the velocity profile can be considered uniform.

* Another example is provided by the equatorial undercurrent. This current can be explained as a mean circulation effect, or as an effect of turbulent eddies near the equator, assuming that potent vorticity is conserved in either case. This is entirely consistent with angular momentum conservation. The boundaries allow a pressure gradient that can accelerate the water eastward. The turbulent friction can be "normal," i.e., produce a force of the same sign as molecular friction. In the corresponding atmospheric case, an eastward jet at the equator cannot be produced by a meridional circulation alone, since this contradicts angular momentum conservation. The eddies can only do the job if the friction becomes anomalous, producing a force with the sign opposite to that of molecular friction.

The classical study by Ekman (1905, 1923) neglects the β-term, as well as lateral friction and inertial (nonlinear) terms. In the study by Stommel (1948), the important β-term is added. In his model the third term in Eq. (1), representing the bottom stress curl, is simply modeled by $r\nabla^2 \psi$, where r is a constant; this approximation is retained in most later works.

The works on the transport problem by Stockman (1946), Sverdrup (1947), and Munk (1950)—although in their general forms derived for a stratified ocean—also apply to the homogeneous, uniform-depth ocean with a slip-bottom. Munk gives the solution in the linear case for a closed rectangular basin. As seen from Figure 1(a,b), the difference between his and Stommel's solution is slight.

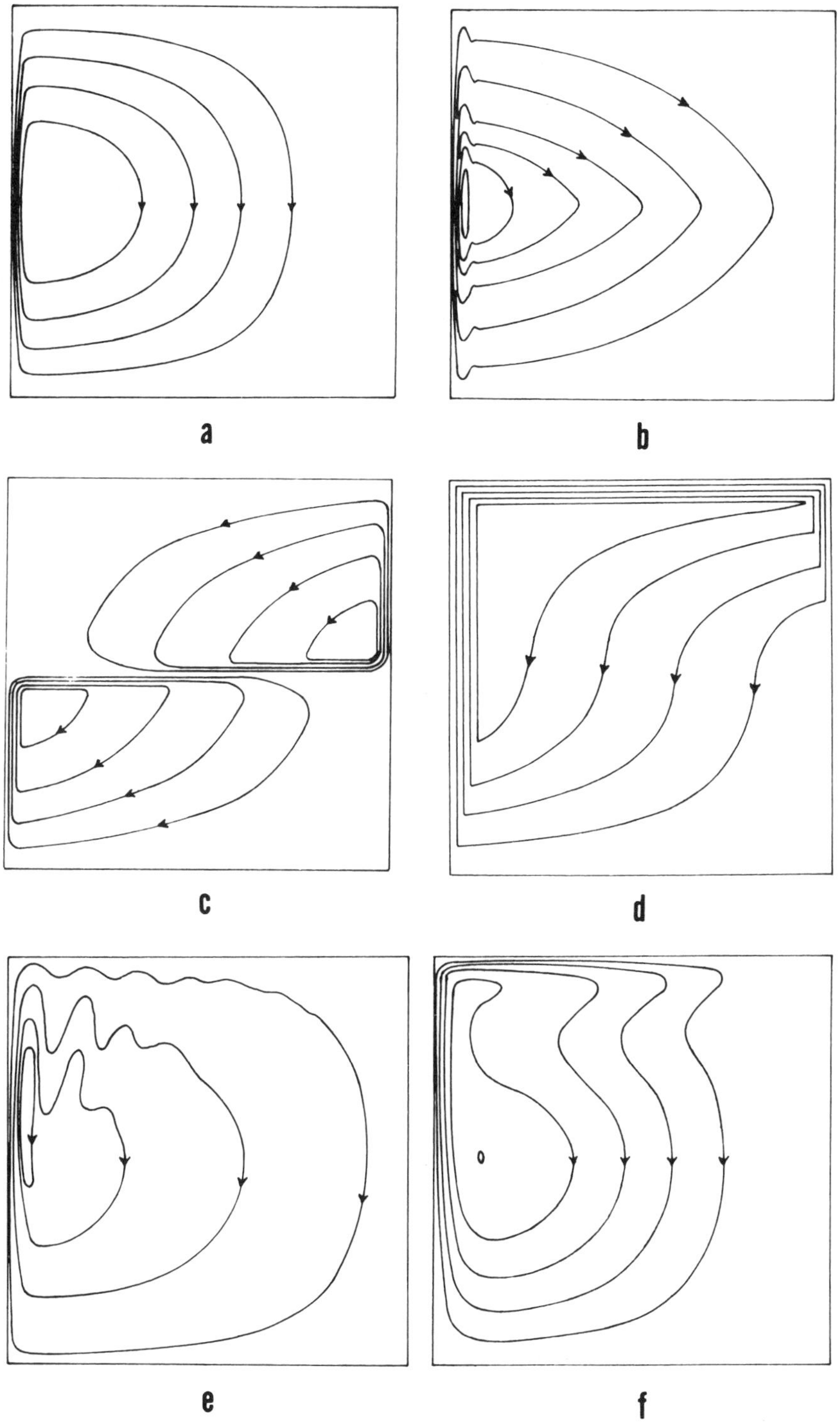

FIGURE 1 Examples of model solutions for the transport stream function: (a) and (b) with bottom and side friction, respectively; (c) and (d) inertially dominated solutions; (e) inertial friction solution in an Oseen approximation; and (f) inertial friction solution from a computer calculation.

(Munk uses the slip condition at the zonal boundaries; if the more proper nonslip condition is used, zonal boundary layers are added, which make the two circulations look more different).

These two linear solutions demonstrate clearly the westward intensification and the formation of a Gulf Stream-like current due to the β-effect; if one sets $\beta = 0$, the transport solutions become symmetric in the east-west direction. The mixed case, with both vertical and horizontal friction, gives a two-scale lateral boundary layer but no essentially new phenomena.

The more difficult inertial case has been studied analytically by a number of investigators. The nature of the nonlinear boundary layer at the western wall was discussed in early works by Charney (1955) and Morgan (1956). These models apply in the region where the boundary current is fed from the interior and thus intensifies. (The above-mentioned models were actually developed for a two-layer ocean; the one-layer case is not essentially different.) The case of a free inertial circulation was studied by Fofonoff (1954), assuming that the existing functional relation between absolute vorticity and stream function is linear. In this case one finds that the β-effect produces a north–south asymmetry rather than an east-west one. The solution is, however, nonunique; and free eastward jets could be added along any latitude circle.

The case of a forced inertial circulation was considered by Carrier and Robinson (1962). As in Fofonoff's free-flow case, they found that the interior flow must be westward. Their suggestion is that the western boundary current separates at the point where the westward interior inflow vanishes, i.e., at the latitude of maximum wind stress curl. The current should proceed eastward along this latitude circle and turn up the eastern boundary, then feeding back to the interior (Figure 1c). The solution is consistent only if a small friction is added to permit a vorticity diffusion; if there acts a wind stress curl of one sign, every stream line must actually pass through a diffusive region. However, again a nonuniqueness arises. It seems possible to let free jets cross the basin also at other latitudes, or the boundary current can continue up to and along the northern wall (Figure 1d). A more complete analysis, which explicitly considers the friction as well as the inertial terms, is needed to solve the problem. Analytically, one can hardly hope to solve the general nonlinear problem; but some information can readily be obtained using nonlinear perturbation techniques. A straightforward expansion after amplitudes produces a first-order correction to the driving force, $-\partial(\psi^o, \nabla^2\psi^o)/\partial(x,y)$, in the right-hand side of Eq. (1), where ψ^o is the appropriate linear solution. The effect is to shift the gyre northward next to the western boundary (Munk *et al.*, 1950; Veronis, 1966a).

Another perturbation method was tried by Moore (1963). If the zonal velocity at the edge of the boundary current is U, the correction term $U\nabla^2\psi_x$ is added in Eq. (1). This Oseen-type calculation does not work well everywhere; at the meridional boundary itself, the correction is not justified. However, some qualitatively correct features seem to come out from this approach.

With bottom friction included, Moore found that the boundary current returns from the western wall to the interior through standing, damped Rossby waves, which ride on the eastward current (see Figure 1e). A similar result is obtained if lateral friction is kept. Obviously friction is needed; neglecting this, the Rossby waves fill the basin at all latitudes of eastward flow.

More detailed analytical studies of the western boundary currents, including inertial terms and friction, have been made by Ilyin and Kamenkovich (1963) and several later investigators. The physical picture of the situation is nicely described in a short article by Stewart (1964). Still, analytical theory has not been able to deal with the problem completely. In particular, the study of the possible separation and instability of the boundary current is missing. If the shear becomes large enough in the boundary current, an instability is expected, at least with lateral friction included, that gives an inflexion point in the velocity profile. If the boundary current separates, as predicted by the Carrier–Robinson model, a further instability of the free jet seems likely.

A number of important numerical model studies of the problem have been carried out,* and some good laboratory experiments that bear directly on the problem also exist (Baker and Robinson, 1969). The applicability of the models described here to the real oceans is quite uncertain. The models obviously are grossly oversimplified when both stratification and bottom topography are left out. However, we actually have a case where two bad approximations add up to something better. The stratification in the real oceans protect the upper layer from the topographic influence; and the model may therefore, to a first approximation, describe the transport field above the main thermocline correctly. It actually can be interpreted as the upper layer of a strongly stratified two-layer model. The real interfaces do slope considerably in reality, but neglecting this slope turns out to be less serious than expected. There are, unfortunately, no good measurements of the transport field in the interior ocean with which the theory can be compared, but a comparison with diagnostic calculations, such as the one reported by Holland (private communication) may be tried. Holland uses the observed density field; the unknown barotropic pressure field is then determined by the top and bottom boundary conditions, including real bottom to-

* Veronis (1966a) has carried out numerical experiments over a large range of parameter values. One solution from this study is shown in Figure 1f. This includes inertial and bottom friction terms of comparable magnitudes.

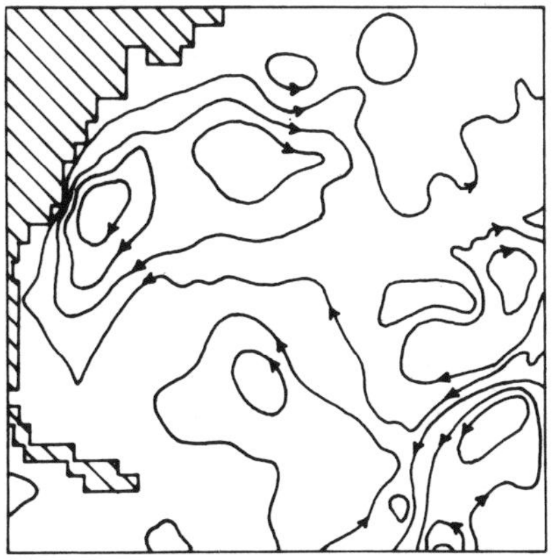

FIGURE 2 The transport stream function in the western North Atlantic obtained in a diagnostic calculation by W. R. Holland.

pography. Figure 2 gives part of his calculated total transport field for the North Atlantic. If this calculation can be trusted, it is obvious that our rectangular oceanic models do not predict the total transport field even qualitatively correctly. On the other hand, the diagnostic transport field for an upper layer has the same qualitative features as the models, with a well-developed subtropical gyre and a strong westward intensification.

The transport for the Gulf Stream has been measured, and the values show consistent variations along the Stream (Knauss, 1969). The maximum transport values are much larger than the ones found from a linear theory, using the wind stress data by Hellerman (1965). Even if only the upper layer is considered, the real Gulf Stream transport is at least double the theoretical value. Gill (1971) has suggested that the recirculation predicted in the numerical calculations by Bryan (1963) and Veronis (1966a) can explain the discrepancy, but unless the main interior Sverdrup regime is abandoned, we merely shift the problem to the eastern coastline. Nothing in the data suggests a strong compensating boundary current at this place. The pressure torque effect appearing through a combination of stratification and bottom topography, which has been recently studied by Holland (private communication), appears to be a more likely explanation. It must also be remembered that the wind stress values may be in error. An estimate of the wind stresses by Holopainen (1967), based on the vorticity budget of the atmosphere, actually suggests values essentially larger than the ones given by Hellerman; it seems important to get this discrepancy settled.

The linear homogeneous model discussed previously in this section can easily be extended to include bottom topography. The role of β is then replaced by that of f/H, where H is the depth and the "westward intensification" is replaced by the "intensification to the left of $\nabla(f/H)$." Some new effects appear along lines where this gradient vanishes, as well as in interior regions of closed f/H-contours. The case of a rectangular ocean with an added topography that makes the effective β change sign in the northern half has been considered by several investigators; the correct mathematical solution has been presented by Kamenkovich (private communication) and Fandry and Leslie (1972). An illustration of this is given in Figure 3.

A general discussion of the topographic effects in rotating homogeneous fluids has been given by Greenspan (1968). Separate analytical studies have been carried out for the flow relative to certain simple obstacles (steps, ridges, sea mounts, etc.). As expected, strong effects of topography are seen when the Rossby number is small. However, as remarked earlier, these topographic models cannot be used for transport predictions; and one may doubt that they apply even for the deep sea separately. The effect of the stratification, measured by the ratio N/f, where N is the Brunt-Vaisala frequency, is appreciable almost everywhere in the oceans.

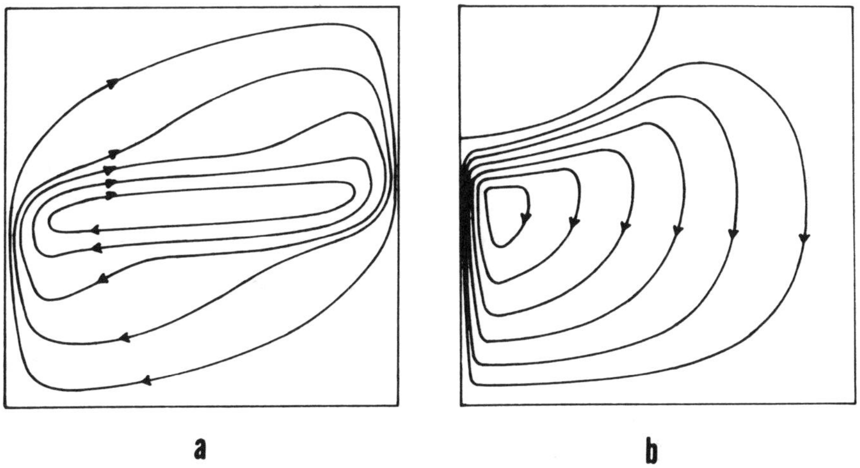

FIGURE 3 Further examples of model solutions for the transport stream function. In (a) a meridional bottom slope is introduced; in (b) there is a lower layer at rest reaching the surface in the northwestern region of the basin. The driving force is the same as in Figure 1.

WIND-DRIVEN CIRCULATION IN STRATIFIED OCEANS

While the complete theory for the oceanic circulation should explain the total velocity and mass fields created by the wind stress and the thermohaline forcings, it may be of interest to look on the partial problem where the wind stress is assumed to act over an ocean of given stratification, neglecting the diffusion of mass. Such a stratified model should give a better prediction of the circulation in the upper layer than the homogeneous model discussed in the previous section. In the thermocline and the deep sea, the thermohaline circulation is, however, expected to play an important role; and it is not clear that the model will work. It should be noted that the circulations induced by the wind stress on the one hand and the thermohaline forcings on the other cannot be separated, except possibly when one process dominates. In particular, a strong nonlinear coupling exists through the temperature and salinity advection terms.

In one special case, the detailed stratification does not affect the transport field, which therefore comes out independent of any existing thermohaline processes. If all motion decays at great depths, the linear frictional model can be directly integrated over the depth to give the transport Eq. (1), with the inertial and bottom friction terms missing. Neglecting the lateral friction, the transport equation by Sverdrup (1947) is obtained, relating the meridional transport directly to the wind stress curl. This equation can be used to calculate the interior transport if a condition for ψ is specified at one meridional boundary; normally it is assumed that the regime applies up to an eastern boundary, where one sets $\psi = 0$. If the lateral friction is retained, the model by Munk (1950) comes out. These transport models cannot, however, be directly generalized to include the inertial terms, unless the (inconsistent) assumption is made that the boundary current is predominantly barotropic.

The Sverdrup–Munk transport models are appealing because of their simplicity. Qualitatively correct predictions seem to come out, with the main gyres and the boundary currents at the right places. It has therefore been felt that the Sverdrup balance represents the correct first-order balance for the interior ocean (still allowing corrections of, say, 20–50 percent). However, as discussed in the previous section, some doubt about this has arisen. The Sverdrup balance probably predicts the upper layer circulation qualitatively correctly but may be an unvalid first approximation for the total transport. Introducing a detailed basic stratification, it should in principle be possible to calculate the wind-driven circulation with correctly applied bottom boundary condition (slip or nonslip condition depending on the type of friction assumed), without making any assumption of a downward decay. The vertical integration would then give a generalized transport equation.

The simplest case is represented by a two-layer model with vertical friction (Welander, 1968). In order to set the lower layer in steady motion the model requires a frictional coupling across the interface in the form of an interface stress. This interface stress seems, however, somewhat arbitrary and cannot easily be identified with processes assumed to work in a real, continuously stratified fluid. In the case of uniform depth, the model predicts a deep western boundary gyre, driven by the upper boundary current. The total transport still agrees closely with that of the one-layer model. If topography is added, an interior deep circulation and a modified total transport field is obtained; but, because of the appearance of the interface stress, which we do not really know how to calculate, any predictions made by this model cannot be trusted.

If the wind stress is strong enough, the interface will reach the surface; this will happen at the western boundary. Thus the western boundary current must separate. The path of the separated current can be calculated if one assumes that the motion in the lower layer is small enough, as described by Parsons (1969). One simply finds the position of the jet at each longitude from the requirement that the interior meridional transport from this longitude up to the eastern wall balances the jet transport, given by $1/2\ \rho g' h_i^2$, where g' is the reduced gravity and h_i is the depth of the interface at the edge of jet; this depth is determined by the interior solution. However, it is not clear that the lower layer motions, induced by direct wind action, can be neglected. At least in the transport calculation the lower layer must certainly be considered. The possibility also exists that the jet will become unstable when it separates. This could perhaps be accounted for in the model by introducing an appropriate lateral friction term. The solution by Parsons is shown in Figure 3b. The two-layer calculations for the Gulf Stream by Charney (1955) and Morgan (1956) have already been mentioned. More recent attempts to model the Gulf Stream in detail have been carried out by Robinson and Niiler (1967). The major aim is the prediction of the path of the current after it passes Cape Hatteras. In this model, an integration across the jet is made, keeping both the continous stratification and the topographic effects. This and other similar studies seem to indicate that the bottom topography has a quite strong steering effect on the Gulf Stream.

A general theory for the wind-induced circulation in a continuously stratified ocean offers certain principal difficulties. If a basic density stratification $\gamma = d\rho/dz$ is introduced, the steady perturbation form of the density conservation equation degenerates to $w = 0$, i.e., a purely horizontal motion is predicted. To obtain nontrivial results, the nonlinear advection must be included, or some new process, such as the density diffusion, must be added. Inclusion of a vertical density diffusion seems sensible, since the turbulent diffusion is expected to play a main role in the formation of the actual stratification in the oceans. However, this approach also leads to some difficulties. A realistic theory seem still to require nonlinear terms.

THERMOCLINE THEORY

To understand the role of the thermohaline forcing in the oceanic circulation, one may start with a model that neglects the wind effect; the entire driving is then associated with the density differences at the ocean surface produced by differential heating, evaporation-precipitation, and other processes that involve normal heat and freshwater transports. This is the so-called "thermocline theory." Such a model hopefully can give some insight into the process by which the interior oceanic density field is produced. However, *a priori* it is not known that the wind effect can be neglected in this problem.

The thermocline problem arising from perturbing around a basic linear density variation supported by diffusion has been dealt with by Lineykin (1955) and has been extended to a β-plane model by Stommel and Veronis (1957). The dynamics is linear with geostrophic and vertical friction terms; the linear heat continuity equation expresses the balance between vertical heat advection of the basic temperature field and vertical heat diffusion.*

The case with horizontal diffusion and friction included has been studied by Pedlosky (1969). He actually considers a closed rectangular ocean and includes also the wind stress driving. This complicated problem, which involves the matching of a number of boundary layers, is worked out in detail. It is of considerable value to have such model problems completely solved; only too often in the thermocline theory are partial solutions considered. However, the linear model is oversimplified in a very fundamental respect. The real oceans have a practically insulated bottom. This condition cannot be met by a model with only a vertical, basic diffusion; in this case, the basic heat flux must obviously be vertically uniform. If lateral diffusion is added, this difficulty is avoided; but the basic state obtained by balancing the vertical and horizontal diffusion will look highly unrealistic, with about half the ocean statically unstable. It must be realized that the thermocline problem is an essentially non-linear one, through the appearance of the advection terms in the heat continuity equation.

The nonlinear thermocline problem described by the heat continuity equation, $\mathbf{v}\cdot\nabla T = \kappa T_{zz}$; plus the geostrophic-hydrostatic balance equations have been studied in several papers, beginning with Robinson and Stommel (1959). Some exact solutions have been found, where the vertical profiles are either of exponential or inverse power types. The exponential solution in particular is capable of describing some features of the real oceanic thermocline quite well; see, for example, Blandford (1965). A more general class of similarity solutions for the temperature field also exists (Robinson and Welander, 1963).

These solutions can be made to fit given surface temperature distributions and also allow the vertical velocity to vanish at the top. On the other hand, bottom conditions cannot be specified freely. It is possible to let the deep temperature approach a constant value, but a barotropic velocity field will exist that cannot be adjusted to satisfy the zero normal valve at the bottom.

The scale-depth predicted by the nonlinear thermocline theory is $S = (\kappa f L^2/g\alpha\Delta T)^{1/3}$, where α is the thermal expansion coefficient and ΔT is the characteristic horizontal temperature variation, which is usually prescribed through the top boundary condition. The value of κ is, of course, at disposal (no direct measurements of this coefficient exist in the thermocline); a value $\kappa \cong 1\ \text{cm}^2\ \text{s}^{-1}$ gives a reasonable fitting to the temperature observations. Special solutions, such as the exponential one, contain a free-scale parameter, and this can be fitted to the observations independent of the κ-value (the associated velocity field changes, however, with κ). In particular, one may consider the case $\kappa = 0$, representing an ideal fluid solution. All the exact solutions found are, however, degenerate ones because of a detailed balancing of terms in the heat continuity equations (for example, in the exponential solution $w_0 T_z$ balances κT_{zz}, where w_0 is the deep vertical velocity; all the other advection terms balance out together).

To obtain the complete solution for a closed ocean, other regimes must obviously be added. Nongeostrophic terms are required at lateral boundaries (otherwise there is a normal thermal wind across these); and, in general, horizontal heat diffusion is also required. Friction is not necessarily needed in the absence of a wind stress. At the high latitudes, a special convective regime should be added, allowing cooled surface water to overturn. This can be achieved by setting $\kappa = \infty$ whenever $T_z < 0$.†

THE GENERAL PROBLEM

The final problem of the circulation induced by wind stress and thermohaline forcing in combination can to some extent be dealt with using a generalized thermocline theory, noting that the wind stress effect can be translated to a condition on the vertical velocity at the bottom of the top Ek-

* The model assumes that salinity effects can be modeled through an "equivalent temperature"; this is correct when the Boussinesq approximation is used and the turbulent diffusion coefficients for heat and salt are assumed to be the same. The same approximation is used in other thermocline models; only in some numerical models are nonlinear equations of state used, requiring an explicit distinction in the problem between the temperature and salinity fields.

† Here is an example of a condition that makes analytical work almost impossible. On the other hand, the condition is quite simply added in numerical model calculations.

man layer $w = w_E = \text{curl}_z(\tau/f)$. The temperature variation across a thin Ekman layer can generally be neglected, but the horizontal heat advection may not necessarily be small. A vertical integration of the heat transport equation over a thin Ekman layer gives $U_E T_x + V_E T_y = q - \kappa T_z$, where $U_E = \tau^y/f$, $V_E = -\tau^x/f$ are the wind drift transport components, and q is the top heat flux; this relation applies at the bottom of the Ekman layer. The heat flux can be prescribed or related to an external temperature, as described in the section, "The General Formulation of the Problem" (pp. 63-65).

The generalized thermocline problem can conveniently be described in terms of a single equation for a function M, which is an integrated pressure function (Welander, 1971). The equation, worked out for a spherical earth, is

$$\kappa \Omega R^2 \sin 2\theta \cdot M_{zzzz} + \frac{\partial(M_{zz}, M_z)}{\partial(\lambda, \theta)} - \cot\theta \cdot M_\lambda M_{zzz} = 0, \qquad (2)$$

where λ, θ are longitude and latitude and R and Ω are the earth's radius and angular speed. The top boundary conditions are $M = M_\theta\ (\lambda, \theta)$, where M_θ is determined by w_E plus the thermal condition, which in the most general case described previously gives a relation between $M_{\lambda zz}$, $M_{\theta zz}$, M_{zz}, and M_{zzz}. The condition of no normal velocity and no normal heat diffusion at the ocean bottom add up to the needed four conditions in the vertical.

This problem will, for small diffusivities, lead to a double-scale thermocline below the Ekman layer. There is one ideal fluid scale-depth, $\delta_1 = (\Omega R^2\ w_E/g\alpha\Delta T)^{1/2}$, and a smaller scale-depth, $\delta_2 = \kappa/w_E$, that represents the required top diffusive layer in the regions of upwelling. For large κ, we come back to the thermocline scale given in the previous section. The value of κ, which marks the transition between these two cases, seems to lie below 1 $cm^2\ s^{-1}$, possibly near 0.1 $cm^2\ s^{-1}$ (Philander, private communication). For still smaller κ, the thermocline is essentially an ideal fluid phenomenon in the subtropical gyre, with water sinking along density surfaces below a convergent Ekman layer. For larger κ, on the other hand, we find a general upwelling through the thermocline, as has been suggested by Stommel.

At present, any detailed knowledge of the solution to the nonlinear problem stated above is missing, even in the simplest case where the depth is assumed uniform (lateral boundaries cannot generally be included at all in this approximation). As in the previous thermocline problem, special exact solutions or similarity form solutions can be found, but these are clearly too restrictive. For example, assuming a similarity form for the temperature $T = A(\lambda, \theta)\ F\{z\ \kappa(\lambda, \theta)\}$, the equations can be satisfied, but not for any functions of A and κ. The permissible functions restrict the boundary conditions and actually require a certain relation between the wind stress, the surface temperature, and the bottom topography fields. The danger is that the restrictions may be forgotten in the course of the discussions. If the functions look reasonable, the solution may be accepted as a rough approximation to the complete solution, at least in some interior parts. However, in the similarity solution the two-scale feature of the thermocline is completely lost. The functional relations required are, of course, just the ones needed to reduce the two scales to one. This again demonstrates the danger of working with partial solutions and using the extra freedom in parameters and functions to obtain mathematically simple cases.

When a laterally closed basin is considered, further regimes must be added, as in the previous thermocline problem. The final problem, including lateral friction and diffusion, clearly is too complicated to be solved analytically. One can look at the linear case worked out by Pedlosky (1969) and imagine how a corresponding nonlinear solution may look.

In the end one wonders, however, whether a theory aimed at a first order understanding and semiquantitative prediction of the general oceanic circulation really needs to be so complicated. The real mean circulation in the interior ocean is poorly known, but we can make some judgment from the observed mean fields of temperature, salinity, and eventually other tracer-type variables. These fields do not look too complicated in a large-scale picture; rather one sees a great deal of regularity in them. In other physical problems, the understanding of even complex phenomena have been achieved through basically simple theoretical models. In particular, it has been possible to deal successfully with some simple steady-type problems (for example, laminar flow), and systems of great disorder (statistical mechanics, kinetics of gases, etc.). In our problem, the existence of turbulence is believed to be the main obstacle for developing a simple and quantitatively good theory, but this is not necessarily the case. The possibility exists that the essential oceanic regimes are ideal fluid-like and that the role of the turbulence is secondary (except for providing the transfers at the top and the necessary overall dissipation). Another possibility is that the turbulent processes dominate the situation. In such a case, one should perhaps look for an understanding that is less mechanistic and more statistic. (The studies by Malkus, Howard, and others on the turbulent processes in certain simple systems such as Rayleigh convection and shear flow represent one interesting alternative line.)

THE CIRCUMPOLAR CURRENT AND THE WORLD OCEAN CIRCULATION

The models discussed previously deal with the circulation in a single, laterally bounded basin. The real oceans are, however, not bounded but connect to form the world ocean. The world ocean is, of course, itself bounded, but it has certain fundamentally new features. Firstly, it is multiconnected, the continents lying as "islands" in a spherical ocean. Secondly, it lacks any meridional barriers in certain latitude ranges. In the Antarctic Sea such a range exists, allowing a circumpolar current that is of critical importance for the world ocean circulation. The Arctic Sea offers another example, but this is considered to be a more isolated problem; the water exchange between this sea and the Atlantic and Pacific Oceans is usually considered negligible in global calculations.

To close the circulation problem, first of all a theory for the Antarctic circumpolar current is needed. The novelty of the circumpolar regime has been pointed out by Munk and Palmen (1951). Attempts to achieve the necessary angular momentum and vorticity balances obviously become difficult when the current is assumed zonally symmetric. For example, if the wind stress torque acting on the current is balanced by lateral friction, friction coefficient values of order 10^{10} cm^2 s^{-1} or more are needed. It seems also difficult to achieve a balance by Ekman bottom friction or by adding the effect of the net water outflow from the Antarctic Continent, which has been attempted. Stommel (1957) discusses the possibility of a nonzonal current. He points out that at least for the deeper water there is only a narrow latitude belt of free zonal passage. The current may be expected to swing north as it passes Drake Passage, allowing a pressure reaction from the South American coast to enter the problem. Mathematical solutions of the problem were later worked out (Kamenkovich, 1962; Gill, 1968), proving the existence of model solutions of this type. The phenomenon can also be reasonably well modeled in laboratory experiments using a rotating table.

In reality, the effect of the bottom topography may be important along much of the current. Pressure torques due to the combined effect of topography and stratification may, for example, play a role. Little analytical work has, however, been done on this problem.

The next step is to connect the circulations of the oceans and the Antarctic Sea. Within the framework of the linear frictional models by Stommel or Munk, the transport field for the world ocean seems to have a unique solution (Ilyin *et al.,* 1969). The nature of the solution is reasonably well understood, although the actual transport streamline field for the real world ocean geometry (assuming still, uniform depth or compensation at great depths) must be determined numerically.

With regard to the nonlinear problem, little has been done. Analytical theory for the three-dimensional world ocean circulation does not exist; as seen from the previous section, the problem is far from its solution, even for the standard rectangular case.

While a precise analytic theory is lacking, a very simple model based on certain plausible assumptions of the vertical circulation has appeared, which has changed our ideas of the deep world ocean circulation in some basic ways. In short, it is assumed that the concentrated sinking of deep and bottom water (in the North Atlantic and the Antarctic Sea) is balanced by a reasonably uniform upwelling through the thermocline. If geostrophic motion is assumed, the relation $\beta v = f w_z$ holds, requiring a general poleward flow in the deep ocean, where w_z by this assumption should be positive. To obtain a mass balance, the sinking water must find a nongeostrophic regime that can carry it toward the equator. The same arguments that apply in the problem of wind-driven circulation suggest a western boundary current. Actually the problem becomes formally much the same, translating the vertical velocity at thermocline depths to an equivalent wind stress. The mass-balance condition is, however, changed by the presence of the sources of deep water. The deep boundary currents actually involve both the source water and a recirculating part of the interior ocean water.

The above model originates from Stommel and has been developed theoretically by Stommel and Arons (1960a,b). It has also tested experimentally (Stommel *et al.,* 1958). The search for the deep western boundary currents in the real oceans has been successful; there are firm indications of currents of this type in all three oceans. The dynamics of these currents is, however, not yet fully understood. It seems likely that topography plays an important role in determining their width and structure; some theoretical calculations based on such an idea are being carried out by Stommel (private communication).

The basic idea that an interior net upwelling under geostrophic constraint will require a deep western boundary current seems to be well demonstrated. However, it must be remembered that the oceans locally may show quite different regimes. It is still possible that the water sinks in the subtropical gyre as predicted by the ideal fluid thermocline model. It is also possible that large deviations from the geostrophic balance occur even in the interior oceans. To get a good quantitative theory, it is necessary, even in the Stommel–Arons model, to know the distribution of the vertical velocity at an interior level. This velocity can only be found by solving the three-dimensional circulation problem in detail, and we are back to all the original difficulties.

CONCLUSION

Looking back on the development of the analytical theory, the major milestones appear to be the first mathematical circulation model by Ekman (1905, 1923), the Sverdrup (1947) transport calculation, and the demonstration of the westward intensification by Stommel (1948). These models seem to give qualitative and possibly semiquantitative descriptions of the circulation of an upper layer in the oceans. Later analytical work has been concentrated on such problems as the effects of nonlinear terms in the boundary currents, the thermocline and the thermohaline circulation, and the role of topography. It must be admitted that these problems have not been satisfactorily solved. The nonlinear models of wind-driven circulation may provide an improved picture of the western boundary currents; they have not been able to predict the total transports correctly. The interior Sverdrup solution provides at most half of the observed Gulf Stream transport, using standard wind stress estimates. The nonlinear models can give an increased boundary current transport, but only by adding an eastern boundary current or allowing a breakdown of the interior linear regime. Neither of these possibilities seem likely.

The effect of bottom topography and stratification in combination is probably the most important feature that needs to be added. Numerical models have included both effects and convincingly demonstrated their importance; analytically, little has been done on this problem.

With regard to the nonlinear thermocline problem, a good start has been made; but at the moment we see a deadlock. It has not been possible to work out the problem completely, even in a rectangular basin. The dependence of the solution on the diffusion parameter is still very incompletely understood, even in the interior regime.

At this stage numerical models may turn out very useful. If the numerical experiments can tell us which processes are of first-order importance for the circulation, and which terms form the first-order balance in the equations, we have already gained much. Analytical theory is probably less restricted by techniques than usually believed. Once the problem is defined and there is an urgent need to solve it, the appropriate techniques usually can be found. If we were convinced that the Gulf Stream separation was the key to the understanding of the Atlantic circulation, this problem would have been tackled and solved by now. If we were convinced that the circulation was an essential effect of turbulence, we may have been able to crack even this problem. In the end, the existence of the proper ideas turns out to be the most important factor for our progress.

REFERENCES

Baker, D. J., and A. R. Robinson. 1969. A laboratory model for the general ocean circulation. Philos. Trans. R. Soc. Lond. Ser. A. 265:533.

Beardsley, R. C. 1969. A laboratory model of the wind-driven ocean circulation. J. Fluid Mech. 38:255.

Blandford, R. R. 1965. Notes on the theory of the thermocline. J. Mar. Res. 23:18.

Bretherton, F. P., and J. S. Turner. 1968. On the mixing of angular momentum in a stirred rotating fluid. J. Fluid Mech. 32:449.

Bryan, K. 1963. A numerical investigation of a non-linear model of wind-driven ocean. J. Atmos. Sci. 20:594.

Carrier, C. F., and A. R. Robinson. 1962. On the theory of the wind-driven ocean circulation. J. Fluid Mech. 12:49–80.

Charney, J. G. 1955. The Gulf Stream as an inertial boundary. Proc. Natl. Acad. Sci. 41:731. Washington, D.C.

Ekman, V. W. 1905. On the influence of the earth's rotation on ocean currents. Ark. Mat. Astron. Fys. 2(11):1–52.

Ekman, V. W. 1923. Über horizontalzirkulation bei Winderzeugten Meeresströmungen. Ark. Mat. Astron. Fys. 17(26), 74 pp.

Fandry, C. B., and L. M. Leslie. 1972. A note on the effect of latitudinally varying bottom topography on the wind-driven ocean circulation. Tellus 24:164.

Fofonoff, N. P. 1954. Steady flow in a frictionless homogeneous ocean. J. Mar. Res. 13:254.

Gill, A. E. 1968. A linear model of the Antarctic circumpolar current. J. Fluid Mech. 32:465.

Gill, A. E. 1971. Ocean models. Philos. Trans. R. Soc. Lond. Ser. A. 270:391.

Gill, A. E. 1972. Equatorial currents. Stenciled preprint.

Greenspan, H. 1968. The Theory of Rotating Fluids. Cambridge University Press, London.

Hellerman, S. 1965. Computation of wind stress fields over the Atlantic Ocean. Mon. Weather Rev. 93:239.

Holopainen, E. O. 1967. A determination of the wind-driven ocean circulation from the vorticity budget of the atmosphere. Pure Appl. Geophys. 67:156.

Ilyin, A. N., and V. M. Kamenkovich. 1963. On the influence of friction on ocean currents. Dokl. Akad. Nauk. USSR 150:1274.

Ilyin, A. N., V. M. Kamenkovich, T. G. Zhugrina, and M. M. Silkina. 1969. On the calculation in the world ocean (stationary problem). Izv. Akad. Nauk. USSR Atmos. Oceanic Phys. 5(11):1160.

Kamenkovich, V. M. 1962. The theory of Antarctic circumpolar current. Inst. Oceanol. Acad. Sci. USSR 56.

Kamenkovich, V. M. 1967. On the coefficients of eddy diffusion and eddy viscosity in large-scale oceanic and atmospheric motions. Izv. Akad. Nauk. USSR Atmos. Oceanic Phys. 3:1326.

Kirwan, A. D., Jr. 1969. Formulation of the constitutive equations for large-scale turbulent mixing. J. Geophys. Res. 74:69.

Knauss, J. A. 1969. A note on the transport of the Gulf Stream. Deep-Sea Res. Suppl. 16:117.

Lighthill, M. J. 1971. Time-varying currents. Philos. Trans. R. Soc. Lond. Ser. A. 270:371.

Lineykin, P. C. 1955. On the determination of the thickness of the baroclinic layer of fluid heated uniformly from below. Dokl. Akad. Nauk. USSR 101:461.

Lorenz, E. N. 1967. The nature and theory of the general circulation of the atmosphere. WMO No. 218. 115 pp.

Manabe, S., and K. Bryan. 1969. Climate calculation with a combined ocean–atmosphere model. J. Atmos. Sci. 26:786.

Moore, D. W. 1963. Rossby waves in ocean circulation. Deep-Sea Res. 10:735–48.

Morgan, G. W. 1956. On the wind-driven circulation. Tellus 8:301.

Munk, W. H. 1950. On the wind-driven ocean circulation. J. Met. 7:79.

Munk, W. H., G. W. Groves, and G. F. Carrier. 1950. Note on the dynamics of the Gulf Stream. J. Mar. Res. 9:218.

Munk, W. H., and E. Palmen. 1951. Notes on the dynamics of the Antarctic circumpolar current. Tellus 3:53.

Niiler, P. P., and W. J. Schmitz, Jr. 1969. A note on the kinetic energy exchange between fluctuations and mean flow in the surface layer of the Florida current. Tellus 21:814.

Parsons, A. T. 1969. A two-layer model of the Gulf Stream separation. J. Fluid Mech. 39(3):511–28.

Pedlosky, J. 1967. Fluctuating winds and the ocean circulation. Tellus 19:250.

Pedlosky, J. 1969. Linear theory of the circulation of a stratified ocean. J. Fluid Mech. 35:185.

Robinson, A. R. 1965. Oceanography, p. 504. *In* Research Frontiers in Fluid Dynamics. Interscience, New York.

Robinson, A. R. 1971. Boundary layers in ocean circulation models. Ann. Rev. Fluid Mech. 3:293.

Robinson, A. R., and H. Stommel. 1959. The oceanic thermocline and the associated thermohaline circulation. Tellus 11:295.

Robinson, A. R., and P. Welander. 1963. Thermal circulation on a rotating sphere, with application to the oceanic thermocline. J. Mar. Res. 21:25.

Robinson, A. R., and P. P. Niiler. 1967. The theory of free inertial currents. I. Path and structure. Tellus 19:269.

Stewart, R. W. 1964. The influence of friction on inertial models of oceanic circulation. *In* Studies in Oceanography. University of Washington Press.

Stockman, W. B. 1946. Equations for a field of total flow induced by the wind in a non-homogeneous sea. Comptes Rendus (Dokl.) de l'acad. Sci. l'URSS 54:403.

Stommel, H. 1948. The westward intensification of wind-driven ocean currents. Trans. Am. Geophys. Union 29(2):202–06.

Stommel, H. 1957. Survey of ocean current theory. Deep-Sea Res. 4:149.

Stommel, H. 1965. The Gulf Stream. University of California Press, Berkeley.

Stommel, H., and G. Veronis. 1957. Steady convective motion in a horizontal layer of fluid heated uniformly above and non-uniformly from below. Tellus 9:401.

Stommel, H., A. B. Arons, and A. J. Faller. 1958. Some examples of stationary planetary flow patterns in bounded basins. Tellus 10:17.

Stommel, H., and A. B. Arons. 1960a. On the abyssal circulation of the world ocean. I. Stationary planetary flow patterns on a sphere. Deep-Sea Res. 6:140.

Stommel, H., and A. B. Arons. 1960b. On the abyssal circulation of the world ocean. II. An idealized model of the circulation pattern and amplitude in oceanic basins. Deep-Sea Res. 6:217.

Sverdrup, H. U. 1947. Wind-driven currents in a baroclinic ocean, with application to the equatorial currents of eastern Pacific. Proc. Natl. Acad. Sci. 33:318. Washington, D.C.

Veronis, G. 1966a. Wind-driven ocean circulation. Part 1: Linear theory and perturbation analysis; Part 2: Numerical solutions of the non-linear problem. Deep-Sea Res. 13:17, 31.

Veronis, G. 1966b. Generation of mean ocean circulation by fluctuating winds. Tellus 18:67.

Veronis, G. 1972a. Large-scale ocean circulation. Unpublished paper.

Veronis, G. 1972b. On the theoretical models of the thermocline circulation. Deep-Sea Res. Suppl. 16:301.

Webster, F. 1961. The effect of meanders on the kinetic energy balance of the Gulf Stream. Tellus 13:392.

Welander, P. 1967. On the oscillatory instability of a differentially heated fluid loop. J. Fluid Mech. 29:17.

Welander, P. 1968. Wind-driven circulation in one and two-layer ocean of variable depth. Tellus 20:1.

Welander, P. 1971. The thermocline problem. Philos. Trans. R. Soc. Lond. Ser. A. 270:415.

Welander, P. 1972. Lateral friction in the oceans as an effect of potential vorticity mixing. Stenciled preprint.

DISCUSSION

PEDLOSKY: Geostrophy and Ekman theory alone are not sufficient to obtain the Sverdrup balance. The latter requires an additional constraint.

NIILER: In a restricted region in the southeastern portion of the North Atlantic, away from cold water eddies and eastern boundary currents, it may be possible to test quantitatively the Sverdrup theory. I have calculated the differences of the integrated pressure as required by the Sverdrup equation and compared them with what one might expect from the Hellerman wind stress data. The comparison is quite good. It might be possible to make similar tests in other parts of the world ocean, such as the South Atlantic.

POND: I seriously question the validity of the Hellerman wind stress data; therefore, you may be getting good agreement with bad data. One of the problems with the Hellerman data is that the drag coefficient that he used may produce unreliable stress estimates for wind speeds at around 8 m/s.

NIILER: The region in which I conducted my study was in the trade wind region of the Atlantic, and I don't think that this was a problem in that particular region.

REVIEW OF NUMERICAL OCEAN CIRCULATION MODELS USING THE OBSERVED DENSITY FIELD

A. S. SARKISYAN and V. P. KEONJIYAN

INTRODUCTION

Until the 1960's, the only methods for solving various problems of sea current dynamics were analytical. However, nonlinearity of ocean-thermohydrodynamic equations, as well as the complicated bottom relief and shore contours, require the use of numerical methods for the investigation of a real sea in a realistic oceanic basin. The first numerical experiments have shown that, even after a number of simplifications, the calculation of the density field involves a large number of calculations in computers (Sarkisyan, 1961, 1962; Sarkisyan and Garmatyuk, 1965).

Oceanographers have accumulated many hydrological observations used in composing atlases of density fields. At the same time, the observations of the horizontal components of the currents are sparse and rather expensive to obtain, while the vertical component is rarely estimated at all. Hence, it appears necessary to derive information about current fields from the available information of the density fields. Until the middle of the 1960's, the only method for obtaining information about current fields was the dynamical method of current calculation, which has a number of drawbacks, the most important of which is that the reference level must be chosen somewhat artificially. This is the reason why numerical methods that use the density field, but eliminate the shortcomings of the dynamical method, must be used to calculate the current velocity, as well as the other hydrodynamical characteristics.

STATEMENT OF THE PROBLEM

The physical nature of the problem is the following. Consider an oceanic basin of arbitrary form and arbitrary bottom relief. If part of the wall of the basin is an open boundary, assume that the normal mass flux is given there. In the basin, the density field is also given as an arbitrary function of the coordinates. At the surface of the basin, the wind stress, which is required to calculate the current velocity and other hydrodynamical characteristics, is given. Under this statement, two problems could be solved: (a) the calculation of stationary or seasonal currents using long-term average annual or seasonal density and wind fields, and (b) the short-range forecast of currents due to nonstationarity of the wind field, but with a stationary density field.

In most of the works mentioned below, the sphericity of the earth is taken into account. A number of calculations have been carried out for the Southern Hemisphere and even for the world ocean. For the sake of simplicity, we shall write all the equations in a cartesian coordinate system for a basin situated in the Northern Hemisphere.

For solving this problem we shall proceed from the following system of equations:

$$\mu \frac{\partial^2 u}{\partial z^2} + lv = \frac{1}{\rho_0} \frac{\partial P}{\partial x} + A, \tag{1}$$

$$\mu \frac{\partial^2 v}{\partial z^2} - lu = \frac{1}{\rho_0} \frac{\partial P}{\partial y} + B, \tag{2}$$

$$\frac{\partial u}{\partial x} + \frac{\partial v}{\partial y} + \frac{\partial w}{\partial z} = 0, \tag{3}$$

$$P = \rho_0 g \left(\zeta + \frac{P_a}{\rho_0 g} \right) + g \int_0^z \rho \, dz \cong \rho_0 g \zeta + g \int_0^z \rho \, dz. \tag{4}$$

Where A and B denote the effects of inertial forces and lateral exchange,

$$A = \frac{\partial u}{\partial t} + u\frac{\partial u}{\partial x} + v\frac{\partial u}{\partial y} - A_l \Delta u, \tag{5}$$

$$B = \frac{\partial v}{\partial t} + u\frac{\partial v}{\partial x} + v\frac{\partial v}{\partial y} - A_l \Delta v. \tag{6}$$

The unknown functions here are the current velocity components for the axes x, y, and z, and the ocean reference level ζ; the axis x is directed to the east, y is to the north, and z is vertically downward.

The boundary conditions are the following:

At the ocean surface,

$$\rho_o \mu \frac{\partial u}{\partial z}\bigg|_{z=0} = -\tau_x^{(o)}; \quad \rho_o \mu \frac{\partial v}{\partial z}\bigg|_{z=0} = -\tau_y^{(o)};$$

$$w\bigg|_{z=0} = 0. \tag{7}$$

At the bottom of the ocean,

$$w(H) = u(H)\frac{\partial H}{\partial x} + v(H)\frac{\partial H}{\partial y}. \tag{8}$$

For the horizontal components of the current velocity, the nonslip conditions are the following:

$$u = v = 0, \tag{9}$$

while the conditions of sliding without friction are,

$$\rho_o \mu \frac{\partial u}{\partial z}\bigg|_{z=H} = \rho_o \mu \frac{\partial v}{\partial z}\bigg|_{z=H} = 0. \tag{10}$$

In the case when the effect of the lateral exchange is not taken into account ($A_l = 0$), the component of the horizontal velocity normal to the boundary is specified; in particular, in the solid parts of the boundary, this velocity equals zero. If the pressure field P were known, it would be possible to find u and v from Eqs. (1) and (2) and w from Eq. (3). Since the density field is given, it is obvious from Eq. (4) that in order to estimate the pressure it is necessary to determine the reference level $\zeta(x, y, t)$.

Thus, the solution of the problem is reduced to determining the field ζ. If the equator is not taken into account, and the components u and v in the expressions for A and B are substituted by geostrophical approximation, after some simple modifications we shall obtain the following equation for ζ (Sarkisyan, 1969b):

$$\overbrace{\frac{1}{2\alpha}\Delta\zeta}^{\text{I}} - \overbrace{\frac{H\beta}{l}\frac{d\zeta}{dx}}^{\text{II}} + \overbrace{J(H,\zeta)}^{\text{III}} + \overbrace{\frac{H}{l}\frac{d}{dt}\Delta\zeta}^{\text{IV}} + \overbrace{\frac{gH}{l^2} J(\zeta, \Delta\zeta)}^{\text{V}}$$

$$- \overbrace{\frac{A_e H}{l}\Delta\Delta\zeta}^{\text{VI}} = \frac{1}{\rho_o g}\text{rot}_z \vec{\tau} - \frac{\beta}{\rho_o g l}\tau_x + f; \tag{11}$$

$$f = -\overbrace{\frac{1}{2\alpha\rho_o}\int_o^H \Delta\rho\, dz}^{1} + \overbrace{\frac{\beta}{\rho_o l}\int_o^H (H - z)\frac{d\rho}{dx} dz}^{2}$$

$$-\overbrace{\frac{1}{\rho_o}\int_o^H J(H, \rho)\, dz}^{3} - \overbrace{\frac{1}{\rho_o l}\int_o^H (H - z)\frac{d}{dt}\Delta\rho\, dz}^{4}$$

$$\overbrace{+\frac{g}{l^2 g_o} J\left[\zeta, \int_o^H (H - z)\Delta\rho\, dz\right] - \frac{g}{l^2 \rho_o} J\left[\Delta\zeta, \int_o^H (H - z)\rho\, dz\right]}^{5}$$

$$-\overbrace{\frac{g}{\rho_o{}^2 l^2}\int_o^H J\left(\int_o^z \rho dz, \int_o^z \Delta\rho\, dz\right)}^{5}$$

$$+\overbrace{\frac{A_e}{\rho_o l}\int_o^H (H - z)\Delta\Delta\rho\, dz}^{6} \tag{12}$$

Using the approximations given in Sarkisyan (1966b), the components of the current velocity are determined according to the following formula:

$$u + iv = \frac{1}{\rho_o l}\left(i\frac{dP}{dx} - \frac{dP}{dy}\right) + \frac{(\tau_x + i\,\tau_y)e^{-\alpha(1+i)z}}{\alpha\,\rho_o\,\nu(1 + \text{i})}$$

$$+\frac{1}{l}(Ai - B) - \frac{\delta}{\rho_o l}\left(i\frac{dP(H)}{dx} - \frac{dP(H)}{dy}\right) e^{(1+i)\,\alpha\,(z - H)}$$

$$-\frac{\delta}{l}\left[iA(H) - B(H)\right] e^{(i+1)\,\alpha\,(z - H)}. \tag{13}$$

Here $\alpha = (l/2\mu)^{1/2}$ and $\delta = 0$ or 1 depending on whether the bottom is slippery or not.

In the right-hand side of Eq. (13), A and B are expressed by the geostrophical approximation through P, while P is expressed by ζ and ρ with the help of Eq. (4). Thus, the unknown functions are expressed by the given field ρ and the unknown field ζ. The presented scheme allows the performance of calculations in a middle-class computer for any basin, since it demands a minimum of the memory block.

For determining ζ on the contour of the boundary of the basin, the relations of Sarkisyan and Ivanov (1972) are used:

$$\frac{\partial \zeta}{\partial x} = \frac{l}{gH}\frac{\partial \psi}{\partial x} - \frac{1}{H\rho_0}\int_0^H (H-z)\frac{\partial \rho}{\partial x}\,dz + \frac{\tau_x}{\rho_0 g H}, \quad (14)$$

$$\frac{\partial \zeta}{\partial y} = \frac{l}{gH}\frac{\partial \psi}{\partial y} - \frac{1}{H\rho_0}\int_0^H (H-z)\frac{\partial \rho}{\partial y}\,dz + \frac{\tau_y}{\rho_0 g H}. \quad (15)$$

If the "softened" boundary conditions are used on the lateral boundaries, i.e., if ψ is considered to be given, then Eqs. (14) and (15) will be relations for determining ζ on the contour confining the basin. The physical sense of the terms in the left-hand side of Eq. (11) is the following. Term I is due to the Ekman bottom friction; II, the β-effect; III, the bottom relief effect; IV, the local derivatives of u and v with respect to time; V, the nonlinear inertial terms; and VI, lateral exchange.

In deriving Eq. (11), we used formula (4). The left-hand side of the former depends upon the first term of the right-hand side of the latter and the expression f upon the second term. For the sake of convenience, we denote the "related" terms of Eq. (12) by the corresponding Arabic numerals. Thus, the 1st is the baroclinic effect of the Ekman bottom friction, the 2d is the baroclinic β-effect, the 3d is the joint effect of baroclinicity and the bottom relief (JEBAR).

REVIEW OF SOME SPECIFIC MODELS AND THEIR RESULTS

Koshlyakov (1961) evaluated the characteristic values of terms I-III, 1-3, $\text{rot}_z\,\boldsymbol{\tau}$, and those of the lateral exchange effect in Eq. (11). The author came to the conclusion that the effects of lateral friction and those of bottom friction could be neglected.

Koshlyakov has also succeeded in building an equation of first order with respect to ζ and suggests that it should be solved using the method of characteristics. He has not yet carried out the concrete calculations, but almost all the evaluations he has performed have proved to be right, with the exception of underestimating the order of magnitude of terms I and 1. According to his evaluations, the bottom friction effect is two orders of magnitude less than that of the wind stress. In what follows we shall see that they are of the same order.

In the left-hand side of Eq. (11) there are four groups of terms that Koshlyakov has not taken into account. These are I, IV, V, and VI. All of them are small values of almost the same order. But if we are going to solve the problem for a closed basin, we should take into consideration at least one of these groups. For solving stationary problems it is convenient to consider group I. Then, we obtain the following simplified equation:

$$\underbrace{\frac{1}{2\alpha}\Delta\zeta}_{\text{I}} - \underbrace{\frac{H\beta}{l}\frac{\partial \zeta}{\partial x}}_{\text{II}} + \underbrace{J(H,\zeta)}_{\text{III}} = \frac{1}{\rho_0 g}\text{rot}_z\,\boldsymbol{\tau} - \frac{\beta}{\rho_0 g l}\tau_x - \underbrace{\frac{1}{2\alpha\rho_0}\int_0^H \Delta\rho\,dz}_{1} + \underbrace{\frac{\beta}{\rho_0 l}\int_0^H (H-z)\frac{\partial \rho}{\partial x}\,dz}_{2} - \underbrace{\frac{1}{\rho_0}\int_0^H J(H,\rho)\,dz}_{3} \quad (16)$$

If the terms of groups I and 1 are neglected, we obtain Koshlyakov's equation from formula (16).

The numerical model and the results of calculations of ζ, u, v, and w on the basis of Eq. (16) have been published (Sarkisyan, 1966b). The values of ζ on the basin's boundary were determined using the relations (14) and (15) and the given water flux. The numerical method is extremely simple: In the left side of Eq. (16), the derivatives of the first order were substituted by directed differences (the approximation of the first order), depending on the signs of their coefficients, in order to retain diagonal dominance. The derived system was then solved with the help of the method of successive approximations of Gauss-Zeidel. The concrete calculations were carried out for five layers of the North Atlantic using the density fields taken from the maps produced by Muromtsev (1963).

Consider in brief the major results of these calculations. As is well known, long before the publication of Sarkisyan (1966b), two different methods of reference level calculations were widely used: (a) the classical method of the homogeneous ocean, $\rho = 0$ in the right side of Eq. (16), the development of which was begun by Ekman (1905, 1906, 1923); and (b) the dynamical method, and the method of Lineikin (1957), in both of which ζ is determined exclusively from the density field with the help of the elementary formula:

$$\zeta = -\frac{1}{\rho_0}\int_0^H \rho\,dz. \quad (17)$$

In the dynamical method, H is the depth of the zero surface, whereas in Lineikin's method it represents the depth of the baroclinic layer. Practically, they are similar, both of them being of the order of 1-1.5 km. Certainly, in the dynamical method there is also the indirect influence of the wind, while in the homogeneous ocean model the only direct influence is that of the wind stress. By solving Eq. (16), we can compare these two opposed methods. The calculations have shown that the homogeneous ocean model leads to extremely small values of the current's velocity (1 cm/s and smaller), whereas considering the baroclinicity of seawater we have obtained velocities of the order of 15-20 cm/s. Therefore, the classical model of a homogeneous ocean cannot be a good first approximation in theories of the ocean or deep-sea currents. So, it is necessary to consider the sea baroclinic. Among the terms of the right side of Eq. (16) containing baroclinicity, the main ones are group 2 (the baroclinic β-effect) and group 3 (JEBAR). As to the bottom friction baroclinic effect (group 1), this factor is of the same order as $\mathrm{rot}_z\tau$, i.e., one order less than the main ones. The direction of the calculated current velocity field is qualitatively correct in representing the familiar notions of large-scale circulation in this basin. According to the observations made by Swallow and Worthington (1961) in the Gulf Stream area, the current, at the depth of 0.5-1.5 km, reverses its direction. The absolute value of the calculated horizontal current's velocity does not attenuate with depth. Calculations with artificial changes in the bottom relief have once again shown the significance of this factor, the influence of which speads nearly up to the ocean surface. The vertical component of the current's velocity has been also calculated and proved to be of the order of 10^{-6}-10^{-5} cm/s, growing with the depth. It is with the relief of the ocean bottom rather than with the wind field that the areas of upwelling and downwelling correlate.

In subsequent years, numerous calculations for a number of basins were carried out with the help of the method described above. In particular, the work of Sarkisyan *et al.* (1967) concerns experiments with changes in the bottom relief. Smoothing down the bottom relief has substantially altered the form of the reference level. The seasonal changes in the reference level, as well as the velocity of the surface currents, have turned out to be small regardless of great changes in the wind field.

The fact is that this factor is not significant, and the seasonal changes in the density anomaly had a rather poor representation in Muromtsev's maps. Using the model mentioned above, Bolgurtsev (1969) and Bolgurtsev *et al.* (1969) calculated the reference level and currents for the Antarctic sector of the Pacific Ocean. These calculations have confirmed those that had pointed out the significance of baroclinicity and the bottom relief and the slow decreasing of the current velocity with depth.

It is worthwhile to note some interesting results of the numerical experiments of calculation of the Caribbean Sea currents (Sarkisyan, 1969c). It is known that a great mass of water passes through this sea, subsequently crossing the Gulf of Mexico to form the Florida current. The question arises whether it is possible to obtain the general pattern of the circulation in this sea only by the specified water flux through the boundaries and the observed field of wind stress. The following experiments have been carried out. Suppose that 30 Sverdrups of water enter the Caribbean Sea through the straits of the Lesser Antilles Islands, coming out through the Yucatan Strait. Considering also the wind stress, we can calculate the current in this sea if it were filled with homogeneous water. In spite of such a great flux through the basin, the currents in the Caribbean proved to be weak and evenly distributed all over the sea. If the baroclinicity of the seawater is taken into consideration, there appear current velocities of the order of 10 cm/s. Thus, for obtaining a correct pattern of currents, it is insufficient to give the real water flux only. We believe that it is much more important to have a good atlas of density fields. In 1970 the maps made by Muromtsev (1963) were used for completing more accurate calculations of the reference level and current velocity in the North Atlantic (Sarkisyan and Pastukhov, 1970). Changes in the model were made; namely, the inertial terms and the lateral exchange effect were included, the horizontal spacing was taken to be half as large as in the previous case (in the area of the Gulf Stream four times smaller), and instead of five levels, the density fields of all the levels available in Muromtsev's atlas were used. The main results of this work are as follows. The effects of the nonlinear inertial terms and lateral exchange (when A_e = 10^8 CGS) turned out to be insignificant. The reason is that the minimal spacing in the area of the Gulf Stream was still rather big (140 km), but subsequent decreasing of the spacing is not advisable because the density maps are rough. The neglect of the wind stress over all parts of the ocean changes the amplitude of ζ only by 10 percent; while, if we neglect the density anomaly only at some points, it will lead to substantial changes in the given region. Hence, the major indicator of currents is the density anomaly. While calculating ζ on the basin boundary, the bottom friction can be neglected. The anomaly of the deep layer density (below 1.5 km) slightly affects ζ, i.e., the surface gradient currents.

Diagnostic calculations of the reference level and the current velocity in the southern Pacific are presented in Sarkisyan and Perederey (1972). They present a table of the absolute values of the terms in the right-hand side of Eq. (16), which shows that both group 1 and $\mathrm{rot}_z\tau$ are one or two orders of magnitude smaller than groups 2 and 3. It has been shown that the consideration of baroclinicity in the upper 100-m layer leads to an amplitude that is seven times larger than that of the reference level in a homogeneous ocean. The maps of ζ given in the work mentioned above have been obtained by the dynamical method, that is using formula (17) with H = 1 km. If Eq. (16) is solved with the baroclinic layer depth equal to 1 km, the picture obtained is in good agreement with the former case, which proves that the dynamical method is a reliable first approximation in calculating ζ.

In the works mentioned above, the problem was to determine the reference level ζ, but the fact is that those problems could also be solved using the function of the total water flux ψ. For passing from ζ to ψ it is sufficient to use the relationships in Eqs. (14) and (15). Then, from formula (11), one can obtain the equation for ψ.

$$\underbrace{\frac{1}{2\alpha H}\Delta\psi}_{\text{I}} + \underbrace{\frac{\beta\partial\psi}{\partial x}}_{\text{II}} \underbrace{-\frac{l}{H}J(H,\psi)}_{\text{III}} + \underbrace{\frac{\partial}{\partial t}\Delta\psi}_{\text{IV}} + \underbrace{\frac{1}{H}J(\psi,\Delta\psi)}_{\text{V}}$$

$$\underbrace{-A_e\Delta\Delta\psi}_{\text{VI}} = \frac{\text{rot}_z\,\tau}{\rho_0} - f_1, \quad (18)$$

$$f_1 = \overbrace{-\frac{g}{2\rho_0\alpha H}\int_0^H z\,\Delta\rho\,dz}^{1} \overbrace{-\frac{g}{\rho H}\int_0^H zJ(H,\rho)\,dz}^{3}$$

$$+\overbrace{\left(\frac{g}{\rho_0 l}\right)^2\left\{\frac{1}{H}J\left[\int_0^H \rho\,dz, \int_0^H (H-z)\,\Delta\rho\,dz\right]\right.}^{5}$$

$$\overbrace{\left.-\int_0^H J\left[\int_0^z \rho\,dz, \int_0^H \Delta\rho\,dz\right]\right\}}^{5}$$

$$+\left(\frac{\partial H}{\partial J} + \frac{H\beta}{l}\right)\frac{\tau_x}{\rho_0 H} - \frac{\partial H}{\partial x}\frac{\tau_J}{\rho_0 H}. \quad (19)$$

First, the similarity of Eqs. (11) and (18) should be noted. The corresponding terms of these equations are denoted by the same number. Here, as in Eq. (11), the left-hand side is formed by the first term of the right-hand side of formula (4), whereas f_1 is formed by the second one. If the last terms in the right-hand sides of Eqs. (14) and (15) are neglected, and parameter l is assumed to be nearly constant, then, using formula (17) we can easily get the formula of the total flux function determined by the dynamical method:

$$\psi = \frac{-g}{lg}\int_0^H z\rho\,dz. \quad (20)$$

The only difference between Eqs. (11) and (18) is the absence of groups with even numbers in f_1. From what follows one can judge whether this difference is significant. Sarkisyan (1969b) presents the derivation of Eqs. (11) and (18), as well as their analysis and the result of preliminary calculations. He also shows the shortcomings of the barotropic models of the oceanic circulation. Before giving the conclusions of this paper, it would be useful to mention some works on the total flux theory.

Stockman (1946) succeeded in deriving the equation of the total flux, according to which the balance between group VI and $\text{rot}_z\tau$ is realized. Sverdrup (1947) suggested that it should be calculated from the balance between II and $\text{rot}_z\tau$. Stommel (1948) calculated ψ from the balance between groups I, II, and $\text{rot}_z\tau$; he was the first to demonstrate the role of the β-effect in the current intensification of the western shore of the ocean. Munk (1950) calculated ψ from the balance between II, VI, and $\text{rot}_z\tau$. Ivanov and Kamenkovich (1959) investigated the balance between I–III and $\text{rot}_z\tau$, while Carrier and Robinson (1962) studied the balance between the terms of II, IV, V, VI, and $\text{rot}_z\tau$, etc. The list could be extended to hundreds of works. Because our task is not to review the articles on the total currents theory, we have enumerated only some of them to show the main drawbacks of this theory. In all of these works, only the first term of the right-hand side of Eq. (18) is taken into account. The only difference between them is that each time some of the terms of the left-hand side of this equation are opposed to $\text{rot}_z\tau$. Moreover, based on the well-known work of Sverdrup (1947) and Stommel (1948), the field ψ beyond the western boundary layer is often calculated thus:

$$\beta\frac{\partial\psi}{\partial x} = \frac{\text{rot}_z\tau}{\rho_0}. \quad (21)$$

Therefore, to obtain the fundamental equation of the total water flux theory, it is first necessary to assume that $f_1 = 0$ in Eq. (18), thus assuming the homogeneity of the seawater. As it was shown above, the homogeneous ocean model leads to unrealistically small values of the current velocity. Sarkisyan (1969b) showed this not only with the example of calculating ζ, but also with calculating ψ. After evaluating the characteristic values, it has been established that when investigating the large-scale currents outside the boundary layers, one can determine ψ with sufficient accuracy from the simplified variant of Eq. (18):

$$\frac{1}{2\alpha H}\Delta\psi + \beta\frac{\partial\psi}{\partial x} + \frac{l}{H}J(H,\psi) = \frac{\text{rot}_z\tau}{\rho_0} - \frac{g}{2\alpha\rho_0 H}\int_0^H z\Delta\rho\,dz$$
$$-\frac{g}{\rho_0 H}\int_0^H zJ(H,\rho)\,dz. \quad (22)$$

The preliminary diagnostic calculations have shown that in right-hand side of Eq. (22), group 3, that is JEBAR, is the major factor, whereas group 1 and $\text{rot}_z\tau$ are the minor ones. Thus, it was found that Sverdrup's relation is not fulfilled, and this is the main shortcoming of the works on the total currents theory.

To get a correct estimate of the integral water flux in the real ocean, the first thing to do is to take into consideration the JEBAR. Here we obtain a flux that is almost one order of magnitude larger than those obtained according to Sverdrup's relation. Eq. (22) was derived by Welander (1959), but until 1969 nobody appreciated the importance of JEBAR in this equation. It is more important to take into account this factor in Eq. (21) than in Eq. (18). If the right-hand side of formula (18) contains two main groups of terms, viz. 2 and 3, then in the right-hand side of Eq. (22) the only dominant factor is the JEBAR. This can also be understood from a physical point of view: The influence of the bottom relief upon the integral water flux is greater than upon the surface current.

A number of diagnostic calculations have been carried out on the basis of the model mentioned above (Ivanov, 1970, 1971; Kozlov, 1971; Sarkisyan and Ivanov, 1971, 1972). The main results of these calculations are the following. Sarkisyan and Ivanov (1971) present the calculations of the fields ζ and ψ, as well as the velocity of horizontal currents on eight levels of the North Atlantic. The density field in the upper 1.5-km layer was taken from Muromtsev's maps (1963a), and below it was extrapolated to the bottom. It has been found that even taking into account the baroclinicity of the upper layer of 1.5 km, a field ψ is obtained that has nothing in common with ψ obtained from Sverdrup's relation. The regard for baroclinicity in the lower layers influences ζ little, but transforms ψ greatly, making the amplitude of one order of magnitude larger than that of Sverdrup's; while in the middle latitudes, we can observe an intensive cyclonic rotation instead of the conventional anticyclonic one (in the total water transport theory). The velocity of the horizontal currents in upper layers calculated with ζ and ψ is practically the same, the differences being more significant at lower depths. The subsequent calculations (Sarkisyan and Ivanov, 1972), with more successful extrapolations, have somewhat decreased the amplitude of ψ; but the main conclusion remains the same: The Sverdrup transport is too small, and the comparison of the integral transport with the surface currents often used in the total flux theory is groundless. At the depth of 0.5–1 km under the Gulf Stream there appears the countercurrent that is the decisive factor in forming the field ψ. It has been shown that changes in the extrapolation method, as well as changes in the bottom relief, transform the field ψ to a great extent, weakly affecting ζ. Simultaneously with Sarkisyan and Ivanov (1971), Kozlov (1971) gave the diagnostic calculations of the ψ field for the Pacific. His conclusions generally coincide with Sarkisyan and Ivanov (1971), namely, that the regard for the JEBAR completely transforms the Sverdrup integral transport. Using the example of current calculation in the North Atlantic, Ivanov (1970) has shown that ψ reacts mostly to the bottom relief changes, but ζ to the changes in the upper layer density. Ivanov (1971) has also calculated the vertical component of the current velocity for this very region. The main conclusions are coincident with those of Sarkisyan (1966), the difference being that Ivanov performed his calculations with smaller horizontal and depth spacings, using a more accurate calculation method.

Concluding the review of the works of this series, it is worthwhile to dwell upon the accuracy of the directed differences method. According to the suggestion made by A. I. Perederey, a very simple and convenient test was built, which can be used in checking the accuracy of any numerical method of solving equations of the type of (11) and (18) and their particular cases (16) and (19). For this purpose, certain simplifications and modifications are performed in the right-hand sides of these equations, the differential operators in the left-hand sides remaining the same. As an example, we can show the method of transformation of the right-hand side of Eq. (16): The wind stress is neglected, the derivatives of X and Y are taken out of the integrals, and the integral $\int_0^H (H - z)\rho \, dz$ is replaced by $\int_0^H \rho \, dz$. Thus, we approach the equations for which the dynamical method expressed by formulas (17) and (20) are the exact solutions. These exact solutions have enabled us to eliminate the errors in calculating the right-hand sides of Eqs. (16) and (18) that existed earlier in many works. After eliminating this shortcoming, the method of directed differences leads to values ζ and ψ that are very close to the exact solutions, the error being less than 1 percent.

The works listed above allow one to calculate ζ, ψ, U, V, and W in the ocean by means of the "through passage" over the equator. This method was used by Friedrich (1966). For special investigations of the equatorial currents and countercurrents, some models have been developed and the first diagnostic calculations have already been carried out (Sarkisyan, 1966a, 1967, 1969a; Sarkisyan and Serebriyakov, 1967). These works are not yet perfect, but they allow one to come to a definite conclusion: While investigating the structure of the equatorial currents, it is absolutely necessary to take into account the baroclinicity of the seawater.

NEW CALCULATIONS OF CIRCULATION IN THE NORTH ATLANTIC

The investigations discussed above were based on the greatly smoothed densities taken, for example, from Muromtsev's atlases. The absence of data for the densities of the lower levels forced the scientists to extrapolate the density somehow, which inevitably led to errors. In particular, this was the reason for failing to show the intense currents in the Gulf Stream area. It is necessary to check the presented results using more accurate calculations, i.e., using more detailed density fields with a higher space resolution and therefore better approximation of the main equations. For this purpose we have used the density fields constructed from observational data by V. F. Sukhovey with a spacing of 1¼° for the levels of 0; 20; 50; 100; 200; 300; 400; 500; 600; 800; 1,000; 1,200; 1,500; 2,000; 3,000; and 4,000 m respectively. The method of reproduction and examples of density maps are available in Sukhovey (1971). These fields provide us with information about the average long-range seasonal (in this particular case summer) density. As a result of performing calculations for the region between 7° and 65° of latitude of the North Atlantic, with an horizontal spacing $\delta\theta = \delta\lambda = 1.25°$, we have obtained about 30,000 points. In addition, the maps of the North Atlantic bottom relief and the average long-range seasonal (summer) field P_a were used. All calculations were performed both with and without regard to the flux on the liquid part of the boundary, the flux being calculated with the help of the dynamical method.

The numerical calculations were carried out using the finite-difference scheme of Ilyin (1969), which, as it has been found, practically coincides with the method of directed differences of Sarkisyan and Ivanov (1972). The evaluation of the values of various terms in the right-hand sides of Eqs. (16) and (22) show that the main contribution to the right-hand side of (16) is made by the JEBAR, with the baroclinic β-effect, the direct contribution of the wind, and the baroclinic effect of the bottom friction being in the average one or two orders of magnitude smaller. All the groups of terms connected with baroclinicity are monotonically growing functions of the baroclinic layer depth (H_o). It is characteristic that when $H_o = 20$, the JEBAR's influence in Eq. (16) is comparable to the direct influence produced by the wind. In the right-hand side of Eq. (22), the only dominant factor is the JEBAR, the thickness of the baroclinic layer at which the JEBAR becomes larger than the wind effect being 500 m.

Figure 1 represents the field $\psi(\theta,\lambda)$ of the homogeneous ocean of a constant depth. In that case, in the right-hand side of Eq. (22), only $\mathrm{rot}_z\tau$ is conserved. Thus, we are kept within the limits of Stommel's problem (1948), i.e., ψ is actually determined from Sverdrup's relationship. Figure 2 shows the function ψ also for the homogeneous ocean without including the JEBAR term. The bottom relief is the main factor taken into account here as compared with Figure 1. It is easy to see that bottom relief competes with such an important factor as the β-effect. In this experiment, as well as in Figure 1, the amplitude of ψ is about 20×10^6 m^3/s. Figure 3 represents the field $\psi(\theta,\lambda)$ obtained from the solution of Eq. (22), including the JEBAR term, the water flux being given on the liquid parts of the boundary. The

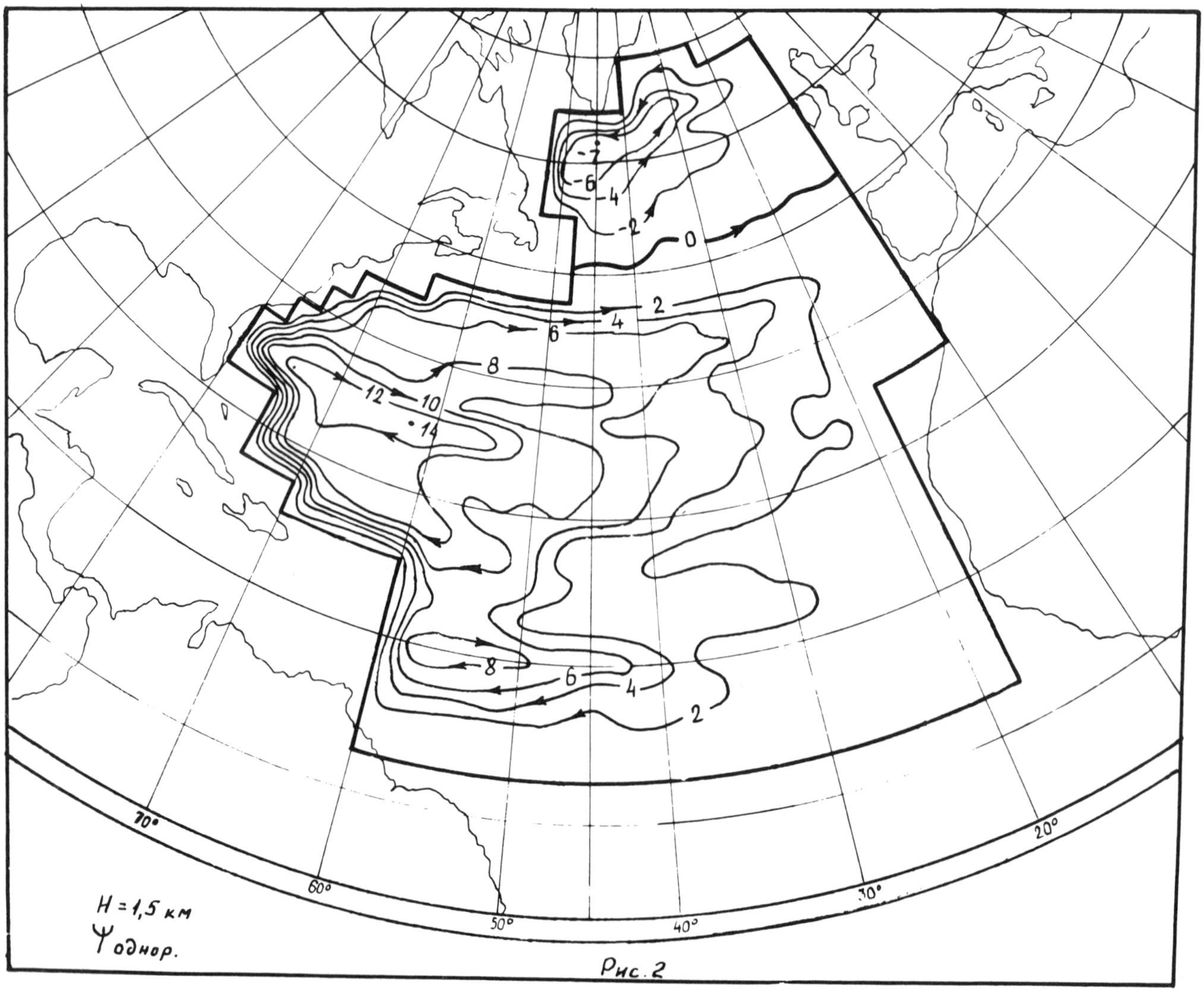

FIGURE 1 The total water flux function $\psi(\theta,\lambda)$ for the homogeneous ocean of constant depth, in units of 10^6 m^3/s.

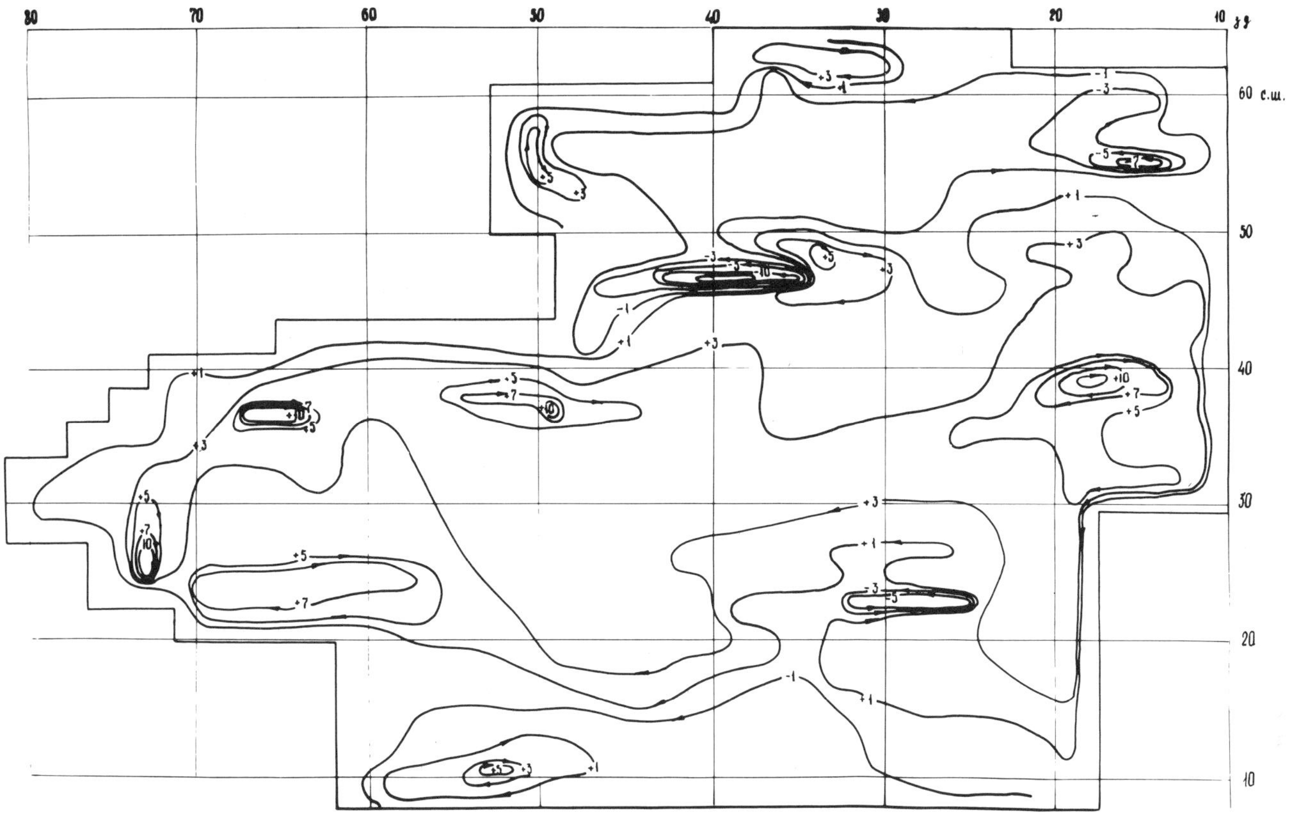

FIGURE 2 The total water flux function $\psi(\theta,\lambda)$ for the homogeneous ocean with real bottom relief.

baroclinicity was regarded up to a depth equal to 2,000 m. The behavior of the total current function is described by a complicated system of small but intensive eddies, the anticyclonic motion being predominant in the southwest, the cyclonic, in the northeast. Note that this map cannot be used for judging either the surface or the depth currents at some definite level, but it can only give a notion of the total water transport in the given ocean region. The obtained solution gives the integral flux near the eastern shore as being of the order of 50-60 $\times 10^6$ m^3/s. In the case of neglecting the flux on the boundary, the pattern greatly changes on the south and a chain of intensive cyclonic eddies can be observed. At the same time, the ocean does not accept any unnecessary flux on the boundary. By varying this flux, we have become convinced of the fact that in approaching a certain value of the inflow the ocean throws away any extra water immediately, the information about the necessary flux being given empirically by the density field. As a whole, Figure 3 strikingly differs from Figures 1 and 2, which once again confirms the real role played by the JEBAR term in the field $\psi(\theta,\lambda)$. Figure 4 shows the field $\psi_d(H_o = 3{,}000$ m) determined by the simple relationship in Eq. (20), analogous to the well-known dynamical formula (17) for ψ. It is clear that this method catches only the general features of the circulation without giving its finer structure. The greatest difference is observed in the regions of weak baroclinicity and in shallow waters. Nevertheless, the function (20) is rather useful, for it serves as the zero approximation of ψ, and it can be used for building tests both for checking the quality of the density field and for estimating the accuracy of the numerical method in solving Eq. (22). The calculations were carried on with various values of the parameter H_o.

Now we turn to the results of the calculations of the reference level ζ. If we assume $\rho \equiv 0$ in Eq. (16), we obtain the fundamental equation of Ekman's theory. In this case the amplitude is only 7 cm. The velocities of the gradient currents connected with such small values of the reference level inclination does not exceed 0.5 cm/s. This smooth field changes slightly due to group 1 in Eq. (16), whereas taking into account the baroclinic β-effect of the terms of the JEBAR group makes the amplitude become more than one order greater. To calculate the unknown field, ζ it is necessary to consider both major terms. The map corresponding to this case (when taking into consideration the flux within the liquid part of the boundary calculated by the dynamical method) is given in Figure 5. As a whole, the circulation here is described by two global eddies: cyclonic on the north and anticyclonic at the middle latitudes. Using this map, one can judge the surface gradient currents: The intensification of the western boundary currents is clearly

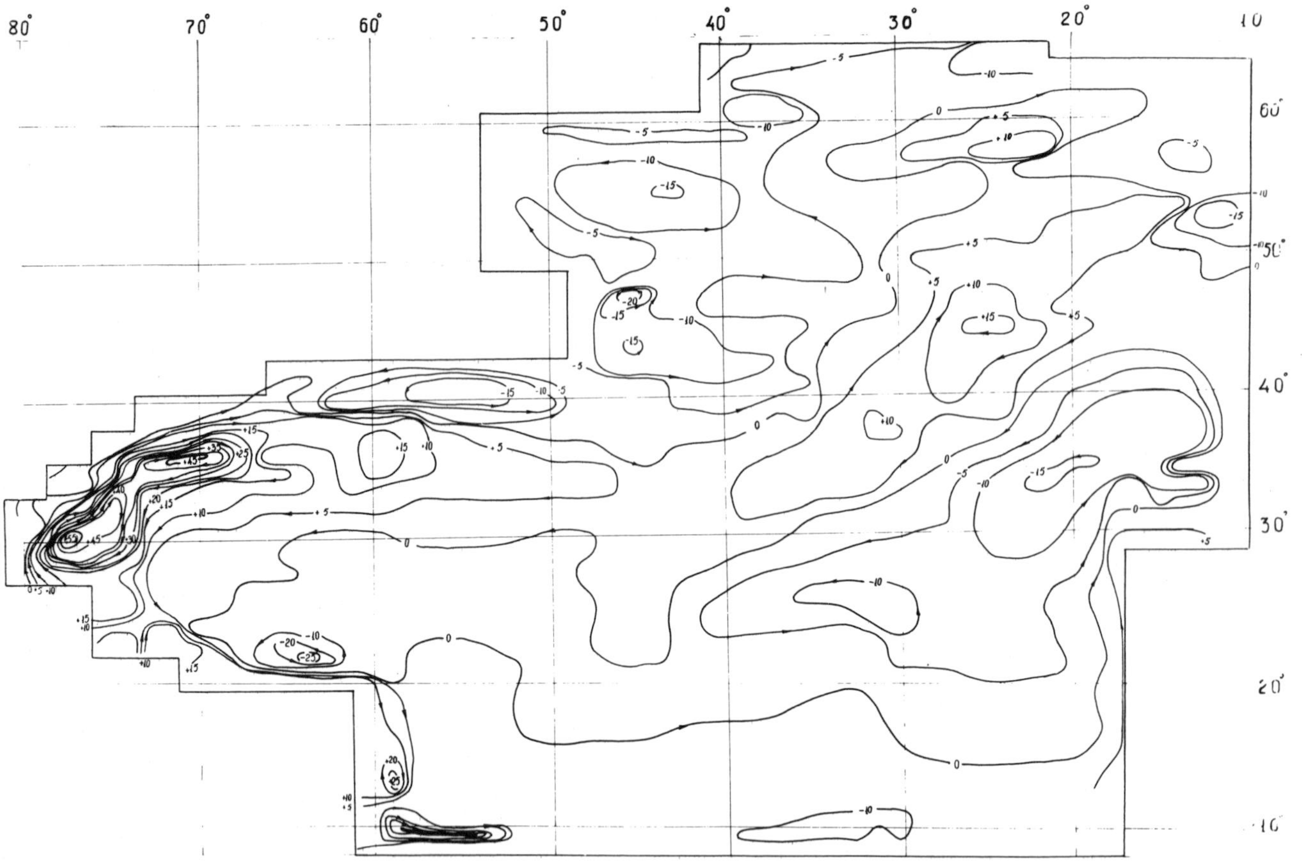

FIGURE 3 The total water flux function $\psi(\theta,\lambda)$ for the baroclinic ocean with real bottom relief.

seen, and the division of the powerful North Atlantic current into separate streams when tearing away from the shore is easily observed. The amplitude is a monotonically growing function of the baroclinic layer depth H_o; when H_o = 3,000 m, it reaches 160 cm, the tendency to saturation being clearly seen. Therefore, when performing calculations we confine ourselves to a baroclinic layer of 2,000 m.

The changes in ζ caused by neglecting the water flux on the liquid part of the boundary take place mainly to the south of the region, being less significant than the analogous changes of the field ψ.

When varying ν and ν' within the limits of order $10^{\pm 1}$, the solutions of Eqs. (16) and (22) did not change qualitatively; changes in the amplitudes of these solutions did not exceed 7 percent.

Figure 6 presents the ζ_d field calculated according to Eq. (17) (H_o = 3,000 m). It is similar to the previous ζ field in the middle latitudes, in the regions where density gradients are significant; but it differs from ζ substantially in the northern shallow waters and in the regions where inhomogeneities in the seawater are not significant. There is no doubt that ζ_d is a good first approach of ζ, more reliable than ψ_d for ψ.

Consider now the results of the calculations of the horizontal velocity components on the basis of the already known fields of $\zeta(\theta,\lambda)$ and $\psi(\theta,\lambda)$, using the familiar formulas available, for example, Sarkisyan and Ivanov (1971). Using about 30,000 points, we were also able to obtain extremely detailed information about the North Atlantic currents.

We have already analyzed the whole material, but we can certainly show only a small part of it. In Figure 7 one can observe the field of the surface current. It fully corresponds to the modern notions of North Atlantic circulation. One can easily see the cyclonic character of the circulation in the north, with the East-Greenland current in the northwest and the Labrador current near the western boundary, with velocities up to 15 cm/s. A large area is occupied by the great anticyclonic rotation that has already been shown in Figure 5. In the previous calculations (Sarkisyan and Pastukhov, 1970; Sarkisyan and Ivanov, 1971, 1972), we could not obtain the intensive currents in the area of the Gulf Stream. On the given map, the Gulf Stream is sufficiently near to its prototype. Here the velocities significantly exceed the values obtained earlier and are of the order of 80-100 cm/s. The stream character of this current, as well as its tendency to split near 40° W, is shown rather well.

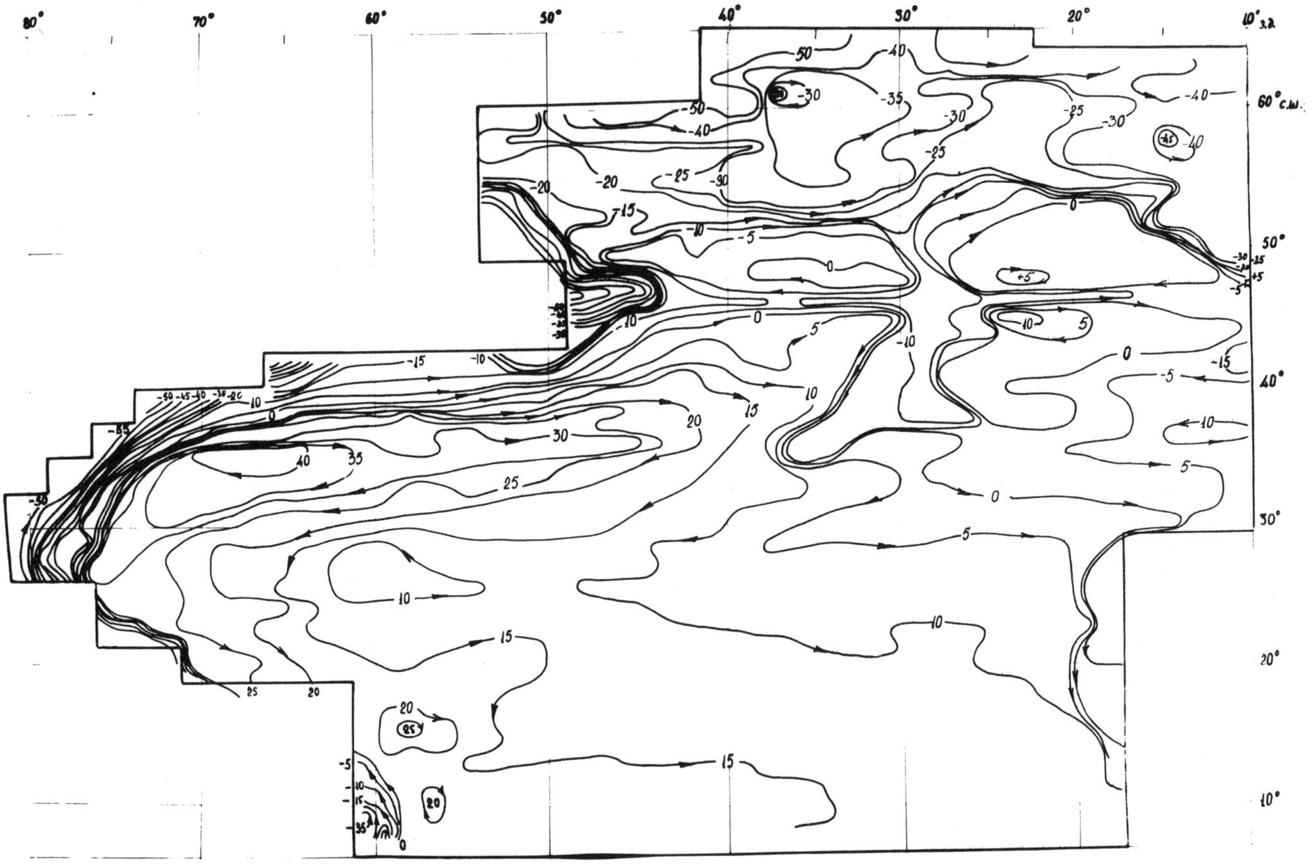

FIGURE 4 The total water flux function $\psi_{d'}$ calculated by the dynamical method.

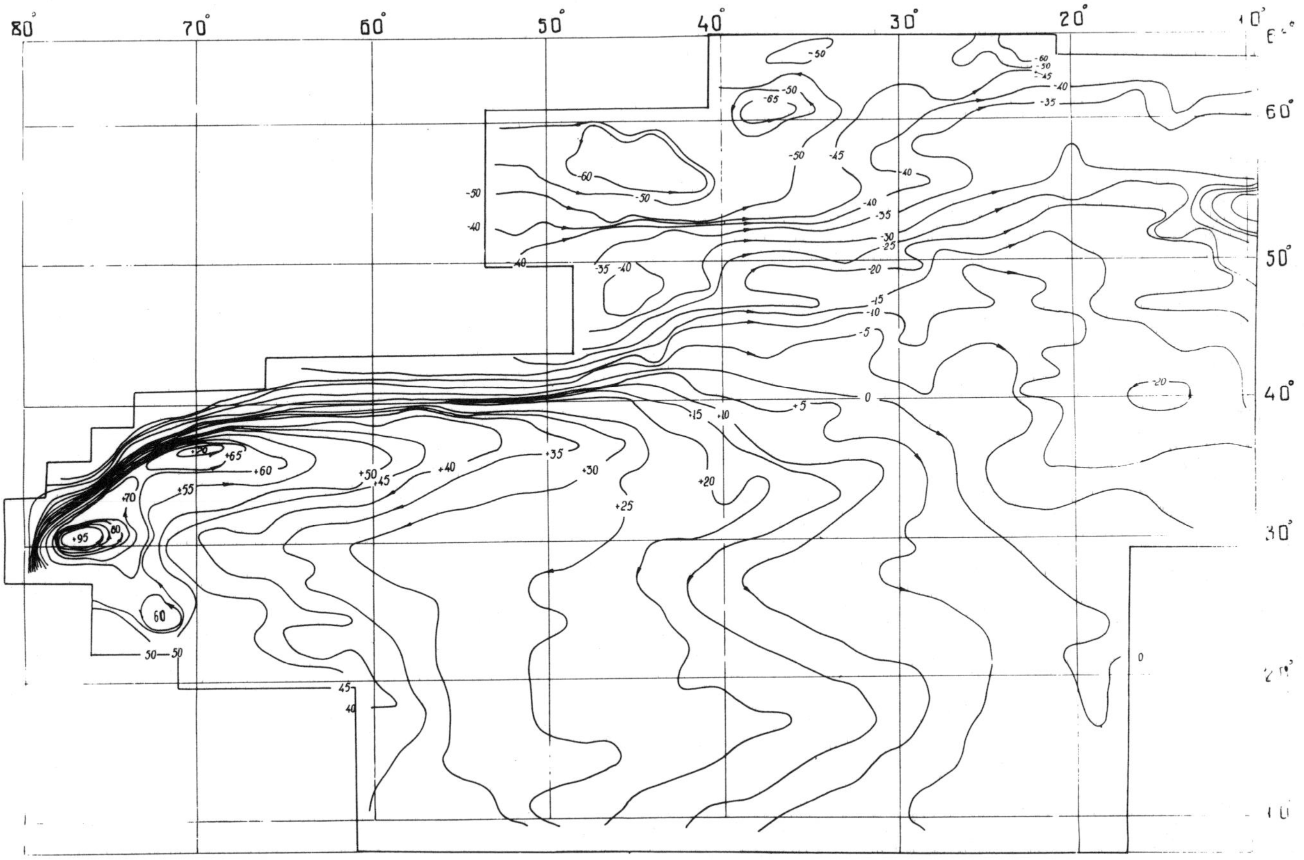

FIGURE 5 The relief of the baroclinic ocean free surface $\zeta(\theta,\lambda)$ in cm with the real bottom relief.

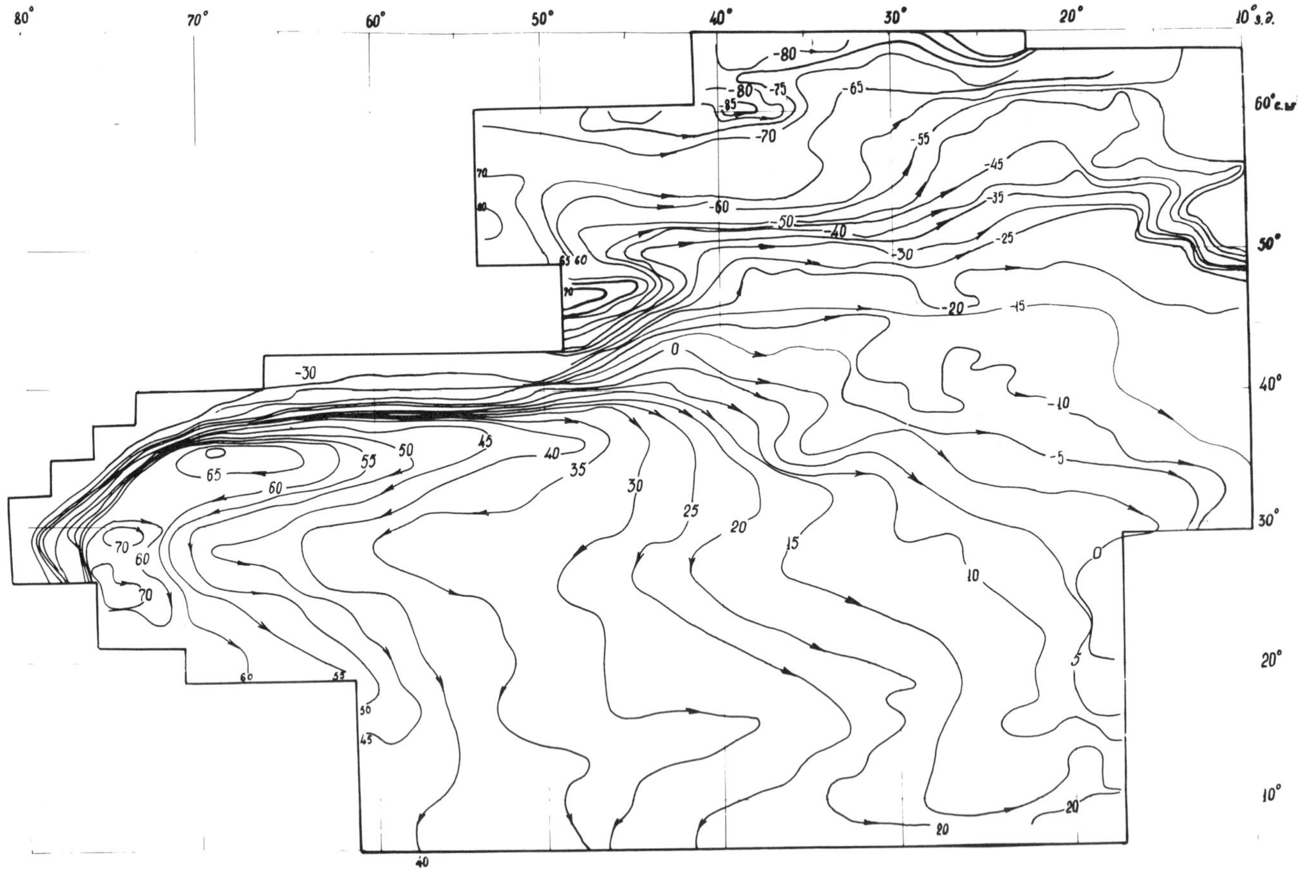

FIGURE 6 The relief of the ocean free surface calculated by means of the dynamical method.

The Antilles current in the southwest part of the basin, and the northern easterlies current in the south of the basin, can be observed, with velocities of 30–60 cm/s. The intensive currents can be observed not only in the west, but also in the east; as an example, we can show the Canary current present on the map. Figure 8 shows the currents at the depth of 500 m; here the Gulf Stream is clearly seen, with velocities reaching 50 cm/s. Figure 9 represents the horizontal current velocity field at Z-1 km. Here one can see the countercurrent under the Gulf Stream with velocities reaching 35 cm/s. Countercurrents are also present at this level under Canary currents.

Current velocities at the level of Z–3 km are represented in Figure 10. Here a huge cyclonic gyre exists, which occupies the whole ocean basin. An idea of the vertical structure of the motions in the ocean is given by the vertical profiles presented in Figure 11. The first profile corresponds to the region of coordinates 33° N, 52° W; the second one, to that of coordinates 33° N, 75° W; and the third, to that of 20° N, 27° W. By means of the vertical cross sections, it is possible to judge qualitatively the magnitude of the total current flux. For example, cross section II allows one to assume that the power of the countercurrent is not correlated to the Gulf Stream itself. The countercurrent appears at different depths in different regions. Roughly, it could be said that the surface of separation between two currents sinks toward the west, from 200 to about 1,000 m. Therefore, it seemed to be interesting to find the total currents $[\psi^{(1)}, \psi^{(2)}]$ for two layers ($0 \leqslant Z \leqslant 800$ m, $800 < Z \leqslant 2{,}000$ m) and compare them with the total integral stream $\psi(\theta,\lambda)$ calculated from the surface to the bottom.

Figures 12 and 13 represent the fields $\psi^{(1,2)}(\theta,\lambda)$ for the layers 0–800 m and 800–2,000 m, respectively. It can be easily seen from these two figures that in the Gulf Stream area, as well as in other places, the integral circulations of the two layers have opposite directions.

In conclusion, it should be noted that the main results of the recent diagnostic calculations made by Holland and Hirschman* based on density fields compiled at the NOAA laboratory at Princeton University are in good agreement with ours.

* Holland, W. R., and A. D. Hirschman. 1972. A numerical calculation of the circulation of the North Atlantic Ocean. J. Phys. Ocean 2:336–54.

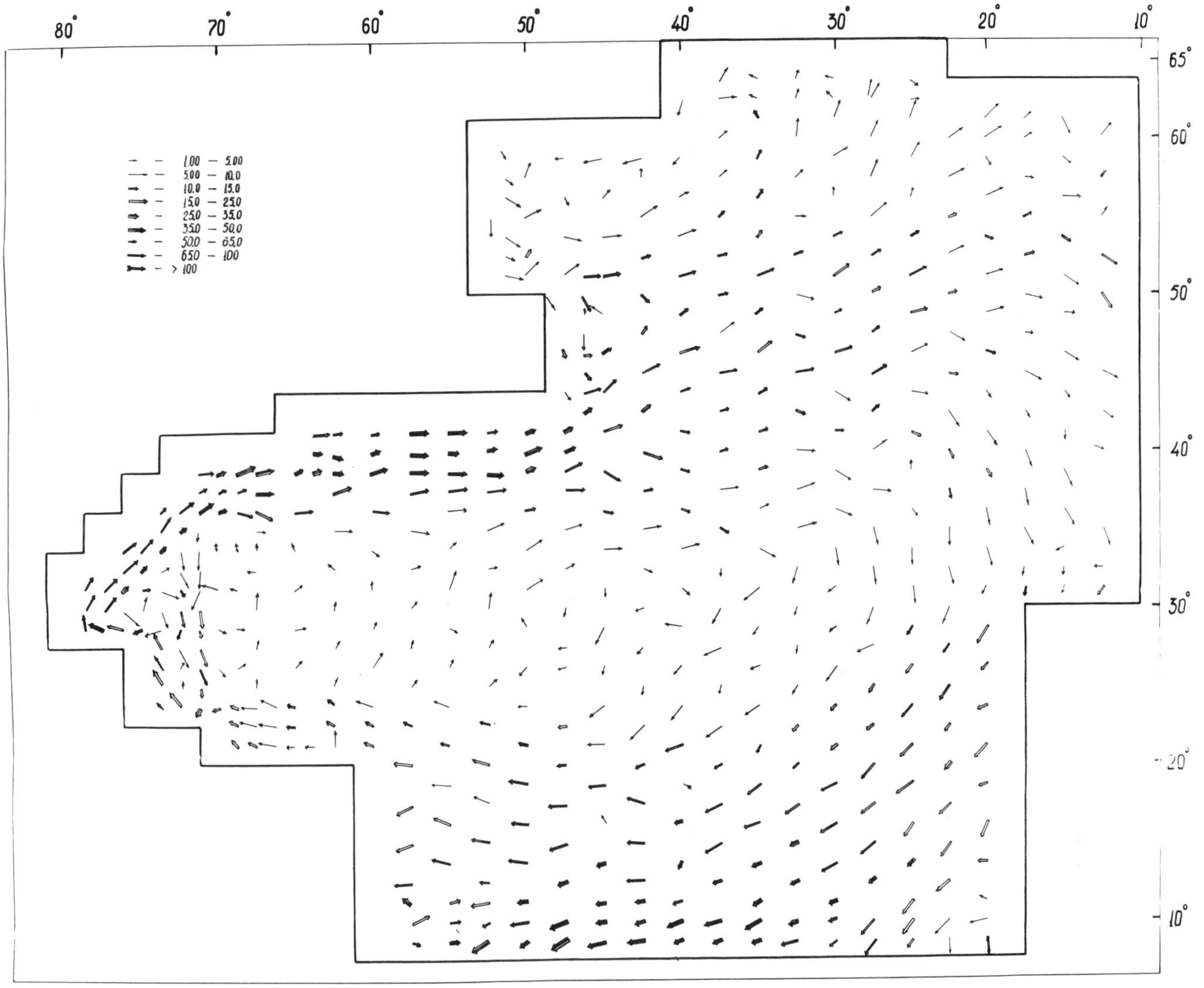

FIGURE 7 Map of the surface currents in the North Atlantic.

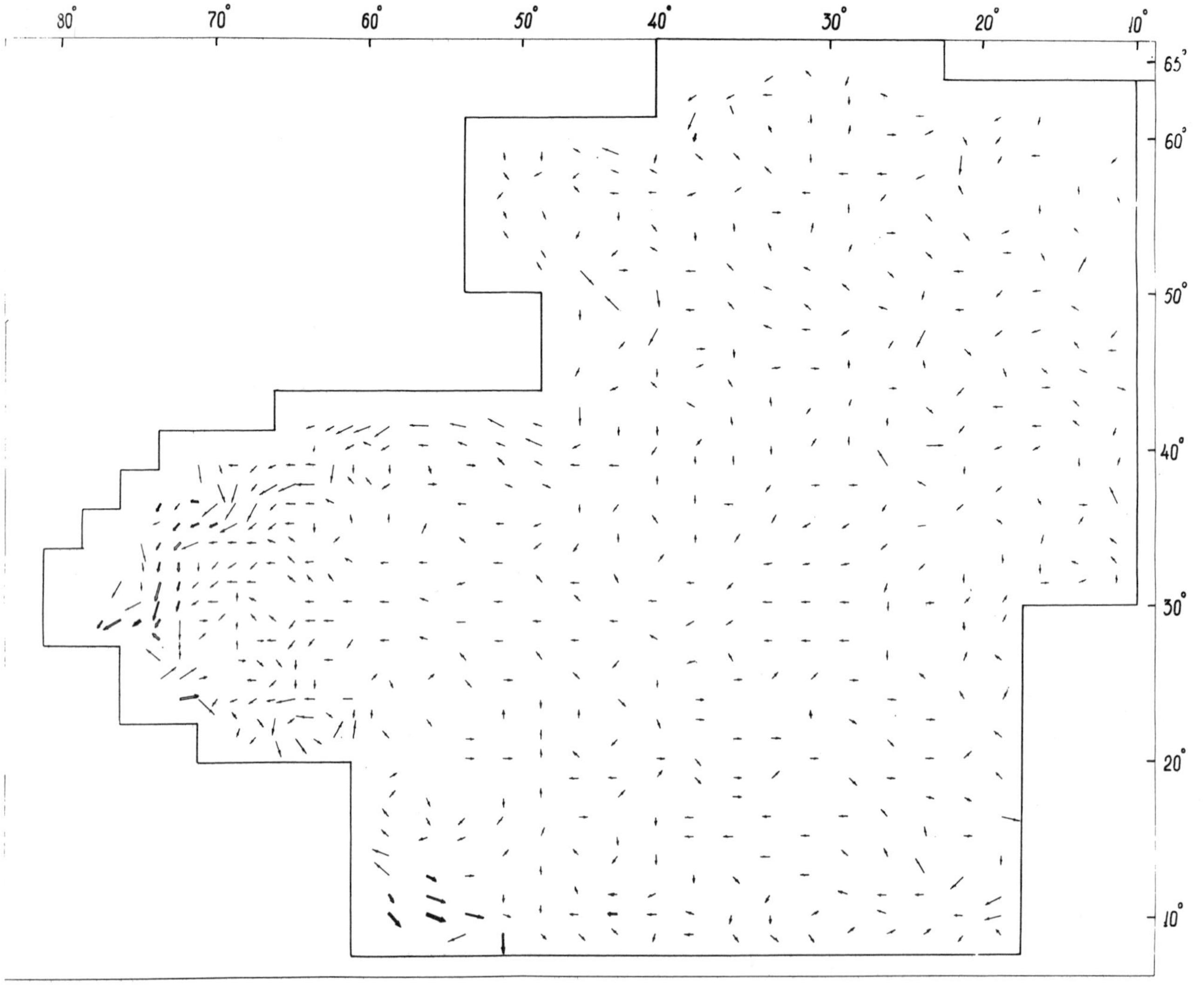

FIGURE 8 Map of the gradient currents in the North Atlantic at the depth of 500 m.

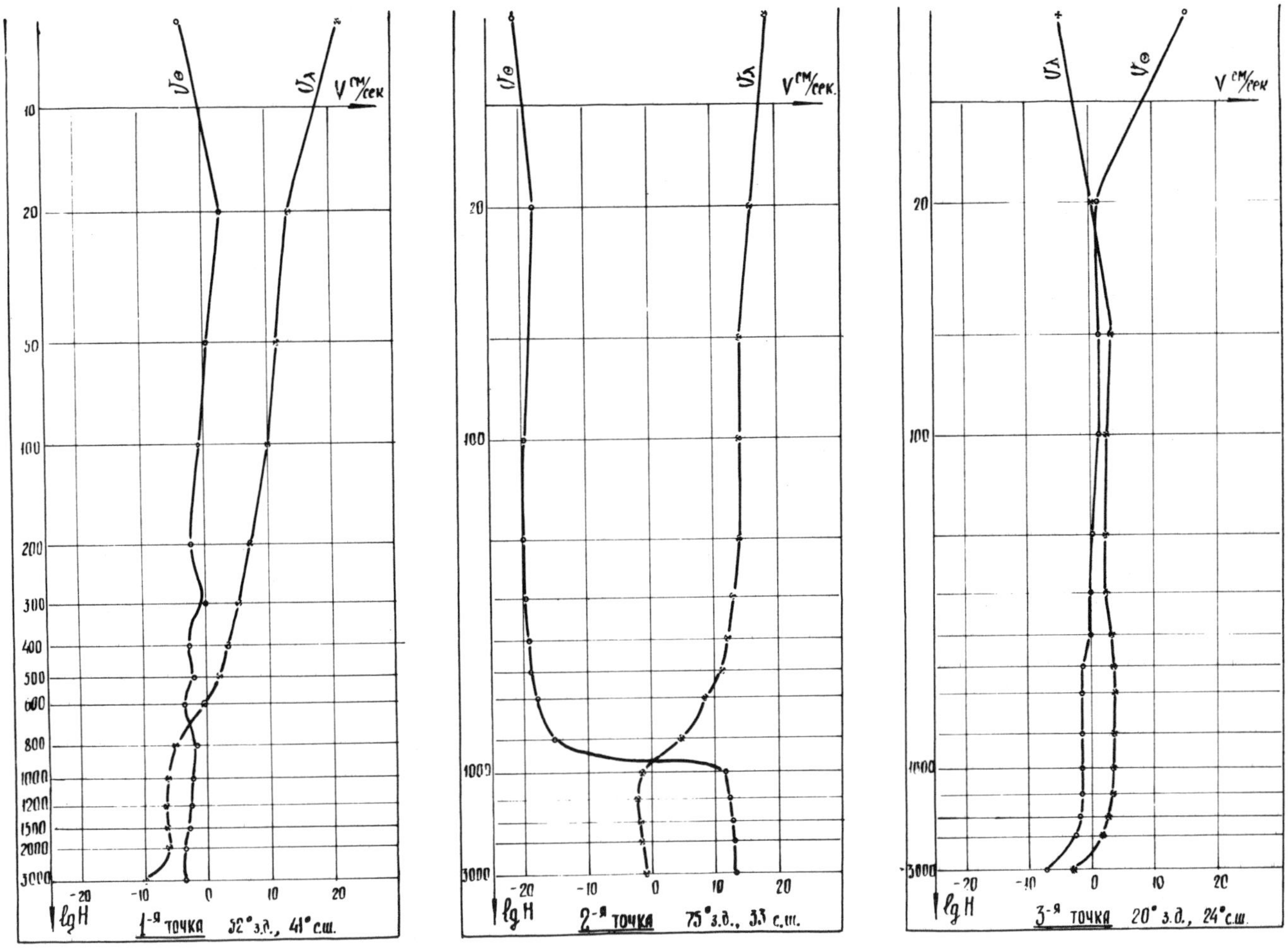

FIGURE 9 Current velocities at $Z = 1$ km.

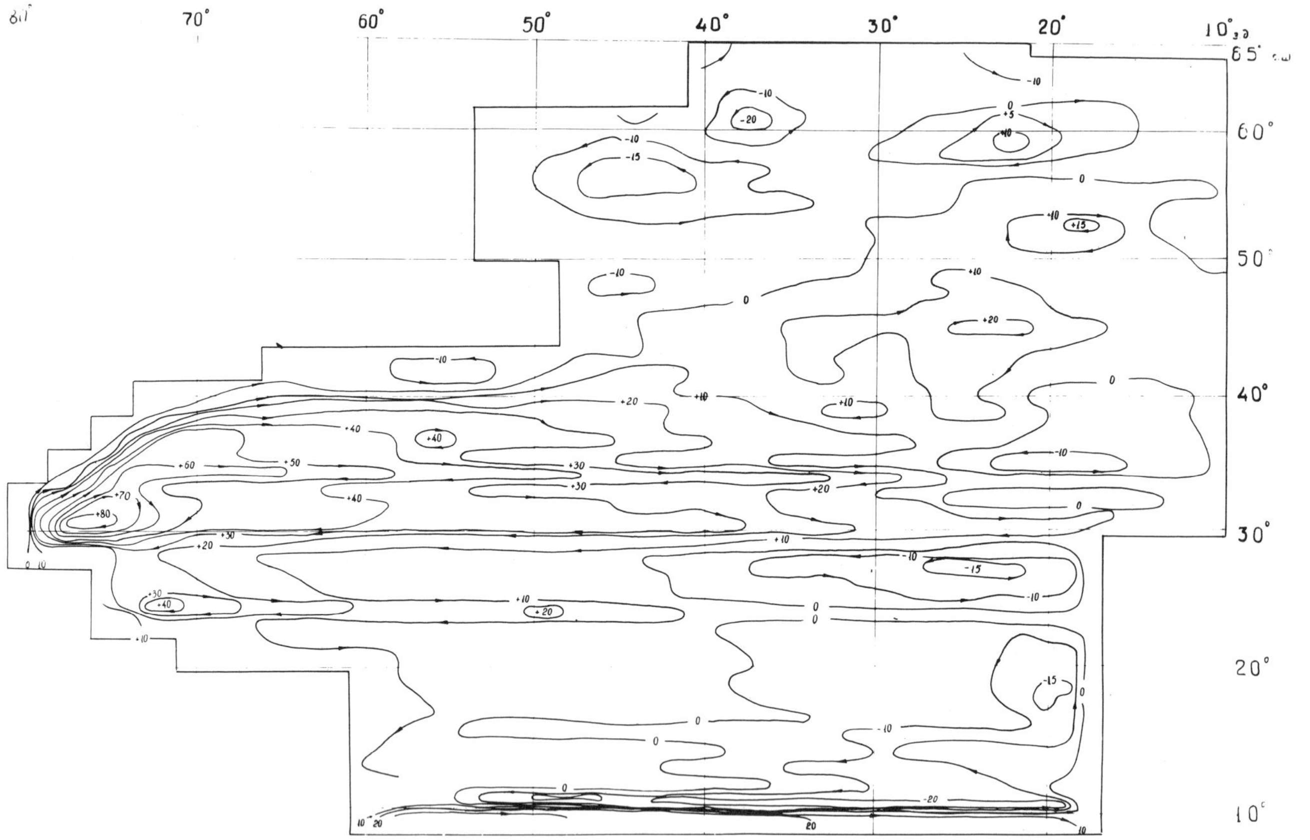

FIGURE 10 Map of current velocities at $Z = 3$ km.

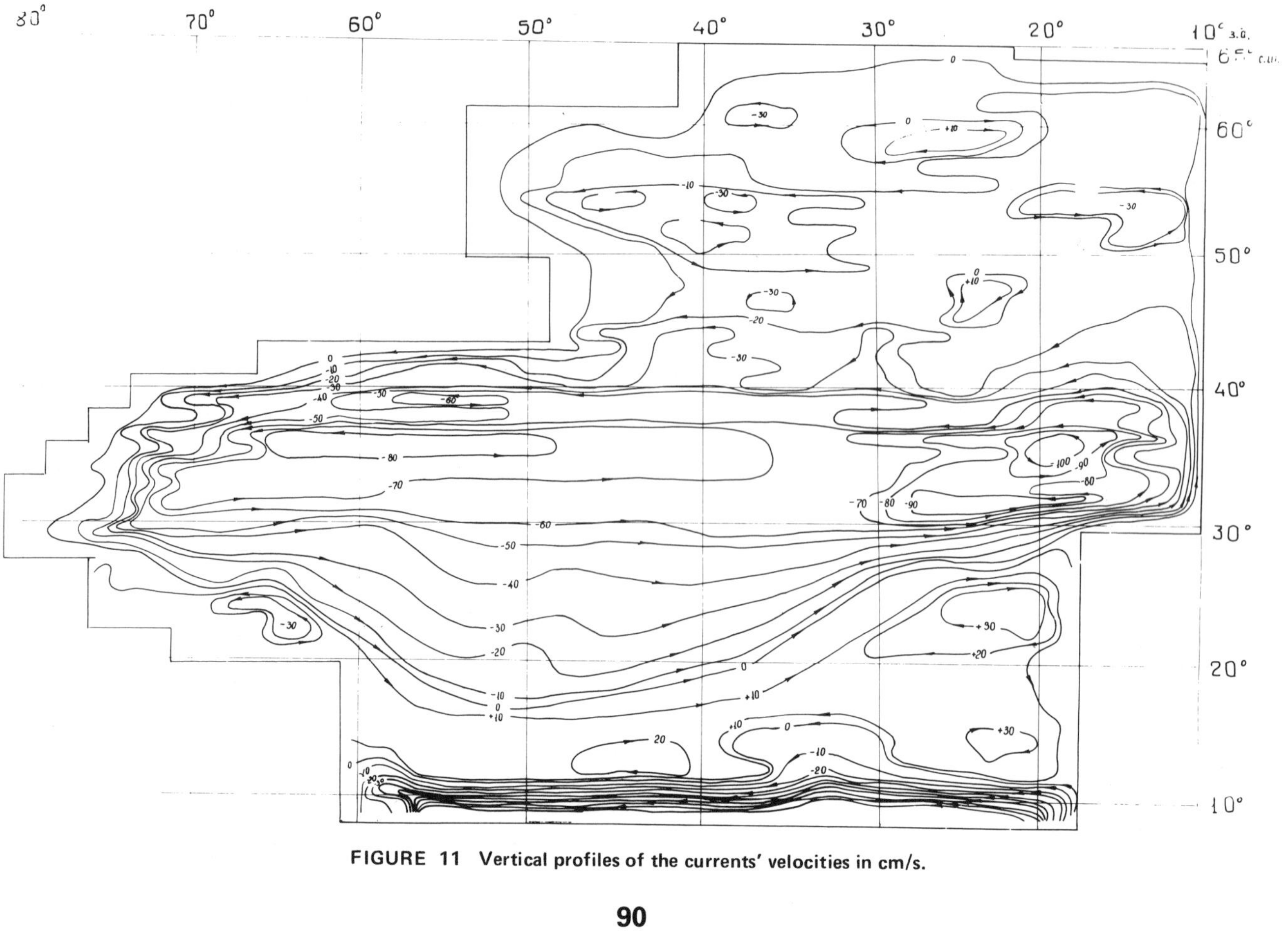

FIGURE 11 Vertical profiles of the currents' velocities in cm/s.

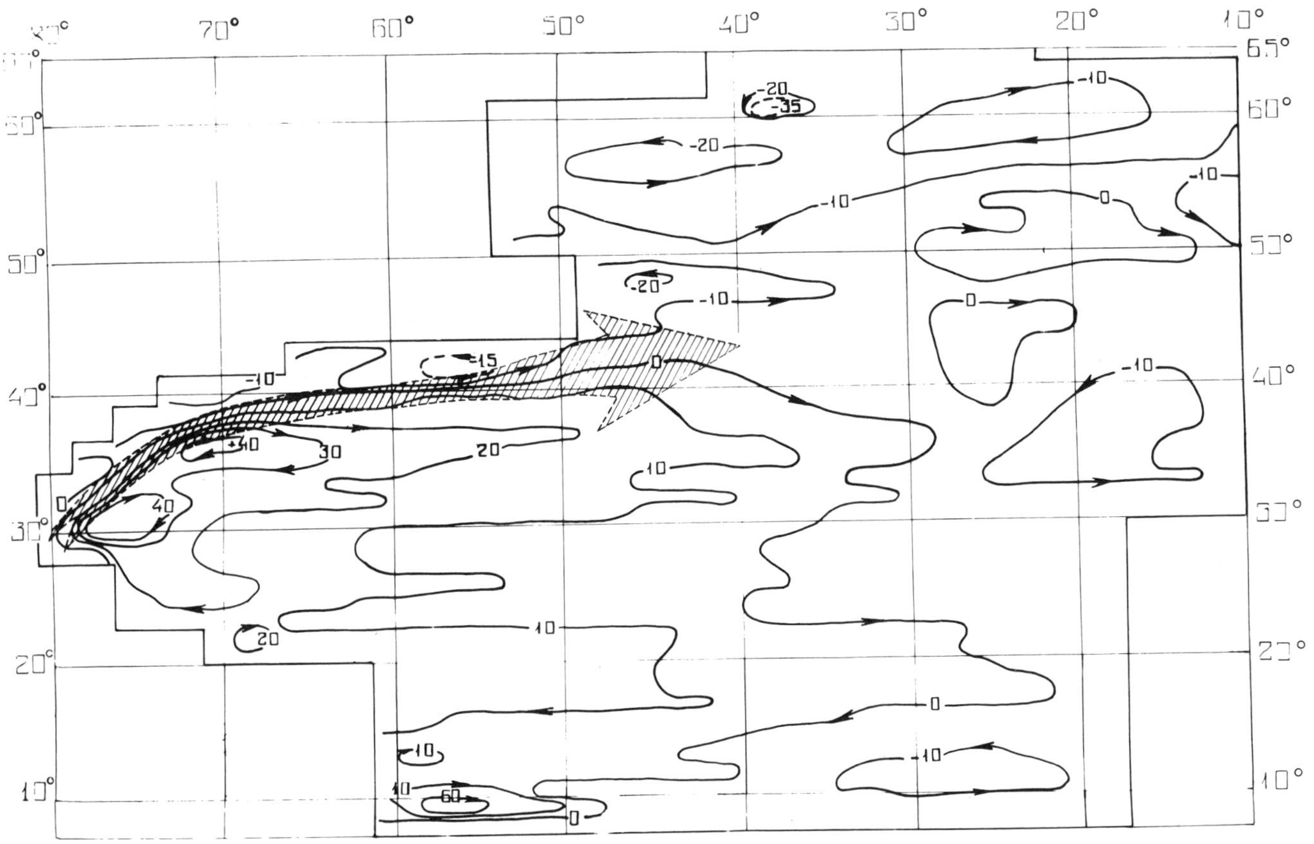

FIGURE 12 The total water flux function $\psi^{(1)}(\theta,\lambda)$ of the layer $0 \leqslant Z \leqslant 800$ m.

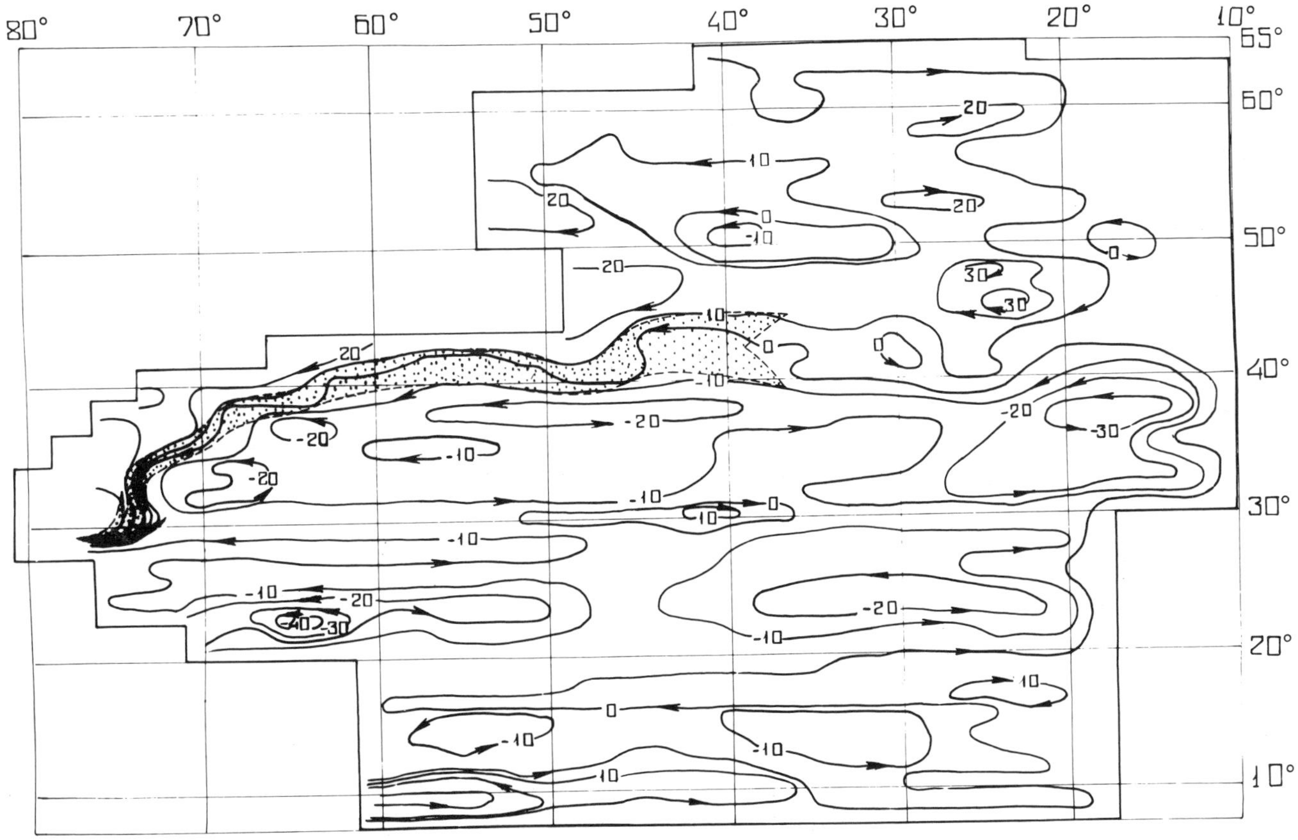

FIGURE 13 The total water flux function $\psi^{(2)}(\theta,\lambda)$ of the layer $800 < Z \leqslant 2{,}000$ m.

CONCLUSIONS

Neither Sverdrup's formula nor any other homogeneous model of the ocean can be used for calculations of large-scale stationary or seasonal currents in the ocean. In middle latitudes the dynamical method can serve as a reliable first approximation in calculating ζ and a less accurate approximation in calculating ψ. In calculating ζ, and especially in calculating ψ, it is necessary to consider the joint effect of the baroclinicity and the ocean bottom relief (JEBAR). The developed numerical models permit one to obtain reliable information about the currents associated with a given density field. Such calculations are of great interest. Their accuracy depends basically on that of the density field, whereas the accuracy of the wind field is not of great importance. The function ψ depicts the deep layer circulation and is extremely sensitive to changes in the bottom relief, water flux through the "liquid shores," and density anomalies at great depths. These anomalies are poorly known so that the field ψ is inaccurate. The reference level ζ representing the surface currents depends considerably less upon the anomaly of the deep layer density (1.5-2 km).

REFERENCES

Bolgurtsev, B. N. 1969. Surface and depth circulation of the Antarctic waters in the Pacific. Izv. Akad. Nauk. USSR Atmos. Oceanic Phys. 5(8).

Bolgurtsev, B. N., V. F. Kozlov, and L. A. Molchanova. 1969. The results of current calculations in the Pacific sector of the Antarctic. Izv. Akad. Nauk. USSR Atmos. Oceanic Phys. 5(8).

Carrier, G. F., and A. R. Robinson. 1962. On the theory of the wind-driven ocean circulation. J. Fluid Mech. 12:49-80.

Ekman, V. W. 1905. On the influence of the earth's rotation on ocean currents. Ark. Mat. Astron. Fys. 2(11):1-52.

Ekman, V. W. 1906. Beitzage zur Theorie Meeresströmun. Ann. Hydrog. Marit. Meteorol. 34(9).

Ekman, V. W. 1923. Über Horizontalzirkulation bei Winderzeugten Meersströmungen. Ark. Mat. Astron. Fys. 17(26), 74 pp.

Friedrich, H. 1966. Numerische Berechnungen der algemeinen Zirkulation im Meere nach einen Differenzenverfahren, vornehm lich für den Atlantischen Ozean. Mitt. Inst. Meereskd. Univ. Hamburg 3.

Ivanov, V. F. 1970. On the role of bottom relief in the stationary circulation of the baroclinic ocean. Sea Hydrophys. Res. 4(50).

Ivanov, V. F. 1971. The vertical velocity calculation in the North Atlantic using the total current function and reference level. Sea Hydrol. Res. 6(56).

Ivanov, Yu. A., and V. M. Kamenkovich. 1959. The bottom relief as the fundamental factor forming nonzonality of the Antarctic circumpolar current. Dokl. Akad. Nauk. USSR 128(6).

Ilyin, A. M. 1969. Difference scheme for differential equation with the small parameter by high-grade derivative. Math. Notes 6(2).

Koshlyakov, M. N. 1961. Calculations of ocean deep circulation. Oceanol. 1.

Kozlov, V. F. 1971. Some results of the approximated calculation in the Pacific circulation. Izv. Akad. Nauk. USSR, Atmos. Oceanic Phys. 7(4).

Lineikin, P. S. 1957. Fundamental questions of the dynamical theory of the baroclinic layer of the ocean. Gidrometizdat, Leningrad, USSR.

Munk, V. H. 1950. On the wind-driven ocean circulation. J. Meteorol. 7(2):79-93.

Muromtsev, A. M. 1963. Fundamental features of the Atlantic Ocean hydrology. Gidrometizdat, Leningrad, USSR.

Muromtsev, A. M. 1963. Atlas of temperature, salinity, and density of the Pacific Ocean. Izv. Akad. Nauk. USSR.

Sarkisyan, A. S. 1961. On the role of the drift advection of the density in the baroclinic ocean. Izv. Akad. Nauk. USSR (9).

Sarkisyan, A. S. 1962. On the dynamics of wind current appearance in the baroclinic ocean. Oceanology 2(3):395-409.

Sarkisyan, A. S. 1966a. On dynamics of currents in the equatorial Atlantic. Proc. Symp. Oceanogr. Fish Res. Trop. Atlantic. Abidjan, Ivory Coast.

Sarkisyan, A. S. 1966b. Theory and calculation of oceanic currents. Gidrometizdat, Leningrad, USSR.

Sarkisyan, A. S. 1967. The problem statement and the scheme of equatorial currents calculation. Express-Information, Izv. Akad. Nauk. USSR (7).

Sarkisyan, A. S. 1969a. Nonstationary model of the equatorial currents. Oceanology 9(1).

Sarkisyan, A. S. 1969b. On the shortcomings of the baroclinic models of the oceanic circulation. Izv. Akad. Nauk. USSR Atmos. Oceanic Phys. 5(8).

Sarkisyan, A. S. 1969c. The experience in calculating the reference level and current velocity in the Caribbean Sea. Meteorol. Hydrol. (3).

Sarkisyan, A. S., and Yu. K. Garmatyuk. 1965. The results of current calculations in the North Atlantic using the four-level model. Izv. Akad. Nauk. USSR Atmos. Oceanic Phys. 1(3).

Sarkisyan, A. S., V. V. Knish, K. I. Vasilyeva, and N. M. Kireeva. 1967. The examples of calculating three components of current velocity in the North Atlantic using the observed density field. Hydrophysical and hydrochemical research in the Atlantic Ocean and in the Black Sea. Nauk. Dumk., pp. 24-35.

Sarkisyan, A. S., and A. A. Serebriyakov. 1967. The results of approximated calculations of equatorial countercurrent Lomonosov. Express-Information 7 Coll.: New Models and Results of Current Calculation in the Baroclinic Ocean. Sevastopol.

Sarkisyan, A. S., and A. F. Pastukhov. 1970. The density field as the fundamental indicator of the stationary sea currents. Izv. Akad. Nauk. USSR Atmos. Oceanic Phys. 6(1).

Sarkisyan, A. S., and V. F. Ivanov. 1971. The joint effect of baroclinicity and the bottom relief as an important factor in the sea current dynamics. Izv. Akad. Sci. USSR Atmos. Oceanic Phys. (2).

Sarkisyan, A. S., and A. I. Perederey. 1972. The dynamical method as the first approximation in calculating the reference level of the baroclinic ocean. Meteorol. Hydrol. 4.

Sarkisyan, A. S., and V. F. Ivanov. 1972. The comparison of various methods of calculating the baroclinic ocean currents. Izv. Akad. Nauk. USSR Atmos. Ocean Phys. 8(4).

Stockman, W. B. 1946. Equations of the wind-driven water flux in the homogeneous sea. Dokl. Acad. Sci. USSR 54(5).

Stommel, H. 1948. The westward intensification of wind-driven ocean currents. Trans. Am. Geophys. Union 29(2):202-06.

Sukhovey, V. F. 1971. The reconstruction of the hydrological element fields by the observational data. Sea Hydrophys. Res. 3(53).

Sverdrup, H. 1947. Wind-driven currents in a baroclinic ocean, with application to the equatorial currents of the eastern Pacific. Contr. Scripps Inst. Oceanogr. July:318–26.

Swallow, J. C., and L. V. Worthington. 1961. An observation of a deep countercurrent in the western North Atlantic. Deep-Sea. Res. 8(1):1–19.

Welander, P. 1959. On the vertically integrated mass transport in the oceans, pp. 95–101. *In* B. Bolin, ed. The Atmosphere and the Sea in Motion. New York.

DISCUSSION

MOORE: In a diagnostic calculation such as you have discussed here, one completely ignores the density equation. What happens if you take your solution and put it into the density equation?

SARKISYAN: The data that we have used so far is not accurate enough to make such a calculation. We have only made these calculations for the density field for summertime conditions. We have not found a good balance in the upper 200–300 m in our calculations, mainly because of the large effect of sea level variation. Only in the region between 400–600 m, where seasonal changes are not important, do we find a good balance. These are only very preliminary results.

VERONIS: I suspect that the observed density field is pretty much in geostrophic balance. In this case, certain terms in the density equation largely cancel each other. If you could somehow eliminate this effect, you might have something more substantial.

SARKISYAN: Our results are only preliminary, and it's too early to make a definitive statement on this effect. But I would like to say that the geostrophic balance is not enough to cause the two advective terms $u(\partial\rho/\partial x)$ and $v(\partial\rho/\partial y)$ to cancel each other.

THREE-DIMENSIONAL NUMERICAL MODELS OF THE OCEAN CIRCULATION

K. BRYAN

INTRODUCTION

There are two possible approaches to constructing models of the ocean circulation. One is to formulate problems in geophysical fluid dynamics that are relevant to ocean circulation but do not contain any elements that are not essential to test a given idea. The other approach is to attempt to simulate the real ocean in such a way that the solutions can be compared directly with observed data. Both methods of attack are important and complement each other. In this review, however, most attention will be given to the first approach, since relatively few solutions are available that actually take into account the geometry of ocean basins.

Welander (pp. 63-75) has reviewed analytic theories of ocean circulation. In certain asymptotic ranges of the parameters, the analytic solutions can be used to test the numerical models for ocean basins with idealized geometry. These tests are essential, since one point of numerical models is to extend results already obtained into parameter ranges that are of physical interest but are not accessible to analytic methods.

GOVERNING EQUATIONS

In an ocean model study we wish to predict the three-dimensional distribution of water mass properties and the flow field within a basin in response to a given set of boundary conditions at the upper surface. In general, the system will be time-dependent due to inherent instabilities, even if the boundary conditions are steady. The intuitive approach to devising model equations is to average the Navier-Stokes equations over some "grid" scale in space and a corresponding interval in time. The new set of averaged equations have the form of Reynolds equations with the effect of small-scale, high-frequency motions represented as Reynolds stresses. Except in the case of pronounced "spectral gap" at the grid scale, this derivation is not rigorous. For continuous spectra, the temperature and velocity fields do not satisfy the so-called Reynolds conditions (Monin and Yaglom, 1971) and these conditions are required to carry out the various manipulations needed to write the equations of motion in Reynolds form. The difficulty is overcome by redefining the averaged quantities as the most probable values for a set of realizations with boundary conditions and initial conditions that differ in detail but have the same large-scale characteristics. The Reynolds conditions are automatically satisfied, if our explicit variables are defined as probabilities rather than space-time averages.

The model is based on the assumptions that the motion is hydrostatic and Boussinesq. These assumptions are quite accurate for large-scale motion in the ocean. A much more difficult problem is the formulation of an accurate closure hypothesis to specify the Reynolds stresses and the equivalent mixing terms in the temperature and salinity equations. At present very little information exists on the momentum transfer by smaller scales (less than 100 km). In the future, experiments such as the Mid-Ocean Dynamics Experiment (MODE) (Hammond, 1972), may provide us with the needed information to formulate realistic closure schemes. The simple "turbulent viscosity" hypothesis used in most of the numerical ocean models to date must be considered a temporary expedience. Let $q = v - kw$, where k is the unit vector normal to the surface of the ocean at rest; and $\mathbf{v}$ is the total velocity vector. The equation of motion for the horizontal component of velocity is

$$q_t + (v \cdot \nabla)q + 2\Omega \sin \phi k \times q$$

$$= -\frac{1}{\rho_o} \nabla p + A_z q_{zz} + A_m F. \qquad (1)$$

A_m and A_z are mixing coefficients required by the closure hypothesis and Ω is the angular velocity of the earth. In Cartesian coordinates,

$$F = i \nabla^2 u + j \nabla^2 v. \qquad (2)$$

In the case of anisotropic mixing on a sphere, a more complicated formula is required (Kamenkovich, 1967). The hydrostatic relation and the continuity relation are

$$\rho g = -p_z, \qquad (3)$$

$$\nabla \cdot v = 0. \qquad (4)$$

An equation of state has the general form

$$\rho = \rho(\Theta, S, p), \qquad (5)$$

where the density is a complicated function of the potential temperature, Θ; salinity, S; and pressure, p. Conservation equations for Θ and S are

$$(\Theta, S)_t + (v \cdot \nabla)(\Theta, S) = A_H \nabla^2 (\Theta, S) + [\eta(\Theta, S)_z]_z. \qquad (6)$$

Compression effects are rather small in the ocean, so that Θ differs by only a small amount from the *in situ* temperature. The difference becomes significant only for very detailed simulation experiments.

For studies of the dynamics of ocean circulation in which it is not important to know the details of the heat and salinity balance, we can use the simplified equation of state,

$$\rho = \rho_o (1 - \alpha\theta), \qquad (7)$$

where θ is an "apparent" temperature. The "apparent" temperature is calculated from an equation of the form in Eq. (6) and boundary conditions that specify the total buoyancy flux at the surface of the model ocean. In this case, Eqs. (1-7) can be put in dimensionless form with the following substitutions:

$$x, y = L(x', y'), \qquad (8)$$

$$z = D z', \qquad (9)$$

$$t = t'L/V^*, \qquad (10)$$

$$p = \Omega V^* L \rho_o p', \qquad (11)$$

$$\theta = 2\Omega V^* L \theta' / g\alpha D, \qquad (12)$$

and

$$w, q = V^* (Dw'/L, q'). \qquad (13)$$

L and D are the horizontal and the vertical length scales, respectively. V^* is the velocity scale that can be defined in terms of the specified boundary conditions at the upper surface. For example, let $\Delta\theta^*$ be a measure of an imposed meridional gradient of density at the upper boundary of the model ocean. The corresponding geostrophic current is

$$V^* = g\,\alpha\,\Delta\theta^* D / 2\Omega L, \qquad (14)$$

where D is a measure of the thermocline depth. The scale depth, D, is usually defined from

η_0 diffusion coefficient? η_0 : vertical mixing

$$V^* \frac{\Delta\theta}{L} = \frac{\eta_0}{D^2} \Delta\theta. \qquad (15)$$

$[\eta_0] = m^2 s^{-1}$

Let γ be the ratio of upwelling in the surface Ekman layer to the vertical velocity connected to the thermal circulation, given as W_e^* and W_T^*, respectively,

$$\gamma = (W_e/W_T)^* = W_e^* L / DV^*. \qquad (16)$$

In the case of the real ocean, γ is nearly unity, which is one reason it is so difficult to separate out the relative contribution of wind and thermal driving to the ocean circulation.

Making use of Eqs. (7-12),

$$R_o [q'_t + (v \cdot \nabla) q'] + \sin \phi\, k \times q' = -\nabla p'$$

$$+ Ek_V q'_{zz} + Ek_H F', \qquad (17)$$

$$\theta' = p_z', \qquad (18)$$

$$\nabla \cdot v' = 0, \qquad (19)$$

$$\theta_t' + (v' \cdot \nabla)\theta' = Pe_H^{-1} \nabla^2 \theta' + (Pe_V^{-1} \theta_z')_z, \qquad (20)$$

where

$$R_o = V^*/2\Omega L, \qquad (21)$$

$$Ek_H, Ek_v, Pe_H^{-1}, Pe_V^{-1},$$

$$= \frac{A_m}{2\Omega L^2}, \frac{A_z}{2\Omega D^2}, \frac{A_H}{V^* L}, \frac{\eta_0}{V^* D}, \qquad (22)$$

R_o, Ek_H, and Ek_V are the Rossby number and the horizontal and vertical Ekman numbers, respectively. *Pe* is the

Péclet number and is the equivalent to the Reynolds number for diffusion. In some studies the Péclet number is written as a combination of the Rossby number, Ekman number, and a Prandtl number (Pedlosky, 1968).

In small-scale convection, where the Richardson number may be negative, the vertical and horizontal scales of motion tend towards isotropy. A hydrostatic model cannot handle such a flow, so convection must be taken care of implicitly through the vertical mixing closure hypothesis. Most of the investigations to be described in the next section use the following rules:

$$Pe_v^{-1} = \eta_o L/V^*D^2, \quad \theta_z' \geqslant 0 \tag{23}$$

$$Pe_v^{-1} \gg \eta_o L/V^*D^2, \quad \theta_z' < 0. \tag{24}$$

This means that vertical mixing η, is equal to η_o for all cases of stable stratification, but jumps to a much higher value when the stratification becomes unstable. Effectively, a constraint is imposed by the vertical mixing formulation, which never allows the stratification to be less than neutral.

Boundary conditions on the lower boundary of the ocean model are,

$$q = w = \theta_z = 0, \quad z = -H = \text{constant}. \tag{25}$$

On the side boundaries we have,

$$q = \boldsymbol{n} \cdot \nabla \theta = 0, \tag{26}$$

where $\boldsymbol{n}$ is the unit vector normal to the boundary. Most investigations of numerical models that have been carried out so far specify momentum flux and the density distribution at the upper boundary. Exceptions are studies by Bryan (1969b) and Haney (1971) for the purpose of investigating large-scale, air–sea interaction. A computational advantage is gained by setting $w = 0$ at the upper surface, filtering out surface gravity waves; but this is not an essential feature of the model.

THE THERMOHALINE CIRCULATION IN A BASIN OF SIMPLE GEOMETRY

The rather small number of published calculations based on ocean circulation models with predicted density structure are listed in Table 1. Several more very interesting studies are in press. The numerical calculations are a cumbersome tool to study the parameter dependence of models, because a solution for each case requires considerable effort to obtain. However, a comparison of the few numerical solutions available provides some interesting insight on the relative importance of the Rossby number and mixing parameters.

In the early studies of Sarkisyan (1962) and Bryan and Cox (1967) the true time scales in the problem were overlooked. As a result, these solutions represent transients not in true equilibrium with the upper boundary conditions. For purposes of estimating time scales one can write Eq. (6) in the following schematic form:

$$\frac{\Delta T}{\Delta t} = -\frac{w^*}{z}\Delta T + \frac{A_H}{L^2}\Delta T + \eta_o\frac{\Delta T}{z^2}. \tag{27}$$

From Eq. (27) we get three time scales:

$$\Delta t_1 = z/w^*, \; w^* = V^*z/L; \tag{28}$$

$$\Delta t_2 = L^2/A_H; \tag{29}$$

$$\Delta t_3 = z^2/\eta_o. \tag{30}$$

The first time scale, Δt_1, is an upwelling time scale that is very important in the time variability of ocean circulation.

TABLE 1 Published Studies of Three-Dimensional Models in Which both Density and Velocity are Predicted

Author	Geometry	Resolution	Density Equilibrium Achieved
Sarkisyan (1962)	North Atlantic	10° by 10°, 6 levels	Tendency only
Schmitz (1964)	Arabian Sea	25 by 25 km, 2 levels	Tendency only
Bryan and Cox (1967)	Idealized	Variable resolution, 6 levels	Partial
Bryan and Cox (1968)	Idealized	Variable resolution, 6 levels	Almost complete
Bolgurtsev *et al.* (1969)	Antarctic, Pacific	5° by 5°, 2-parameter model	Exponential density profile assumed
Cox (1970)	Indian Ocean bottom topography	1° by 1°, 7 levels	Almost complete
Friedrich (1970)	North Atlantic bottom topography	2½° by 2½°, 18 levels	Almost complete
Gill and Bryan (1971)	Idealized	Variable grid, 8 levels	Almost complete
Holland (1971)	Idealized	Variable, 18 levels	Almost complete
Haney (1971)	Idealized	3° by 2½°, 6 levels	Almost complete

Near the boundary where upwelling is intense Δt_1 can be quite short as shown by Charney (1955). In Bryan and Cox (1968) an initial value problem is solved by numerical integration starting from a state of complete rest and horizontally uniform fields of apparent temperature at each level. A longer and longer period was required for transient changes in the temperature field to die away as depth increased and in spite of many other factors in the problem, the time required for equilibrium to be reached could be predicted quite closely by z^2/η_o.

The degree to which this equilibrium in the deep water has been achieved is indicated in the last column of Table 1. To reach an equilibrium by straightforward numerical integration usually requires a great deal of computation. There is scope for a great deal of ingenuity to overcome this problem. Bryan and Cox (1968) and Cox (1970) carried out a numerical integration on a very coarse mesh and then interpolated the results on to a finer mesh as equilibrium was approached. Gill and Bryan (1971) carried out computations for a Rossby number much larger than that appropriate for an actual ocean basin, but at the same time much less than 1. The effect was to produce a very vigorous circulation with a shortened time scale and relatively broad and easy to resolve boundary currents. Holland (1971) abandoned the pure initial-value problem approach and used a judicious combination of time-stepping and interpolation.

The geometries that are indicated as "idealized" in Table 1 correspond to the basin shown in Figure 1. The depth is uniform, and the side walls correspond to lines of constant latitude or longitude. In all cases except Bryan and Cox (1967) a condition of symmetry is assumed across the equator. This condition corresponds to the existence of a mirror-image solution across the equator exactly matching the main solution.

In the discussion that follows, three cases with idealized geometry have been selected for comparison. The parameters for these three cases are given in Table 2. The study by Gill and Bryan (1971) was designed to study the effects of an idealized Drake Passage, but one control case (14I) had a geometry similar to Figure 1. Two parameters appearing in Table 2, which are not defined in the previous section, are the Reynolds number Re and γ. The Reynolds number is simply the ratio R_o/Ek_H in this context, and γ is the ratio of suitably defined scale velocities depending on the boundary conditions and on the surface stress and density distribution at the surface. The estimate of the nondimensional parameters in the case of Holland's (1971) study is somewhat approximate.

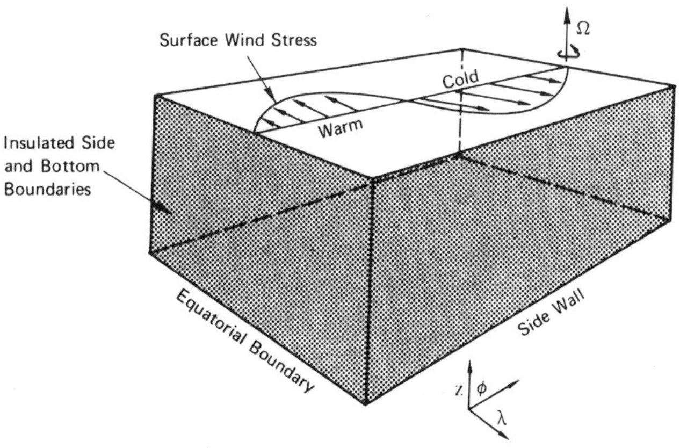

FIGURE 1 A sketch of an idealized ocean basin with an indication of the wind stress pattern and temperature gradient at the upper surface.

The types of boundary layers that arise in this problem have been discussed by Pedlosky (1968), Robinson (1970), and Gill (1971). Table 3 indicates some of the more important boundary scales that must be considered in constructing a numerical model. The estimates from Table 3 specify the minimum resolution needed at the side walls. In the three cases shown in Table 2, the numerical grid has a variable spacing with increased resolution at the lateral boundaries. In a similar context Schulman (pp. 147-167) has obtained excellent results using a stretched coordinate near the walls.

The variation of the Rossby number is probably the most significant feature in Table 2. The Reynolds number also varies over a wide range, but this is not really an independent parameter, since it may be expressed as the ratio of the Rossby number and Ekman number. In spite of the differences in the Rossby number, the circulation in all three cases has many features in common. Some of these common features are shown in a schematic diagram in Figure 2. The circulation pattern corresponds to that predicted by Stommel (1965) from simple vorticity arguments. There is an anticyclonic gyre in the upper part of the basin and an anticyclonic gyre in the lower part with western intensification in both cases. The upper and lower circulations are joined by a concentrated sinking along the poleward wall and upwelling at lower latitudes. In all three solutions cited in Table 2, a certain amount of upwelling takes place in the interior; but an unexpected feature is that an equal

TABLE 2 Parameters for Three Ocean Circulation Model Solutions

		Holland (1971)	Bryan and Cox (1968)	Gill and Bryan (1971)
R_o	$V^*/2\Omega L$	1.5×10^{-5}	2×10^{-4}	2×10^{-3}
Ek_H	$A_M/2\Omega L^2$	8×10^{-5}	1.3×10^{-6}	9×10^{-5}
Ek_V	$A_V/2\Omega D^2$	4×10^{-8}	2×10^{-6}	2.4×10^{-5}
Re	V^*L/A_M	1.8	150	22
Pe_H	V^*L/A_H	18	150	32
Pe_V	$V^*L/\eta_o D^2$	2×10^{-3}	1×10^{-2}	1.2×10^{-2}
γ	–	3.4	1.0	1.1

TABLE 3 Boundary Layers in an Ocean Circulation Solution for the Geometry Shown in Figure 1

Name	Terms Involved	Equation	Non	Reference
Munk layer	$\cos\phi V = Ek_H V_{xxx}$	vorticity	$Ek_H^{1/3}$	Munk (1950)
Inertial layer	$\cos\phi V = R_o V_{xx}$	vorticity	$R_o^{1/2}$	
Diffusive layer	$U\theta x = Pe^{-1}\,\theta_{xx}$	density	Pe^{-1}	
Equatorial viscous layer	$yk \times q = Ek_H q_{yy}$	momentum	$Ek_H^{1/3}$	Gill (1971)
Planetary boundary layer	$\sin\phi k \times q = Ek_V q_{zz}$	momentum	$Ek_V^{1/2}$	

or greater amount takes place in the western boundary current. This point will be discussed in more detail later in connection with the heat balance.

The effects of increasing the Rossby number and variations in Reynolds number may be seen in Figure 3. The pattern of the mass transport stream function is shown corresponding to the three cases given in Table 2. Holland's (1971) solution is in units of 10^6 tons/s, while the other patterns are in dimensionless transport units. In Figure 3a nonlinear terms are practically negligible in the momentum equations. In the case of uniform depth this means that there is no way for baroclinicity to influence the total transport pattern. As a result Holland's (1971) transport pattern corresponds closely to Munk's (1950) solution from the wind-driven ocean theory. There are two regular gyres in Figure 3a that are nearly symmetric in the north-south direction. For the parameter range of Holland's (1971) solution, the pattern is nearly stationary. In contrast, both the patterns of Figure 3b and 3c represent the averages of fluctuating solutions. The fluctuations are strong in the Bryan and Cox (1968) solution in which the Reynolds number is particularly high. The baroclinic solutions shown in Figure 3b and 3c confirm predictions about the mass transport streamline pattern based on simpler, nonlinear barotropic models (Bryan, 1963; Veronis, 1966). In

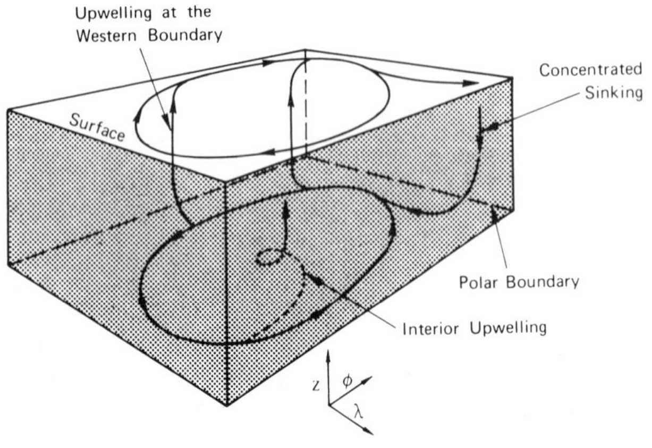

FIGURE 2 A schematic drawing of the thermohaline circulation found in numerical models.

the barotropic models, however, the nonlinear effects are negligible unless the thermocline is included implicitly by making the depth of the wind-driven model very shallow. In the baroclinic cases shown in Figure 3, the nonlinearity arises in a natural way due to the concentration of transport above the thermocline. In the case of Figure 3b the total transport of the western boundary current is enhanced by a factor of about 50 percent over that expected from linear theory.

The streamlines of total transport in the vertical-meridional plane are shown in Figure 4 for the same three cases given in Table 2. Note that the units are the same and the total magnitude of the circulation is nearly the same as in Figure 3. All of the patterns indicate a concentrated downward motion in the poleward end of the basin and a general upwelling over the remainder of the basin. Other experiments show that the shallow subcell near the equator is only present where there is a wind stress specified at the surface. The principle effect of a decrease in Rossby number appears to be a tendency to squeeze the downward flow into a smaller area near the northern boundary. Otherwise the patterns are much alike. The total circulation in the zonal plane is shown in Figure 5 for two of the three cases. The units are the same as in Figures 3 and 4. We see that downward motion is very much compressed to the eastern wall, and in Holland's (1971) solution the upward motion is also concentrated at the western wall. An examination of the horizontal patterns of vertical motion in Holland's (1971) solution indicate that vertical motions at low and high latitudes in the interior are of opposite sign and therefore tend to cancel out when a meridional integral is taken.

An idea of the effect of wind can be obtained by examining Figure 6, consisting of several vertical cross sections showing the meridional component of velocity. Figure 6b is based on Bryan and Cox (1968) and Figure 6a is an unpublished solution for an identical case with no wind driving. For comparison, a velocity section off Cape Hatteras calculated by Swallow and Worthington (1961) is shown in Figure 6c. Note that a strong western boundary current is present in both cases. The main effect of the wind is to greatly enhance the western boundary current and to produce a net northward transport. There is a major discrepancy in the calculated and "observed" width of the western boun-

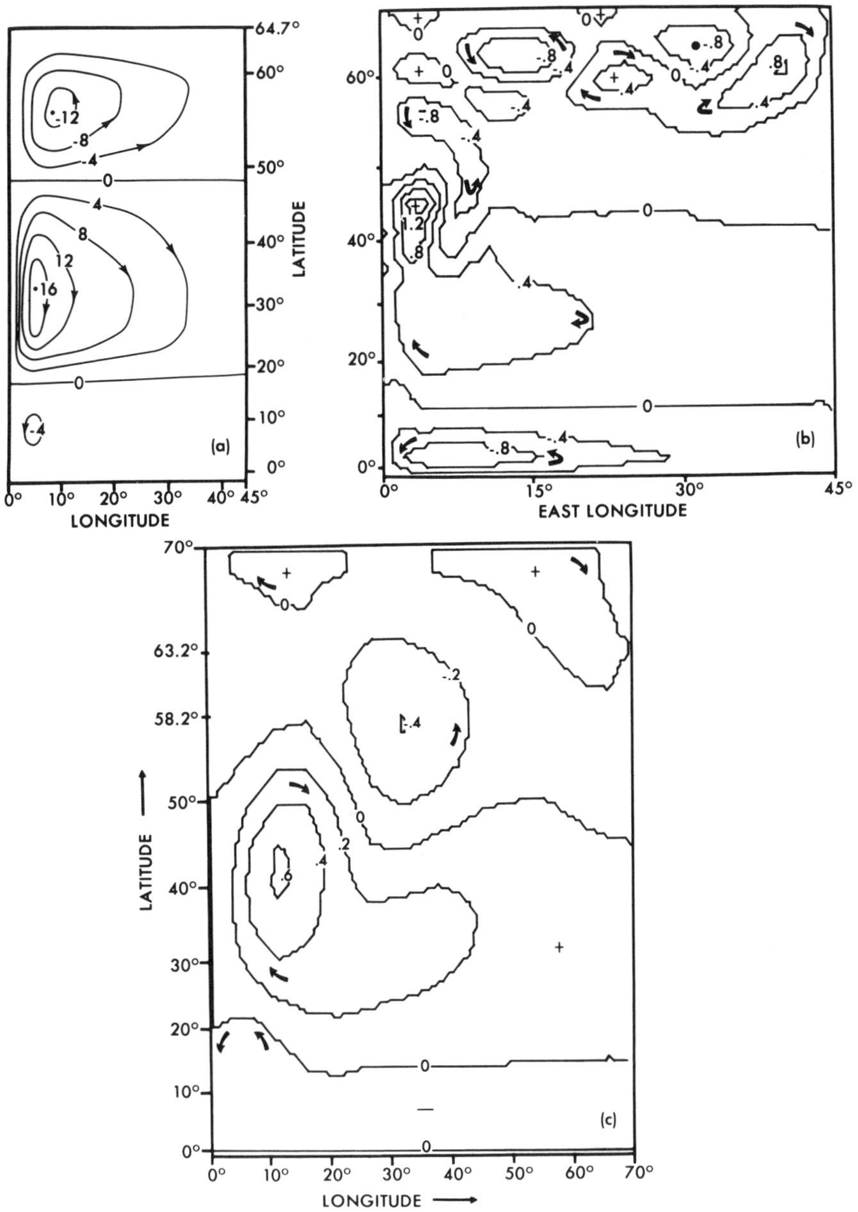

FIGURE 3 The pattern of mass transport stream function, giving the vertically integrated flow. (a) Holland (1971) in units of million tons/s, (b) Bryan and Cox (1968), (c) Gill and Bryan (1971).

dary current. Swallow and Worthington's (1961) section indicates a width of about 3/4° of longitude, while Figure 6b shows that the Bryan and Cox (1968) boundary current is about 2 1/2° wide. However, Table 2 indicates that there is an order of magnitude difference between the Rossby number used by Bryan and Cox (1968) and the more appropriate value for the real ocean used by Holland (1971). Since nonlinear effects are important in the Bryan and Cox (1968) solution, it seems realistic to use the inertial width scale, $R_o{}^{1/2}$ (see Table 3). This scale would predict a difference of approximately $\sqrt{10}$ between the width of the current computed in Bryan and Cox (1968) and the observed current, which is in fair agreement with Figure 6. Note that R_o depends only on the rotation and the density gradient imposed at the surface, and is independent of mixing parameters.

Welander has already reviewed analytic theories. Among the most remarkable developments are the similarity solutions for the thermocline. The solutions are for simple geostrophic models without lateral mixing. The nonlinearity enters through the advection terms in the density equation. In Bryan and Cox (1967), this theory is used to test the numerical model. A convenient exact solution for a special case has been found by Blandford (1965). Blandford's solution corresponds to a nonzonal temperature distribution at the surface, and all variables except the vertical velocity decay with depth. In contrast the Bryan and Cox (1968) solution corresponds to a strictly zonal distribution of apparent

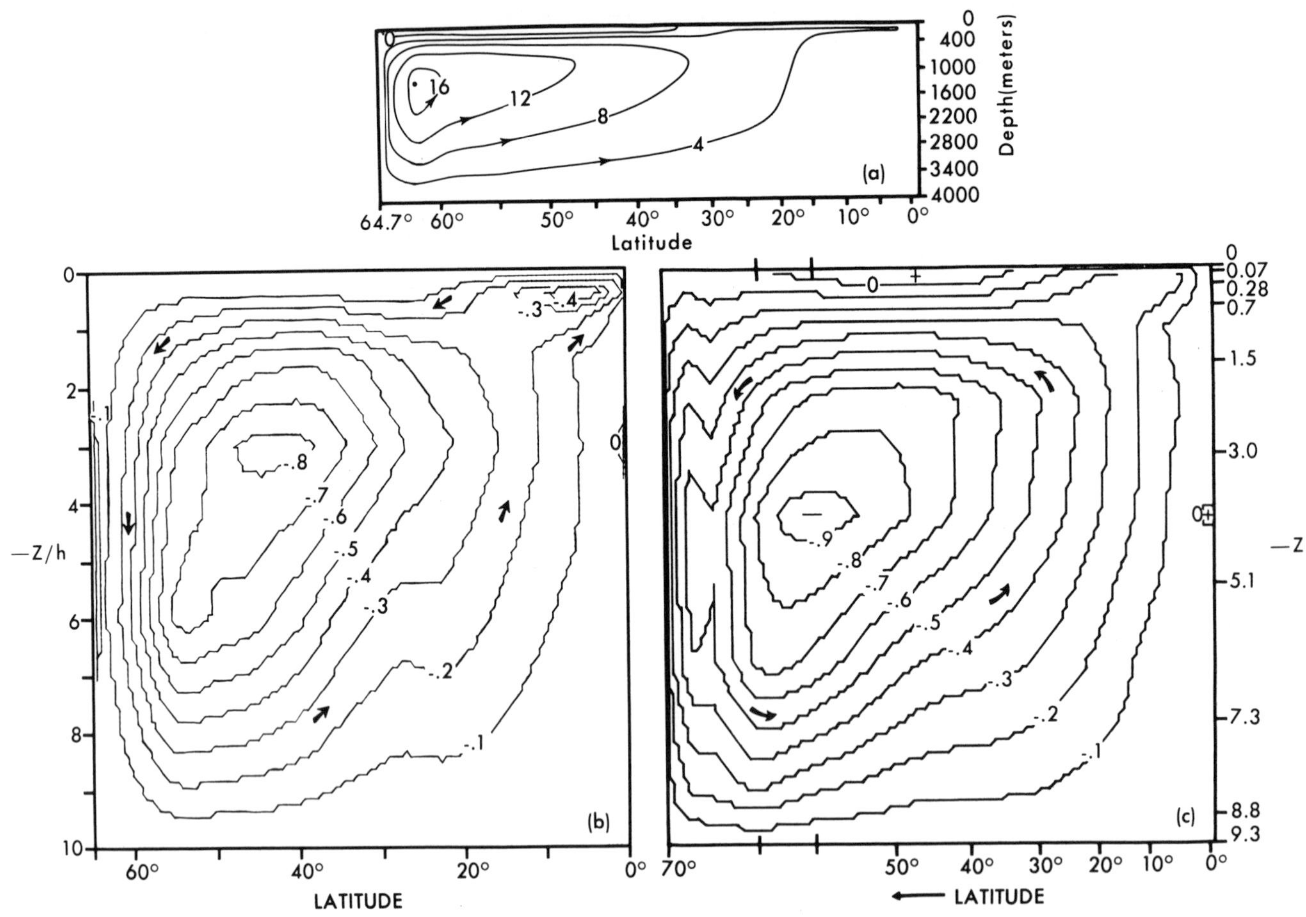

FIGURE 4 The streamlines of total transport in the vertical-meridional plane. The circulation is counterclockwise in all cases. (a) Holland (1971), (b) Bryan and Cox (1968), (c) Gill and Bryan (1971).

temperature at the upper boundary, and currents exist right to the bottom. In spite of these differences, the heat balance of the interior subtropical gyre region for the analytic and numerical solutions are remarkably similar. The patterns are shown in Figure 7(a and b). In the upper part of the water column, there is a strong cooling due to the general southward flow of water in the presence of a poleward temperature gradient. The cooling effect is balanced by downward diffusion of heat from the surface and downward motion connected with Ekman pumping in the subtropical wind gyre. Well below the thermocline, the heat balance changes due to a reversal in sign of the vertical velocity and the great attenuation with depth of horizontal advection. Only in the deep water can the heat balance be considered local since diffusion is almost entirely balanced by upwelling.

Although the lateral diffusion of heat plays an insignificant role in the interior, it has a crucial role along the western boundary. The heat balance for the western wall is shown in Figure 8 for a level corresponding to the upper thermocline. As the western boundary current moves northward along the wall, it intensifies through inflow and upwelling. Poleward flow in the presence of a poleward temperature gradient produces a warming effect that is balanced by upward motion and inflow of colder water. As indicated in Figure 8, lateral and vertical advection of apparent temperature are almost exactly balanced away from the wall. Vertical diffusion is relatively insignificant in the boundary current. This balance of terms cannot hold right at the wall, however, as horizontal advection must go to zero to satisfy the boundary conditions of the horizontal velocity. On the other hand, the vertical velocity may be a maximum at the wall. The end result is that a diffusive layer is required close to the wall. Some of the consequences of this diffusive layer are discussed by Veronis (pp. 133–146) in this symposium. As he points out, the strong mixing in this lateral diffusive layer permits upward motion through the thermocline, reducing the amount of upwelling required in the interior. He predicts that the ratio of upwelling in the interior to upwelling in the western boundary current is proportional to the horizontal Péclet number.

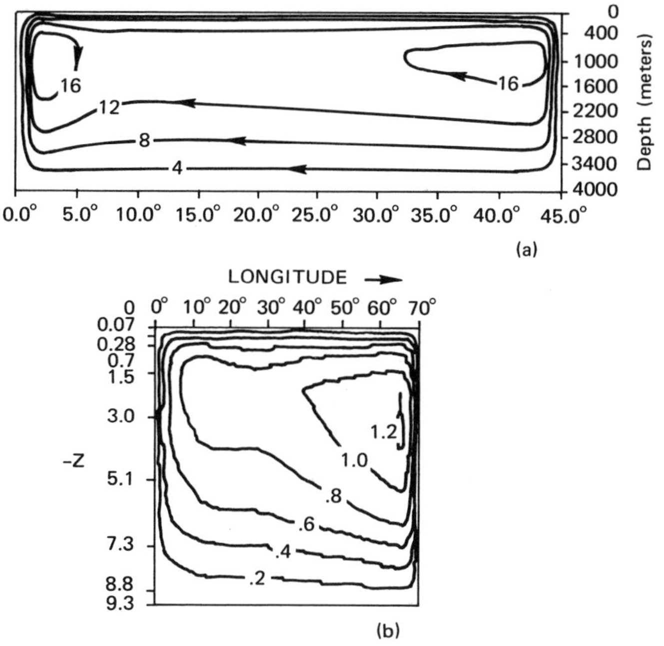

FIGURE 5 The total transport in the vertical-zonal plane. The circulation is clockwise in both cases. (a) Holland (1971), (b) Gill and Bryan (1971).

COX'S INDIAN OCEAN MODEL

Turning to models that include the actual geometry of an ocean basin, we find very little published work aside from the "diagnostic" studies carried out by Sarkisyan and co-workers in the Soviet Union. One of the few studies that predicts the evolution of the density field as well as the velocity field for a realistic geometry is Cox's (1970) study of the Indian Ocean. This study is also of special interest because it attempts to model the seasonal variability of a large-scale current.

Cox's model extends over the Indian Ocean region with an open boundary at latitude 20° S. Temperature, salinity, and two components of velocity are predicted at each of seven levels along the vertical coordinate. The levels are positioned to give the maximum resolution in the upper thermocline. Temperature, salinity, and wind stress are specified as a function of season at the surface. Hydrographic data are used to determine the distribution of temperature and salinity on the vertical section at the open boundary. The inflow and outflow at different levels along this section is free to adjust itself to the density field; but in the absence of better information, the total transport is simply set equal to zero. In other words, the shape of the vertical profile can adjust to the density field with the constraint that the vertically integrated flow in and out of the region is zero.

Starting with horizontally uniform fields of temperature and salinity, a numerical integration with respect to time is carried out over the equivalent of 192 years. Details of the construction of the numerical model are given in Bryan (1969a). To make such an extended integration feasible the calculation is carried out in three stages. In the initial stage, a 4° by 4° horizontal resolution is used. The final results of this stage are interpolated onto a 2° by 2° grid, and finally onto a 1° by 1° grid. The layout of the grid in the second and third stages is shown in Figure 9. A table of parameters from Cox's (1970) paper is reproduced as Table 4.

The numerical method requires a closure scheme that will damp out small-scale components. As the grid is refined, less damping is required, which allows A_H for momentum to be reduced substantially for each segment. On the other hand, A_H for the temperature and salinity fields is only changed by a factor of two in order to minimize changes in

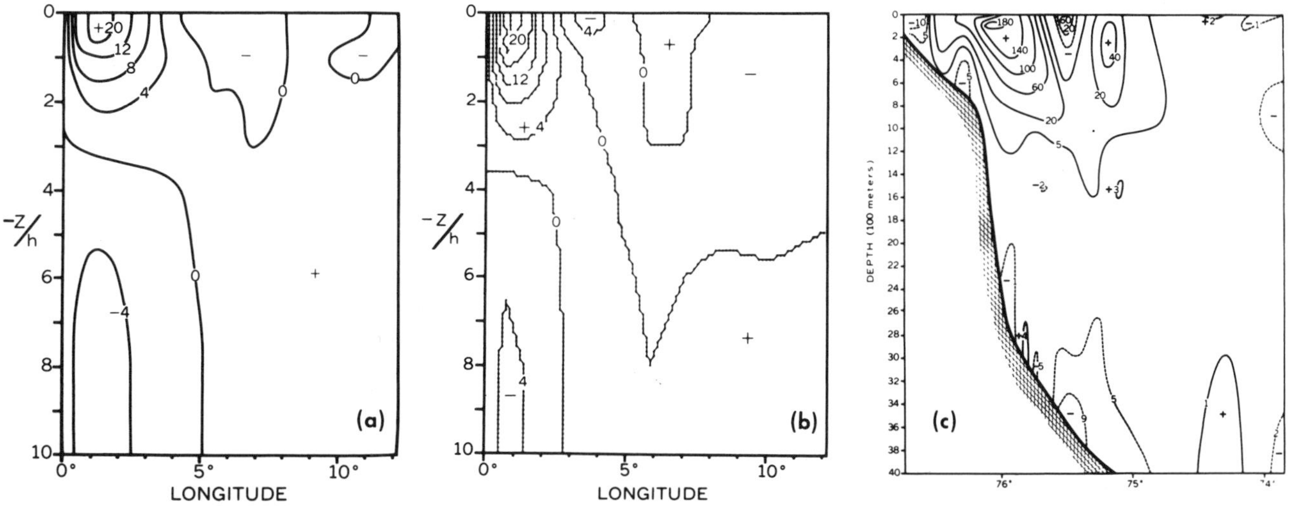

FIGURE 6 The meridional component of velocity near the western wall in nondimensional units. (a) no wind, (b) with wind, (c) velocity section off Cape Hatteras in units cm/s (Swallow and Worthington, 1961).

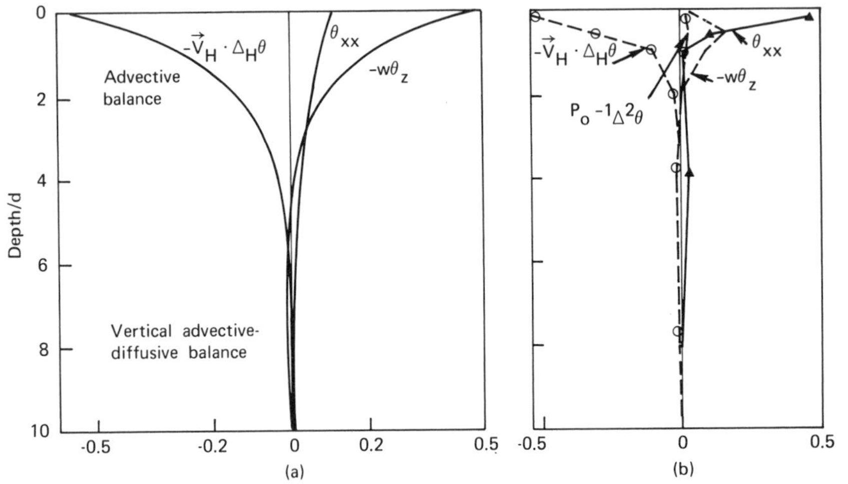

FIGURE 7 Heat balance components in the interior of the subtropical gyre. (a) Blandford's (1965) analytic model, (b) numerical model (Bryan and Cox, 1968) (diagram from Alexander, 1971).

the heat and salt balance. Vertical mixing of heat, salinity, and momentum are kept at a constant value of 1 cm^2/s throughout.

The thermocline in Cox's final solution is uniformly deeper than observed, indicating that the vertical mixing in the model is too large, at least in the upper thermocline. The most interesting results relate to the seasonal variations of the Somali current. Figure 10 shows the long shore velocity component calculated by the model for the summer and winter season. While the peak intensity is much less than what was observed, the results are in qualitative agreement with measurements made during the Indian Ocean expedition. During the southwest monsoon there is a shallow intense northward-flowing current along the African coast. The currents reverse, but it is much weaker during the northeast monsoon. It is a matter of considerable interest to understand how the Somali current responds so rapidly to the wind, while the other major western boundary currents such as the Gulf Stream and the Kuroshio are relatively steady. Lighthill (1969) has suggested a mechanism involving a rapid response due to mixed baroclinic Rossby gravity waves at the equator.

Based on an analysis of the results shown in Figure 10, Cox (1970) concludes that most of the coastal upwelling can be directly accounted for by an Ekman transport away

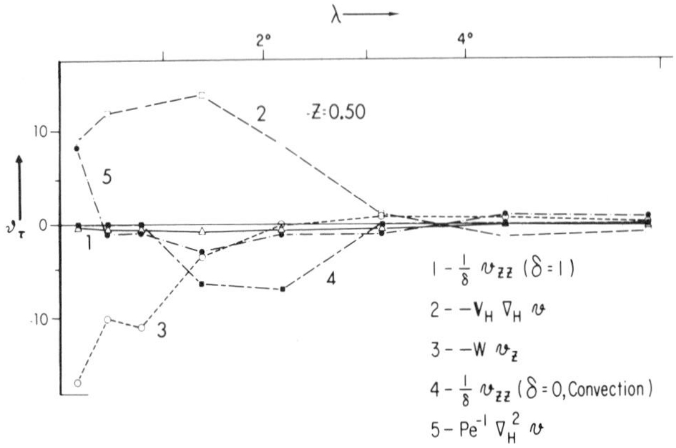

FIGURE 8 Heat balance at the western wall in the Bryan and Cox (1968) solution. Note the diffusive layer immediately adjacent to the wall.

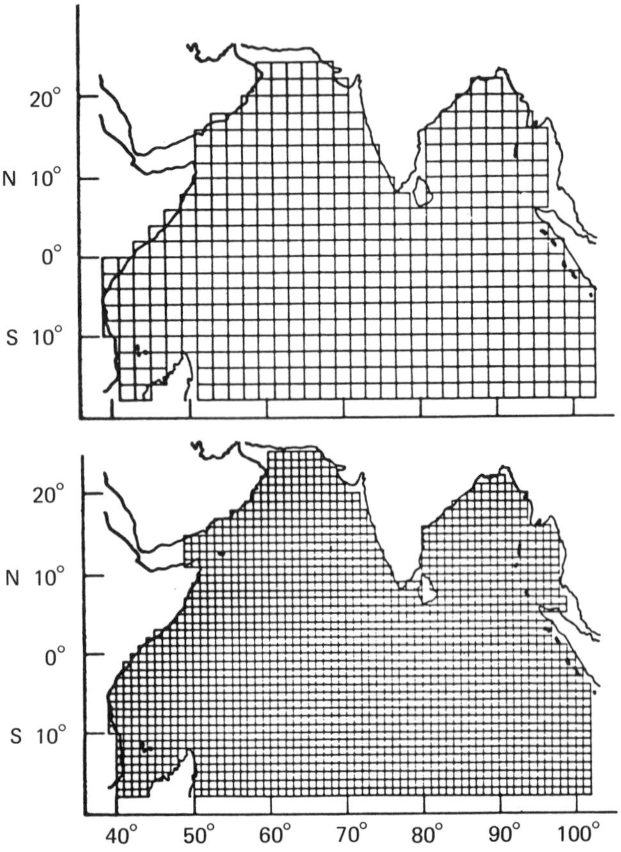

FIGURE 9 A layout of the horizontal numerical grid used in the second and third stages of Cox's (1970) Indian Ocean computation.

TABLE 4 Parameters and Other Information for the Three Stages of Numerical Integration in Cox's (1970) Indian Ocean Model

	Segment 1	Segment 2	Segment 3
Resolution	4° square	2° square	1° square
A_M	2×10^9 cm²/s	2×10^8 cm²/s	5×10^7 cm²/s
A_H	10^8 cm²/s	10^8 cm²/s	5×10^7 cm²/s
η_0	1 cm²/s	1 cm²/s	1 cm²/s
Interval of integration	0–130 yr	130–185 yr	185–192 yr
$\Delta\tau$	0.6 day	0.3 day	0.1 day
Computer time (UNIVAC 1108)	0.2 h/yr	1.7 h/yr	22 h/yr

from the coast during the southwest monsoon. A cooling due to upwelling alone would produce a long shore baroclinic current 90° or 3 months out of phase with the seasonal wind cycle. The numerical solution indicates that, after the onset of the southwest monsoon, the net cooling near the Somali coast is due to a small difference between the effects of upwelling and horizontal advection. In analogy with other vibrating systems, the lateral advection operates as a damping mechanism that reduces the difference in phase angle between the forcing and response. The model predicts a phase lag of only 10–20 days, which is close to that shown in the climatological atlases for the area. The model indicates that the Somali current has much in common with eastern boundary currents. In order to get a better verification with actual current measurements made during the Indian Ocean expedition, it would be of great interest to repeat Cox's calculation with much finer resolution near the Somali coast.

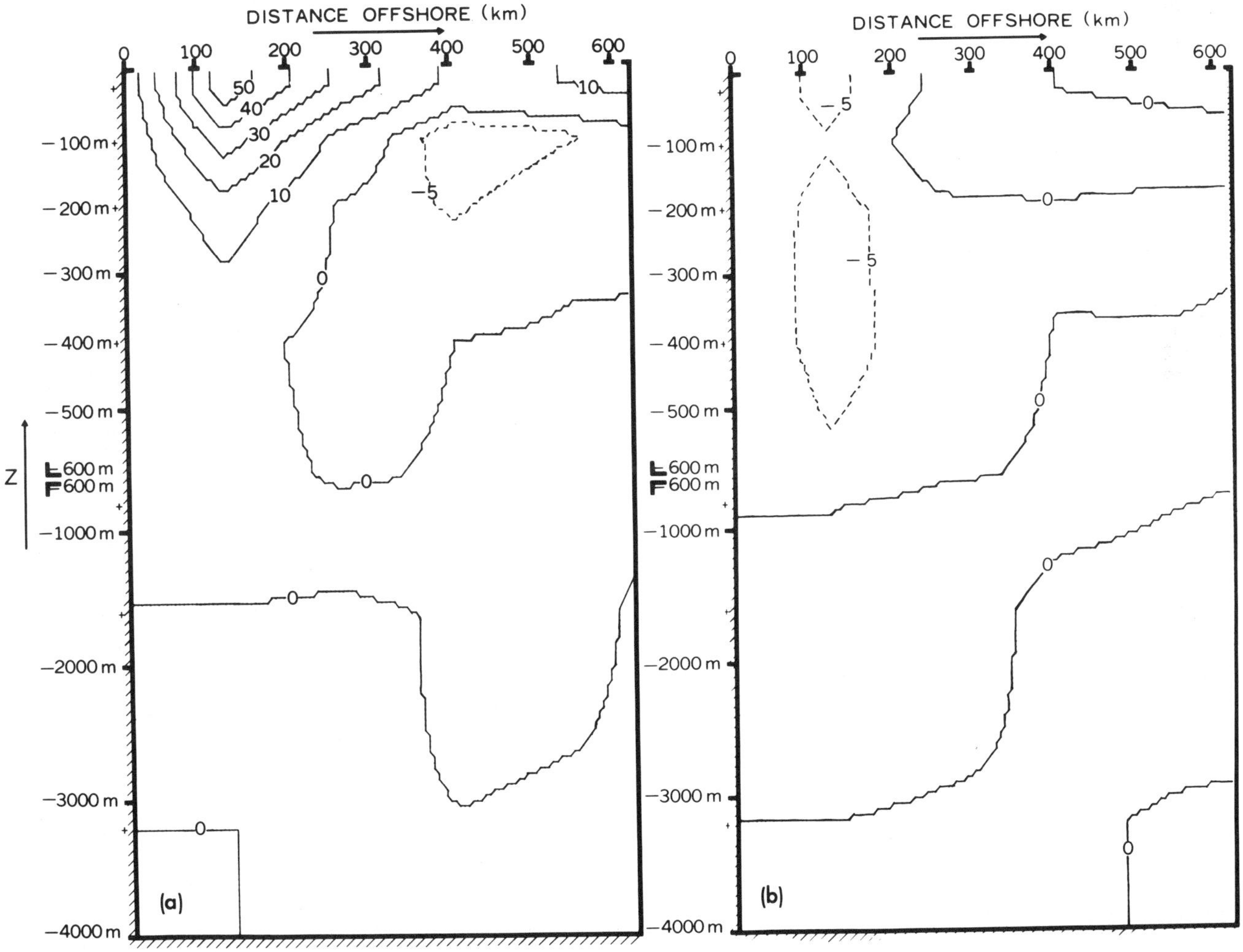

FIGURE 10 The longshore component of velocity in Cox's model. (a) southwest monsoon, (b) northwest monsoon (units, cm/s).

SUGGESTIONS FOR FUTURE WORK

In this review we have discussed two kinds of numerical experiments. One type is aimed at illuminating the physics of ocean circulation through idealized models. Only a minimum amount of detail is considered in each case. The second type involves a model that will allow direct comparison with oceanographic data. Cox's (1970) study of the Indian Ocean is taken as an example. In the future other types of models should be considered for the analysis and extrapolation of data. For example, there is no reason why a mixed "diagnostic" and predictive calculation cannot be carried out for an ocean model. In this case densities and velocities would be held fixed at certain points where data is available, and predictions would be made in all surrounding areas. In this way the numerical model could be used to extrapolate scattered observations in such a way that the constraints associated with the dynamics and continuity of large-scale flow would be taken into account. Some pioneering work along these lines is presently being carried out by Bretherton (pp. 237-249) in connection with MODE.

Once the validity of ocean circulation models has been established by repeated comparisons of different solutions with the real ocean, the way is open for many practical applications. As times goes on, numerical models may become the major means by which fruitful interaction can take place between geochemists, fisheries experts, meteorologists, and physical oceanographers primarily concerned with ocean circulation.

REVIEW: BY C. E. LEITH

In this paper the author reviews recent work with numerical ocean models. In a section dealing with the derivation of the hydrostatic Boussinesq equations, he describes the common problem of simulating the average influence of subgrid motions through some sort of eddy diffusion coefficient. For the models discussed, the horizontal eddy diffusion coefficient has been taken as a specified constant, but in the vertical direction an additional mixing mechanism is provided through a convective adjustment that prevents the development of unstable stratification. For computing a thermohaline circulation, it is often convenient to combine temperature and salinity into a single buoyancy variable.

The important problem of time scale is discussed at length. Many early model experiments were not carried beyond an initial transient regime. The vertical diffusive time scale seems to be the critical one—and this is typically hundreds of years—yet the description of more rapid motions requires computational time steps of tenths of days. A similar difficulty arises for space scales. The circulation in an ocean basin is largely to be found in narrow boundary layers of one sort or another. We have, then, in ocean models a great range of important space as well as time scales, the resolution of which requires at least as much computational power as current technology can provide.

Some results of numerical model experiments in ideal basins are described. These seem to be in qualitative agreement with simple models of the thermohaline circulation. The boundary layers are not necessarily of small enough scale in the numerical models, but this error may have little influence on the circulation in the large. The boundary layers are required to complete mass, momentum, and buoyancy budgets and in simple models have been treated almost symbolically. It may be no worse to trifle with their detail in numerical models.

The example of a real ocean basin problem given in the paper is of a model of the Indian Ocean. Here there has been considerable success in describing the remarkably rapid response of the Somali current to the changing wind stress associated with changing monsoon regimes.

The main problem of ocean circulation models seems to be that much computation must be executed to describe small space and time scales of motion, which in themselves are not of interest, but whose influence on larger and slower motions is important. This is like the usual problem of the treatment of subgrid-scale motions and requires for its solution some statistical theory of the average influence of the uninteresting scales on those of interest. Unfortunately, the simple statistical ideas from turbulence theory that have been used in atmospheric models do not seem to be as useful here, where in fact motions of small time and space scales tend to be localized in boundary layers rather than distributed homogeneously throughout the fluid.

REFERENCES

Alexander, R. C. 1971. On the advective and diffusive heat balance in the interior of a subtropical ocean. Tellus 23:393–403.

Blandford, R. 1965. Notes on the theory of the thermocline. J. Mar. Res. 23:18–29.

Bolgurtsev, B. N., V. F. Kozlov, and L. A. Molchanova. 1969. Results of calculation of the currents in the Pacific Ocean sector of the Antarctic. Izv. Akad. Nauk. USSR Atmos. Oceanic Phys. 8:846–59.

Bryan, K. 1963. A numerical investigation of a nonlinear model of a wind-driven ocean. J. Atmos. Sci. 20:594–606.

Bryan, K. 1969a. A numerical method for the study of the circulation of the world ocean. J. Comp. Phys. 3:347–76.

Bryan, K. 1969b. Climate and ocean circulation. Part III: The ocean model. Mon. Weather Rev. 97:806–27.

Bryan, K., and M. D. Cox. 1967. A numerical investigation of the oceanic general circulation. Tellus 19:54–80.

Bryan, K., and M. D. Cox. 1968. A nonlinear model of an ocean driven by wind and differential heating. Parts I and II. J. Atmos. Sci. 25:945–78.

Charney, J. G. 1955. The generation of ocean currents by wind. J. Mar. Res. 14:477–98.

Cox, M. D. 1970. A mathematical model of the Indian Ocean. Deep-Sea Res. 17:45–75.

Friedrich, H. J. 1970. Preliminary results from a numerical multilayer model for the circulation in the North Atlantic. Dtsch. Hydrogr. Z. 23:145–64.

Gill, A. E. 1971. The equatorial current in a homogeneous ocean. Deep-Sea Res. 18:421–31.

Gill, A. E., and K. Bryan. 1971. Effects of geometry on the circulation of a three-dimensional southern-hemisphere ocean model. Deep-Sea Res. 18:685–721.

Hammond, A. L. 1972. Planning for a major experiment. Science 176:268–69.

Haney, R. L. 1971. A numerical study of the large scale response of an ocean circulation to surface heat and momentum flux. Ph.D. Dissertation. Department of Meteorology, University of California, Los Angeles.

Haney, R. L. 1974. A numerical study of the response of an idealized ocean to large-scale surface heat and momentum flux. J. Phys. Ocean. 2:145–67.

Holland, W. R. 1971. Ocean tracer distributions. Part I: A preliminary numerical experiment. Tellus 23:371–92.

Kamenkovich, V. M. 1967. On the coefficients of eddy diffusion and eddy viscosity in large-scale oceanic and atmospheric motions. Izv. Akad. Nauk. USSR Atmos. Oceanic Phys. 3:1326–33.

Lighthill, M. J. 1969. Dynamic response of the Indian Ocean to onset of the southwest monsoon. Philos. Trans. R. Soc. Lond. Ser. A 265:45–92.

Monin, A. S., and A. M. Yaglom. 1971. Statistical Fluid Mechanics. MIT Press, Cambridge. 769 pp.

Munk, W. H. 1950. On the wind-driven ocean circulation. J. Meteorol. 7:79–93.

Pedlosky, J. 1968. An overlooked aspect of the wind-driven oceanic circulation. J. Fluid Mech. 32:809–21.

Robinson, A. R. 1970. Boundary layers in ocean circulation models. Annu. Rev. Fluid Mech. 2:293–312.

Sarkisyan, A. S. 1962. On the dynamics of the origin of wind currents in the baroclinic ocean. Okeanologia 11:393–409.

Schmitz, H. P. 1964. Modellrechnungen zu wind-erzeugten Bewegungen in einen Meer mit Sprungschicht. Dtsch. Hydrogr. Z. 17:201–31.

Stommel, H. 1965. The Gulf Stream (2d. Ed.) University of California Press, Berkeley. 240 pp.

Swallow, J. C., and L. V. Worthington. 1961. An observation of a deep countercurrent in the Western North Atlantic. Deep-Sea Res. 8:1–19.

Veronis, G. 1966. Wind-driven ocean circulation. Parts I and II. Deep-Sea Res. 13:17–55.

DISCUSSION

PEDLOSKY: The discussion with Leith indicates that scale separation in the oceans is a major problem. Perhaps this is something that can be exploited rather than being treated as a problem. By this, I mean that a full-blown theory for these processes would have to be developed.

BRETHERTON: The evidence seems to be that there are small-scale eddies in the ocean with velocities in the order of 10 cm/s, which may be as large or larger than general circulation features. In these eddies, topographic effects are extremely important, as is baroclinic instability. To account for these eddies in general circulation models, one would have to have a grid spacing of 20 km. Anything greater would be far too large.

ROBINSON: In the presence of such large-scale fluctuations associated with mesoscale eddies with velocities on the order of 10 cm/s, it is not clear that present numerical models can treat the residual (presumably associated with the general circulation features) in a meaningful way.

CHARNEY: I would like to return to the point that Pedlosky made earlier. Perhaps it will be possible to turn to advantage the fact that in the ocean the radius of deformation is small compared to the geometry of the system. In the kinetic theory gases, the RMS molecular velocities are much greater than the streaming velocities, and it is here that the mixing-length ideas seem to work very well. I think that there is some hope of parameterizing the eddies in the ocean. I don't see much chance of getting the sort of horizontal resolution Bretherton calls for.

SARKISYAN: I would like to comment on two aspects of Bryan's paper. The first is his numerical scheme. In Bryan's model, whenever the density field is statistically unstable, there is infinite mixing and this instability is not carried forward to the next time step. Our calculations suggest that it may not be necessary to do this correction. The instabilities, when they occur, occur only at a few grid points. Horizontal mixing usually gets rid of the instability after a few time steps, and no serious error is propagated in the solution. It is very important to learn more about the physics of this instability. A second point concerns the calculation or use of the density field. At present, predictive models cannot calculate the density with sufficient accuracy to be compared with observations. However, over much of the ocean there is insufficient data on the density field. Perhaps it will be possible in this case to make hydrodynamical interpolations using both diagnostic and predictive techniques for these regions.

BRYAN: I would like to comment on Sarkisyan's first point. I feel that our whole system of equations depends on the use of the hydrostatic equation and that it is wrong in principle to apply these equations to the unstable case. For this reason, I think it is important that we constrain the model equations so that there is no static instability.

PHILLIPS: I would like to comment on the use of a Richardson number for rapid mixing of an instability. The Richardson number is a local number, whereas the general circulation models require large-scale characteristics. In fact, there may be mesoscale eddies sloshing around and internal waves breaking that can produce strong mixing effects.

A BAROCLINIC NUMERICAL MODEL OF THE WORLD OCEAN: PRELIMINARY RESULTS

M. D. COX

INTRODUCTION

The communication between the major ocean basins is generally believed to be very important in the dynamics of the interiors of the separate basins. Recently, baroclinic numerical models have been used to study the dynamics of separate oceans (Cox, 1970; Friedrich, 1970; Holland and Hirschman, in press). In these studies, the communication with neighboring oceans is accomplished primarily by the specification of prognostic variables along all open lateral boundaries using observed data. Extending the region of solution of the model to include the entire world ocean makes such *a priori* assumptions concerning water-mass exchange unnecessary, and the circulation may be predicted from the sea-surface driving alone. Another decrease in total information input to the predictive system is accomplished by the combination of global oceanic and atmospheric models, where the incident solar energy only must be specified. This approach will be taken up in separate investigations.

Unfortunately, the prediction of the steady-state configuration of the density structure in the world ocean from an arbitrary initial state is rendered impractical at this time, by the immensity of the computational effort involved. However, various simpler predictions of shorter characteristic time scale are feasible; it is these preliminary experiments that will be described here.

The first experiment assumes that the density is completely homogeneous over the entire volume. A similar study has been performed by Leichtmann *et al.* (1971). This case is a good test of the model, because comparisons may be made with familiar analytic results from the theory of wind-driven oceans and the theory of topographic influence on barotropic flow. In the second experiment, the density is specified using observed data. The resulting baroclinic driving augments the driving of the previous case to yield a new solution. This approach has been suggested by Sarkisyan (1966) and applied to the North Pacific by Kozlov (1971).

In both of the experiments, the density is held fixed. This greatly reduces the characteristic time scale of adjustment within the model, and a steady-state solution can be reached. In the third experiment, the density (i.e., T and S) is treated as a prognostic variable with initial values corresponding to those of the second experiment. In this case, the longer characteristic time scale involved in the adjustment of the density structure makes the computational effort to obtain a steady-state solution impractical. As an alternative, the adjustment that takes place—in the observed initial conditions—over the first few years of integration is investigated.

THE MODEL

The model is basically the same as that described by Bryan (1969) and used by Cox (1970). The Navier-Stokes equations for a rotating spherical coordinate system are used with three basic simplifications. The Boussinesq approximation is made in which variations in density are neglected except in the bouyancy term. Hydrostatic balance is assumed. Viscosity and conductivity are replaced by new terms representing the diffusion of momentum and heat by small-scale, transient disturbances.

Let $m = \sec\phi$, $n = \sin\phi$, $u = a\dot{\lambda}m^{-1}$, and $v = a\dot{\phi}$, where a

is the radius of the earth, λ is longitude, and ϕ is latitude. The two equations of motion are

$$u_t - 2\Omega n(v) = -\frac{m}{a}(P/\rho_o)_\lambda + G^\lambda, \qquad (1)$$

$$v_t + 2\Omega n(u) = -\frac{1}{a}(P/\rho_o)_\phi + G^\phi, \qquad (2)$$

where Ω is the angular velocity of the earth, P is pressure, and ρ_o is average density.

$$G^\lambda = -\frac{m}{a}[(u^2)_\lambda + (uv/m)_\phi] - (wu)_z + mnuv/a$$
$$+ A_v u_{zz} + A_m a^{-2}[\Delta u + (1 - m^2n^2)u - 2nm^2 v_\lambda], \qquad (3)$$

$$G^\phi = -\frac{m}{a}[(uv)_\lambda + (v^2/m)_\phi] - (wv)_z - mnu^2/a$$
$$+ A_v v_{zz} + A_m a^{-2}[\Delta v + (1 - m^2n^2)v + 2nm^2 u_\lambda], \qquad (4)$$

$$\Delta(\ ) = m^2(\ )_{\lambda\lambda} + m[(\ )_\phi m^{-1}]_\phi. \qquad (5)$$

A_v and A_m are constant "eddy viscosity" coefficients in the vertical and horizontal directions, respectively.

The hydrostatic relation is

$$\rho g = -P_z. \qquad (6)$$

The continuity equation is

$$w_z = -\frac{m}{a}[u_\lambda + (v/m)_\phi]. \qquad (7)$$

When temperature and salinity are treated as prognostic variables, they are computed from their conservation equations,

$$T_t + \frac{m}{a}[(uT)_\lambda + (vT/m)_\phi] + (wT)_z = \frac{A_v}{\delta}T_{zz} + \frac{A_h}{a^2}\Delta T, \qquad (8)$$

$$S_t + \frac{m}{a}[(uS)_\lambda + (vS/m)_\phi] + (wS)_z = \frac{A_v}{\delta}S_{zz} + \frac{A_h}{a^2}\Delta S. \qquad (9)$$

A_h is the horizontal eddy diffusion coefficient for heat and salinity, and A_v is as defined above, retaining the same value as in the momentum equations. (In vertically stable cases, vertical mixing is uniform and in unstable cases, it is infinite.) Let ρ' be the density that a parcel of water would have if it were transferred adiabatically to the surface.

$$\delta = \begin{cases} 1 & \text{if } \rho_z' < 0 \\ 0 & \text{if } \rho_z' > 0. \end{cases} \qquad (10)$$

Boundary conditions at the lateral walls are

$$u = v = T_n = S_n = 0, \qquad (11)$$

where T_n indicates a local derivative with respect to the coordinate normal to the wall. At the upper boundary,

$$\left.\begin{array}{l} W = 0 \\ \rho_o A_v(u_z, v_z) = \tau^\lambda, \tau^\phi \\ T = T_{SUR} \\ S = S_{SUR} \end{array}\right\} z = 0, \qquad (12)$$

where T_{SUR} and S_{SUR} are specified surface temperature and salinity, and τ^λ and τ^ϕ are the zonal and meridional components of the surface stress. Setting the surface vertical velocity to zero ("rigid-lid" approximation) filters out external inertia-gravitational oscillations that would seriously limit the time step of integration. This approximation causes the loss of the kinematic effect of variations of the sea surface. At the lower boundary,

$$\left.\begin{array}{l} w = -ua^{-1}mH_\lambda - va^{-1}H_\phi \\ u_z = v_z = 0 \end{array}\right\} z = -H. \qquad (13)$$

The preceding equations form a complete description of the model. However, further manipulation is required to obtain the form of the equations that serves as the basis for the numerical model. In order to eliminate pressure, Eqs. (1-2) are differentiated with respect to z,

$$u_{tz} - 2\Omega n v_z = \frac{mg}{a}\frac{\rho\lambda}{\rho_o} + (G^\lambda)_z, \qquad (14)$$

$$v_{tz} + 2\Omega n u_z = \frac{1g}{a}\frac{\rho\phi}{\rho_o} + (G^\phi)_z. \qquad (15)$$

Making use of the boundary conditions in Eqs. (12-13), it is possible to obtain a transport stream function,

$$\psi_\lambda, \quad \psi_\phi = m^{-1}a\int_{-H}^{O}\rho_o v\,dz, \quad -a\int_{-H}^{O}\rho_o u\,dz. \qquad (16)$$

Taking the vertical integral of formulas (1-2) and making use of the hydrostatic relation yields

$$\frac{1}{a}(-\psi_{\phi t} - 2\Omega mn\psi_\lambda) = \frac{-mH}{a}(P^s)_\lambda$$
$$+ \int_{-H}^{O}(\rho_o G^\lambda - a^{-1}\int_{Z}^{O} mg\rho_\lambda\,dz')\,dz, \qquad (17)$$

$$\frac{1}{a}(m\psi_{\lambda t} - 2\Omega n\psi_\phi) = \frac{-H}{a}(P^s)_\phi$$

$$+ \int_{-H}^{O} (\rho_o G^\phi - \int_{Z}^{O} ga^{-1} \rho_\phi \, dz') \, dz. \qquad (18)$$

Here P^s is the surface pressure. Density can be measured directly, but P^s cannot. To eliminate this term, Eqs. (17–18) are divided by H and cross-differentiated to form a single transport vorticity equation,

$$a^{-1}(m\psi_{\lambda t}H^{-1})_\lambda + a^{-1}[\psi_{\phi t}(mH)^{-1}]_\phi = [2\Omega n\psi_\phi(aH)^{-1}$$

$$+ H^{-1}\int_{-H}^{O} (\rho_o G^\phi - \int_{Z}^{O} ga^{-1}\rho_\phi \, dz') \, dz]_\lambda$$

$$- [2\Omega n\psi_\lambda(aH)^{-1} + (mH)^{-1}\int_{-H}^{O} (\rho_o G^\lambda$$

$$- \int_{Z}^{O} gma^{-1}\rho_\lambda \, dz') \, dz]_\phi. \qquad (19)$$

The lateral boundary condition on ψ corresponding to Eq. (11) is that the boundary coincides with a streamline. The relations (14–15) predict the shape of the velocity profile in the vertical, and (19) predicts a reference velocity by specifying the total integrated transport.)

A description of the finite-difference method and a discussion of its important properties is given in Bryan (1969).

EXECUTION OF THE EXPERIMENTS

The numerical grid used in previous applications of this model has been defined on a simple spherical geometry, with grid points on latitude and longitude lines. Therefore, the grid spacing in the east-west direction becomes smaller at higher latitudes, converging towards zero at the poles. In this study, the very small grid spacing near the pole would seriously limit the length of the maximum stable time step. To avoid this problem, the sphere is covered by a system of overlapping grids, none of which have such a singular point. The central and largest grid is similar to those used in previous studies and centers on the equator. It is 2° by 2° on spherical geometry and it extends to 62° north and south. Cyclic boundaries are imposed at the longitudinal break. To complete the coverage, separate 2° by 2° spherical grids are used for the polar regions, with the difference that the line of symmetry of the grid passes through the pole rather than along the equator as in the central grid.

In Figure 1, the three grids appear as they would on a mercator projection. The two polar grids are not similar in shape, because of the different land distribution. The north polar grid can be smaller and nonsquare to save computer space. The three grids overlap considerably. This tends to minimize the numerical difficulties normally encountered in splicing grids together. As the experiment is performed, the equations are integrated separately for each grid over a specified number of time steps equalling a fraction of a day. For subsequent integration, boundary conditions along open boundaries for the adjoining grid are then set. The stream function and, when appropriate, T and S are interpolated directly. Because the flow is generally highly geostrophic, the specification of T and S establishes the vertical profile of velocity to a large extent. The following is the only weak condition placed on it:

$$\frac{\partial}{\partial n'}\left[(u,v) - \frac{1}{H}\int_{-H}^{O}(u,v)\,dz\right] = 0, \qquad (20)$$

where n' is the coordinate normal to the open boundary in question.

The distribution of grid points in the vertical is the same in all three grids and varies from a spacing of about 40 m at the top to 1,500 m in deep water. There are nine levels in deep basins and fewer in others, depending upon the real depth. The surface boundary condition on momentum was established using the observed annual mean wind stresses, as compiled by Hellerman (1967) with an extension to polar regions. At this relatively coarse resolution, the horizontal eddy viscosity coefficient is determined by considerations of numerical stability. Empirically, it was found that a value of 8×10^8 cm^2/s is needed to suppress grid-point alternation in the solutions, particularly at certain points where critical combinations of flow and bottom topography tend to generate small-scale disturbances. This mixing causes a Munk viscous boundary layer of around 400 km, some six times more than that observed. A better treatment of smaller-scale features in world ocean studies will have to wait for larger computers. In accordance with estimates based upon observations, the value of the vertical eddy viscosity coefficient is set at 1 cm^2/s. This simple linear closure scheme, representing interactions with small-scale motions, hopefully will be replaced by a more sophisticated one in the future.

The system of equations of the model is solved as an initial value problem, starting at a state of rest and integrating numerically with respect to time. The three experiments are performed with the same grid and parameters and differ only in the role that density plays.

RESULTS OF THE EXPERIMENTS

Experiment I

In the first experiment, T and S are set constant throughout the region and are not allowed to change in time. All terms involving derivatives of ρ vanish from Eqs. (14), (15), and (19). With such a large viscosity, essentially the same results could be achieved using a vertically integrated model, with possible exceptions in equatorial regions. The response time of this system is given by the time needed for a Rossby wave to move between longitudinal barriers. In the southern

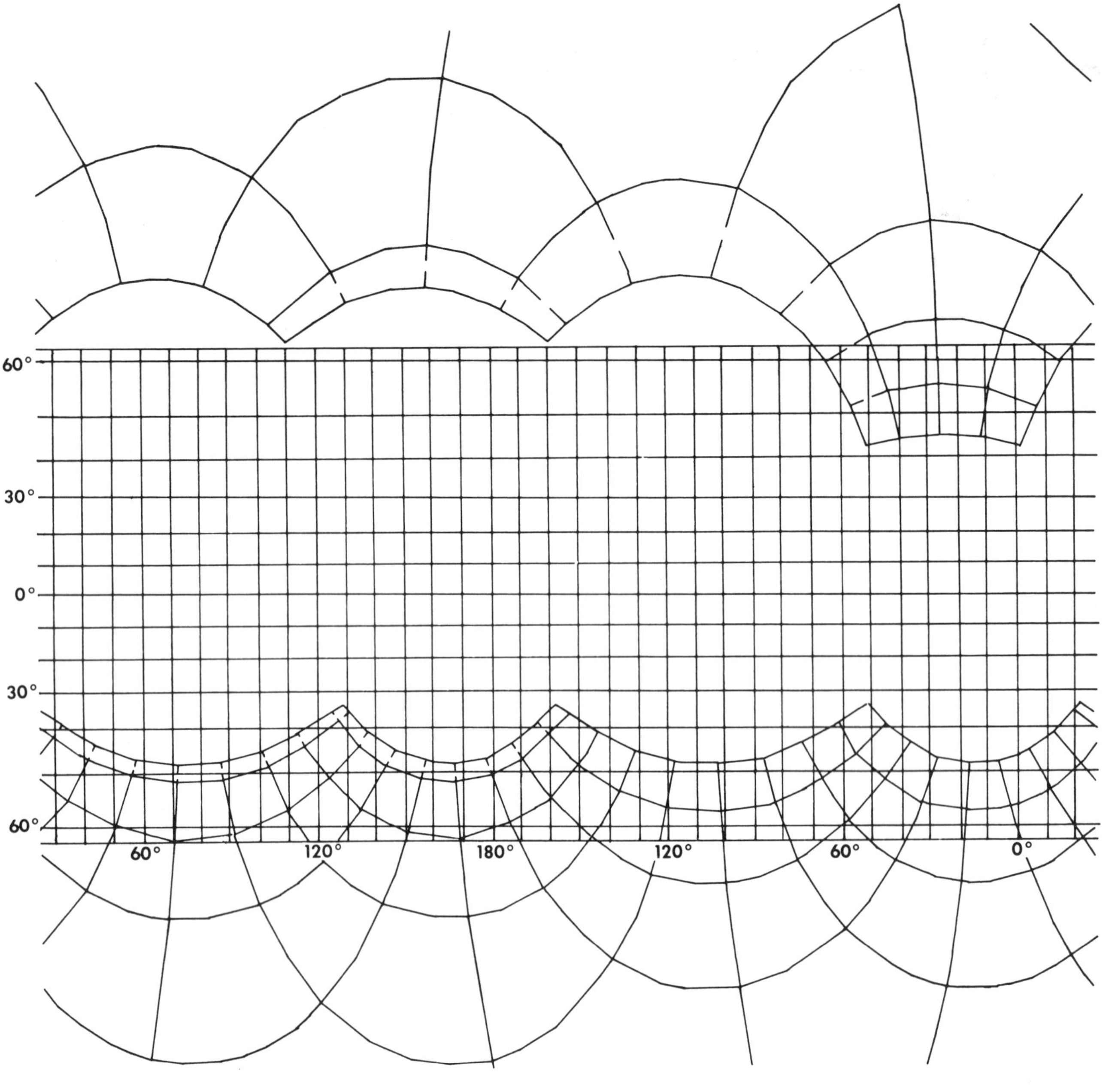

FIGURE 1 A mercator projection of the three grids used in the model.

ocean, this amounts to about two days. However, the absence of definite longitudinal barriers south of Cape Horn and the frictional transfer of energy between neighboring gyres appear to lengthen the response time. Thus, a total of several months must be allowed in the integration to reach a steady state.

In areas of the world ocean away from frictional boundary layers and strong wind-forcing, barotropic flow is expected to take place along lines of constant H cosecϕ for total potential vorticity to be conserved. In Figure 2, the steady-state solution of the homogeneous case is illustrated by the mass transport stream function. A sample line of constant H cosecϕ is superimposed on this pattern. Except in frictional boundary layers, the streamlines generally follow this contour. Bottom topography has a very definite effect in distorting the zonally symmetric gyres predicted by the Sverdrup relation for homogeneous flow over a flat bottom (Welander, 1959). The gyres are also suppressed in magnitude. Leichtmann *et al.* (1971) performed a similar study for a resolution of 5° by 5°, where similar effects of topography were observed. In both studies the Antarctic circumpolar current is deflected northward by the various ridges in

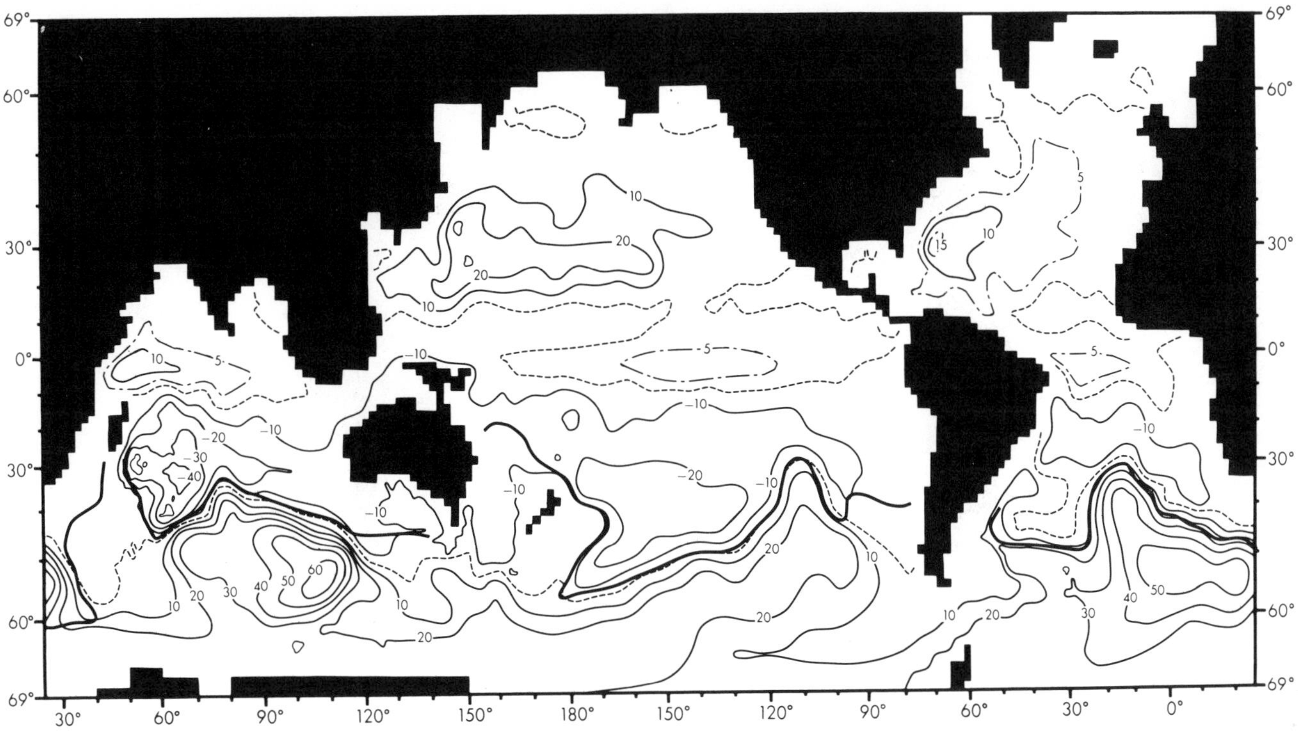

FIGURE 2 Horizontal mass transport stream function (× 10^6 m^3/s), Experiment I. Positive values represent clockwise flow. Heavy line represents H cosec ϕ = 6 km. Transport through Drake Passage = 22.

its path. Also, the western boundary current off Australia predicted by the Sverdrup relation is suppressed by the shallow topography to the east.

Experiment II

The T and S in the second experiment are again specified, and not allowed to change in time. However, they are now equal to observed mean values taken from the raw data file of the National Oceanographic Data Center (NODC). This data was first interpolated to a 1° by 1° grid for all standard levels and then interpolated to the grid of the model. This provides internal driving of momentum through the density terms of the equations of motion. A similar approach has been suggested by Sarkisyan (1966) and applied to the North Pacific by Kozlov (1971). The limiting time scale remains that of the first experiment, because the response of the momentum equations to the imposed density structure is much faster than that of the barotropic mode.

For purposes of comparison with Experiment I, the steady-state solution for Experiment II is represented in part by the mass transport stream function in Figure 3. In this case, the density terms in Eq. (19) dominate. All gyres are amplified over the homogeneous case, some by a factor of two to three. Others, including the Antarctic circumpolar current are increased by a factor of as much as 10. The effect of baroclinicity in conjunction with topographic variation has been discussed by Welander (1959), where he points out the possibility of compensation of dynamic effects of bottom slopes by variations in density. Thus, the same Sverdrup transport would take place in the baroclinic, topographic case as occurs in the barotropic, flat bottom case. Holland (in press) has studied this effect using the present model on an idealized basin with a continental shelf and found that density variations tend to overcompensate for bottom slope and the resulting bottom torques act to amplify the net horizontal transport. It is this same effect which augments the transport of Experiment II. If the path of the Antarctic circumpolar current is again compared to the sample line of H cosecϕ, we see that the current is not deflected nearly as strongly by the bottom slope as before but, aided by the baroclinic effects, passes more readily across ridges.

Experiment III

In the third experiment, the initial conditions are the same as Experiment II. T and S are then treated as prognostic variables, adjusting in response to the velocity patterns through their respective conservation equations (8,9). The parameter A_v in these equations is taken to be equal that of the momentum equations (1 cm^2/s). However, in order to reduce transport of heat by horizontal diffusion, the parameter A_H is taken to be 10^7; a factor of 80 less than that of

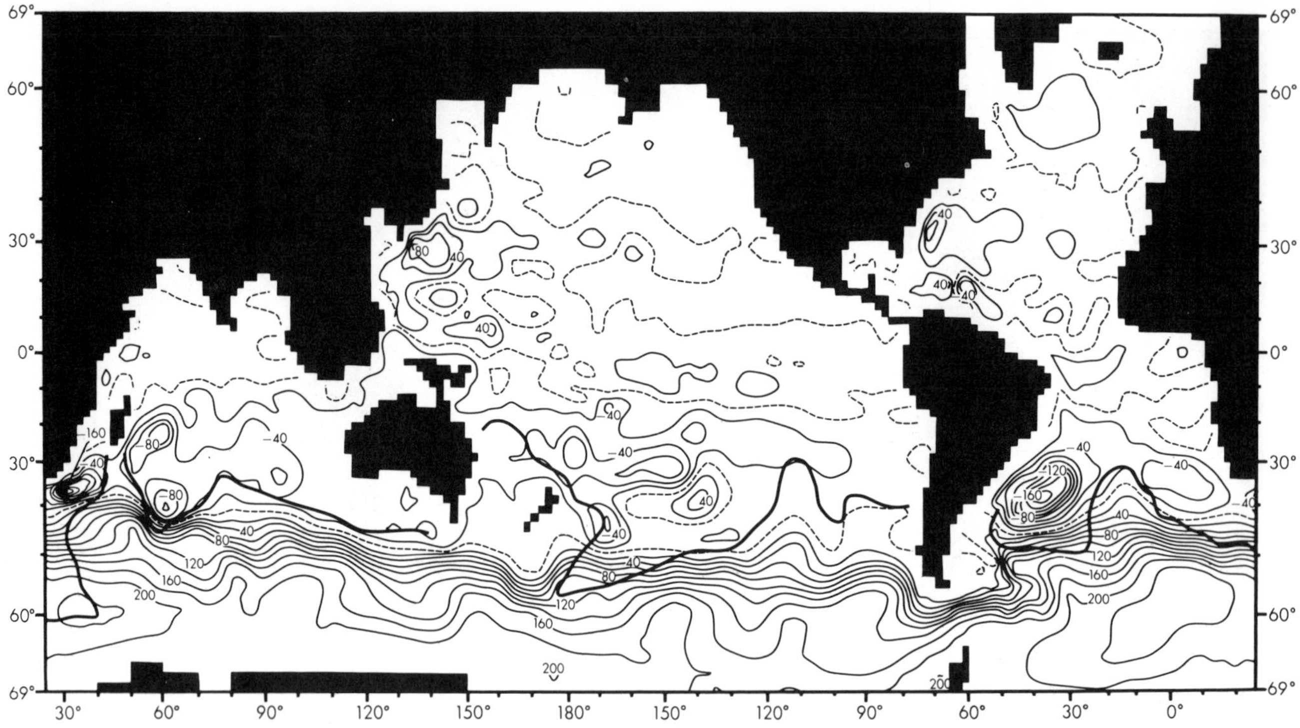

FIGURE 3 Horizontal mass transport stream function, Experiment II. Transport through Drake Passage = 184.

the momentum equations. The longest time scale in this system of equations is that of the establishment of a steady balance between the vertical advection and diffusion of heat. This time scale has been determined to be on the order of centuries (Bryan and Cox, 1968). Since the integration takes place at a speed of just less than 10 hours of computer time per year of ocean time, a steady-state solution is not a practical goal and, instead, the initial response of the model to the additional degrees of freedom is investigated here.

The temporal response of the model may be monitored by various integrals, two of which are illustrated in Figure 4. The root mean square value of vertical velocity has been computed for the entire volume of both the central and south polar sectors of the model. This integral tends to be sensitive to the large values of w that occur along the equator and near boundaries. Its temporal variation is therefore an efficient indicator of the diminution of unsupportable density configurations present in the initial data in these areas. Such imbalances are due to simplified methods of interpolation of the observed data, truncation error and other nonphysical mechanisms in the model, or errors of observation. This adjustment appears to occur within the first year of integration. Thereafter, the vertical velocities change much more slowly as the system enters the long-scale adjustment.

Another integral, which reflects the response of the interior to a higher degree, is the average of the absolute value of temperature tendency for each grid point over the central

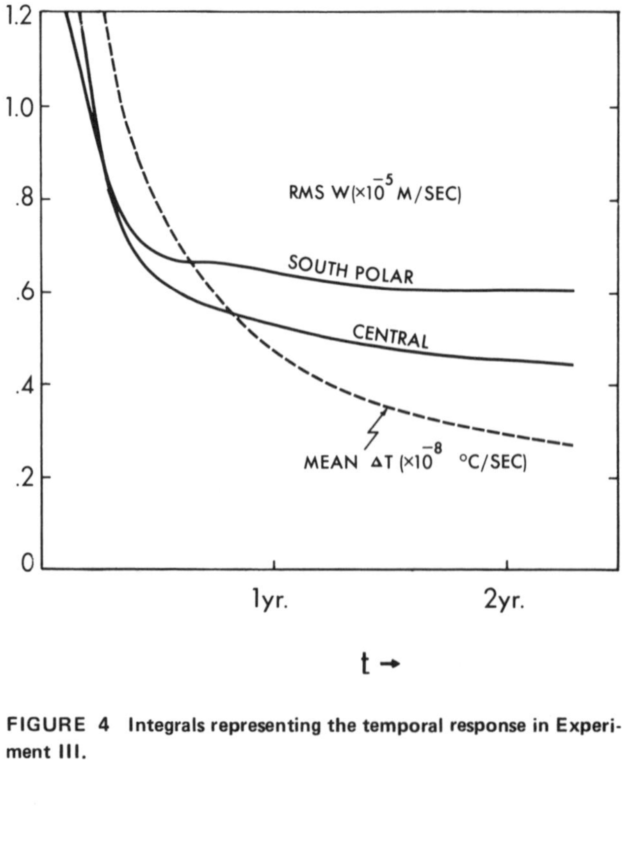

FIGURE 4 Integrals representing the temporal response in Experiment III.

sector. This integral also reveals a rapid initial adjustment followed by an apparent slow convergence to the steady state. Together, these integrals indicate that the initial adjustment, which takes place in the density patterns primarily in boundary current and equatorial regions, occurs within the first year.

The regime that has evolved over a period of 2.3 years of integration is presented in part in Figure 5. The various small subgyres of Figure 3 are almost completely diminished and the integrated transport is much simpler, having been organized into the more familiar primary gyres predicted from Sverdrup theory (Welander, 1959). The transports of these gyres have been affected differently by the adjustment of the density patterns. Most have decreased, with the exception of the Antarctic circumpolar current, which has remained practically constant in magnitude. It has become broader and less intense in some areas, i.e., the southeast Indian and South Pacific Oceans. Recent estimates of the transport through the Drake Passage have varied greatly. Unpublished estimates by the Bedford Institute of Canada, using current meter and geostrophic calculations, indicate a transport near zero. Reid and Nowlin (1971), using the same technique, have found the flow to be 237 × 10^6 tons/s. The latter value is more in agreement with that predicted by the model (186 × 10^6 tons/s).

The integrated meridional circulation for the entire central sector is shown in Figure 6. The large counterclockwise gyre of the Northern Hemisphere is mainly a reflection of the circulation of the North Atlantic, with only about one-fourth of the transport occurring in the North Pacific. Most of the volume of the central sector is predicted to have counterclockwise meridional circulation, with exceptions just south of the equator in the upper 300 m and below 3,000 m. Both of these clockwise transports occur mainly in the Pacific, but are also present in the other oceans.

CIRCULATION OF THE SOUTH PACIFIC

According to Welander (1959), the prevailing wind patterns over the South Pacific produce a Sverdrup transport regime in the subtropics similar to those in the Northern Hemisphere, with a resulting western boundary current flowing southward along eastern Australia of approximately 28 × 10^6 tons/s. However, Hamon (1970) discovered that the East Australian current is most often the western segment of southward-moving, counterclockwise eddies, and is therefore largely compensated by northward flow to the east. The character of the net southward transport that is necessary to balance the Sverdrup transport of the interior remains in doubt. The following is a description of the mass budget for this area of the solution of Experiment III.

In Figure 5 there is a total northward transport of 40 × 10^6 tons/s in the subtropical gyre of the South Pacific. After being carried westward in the south equatorial current, this water divides, and some 18 × 10^6 tons/s proceeds northward into a small clockwise gyre east of New Guinea.

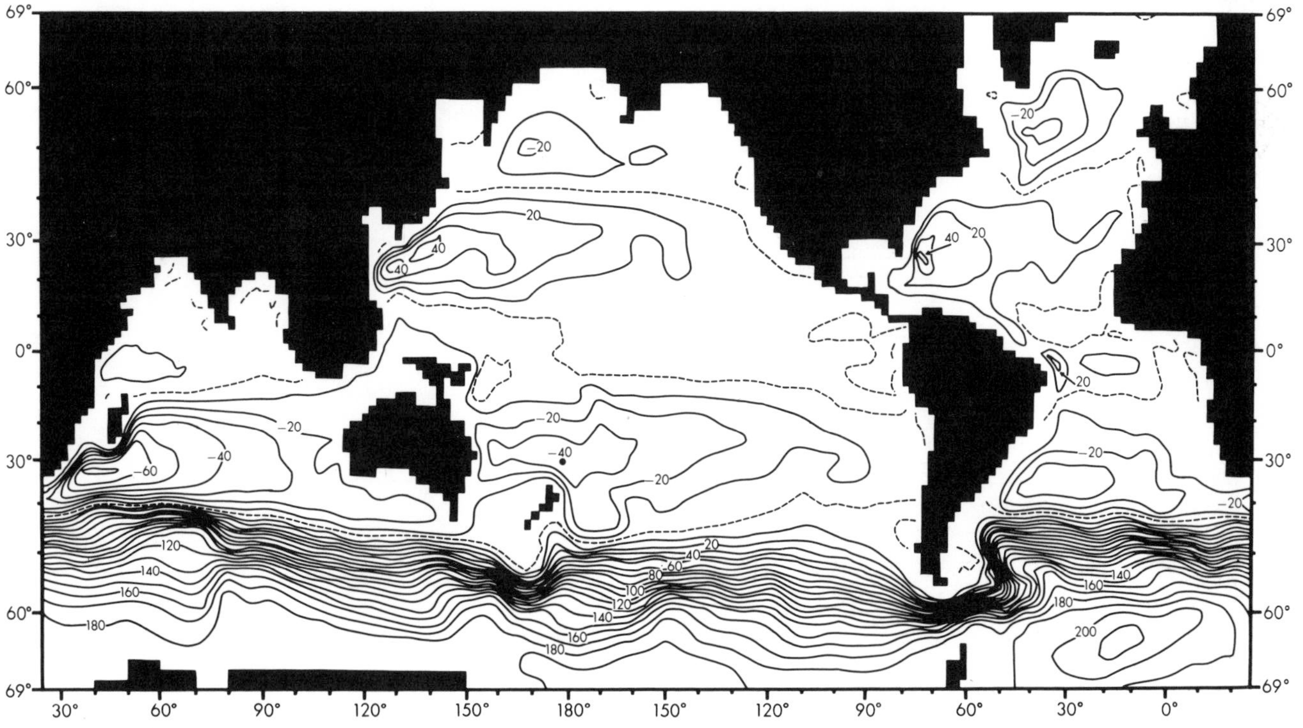

FIGURE 5 Horizontal mass transport stream function, Experiment III. Transport through Drake Passage = 186.

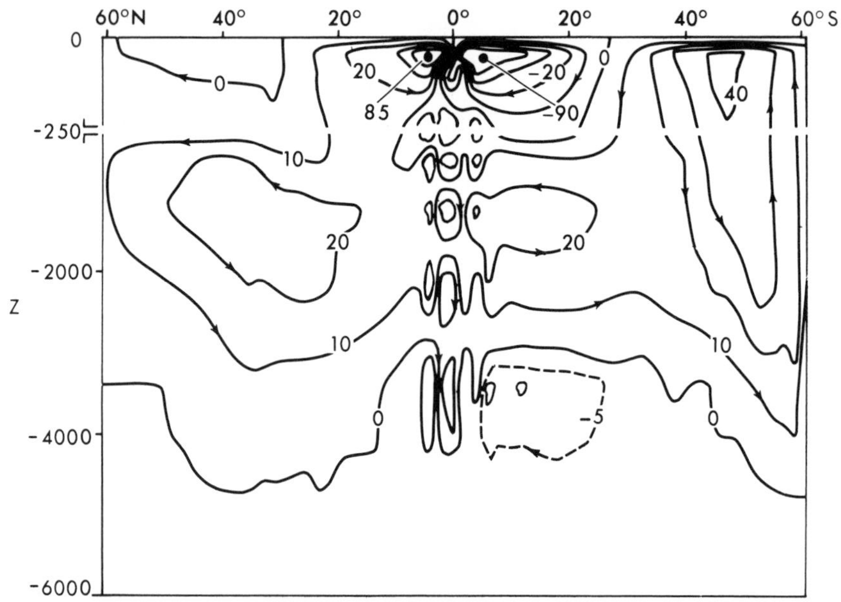

FIGURE 6 Meridional mass transport stream function (× 10^6 m^3/s), Experiment III, integrated zonally around the globe.

It flows through the passage between New Guinea and Southeast Asia, to be picked up by the gyre of the South Indian Ocean and transported southward to the Antarctic circumpolar current. The remaining 22 × 10^6 tons/s flows southward, east of Australia. However, this flow does not take the form of a typical western boundary current. The various meridional ridges between Australia and the Tonga Trench, some 3,000 km to the east, each act as partial western boundaries. The southward transport is spread over a considerably wider zone than in other major gyres of the world ocean. As predicted by Warren (1970), this flow does not continue southward between Australia and New Zealand, but turns sharply eastward at the latitude of the northern tip of North Island. It then joins with a northward-flowing western boundary current of 13 × 10^6 tons/s from the Tasman Sea to the south and proceeds in an intense flow around the tip of North Island and southward to complete the gyre. In the model, the latter is by far the most intense vertically averaged flow in the subtropical gyre of the South Pacific.

The topography to the east and north of Australia is very complex and impossible to incorporate explicitly into a 2° by 2° model. The large features such as the Tonga, Kermadec, and Lord Howe Ridges have been included, however; the effect of the deletion of smaller scales is left to further study.

In Figure 7 the meridional circulation is shown for this region. These values represent the net northward transport,

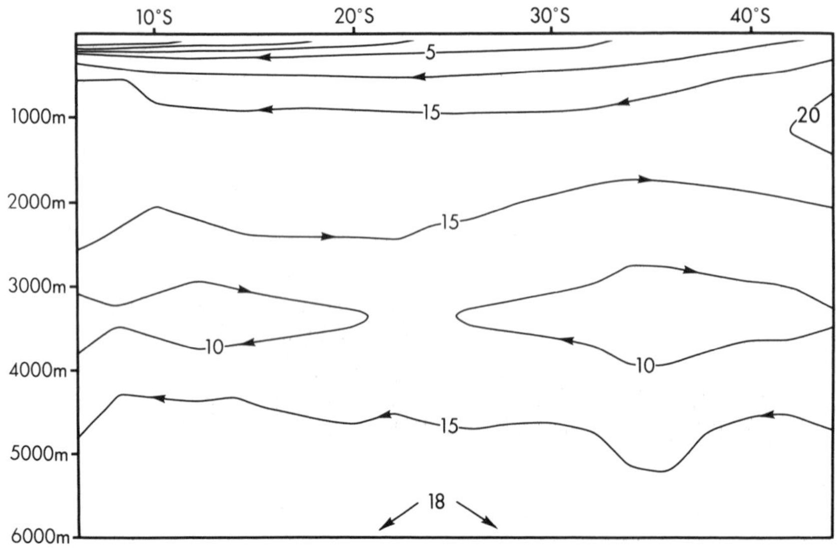

FIGURE 7 Meridional mass transport stream function, Experiment III, integrated zonally across the South Pacific only.

integrated from the surface downward and from Australia–New Guinea to South America. The transport at the bottom is therefore 18 × 10^6 tons/s, the same as the outflow from the Pacific north of Australia. There is strong northward flow between the surface and 1,100 m that accounts for the entire mass flux required. The circulation below 1,100 m consists essentially of two compensating flows, one of roughly 10^7 tons/s to the south between 1,100 and 3,400 in and the other of the same magnitude to the north below 3,400 m. This regime is in good agreement with the meridional oxygen section of Reid (1965) taken along 160° W that shows high oxygen water deriving from the Antarctic above 1,200 m and below 3,400 m, as far north as 20° S. In between there is a core of oxygen-minimum water that appears to be traceable to northern areas. To provide information on the zonal structure of this flow, Warren (1970) has constructed zonal cross sections of temperature and salinity at 28° S and 43° S. These profiles indicate that the northward flow tends to take place along the western boundary of the deep basin at a depth of 2,500–4,500 m. This supports the prediction of Stommel and Arons (1960), whose linear geostrophic model of abyssal circulation requires that the deep interior flow have a meridional component toward the pole, with all northward flow confined to a western boundary current. Warren points out, however, that the width of the northward flow indicated by his data (900–1,000 km) is considerably greater than the northward flow usually associated with western boundary currents.

The meridional component of the flow predicted in Experiment III is shown in Figure 8 for latitude 42° S across the Southwest Pacific basin. The flow is depicted by quantities of northward mass flux through partitioned interfaces as indicated. The northward mass flux in deep layers (eight and nine) is almost totally accounted for by a current some 1,000 km wide, near but not adjoining the western boundary. The position of this current in the west, therefore, appears to be caused by the fact that it is being fed from the west and south by the Antarctic circumpolar current and not due to western intensification. The wedge of southward-moving water adjacent to the western boundary and penetrating to the bottom is in singular disagreement with the theory and observations cited.

The net southward transport at middle depths indicated in Figure 7 and occurring in layers six and seven is seen to take place along eastern New Zealand and east of the East Pacific rise, with a return flow west of the rise. Above this

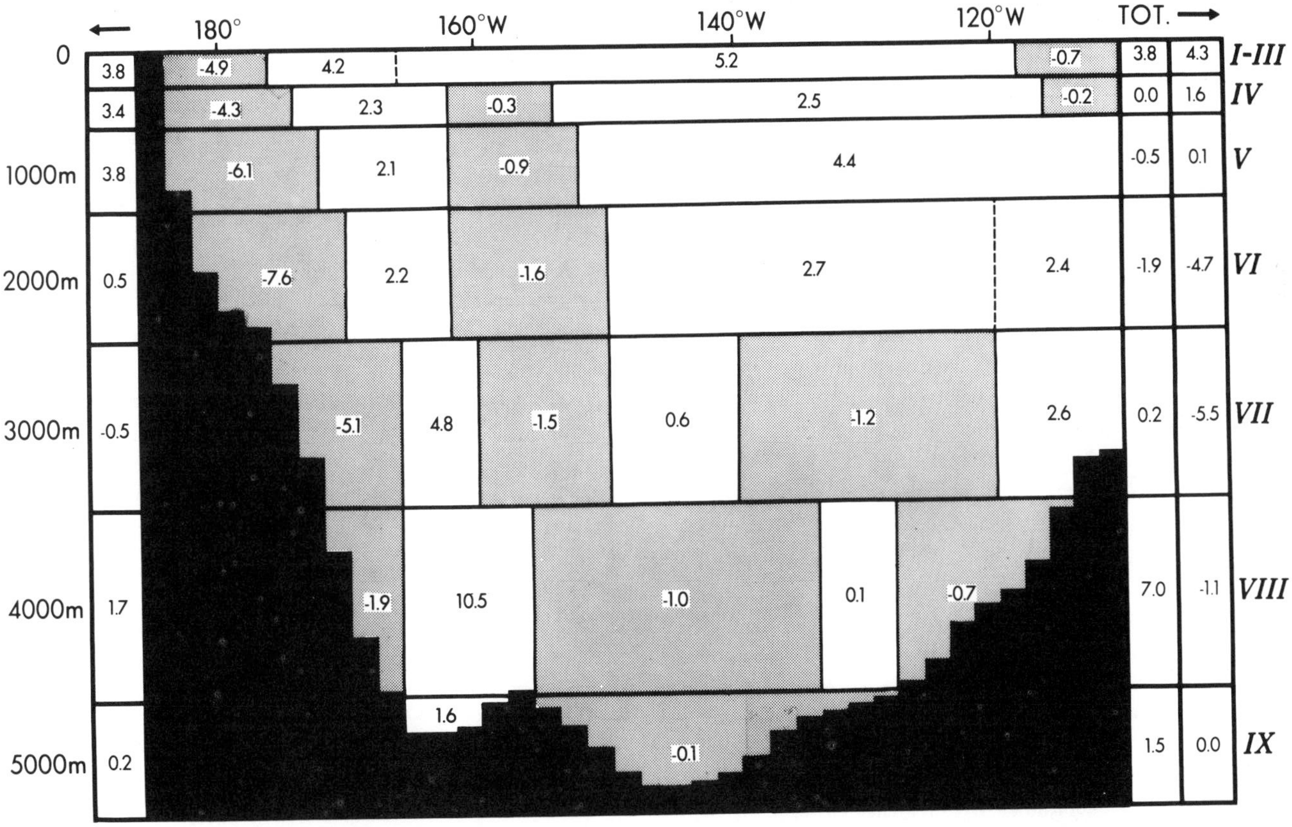

FIGURE 8 A zonal cross section of the Southwest Pacific basin at 42° S showing the net northward mass flux through the indicated partitions (× 10^6 m^3/s). Vertical sides of partitions represent points of change of direction except when dashed, indicating areas of more intense flow. The total flow for each layer is given on the right; and the flow to the west and east, beneath the arrows.

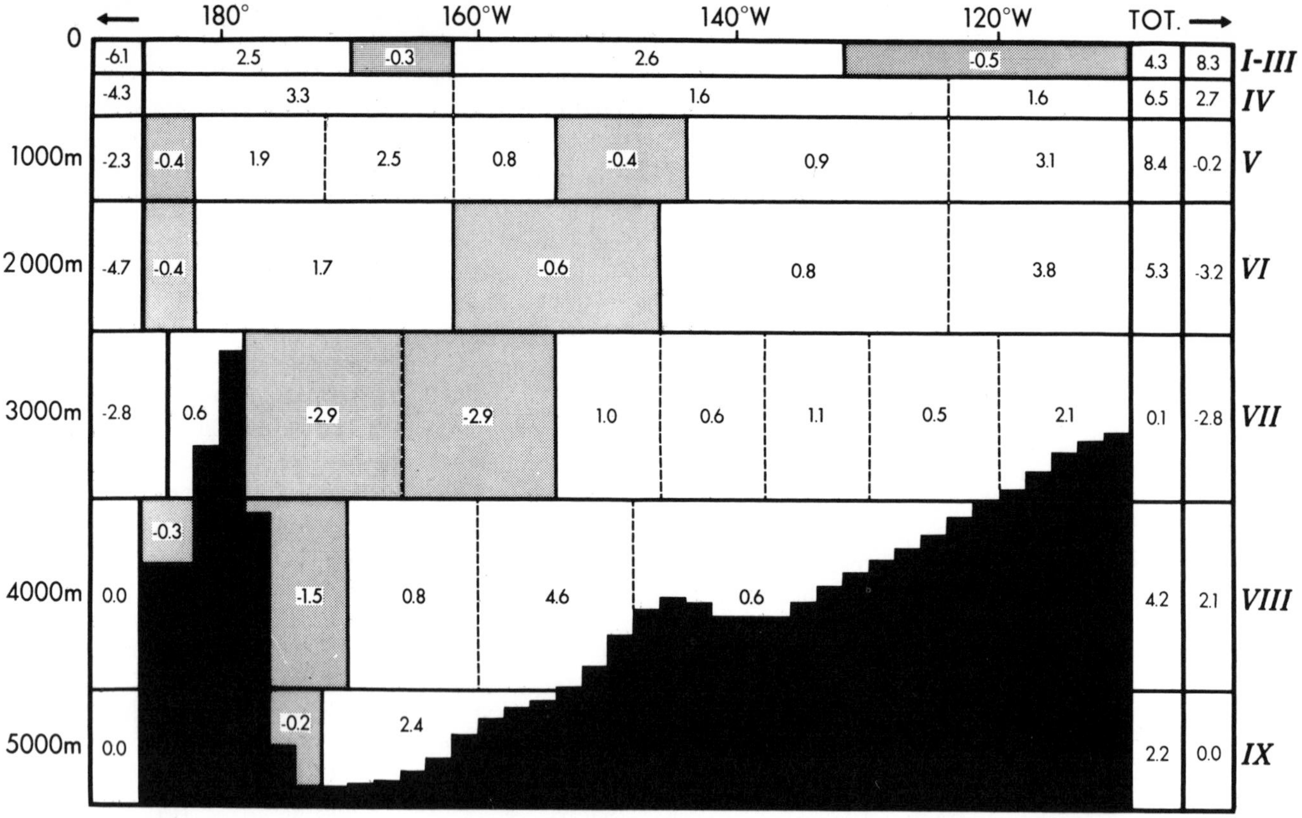

FIGURE 9 A zonal cross section of the Southwest Pacific basin at 28° S showing the net northward mass flux through the indicated partitions.

depth, the flow consists of the familiar broad drift in the interior, compensated in part by the western boundary current. A similar profile is shown in Figure 9 for latitude 28° S. The core of the northward abyssal flow is even further to the east at this point, and the southward flow along the western boundary persists. The total northward flow at this latitude in the two deepest layers is about 2×10^6 tons/s less than that of 42° S, revealing a net upwelling of this magnitude across the 3,400-m level.

The southward flow in middle depths is similar to that at 42° S, taking place along the western boundaries of the several basins at this latitude, with return flow along the western slope of the East Pacific rise. The flow in the upper layers is primarily northward in the interior with the return flow taking place to the west of the Kermadec Ridge. Reid's meridional configuration of oxygen described earlier is in general support of the flow indicated at 160° W. However, the density structure presented by Warren at this latitude, indicating northward flow along the Kermadec Ridge, is not in agreement with the model.

Finally, the solution presented for Experiment III is not a steady-state solution, but one that is undergoing a very long-term adjustment from the observed initial conditions that were imposed. After only 2 years of adjustment, the solution remains under the strong influence of these observations, particularly in the lower layers. Unfortunately, the observations of Warren are not included in the data set used in these experiments.

REVIEW: W. L. GATES

Although there have been numerous studies of the effects of topography, baroclinicity, viscosity, and wind stress on the circulation in idealized ocean basins, it is only recently that such effects have been studied with realistic ocean geometry. Cox presents the first systematic study of the role of baroclinicity in the circulation of the world ocean, in which the complete quasi-static dynamical equations are used to predict the velocity and density distributions. The present results are thus a preliminary view of the most ambitious oceanic simulation so far carried out.

Of the several possible approaches to the fully time-dependent problem, Cox has chosen to examine the progression from a homogeneous model to a baroclinic model with observed (prescribed) density, and thence to a baroclinic model with predicted (time-dependent) density. Each of these cases is examined with the aid of the basic three-dimensional (nine-level) model used earlier by Cox (1970) in his study of the Indian Ocean, and each employs the observed lateral and bottom geometry of the world ocean as seen with 2° spherical resolution.

The principal scientific concern of this paper is the interaction of baroclinic and topographic effects in a model of relatively modest levels of viscosity. Here the horizontal and vertical Ekman numbers (given by $A_m/\Omega a^2$ and $A_v/\Omega H^2$ in Cox's notation) are 2.7×10^{-5} and 3.6×10^{-8} (for the deepest water). These in turn give about 190 km and 1.1 m, respectively, for the width of the (viscous) lateral boundary layer and the thickness of the surface (Ekman) layer. Since the interior Rossby number is here of the order 10^{-5}, the bulk of the ocean is under strong rotational constraint and the currents may be expected to be nearly geostrophic. The significant vertical motions are thus those induced in the surface layer by the imposed wind stress, those occurring in higher latitudes with convective overturning, and those occurring near the equator (where the rotational constraint is relaxed). Presumably there are also significant vertical motions induced by the flow over irregular submarine topography, although this feature is not given separate consideration.

The first major result of the present work is that the introduction of the observed average density distribution (Figure 3) in place of a uniform density (Figure 2) results in a general increase of the strength of the mid-latitude gyres by a factor of about three, while the transport stream function pattern becomes somewhat more cellular. Use of the observed density field also produces an increase in the strength of the Antarctic circumpolar current by nearly an order of magnitude, as well as introducing noticeable departures of its path from the isolines of H cosecϕ (which are closely followed in the homogeneous solution). While there is apparently no other such calculation for the world ocean with bottom topography yet published, Sarkisyan and Ivanov (1971) have considered the joint effect of baroclinicity and bottom relief in the North Atlantic. Using a steady-state model, they also find that the introduction of the observed density field completely alters the total transport stream function. In their case not only is the flow intensified approximately tenfold, but is actually reversed relative to that with uniform density in the principal gyres of the North Atlantic. This is a somewhat more drastic change than that found by Cox, and may be due to the differences in the two formulations. In this regard we note that Sarkisyan and Ivanov use a vertical eddy viscosity 100 times larger than Cox's and neglect lateral eddy viscosity altogether. These authors have also used different internal density data and different lateral boundary conditions.

The second major result presented by Cox is that in allowing the internal density distribution to be determined by the model itself (from the appropriate conservation equations for heat and salt), the mid-latitude gyres are intensified (relative to the homogeneous case) by a factor of about two. At the same time the transport stream function assumes an organized large-scale structure with clearly marked western intensification, although not yet in complete equilibrium (after 2.3 years of simulation). This effect is in marked contrast to that produced by use of the observed density field cited above, and is more in accord with the commonly-accepted notion of what the circulation "should" look like. The Antarctic circumpolar current, on the other hand, is similar in position and intensity to that found with the observed density, i.e., it is about 10 times stronger than that found in the homogeneous case.

In comparing the solutions with prescribed (observed) density (Figure 3) and internally computed density (Figure 5), one is led to speculate why the observed density distribution in the southern ocean is so much more compatible with the model's total transport than is that prescribed elsewhere. One hypothesis is that smaller-scale transient disturbances not well described by the present model play an essentially different role in the general circulation of the zonally bounded Atlantic, Pacific, and Indian Oceans than they do in the circumpolar ocean surrounding Antarctica. Such disturbances would be critically affected by the topographic gradients and the irregular lateral boundaries of the three northern oceans. Hopefully the MODE program will provide evidence of such disturbances if they exist, and they could then presumably be simulated with a model of higher resolution.

A further question raised by Cox's results is the degree to which compensation occurs between topographic and baroclinic contributions to the total transport. Although Cox does not present the results for a homogeneous world ocean of uniform depth, such a solution is given by Bryan and Cox (1972) for the same basic model used here. With the exception of the Antarctic circumpolar current (and the associated gyres southeast of Australia and South America), their solution for the transport stream function in a 5-km homogeneous ocean closely resembles that of Cox for the topographic time-dependent density case (Figure 5) in both pattern and intensity. In most of the Atlantic, Pacific, and Indian Oceans there is, therefore, an effective topographic-baroclinic compensation, at least in the model. We may note in Figure 6 that north of about 25° S the meridional circulation is characteristically reversed above and below about 1 km in depth, while in the southern ocean there is a more or less uniform southward flow at all levels below the surface layer. The total transport thus resembles the surface circulation in the Atlantic, Pacific, and Indian Oceans, while the Antarctic circumpolar current is less compensated and extends to the bottom. This current may therefore show a stronger than ordinary topographic dependence.

The mean meridional circulation shown in Figure 6 also

makes it clear that the present model's resolution should be increased near the equator. At each of the discrete levels used in the model (42; 90; 257; 555; 1,164; 2,131; 3,358; 4,741; and 6,186 m) and at each of the low-latitude grid points (4° S, 2° S, 0°, 2° N, 4° N), there appears to be a mode in the computed circulation pattern. A graded mesh, such as that used by Bryan and Cox (1968) in their earlier studies of an idealized ocean basin, would more adequately resolve the details of this current structure.

While the method of numerical solution is presumably that described by Bryan (1969), two points deserve further comment. First is the problem of determining the transport stream function around islands, of which Antarctica and Australia are the most important examples. The finite-difference method given by Bryan (1969) for the calculation of the time-dependent stream function around an island will not necessarily satisfy the Stokes circulation theorem. It is not clear whether Cox has here used this method or has adopted the newer and more accurate technique described by Bryan and Cox (1972). This problem can be avoided by integrating the primitive equations of motion with a free upper surface, but then a somewhat smaller time step must be used to maintain linear computational stability.

A second point of interest is Cox's imposition of a zero stress condition at the ocean bottom. Since the current is computed only at the nine levels cited earlier, this may have resulted in the enforcement of zero vertical shear over an excessively deep bottom layer in many regions of the world ocean. The presence of a bottom Ekman stress in such a model without topography is known to reduce the amplitude of the current fluctuations, for example (Bryan and Cox, 1968), and may play an even more important role in the presence of topography. We may also note that the previous calculations with this model have included bottom stress (Cox, 1970; Bryan and Cox, 1972).

While it is relatively easy to suggest ways in which the present solutions could be extended, sight should not be lost of the pioneering nature of Cox's work. When further results are available, various components of the oceanic energy and momentum balance can be evaluated, in which the roles of variable density and topography will be of particular interest. It is to be hoped that the already impressive series of studies by Cox and Bryan will be continued, and lead ultimately to the examination of fully coupled global atmospheric and world ocean models.

REFERENCES

Bryan, K. 1969. A numerical method for the study of the circulation of the world ocean. J. Comp. Phys. 4(3):347–76.

Bryan, K., and M. D. Cox. 1968. A nonlinear model of an ocean driven by wind and differential heating. Part 1. J. Atmos. Sci. 25(6):945–78.

Bryan, K., and M. D. Cox, 1972. The circulation of the world ocean: A numerical study. Part I: A homogeneous model. Geophysical Fluid Dynamics Laboratory/NOAA, Princeton, N. J. Unpublished manuscript.

Cox, M. D. 1970. A mathematical model of the Indian Ocean. Deep-Sea Res. 17(1):47–75.

Friedrich, H. J. 1970. Preliminary results from a numerical multi-layer model for the circulation in the North Atlantic. Dtsh. Hydrogr. Z. 23(4):145–64.

Hamon, B. V. 1970. Western boundary currents in the South Pacific, pp. 50–59. *In* Scientific Exploration of the South Pacific. National Academy of Sciences, Washington, D. C.

Hellerman, S. 1967. An updated estimate of the wind stress on the world ocean. Mon. Weather Rev. 95(9):607–26. (See correction, 1968, 96(1):63–74).

Holland, W. L. (In press.) Baroclinic and topographic influences on the transport in western boundary currents.

Holland, W. L., and A. D. Hirschman. (In press.) A numerical calculation of the circulation in the North Atlantic.

Kozlov, V. F. 1971. Geostrophic currents in the North Pacific. Oceanology 2(2):173–77.

Leichtmann, D. L., B. A. Kagan, L. A. Oganesian, and R. V. Piaskovsky. 1971. On the global circulation of an ocean with variable depth. Dokl., Akad. Nauk., USSR 198(2):333–36.

Reid, J. L., Jr. 1965. Intermediate waters of the Pacific Ocean. Johns Hopkins Oceanogr. Stud. No. 2. Johns Hopkins Press, Baltimore. 85 pp.

Reid, J. L., Jr., and W. D. Nowlin. 1971. Transport of water through the Drake Passage. Deep-Sea Res. 18(1):51–64.

Sarkisyan, A. S. 1966. Fundamentals of the theory and computation of oceanic currents. Gidrometeoizdat. Leningrad.

Sarkisyan, A. S., and V. F. Ivanov. 1971. Joint effect of baroclinicity and bottom relief as an important factor in the dynamics of sea currents. Izv. Akad. Nauk. USSR Atmos. Oceanic Phys. 7(2):173–88.

Stommel, H., and A. B. Arons. 1960. On the abyssal circulation of the world ocean. Part 2: An idealized model of the circulation pattern and amplitude in oceanic basins. Deep-Sea Res. 6(3):217–33.

Warren, B. A. 1970. General circulation of the South Pacific, pp. 33–49. *In* Scientific Exploration of the South Pacific. National Academy of Sciences, Washington, D. C.

Welander, P. 1959. On the vertically integrated mass transport in the oceans, pp. 95–101. *In* B. Bolin, ed. The Atmosphere and the Sea in Motion. Rockefeller Institute Press and Oxford University Press, New York–London.

DISCUSSION

UNIDENTIFIED: A couple of things struck me in reading Cox's paper. One supports the important joint effects of baroclinicity and topography reported on earlier by Sarkisyan, in that in changing the density field from a homogeneous value to the observed field, a very great change is produced in the final transport stream function.

GATES: The flow became, as you saw, several times stronger. Even more interesting is the case in which Cox replaces the observed density by the internally computed density. I think that it's quite clear, as you pointed out, that the flow is much more organized. And since the starting point in this calculation was the observed density, the whole change in the transport in your last calculation is a measure of how unhappy the model is with the observed density.

NIILER: This must be so, and it must indicate that the model is handling the density distribution and the total transport in a way that is different from that in nature. This may be due to the high level of lateral viscosity.

GATES: I also was struck by the large-scale transport picture in your last calculation with internally computed density in that it appears similar to the calculations that you get in the flat-bottom, homogeneous density, world ocean model. It is nearly the same large-scale type of picture that indicates that in the middle- and low-latitude basins there apparently is an effective compensation between the baroclinic and topographic effects. Next I'd like to ask about your use here of zero bottom stress, whereas previously you used bottom friction. Now, in models of uniform depth, I think your earlier work has shown that bottom stress of the friction will reduce the total magnitude of the transport. So in a model of nonuniform depth, particularly where you have large shallow-water regions, isn't it possible that bottom friction would have an important effect?

COX: I think that the system should change the density structure to a fairly high degree. I think it's probably predictable by the fact that the Munk viscous boundary layers are about six times wider than what is observed. So I think it's a little foolhardy to expect that a great deal of smoothing wouldn't take place under these conditions. I think with additional resolution we can alleviate this problem somewhat. About the bottom friction, it turns out in this particular scheme that it was very difficult to incorporate because of the variable thickness of our bottom layer and that is why we didn't use it. Also, I believe that the role of bottom friction is a question that needs a great deal more investigation. We don't, or at least I don't, have a very good feel for what the bottom friction does, and I think I'd rather not have it in than to have an extra parameter that I don't understand.

VERONIS: One of the restrictions that we all know in numerical calculations of this type is that the grid must necessarily be coarse, because a much more precise grid cannot be handled on the computer. With such a grid network, one must choose a very large horizontal mixing coefficient to have the flow resolved on the scale of the grid. With sloping density surfaces this effect sucks out a large amount of fluid. If one looks at the upwelling velocity on a meridional cross section averaged across a latitude circle, one sees from these calculations the importance of the boundary layers. The reason for this is that the density lines are sloping in the boundary layer and that horizontal mixing mixes a large amount of water normal to the density surfaces. This changes, in my opinion, the character of the entire circulation. I think that all of these models have such an approximation made because of the unavoidable constraint of the coarse grid network. I recall Holland's work in connection with tracers. I talked to him about his calculations made with a small diffusion coefficient. As he reduced the diffusion coefficient, upwelling started to become stronger in the interior. In fact, in the beginning he was getting interior downwelling, which is a surprising result. Everything that has been done analytically has assumed a basic upwelling in the interior. The explanation is that as horizontal mixing becomes smaller in the boundary layer, then less water is sucked in. I have a suspicion that this kind of relaxation of the system away from the observed profiles must be in large part controlled by the boundary layer process. It's something like having a plunger in the western boundary layer that is controlling the entire situation.

WARREN: I'm not really surprised to see such bad agreement in the deep-flow pattern in the South Pacific between Cox's calculations and what was observed in the *Scorpio* expedition. For some reason, you don't seem to have the *Scorpio* data from NODC. There's no trace of the undercurrent structure in the older data and, therefore, it was not surprising to see that you get something very different.

COX: That's true, but we had hoped that possibly the tendency toward reality would be there in those 2–3 years, which it didn't seem to be.

BEARDSLEY: Would you expect to get a bottom boundary current out of this new model without bottom friction?

BRYAN: In other models bottom friction doesn't seem to be an essential mechanism. It changes the solution somewhat, but it's not essential for the bottom circulation.

RATTRAY: It may very well be that some of this change is due to the fact that the grid scales for the bottom topography and the density fields were lined up in a way that might not be realistic. As the model ran, there could be a change in the bottom baroclinic topographic driving forces. I wonder if you had a measure of the change of those with time.

COX: No, we never pursued that. That's certainly a possibility.

RATTRAY: One would expect that the initial state might not be lined up with the general trend.

COX: There are errors in the topography due to the fact that it has to be stepwise and also errors in density due to interpolation. So, in such a sensitive term, there certainly is a possibility that the effect you mentioned might be a factor.

SARKISYAN: The diagnostic result is very interesting, but I am much more interested in the prognostic calculation.

Predictive calculations will help give us a more exact answer to Veronis' question. It is going to adjust the density field to the flow velocity. It is an interesting idea to begin from the observation of data to investigate what this numerical scheme is doing with observational data. It must be smooth of course, because the scale's horizontal grid mesh is more than 200-300 km—it's too much to describe with jetlike currents near boundaries. But I think this scheme has one drawback—it is regular. The calculations are not yet completed and are continued only up to 2.3 years. For example, the real cause of this regular smoothing is a too-large coefficient of horizontal viscosity. It is one or two orders larger than real viscosity in the ocean. This question must be faced in the future. Every numerical scheme has its own numerical viscosity, and in general this viscosity is much larger than the physical one. So this is, I think, the main problem with this numerical scheme.

A NUMERICAL SIMULATION OF THE WORLD OCEAN CIRCULATION: PRELIMINARY RESULTS

K. TAKANO

MODEL

The ultimate goal of the present work is to develop a numerical model of the world ocean circulation that will be coupled to the UCLA Mintz-Arakawa atmospheric general circulation model and to use that joint atmosphere-ocean model to study the dynamics of climate and climate changes. Here, we confine ourself to showing some of the results of a preliminary test of the ocean model.

The basic assumptions are as follows:

1. The circulation is driven by differential heating and wind stress.
2. The Arctic Ocean is excluded.
3. The ice phase and the salinity are excluded.
4. The ocean has a constant depth.
5. The momentum advection is negligible.
6. Water density is taken as a linear function of temperature.
7. The heat flux across the ocean surface is computed and used as a boundary condition. This flux is made proportional to the difference between the predicted surface water temperature and a prescribed atmospheric temperature that is only a function of latitude, as is assumed by Haney (1971a,b).

The thermal condition at the upper boundary is thus written as

$$c\rho K \frac{\partial T}{\partial z} = d\,(T_A - T_s), \tag{1}$$

where ρ is the density, c is the specific heat, K is the coefficient of vertical eddy diffusivity, T is the temperature, T_s is the predicted ocean surface temperature, T_A is the prescribed atmospheric temperature, d is a constant, and the z axis is positive upward.

All the processes affecting the heat exchange between the atmosphere and the ocean are incorporated in the right-hand side of Eq. (1). The atmospheric temperature T_A, which varies with latitude only, is shown in Figure 1. The constant d is taken as 16.8 ly deg^{-1} day^{-1}

The other conditions at the upper boundary are

$$\rho K \frac{\partial u}{\partial z} = \tau_\lambda, \tag{2}$$

$$\rho K \frac{\partial v}{\partial z} = \tau_\phi, \tag{3}$$

$$w = 0, \tag{4}$$

where u, v, and w are the eastward, northward and upward components of the velocity, respectively; τ_λ and τ_ϕ are the eastward and northward components of the wind stress, respectively; and K is the coefficient of vertical eddy viscosity, assumed to be equal to the coefficient of vertical eddy diffusivity.

The wind stress is prescribed by a climatological mean (Hellerman, 1967), which is constant in time but variable with both latitude and longitude.

There is no friction, no heat flux at the bottom; no slip, no heat flux at the lateral walls.

By the assumptions of constant depth, no momentum advection, and free-slip condition at the bottom, the veloc-

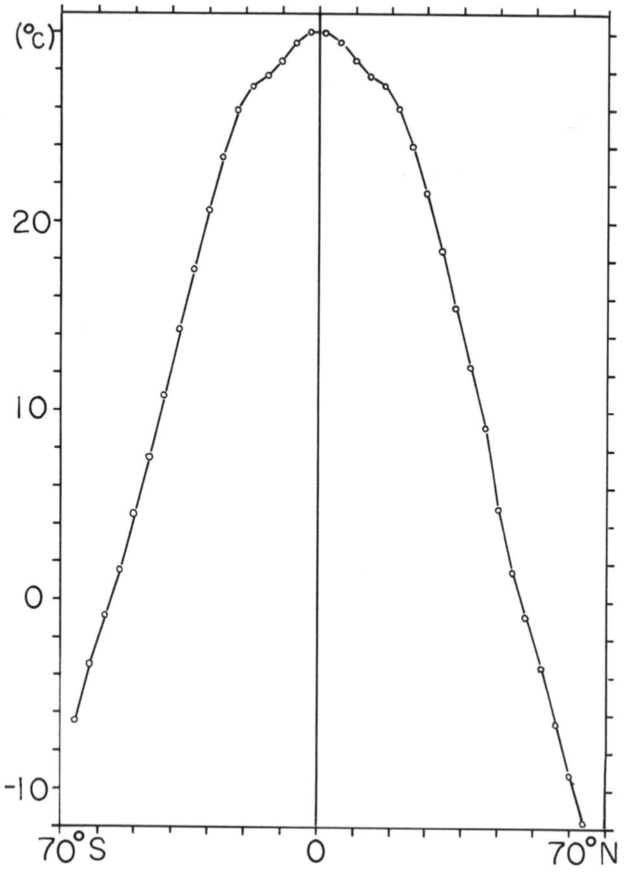

FIGURE 1 Prescribed atmospheric temperature as a function of latitude.

ity field is divided into two separate parts: one is the barotropic component (vertical mean of the horizontal velocity), which is governed by the wind stress curl; and the other is the baroclinic component (deviation of the horizontal velocity from its vertical mean), which is mainly governed by the heating. No interaction exists between these two components, although the former affects the latter through the horizontal advection of heat.

The barotropic component is readily obtained as a solution of the vorticity equation derived from the equations of motion and the equation of continuity.

GRID STRUCTURE

The grid structure is the same as the one used by Haney (1971a). Figure 2 shows the arrangement of the dependent variables. The coastlines are defined by T, w, p (pressure), and Φ (stream function of the barotropic component of the velocity) points. The grid size is 4° in latitude and 2.5° in longitude.

The southern boundary is located at the annual mean position of the northern boundary of the Antarctic ice.

Five levels are set up in the vertical to calculate T, u, v, and p at depths of 20; 120; 640; 1,280; and 2,760 m and w at depths of 70; 380; 960; and 2,020 m. The depth of the ocean is 4,000 m.

The finite-differencing scheme is almost the same as the one used by Haney (1971a).

RESULTS

The numerical values of principal parameters are as follows:

Acceleration of gravity	980 cm s^{-2}
Radius of the earth	6.37×10^8 cm
Angular velocity of the earth	0.729×10^{-4} s^{-1}
Specific heat of water	0.93 cal gm^{-1} deg^{-1}
Coefficient of thermal expansion	2.5×10^{-4} deg^{-1}
Coefficient of horizontal eddy viscosity	10^9 cm^2 s^{-1}
Coefficient of horizontal eddy diffusivity	2.5×10^7 cm^2 s^{-1}
Coefficient of vertical eddy viscosity and diffusivity	1 cm^2 s^{-1}

The vorticity equation is resolved by means of the "hole relaxation," which is a very useful tool in such a multiconnected domain as the world ocean. Figure 3 illustrates the streamlines. The contour interval is 2.5×10^7 cm^2 s^{-1}. The Antarctic circumpolar current transports 35×10^{12} cm^3 s^{-1}. Although the estimate of it based on the observation is sparse and uncertain, this computed transport may be too small, because of the large coefficient of horizontal eddy viscosity and of the location and shape of the southern

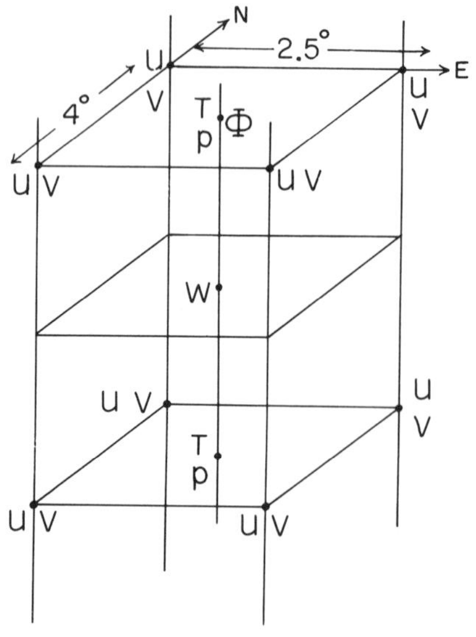

FIGURE 2 Grid structure.

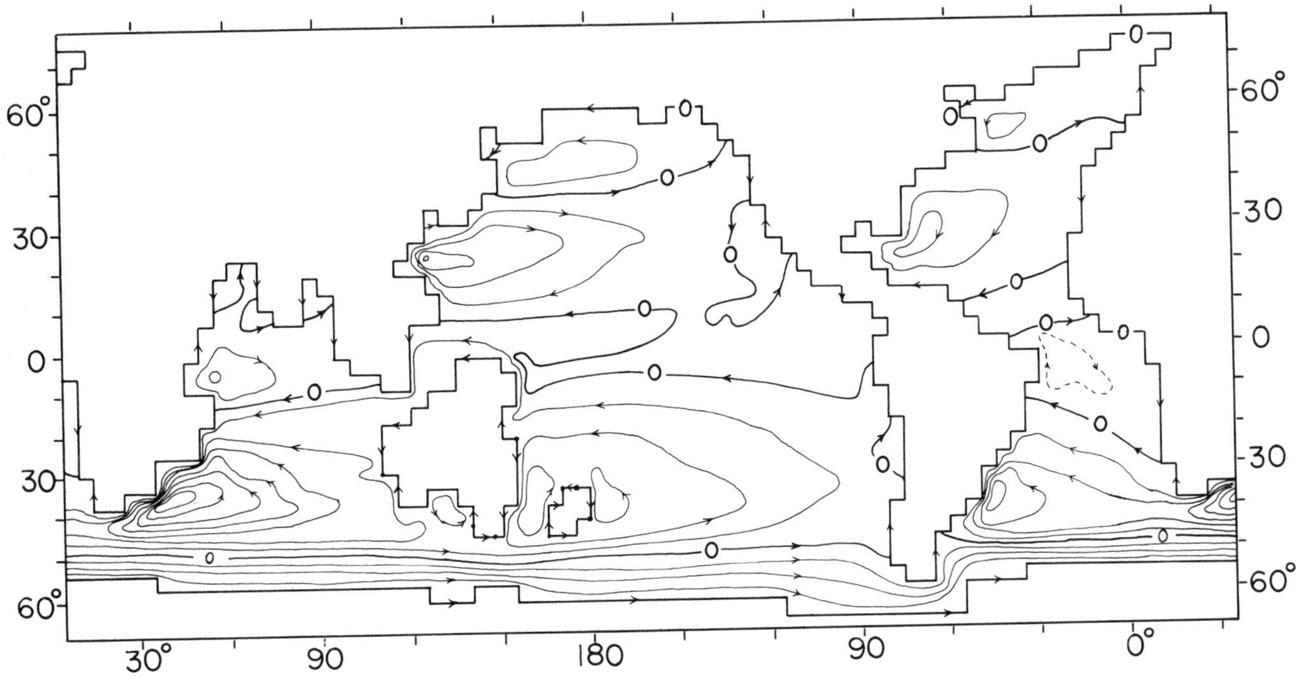

FIGURE 3 Streamlines of the barotropic component of the velocity. The contour interval is $2.5 \times 10^7 cm^2 s^{-1}$.

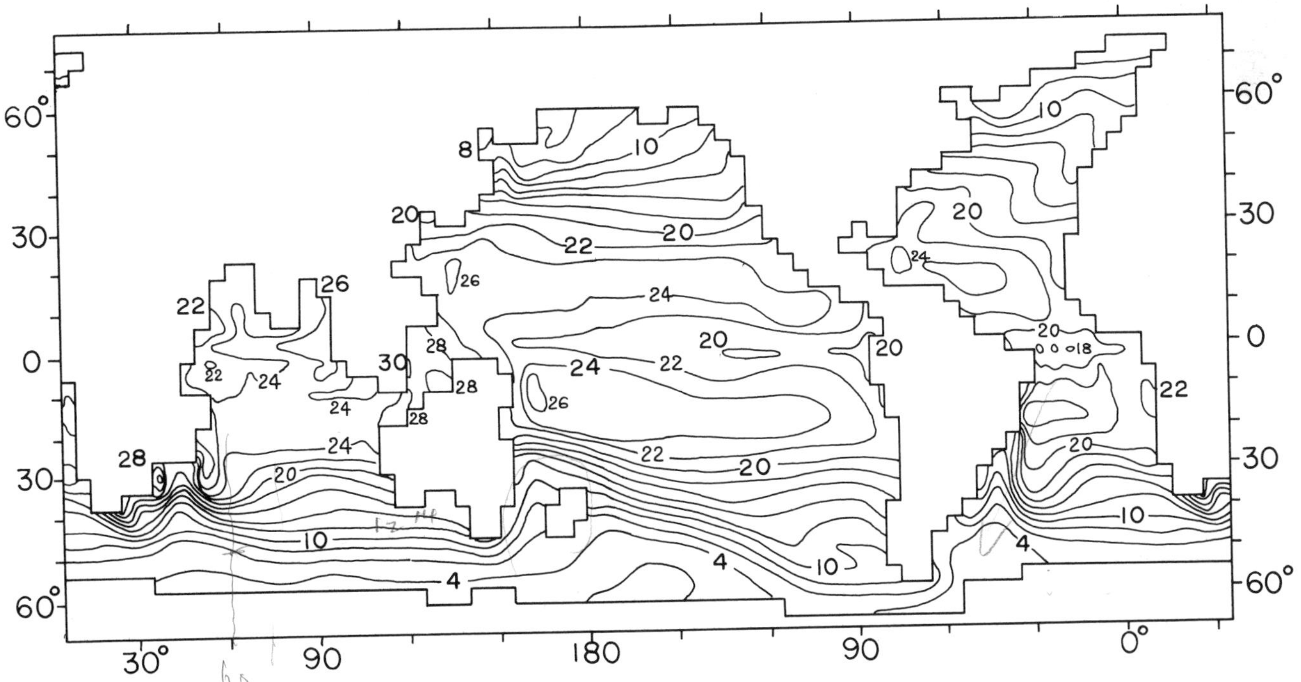

FIGURE 4 Temperature distribution at a depth of 20 m.

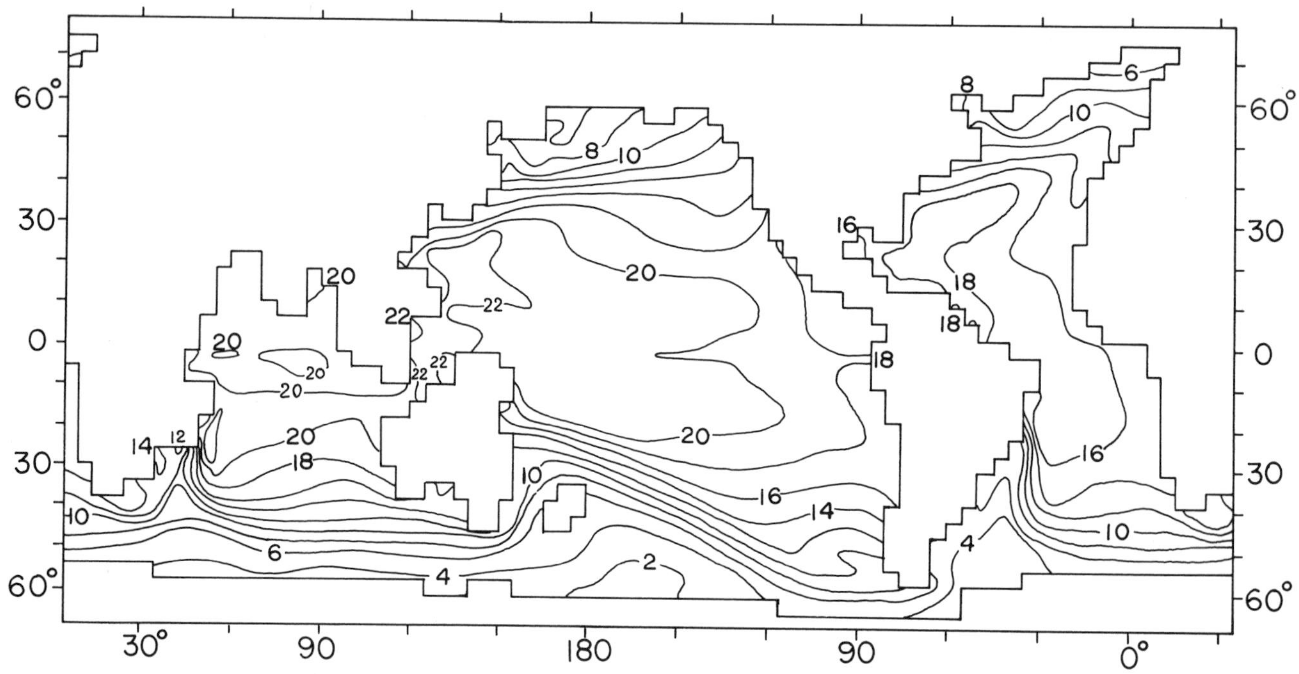

FIGURE 5 Temperature distribution at a depth of 120 m.

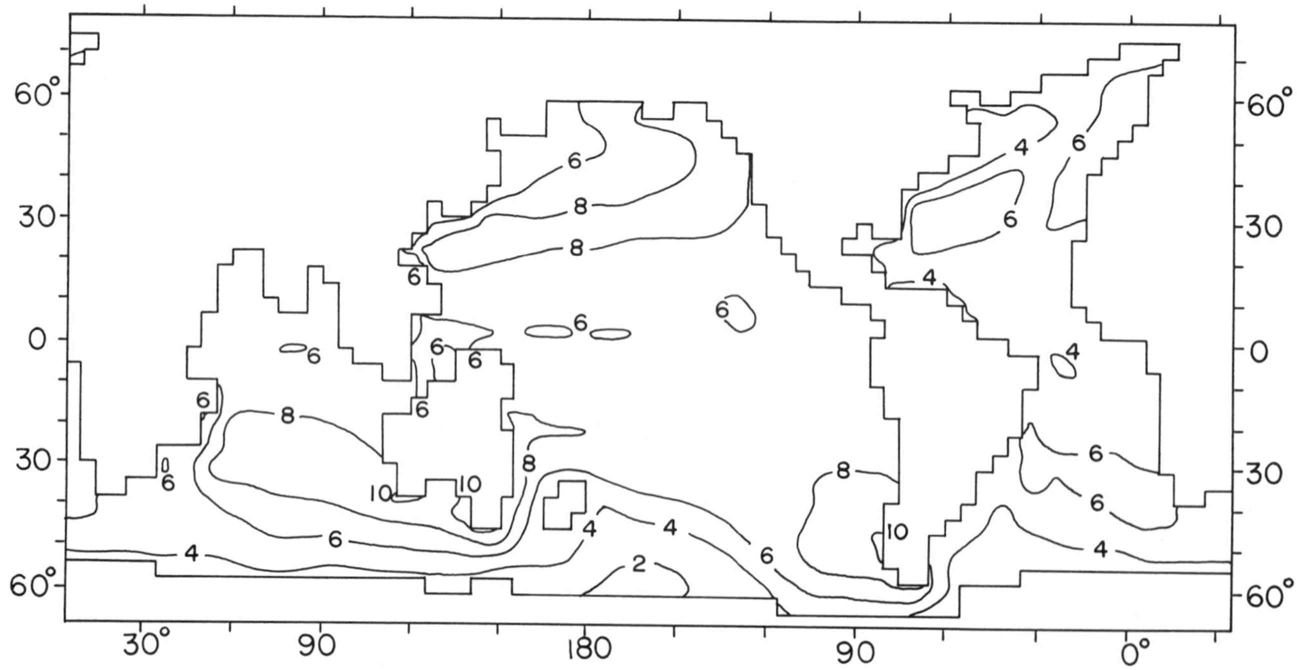

FIGURE 6 Temperature distribution at a depth of 640 m.

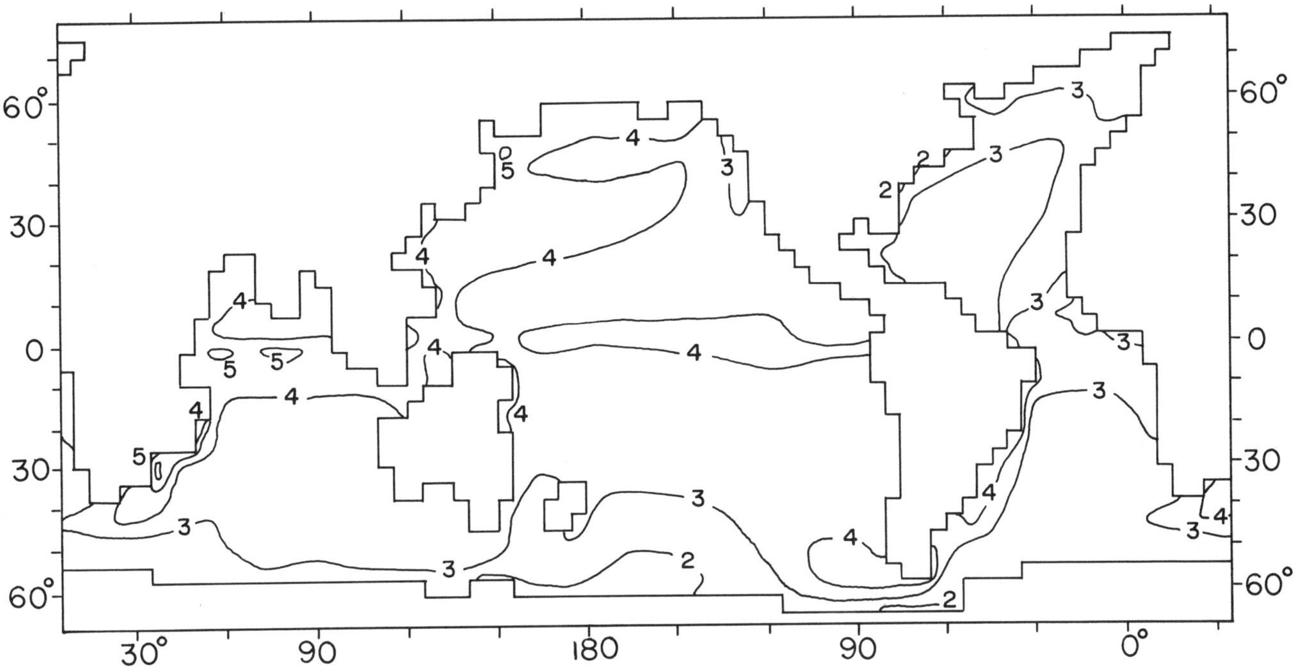

FIGURE 7 Temperature distribution at a depth of 1,280 m.

boundary. To examine how the transport through the Drake Passage depends on them, additional computations are carried out in three cases. (a) The southern boundary is shifted southward to be located along the 66° S parallel. The wind stress curl is put as 0 on the water surface recovered by this shift. The coefficient of horizontal eddy viscosity is unchanged ($10^9\,cm^2\ s^{-1}$). (b) The southern boundary is unchanged, but the coefficient of horizontal eddy viscosity is reduced to $3 \times 10^8\,cm^2\ s^{-1}$. (c) The southern boundary is shifted southward to be located along the 66° S parallel, and the wind stress curl is 0 on the surface recovered, just as in case (a), but the coefficient of horizontal eddy viscosity is $3 \times 10^8\,cm^2\ s^{-1}$. The transport of the Antarctic circumpolar current is

$$46 \times 10^{12}\,cm^3\ s^{-1} \text{ in case (a),}$$
$$59 \times 10^{12}\,cm^3\ s^{-1} \text{ in case (b),}$$
$$87 \times 10^{12}\,cm^3\ s^{-1} \text{ in case (c).}$$

A more substantial discussion would be possible if the bottom topography and ice motion were taken into account.

To save the machine time for the baroclinic component and the temperature, an initial temperature field that is not far from the observed one is given as a function of latitude and depth. The corresponding geostrophic shear current is used together with the barotropic component as the initial velocity field. The integration in time is carried forward for about 12 years in simulated time. Although this is not long enough for the deeper layers, a quasi-steady state is reached in the upper layers.

Figures 4–7 show the horizontal distribution of temperature at depths of 20; 120; 640; and 1,280 m, respectively. The vertical distribution of temperature at two selected points is given in Figure 8 with that in the initial state.

Figure 9 shows the heat flux across the surface computed from the surface water temperature (Figure 4) and the right-hand side of Eq. (1).

The computed temperature field agrees fairly well with the observed one, in spite of the crude formulation of the heat flux at the surface.

The major features in the velocity field are in fairly good agreement with the observed ones, except for the equatorial counter-current, which is almost completely missing, although the currents are too weak due to the large coefficient of horizontal eddy viscosity and to the coarse grid. The maximum speed is 35 cm s^{-1} for the Gulf Stream and 30 cm s^{-1} for the Kuroshio current.

Figures 10 and 11 show the vertical distribution of the horizontal velocity at four selected points. The direction of the vertical component of the velocity is shown in Figures 12 and 13. It is upward in the shaded areas.

ACKNOWLEDGMENTS

I wish to express my gratitude to Professors Y. Mintz and A. Arakawa for their support and valuable suggestions during all phases of this work. I also wish to thank Dr. T. Matsuno of the Geophysical Institute of the University of Tokyo and Dr. R. Haney of the Naval Postgraduate School for valuable discussions. Assistance of Mrs. D. Hollingworth, Mr. C. Kurasch, and Mrs. D. Conti in carrying the computation is appreciated.

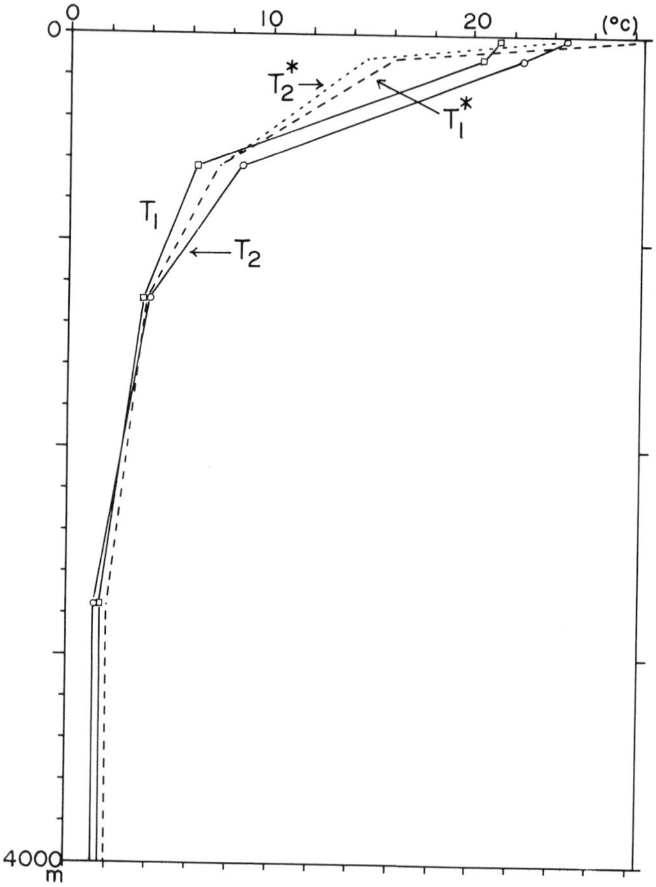

FIGURE 8 Vertical distribution of temperature. T_1 is the computed temperature and T_1* is the initial temperature at 147.5°W, 6°N. T_2 is the computed temperature and T_2* is the initial temperature at 125°E, 22°N.

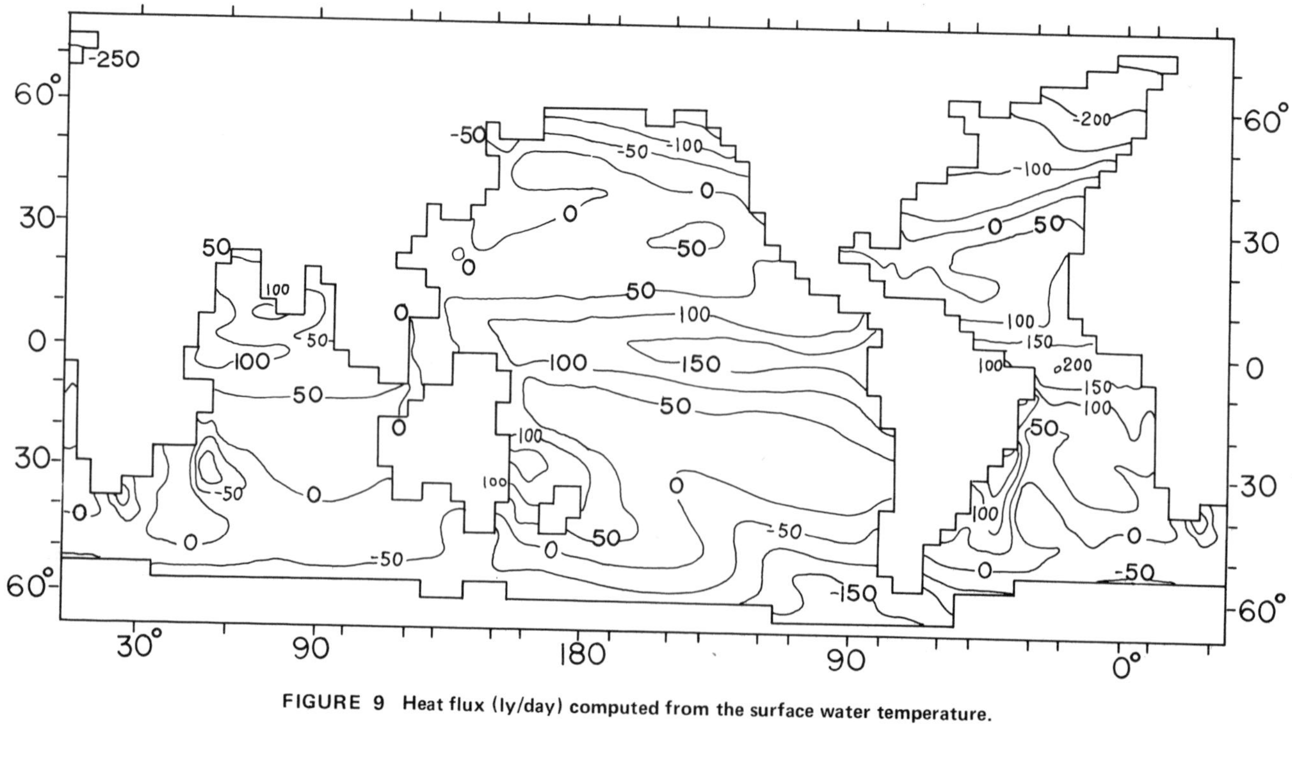

FIGURE 9 Heat flux (ly/day) computed from the surface water temperature.

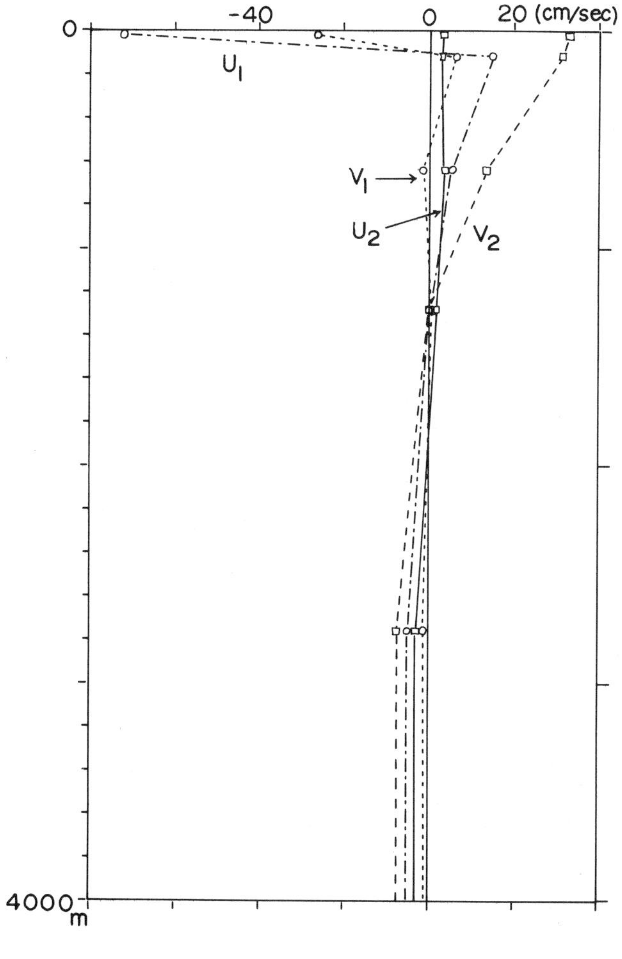

FIGURE 10 Vertical distribution of the horizontal velocity. u_1 and v_1 are the eastward and northward components at 146.25° W, 4° N; u_2 and v_2 are those at 126.25° E, 20° N.

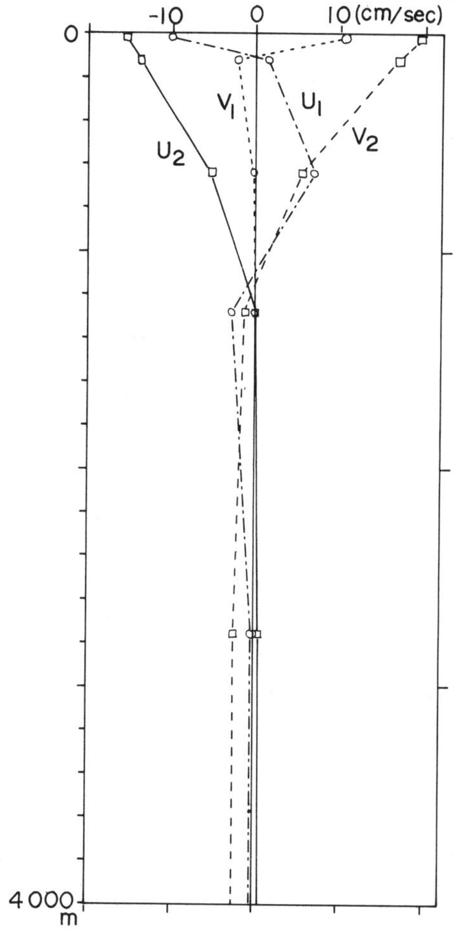

FIGURE 11 Vertical distribution of the horizontal velocity. u_1 and v_1 are the eastward and northward components at 146.25° W, 0° N; u_2 and v_2 are those at 73.75° W, 28° N.

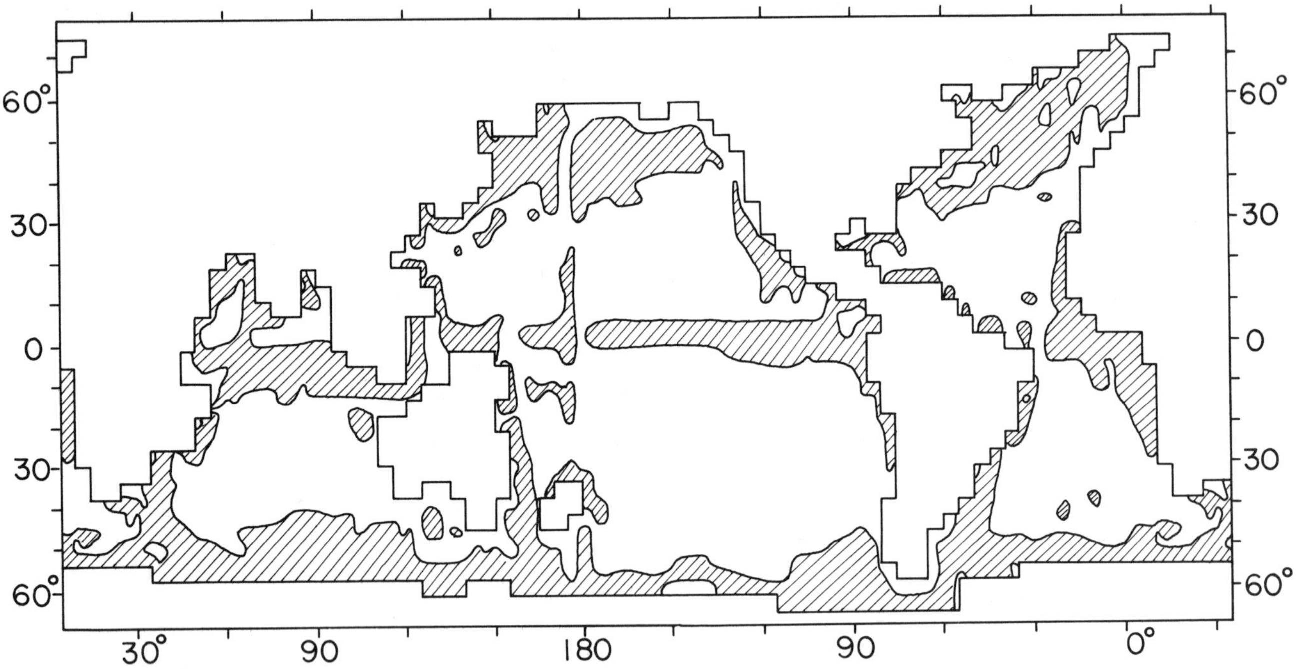

FIGURE 12 Vertical component of velocity at a depth of 70 m.

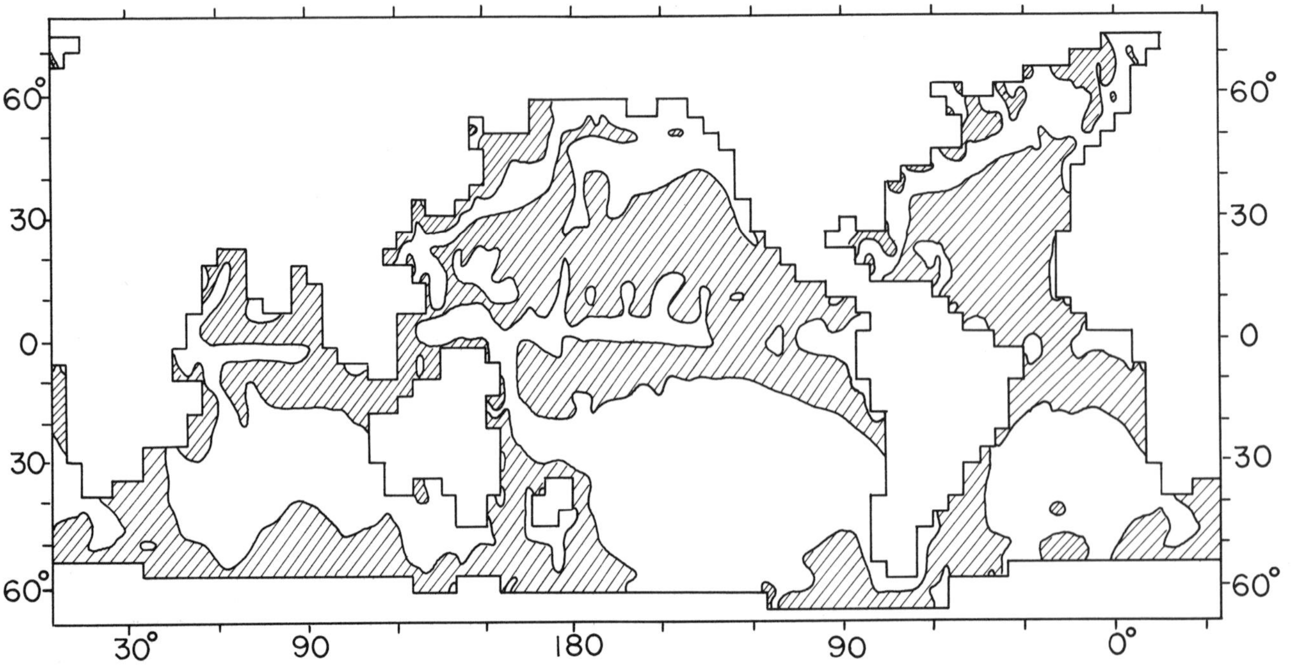

FIGURE 13 Vertical component of velocity at a depth of 380 m.

This work was supported by the U.S.-Japan Cooperative Science Program of the National Science Foundation under Grant GF369 and the Atmospheric Sciences Section of the National Science Foundation under Grants GA778, GA1470, and GA22756.

REFERENCES

Haney, R. L. 1971a. A numerical study of the large scale response of an ocean circulation to surface heat flux and momentum flux. Ph.D. Dissertation. Department of Meteorology, University of California, Los Angeles.

Haney, R. L. 1971b. Surface boundary condition for ocean circulation models. J. Phys. Oceanogr. 1:241–48.

Hellerman, S. 1967. An updated estimate of the wind stress on the world ocean. Mon. Weather Rev. 95:607–26 (correction, 1968, 96:63–74).

IV SPECIAL STUDIES USING NUMERICAL MODELS

THE ROLE OF MODELS IN TRACER STUDIES

G. VERONIS

INTRODUCTION

This paper contains a review of some recent studies of the use of tracers in determining features of ocean circulation. The models discussed range from the mathematically simple box models to models involving mathematically complex three-dimensional numerical integrations. Between these extremes are vertical advective-diffusive models and studies using simple dynamical models together with tracer distributions.

Although the mathematics becomes increasingly involved in this heirarchy of models, the subtlety and sophistication required to produce significant results varies perhaps in the reverse order. Box models require particularly careful formulation because the principal constraints on the system are included in the formulation. The special advantage of the box model is that results can be obtained quickly, with relative ease, and the parameters of the system can be varied over enormous ranges.

Vertical advective-diffusive models are also relatively simple mathematically. The most straightforward use of these models yields estimates of the vertical velocity and the vertical diffusion coefficient, which have formed the basis for more complex studies. However, these estimates include the effects of processes that are excluded from the model itself but may determine the observed vertical distributions. In a recent study of tritium distributions, Rooth and Östlund (1972) have adopted a novel and interesting approach to these models and they have concluded that the vertical mixing coefficient K, is nearly an order of magnitude smaller than the usually accepted value. These results and their implications are discussed in the section, "Vertical Exchange Models" (pp. 135-137).

Stommel's (1958) *tour de force* circulation model for abyssal waters serves as a dynamical basis for studies of distributions of tracers in the abyss. The lateral advective-diffusive equation for tracers with the abyssal circulation velocities incorporated can be solved to determine the tracer distribution consistent with assumed sources and decay processes. The results of a study by Kuo and Veronis (1970) are mentioned in the section, "Lateral Advective-Diffusive Models for the Abyss" (pp. 137-139), and a brief discussion of extensions of this work is given.

The paper ends with a critique of Holland's calculation for a three-dimensional model of the North Atlantic in which temperature, salinity, oxygen, and radiocarbon distributions are calculated along with the velocity fields. The importance of the assumed magnitude of mixing parameters is clearly brought out by a simple analysis of the western boundary region where Holland's results are used to determine the balance of processes.

BOX MODELS

Mathematically, the simplest tracer model for deducing some features of ocean circulation is the box, or reservoir, model. The simplest of box models is shown in Figure 1. Box 1 receives fluid at a rate F_2 (>0) from Box 2 and loses fluid at a rate of F_1 (>0) to an undetermined sink. Associated with the flow is a property P, which for incoming fluid from Box 2 has the known value P_2 and for outgoing fluid has the known value P_1. In addition, there may be a source or a sink of property P, whose rate is given by cP_s. For a steady state, F_1 and F_2 must balance and the conservation equations for Box 1 corresponding to mass flow and flux of property P are

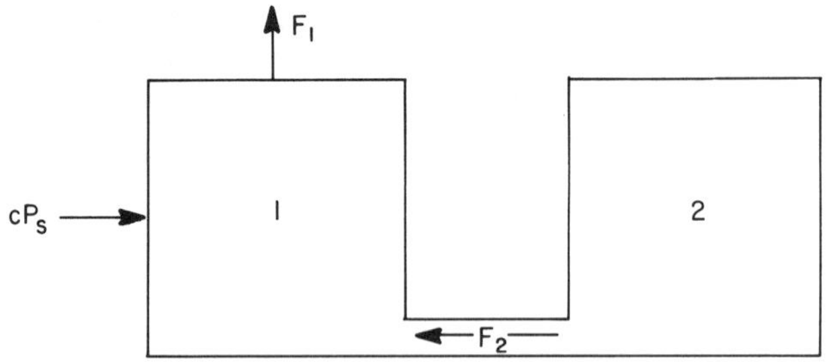

FIGURE 1 Two boxes, 1 and 2, are connected by a pipe, where the flux of fluid from box 2 to box 1 is given by F_2. The flux of fluid out of box 1 is F_1. A property P is associated with the fluid in each box. The quantity cP_S is the rate of flux of property P into box 1 from a source or sink.

$$F_2 - F_1 = 0, \tag{1}$$

$$F_2 P_2 - F_1 P_1 = cP_S. \tag{2}$$

The fluxes F_1 and F_2 may be expressed in terms of the known values P_1, P_2, and cP_S as

$$F_1 = F_2 = cP_S/(P_2 - P_1). \tag{3}$$

The box models discussed in the literature (e.g., Broecker *et al.*, 1960; Bolin and Stommel, 1961; Keeling and Bolin, 1968) are elaborations of the simple model given by Eqs. (1) and (2), with the numbers of boxes and of properties increased. Also included in some models are decay or consumption of properties.

The simplicity of box models is restricted to the ease with which one can obtain numerical results. The difficulties arise in connection with the formulation, because there is considerable subtlety in constructing a really meaningful box model and there are several pitfalls that must be avoided.

First, the idea of a box or reservoir appears to stem from the identification of water masses that are commonly referred to by oceanographers. As Sverdrup *et al.* (1942) point out, a water mass is identified by a characteristic curve in the *TS* plane. In a box model, single values of T, S, and other properties are taken to represent the water in a particular box. Such a procedure would be acceptable if the waters of the oceans were distributed in the *TS* plane in a way that "box" values were associated with distributional peaks separated by low valleys. Yet, it is evident from the distributions of properties in the oceans (Cochrane, 1958; Montgomery, 1958; Pollack, 1958; Bolin and Stommel, 1961) that there is a continuous transition in the distribution from one water mass to another. Nevertheless, it has become customery to think in terms of identifiable reservoirs (indeed, the accepted nomenclature simply reflects that fact) and to discuss the exchanges from one to another. One difficulty with which one is confronted from the outset is to assign appropriate values to the properties for a particular box. This is a particularly important point if the final model is sensitive to small changes in the chosen values of the properties.

A second point, rather closely related to the first, is that the reservoirs are joined not by insulated pipes but by dynamically active bodies of water. Thus, if one box represents Antarctic bottom water and another the common water of the Pacific and Indian Oceans, the joining region is the Antarctic circumpolar current, which is certainly not a passive carrier. If the exchange of the latter is left out of consideration, the reliability of the results is going to be limited to a certain extent.

A third point is one made by Defant (1936) and later discussed by Bolin and Stommel (1961). Mathematically, the box model reduces to the solution of a set of linear equations. If the determinant of the coefficient matrix nearly vanishes, the system is sensitive to small changes in the coefficients. Such ill-conditioned equations can yield results that vary widely and are not reliable. Bolin and Stommel show how the elaboration of a simple four-box system, incorporating North Atlantic deep water, Antarctic bottom water, Pacific and Indian intermediate water, and common water, to one that includes a fifth box (Antarctic surface water) and a larger number of constraints, leads to a system that is ill-conditioned with respect to the added components. Thus, a more elaborate model need not be an improvement and may even lead to greater uncertainty. Although this point is simple in concept, it is often disregarded.

In spite of the difficulties mentioned above, properly constructed box models serve a very useful purpose in providing gross, zeroth-order pictures of exchanges between different water masses. The principal results which emerge from these simple models are the average flow rates into and out of a reservoir from other reservoirs and the residence times of water in any given reservoir. Careful interpretation of the direct results can lead to estimates of quantities, such as vertical motions across the top or bottom of a reservoir, which are not observable and cannot be deduced quantitatively without resorting to much more elaborate models.

An added advantage of box models is that they may test ideas about additional processes and mechanisms that affect the distribution or exchange of properties. Although the tests in such cases are often too crude to be decisive, there are situations where these simple models are effective means of making the tests. In a recent careful analysis using box models, Craig (private communication) has shown that a source term associated with the input of a property via particulate matter can drastically alter the results of earlier studies. In a situation such as this, the usefulness of a box model is undeniable because of the extreme economy of computations.

However, the nature of the box model is such that mechanisms per se cannot really be studied. In order to obtain information, it is necessary to construct more mechanistically oriented models, a key feature of which is the lateral and vertical exchanges associated with large-scale mixing. Before proceeding to a discussion of more elaborate numerical models, we shall look into some of the attempts to establish quantitative measures of the mixing processes.

VERTICAL EXCHANGE MODELS

The basis for estimates of the intensity of vertical-mixing processes in the oceans is the observation that the main thermocline is a more or less steady, global feature of the oceans. The thermal structure of the thermocline implies that any small-scale, vertical-mixing processes must transport heat downward. For a steady temperature field it is necessary that the heat accumulated via this downward transfer be removed by some other mechanism. Stommel (1958) made the reasonable conjecture that the downward heat flux is balanced by an upwelling of cold, abyssal water into the thermocline. For the past 15 years, this vertical diffusive-convective model has played an important part in many of the thermohaline circulation models and in the studies of distribution of properties in the ocean. In this section, our purposes are to assess the reliability of this basic balance and to obtain reasonable estimates of the vertical diffusion coefficient.

A generalization of the model is used when the distribution of radioactive tracers is incorporated into the description. For example, for the dissolved concentration of a tracer between two reference levels $z = 0$ and $z = z_m$, the vertical exchange model becomes (Craig, 1969)

$$w \frac{\partial C}{\partial z} = K \frac{\partial^2 C}{\partial z^2} - \lambda C + J, \tag{4}$$

where w is the vertical velocity, K is the vertical eddy diffusion coefficient, λ is the decay of the radioactive tracer, and J is a source term. The latter may be the result of particulate matter containing the tracer and carried into the layer by some process. All four of the coefficients in Eq. (4) are assumed constant and the solution, with $C = C_o$ at $z = 0$ and $C = C_m$ at $z = z_m$, is (in Craig's notation)

$$C - J/\lambda = [\sinh (Az_m/2z^*)]^{-1} \; [(C_m - J/\lambda) \exp (z - z_m)/2z^*]$$
$$\sinh(Az/2z^*)^{-h}(C_o - J/\lambda) \exp (z/2\, z^*)$$
$$\sinh\, [A(z - z_m)/2z^*], \tag{5}$$

where $z^* = K/w, A = \; [1 + 4z^*\lambda/w]^{1/2}$.

Craig (1969), who extended the work of Munk (1966) by introducing the production term J, has discussed the implications of the result of Eq. (5) when used in concert with observed distributions of several tracers. Wyrtki (1962) had used the same model (without J) to analyze the vertical distribution of oxygen and, in particular, to discuss the observed oxygen minima. Although there is considerable controversy, some of it scientific, about the importance of the roles played by the different processes included in the model, there is general agreement about the implications of the model when it is applied to the layer of ocean extending from the base of the thermocline down to a deep level (4,000 m).

Using different physical models and observed distributions of temperature and salinity, Stommel and Arons (1960) chose a value $K = 0.7$ cm^2 s^{-1} and concluded that the range of vertical velocity required to provide consistency with observed features is between 0.5 and 3.0 cm day^{-1}. Hence, the scale height $z^* = K/w$ ranges from 0.3 km to 1.4 km. Vertical temperature profiles from different regions of the oceans can be used to support a choice of z^* anywhere within this range. Wyrtki (1961) has obtained similar values from vertical temperature profiles in the South Pacific. Munk (1966) has used profiles of salinity and temperature together with distributions of other tracers in the Pacific Ocean to conclude that these distributions "are not inconsistent with a simple model involving a constant upward vertical velocity $w \simeq 1.2$ cm day^{-1} and eddy diffusivity $K \simeq 1.3$ cm^2 s^{-1}." Craig, in a series of papers beginning with the abyssal carbon paper cited above, has arrived at similar conclusions for the water in the depth range of 1 to 4 km. Hence, all of these investigators are in agreement that the rough estimates—$w = 1$ cm day^{-1}, $K = 1$ cm^2 s^{-1}, $z^* =$ 1 km—are characteristic values for the layer of water between 1 and 4 km.

Although it is comforting to obtain a concensus on the estimated global magnitudes of quantities such as w and K, which defy direct measurement, there are several disquieting aspects of this approach. One is that vertical profiles exhibit different scale heights from station to station, and even at a single station it is necessary to use different scale heights for different vertical ranges. This observation introduces considerable uncertainty into the wisdom of using constant values for w and K. Although most investigators are cautious about too liberal a use of the simple balances proposed above, nevertheless, it is tempting to try to patch up the picture within the given context when conflicting evidence appears. A second point is the role of horizontal exchange, which has seldom been seriously considered in combination with the vertical-exchange process. The reasons for this are obvious when one considers the magnitude of the problem introduced by bringing in horizontal advection and diffusion. There are too many unknown parameters to be considered in a problem that is far from trivial, and the task of exploring the different ranges of parameters is truly formidable.

An additional difficulty with the present problem is one that often confronts oceanographers. The observations can be shown to be consistent with models that take into account mutually exclusive processes or that appear to differ from each other in some fundamental fashion. No single feature of these models seems to be more successful or plays a more important role in "explaining" the observations than the vertical diffusion coefficient, K, perhaps the least understood of all of the parameters in use in oceanography at the present time.

An important step in determining the respective importance of vertical and lateral exchange processes has recently been taken by Rooth and Östlund (1972), who have used observations of tritium in the Sargasso Sea and a novel approach to the problem. They observed that soundings made on R/V *Pillsbury* cruise P-6910 in October 1969, over a region in the Sargasso Sea from 20°30′ N to 30°25′ N show a temperature versus depth profile in the range 9.3 °C $< T <$ 17.3 °C that is very closely approximated by an exponential curve with a scale height of 440 m. A log-log plot of observed tritium units (the tritium unit is 10^{18} times the mole fraction of tritium in total hydrogen) versus temperature in the range cited above shows that the data points for higher temperatures cluster along a line for which

$$\phi = \mu\theta + \text{const}, \tag{6}$$

where $\phi = ln$ (tritium concentration) and $\theta = ln$ (temperature minus reference temperature). The constant μ is approximately equal to 5 for temperatures above 14 °C.

On the assumption that temperature, T, and concentration, C, are determined by advective-diffusive equations with anisotropic diffusive processes governed by the coefficients, K and K_H, in the vertical and horizontal directions, respectively, Rooth and Östlund write

$$C_t + \nu\cdot\nabla C + \lambda C = KC_{zz} + K_z C_z + K_H \nabla_H{}^2 C, \tag{7}$$

$$\nu\cdot\nabla T = KT_{zz} + K_z T_z + K_H \nabla_H{}^2 T, \tag{8}$$

where subscripts t and z correspond to partial derivatives and λ is the decay rate for the radioactive substance, C. The temperature is taken to be steady, whereas the concentration C will generally exhibit transient behavior. Because a relatively massive amount of tritium was injected into the atmosphere from the fusion bomb explosions during the years 1956 to1962, a secular change of tritium (with a half-life of 12 years) can be expected.

The substitutions $\phi = lnC$, $\theta = ln(T - T_c)$ into Eqs. (7) and (8) yield

$$\phi_t + V\cdot\nabla\phi + \lambda = K[(\phi_z)^2 + \phi_{zz}] + K_z\phi_z + K_H[(\nabla_H\phi)^2 + \nabla_H{}^2\phi], \tag{9}$$

$$\nu\cdot\nabla\theta = K[(\theta_z)^2 + \theta_{zz}] + K_z\theta_z + K_H[(\nabla_H\theta)^2 + \nabla_H{}^2\theta]. \tag{10}$$

Now, if the empirical relation (6) is used, Eqs. (9) and (10) combine to form the balance

$$\phi_t + \lambda = (\mu^2 - \mu)\,[K(\theta_z)^2 + K_H(\nabla_H\theta)^2] = (\mu^2 - \mu)(KH^{-2} + K_H L^{-2}), \tag{11}$$

where H and L are characteristic vertical and horizontal scale lengths in the thermocline region of the measurements. Eq. (11) describes a weighted diffusion time scale in terms of the local rate of change and the decay coefficient λ. The use of the observed power law (Eq. 6) provides the balance (Eq. 11) irrespective of boundary conditions and convective effects.

Preliminary analysis of water samples from a 1971 cruise have been made by Rooth and Östlund, who have concluded that the tritium concentration is stationary to within 4 percent (the accuracy of the tritium determinations). Hence, over the 3-year period the estimate is $|\phi_t| \leqslant 5 \times 10^{-10}\ s^{-1}$. Using $\lambda = 1.8 \times 10^{-9}\ s^{-1}$, together with the observed scale height $H = 440$ m and the fact that $K_H L^{-2} > 0$, they arrive at the important conclusion

$$K < 0.2\ \text{cm}^2\ s^{-1}. \tag{12}$$

The measured temperature scale height of 440 m, together with Eq. (12) yields

$$w = \frac{K}{H} < 0.45 \times 10^{-5}\ \text{cm s}^{-1} = 1.4\ \text{m yr}^{-1}. \tag{13}$$

The values deduced are at the lower extremes of the ranges given by earlier workers.

A crude estimate by Rooth and Östlund of horizontal diffusive exchange along isopycnic surfaces indicates that a coefficient $K_H = 10^8\ \text{cm}^2\ s^{-1}$ would be required to dominate the exchange process. This value is rather large and the conclusion is that local vertical diffusion is dominant in the region under consideration.

In an earlier analysis of the tritium distribution at 28°29′ N, 121°32′ W in the North Pacific, Roether *et al.* (1970) have used the vertical diffusive-advective model to arrive at the value $K = 0.2\ \text{cm}^2\ s^{-1}$, when a vertical velocity of 10 m yr^{-1} is assumed. A lower value of w would yield a proportionately lower value of K. Hence, a rather low upper bound for K is provided by this independent measurement. [An additional indication of a low value for K was given in an earlier paper by Veronis (1969), where the inverse power law solution to the thermocline model yielded the value $K = 0.15\ \text{cm}^2\ s^{-1}$ for a station in the cyclonic gyre north of the Gulf Stream.]

Another interesting result emerging from the Rooth-

Östlund paper is that for temperatures below 14 °C the data show a tritium concentration that is higher at lower temperatures and the points fall on a line with $\mu = 3$ in Eq. (6). The authors point out that the sources of the water for which this happens are peripheral to the Sargasso Sea and they offer the conjecture that the water at these deeper levels has its origin in more distant regions and is advected into the main thermocline region below the Sargasso Sea. On the basis of their rather limited evidence, they suggest that lateral exchange processes dominate over vertical exchange processes in the major part of the main thermocline. Now when $\mu = 3$ is used in conjunction with Eq. (11) and the associated argument, the values that emerge are $w = 5.2$ m yr^{-1} and $K = 0.75$ cm^2 s^{-1}. These values are close to the traditionally accepted ones. If Rooth and Östlund are correct in their conjecture, the implication is that the "traditional" values for w and K are arrived at from analyses that omit the important and presumably dominant process of lateral exchange. In other words, the vertical advective-diffusive model may not be pertinent in the main thermocline region, although formal use of it may lead to values of w and K that are "reasonable."

In the past few years there has been a trend toward exploring thermocline models that do not rest heavily on the assumption of vertical diffusion as a dominant process. Welander's (1959) original thermocline model treated the ocean as an ideal fluid, and he was able to reproduce observed oceanic features without the use of vertical diffusion. Veronis (1969) showed that the role of vertical eddy diffusion in the exponential solution of the thermocline model cannot be tested, because a vertical motion field, independent of the dynamical problem, can be arbitrarily superimposed to balance the effect of vertical diffusion. Welander (1971a) has analyzed a more general ideal fluid model of the thermocline with the result that he is able to extend the consistency of the analysis with observed data. In his most recent paper on the subject, Welander (1971b) has proposed a model that is dominated by advective processes in anticyclonic regions (where the wind stress curl is negative so that the vertical velocity out of the Ekman layer is downward) but with significant vertical diffusion in upwelling regions. This last model is consistent with the Rooth–Östlund results, because their analysis leading to the low value of K is confined to a rather thin layer just below the 18° water in the Sargasso Sea; and, according to their conjecture, the thermocline region below that layer is dominated by horizontal exchange processes.

It remains to be seen whether the more extensive survey of tritium distribution now being undertaken will add further support to the findings reported by Rooth and Östlund. What appears to be emerging, however, is a picture that shows substantially more complicated balances than the simple vertical advective-diffusive one, at least in some oceanic regions.

LATERAL ADVECTIVE-DIFFUSIVE MODELS FOR THE ABYSS

The basic premise leading to Stommel's (1958) abyssal circulation for the world ocean is uniform upwelling at the base of the thermocline to balance the downward diffusion of heat associated with the stably stratified thermocline region. Although this premise may be questioned as a result of the recent developments mentioned in the foregoing section, Stommel's *tour de force* is still the only simple, complete model for the abyssal circulation. A few modifications, incorporating the effects of bottom topography, have been attempted; but these have also been based on the assumption of a uniform upwelling.

Two calculations have been made of the abyssal distribution of tracers based on Stommel's circulation model of a homogeneous abyssal ocean. The first of these, by Arons and Stommel (1967), fits somewhere between box models and continuous circulation models. The analysis is restricted to the abyssal North Atlantic, which is treated as two strips, one representing the latitude band from 0 to 30° N, the other from 30° N to 60° N. Continuous variation of properties is allowed in the east-west direction; but north-south variations, expressed in terms of incremental changes between the two strips, are determined largely by imposed differences at the western edges of the strips, where input from the western boundary current is prescribed. Because the latitudinal direction is thus treated as a half-dimension, in the sense of admitting only restricted incremental changes, the dynamics of the basic circulation model cannot be fully incorporated into the tracer model and some freedom is allowed in what would otherwise be determined quantities. For example, in the global abyssal circulation model, prescribing the strength of the source of abyssal water automatically determines the magnitude of the upwelling velocity (by mass conservation); the transport in the western boundary layer, as well as the recirculation intensity, is also a result of the dynamics. In addition, prescribing the concentration of tracer in the source water and the decay rate of tracer should suffice for the analysis of the global distribution of tracer concentration.

In the Arons–Stommel analysis, the North Atlantic is treated as an open basin, because water can flow out of it via the western boundary layer. Hence, only a fraction of the source water is advected from the western boundary layer into the basin. Of that fraction, a portion is recirculated and the remainder provides the upwelling velocity through the base of the thermocline. Using observed east-west distributions of dissolved oxygen as a guide, Arons and Stommel calculated a series of models and chose the values of their undetermined parameters to give the best fit to the observed data in the strips. They then turned to a similar (simplified) model for the distribution of radiocarbon to obtain additional information in order to determine the mass transport into the basin from the western boundary layer. As part of their argument, it was necessary to obtain an independent estimate (from observed data) of the oxygen content of the recirculated water versus the content of the source water. By means of their quasi-analytic approach, they were able to deduce estimates of the horizontal mixing coefficient K_H and of the decay rate ν of oxygen. They concluded that K_H is in the range 6.0 to 7.4 × 10^6 cm^2 s^{-1} with ν between 2.0 and 2.5 × 10^{-3} ml l^{-1} yr^{-1}. These are consistent with other estimates of K_H and ν based on different considerations.

The observed eastward decrease of dissolved oxygen (in both strips) emerges from the calculation, although there is more structure in the observed data than in the derived profiles. The simplicity of the model is such that the calculation time is relatively trivial, and one can experiment with wide ranges of parameters. As it turns out, the results are rather sensitive to choices of the Péclet number (the ratio of advection to diffusion time), as well as to the ratio of diffusion to decay time for oxygen. The supplementary data from the radioactive decay model required to determine the mass transport from the western boundary layer into the basin turns out to be noncritical, because only an average value of ^{14}C for the entire North Atlantic basin is used in the calculation.

The reasonable findings of the Arons-Stommel study encouraged Kuo and Veronis (1970) to apply a more critical test to the hypotheses of the basic circulation model. The ocean basin was extended to include an idealized model of the world ocean with the Atlantic, Indian, and Pacific Oceans connected at their southern extremities by the Antarctic circumpolar current. Sources of equal strength were assumed in the polar regions of the Atlantic, corresponding to the sinking regions in the Greenland and Weddell Seas. A recirculation R of water around the Antarctic circumpolar current was also assumed. On the basis of these conditions and geostrophic, hydrostatic dynamics, plus a uniform upwelling velocity through the upper surface of the abyssal water, a circulation (essentially Stommel's *tour de force*) can be determined if western boundary currents are appended where needed to provide mass conservation. The circulation picture is shown in Figure 2.

The lateral advective-diffusive equation for oxygen, derived by integrating the three-dimensional advective-diffusive equation in the vertical direction, becomes

$$K_H \nabla_H{}^2 \bar{C} - \nu_H \cdot \nabla_H \bar{C} - \nu = 0, \qquad (14)$$

where subscript H corresponds to "horizontal" components and the overbar to a vertical average. Given the velocity field

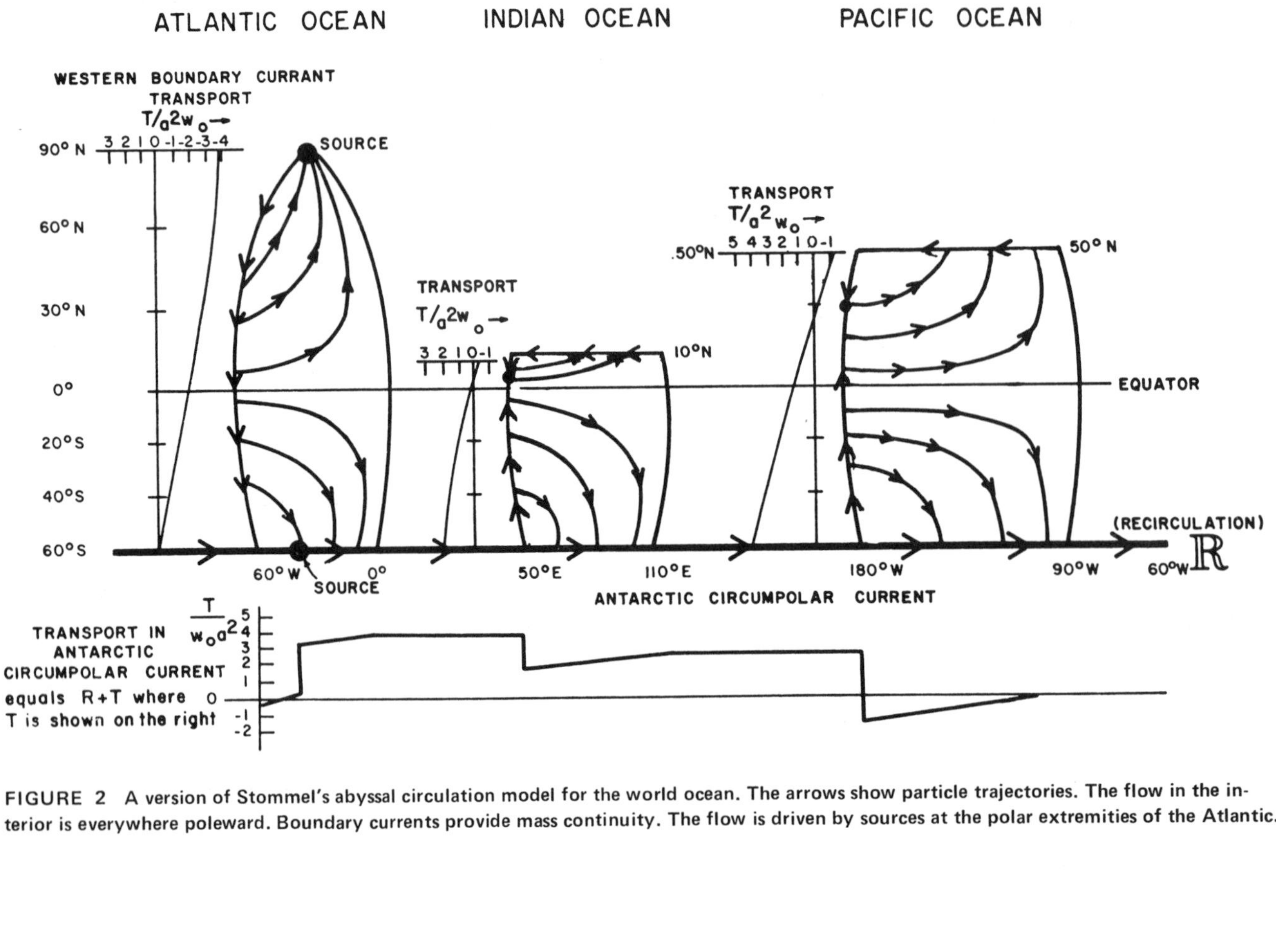

FIGURE 2 A version of Stommel's abyssal circulation model for the world ocean. The arrows show particle trajectories. The flow in the interior is everywhere poleward. Boundary currents provide mass continuity. The flow is driven by sources at the polar extremities of the Atlantic.

as determined by the abyssal circulation model and the concentration $\bar{C}$ at the source points, the task is to determine $\bar{C}$ everywhere. Boundary conditions are that the normal derivative of $\bar{C}$ vanish at all solid boundaries. The values of K_H, ν, and the strengths of the sources, as well as of the recirculation, are parameters that can be adjusted to derive the best fit with observed oxygen data.

The present model includes a consistent dynamical description of the flow field, and the solutions that emerge must be consistent with the dynamics. Mathematically the model is a simple one, but the shapes of the boundaries necessitate a numerical treatment. Because Eq. (14) is an elliptic one, the solution can be obtained by relaxation as long as $K_H/|\nu_H|$ is sufficiently large. The latter condition is equivalent to requiring that the Péclet number, $w_o a^2/HK_H$, where w_o is the magnitude of the upwelling and H is the depth of the abyssal ocean, is not larger than order unity. Solution by relaxation takes about 2 minutes on an IBM 7090-40 for a grid network with 10° intervals. Hence, it is possible to explore the changes in concentration introduced by different values of the parameters.

The observed abyssal (at 4,000 m in depth) oxygen distribution, as determined by Stommel and Stroup (unpublished, but reported by Stommel and Arons, 1960), is shown in Figure 3. The best fit to this data obtained by the present model is shown in Figure 4. The values of the parameters are $\nu = 2 \times 10^{-3}$ ml l^{-1} yr^{-1}, $w_o = 1.25 \times 10^{-5}$ cm s^{-1}, $K_H = 10^7$ cm^2 s^{-1}, and $R = 10^7$ m^3 s^{-1}.

The principal conclusion to emerge from the calculation is that horizontal mixing must be important in determining the distribution of dissolved oxygen. Simple advection would show a decrease of concentration along the trajectories of Figure 2. That is, one would expect to see the highest concentration in the equatorial regions of the Indian and Pacific basins. However, there is an overall northward decrease of concentration in the Pacific and Indian Oceans, which, in the present model, have no sources of abyssal water other than the western boundary current. Hence, horizontal mixing processes must serve to mix newer water northward into these basins from the Antarctic circumpolar current. This distribution of dissolved oxygen is also observed.

Of course, consistency with observation does not constitute proof that the assumptions of the basic model are valid, because it is clearly possible that a model with different dynamics may also reproduce the observed distribution. Nevertheless, the model has satisfied this necessary condition of consistency and deserves further study. Some progress has been made in extending the investigation to a wider range of parametric values. The relaxation method breaks down when the Péclet number exceeds the value two. When derivatives are written in terms of finite difference that are weighted on one side to allow for the advective effects, the solution can be obtained for all Péclet numbers. The calculation is being carried out with the altered scheme, so that a better set of results should soon be available.*

The effects of bottom topography on the abyssal circulation have been incorporated into a model of the Pacific Ocean. Because of the strong constraint of rotation in the nearly homogeneous abyssal waters, bottom topographic effects alter the circulation picture substantially. Horizontal diffusion may be expected to smooth out some of the differences in the tracer distribution introduced by the altered flow field.

A THREE-DIMENSIONAL NUMERICAL CALCULATION

Holland (1971) has published a report of a numerical calculation to determine the three-dimensional distributions of temperature (T), salinity (S), dissolved oxygen (O), and radiocarbon (^{14}C), as well as the field of motion, for an ocean basin representing the North Atlantic. The ocean is driven by wind and thermohaline processes. The model includes anisotropic eddy diffusive processes for momentum and concentration properties, an estimated consumption rate for oxygen (given as a function of depth), the known radioactive decay of ^{14}C, and observed surface values for salinity, temperature, oxygen, and radiocarbon.

The dynamical model is similar to Bryan's (1969), but with a somewhat larger value for the horizontal momentum diffusion coefficient. When the density becomes unstably stratified, vertical mixing is taken to be infinite so that the unstable vertical gradients are wiped out. Otherwise, constant eddy coefficients are assumed to provide horizontal and vertical exchange associated with scales smaller than those that can be calculated directly.

The most important results from Holland's model are given here, together with a modest attempt to understand the primary result of his calculation, viz., the fact that downwelling occurs over a great part of the ocean, in contrast to the assumed upwelling of Stommel's *tour de force* circulation.

The principal parameters that appear to determine the important balances in the calculation are the mixing coefficients. The horizontal eddy diffusion coefficient for momentum A_m was chosen to be 5×10^8 cm^2 s^{-1}, a large value necessitated by the rather coarse grid used for the calculations. The vertical and horizontal eddy diffusion coefficients for the four tracer properties (T, S, O, and ^{14}C) were respectively, $K = 1$ cm^2 s^{-1} and $K_H = 5 \times 10^7$ cm^2 s^{-1}. (Holland's notation for K_H is A_H.) Temperature and salinity combine to determine the density (via the equation of state) so that K and K_H contribute also to the dynamical balances.

Holland has presented a fairly comprehensive picture of the results obtained from his model. Only those that can be

* The results of this work are reported by Kuo and Veronis, 1973, Deep-Sea Res., 20:871–88.

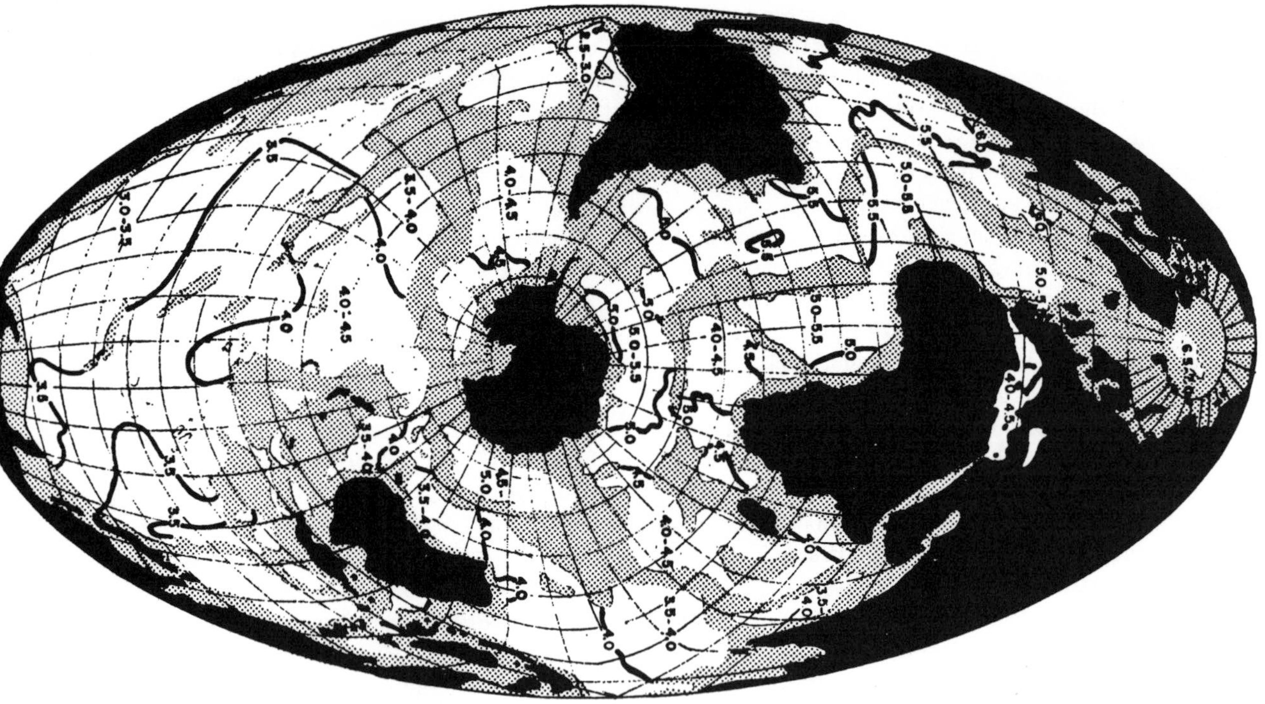

FIGURE 3 A sketch of the distribution of dissolved oxygen (ml/liter) at a depth of 4,000 m in the oceans of the world. (Reproduced from Figure 3 in Stommel and Arons, 1960.)

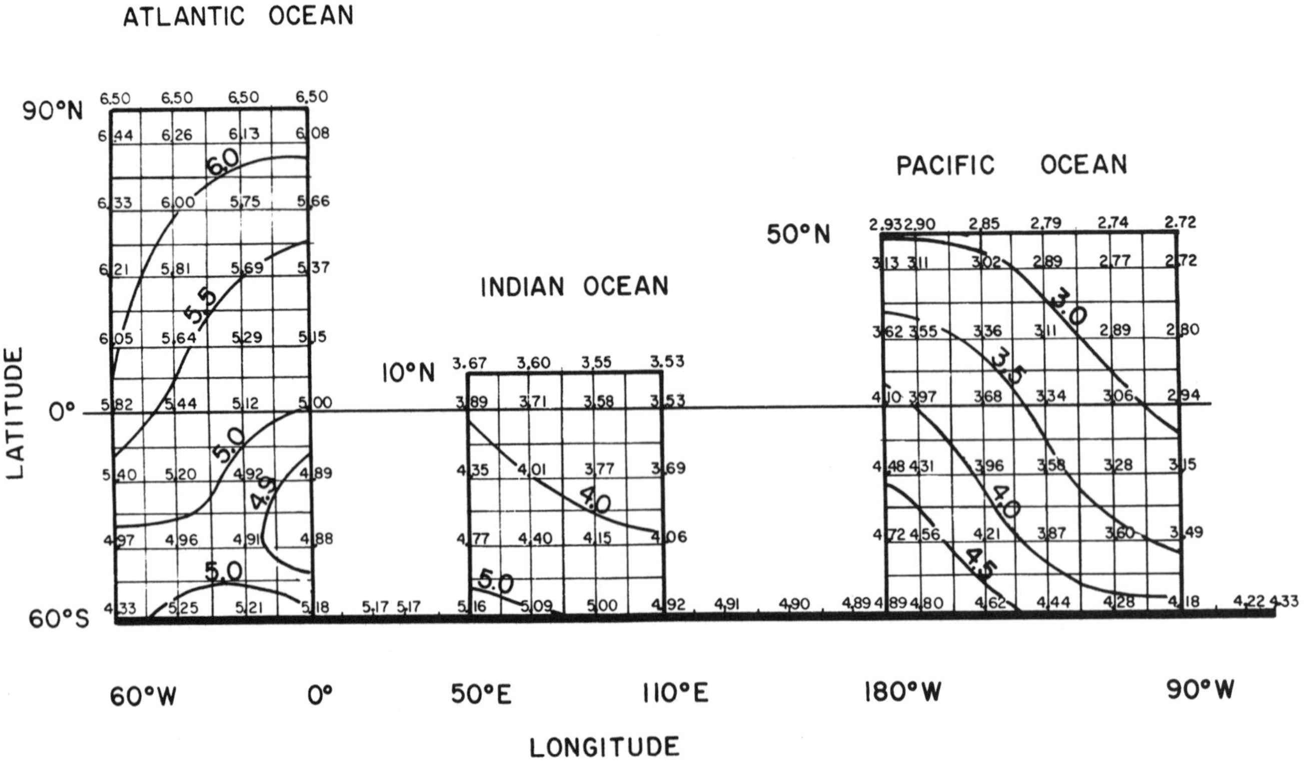

FIGURE 4 Dissolved oxygen in the abyssal oceans of the world as calculated from Eq. (14). The upwelling velocity is $w = 1.25 \times 10^{-5}$ cm s^{-1}, the horizontal eddy diffusion coefficient is $K_h = 10^7$ cm^2 s^{-1}, and the recirculation in the Antarctic circumpolar current is 10^7 m^3 s^{-1}.

compared to the results of the simpler Kuo-Veronis calculation are discussed here, because the reasons for agreement and disparity can be analyzed. The many other results of the calculation are intimately related to the ones discussed here, and their plausibility increases along with that of the ones to be discussed.

The boundary conditions prescribed at the surface of the model were zonally uniform values of *T, S, O,* wind stress, and a constant value of ^{14}C. The system was taken to be symmetric across the equator.

The values of the parameters were such that the final solution was steady, hence, vertical sections and horizontal contour charts summarize some of the findings. The principal results to be discussed here are shown in Figures 5-8. Exhibited in Figure 5 are horizontal contours of the horizontal transport stream function in the steady state. This figure shows that the solution is linear (frictionally controlled at the western boundary layer) and that the Sverdrup solution, giving a balance between wind stress curl and β-effect, is applicable to the interior flow.

In Figure 6 the associated vertical velocity field is shown at three levels with the stippled regions representing downwelling. Even at great depth, the calculations show downward flow over the bulk of the ocean. This result marks a point of departure from Stommel's *tour de force* where an upwelling at the base of the thermocline is assumed. Hence, either the latter assumption is basically incorrect or the downwelling is the product of a process that is peculiar to the choice of parameters of Holland's model.

Figure 7 shows the horizontal distributions of *T, S,* and *O* at 1,800 m. The temperatures are on the low side for the North Atlantic and the salinities are rather uniform, except for the distribution in the northeast corner. In the latter region, there is intense downwelling of water of low salinity and higher temperature. The mechanism for sinking of water of lower density does not make sense from the point of view of convective overturning. It is apparently associated with the use of an infinite vertical diffusion coefficient invoked in regions of unstably stratified water, although how warm, fresh water sinks as a result is somewhat of a mystery.

The oxygen distribution shows that oldest water occurs at the southwest corner of the basin. Sinking water at the north has high oxygen content, and rapid southward advection tends to keep the oxygen content high along the western boundary layer. Elsewhere, consumption of oxygen reduces the concentration; and the southwest corner, farthest removed from the source region, has lowest concentration. In the interior of the ocean, the horizontal velocities are rather low at the 1,800-m level and the oxygen content is dominated by consumption and horizontal diffusion.

Qualitatively, Holland's oxygen distribution at 1,800 m agrees with that obtained by Kuo and Veronis for the abyssal waters with $K_H = 10^8$ cm^2 s^{-1}, $w = 1.25 \times 10^{-5}$ cm s^{-1}. Detailed comparison is not meaningful because Holland assumed a condition of north-south symmetry at the equator, and the Kuo-Veronis calculation shows a monotonic trend there.

Certainly the principal difference between the two calculations is in the distribution of vertical velocities, which affects the horizontal velocities and, consequently, the oxygen distribution. The uniform upwelling at the surface of the abyss is an assumed part of Stommel's circulation model and is a fundamental part of the Kuo-Veronis calculation. In Holland's calculation, the downward vertical velocity in the interior is a dynamical consequence of his assumed processes.

By considering the balances in the western boundary layer, it is possible to obtain a physical feeling for the reason for the downwelling in Holland's model. In all of the general ocean circulation models, the north-south flow in the western boundary layer is geostrophic. Because Holland's dynamical model is one with frictional control in the western boundary layer, the inertial terms are not important, even in the remaining horizontal momentum equation.

The principal balances in the western boundary layer can thus be summarized by the following set of equations:

$$fv = \frac{-\partial P}{\partial x}, \tag{15}$$

$$fu = \frac{-\partial P}{\partial y} + \frac{A_h}{f}\frac{\partial^2 v}{\partial x^2} = \frac{-\partial P}{\partial y} + \frac{A_h}{f}\frac{\partial^3 P}{\partial x^3}, \tag{16}$$

$$\frac{\partial P}{\partial z} = -g\hat{\rho}, \tag{17}$$

$$u\frac{\partial \hat{\rho}}{\partial x} + v\frac{\partial \hat{\rho}}{\partial y} + w\frac{\partial \hat{\rho}}{\partial z} = K\frac{\partial^2 \hat{\rho}}{\partial z^2} + K_h\frac{\partial^2 \hat{\rho}}{\partial x^2}, \tag{18}$$

$$\frac{\partial u}{\partial x} + \frac{\partial v}{\partial y} + \frac{\partial w}{\partial z} = 0, \tag{19}$$

where the rectangular coordinates, x(eastward), y(northward), and z(upward) are used because we are concentrating on the local behavior in the western boundary layer; P is p/ρ_o; $\hat{\rho}$ is ρ/ρ_o; and ρ_o is the mean density. In the diffusion terms, derivatives with respect to y are neglected as is customary in the boundary layer. Also, vertical momentum transfer by mixing is not important outside the surface and bottom Ekman layers.

Eliminating pressure from the first two equations and using the last equation gives the planetary vorticity equation (with $\beta = df/dy$)

$$f^2\frac{\partial w}{\partial z} = \beta\frac{\partial P}{\partial x} - A_h\frac{\partial^4 P}{\partial x^4}. \tag{20}$$

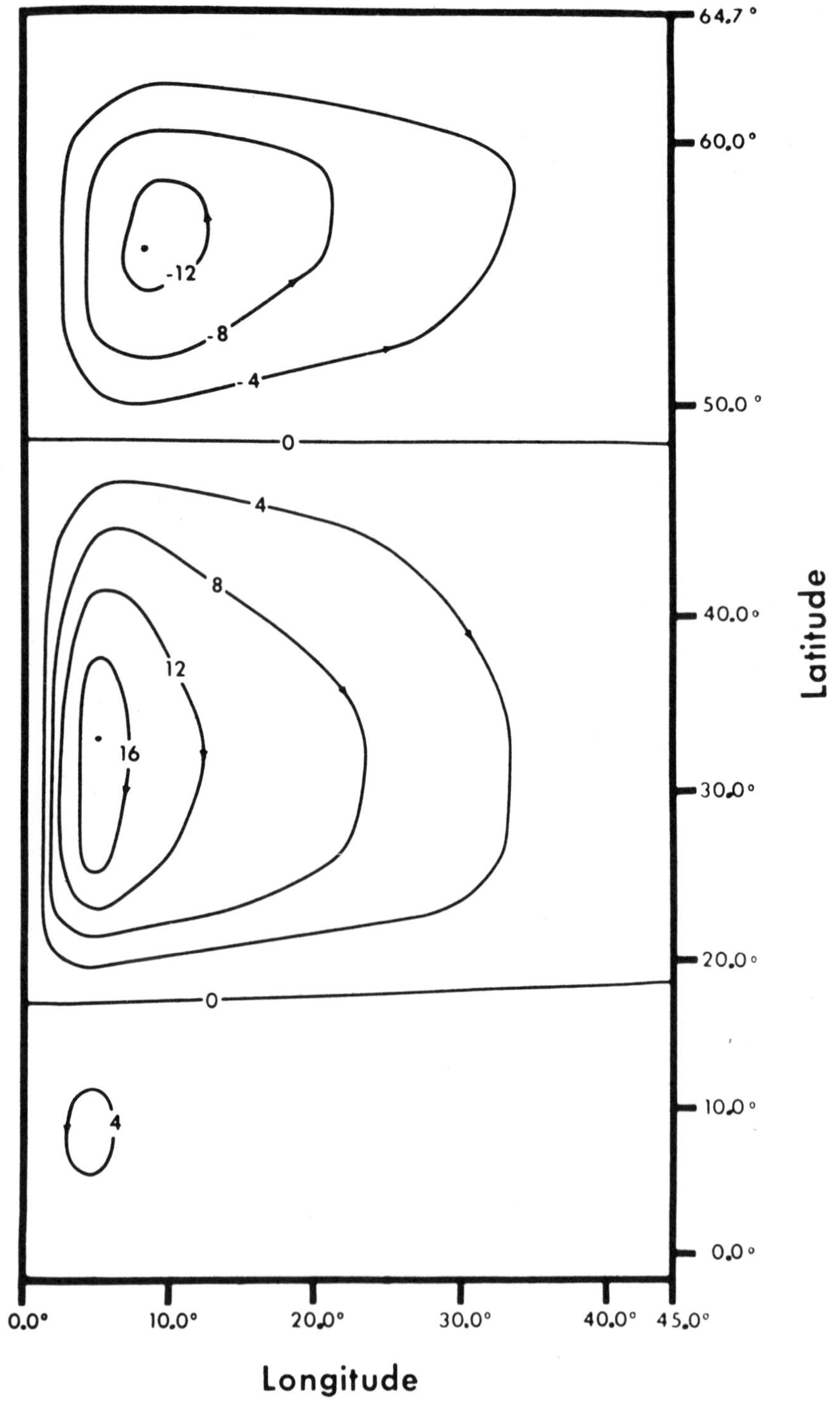

FIGURE 5 Contours of the vertically integrated transport in the North Atlantic Ocean as calculated by Holland (1971) by a three-dimensional numerical integration. Units are $10^6\ m^3\ s^{-1}$. This figure, as well as Figures 6, 7, and 8, was reproduced from Holland.

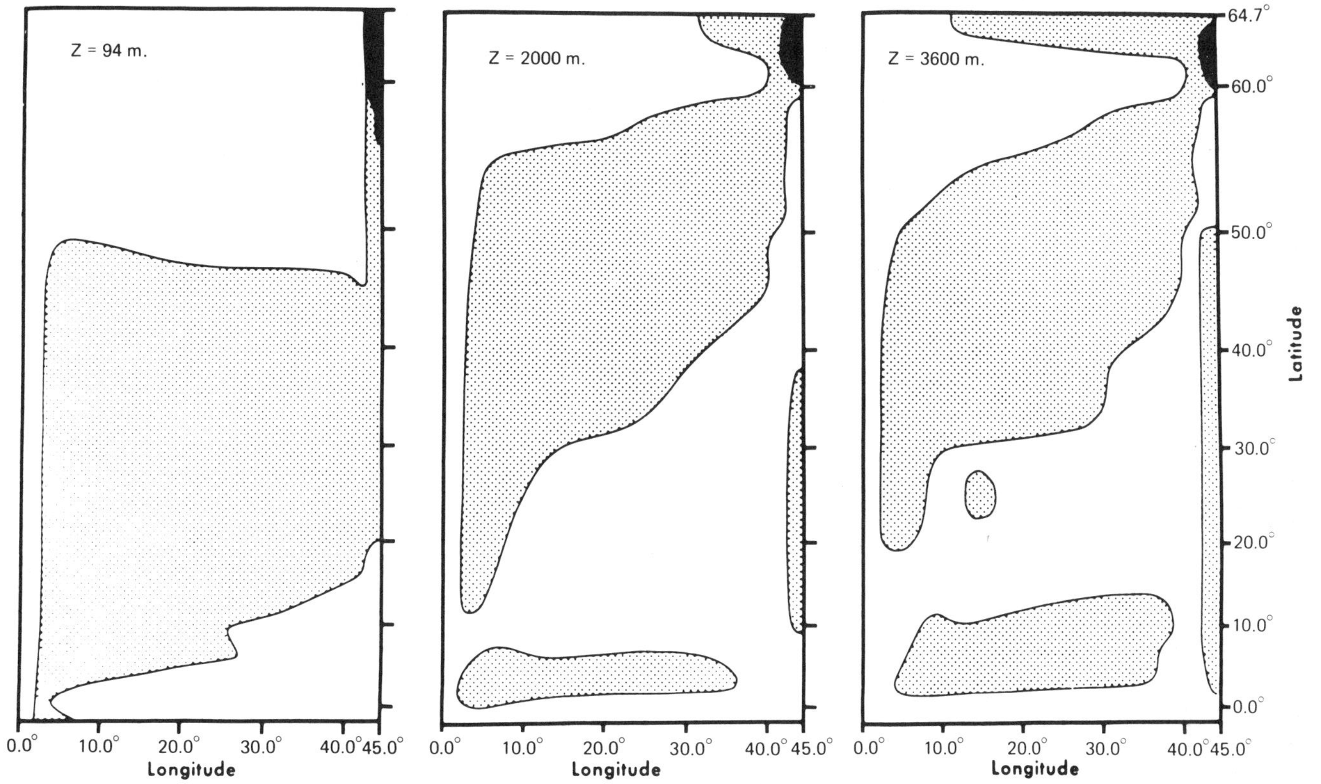

FIGURE 6 The vertical velocity, positive in white regions and negative in stippled regions, as calculated by Holland (1971) for three levels—94 m; 2,000 m; and 3,600 m below the surface in the North Atlantic Ocean.

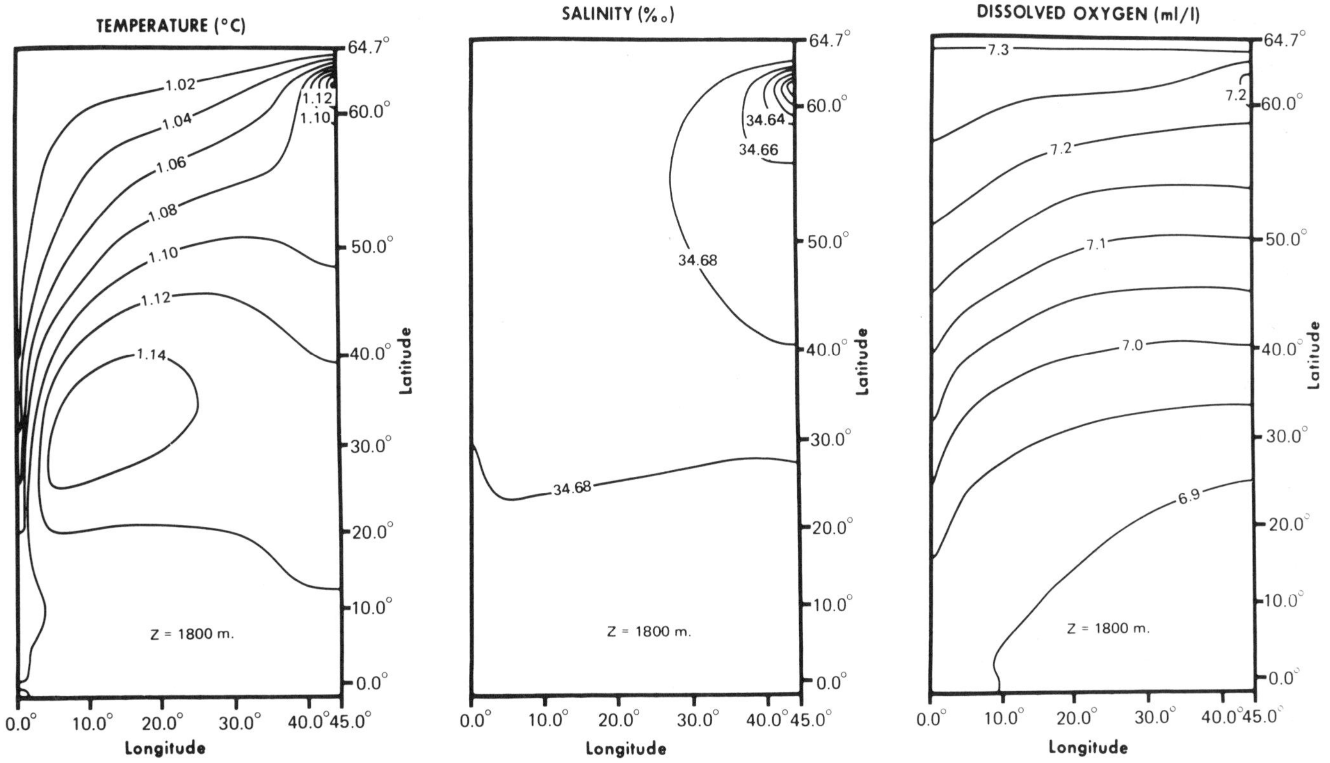

FIGURE 7 Horizontal contours of temperature, salinity, and oxygen calculated at the 1,800-m level by Holland for the North Atlantic Ocean.

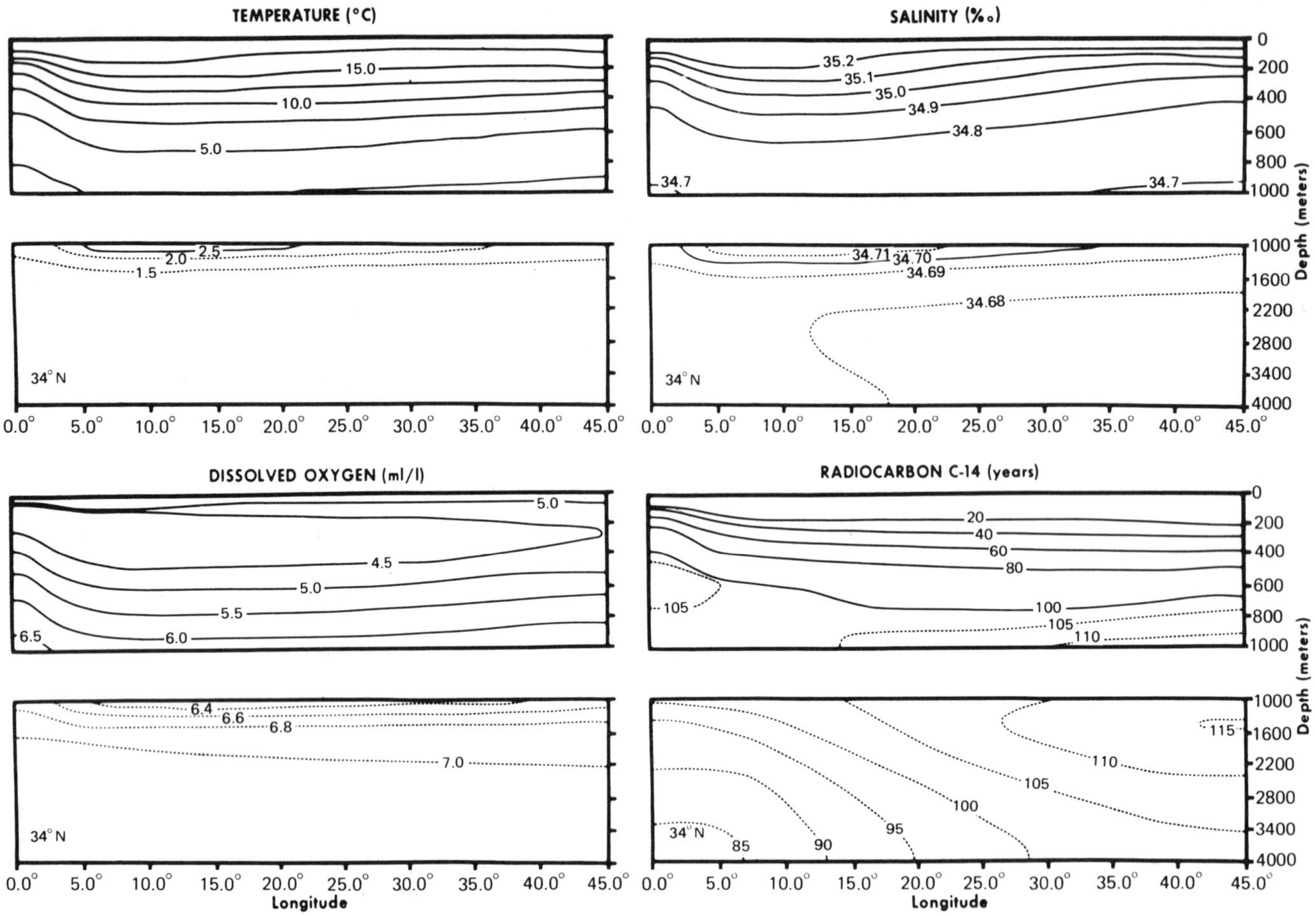

FIGURE 8 Zonal sections of temperature, salinity, oxygen, and ^{14}C at 34° N in Holland's model. The upper kilometer has an expanded vertical scale in each figure.

Using the first three equations to express u, v, and $\hat{\rho}$ in terms of P yields for the fourth equation

$$\frac{1}{f}\left[\frac{-\partial P}{\partial y}+\frac{A_h}{f}\frac{\partial^3 P}{\partial x^3}\right]\frac{\partial^2 P}{\partial x \partial z}+\frac{1}{f}\frac{\partial P}{\partial x}\frac{\partial^2 P}{\partial z \partial y}+w\frac{\partial^2 P}{\partial z^2}$$

$$=K\frac{\partial^3 P}{\partial z^3}+K_h\frac{\partial^3 P}{\partial z \partial x^3}. \quad (21)$$

Now w can be eliminated from Eqs. (20) and (21) to give a single equation in P. Hence, individual terms can be compared by using Holland's published results to evaluate each term.

It is evident from Figure 8 that T and S slope more or less uniformly down to the right in the western boundary layer. At a depth of 400 m, the horizontal scale is about 5° longitude or 450 km and the vertical scale is 400 m. Over these scales, the change in density is approximately 5×10^{-4} g cm^{-3}. Thus, from the hydrostatic equation one obtains

$$\frac{\partial P}{\partial z} \sim \frac{\Delta P}{H} = -g\hat{\rho}, \quad (22)$$

and with $H \sim 400$ m, $g = 10^3$ cm s^{-2}, and $\hat{\rho} \sim 5 \times 10^{-4}$ the conclusion is

$$\Delta P \sim 2 \times 10^4 \text{ cm}^2 \text{ s}^{-2}. \quad (23)$$

With this scale analysis the geostrophic terms, $-1/f$ $(\partial P/\partial y)\,\partial^2 P/\partial x \partial z$ and $1/f\,(\partial P/\partial x)\,\partial^2 P/\partial y \partial z$ cancel and the remaining terms in Eq. (21) can be evaluated once a magnitude of w is obtained from Eq. (20). It is easy to verify (using the above values) that within 1 percent the balance of terms in (21) is

$$w\frac{\partial \hat{\rho}}{\partial z} = K_h \frac{\partial^2 \hat{\rho}}{\partial x^2}, \quad (24)$$

where P has been replaced by its equivalent term in $\hat{\rho}$. Now substituting $K_h = 5 \times 10^7$ cm^2 s^{-1} and the foregoing values for $\hat{\rho}$, the horizontal and vertical scale heights yield

$$w \sim 10^{-3} \text{ cm s}^{-1}, \quad (25)$$

a very large value for the steady vertical velocity of the thermohaline circulation.

The mechanism for the large vertical velocity is now evident. There is a large lateral divergence of heat flux from the interior into the western boundary layer because of intense horizontal diffusion of heat. Because there is no heat flux through the boundary, it is necessary in a steady-state system that the heat be removed by some process. The relatively intense upwelling of cold water serves this purpose. However, the net effect is more than just a local one. The intense upwelling in the boundary layer requires that abyssal water be formed elsewhere, and the result is that the horizontal flow in the interior has a small downward component over the bulk of the ocean. The western boundary layer serves as a sink for abyssal water, the source being most of the rest of the ocean.

In a model such as Holland's, the use of horizontal mixing along a level surface should perhaps be replaced by mixing parallel to potential density surfaces. In the interior, the distinction is slight because potential density surfaces are nearly flat. However, in the western boundary layer, where the density surfaces have significant slopes, mixing along constant z implies some mixing normal to density surfaces. For example, in Holland's calculation, if $K_h \partial^2 \rho/\partial x^2$ is replaced by $K \partial^2 \rho/\partial z_\sigma{}^2$ where z_σ is the level of a constant density surface, and if the vertical and horizontal scales cited above are used in place of the derivatives, the effective vertical (normal to constant density surfaces) diffusion coefficient is 50 $cm^2\ s^{-1}$. Thus, the balance in the western boundary layer is a vertical diffusive-advective one with a very large vertical diffusion coefficient.

The foregoing argument accounts for the principal discrepancy between Stommel's *tour de force* circulation and Holland's circulation pattern. In a more recent calculation Holland (private communication) has used a smaller horizontal diffusion coefficient for heat ($K_h = 10^7\ cm^2\ s^{-1}$) and the results show a weaker upwelling in the western boundary layer and an upwelling almost everywhere in the interior. In this last calculation, support is provided for the basic assumption in Stommel's *tour de force.* Flux boundary conditions for T and S, also included in a more recent (unpublished) calculation by Holland, provide more realistic distributions for T and S and also serve to broaden the region of sinking motion in the northeast corner.

ACKNOWLEDGMENTS

In a discussion about the Holland model, Henry Stommel pointed out to me the effective vertical diffusion associated with horizontal mixing along level surfaces. I wish to thank him for a very helpful discussion about these numerical models. The National Science Foundation provided support through Grant 25723.

REVIEW: W. S. BROECKER

The following comments and questions come to mind while reading Veronis' paper:

1. The Rooth-Östlund thermocline model treats the tritium distribution as if it were at steady state. Based on Roether's observation that the ratio of bomb ^{14}C (half-life 5,700 years) to bomb H^3 (half-life 12 years) is nearly constant with depth in the thermocline. I seriously doubt that this is the case. The H^3 distribution is very likely still in a transient state. Therefore the time constant (17 years) used in the calculation is very likely an upper limit. This means that all values of K derived from the model must be lower limits. Indeed, is there any significance at all to dynamic parameters calculated from a transient distribution using a steady-state model?

2. How sacred is the uniform upwelling rate? Evidence from the opal distribution in marine sediments certainly is in direct contradiction to such a concept. The productivity of siliceous material (and hence the amount of SiO_2 reaching the sea surface) must be at least an order of magnitude greater along the perimeter of the Pacific Ocean basins (including the equator) than in the interior.

3. Although three-dimensional models must ultimately be used, I suspect that at present they are obscuring some of the real problems we face. (a) They fail to take into account the distinct layering within the deep sea. There seems to be little room for abyssal fronts. (b) Special assumptions are either specifically made or built into the model with regard to transport between the major ocean basins, i.e., the fraction of the deep-source water upwelling in each basin, the ratio of input from the two major deep water source regions, and transport across the equator (can the same coefficients of horizontal mixing be used there as elsewhere). (c) How much ^{14}C reaches the deep sea via the Antarctic Ocean surface? (d) Is there in any sense spacial uniformity in the consumption of O_2 or in the release of particulate ^{14}C in the deep sea?

The day of the box model is not over. Its advantage is that it focuses attention on these critical boundary problems. Until some limits are placed on these questions, I am very dubious about the significance of *tour de force* continuous circulation modeling to the real ocean.

In this connection I am disappointed that Veronis did not refer to the Broecker-Li mixing cross model (J. Geophys. Res. 75:3553-57, 1970). We attempted to delineate some of these basic questions.

REFERENCES

Arons, A. B., and H. Stommel. 1967. On the abyssal circulation of the world ocean. III. An advective lateral mixing model of the distribution of a tracer property in an ocean basin. Deep-Sea Res. 14:441-57.

Bolin, B., and H. Stommel. 1961. On the abyssal circulation of the world ocean. IV. Origin and rate of circulation of deep waters as determined with aid of tracers. Deep-Sea Res. 8:95-110.

Broecker, W. S., R. Gerard, M. Ewing, and B. C. Heezen. 1960. Natural radiocarbon in the Atlantic Ocean. J. Geophys. Res. 65:2903-31.

Bryan, K. 1969. A numerical method for the study of ocean circulation. J. Comp. Phys. 4:347-76.

Cochrane, J. D. 1958. The frequency distribution of water characteristics in the Pacific Ocean. Deep-Sea Res. 5:111-27.

Craig, H. 1969. Abyssal carbon and radiocarbon in the Pacific. J. Geophys. Res. 74:5491-5506.

Defant, A. 1936. Quantitative Untersuchungen zür Statik und Dynamik des Atlantischen Ozeans: Ausbreitungs–und Vermischungsvorgänge im antarktischen Bodenstrom und im subantarktischen Zwischenwasser. "Meteor" Exped. Wiss. Ergeb. Bd. VI, Teil II, 2 Lief.

Holland, W. 1971. Ocean tracer distributions–a preliminary numerical experiment. Tellus 23:371-92.

Keeling, C. D., and B. Bolin. 1968. The simultaneous use of chemical tracers in ocean studies. II. A three reservoir model of the North and South Pacific Oceans. Tellus 20:17-54.

Kuo, H., and G. Veronis. 1970. Distribution of tracers in the deep oceans of the world. Deep-Sea Res. 17:29-46.

Montgomery, R. B. 1958. Water characteristics of Atlantic Ocean and world ocean. Deep-Sea Res. 5:134-48.

Munk, W. H. 1966. Abyssal recipes. Deep-Sea Res. 13:707-30.

Pollak, M. J. 1958. Frequency distribution of potential temperatures and salinities in the Indian Ocean. Deep-Sea Res. 5:128-33.

Roether, Münnich, and Östlund. 1970. Tritium profile of the North Pacific (1969) Geosecs Interceliliration Station. J. Geophys. Res. 75:7672-75.

Rooth, C., and G. Östlund. 1972. Penetration of tritium into the Atlantic thermocline. Deep-Sea Res. (In press.)

Stommel, H. 1958. The abyssal circulation. Deep-Sea Res. 5:80-82.

Stommel, H., and Arons, A. B. 1960. On the abyssal circulation of the world ocean. II. An idealized model of the circulation pattern and amplitude in oceanic basins. Deep-Sea Res. 6:217-33.

Sverdrup, H. U., M. W. Johnson, and R. H. Fleming. 1942. The Oceans: Their Physics, Chemistry and General Biology. Prentice-Hall, New York. 1087 pp.

Veronis, G. 1969. On theoretical models of the thermohaline circulation. Deep-Sea Res. 16(suppl.):301-23.

Welander, P. 1959. An advective model of the thermohaline circulation. Tellus 11:309-18.

Welander, P. 1971a. Some exact solutions to the equations describing an ideal fluid thermocline. J. Mar. Res. 29:60-68.

Welander, P. 1971b. The thermocline problem. Philos. Trans. R. Soc. Lond. Ser. A. 270:69-73.

Wyrtki, K. 1961. The thermohaline circulation in relation to the general circulation in the oceans. Deep-Sea Res. 8:39-64.

Wyrtki, K. 1962. The oxygen minimum in relation to ocean circulation. Deep-Sea Res. 9:11-28.

A STUDY OF TOPOGRAPHIC EFFECTS

E. E. SCHULMAN

INTRODUCTION

Historically, the role of bottom relief has been considered to be of secondary importance in the dynamics of large-scale ocean circulations. In fact, if it is assumed that the total transport field is similar to the surface-current pattern, inclusion of bottom topography seems to degrade the results. Because homogeneous, wind-driven models seemed to conform so well with our preconceived notions of the general circulation, many studies have been made of such flows. In this paper, it will be shown that baroclinic and topographic features are at least as important as the direct effect of surface wind and that neglecting these cannot be justified on any reasonable physical basis.

It has been recognized, however, that bottom relief can be significant in certain regions of intense flow. There is a close correlation between the nonzonality of the Antarctic circumpolar current and bottom topography (Kamenkovich, 1962).

Warren (1963) was the first to show that variations of topography are significant in determining the course of the Gulf Stream. Robinson and Niiler (1967) developed a general theory of free inertial currents that was then applied to Gulf Stream meanders (Niiler and Robinson, 1967), the east Australian current (Godfrey and Robinson, 1971), and the Kuroshio current (Robinson and Taft, 1972). In all cases, topographic effects are particularly important in determining the path of western boundary currents, because they tend to follow constant isobaths. Furthermore, theoretical studies indicate that bottom relief is important for the existence, separation, and meandering of the Gulf Stream (Greenspan, 1963) and that it may cause the splitting of a stream into two branches near the Grand Banks of Newfoundland (Warren, 1969) and baroclinically destabilize the Gulf Stream (Orlanski, 1969). This paper is concerned primarily with large-scale open ocean effects and specialized studies will not be discussed.

HOMOGENEOUS SYSTEMS

Although the oceans are baroclinic, some insight into the role played by topography can be gained by considering a barotropic fluid. The equations for a homogeneous fluid over arbitrary relief are

$$\frac{D}{Dt}u - fv = \frac{-1}{\rho_o}P_x + \nu u_{zz} + A\nabla^2 u, \tag{1}$$

$$\frac{D}{Dt}v + fu = \frac{-1}{\rho_o}P_y + \nu v_{zz} + A\nabla^2 v, \tag{2}$$

$$u_x + v_y + w_z = 0, \tag{3}$$

$$-g = \frac{1}{\rho_o}P_z, \tag{4}$$

where $D/Dt = \partial/\partial t + u(\partial/\partial x) + v(\partial/\partial y)$. The boundary conditions are

$$\nu u_z = \frac{\tau^{(x)}}{\rho_o},$$

$$\nu v_z \frac{\tau^{(y)}}{\rho_o} \quad \text{at } z = \eta,$$

$$w = u\eta_x + v\eta_y + \eta_t, \tag{5}$$

$$\nu u_z = \frac{\tau_b{}^{(x)}}{\rho_o},$$

$$\nu v_z = \frac{\tau_b{}^{(y)}}{\rho_o} \quad \text{at } z = -H,$$

$$w = -(uH_x + vH_y). \tag{6}$$

In the above, η is the free surface elevation; H is the depth of the ocean; and $\tau_b{}^x$, $\tau_b{}^y$ are the bottom stress components. The momentum Eqs. (1) and (2) are integrated from $-H$ to η to yield

$$\frac{D}{Dt}u - fv = -g\eta_x + \frac{[\tau^{(x)} - \tau_b{}^{(x)}]}{\rho_o H + A_u \nabla^2 u}, \tag{7}$$

$$\frac{D}{Dt}v + fu = -g\eta_y + \frac{[\tau^{(y)} - \tau_b{}^{(y)}]}{\rho_o H + A_H \nabla^2 u}. \tag{8}$$

In the above, the velocities are assumed to be independent of z. Alternatively, formulas (7) and (8) may be considered the fundamental momentum equations with the surface and bottom stresses assuming the role of body forces. Cross-differentiation of them eliminates η:

$$\frac{D}{Dt}(\zeta + f) = -(\zeta + f)(u_x + v_y) + \text{curl}\,\frac{\tau}{\rho_o H} - \text{curl}\,\frac{\tau_b}{\rho_o H} + A_H \nabla^2 \zeta, \tag{9}$$

where $\zeta = u_x - v_y$ is the relative vorticity.

Integration of the continuity Eq. (3) with boundary conditions on w yields

$$u_x + v_y = \frac{-1}{H + \eta}\frac{D}{Dt}(H + \eta). \tag{10}$$

Substitution into Eq. (9) provides the vorticity equation

$$(H + \eta)\frac{D}{Dt}\left(\frac{\zeta + f}{H + \eta}\right) = \text{curl}\,\frac{\tau}{\rho_o H} - \text{curl}\,\frac{\tau_b}{\rho_o H} + A_H \nabla^2 \zeta. \tag{11}$$

In the absence of wind and friction, this reduces to

$$\frac{D}{Dt}\left(\frac{\zeta + f}{H + \eta}\right) = 0. \tag{12}$$

The quantity $(\zeta + f)/(H + \eta)$ is referred to as the potential vorticity. Under the assumed conditions (ignoring wind stress, friction, and baroclinicity), potential vorticity is conserved along streamlines.

For linear motion, the contribution due to ζ is eliminated and this simple expression further reduces (with $\eta \ll H$) to

$$\frac{D}{Dt}\left(\frac{f}{H}\right) = 0. \tag{13}$$

There is a tendency for the fluid to follow contours of f/H. Over a flat bottom and in equatorial regions, these isolines are zonal; at high latitudes, they are nearly parallel to the isobaths. Thus, flow approaching a shallowing bottom is deflected toward the equator; a deepening bottom causes poleward flow. Welander (1968) discusses the features of slow circulation in one- and two-layer models and demonstrates the importance of f/H contours in controlling the flow. Kamenkovich (1962) related the trajectory of the Antarctic circumpolar current to these contours.

For steady flow, a stream function can be defined by

$$u(h + \eta) = -\psi_y, \qquad v(h + \eta) = \psi_x, \tag{14}$$

and, in terms of ψ, the conservation of potential vorticity, Eq. (12) becomes

$$\frac{D}{Dt}\left[\frac{\nabla(1/H\nabla\psi) + f}{H}\right] = 0. \tag{15}$$

Porter and Rattray (1964) obtained solutions to this equation for various zonally varying bathymetric features with initially zonal flow. For flow to the east, infinite deflection, or stationary, undamped Rossby waves may occur downstream, i.e., local topographic features can disturb the flow at long distances away. Clarke and Fofonoff (1969) generalized these results for initial zonal flow entering a region where depth variations occur in a direction inclined to latitude circles. Large meanders are predicted whose amplitude increases downstream, even in regions of constant depth. In both models, bathymetric features have a rather large effect on a uniform current. Although direct application to the real oceans is questionable because baroclinicity is suppressed, they do provide plausible explanation for Gulf Stream meanders and the possible distortion of streamlines near mid-ocean ridges.

Two forms of bottom friction have been commonly used:

$$\tau_b{}^{(x)} = RH_u, \qquad \tau_b{}^{(y)} = RH_v, \tag{16}$$

i.e., the bottom stress is proportional to the transport; and

$$\tau_b{}^{(x)} = ru, \qquad \tau_b{}^{(y)} = rv, \tag{17}$$

i.e., the bottom stress is proportional to the velocity. On physical grounds (Ekman theory), the latter formulation is better. In the above, R and r are the coefficients of bottom friction.

In terms of the stream function, Eq. (11) has the form

$$\frac{\partial}{\partial t}\zeta - \psi_y \frac{\partial}{\partial x}\left(\frac{g+f}{H}\right) + \psi_x \frac{\partial}{\partial y}\left(\frac{g+f}{H}\right) = \text{curl}\,\frac{\tau}{\rho_o H} + A_H \nabla^2 \zeta - R\zeta - r\nabla\left(\frac{\psi}{H^2}\right), \quad (18)$$

where $\zeta = \nabla(\nabla\psi/H)$. This may be expressed in the more convenient form

$$-A_H \nabla^2 \zeta + R\zeta + r\nabla\left(\frac{\nabla\psi}{H^2}\right) + \frac{1}{H} J(\psi_1 \zeta) + \beta\psi_x - \frac{(f+g)}{H} J(\psi_1 H) + \frac{\partial}{\partial t} = \text{curl}\,\frac{\tau}{\rho_o H}. \quad (19)$$

The individual contributions can be identified as follows: The first term is the dissipation of vorticity due to lateral friction; the second and third terms are alternate forms of bottom friction; the fourth is the nonlinear advection of vorticity; the fifth is the planetary vorticity tendency; and the sixth is the topographic vorticity tendency. The right-hand side is the wind stress curl modified by topography. For most investigations, only one of the quantities A_H, R, and r is nonzero; under no circumstances are both r and R nonzero.

If H is assumed level and bottom friction is discarded, Eq. (19) then becomes

$$-A_H \nabla^\psi \psi + \frac{1}{H} J(\psi_1 \nabla^2 \psi) + \beta\psi_x + \frac{\partial}{\partial t}\nabla^2 \psi = \frac{1}{H}\,\text{curl}\,\frac{\tau}{\rho_o}. \quad (20)$$

This is the nonlinear equation considered by Carrier and Robinson (1962) in the study of wind-driven ocean circulations. It may also be derived for a baroclinic system provided $\nabla H = 0$.

A linearized version of this with only transport-type bottom friction is

$$R\nabla^2\psi + \left(\beta - \frac{R}{H}H_x - \frac{f}{H}H_y\right)\psi_x + \left(\frac{f}{H}H_x - \frac{R}{H}H_y\right)\psi_y = \frac{\partial}{\partial x}\left(\frac{\tau^{b1}}{\rho_o}\right) - \frac{\partial}{\partial x}\left(\frac{\tau^x}{\rho_o}\right) - \frac{\tau^{b1}}{\rho_o}\left(\frac{H_x}{H}\right) + \frac{\tau^x}{\rho_o}\left(\frac{H_y}{H}\right). \quad (21)$$

The right-hand side of this equation contains, in addition to the curl of the tangential wind stress, terms that depend on slopes. All other things being equal, the same wind stress should generate different current systems in basins with level and inclined bottoms. In particular, a uniform wind results in zero integral flow over an ocean of constant depth—this is not true for a basin of variable depth.

Looking at the coefficient of ψ_x, it can be seen that bottom slopes can either intensify or diminish the β-effect. Because $R \ll f$, meridional depth gradients are more important. If the basin depth increases to the north, this reduces the β-effect and may even cause current intensification along the eastern shore instead of near the western coast.

The principal term in the coefficient of ψ_y is due to zonal bottom slopes, which cause meridional displacement of the circulation. If the basin depth increases to the east, southern intensification of currents can be expected. Depth increasing to the west may cause northern boundary intensification.

If the wind is zonal of the form $\tau^x = -A \cos \pi y/L$ and the bottom varies only in the meridional direction, the right-hand side can be written in the form (Fomin, 1969)

$$\frac{-A}{\rho_o}\left[\frac{\pi^2}{L^2} + \left(\frac{H_y}{H}\right)^2\right]^{1/2} \sin\frac{\pi}{L}(y+\gamma), \quad (22)$$

where $\gamma = L/\pi \tan^{-1} [(L/\pi)(H_y/H)]$, which is equivalent to having a tangential wind stress

$$T^x = -A\left[1 + \frac{L^2}{\pi^2}\left(\frac{H_y}{H}\right)^2\right]^{1/2} \cos\frac{\pi}{L}(y+\gamma). \quad (23)$$

It is noted that $T^{(x)}$ is very different from $\tau^{(x)}$. For example, when $\gamma = 0.5\,L$, two gyres are expected instead of one. The last two terms on the right-hand side of Eq. (21) are of the form $1/\rho_o H(\tau^x \nabla H)$. If the direction of the wind is parallel to depth variations, the contribution of bottom slope on the right-hand side vanishes. Thus, the wind-generated current systems depend on the angle between the wind direction and the dominant bottom slope.

In conclusion, bottom relief modifies the circulation as much as the wind stress. Bottom relief also produces a tendency for displacement of circulation centers such that intensification of currents is expected near boundaries, not necessarily the western one.

Schulman and Niiler (1970) considered the effect of zonally varying topography on linear, wind-driven homogeneous circulation. With bottom friction proportional to the velocity, the determining equation is

$$\frac{\partial}{\partial x}\left(\frac{r}{H^2}\psi_x\right) + \frac{\partial}{\partial y}\left(\frac{r}{H^2}\psi_y\right) + \psi_x\frac{\partial}{\partial y}\left(\frac{f}{H}\right) - \psi_y\frac{\partial}{\partial x}\left(\frac{f}{H}\right) = \text{curl}\,\frac{\tau}{\rho_o H}. \quad (24)$$

Note that bottom friction and wind stress are ignored; ψ is a factor solely of f/H. A previous result is that flow will follow contours of f/H. In the absence of friction, analytic solutions can be obtained to Eq. (24) where the zonal wind stress is

$$\frac{1}{\rho_0}\tau^x(y) = \frac{-1}{\pi}\cos\pi y \,. \tag{25}$$

Writing $\psi = Im\,[\phi(x)e^{i\pi y}]$, the explicit dependence on y disappears and in nondimensional form, producing

$$H\frac{d\phi}{dx} + \frac{i\pi}{\beta^*}\frac{dH}{dx}\phi = -H \tag{26}$$

where $\beta^* = \beta L/f_0$. The solution to Eq. (26) satisfying $\phi(1) = 0$ is

$$\Phi = H^{-i\pi/\beta^*}\int_x^1 H^{i\pi/\beta^*}\,dx, \tag{27}$$

which should be regarded as a topographic extension to the Sverdrup relationship.

The boundary condition is taken on the eastern side of the boundary, because the inviscid solution is valid only outside the western boundary layer (the only one present in the chosen topography). Friction must be included to satisfy the boundary condition at the western wall. In the above derivation of Eq. (26), set $f - 1$ and all terms that resulted from previous differentiation have been retained. This commonly-used artifice results in the important topographic variable being $f = lnH$ and not f/H. Qualitatively, the two are similar and major discrepancies should arise only for large y.

The stream function can be obtained by quadrature of Eq. (27) for arbitrary oceanic relief. Figure 1 illustrates the results for a variety of different topographies. It is no understatement that topography completely alters the homogeneous flow distribution.

When friction is included, Eq. (24) assumes the form

$$r'\phi_{xx} + \left(H - 2r'\frac{H_x}{H}\right)\phi_x + \frac{i\pi}{\beta^*}H_x\phi = -H, \tag{28}$$

where $r' = r/_{\beta}H_0L \ll 1$. This is solved numerically utilizing $\phi(0) = 0$ for the case $r' = 10^{-3}$ in Figure 2. The effect of friction is confined mainly to the western edge where the circulation has been diminished.

One rather interesting point bears mention. In the special case where the length-scale of topographic variations on the continental shelf is much smaller than the width of the frictional layer, the solution in the westernmost (topographic) layer is

$$\psi = \frac{\sin\pi y}{r'}\int_0^x H^2\,dx\,. \tag{29}$$

Then the integrated transport $V = H^2/r'\sin\pi y$ and the depth-averaged velocity is

$$v = \frac{H}{r'}\sin\pi y\,. \tag{30}$$

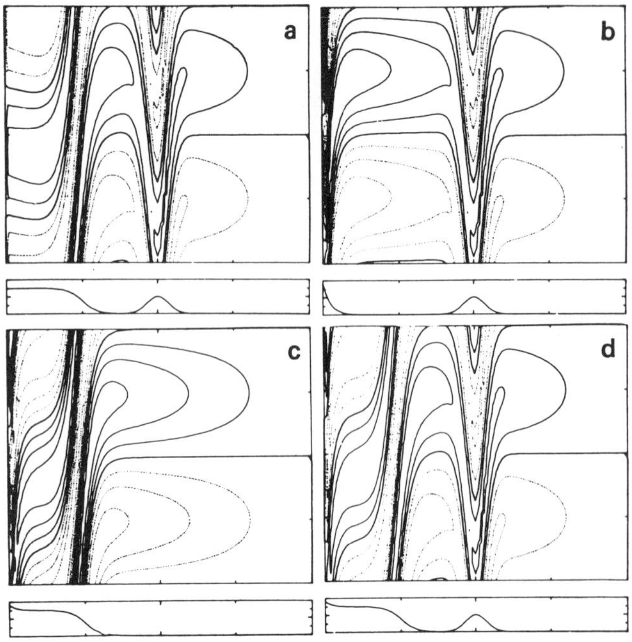

FIGURE 1 Frictionless flow over composite topography. (a) Plateau and ridge; (b) continental rise and ridge; (c) continental rise and plateau; and (d) continental rise, plateau, and ridge (from Schulman and Niiler, 1970).

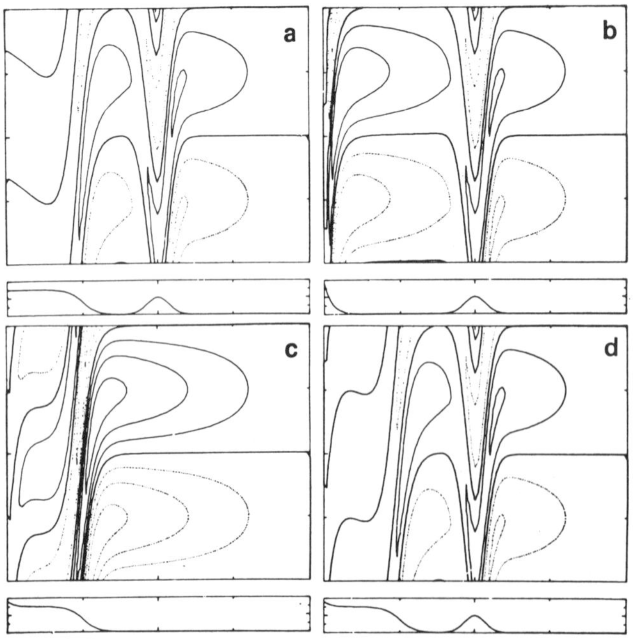

FIGURE 2 Frictional flow over composite topography with $r' = 10^{-3}$. Same topographic parameters as in Figure 1 (from Schulman and Niiler, 1970).

Eq. (30) has rather striking geophysical importance. Although, in principle, the solutions allow free slip above the boundaries, there can be no tangential velocity along the wall for steep topographies if $H(0) = 0$, as if a no-slip boundary condition had been imposed *a priori.* Furthermore, the mass transport and velocity increase away from the wall until the abyssal plain is reached, where friction will act. The maximum velocity is thus predicted to appear near the base of the continental rise, which is confirmed by Gulf Stream observations in the Florida Straits (Richardson *et al.*, 1969).

A somewhat similar numerical experiment was performed by Kochergin and Klimok (1971). Using velocity-type bottom friction, an equation equivalent to Eq. (24) was solved in a closed ocean basin with rather complicated two-dimensional relief. Figure 3 contrasts the flat bottom case (Stommel, 1948) with one in which the depth increases to the north. Topography completely overwhelms the β-effect, and an eastern coastal current, as predicted earlier, appears instead of a western one. The authors find that the direction of the circulation in various experiments depends on the sign of $\partial/\partial y\,[\tau^{(x)}/H]$ and the sign of $\partial/\partial y(f/H)$ determines which shore the flow is pressed against. These results follow from the discussion of Eq. (21). In Figures 4 and 5, flow in the North Atlantic is contrasted for flat bottom and real topography. The Gulf Stream is weakened, and the mid-Atlantic ridge apparently divides the circulation in two with a strong cyclonic eddy in the lower right-hand corner.

Holland (1967) solved Eq. (19), including the nonlinear terms but with no bottom friction, for some simple topographies. Numerical solutions are compared for level bottom and the topography indicated in Figure 6. In Figures 7 and 8, the nondimensional friction boundary layer width is $W_F = (A_H/\beta L^3)^{1/3} = 0.025$ and the inertial boundary layer width, $W_I = (\tau_0\pi/\rho_0\beta^2 HL^2)^{1/2}$, is varied for all cases.

For all cases with this topographic regime, the boundary

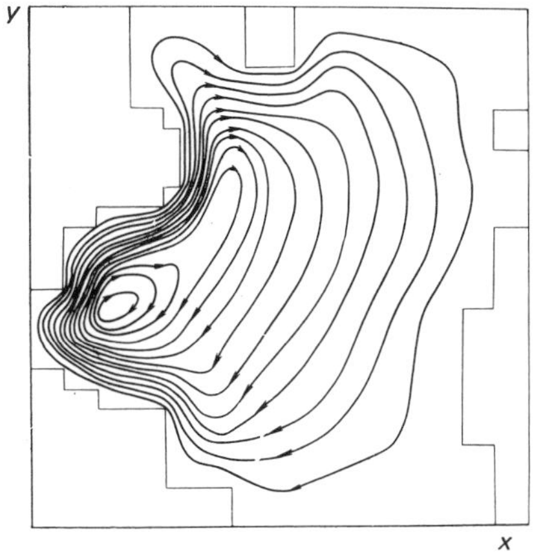

FIGURE 4 Homogeneous circulation over flat bottom for the North Atlantic area (from Kochergin and Klimok, 1971).

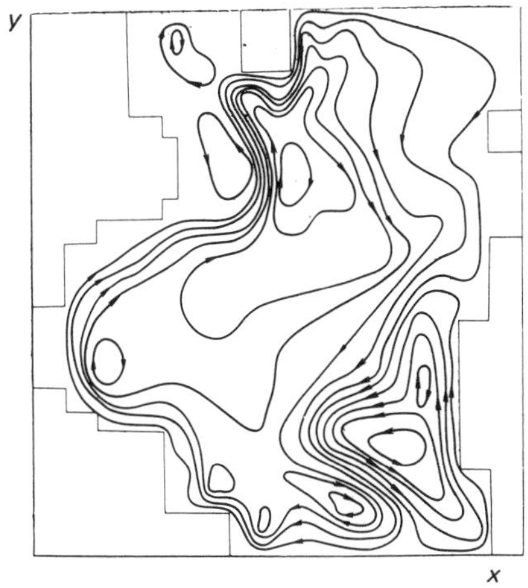

FIGURE 5 Homogeneous circulation over real bottom relief for the North Atlantic area (from Kochergin and Klimok, 1971).

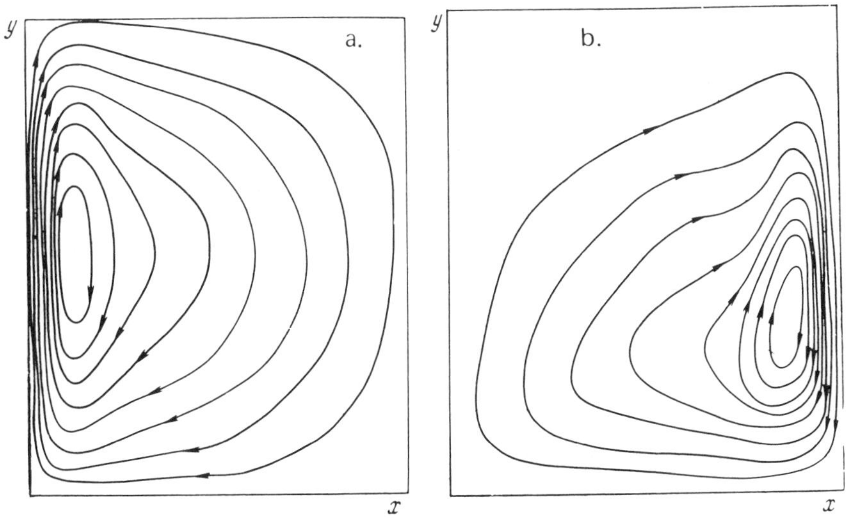

FIGURE 3 Transport stream function for homogeneous circulation for (a) H = const and (b) H proportional to exp(1. 3y) (from Kochergin and Klimok, 1971).

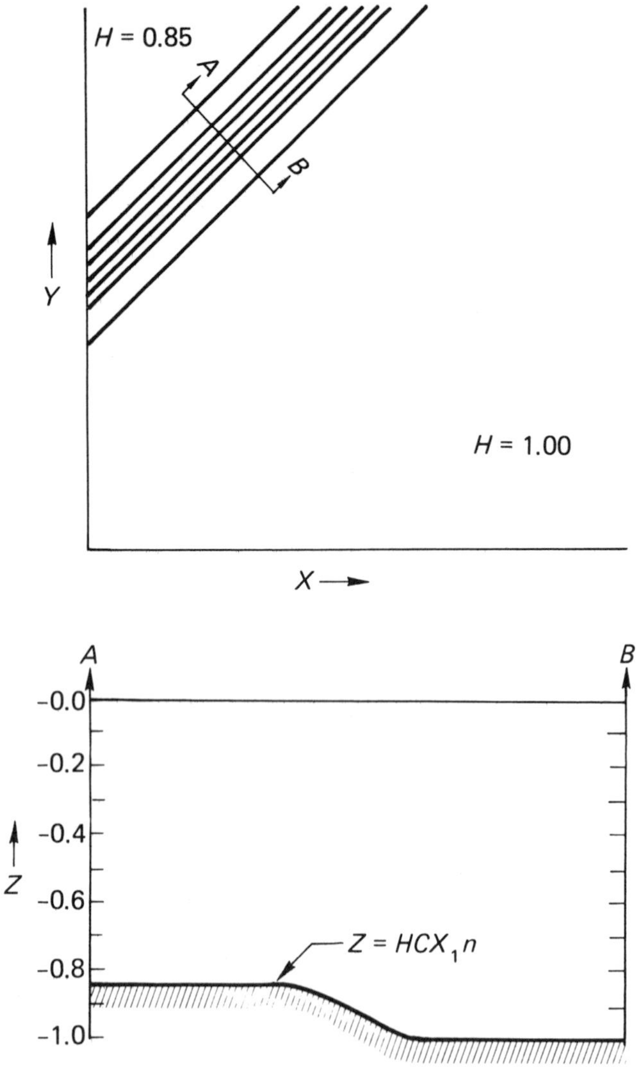

FIGURE 6 The topographic regime considered by Holland (1967). $H = 0.925 + 0.075 \tanh [10(x - y - 0.5)]$.

current leaves the coast, but never when the bottom is level. Thus, topographic factors play a dominant role in western boundary current separation in both the frictional and inertial extremes. In the highly frictional cases, the intense stream upon separation follows lines of constant f/H. For the more inertial cases, meandering about f/H contours is apparent. This meandering is related to the oscillatory nature of inertial flow in the northern halves of the basins.

Schulman (1970) developed a numerical model of homogeneous flow in the southern ocean to study the effects of different kinds of bottom relief and nonlinearity on the Antarctic circumpolar current. The spherical geometry forms of Eqs. (7-10), with $A_H = R = 0$ were integrated until a steady state was reached. Several regions are encountered in the solution to the system where gradients are large, *viz.*, the western boundary layer off South America, the area in the vicinity of the narrow Drake Passage, and places near rapidly varying topography. These regions are difficult to resolve and would require considerable increase in computational time, even for fine uniform grids. Instead, a transformation of coordinates is made of the form

$$\xi = c\left[\alpha x + \sum_{L=1}^{N} \tanh\left(\frac{x - x_i}{S_i}\right) + b\right], \qquad (31)$$

where x is the physical variable, and ξ is the "stretched" variable. The quantities b and c are chosen such that x and ξ have the same range. Greater resolution is obtained at the points x_i; S_i determines the amount of added resolution at these points; and α affects the ratio between the number of grid points in the interior and boundary layer regions.

Figure 9 illustrates the flow for level relief (5 km) for the case $\delta = r/2\Omega H_0 = 0.1$, where $H_0 = 1$ km. Some of the major features of the observed calculations are reproduced: The constriction of the Antarctic circumpolar current through the Drake Passage (South America and the Antarctic Peninsula are idealized as straight meridional line segments), the northward deflection of the stream into the Falkland current, and an indication of the southward-flowing Brazil current.

In the following Figures 10–14, various types of localized topography are included: shallowing regions on both sides of the Antarctic Peninsula (10), the inverse C-shaped Scotia Ridge lying east of the Drake Passage (11), shallowing of the Drake Passage (12), the rather broad continental shelf east of South America (13), and a composite of all the above (14).

Again, the strong tendency of the fluid to follow isolines of f/H from its deflection away from the Antarctic Peninsula (Figure 10), the tendency to flow around the Scotia Ridge (Figure 11), and its eastward displacement from South America (Figure 13) are seen. In these cases, the transport through the Drake Passage is diminished by 10–30 percent, and there is a tendency for increased transport in the Brazil current.

The most striking effect is that resulting from the variable relief in the Drake Passage (Figure 12). The transport has been reduced by 80 percent. From the level bottom case, gyres have been formed southwest and northeast of the passage, and the Brazil current and northern gyre have significantly increased in transport and southward penetration.

BAROCLINIC SYSTEMS

To demonstrate the modification due to baroclinicity in the oceans in its simplest form, the equations for linear, steady

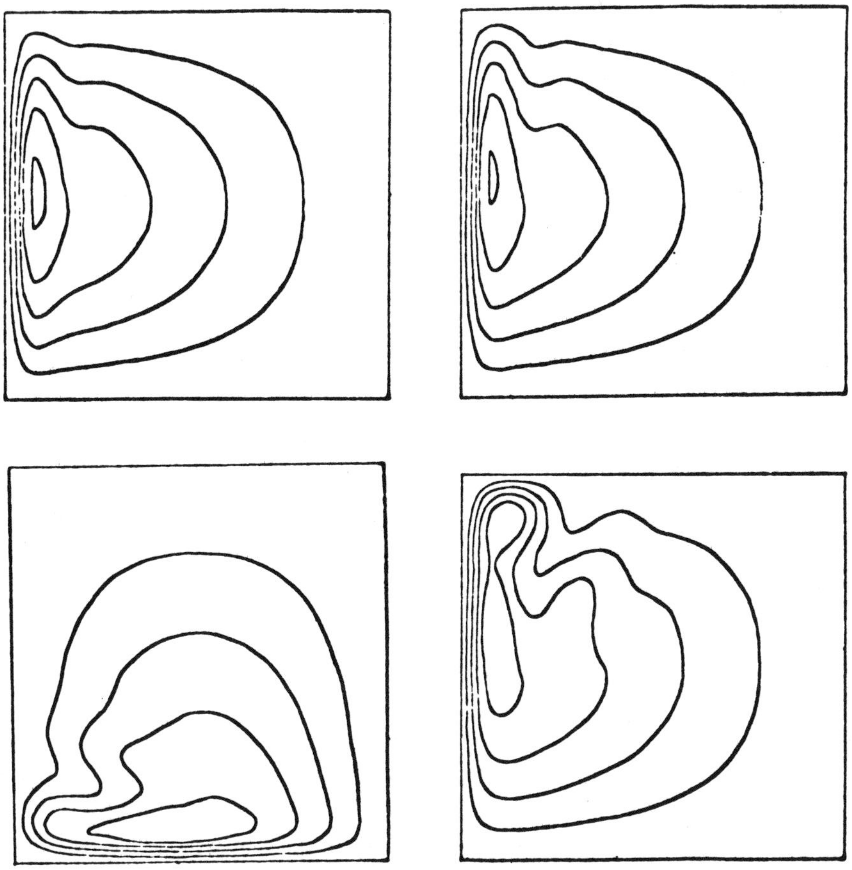

FIGURE 7 Transport streamlines for homogeneous, nonlinear circulation over level bottom. $W_F = (A_H/\beta L^3)^{1/3} = 0.25$. Upper left, $W_I = (\tau_0\pi/\rho_0 HL^2)^{1/2} = 0.010$; upper right, $W_I = 0.015$; lower left, $W_I = 0.020$; lower right, $W_I = 0.025$ (from Holland, 1967).

flow without lateral exchange of momentum will be considered. Eqs. (1) and (2) reduce to

$$-fv + \frac{1}{\rho_0} P_x = \nu u_{zz}, \tag{32}$$

$$fu + \frac{1}{\rho_0} P_y = \nu v_{zz}. \tag{33}$$

Eqs. (32) and (33) are integrated from $z = -H$ to $z = \eta$, and the bottom stress is proportional to the transport. (This is physically questionable, but it is expected that the details of bottom friction are unimportant for mid-ocean flow.) This integration yields.

$$-fV + \frac{1}{\rho_0}\int_{-H}^{\eta} P_x\, dz = \tau^{(x)} - RU, \tag{34}$$

$$fU + \frac{1}{\rho_0}\int_{-H}^{\eta} P_y\, dz = \tau^{(y)} - RV, \tag{35}$$

where

$$U = \int_{-H}^{\eta} u\, dz = -\psi_y, \tag{36}$$

$$V = \int_{-H}^{\eta} v\, dz = \psi_x. \tag{37}$$

Eqs. (34) and (35) are cross-differentiated and Eqs. (36) and (37) are substituted. The vorticity equation assumes the form

$$R\nabla^2\psi + \beta\psi_x + \frac{1}{\rho_0}\left[H_x\frac{\partial\rho}{\partial y}(-H) - H_y\frac{\partial\rho}{\partial x}(-H)\right] = \operatorname{curl}\frac{\tau}{\rho_0} \tag{38}$$

and the problem reduces to finding the horizontal pressure gradients at the ocean bottom. According to Fomin (1969), the density distribution can be written in the form

$$\rho(x,y,z) = S - q(x,y)\delta(z), \qquad S = \text{const.} \tag{39}$$

An analytic form for $\delta(z)$ must be assumed that is valid for all z including $z < -H$. This can be accomplished by choosing an expression provided by theory or values of density extrapolated to beneath the ocean bottom.

Integration of the hydrostatic Eq. (4) yields the pressure distribution

$$p(x,y,z) = gS(\eta - z) - gq(x,y)\int_z^{\eta}\delta(z)\, dz, \tag{40}$$

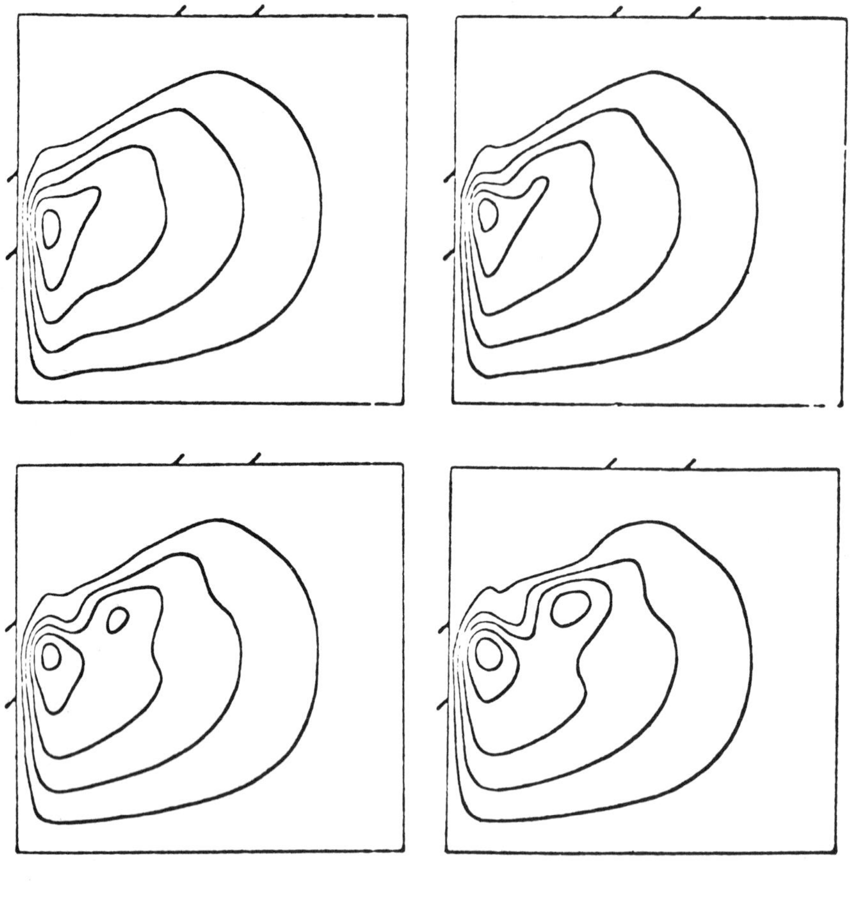

FIGURE 8 Transport streamlines for homogeneous, nonlinear circulation over topography shown in Figure 8. $W_F = 0.025$. Upper left, $W_I = 0.05$; upper right, $W_I = 0.10$; lower left, $W_I = 0.15$; lower right, $W_I = 0.20$.

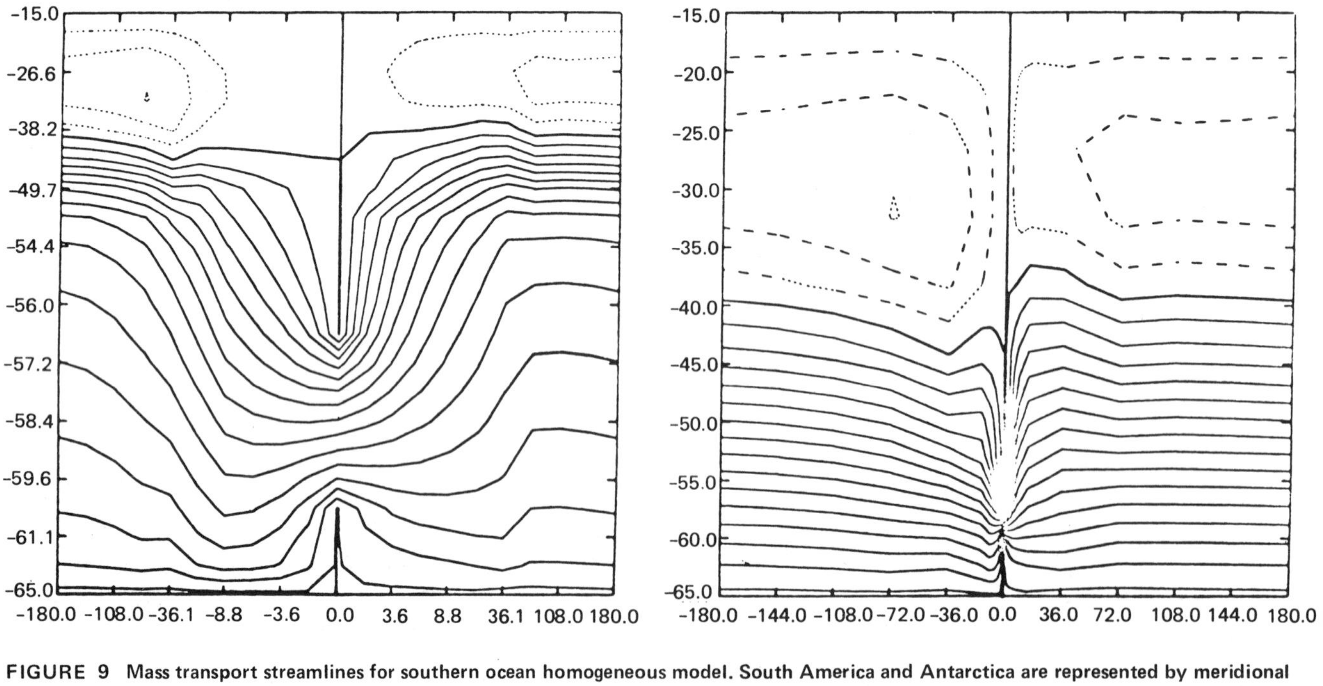

FIGURE 9 Mass transport streamlines for southern ocean homogeneous model. South America and Antarctica are represented by meridional line segments. On the left is the flow computed in stretched coordinates. On the right, the streamlines are transformed to physical space. Flat topography, $H = 5$ km. $r' = r/fH_0 = 0.2$, where $H_0 = 1$ km. Transport = 70 Sverdrups (from Schulman, 1970).

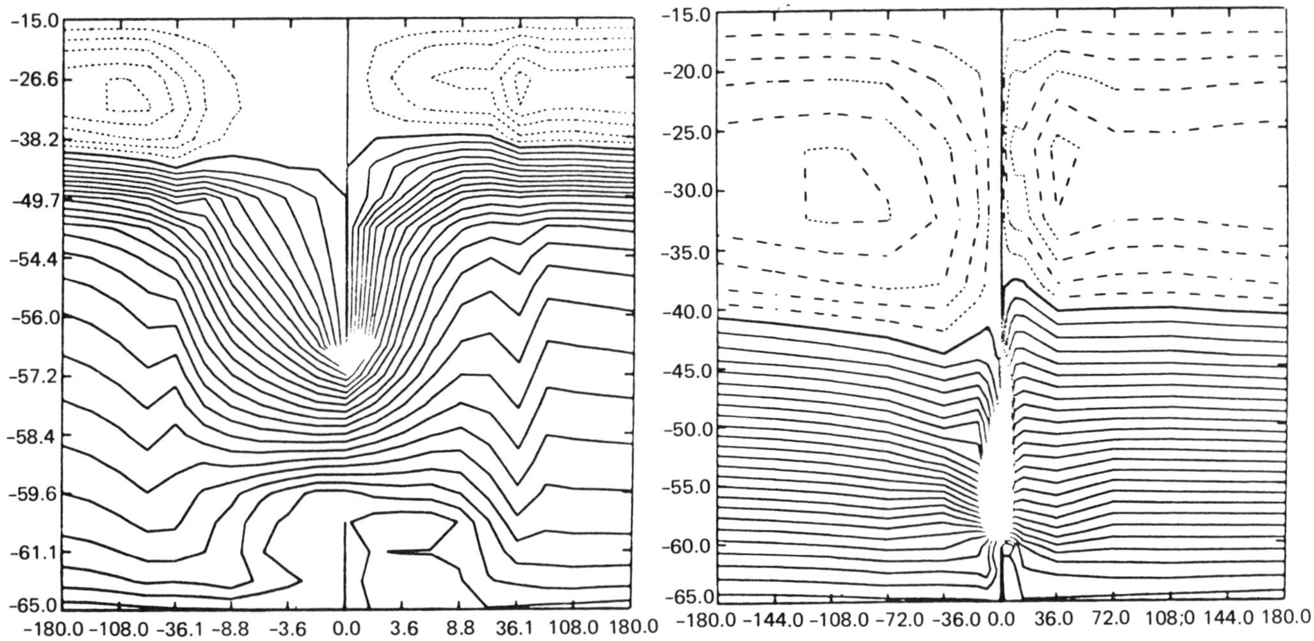

FIGURE 10 Streamlines for Antarctic Peninsula topography, $r' = 0.1$. $H = 1 + 4/12° \; |\lambda|$, $|\lambda| \leqslant 12°$, $\theta° \leqslant -61°$; $H = 5$ elsewhere. Transport = 115 Sverdrups.

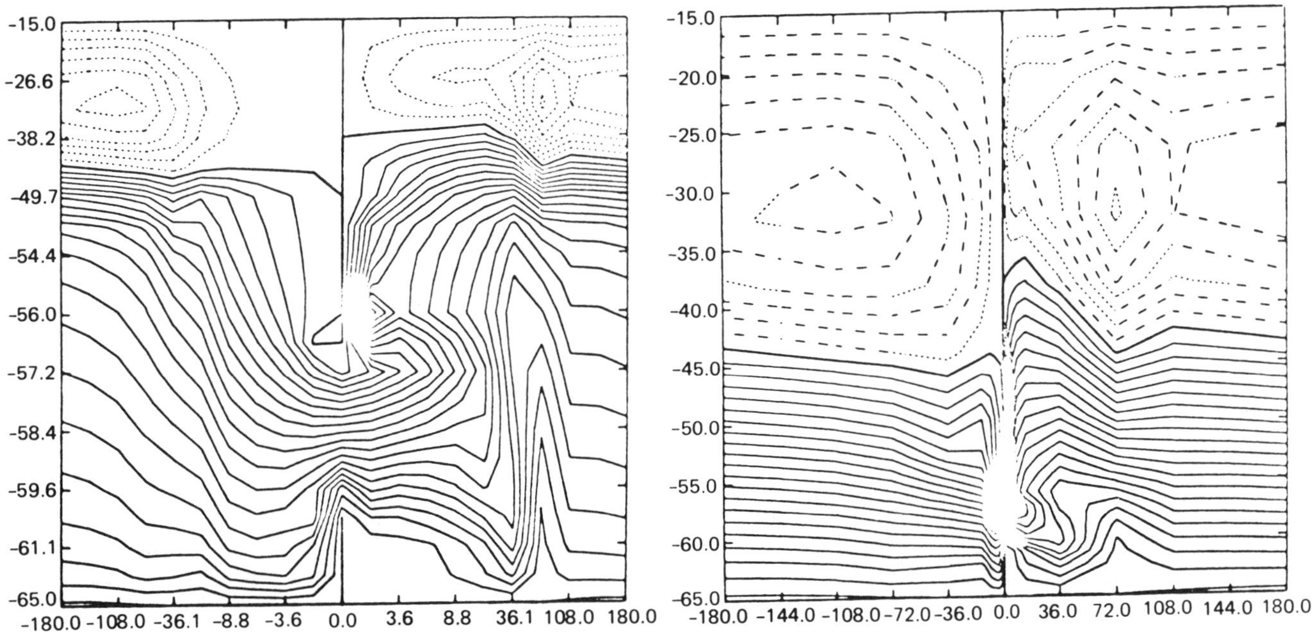

FIGURE 11 Streamlines for Scotia Ridge topography, $r' = 0.1$. $H = 3$ for $\lambda \geqslant 35°$, $\theta = -56.6°$, $-61°$; $H = 1$ at $\lambda = 35°$, $-61.0° \leqslant \theta \leqslant -56.6°$; $H = 5$ elsewhere. Transport = 90 Sverdrups.

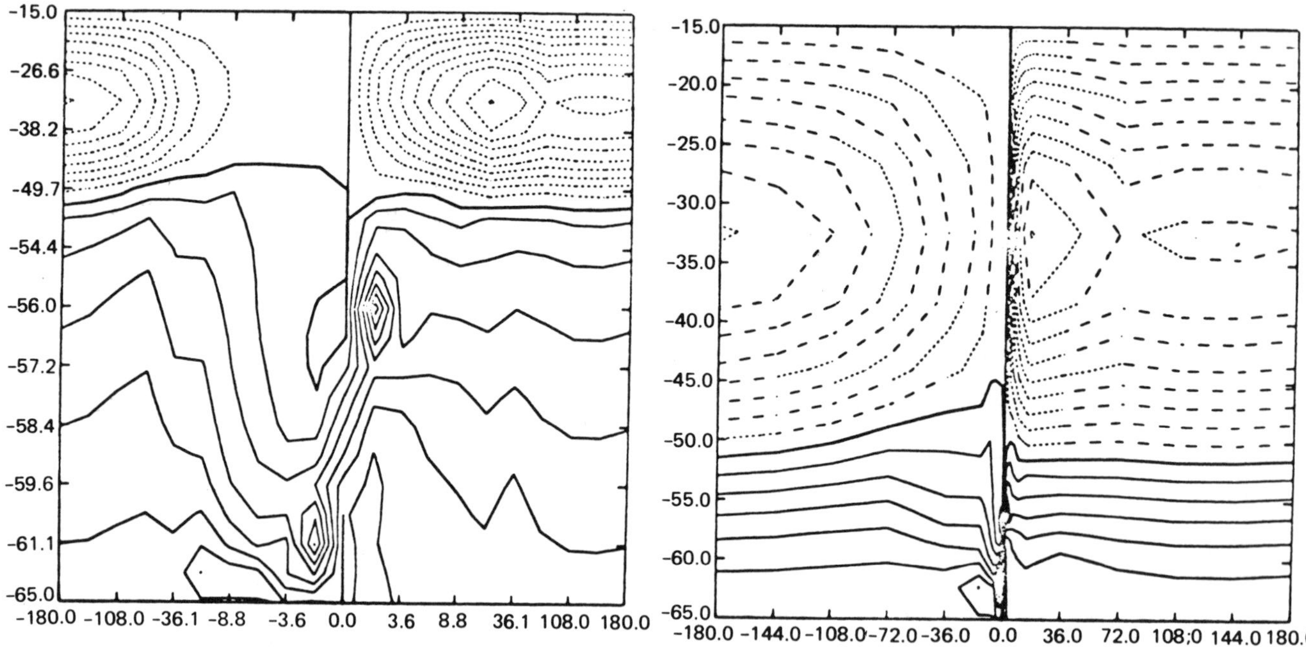

FIGURE 12 Streamlines for Drake Passage topography, $r' = 0.1$. $H = 2 + 3/5^\circ |\lambda|$, $|\lambda| \leqslant 5^\circ$, $-61.0^\circ \leqslant \theta \leqslant -56.5^\circ$; $H = 5$ elsewhere. Transport = 25 Sverdrups.

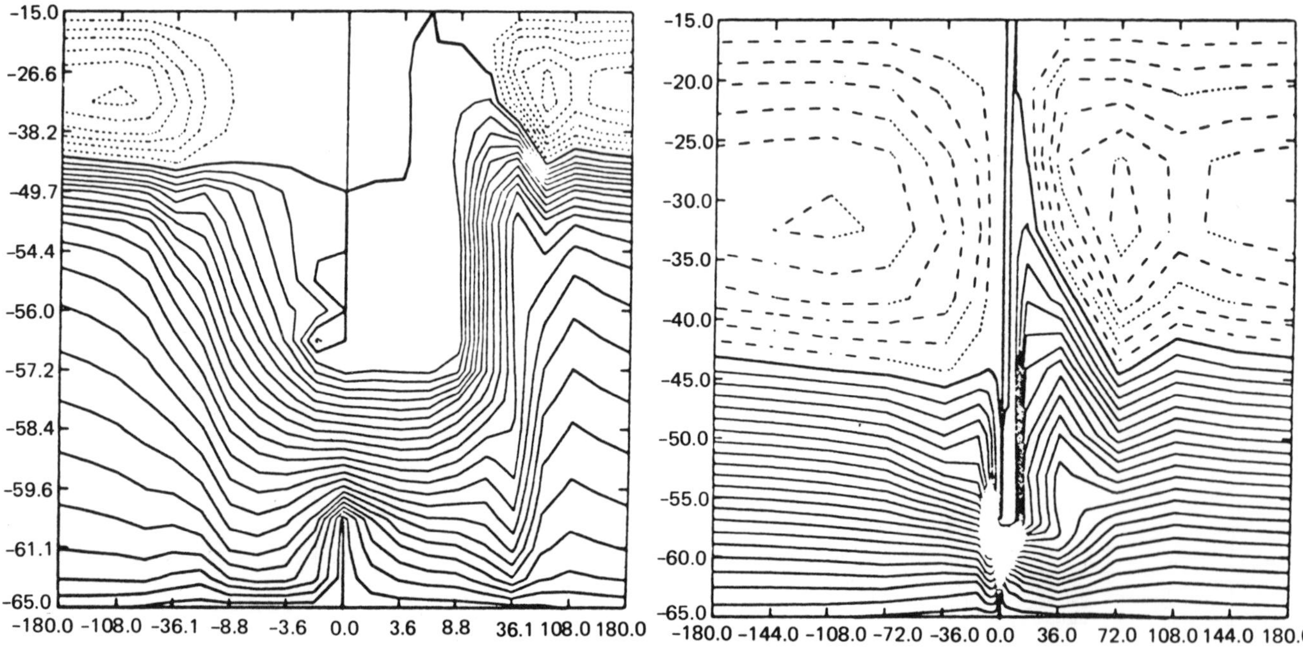

FIGURE 13 Streamlines for continental shelf topography, $r' = 0.1$. $H = 0.1$, $\lambda \leqslant 5^\circ$, $\theta \geqslant -56.5^\circ$; $H = 4.9/7^\circ\ (\lambda - 5^\circ)$, $5^\circ \leqslant \lambda \leqslant 12^\circ$. $\theta \geqslant -56.5^\circ$; $H = 5$ elsewhere. Transport = 105 Sverdrups.

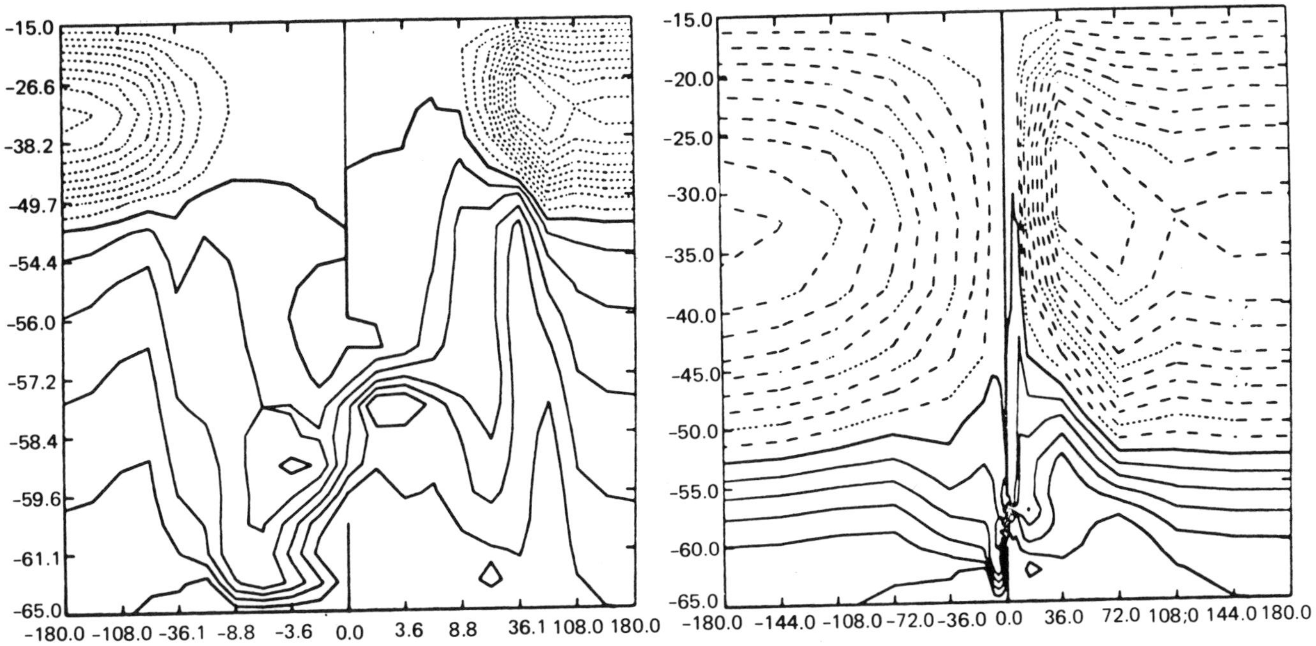

FIGURE 14 Streamlines for composite topography, $r' = 0.1$. H = minimum of depths computed in Figures 10-13. Transport = 20 Sverdrups.

and taking the horizontal gradient of Eq. (40), we obtain

$$\nabla p = g[S - q\delta(\eta)]\nabla\eta - g\nabla q \int_z^\eta \delta(z)\,dz. \qquad (41)$$

It is further assumed that at some surface $z = -D(x,y)$, the horizontal pressure gradient vanishes. No constraints on the form of D are assumed, and included is the possibility that D may be greater than H, in which case stratification reduces but does not cancel the deep-pressure gradient. The assumption of such a surface depends only on the gradient of the current velocity decreasing with depth, which is confirmed by oceanic calculations. This yields

$$g\nabla q = \frac{q}{\rho_o}[S - q\delta(\eta)]\nabla\eta / \int_{-D}^\eta \delta(z)\,dz. \qquad (42)$$

Substitution of the pressure gradient from Eq. (41) into Eqs. (32) and (33) and integration over the depth yields

$$\frac{g}{\rho_o}(H+\eta)[S - q\delta(\eta)]\,\eta_x - gq_x \int_{-H}^\eta \int_z^\eta \delta(z)\,dz^2 = \tau^x + f\psi_x + R\psi_y, \qquad (43)$$

$$\frac{g}{\rho_o}(H+\eta)[S - q\delta(\eta)]\,\eta_y - gq_y \int_{-H} \int_z \delta(z)\,dz^2 = \tau^y + f\psi_y - r\psi_x. \qquad (44)$$

Eliminate q_x, q_y with formula (42) and an expression for η_x, η_y in terms of τ and ψ is obtained. This allows the solution for the pressure gradient of the ocean bottom, which, when substituted into Eq. (38) results in the equation

$$R\nabla^2\psi + \left(\beta - \frac{R}{M}H_x - \frac{f}{M}H_y\right)\psi_x + \left(\frac{f}{M}H_x - \frac{R}{M}H_y\right)\psi_y = \frac{\partial}{\partial x}\left[\frac{\tau^{(y)}}{\rho_o}\right] - \frac{\partial}{\partial y}\left[\frac{\tau^{(x)}}{\rho_o}\right] - \frac{\tau^{(y)}}{\rho_o M}H_x + \frac{\tau^{(x)}}{\rho_o M}H_y, \qquad (45)$$

where

$$M = H + \left[H\int_{-H}^0 \delta(z)\,dz - \int_{-H}^0 \int_z^0 \delta(z)\,dz^2\right] \Big/ \int_{-D}^{-H} \delta(z)\,dz. \qquad (46)$$

Eq. (45) has an identical form to Eq. (21), which controlled the transport of wind-driven circulation in a homogeneous ocean. They differ only in the replacement of H in certain terms by the function M. Because of the similarity of the equations, previous conclusions regarding the effect of bottom topography are still valid.

In the special case $D = H$, M is infinite and all topographic effects are eliminated, leaving Stommel's equation. The term in brackets in Eq. (46), expressing the difference of two integrals, is always positive. Thus if $D < H$, i.e., the zero, pressure gradient surface lies within the ocean, the pressure gradient has reversed direction at the bottom and $M < H$, in which case topographic effects are magnified. The possibility exists that $M < 0$, in which case baroclinicity reverses the topographically influenced currents, or that M is nearly zero, in which case a very different balance of forces ensues where β does not contribute.

If $D > H$, then $M > H$, and this latter inequality intensifies as the stratification increases. For this case, the influence of bottom irregularities upon a circulation should be weaker than bottom influence in a uniform area. However, the last integral in Eq. (46) is unusual because it involves integrating the density of the ocean below the sea floor. Perhaps the proper interpretation is a symbolic one: The quantity $D - H$ should express the baroclinicity of the circulation. If $D \to \infty$ and $\int_{-D}^{-H} \delta(z)\, dz \to \infty$, then $M \to H$, and the homogeneous result is established. As $D \to H$, topography becomes less important on the sea floor. If $D > H$, the effect of stratification is to weaken the topographic influence, but the latter is nevertheless comparable to the β-effect.

Eqs. (45) and (46) show that the density distribution at lower levels may have a significant effect on the transport. Density data below $h - 1{,}000$-$2{,}000$ m are scarce. To test the importance of deep-density anomalies, Kozlov (1969) tried three different distributions below h in calculations of the Pacific Ocean with variable topography: [a] $\nabla\rho(z) = 0$, [b] $\nabla\rho(z) = \nabla\rho(h)$, and [c] $\nabla\rho(z) = \nabla\rho(h)\cdot(H - z)/(H - h)$.

The vertical variations of horizontal velocities were calculated and compared for the three cases. Cases [b] and [c] are similar, with an average difference of only 0.1 cm/s. However, case [a] is qualitatively and quantitatively different. From this study, it is concluded that models incorporating variable topography with a uniform lower layer are highly suspect.

The calculations were repeated without wind stress and the average velocity changed by only 0.3 cm/s. Thus, deep motion is determined mainly by thermohaline factors. The effect of wind is confined to a thin surface layer and is not transmitted downward by vertical motion.

The calculations were also performed with level bottom. The major changes were recorded in middle and high latitudes. Variations of topography have practically no effect on the current field in equatorial regions.

Thus, the baroclinicity of an ocean with variable depth may be of great significance. To evaluate the importance of the contribution, the problem of calculating currents in an ocean of arbitrary bottom relief, with the density field given from observations, will be considered. Following Sarkisyan (1969), the equations are written in the form

$$-fv = \frac{-1}{\rho_o} P_x + \nu v_{zz} - A, \tag{47}$$

$$fu = \frac{-1}{\rho_o} P_y + \nu v_{zz} - B, \tag{48}$$

where

$$A = u_t + uu_x + vu_y - A_H \nabla^2 u, \tag{49}$$

$$B = v_t + uv_x + vv_y - A_H \nabla^2 v \tag{50}$$

represent the effects of inertial forces and lateral mixing. Eqs. (47) and (48) are integrated to obtain

$$V = \frac{1}{\rho_o f} \int_{-u}^{0} P_x\, dz - \frac{\tau(x)}{f\rho_o} - \frac{\delta}{2\rho_o f\alpha}\left(\frac{\partial}{\partial x}P_u + \frac{\partial}{\partial y}P_H\right) + \frac{1}{f}\int_{-H}^{0} A\, dz, \tag{51}$$

$$U = -\frac{1}{\rho_o f} \int_{-K}^{0} P_y\, dz + \frac{\tau(y)}{\rho_o f} + \frac{\delta}{2\rho_o f\alpha}\left(\frac{\partial}{\partial y}P_H - \frac{\partial}{\partial x}P_H\right) - \frac{1}{f}\int_{-\alpha}^{0} B\, dz. \tag{52}$$

In the above, P_H is the pressure at depth H, $\alpha = \sqrt{f/2}$, and δ signifies bottom frictional terms.

From the hydrostatic equation, the pressure is written as

$$P = g\rho_o\eta + g\int_z^0 \rho\, dz. \tag{53}$$

Substituting Eq. (53) into Eqs. (51) and (52), the primary balance is geostrophic. Employing oceanographic data and previous work, Sarkisyan estimates that the first term of the right-hand side of Eq. (51) is about 9×10^5 cm^2/s with values up to 10^7 in boundary flow. The direct wind action, the second terms in Eqs. (5) and (6), is of the order of 10^4 cm^2/s, more than an order of magnitude less. The effect of bottom friction is at most this amount, and the last term is much smaller than the pressure gradient, even in coastal areas.

Eqs. (51) and (52) are cross-differentiated and yield

$$\beta V = \frac{1}{\rho_o} J(P_H, H) + \frac{1}{\rho_o}\,\text{curl}\,\tau - \frac{\delta}{2\alpha\rho_o}\nabla^2 P_H + \frac{\partial}{\partial y}\int_{-H}^{0} A\, dz - \frac{\partial}{\partial z}\int_{-H}^{0} B\, dz. \tag{54}$$

Sarkisyan, in evaluating the terms, concludes that the primary balance is between the left-hand side and the first term of the right. They have a mean value of about 2×10^{-7} cm/s with values of about 5×10^{-6} in boundary regions. However, curl τ is only 10^{-8}, and the inertial terms are important only in coastal regions.

Using these primary balances, including wind stress wherever it appears, and making certain simplifying but reasonable assumptions regarding the variability of H and f

(Sarkisyan, 1969), the following equation for the total transport stream function is obtained:

$$A_H \nabla^4 \psi - \frac{\partial}{\partial f} \nabla^2 \psi - \frac{1}{H} J(\psi_1 \nabla^2 \psi)$$

$$- \frac{f}{2\alpha H} \nabla^2 \psi + \left(\frac{f}{H} H_y - \beta\right) \psi_x - \frac{f}{H} H_x \psi_y = \frac{-1}{\rho_o} \text{curl } \tau$$

$$- \left(H_y + \frac{\beta H}{f}\right) \frac{\tau^{(x)}}{\rho_o H} + \frac{H_x \tau^{(y)}}{\rho_o H} + f_1, \qquad (55)$$

where

$$f_1 = \frac{-1}{H} \left(\frac{g}{\rho_o f}\right)^2 J\left[\int_0^H (H-z)\rho \, dz, \quad \int_0^H (H-z)\nabla^2 \rho \, dz\right]$$

$$+ \left(\frac{g}{\rho_o f}\right)^2 \int_0^H J\left[\int_0^z \rho \, dz, \quad \int_0^z \nabla^2 \rho \, dz\right] dz$$

$$+ \frac{g}{2\rho_o \alpha H} \int_0^H z \nabla^2 \rho \, dz - \frac{g}{\rho_o} H_y \int_0^H \frac{z}{H} \frac{\partial \rho}{\partial x} dz$$

$$+ \frac{g}{\rho_o} H_x \int_0^H \frac{z}{H} \frac{\partial \rho}{\partial y} dz. \qquad (56)$$

In Eq. (55), Sarkisyan's coordinate frame has been used where z is the direction downward from the surface $z = 0$. It is instructive to compare this to Carrier and Robinson's (1962) Eq. (20). In the latter, curl τ plays a decisive role, because more important factors (baroclinicity and topography) have not been included.

The geostrophic transport is of the order of 5×10^5 cm^2/s, but the Sverdrup flow is only about 10^4 cm^2/s. If the validity of the conflicting theories was based on how accurately they predict the average velocities, we must conclude that the utility of homogeneous flow is limited only to shallow seas of about 100 m in depth.

For homogeneous flow, $\rho = 0$ is set in Eq. (55). Eq. (20) then follows if we set H = constant (a highly idealized situation) and neglect bottom friction (physically unjustified) and discard some small terms. Eq. (20) is valid for a homogeneous fluid, but this assumption is not necessary in its derivation. This is because an alternative way of getting from (55) to (20) is to neglect the following terms with corresponding indices in (55): (a) bottom friction, (b) replace integrals of products by products of in integrals, and (c) assume depth of ocean is constant.

Through these three assumptions, baroclinicity is completely removed from the system. For flow away from the boundary layer regions, Eqs. (1) and (2) can be justified, but Eq. (3), representing bottom topography and baroclinicity, cannot be ignored. The major problem of homogeneous models that attempt to represent the real ocean is their failure to include the joint effect of baroclinicity and bottom relief.

To test these conclusions, Sarkisyan and Ivanov (1971) performed a series of numerical experiments. Direct calculations of ψ, using the equivalent of Eq. (55) on a sphere, were made for the North Atlantic; and the direct influence of bottom relief and baroclinicity on the dynamics of the current was investigated. In these calculations, inertial terms and lateral mixing are neglected. The density distribution and wind are specified, and mass transport of water across all boundaries is set equal to zero. The experiments were as follows:

1. Homogeneous ocean of constant depth 1,500 m (Figure 15)—the transport in the Gulf Stream is only 10–12 Sverdrups, an underestimate by an order of magnitude. The figure can be increased by decreasing the frictional coefficient, but it is capricious to attempt reasonable values of Gulf Stream transport using wind-driven homogeneous models. However, the flow pattern is in agreement with our knowledge of the surface circulation in the Atlantic.
2. Homogeneous ocean with variable depth (Figure 16). This differs considerably from Eq. (1), with bottom relief now competing with the β-effect. Inclusion of bottom topography adversely affects the results, probably because of preconceived notions of total circulation having been erroneously based on surface velocities.
3. Joint effect of baroclinicity and topography (Figure 17). Because the density field is not known in deep water, it was linearly extrapolated to zero at the bottom from

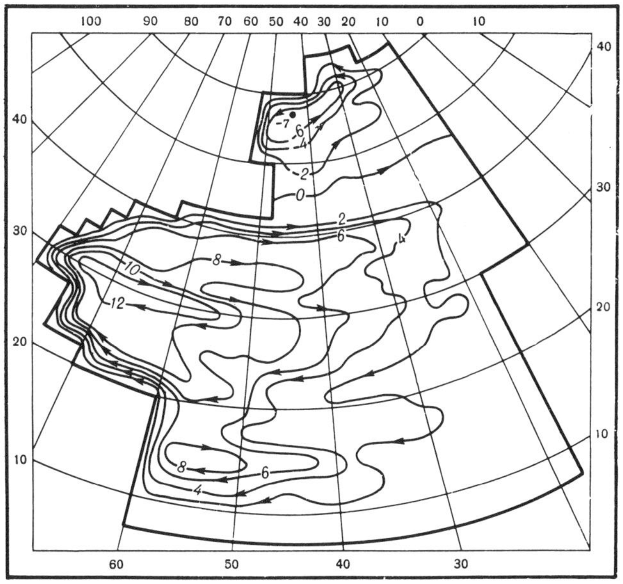

FIGURE 15 Transport stream function (in Sverdrups) of homogeneous ocean of constant depth 1,500 m (from Sarkisyan and Ivanov, 1971).

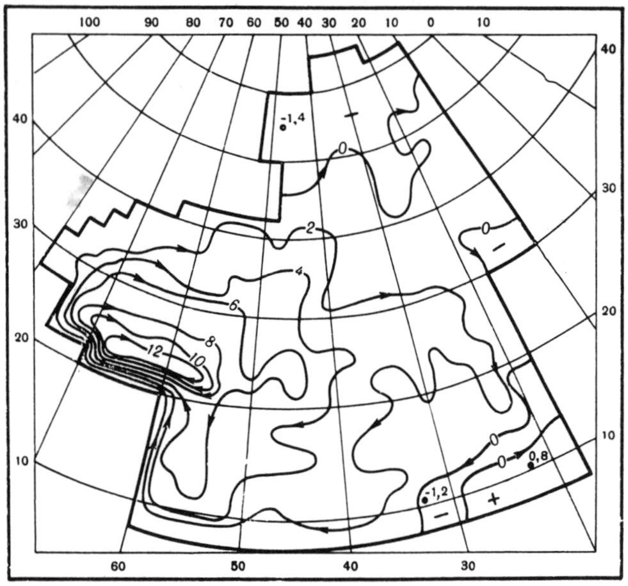

FIGURE 16 Transport stream function of homogeneous ocean with real topography (from Sarkisyan and Ivanov, 1971).

known values. A new pattern emerges, completely different from Eqs. (1) and (2). The transport has risen by an order of magnitude, and the anticyclonic eddies are replaced by cyclonic ones, perhaps because $D < H$ and $M < 0$ in Eq. (45). Several small eddies induced by topography appear, and closed gyres are located in deep portions on each side of the mid-Atlantic ridge.

4. Same as experiment 3 but density anomalies below 1,500 m are neglected (Figure 18). These results differ considerably from Eq. (3). Now, the flow consists of individual eddies whose strength is an order of magnitude less. This result—that deep density variations can have a crucial effect on the transport—is in agreement with Kozlov (1969).

Kozlov (1971) performed a similar numerical experiment for circulation in the Pacific Ocean. Because present knowledge of the deep-density distribution is deficient, a single-parameter model is assumed. Given the density distribution at a single level, we compute the density everywhere by an analytic formula. A simplified version of Eq. (55) was solved for the following series of numerical experiments:

1. Circulation over bottom of constant depth (Figure 19). Resulting from the approximations made, baroclinicity has been suppressed and the resultant flow is effectively homogeneous. This is Stommel's model with a Sverdrup interior.
2. Homogeneous circulation with variable topography (Figure 20). The currents are shaped by large-scale relief features, and the effect is most pronounced in the Southern Hemisphere. The east Australian current is shifted eastward to deeper water and an anticyclonic circulation appears near South America.
3. Joint effect of topography and baroclinicity (Figures 21 and 22). These two circulations are based on different formulas for the density distribution. Except in equatorial regions, there is good agreement; and they are both quite different from Eqs. (1) and (2). However, the considerable increase in transports and the reversal of gyres due to baro-

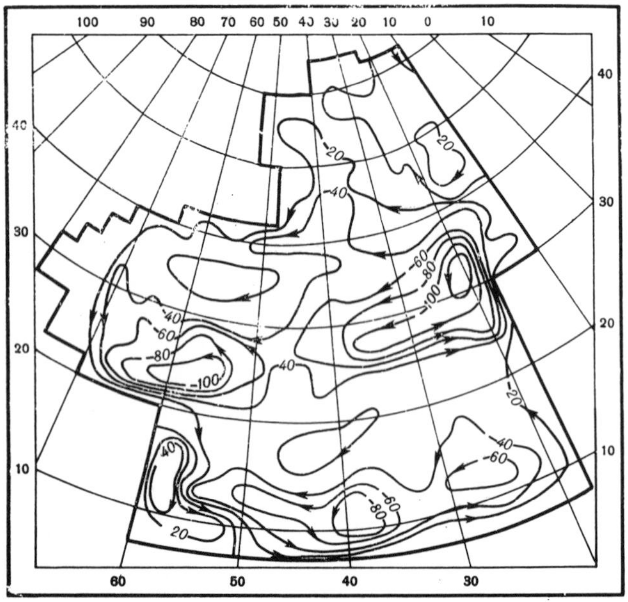

FIGURE 17 Transport stream function when joint effect of bottom relief and baroclinicity are taken into account (from Sarkisyan and Ivanov, 1971).

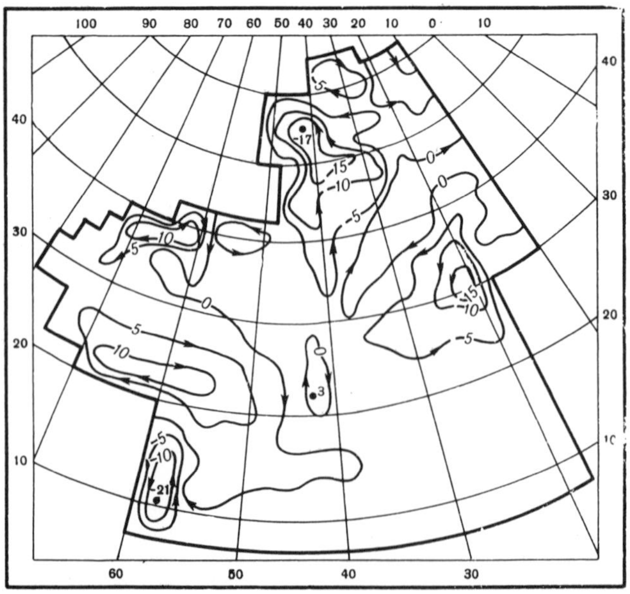

FIGURE 18 Same as Figure 17 with homogeneous ocean below 1,500 m (from Sarkisyan and Ivanov, 1971).

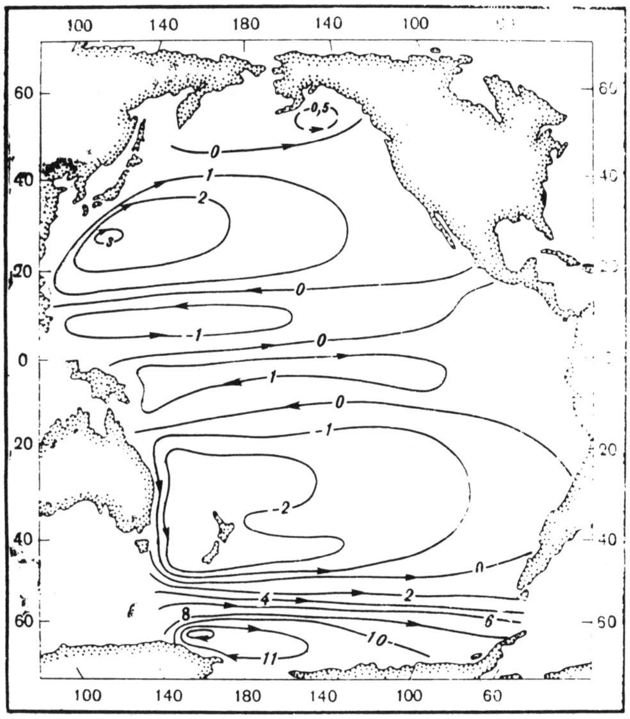

FIGURE 19 Transport stream function for horizontal ocean bottom. Each unit is 10 Sverdrups (from Kozlov, 1971).

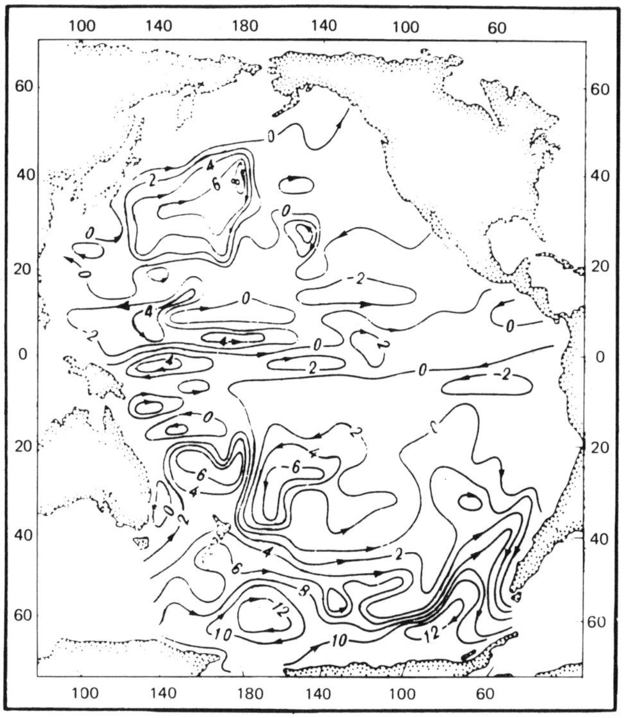

FIGURE 21 Transport stream function when joint effect of baroclinicity and topography are taken into account (from Kozlov, 1971).

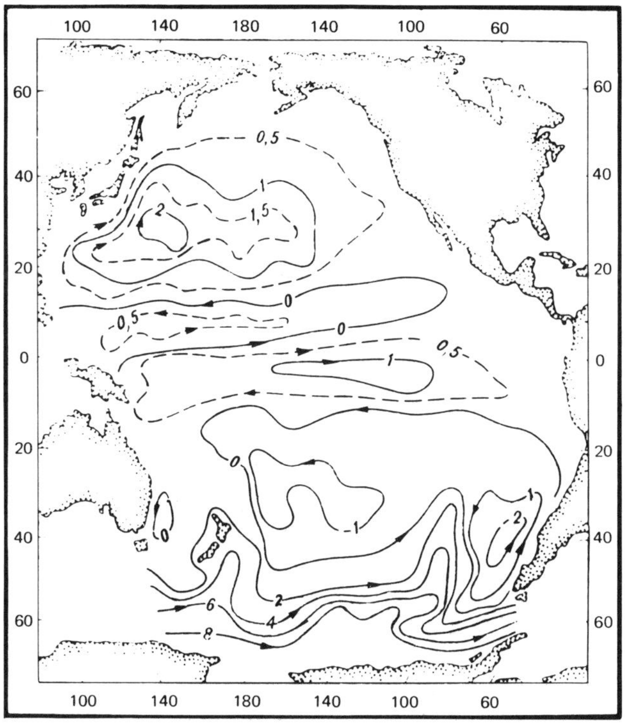

FIGURE 20 Transport stream function for homogeneous ocean with real topography (from Kozlov, 1971).

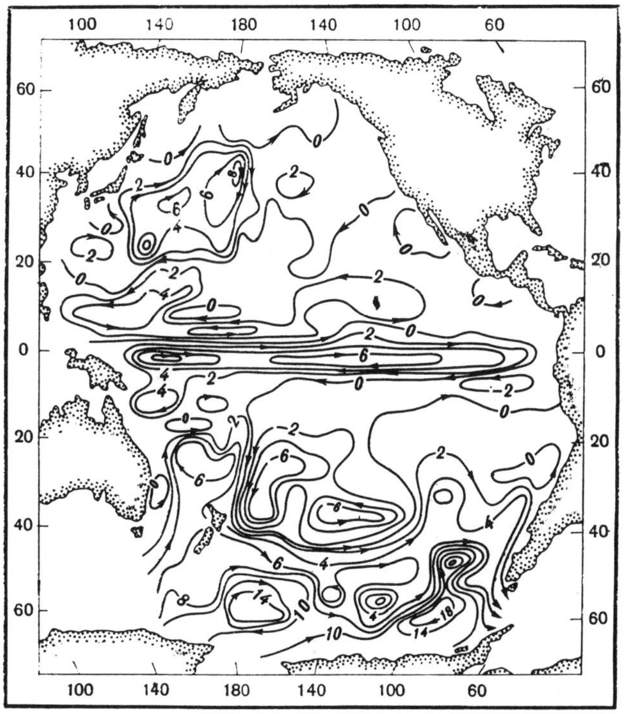

FIGURE 22 Same as Figure 21 with different formula for stratification (from Kozlov, 1971).

clinicity obtained by Sarkisyan and Ivanov are not produced in these calculations.

Gill and Bryan (1971) have treated the full three-dimensional circulation in the Southern Hemisphere. Although the bottom was assumed level, effective topography was included by varying the depth of the sill in the Drake Passage. Figure 23 shows the dramatic effect caused by varying this topographic feature. In *a*, the gap is closed and there is no circumpolar current. In *b*, the gap is open and as deep as the ocean basin. In *e*, the depth at the passage is one-half the total depth. The transport is increased for the shallow gap situation by a factor of three. By examining the balance of forces, it is noted that the east–west pressure difference just below the sill is driving the current in the same direction as the wind-force and is four times as great. Clearly this contribution is lacking in the deep-gap case. This effect is entirely due to baroclinicity and stands in contrast to Schulman (1970), who predicted shallowing in the Drake Passage should decrease the flow. This experiment by Gill

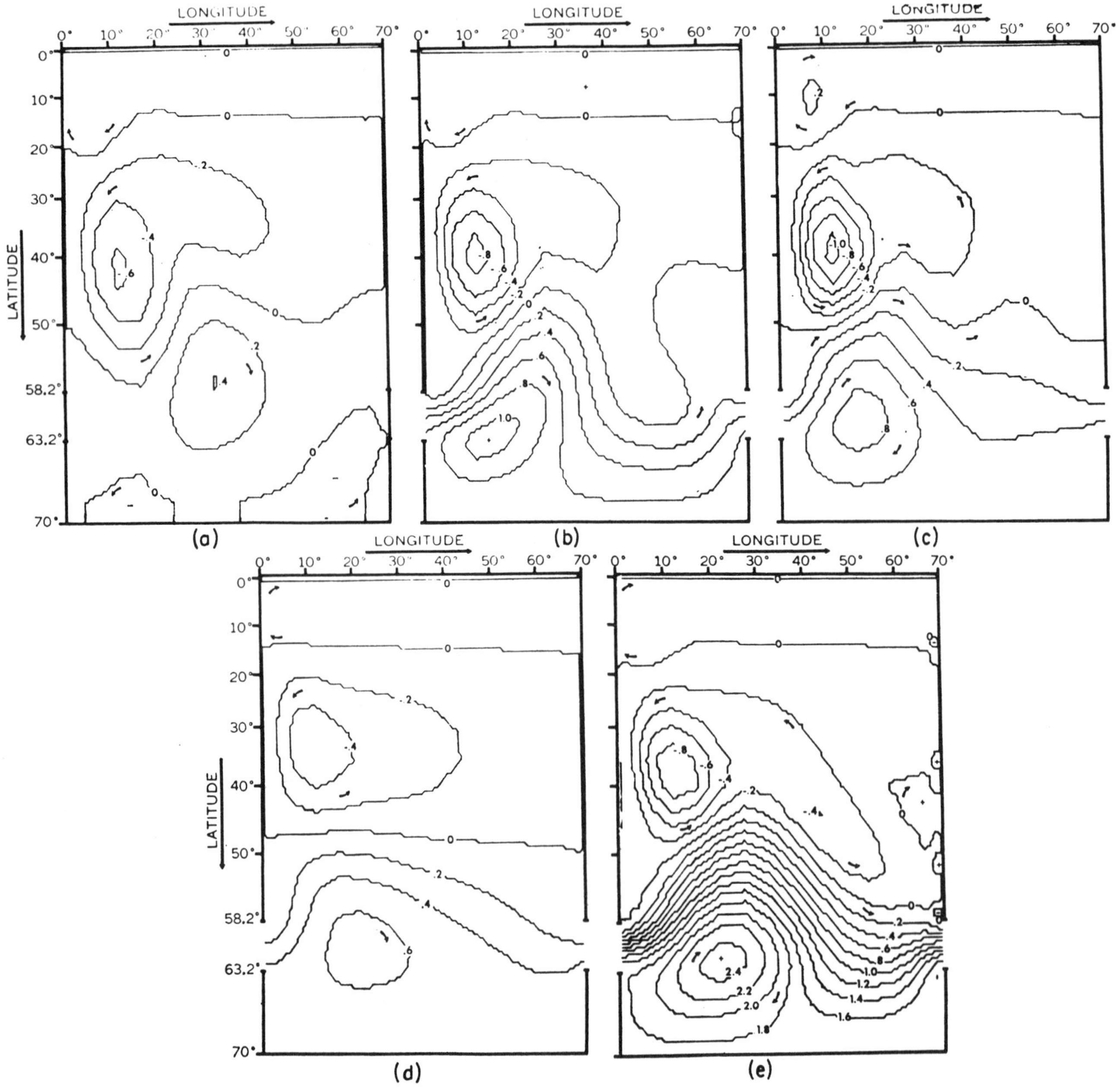

FIGURE 23 Transport stream function for baroclinic southern ocean model. (a) closed basin; (b) deep gap, linear surface-temperature distribution; (c) deep-gap, curved surface-temperature distribution; (d) deep-gap, barotropic case; (e) shallow gap, linear surface-temperature distribution. The nondimensional transports through the passage are: (b) 0.64, (c) 0.48, (d) 0.42, (e) 1.78 (from Gill and Bryan, 1971).

and Bryan demonstrates both the importance of bottom topography and the joint effect of baroclinicity and topography.

Two main methods of integration have been illustrated above. The first, used by Sarkisyan (1969), Kozlov (1969), and others, is to specify completely the density field from observations or theory. The difficulty here is that the density field is not known below 1,000–2,000 m, and slight errors could lead to significant changes in the circulation. The second method, employed by Bryan (1969) and his colleagues, involves the time-integration of all dependent variables over the three-dimensional volume. Unfortunately, this requires considerable computational facilities.

The use of single-parameter density models is a compromise approach to solving three-dimensional baroclinic circulations with arbitrary relief. Because the density field has a simple and regular pattern for most of the world ocean, the vertical stratification can be approximated by an analytical function of the quantity $z/h(x,y)$. The parameter $h(x,y)$ is determined in solving the equations. This method reduces the solution of the three-dimensional problem to a two-dimensional one. The details of this method are discussed by Bolgurtsev and Kozlov (1969) and Bolgurtsev *et al.* (1969).

CONCLUSIONS

This paper has shown that topography significantly changes the circulation of a homogeneous ocean via the tendency of the fluid to conserve potential vorticity. Not only is bottom relief comparable to the β-effect, but may even overwhelm it; as, for example, transforming a western intensified flow into an eastern coastal current.

However, the basic conclusion regarding the applicability of homogeneous ocean circulations to the real ocean is highly questionable. The influence of variable topography cannot be treated independently of baroclinicity in any physically consistent manner. Small-density anomalies at large depths significantly alter the transport. The resultant flow is considerably different from the surface currents and there is no correlation between the two.

To understand the real nature of the oceans and, in particular, the important effect of topography, the three-dimensional structure of currents and density must be studied. Although the mathematical formulation of the problem is rather straightforward, the solution of the equations is greatly complicated by numerical difficulties requiring the most sophisticated high-speed computers.

Except for the pioneering work of Bryan (1969) and his colleagues, there are no examples of the simultaneous computation of the velocity and density fields encompassing physical conditions. Furthermore, no such calculations have been made for the world ocean in which bottom relief has been taken into account in a systematic study. It is expected that numerical studies of baroclinic flow over variable relief will be the focus of considerable oceanographic research in the near future as high-speed, large-core computers are made available for research purposes.

REVIEW: WILLIAM R. HOLLAND

The effects of bottom topography were neglected in early models of the large-scale ocean circulation for the sake of a simplicity of interpretation, but numerous studies in the last few years have suggested that bottom relief may play an extremely important role in determining the general circulation of the ocean. Schulman reviews in some detail the results of numerical experiments concerned with such effects. These studies have dealt for the most part with the two-dimensional mass transport field in the ocean (obtained by vertically averaging the three-dimensional model equations). Schulman first reviews the homogeneous ocean results and then the baroclinic ones. His discussion of the manner in which the baroclinic mass transport equation (45) is related to the homogeneous one (21) is a nice illustration of how compensation by the density field can affect the transport pattern. In particular the M-equation (46) displays explicitly how topographic effects can be magnified over what they are in the homogeneous case. The computations, done with a fixed (observed) density field, confirm this as a possbility (Kozlov, 1969; Sarkisyan and Ivanov, 1971).

Using the Bryan (1969) numerical ocean model, Holland and Hirschman (1972) have carried out some experiments on the circulation in the North Atlantic using mean density data obtained from the data files at the National Oceanographic Data Center. The results may be compared with those of Sarkisyan and Ivanov (1971) for the same region (see Figures 15–18). Eq. (1) (in this review) shows the mass transport results from three cases: (a) a homogeneous ocean with bottom topography, (b) a baroclinic ocean with a flat bottom (put at 1,200 m), and (c) a baroclinic ocean with bottom topography. The dynamics of (b) are simply those of Munk (1950); that is, the boundary currents here are highly frictional and inertial effects play a little role. The interior flow is governed entirely by the wind stress curl. In the other two cases, topography plays an important and even dominating role in the interior of the ocean. Note especially the very strong magnification of the transport by the Gulf Stream in case (c).

The investigations discussed by Schulman rely for the most part on two-dimensional vorticity theory. Thus, for example, in Eq. (38) the "new" effect introduced by bottom topography comes in as a bottom pressure torque,

$1/\rho_o J[H, p(-H)]$. The vorticity associated with the vertically averaged flow may be changed by a horizontally varying pressure distribution at the sea bottom acting against changes in bottom relief. This effect results from the horizontal divergence induced by bottom topography. For instance, in the simple case of geostrophic flow it can be shown that

$$J(p_{-H},H) = -\rho_o f\, w_{-H} = +\rho_o f \int_{-H}^{0} w_z\, dz. \quad (1)$$

Another way to get some insight into the bottom topography problem is to examine a circulation theorem associated with the vorticity equation. We write the vorticity equation in the form

$$\nabla^2 \psi_t = \boldsymbol{k}\cdot\nabla x(f\nabla\psi + \tau^S + p_{-H}\nabla H + \boldsymbol{F} + \boldsymbol{N} - \tau^B), \quad (2)$$

where f is the Coriolis parameter and $\boldsymbol{F}$ and $\boldsymbol{N}$ are vertical integrals of the frictional and nonlinear advection terms in the equations of motion. Then computing a two-dimensional area integral of these terms and using Green's theorem to transform into line integrals along the path surrounding the region, we find

$$\frac{\partial}{\partial t}\int_S \nabla\psi\cdot{}_n\, dl = \int_S (f\nabla\psi + \tau^S + p_{-H}\nabla H + \boldsymbol{F} + \boldsymbol{N} - \tau^B)\cdot{}_S\, dl. \quad (3)$$

If the contour S is chosen to coincide with a streamline, the first term on the right is zero. The left hand side of the equation is the rate of change with time of the mass transport averaged around the closed circuit per unit width of path. In the steady state, the terms on the right side balance one another and the time change is zero. These terms describe the balance of forces per unit width of path averaged around the circuit. The mean forces per unit width are respectively (a) the Coriolis force, (b) the wind stress, (c) the force exerted by the solid earth on the water column through the action of pressure forces pushing against vertical changes in topography, (d) the lateral friction force, (e) advective forces, and (f) the bottom stress. Note that the bottom pressure forcing (c) would be zero if either the depth were constant or the ocean were barotropic.

Table 1 shows the various balances for the experiment (c); Eq. (1), for the region encompassed by the ψ contour equal to 20×10^6 m^3/s in the Gulf Stream gyre. When the forces per unit width are added up around this particular closed path, the bottom pressure forcing is 25 times stronger than the wind stress. Note that the summation of $p_{-H}\Delta H\cdot{}_S\, dl$ is similar to atmospheric computations of mountain torque contributions to the angular momentum balance of the atmosphere.

While this clarifies somewhat the appropriate forcing that leads to enhanced transports when baroclinicity and topographic relief are jointly present in the model, the energetics are still a bit obscure. If we take the simplest model discussed by Schulman, as expressed in Eqs. (32) and (33), we can construct some energy integrals that suggest the nature of the energy flow between various reservoirs in the model. The model equations we shall use for this purpose are

TABLE 1 Magnitude of the Mean Forces per Unit Width Driving the Flow Around the Path *S*

Coriolis force	0.000
Wind stress	.005
Bottom pressure	.126
Lateral friction	−.127
Advective forcing	−.007
Bottom friction	−.002

$$U_t - fV = \frac{-1}{\rho_o} p_x + \nu U_{zz}, \quad (4)$$

$$V_t + fu = \frac{-1}{\rho_o} p_y + \nu V_{zz}, \quad (5)$$

$$U_x + V_y + w_z = 0, \quad (6)$$

$$P_z = -\rho g. \quad (7)$$

Then the rate of change of kinetic energy per unit volume is given by

$$\frac{\partial}{\partial t}\left(\rho_o \frac{u^2+v^2}{2}\right) = -(up_x + vp_y) + \rho_o \nu(uu_{zz} + vv_{zz})$$

$$= (up_x + vp_y + wp_z) - \rho g w$$

$$+ \rho_o \nu(uu_{zz} + vv_{zz}). \quad (8)$$

If we integrate over a closed basin (with no inflow or outflow), letting $\{\quad\} = \iiint(\quad)\, dx\, dy\, dz$,

$$\frac{\partial}{\partial t}\left\{\rho_o \frac{u^2+v^2}{2}\right\} = -\left\{\rho g w\right\} + \iint V\cdot(\tau^W - \tau^B)\,dx\,dy - \left\{\rho_o \nu\, V_z\cdot V_z\right\}. \quad (9)$$

Thus the total kinetic energy can change in consequence of work done by buoyancy forces that convert potential energy to kinetic energy (or vice versa), work done by the wind stress and by the bottom stress, and internal dissipation.

For the purpose of understanding the mass transport problem, it is necessary to examine the energy associated with the vertically averaged flow. Then if the momentum equations (4) and (5) are averaged vertically [let the bar operator mean $\overline{(\ )} = 1/H\int_{-H}^{0}(\ )\,dz$] and the kinetic energy equation formed, we find

$$\frac{\partial}{\partial t}\left\{\rho_o \frac{\overline{u}^2 + \overline{v}^2}{2}\right\} = -\iint (H\overline{V}\cdot\nabla\overline{P}_x)dx\,dy + \iint \overline{V}\cdot(\tau^S - \tau^B)dx\,dy. \quad (10)$$

The kinetic energy of the vertically averaged flow can be changed by the action of pressure forces and by the work done by the wind and bottom stresses.

Let us look further at the first term on the right. Using the hydrostatic relation, this term can be put in the form

$$-\iint \frac{\overline{p} - p_{-H}}{H} J(\psi,H)dx\,dy, \quad (11)$$

where ψ is the mass transport stream function, $\psi_x = \overline{v}H$, $\psi_y = -\overline{u}H$. Now we can see how the joint effect of baroclinicity and bottom relief come into play. If either the depth or the density is constant, then work done by this term is identically zero. It is only in the presence of both variable density and variable topography that the work done on the vertically averaged flow can be enhanced over that due to the wind stress alone.

REFERENCES

Bolgurtsev, B. N., and V. F. Kozlov. 1969. An approximate method of calculating current and density fields in a baroclinic ocean. Izv. Akad. Nauk. Atmos. Oceanic Phys. 5(7):704–13.

Bolgurtsev, B. N., V. F. Kozlov, and L. A. Molchanova. 1969. Results of calculation of the currents in the Pacific Ocean section of the Antarctic. Izv. Akad. Nauk. Atmos. Oceanic Phys. 5(8): 846–59.

Bryan, K. 1969. A numerical method for the study of ocean circulation. J. Comput. Phys. 4:347–76.

Carrier, G. F., and A. R. Robinson. 1962. On the theory of the wind-driven ocean circulation. J. Fluid Mech. 12(1):49–80.

Clarke, R. A., and N. P. Fofonoff. 1969. Oceanic flow over varying bottom topography. J. Mar. Res. 27(2):226–40.

Fomin, L. M. 1969. V. B. Shtokman's method of mass transport for an ocean of variable depth. Okeanologiya 9:92–96.

Gill, A. E., and K. Bryan. 1971. Effects of geometry on the circulation of a three-dimensional southern-hemisphere ocean model. Deep-Sea Res. 18(4):685–721.

Godfrey, J. S., and A. R. Robinson. 1971. The East Australian Current as a free inertial jet. J. Mar. Res. 29(3):256–80.

Greenspan, H. P. 1963. A note concerning topography and inertial currents. J. Mar. Res. 21(3):147–54.

Holland, W. R. 1967. On the wind-driven circulation in an ocean with bottom topography. Tellus 19(4):582–600.

Holland, W. R., and A. D. Hirschman. 1972. A numerical calculation of the circulation in the North Atlantic Ocean. (Unpublished paper.)

Kamenkovich, V. M. 1962. On the theory of the Antarctic circular current. Trudy Inst. Okeanol. 56:241–93.

Kochergin, V. P., and V. I. Klimok. 1971. Effect of bottom relief on oceanic circulation. Izv. Akad. Nauk. Atmos. Oceanic Phys. 7(8): 885–91.

Kozlov, V. F. 1969. Effect of bottom topography on geostrophic currents in the Pacific Ocean. Okeanologiya 9:496–502.

Kozlov, V. F. 1971. Some results of an approximate calculation of the circulation in the Pacific Ocean. Izv. Akad. Nauk. Atmos. Oceanic Phys. 7(4):421–30.

Niiler, P. P., and A. R. Robinson. 1967. The theory of free inertial jets. II. A numerical experiment for the path of the Gulf Stream. Tellus 19(4):601–19.

Orlanski, I. 1969. The influence of bottom topography on the stability of jets in a baroclinic fluid. J. Atmos. Sci. 26(11):1216–32.

Porter, G. H., and M. Rattray. 1964. The influence of variable depth on steady zonal barotropic flow. Dtsh. Hydrogr. Z. 17(4):164–74.

Richardson, W. S., W. S. Schmitz, Jr., and P. P. Niiler. 1969. The velocity structure of the Florida current from the Straits of Florida to Cape Fear. Deep-Sea Res. 16(suppl.):225–31.

Robinson, A. R., and P. P. Niiler. 1967. Theory of free inertial currents. I. Path and structure. Tellus 19(2):269–91.

Robinson, A. R., and B. A. Taft. 1972. A numerical experiment for the path of the Kuroshio. J. Mar. Res. 30(1):65–101.

Sarkisyan, A. S. 1969. Deficiencies of barotropic models of ocean circulation. Izv. Akad. Nauk. Atmos. Oceanic Phys. 5(8):818–35.

Sarkisyan, A. S., and V. F. Ivanov. 1971. Joint effect of baroclinicity and bottom relief as an important factor in the dynamics of sea currents. Izv. Akad. Nauk. Atmos. Oceanic Phys. 7(2):173–88.

Schulman, E. E. 1970. The Antarctic circumpolar current, pp. 955–68. Proc. Comput. Simul. Conf., 6–12 June 1970, Denver, Colo.

Schulman, E. E., and P. P. Niiler. 1970. Topographic effects on the wind-driven ocean circulation. Geophys. Fluid Dyn. 1(4):439–62.

Stommel, H. M. 1948. The westward intensification of wind driven ocean currents. Trans. Am. Geophys. Union 29:202–6.

Warren, B. A. 1963. Topographic influences on the path of the Gulf Stream. Tellus 15(2):167–83.

Warren, B. A. 1969. Divergence of isobaths as a cause of current branching. Deep-Sea Res. 6(suppl.):339–55.

Welander, P. 1968. Wind-driven circulation in one and two layer oceans of variable depth. Tellus 20(1):1–15.

DISCUSSION

HOLLAND: If you look at the energetics of a baroclinic ocean, then you can show that it's only with variable density and variable topography that you can pump extra energy into the external mode by pressure forces. This is an experiment in which you can put energy into the vertically averaged part of the kinetic energy in a way that's not present in a constant-density ocean.

BRETHERTON: What strikes me most about this discussion, and indeed all of yesterday, is that we've been talking as if the density field and the topography field are things that are given. Now the fact is they're not. Take the topography, for example; I can vary the data quite substantially. But above all, how I smooth that topography can be absolutely critical. One of the most notable things about Sarkisyan's calculations and equally about this is that it does give rise to a lot of small-scale eddies and gyres. Indeed, all of the energy is on the very smallest scale as a result of running the model. And maybe that should give us pause to think that maybe the smoothing that we're doing in putting in these fields may in fact be critically important; and what really all this is pointing to is that we may be missing the whole essence of the thing, which is on smaller scales than we are actually resolving. That's why we keep running into these troubles.

GALT: If you run into the case where the level of no motion is somehow below the bottom (this would be the case if you had very weak stratification or very severe bathymetry), it would mean that the level of no motion had not been reached. In this case, from the simulation point of view, the ocean can be considered homogeneous and a reduced bathymetry used. I tried this for the Arctic Ocean, and the results look quite reasonable.

SCHULMAN: That's ostensibly what you get out of this equation. Galt is telling us that D is greater than H. Then the effect of baroclinicity is to reduce the effect to topography.

GALT: It reduces the stretching somewhat; for an Arctic circulation model, reducing the variations in the bathymetry to 15 percent of the actual values gave reasonable results in terms of circulation patterns.

PHILLIPS: I would interpret your taking Δ as an independently prescribed quantity as really defining what vertical wave number you're assigning to the flow. That assigns the same wave number to the density variation, pressure variation, and the vertical velocity and, therefore, also the horizontal velocity. It's a very dangerous thing to do, especially with respect to flow over a ridge. The vertical wave number is determined by the dispersion equation, and it's the type of flow we're interested in here. Let's take, for example, the Rossby wave response due to flow over a ridge. You will get quite different results depending on whether the flow is east or west; the vertical wave number could be imaginary or, in this case, real.

SCHULMAN: I think that would also have to do with Bretherton's point about how you average your density and topography. If you have a coarse enough average, than delta z will be somewhat uniform.

RATTRAY: This delta z may not be very critical. Consider the vertical profile of the horizontal velocity. If one breaks the profile up into a baroclinic part and barotropic part (as Fofonoff does), then it is quite possible to have a positive net transport in this way, while you have actually a negative barotropic velocity defined as above. This is opposite to what you would have if you defined the barotropic velocity to give the total transport. With small vertical gradients of velocity over the depth range of bottom features, it is Fofonoff barotropic velocity that responds to the bathymetry. With $D < H$, this velocity may be reversed from the total transport. If you go to the other situation, where you have $D > H$, this means you have a velocity profile without a flow reversal. We have a barotropic part again; and a baroclinic that doesn't feel the bottom acts on the reduced barotropic transport and is therefore less effective. The Fofonoff of the transport feels the bottoms; the rest of the transport doesn't. This is one convenient way to look at the bathymetry or bottom effects on various velocity profiles, I think. And really that is the essence of Fofonoff's decomposition between barotropic and baroclinic, with the barotropic being defined for his purposes by the bottom velocity.

RATTRAY: The effect of bottom topography depends on the kind of vertical velocity profile you have, which is implicitly in the kind of delta z that is chosen.

UNIDENTIFIED: How do you get these enormous increases in the transport with that kind of interpretation?

RATTRAY: I think it was stated that the Jacobian was the difference between two big numbers—each depending on gradients of depth and of density almost universally taken from different sources. Using the wind stress and the density field in the eastern North Pacific, the more carefully I tried to determine the flow near the bottom, the more parallel the streamlines at the bottom were the bathymetry. And it's really not clear to me what the effects would be of smoothing bathymetry in one way and smoothing the density field in another, and then taking the Jacobian of the two fields.

UNIDENTIFIED: In other words, you're saying that the observations that we presently have are not sufficiently good to estimate the order of magnitude of that number. In other words, the uncertainty is bigger than the size of the number.

RATTRAY: I am open-minded on that possibility.

BRYAN: We have concentrated our attention on the problem of evaluating this term from data. And I think it might be valuable to bring up a calculation that Bill Holland has made. He has calculated the bottom pressure torque from a predictive calculation with a numerical model, starting out from arbitrary initial conditions.

HOLLAND: I'll try and summarize it very briefly. Vorticity arguments imply that the southward-flowing undercurrent along the base of the continental slope is associated with vertical motion that is induced there. It essentially turns out that all you need is a very slight upslope flow of the undercurrent to produce the effect.

BRYAN: Less than a 5° angle to the isobaths, isn't it?

HOLLAND: Less than 5°. The vertical velocities are not overly large. They're larger than the interior by a factor of 10 or so, but they're not enormous. In that calculation, the density is predicted and it takes on its configuration from the dynamics of the flow. The dynamics determines the fact that the pressure lines intersect the topography in the calculation; whereas in the diagnostic cases, there is the problem of just what the density field really does look like.

UNIDENTIFIED: Is the countercurrent essential?

HOLLAND: It's intimately tied up with the meridional transport.

CHARNEY: In your model, where you don't make any *ad hoc* assumptions but actually carry out an integration, what kind of initial conditions do you start out with? Do you start out with nothing, or do you start with some of the presumed observed system, because it takes a long time to reach equilibrium.

HOLLAND: In that experiment, there is a very long integration. In the initial stage I have a uniform stratification, but it is not similar to that at the end of the calculation.

CHARNEY: But have you reached anything like equilibrium?

HOLLAND: Oh, yes.

CHARNEY: In the deep water?

HOLLAND: In the deep water.

CHARNEY: With a time scale of 1,000 years?

HOLLAND: That particular calculation was not done purely as an initial value problem; there were some extrapolation techniques. So, the only way I can really say how steady it was is to look at the balance of terms, which were very near equilibrium. I tried to look at that as carefully as possible, and it's quite difficult. I think the question gets to the important point; it is a fairly delicate balance between these two terms, the surface pressure and the density field.

CHARNEY: Would you be in a position to say that there are strong barotropic currents in the deep water?

HOLLAND: Yes, I think so.

CHARNEY: But if that were the case, what would happen to the whole abyssal circulation, which is very weak?

HOLLAND: The particular effect that I find in my experiment is confined to the topographic region and is not connected with the interior.

CHARNEY: Oh, I see; so this is near the continental shelf. I really mean deep water, about 4,000 m.

NIILER: Would someone who does these numerical models please tell me on what diffusive parameters does the meridional overturning depend? I suspect that it depends on what the vertical coefficient of heat diffusion is. Would you explain to me what it does depend upon? Because, you see, the topographic effect is very strongly tied, at least in Holland's model, to the fact that there is an overturning and then a northerly undercurrent is driven into the shelf to join the Gulf Stream flow on the surface. Has there been a parameter study in these models—on what the strength of the sinking and the overturning depend?

BRYAN: I did a study of that kind and never got around to publishing it. But I found results that are roughly similar to what you'd expect from thermocline theory. There's a dependency on the vertical mixing such that if the vertical mixing is very intense, you will get much more intense thermoplane circulation. This is the case where the temperature at the surface is fixed.

UNIDENTIFIED: I just wanted to point out that in the summer of 1971, we had a current metered down. We had seven current meters down west of the New England seamount; they were 15 miles apart, hopefully across the stream. And the northern two current meters practically throughout the entire month that we had them down showed very strong countercurrent, sometimes carrying 30 cm/s over a period of days, while 30 miles south there were currents that were going the opposite direction.

BRYAN: I don't think there's any dispute that a countercurrent exists; it's a question of upslope motion. I don't think this can be determined from the current meters, because the very small crossing of contour lines is obscured by sampling error, if you put a current meter in any one of these locations. What we need is a study with floats that simply drift near the bottom along the slope and sample over a larger area.

BRETHERTON: But having looked at their data too, I think he has a very valid point. That is, that if you move 30 miles away, the current was in a totally opposite direction, and very, very, very different.

ENERGETICS OF BARCOCLINIC OCEANS

W. R. HOLLAND

INTRODUCTION

In this paper we will examine the energetic characteristics of several numerical experiments that have been carried out by various investigators, using the Bryan (1969) general circulation model, which is constructed with certain energy-conserving properties incorporated into finite-difference equations. Certain fundamental properties of the model that are not apparent from examining the velocity and density distributions themselves may be ascertained by summarizing the result of these experiments with respect to the energetics.

Models of the general ocean circulation have not reached the stage attained by atmospheric models, which treat explicitly the eddy processes that can naturally occur in the atmosphere. This is largely due to resolution problems, because atmospheric eddies typically have wave lengths of several thousand kilometers, while those observed in the ocean are about several hundred kilometers. For this reason most ocean models of the large-scale circulation have entirely parameterized the effect of transient eddies in terms of an eddy-mixing hypothesis. In the near future, however, general circulation calculations will have enough resolution to include such eddy scales even in entire ocean basins; and detailed studies of the fluxes of momentum, heat, salt, and other constituents throughout the ocean will be made. Then, as with similar developments in atmospheric dynamics, an understanding of the oceanic mean circulation will require an understanding of the energetic properties of the system. Here we can lay some of the groundwork by examining from a new point of view some numerical experiments already carried out, even though the eddy-mixing is parameterized and is probably quite unrealistic.

The experiments we are going to discuss are those by Bryan and Cox (1968), Cox (1970), and Holland (1971, 1973). The energetic properties associated with these and other experiments carried out in conjunction with them have largely been ignored. We shall summarize some of the energetic properties and suggest fundamental mechanisms that operate in the various experiments and may be important in the actual ocean.

THE BASIC EQUATIONS OF THE MODEL

In the numerical model developed by Bryan (1969), the equations of motion are the Navier-Stokes equations with several basic modifications: (a) The boussinesq approximation is made in which density variations are ignored, except in the buoyancy term; (b) a hydrostatic balance is assumed; and (c) the diffusion of momentum, heat, and salt by small-scale transient disturbances is parameterized by an eddy-mixing hypothesis.

Let V be the horizontal velocity vector (with eastward and northward components u and v), let w be the vertical velocity, and let ω be the horizontal grad operator. The equations of motion and continuity are

$$\rho_o V_t + \rho_o V \cdot \nabla V \rho_o + \omega V_z + \rho_o f x \; V$$

$$= -\nabla p + F + \rho_o K_m V_{zz}, \qquad (1)$$

$$\rho g = -p_z, \qquad (2)$$

$$\nabla \cdot V + \omega_z = 0. \quad (3)$$

Here K_m is the vertical eddy viscosity and F is a horizontal body force caused by lateral friction. In Bryan's model

$$F^\lambda = \rho_o A_m \left[\nabla^2 u + \frac{(1-\tan^2\theta)}{a^2} u - \frac{2\tan\theta}{a^2 \cos\theta} v_\lambda \right], \quad (4)$$

$$F^\theta = \rho_o A_m \left[\nabla^2 v + \frac{(1-\tan^2\theta)}{a^2} v + \frac{2\tan\theta}{a^2 \cos\theta} u_\lambda \right], \quad (5)$$

where λ and θ are longitude and latitude, a is the radius of the earth, and A_m is the coefficient of lateral mixing of momentum.

In some of the experiments we shall discuss, the density is itself predicted, while in others, the temperature and salinity are predicted and the density is obtained from an equation of state. Because the latter complicates somewhat the discussion of the potential energy of the system, we shall assume that the density is predicted. The conservation equation is then

$$\rho_t + V \cdot \nabla \rho + \omega \rho_z = \frac{K_h}{\delta} \rho_{zz} + A_h \nabla^2 \rho, \quad (6)$$

where $\delta = 1$ when $\rho_z < 0$ and $\delta = 0$ when $\rho_z > 0$. Thus vertical mixing can occur either by ordinary diffusion when the water column is stable or by "convective mixing" when the water column is unstable. The "convective-mixing" process restores the water column to neutral stability by a downward density flux. This implicit treatment of the vertical-mixing process is discussed in Bryan and Cox (1968).

To compare results from several numerical experiments, certain nondimensional numbers based on these equations may be calculated. Following Gill and Bryan (1971), a velocity scale V^* and a depth scale d are defined on the basis of the thermal wind and density prediction equations: $2\Omega V^*/d = g\Delta\rho/a$ and $V^*/a = K_h/d^2$. Here $\Delta\rho$ is the density scale based on the north-south density contrast at the sea surface. A second horizontal velocity scale V^{**} may be defined based on wind forcing: $V^{**} d = \tau^*/2\Omega\rho_o$. Several independent nondimensional parameters can be defined, four of which are relevant to our discussion. These are the Rossby number ($Ro = V^*/2\Omega a$), the Reynolds number ($Re = V^* a/A_m$), the Peclet number ($Pe = V^* a/A_h$), and the ratio of the velocity scales ($\gamma = V^{**}/V^*$). We can relate Ro, Re, and Pe to three other nondimensional numbers that are associated with the width of the western boundary layer (Bryan and Cox, 1968): $L_F = (Ro/Re)^{1/3}$, $L_I = Ro^{1/2}$, and $L_M = Pe^{-1}$. These correspond to boundary layers in which there are important effects caused by lateral friction, inertia, and lateral diffusion of density. The values of these parameters are shown in Table 1 for the experiments to be discussed.

THE ENERGY EQUATIONS

In studies of the atmosphere, a comparison of the energy budget based on observations with the energetics of numerical models has contributed a great deal to the present understanding of large-scale motions. Although comparable observations in the ocean do not yet exist, comparison of the energetic budgets from alternative numerical experiments is useful. To do so we must develop the relevant energy equations.

If the kinetic energy per unit volume is $e = \rho_o (V \cdot V)/2$, then the time rate of change of kinetic energy is found by forming the scalar product of V with the terms in the horizontal momentum equation (1). The result can be put in the form

$$e_t = -\nabla \cdot [V(e+p)] - [\omega(e+p)]_z + g\rho\,\omega + V \cdot F + \rho_o K_m (V \cdot V_z)_z - \rho_o K_m (V_z \cdot V_z). \quad (7)$$

TABLE 1 Nondimensional Parameters Describing the Experiments

Experiment	Bryan and Cox (1968)	Cox (1970)	Holland (1971)	Holland (unpublished)	Holland (1973)	Holland (unpublished)
Ro	2×10^{-4}	1.5×10^{-5}	1.5×10^{-5}	1.5×10^{-5}	1.5×10^{-5}	1.5×10^{-5}
Re	150	18	1.8	0.9	1.8	1.8
Pe	150	18	18	90	18	18
γ	1	4.6	3.4	3.4	3.4	0
L_F	.011	.009	.020	.026	.020	.020
L_I	.014	.004	.004	.004	.004	.004
L_M	.007	.056	.056	.011	.056	.056
Nature of driving	steady wind and thermohaline	transient wind and thermohaline	steady wind and thermohaline	steady wind and thermohaline	steady wind and thermohaline	steady thermohaline only
Nature of solution	transient	transient	steady	steady	steady	steady
Depth	constant	variable	constant	constant	variable	variable

Integrating over a fixed volume; dividing by the surface area of the ocean, A_s; and defining $<>$ as $A_s^{-1} \iiint (\;) \, dV$ and E as $<e>$, we have

$$E_t = \frac{1}{A_s}\iint (e+p)V_n dS - <g\rho\omega> + <V\cdot F>$$
$$+\frac{1}{A_s}\iint V\cdot\tau^\omega \, dx\, dy - \frac{1}{A_s}\iint V\cdot\tau^b \, dx\, dy$$
$$-<\rho_0 K_m V_z\cdot V_z>. \tag{8}$$

The term on the left is the rate of change of kinetic energy per unit area per unit time (ergs/cm^2/s) and the terms on the right are the work done per unit area.

Let us now interpret the terms in Eq. (8). The total kinetic energy in a fixed region may be changed in several ways:

1. By the advection of kinetic energy into the region across the boundary (V_n = inward normal). Call this

$$A = \frac{1}{A_s}\iint eV_n \, dS. \tag{9}$$

This is a redistribution of the kinetic energy.

2. By the performance of work by pressure forces at the boundary as a consequence of flow across the boundary. This is represented by

$$G = \frac{1}{A_s}\iint pV_n \, dS. \tag{10}$$

This also is a redistribution of kinetic energy. Note that $A = G = 0$ for a closed region, that is, one that has no flow across the boundary.

3. By the performance of work done by the surface wind stress. Here the integral is taken over the area of the ocean's surface:

$$W = \frac{1}{A_s}\iint V\cdot\tau^\omega \, dx\, dy. \tag{11}$$

4. By the performance of work done by buoyancy forces in the interior of the fluid:

$$B = -<g\rho\omega>. \tag{12}$$

The kinetic energy will increase if ρ and ω are negatively correlated (ρ small in upward motion, large in downward motion) and will decrease if ρ and ω are positively correlated. This represents a conversion of potential to kinetic energy or vice versa.

5. By the loss of energy due to dissipation distributed throughout the fluid and due to work performed by tangential stresses at the lateral walls and bottom:

$$D = <V\cdot F> - <\rho_0 K_m V_z\cdot V_z>$$
$$-\frac{1}{A_s}\iint V\cdot\tau^b \, dx\, dy. \tag{13}$$

Now the general equation can be written

$$\frac{dE}{dt} = A + G + B + W + D. \tag{14}$$

If the volume integral is taken over a mechanically closed region (where the velocity component normal to the boundary is zero),

$$\frac{dE}{dt} = B + W + D. \tag{15}$$

It is useful to add one more degree of complexity to the energy diagram in order to describe another aspect of energy transformations that help clarify the results of various numerical experiments. Let the kinetic energy per unit area E be divided into two principal components,

$$\bar{E} = <\rho_0(\bar{V}\cdot\bar{V}/2>, \tag{16}$$

$$\hat{E} = <\rho_0(\hat{V}\cdot\hat{V})/2>, \tag{17}$$

where the overbar ($\bar{\;}$) and caret ($\hat{\;}$) indicate the vertical average and the deviation from the vertical average respectively. $\bar{E}$ and $\hat{E}$ will be referred to as the external and internal mode kinetic energies. The rate of change of $\bar{E}$ is obtained directly by averaging the equations of motion (1, 2, and 3) with respect to depth and forming the product $\rho_o\, \bar{V}\cdot\bar{V}_t$. Then

$$\bar{E}_t = N_e + B_e + W_e + D_e, \tag{18}$$

where

$$N_e = -<\rho_o\bar{V}\cdot\overline{(V\cdot\nabla V + \omega V_z)}>, \tag{19}$$

$$B_e = -<\bar{V}\cdot\overline{\nabla p}>, \tag{20}$$

$$W_e = \frac{1}{A_s}\iint (\bar{V}\cdot\tau^\omega) \, dx\, dy, \tag{21}$$

$$D_e = -\frac{1}{A_s}\iint (\bar{V}\cdot\tau^b) \, dx\, dy + <\bar{V}\cdot\bar{F}>. \tag{22}$$

These are respectively the work done per unit area on the external mode by the nonlinear terms, the pressure forces, the wind stress, and the dissipative forces.

The rate of change of $\hat{E}$ is obtained by subtracting Eq. (18) from Eq. (14),

$$\hat{E}_t = N_i + B_i + W_i + D_i, \qquad (23)$$

where

$$N_i = A - N_e, \qquad (24)$$

$$B_i = G + B - B_e, \qquad (25)$$

$$W_i = W - W_e, \qquad (26)$$

$$D_i = D - D_e. \qquad (27)$$

Because in a mechanically closed basin, $A = G = 0$,

$$N_e + N_i = 0, \qquad (28)$$

$$B_e + B_i = -<g\rho\omega> = B. \qquad (29)$$

Eq. (28) may be interpreted as a statement that the nonlinear advective terms provide an exchange of energy between the internal and external modes, but do not lead to a net increase in kinetic energy. Eq. (29) states that, in general, there is a conversion of potential energy to (or from) the kinetic energy of both the external and internal modes by the action of buoyancy forces. An important point to mention here, which will be dealt with more fully later, is that for a flat-bottom ocean, $B_e = 0$. This is easily shown because

$$B_e = -<\bar{V} \cdot \overline{\nabla p}> = -<\bar{V} \cdot \nabla \bar{p}> - <(\bar{p} - p_b)\, \bar{V} \cdot \nabla H/H>. \qquad (30)$$

The first term on the right is zero for a closed basin. The second term is zero if either the bottom is flat or the ocean is homogeneous. Thus, unless the ocean has variable density *and* variable topography, the link between potential and external mode kinetic energy is not present. The pressure forces can do work on the external mode only in the presence of variable depth.

An equation governing the rate of change of the potential energy of the system is derived by multiplying the density equation (6) by z [z is the depth that varies from $-H(\lambda, \theta)$ at the bottom to zero at the top] to find

$$\phi_t + V \cdot \nabla \phi + \omega\phi_z - g\rho\omega = \frac{K_h}{\delta} gz\rho_{zz} + A_H \nabla^2 \phi, \qquad (31)$$

where $\phi = g\rho z$. Letting $P = <\phi>$, integrating Eq. (31) over the volume, and dividing by the ocean surface area,

$$P_t = -<V \cdot \nabla \phi + \omega\phi_z> + <g\rho\omega> + <\frac{K_H}{\delta} gz\rho_{zz} + A_h \nabla^2 \phi> \qquad (32)$$

or

$$\frac{dP}{dt} = Q - B + M, \qquad (33)$$

where $Q = -<V \cdot \nabla\phi + \omega\phi_z>$ is the advection of potential energy. If the volume integration is taken over a mechanically closed region, the first term on the right vanishes and Eq. (33) can be written

$$\frac{dP}{dt} = -B + M. \qquad (34)$$

Here B is the work done per unit area by buoyancy forces and M is the work done per unit area by eddy-mixing processes:

$$M = <\frac{K_h}{\delta} gz\, \rho_{zz} + A_h \nabla^2 \phi>. \qquad (35)$$

Note that M includes horizontal and vertical diffusive effects, as well as the convective-mixing process that occurs when fluid columns tend to become statically unstable.

Eqs. (15) and (34) describe the rates of change of kinetic and potential energies per unit area of ocean surface for a closed system. The importance of the work done by buoyancy forces (B) is apparent. It describes the conversion of potential to kinetic energy or vice versa. The other terms describe the rates at which work is done by stresses and by diffusive mixing on the boundaries and in the interior of the ocean.

ENERGETIC BALANCES

Let us now discuss the energetic balances for the various experiments listed in Table 1. It will be convenient to discuss them according to their fundamental physical characteristics (and increasing complexity) rather than in the order in which they were done.

Constant Depth Oceans with Steady Driving

We will first examine the cases where the ocean is of constant depth and is driven by wind stress and surface density distributions that are steady. Figure 1 shows the energy diagrams for two experiments by Holland in Table 1. The arrows indicate the direction of energy flow. The values show the magnitudes of work performed per unit area in units of ergs/cm^2/s. These experiments describe the behavior of an ocean where the inertial terms are not important, as measured

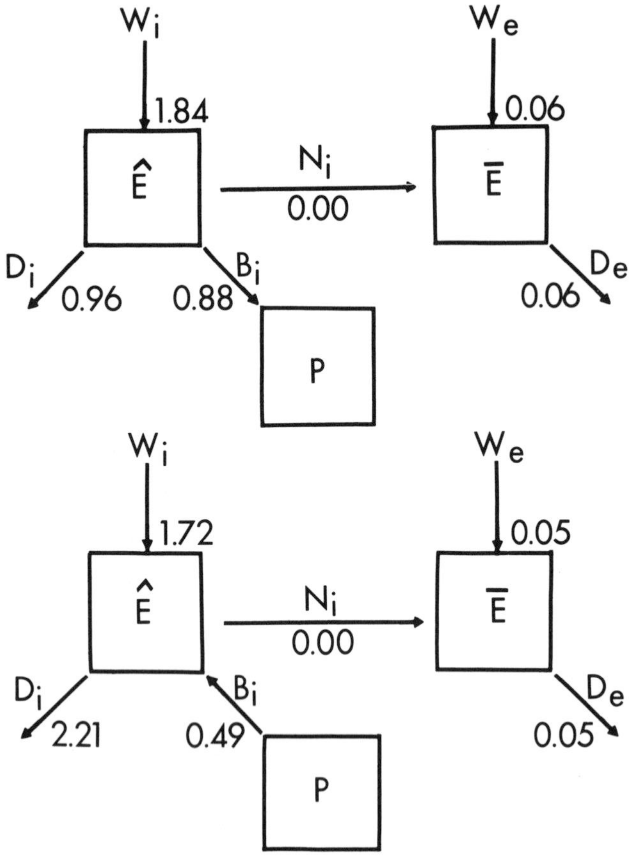

FIGURE 1 Energy diagrams showing the magnitude and direction of the work done per unit area of the ocean's surface (in units ergs/cm^2/s). In the first case, $L_F/L_M = 0.36$, and in the second, $L_F/L_M = 2.3$. The eddy Prandtl numbers ($A_M/A_H = Pe/Re$) are 10 and 100, respectively. These experiments correspond to the third and fourth columns in Table 1.

by the fact that $L_I \ll L_F$. Thus, the energy conversion term, N, which describes the transfer from internal to external mode kinetic energy, is very small. Because the ocean depth is constant, the pressure forces do no net work on the external mode ($B_e = 0$). Thus, the energy $\bar{E}$ is isolated from the energy pool, $\hat{E} + P$. The external mode is driven by the wind alone, and the energy of the wind is dissipated there. As far as the external mode is concerned, thermohaline processes play no important role in viscous, constant-depth oceans.

There is an important difference between these two experiments. In the first case, buoyancy forces act to transfer energy from the internal mode kinetic energy to the potential energy of the system. Thus, the wind does work to maintain the density configuration. In the other case, the result is reversed; potential energy is converted into kinetic energy of the system. As shown in Table 1, these experiments differ in the ratio of L_F/L_M. In the first case it is 0.36; in the second, 2.3. Another way of stating this is that these experiments have different eddy Prandtl numbers, A_M/A_H. In the first case, lateral heat diffusion is important in the western boundary current, and, in the second case, the boundary layer is dominated by the diffusion of momentum. The sign of the net work by the buoyancy forces depends upon the details of the boundary layer, and energetic considerations suggest there is an important transition in behavior near $L_F/L_M = 1$ (at least when $L_I \ll L_F$).

The computation by Bryan and Cox (1968) gives an example of the nature of the energetic processes for a different parameter range. In this case, the external parameters have been chosen to give an artificially large Rossby number so that inertial effects would be important. Thus, in this case $L_I/L_F > 1$, while L_M is relatively small. Although the wind and thermohaline driving are steady, the solution contains transient eddies that presumably are due to a physical instability of some kind. It would be of interest to compile the energetics of these eddies to determine if their energy source is the potential energy of the mean flow, that is, whether the eddies are due to baroclinic instability like cyclone waves in the atmosphere. This has not been done here. Instead, we will consider only the energetic properties of the flow averaged over a certain period of time [see Bryan and Cox (1968) for a discussion of these transients and of the averaged solution].

Figure 2 shows a diagram describing the energy flow. B_e is zero, because the ocean has constant depth. But, in this case, there is an important link between the energy pool $\hat{E} + P$ and $\bar{E}$, because of the nonlinear terms, N. Seventy percent of the energy input to the external mode is by way of nonlinear processes, and only 30 percent is due to work done directly by the wind. In this case, the buoyancy forces transfer energy from potential to kinetic energy, $L_m < L_f$; and the buoyancy forces are almost as effective quantitatively as the surface wind stress in creating net kinetic energy.

Variable-Depth Oceans with Steady Driving

In a series of experiments, Holland (1973) examined the effect of bottom topography on the horizontal mass transport in oceans driven by both wind and thermohaline processes. The results suggest that in a baroclinic ocean with variable depth, the transport in the western boundary current may be enhanced over that found when the ocean floor is flat or the density is constant. In terms of vorticity arguments, it was shown that the bottom-pressure torque term in the vorticity equation for the vertically averaged flow puts in vorticity of the same sign as the wind stress curl in the subtropical gyre. The energetics of those experiments will be examined to get at the fundamental causes of the enhancement.

Figure 3 shows energetic diagrams for three cases: a baroclinic ocean of constant depth [Holland (1971) in

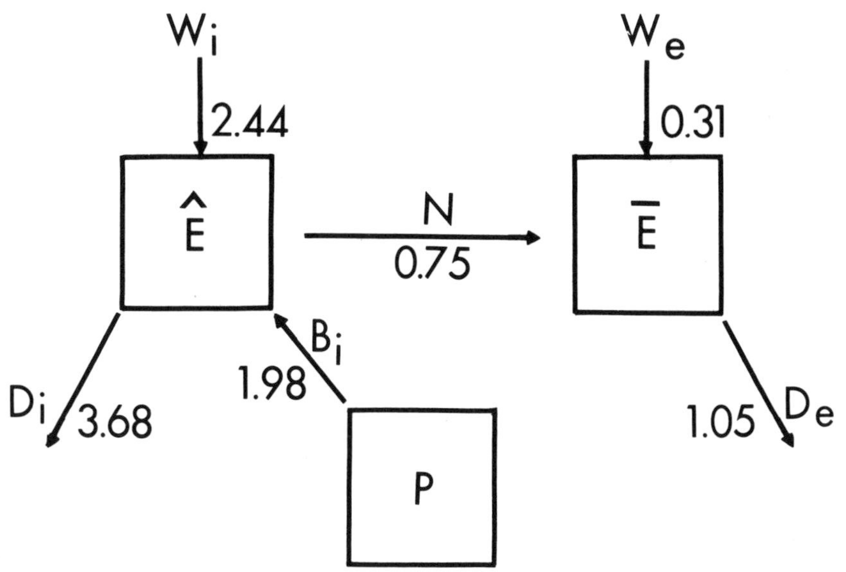

FIGURE 2 Energy diagram showing the magnitude and direction of the work done per unit area of the ocean's surface ($ergs/cm^2/s$) for the large Rossby number case (column one in Table 1). The inertial boundary width, L_I, is greater than the frictional width, L_F.

Table 1], a homogeneous ocean with variable depth (not shown in Table 1), and a baroclinic ocean with variable depth [Holland (1973) in Table 1]. In the first of these, B_e is zero because the depth is constant; the energy of the external mode is maintained by direct wind driving only. $\bar{E}$ is calculated to be 1.7×10^4 $ergs/cm^2$. In the second case, the density is constant so B_e is again zero. In this case, $\bar{E}$ is 1.1×10^4 $ergs/cm^2$. In the baroclinic case with variable topography, B_e is not zero and supplies energy to the external mode at a rate of 0.71 $ergs/cm^2/s$, a factor of five larger than the direct work on the external mode by the wind stress. The average kinetic energy of the external mode, $\bar{E}$, is 2.0×10^5 $ergs/cm^2$. The total kinetic energy ($\hat{E} + \bar{E}$) is 3.7×10^5 $ergs/cm^2$, compared to a value of 2.6 $\times$ 10^5 $ergs/cm^2$ for the flat-bottom case. These results show why topography can play such an important role in the dynamics of steady ocean currents: The pressure forces in a variable-depth ocean can redistribute energy so that the external mode receives energy from potential and internal mode kinetic energy.

A fourth experiment (the last column in Table 1) allows us to discuss the question of wind versus thermohaline driving. The wind driving has been set at zero; in other respects the experiment is identical to the third case discussed above. Figure 4 shows the energetic results for these two cases. When there is no wind, work is done on the internal mode by the pressure forces (as it must be, because there is no other energy source for the internal mode). In the wind-driven case, the energy flux is in the opposite direction. Thus the relative strengths of driving by wind and thermohaline effects, as measured by the parameter γ, is an important parameter in governing the energetics. Note that the energetics of the external mode are relatively insensitive to the action of the wind. If the depth is variable, the external mode can be quite vigorous without wind driving.

The time scales suggested by the work and energy values found in these experiments are of interest. If the external driving by wind and thermohaline processes were turned off in the constant depth ocean (column 3, Table 1), the kinetic energy of the external mode would be dissipated in a time

$$\bar{E}/D_e = \frac{1.7 \times 10^4 \text{ ergs/cm}^2}{0.06 \text{ ergs/cm}^2/\text{s}} = 3.3 \text{ days.}$$

Because there are no other energy inputs (B_e equals zero and N_i is very small), the energy would be dissipated very rapidly. If the external driving by wind and thermohaline processes were turned off in the variable depth ocean (column 5, Table 1), the external mode would still be driven by the energy flux, B_e. Thus, before the external mode kinetic energy could be entirely dissipated, the energy stored in the potential energy field would have to be dissipated as well. Estimating the available potential energy as $\langle(\rho - \rho_m)gz\rangle$, where ρ_m is the averaged density, we find for Holland's (1973) experiment that $P = 5.2 \times 10^7$ $ergs/cm^2$. Thus, the relevant dissipation time scale is

$$\frac{P+E}{D_e} = \frac{5.2 \times 10^7 \text{ ergs/cm}^2}{0.84 \text{ ergs/cm}^2/\text{s}} = 720 \text{ days.}$$

Stommel (1960) estimated that the potential energy stored in the Noth Atlantic is sufficient to maintain the current system for 1,700 days in the absence of the driving stress of the winds.

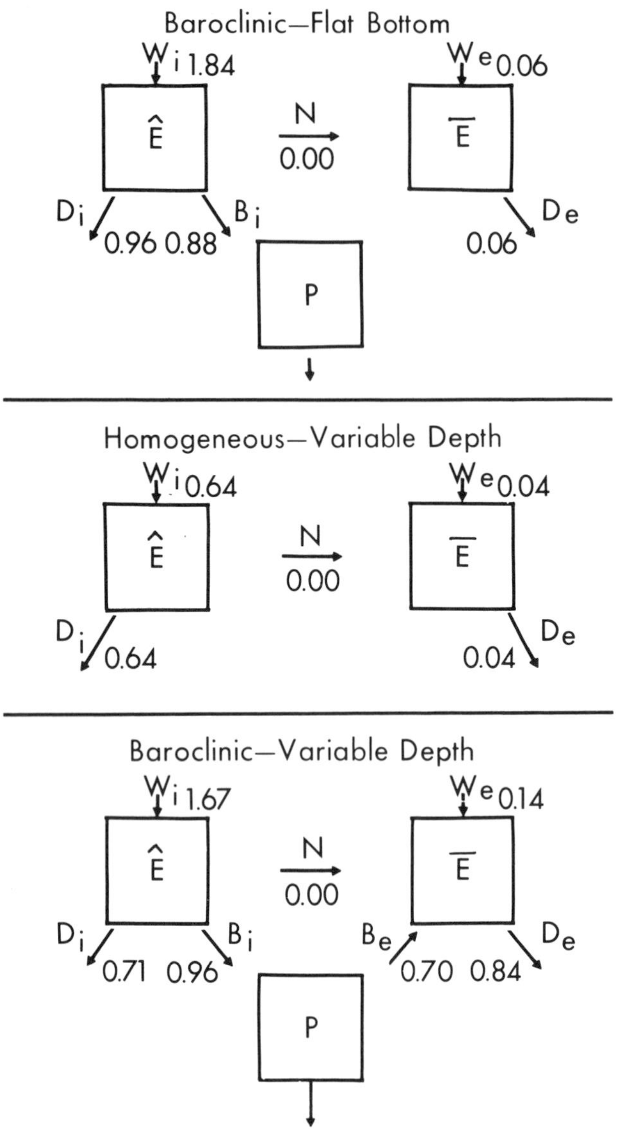

FIGURE 3 A comparison of the energetics for cases with and without variable bottom topography. There are three cases: (a) a baroclinic ocean of constant depth (column three in Table 1), (b) a homogeneous ocean of variable depth (not shown in Table 1), and (c) a baroclinic ocean with variable depth (column five in Table 1). Note that the work done by pressure forces on the external mode, B_e, is identically zero for (a) and (b).

Time-Dependent Driving—The Indian Ocean

In most of the three-dimensional numerical experiments that have been performed, the driving by wind and thermohaline processes has been steady. Depending on the parameters, the solution may either (a) reach a steady state, or (b) reach a state where various transient eddies are a naturally occurring phenomenon. These cases are treated above. We shall now consider the experiment by Cox (1970), where the Indian Ocean is driven by seasonal wind and thermohaline driving associated with the monsoons.

Cox's experiment was carried out by spinning up the ocean in three stages with successively finer grids (4°, 2°, 1° horizontal resolutions). The final stage of the computation, with 1° horizontal resolution, was run for 7 years of ocean time to allow transients associated with initial conditions and changes in grid size to die out. However, there were still some adjustments occurring when the experiment was concluded. We shall examine the time-dependent behavior associated with the final 15 months of the experiment (January, year 192, to March, year 193) although data needed to calculate the potential energy was available only for the period April, year 192, through March, year 193. The picture of the annually averaged energetics is based upon the final complete year, January-December, year 192.

The various terms describing the work done on this portion of the Indian Ocean as a function of time of year are shown in Figure 5. The total kinetic and potential energies per unit area are also shown. *P* is defined here only to within an arbitrary constant, and only the variation with time and not the absolute magnitude is significant. The total available potential energy, as mentioned earlier, is several orders of magnitude greater than the kinetic energy. The left and middle panels of Figure 5 show the various rates at which

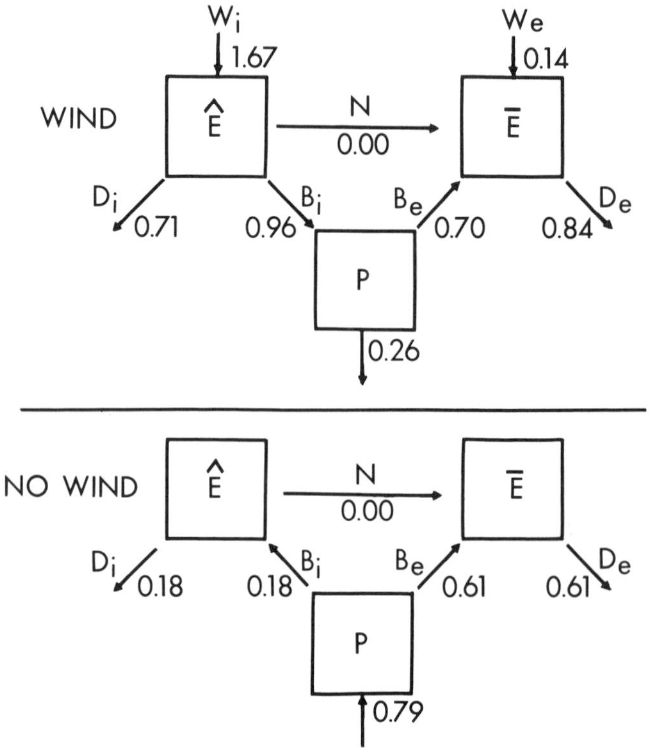

FIGURE 4 A comparison of the energetics for cases with and without wind driving. These oceans have variable depth and correspond to experiments five and six in Table 1.

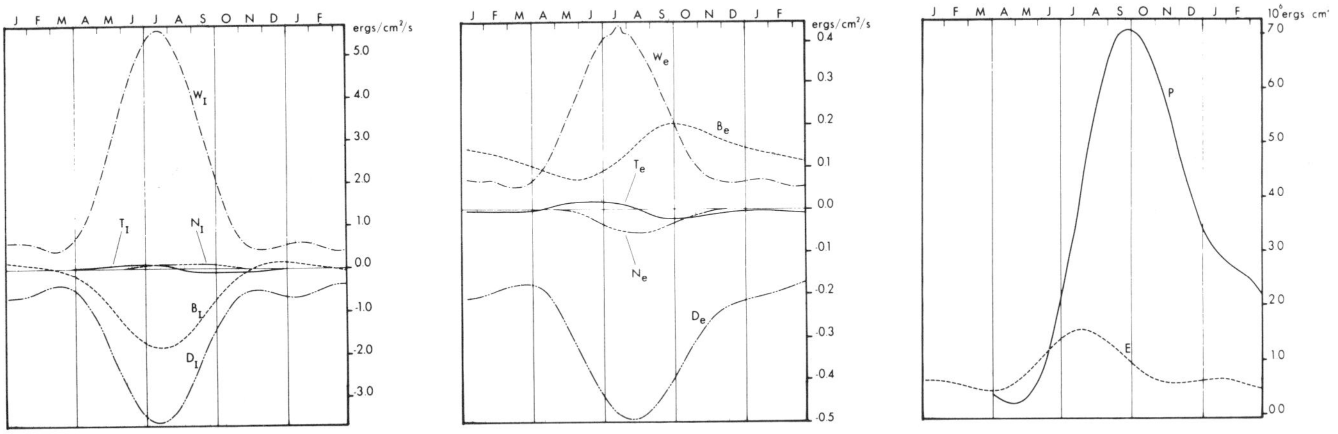

FIGURE 5 The energetics of the Indian Ocean. Left: the work done per unit area on the internal mode by wind (W_i), pressure forces (B_i), advection terms (N_i), and dissipation (D_i). The sum of these gives the time rate of change of internal mode kinetic energy ($T_i = E_t$). Middle: the work done per unit area on the external mode. Right: the time-dependent behavior of the total kinetic and potential energies, E and P. The letters on the top denote months of the year.

work is done. The time rate of change term, T, for the internal and external mode kinetic energies is also shown. The seasonal behavior of these energy fluxes shows the nature of the response to the monsoon winds. With the onset of the southwest monsoons in April, the wind driving begins to increase and reaches a maximum value in mid-July. By November it has decreased to its winter minimum value. The internal mode response shows that the dissipation, D_i, and the work done by pressure forces, B_i, are very nearly in phase with the wind driving, W_i, and almost balance it. The sum ($T_i = W_i + B_i + N_i + D_i$) indicates, however, that the internal mode kinetic energy increases from April through July and decreases from August until December. The rate of change of external mode kinetic energy, T_e, shows similar behavior; and the two together result in the time dependence of the total kinetic energy, E, in the right-hand panel of Figure 5.

The maximum in the external mode dissipation term, D_e, lags about 2 weeks behind the maximum in the wind driving, W_e. The work per unit area by the pressure forces, B_e, is out of phase with the wind driving, reaching a peak in late September. During the winter months, it provides the major input to the maintenance of the kinetic energy of the external mode. Because B_e and B_i are both positive during the winter, the kinetic energy of the entire ocean is maintained at that time by the available potential energy stored in the density field.

This computation is not carried out for a mechanically closed basin. The southern boundary is an open one, and Eqs. (18), (23), and (33) are the relevant energy equations. Thus there are contributions to the rate of change of total kinetic energy as a consequence of (a) the advection of kinetic energy into the basin across the southern boundary [terms A, Eq. (14)], and (b) the performance of work by pressure forces at the southern boundary as a consequence of flow across it [term G, Eq. (14)]. Similarly, the advection of potential energy, Q, in Eq. (33) must be taken into account. Figure 6 shows the energy diagram for the annually averaged energy fluxes. The external mode kinetic energy is maintained almost equally by wind work (0.18 ergs/cm^2/s) and by the pressure forces (0.13 ergs/cm^2/s). The nonlinear terms, N_e and N_i, are quite small and do not balance as they did in closed basins. This is the result of a very small loss of kinetic energy because of advection (A) across the southern boundary. There is also a net loss of total kinetic energy by pressure forces, $B_e + B_i$. Part of this goes into work by buoyancy forces (B) and part into work by pressure forces as a result of flow across the southern boundary (G). The energy fluxes G, B, and Q are quite large because, for an ocean with an open boundary, there can be a net vertical flux of water that is replaced by lateral flow through the boundary.

CONCLUSIONS

The energetics of the large-scale ocean circulation has received little attention in the past, because observations are not available to compute the various components of the energetic cycle. The development of numerical models, however, allows us to perform controlled experiments where the energetic terms can be computed and examined in various ways. Such a process is a useful way of understanding these numerical oceans (if not the real one), and it is possible to develop a deeper insight into the results than can be gotten by examining the velocity, temperature, and salinity fields themselves.

The several results pointed out in previous sections confirm the usefulness of looking at the experiments from the energetic point of view. For instance, the fundamental causes of the enhanced mass transport, when the Rossby number is large or when variable bottom topography is

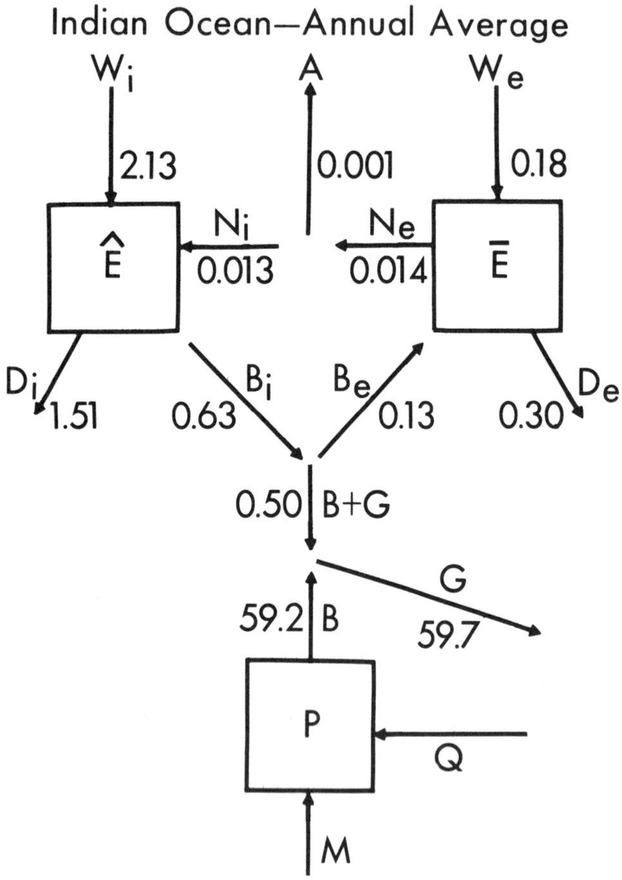

FIGURE 6 The annually averaged work done per unit area on the Indian Ocean (ergs/cm²/s). Note that since this ocean has an open southern boundary, three additional energy fluxes arise. These are due to (a) the advection of kinetic energy into the basin (*A*), (b) the work done by pressure forces as a result of flow across the southern boundary (*G*), and (c) the advection of potential energy into the basin (*Q*).

taken into account, are apparent. Work is done on the external mode in addition to that by the wind, in the first case by nonlinear processes and in the second by pressure forces. Similarly, the seasonal calculation for the Indian Ocean suggests some intriguing questions regarding the possibility that wind energy is stored in the density field ($B_e + B_i < 0$) during part of the year and is released ($B_e + B_i > 0$) during periods when the wind is too weak to maintain the circulation.

It is necessary that oceanographers eventually move away from the strong dependence of results upon the eddy viscosity hypotheses and allow the fluid to determine its own eddy mixing of momentum and other properties. This can be done through the development of models that explicitly treat transient eddies in much the same way that atmospheric models do today. Since energetic considerations have played such a fundamental role in developing an understanding of such atmospheric processes, it is useful for us to begin to lay the foundation for similar studies of the oceanic circulation.

REFERENCES

Bryan, K. 1969. A numerical method for the study of ocean circulation. J. Comput. Phys. 4:347–76.

Bryan, K., and M. D. Cox. 1968. A nonlinear model of an ocean driven by wind and differential heating. Parts I and II. J. Atmos. Sci. 25:945–78.

Cox, M. D. 1970. A mathematical model of the Indian Ocean. Deep-Sea Res. 17:47–75.

Gill, A. E., and K. Bryan. 1971. Effects of geometry on the circulation of a three-dimensional Southern Hemisphere ocean model. Deep-Sea Res. 18:685–721.

Holland, W. R. 1971. Ocean tracer distributions. Part I. Tellus 23: 371–92.

Holland, W. R. 1973. Baroclinic and topographic influences on the transport in western boundary currents. Geophys. Fluid Dyn. 187–210.

Stommel, H. 1960. The Gulf Stream. University of California Press, Berkeley. 202 pp.

DISCUSSION

KAMENKOVICH: I think that these results have very important discrepancies with earlier results concerning the joint effect of baroclinicity and bottom relief.

BRETHERTON: I'm sorry to keep hammering at it, but if you look at those figures, am I mistaken, do they not indicate an rms velocity of 1.5 mm/s?

HOLLAND: Yes, I think they do.

BRETHERTON: In contrast with the observed kinetic energies of 5 and 10 cm/s.

HOLLAND: For the transient processes.

BRETHERTON: The transient processes have an energy level that is several hundred times larger than those figures.

HOLLAND: I agree with what you're saying, but that is not the point that the model is addressing.

RATTRAY: Two comments. First, the split-up into barotropic and baroclinic is wave-like here; both of them have velocities at the bottom, as opposed to the steady-state breakup of Fofonoff. Secondly, bottom velocity or flow over ridges often give rise to energetic, standing wave patterns. It has also been shown that there's a tendency for concentration along the western boundary. I wonder if some of this can be interpreted in terms of standing baroclinic and barotropic Rossby waves in this region where lines of f/h are skewed because of the bottom slope in the boundary region. Obviously there would be more energy in the model if you had standing waves present.

HOLLAND: I can't say offhand.

ROBINSON: I think this kind of study is particularly important in that it uses simulated data, provided by big numerical models to explore processes that happen under different parametric assumptions. In this way, the results do contribute towards an ultimate understanding of the ocean circulation. It is a very appropriate way to use the data that's generated in these numerical experiments, perhaps even more useful at this time than a direct comparison with field data. We learn a lot by this kind of in-depth analysis.

V MODELING OF TRANSIENT OR INTERMEDIATE SCALE PHENOMENA

MODELS OF EQUATORIAL CURRENTS

A. E. GILL

BASIC IDEAS

The most striking feature of the ocean current system in the tropics is the equatorial undercurrent. This is a strong, shallow, subsurface current that runs eastward along the equator. It has a half-width of 100 km, a half-depth of 100 m, and a maximum current of 1 m s^{-1}. It appears to be a permanent feature in the Atlantic and Pacific Oceans, but is only present part of the time in the Indian Ocean because of the variation in wind direction with the coming and going of the monsoon. Figure 1 shows some sections across the current and the associated thermal structure. A compilation of data by Tsuchiya (1968) shows the relationship of the undercurrent in the Pacific with other features.

There are two main physical ideas about this current. The first (Fofonoff and Montgomery, 1955; Veronis, 1960) is simply that the ocean surface tilts in response to the wind so that (Figure 2) the force (westward) of the wind on the surface is opposed by the difference in pressure forces acting on the eastern and western ends. Since the ocean is stratified, the pressure gradient is taken up almost entirely in the upper layers. Thus, as the surface tilts upward towards the west, isopycnals near the surface tilt upwards towards the east, while deeper isopycnals are hardly affected. Figure 3 (from Lemasson and Piton, 1968) shows these effects in a section along the equator in the Pacific. Away from the equator, such a pressure gradient would be balanced geostrophically by a flow toward the equator. At the equator itself, however, the Coriolis parameter vanishes; and so the fluid simply flows down the pressure gradient, giving the observed eastward flow.

The wind drag (westward) on the surface creates a region of strong shear above the undercurrent. The surface current is always strongly westward relative to the undercurrent and usually (but not always) westward relative to the earth.

The second basic idea (Cromwell, 1953) has to do with the associated meridional circulation. The westward wind produces an Ekman flux, which is directed away from the equator. At the same time, the pressure gradient set up in response to the wind produces a geostrophic flow towards the equator below the surface. Thus, the region close to the equator may be expected to be one of strong upwelling. Cromwell (1953) and Knauss (1966) discussed indirect evidence for this feature. More recently, Taft and Jones (1973) have reported an instance where direct measurements of surface divergence were consistent with Ekman theory and calculated that an upwelling velocity of 10^{-4} m s^{-1} (10 m/day) was required to balance the observed surface-layer divergence.

Very simple models can show the above two basic features. However, it is very much more difficult to obtain a model that can be directly related to observation because of the many effects, such as inertia and stratification, which are known to be important. Also, if the origin of the water in the undercurrent is in question, it needs to be studied in terms of an extensive three-dimensional model. There are also more fundamental questions. What process limits the flow down the pressure gradient? One would like to model the turbulence better than by imposing a friction coefficient. Also, the meridional circulation brings up heavy water and tends to force it over lighter water. What mixing processes occur to keep the system gravitationally stable?

LINEAR MODELS FOR A HOMOGENEOUS OCEAN

The two basic ideas introduced in the previous section can be illustrated by simple linear models for a homogeneous ocean. These have the virtue of showing the flow down the pressure gradient and the meridional circulation in a straight-

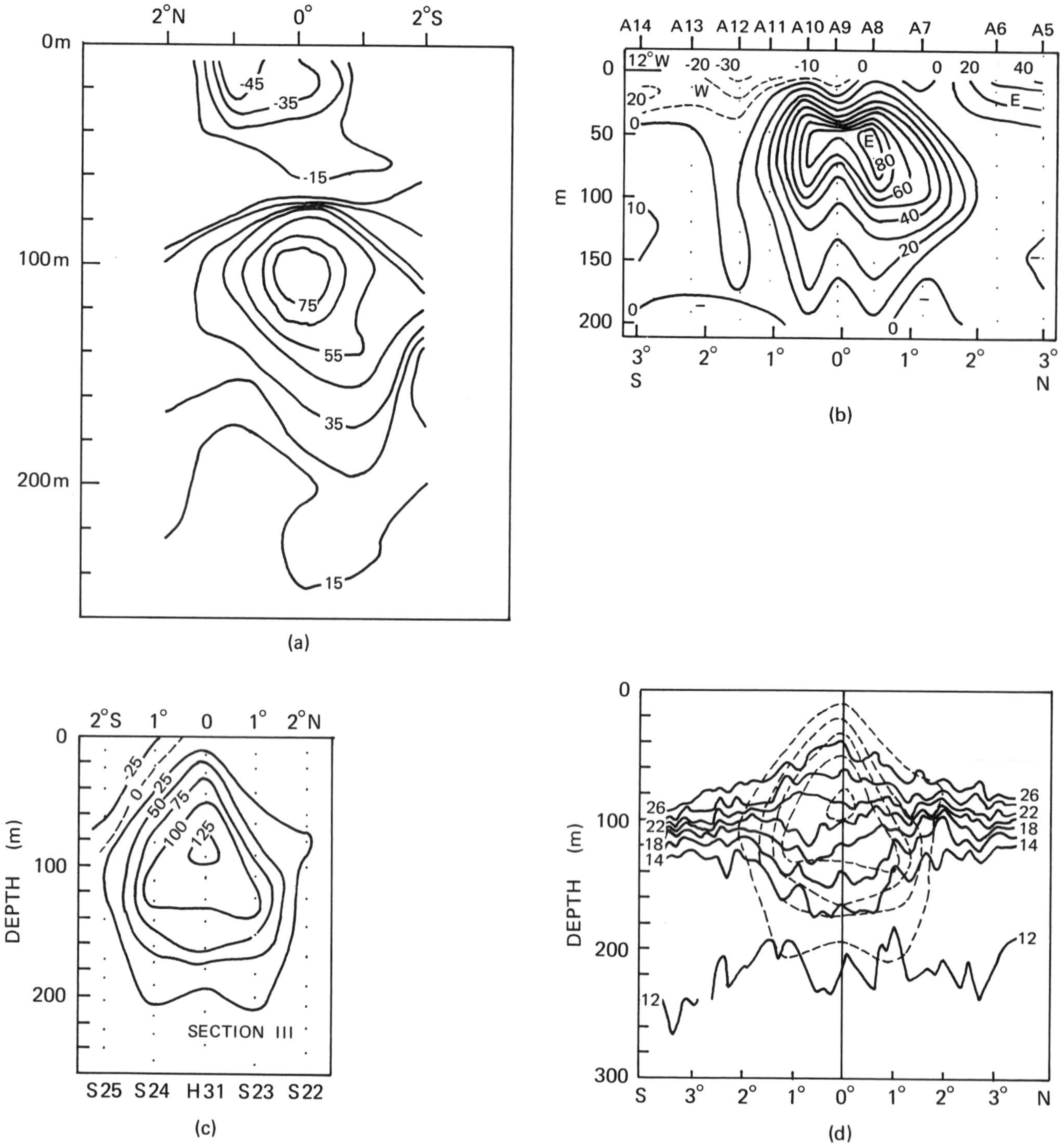

FIGURE 1 Meridional sections of eastward velocity in cm s^{-1} in (a) the Indian Ocean at 92° E (from Taft, 1967); (b) the Atlantic Ocean at 12° W (from Sturm and Voigt, 1966); and (c) the Pacific Ocean at 140° W (from Knauss, 1960). (d) the velocity contours from (c) superimposed on temperature contours for the same section (from Knauss, 1960).

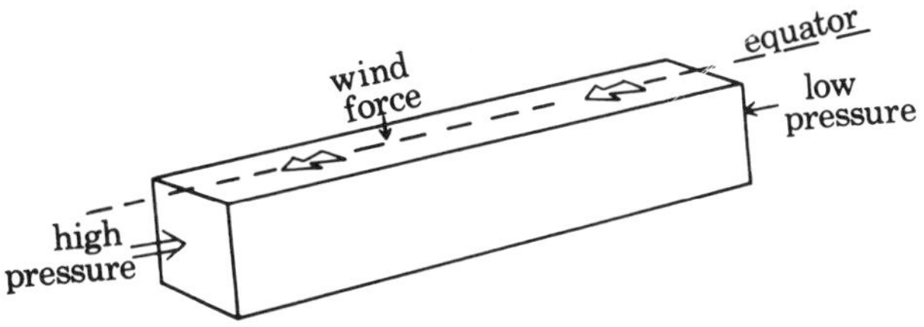

FIGURE 2 A sketch showing how the equatorial undercurrent is driven. At the equator, the force of the wind on the surface is balanced by the difference in pressure forces on the two ends. The undercurrent is directly driven by the resulting pressure gradient.

forward way, thus giving an insight into the physics of the more complicated situation that is observed. Stommel (1960) was the first to propose such a model, the process limiting the flow down the pressure gradient in his model being vertical friction; the eddy viscosity coefficient, ν, being taken as a constant. Because Ekman's solution for the surface layer breaks down at the equator, a singularity might be expected there; but Stommel showed that, for an ocean of finite depth, no such singularity exists. In fact, since there is no lateral friction, the solution at the equator is independent of the solution elsewhere. The velocity profile is simply the parabolic profile (see Figure 4) obtained for flow in a (nonrotating) channel with a wind stress pushing one way and a pressure gradient opposing. Stommel worked out the solution for zero stress at the bottom, the latter being identified with the thermocline rather than the bottom of the ocean.

Felsenbaum and Shapiro (1966) calculated the solution for a complete ocean basin with no slip allowed at the bottom; Muzylev and Felsenbaum (1970), Korotaev (1970), and Philander (1971) have developed the theory for this case in the limit of vanishing friction. In this limit, the solution does *not* give an undercurrent at the equator; and bottom friction plays an important role in determining details of the solution.

Another simple model (Hidaka, 1961; Gill, 1971a) is obtained if lateral friction is assumed to be the process limiting the flow down the pressure gradient. If the lateral eddy viscosity (A) is large enough, the Ekman layer does not extend to the bottom at the equator, as in Stommel's solution, the singularity at the equator being avoided because of the lateral friction effects. The fluxes in the Ekman layer and the flow below can be found analytically. The variation, below the Ekman layer (u, v, w) with latitude is shown in Figure 5. An interesting property of this solution is that the transport of the undercurrent is independent of A and given by

$$\text{mass transport of undercurrent} = -\pi\tau^x/\beta, \qquad (1)$$

where τ^x is the wind stress, $\beta = 2\Omega/a$ is the rate of change of the Coriolis parameter with latitude, Ω is the earth's rotation rate, and a is the earth's radius. An order of magnitude calculation shows that the transport of the undercurrent in Stommel's model is also proportional to τ^x/β. Eq. (1) underestimates the transport of the undercurrent by a factor of around five; but, as will be discussed later, nonlinear effects can account for this discrepancy.

An even simpler model has been suggested by McKee (private communication, 1971). In this, the flow down the pressure gradient is limited by a (rather peculiar) body friction proportional to the local velocity. This model is so simple and illuminating that it is worth giving details. Let x, y, and z be coordinates such that x measures distance eastwards; y, the distance northwards from the equator; and z, distance upwards from the ocean surface; and u, v, and w are the corresponding velocity components. The equations (cf., Mikhailova and Shapiro, 1970) of the model are

$$-\beta y v = -p_x + \nu u_{zz} - ru, \qquad (2)$$

$$\beta y u = -p_y + \nu v_{zz} - rv, \qquad (3)$$

$$u_x + v_y + w_z = 0, \qquad (4)$$

where r is a constant and the pressure gradient p_x, p_y is independent of depth. The boundary conditions are

$$\nu u_z = \tau^x, \quad \nu v_z = \tau^y \quad \text{at} \quad z = 0, \qquad (5)$$

and the stresses νu_z and νv_z are assumed to vanish below the Ekman layer, whose thickness is assumed to be much less than the depth, H.

The vertical integral of Eq. (4) allows the introduction of a stream function, ψ, such that

$$\int_{-H}^{0} u\, dz = -\psi_y, \quad \int_{-H}^{0} v\, dz = \psi_x. \qquad (6)$$

Elimination of pressure from the vertically integrated equation leads to Stommel's (personal communication) equation for the stream function, that is

$$r(\psi_{xx} + \psi_{yy}) + \beta\psi_x = \tau_x{}^y - \tau_y{}^x. \qquad (7)$$

This has no singularity or special behavior at the equator; and since the wind stress varies on a large scale compared with the undercurrent, the first-order local behavior can be obtained by taking τ^x, τ^y to be a constant and so the solution of Eq. (7) is

$$\psi = 0. \qquad (8)$$

The corresponding solution for the pressure gradient is

$$Hp_x = \tau^x, \quad Hp_y = \tau^y. \qquad (9)$$

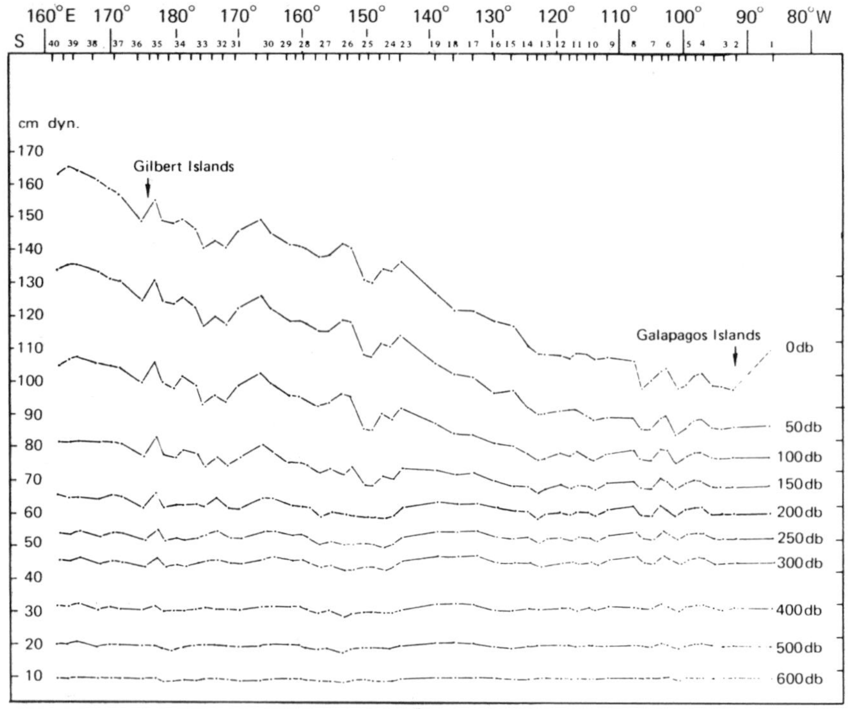

a.

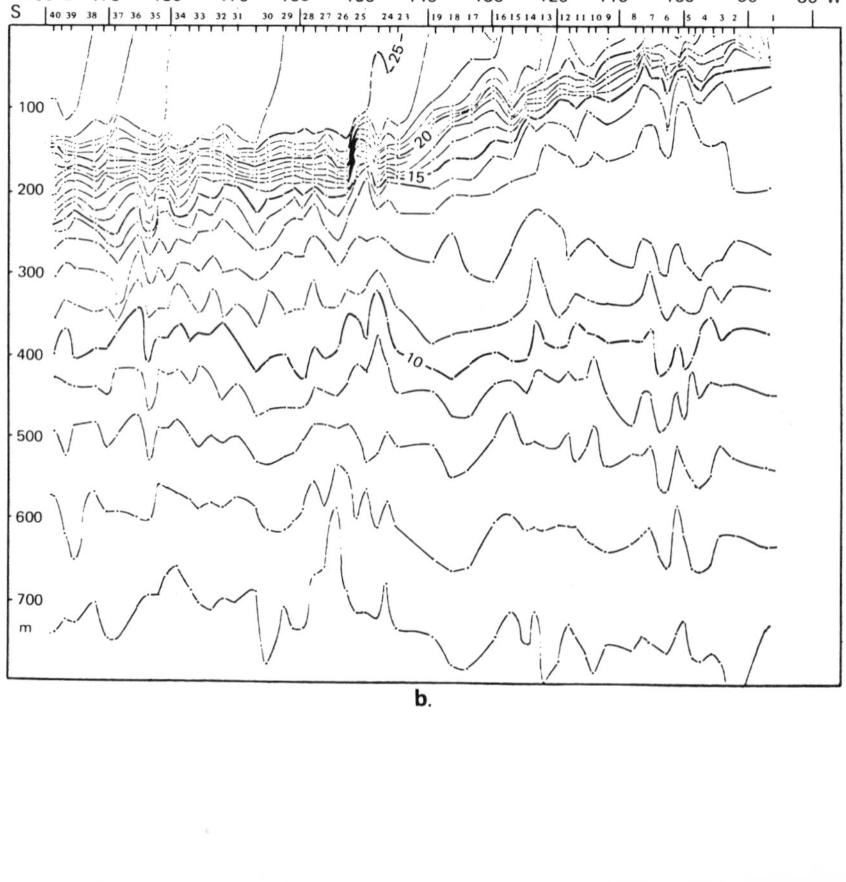

b.

FIGURE 3 (a) Variation of dynamic height, relative to 700 decibars, along the equator in the Pacific Ocean. The pressure decreases toward the west, the pressure gradient being confined to the upper 200 m (from Lemasson and Piton, 1968). (b) Temperature distribution along the same section (from Lemasson and Piton, 1968). The upward tilt of the thermocline toward the west is associated with the pressure gradient. The tilt of the thermocline is seen to result in a thick surface-mixed layer toward the west, and a thick layer of "13° water" under the thermocline toward the east.

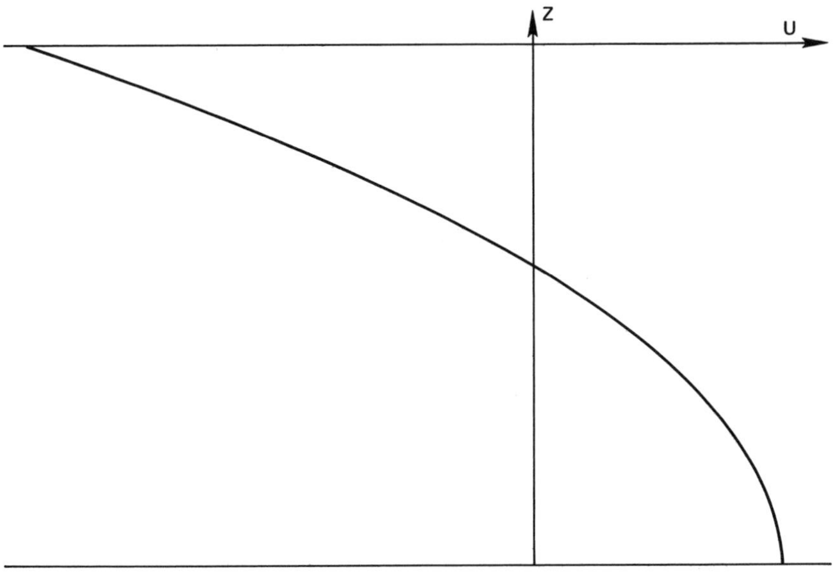

FIGURE 4 Vertical profile of eastward velocity at the equator obtained in Stommel's (1960) linear model.

Below the Ekman layer, the terms νu_{zz} and νv_{zz} in Eqs. (2-3) vanish. So, using Eq. (9) for the pressure gradient, it follows that the velocity (u,v) of the undercurrent satisfies

$$-\beta y v = -\tau^x/H - ru, \tag{10}$$

and

$$\beta y u = \tau^y/H - rv. \tag{11}$$

Solving for u, v gives

$$u = \frac{-r\tau^x - \beta y \tau^y}{H(r^2 + \beta^2 y^2)}, \qquad v = \frac{\beta y \tau^x - r\tau^y}{H(r^2 + \beta^2 y^2)}. \tag{12}$$

By continuity, the vertical velocity below the Ekman layer is given by

$$w = -\left(\frac{z+H}{H}\right) \cdot \frac{\beta(r^2 - \beta^2 y^2)\tau^x + 2r\beta^2 y \tau^y}{(r^2 + \beta^2 y^2)^2}. \tag{13}$$

These solutions are useful in indicating the type of flow that occurs for winds from different directions; e.g., for a wind from the southeast, the undercurrent at the equator flows down the pressure gradient towards the southeast (see Figure 6). The maximum value of u is south of the equator, because the geostrophic current associated with high pressure to the north enhances the current there. The maximum value of w is also south of the equator, because the Ekman flux at the equator is downwind; i.e., it has a northward component, which enhances the divergence to the south. The same effect is found in nonlinear models, e.g., Charney and Spiegel (1971). For variables τ^x and τ^y, the above type of solution represents only the local behavior relative to the larger-scale circulation, obtained by solving Eq. (7). For instance, if the large-scale circulation gives rise to a westward flow near the equator, the undercurrent will appear to be weaker.

Another property of the linear homogeneous-ocean models is their simple behavior at the eastern and western edges of the basin. For the models with no bottom friction, there is a boundary layer in which the flow in the equatorial plane adjusts; e.g., at the eastern end there is upwelling so that water from the undercurrent rises and returns in the westward flow nearer the surface. In the lateral friction model, this boundary layer has the same thickness as the undercurrent (Gill, 1971b).

NONLINEAR EFFECTS FOR A HOMOGENEOUS OCEAN

Knauss (1966) has shown from observations that nonlinear effects in the undercurrent are important. For instance, he

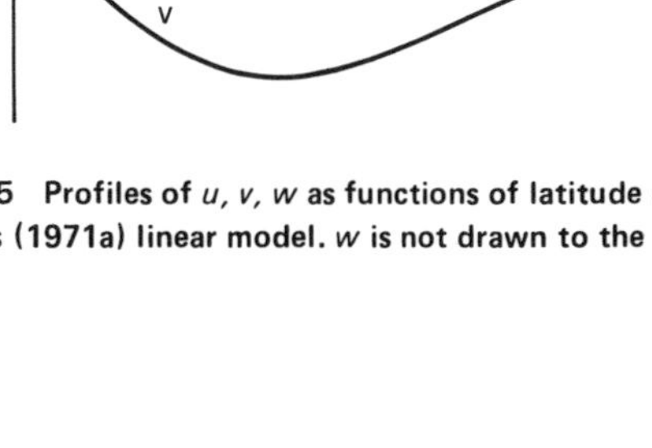

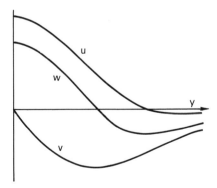

FIGURE 5 Profiles of u, v, w as functions of latitude obtained from Gill's (1971a) linear model. w is not drawn to the same scale as u and v.

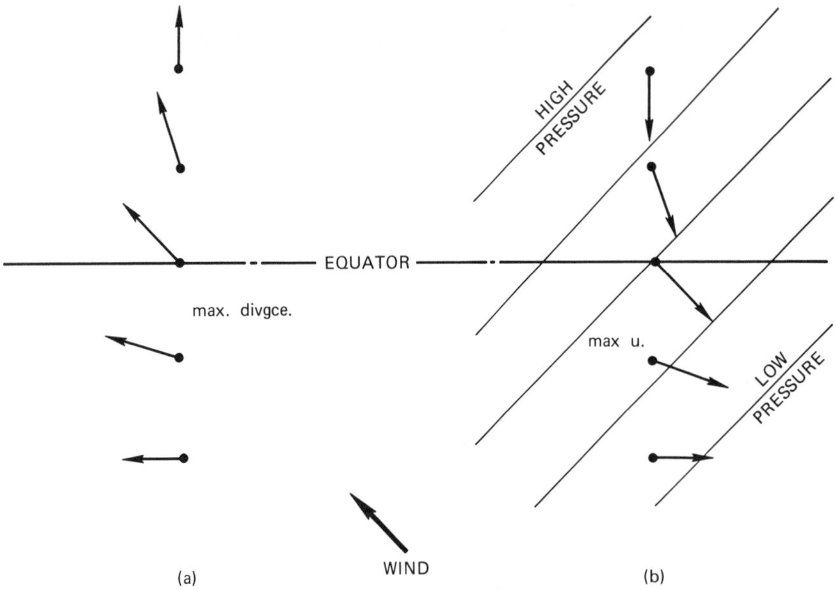

FIGURE 6 (a) Ekman flux at various distances from the equator for a wind from the southeast. At the equator, the flux is downwind. To the north, it is to the right of the wind. The greatest divergence, and hence the strongest upwelling, is south of the equator. (b) Velocity below the Ekman layer at various distances from the equator for a wind from the southeast. At the equator, the flow is down the pressure gradient. The pressure is high to the north, so the geostrophic current has an eastward component south of the equator and a westward component north of the the equator. Hence, the maximum eastward current is south of the equator.

gives as an average value of u_y between 0° and 1°,

$$u_y \sim 5 \times 10^{-6}/s^{-1}.$$

This is about four times the average value of the Coriolis parameter, βy, in the same range of latitudes; i.e., the local Rossby number is large. It is not surprising, therefore, that calculations of nonlinear terms based on the results of linear models show that neglect of these terms is unjustified.

Charney (1960) was the first to make quantitative calculations of nonlinear effects. His model included vertical friction (ν constant) but no lateral friction, and a no-slip condition was applied at the bottom. If symmetry is assumed around the equator, the velocity profile at the equator can

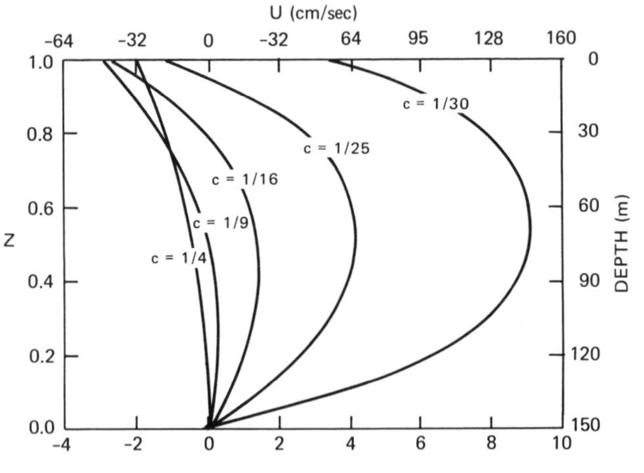

FIGURE 7 Vertical profiles of eastward velocity, u, obtained from Charney's (1960) nonlinear model. c is the parameter $\nu H^{-5/3}(-\tau^x\beta/\rho)^{-1/3}$, which decreases as nonlinear effects become more important.

be calculated independently of the flow elsewhere; and Charney did this by numerical integration of a time-dependent system to a steady state. Figure 7 shows his results. In the linear case (c large), the flow is entirely westwards and there is no undercurrent. As nonlinear effects increase (c decreasing), an undercurrent develops; but, as c decreases further, the flow becomes entirely eastward. Robinson (1966) showed that the first correction to u for small nonlinearity is eastward, whatever the direction of the wind; Mikhailova (1966), Mikhailova, Felsenbaum, and Shapiro (1967), and Charney and Spiegel (1971) confirmed this numerically. Robinson (1966) showed that this striking effect is, at least for small nonlinearity, the result of divergence of zonal momentum flux. The effect can be explained in more general terms as follows. First take the vertical average (denoted by an overbar) of the x-component of the momentum equation. This gives

$$\bar{u}_t + (\overline{uu})_x + (\overline{uv})_y - \beta y\bar{v} = -p_x + \tau^x/H - (\nu u_z)_b/H + A(\bar{u}_{xx} + \bar{u}_{yy}), \qquad (14)$$

where the suffix b indicates the value at the bottom. Applying the equation outside the equatorial boundary layer gives

$$p_x = \tau^x/H. \qquad (15)$$

Thus if x-derivatives are assumed small, continuity gives $\bar{v} = 0$ and Eq. (14) becomes

$$\bar{u}_t = -(\overline{uv})_y - (\nu u_z)_b/H + A\bar{u}_{yy}. \qquad (16)$$

The quantity $\overline{uv}$ (when multiplied by ρ) is the average northward flux of eastward momentum. If this decreases towards the north, i.e., $(\overline{uv})_y < 0$, there is a convergence of eastward momentum that has the same effect on the vertically averaged flow as the application of an eastward force.

Figures 8a and 8b show typical variations of u and v with latitude and depth for a linear case with a westward wind. Figure 8c shows the corresponding variation of $\overline{uv}$ with latitude. If the wind is eastward, u and v are both reversed, so $\overline{uv}$ is unchanged. In nonlinear cases, similar variations of $\overline{uv}$ are also found.

At the equator, $(\overline{uv})_y$ is negative, and so eastward momentum is generated. If this effect were suddenly turned on, Eq. (16) shows that $\overline{u}_t$ would be positive; i.e., the fluid would accelerate eastwards until friction produced a balance. If $A = 0$ (as in Charney's model), the balance is struck with bottom friction; and so, by Eq. (16),

$$(u_z)_b > 0.$$

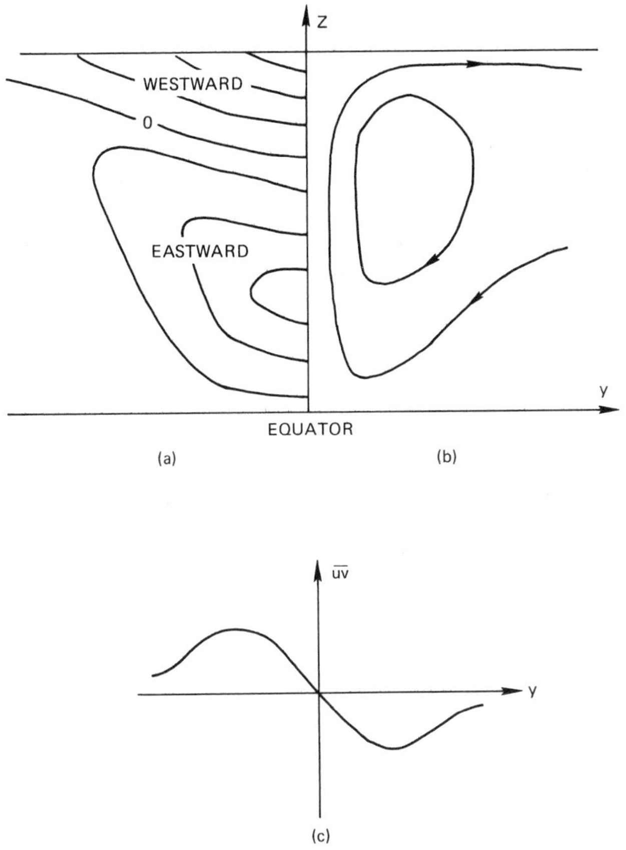

FIGURE 8 Typical variations of (a) eastward velocity and (b) northward velocity for a linear model with a westward wind. In (a) contours of u are drawn, while (b) shows streamlines of the meridional circulation and (c) shows the resulting variation of $\overline{uv}$. For an eastward wind, the signs of u and v are reversed, but $\overline{uv}$ remains the same.

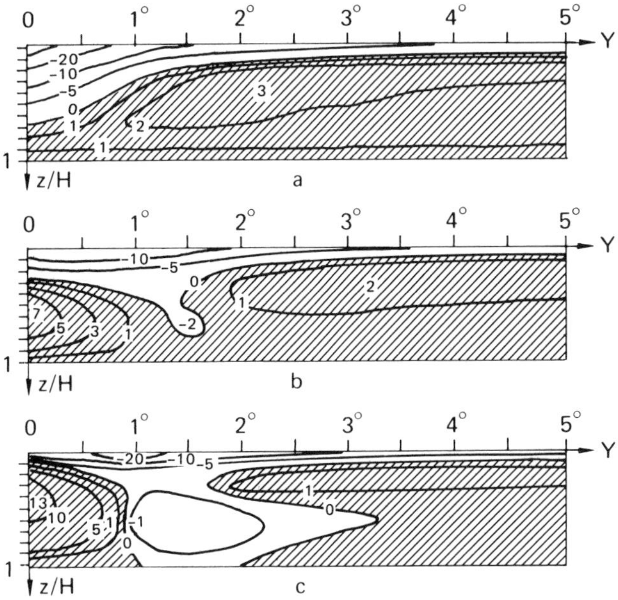

FIGURE 9 Effects of increasing nonlinearity (decreasing friction coefficient) on the distribution of eastward velocity (from Mikhailova *et al.*, 1967). The westward wind stress was 0.02 Nm^{-2} (0.2 dyn cm^{-2}) and the depth 200 m. (a) is the linear calculation and (b) the nonlinear calculation for $\nu = 5 \times 10^{-3}$ m^2 s^{-1} (50 cm^2 s^{-1}). (c) is the nonlinear case for $\nu = 3 \times 10^{-3}$ m^2 s^{-1} (30 cm^2 s^{-1}). The nonlinear effect may be ascribed to the poleward advection of the westerly momentum fed in through the surface by the westward wind. This produces the westward currents found at 1.5° latitude (not hatched) and intensifies the eastward flow (shown hatched) at the equator.

Since $u = 0$ at the bottom, an eastward flow near the bottom is implied. If lateral friction is the balancing effect $\nu = 0$, integration of Eq. (16) across the boundary layer implies $\overline{u} > 0$ at the equator; i.e., there is a net eastward flow there.

This result is important and physically simple enough to add to the two basic ideas discussed in the first section of this paper. This third basic idea is that the meridional circulation gives a net transport of eastward momentum toward the equator and so generates a net eastward flow at the equator. Another way of putting it, for the case of a westward wind, is as follows: Westward momentum fed into the surface layers by the wind is advected away from the equator by the Ekman flux. This makes the flow at the equator more strongly eastward than in the linear case and the flow at some distance more strongly westward. The results of Mikhailova and Felsenbaum (1967), reproduced in Figure 9, show the effect of increasing nonlinearity rather well. Charney and Spiegel's (1971) solutions show the results of even stronger nonlinearity. The westward currents on either side of the undercurrent are often observed, and an example from Hisard *et al.* (1970) is shown in Figure 10.

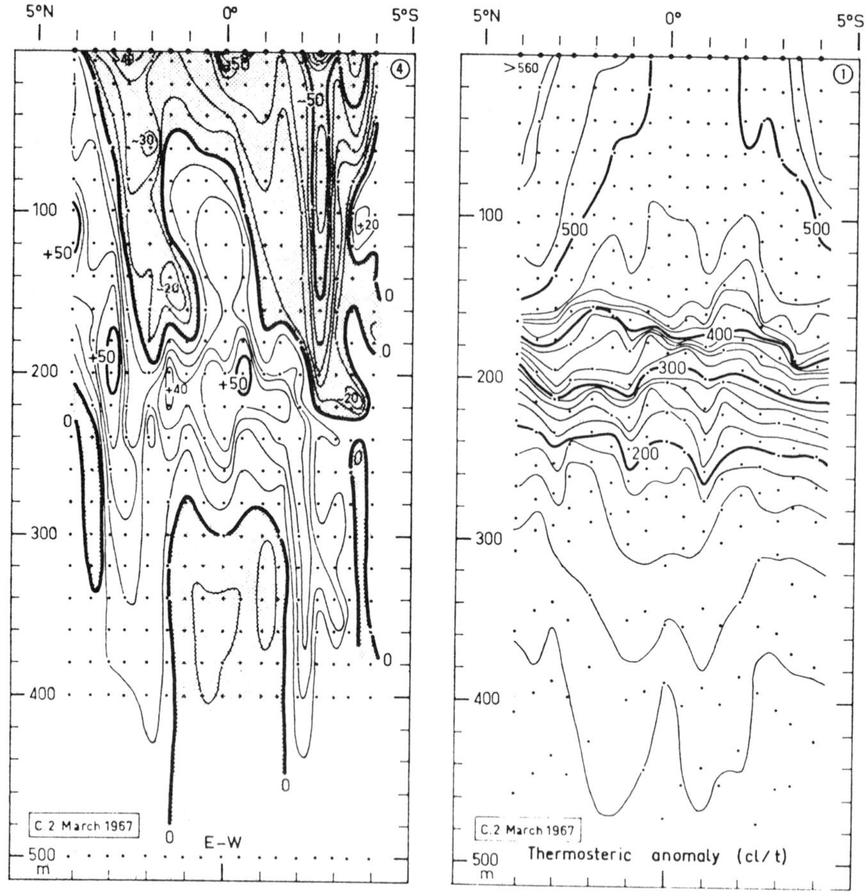

a. b.

FIGURE 10 A meridional section of (a) eastward velocity in cm s^{-1} and (b) thermosteric anomaly in cl/t at 170° E in March 1967 (from Hisard *et al.*, 1970). The shaded area represents westward currents (in contrast to the previous figure).

NONLINEAR EFFECTS: A LATERAL FRICTION MODEL

Charney and Spiegel's (1971) solutions have a discontinuity in u_y at the core of the undercurrent. The explanation follows from a qualitative discussion of Fofonoff and Montgomery (1955); namely, that in an inertial jet, the value of $-u_y$ at the core will equal the planetary vorticity f at the point of origin of the water particle in the core. Thus u_y is negative and finite on the north side of the core and positive and finite on the south side. Another difficulty in their model is that the maximum value of u is very sensitive to the parameter, c, of the model, e.g., u_{max} increases by a factor of 15 when c is reduced from one-thirtieth to one-thirty-second.

Such difficulties are avoided in a model where lateral friction is included. McKee (1970) has calculated nonlinear solutions for the case of zero stress at the bottom. As did Charney and Spiegel (1971), he calculated the steady state as the final outcome of a time integration with forward time differences. The results for the lateral friction model depend on the relative importance of the two friction coefficients ν and A, as measured by the parameter

$$E = \nu A^{-1/3} \beta^{-2/3} H^{-2}. \tag{17}$$

McKee made a series of calculations for different degrees of nonlinearity, as measured by the parameter

$$R = \tau/(\rho\beta A H). \tag{18}$$

For R in the range 0 to 1.25, the results for a fixed value of $E = .01$ showed an approximately linear trend in the mass transport, given roughly by

$$\text{mass transport} = \frac{\pi\tau}{\beta}\left(1 + \frac{3\tau}{\rho\beta A H}\right). \tag{19}$$

Thus the fact that the linear result underestimates the transport can easily be accounted for. McKee also found that as R increased, the undercurrent appeared to thicken. In addition, the meridional circulation was weakened. The increase in u and decrease in ν also meant that currents were more nearly parallel to the equator than in the linear case. McKee examined the balance of terms in the undercurrent for $R = 1$ and found (a) that the undercurrent was in geostrophic balance; and (b) in the east-west momentum equation, the Coriolis term, the friction term, and the nonlinear term vu_y were all important. Result (a) contrasts with the linear case where the undercurrent is *not* in geostrophic balance. Observations indicate that, on occasions at least, the undercurrent is in approximate geostrophic balance (Knauss, 1960, 1966; Montgomery and Stroup, 1962; Hisard *et al.*, 1970).

A difficulty with McKee's model is that an entirely consistent solution cannot be obtained without allowing variations in the x-direction. The same is true of the bottom friction model (see Philander, 1971). The nature of the difficulty in the lateral friction case can be seen from Eq. (16) with $\nu = 0$. If one is far enough from the equator, the main contribution to $\overline{uv}$ comes from the Ekman layer; and use of the classical Ekman solution gives (for $\tau^y = 0$)

$$\overline{uv} = -(\tau^x)^2/2^{5/2}H\nu^{1/2}(\beta y)^{3/2}. \tag{20}$$

Integration of Eq. (16) shows that $u \sim y^{-1/2}$ as $y \to \infty$, and so the transport is infinite.

Before discussing how this difficulty is resolved, one can see that an important principle is raised. Nonlinear effects give rise to a net eastward transport at the equator, requiring a return westward transport somewhere else in the ocean. The ocean generally doesn't allow strong currents along the eastern boundary to remove the flux, and a slow return flow a long way from the equator is not consistent with Sverdrup's solution. It follows that westward-flowing currents near the equator are required and that these currents are intimately associated with the undercurrent. Their existence depends on the fact that eastward momentum is transported towards the equator by the meridional circulation, thus producing a net eastward flow at the equator, which returns as westward-flowing currents near the equator.

To resolve the difficulty raised in the lateral friction model, consider the vertically average momentum equations for the case of no bottom friction. One of these is Eq. (14) and the other is

$$\bar{v}_t + (\overline{uv})_x + (\overline{vv})_y + \beta y\bar{u} = -p_y + \tau^y/H + A(\bar{v}_{xx} + \bar{v}_{yy}). \tag{21}$$

Introducing the stream functions $Hu = -\psi_y$ and $Hv = \psi_x$ and eliminating p gives, for the steady case,

$$A\nabla^4\psi - \beta\psi_x = \tau^x{}_y - \tau^y{}_x - H[(\overline{uv})_{yy} - (\overline{uv})_{xx} + (\overline{uu} - \overline{vv})_{xy}]. \tag{22}$$

McKee's solution for the cases τ^x = constant and $\tau^y = 0$ is valid as an inner solution for small y and satisfies

$$A\psi_{yyyy} = -H(\overline{uv})_{yy}. \tag{23}$$

The right-hand side in McKee's solution is calculated from the solution for the flow relative to the vertical average. For y large, $\overline{uv}$ is given by Eq. (20) and satisfies

$$\psi \sim -y^{1/2}(\tau^x)^2/A(2\nu)^{1/2}\beta^{3/2}, \tag{24}$$

By Eq. (21), p_y satisfies

$$p_y \sim -(2y)^{1/2}(\tau^x)^2/AH\nu^{1/2}\beta^{1/2}, \tag{25}$$

and the flow is geostrophic. The resolution of the difficulty comes from matching Eq. (24) to an outer solution. Assuming that this has a boundary-layer character, Eq. (22) becomes

$$A\psi_{yyyy} - \beta\psi_x = -H(\overline{uv})_{yy}. \tag{26}$$

A solution that matches Eq. (24) can be found of the form

$$\psi = (L-x)^{1/8}F[y(L-x)^{-1/4}] \tag{27}$$

where $x = L$ represents the eastern boundary of the ocean basin. This solution provides a transition from Eq. (24) to the Sverdrup solution of Eq. (26), i.e., the solution for $A = 0$, viz.

$$\psi = -H(\overline{uv})_{yy}(L-x)/\beta. \tag{28}$$

The width of the transition layer is of order $(AL/\beta)^{1/4}$, i.e., about 200 km when $A = 10^4\ \mathrm{m^2\ s^{-1}}$. This is not much wider than the undercurrent itself, so the separation into an inner and outer zone is not completely justified, nor are the assumptions that led to the separation. However, the above argument gives an indication of the type of vertically integrated flow pattern to expect (see Figure 11). Perhaps the main lesson to be learned is that with nonlinear models, one has to take account of the variations in all three dimensions. One can also see that the interaction of the equatorial system with the general circulation (e.g., where the western boundary currents cross the equator) will be more complicated than in the linear models. This is an aspect of the nonlinear problem that has not yet been studied.

EFFECTS OF STRATIFICATION

Some simple stratification effects can be deduced by a reinterpretation of the results of homogeneous models. If the homogeneous layer is now regarded as being the upper of two layers, the lower one being relatively motionless, then the pressure gradients found in the homogeneous models can be related to the slope of the interface. (This is a consistent assumption, at least in those cases where the stress

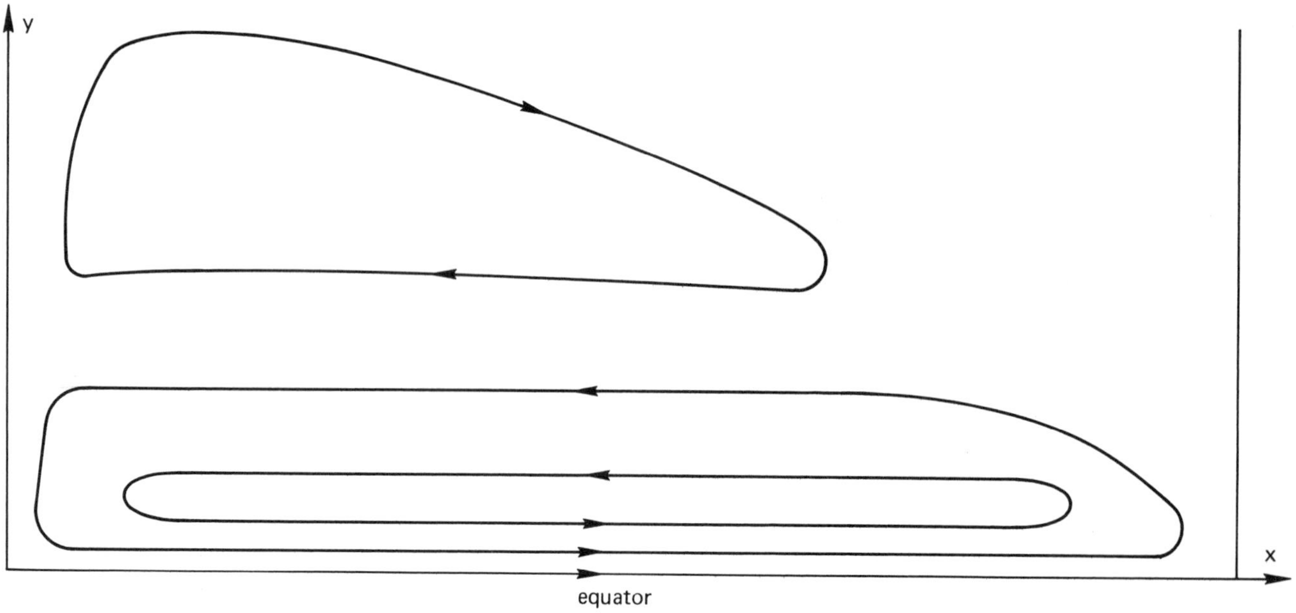

FIGURE 11 Sketch of expected form of variation of transport stream function ψ for a constant westward stress when nonlinear effects are important. The flux of eastward momentum towards the equator results in a term $C(y) = -\rho H(\overline{uv})_{yy}$, which plays the role of a wind stress curl in the vertically integrated Eq. (22). In McKee's (1970) nonlinear solution, this reaches a magnitude of 3×10^{-7} Nm^{-3} (3×10^{-8} dyn cm^{-3}) close to the equator, i.e., a value much bigger than typical values of the wind stress curl itself.

vanishes at the bottom of the homogeneous layer). As Stommel (1960) pointed out, the east-west pressure gradient implies that the thermocline rises towards the east (as can be seen in Figure 3). This implies that, if the transport and width of the undercurrent remain fairly independent of longitude, then the velocity of the undercurrent will increase toward the east.

The homogeneous nonlinear models also produce a pressure gradient across the current, which may be related to the slope of an isopycnal. Both McKee (1970) and Charney and Spiegel (1971) find a high pressure at the equator, as is required for geostrophic balance with an eastward current. This corresponds to *downward* bowing of the interface. In practice, the isopycnals do show downward bowing below the core of the undercurrent, but bow upwards above the core. This, of course, is consistent with the "thermal wind" relation

$$\beta y u_z = g\rho_y, \qquad (29)$$

i.e., isopycnals are flat at the core where $u_z = 0$, and the "spreading" of the isopycnals about the core is determined from the sign of u_{zz}. Howard and Veronis (see Veronis, 1960) noted another property of the stratified solution. This property comes from the balance between the wind stress and integrated pressure gradient at the equator,

$$\int_{-H}^{0} p_x \, dz = \tau^x, \qquad (30)$$

and the hydrostatic equation. If $\Delta\rho$ is a typical density difference, the east-west change, h^2, in the square of the depth of the thermocline is given by

$$g \cdot \Delta\rho \cdot h^2 \sim \tau^x \cdot L. \qquad (31)$$

Robinson (1960) suggested that the equatorial current system is not purely a response to winds near the equator, but is partly a response to the general thermohaline circulation of the ocean. He pointed out that the equations used to describe the thermohaline circulation at mid-latitudes are not valid at the equator, and derived the appropriate modifications. He inferred a much stronger coupling between thermally driven and wind-driven motions at the equator than at mid-latitudes. He also deduced from a scale analysis a velocity scale and width of the undercurrent in agreement with observation. (In fact, since so many effects are important at the equator, estimates based on a variety of balances give the right orders of magnitude.) Philander (1971) went further to deduce signs for various components of the thermally driven motion. He assumed a deep upwelling below the thermocline away from the equator, which implies equatorward motion in the thermocline. The westward increase in surface temperature at the equator then implies an eastward undercurrent. The model also requires downwelling at the equator, and Philander associates this with the region below the core. The model, however, is based on the assumption that the equatorial boundary layer is "passive" in the sense that the flow away from the equator can be deduced without reference to conditions at the equator and that the solution can then be patched up by adding a boundary layer at the equator. This may not be so.

Two-layer models with vertical friction (only) in each layer have been studied by Dvoryaninov and Felsenbaum (1969), Korotaev (1970), Dvoryaninov (1970), and Mikhailova and Shapiro (1971). These models produce strong narrow undercurrents with a great variety of profiles dependent on the parameter range studied. A key ingredient in the models is the interface friction, which provides the coupling between the two layers (stress and velocity are continuous across the interface). My impression is that the interface friction plays too prominent a role for the results to be realistic and that studies of continuously stratified models will be more rewarding.

Because so many effects are important at the equator—stratification, nonlinearity, etc.—there is much to be learned from three-dimensional numerical models that can readily combine all the effects. The problem is not merely one of *simulation* of the observed current system, but of gaining physical insight from the analysis and interpretation of the solutions. Holland (private communication, 1970) has made some three-dimensional calculations which are very promising. Figure 12 shows some results for a case where lateral friction is rather too large, resulting in a rather broad, slow undercurrent. However, the characteristic spreading of the isotherms above and below the core is found to change sign at about the level of the core (upwelling above, downwelling below). Further experiments on these lines should be of great value.

STABILITY OF THE UNDERCURRENT

No specific studies of the stability of the undercurrent appear to have been made; but there are a few remarks in the literature that are pertinent, and it is worth drawing attention to them. Charney and Spiegel (1971) point out that the undercurrent could be unstable in the Rayleigh sense, i.e., be "barotropically" unstable, because the absolute vorticity

$$|\beta y - u_y| \qquad (32)$$

has a maximum. Figure 13 shows a sketch of the function

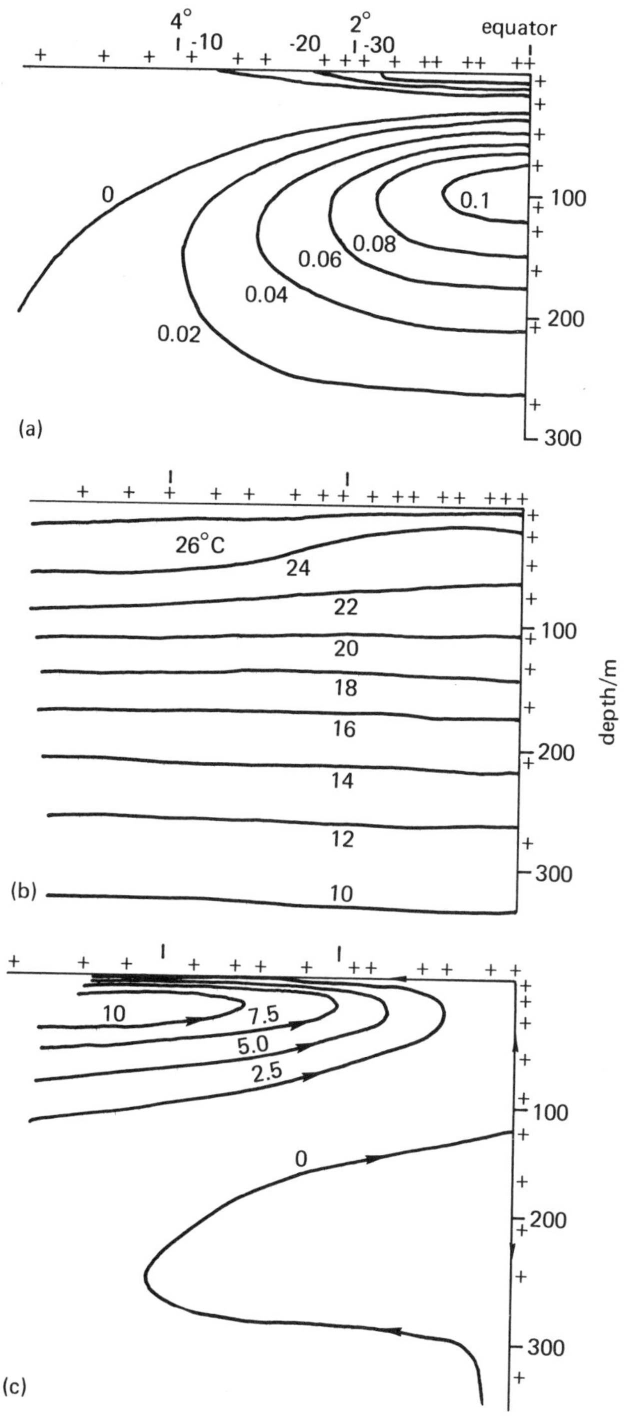

FIGURE 12 Some preliminary results of W. R. Holland (private communication) for the equatorial region showing meridional sections with (a) contours of eastward velocity in m s^{-1}, (b) temperatures in °C, and (c) contours of meridional transport stream function in units of 10^6 m^3 s^{-1}.

A model like that of Bryan (1969) has been used with the following values of the parameters: $A_M = 5 \times 10^4$ m^2 s^{-1}, $A_H = 5 \times 10^3$ m^2 s^{-1}, $K = 10^{-4}$ m^2 s^{-1}, $\nu = 10^{-3}$ m^2 s^{-1}. The wind stress distribution is a zonal average of Hellerman's (1967, 1968) wind data. The wind stress at the equator was 0.029 Nm^{-2} (0.29 dyn cm^{-2}) westward. The position of the grid points is marked. The computations were made for the northern half of a basin 4 km deep occupying 20° of latitude at each side of the equator and 45° of longitude. Symmetry was assumed around the equator. At the surface, wind stress, temperature, and salinity were specified. At the northern boundary, temperature and salinity were specified and the vertically integrated northward velocity was set at zero.

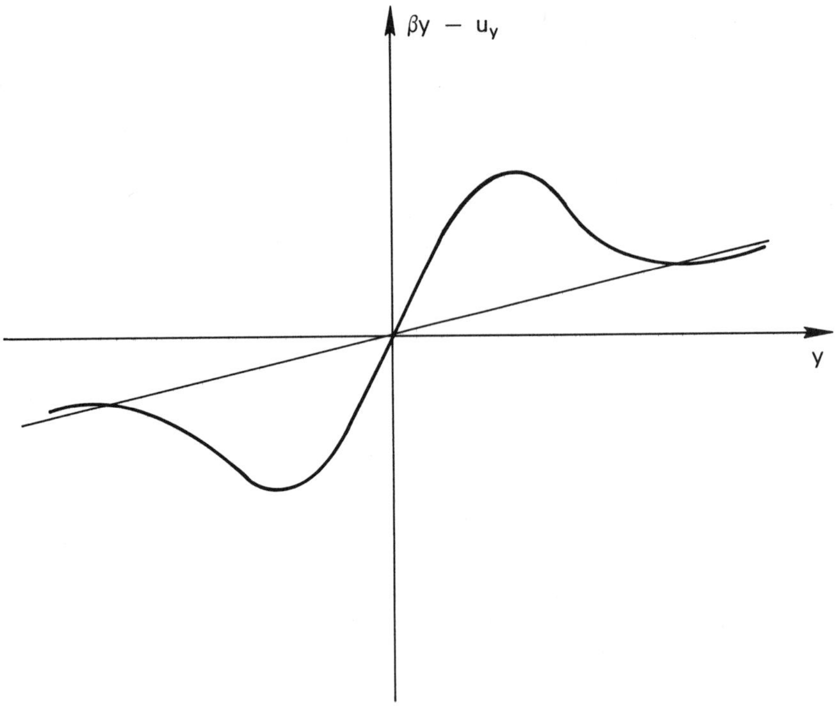

FIGURE 13 Sketch showing the vertical component, $\beta y - u_y$, of total vorticity as a function of latitude at the depth where the undercurrent is strongest.

$\beta y - u_y$ at the level of the core. For a Gaussian velocity profile

$$u = u_o e^{-(y/\delta)^2}$$

with width δ of 100 km, an eastward current can satisfy Eq. (19) when u_o is greater than 0.26 m s^{-1}. For a westward jet, Eq. (32) is satisfied at a lower speed, in accordance with a remark of Lin's (see Veronis, 1960). For the Gaussian profile, the same formula is satisfied when $-u_o$ is greater than 0.12 m s^{-1}. Although Eq. (32) is a useful guide, it should be pointed out that it is only a necessary condition for instability for a flow that is independent of y and z. There appears to be no observational evidence available to support the idea that the undercurrent is unstable because of the north–south shear.

The criterion for the vertical gradient of u to produce instability is that the Richardson number be sufficiently small. Some observations reported by Jones (1971) indicated a near-critical Richardson number at the equator at all levels down to 300 m, except for those where the shear vanished. This suggests that turbulence generated by the shear is playing an important role in establishing the vertical profile of horizontal velocity.

TURBULENT PROCESSES

On the basis of the above remark about stability, it seems that if accurate simulation of the undercurrent is required, a suitable parameterization of turbulent processes is necessary. Robinson (1966) explored a model in which ν was a function of Richardson number (the stratification was taken to be constant) and found that the turbulent eddy viscosity model is capable of giving more realistic velocity profiles than the constant eddy viscosity model. Jones' observations, referred to above, certainly indicate that the Richardson number is a key parameter and that observations could well be directed at finding a suitable empirical relation for representing the turbulence in large-scale models.

Gibson and Williams (1972) give a preliminary report on direct measurements of turbulence at a depth of 100 m at 1° N, 150° W. The level of turbulence is very high compared with other parts of the ocean, e.g., the estimated viscous dissipation rate is about 10^{-5} m^2 s^{-3} (0.1 cm^2 s^{-3}) and the temperature dissipation rate about 10^{-5} °C^2 s^{-1}. Further work is in progress to see if these results are representative of more than one location and time. The consequences of such estimates for model studies have yet to be evaluated.

Munk and Moore (1968) discussed the possibility that planetary-gravity waves might drive an undercurrent. It turned out, however, that their model gave no rectified Lagrangian mean flow. All the same, they pointed out that the wave solutions give the strongest currents where the Brunt–Vaisala frequency is largest and sought thereby to explain the concentration of the mean flow in the thermocline. Perhaps this idea is worthy of further exploration. Bretherton and Moore (private communication, 1968) subsequently showed that planetary-gravity waves can give up momentum to the undercurrent at the place where their

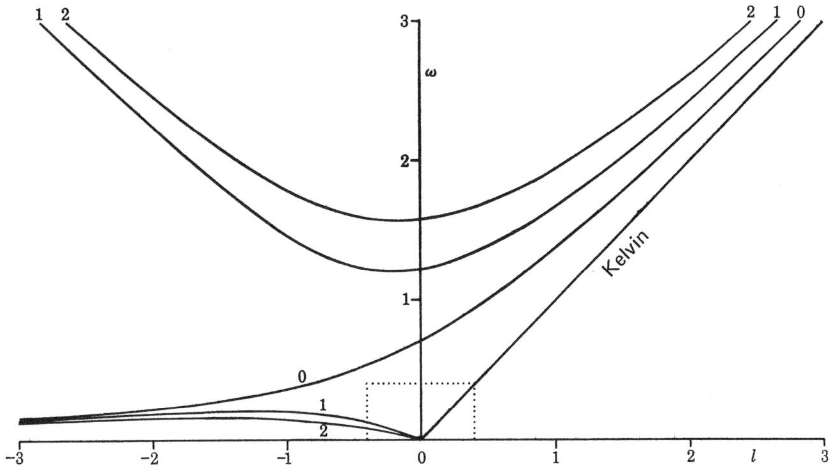

FIGURE 14 Dispersion curves for equatorial waves showing the relation between frequency ω and the eastward component, l, of wave number. The curves have been normalized by using the length scale $(c_n/2\beta)^{1/2}$ and the time scale $(2\beta c_n)^{-1/2}$.

phase velocity has the same eastward component as the velocity of the undercurrent. This process, known as "critical-layer absorption," feeds momentum to the undercurrent of the same sign as already exists and has been found to be significant in the dynamics of the stratospheric jet that occurs in low latitudes. Clearly there is a need of observational information about the nature of eddy processes at the equator.

TIME-DEPENDENT SOLUTIONS

A body of literature on time-dependent solutions for motion near the equator exists. These solutions are mainly linear* and analytical in character. McKee (1970) considered the time development of the undercurrent in a linear homogeneous model. The main point about the model was that the time scale for setting up the undercurrent was f^{-1}, where f is the Coriolis parameter, say a half-width away from the equator. This time scale is of order 10 days. Charney (1960), McKee (1970), and Charney and Spiegel (1971) used time-dependent schemes to calculate steady nonlinear solutions. They found that the nonlinear solution could take much longer to reach equilibrium. In McKee's case, the long time was found to be associated with the establishment of the time-integrated flow generated by the nonlinear terms, the vertical derivatives of velocity reaching equilibrium much more quickly.

Several authors (e.g., Blandford, 1966; Matsuno, 1966) have studied free waves, which can be trapped at the equator. The vertical structure of the waves depends only on the density profile, each mode being characterized by a wave speed, c_n, and a velocity profile, $\hat{u}_n(z)$. For the first baroclinic mode, c_1 is about 2.5 m s^{-1}. For the second baroclinic mode, c_2 is about 0.5 ms^{-1} and for the higher modes, c_n varies roughly like n^{-1}.

*However, Mikhailova and Shapiro (1972) have considered nonlinear effects of oscillatory forcing.

For each n, there is an infinite set of solutions, each with a different variation of u and v with latitude. The dispersion curves are shown in Figure 14. They are the same for each n, apart from scale. If we confine attention to zonal wavelengths comparable with the size of ocean basins and to periods of more than a week, we are interested only in the region near the origin, marked by a dotted line in Figure 14. The waves in this region consist of:

(a) An eastward propogating Kelvin wave, which propogates with speed c_n. The solution for this wave is

$$u = F(x - c_n t) D_0(\eta_n) \hat{u}_n(z), \qquad (33)$$

$$v = 0, \qquad (34)$$

where

$$\eta_n = (2\beta/c_n)^{1/2} y \qquad (35)$$

and $D_m(\eta)$ is a parabolic cylinder function, in this case $(m = 0)$ a Gaussian function.

(b) An infinite set of westward-propagating planetary waves that propagate with speed $c_n/(2m+1)$, where $m =$ 1,2,3, etc. The north–south scale is $(2c_n/\beta)^{1/2}$, i.e., 500 km for the first baroclinic mode and 200 km for the second baroclinic mode. The solutions for these waves are

$$u = F\left(x + \frac{c_n t}{2m+1}\right)\left[D_{m+1}(\eta_n) - (m+1)D_{m-1}(\eta_n)\right] \hat{u}_n(z), \qquad (36)$$

$$v = \frac{4(m+1)}{(2m+1)}\left(\frac{c_n}{2\beta}\right)^{1/2} F'\left(x + \frac{c_n t}{2m+1}\right) D_n(\eta_n)\hat{u}_n(z), \qquad (37)$$

where $m = 1, 2, 3,$ etc.

For the first baroclinic mode, the Kelvin wave travels

60° of longitude eastward in a month, while the planetary waves travel distances of 20°, 12°, etc. westward. For the second baroclinic mode, the Kelvin wave travels about 12° in a month and the first planetary wave travels only about 4°.

Lighthill (1969) considered the generation of equatorial waves by a wind stress distribution that is suddenly applied in a limited area. He pointed out the importance of the rapid propagation of baroclinic waves at the equator relative to mid-latitudes and applied his calculations to the response of the Indian Ocean following the onset of the southwest monsoon.

There is some observational evidence about time-dependent currents, the most ambitious experiment to date (Stalcup and Metcalf, 1966) involving the use of moored current meters, one mooring operating for 60 days and the others mainly for 6 days. This mooring was at 35° W on the equator, and a marked 12.4 h periodicity was observed (it is not stated whether the associated motion was barotropic or baroclinic). Although the mean flow was quite strong, there were significant changes in the daily mean current over the 60-day period (Figure 15).

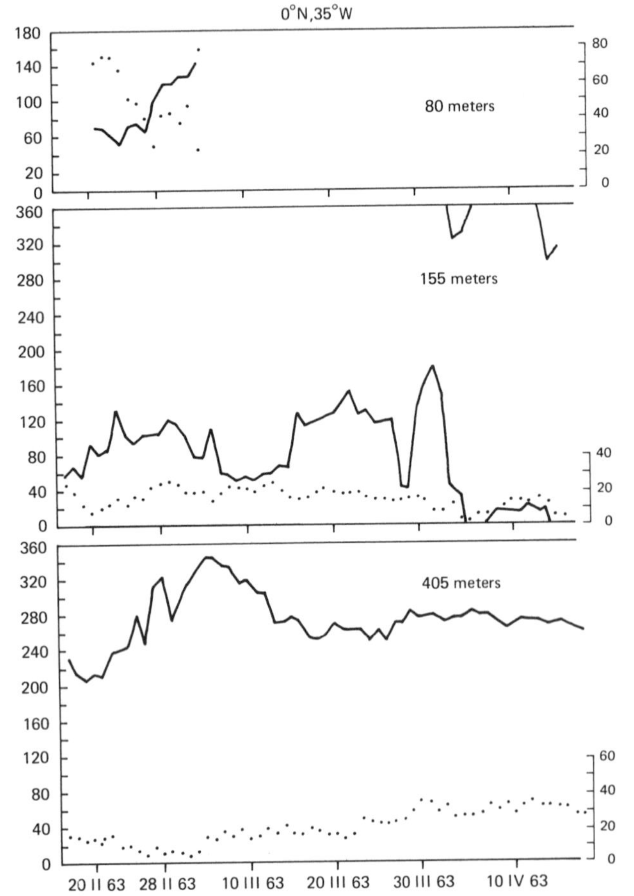

FIGURE 15 Daily mean direction (solid line) and speed (dotted line) on the equator at 35° W and at the indicated depths over a 60-day period (from Stalcup and Metcalf, 1966).

THE CLOSE RELATIONSHIP WITH PROBLEMS OF COASTAL DYNAMICS

A close relationship exists between many problems associated with the equatorial boundary layer and problems associated with coastal dynamics, as pointed out by Yoshida (1959). It is important to realize this, because physical insight gained from a study of one problem may be applicable to another and because models developed for, say, coastal studies may be easily adapted for studies of the equatorial system. Two examples will be discussed.

The Steady Flow in a Homogeneous Ocean

The wind stress acting on the surface of the ocean drives an Ekman flux normal to the wind stress. Where this flux has a component normal to the coast, upwelling or downwelling must occur; and this is confined to a coastal boundary layer. At the equator the Ekman flux changes sign, so upwelling or downwelling also occurs here, and again in a boundary layer. If the boundary layer is dominated by lateral friction, the relevant equations in both cases are the real and imaginary parts of

$$A(u + iv)_{yy} - if(u + iv) = (\tau^x + i\tau^y)/H. \qquad (38)$$

For the coastal upwelling layer studied by Hidaka (1954), Pedlosky (1968), and Garvine (1971), f is taken as a constant and the boundary layer has thickness $(A/f)^{1/2}$. In the case of the equatorial upwelling layer studied by Hidaka (1961) and Gill (1971a), $f = \beta y$ and the thickness of the layer is $(A/\beta)^{1/3}$.

The Response of an Inviscid Stratified Ocean to the Imposition of a Wind Stress at a Particular Time

The wind generates Ekman fluxes in the surface layers. Near the coastline, this will lead to upward or downward movement of the isotherms, which is mainly confined to within a distance c/f (the radius of deformation, typically 10–30 km) of the coast, where c is the speed of long internal waves. The slope of the isotherms is associated with a "coastal jet" (Charney, 1955). The disturbance to the density field at one point on the coast tends to propagate along the coast as an internal Kelvin wave (Csanady, 1968, 1971; Walin 1972a,b). Similarly, the density field near the equator responds to the Ekman flux, tending to be either away from or toward the equator on both sides. The disturbance, which is mainly confined to a distance $(c/\beta)^{1/2}$ of the equator, can propagate along the equator either as a planetary wave or as a Kelvin wave (Lighthill, 1969).

As a particular case, consider the baroclinic motion that is generated in a two-layer ocean by the imposition at time ($t = 0$) of a constant wind stress (τ^x) parallel to (a) an infinite straight coastline, $y = 0$; or (b) the equator, $y = 0$. Let the suffix 1 refer to the upper layer, which has thickness, H_1; density, ρ_1; and velocity components, u_1 and v_1. Let suffix 2 refer to the lower layer. The stress is treated as if it is distributed over the entire upper layer, this condition resulting from vertical averaging of the equations of the upper layer. In the initial stages, the upward displacement (h) of the interface is small, and a linear approximation can be used. The equations for the baroclinic mode involve only the differences $u = u_1 - u_2$ and $v = v_1 - v_2$ between the velocities of the two layers. The equations are

$$u_t - fv = \tau^x/\rho_1 H_1, \quad (39)$$

$$v_t + fu = g' h_y, \quad (40)$$

$$\left(\frac{1}{H_1} + \frac{1}{H_2}\right) h_t = v_y, \quad (41)$$

where $g' = g(\rho_2 - \rho_1)/\rho_2$ and g is the acceleration due to gravity. For the coastal problem, f is taken as a constant; and for the equatorial problem, $f = \beta y$. The solution has the property that u and h are proportional to t, while v is independent of t; so the term v_t can be omitted from the second equation. Elimination of u and h leads to

$$f^{-1} c^2 v_{yy} - fv = \tau^x/\rho_1 H_1, \quad (42)$$

where $c^2 = g' H_1 H_2 (H_1 + H_2)$ is the square of the speed of long internal waves. In the coastal case, the solution is

$$v = h - \tau^x (\rho_1 H_1 f)^{-1} (1 - e^{-fy/c}), \quad (43)$$

$$u = t\tau^x (\rho_1 H_1)^{-1} e^{-fy/c}, \quad (44)$$

$$g'h = -ct\tau^x (\rho_1 H_1)^{-1} e^{-fy/c}. \quad (45)$$

Throughout the motion the potential vorticity remains constant [c.f. the solution discussed by Stommel (1960, p. 111) in connection with the Gulf Stream], and the energy of the coastal jet is equally divided between kinetic and potential energy.

In the equatorial case, the solution is

$$v = -\tau^x (\rho_1 H_1)^{-1} (2/\beta c)^{1/2} P(\eta), \quad (46)$$

$$u = t\tau^x (\rho_1 H_1)^{-1} [1 - \eta P(\eta)], \quad (47)$$

$$g'h = -ct\tau^x (\rho_1 H_1)^{-1} P'(\eta), \quad (48)$$

where η is defined by Eq. (35) and $\eta^{-1/2} P$ is a modified Lommel function of order one-fourth. P satisfies the differential equation

$$P'' - \frac{1}{4}\eta^2 P = -\frac{1}{4}\eta \quad (49)$$

and is defined by the power series

$$P = \frac{\eta}{2}\left[a\left(1 + \frac{\eta^4}{5.4.2^2} + \frac{\eta^8}{9.8.5.4.2^4} + \frac{\eta^{12}}{13.12.9.8.5.4.2^6} + \ldots\right) + \left(\frac{\eta^2}{3.2.2} + \frac{\eta^6}{7.6.3.2.2^3} + \frac{\eta^{10}}{11.10.7.6.3.2.2^5} + \ldots\right)\right], \quad (50)$$

where

$$a = (\pi/2)^{3/2}\left[2\Gamma\left(\frac{5}{4}\right)\right]^{-2} \simeq 0.59907. \quad (51)$$

For large (positive or negative) η, P has asymptotic expansion

$$P \sim \frac{1}{\eta}\left(1 + \frac{2.1.2^2}{\eta^4} + \frac{6.5.2.1.2^4}{\eta^8} + \ldots\right). \quad (52)$$

Graphs of the functions P, $1 - \eta P$, and P' are displayed in Yoshida (1959). (Note: Yoshida's $\xi = 2^{-1/2}\eta$ and his function P is $2^{1/2}$ times the above function P).

The solutions of the above problems are only of value for a finite time. They ignore, for instance, variations in the x-direction and, therefore, the effect of barriers and the establishment of east–west variations of h. The speed of wave propagation and the distances in the x-direction involved will presumably determine the time scales that are relevant. The above solutions also become invalid when nonlinear effects become important. This happens in a time of order $t \sim \rho_1 H_1 c/\tau^x$ (typically 10–30 days), when $u \sim c$, $u_y \sim f$, and $h \sim H_1$ or H_2. For the coastal upwelling problem, this is the time for the pycnocline to reach the surface. O'Brien and Hurlburt (1972) numerically integrated a solution of such a problem into the nonlinear regime, but there was no obvious change in behavior before the pycnocline reached the surface (beyond which stage the numerical solution could not be taken). There is also a question of stability, or of the effects of disturbances on the solution. It seems that with regard to time-dependent effects, there is still much "territory" to be explored, both in the equatorial problem and in the coastal problem.

DEVELOPMENT OF AN UNDERCURRENT FROM REST

A major problem connected with the undercurrent is that of understanding why the core of the undercurrent lies in the themocline. Munk and Moore (1968) noted that time-dependent solutions can show the correct relationship between current and density structure, suggesting that study of the development of the undercurrent with time will aid in understanding this relationship. We, therefore, consider the development of flow in a stratified ocean. At time zero, the density is taken to be a function of depth only. Then a uniform westward stress is applied in a surface homogeneous layer and held at a fixed value. This differs from the problem considered by Lighthill (1969) in that (a) the stress is applied over the whole ocean rather than in a limited area and (b) the motion is studied at an interior point rather than at points near the boundary.

There seems little point in carrying the solution far beyond the time for friction and diffusion effects to dominate. The measurement of viscous dissipation rate reported by Gibson and Williams (1972) can hardly be typical, as this would remove the energy from the current in a day or so. Values estimated from steady-state models vary between 10 and 100 days, so perhaps it is worthwhile to consider the development that takes place in the first 100 days.

A convenient model of the stratification (Lighthill, 1969) for finding solutions analytically consists of an upper homogeneous layer of thickness h_m, below which is a uniformly stratified layer with thickness h_s and Brunt-Vaisala frequency N. Below this lies a deep homogeneous layer. If this is very deep compared with h_s and h_m, the velocities in this layer are very small and the modes are given by

$$\hat{u}_n(z) = \begin{cases} \sin(Nz/c_n) & 0<z<h_s \\ \sin(Nh_s/c_n) & h_s<z<h_s+h_m, \end{cases} \tag{53}$$

where c_n satisfies

$$\cot(Nh_s/c_n) = Nh_m/c_n, \tag{54}$$

and the origin $z = 0$ has been placed at the base of the stratified layer.

In the interior, the solution will be independent of x until enough time has elapsed for boundary effects to have propagated. The x-independent solution is the same as that derived in the second part of the previous section, except that now there are an infinite number of modes $\hat{u}_n(z)$. The method of finding the amplitude of each mode when the stress is applied uniformly over the upper mixed layer is given by Lighthill (1969). The solution has the form

$$u = t\tau^x(\rho_1 h_m)^{-1} \sum_{n=1}^{\infty} a_n \hat{u}_n(z)\left[1 - \eta_n P(\eta_n)\right], \tag{55}$$

where

$$a_n = 2h_m(Nh_s/c_n)[h_s + h_m \sin(Nh_s/c_n)]^{-1}, \tag{56}$$

and η_n is defined by Eq. (35).

The solution of Eq. (55) does not satisfy the boundary condition $u = 0$ at the eastern and western boundaries, so it is necessary to add a set of free modes such that the sum satisfies the boundary conditions. The free modes will begin propagating from the boundaries at time $t = 0$ and arrive at a given point, x, in a sequence determined by the propagation speeds of the different modes and the distances of the point from the two boundaries. The set of free modes will include (see Figure 14) some high-frequency gravity waves of small amplitude that will be ignored. The free modes also include some small-scale planetary waves whose effect at interior points will also be ignored. The remaining free modes are those given by Eqs. (33-34) and (36-37).

To find the magnitudes of the free waves involved, it is necessary to expand the function $1 - \eta P(\eta)$, which appears in Eq. (45) in terms of the parabolic cylinder functions, which appear in Eqs. (33-34) and (36-37). The appropriate expansion is

$$1 - \eta P(\eta) = 2^{-1/2}\left\{D_o(\eta) - \sum_{m=1}^{\infty} [D_{2m}(\eta) - 2mD_{2m}(\eta)]/(4m-1)2^m mm\right\}. \tag{57}$$

This can be proved by taking the scalar product of this equation with $D_q(\eta)$ and using the result with Eq. (49) satisfied by P.

At the western boundary, only modes with eastward group velocity can be generated for low frequencies (see Figure 14). These consist of the Kelvin wave and a set of small-scale planetary waves, for which u varies like

$$D_{2m}(\eta) - (2m-1)D_{2m-2}(\eta). \tag{58}$$

Thus an expansion in terms of $D_o(\eta)$ (the Kelvin wave) and these functions is required. From Eq. (57), it follows that

$$1 - \eta P(\eta) = bD_o(\eta) - \sum_{m=1}^{\infty} b_m [D_{2m}(\eta) - (2m-1)D_{2m-2}(\eta)], \tag{59}$$

where

$$b = 2^{-1/2}(1 + \sum_{m=1}^{\infty} [(4m-1)\, 2^m(mm)^{-1}] \simeq 0.839. \tag{60}$$

The values of b_1, b_2, etc., which are not required as the contributions of the small-scale waves at interior points, will be ignored.

At the eastern boundary, only modes with westward group velocity can be generated. At low frequencies, the appropriate modes are the long planetary waves given by Eqs. (36-37). These do not form a complete set, however, and one needs to include a set of Kelvin waves, which propagate away from the equator along the eastern boundary.

An Example: The Undercurrent at 170° E

As an example, take the section at 170° E shown in Figure 10. The basic stratification will be modeled by an upper homogeneous layer of thickness, h_m = 150 m, below which is a uniformly stratified layer (thickness 100 m) across which the thermosteric anomaly changes from 480 to 180 cl/t, i.e., $N = 3^{1/2} \times 10^{-2}\ s^{-1}$. The region below 250 m is modeled by a deep homogeneous layer. The modes have the structure given by Eq. (51) with $c_1 = 2{\cdot}35\ m\ s^{-1}$, $c_2 = 0{\cdot}51\ m\ s^{-1}$, $c_3 = 0{\cdot}27\ m\ s^{-1}$, etc. Thus, the first boundary effect to reach 170° E will be the arrival of the Kelvin wave associated with the first mode after 20 days. The second boundary effect will be the arrival of the Kelvin wave associated with the second mode after 100 days. Since the solution will only be considered for 100 days, the contribution of this Kelvin wave and of all effects of the eastern boundary will not be felt.

For the first 20 days, the solution at 170° E is given by Eq. (55). Figure 16a shows the solution at 20 days for a wind stress $\tau^x = -0.035\ Nm^{-2}(-0.35$ dyne $cm^{-2})$, computed as the sum of the first 25 terms in the same formula. The diagram is drawn with the same vertical exaggeration as Figure 10. The main effects observed are the generation of a westward current at the equator by direct wind driving and the raising of the thermocline through Ekman fluxes away from the equator.

Between 20 and 100 days, the solution is the sum of Eq. (55) and the appropriate Kelvin wave solution [cf. Eqs. (33-34)]

$$-\tau^x(\rho_1 h_m)^{-1} F(t - x/c_1) a_1 b\hat{u}_1(z) D_o(\eta_1), \qquad (61)$$

where a_1 is given by Eq. (56), b by Eq. (60), and F is the function defined by

$$F(w) = \begin{cases} w & w>0 \\ 0 & w<0. \end{cases} \qquad (62)$$

Figure 16b shows the solution calculated in this manner for t = 50 days and Figure 16c shows the solution for t = 100 days. One can see the development of an eastward undercurrent and the corresponding spreading of the isopycnals. The current has the correct width and is correctly placed in the thermocline. It has this structure because the Kelvin wave removes a large part of the first mode, leaving a structure in which the second baroclinic mode is an important element. This mode has a width and velocity structure very similar to the observed undercurrent.

The Kelvin wave also brings with it a pressure gradient given by

$$p_x = \tau^x h_m^{-1} a_1 b\hat{u}_1(z) D_o(\eta_1), \qquad (63)$$

whose distribution with depth, as shown in Figure 17, is also close to that observed. This pressure gradient falls off with distance from the equator on the scale of the first baroclinic mode, i.e., is reduced by a factor e in 500 km.

Friction Effects

One can argue that friction and diffusion will smooth out the profile in the upper layer, giving something closer to that observed. Yoshida (1959) considered a steady-state model in which the operator $\partial/\partial t$ in the equations that lead to Eq. (59) is replaced by $\nu\partial^2/\partial z^2$. This set of equations has separable solutions with the same y-dependence. The z-dependence, however, is different; and there is difficulty in satisfying boundary conditions, because the term νv_{zz} is ignored and Ekman layers can not be reproduced. Mikhailova and Shapiro (1970) also considered a steady-state stratified model. In their model, friction is proportional to velocity; and a constant eddy diffusivity is incorporated. They found some numerical solutions that show raising of isopycnals by Ekman-induced upwelling at the equator. A model considered by Yoshida (1967) is similar to one that would be obtained if ρ_t in the density equation is replaced by $-r\rho$.

Related Problems

Studies like that above of time development in a stratified ocean would be useful for understanding the behavior near tropical coastlines. If the wind has a component parallel to the coast, upwelling will take place away from the equator [Eqs. (43-45)] in a layer of width c/f. This layer becomes wider as the equator is approached until it merges with the equatorial layer of thickness $(c/\beta)^{1/2}$. On the western boundary, variations of upwelling with distance from the equator will lead to the generation of Kelvin waves that propagate towards the equator. The solution will be rather complicated in the region where the upwelling layer and equatorial layer merge. Leetma (1972) reports on observations in this region.

A similar model applied at an eastern boundary (Yoshida, 1967) could be studied in relation to Peruvian upwelling. This case is complicated by the Kelvin waves, which

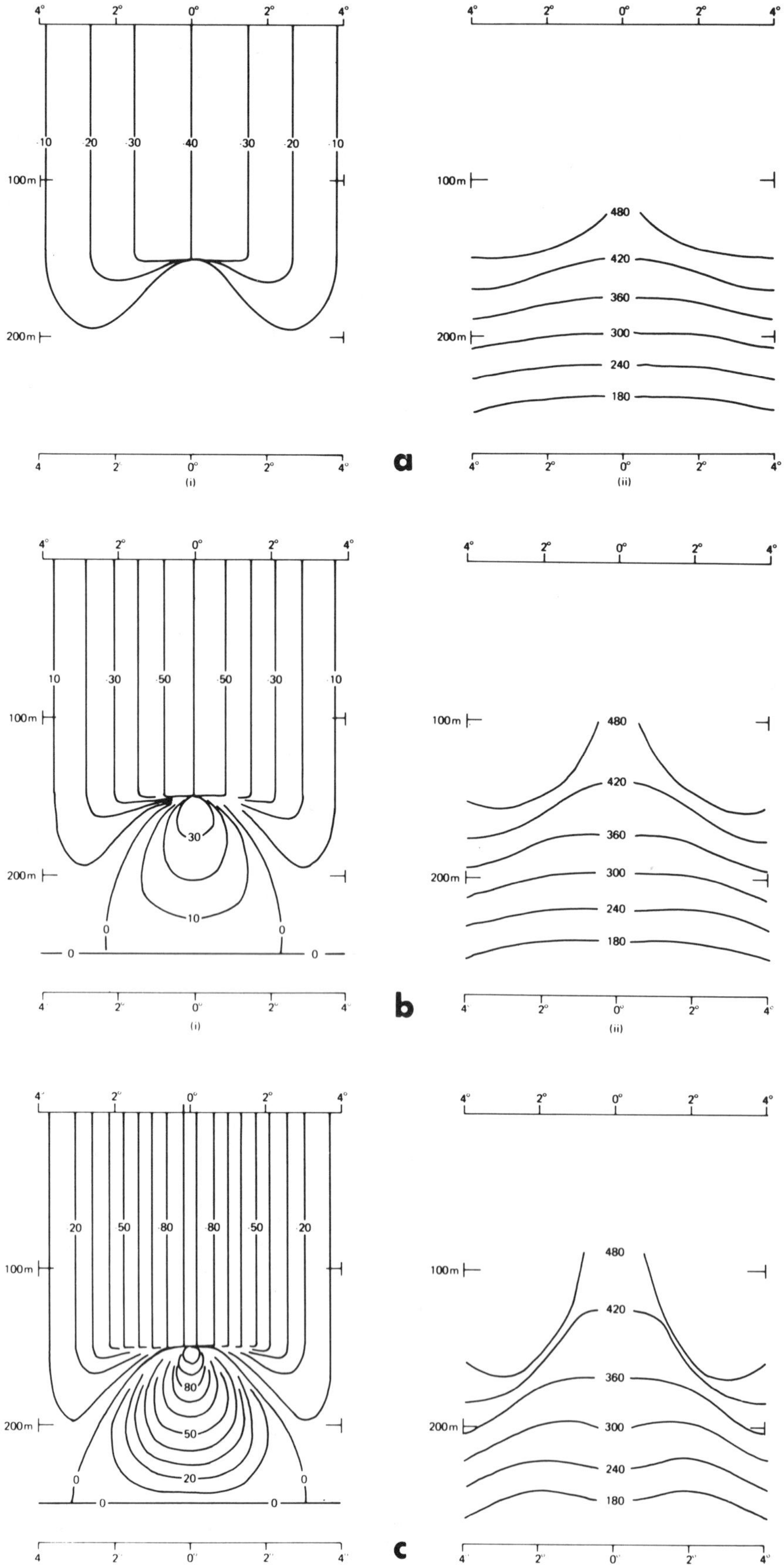

FIGURE 16 Contours of (i) eastward velocity in cm/s and (ii) thermosteric anomaly in cl/t at 170° E from a model calculation. The same vertical exaggeration as in Figure 10 is used. A uniform westward wind stress of 0.35 dyn/cm² is switched on at time $t = 0$, the stress acting as a body force distributed uniformly over the upper homogeneous layer of thickness 150 m. The region between 150 m and 250 m is initially uniformly stratified, and there is a very deep homogeneous layer below 250 m. The curves shown in (ii) are drawn using the expression for the displacement of each isopycnal derived from the (linear) theory. (a) shows the situation at $t = 20$ days, just before boundary effects have propagated as far as 170° E; (b) at 50 days and (c) at 100 days show the effect of the Kelvin wave associated with the first baroclinic mode. There is a singularity at 0° and 150 m, where both u_z and the displacement of the isopycnal are infinite. The development of the undercurrent and associated spread of the isopycnals can be seen in (b) and (c).

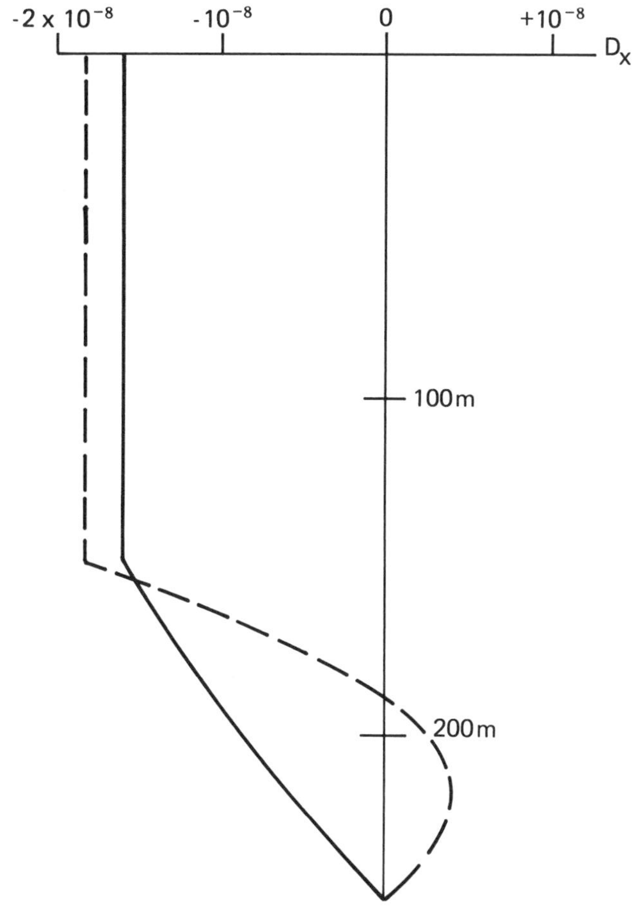

FIGURE 17 The eastward slope of the isobaric surfaces at the equator at 170° E as a function of depth according to the model calculation. Before the arrival, at 20 days, of the Kelvin wave associated with the first baroclinic mode, the pressure gradient is zero. Between 20 days and 100 days, the pressure gradient is shown as a solid curve. The broken line shows the pressure gradient just after the arrival, at 100 days, of the Kelvin wave associated with the second baroclinic mode.

are generated at the equator and propagate along the coastline away from the equator.

THE PRESENT POSITION AND SUGGESTIONS ABOUT FUTURE WORK

From simple analytical theories, it can be seen why an undercurrent should exist at the equator and be of limited horizontal extent. These models show the undercurrent as a flow down the pressure gradient, and this is in accord with observation. The models also show a meridional circulation with upwelling at the equator, about which further observational evidence is desirable. Nonlinear theories show how a net eastward transport is generated at the equator by advection of eastward momentum, and consequently nearby westward flows are required to return the fluid. The nonlinear theories show the need for understanding the equatorial system of currents as a whole, and the relation of the undercurrent, for instance, with the western boundary currents near the equator. Some useful ideas about the relation of the undercurrent with stratification come from a time-dependent study. Three-dimensional numerical models can produce currents and density fields similar to those observed; but their use is still at an early stage, and we must look to the main benefits of their use in the future.

There is a need to understand the nature of turbulent processes, both "vertical" and "horizontal" (if such a separation is appropriate) by whatever means are available—observation, numerical and laboratory models, etc. There are many time-dependent effects that need to be studied. The seasonal changes in the Indian Ocean are of great interest (observations are reported by Knauss and Taft, 1964; Taft, 1967; Taft and Knauss, 1967; and Swallow, 1967), but there are also interesting changes in the Western Pacific, where there are some monsoon effects. It appears that at 170° E (Hisard *et al.*, 1970) and near New Guinea (Colin *et al.*, 1971) the undercurrent has a double-cell structure. The upper cell in the mixed layer (about 150 m deep in those parts) is not in geostrophic balance and appears to change signs with changes in the wind, rather like in the linear homogeneous models. The lower cell, in the thermocline, is geostrophically balanced and apparently permanent. (Perhaps the time scale of the latter is associated with the time for a higher baroclinic mode to travel across the Pacific and back—several months.) There are also interesting effects observed east of the Galapagos Islands (Stevenson and Taft, 1971), which partly block the undercurrent; and there is interest in the behavior near an eastern boundary (Sturm and Voigt, 1966). Models that could predict surface temperature near the equator would be immensely valuable for studies of air-sea interaction, particularly as upwelling near the equator is thought to have important effects for the whole atmosphere (Bjerknes, 1966, 1969). Other interesting phenomena can be expected because of the existence in the atmosphere of the intertropical convergence zone. In short, there is no lack of interesting problems, and numerical models seem likely to play an important part in solving many of them.

REFERENCES

Bjerknes, J. 1966. A possible response of the Hadley circulation to variations in the heat supply from the equatorial Pacific. Tellus 18:820–29.

Bjerknes, J. 1969. Atmospheric teleconnections from the equatorial Pacific. Mon. Weather Rev. 97:163–72.

Blandford, R. 1966. Mixed gravity-Rossby waves in the ocean. Deep-

Sea Res. 13:941–61.
Charney, J. G. 1955. The generation of oceanic currents by the wind. J. Mar. Res. 14:477–98.
Charney, J. G. 1960. Non-linear theory of a wind-driven homogeneous layer near the equator. Deep-Sea Res. 6:303–10.
Charney, J. G., and S. L. Spiegel. 1971. Structure of wind-driven equatorial currents in homogeneous oceans. J. Phys. Oceanogr. 1:149–60.
Colin, C., C. Henin, P. Hisard, and C. Oudot. 1971. Le Courant de Cromwell dans le Pacifique centrale en Fevrier 1970. Cah. ORSTOM, Ser. Oceanogr. 9:167–86.
Cromwell, T. 1953. Circulation in a meridional plane in the central equatorial Pacific. J. Mar. Res. 12:196–213.
Csanady, G. T. 1968. Motions in a model Great Lake due to a suddenly imposed wind. J. Geophys. Res. 73:6435–47.
Csanady, G. T. 1971. Baroclinic boundary currents and long edge waves in basins with sloping shores. J. Phys. Oceanogr. 1:92–104.
Dvoryaninov, G. S. 1971. The effect of stratification on the planetary boundary layer in the ocean. Izv. Akad. Nauk. USSR Atmos. Oceanic Phys. 7:214–19.
Dvoryaninov, G. S., and A. I. Felsenbaum. 1969. Linear theory of the Cromwell and Lomonosov currents. Morsk. Gidrofiz. Issledovaniya, Sebastopol 3:27–43.
Felsenbaum, A. I., and N. B. Shapiro. 1966. Steady wind circulation in a homogeneous ocean. Dokl. Akad. Nauk. USSR 168: 569–72.
Fofonoff, N. P., and R. B. Montgomery. 1955. The equatorial current in the light of the vorticity equation. Tellus 7:518–21.
Garvine, R. W. 1971. A simple model of coastal upwelling dynamics. J. Phys. Oceanogr. 1:169–79.
Gibson, C. H., and R. B. Williams. 1972. Measurements of turbulence and turbulence mixing in the Pacific equatorial undercurrent. Paper presented at International Symposium on Oceanography of the South Pacific, Wellington, N.Z., 1972.
Gill, A. E. 1971a. The equatorial current in a homogeneous ocean. Deep-Sea Res. 18:421–31.
Gill, A. E. 1971b. Ocean models. Philos. Trans. R. Soc. Lond. Ser. A 270:391–413.
Hidaka, K. 1954. A contribution to the theory of upwelling and coastal currents. Trans. Am. Geophys. Union 35:431–44.
Hidaka, K. 1961. Equatorial upwelling and sinking in a zonal ocean with lateral mixing. Geophys. J. R. Astr. Soc. 4:359–71.
Hisard, P., J. Merle, and B. Voituriez. 1970. The equatorial undercurrent at 170° E in March and April 1967. J. Mar. Res. 28:281–303.
Jones, J. H. 1971. Recent observations of the current structure in the eastern equatorial Pacific Ocean. The Ocean World (Proc. Joint Oceanogr. Assoc. Tokyo 1970), Jap. Soc. Promotion Sci. 225- 26.
Knauss, J. A. 1960. Measurements of the Cromwell current. Deep-Sea Res. 6:265–86.
Knauss, J. A. 1966. Further measurements and observations of the Cromwell current. J. Mar. Res. 24:205–40.
Knauss, J. A., and B. A. Taft. 1964. Equatorial undercurrent of the Indian Ocean. Science 143:354–56.
Korotaev, G. K. 1970. Some problems of the theory of currents in an ocean including the equatorial zone. Sebastopol 4:21–33.
Leetmaa, A. 1972. The response of the Somali current to the southwest monsoon of 1970. Deep-Sea Res. 19:319–25.
Lemasson, L., and B. Piton. 1968. Cah. ORSTOM, Ser. Oceanogr. 6:39–46.
Lighthill, M. J. 1969. Dynamic response of the Indian Ocean to the onset of the southwest monsoon. Philos. Trans. R. Soc. Lond. Ser. A 265:45–92.
McKee, W. D. 1970. Some topics in dynamical oceanography. Ph.D. Thesis. University of Cambridge, U.K. 143 pp.
Matsuno, T. 1966. Quasi-geostrophic motions in the equatorial area. J. Meterol. Soc. Jap. 44:25–43.
Mikhailova, E. N. 1966. Certain problems in the theory of non-linear currents. *In* Problems of the Theory of Ocean Currents. Navkova Dumlea Press.
Mikhailova, E. N., A. I. Felsenbaum, and N. E. Shapiro. 1967. A contribution to the non-linear theory of currents at the equator. Dokl. Akad. Nauk. USSR 175:574–77.
Mikhailova, E. N., and N. E. Shapiro. 1970. On the effect of baroclinicity on currents in the equatorial zone of the ocean. Morsk. Gidrofiz. Issledovaniya, Sebastopol 3:28–38.
Mikhailova, E. N., and N. E. Shapiro. 1971. A 2-layer model of currents at the equator with due regard for non-linear accelerations. Morsk. Gidrofiz. Issledovaniya, Sebastopol 5:87–107.
Mikhailova, E. N., and N. E. Shapiro. 1972. Certain problems in the non-linear theroy of equatorial currents. Izv. Akad. Nauk. USSR, Atmos. Oceanic Phys. 8:409–18.
Montgomery, R. B., and E. D. Stroup. 1962. Equatorial waters and currents at 150° W in July–August 1952. Johns Hopkins Oceanogr. Stud. No. 1. 68 pp.
Munk, W., and D. Moore. 1968. Is the Cromwell current driven by equatorial Rossby waves? J. Fluid Mech. 33:241–59. (Corrigendum, J. Fluid Mech. 35:828)
Muzylev, S. V., and A. I. Felsenbaum. 1970. An analytical study of stationary wind-driven circulation in a uniform ocean including the equatorial zone (a linear problem). Morsk. Gidrofiz. Issledovaniya, Sebastopol 4:5–15.
O'Brien, J. J., and H. E. Hurlburt. 1972. A numerical model of coastal upwelling. J. Phys. Oceanogr. 2:14–26.
Pedlosky, J. 1968. An overlooked aspect of the wind-driven oceanic circulation. J. Fluid Mech. 32:809–21.
Philander, S. G. H. 1971. The equatorial dynamics of a shallow, homogeneous ocean. Geophys. Fluid Dyn. 2:219–45.
Robinson, A. R. 1960. The general thermal circulation in equatorial regions. Deep-Sea Res. 6:311–17.
Robinson, A. R. 1966. An investigation into the wind as the cause of equatorial undercurrent. J. Mar. Res. 24:179–204.
Stalcup, M. C., and W. G. Metcalf. 1966. Direct measurements of the Atlantic equatorial undercurrent. J. Mar. Res. 24:44–55.
Stevenson, M. R., and B. A. Taft. 1971. New evidence of the equatorial undercurrent east of the Galapagos Islands. J. Mar. Res. 29:103–15.
Stommel, H. 1960. Wind-drift near the equator. Deep-Sea Res. 6:298–302.
Stommel, H. 1965. The Gulf Stream. University of California Press, Berkeley, and C. V. P. 248 pp.
Sturm, M., and K. Voigt. 1966. Observations of the structure of the equatorial undercurrent in the Gulf of Guinea in 1964. J. Geophys. Res. 71:3105–8.
Swallow, J. C. 1967. The equatorial undercurrent in the western Indian Ocean in 1964. Stud. Trop. Ocean. No. 5 (Proc. Int. Conf. Trop. Ocean. Miami):15–36. University of Miami, Fla.
Taft, B. A. 1967. Equatorial undercurrent of the Indian Ocean, 1963. Stud. Trop. Ocean. No. 5 (Proc. Int. Conf. Trop. Ocean. Miami):3–14. University of Miami, Fla.
Taft, B. A., and J. A. Knauss. 1967. The equatorial undercurrent of the Indian Ocean as observed by the Lusiad Expedition. Bull. Scripps Inst. Oceanogr. 9:1–163.
Taft, B. A., and J. H. Jones. 1973. Measurements of the equatorial undercurrent in the eastern Pacific. *In*: Progress in Oceanography 6:47–111, ed. by B. A. Warren. Oxford, Pergamon Press.
Tsuchiya, M. 1968. Upper waters of the intertropical Pacific Ocean. Johns Hopkins Oceanogr. Stud. 4. 50 pp.
Veronis, G. 1960. An approximate theoretical analysis of the equa-

torial undercurrent. Deep-Sea Res. 6:318–27.
Walin, G. 1972a. On the hydrographic response to transient meteorological disturbances in the Baltic. Tellus 24:169–86.
Walin, G. 1972b. Some observations of temperature fluctuations in the coastal region of the Baltic. Tellus 24:187–98.
Yoshida, K. 1959. A theory of the Cromwell current (the equatorial undercurrent) and of the equatorial upwelling–an interpretation in a similarity to a coastal circulation. J. Oceanogr. Soc. Jap. 15:159–70.
Yoshida, K. 1967. Circulation in the eastern tropical oceans with special references to upwelling and undercurrents. Jap. J. Geophys. 4(2):1–75.

DISCUSSION

PEDLOSKY: I wish you had commented in your paper on the role of the approximation of no downstream variation, which is built into the theory in a very intricate kind of way. What is usually done is to assume a similar scale between the north-south velocity and the east-west velocity, but a disparity of scale between north-south and east-west.

GILL: One can justify this easily for a linear model; for a nonlinear model one can't. In fact, you can't construct a consistent nonlinear model incorporating the effects of the meridional boundaries without taking account of east-west variations in some way.

CHARNEY: I think that if you have a homogeneous model, you do get a consistent scaling with no downstream variation. But in a stratified ocean, where the flow must fit an extra-equatorial thermohaline solution, *a la* Robinson–Welander, or something like that, you definitely have to have a downstream variation.

GILL: To begin with, we have the thermocline tilting up toward the east in the stratified ocean, which introduces x-variation. Secondly, if the momentum equations are vertically integrated, you have a nonlinear term, the y-derivative of the integral over depth of the momentum flux, which appears in the equation in the same way as does the wind stress. The nonlinear term is equivalent to a strong wind stress confined to a narrow band around the equator. So to calculate the effect of this on the vertically integrated flow is equivalent to solving the problem of a wind stress confined to a narrow equatorial band. The solution has x-variations and results in a westward current along the equator and eastward currents a few degrees to the north or south. The entire vertically integrated flow is driven by the transport of eastward momentum toward the equator via the meridional circulation. Bill Holland has done some calculations with a constant wind stress that produce a circulation rather like this. It seems to be a real effect.

MUNK: You can accomodate the discrepancy of three or four between observed and linearly computed wind stress by the number given, essentially. Is that correct?

GILL: Yes.

ROBINSON: I have one comment based on a simplified two-layer model in which the layer depth is free to adjust itself with the flow. I was working on this model, because it wasn't clear to me that we had theories that properly related the equatorial undercurrent to all the possible driving terms, for example, local winds, or winds of greater meridional extent, or the thermohaline circulation, etc. In terms of the simple model, I was hoping to trace the forcing. The first solution I took was a purely thermohaline case with no wind. And I was very surprised to find that there was no equatorial undercurrent under the boundary conditions of no east coast transport. This was surprising, because similarity theories indicate that there is a purely thermal undercurrent. So, to investigate this a little further, I tried to force a similarity-like structure on this model; instead of an east coast condition, I brought the bottom layer up to zero along some virtual line of constant longitude to the east. Indeed, I do get an equatorial undercurrent much like that seen in the similarity solutions.

WELANDER: The only one that we still do not understand is the model in which the wind blows from east to west, piling up water and then having it going back along the equator. I don't know if there is something wrong with that model, because it is still difficult to understand. If you have a meridional circulation, what does make a particle go eastward at the equator? Now I understand that there are models where you don't have east-west variation, but they don't have a meridional circulation either. Is that correct?

GILL: They still have a pressure gradient and it's assumed constant.

PHILLIPS: The center of the current seems to be roughly at the level where the thermocline exists, at, let's say, 5° south or north of the equator. Do these theories give a clear explanation of why the undercurrent doesn't extend much deeper?

GILL: That's one feature that we'd like to explain. Munk produced a very nice explanation of it, but unfortunately–

MUNK: It's wrong.

GILL: So I don't know that there is a nice theory. Bill Holland has done some interesting calculations that agree with this. A result of one of his calculations is in the manuscript.

ROBINSON: Of course, a scale analysis does indicate the general character of the model in a correct way by assuming a value for the vertical-mixing coefficient. If this is done, the scale depth comes out right, doesn't it?

GILL: It does. The Princeton model, a fully predictive model, was shown during this meeting. This is a case with a very large eddy friction; so it gives a rather broad, weak undercurrent. But you can see that the undercurrent has its core at about 100 m; and you can see how this fits in with the thermocline some distance away, so that sort of feature is reproduced. Holland has done calculations with less friction, but he hasn't analyzed them fully yet.

VERONIS: Is there any evidence that the global undercurrent has any effect outside of the vicinity of the equator, or is it essentially more or less confined to the equatorial region?

GILL: I think that it does have an effect outside the equatorial region. One factor is the one that I mentioned here about the nonlinear effects driving the net eastward transport along the equator, which has to be balanced by a return flow just a little bit to the north or south. So you have to have a westward transport north or south to complete the circulation.

VERONIS: That's consistent with the wind distribution just off the equator—that you get a divergent flow north and south away from the equator. So, in a sense you could conceivably account for that without an equatorial undercurrent.

GILL: Yes, you're saying that the linear circulation models all produce the westward current there anyway.

O'BRIEN: The thing is that observations tend to show us that this large flux of water in the undercurrent apparently flows mostly to the south, and it is the water that then separates the Peru current into two branches—a nearshore and an offshore equatorial current.

NIILER: We know that there is quite a broad-surface, westward flow at the equator that persists through considerable depth away from the undercurrent. This is the flow that feeds the north equatorial countercurrent and that then ends up in the north equatorial current. So, in a sense, if there were no undercurrent here, the transport of this current would be much stronger to the west. In particular, what happens then around Mindanao and the Bay of the Philippines would immediately be reflected as to how this western boundary current feeds mass back into the whole North Pacific.

MUNK: Norman Phillips' question encourages me to ask a question of Francis Bretherton. The paper of Dennis Moore and myself, which confused Eulerian and Lagrangian flow, has two messages. One is that it naturally gave a maximum for the thermocline depth strictly in terms of the wave function—it tried to explain the undercurrent in terms of the radiation stresses of Rossby waves. And it has the nice feature that the wave energy of Rossby waves is peaked where the Vaisala frequency is a maximum; it also gives some possible insight into why the undercurrent should move eastward instead of westward. But that was wrong. But, then I heard that Francis Bretherton was possibly thinking of an alternative point of view, which had to do with the critical layer reflection of Rossby waves by an equatorial undercurrent while being formed. Am I correct? Was there some merit to that?

BRETHERTON: I still don't think so. I must admit that I had been planning not to put this forward into the discussion at this time, but obviously I have to. Basically, this was just another conceivable theory of the undercurrent. It is based on the remark that if you have ordinary internal gravity waves produced more or less isotropically in the regions to the north and south of the equator, some of them are bound across the equator. And if they do cross the equator, they start interacting with the undercurrent, which is one of the strongest features present. If their component of phase velocity towards the east is less than the maximum speed of the current, there will be a critical layer. The implication is that the wave is almost certain to be absorbed when it passes out of the current. Waves, on the other hand, that have a component of phase velocity towards the west will get through relatively unscathed. Now waves that have a phase-component velocity towards the east carry momentum towards the east, and all the rational arguments that have been put forth suggest that that momentum ends up essentially as a net force on the body of water where the current is. We therefore have a slightly peculiar situation. Once you get a current headed towards the east, it can selectively extract momentum from the wave-energy field to keep it going towards the east. This says nothing about the distribution or the width of the current. Dennis and I did some calculations on this a number of years ago, but we never published them because of our total ignorance about the magnitude of the internal wave spectrum in most parts of the world and our real inability to put the hard numbers in—the numbers that define what the contribution to the actual driving forces might really be. The sort of very crude numbers that we invented more or less off the top of our heads did suggest that you could get net stresses toward the east on the average around .2 dyn/cm^2 or something like that. But this is I agree a subject that perhaps we ought to take up again, and I must admit I'm rather embarrassed to have to talk about it at this state without having that much work.

PEDLOSKY: Would the mechanism continuously broaden the current?

BRETHERTON: Let's say this—insofar as you can localize the absorption region, the strongest conclusion is that absorption will take place as the wave goes through. The next strongest conclusion is that the actual stress will be applied towards the flanks of the current on the other side. But, of course, as soon as you start applying stress towards the east, the Coriolis force starts acting and essentially tends to pull the current together and narrow it. So what the final distribution would be, in other words, what the effects of such a stress would be on the current itself, I have no view at the moment.

PEDLOSKY: I was just thinking that it's the same thing as the Lindzen and Holton model. As the thing comes in, the position of the critical layer will then continuously move outward from the center.

BRETHERTON: It's far from obvious to me that the position of the critical layer will in fact move out toward the center.

PEDLOSKY: Well, as the momentum is absorbed, the current there would speed up, so it would seem then that you're saying you'd have to get further out to find the critical layer.

BRETHERTON: Except insofar as you get direct nonlinear advective effects pulling it in. If you speed up current towards the east, in the presence of a Coriolis force, it moves toward the equator, if you don't do anything else to stop it.

MODELS OF COASTAL UPWELLING

J. J. O'BRIEN

INTRODUCTION

Along the western coasts of the continents, a narrow strip, 0 (100 km), of cold coastal water is observed (Figure 1). This anomaly is explained by the phenomenon called coastal upwelling. The phenomenon is important physically, ecologically, and climatologically. The strong upwelling of nutrient-rich water increases the total productivity of the coastal region.

Upwelling to an oceanographer means positive (upward) vertical velocity. Coastal upwelling is the process in which water from depths of up to a few hundred meters is pumped into the upper several meters near shore. The classic Ekman (1905) explanation states that, due to the earth's rotation, equatorward winds along the eastern boundary of the ocean produce an offshore mass transport in a surface Ekman layer, thereby creating an upwelling of water near the coast. In a review article, Smith (1968) discusses the research on upwelling up to 1967. Compared to research on the western boundary layer, there has been relatively little theoretical and observational work on coastal upwelling.

The regions of strong, reoccurring coastal upwelling are off the western United States, Peru, Morocco, South Africa, northwest Africa, and western Australia. Coastal upwelling is created by seasonal monsoon winds off the coasts of Somaliland. A world map of areas of high organic production is essentially a map of strong upwelling. Ryther (1969) estimates that more than half of the world's fish food supply may be produced in coastal upwelling regions.

Coastal upwelling is found observationally to be a time-dependent, nonlinear, three-dimensional, boundary-layer phenomenon. Most models of coastal upwelling are steady, linear, and two-dimensional. Based on series of mesoscale measurements of the coastal upwelling region off the Oregon coast, Smith *et al.* (1971) following Mooers (1969) present the following verbal description of steady-state coastal upwelling (Figure 2):

1. In the summer season, the mean north-northwesterly winds cause a net offshore transport of water in the surface Ekman layer, which is of the order of 10 meters thick. They also cause a southward flow in the alongshore direction, which can be thought of as the barotropic component of the alongshore flow, to a depth of about 40 m.
2. Mass compensation requires a net onshore transport of water below the surface Ekman layer. The flow is onshore in the upper portion of the permanent pycnocline, and presumably in a bottom Ekman layer, 10 to 20 m thick.
3. Since the water of the open ocean reservoir is density stratified with a permanent pycnocline at a depth of about 100 meters, the net offshore transport of light water near the surface and the net onshore transport of heavy water near the bottom cause the permanent pycnocline to rise inshore, forming an inclined frontal layer.
4. The inclined frontal layer induces a "thermal wind." Thus, there is a baroclinic component to the alongshore flow such that the flow in the inclined frontal layer is increasingly poleward relative to the surface flow as the depth increases. To the extent that the barotropic and baroclinic flow components can be considered linearly superimposed, the barotropic flow induced by the wind, or inclination of the sea surface, either operates to reinforce or to cancel the baroclinic flow in the frontal layer. For instance, with the permanent pycnocline at a fixed intensity and inclination, if the barotropic flow is sufficiently southerly, the lower layer can come to a standstill or be reversed to equatorward flow, while the surface layer continues to flow equatorward. On the other hand, if the barotropic component relaxes, or reverses, the upper layer can come to a standstill or be reversed to poleward flow, while the lower layer continues to flow poleward. Reversals similar to those described are observed to occur on a time scale of several days to weeks.
5. The inclined frontal layer is a region where the processes of frontogenesis, necessary for the development and the sustenances of the frontal layer, and of frontolysis, necessary for the destruction of the frontal layer, are of significance. Appreciable mixing occurs in the frontal zone. If mixing is sufficiently intense, the isopycnals in the layer beneath the inclined frontal layer become downwarped, intensifying the tendency for northward flow there. The mixing of warm, fresh waters derived from the surface layer with cold, saline waters upwelled from the lower layer near the surface front replenishes the water mass of the frontal layer. The freshly formed water mass of the frontal layer sinks to the lower half of the inclined frontal layer and below and then flows seaward, adding to the volume

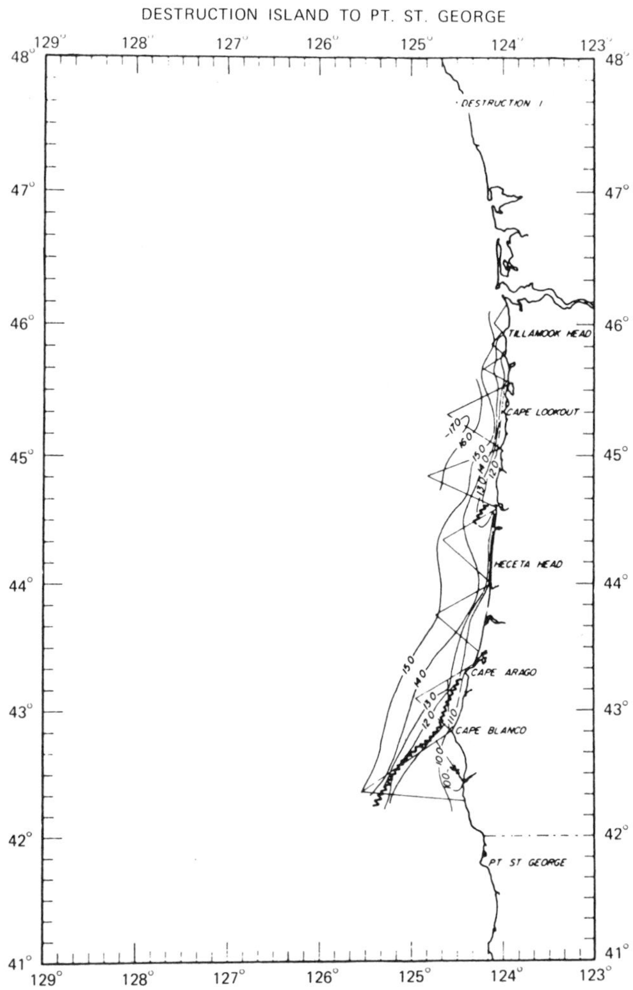

FIGURE 1 Sea-surface temperature (°C) from ART along Oregon coast 12 August 1969 (from Smith *et al.*, 1971).

of the permanent pycnocline. The modified, or mixed, upwelled water is warmer, but more saline, than water of similar densities offshore and thus appears as a temperature inversion. The temperature inversion water is presumably 'leaked' through the current meter array, due to the large separation between current meters. The hydrological-optical investigation of Pak *et al.* (1970) supports the deduced cross-stream flow pattern.

6. The seasonal pycnocline develops at the base of the surface Ekman layer. It is formed by the seasonal thermocline, which develops from summer heating, and by the seasonal halocline, which is derived from the mixing of surface layer water with the relatively fresh water of the Columbia River plume. The seasonal pycnocline breaks the sea surface to form a surface front, which tends to block the offshore flow of lower layer water that has been supplied from the upper portion of the permanent pycnocline to the surface Ekman layer inshore.

7. The above remarks present only a steady-state model. When the winds accelerate sufficiently, the permanent pycnocline becomes more steeply inclined and breaks the surface, forming a surface front, while the surface front formed by the seasonal pycnocline propagates offshore, causing a strong surface divergence to develop. The acceleration process may be largely advective. When the winds decelerate, the response is less rapid because the process of developing an inclined frontal layer is essentially irreversible on the short time scale, requiring mixing for its destruction.

This picture developed by seagoing oceanographers is complicated. Except for some preliminary theoretical work by Mooers (1969) and Csanady (1972), the modelers of upwelling have ignored the theoretical complications introduced by the formation of a surface front.

This paper will review the dynamics of coastal upwelling as seen through the pen of the theoretician. There is considerable room for improved explanation. When more supporting observational evidence of the mesoscale circulation is obtained in coastal upwelling regions, the theoretical physical oceanographer will, no doubt, contribute more encompassing and plausible explanations than presently exist.

THE CLASSICAL EKMAN-SVERDRUP MODEL OF COASTAL UPWELLING

The equations of motion for a steady, homogeneous ocean are assumed to be

$$0 = fv + \frac{1}{\rho}\frac{\partial}{\partial z}\left(A_v \frac{\partial u}{\partial z}\right), \tag{1}$$

$$0 = -fu + \frac{1}{\rho}\frac{\partial}{\partial z}\left(A_v \frac{\partial v}{\partial z}\right). \tag{2}$$

The integrated mass transports are defined in the usual way,

$$M_x = \int_{-\infty}^{0} \rho u \, dz, \tag{3}$$

$$M_y = \int_{-\infty}^{0} \rho v \, dz, \tag{4}$$

and we assume that the stresses vanish at some depth in the ocean. Sverdrup (1938), Sverdrup and Fleming (1941), and Yoshida (1955) assume that away from the eastern boundary the surface transport is

$$M_x = \tau_y/f, \tag{5}$$

where τ_y is the longshore wind stress. By neglecting longshore variations in the velocity field, the continuity equation yields at some distance from the shore (L)

$$u(-L) = -\int_0^{-L} \frac{\partial w}{\partial z} \, dx. \tag{6}$$

In addition, if w at the sea surface is zero, then

$$M_x = \int_0^{L} \rho w_{-H} \, dx, \tag{7}$$

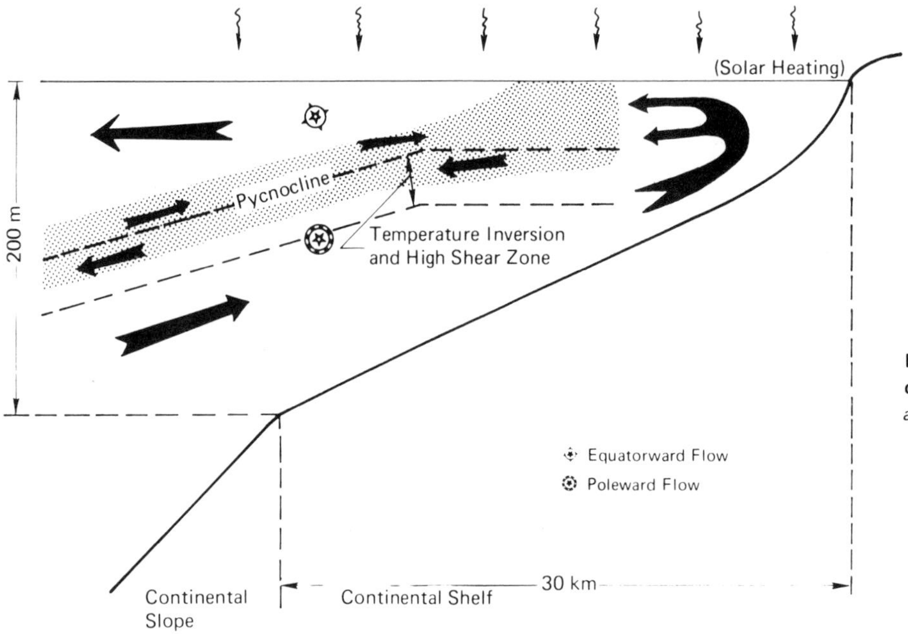

FIGURE 2 Schematic of mean circulation during upwelling off Oregon (from Smith *et al.*, 1971).

where H is the depth of the Ekman layer, which has been classically (but perhaps erroneously) assumed to be the depth of the mixed layer.

LOCAL, STEADY, HOMOGENEOUS MODELS

Hidaka (1954) attempted to deduce the three-dimensional flow using a steady-state, homogeneous, infinitely-deep hydrostatic ocean. His equations of motion were

$$0 = -g\frac{\partial \eta}{\partial x} + fv + K_H\frac{\partial^2 u}{\partial x^2} + K_v\frac{\partial^2 u}{\partial z^2}, \tag{8}$$

$$0 = -fu + K_H\frac{\partial^2 v}{\partial x^2} + K_v\frac{\partial^2 v}{\partial z^2}, \tag{9}$$

where η_x is the sea surface slope and K_H and K_v are constant eddy viscosities. If D_H and D_v are defined

$$D_H = (K_H/f)^{1/2}, \tag{10}$$

$$D_v = (K_v/f)^{1/2}, \tag{11}$$

then Hidaka calculated the solution for the special case where the constant wind stress vanishes at $L = -2\pi D_H$. This arbitrary choice results in strong downwelling centered at $-L$ offshore due to simple Ekman pumping.

The circulation calculated by Hidaka is quite simple. The offshore mass transport, τ_y/f, occurs in a surface Ekman layer of thickness, D_v; upwelling at the coast occurs in a thickness, D_H. Since the ocean is homogeneous, the upwelled water comes from infinite depth. An estimate of the vertical velocity obtained from continuity is

$$\frac{w}{u} = \frac{D_v}{D_H} = (K_v/K_H)^{1/2}. \tag{12}$$

Since we expect K_v/K_H to be $0(10^{-6})$ and u of $0(1 \text{ cm s}^{-1})$, w is 10^{-3} cm s^{-1}. Saito (1956) extended Hidaka's theory to the transient problem when an ocean initially at rest is subjected to a suddenly applied (step function) wind stress.

Pedlosky (1968) and Johnson (1968) independently comment briefly on coastal upwelling, which is required for closure of the circulation in a three-dimensional, linear, homogeneous ocean. Garvine (1971) analyzes more completely the motion due to surface wind stress acting on homogeneous water of constant depth. His fundamental contribution is demonstrating that the north-south pressure gradient must be retained in the dynamics. His model equations are

$$\frac{\partial u}{\partial x} + \frac{\partial w}{\partial z} = 0, \tag{13}$$

$$-fv = -g\frac{\partial \eta}{\partial x} + K_H\frac{\partial^2 u}{\partial x^2} + K_v\frac{\partial^2 u}{\partial z^2}, \tag{14}$$

$$fu = -g\frac{\partial \eta}{\partial y} + K_H\frac{\partial^2 v}{\partial x^2} + K_v\frac{\partial v}{\partial z^2}. \tag{15}$$

The velocity (u,v) vanishes at the straight north-south coastline $(w = 0)$ at top and bottom, and a constant wind stress is applied at the surface. The parameters are chosen such that the depth of the ocean (H) is much greater than

D_v, the depth of the surface Ekman layer. The onshore mass flux must balance the Ekman flux, τ_y/f. Garvine argues that based on observations this onshore flux must be uniformly distributed over depth below the surface Ekman layer, thereby removing any role for a bottom Ekman layer. Thus, away from any boundary layer,

$$fu = -g \frac{\partial \eta}{\partial y}, \qquad (16)$$

or the return flow is geostrophic. In addition, as a result of mass continuity,

$$\int_{-H}^{o} u \, dz = 0, \qquad (17)$$

he obtains

$$\frac{\partial \eta}{\partial y} = \tau_y/(\rho g H), \qquad (18)$$

as $x \to -\infty$. Since the wind stress and the depth are constant, the long-shore pressure gradient is independent of distance offshore. Further analysis (not detailed here) reveals that

$$\int_{-H}^{o} v \, dz = 0. \qquad (19)$$

This is an important result; the entire vertically integrated flow vanishes. Consequently, there must be a poleward undercurrent beneath the equatorward surface current. This is similar to the results of Durance and Johnson (1970).

The upwelling circulation that emerges from this paper is as follows. The wind stress drives a thin Ekman layer when $D_v/H < 1$ with offshore transport τ_y/f. The return flow is geostrophically balanced in the interior by a longshore pressure gradient. As the onshore flow enters the sidewall Ekman layer of thickness, D_H, the fluid rises to the surface. It is important to recognize that no bottom Ekman layer is required.

In a recent contribution, Garvine (1972) includes bathymetry in this model. He concludes that shoaling uplifts and accelerates the return onshore flow, thereby inducing a jet in the longshore velocity field in the subsurface layer. A net equatorward longshore mass flux results for $|\tau| = \tau_y$.

Hsueh and O'Brien (1971) investigate a somewhat different problem. They consider the circulation on a broad, flat shelf driven by a strong offshore current such as the loop current in the Gulf of Mexico. Their model predicts that the geostrophic interior current will respond to the shelf by transporting a bottom Ekman flux onto the shelf due to friction. The resulting circulation produces a weak upwelling circulation on the shelf; the structure of the circulation depends critically on the vertical profile of the exterior flow. This phenomenon, called current-induced upwelling, seems to have been observed off southwest Africa (Bang, 1971) and west Florida (Austin, 1971; Wroblewski, 1972). When a poleward undercurrent exists in the exterior flow, a two-gyre circulation develops with upwelling displaced offshore but on-the-shelf and weak downwelling at the coastline.

The main weakness of these homogeneous models is the neglect of stratification. The waters on the continental shelf in upwelling regions are almost always strongly stratified.

TWO-LAYER STRATIFIED MODELS

Two-layer ocean models have been a useful tool for studying most ocean circulation models. When the ratio of vertical to horizontal length scales is much less than unity, the hydrostatic approximation permits the modeler to formulate "reduced gravity" models. This is appropriate for coastal upwelling.

Consider a stably stratified, rotating, incompressible fluid on a continental shelf-slope cross section near a north-south coastline.

The equations of motion are

$$\frac{\partial u_1}{\partial t} + u_1 \frac{\partial u_1}{\partial x} - f v_1 = -g \frac{\partial}{\partial x}(h_1 + h_2 + D) + \frac{(\tau_{sx} - \tau_{Ix})}{\rho h_1} + K_H \frac{\partial^2 u_1}{\partial x^2}, \qquad (20)$$

$$\frac{\partial v_1}{\partial t} + u_1 \frac{\partial v_1}{\partial x} + f u_1 = -g \frac{\partial}{\partial y}(h_1 + h_2 + D) + \frac{(\tau_{sy} - \tau_{Iy})}{\rho h_1} + K_H \frac{\partial^2 v_1}{\partial x^2}, \qquad (21)$$

$$\frac{\partial h_1}{\partial t} + \frac{\partial}{\partial x}(u_1 h_1) = 0, \qquad (22)$$

$$\frac{\partial u_2}{\partial t} + u_2 \frac{\partial u_2}{\partial x} - f v_2 = -g \frac{\partial}{\partial x}(h_1 + h_2 + D) + g' \frac{\partial h_1}{\partial x} + \frac{(\tau_{Ix} - \tau_{Bx})}{\rho h_2} + K_H \frac{\partial^2 u_2}{\partial x^2}, \qquad (23)$$

$$\frac{\partial v_2}{\partial t} + u_2 \frac{\partial v_2}{\partial x} + f u_2 = -g \frac{\partial}{\partial y}(h_1 + h_2 + D) + g' \frac{\partial h_1}{\partial y} + \frac{(\tau_{Iy} - \tau_{By})}{\rho h_2} + K_H \frac{\partial^2 v_2}{\partial x^2}, \qquad (24)$$

$$\frac{\partial h_2}{\partial t} + \frac{\partial}{\partial x}(u_2 h_2) = 0, \qquad (25)$$

$$g' = \frac{\rho_2 - \rho_1}{\rho_2} g. \tag{26}$$

The subscripts 1 and 2 refer to upper and lower layers. The usual notation and right-handed coordinate system is used. The stresses carry subscripts *s, I,* and *B,* denoting surface, interior, and bottom. These equations are equivalent to those used by Charney (1955), Yoshida (1967), Hurlburt and Thompson (1972), McNider and O'Brien (1972), O'Brien and Hurlburt (1972), and Thompson and O'Brien (1972). In each paper the velocity field is considered independent of y. However, major differences exist in the analysis. These will be indicated subsequently. (Yoshida has a number of the papers prior to 1967 that are not referenced here, since the 1967 paper is a masterful integration of his earlier work. Unfortunately, this paper is not readily available in many U.S. libraries. It is essential reading for studying upwelling. In particular, Yoshida does consider the case $\partial/\partial y \neq 0$.)

In the model equations, we may invoke an f-plane or a β-plane analysis. For the former, it is easily shown that the north–south pressure gradient is identically zero or a constant. Yoshida (1955) and Charney (1955), using analytical methods, and O'Brien and Hurlburt (1972), using numerical methods, have shown that a coastal upwelling, equatorward, surface jet occurs during active upwelling. This has been confirmed observationally by Mooers *et al.* (1975). Since the jet occurs in the β-plane models also, we shall only explore in detail the dynamics of the β-plane model.

In contrast to the steady homogeneous models, the two-layer stratified models have no interesting steady state. Thermodynamic mixing is neglected by all authors (except Yoshida, 1967) under the assumption that it has a long time scale compared to the upwelling time scale of several days to two weeks. For a steady state, Eqs. (22) and (25) imply $\partial/\partial x\,(u_i h_i) = 0$. However, since u_i vanishes at the coast, u_1 and u_2 are zero everywhere; and consequently, w is zero at the interfaces. Some analysis shows that v_1 and v_2 are balanced geostrophically by the east–west pressure gradients, if bottom friction is strong enough to balance the surface wind stress, τ_y. This is an uninteresting solution.

If the time scale for the interface to surface is the order of several days, the changes over a day are small and we may look at the essential balances in the equations. These may be derived by scale analysis or empirically from a numerical solution. Let us assume, for simplicity, an equatorward wind stress that may be a function of x or t and that flat, wide-ocean shelf, quasi-balanced equations for the β-plane model are

$$fv_1 = g\frac{\partial}{\partial x}(h_1 + h_2), \tag{27}$$

$$fu_1 = -g\frac{\partial}{\partial y}(h_1 + h_2) + \frac{\tau_{sy}}{\rho h_1} + K_H\frac{\partial^2 v_1}{\partial x^2}, \tag{28}$$

$$fv_2 = g\frac{\partial}{\partial x}(h_1 + h_2) - g'\frac{\partial h_1}{\partial x}, \tag{29}$$

$$fu_2 = -g\frac{\partial}{\partial y}(h_1 + h_2) + K_H\frac{\partial^2 v_2}{\partial x^2}. \tag{30}$$

One may also argue that the tendency terms must be retained in Eqs. (28) and (30). The continuity equations yield

$$u_1 h_1 + u_2 h_2 = 0. \tag{31}$$

The sidewall friction terms are only important within a distance (O'Brien and Hurlburt, 1972)

$$D_H = \left(\frac{K_H v_1}{fu_1}\right)^{1/2} \geqslant 5 \text{ km}, \tag{32}$$

where v_1 is determined by Eq. (27) and the Ekman transport. These horizontal friction terms serve only to bring the longshore flow to zero. In contrast to the steady, homogeneous models, each investigator of two-layer models has chosen to minimize the role of sidewall friction. In these models, w does not vanish at the coast. A thin nonhydrostatic layer of the order of a few meters thick is required to bring w to zero at the wall; this boundary layer is ignored in two-layer models.

If $h_2 > h_1$, the usual case considered, the equatorward wind stress drives a reduced Ekman transport offshore,

$$\rho u_1 h_1 = \frac{\tau_{sy}}{f} - \frac{\rho g h_1}{f}\frac{\partial}{\partial y}(h_1 + h_2). \tag{33}$$

The return flow is balanced geostrophically by the north–south barotropic pressure gradient

$$\rho u_2 h_2 = -\frac{\rho g h_2}{f}\frac{\partial}{\partial y}(h_1 + h_2). \tag{34}$$

The longshore flow is geostrophically balanced [Eqs. (27) and (29)]. If the north–south pressure gradient is not retained in the problem, the return flow must be balanced by the tendency of v_2, or bottom friction. Interior friction and the field accelerations do not seem to be important. It appears from Yoshida (1967), Hurlburt and Thompson (1972), and Garvine (1971) that a small north–south barotropic pressure gradient is an essential dynamic ingredient of coastal upwelling. For a wind stress of 1 dyn cm^{-2} and a shelf depth of 300 m, the sea slope is approximately 3 cm in 1,000 km. This result is independent of latitude.

The existence of the coastal upwelling surface jet is seen using a potential vorticity argument (Charney, 1955; O'Brien and Hurlburt, 1972). If τ_y is a constant for a hundred kilometers or more offshore, the frictionless potential vorticity equations are

$$\frac{d}{dt}\frac{\left(\frac{\partial v_1}{\partial x}+f\right)}{h_1}=0, \qquad (35)$$

$$\frac{d}{dt}\frac{\left(\frac{\partial v_2}{\partial x}+f\right)}{h_2}=0. \qquad (36)$$

If the fluid is at rest initially, we may integrate once and obtain

$$\frac{\partial v_1}{\partial x}=f\frac{(h_1-H_1)}{H_1}, \qquad (37)$$

$$\frac{\partial v_1}{\partial x}=f\frac{(h_2-H_2)}{H_2}, \qquad (38)$$

where H_1 and H_2 are the undisturbed thicknesses. When upwelling occurs near the coast, $h_1/H_1 < 1$ and $h_2/H_2 > 1$. Therefore, v_1 must be a minimum near the coast and v_2 a maximum. The influence of horizontal friction displaces the jet maximum away from the coast. If D_H is as large as the upwelling length scale, the jet will not be as evident in a numerical or analytical model.

Hurlburt and Thompson (1972) demonstrate that if the wind stress curl vanishes over the upwelling region and the bottom is flat, then the integrated longshore transport is zero or

$$v_1 h_1 + v_2 h_2 = 0. \qquad (39)$$

McNider and O'Brien (1972) find this result of zero longshore transport holds for a four-layer extension of this problem. Yoshida (1967) also derives this result. Eq. (39) implies the existence of a subsurface poleward countercurrent! Eqs. (27), (29), and (39) may be combined to yield the useful diagnostic relations (Hurlburt and Thompson, 1972),

$$v_1=\frac{g'}{f}\left(\frac{h_2}{h_1+h_2}\right)\frac{\partial h_1}{\partial x}, \qquad (40)$$

$$v_2=-\frac{g'}{f}\left(\frac{h_1}{h_1+h_2}\right)\frac{\partial h_1}{\partial x}. \qquad (41)$$

These diagnostic relations agree within 5 percent with the solutions found numerically by Hurlburt and Thompson.

Coastal upwelling occurs in a narrow boundary zone. Following Yoshida (1955), several authors have shown that the appropriate horizontal length scale is the baroclinic radius of deformation. In a two-layer fluid, this is

$$\lambda=\left[\frac{g'H_1H_2}{f^2(H_1+H_2)}\right]^{1/2}. \qquad (42)$$

At mid-latitudes, λ is 0(10 km). This is an order of magnitude less than the textbook value of a 100-km length scale. We expect that upwelling will occur within 10 km of the coast.

The time scale, T, for the surfacing of the interface, can be estimated from continuity and the Ekman drift relation,

$$T=\rho H_1\lambda f/\tau_y. \qquad (43)$$

A typical vertical velocity, W, is

$$W=\tau_y/(\rho\lambda f). \qquad (44)$$

At mid-latitudes and with a wind stress of 1 dyn cm^{-2}, W is 10^{-2} cm s^{-1}, an order of magnitude higher than that estimated from homogeneous models. Note that W is independent of latitude, since λ is proportional to f^{-1}. If $H_1 < H_2$, we obtain

$$W=\tau_y/\rho(g'H_1)^{1/2}. \qquad (45)$$

Thus a parcel at 50 m is expected to rise to the surface in approximately 5 days due to a steady wind stress of 1 dyn cm^{-2}. The expressions for T and W were derived first by Yoshida (1955).

CONTINUOUSLY STRATIFIED MODELS

Since coastal upwelling is a mesoscale boundary phenomenon, it is rarely resolved in large-scale numerical ocean models. An exception is Cox (1970), who calculates strong upwelling shoreward of the northern part of the Somali current in his Indian Ocean model.

Boundary-layer analysis has, in my opinion, not been highly successful in deducing the dynamics of coastal upwelling. For example, the coastal jet and the strong poleward undercurrent system are not explained in the literature. These phenomena appear in the so-called corner region, which is difficult to analyze due to singularities. Johnson (1968) uses simple Ekman theory in discussing the eastern boundary layer. He says that "a full description of the flow in the eastern boundary layer must await an analysis of this layer." Gill (1970) has a similar result.

An important result from boundary-layer analysis is the identification of two vertical length scales—the Ekman-layer thickness and the Lineykin-layer thickness. The latter was recognized by Lineykin (1955). Tomczak (1970), Leetmaa (1971), Blumsak (1972), Hsueh and Kenney (1972), and Allen (1972 a,b) have contributed to the linear theory of stratified, two-dimensional, rotating, incompressible Boussinesq fluids near an upwelling sidewall.

The analysis (and notation) of Leetmaa (1971) is useful for displaying the essential results. Leetmaa assumes σ = 0(1) and $Ro \ll E \ll 0(1)$, where $\sigma \equiv$ Prandtl number = ν/κ,

$E \equiv$ Ekman number $= \nu/fD^2$, and $Ro \equiv$ Rossby number $= U/fL$. The resulting nondimensional equations are

$$-v = -p_x + E\nabla^2 u, \tag{46}$$

$$u = E\nabla^2 v, \tag{47}$$

$$o = -p_z + T, \tag{48}$$

$$o = u_x + w_z, \tag{49}$$

$$(\sigma s\delta)w = E\nabla^2 T. \tag{50}$$

The notation is standard for geophysical fluid dynamics: $\delta \equiv$ aspect ratio $= D/L$ and $s \equiv g\alpha\Delta T/f^2 L$. The two vertical scales that result from the analysis are $E^{1/2}$, the Ekman layer thickness, and the Lineykin layer thickness, $\lambda_L = (\sigma s\delta)^{-1/2}$. The appropriate value of λ_L is important to the character of the circulation. Allen (1972a) shows that if $\lambda_L < D$, the upwelling circulation in the plane perpendicular to the coast is confined to the depth λ_L. Tomczak (1970) and Hsueh and Kenney (1972) estimate that $\lambda_L > D$ for the real ocean. In other words, the Lineykin depth is thicker than the depth of the ocean for typical values of the parameters. This controversy needs to be resolved.

Tomczak (1970) also demonstrates that the type of circulation depends essentially on the form (curl) of the wind field, while the magnitude of the wind stress influences only the intensity of the circulation. The depth of upwelling is inversely proportional to the square root of the Brunt-Vaisala frequency.

Much more analytical work needs to be done for coastal upwelling boundary layers if the complete dynamics is to be understood.

GEOMETRY MODIFICATION

Following the tradition of "square basin" oceanography, modelers of coastal upwelling have assumed simple geometry: infinitely deep ocean or flat-bottom and north-south coastline. However, the descriptive oceanographers frequently refer to occurrences of centers of upwelling and upwelling plumes. Marine biologists observe large discrete patches of phytoplankton in upwelling regions. An example of a plume is shown in Figure 3 from Walsh *et al.* (1971). Reid *et al.*

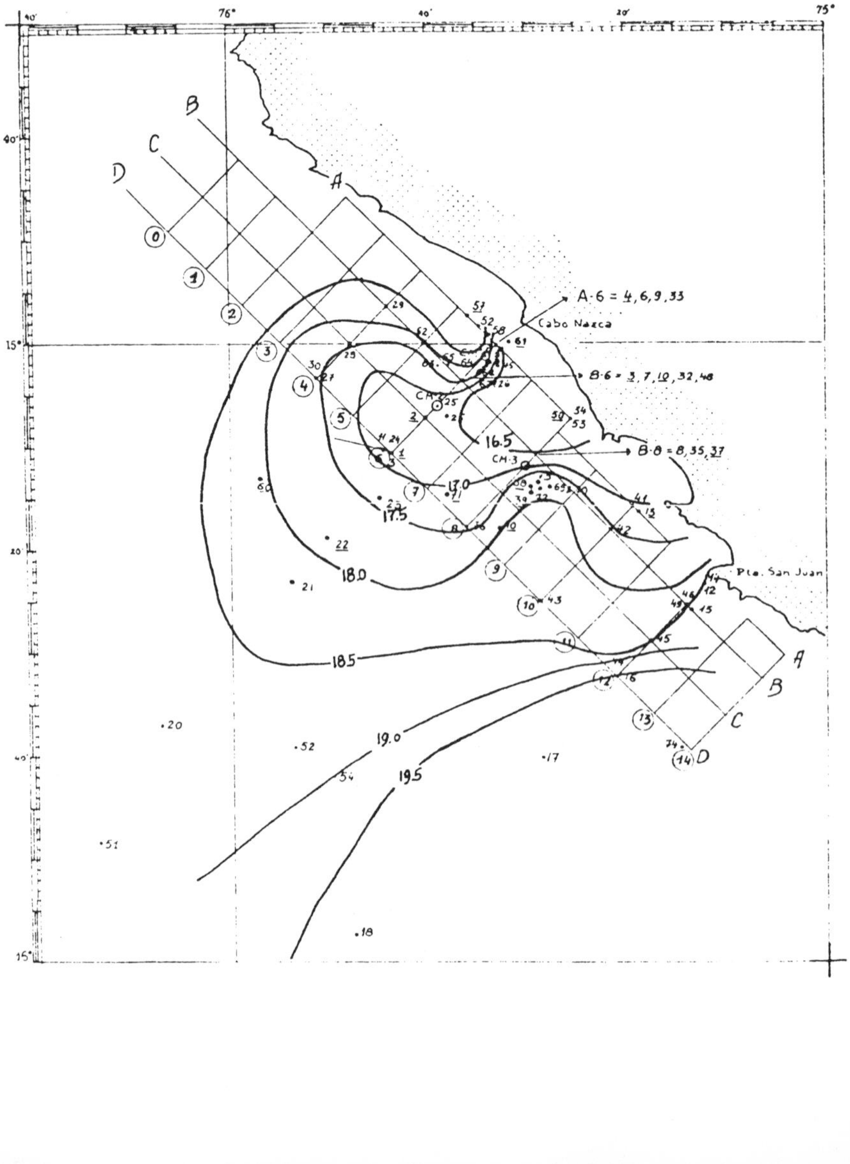

FIGURE 3 Day-temperature distribution (°C) at 3-m depth (from Walsh *et al.*, 1971).

(1958) have commented on the intensification of upwelling south of capes and points that extend out into coastal currents.

Arthur (1965) and Yoshida (1967) have contributed to explaining the increased upwelling south of capes. The mechanism is quite simple. Consider a longshore current flowing past a cape toward the equator. Since the current must follow the curved shoreline, Yoshida (1967) observes that there must be horizontal divergence south of the cape that will create upwelling. Arthur (1965) uses a simple vorticity equation and observes that there will be increased cyclonic relative vorticity, which also leads to upwelling. Considerably more research is required to understand these dynamics. Observational programs now being designed should provide data that will encourage theoreticians to work on this problem.

The effect of shelf geometry is less understood. Observations tend to indicate that weak upwelling may occur at the shelf-slope break (Bang, 1971). Yoshida (1967), O'Brien and Hurlburt (1972), and Hsueh and O'Brien (1971) have shown that this is possible. The shelf geometry and/or boundary conditions used by these investigators are controversial and much more research is needed to elucidate the role of shelf topography.

CONCLUSIONS

Much more analytical and numerical work is required to understand completely the dynamics of coastal upwelling. The reader who rereads the observational description of upwelling in the Introduction will be struck by the inadequacy of present theory. On the other hand, the sea-going physical oceanographer must obtain a more detailed observational picture of coastal upwelling. It seems clear to me that it would be fruitful for theoreticians in the next few years to explore the following:

(a) the time-dependent aspects of coastal upwelling on both the several day and the seasonal time scales,
(b) the dynamics of an inclined frontal layer in the ocean,
(c) the influence of topography on coastal upwelling,
(d) the role of mixing processes during active upwelling, and
(e) the role of semipermanent large-scale ocean currents (such as the California current).

ACKNOWLEDGMENTS

Support for this work has been provided by the Office of Naval Research, Oceanography Section of the National Science Foundation (Grant GA-29734), and the International Decade of Ocean Exploration Program of NSF (Grant GX-28746). This is a theoretical contribution to CUEA, which is an IDOE/NSF-sponsored project. I wish to thank John Allen, Phil Hsueh, Harley Hurlburt, Bob Smith, and Dana Thompson for helpful suggestions. Contribution 97 of the Geophysical Fluid Dynamics Institute, Florida State University.

REVIEW: J. S. ALLEN

Dr. O'Brien has pointed out clearly that more analytical and numerical work is required to elucidate the dynamics of coastal upwelling. The difference between the results from the presently available theory of coastal upwelling and a conceptual model of upwelling off the Oregon coast, based on observations (Smith *et al.,* 1971) has been emphasized. It has been noted that the description of the possible formation of surface fronts is not included in the present analytical or numerical models. Clearly, work in the future will have to be directed toward the improvement of upwelling models so that they have the capability to describe this type of process. Because of the rather complicated nature of the phenomena, it can be expected that numerical, finite-difference solutions will play a role in the studies. Obviously, in that case a great deal of care will have to be given to the methods of modeling the effects of turbulent diffusion.

The results from analytical and numerical studies of upwelling in homogeneous, two-layer, and continuously stratified models have been reviewed. In connection with continuously stratified models, it is stated that boundary-layer analysis has not been highly successful in explaining the dynamics of upwelling. One reason for this, however, is that the appropriate theories have not as yet been worked out. If it is agreed that it is possible for studies with simplified models to give insight into the behavior of the real ocean, then a set of idealized, linear problems, which should be accessible to analytical or numerical treatment and which should yield useful results, can be identified. Some of these have been worked out; several have not. This set includes models with homogeneous, two-layer, and continuously stratified fluids that are adjacent to a coast and that are acted upon by a wind stress. For each of the three types of fluids, the models further subdivide into those on an f-plane or on a β-plane and those with simplified and with realistic bottom topography. Both time-dependent processes, due to an impulsively applied or time-varying wind stress, and steady-state features should be examined. The previous work on some of these problems has been described by Dr. O'Brien. The problems that remain include, for the most part, those with continuous stratification.

Dr. O'Brien has emphasized the time-dependent nature of upwelling. However, it should be remembered that some aspects of upwelling appear to be characterized by a quasi-steady balance. Observations off the Oregon coast (Mooers *et al.*, 1972) show that, at the beginning of the upwelling season after the onset of northerly winds, the density surfaces near the coast begin to rise and in some cases can be thought of as eventually intersecting the sea surface. Later in the upwelling season, with the winds still from the north, it seems that some type of equilibrium situation is reached, such that the position of the density surfaces essentially stabilizes. At least the density surfaces that have intersected the sea surface do not keep propagating out to sea. This situation appears to reflect some type of quasi-steady balance, perhaps of the frontal type referred to before. The nature of this apparent quasi-steady state should be investigated.

Further investigations of upwelling in linear, continuously stratified models is bound to involve a set of corner and/or boundary-layer regions that might be viewed skeptically with respect to their direct relation to the real ocean. Each different region will be governed by different physics, however, and hopefully some insight into controlling mechanisms might be obtained from the solutions. It appears to this reviewer that there are features of upwelling—such as the coastal jet, the poleward undercurrent, and the effect of the continental shelf break—that could be profitably investigated within the framework of simple, continuously stratified models. Certainly, the results from these studies will be helpful in guiding the construction of more complicated models.

With regard to boundary-layer regions, the consequences of boundary-layer scalings, where dimensionless variables are often expanded in terms of complicated combinations of parameters, should be clearly pointed out by those who use them. For example, the scaling of the velocities in the upwelling region in the homogeneous model of Durance and Johnson (1970) implies that the dimensional vertical velocity is of the same order of magnitude as the alongshore velocity. This certainly conflicts with observations.

Dr. O'Brien has discussed the results from two-layer models in some detail. These models have certainly provided some important information on the upwelling process and are useful because of their relative simplicity. However, the extent to which two-layer, depth-integrated models are capable of modeling upwelling and the limits on the type of information they can provide have not been clearly discussed. It seems that to understand the nature of the representation of upwelling in a two-layer model, the behavior of the fluid inside the two homogeneous layers has to be examined. Consider, for example, a two-layer fluid in a two-dimensional, f-plane model of upwelling in a rectangular geometry (i.e., with a finite dimension in the offshore direction) similar to the geometry of the model used by O'Brien and Hurlburt (1972). Further, consider an initial-value problem due to the impulsive application of a constant alongshore surface stress so that there is upwelling near one of the vertical walls that represents a coast. It is clear that the initial motion of the interface near the coast represents the vertical upwelling velocity of the fluid. However, as time increases, an Ekman layer will develop at the interface that will recirculate fluid in the upper layer—up the coastal sidewall—to feed the offshore flow in the surface Ekman layer. As a result, the motion of the interface no longer represents the total upwelling velocity. A steady state is possible, with a stationary interface that might intersect the sea surface. Upwelling still takes place within the two layers. The fluid moves upward in sidewall boundary layers between Ekman layers on the top and bottom surface and at the interface (see Carrier, 1965). The spin-up time for the linear problem, where the interface does not intersect the surface, is $O(E_\nu^{-1/2})$ (Pedlosky, 1967), where E_ν is the vertical Ekman number. The question arises, for what time scales do depth-integrated, two-layer models, where the motion of the interface is supposed to reflect the upwelling velocities, give a useful representation of upwelling? Are the steady-state solutions of any value? In connection with the question on steady-state solutions, it should be mentioned that the resulting steady upwelling circulation pattern in the two homogeneous layers of a two-layer fluid model is qualitatively similar to the conceptual circulation pattern from Smith *et al.* (1971), reproduced in Figure 2.

The results from studies with two-layer models should serve as guides for more detailed analytical or numerical studies with continuously stratified models. For example, the coastal jet found in the two-layer model should appear in a linear, continuously stratified model. The jet should have a horizontal scale $\lambda = DN/f$, where D is the depth, N is the Brunt-Vaisala frequency, and f is the Coriolis parameter. Important differences that might appear in the continuously stratified case are a qualitative change in spin-up time [from $O(E_\nu^{-1/2})$ to $O(E_\nu^{-1})$] and, of course, a change in the final steady-state structure.

A point that was not made by Dr. O'Brien, which this reviewer feels is important, is the following. Coastal upwelling investigations naturally concentrate on the motion near a coastal boundary. This leads, in many cases, to a local analysis with boundary or matching conditions provided by the fluid surrounding the upwelling area. Care should be taken by those studying the local upwelling region, first, to insure that the boundary conditions used are compatible with a model of the flow in the interior that is consistent with the model in the upwelling region and, second, to try to assess and explain any implication of those boundary conditions. For example, in the analysis of upwelling in a homogeneous fluid by Hsueh and O'Brien (1971), an alongshore velocity, which has a vertical gradient, is specified at the offshore edge of the upwelling region. It is rather hard to understand how a homogeneous interior flow would lead to that type of condition or how a stratified interior flow would adjoin a homogeneous upwelling region. As another example, in the thorough analysis by Garvine (1971) of steady-state upwelling in a homogeneous fluid, the rotation is taken to be locally constant (f-plane) in the upwelling region. The boundary conditions that were used on the subsurface onshore flow into the upwelling layer are, however, completely consistent for a general wind stress distribution with a β-plane interior flow. The analysis is correct for an upwelling layer in a homogeneous β-plane model. The β-effect does not enter locally in the upwelling region, but it is important in determining the form of the interior flow that feeds the upwelling boundary layer.

The consideration of boundary conditions for a local upwelling region will also be important in the future in connection with the formulation of three-dimensional numerical models of coastal upwelling.

Finally, with regard to the recommendation of topics that should be explored in the future, the surface layer should be included. Upwelling is thought to be driven directly by the wind, through a turbulent Ekman layer at the sea surface. There is a great deal yet to be learned about the surface Ekman layer, both from observation and, hopefully, from analytical and numerical studies.

This work was supported by the Oceanography Section, National Science Foundation, under NSF Grant GA-30592.

REFERENCES

Allen, J. S. 1972a. Upwelling of a stratified fluid in a rotating annulus: Steady state. Part I: Linear theory. Unpublished manuscript.

Allen, J. S. 1972b. Upwelling of a stratified fluid in a rotating annulus: Steady state. Part II: Numerical solutions. Unpublished manuscript.

Arthur, R. S. 1965. On the calculation of vertical motion in eastern boundary currents from determinations of horizontal motion. J. Geophys. Res. 70:2794–2803.

Austin, H. M. 1971. The characteristics and relationships between the calculated geostrophic current component and selected indicator organisms in the Gulf of Mexico loop current system. Ph.D. Dissertation. Florida State University, Tallahassee. 172 pp.

Bang, N. D. 1971. The southern Benguela current region in February 1966: Part II: Bathythermography and air–sea interactions. Deep-Sea Res. 18:204–24.

Blumsack, S. L. 1972. The transverse circulation near a coast. J. Phys. Oceanogr. 2:34–40.

Carrier, G. F. 1970. Some effects of stratification and geometry in rotating fluids. J. Fluid Mech. 23:145–72.

Charney, J. G. 1955. The generation of oceanic currents by wind. J. Mar. Res. 14:477–98.

Cox, M. D. 1970. A mathematical model of the Indian Ocean. Deep-Sea Res. 17:47–75.

Csanady, G. T. 1972. Frictional secondary circulation near an upwelled thermocline. Unpublished manuscript.

Durance, J. A., and J. A. Johnson. 1970. East coast ocean currents. J. Fluid Mech. 44:161–72.

Ekman, V. W. 1905. On the influence of the earth's rotation on ocean currents. Ark. Mat. Astron. Fys. 12:1–52.

Garvine, R. W. 1971. A simple model of coastal upwelling dynamics. J. Phys. Oceanogr. 1:169–79.

Garvine, R. W. 1972. The effect of bathymetry on the coastal upwelling of homogeneous water. Unpublished manuscript.

Gill, A. E. 1970. Ocean models. Philos. Trans. R. Soc. Lond. Ser. A 270:391–413.

Hidaka, K. 1954. A contribution to the theory of upwelling and coastal currents. Trans. Am. Geophys. Union 35:431–44.

Hsueh, Y., and J. J. O'Brien. 1971. Steady coastal upwelling induced by an alongshore current. J. Phys. Oceanogr. 1:180–86.

Hsueh, Y., and R. N. Kenney, III. 1972. Steady coastal upwelling in a continuously stratified ocean. J. Phys. Oceanogr. 2:27–33.

Hurlburt, H. E., and J. D. Thompson. 1972. Coastal upwelling on a β-plane. Unpublished manuscript.

Johnson, J. A. 1968. A three-dimensional model of the wind-driven ocean circulation. J. Fluid Mech. 34:721–34.

Leetmaa, A. 1971. Some effects of stratification on rotating fluids. J. Atmos. Sci. 28:65–71.

Lineykin, P. S. 1955. On the determination of the thickness of the baroclinic layer in the ocean. Dokl. Akad. Nauk. USSR 101: 461–64.

McNider, R. T., and J. J. O'Brien. 1972. A multi-layer model of coastal upwelling. Unpublished manuscript.

Mooers, C. N. K. 1969. The interaction of an internal tide with the frontal zone of a coastal upwelling region. Ph.D. Dissertation. Oregon State University, Corvallis.

Mooers, C. N. K., C. A. Collins, and R. L. Smith. 1975. The dynamic structure of the frontal zone in the coastal upwelling region off Oregon. Unpublished manuscript.

O'Brien, J. J., and H. E. Hurlburt. 1972. A numerical model of coastal upwelling. J. Phys. Oceanogr. 2:14–26.

Pak, H., G. F. Beardsley, and R. L. Smith. 1970. An optical and hydrographic study of a temperature inversion off Oregon during upwelling. J. Geophys. Res. 75:629–36.

Pedlosky, J. 1967. Spin-up of a stratified fluid. J. Fluid Mech. 28:463–80.

Pedlosky, J. 1968. An overlooked aspect of the wind-driven oceanic circulation. J. Fluid Mech. 32:809–21.

Reid, J. L., Jr., G. I. Roden, and J. G. Wylie. 1958. Studies of the California current system. Calif. Coop. Oceanic Fish. Invest. Prog. Rep. Vol. VI:27-57.

Ryther, J. H. 1969. Photosynthesis and fish production in the sea. Science 166:72–76.

Saito, Y. 1956. The theory of the transient state concerning upwelling and coastal current. Trans. Am. Geophys. Union 37:38–42.

Smith, R. L. 1968. Upwelling. Oceanogr. Mar. Biol. Annu. Rev. 6:11–47. Geo. Allen and Unwin, Ltd., London.

Smith, R. L., C. N. K. Mooers, and D. B. Enfield. 1971. Mesoscale studies of the physical oceanography in two coastal upwelling regions: Oregon and Peru, pp. 513–35. *In* Fertility of the Sea. Vol. 2. Gordon and Breach, New York.

Sverdrup, H. U. 1938. On the process of upwelling. J. Mar. Res. 1:155–64.

Sverdrup, H. U., and R. H. Fleming. 1941. The waters off the coast of southern California, March to July 1937. Scripps Inst. Oceanogr. Bull. 4:261-378.

Thompson, J. D., and J. J. O'Brien. 1972. Time-dependent coastal upwelling. Unpublished manuscript.

Tomczak, M., Jr. 1970. Eine lineare Theorie des stationaren Auftriebs im stetig geschichteten Meer. Dtsh. Hydrogr. Z. 5:214–34.

Walsh, J. J., J. C. Kelley, R. C. Dugdale, and B. C. Frost. 1971. Gross features of the Peruvian upwelling system with special reference to possible diel variation. Invest. Pesq. 35:25–42.

Wroblewski, J. S. 1972. An ecological model of the lower marine trophic levels on the continental shelf off West Florida. Master's Thesis. Florida State University, Tallahassee.

Yoshida, K. 1955. Coastal upwelling off the California coast. Rec. Oceanogr. Works Jap. 2(2):1–13.

Yoshida, K. 1967. Circulation in the eastern tropical oceans with special reference to upwelling and undercurrents. Jap. J. Geophys. 4(2):1–75.

DISCUSSION

MUNK: I should think the progressive vector diagram is *not* among the oceanographic concepts that should be exported to the meteorologists.

O'BRIEN: That's the first time I've ever seen a wind diagram done that way.

BRETHERTON: The Woods Hole people have been doing them routinely for a long time.

O'BRIEN: On winds?

MOORE: Yes, because the wind recorders on their buoys are current meters turned upside down.

O'BRIEN: The advantage of a several-day progressive diagram is that if you're interested in a several-day time scale, then you get to see that very nicely; whereas, if I showed you a similar picture of u and v, you see all the high-frequency motions and this is not interesting to us for this mesoscale problem now.

KIRWAN: Jim, in your two-layer model, that simple calculation that you showed in your last figure, the poleward velocity, is about 5 cm/s. How closely does that match the mean current meter observations?

O'BRIEN: The model gives about half of what's observed in the mean.

MUNK: That's within the accuracy of measurements, isn't it?

O'BRIEN: No, I don't think so. The mean for the surface flow is probably more like 30, and mine is about 25, so that's within the accuracy. But I think we can tell the difference between a mean of 5 or 10 for the deeper poleward undercurrent.

VERONIS: In one of the diagrams, you showed that the water temperature is as cold as 8°. What's the normal depth for that?

O'BRIEN: The normal depth of that water would be 100 m when you're off the shelf away from the boundary layer.

VERONIS: Oh, so it's not on the shelf to begin with?

O'BRIEN: Oh, yes, it's on the shelf in this season, but I'm saying outside the first 10 km.

VERONIS: I wonder about what happens before the upwelling takes place.

O'BRIEN: In the time scale that we looked at here, that water is somewhere between 50 and 100 m deep on the shelf.

MOORE: What sort of moorings were those current meters on, Jim?

O'BRIEN: Subsurface taut wire moorings with the top being at 17 m below the surface.

CHARNEY: Some of O'Brien's remarks have touched off a different train of thought, however, which has to do with an upwelling phenomenon of considerable meteorological interest, namely the equatorial upwelling with easterly winds that has already been referred to by Gill. This upwelling does bring cold water to the equator and is thought by a number of people, especially Bjerknes, to have a considerable influence on the atmospheric circulation. There's another place where you expect upwelling, but the cold water doesn't come to the surface. This suggests that there may be more complicated cellular circulations and mixing processes there.

RATTRAY: First, just a comment on this last point. Situations off the coast of Oregon and Washington are pretty much the same, except for one thing—off the coast of Washington, there's a rather large freshwater outflow at this time, and the same sort of things happen—the isotherms rise but do not get to the surface because of the much stronger density gradient in that upper layer. Well, nevertheless, there is a possibility of field observations for starting to compare where you get one and where you get the other. And then, secondly, I want to mention that we have in fact developed and are getting a preliminary look at some similarity solutions to this from a model that is continuously stratified and that has the capability of varying the stratification in the ocean, heat flux on the surface, freshwater flow in the surface and at the sloping shelf, and width of the shelf. In fact, we have been able to get two-cell or one-cell circulations for the upwelling. Depending on the range of parameters, we get a surface flow with the wind, a countercurrent, and another bottom countercurrent in some cases; in other cases, we get the flow all in the direction of the wind. So there is a wide range of possibilities, depending on the range of parameters.

GALT: Is that model steady-state?

RATTRAY: The steady-state about which the fluctuations vary. There is a climatic upwelling. In this steady-state model you have to put in diffusion and these sort of things, as opposed to the wave-type solutions, where you can say that for a short period of time maybe diffusion doesn't change the distribution of properties compared to these advective effects.

NIILER: I did have a comment on Charney's comment. It turns out that right underneath the intertropical convergence, in the Pacific, at least, there's a very strong countercurrent. The ocean current runs as fast as 60 cm/s, at times, against the wind. The thermal structure is a very well-mixed layer down to about 100 m, and it's there almost all year. There's a great deal of turbulent mixing in that surface layer, and the situation is dynamically completely within a different parameter range. Below the mixed layer is a very sharp thermocline. The depth of the thermocline there is only another 200 m, and the O_t jump across that is almost 2½ units. So it's one unit larger than the North Atlantic thermocline. It is difficult to produce upwelling, for vigorous wind mixing will quickly mix surface anomalies to a deeper depth.

WARREN: I have yet to see a model that did not produce upwelling all the way to the bottom, no matter how deep one made the bottom. Although hydrographic observations on this aren't perfectly clear, I think they do suggest that the upwelling does not come from depths greater than 300 m.

ALLEN: One way that you can get an upwelling from intermediate depths is by having a heavy stratification in an f-plane model. Another possibility involves an unsolved problem, a stratified model with the β-effect. If you look at a two-dimensional homogeneous fluid on an f-plane model, you find that there is flow-out in the top surface Ekman layer, flow-in in the bottom surface Ekman layer, and flow-up in the sidewall. Now this could model upwelling in a homogeneous lake, for example. There is a possibility of some inflow, but most of the flow can come from the bottom Ekman layer. Now, however, if the interior is governed by β-plane dynamics, then, although the boundary layer is independent of the β-effect, you find that the inflow to the boundary layer is distributed uniformly—same dynamics of the boundary layer, different in the interior, and a completely different picture of upwelling because the flow comes in uniformly distributed over the depth. In the case of stratification, we are looking forward to seeing what a β-plane model can give, as compared to an f-plane, stratified model.

WARREN: But that model still has water coming from the bottom!

ALLEN: No, no water can come from the bottom.

PEDLOSKY: I don't think too much of this. The models I worked out were very simple. They were linear models of the β-plane dynamics. At least it appeared in that case that with the stratification the upwelling was limited.

ALLEN: What happens in the stratified model is that you get a series of one-quarter regions. It doesn't come off the bottom and the inflow can't either. But then one asks, what if there's a shallow shelf, and you might have to modify your considerations to take into account β-dynamics in the shelf.

O'BRIEN: Walter, I think maybe we've left the impression that there's a lot of work for a lot of people to do.

MUNK: Oh, you did.

BRYAN: Regarding Cox's numerical model for the Indian Ocean, the offshore Ekman transport was compensated by a flow at a fairly shallow depth, say 300–400 m.

MUNK: Could I ask Dr. O'Brien whether one is supposed to be surprised by your illustration of floats that were photographed during the critical period, which seem to all drift parallel and show no convergence at all?

O'BRIEN: In that period, the front was below the surface. It surfaced shortly after that.

MUNK: And after it surfaced, would one find that the floats do converge?

O'BRIEN: Oh, yes. In fact, let me tell you about a second drogue experiment. A line of drogues was put out about a third of a mile apart; within 24 h, this line of drogues rotated into the front.

VARIABILITY IN WESTERN BOUNDARY CURRENTS

P. P. NIILER

GENERAL DISCUSSION

The most voluminous and comprehensive description of ocean circulation deals with the currents that hug the eastern shores of the major subtropical continents of the world. These currents are narrow and intense and can be clearly identified as persistent features of the density structure near the ocean surface (Figure 1), as the northwestern front of the warm lens of subtropical water. Typically, they flow against the eastern boundaries of the continental landmasses for a short distance and subsequently meander eastward as intense, mid-oceanic flows. It is known that each current is somewhat different in intensity, width, and seasonal persistence; however, their short-scale spatial varability and shorter-term temporal variability are not well documented. Hence, the east Australian current is found at the latitude of Sydney as often as it is not (Hamon, 1965, 1969). It is known that the surface flow in the Somali current off the coast of South Africa reverses seasonally (Lighthill, 1971; Duing, 1970). Similar reversals should be apparent in the Brazil current, which is in a wind regime that seasonally reverses its vorticity distribution (Van Loon, 1972). The seaward extension of the Benguela current (Shannon, 1970) is characterized by 1,000-km-long meanders, while the seaward Gulf Stream meanders are normally 200–300 km long. The location of the Kuroshio is shifted every few years from the continental shelf to the abyssal plain (Robinson and Taft, 1972). The circulation and variability of the Argentine current is strongly linked to the circumpolar current (Schulman, 1970). It is commonly held that the existence of the western boundary current along the continental boundaries has a common underlying physical reason (Stommel, 1965), and that they are an integral part of a wind-driven gyre; whatever the physical processes that lead to their separation from the coast, their subsequent mid-oceanic meandering is the topic of much controversy.

At the present time, there is no adequate documentation of the dynamical structure of these currents, nor a clear delineation of their role in the dynamics of general ocean circulation. The difficulty lies in the fact that western boundary currents are "variable," such that observational programs have not been extensive enough, and the hydrodynamic models have been too simplistic in describing their circulation. Consider the Gulf Stream.

Unquestionably, the Gulf Stream (including the Florida current) is the most intensely documented flow. It is relatively simple to measure its velocity and density structure from ships or aircraft (W. S. Richardson and Schmitz, 1965; Barret and Schmitz, 1971; P. L. Richardson, 1972). This reviewer is aware that in the past 10 years at least 130 hydrographic sections of the Gulf Stream have been logged, and more than 150 sections that describe the horizontal velocity structure to 1,000 m have been reported. The U.S. Naval Oceanographic Office, the National Oceanic and Atmospheric Administration, and the Woods Hole Oceanographic Institution have gathered more than 90 tracks of cold-water penetration into the Sargasso Sea, which forms the northern edge of the Gulf Stream system (Naval Oceanographic Office Gulf Stream report by Hansen, 1970; Niiler and Robinson, 1967). Figures 1–8 display a subset of this data and illustrate the degree of variability in the Gulf Stream system.

During the years 1967–70, W. S. Richardson and his colleagues (1969) measured the horizontal velocity structure and the density structure of the Florida current at seven different sections along the eastern coast of North America

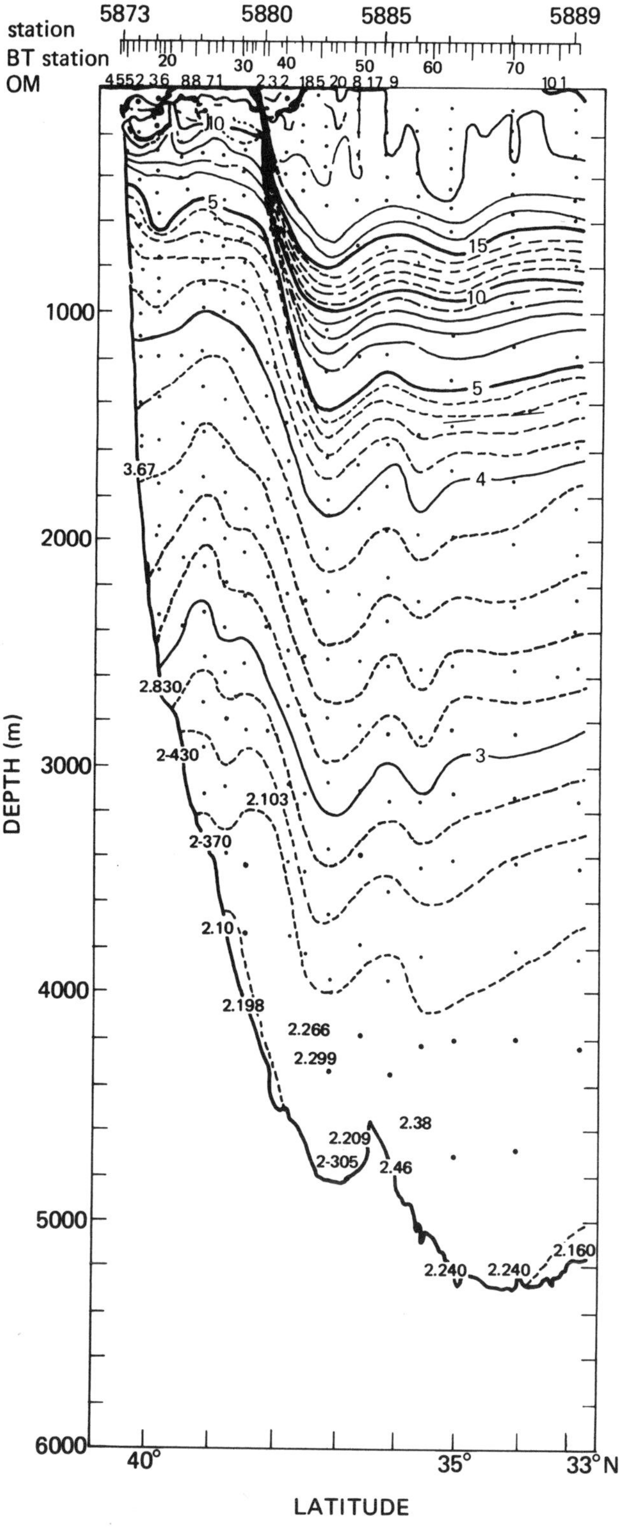

FIGURE 1 Temperature section across the Gulf Stream taken on April 9, 1960, at 62° 30′ W longitude (Fuglister, 1963). Units are °C.

(Figure 2). A compilation of the summertime surface current data from measurements over a 6-week period from Sections III and VII is shown in Figure 3. Figure 4 gives plots of depths of the 25 σ_t and 27 σ_t surfaces at Section VI (from hydrographic data gathered by Woods Hole Oceanographic Institution, November, 1961). In the summer of 1968, the U.S. Naval Oceanographic Office, Woods Hole Oceanographic Institution, and Harvard University cooperated in a program to determine the synoptic structure of the cold edge of the Gulf Stream northeast of Cape Hatteras, North Carolina (northeast of Section VII, Figure 2). The results of this 8-week observation are presented in Figure 5. The largest ensemble of data is from Section III at the Miami latitude.

The compendium of 78 directly measured values of transport between Miami and Bimini, in the Bahamas, is shown in Figure 6. It takes 8 h to complete a transect, and these samples represent ½-day means. It is seen that the seasonal variability is as large as the shorter-term changes. The seasonal range of the transport variability is estimated at 8.8×10^6 m^3/s. At the moment, there are no observations of sufficient duration to give spectral energy estimates for periods longer than 4 weeks. Records lasting 5 years or longer are required for reliable estimates of seasonal components of the spectrum.

Currently, the longest continuous analyzed record of the variability in the western boundary current is from a short segment of electromagnetic cable at the westernmost edge of the Florida current. The cable segment was in operation for 6 months, beginning on May 5, 1969, and had been calibrated by direct measurements. The potential difference across the cable is a measure of the total water flux above the section. The spectrum from this 6 months of data is reproduced in Figure 7. The data has been band-passed between 20 days and ½ day. Besides the tidal motions, the most energetic portion is between 4 and 7 days; and a second peak in the spectrum is centered at 2 weeks. Similar spectra are reported by Lee (1972) from a 4-month current meter record in the shallow water (50 ft) off Palm Beach, Florida, and by Sanford (1972) from the potential difference of the cable between Palm Beach and West End, in the Bahamas. It is most likely that these intense, nonseasonal fluctuations are endemic to the Gulf Stream. Schmitz (1971) has reported that along the 70° W longitude 3- to 14-day fluctuations near the ocean bottom diminish by a factor of four from a location under the Gulf Stream to 31° S (see Schmitz *et al.*, 1970, for a record of the bottom currents under the Gulf Stream). The energy level in these latter records is no longer in a narrow frequency band as in the Florida current, and it obviously contains components of the mid-oceanic variability.

To understand the energetics of the Gulf Stream system, it is quite apparent that the mean flow needs to be described; but it is not altogether obvious that the fluctua-

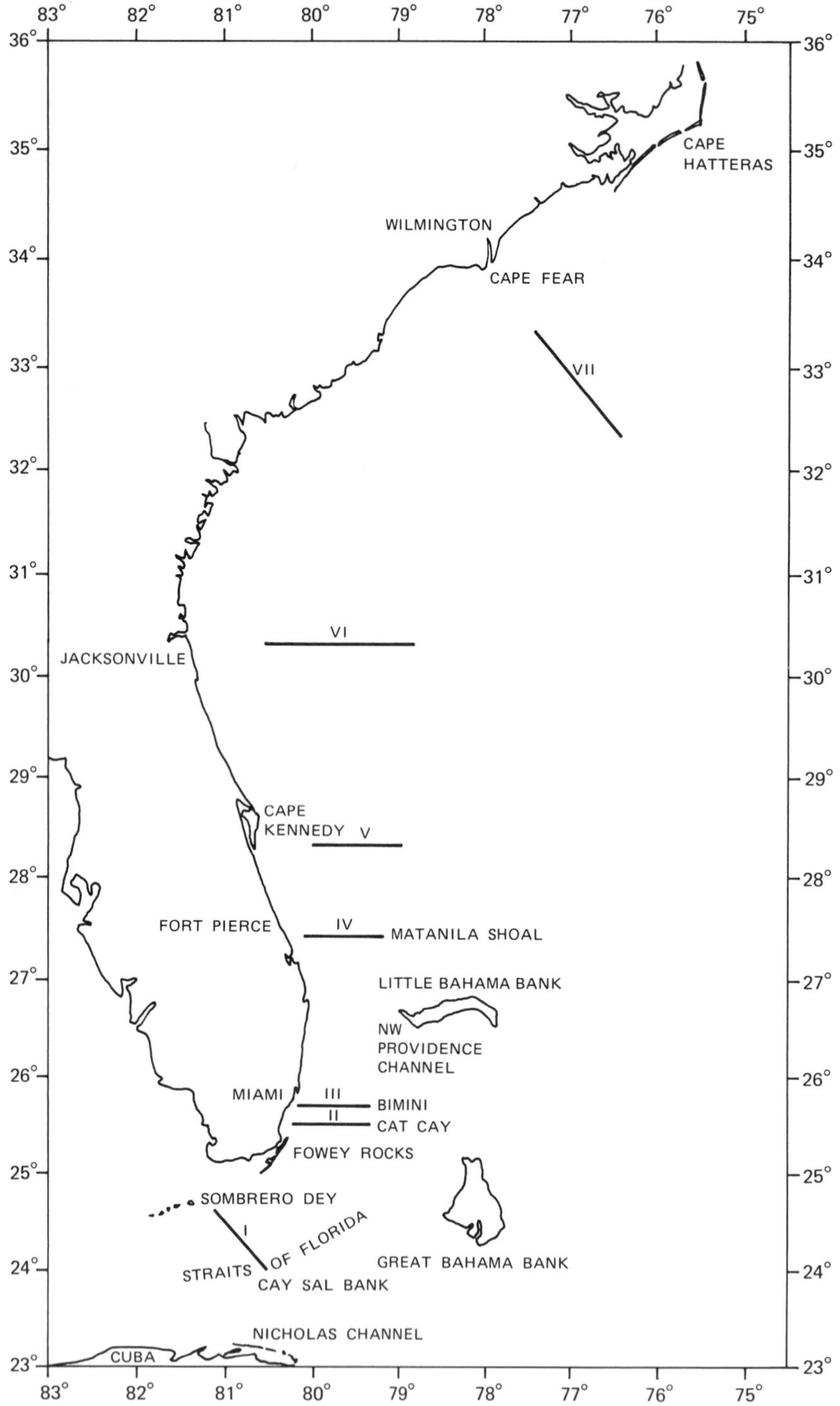

FIGURE 2 Location of sections of the Florida current along which measurements of the horizontal velocity structure have been made by W. S. Richardson *et al.* (1969).

tions of the scale described above are energetically active. The only partial estimate of the fluctuation energetics is from the ensemble of the surface current observations. It is found that the horizontal Reynolds stresses in the surface layer can transfer energy both to and from the mean flow (Webster, 1961; Schmitz and Niiler, 1969). Over the entire length of the Gulf Stream system, this rate of transfer can locally double the kinetic energy of the flow. No such acceleration is observed, and it is quite possible that this input is balanced by an opposite potential energy transfer such that a persistent current is maintained.

Complete estimates of potential energy transfer (or vertical transfer of kinetic energy) cannot be made from the existing data. A complete description of the fluctuation

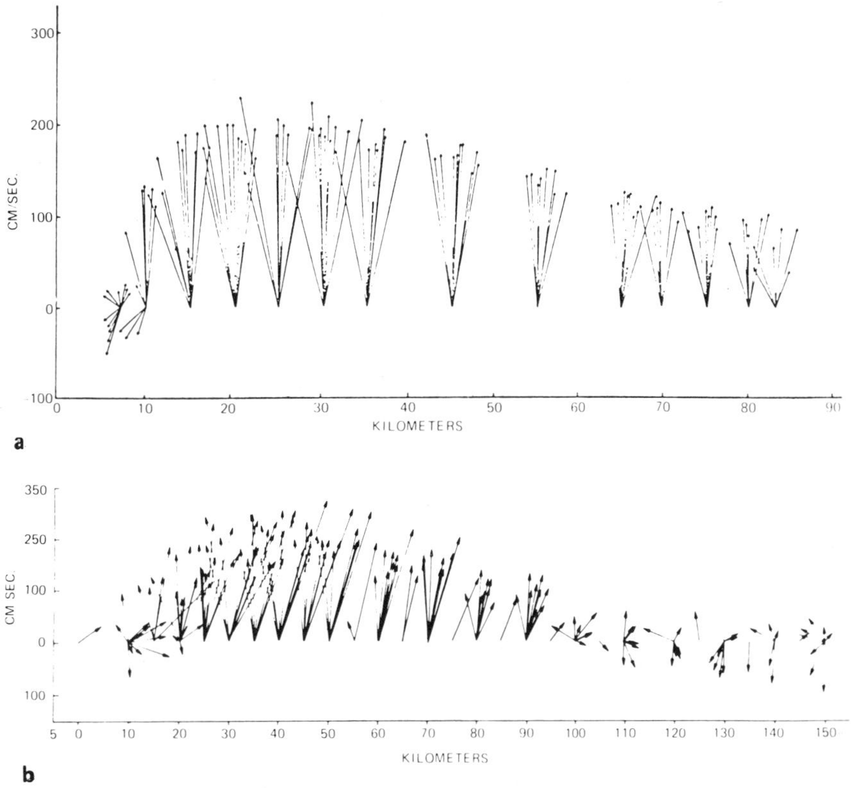

FIGURE 3 Variability of directly measured surface currents of the Florida current. Measurements in (a) were gathered in the summer of 1969 at the Miami latitude (Section III, Figure 2) and those in (b) were gathered in the summer of 1968 southeast of Cape Fear, North Carolina (Section VII, Figure 2).

energetics requires the simultaneous measurement of both density and velocity variability at a large number of horizontally and vertically separated points, of which only rudimentary records are available.

Potentially, the best such records of Gulf Stream fluctuations are the contours of the mature, large-scale, meander patterns northeast of Cape Hatteras and the recent acquisitions of near-stream current meter records by Woods Hole Oceanographic Institution.

A corollary to the above is that when the fluctuation energetics cannot be resolved by a data base neither can the dynamics of the mean flow be described adequately.

If an average dynamical distribution, such as the mean vorticity structure along isopycnal surfaces, is desired, a sufficiently large number of measurements must be obtained at a number of locations, so that statistically significant averages of the velocity and density structure can be computed. Fifteen ship crossings can easily be carried out in 6 weeks, and the kinematic description (the total flux of mass and heat) can be defined quite adequately (within 10 percent) by such a seasonal experiment. However, the data from such an observational program implies an average potential vorticity structure that has an rms error of 30 percent; this data will represent a seasonal mean, but is not suf-

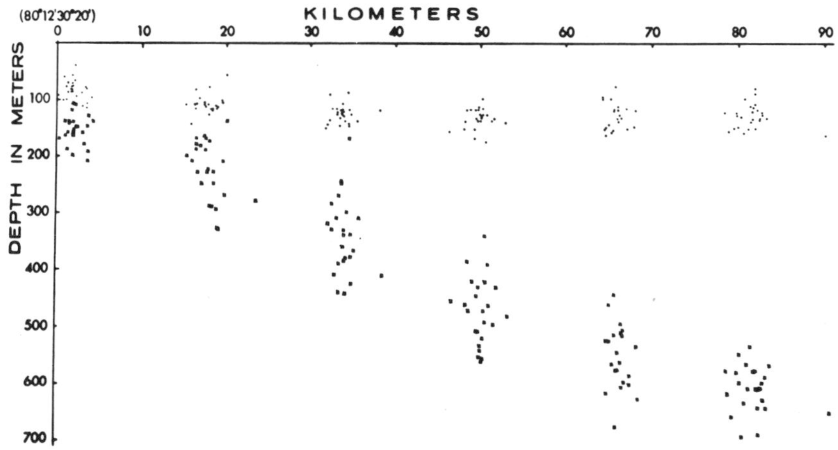

FIGURE 4 The variability of the depth of the $25\sigma_t$(•) and $27\sigma_t$(▪) isopycnals in the Florida current, east of Jacksonville (Section VI, Figure 2). The data were gathered in November 1961 by WHOI, *Crawford* cruise No. 70.

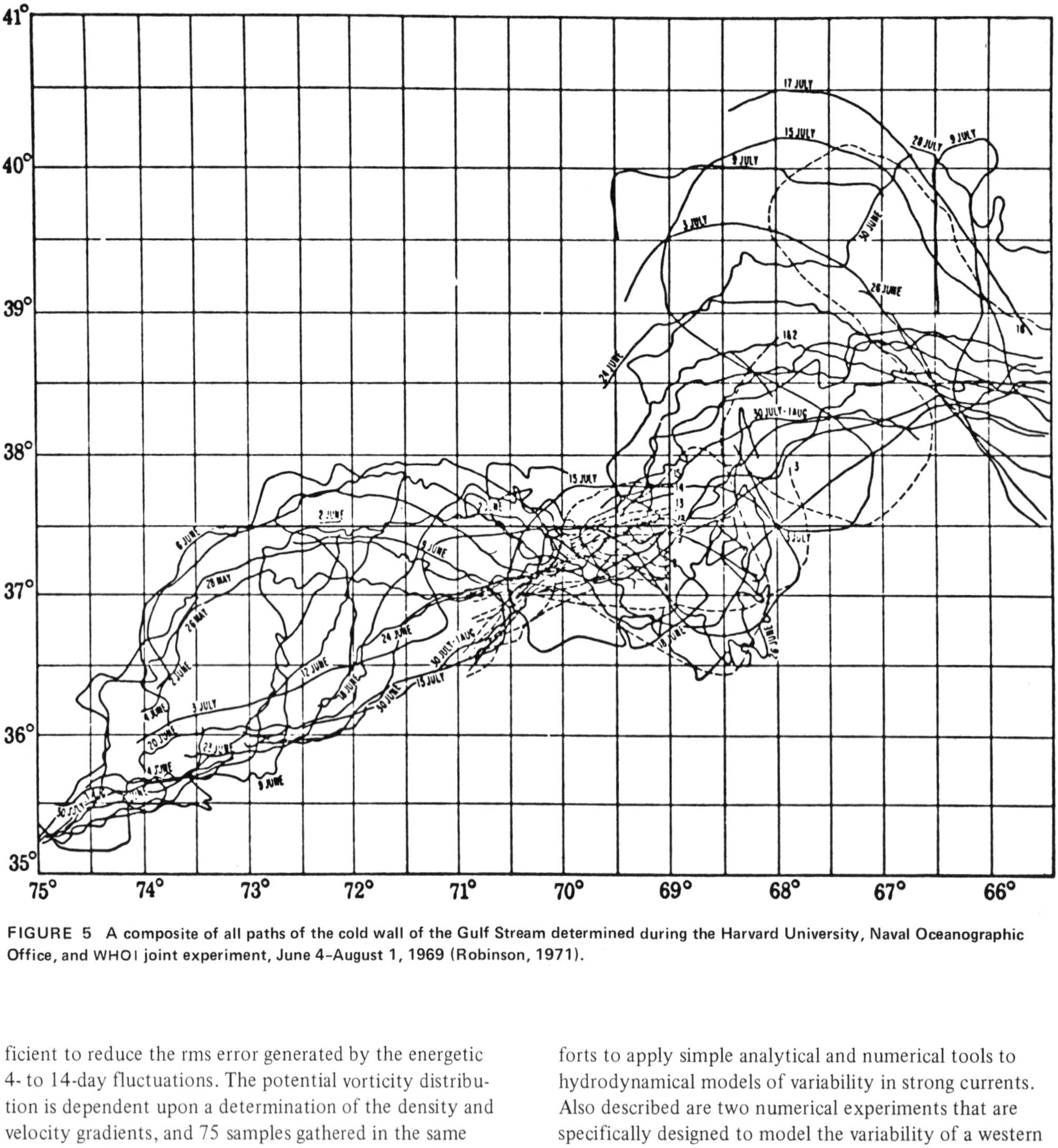

FIGURE 5 A composite of all paths of the cold wall of the Gulf Stream determined during the Harvard University, Naval Oceanographic Office, and WHOI joint experiment, June 4–August 1, 1969 (Robinson, 1971).

ficient to reduce the rms error generated by the energetic 4- to 14-day fluctuations. The potential vorticity distribution is dependent upon a determination of the density and velocity gradients, and 75 samples gathered in the same season in different years are needed to form a significant average with a 10 percent rms error. Because vorticity tends to be conserved in the Gulf Stream system (Figure 8), such a precise determination must be made before the establishment of a conservation law can be made at a significant level. The role of the boundary current in the general circulation crucially depends upon the degree to which potential vorticity is conserved in this intense flow.

This paper continues with a brief review of recent theories of western boundary current variability and of efforts to apply simple analytical and numerical tools to hydrodynamical models of variability in strong currents. Also described are two numerical experiments that are specifically designed to model the variability of a western boundary current and its interaction with the variability in the open ocean. The reader may anticipate that the fluctuation theories are no further advanced than the observations, whence a ripe time is at hand for progress.

STATIONARY MEANDERING OF STRONG CURRENTS IN THE OPEN OCEAN

The variability of the structure of a specific region of the ocean reflects the variability associated with the entire

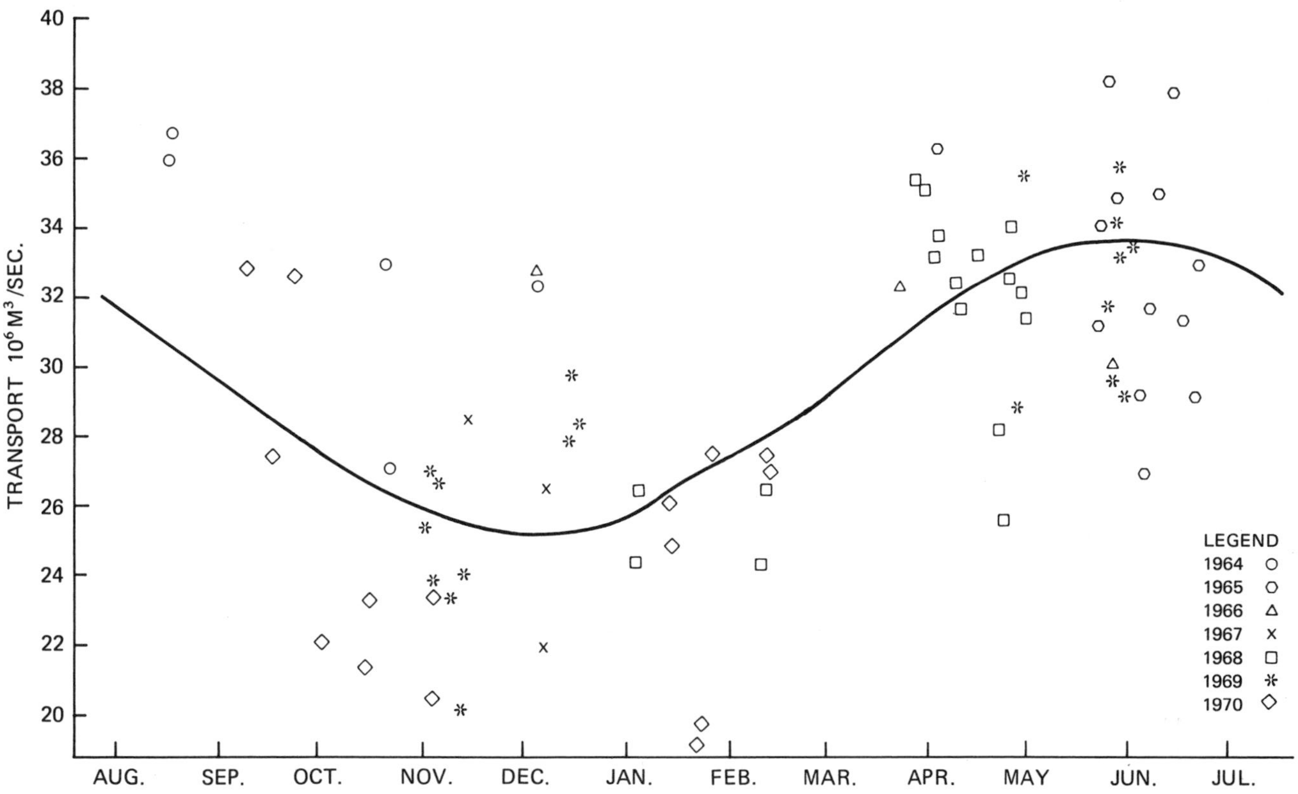

FIGURE 6 Directly measured Florida current transport at the Miami latitude (Section III, Figure 2) (Niiler and Richardson, 1972).

ocean basin, for long gravity waves and Rossby waves can transport energy over great distances. For the moment, however, concentrate on the class of motions and scales that can be maintained by western boundary currents and that could not exist in the broad ocean basins in their absence. In particular, consider the problem in the region where the boundary current no longer hugs a landmass, but forms the northwestern (poleward) edge of the warm-water gyre.

A multiple-ship survey of the Gulf Stream in the summer

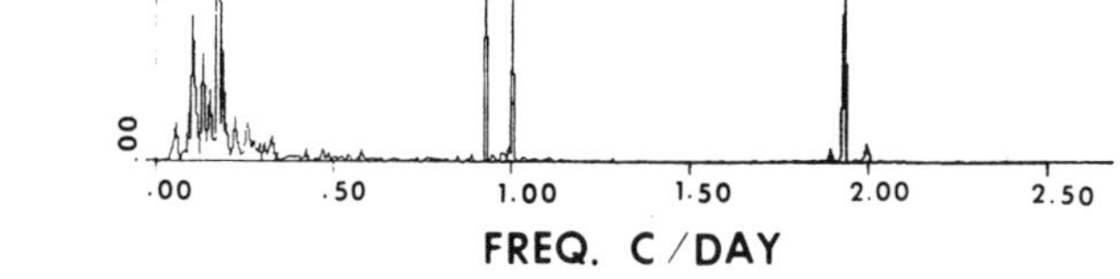

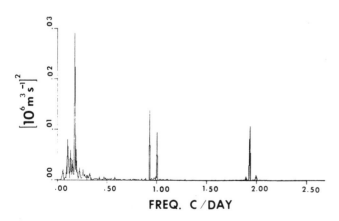

FIGURE 7 Spectrum of the calibrated potential difference across a short segment of a cable along the western side of Section II, Figure 2 (Ferrara, 1970).

of 1960 created a strong impetus for a study of these slowly variable motions. Two remarkable features of the circulation pattern were discovered (Figure 9). For the first time, large meander patterns of the cold edge of the warm Sargasso Sea water were mapped, which suggested that this pattern along the continental rise between 70°-50° W remained stationary during the 2-month cruise. Although this interpretation later was proved to be an exception rather than the rule (Figure 10), it did suggest that the meander phenomenon might in fact be governed by quasi-steady dynamics. First attempts at developing the theory of quasi-steady meanders over a continental slope were made by Warren (1963); a rigorous derivation of Warren's model, together with the subsequent coupling of the meander pattern to the circulation in the open ocean, was carried out by Robinson and Niiler (1967). The physical idea behind determining the location of such a strong, mid-oceanic current is simply an application of the conservation of the vertical component of vorticity within a narrow current filament that is imbedded in a more sluggish flow. The average value of the rate of change of the relative vorticity of such an intense current is

$$\partial/\partial y \left(\iint_A Kv^2 \, dx \, dz \right),$$

where the integration is carried out over the effective cross

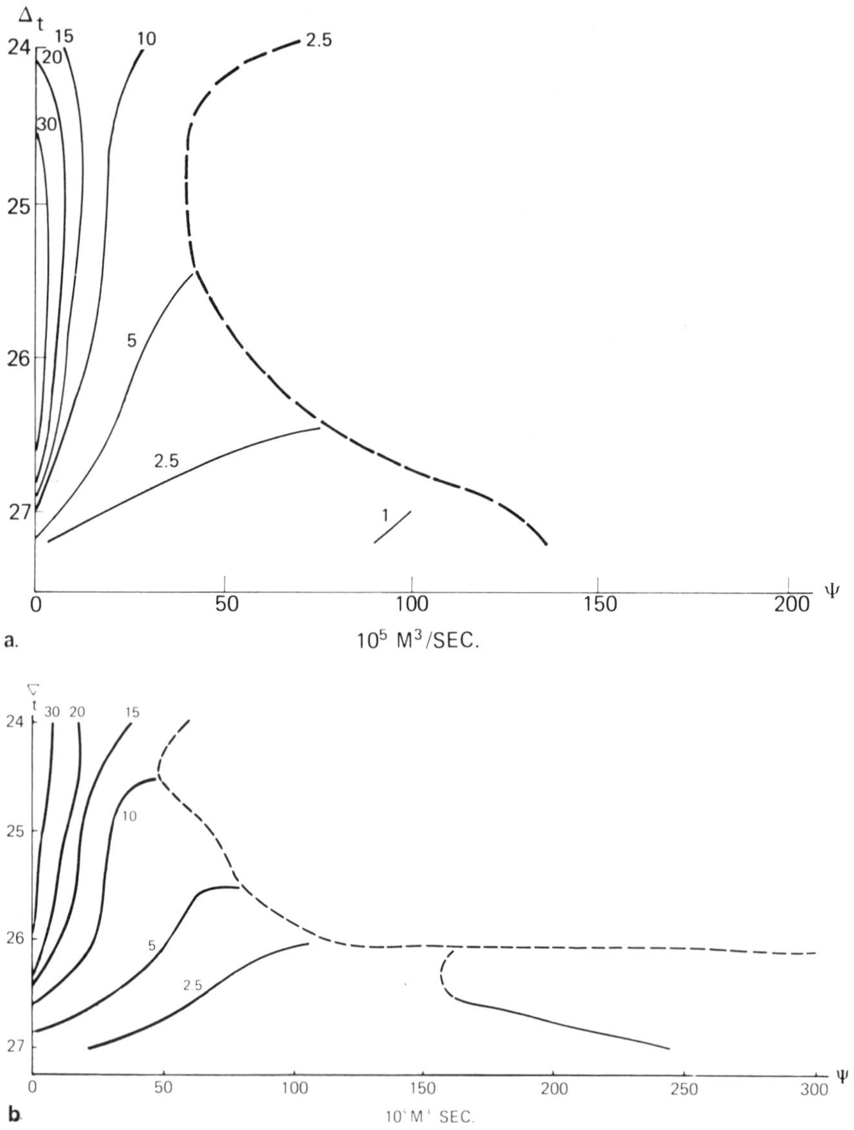

FIGURE 8 Potential vorticity distribution of the Florida current at (a) Section III and (b) Section VII, Figure 2.

sectional area of the current, axial velocity is v, and y measures distance along the sinuous axis. The curvature of the filament is $K = (d^2y/dx_2)/[(1 + dy/dx)^2]^{3/2}$, where $Y(X)$ is the geographical location of the axis. The rate of change of planetary vorticity is the sum of the rate due to the β-effect,

$$\iint_A \partial f/\partial y \; v \, dx \, dz,$$

and the rate at which the planetary vortex filaments are stretched by changes in the topography,

$$\int_L fv(B)\partial B/\partial y \, dx,$$

the Coriolis parameter is $f = f_0 + \beta Y$; and B is the depth of the ocean under the axis. If v_0 is known at a location (X_0, Y_0) and the bottom changes as well as the maximum excursion of the jet from that latitude are small, then $v \cong v_O(z,x)$, and the conservation of vorticity of the filament is expressed as

$$(K - K_0)\iint_A v_0^{\,2} \, dx \, dz + \beta(Y - Y_0)\iint_A v_0 \, dx \, dz$$

$$+ f_0(B - B_0) \int_L v_0(B) \, dx = 0. \quad (1)$$

The integration in the last term of Eq. (1) is carried out across the stream of width L. The terms with subscripts $_0$ are evaluated at the location (X_0, Y_0). Eq. (1) is seen to be a second-order differential equation for the path, $Y(X)$, which describes the location of the vortex filament.

Three specific applications of this quasi-steady theory have been worked out in great detail. In an extensive set of calcu-

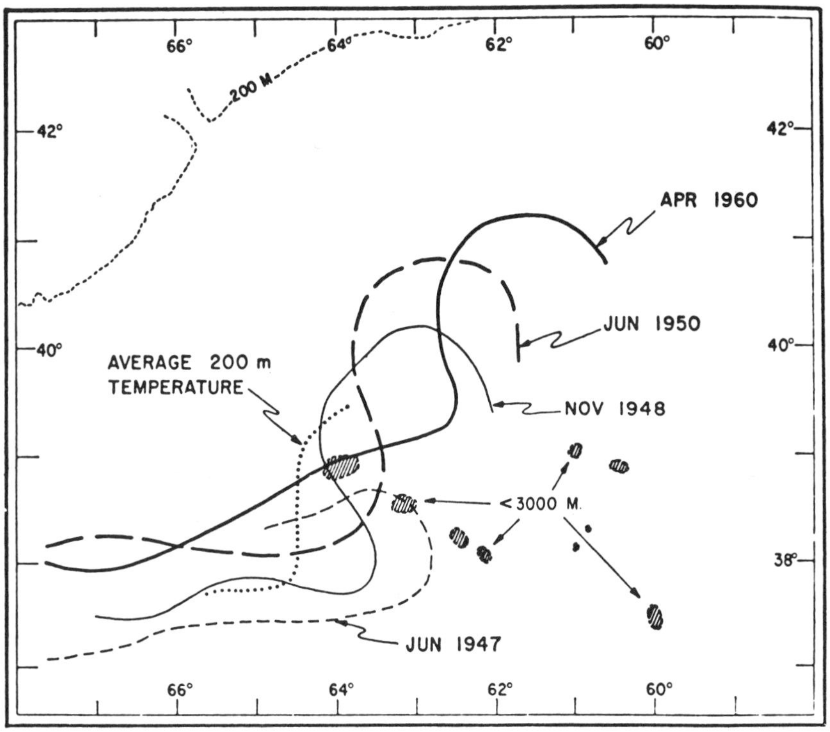

FIGURE 9 Quasi-stationary positions of the abrupt change in Gulf Stream meanders (Fuglister, 1963).

lations of the meandering path of the Gulf Stream, Niiler and Robinson (1967) found that while the mean path of the Gulf Stream followed that which was predicted by the above, the wavelength of observed meanders about this path was significantly less than the predicted value. At the same time, Hansen (1970) carried out a set of consecutive monthly trackings of the Gulf Stream. Relatively coherent eastward propagation of the meander patterns was found to occur (Figure 10), and Hansen estimated that the local time variability in the vorticity of the stream was as large as the rate at which planetary vorticity was advected along the stream. It was found that the quasi-steady meander phenomenon is not appropriate for describing the detail of statistics, of the meander pattern. Furthermore, this quasi-steady theory has no mechanism for tracing the time evolution of a meander or the evolution from one meander to another: It implies an infinite signal propagation speed—a change in the initial conditions of the meander at $X = X_0$ and $Y = Y_0$ is felt instantaneously at all X.

In spite of the failure of this theory to describe the detailed structure of the meander pattern, it is instructive to consider the role that vorticity conservation plays in other

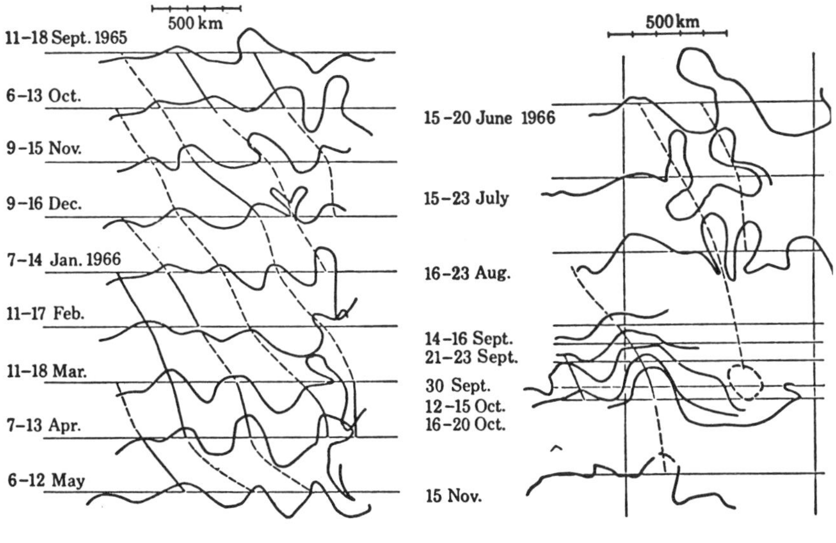

FIGURE 10 Phase propagation interpretation of successive Gulf Stream positions (Hansen, 1970).

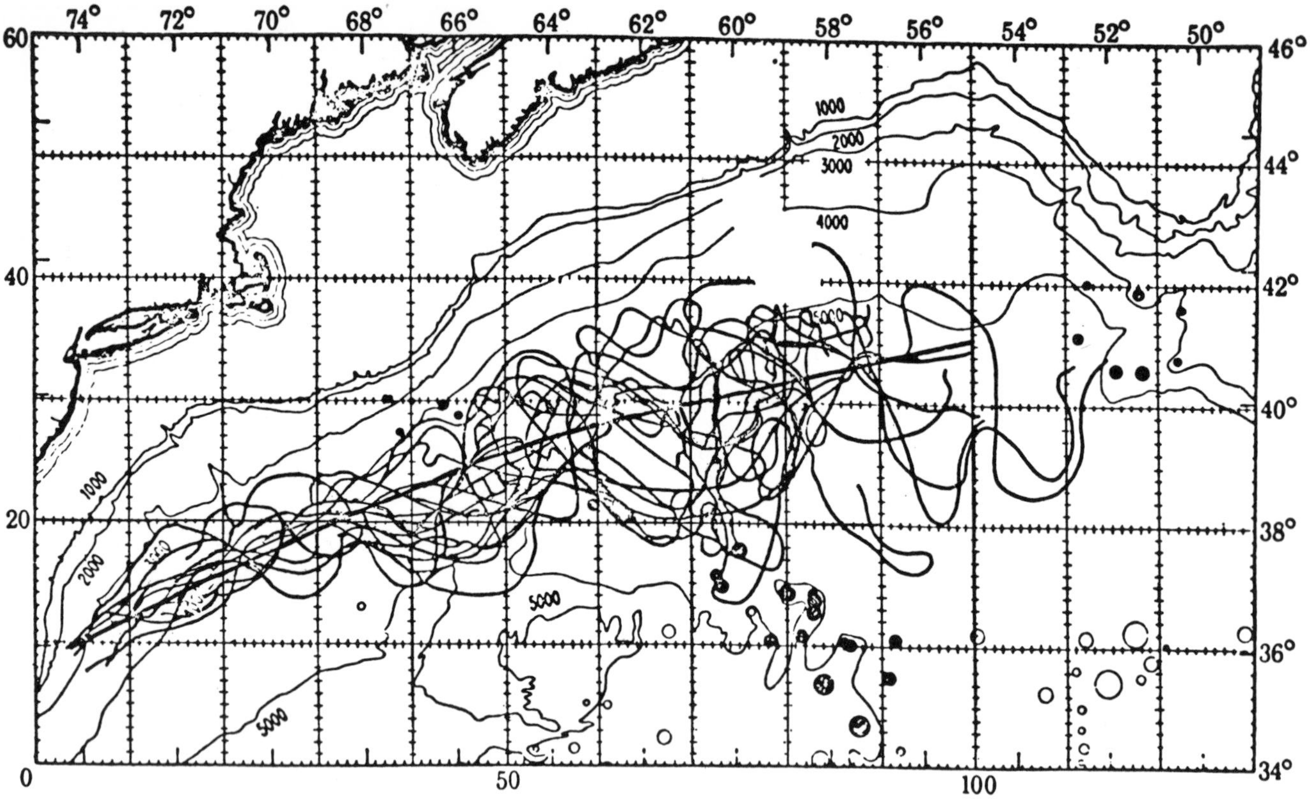

FIGURE 11 Composite of all available Gulf Stream paths through May 1966; a solid line is the mean position (Niiler and Robinson, 1967).

boundary currents, whose locations and seaward extensions have been mapped. Godfrey and Robinson (1971) and Robinson and Taft (1972) have shown that segments of the east Australian, as well as the Kuroshio current, are most likely nondivergent and conserve planetary vorticity in their gentle fall off the continental slope. The mean path of these currents can be described within the confines of this theory. Simply, if a y average of Eq. (1) is taken in which

$$\bar{K} \equiv \int_{y_0}^{y} K\,dy = 0,$$

then the control path (Robinson and Niiler, 1967) (Figure 11) of the nondivergent stream is determined from

$$K_0 \iint_A v_0{}^2\,dA + \beta(\bar{Y} - Y_0) \iint_A v_0\,dA + f_0 \int_L \bar{B} v_0(\bar{B})\,dx = 0. \quad (2)$$

The Gulf Stream follows a well-determined mean path, as do the east Australian and the Kuroshio currents, provided that short-scale meander patterns remain sufficiently small. Godfrey and Robinson (1971) and Robinson and Taft (1972) showed that if the current were initially directed at a large angle off the curve $\bar{Y}$, the east Australian current would leave the continental rise abruptly and the Kuroshio, if it loses contact with the bottom, could be steered back onto the continental shelf (Figures 11, 12, and 13).

Parsons (1969) and Kutalo (1971) have discussed the mean, steady path of a free boundary current in a two-layer model of the ocean in which the meander mechanism has been averaged from the dynamics, *a priori.* This approach must be carried out very cautiously, for the existence of the coherent current itself depends upon the detailed meander path. Robinson and Niiler (1967) have shown that quasi-steady meanders about a mean path, as postulated by Parsons, eventually would form closed loops. In the final analysis, the small, quasi-geostrophic changes of the filament structure determine the existence of and the extent of the entire western boundary current. This is true in these models of quasi-steady jets and for all existing models of time-space varying perturbations.

THEORY OF SMALL AMPLITUDE FLUCTUATIONS AND INITIATION OF MEANDERS

A remarkable feature of the boundary currents is that they persist over distances equal to many stream widths (Figure 14). In particular, when the Gulf Stream is flowing northward against the continental landmass, its persistence is so strong that the Eulerian fluctuations of the axial velocity

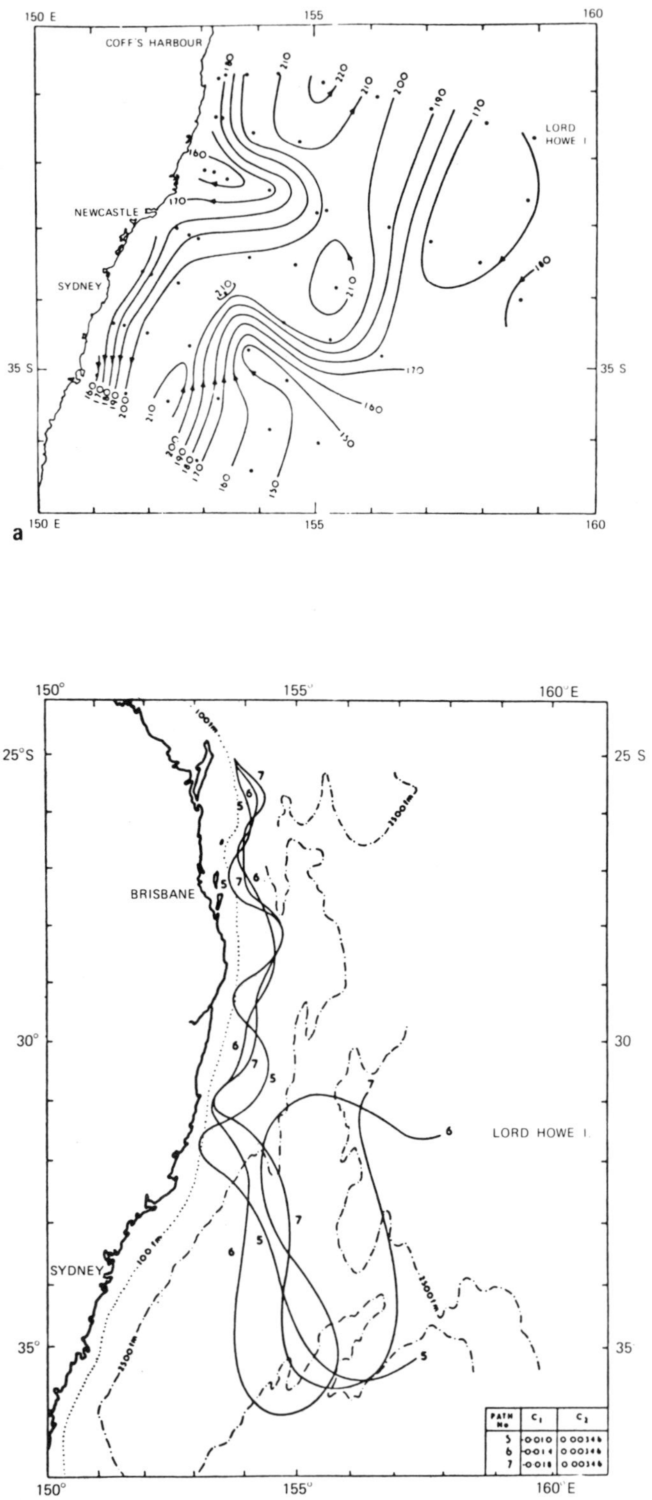

FIGURE 12 (a) Surface dynamic topography relative to 1,300 db, for cruise 64/65 (March 8-22, 1965) (Boland and Hamon, 1970); (b) Series of nondivergent paths whose control curves reach 4,740 m at 34° S. Each path has a different initial curvature: $C_0 = 10^6 K_0$; $C_1 = 10^{10} F_0 \int_L V_0(x,-B)\,dx / \int_A\int V_0^2\,dA$; $C_2 = 10^{12} B \int_A\int V_0\,dA / \int_A\int V_0^2\,dA$.

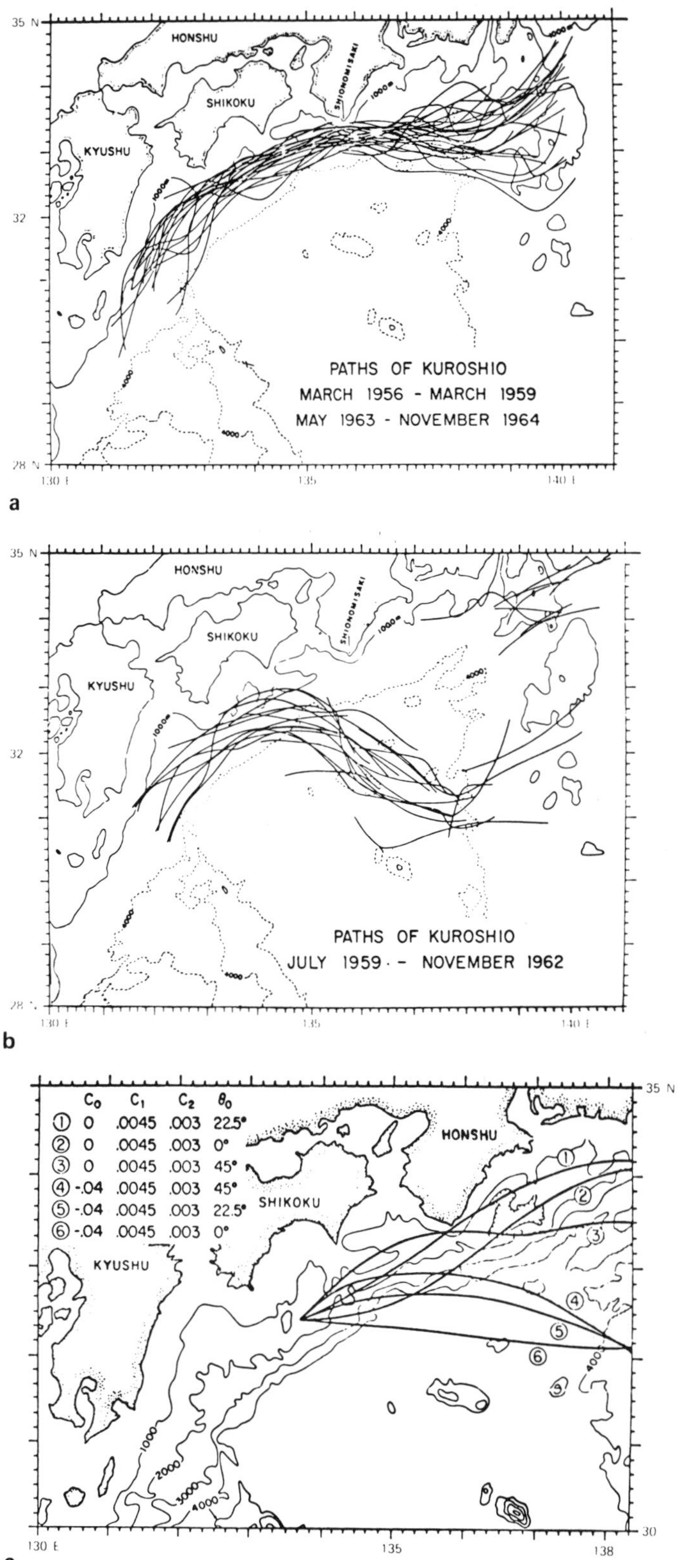

FIGURE 13 (a) Paths of Kuroshio along continental shelf; (b) Paths of Kuroshio along continental rise; and (c) Numerical paths that remain on the shelf (1, 2, 3) and those which are steered into deep water (4, 5, 6). (See Figure 12 for definitions of C_0, C_1, C_2.) (Robinson and Taft, 1972).

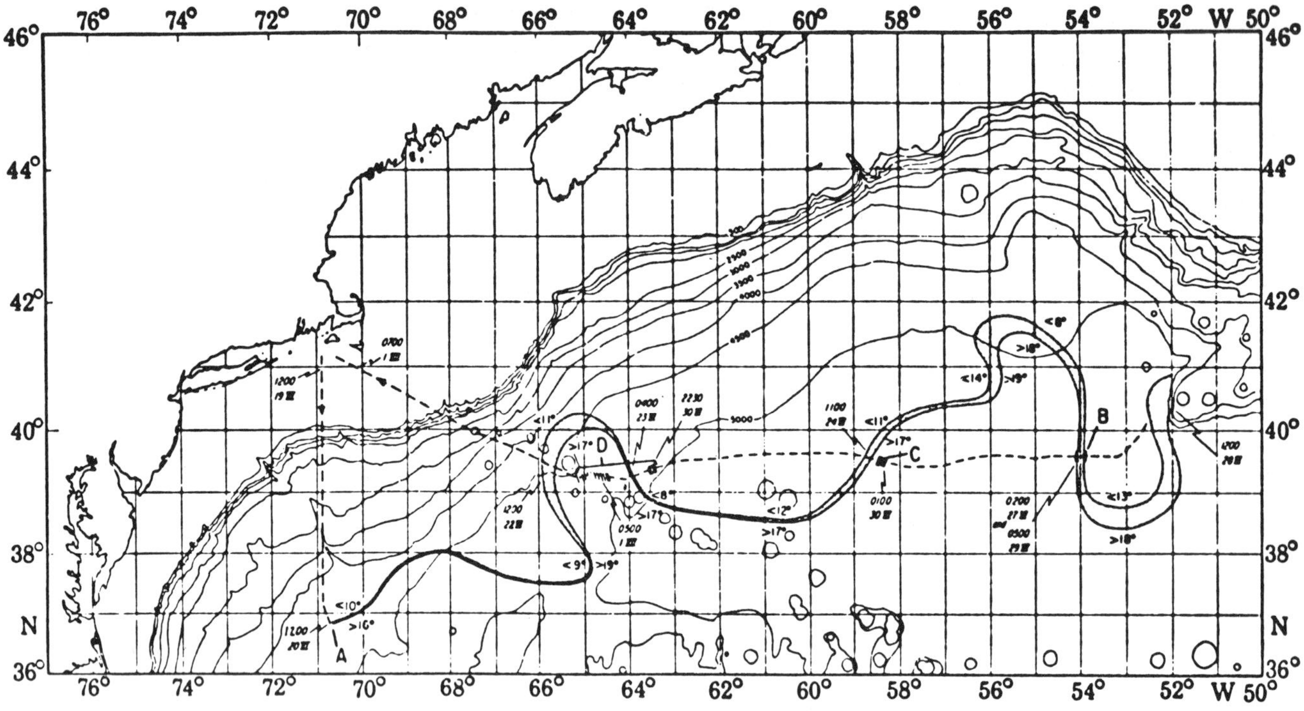

FIGURE 14 Path of the Gulf Stream in late June 1964, inferred from temperatures at a depth of 200 m (Fuglister and Voorhis, 1965).

structure never destroy its identity. (Contrast this with the problem of the atmospheric westerlies, where the fluctuations are larger than the mean.)

Even when the Gulf Stream can be clearly identified as flowing eastward in the deep ocean, the changes in its axial speed above the main thermocline are not large. The mean currents are baroclinic, and it is clear that below the thermocline the fluctuations are larger than the mean flow (Schmitz *et al.*, 1970). At a fixed longitude, the position of the Gulf Stream is reflected in the variable meander patterns, while changes in the axial current associated with this meandering appear more subdued. Strictly, the Eulerian variability along the mean location of the stream is as large as the mean flow itself; in the reference frame of the meander, the time variability appears to be the same order as when the currents hug the continental shelf. The problem of observationally or theoretically modeling the finite amplitude variability along the continental boundary is quite different from the problem of describing the variable flow in the open ocean.

The theory of the propagation and generation of small-amplitude variability of a nondivergent current, whose location is known at an initial time, sheds some light on the scales of variability that can be initiated in the current. The problem of generation of stable or unstable fluctuations must not be overlooked, for a perturbation in the current cannot reinforce itself by traveling around the oceanic gyre, as can a long atmospheric wave around the earth. The horizontal scales of the observed features that are the most energetic are nearly 50 times smaller than the circumference of a basin, while only 4 to 11 wave numbers normally fit around the entire globe when an atmospheric baroclinic wave is observed. While it is true that some energy can be fed into all wave numbers of the ocean current modes, the observed wave packets would depend not only on the growth but also on the level at which they can be excited, or destroyed, by atmospheric or mid-oceanic interactions.

The reader indubitably is aware of the proliferation of studies of fluctuations in atmospheric flows. However, there is a fundamental problem in extending these calculations directly to the oceanic situation, because the western boundary currents are not dynamically similar to the atmospheric westerlies. In both cases, one is interested in modeling the energetic subinertial frequency band in a stratified, swiftly flowing current on a shelf. In both currents the suitably defined Richardson number is larger than unity. The radius of deformation in the atmospheric current is less than its width, while that in the ocean is equal to its width. In other words, the Rossby number of the atmospheric flow is less than unity, while the persistent oceanic jets are characterized by a flow where the Rossby number varies from one-fourth to three. The second fundamental difference is that the slopes of the continental rise under strong oceanic currents are as large as the isopycnal slopes, a dynamically important condition that is not found in the terrestrial contours of the earth's surface.

A number of investigations have direct application to small variability in the Gulf Stream system. Orlanski (1969) carried out numerical integrations of the complex dispersion curve for a two-layer model of small-amplitude waves on a baroclinic boundary current that rides over the continental slope. The study was carried out in an effort to compute the effect of topographic slopes on the baroclinic stability of confined ocean currents of small Rossby number. Orlanski shows that the most unstable waves on the deep shelf have a wavelength of 365 km, a period of 38 days, and an exponential doubling time of 5 days. These waves are retrogressive, and a group of waves that grows in amplitude travels only 36 km before its amplitude doubles. The waves are maintained by a release of available potential energy in the main thermocline and, as such, behave very much like baroclinic waves in the atmosphere. The topographic slope contours used in these calculations destabilize the waves.

Robinson and Gadgil (1970) have studied a continuous model of fluctuations of a broad baroclinic current that overlies a mild topographic slope. The singular feature of this calculation is that the broad flow has horizontal and vertical density contrasts of the same order. It can be shown that this analysis is pertinent only to long waves (waves longer than the baroclinic deformation radius) and cannot describe the maximum growth rates, which typically are of a length comparable to the radius of deformation. In this theory, the shorter the wave, the more rapid its growth. A class of initial value problems is considered in which it is found that waves grow while they propagate as coherent groups of decreasing wavelength; the instability is bounded to a space-time domain (Gadgil, 1970). It can easily be shown that these waves are maintained by the release of available potential energy. In this model, the longest waves are stable and, in effect, are topographic Rossby waves in a uniform barotropic current over a gentle slope.

Robinson and Luyten (1972) have developed the theory of the finite-amplitude long waves on a narrow vortex filament. The description of the dynamics is written in a variable coordinate system whose time-varying generatrix is the sinuous axis of the swift current. It is postulated that the wave energy is not trapped in the current and that the fluctuations in the jet are related only to the movement of the filament and are independent of the distance across the local current. In this model, the meander is felt a large distance away from the meandering current. Hence, quite simply, when the amplitude of the meanders is small, the theory of Gadgil (1970) is recovered, for the interaction phenomenon with the ocean basin is identical to the latter theory.

The essential analysis of these long-wave models is attributed to Tareev (1965). Let $V_0(x,z)$ be the geostrophically balanced velocity component of the oceanic current, $p'(x,z)e^{i\sigma t - iky}$ is the perturbation pressure associated with the traveling wave motion, x is the cross-stream distance, y is the downstream distance, and z is the vertical coordinate. In the boundary currents, the horizontal and vertical density gradients are the same order of magnitude, whence the conservation of the perturbation density is approximated by

$$\left(V_o - \frac{\sigma}{K}\right)p_z' - V_{oz}p' = 0. \qquad (3)$$

The conservation of potential vorticity, however, is expressed as

$$-\int_{-B}^{0} [(i\sigma - ikV_o)\ (p_{xx}' - k^2 p') + \beta p_x' \ + ikp' V_{oxx}]\ dz$$
$$+\frac{f^2}{g}\int_{-B}^{0} (w_z)\ dz\ e^{-i\sigma t + ikx} = 0. \qquad (4)$$

The last term of Eq. (4) can be integrated; and, if there is a cross-stream bottom slope underneath the stream, then $(f/g)w(x,-B) = ikB_x p'\ e^{-ikx + i\sigma t}$; on the free ocean surface, $w(x,y,\sigma) = 0$.

The general solution of Eq. (3) is

$$p' = \left[V_o\ (x,z) - \frac{\sigma}{k}\right] \phi_o\ (x). \qquad (5)$$

Tareev (1965) (and later Robinson and Gadgil, 1970) assumed that ϕ_o was linear in x only, and that v' was independent of x. This is not consistent with parameterizing wave coupling to the general ocean circulation, for the pressure perturbation would increase without bound on either side of the Gulf Stream. Now, substituting Eq. (5) and the boundary condition on w into Eq. (4), one obtains the equation for $\phi_o(x)$, with $c = (\sigma/k)$.

$$\int_{-B}^{0} [(V_o - C)^2 \phi_{ox}]\ dz + \frac{i\beta}{k} \int_{-B}^{0} [(V_o - C)\phi_o]\ dz$$
$$-\left\{\int_{-B}^{0} [(V_o - c)^2 k^2]\ dz - B_x v_o(x,-B)\ [v_o - c]\right\} \phi_o = 0. \qquad (6)$$

The complex dispersion diagram for trapped waves must be obtained by solving Eq. (6) under the condition that $\phi_o \to 0$ as $x \to \pm\infty$. It is clear that the leaky meanders are barotropic topographic Rossby waves, which can exist even where $v_o \to 0$. The proper problem for oscillations is an initial boundary value problem in two dimensions; it is an aspect of the linear problem of Tareev (1965) and Robinson and Gadgil (1970) that has not been carried out. A simple modification as expressed in Eq. (6) would render the small-amplitude theories more plausible in that the interaction with the open ocean is more adequately parameterized. [Munk *et al.* (1970) have successfully described tidal oscillations in the eastern North Pacific in terms of trapped and leaky modes of planetary gravity waves.]

Because of lack of adequate observations, it is not clear whether baroclinic, unstable waves are fundamentally responsible for the most energetic fluctuations. Eq. (6) contains the energetics that can release perturbation kinetic energy from the lateral shear as well. It has been demonstrated by Niiler and Mysak (1971) and Jacobs and Sela (1971) that barotropic waves can grow on the Gulf Stream, and the most unstable wavelength, group velocity, and maximum growth rate are similar to those of the baroclinic meanders discussed above. In the latter case, the waves are strongly stabilized by an underlying topographic slope and exist only within the strong current.

Mysak (1971) has solved an initial value problem for these barotropic waves that could be generated by strong meteorological cyclones. He found that very little energy is fed into the short, most unstable waves (as compared with more stable, longer wavelength patterns), and only after many *e*-folding growth times is the most unstable wave recognizable. In all the before-mentioned work, the growth rates for waves in the Gulf Stream lie between 3 and 12 days, in which time the group can travel only a few meander lengths. Pedlosky (1972) has pointed out quite clearly in his studies of finite-amplitude, quasi-geostrophic, baroclinic waves that within the doubling time of an infinitesimal wave (in the case that the frequency is large compared to the growth rate), the baroclinic energy source for the waves can be reduced through nonlinear interactions; the linear growth rate is maintained only until the wave amplitude doubles, and finite-amplitude groups travel faster than infinitesimal waves.

NUMERICAL MODELS OF BOUNDARY VARIABILITY

A simple numerical model of western boundary current variability has been carried out by Parrish (1975). In this model, an initial quasi-geostrophic vorticity distribution is specified in a basin; it consists of a small mid-ocean vortex, and the general circulation is parameterized as a barotropic, constant-potential, vorticity gyre whose mid-oceanic Rossby number is much less than unity (Fofonoff, 1954). Both baroclinic and barotropic oscillations are considered. The equation for the simplest problem is

$$\left(\frac{\partial}{\partial t} + \psi_x \frac{\partial}{\partial y} - \psi_y \frac{\partial}{\partial x}\right)(\epsilon\nabla^2\psi) + \beta\psi_x = 0, \qquad (7)$$

where ψ is the barotropic stream function and $\epsilon \sim 10^{-2}$ or 10^{-3}, $\beta = 1$. Figure 14 shows the initial vorticity distribution. A conservative numerical scheme has been developed to resolve the pertinent scales in a leap-frog integration of Eq. (7). Orszag's (1971) method of finite fourier sine transforms is used, and a 64 by 64 element grid is utilized [32 by 32 terms of the series $\psi = \Sigma A_{mn}(t) \sin mx \sin ny$] to represent the solution. The general circulation is of maximum-amplitude unity and the vortex is of amplitude one-half. The general circulation is absolutely stable (Blumen, 1968, 1971); and, without the small mid-oceanic vortex, the numerical scheme is stable for 5 years of integration.

The sequence of diagrams in Figures 15 and 16 shows the history of the development of the wave pattern in the gyre. The eddy propagates to the west as a dispersive Rossby wave train and joins the western boundary current as a coherent meander pattern. A large number of experiments of baroclinic Rossby wave propagation have been made as well. In these latter experiments, the wave pattern makes many excursions around the gyre without a change of form; however, a more extensive discussion of the baroclinic patterns is not appropriate to this paper. Parrish has found that short-scale horizontal patterns that are absorbed by the boundary current travel eastward essentially with the speed of the northern boundary jet; however, large-scale meanders move slowly to the east, because their westward group velocity is comparable to the mean speed of the current. It is of interest to note that Richardson *et al.* (1972) recently reported tracking a detached Gulf Stream eddy to 30° N latitude, at which time the vortex was being reabsorbed into the Gulf Stream. Might the large-amplitude meandering mechanism be more directly linked to a recirculation of the vorticity of the Gulf Stream system in the northwest part of the North Atlantic gyre than to the generation of unstable waves in the Gulf Stream itself?

A second numerical study of interest has been initiated by Orlanski and Cox (1972). They used the Princeton GFD 15-level model, which employs Navier–Stokes friction laws to parameterize small-scale turbulent diffusion ($k_H \sim 10^6$, $k_v \sim 10$ cm^2/s^2). At an initial time, a geostrophically balanced north–south current and the associated nonuniform density distribution over a 4-km-deep channel is specified. The initial state is not an exact solution of the steady equations of motion, but it quickly adjusts to the frictional torques within the channel. The equilibrium solution is then perturbed in all the fields everywhere along the channel with a small random perturbation. Within 3 days, a baroclinic wavelength pattern of 100 km is formed and slowly grows after that at a much reduced growth rate. The phase velocity of these most unstable waves is very nearly equal to the velocity of the flow in the layer of maximum baroclinicity (1.5 m/s). Intense, short, and rapidly moving waves have been reported in the Gulf Stream (Robinson, 1971). These waves convert potential energy to kinetic energy (even in the presence of small-scale diffusion) and transfer kinetic energy to the mean flow along a continental shelf. Nevertheless, the "effective diffusivity" is as large as that normally attributed to small-scale processes. The Gulf Stream meander pattern is observed to grow eastward; it would be of considerable interest to carry out a numerical experiment

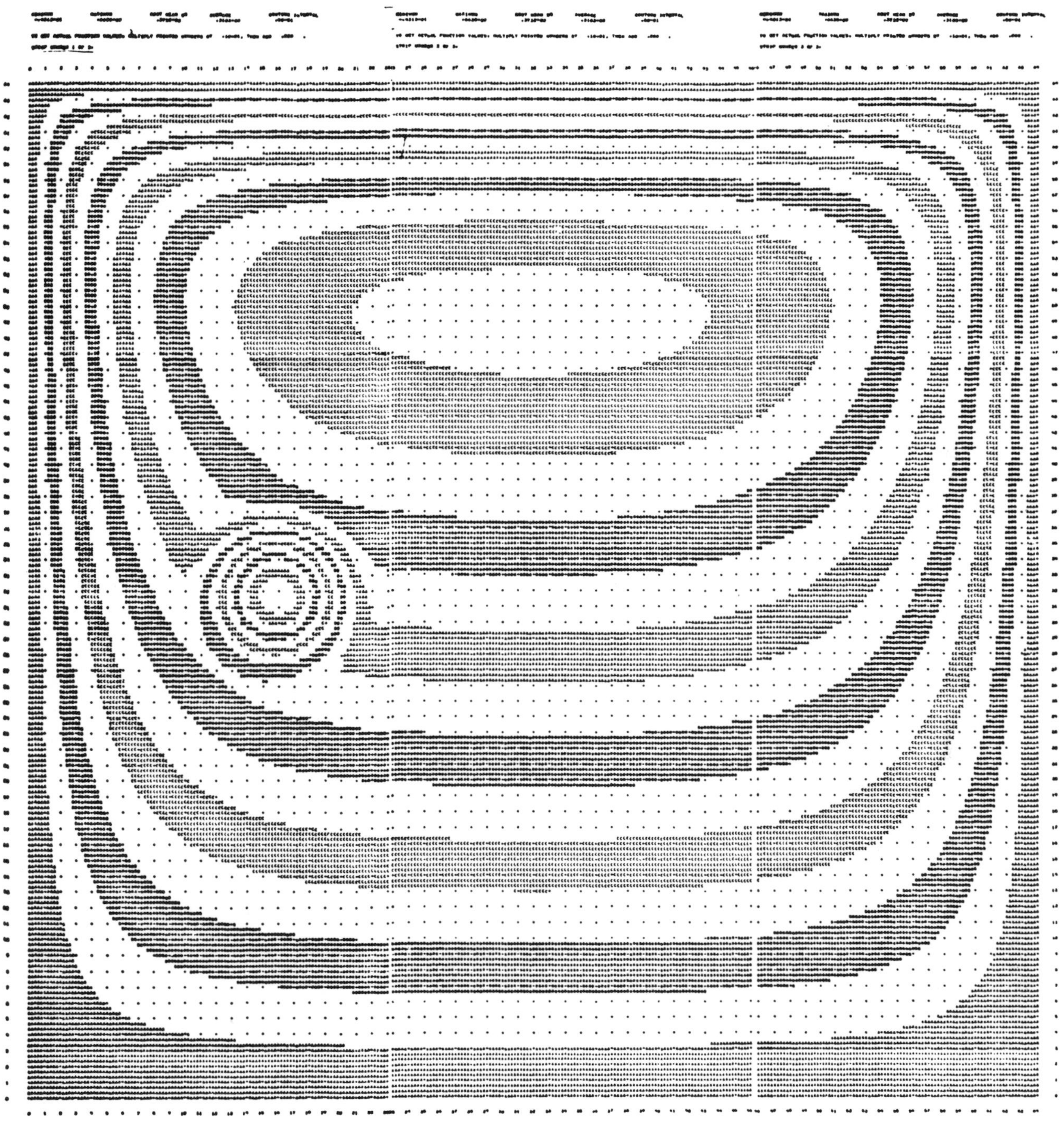

FIGURE 15 Initial streamline pattern in a calculation of the interaction of Rossby waves with a midlatitude inviscid ocean gyre (Parrish, 1972).

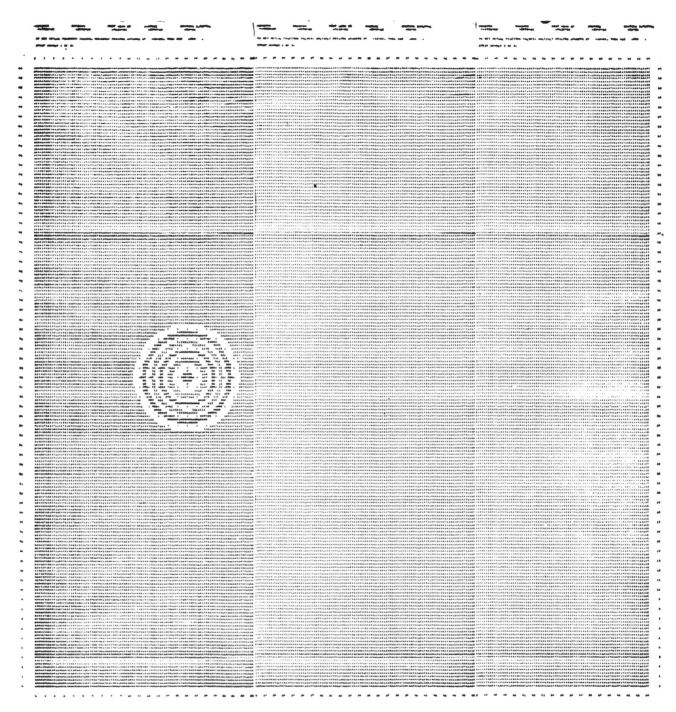

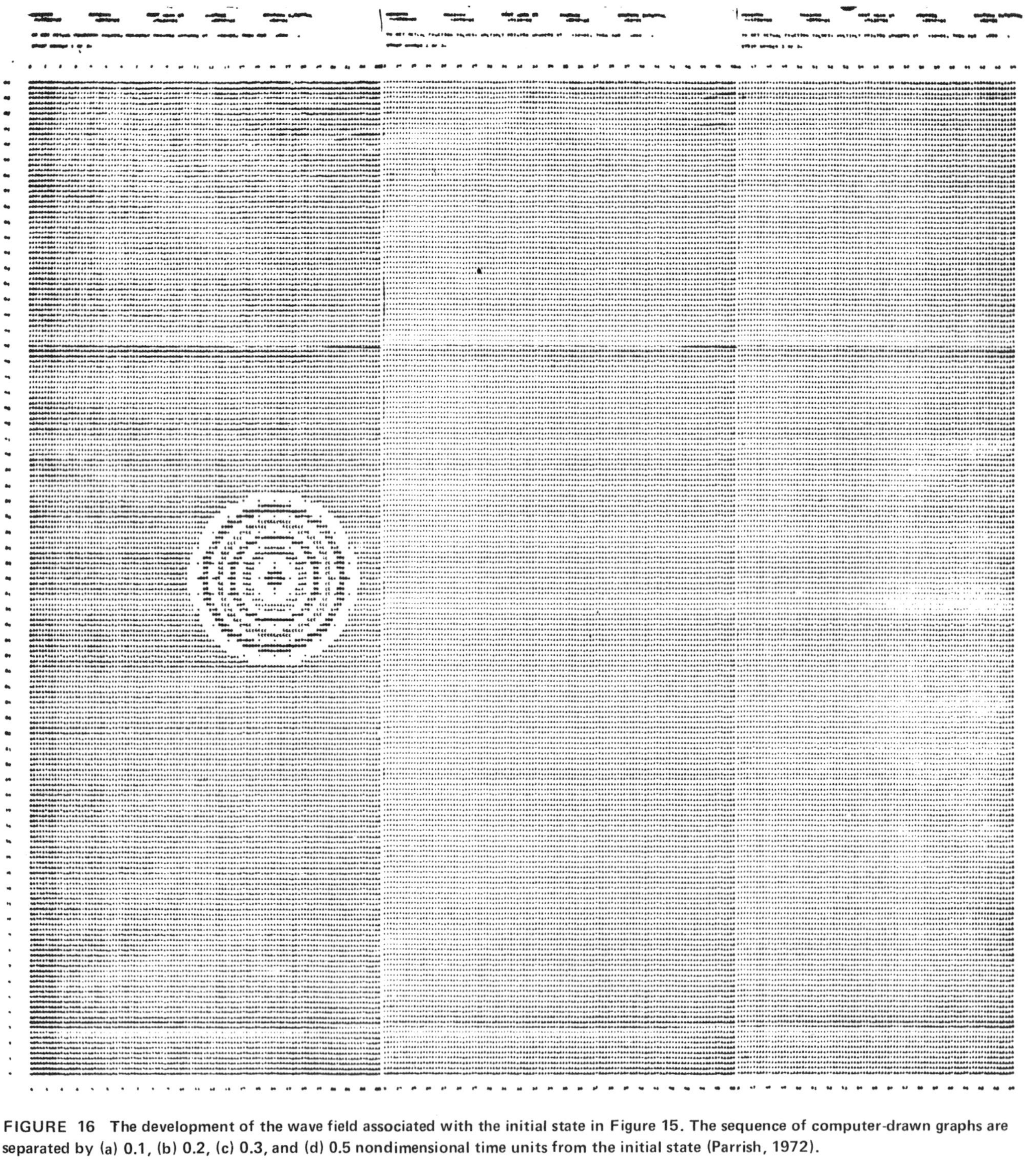

FIGURE 16 The development of the wave field associated with the initial state in Figure 15. The sequence of computer-drawn graphs are separated by (a) 0.1, (b) 0.2, (c) 0.3, and (d) 0.5 nondimensional time units from the initial state (Parrish, 1972).

FIGURE 16–Continued

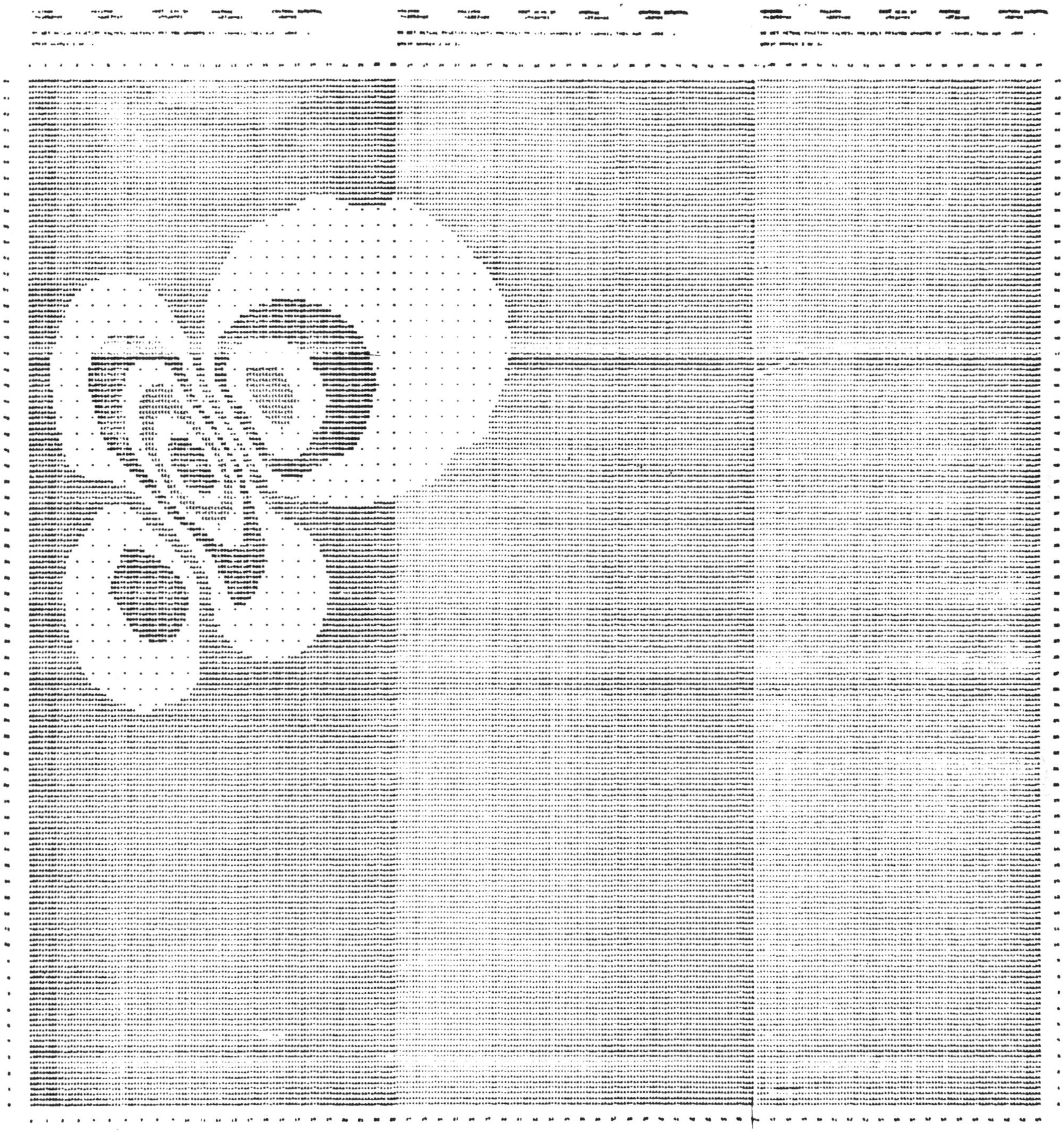

FIGURE 16—Continued

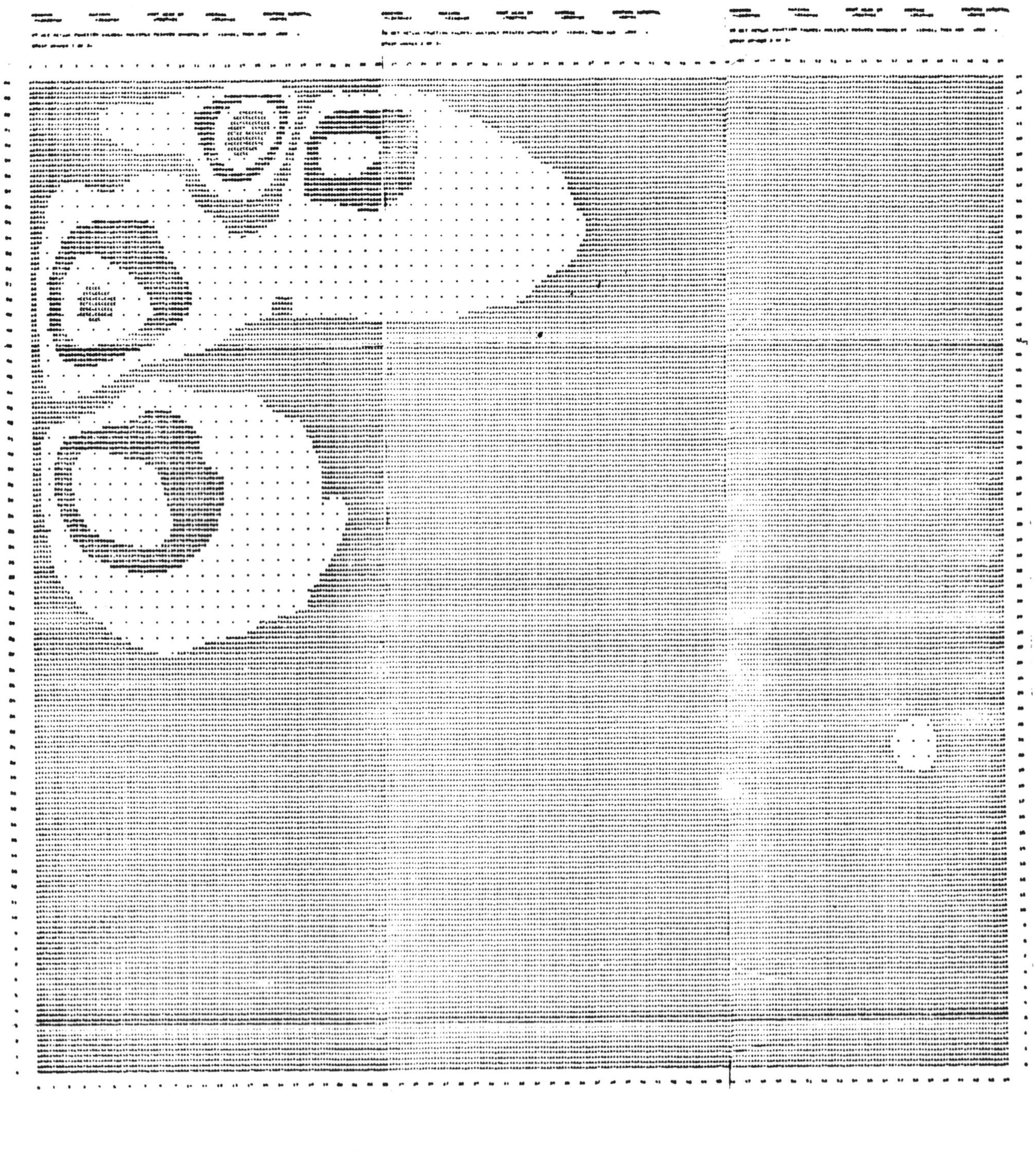

FIGURE 16—Continued

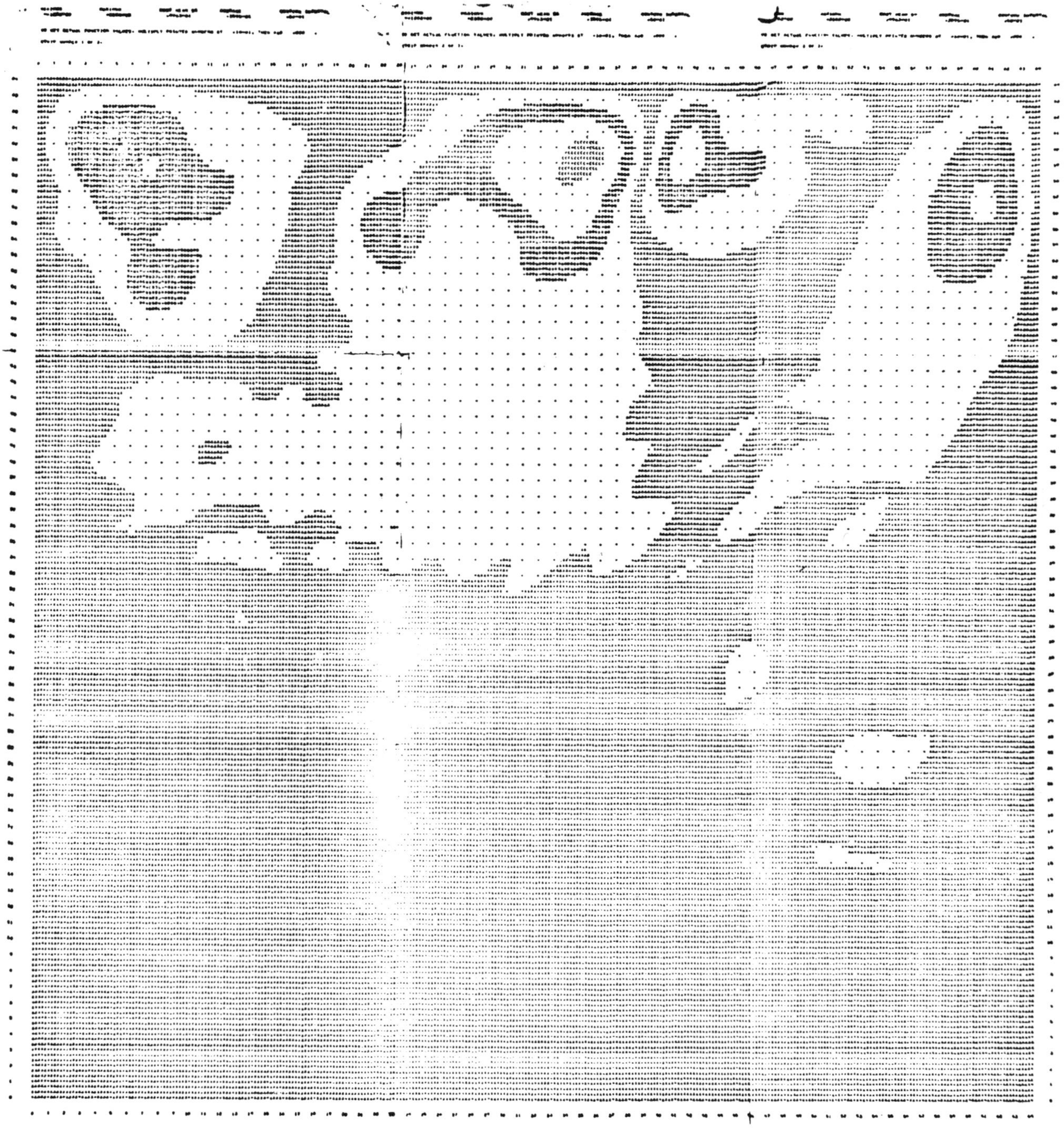

in which a wave-packet of 200-100 km is prescribed at some initial time and location and is followed downstream. In Orlanski's model, the boundary conditions downstream are again periodic, whence the wave can run through the system in phase many times as it grows.

ACKNOWLEDGMENTS

The author is grateful for the support of National Science Foundation, Grant GA-14688 during the tenure of this study. Drs. William Schmitz, Dennis Moore, and Mark Wimbush conscientiously extended their advice in the preparation and presentation of this material.

REVIEW: M. RATTRAY

The western boundary currents are the most dramatic feature of the ocean circulations, but they should not be viewed as a separate entity. They are, in fact, part of an asymmetrical gyre that is intensified at its western edge. But for many purposes, the western boundary currents can be considered as a special problem, and Niiler's paper deals with the space-time fluctuations.

At the outset Niiler states that "When the data base cannot resolve the fluctuation energetics, neither can it describe the dynamics of the mean flow." He then goes on to say that "The fluctuation theories are no further advanced than the observations." We agree. There will be no adequate theory of the western boundary currents on the average until the dynamics of the fluctuations is understood.

It is disappointing that even here the observations have not resolved the problem. The Gulf Stream is the most intensely studied ocean area in the world, and its meandering currents (as deduced largely from aerial radiation measurements) densely cover the maps of the northwestern Atlantic. The meanders are very pronounced. When they were discovered, they were thought to be quasi-stationary, possibly hooked to bottom features. We now know that they move on the average eastward (downstream). Typical wavelengths are 300 km. The amplitudes are of the same order as the wavelengths, certainly not good material for linearized theory.

This has not stopped people from attempting linearized theory. Orlanski (1969) observed a most unstable wavelength of 365 km, a period of 38 days, and an *e*-folding time of 5 days! This is again indicating the inadequacy of linearization. There has been intensive development of finite-amplitude theories under the leadership of Robinson and Niiler. Early work with stationary waves led to wavelengths significantly shorter than the observed value, but more recent theory has led to more satisfactory results. A recent numerical model (Parrish, 1975) showed the development of an unstable wave pattern in the gyre leading to westward propagation of dispersive Rossby waves, which eventually joined the western boundary current. This work, plus recent observations by Richardson, suggests that unstable vortices are eventually reabsorbed into the Gulf Stream and that meandering might, in fact, be closely related to such recirculation of vorticity.

All this suggests the shortcomings of steady-state models with very large eddy friction. Numerical calculations of the mean circulation have, in fact, indicated a fascinating instability that might be related to Rossby waves. The computer is trying to tell us that the steady state is unstable and that we should not attempt to stabilize it by enormous eddy friction, but that we should let it oscillate and properly take into account the associated eddy fluxes.

It is in this sense that the steady circulation may not be understood until we have made progress in understanding the oscillations of the western boundary currents.

REFERENCES

Barret, J., and W. Schmitz, Jr. 1971. Transport float measurements and hydrographic data from three sections across the Gulf Stream near 67° W. WHOI Rep. No. 71-66.

Blumen, W. 1968. On the stability of quasi-geostrophic flow. J. Atmos. Sci. 25:929-31.

Blumen, W. 1971. On the stability of plane flow with horizontal shear to three-dimensional non-divergent disturbances. Geophys. Fluid Dyn. 2:189-200.

Boland, F. M., and B. V. Hamon. 1970. The east Australian current, 1965-1968. Deep-Sea Res. 17:777-94.

Duing, W. 1970. The Monsoon Regime of the Currents in the Indian Ocean. East-West Center Press, Honolulu, Hawaii. 68 pp.

Ferrara, A. 1970. Dynamically induced fluctuations in acoustic transmission. Univ. Miami Rep. No. ML 70-116.

Fofonoff, H. 1954. Steady flow in a frictionless homogenous ocean. J. Mar. Res. 13:254-62.

Fuglister, F. C. 1963. Gulf Stream '60. Prog. Oceanogr. 1:265-383.

Fuglister, F. C., and A. D. Voorhis. 1965. A new method of tracking the Gulf Stream. Limnol. Oceanogr. Suppl. 10:115-24.

Gadgil, S. 1970. Time dependent topographic meandering and jets in rotating systems. Ph.D. Thesis. Harvard University, Cambridge, Mass.

Godfrey, T., and A. R. Robinson. 1971. The east Australian current as a free inertial jet. J. Mar. Res. 29(3):256-80.

Hamon, B. V. 1965. The east Australian current, 1960-64. Deep-Sea Res. 12:899-921.

Hansen, D. V. 1970. Gulf Stream meanders between Cape Hatteras and the Grand Banks. Deep-Sea Res. 17:495-511.

Jacobs, S. J. 1971. Ageostrophic stability of divergent jets. J. Atmos. Sci. 28(6):962-67.

Jacobs, S. J., and J. Sela. 1971. Ageostrophic effects on baroclinic instability. J. Atmos. Sci. 28(6):944-53.

Kutalo, A. A. 1971. On seasonal changes in the North Atlantic circulation. Izv. Akad. Nauk. USSR Atmos. Oceanic Phys. 7(3): 208-13.

Lee, T. 1972. Ph.D. Thesis. Florida State University, Tallahassee.

Lighthill, M. J. 1971. Time-varying currents. Philos. Trans. R. Soc. Lond. Ser. A, pp. 371-90.

Munk, W., F. Snodgrass, and M. Wimbush. 1970. Tides off-shore: Transition from California coastal to deep-sea waters. Geophys. Fluid Dyn. 1:161–235.
Mysak, L. A. 1971. Private communication.
Niiler, P. P., and A. R. Robinson. 1967. The theory of free inertial jets. II. A numerical experiment for the path of the Gulf Stream. Tellus 19:269–91.
Niiler, P. P., and L. A. Mysak. 1971. Barotropic waves along eastern continental shelf. Geophys. Fluid Dyn. 2:273–88.
Niiler, P. P., and W. S. Richardson. 1972. Seasonal variability in the Florida current. Unpublished manuscript.
Orlanski, I. 1969. The influence of bottom topography on the stability of jets in a baroclinic fluid. J. Atmos. Sci. 26:1216–32.
Orlanski, I., and M. D. Cox. 1972. Baroclinic instability in ocean currents. Unpublished manuscript.
Orszag, S. 1971. Numerical simulation of incompressible flows within simple boundaries: Accuracy. J. Fluid Mech. 49(1):75–112.
Parrish, D. 1975. Ph.D. Thesis. Nova University, Fort Lauderdale, Fla.
Parsons, A. T. 1969. A two-layer model of the Gulf Stream separation. J. Fluid Mech. 39(3):511–28.
Pedlosky, J. 1972. Finite amplitude baroclinic wave packets. Unpublished manuscript.
Richardson, P. L. 1972. Observations of a cyclonic eddy southeast of Cape Hatteras. Trans. Am. Geophys. Union 53(4):393.(A)
Richardson, W. S., and W. J. Schmitz, Jr. 1965. A technique for the direct measurement of transport with application to the Straits of Florida. J. Mar. Res. 23:172–85.
Richardson, W. S., A. R. Carr, and H. J. White. 1969. Description of a freely dropped instrument for measuring current velocity. J. Mar. Res. 27(1):153–57.
Richardson, W. S., H. J. White, and L. Nemeth. 1972. A technique for the direct measurement of ocean currents from aircraft. Unpublished manuscript.
Robinson, A. R. 1971. The Gulf Stream. Philos. Trans. R. Soc. Lond. Ser. A., p. 270.
Robinson, A. R., and P. P. Niiler. 1967. The theory of free inertial currents. I. Path and structure. Tellus 19:269–91.
Robinson, A. R., and S. Gadgil. 1970. Time dependent topographic meandering. Geophys. Fluid Dyn. 1:411–38.
Robinson, A. R., and J. R. Luyten. 1972. Theory of quasi-geostrophic meanders of a baroclinic jet. Unpublished manuscript.
Robinson, A. R., and B. A. Taft. 1972. A numerical experiment for the path of the Kuroshio. J. Mar. Res. 30(1):65–101.
Sanford, T. 1972. Private communication.
Schmitz, W. J., Jr. 1971. Private communication.
Schmitz, W. J., Jr., and P. P. Niiler. 1969. A note on the kinetic energy exchange between fluctuations and mean flow in the surface layer of the Florida current. Tellus 11:814–19.
Schmitz, W. J., Jr., A. R. Robinson, and F. C. Fuglister. 1970. Bottom velocity observations directly under the Gulf Stream. Science 170:1192–94.
Schulman, E. E. 1970. The Antarctic circumpolar current. Proc. Comput. Simul. Conf., 6–12 June 1970, Denver, Colorado, pp. 955–68.
Sela, J., and S. J. Jacobs. 1971. Ageostrophic effects on Gulf Stream instability. J. Atmos. Sci. 28(6):962–67.
Shannon, L. V. 1970. Oceanic circulation off South Africa. S. Afr. Fish. Bull. No. 6, pp. 27–33.
Stommel, H. 1965. The Gulf Stream. Univ. Calif. Press, Los Angeles. 243 pp.
Tareev, B. A. 1965. Unstable Rossby waves and the instability of ocean currents. Izv. Akad. Nauk. USSR Atmos. Oceanic Phys. 1:250–56.
Van Loon, H. 1972. A half-yearly variation of the circumpolar surface drift in the Southern Hemisphere. Tellus 23(6):511–16.
Warren, B. A. 1963. Topographical influences on the path of the Gulf Stream. Tellus 15:167–83.
Webster, F. 1961. The effect of meanders on the kinetic energy balance of the Gulf Stream. Tellus 12:397–401.

DISCUSSION

RATTRAY: I thought the last numerical experiment that you showed was very elucidating.

NIILER: David Parrish has used a model of Fofonoff's gyre, and calculated by Orszag's method, on a 64 by 64 element grid for which the initial condition in a computational scheme remains stable for 5 years. The potential vorticity at $t = 0$ is such that no horizontal shear instabilities can grow in the system. Now what Parrish does is to put in a mesoscale vortex as a perturbation of the entire system. The vortex breaks into a Rossby wave train, is dispersive and, consequently, is being sucked into the western boundary current as a series of intense meanders.

CHARNEY: How does that change the mean flow?

NIILER: It eventually breaks up so that the energy gets into all the smaller scales and eventually fills the whole basin.

CHARNEY: Would you say the mean flow breaks up too?

NIILER: It depends on how strong the initial perturbation is, how much extra vorticity you put in. But it is conservative and will keep oscillating in the box.

RATTRAY: The point I really wanted to make is that if we're talking about time-dependent dynamics, we're simply talking about modified Rossby wave dynamics. This thing that most oceanographers would call an eddy when it began showed its wave features as time progressed. In fact, it looks like it might take momentum from one part of the mean stream to another part. This seems to appear several times in your paper.

MUNK: I want to comment on the very great importance of variability. Also, it is amazing that the most characteristic numbers that you mentioned, namely 2 months and 300 km, happened to be the scales that MODE has adopted as being the most meaningful.

NIILER: Can I say one thing about the scales. You see, this boundary current is a very strong inertial motion. Therefore, the radius of its deformation is the same as in the middle of the ocean. The most unstable waves are a combination of baroclinic and barotropic scales, because the deformation radius is the width of the stream. The most unstable waves on a boundary current like this are again on the order of the Rossby radius of deformation themselves. Hence, these waves can effectively radiate back to the waves on the scale of the Rossby radius of deformation in the center of the ocean. The deformation radius is conserved within the Gulf Stream, but the growth rates of instabilities are an order of magnitude larger than in the middle of the ocean.

ROBINSON: I would like to mention that the filament theory Peter here mentioned is a steady-state one, and that over the past couple of years Jim Luyten and I have developed the time-dependent version, which is coupled directly to the open ocean. The reason we're doing it is to try to pin down the dynamics of this mesoscale phenomenon. I've also begun to develop a predictive model to show that we have in fact rationalized the local dynamics. Our 1969 Gulf Stream cruise showed the great variety of data that was taken—hydrographic data; bottom current meter data; ship-tracking data to position the stream; and long-time, long-distance, aircraft data. We've been going after that data with our kind of predictive scheme, but I would like to draw this very rich data base to the attention of people who may wish to use it in their more standard numerical models.

GILL: I just want to mention some recent merchant ship data on the east Australia current that Bruce Hamon has been collecting, which shows these same sort of time and space scales. As a function of latitude and time, if you plot the current velocity that you get from ship's drift, you get a contour pattern of diagonal stripes with a time scale of about 4 months and a space scale of about 1,000 km. You also see that these time scales in the spectrum of sea level at Lord Howe Island have an unusually vigorous spectrum in the low frequencies. The variance comes mainly from the frequency band corresponding to periods of a few months.

NIILER: Might I say that we know now that the initiation process down the Florida Straits happens in frequency on the order of between 5 and 7 days. There's a very strong peak in the spectrum of almost any measurement. We know also, from Robinson's 1969 cruise and from my own observations, that very intense short-scale meanders can come shooting through the system at a speed of almost 100 cm/s. These are of a width that is on the order of the stream itself, and a length scale of about 100 km. So there is the Gulf Stream system, at least in the Florida current system, where we're beginning to be able to identify a peak and a number of events in addition.

MID-OCEAN MESOSCALE MODELING

F. P. BRETHERTON and M. KARWEIT

INTRODUCTION

The oceanic mesoscale here refers to a range surrounding the Rossby radius of deformation ($\sim$ 50 km) with associated time scales from a few days upwards. In flow patterns on substantially smaller horizontal scales, the deep currents are dynamically isolated from those above the main thermocline, whereas on larger ones there is a strong geostrophic coupling throughout a vertical water column. These concepts of space and time scale refer to typical values over which the flow field changes by a significant fraction. For a sinusoidal pattern, they should be multiplied by 2π to obtain the wavelength and period.

Pioneer observations by Crease (1962) and others disclosed currents below the main thermocline in mid-ocean as large as 5-10 cm/s, which change completely in magnitude and direction over intervals of a month or so. Recent data from arrays of moored current meters in the western North Atlantic [part of the Mid Ocean Dynamics Experiment (MODE)] have confirmed these observations and indicate a dominant horizontal scale of 50-100 km.

Before discussing numerical models, some preliminary scale analysis is helpful. At a speed $U \sim$ 5 cm/s and a length scale $L \sim$ 50 km at latitude 30° N, the Rossby number is $Ro = U/Lf \sim 0.01$, indicating that such currents should be in geostrophic balance to a high degree of approximation. However, the nonlinear terms in the vorticity equation cannot be ignored, because the advective time scale, $L/U \sim 10$ days, is comparable to that observed. The dynamical importance of the stable stratification has already been mentioned. Irregularities of magnitude h in the depth (H) of the ocean on this length scale will cause stretching of vortex lines and changes of relative vorticity of magnitude around $f(h/H)$. With $H \sim$ 5 km this exceeds observed values of U/L if h is greater than about 50 m. Topographic charts show that such irregularities are normal over almost all the deep-ocean floor. The effects of the variation β of the Coriolis parameter with latitude are measured by the ratio $\beta L^2/U \sim 1$, indicating that they too must be included in any comprehensive study of mesoscale dynamics. On the other hand, the magnitude of the frictional dissipation in the bottom Ekman layer above smooth sediment may be estimated from recent measurements by Weatherly (1972) below the Florida current—in agreement with semiempirical theories of the neutral Ekman layer (Gill, 1968) using atmospheric data. These indicate a spin-down time for motion in the barotropic mode in excess of 500 days, which is sufficiently greater than the other time scales involved in mesoscale motion to suggest that bottom friction is not of first order importance in the dynamics, though it may of course be critical for the long-term statistical behavior. Vertical fluxes of momentum in the interior associated with turbulence and internal waves are presumably also negligible. The surface wind stress probably acts mainly on the space and time scales of the atmospheric disturbances—predominantly larger, but shorter than those we are concentrating on. Apparently, no adequate analysis has yet been made of just how much direct forcing is to be expected into the oceanic mesoscale motions; but an important question is whether the latter might be driven indirectly, by large-scale, wind-driven currents interacting with topographic features.

In this paper we present some preliminary results from a numerical model designed to simulate the mesoscale dynamics suggested by the above scale analysis with sufficient flexibility to permit a wide range of exploratory investigations. After development at The Johns Hopkins University, this model is presently implemented using the CDC 7600 at the National Center for Atmospheric Research, Boulder,

Colorado, without whose generous hospitality and cooperation the project would have been severely restricted. Priorities have been influenced by the time table for the design of the field program of MODE-I, which is expected to take place in a 250-km square centered near 28° N, 69°20′ W during early summer 1973. Using the background stratification and bottom topography appropriated to the MODE area, several different forcing mechanisms have been investigated; but so far attention has been largely concentrated on finding situations that yield flow patterns qualitatively resembling those already revealed in a fragmentary manner by the preliminary observational program. These are being used to generate simulated data for design studies on instrument deployment and data analysis techniques.

A second objective has been to describe the "synoptic signatures" of these different mechanisms so that, following the main field program, we may be better able to identify which one is probably responsible for the mesoscale eddies. Meanwhile, several interesting theoretical questions raised by the calculations have been shelved for the time being.

THE MODEL

This project involves integrations forward in time of a six-level, quasi-geostrophic model using observed stratification and bottom topography within a horizontal square of side *LL* divided into a 32 by 32 or 64 by 64 grid. *LL* in different studies has been variously 480 km; 1,000 km; and 1,920 km, giving a minimum grid spacing of 15 km. Geostrophic velocities and bottom roughness are effectively extended periodically outside the area of integration, simulating a "typical" region in mid-ocean rather than an enclosed basin. The flow field is driven either by following the development with time of an initially given "eddy" field or by an imposed "large-scale" velocity interacting with bottom roughness. "Large scale" here means the horizontal average over the area of integration; "eddies" are any departures from this instantaneous large-scale velocity. Bottom friction, linear so far, is allowed for, together with a weak but highly selective damping to prevent accumulation of entrophy of the smallest horizontal scales resolvable in the model. There is no vertical diffusivity.

The quasi-geostrophic equations were first enunciated for the atmosphere by Charney (see Pedlosky, 1964) and are a consistent approximation, valid as the Rossby number tends to zero. The model is on a β-plane, axes Oxy towards the east and north, respectively, with the Coriolis parameter taken as $f + \beta y$. The ocean is represented by M, discrete layers of known density $\rho(1 + \sigma_r)$, and mean thickness Δ_r $(r = 1, \ldots M)$. The structure used for simulations in the MODE area is shown in Figure 1. In each layer the horizontal velocities are independent of depth and are in approximate geostrophic balance. The dominant nondivergent part may be derived from a stream function, $\psi_r(x,y,t)$,

$$u = -\frac{\partial \psi}{\partial y}, \qquad v = \frac{\partial \psi}{\partial x}. \tag{1}$$

The small vertical displacement $\zeta(x,y,t)$ of the interface between the layers r and $r + 1$ is given by the hydrostatic relation

$$\zeta = \frac{f}{g\delta\sigma}\,\delta\psi, \tag{2}$$

where δ is the vertical finite-difference operator $(\ )_{r+1} - (\ )_r$. The instantaneous thickness of each layer is thus $\Delta - \delta\zeta$. The small (of order Ro) changes from the mean

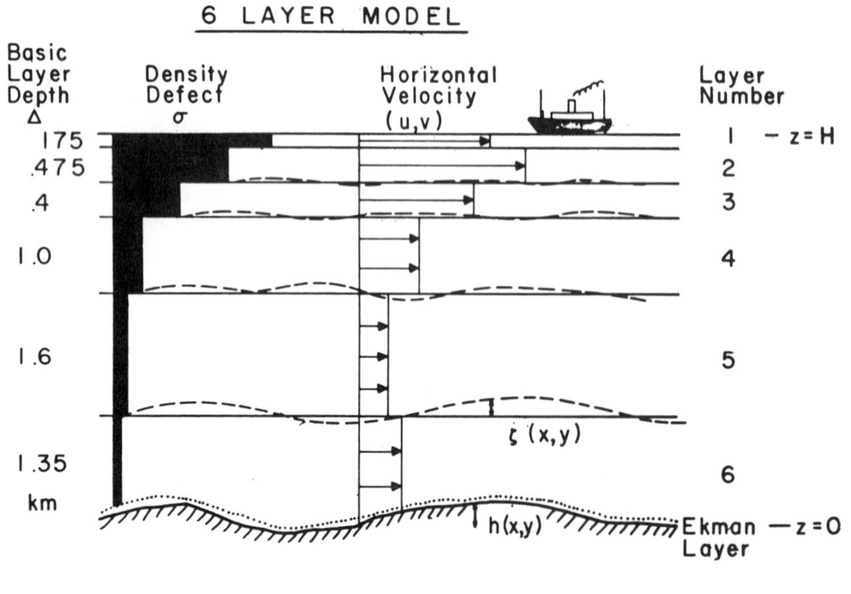

FIGURE 1 The vertical structure for the six-layer model in the MODE area.

value Δ imply slight horizontal convergences and corresponding changes in absolute vorticity. Neglecting terms (of order Ro) smaller than those retained, the potential vorticity equation for each layer becomes

$$\frac{D}{Dt}\left[\Delta\left(\frac{\partial^2\psi}{\partial x^2}+\frac{\partial^2\psi}{\partial y^2}\right)+\delta\left(\frac{f^2}{g\delta\sigma}\delta\psi\right)\right]+\beta\Delta\frac{\partial\psi}{\partial x}=0, \quad (3)$$

where

$$\frac{D}{Dt}=\frac{\partial}{\partial t}-\frac{\partial\psi}{\partial y}\frac{\partial}{\partial x}+\frac{\partial\psi}{\partial x}\frac{\partial}{\partial y}. \quad (4)$$

Here

$$\left[\delta\left(\frac{f^2}{g\delta\sigma}\delta\psi\right)\right]_r=\frac{f^2}{g}\left[\frac{1}{\sigma_{r+1}-\sigma_r}(\psi_{r+1}-\psi_r)-\frac{1}{\sigma_r-\sigma_{r-1}}(\psi_r-\psi_{r-1})\right].$$

At the ocean surface above layer 1 the boundary condition is

$$\frac{D}{Dt}\zeta=0, \quad (5)$$

i.e., the vertical velocities vanish and a surface Ekman layer is ignored. This is simply implemented by ignoring the term containing the implied reference to σ_o, ψ_o in Eq. (3).

Similarly, all the ocean floor below layer M,

$$\frac{D}{Dt}\left[\zeta-h(x,y)\right]=-\epsilon\left(\frac{\partial^2\psi}{\partial x^2}+\frac{\partial^2\psi}{\partial y^2}\right). \quad (6)$$

This states that fluid particles just above the Ekman layer of effective thickness ϵ move over topography $h(x,y)$. This assumption of a linear bottom friction is for convenience rather than necessity (though required hitherto to save core storage), and in further developments the correct nonlinear form should be incorporated. For layer M, Eq. (6) is subtracted from Eq. (3), eliminating reference to σ_{M+1} and ψ_{M+1}, but requiring $f[h(x,y)]$ to be added to the potential vorticity just before computing the advective term in D/Dt. It should be noted that according to this procedure the lower boundary condition is always applied to the lowest layer, regardless of how high the topography $h(x,y)$ may be. This is a good approximation over much of the ocean, but areas like the continental slope cannot consistently be treated in this way.

Eqs. (3) and (4), modified by the upper and lower boundary conditions, comprise M-linked partial differential equations for the M variables $\psi_r(x,y,t)$. However, the horizontal boundary condition is yet to be stated. The particular form for this is the main innovative feature of this model, which permits the embedding of a mesoscale structure within a "large-scale" circulation and is built into the numerical methods in a deep-seated manner. It is that the velocity (not the stream function ψ) should be a periodic function of x and y with period L in each direction. If we write

$$\psi=-Uy+Vx+\psi'(x,y,t) \quad (7)$$

$$h=ax+by+h'(x,y), \quad (8)$$

where ψ' and h' are periodic; (U,V) and (a,b) are the "large-scale" current and bottom slope respectively. These are by definition uniform over the area under consideration. By contrast the "eddies" (ψ') and "roughness" (h') are the mesoscale structures. If we substitute into Eq. (3), we obtain two important constraints necessary for the consistency of this separation,

$$\frac{\partial}{\partial t}(\delta U)=\frac{\partial}{\partial t}(\delta V)=0, \quad (9)$$

$$f(aU_M+bV_M)+\sum_{r=1}^{M}\beta\Delta_r V_r=0. \quad (10)$$

Eq. (9) states that the baroclinic part of the large-scale current cannot change with time. Eq. (10) is a diagnostic statement roughly equivalent to "the large-scale barotropic flow is parallel to contours of constant Coriolis parameter divided by large-scale depth." However, these equations still permit

$$\frac{\partial U_r}{\partial t}=\cos\phi\frac{d\widetilde{W}}{dt},\quad \frac{\partial V_r}{\partial t}=\sin\phi\frac{d\widetilde{W}}{dt},\quad r=1,\ldots M, \quad (11)$$

where

$$\cos\phi=fb+\beta H/[f^2a^2+(fb+\beta H)^2]^{1/2},$$

$$\sin\phi=-fa/[f^2a^2+(fb+\beta H)^2]^{1/2}, \quad (12)$$

and where $\widetilde{W}(t)$ is a single undetermined function of time—the component of barotropic current perpendicular to the large-scale gradient of vertically integrated potential vorticity. The latter is the external forcing applied to the mesoscale, and a formula defining $d\widetilde{W}/dt$ must be supplied by the experimenter. It may be prescribed *a priori* (as if an arbitrarily great large-scale stress were available) or allowed to change freely in response to the topographically induced drag associated with the bottom roughness within the model (so that the total energy is constant); or some intermediate principle may be adopted. This topographically induced drag arises because the pressure on one slope of a roughness element is not necessarily the same as that on the opposing slope. It is computed at each time step by a method to be described below.

To solve Eq. (3), ψ is separated, according to Eq. (7), into eddies $\psi_r'(x,y,t)$ and large-scale flow (U_r, V_r) $(r = 1 \ldots M)$. At each time step, Poisson's equation has to be solved

$$\Delta\left(\frac{\partial^2 \psi'}{\partial x^2} + \frac{\partial^2 \psi'}{\partial y^2}\right) + \delta\left(\frac{f^2}{g\delta\sigma}\delta\psi'\right) = q', \qquad (13)$$

where at and between each level $\Delta, f^2/g\delta\sigma$ are given constants. This is accomplished by discrete Fourier transforming with respect to x and y; and, for each wave number (k,l), solving M simultaneous equations for the Fourier components $\hat{\psi}_r(k,l)$ in terms of $\hat{q}_r(k,l)$. The necessary matrix coefficients are computed at the outset and then stored. $\partial\hat{q}/\partial t$ is also evaluated in wave number space, except for the Jacobian $\partial(\psi',q')/\partial(x,y)$, which is evaluated at each level at the grid points using Arakawa's (1966) fourth-order scheme and then Fourier transformed. In the advection of each component $\hat{q}_r(k,l)$ by the large-scale velocity (U_r, V_r), a formula consonant with Arakawa's scheme is used, thus preserving its important energy- and vorticity-conserving features. A small artificial damping proportional to $(k^2 + l^2)^2\, \hat{q}_r$ controls unwanted buildup of energy in the highest wave numbers. $\partial U_r/\partial t$ and $\partial V_r/\partial t$ follow from Eq. (11). Centered differences in time (leap frog) were used throughout, with a forward difference initially and every 50 time steps thereafter. The time step dt was chosen to keep the Courant-Friedrichs-Lewy parameter (the local maximum speed times dt divided by the grid spacing) between 0.2 and 0.8, except where that implied $\omega\, dt > 1$, where ω is the angular frequency of the barotropic Rossby wave in wave number (1,0). Neglect of this last exception resulted occasionally in catastrophic instability, but otherwise no problems were encountered. A typical dt would be 0.5 days. On a 32 by 32 grid, the computation takes 0.6 s per time step on the NCAR CDC 7600, making extensive use of the large-core memory for rapid access storage.

The units used are kilometers and days throughout, with stresses and energy-per-unit volume being divided by the density to be in units of (km/day)^2. Note that 1 km/day = 1.16 cm/s, and near 30°N, $f = 6.3$ day^{-1}, $\beta = 0.002$ km^{-1}/day^{-1}. A stress of one unit corresponds to 1.35 dyn/cm^2.

Two versions of the bottom topography have been used—appropriate to a 480 km square and a 1,000 km square, respectively. The latter (the extended MODE area) was digitized by Miss Pat Jaskyn from all available soundings and kindly made available to the authors by Prof. Allan Robinson. It was processed by subtracting a linear trend ($ax + by$ in Eq. 8), modifying the residual around the edges of the area of interest to make it match smoothly across the west and east boundaries and across the south and north boundaries, Fourier transforming the result, discarding all components with wave number $|k|$ or $|l| \geq 8$ (wavelength < 125 km), and reconstituting. The result is shown in Figure 2. The large-scale slope (a,b) is -7.4×10^{-5} and 5.6×10^{-4}, i.e., essentially north-south and with magnitude and sign equivalent to about 35 percent of the β-effect for the barotropic mode. The one-dimensional power spectrum of the roughness elements (before filtering) is roughly proportional to k^{-m}, where m lies between 1.5 and 2, though substantial anisotropy is detectable over this area with ridges and troughs tending to be oriented northwest-southwest. The smaller area, a subset of the larger, centered on 67° W, 25°50′ N, processed in a similar manner. The mean slope was also (fortuitously) approximately north-south.

The layer thicknesses Δ_r and densities σ_r were selected to match the Rossby radius of deformation L_o for the external and first two internal modes to the values for the continuous distribution of density observed on the Crawford cruise (Stations #315, 317; Fuglister, 1960). L_o is defined in the model by the matrix eigenvalue problem

$$\delta\left(\frac{f^2}{g\delta\sigma}\delta\hat{\psi}\right) + L_o^{-2}\,\hat{\psi} = 0, \qquad (14)$$

being infinite for the external mode. In addition, attention was paid to the concept of bottom trapping on scales $L \ll L_o$. This arises within quasi-geostrophic theory from a combination of the rotation and stratification. If the potential vorticity were uniform ($q' = 0$), the velocity in a con-

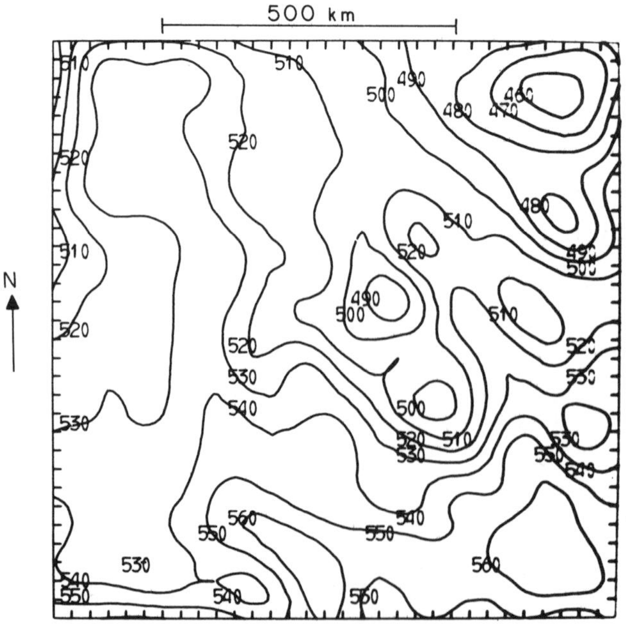

FIGURE 2 The bottom topography used in the experiments, with LL = 1,000 km; contour interval is 10 m.

tinuously stratified fluid with Brunt-Vaisala frequency N above a sinusoidal topographic feature,

$$h'(x) = \hat{h} \sin x/L, \tag{15}$$

would be

$$v = Nh'(x)e^{-Nz/fL}. \tag{16}$$

Different Fourier components may be superimposed, so that the topography is directly reflected in the velocity field above, but filtered. Using an appropriate value of N ($\sim 5f$), the exponent is unity at a height 1 km above the bottom for $L = 5$ km—so that wavelengths shorter than 30 km are greatly attenuated. Note that just above the bottom Ekman layer this would indicate speeds of 3 km/day associated with a bump of height 100 m. For much larger scales, the penetration extends up to the main thermocline; and N cannot be taken as uniform. Of course, in practice the potential vorticity is not uniform; but a strong large-scale current tends to dissociate fluctuations from particular small-scale topographic features, so this pattern may show through in the time average of the flow field. Δ_r and σ_r in the model were chosen so that on the smallest horizontal scale, well resolved by the finite-difference scheme (wavelength = 4 grid spaces, $L = 10$ km), the filter ratio between adjacent layers for bottom induced effects is about 2:5.

EXPERIMENTS

The experiments reported here fall into three main categories: (a) interaction between a large-scale barotropic current and bottom roughness, (b) baroclinic instability, and (c) isolated eddies. In addition, pilot studies have been made of the reflection of Rossby waves from the Blake-Bahama outer bank, driven by variations in the large-scale, wind stress curl.

Large-Scale Barotropic Forcing

In experiments one and two, the motion was started from rest on a 32 by 32 grid by a steady barotropic current from the west, $U = 3$ km/day. Thus, $d\widetilde{W}/dt$ in Eq. (11) was identically zero. The bottom topography and stratification were from the MODE area, using $LL = 480$ km and 1,000 km, respectively.

The results in the two experiments were essentially similar, and we will give them in detail only for the second. There was a large systematic transfer of energy into primarily barotropic unsteady eddies with speeds increasing systematically downwards (being at the bottom about 50 percent greater than at the surface). Vertical displacements of the main thermocline were negligible—the ratio of eddy potential energy to kinetic energy was 0:3. This energy transfer continued at an approximately uniform rate, even though the rms eddy speeds (17 km/day after 300 days) became much larger than the large-scale velocity U. The topographic drag P fluctuated around an average value of 1.7 km^2/day^2, corresponding to a stress of 2 dyn/cm^2, in a direction opposing the large-scale current U—so the maintainence of the latter implied a large source of energy. Extrapolating somewhat, a statistically steady state would have been reached after about 400 days, with rms velocities in the deep water around 22 km/day, this value being set by the coefficient of bottom friction.

The flow patterns after 167 days at levels two (mid-depth 400 m) and six (mid-depth 4,325 m) are shown in Figure 3. The dominant scale of these eddies (as measured by the zero crossing of the transverse velocity correlation function) is 115 km at level two and 75 km at level six. These values tended to increase during the experiment as the eddies grew stronger, being 135 km and 100 km, respectively, after 300 days. The flow features drifted irregularly—a subjectively estimated time scale for substantial changes being 30 days—except that in experiment one, a single large stationary eddy came to dominate.

In experiment three, the large-scale current was reduced to $U = 1$ km/day ($LL = 480$ km). In this case the eddy energy stopped increasing after 150 days, when the rms velocity was only about 2 km/day and the structure was much more baroclinic (see Figure 4). The average topographic drag was only 0.2 (km/day)^2, so that the energy input is reduced by a factor of 25 by this change in U. The deep flow formed a marked quasi-steady jet with maximum velocities at 6 km/day, whereas that above the thermocline was distributed among eddies comparable in size to the previous example.

These three experiments demonstrate the strength of the interaction between bottom roughness on the scale of the Rossby radius of deformation and a large-scale barotropic current, being sufficient to transfer energy into the eddies equal in magnitude to the kinetic energy of the large-scale current during a time span of only 5-15 days. The consequent increase in rms velocity near the bottom greatly enhances the rate of frictional dissipation. The dominance of smaller length scales in the deep water is qualitatively consistent with the concept of bottom trapping outlined in Eq. (2), though a quantitative comparison has yet to be undertaken. The jet in experiment three is similar to a feature in some of the later baroclinic instability studies—though over different topography.

When the large-scale flow is from the east, the time average, topographic drag P virtually disappears. In experiment four, an initial barotropic current, $U = 10$ km/day, from the west was allowed to vary with time in response to the drag

$$\frac{d\widetilde{W}}{dt} = -P/H, \tag{16}$$

where H is the total water depth (5 km), thus conserving the

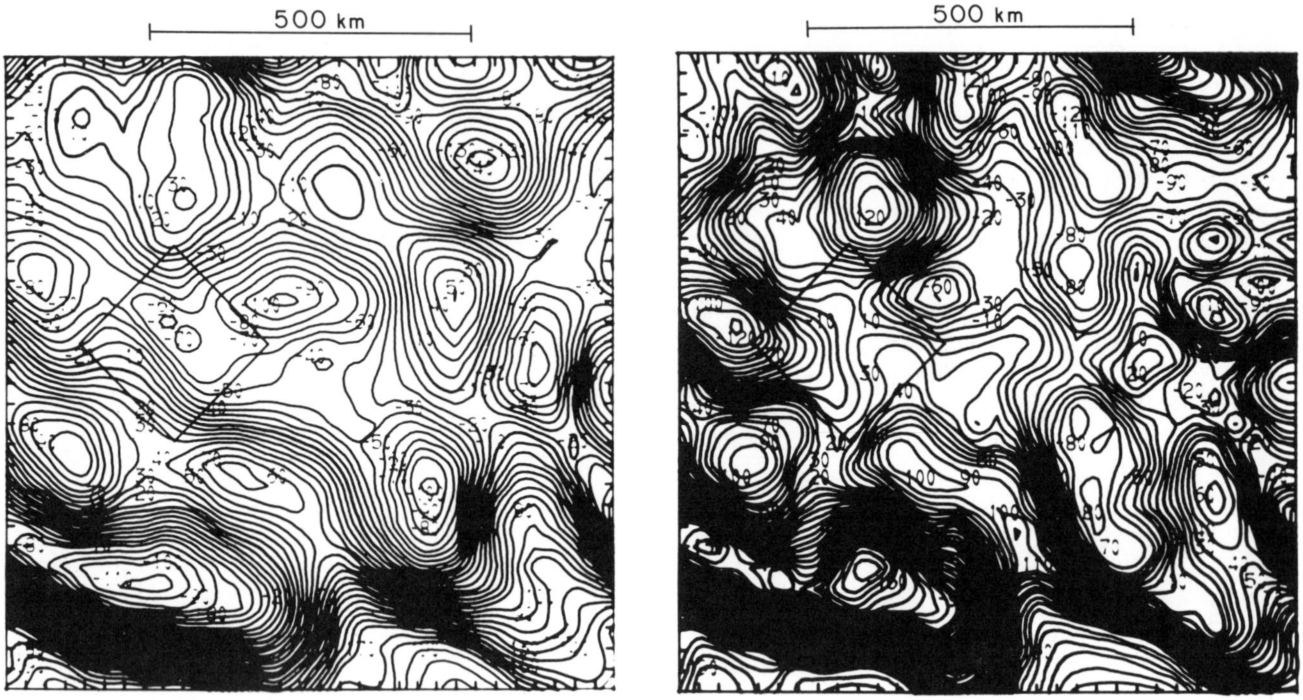

FIGURE 3 Steamline patterns in experiment two after 167 days: (a) level two, above the main thermocline, (b) level six, near the ocean floor. Contour interval is 100 km^2/day.

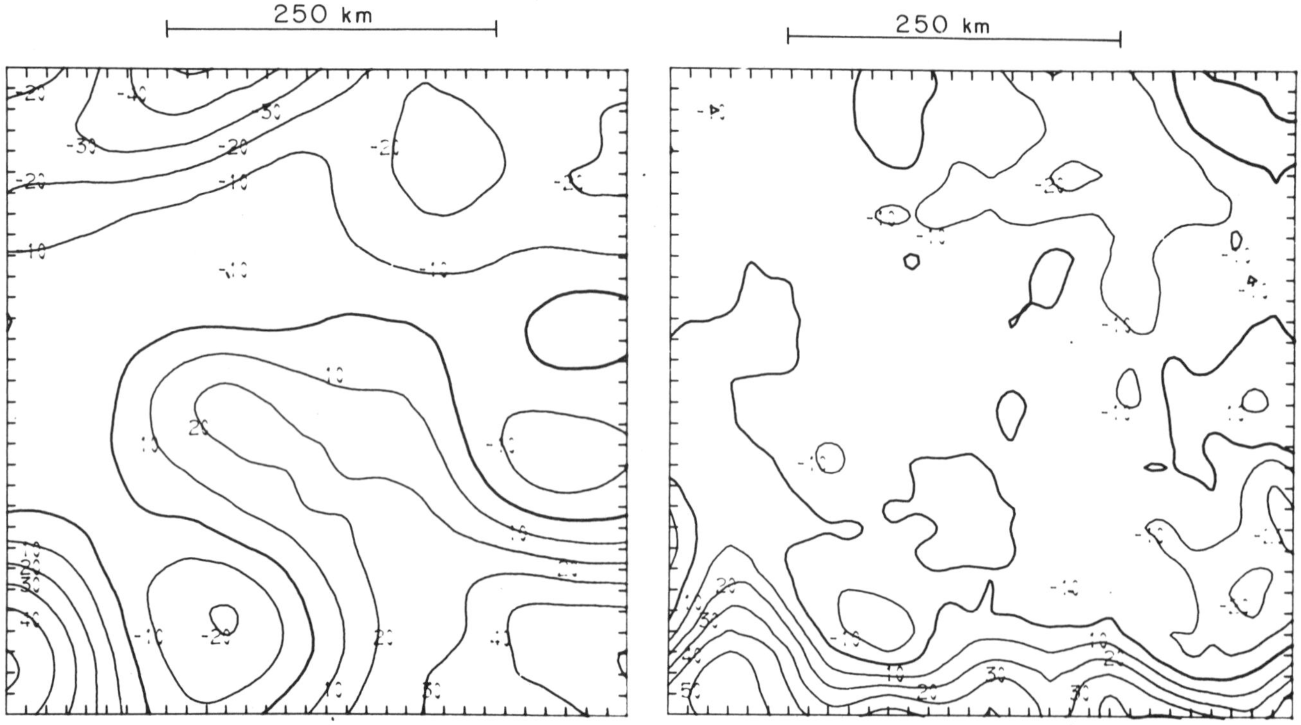

FIGURE 4 Streamline patterns in experiment three after 350 days: (a) level two, (b) level six. Contour interval is 100 km^2/day. The horizontal scale is different from Figure 3.

total energy (except for friction). Within 100 days it had become 5 km/day from the east, after which it settled down to a slow, quasi-exponential, frictional decay in which the whole flow pattern was stationary but decreasing in magnitude. The corresponding drag P is illustrated in Figure 5(a), showing clearly the positive average while U was from the west, but fluctuating about zero thereafter. These oscillations in $P(t)$ are characteristic of all the integrations with this model. This period of about 15 days does not appear to correspond to any of the natural frequencies of the system. Experiment five was identical to four, except that initially $U = -10$ km/day. The reversal did not occur, and in the later stages (after about 100 days) the flow pattern was similar in experiment four, but of greater magnitude. The average drag was close to zero throughout [Figure 5(b)].

This behavior may be explained qualitatively by concentrating on the Rossby waves forced by the large-scale flow over the bottom roughness, but neglecting the nonlinear interaction between the different Fourier components in the eddy pattern thus generated. These nonlinear terms are certainly important in determining the details of the flow pattern and probably profoundly influence the statistics, but they will be ignored here. The complete theory for the spectral distribution of eddy energy for a given topography spectrum and a stationary random forcing, $U(t)$, will be presented elsewhere. The eddies may be divided into those locked to given stationary topographic features and bottom trapped to a degree depending on their scale and into Rossby waves (in the external or internal modes) freely propagating with the appropriate phase speed towards the west relative to the instantaneous value of $U(t)$. These may be excited resonantly by a disturbance of appropriate wave number and frequency. This excitation is particularly strong if U is constant and equal and opposite to the phase speed—so that the wave is approximately stationary relative to the topography, although random fluctuations in $U(t)$ will also contain some power at the appropriate frequency. The generation efficiency is also greatest for the barotropic mode. This resonance process leads to a systematic feeding of energy into the eddies—so that they grow until the frictional dissipation becomes large enough to balance. Since every Rossby wave carries westerly momentum, the process also implies a systematic topographic drag in the same sense, even after friction has become limiting. When U is steady, positive, and greater than 3 km/day, only barotropic waves can resonate. When U is steady and negative, none can; and the free waves and topographic drag are entirely absent.

Baroclinic Instability

The experiments in this category were undertaken to investigate the effects of bottom roughness on the process of baroclinic instability—whereby the available potential energy associated with large-scale horizontal gradients of density may become converted into eddy kinetic and potential energy on scales comparable to or greater than the Rossby radius of

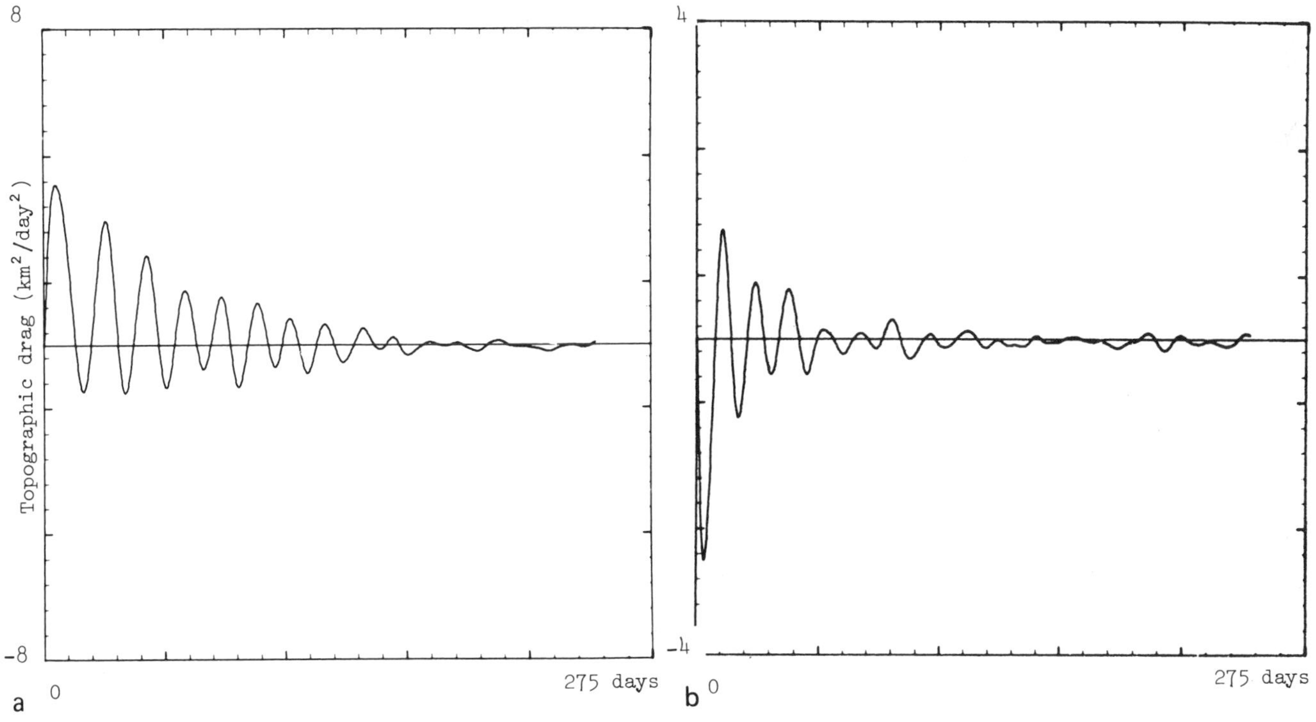

FIGURE 5 Westward component of topographic drag as a function of time in (a) experiment four, and (b) experiment five.

deformation. Since the pioneering studies of Eady (1949) and Charney (1947), an extensive literature on this process above a smooth bottom has arisen; although applications in the oceanic context have been few (e.g., Schulman, 1967). More extensive recent studies by Robinson and McWilliams (unpublished) have shown that in the presence of large-scale bottom slopes of order 1×10^{-3}, shears across the main thermocline of 5 km/day may result in unstable disturbances growing with *e*-folding times of 50–100 days. No theory exists to show whether topographic irregularities on the scale of the disturbances themselves inhibit or enhance the instability, or what should be the typical eddy pattern for finite-amplitude disturbances under such conditions.

The horizontal boundary conditions in the model permit a large-scale baroclinic current in any direction, though Eq. (9) requires that it be maintained constant with time throughout the integration. In these experiments, the vertical structure was always that for the first internal mode, with the maximum shear across the main thermocline. A shear of 2 km/day between levels two and four (mid-depths 400 m and 1,550 m) corresponds in the MODE area to slopes of the interfaces between two and three (basic depth 650 m) and between three and four (basic depth 1,050 m) of 127 m/1,000 km and 163 m/1,000 km, respectively. For comparison, the upward large-scale slope of the surface $\sigma_t = 27.0$ between 20° and 30° N along 65° W (estimated from Crawford 313, 324; Fuglister, 1960) is −134 m/1,000 km, at an average depth of 650 m, though at $\sigma_t = 27.4$ (925 m) this slope is +18 m/1,000 km. In the east-west direction (Discovery II 3593-3621), they are 58 m/1,000 km and 28 m/1,000 km, respectively.

The model was first tested using large shears (10 km/day), with the surface flow from the west above a nearly flat bottom, and verified the predictions of classical linear baroclinic instability theory, provided that the latter was computed for the finite-layer thickness and stratification actually used in the model. The inclusion of full-height bottom roughness appeared to make little difference to the stability boundary or the structure of the growing eddies. However, when the large-scale shears were reduced to magnitudes about twice those observed in the ocean, the picture became more confused. In experiment one a north-south shear ($V_2 = -2.2$, $V_4 = 0.06$ km/day) over the extended MODE topography resulted in an increasing (but not exponential) rate of transfer of energy into a pattern dominated by wave numbers (0,2) above the main thermocline but very irregular and confused below (Figure 6). After 600 days, typical speeds are 8 km/day at level two, but only 2 km/day near the bottom. During this time the topographic drag was always positive, averaging 0.15 km^2/day^2. If the large-scale velocity was allowed to respond to this stress (experiment two) according to Eq. (16), a quite different pattern emerged in the deep water (Figure 7) with a stationary easterly jet dominating the flow. This feature is associated with a marked stationary trough in the upper levels and is linked to the topography, because, when the latter was shifted northwards, the jet moved as well.

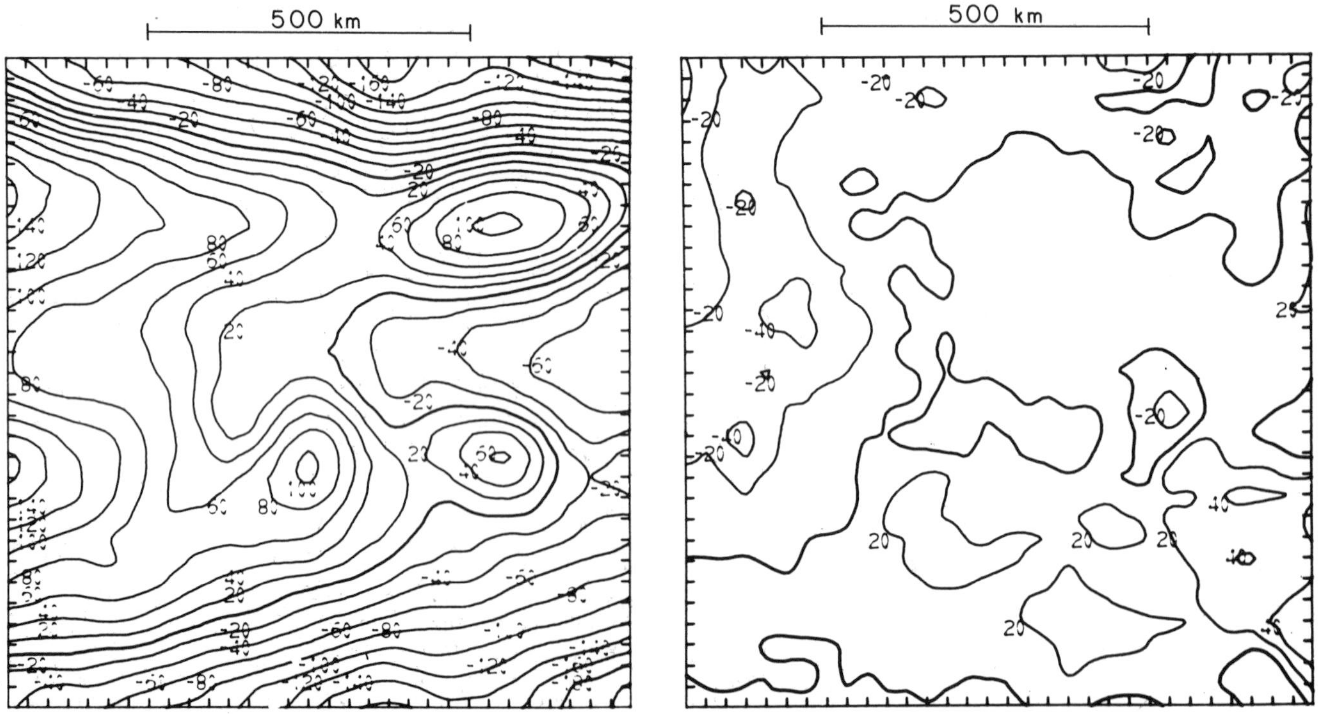

FIGURE 6 Streamline patterns in experiment one after 595 days: (a) level two, (b) level six. Contour interval, 200 km^2/day.

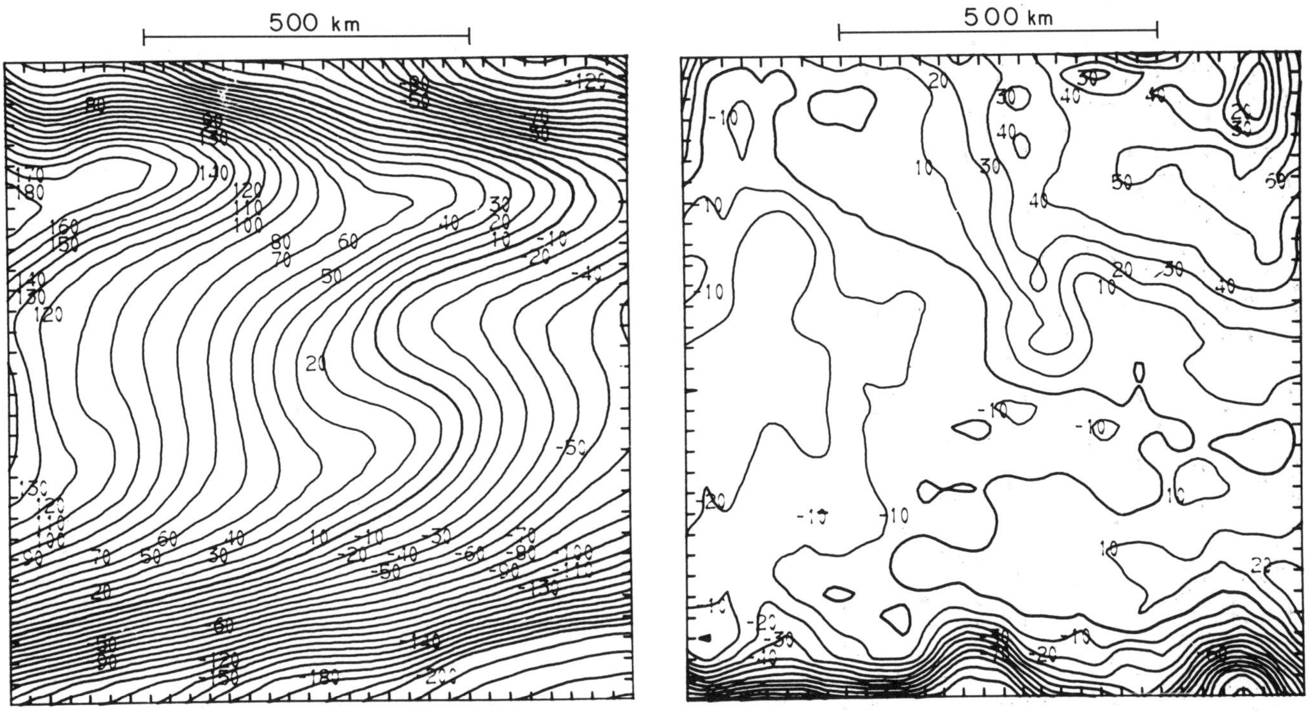

FIGURE 7 Streamline patterns in experiment two after 300 days: (a) level two, (b) level six. Contour interval is 100 km^2/day. Conditions for this experiment were identical to experiment one (Figure 6), except for the growth of a large scale westward barotropic velocity according to Eq. (16).

This numerical configuration suffers from the disadvantage that the available potential energy associated with horizontally uniform and unbounded shear flow is infinite. Since, with a linear bottom friction, both the rate of conversion of this into eddy energy and the rate of dissipation of eddy energy are proportional to the square of the amplitude, unstable eddies can apparently grow in magnitude without limit; and no statistical equilibrium exists. In order to generate more realistic simulated data for other studies, a finite magnitude was arbitrarily assigned to the total available energy; and, as the eddies increased, the shear was reduced accordingly. Strictly speaking, this contravenes Eq. (9); but it may be rationalized by arguing that in a bounded nonperiodic flow, slow changes of this sort must occur. The conditions determining the equilibrium level of eddy kinetic energy are still under investigation, but in experiments three and four the rms velocity in level six (near the bottom) became 4.5 and 11.5 km/day, respectively; whereas the driving shear $(V_2 - V_4)$ was −1.5 and −2.5 km/day, respectively.

It appears that shears corresponding to large-scale slopes of the main thermocline of about 150 m/1,000 km upwards towards the E may mark a threshold above which the rate of conversion to eddy energy accelerates very rapidly, resulting in unrealistically large eddy speeds; whereas below this value a much more quiescent (though unsteady) situation results.

A typical pattern of vertical displacements at the interface 2–3 (mean depth 650 m) in experiment three is shown in Figure 8. These features tend to drift westward at 2–3 km/day. A set of simulated float trajectories (at level four) computed during this experiment is shown in Figure 9. The ratio of eddy potential energy to kinetic energy under these circumstances is rather large (about 5 : 1), in complete contrast to the value for barotropic forcing. The rate of energy conversion from the large-scale, available potential energy is about 0.25 units (0.35 ergs/cm^2/s). In experiment four the velocities and vertical displacements were about 2.5 times these values, and the energy conversions eight times as large. The dominant scale of the eddies (as measured by the distance r_c at which the transverse velocity correlation function changes sign) decreases with depth, being 110 km and 60 km at levels two and six respectively, in experiment two, though the deep scale was substantially larger in experiment four. For comparison, it should be noted that a steady large-scale wind stress of 1 dyn/cm^2 during a Sverdrup transport above the main thermocline of perhaps 1 cm/s, is supplying energy to the large-scale ocean circulation at around 1 erg/cm^2 s.

Isolated Eddies

Meanders in the Gulf Stream frequently grow to such an extent that they form detached closed eddies that drift separately from the main current for many months (Fuglister, 1971). Experiment one was intended to show whether an

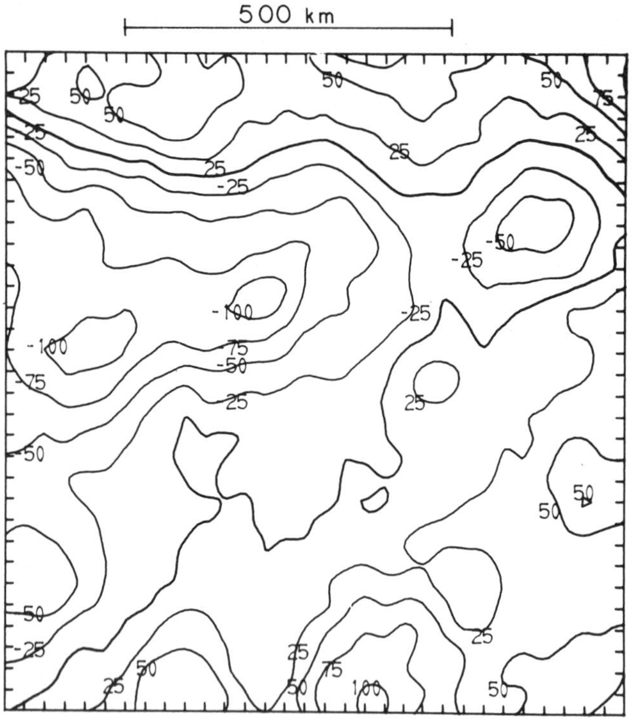

FIGURE 8 Vertical displacement $\zeta(x,y)$ of the interface between layers two and three in experiment three after 1,025 days. Contour interval, 25 m.

intense isolated circular vortex initially concentrated above the main thermocline is a stable configuration, how it will move, and how it will eventually decay. An initial stream function,

$$\psi = -A_r UL \exp - \tfrac{1}{2}\left(\frac{x^2 + y^2}{L^2}\right), \tag{17}$$

[with $U = 33$ km/day, $L = 45$ km, $A_r = (1, 0.9, 0.5, 0.1, 0, 0)$] was inserted into the MODE stratification and bottom topography ($LL = 480$ km), the friction coefficient being set as usual for a barotropic decay time of 500 days (Figure 10). This implies a cyclonic eddy with a maximum orbital speed of 33 km/day at a radius of 45 km at the surface, decreasing to 3.3 km/day at 1,500 m and nothing below 2 km. The subsequent development is shown in Figures 11 and 12. Note that the eddy has continued to move west by northwest throughout this period, but has reappeared at the bottom right of the diagram because of the periodic boundary conditions. The average velocities were −2.4 and 1.5 km/day. No persistent or remarkable structure appeared below the vortex in the deep water at any stage.

This result shows that an intense circular baroclinic vortex is quite stable and is largely unaffected by topographic irregularities. Because of the variation of Coriolis parameter with latitude, it suffers a slow erosion with time as secondary vortices on the periphery gain in strength. The extensive

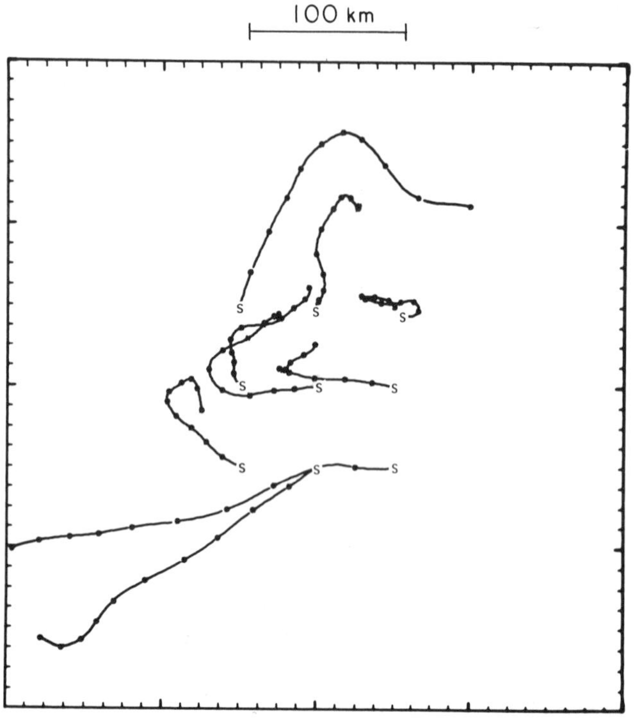

FIGURE 9 Simulated float trajectories for experiment three. Nine floats were placed at the points marked *S* after 932 days. Cross hatches indicate every 7.5 days thereafter.

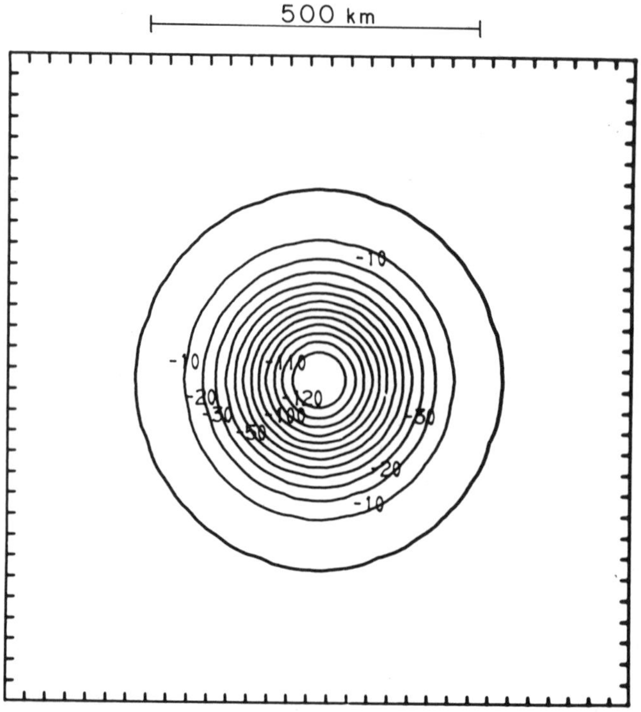

FIGURE 10 Initial streamline pattern for experiment one at level two. Contour interval, 100 km²/day.

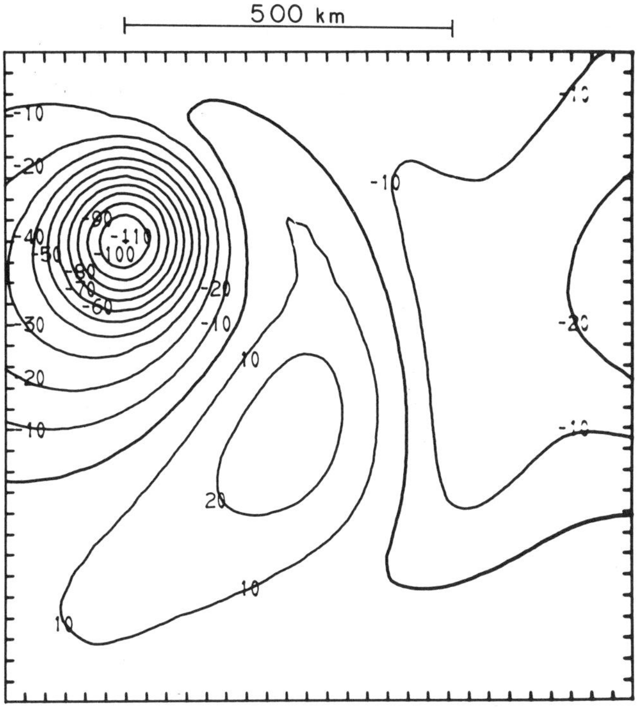

FIGURE 11 Streamline pattern, as Figure 10, after 75 days.

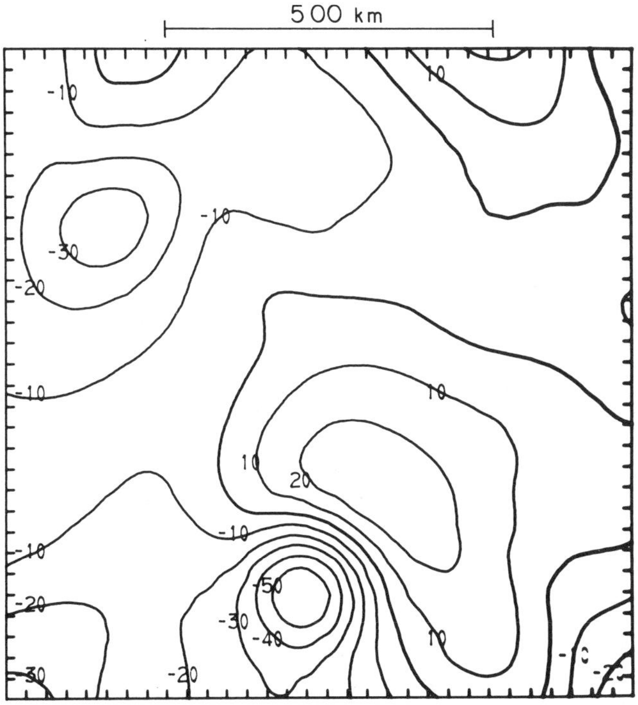

FIGURE 12 Streamline pattern, as Figure 10, after 200 days.

anticyclone to the south and east of the vortex center in Figure 12 is consistent with the net northward displacement on a β-plane of fluid particles in this area since the integration began. A corresponding cyclonic area to the southwest and west of the center appears as a relative spreading of the vortex lines (also extending by periodicity into the right-hand side of the diagram. The resulting velocity induced between these two areas is apparently responsible for the northward drift of the primary vortex. The secondary areas appear only on the periphery of the vortex, because near the core the β-induced vorticity is rapidly wound into a tight spiral of alternating positive and negative bands, with little net result. The westward drift, on the other hand, appears to be essentially an average-speed propagation of Rossby waves.

A pilot study with a somewhat less intense anticyclonic vortex showed essentially similar slow erosion, though the secondary vortices had the opposite sign. The vortex drifted southwest at about 1.5 km/day, thus tending to confirm the above dynamical picture.

A simulation (reported in detail elsewhere) has also been completed for the anticyclonic eddy observed in the Polygon experiment in the subtropical North Atlantic (Koshlyakov and Grachev, 1972). This was approximately elliptical, with maximum orbital speeds of 20 cm/s at a distance 90 km from the center. It was observed to drift slightly south of west at about 4 km/day, a feature well confirmed in the simulation. When the nonlinear advection terms were omitted in the model, the flow pattern was not greatly altered—except that the center moved due west. The eddy eroded and was largely dispersed after about 150 days.

Because of the larger scale of the Polygon eddy, the parameter $U/\beta L^2$, which measures the relative magnitudes of the advective terms and the variation of the Coriolis parameter with latitude, was substantially smaller (1.2) than in the MODE experiment (where it was 8). The radius of deformation $L_0 \doteq 70$ km was also greater. A tentative conclusion from these studies is that the westward movement is a feature of all such eddies (linear or not), whereas the northward or southward drift is a nonlinear effect for a concentrated intense vortex in the cyclonic or anticyclonic sense.

CONCLUSIONS

A six-level, quasi-geostrophic model of a limited area of the deep ocean may be used to investigate realistically the simultaneous dynamical effects of stratification, bottom topography, nonlinear advection, and the variation of the Coriolis parameter with latitude for a variety of configurations emphasizing different forcing mechanisms. These can generate mesoscale eddies with speeds of 5-20 cm/s with a dominant length scale consistently about twice the Rossby radius of deformation (about 50 km at 30° N), though with a tendency to smaller scales and somewhat increased speeds near the ocean floor. Over typical bottom irregularities, a large-scale barotropic current from the west is associated with a topographically induced drag that averages more than 1 dyn/cm^2 at 3 cm/s, and about 0.2 dyn/cm^2 at 1 cm/s; whereas, when the corresponding current is from the east, the average drag is greatly reduced or entirely absent. This drag is apparently associated with the generation of Rossby waves having a westward component of phase velocity. The induced eddies are largely barotropic at the larger forcing velocity and baroclinic for the smaller, but in the latter case the speeds are much smaller than those observed in the field.

Baroclinic instability, on the other hand, does provide a mechanism potentially responsible for the observed mesoscale eddies; although the requirements on the magnitude and direction of the large-scale slope of the thermocline are rather stringent. Baroclinic eddies of approximately the correct strength, length, and time scales then arise naturally. Further numerical studies are needed to determine the precise conditions needed.

An initially circular, isolated vortex above the main thermocline (simulating a cut-off Gulf Stream eddy) erodes slowly by the formation of secondary circulations to the east and west of its center. Under the conditions chosen, the lifetime was about 200 days, during which time the vortex drifted west at about 4 km/day. Due to nonlinear advection terms in the equation of motion, a cyclonic vortex tends to move north, an anticyclonic one south, i.e., towards the main axis of the current if the vortex is generated by a cut-off meander in the Gulf Stream. Bottom irregularities appear to be relatively unimportant for this mechanism.

These crude "synoptic signatures" need to be developed further into discriminating statistical measures that may be determined quantitatively from a limited instrumentation system in the real ocean, and this study is continuing. The limitations of the periodic boundary conditions should be explored further by comparison studies on the same resolution but extending over a larger area and by developing the theory for embedding the mesoscale in the large circulation. Also, refinements of the differencing techniques, the modeling of friction, etc., should be undertaken in order to determine the sensitivity of the results to these apparently minor aspects.

ACKNOWLEDGMENTS

This project was supported by the National Science Foundation (Office of the Decade of Ocean Exploration) Grant GX-30119. We are also indebted to the National Center for Atmospheric Research (also sponsored by the National Science Foundation) for their hospitality and the use of their computing facility and to the other participants in the Mid-Ocean Dynamics Experiment for continuous stimulation, encouragement, and criticism.

REVIEW: A. ROBINSON

I'd like to take this opportunity as a reviewer to explain aspects of this model that are novel. It is a local model, imbedded into the surrounding ocean by the use of periodic boundary conditions. In order to do this, the quasi-geostrophic fields must be decomposed into (area-averaged) mean fields and periodic parts. The quasi-geostrophic equations then yield equations of special form to be integrated numerically for the periodic fields plus certain consistency relationships. These consistency relationships are what Dr. Bretherton has called the specifiable large-scale flow and represent important coupling parameters to the rest of the ocean. They allow the specification of a somewhat arbitrary time-dependent barotropic field, essentially the part of the deep flow that is parallel to the contours of f/H, which can be specified in terms of a single arbitrary function. In addition to this, a baroclinic part must be specified, which, for consistency, is steady. A relative weakness of this model is the rather strong dependence on these external parameters. Now what was called the barotropic eddy experiment consists of not specifying any baroclinic part, but prescribing, in a certain time-dependent way, the barotropic function. In one such experiment there was a big buildup of eddy energy: in another there was none. In the latter case, the time-dependent barotropic parameter was specified precisely to prevent energy accumulation. Now, in fact, the energy in local regions may exhibit low-frequency fluctuations; and there is, therefore, a strong control on the basic processes in this parameterization. Dr. Bretherton did mention the buildup of baroclinic energy in a later experiment. This he controlled by an arbitrary time-variation of the area-averaged baroclinic part of the flow, which, however, violates his consistency condition. Thus what he has is not a real solution to the quasi-geostrophic equations. We are beginning to gain insight into local dynamical processes, but further investigation of the imbedding problem is necessary. Nonetheless, the virtues of the model have already been mentioned. It allows one to make local time-dependent extrapolations and investigations of initial conditions and of eddy processes. The model also allows the production of simulated data, which has enhanced our quasi-geostrophic intuition and has aided in the design of the MODE-I experiment. Perhaps most importantly, these computations allow for direct comparison with measurements that can be made by specific instruments. This study is supported in the MODE theoretical program by other and different numerical models and also by a base of analytical theory. In conclusion, I remark that this is an embryonic example of a local model, the first step toward a regional model that will evolve towards an ocean basin model. This represents an alternative philosophy of construction of a general circulation model, starting with whatever size restrictions are necessary to resolve the eddies and then building successively larger models.

REFERENCES

Arakawa, A. 1966. J. Comp. Phys. 1:119–43.
Charney, J. G. 1947. J. Meteorol. 4:135–62.
Crease, J. 1962. J. Geophys. Res. 3173–76.
Eady, E. T. 1949. Tellus 1(3):33–52.
Fuglister, F. C. 1960. Atlantic Ocean Atlas. Woods Hole Oceanographic Institution, Woods Hole, Mass.
Fuglister, F. C. 1971. Cyclonic rings formed by the Gulf Stream 1965–66. *In* Studies in Physical Oceanography. Gordon & Breach, New York.
Gill, A. E. 1968. Quart. J. R. Meteorol. Soc. 94:586–88.
Koshlyakov, M. N., and Y. M. Grachev. 1972. Mesoscale currents at a hydrophysical polygon in the tropical Atlantic. Unpublished manuscript.
Pedlosky, J. 1964. J. Atmos. Sci. 21:201–19.
Schulman, E. 1967. Tellus 19:292–305.
Weatherly, G. L. 1972. J. Phys. Ocean 2:54–72.

DISCUSSION

VERONIS: I'm not very clear about where all this energy is coming from for the growth of these eddies. Is it a resonant interaction that you're getting?

BRETHERTON: Are you talking about the barotropic or the baroclinic case?

VERONIS: When you say barotropic, you mean you impose the barotropic conditions; and of course you get baroclinic effects. That's the case I mean.

BRETHERTON: To maintain a large-scale current heading this way in the presence of a bottom-induced drag, you've got to do work. What that means is that there has to be an ageostrophic northward drift across the downward pressure gradient. Where that is coming from ultimately is exactly the question that Allan is raising. This is the problem of the imbedding in the large-scale circulation. We did some experiments whereby, instead of maintaining that current, we let the large-scale velocity change in response to the bottom-induced drag. We went to the other extreme by saying that we don't force a large-scale flow; we let the large-scale flow respond completely to the averaged properties of the small-scale flow. What happened then was that within 25 days the large-scale current had reversed and headed eastward.

O'BRIEN: I'm looking forward to reading about the details of your model, because your model is quite similar in that we've also used a layered approach. When one uses doubly periodic conditions like this on a β-plane, a very basic question is: If the planetary vorticity advection in the vorticity balance is important in the interior, and an eddy goes out to the north or south end, it must come back in through the other side because of the periodic conditions. Does this cause a problem, and have you considered it in the consistency relationship?

BRETHERTON: It does not cause a problem, because we are using quasi-geostrophic equations, where what is assumed to be periodic is the nondivergent part of the velocity field. The various ageostrophic components that are necessary to account for β and that sort of thing are not periodic, but they are implicit in the model. The explicit fields are forced to be periodic.

O'BRIEN: One last question. Looking at the intense eddies that you have here, "Do you have conservation of energy in your model?"

BRETHERTON: In the absence of bottom friction and the small lateral numerical friction that I mentioned, the numerical scheme that we have is totally energy-preserving.

PEDLOSKY: As I understand it, in your baroclinic experiment you held the large-scale horizontal temperature gradient fixed during the course of the experiment. According to what Allan said, is this required in some sense for consistency? Because, it seems to me, you know, that when you get growth of baroclinic eddies, the first thing you're going to do is change the mean vertical shear.

CHARNEY: Isn't this the stability analysis?

BRETHERTON: If you consider the eddy problem in an infinite fluid unbounded on the north and south, then the available source of potential energy is infinite. If you do the small-amplitude, baroclinic instability solution, the infinitesimal-amplitude solution then grows exponentially; but it is an exact solution of the nonlinear, quasi-geostrophic equation, however large the amplitude gets. The reason is the infinite source of available potential energy; and, unless you bound the fluid, you've lost that feedback that we've been talking about.

PEDLOSKY: Only if the mode that you're looking at is a very particular kind of plane wave and only if the mode, not the mean field, has no horizontal structure.

MODELING THE BENTHIC PLANETARY BOUNDARY LAYER OF THE OCEAN

S. S. ZILITINKEVICH

The main effect of the benthic boundary layer is the drag of oceanic currents due to the associated friction and the energy dissipation. As a rule, heat and salinity exchange with the bottom do not play any role; and it is permissible to investigate the large-scale oceanic circulations, considering vertical heat and salinity fluxes in the benthic layer as being equal to zero. This layer appears to be neutrally stratified. All that is necessary for a mathematical description of large-scale processes is information on the turbulent fluxes of the momentum horizontal components τ_x and τ_y, which assume their maximum values near the bottom and decrease to zero at the top of the boundary layer. It is necessary to be able to calculate these fluxes using mean values of velocity components.

As we shall see later, the order of magnitude of the thickness of the benthic boundary layer does not exceed 10 m. In numerical models with a more rough vertical resolution, it is advisable not to calculate the vertical structure of the boundary layer, but to consider it entirely immersed into the lower computational layer, where the upper limit τ_x and τ_y will appear to be equal to zero. The explanation of the boundary layer effect is achieved by including the bottom values of the fluxes under consideration (τ_{xo} and τ_{yo}) into the right-hand sides of the horizontal velocity component equations for the lower computational layer.

In most cases, when the statistically stationary and horizontally homogenous turbulent Ekman layer under the flat surface is not very close to the equator, it may serve as a good model of the benthic layer. The averaged dynamic equations are:

$$f(v - V) + \frac{1}{\rho}\frac{\partial \tau_x}{\partial z} = 0, \quad -f(u - U) + \frac{1}{\rho}\frac{\partial \tau_y}{\partial z} = 0, \tag{1}$$

where ρ is the water density, f is the Coriolis parameter, z is the vertical coordinate counter from the bottom upwards, u and v are the mean velocity components corresponding to the horizontal axes x and y, and U and V are the respective velocity components in the free flow (i.e., beyond the boundary layer). The velocity and momentum flux components must meet the following boundary conditions:

$$u = v = 0 \quad \text{at} \quad z = z_o \tag{2}$$

$$u \to U, \ v \to V, \ \tau_x \to 0, \ \tau \to 0 \quad \text{at} \quad z \to \infty, \tag{3}$$

where $z \to \infty$ is the roughness parameter of the bottom. A condition similar to Eq. (3) can be used at some finite height, playing the role of an upper limit to the Ekman boundary layer.

We shall assume that the x axis is directed towards the momentum flux vector at the bottom, τ_{yo} then becomes zero; and instead of τ_{xo}, it is convenient to consider the friction velocity $U_* = (\tau_{xo}/\rho)^{1/2}$. Designating by α the angle between the axis and the direction of the free flow current (i.e., the angle of a total turn of the current in the benthic boundary layer), we obtain $U = G \cos\alpha$, $V = G \sin\alpha$, where G is the modulus of the velocity in the free flow. The problem of parameterization is now reduced to determining the connection between U_* and α on one hand, and G and z_o on the other. The latter is expressed by the resistance law for the turbulent Ekman layer:

$$ln\, R_o = B - ln\,\frac{U_*}{G} + \left[\frac{k^2}{(U_*/G)^2}\right]^{1/2} - A^2,$$

$$\sin\alpha = -\frac{A}{k}\frac{U_*}{G}\sin f, \tag{4}$$

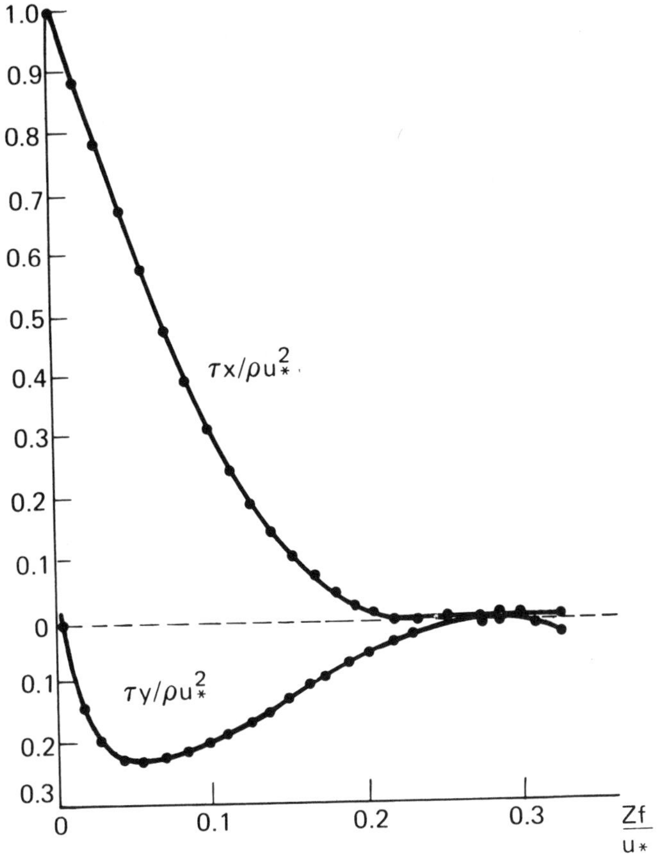

FIGURE 1 τ_x and τ_y profiles using measured velocity defects *u-U* and *v-V*.

where $R_o = G/|f|z_o$ is the surface Rossby number, $k \approx 0.4$ is the Karman constant, and A and B are nondimensional constants of the same type.* Based on a detailed review of empirical data, $A \approx 4.5$ and $B \approx 1$. Assuming that typical velocities over the ocean make the average $G \approx 5$ cm/s and $G \approx 100$ cm/s in the areas of strong currents and taking into account the typical value of 0.2 cm for the roughness parameter, the range for the Rossby number is obtained as $2 \cdot 10^5 < R_o < 5 \cdot 10^6$. According to Figure 1, this corresponds to $C_f \approx 0.04$; and, therefore, the values of the friction velocity U_* are from 0.2 to 4 cm/s.

The turbulent Ekman layer, as is usual for boundary layers over flat planes, has not indicated sufficiently upper limits. Therefore, its thickness may be determined only approximately by different methods. Regarding the influence of the bottom friction upon large-scale currents, we are interested mainly in the layer thickness, on whose upper limit ($z = h_\tau$) the momentum flux becomes negligibly small in comparison with its value at the bottom. Under conditions of neutral stratification, the structure of the layer under consideration is governed only by the parameters U_* and f; and the length scale $U_*/|f|$ is determined by them in a unique manner. Thus, for h, by dimensional considerations, we obtain the formula:

$$h_\tau = aU_*/|f|, \tag{5}$$

where the factor A depends upon a tolerable error, i.e., upon what we imply when we speak of neglibly small values of T_x and T_y at the $Z = h_\tau$ level. According to atmospheric data for neutral stratification (where the role of a tolerable error is played by the available accuracy of the momentum flux measurements) we have $a \approx 0.3$ (see the T_x and T_y profiles at Figure 1, constructed by means of Eq. (1) using the measured velocity defects $u - U$ and $v - V$). So, taking into account the fact that velocities near the bottom do not exceed several centimeters per second, we obtain for moderate latitudes the evaluation $h_\tau < 10$ m mentioned above.

In the resistance law (4), the velocity G at the top of the boundary layer appears; while, in numerical models of oceanic circulations, we can use velocities that are averaged in grid scales, i.e., in the vertical totally over the lower computational layer. This, however, does not cause additional difficulties, because the vertically averaged velocities and the velocities at the top of the boundary layer become approximately equal. Integrating Eq. (1) over the layer $z_o < z < h_\tau$, taking into account the orientation of the coordinate axes chosen in the boundary condition similar to Eq. (3) at the $z = h_\tau$ level; and also using the second formulas in Eqs. (4) and (5), the following is obtained:

$$(\widetilde{U}^2 + \widetilde{V}^2)^{1/2} \approx G\left(1 - \frac{A}{k}\frac{C_\tau^2}{a}\right), \tag{6}$$

where $\widetilde{U}$ and $\widetilde{V}$ are the integrals of u and v over the layer $z_o < z < h_\tau$. Thus, the error in the determination of G as velocity, averaged over the entire boundary layer, does not exceed several percent (with $R_o \approx 10^5 - 10^6$, we have $C_f \approx 0.04$ and $Ac_f^2/k \approx 0.06$).

As an application of the approach stated above, we shall evaluate the dissipation rate of the kinetic energy of ocean currents due to bottom friction. Proceeding from the usual definition of the local dissipation rate ϵ of mean motion energy; $\rho\epsilon = -u\partial(\tau x/\partial z) - v\partial(\tau y/\partial z)$, and using Ekman's Eq. (1), we obtain

$$\int_{z_o}^{h_\tau} \epsilon\, dz = G^3 C_f^2 \cos\alpha, \tag{7}$$

In order to find the global dissipation rate, we have to multiply the right-hand side of Eq. (7) by the water density, ρ, and integrate it over the entire area of the world ocean (this is the way it can be calculated in numerical models). For a rough evaluation we assume as typical the value $G \approx 5$ cm/s, and accordingly $C_f^2 \cos\alpha = 0.15 \cdot 10^{-2}$; the global dissipation rate will then be $3 \cdot 10^{19}$ erg/s, i.e., it will appear rather close to the astronomical estimate of $2.76 \cdot 10^{19}$ erg/s of the dissipation rate of tidal energy.

* The case of neutral stratification is implied here. The resistance law (4) is also true in the stratified Ekman layer; the coefficients A and B in this case are not constants, but are universal functions of the dimensionless hydrostatic stability parameter.

VI NUMERICAL METHODS

A COMPARISON OF NUMERICAL METHODS USED IN ATMOSPHERIC AND OCEANOGRAPHIC APPLICATIONS

H.-O. KREISS

INTRODUCTION

Regarding the atmosphere as well as the oceans, two of the more important physical processes that can be considered are those of wave propagation and diffusion. Hyperbolic equations describe wave propagation phenomena, while diffusive processes can be represented by parabolic differential equations. Of course, these two processes can be found together. Diffusion is often small compared to convection. Then, we have mainly processes of wave propagation and can apply results obtained for hyperbolic equations. We shall therefore only consider hyperbolic equations.

There would be no problem in evaluating different methods if one only had to deal with mixed initial boundary value problems where the boundary conditions are periodic. Though the theoretical basis for more general problems is now available, much needs to be done to develop practical procedures.

It is still worthwhile to compare different methods for the periodic case. This narrows down the number of good methods. For these methods, we shall then discuss extensions to more general problems.

TIME INTEGRATION

For all the methods that we discuss, time integration is by finite differences. As explained in the Global Atmospheric Research Project Report (1971), the best that one can do is to use a second-order procedure. The reason is that first-order methods are not accurate enough and must very often be stabilized by adding dissipative terms. Third- and higher-order methods are either too complicated or need too much storage capacity to be useful. There are essentially three different second-order procedures that are commonly used.

Consider the operator equation, $B du/dt = Au$. Then these three methods are: the leap-frog scheme, $B[v(t+\Delta t) - v(t-\Delta t)] = 2\Delta t A v(t)$; the Crank-Nicholson scheme, $B[v(t+\Delta t) - v(t)] = \frac{1}{2}\Delta t A[v(t+\Delta t) + v(t)]$; and the Taylor expansion (or Lax-Wendroff), $Bv(t+\Delta t) = [B + \Delta t A + \frac{1}{2}(\Delta t)^2 A B^{-1} A] v(t)$.

The leap-frog scheme is stable for hyperbolic equations but not for parabolic. For genuine parabolic equations the Crank-Nicholson scheme is appropriate. There is a combination of the leap-frog and the Crank-Nicholson scheme (Johansson and Kreiss, 1963; Elvins and Sundström, 1972), which handle problems where both diffusion and convection occur. If the diffusion is small, then one can combine the leap-frog scheme with an explicit first-order scheme or a Du Fort–Frankle procedure for the diffusion process. For the Lax-Wendroff method, there is a two-step version that diminishes the amount of work per time step. In my opinion, the first two methods or a combination of them are superior to the Lax-Wendroff method.

If $B = I$ = the unit matrix operator, the first and the last method are explicit methods, while the second is implicit. For problems in more than one space dimension, one has often to combine the second method with an alternating-direction procedure to arrive at fast methods. If B is not a unit matrix operator, then all methods are implicit methods; and integration can become very slow if they cannot be combined with an alternating-direction procedure. This is one of the reasons why I have doubts about using the finite-element method for equations that are essentially hyperbolic.

In the following section we shall not concern ourselves

with discretizing the time direction. This makes the formalism somewhat easier, and nothing essential is lost.

HYPERBOLIC DIFFERENTIAL EQUATIONS AND PERIODIC PROBLEMS

The most simple hyperbolic differential equation is

$$\partial u/\partial t = \partial u/\partial x. \tag{1}$$

We consider the strips $0 \leqslant x \leqslant 1$ and $t \geqslant 0$ with initial condition,

$$u(x,0) = f(x), \tag{2}$$

and periodic boundary conditions,

$$u(0,t) = u(1,t). \tag{3}$$

If $f(x) = e^{2\pi i\omega x}$, then the solution to the above is given by

$$u(x,t) = e^{2\pi i\omega(x+t)}. \tag{4}$$

Thus, the result is a wave whose speed of propagation is unity, independent of the frequency ω; i.e., there is no dispersion. The general solution of Eqs. (1-3) can be described as a superposition of waves.

Let us now discuss the problem in the x-direction. We introduce a grid and grid functions $v_\nu(t)$ by

$$x_\nu = \nu h,\quad \nu = 0,1,2,\ldots,N+1,\quad h = N^{-1},\quad v,(t) = v(x_\nu,t),$$

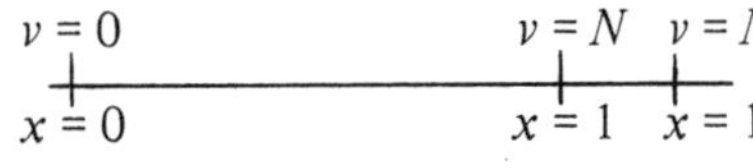

(5)

and replace the above problem by a system of ordinary differential equations,

$$dv_\nu/dt = D_0(h)v_\nu(t),\qquad \nu = 1,2,\ldots,N, \tag{6}$$

with the initial condition,

$$v_\nu(0) = Hf\nu, \tag{7}$$

and periodic boundary conditions,

$$v_0(t) = v_N(t),\qquad v_1(t) = v_{N+1}(t). \tag{8}$$

Here $D_0(h)$ denotes the central difference operator,

$$2hD_0(h)v_\nu = v_{\nu+1} - v_{\nu-1}. \tag{9}$$

The solution of Eqs. (6-8) is

$$v(x,t) = e^{2\pi i\omega[x - c_1(\omega)t]},\qquad x = x_\nu, \tag{10}$$

where

$$c_1(\omega) = \frac{\sin 2\pi\omega h}{2\pi\omega h} \pm \frac{\sin 2\pi(\omega/N)}{2\pi(\omega/N)}. \tag{11}$$

Thus the wave speed depends on the frequency; i.e., dispersion takes place. A comparison of u with v gives us the phase error at time $t = j\omega$, i.e., after j periods in time,

$$e_1 = e_1(\omega) = 2\pi\omega t(1 - c_1\omega) \approx \frac{1}{6}\left(\frac{2\pi\omega}{N}\right)^2 2\pi j. \tag{12}$$

Let e_{1max} be the maximum phase error allowed; then the number of points per wave length, $N_1 = (N/\omega H)$, must at least be

$$N_1 = N/\omega H = 2\pi\left(\frac{2\pi j}{6e_{1max}}\right)^{1/2}$$

$$(e_{1max} = 0.1, 0.01;\qquad N_1 = 20j^{1/2}, 64j^{1/2}). \tag{13}$$

This shows that, to achieve a reasonable accuracy, the number of points per wave length should be considerable. Observe that the method in Eqs. (6-8) is second-order. (For first-order methods, the situation is completely hopeless.)

Consider now the fourth-order method,

$$dv_\nu/dt = \frac{1}{3}[4D_0(h) - D_0(2h)]\,v_\nu(t). \tag{14}$$

In this case, corresponding to Eq. (13), we obtain

$$N_2 = N/\omega - 2\pi\left(\frac{2\pi j}{30e_{2max}}\right)^{1/4},$$

$$(e_{2max} = 0.1, 0.01;\qquad N_2 = 7j^{1/4}, 13j^{1/4}). \tag{15}$$

Thus a considerable improvement over the second-order method is apparent.

One could think of using methods of higher and higher order. Fornberg (1972) estimated the amount of work that is necessary to compute the solution up to time T such that the phase error for the first ν frequencies is smaller than e_{max} (Figure 1). He shows that the greatest gain is reached when using a fourth-order method instead of a second-order method.

The formal limit-of-difference method of higher and higher order is called the "generalized-difference method." Consider the problem (1-3) again and let $v_\nu(t)$ ($\nu = 0, 1, \ldots, N - 1$) be a periodic approximation at time t. For simplicity, we assume that $N = 2p + 1$ is an odd number. Then we can expand $v_\nu(t)$ in a Fourier series,

$$w(x,y) = \sum_{\omega=-\rho}^{\rho} \hat{w}(\omega,t)e^{2\pi i\omega x}, \tag{16}$$

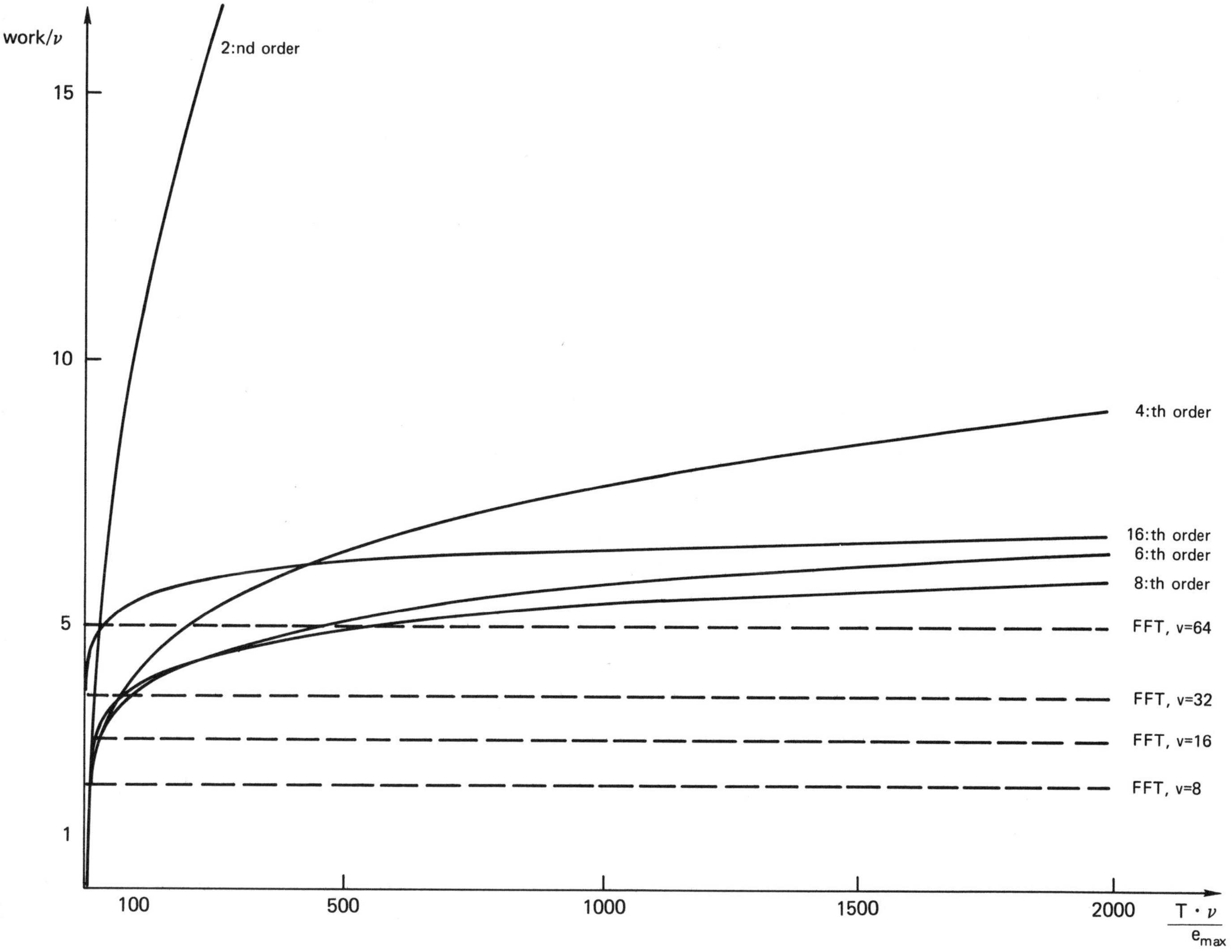

FIGURE 1 Method for estimating amount of work necessary to compute phase error less than e_{max} (Fornberg, 1972).

with

$$w(x_\nu, t) = v_\nu(t). \qquad (17)$$

The derivative of (16) is

$$dw(x,t)/dx = \sum_{\omega=-\rho}^{\rho} 2\pi i\omega \hat{w}(\omega,t)e^{2\pi ix}, \qquad (18)$$

and we define the derivative of $v_\nu(t)$ in the point x_ν by

$$dv_\nu/dx = dw(x_\nu t)/dx_\nu. \qquad (19)$$

The values dv_ν/dx can be computed from the point values $v_\nu(t)$ by two FFT's (Fast Fourier Transforms) and N multiplications. It is a linear operation and can therefore be represented by a linear operator S. We approximate the problem (1-3) by

$$dv/dt = Sv. \qquad (20)$$

Here $v = (v_0, v_1, \ldots, v_{N-1})$ denotes the column vector of all independent point values. It follows from Figure 1 that this method is even faster than the best difference method, provided we do not need to compute more than 64 frequencies. The reason is that the number of necessary points per wave length is optimal, namely two. This compensates the slowness of the FFT.

It is not difficult to generalize the method to equations with variable coefficients and to problems in more than one space dimension (Fornberg, 1972; Kreiss and Oliger, 1972, unpublished). The reason is that we only use the interpolation procedure to compute derivatives. This is a one-dimensional process. However, for equations with variable coefficients, one needs more than two points per wave length. This is caused by the convolution effect between the Fourier modes of the variable coefficients and the solution (Fornberg, 1972). Furthermore, the method is not always stable but the instability can easily be controlled (Kreiss and Oliger, 1972, unpublished).

For equations with constant coefficients, the last method is identical with the spectral method. For variable coefficients, the two methods differ. Let us explain the difference with an example. Consider

$$\partial u/\partial t = \frac{1}{2}\{a(x)\partial u/\partial x + \partial\,[a(x)u]\,/\partial x\}\,. \tag{21}$$

The generalized-difference method has the form

$$dv/dt = \frac{1}{2}\{A(x)Sv + S[A(x)v]\}\,, \tag{22}$$

where

$$A(x) = \begin{bmatrix} a(x_1)0 \ldots 0 & \\ 0 \ldots a(x_2)0 \ldots 0 & \\ \ldots\ldots\ldots\ldots\ldots & \\ 0 \ldots 0 & a(x_{N-1}) \end{bmatrix}. \tag{23}$$

For the spectral method we make an expansion,

$$v(x,t) = \sum_{\omega=-p}^{p} \hat{v}(\omega,t)e^{2\pi i\omega x}, \tag{24}$$

assuming that

$$a(x) = \sum_{u=-\infty}^{\infty} \hat{a}(u)e^{2\pi iux}\,. \tag{25}$$

We introduce Eqs. (24–25) into (21) and develop both sides into Fourier series by forming the necessary convolutions. Neglect of all frequencies higher than p gives us a system of ordinary differential equations for the Fourier components $\hat{v}(\omega,t)$. This method has been advocated by Orszag (1969; 1971a, b), who succeeded in making it remarkably efficient by using a number of tricks in the computation of the convolution sums. As is shown in Kreiss and Oliger (1972), I, nonetheless, believe the method to be less efficient and more complicated than the generalized difference method.

The advantage of the spectral method is that it is always stable provided that there is an energy estimate for the solution of the differential equation. This is so, because the spectral method is an example of the Galerkin method, which we shall now describe (Swartz and Wendroff, 1969).

Let ϕ_j ($j = 1, 2, \ldots, N$) denote a system of linear independent functions. We approximate the solution of (21) by an expression,

$$v(x,t) = \sum_{j=1}^{N} c_j(t)\phi_j(x), \tag{26}$$

where $c_j(t)$ are determined by the ordinary system of differential equations,

$$(\phi_\nu, \partial v/\partial t) = (\phi_\nu, Pv), \qquad \nu = 1, 2, \ldots, N. \tag{27}$$

Here (f,g) denotes the scalar product,

$$(f,g) = \int_0^1 fg\,dx \tag{28}$$

and

$$Pv = \frac{1}{2}(a\partial v/\partial x + \partial(av)/\partial x). \tag{29}$$

We can also write (27) in the form

$$B\frac{dc}{dt} = Ac, \tag{30}$$

where

$$B = \begin{bmatrix} b_{11} \ldots b_{1N} \\ \ldots\ldots\ldots \\ b_{N1} \ldots b_{NN} \end{bmatrix}, \quad A = \begin{bmatrix} a_{11} \ldots a_{1N} \\ \ldots\ldots\ldots \\ a_{N1} \ldots a_{NN} \end{bmatrix}, \quad c = \begin{bmatrix} C_1 \\ \ldots \\ C_N \end{bmatrix},$$

with

$$b_{\nu\mu} = (\phi_\nu, \phi_\mu), \qquad a_{\nu\mu} = (\phi_\nu, P\phi_\mu).$$

For the spectral method, $\phi_j = e^{2\pi ijx}$ forms an orthonormal base. Therefore, $B = I$. If the base is not orthonormal, then B is not the unit matrix; and, in general, the amount of work to invert B makes the method inferior to the methods discussed earlier. The finite-element method is a Galerkin method that uses as base functions piecewise polynomials. In one space dimension, B will be a tridiagonal or five-diagonal matrix, which is easily invertable. In more space dimensions, this is not so; and the inversion is slow.

We have considered the different methods for model equations only. Essentially all results hold also for systems with variable coefficients in many space dimensions. This is obvious for systems with constant coefficients, because they can be solved by the Fourier method. Furthermore, hyperbolic systems with variable coefficients behave essentially in the same way as equations with constant coefficients.

In my opinion the conclusions we can draw are the following:

1. If difference methods are used, they should be at least fourth-order accurate.

2. The generalized-difference method is slightly more economical than fourth-order methods. Instabilities can occur, but they can be overcome.

3. The spectral method has no stability problems but is much more complicated and slower than the generalized-difference method.

4. It is doubtful whether the finite-element method, based on piecewise polynomials, can compete with the above methods.

HYPERBOLIC EQUATIONS; MIXED INITIAL BOUNDARY VALUE PROBLEMS

The main problem for the difference, or generalized-difference method, is to find approximations to the boundary conditions that are sufficiently accurate and stable. This problem has only been solved in one space dimension (Kreiss, 1968; Gustafsson *et al.,* 1972). In more space dimensions, only second-order methods have been investigated (Elvins and Sundström, 1972). Furthermore, only boundaries parallel to the coordinate axis have been investigated in detail. However, curved boundaries can and should be treated by curved nets (Björn, unpublished).

In certain cases the spectral method can be adjusted to initial boundary value problems. We must, however, expect it to lose its high accuracy or to become very slow. For curved boundaries it seems to be impractical.

The only method for which there is no problem with the boundary is the finite-element method. As we explained earlier, its implicit character makes it slow.

Great effort should be directed in overcoming the stability problems for the difference or generalized-difference method.

REFERENCES

Elvins, T., and A. Sundström. 1972. Computationally efficient schemes and boundary conditions for a fine-mesh barotropic model based on the shallow-water equations. Unpublished manuscript.

Enquist, B. On the interpolation of nets. Unpublished manuscript.

Fornberg, B. 1972. On high order approximations of hyperbolic partial differential equations by a Fourier method. Dept. Comp. Sci. Rep. No. 39. Uppsala University, Sweden.

Gustafsson, B., H.-O. Kreiss, and A. Sundström. 1972. Stability theory of difference approximations for mixed initial boundary-value problems. II. Math. Comp. 26.

Johansson, O., and H.-O. Kreiss. 1963. Über das Verfahren der zentralen differenzen zur Löaung des Cauchy-problems für partielle differentialgleichungen. Nordisk Tidskr. Inf. Behandl. 3:97–107.

Kreiss, H.-O. 1968. Stability theory for difference approximations of mixed initial boundary value problems. I. Math. Comp. 22: 703–14.

Kreiss, H.-O., and J. Oliger. Time dependent problems and their approximate solutions. Unpublished manuscript.

Kreiss, H.-O., and J. Oliger. 1972. Comparison of accurate methods for the integration of hyperbolic equations. Tellus 24.

Methods for the approximate solution of time dependent problems. Global Atmospheric Research Project Report, Geneva. Unpublished manuscript.

Orszag, S. A. 1969. Numerical methods for the simulation of turbulence. High-Speed Computing in Fluid Dynamics. The Physics of Fluids, Supplement II.

Orszag, S. A. 1971a. Numerical simulation of incompressible flows within simple boundaries: Accuracy. J. Fluid Mech. 49:75–112.

Orszag, S. A. 1971b. Numerical simulation of incompressible flows within simple boundaries. I. Galerkin (spectral) representations. Stud. Appl. Math. 50:293–327.

Swartz, B., and B. Wendroff. 1969. Generalized finite-difference schemes. Math. Comp. 23:37–49.

PROBLEMS OF ACCURACY WITH CONVENTIONAL FINITE-DIFFERENCE METHODS

B. WENDROFF

FINITE-DIFFERENCE OPERATORS

The basic element in a finite-difference operator is the translation operator. From a given function $u(x)$ of the real variable x, we can form a new function $v(x) = u(x + h)$ by shifting the argument by the amount h. The operation relating u to v is called translation and is usually written as T, provided there is no confusion caused by the dependence on h. Thus, $v = Tu$ means $v(x) = u(x + h)$. Note that $T^k u(x) = u(x + kh)$ for k, an integer (positive or negative).

A two-level difference equation relating two functions, $v(x)$ and $u(x)$, is an equation of the form

$$\sum_{-M}^{M} a_\alpha T^\alpha v = \sum_{-N}^{N} b_\beta T^\beta u. \qquad (1)$$

The functions v and u, appearing in Eq. (1), could just as well be vector-valued functions, in which case the coefficients a_α and b_β are matrices and the translation operators are applied componentwise.

These ideas are easily extended to functions of n variables; that is, if $x = (x^1, \ldots, x^n)$. We introduce partial translation operators T_i by $T_i u(x) = u(x^1, \ldots, x^i + h_i, \ldots, x^n)$. By using multi-indices $\alpha = (\alpha_1, \ldots, \alpha_n)$, with $|\alpha| = |\alpha_1| + \ldots + |\alpha_n|$, and defining $T^\alpha = T_1{}^{\alpha_1}, \ldots, T_n{}^{\alpha_n}$, we may again write a two-level difference equation:

$$\sum_{|\alpha| \leqslant M} a_\alpha T^\alpha v = \sum_{|\beta| \leqslant N} b_\beta T^\beta u. \qquad (2)$$

A two-level equation of the form

$$v = \sum_{|\beta| \leqslant N} b_\beta T^\beta u \qquad (3)$$

is called explicit, and the right-hand side of the equation is an explicit difference operator.

If Eq. (2) is not of the form of Eq. (3), it is implicit. If v is uniquely determined by u, we put

$$v = \left(\sum_{|\alpha| \leqslant M} a_\alpha T^\alpha\right)^{-1} \left(\sum_{|\beta| \leqslant N} b_\beta T^\beta\right) u \equiv Su. \qquad (4)$$

The operator S is a difference operator.

Although two-level difference equations are very common, multilevel equations also occur. A k-level difference equation relates k functions $u^{(l)}, \ldots, u^{(k)}$ as follows:

$$\sum_{i=1}^{k} \sum_{|\alpha| \leqslant N_i} a_\alpha{}^{(i)} T^\alpha u^{(i)} = 0. \qquad (5)$$

The usual situation is that $u^{(1)}, \ldots, u^{(k-1)}$ are given. Put

$$S_i = \sum_{|\alpha| \leqslant N_i} a_\alpha{}^{(i)} T^\alpha. \qquad (6)$$

If Eq. (4) uniquely determines $u^{(k)}$, we put

$$Q_i = S_k^{-1} S_i, \qquad i = 1, 2, \ldots, k-1, \qquad (7)$$

so that

$$u^{(k)} = \sum_{i=1}^{k-1} Q_i u^{(i)}. \qquad (8)$$

The multilevel equation can be written as a larger two-level system by defining compound vectors and matrices as follows:

$$\boldsymbol{u} = \begin{vmatrix} u^{(k-1)} \\ \cdot \\ \cdot \\ \cdot \\ u^{(1)} \end{vmatrix}$$

$$\boldsymbol{v} = \begin{vmatrix} u^{(k)} \\ \cdot \\ \cdot \\ \cdot \\ u^{(2)} \end{vmatrix}$$

$$Q = \begin{bmatrix} Q_{k-1} & Q_{k-2} & \ldots Q_1 \\ I & 0 & \ldots 0 \\ 0 & I & \ldots 0 \\ \ldots & \ldots & \ldots \\ 0 & \ldots & \ldots I\, 0 \end{bmatrix}$$

Then Eq. (8) becomes

$$\boldsymbol{v} = Q\boldsymbol{u}, \tag{9}$$

where Q is now a matrix of difference operators.

Difference equations such as Eq. (1) are associated with the time evolution of systems. If we replace u by $U(t)$, the state at time t, and if we replace v by $U(t + \Delta t)$, then

$$\sum_{|\alpha| \leqslant N} a_\alpha T^\alpha U(t + \Delta t) = \sum_{|\beta| \leqslant M} b_\beta T^\beta U(t). \tag{10}$$

The coefficients a_α and b_β may depend on x, t, h, and Δt if the equation is linear and also on $U(t + \Delta t)$ and $U(t)$ if it is nonlinear.

ACCURACY

We consider equations of evolution, which are systems of the form

$$\frac{\partial u}{\partial t} = F(t,u). \tag{11}$$

For example, in the system $u_t = -\partial/\partial x\,[P(V)]$, $V_t = U_x$, we have $F = -P_x/U_x$. Eq. (10) is consistent with Eq. (11) if

$$\sum_{|\alpha| \leqslant N} a_\alpha T^\alpha u(t + \Delta t) = \sum_{|\beta| \leqslant M} b_\beta T^\beta u(t) + o(\Delta t) \tag{12}$$

for all sufficiently smooth (that is, sufficiently often differentiable) solutions u of Eq. (11). Eq. (10), or the associated difference operator in $U(t + \Delta t) = SU(t)$, has degree of accuracy μ if the term $o(\Delta t)$ can be replaced by $\Delta t 0(h)$.

To check consistency we do not need to know any solutions of Eq. (11); we merely need to assume that u is smooth and satisfies it. The analytical tool used is Taylor's theorem with remainder. We have first that

$$u(t + \Delta t) = u(t) + \frac{\partial u(t)}{\partial t}\Delta t + \ldots + \frac{\partial^k u(t)}{\partial t^k}\frac{\Delta t^k}{k!} + 0(\Delta t)^{k+1}, \tag{13}$$

and then using Eq. (11),

$$u(t + \Delta t) = u(t) + F\Delta t + \frac{dF}{dt}\frac{\Delta t^2}{2!} + \ldots + \frac{d^{k-1}F}{dt^{k-1}}\frac{\Delta t}{j!} + 0(\Delta t)^{j+1}, \tag{14}$$

where dF/dt is $F_t + F_u u_t = F_t + F_u F$, etc. For example, if $F(t,u) = Au_x$, then $dF/dt = A^2 u_{xx}$, $d^2F/dt^2 = A^3 u_{xxx}$, etc., if A is constant. Now substitute the right side of the above into Eq. (10). At this point we assume that

$$\Delta t = \lambda h^L, \quad \lambda \text{ fixed.} \tag{15}$$

The integer L is usually set equal to the order of the differential equation. The result is, considering the function u fixed, an equation of the form $G(h) = 0$. Consistency requires that $G(0) = 0$. To have degree of accuracy μ, we need

$$\frac{d^r C(0)}{dh^r} = 0, \quad r = 0,1,\ldots,L + \mu - 1, \tag{16}$$

which results from a Taylor expansion of $G(h)$ about $h = 0$.

CONSTRUCTING ACCURATE SCHEMES

Consistent difference schemes can be constructed by approximating the coefficients $F(t,u)$; $dF/dt(t,u)$; etc., appearing in Eq. (14). For example, using the fact that $\partial/\partial x = T - T^{-1}/2h + 0(h^2)$ and $\partial^2/\partial x^2 = 1/h^2\,(T - 2I + T^{-1}) + 0(h^2)$, we obtain the Lax-Wendroff scheme,

$$U_k^{n+1} = U_k^n + A\frac{\lambda}{2}(U_{k+1}{}^n - U_{k-1}{}^n) + A^2\frac{\lambda^2}{2}(U_{k+1}{}^n - 2U_k{}^n + U_{k-1}{}^n), \tag{17}$$

which has degree of accuracy 2 for the equation $U_t = AU_x$, A constant, with $L = 1$ (see Pereyra, 1970).

It is sometimes profitable to think of Eq. (11) as an ordinary differential equation in the variable t. If the equation has the form $U_t = Pu$, $P = \Sigma\, a_j(x)\, \partial^j/\partial x^j$, then $U(t + \Delta t) = e^{P\Delta t}\, U(t)$ ($e^{P\Delta t}$ can be rigorously defined, but here we consider it only formally). Then we can use the Padé table to approximate e^z by a rational function, say

$$e^z = \frac{Q(z)}{R(z)} + 0(z), \tag{18}$$

where $Q(z)$ and $R(z)$ are polynomials. Then $R(P\Delta t)U(t + \Delta t) = Q(P\Delta t)U(t) + 0(\Delta t)$. Now if the spatial differential operators are approximated by difference operators with suitable accuracy, the result is a consistent implicit-difference equation. This method is presented in Birkhoff *et al.* (1965).

Single-step Runge-Kutta methods also provide consistent difference equations. For example, Heun's method,

$$U(t + \Delta t) = U(t) + \Delta t\, F\left\{t + \frac{\Delta t}{2}, U(t) + \frac{\Delta t}{2} F[t, U(t)]\right\}, \quad (19)$$

leads to the two-step Lax-Wendroff scheme for the equation $U_t = \partial/\partial x\,[f(u)]$, as follows. Put

$$W_{i+1/2} = \frac{1}{2}(U_{i+1}{}^n + U_i{}^n) + \frac{\Delta t}{2h}\,[f(U_{i+1}{}^n) - f(U_i{}^n)], \quad (20)$$

and then

$$U_i^{n+1} = U_i^n + \frac{\Delta t}{h}\,[f(W_{i+1/2}) - f(W_{i-1/2})]. \quad (21)$$

This has degree of accuracy two.

The method of characteristics can be used to construct consistent difference schemes in special cases. The single equation $u_t + au_x = 0$ has the property that $u(x,t)$ is constant on any line with equation $x - at$ = constant. Thus, if A and B are two points on such a line, then $u(A) = u(B)$. Now choose A to be a mesh point (x_i, t_{n+1}) and let B be the intersection of the characteristic line $x - at$ = constant passing through A with the line $t = t_n$, as in Figure 1. Now approximate $u(B)$ by Lagrange interpolation. Quadratic interpolation using x_{i-1}, x_i, x_{i+1} leads to the Lax-Wendroff scheme. It is easy to see that the degree of accuracy is equal to the degree of the Lagrange interpolating polynomial. Variations on this theme are given in Wendroff (1961), and a theoretical discussion is found in Strang (1962).

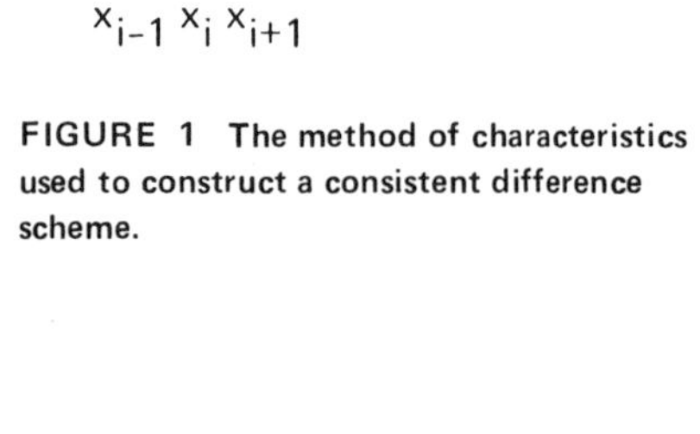

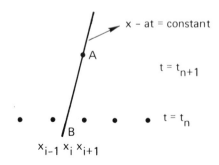

FIGURE 1 The method of characteristics used to construct a consistent difference scheme.

Many partial differential equations are derived from integral conservation laws. It is sometimes advantageous to use these laws to construct difference equations approximating the differential equation. These difference equations will then obey certain discrete conservation laws. We will illustrate this with some examples.

The transport equation $\partial u/\partial t + a(\partial u/\partial x) = 0$ lends itself to this process. Calling u the density of particles per unit volume, particles are conserved if

$$\int_V u\,dv\bigg|_{t+\Delta t} - \int_V u\,dv\bigg|_t = \int_t^{t+\Delta t} F\,ds, \quad (22)$$

where F is the rate at which particles flow across the boundary of the volume element V. Taking V to be the interval x_i, x_{i+1}, we have

$$\int_{x_i}^{x_{i+1}} u(x, t + \Delta t)\,dx - \int_{x_i}^{x_{i+1}} u(x, t)\,dt = \int_t^{t+\Delta t} f(x_{i+1}, s)\,ds - \int_t^{t+\Delta t} F(x_i, s)\,ds. \quad (23)$$

This is an exact integral conservation law. Now, put

$$U_{i+1/2}{}^n = \frac{1}{h}\int_{x_i}^{x_{i+1}} u(x, t_n)\,dx,$$

$$F_i{}^{n+1/2} = \frac{1}{\Delta t}\int_{t_n}^{t_{n+1}} F(x_i, t)\,dt, \quad (24)$$

so that

$$U_{i+1/2}{}^{n+1} - U_{i+1/2}{}^n = \frac{\Delta t}{h}\left(F_{i+1}{}^{n+1/2} - F_i{}^{n+1/2}\right), \quad (25)$$

A physical equation of state will relate F to u; and when this is approximated, a difference equation will result. No matter how this is done, Eq. (25) shows that the quantity $\Sigma\, U_{i+1/2}{}^n$ is conserved, apart from changes due to the boundaries of the system.

In case u is the density of particles moving with speed a, we have $F = -au$. A simple approximation leads to

$$U_{i+1/2}{}^{n+1} - U_{i+1/2}{}^n = \frac{-\Delta t}{h}a\left(U_{i+1}{}^{n+1/2} - U_i{}^{n+1/2}\right), \quad (26)$$

which is called the leap-frog scheme and which has degree of accuracy two. To use this idea in other geometries, see Carlson and Lathrop (1968).

Many physical quantities obey Eq. (25). If u is the heat in a body with temperature ϕ, specific heat is C_v, and conductivity is σ, then $U = C_v\phi$, $F = \sigma\,(\partial\phi/\partial x)$. A preliminary difference equation can be obtained by defining

$$F_i{}^{n+1/2} = \left(\sigma\frac{\partial\phi}{\partial x}\right)_i^{n+1/2} = \frac{1}{2}\left[\sigma\frac{\partial}{\partial x}(\phi^{n+1} + \phi^n)\right]_i. \quad (27)$$

The following prescription has been found useful in case there are discontinuities in σ. Take σ to be a step function with values $\sigma_{i+1/2}$ associated with the interval x_i, x_{i+1}. Call the temperature at x_i, ϕ^*, and put

$$\frac{h}{2}F_i = \sigma_{i-1/2}(\phi^* - \phi_{i-1/2}) = \sigma_{i+1/2}(\phi_{i+1/2} - \phi^*). \quad (28)$$

This determines ϕ^*, and F_i becomes

$$\frac{h}{2}F_i = \sigma_{i-1/2}\sigma_{i+1/2}(\sigma_{i-1/2} + \sigma_{i+1/2})^{-1}\,(\phi_{i+1/2} - \phi_{i-1/2}), \quad (29)$$

so the difference equation is

$$(C_v\phi)_{i+1/2}{}^{n+1} - (C_v\phi)_{i+1/2}{}^{n} = \frac{\Delta t}{h^2}[\sigma_{i+3/2}\sigma_{i+1/2}(\sigma_{i+3/2} + \sigma_{i+1/2})^{-1}\,(\sigma_{i+3/2} - \sigma_{i+1/2}) - \sigma_{i+1/2}\sigma_{i-1/2}(\sigma_{i+1/2} + \sigma_{i-1/2})^{-1}\,(\phi_{i+1/2} - \phi_{i-1/2})]^{n+1/2}. \quad (30)$$

The three unknowns, $\phi_{i-1/2}{}^{n+1}$, $\phi_{i+1/2}{}^{n+1}$, and $\phi_{i+3/2}{}^{n+1}$, appear in each equation. This is the Crank–Nicholson scheme. Note that we could have defined an explicit scheme simply by defining $F^{n+1/2} = (\sigma\,\partial\phi/\partial x)^n$. This method of treating discontinuous coefficients is a special case of a homogeneous difference scheme, discussed in Samarskij and Tihonov (1965).

Integral relations provide a means of constructing difference equations for complicated geometries. The system of conservation laws, $u_t + f_x + g_y = 0$, where $f = f(u,x,y,t)$ and $g = g(u,x,y,t)$, comes from the integral conservation law,

$$\int_R u\,dv\Big|_{t+\Delta t} - u\,dv\Big|_t + \int_t^{t+\Delta t}\left[\int_{\partial R}(f\,dy - g\,dx)\right] ds = 0, \quad (31)$$

where R is any two-dimensional region with boundary ∂R. If the region is covered by cells, R_j, which are polygonal, e.g., triangular, we can approximate $\int_{\partial R_j} f\,dy$ as follows: Suppose u is given at the vertices A, B, C (see Figure 2). Then define $f(u)$ on the edges by linear interpolation to $f(u_A)$, $f(u_B)$, and $f(u_C)$; and then compute $\oint_{\partial R_j} f\,dy$, and similarly $\oint_{\partial R_j} g\,dx$. Putting f_A for $f[u(A)]$, etc., we have

$$2\oint_{\partial R_j} f\,dy = (f_C + f_B)(u_C - y_B) + (f_C + f_A)(u_A - y_C) + (f_A + f_B)(y_A - y_B). \quad (32)$$

Since the line integrals over the edges of adjacent triangles

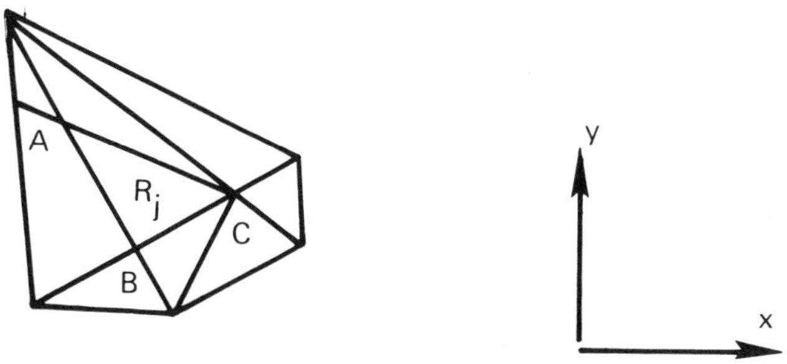

FIGURE 2 **Complex geometry with triangular cells R_j for which a difference equation can be constructed using the integral conservation law.**

are in opposite directions, we have the discrete conservation law,

$$\sum_j \int_{R_j} u\,dv\Big|_{t+\Delta t} = \sum_j \int_{R_j} u\,dv\Big|_t + \text{boundary terms}. \quad (33)$$

For more details see Noh (1964). It is clear that this can be done in curvilinear coordinates.

STABILITY

The equation of evolution (11) defines a function $u(x,t)$ that also satisfies an initial condition $u(x,0) = u_0(x)$ and perhaps certain boundary conditions. The difference equation (10) defines a mesh function $U(x_i, t_n)$, also with an initial condition $U(x_i, 0) = U_0(x_i)$, and some boundary conditions.

Stability theory provides criteria for deciding when U will be arbitrarily close to u if the mesh size is sufficiently small. The fundamental criterion is that U should be bounded independently of the mesh size. If this is true, the difference operator is said to be stable. If the degree of accuracy is μ, then $U - u$ behaves like h^μ as $h \to 0$, if the data is smooth enough. Mathematical stability theory is reviewed in Thomée (1969), and we shall not attempt to give any kind of survey here.

Stability theory tells us something about the behavior of the error as the mesh is refined, but it is of little help in describing the behavior of difference schemes on a fixed, possibly coarse, mesh. A heuristic technique involving a closer look at the truncation error can be helpful in this context. Consider the single equation $u_t = Au_x$, where A is constant and the difference operator is $F_\Delta = 1/2\,(T + T^{-1}) + 1/2\lambda A\,(T - T^{-1})$. This is called Friedrich's scheme. It has degree of accuracy one. For any function $v(x, t)$, $F_\Delta v = v + 1/2\,h^2\,v_{xx} + A\,\Delta t\,v_x + 0(h^3)$, so $v(s, t + \Delta t) - F_\Delta v(x, t) = (v_t - Av_x)\,\Delta t + (v_{tt} - v_{xx}\,\lambda^{-2})\,\Delta t^2/2 + 0(h^3)$, $\lambda = \Delta t/h$. Now let $v_t = Av_x + \Delta t Qv$, where Q is an operator to be determined. The coefficient of Δt^2 is now $Qv + 1/2\,A^2\,v_{xx} - 1/2\,\lambda^{-2}\,v_{xx}$. Thus, if we put $2Qv = (\lambda^{-2} - A^2)\,v_{xx}$, the coefficient of Δt^2 is zero and the truncation error is now $0(h^3)$ instead of $0(h^2)$. Indeed, solutions of Friedrich's scheme behave like v. In particular, if the stability condition $\lambda^2 A^2 \leqslant 1$ is violated, $v(x, t)$ increases exponentially with t; while, if it is satisfied, we are solving the heat equation, obtaining smooth decaying functions.

The same reasoning has been applied to the Lax-Wendroff scheme in Richtmeyer and Morton (1967). The associated differential equation is $v_t = Av_x + \Delta t^2\, Qv + \Delta t^3\, Q^1 v$, where $Qv = 1/6\, A\, [\lambda^{-2} - A^2]\, \partial^3 v/\partial x^3$, $Q^1 v = 1/8\, A^2\, [\lambda^{-2} - A^2]\, \partial^4 v/\partial x^4$. Again, if $A^2\lambda^2 \leqslant 1$, the fourth-order term provides decay or dissipation. The third-order term produces dispersion, accounting for the oscillatory behavior, which has been observed for this scheme.

The above procedure identifies terms that have been added to the differential equation. This suggests the possibility of first perturbing the differential equation to produce an equation with some desired property, such as dissipation (in the physical sense), and then constructing a difference equation. This is the basis of the pseudoviscosity method for computing the flow of compressible nonviscous gases. The presence of shock waves in such flows causes difficulties for finite-difference methods whose very derivations assume smooth functions. By adding small viscous terms to the compressible flow equations, these shock waves are smoothed out, yet retain much of their qualitative behavior. See Richtmeyer and Morton (1967), for details.

A more versatile method is to directly perturb the difference equation. It is shown in Wendroff (1968) that, for well-posed problems with constant coefficients, it is possible to stabilize any consistent difference operator. The Lax-Wendroff treatment of shock waves is a nonlinear analogue of this idea. As described in Richtmeyer and Morton (1967), the procedure is to add nonlinear terms to the Lax-Wendroff scheme. These terms are designed to be negligible where the solution is slowly varying but to have a strong smoothing effect across a shock.

TWO-DIMENSIONAL TECHNIQUES

In dealing with equations of evolution in one space variable, questions of efficiency rarely play a role because of the great speed and capacity of modern digital computers. For two-dimensional problems, efficiency is crucial. A powerful technique for deriving efficient finite-difference methods in several space variables is provided by the method of splitting, or alternating, directions.

Efficient alternating-direction methods have been developed for hyperbolic equations through the pioneering work of Strang (1968). We consider a nonlinear hyperbolic system,

$$u_t = f_x + g_y, \tag{34}$$

where f and g are vector-valued functions of the vector $\boldsymbol{u}$, and we seek a scheme that is accurate of degree two. Such a scheme is proposed in Hubbard (1967), but this scheme has two weaknesses. One is that the matrices $A = \text{grad}_u f$ and $B = \text{grad}_u g$ appear explicitly, necessitating a large number of nonlinear function evaluations at each mesh point. The other is that the stability condition, derived from Lax and Wendroff (1964), that $\lambda\rho(A) \leqslant 8^{-1/2}$ and $\mu\rho(B) \leqslant 8^{-1/2}$ ($\lambda = \Delta t/\Delta x$, $\mu = \Delta t/\Delta y$) is not the best possible.

For simplicity, let us put $\Delta x = \Delta y$ and $\lambda = \mu$, and let

$$\sigma = \max[\rho(A), \rho(B)]. \tag{35}$$

Now, let λ_0 be the maximum allowable mesh ratio for a given scheme. In the above paragraph, $\lambda_0 = [(8)^{1/2} \cdot \sigma]^{-1}$. It is known that, for any explicit scheme, $\lambda_0 \leqslant \sigma^{-1}$. Strang has shown us how to construct difference operators with $\lambda_0 = \sigma^{-1}$, and Gourlay and Morris (1968) have shown how to extend the two-step idea in Eqs. (20-21) so as to avoid matrix evaluations. Several variations have been tested in Eilon *et al.* (1968), and the one which was most efficient for a given level of accuracy is the following, in which we have used

$$\mu_i = \frac{1}{2}\left[T_i\left(\frac{h}{2}\right) + T_i^{-1}\left(\frac{h}{2}\right)\right],$$

$$\delta_i = T_i\left(\frac{h}{2}\right) - T_i^{-1}\left(\frac{h}{2}\right). \tag{36}$$

Let

$$\begin{aligned}
V_1 &= \mu_2\, U^n + \frac{\lambda}{2}\delta_2\, g(U^n),\\
V_2 &= U^n + \lambda\,\delta_2\, g(V_1),\\
V_3 &= \mu_1\, V_2 + \frac{\lambda}{2}\delta_1\, f(V_2),\\
U^{n+1} &= V_2 + \lambda\,\delta_1\, f(V_3),\\
V_4 &= \mu_1\, U^{n+1} + \frac{\lambda}{2}\delta_1\, f(U^{n+1}),\\
V_5 &= U^{n+1} + \lambda\,\delta_1\, f(V_4),\\
V_6 &= \mu_2\, V_5 + \frac{\lambda}{2}\delta_2\, g(V_5),\\
U^{n+2} &= V_5 + \lambda\,\delta_2\, g(V_6).
\end{aligned} \tag{37}$$

It is important to note that this has degree of accuracy two only at every second time step. There are two functional evaluations of f or g in each intermediate step of this scheme, so eight functional evaluations are required to advance the solution at any mesh point.

POISSON'S EQUATION

Physical systems that have reached equilibrium or steady state are usually described by elliptic differential equations, the archetypal such equation being Poisson's equation,

$$\frac{\partial^2 u}{\partial x^2} + \frac{\partial^2 u}{\partial y^2} = f(x,y). \tag{38}$$

The Dirichlet problem for this equation is to find u satisfying the equation in some bounded, simply connected region Ω, with piecewise analytic boundary, such that on the boundary $\partial\Omega$, the values of u are specified, say

$$u = g, \qquad (x, y) \epsilon\, \partial\Omega. \tag{39}$$

The discrete Laplacian is a finite-difference operator that approximates $L = \partial^2/\partial x^2 + \partial^2/\partial y^2$. To define it, place a square mesh with mesh spacing h on Ω, as in Figure 3. Let $\overline{\Omega} = \partial\Omega \cup \Omega$. Let the points at which $\partial\Omega$ crosses a mesh line be $\dot{\Omega}_h$. Let the set of mesh points contained in Ω be Ω_h. Now each point (x, y) has four neighbors: $(x + h, y)$, $(x - h, y)$, $(x, y + h)$, and $(x, y - h)$. Let $\Omega_h{}^*$ be the set of mesh points in Ω_h that have at least one neighbor outside $\overline{\Omega}$. The other mesh points in Ω_h form the set $\Omega_h{}'$, so $\Omega_h = \Omega_h{}^* \cup \Omega_h{}'$.

For any mesh function W, we define the discrete Laplacian $L_h W$ as follows. If $p = (x, y)$ is in $\Omega_h{}'$, then

$$L_h W(p) = h^{-2}\,[W(x + h, y) + W(x - h, y) + W(x, y + h) + W(x, y - h) - 4W(x, y)]. \tag{40}$$

If $p \epsilon \Omega_h{}^*$, suppose that there are two neighbors outside of Ω, say $(x - h, y)$ and $(x, y - h)$. Then there exist α, β, $0 < \alpha \leqslant 1$, $0 < \beta \leqslant 1$, such that $(x - \alpha h, y) \epsilon \dot{\Omega}_h$, $(x, y - \beta h) \epsilon \dot{\Omega}_h$. Then let

$$L_h W(p) = h^{-2}\,\left[\alpha^{-1}\, W(x - \alpha h, y) + \beta^{-1}\, W(x, y - \beta h) + W(x + h, y) + W(x, y + h) - \left[\left(\frac{\alpha+1}{\alpha}\right) + \left[\left(\frac{\beta+1}{\beta}\right)\right] W(x, y)\right]\right]. \tag{41}$$

The approximation to Eq. (38) is

$$L_h\, U(p) = f(p),\ p \epsilon\, \Omega_h, \tag{42}$$

$$U(p) = g(p),\ p \epsilon\, \dot{\Omega}_h. \tag{43}$$

This linear system of equations has a unique solution, $U(p)$, and if $u \epsilon\, C^4(\overline{\Omega})$ (u is four times continuously differentiable in $\overline{\Omega}$), then

$$\max_{p\epsilon\Omega_h} |U(p) - u(p)| = 0(h^2). \tag{44}$$

This theorem is proved in Hubbard (1967).

If the region Ω has a corner point σ with interior angle greater than π, as in Figure 4, then u is no longer in $C^4(\overline{\Omega})$. In this case, if Ω has a corner with interior angle π/α, $1/2 \leqslant \alpha \leqslant \infty$, then

$$\max_{p\epsilon\Omega_h} |U(p) - u(p)| = 0(h^{\alpha-\epsilon} + h^2) \tag{45}$$

for every $\epsilon > 0$.

The simple discrete Laplacian is often too inaccurate. Two methods are known for improving the accuracy, while still retaining the simple structure of the Laplacian. The first of these is Richardson extrapolation and uses the fact that if u is sufficiently smooth there exists a function $\phi(p)$ such that

$$U(h, p) = u(p) + \phi(p)h^2 + 0(h^3), \tag{46}$$

where $U(h,p)$ is the solution of Eqs. (42–43) for a given h. If we let

$$V(p) = \frac{1}{3}\left[4U\left(\frac{h}{2}, p\right) - U(h, p)\right], \tag{47}$$

then

$$V(p) = u(p) + 0(h^3). \tag{48}$$

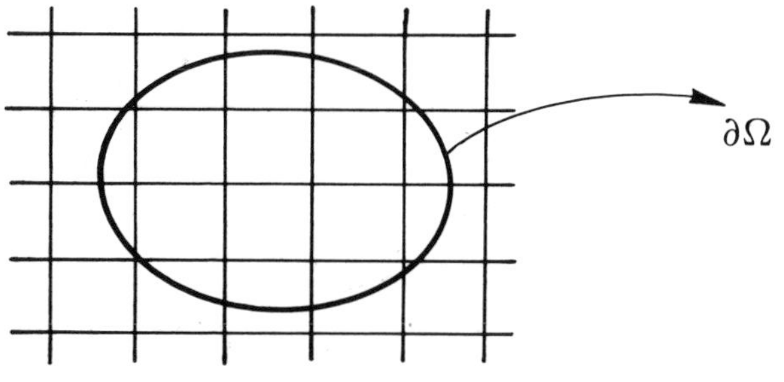

FIGURE 3 Graphic definition of the discrete Laplacian finite-difference operator, with mesh spacing h on Ω.

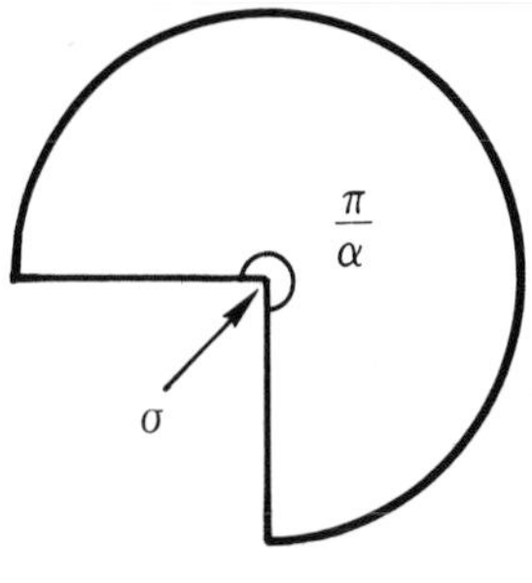

FIGURE 4 Discrete Laplacian when the interior angle at corner point σ is greater than π.

Thus, by doing the calculation first with mesh width h and then repeating it with mesh width $h/2$, we can use Eq. (47) to obtain accuracy $0(h^3)$ on the mesh with width h.

This process could be continued if we knew that $V(p) = u(p) + \psi(p)h^3 + 0(h^4)$. However, each time the mesh size is halved, the work required to solve the equations increases by a power of two. In the ideal case, in which the region is a rectangle, solving Eq. (42) with mesh width $h/2$ takes four times as much work as with h.

The second method is an extension of the method of iterated improvement for correcting the solution of a linear system of equations. It is based on the fact that if $L = \partial^2/\partial x^2 + \partial^2/\partial y^2$, then for any smooth function u we can write,

$$h^2 L_h u = h^2 Lu + \sum_{i=2}^{N} Q_{2i} u \frac{h^{2i+2}}{i!} + 0(h)^{M+2}, \qquad (49)$$

where $M = 2N - 1$ and

$$Q_i = 2\left[\left(\frac{\partial}{\partial x}\right)^i + \left(\frac{\partial}{\partial y}\right)^i\right]. \qquad (50)$$

Now suppose there exist difference operators S_k such that

$$S_k u = \sum_{i=1}^{k} Q_{2i+2} \frac{h^{2i+2}}{(2i+2)!} + 0(h^{2k+4}) \qquad (51)$$

for $k = 1, 2, \ldots, N - 1$. We shall show below that the S_k can be constructed if the boundary of the region intersects the mesh lines only at the mesh points. The iterated improvement or deferred correction algorithm, as described in Pereyra (1970), is the following:

(a) Define U^0 as the solution of Eqs. 42–43.

(b) Compute $S_1 U^0$.

(c) Let V^0 be the solution of

$$h^2 L_h V^0(p) = S_1 U^0(p), \quad p \in \Omega_h,$$

$$V^0(p) = 0, \quad p \in \dot{\Omega}_h. \qquad (52)$$

(d) Define U^1 by $U^1 = U^0 + V^0$.

(e) Having found U^{k-1}, let

$$h^2 L_h V^{k-1}(p) = S_k U^{k-1}(p) - S_{k-1} U^{k-1}(p), \quad p \in \Omega_h$$

$$V^{k-1}(p) = 0, \quad p \in \dot{\Omega}_h, \qquad (53)$$

and define U^k as $U^k = U^{k-1} + V^{k-1}$.

It is shown in Pereyra (1970) that

$$\max_{p \in \Omega_h} |u(p) - U^{k-1}(p)| = 0(h^{2k}) = \max_{p \in \Omega_h} |V^{k-1}(p)| + 0(h^{2k+2}), \qquad (54)$$

so that V^{k-1} provides a good estimate for the error in U^{k-1}. Of course, V^{k-1} can be discarded when proceeding to the next step.

The obviously attractive feature of this method is that only the known right-hand sides in step (e) change when computing V^k at each step, but the matrix remains the same.

Calculations reported in Pereyra (1970) show that just a few iterations give significant improvement in accuracy. The calculations were done in double precision, which is clearly indicated, at least for the right sides in (e). The decision procedure for terminating the iterations is based on the quantity

$$EST_k = \max[|U^{k+1} - U^k| / |U^{k+1}|]. \qquad (55)$$

The iteration is stopped if either $EST_k \geqslant EST_{k-1}$ or EST_k is less than some preassigned tolerance. The V^k were determined by SOR (successive overrelaxation).

We consider now the difference operators S_k. If T is the operation of translation by h, then we must find coefficients α_j such that

$$\sum \alpha_j T^j = \sum_{i=1}^{k} \left(\frac{\partial}{\partial x}\right)^{2i+2} \frac{2}{(2i+2)!} h^{2i+2} + 0(h^{2k+4}). \qquad (56)$$

By Taylor's theorem we have

$$\sum_{\ell} \left(\sum \alpha_j \frac{j^\ell}{\ell!}\right) \left(h\frac{\partial}{\partial x}\right)^\ell = \sum_{i=1}^{k} \frac{2}{(2i+2)!} \left(h\frac{\partial}{\partial x}\right)^{2i+2} + 0(h^{2k+4}). \qquad (57)$$

Equating coefficients of $[h(\partial/\partial x)]^\ell$, we get

$$\sum \alpha_j j^\ell = \tau_\ell \equiv \begin{cases} 0, & \ell < 4, \\ 2, & \ell = 4, 6, \ldots, 2k+2, \\ 0, & \ell = 5, 7, \ldots, 2k+3. \end{cases} \qquad (58)$$

The extent of the summation in Eq. (58) depends on the position of the mesh point at which Eq. (56) is to hold. If the point has $k + 1$ neighbors on either side that are in Ω or on the boundary of Ω, then we can take $\alpha_j = \alpha_{-j}$, so we only need to solve

$$\sum_{j=1}^{k+1} \alpha_j j^\ell = \tau_\ell, \quad \ell = 0, 2, 4, \ldots, 2k+2. \qquad (59)$$

If the point is closer to the boundary, then an unsymmetric formula must be used. In that case, there will be $2k + 4$ unknown coefficients in Eq. (58). The sum in Eq. (56) should then extend right up to the boundary. The y-derivative is handled similarly.

An algorithm for solving Eq. (58) is given in Björck and Pereyra (1970).

The method of deferred corrections can be applied to more general elliptic equations, as shown in Pereyra (1970).

REFERENCES

Birkhoff, G., and R. S. Varga. 1965. Discretization errors for well set Cauchy problems. I. J. Math. Phys. 44:1–23.

Björck, A., and V. Pereyra. 1970. Solution of Vandermonde systems of equations. Math. Comp. 24:893–903.

Carlson, B., and K. D. Lathrop. 1968. Transport theory–The method of discrete ordinates. *In* H. Greenspan, C. N. Kelber, and D. Orkent, eds. Computing Methods in Reactor Physics. Gordon and Breach, New York.

Eilon, B., D. Gottlieb, and G. Zwas. 1968. Numerical stabilizers and computing time for second order accurate schemes. J. Comp. Phys.

Gourlay, A. R., and J. L. Morris. 1968. A multistep formulation of the optimized Lax-Wendroff method for nonlinear hyperbolic systems in two space variables. Math. Comp. 22:715–19.

Hubbard, B. 1967. Remarks on the order of convergence in the discrete Dirichlet problem. *In* J. H. Bramble, ed. Numerical Solution of Partial Differential Equations. Academic Press, New York and London.

Lax, P. D., and B. Wendroff. 1960. Systems of conservation laws. Comm. Pure Appl. Math. 13:217–37.

Lax, P. D., and B. Wendroff. 1964. Difference schemes for hyperbolic equations with high order of accuracy. Comm. Pure Appl. Math. 17:381–98.

Noh, W. F. 1964. CEL: A time-dependent two-space-dimensional, coupled Eulerian-Lagrangian code. *In* Methods in Computational Physics. Vol. 3. Academic Press, New York.

Pereyra, V. 1970. Highly accurate numerical solution of casilinear elliptic boundary-value problems in n dimensions. Math. Comp. 24:771–83.

Richtmeyer, R. D., and K. W. Morton. 1967. Difference Methods for Initial-Value Problems. 2d ed. Interscience, New York.

Samarskij, A. A., and A. N. Tihonov. 1961. On homogeneous difference schemes. ZH. Vychisl. Mat. I. Mat. Fiz. 1:5–63; Math. Rev. 29(1965):5391A.

Strang, G. 1962. Trigonometric polynomials and difference methods of maximum accuracy. J. Math. Phys. 41:147–54.

Strang, G. 1968. On the construction and comparison of difference schemes. J. SIAM Numer. Anal. 5:506–17.

Thomée, V. 1969. Stability theory for partial difference operators. SIAM Rev. 11:152–95.

Wendroff, B. 1961. The structure of certain finite difference schemes. SIAM Rev. 3:237–42.

Wendroff, B. 1968. Well-posed problems and stable difference operators. J. SIAM Numer. Anal. 5:71–82.

A SURVEY OF NUMERICAL METHODS FOR SELECTED PROBLEMS IN CONTINUUM MECHANICS

G. J. FIX

INTRODUCTION

In this paper a selected survey is given of numerical methods used in continuum mechanics to solve partial differential equations. Emphasis will be on current trends and, in particular, on the extent that variational methods using splines and other piecewise polynomial functions are replacing difference methods.

Since the advent of high speed computing machines, in most fields in continuum physics, finite differences have played a dominant role in the numerical solution of partial differential equations. Excellent accounts of this material are found in Forsythe and Wasow (1960), Richtmeyer and Morton (1967), and Thomée (1969). Solid mechanics, on the other hand, is a major exception; and the finite-difference tradition, as it were, has had a minimal impact. For the most part, variational rather than difference methods are used (Zienkiewicz, 1970, 1971; Strang and Fix, 1973). The reason for this is partly physical. The equations of elasticity can be put in a variational form and engineers have found this to be the most physically natural setting to formulate approximations. In addition, the variational approximations—commonly called finite elements—have other properties that are of great value in practice. Complicated boundaries can easily be treated in this setting; singularities in the solution can be modeled in the approximation; and, in dealing with higher-order methods with increased resolving power, the practical problems are much less troublesome than with difference schemes.

The desirable properties of the finite-element method, plus the striking success engineers have had using this method with equilibrium problems, leads one to ask whether it can also be used to advantage for other types of problems. Perhaps the most noncontroversial extension of the finite-element ideas has been with diffusion problems. The advantages cited above for finite elements are certainly present, but these approximations are far more complicated than the usual difference approximations.

Finally, we will consider the extension of the finite-element ideas to hyperbolic problems. Unfortunately, mathematical and numerical experience with these approximations is quite limited. However, the partial understanding of the finite-element method for hyperbolic systems suggests that comparison between finite elements and finite differences is by no means a simple matter.

EQUILIBRIUM PROBLEMS IN ELASTICITY

A convenient and representative model of a boundary value problem in solid mechanics is provided by the bending of a loaded elastically supported plate, Ω (Timoshenho and Goodier, 1951). Letting $f(x, y)$ denote the load function, the associated differential equation for the stress function u is

$$\Delta^2 u(x, y) = \left(\frac{\partial^4}{\partial x^4} + 2\frac{\partial^4}{\partial x^2 \partial y^2} + \frac{\partial^4}{\partial y^4}\right) u(x, y) = f(x, y) \quad \text{for } (x, y) \quad \text{in } \Omega. \quad (1)$$

Because the plate is elastically supported, for (x, y) on the boundary Γ of Ω, we have

$$u(x, y) = 0, \quad (2)$$

$$\Delta u(x, y) + \sigma(x, y)\frac{\partial u(x, y)}{\partial n} = 0, \quad (3)$$

where n denotes the outer normal to Γ and $\sigma(x, y)$ is a positive coefficient: $\sigma(x, y) \geqslant \sigma_o > 0$ for $(x, y) \epsilon \Gamma$.

In order to define difference approximations, let us suppose that Ω is a rectangle and that the solution $u(x, y)$ is smooth throughout $\Omega \cup \Gamma$. For such a circumstance, it is appropriate to use uniform meshes, and we subdivide Ω into squares with side length h and nodes at (jh, kh) (see Figure 1). Letting the mesh vector $u_{jk}{}^h$ denote the approximation to $u(jh, kh)$, we define the difference operator Δ_h by

$$(\Delta_h u^h)_{jk} = h^{-2}\ (u_{j+1,k}{}^h + u_{j-1,k}{}^h + u_{j,k+1}{}^h + u_{j,k-1}{}^h - 4u_{jk}{}^h). \quad (4)$$

Then on the set Ω_h of nodes (jh, kh) in the interior of Ω, the differential equation (1) is replaced with

$$(\Delta_h{}^2 u^h)_{jk} = f(jh, kh), \qquad (jh, kh) \in \Omega_h. \quad (5)$$

For the set Ω_h of nodes (jh, kh) on the boundary Γ, (2) is replaced with

$$u^h(jh, kh) = 0, \quad (6)$$

and (3) with

$$(\Delta_h u^h)_{jk} + \sigma(jh, kh)\ (D_n{}^h u^h)_{jk} = 0, \quad (7)$$

where $D_n{}^h$ is a central difference approximation to the normal derivative $\partial/\partial n$. Thus on a horizontal line,

$$(D_n{}^h u^h)_{jk} = h^{-1}\ (u_{j,k+1}{}^h - u_{j,k-1}{}^h). \quad (8)$$

The set of Eqs. (5-7) is nonsingular (Strang and Fix, 1973) and therefore can be solved for $u_{jk}{}^h$, $(jh, kh) \in \Omega_h$. Unfortunately, iterative techniques (Varga, 1962; Young, 1972) such as SOR work quite poorly for systems like (5-7), arising from fourth-order problems; and the most efficient method for computing $u_{jk}{}^h$ is by elimination (see, for example, Fix and Larson, 1971). Of special interest is the nested-ordering technique of George (1971), which is quite effective for such systems.

The approximation $u_{jk}{}^h$ will converge quadratically (Strang and Fix, 1973), i.e.,

$$\max_{j,\,k}\ |u_{jk}{}^h - u(jh, kh)| \leqslant Ch^2, \quad (9)$$

provided u is sufficiently smooth. Moreover, the error $u^h - u$ is regular throughout Ω; hence, extrapolation techniques (Thomée, 1969) can be used to obtain an arbitrary high order of convergence.

The setting described, however, is somewhat unrealistic, and the more "realistic" aspects of the problem provide the key to why difference methods are rarely used. First, the boundary Γ of Ω is invariably curved. As a consequence, the boundary condition (3) becomes quite troublesome to approximate accurately with finite differences. In addition, the solution u is not always smooth throughout $\Omega \cup \Gamma$. For example, in fracture mechanics problems, the region Ω is typically slit (Figure 2), and the solution u has singular derivatives at the tip P of the slit (Kondrat'ev, 1968; Kellogg, 1970, 1971). As a consequence, it is necessary to refine the mesh near P. Because rectangular subdivisions are used, this means unnecessary refinements on horizontal and vertical lines drawn through P and an unnecessary increase in the number of unknowns.

To see how a finite-element method deals with these problems, recall that the solution u of (1-3) minimizes

$$\Phi(w) = \int_\Omega |\Delta w|^2 + \int_\Gamma \sigma \left|\frac{\partial w}{\partial n}\right|^2 - 2 \int_\Omega fw \quad (10)$$

over the class H_A of functions w such that $\Phi(w) < \infty$ and

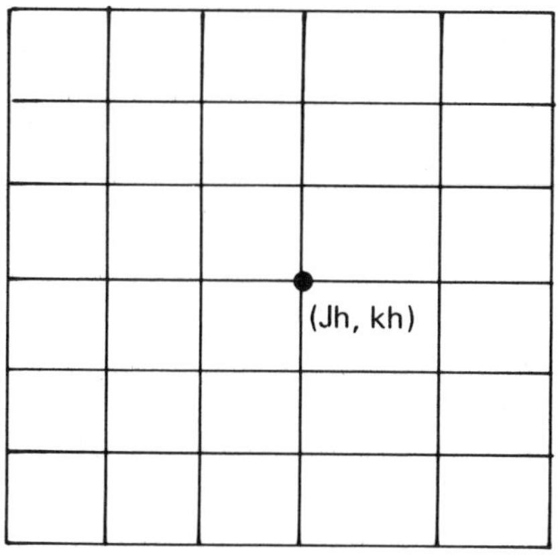

FIGURE 1 Uniform subdivision of Ω.

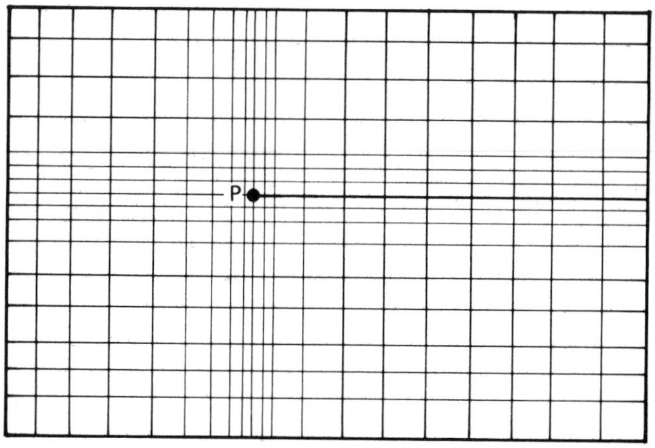

FIGURE 2 A slit region Ω.

$w = 0$ on Γ (Strang and Fix, 1973). Physically, $\Phi(w)$ is proportional to the strain energy associated with the admissible stress function $w \in H_A$, and the variational principle states that the solution u has the least strain energy among all admissible $w \in H_A$.

In general, (10) cannot be minimized over the infinite dimensional space H_A. Nevertheless, the minimum over finite dimensional subspaces of H_A can be computed, and this provides a technique for approximating u. This idea has, however, been around for a very long time (Kantorovic and Krylov, 1952; Courant and Hilbert, 1953; Mikhlin, 1964). What is new about the finite-element technique is the distinguished choice of subspaces to use in the approximation.

In the precomputer era, this variational method was primarily envisioned for subspaces of polynomials (see, for example, Kantorovic and Krylov, 1952). For problems whose solutions do not vary drastically over the region Ω, such spaces work quite well because only low-degree polynomials need be used. However, for problems whose solutions are more complicated, high-degree polynomials are needed to obtain a fixed degree of accuracy; and this invariably leads to problems of numerical stability (Strang and Fix, 1973). In the finite-element method, polynomials are retained but are used only locally. The idea is to subdivide the region Ω and approximate the solution on each subdivision (or element) by a (possibly different) polynomial. The desired accuracy is obtained not by increasing the degree of the polynomial—this would be numerically unstable—but rather by reducing the size of the elements.

There are two important cases that deserve mention for planar problems resembling Eqs. (1-3). One is based on triangular subdivisions and the other on rectangular subdivisions. Starting with the former let Ω be a polygon. The first step is to subdivide Ω into triangles with nodes at $\mathbf{z}_j$ and maximum diameter $h > 0$ (Figure 3). We wish to consider a space of functions that reduce to polynomials on each triangular subdivision. The major problem here is to insure that each such function is admissible,* i.e., vanishes on Γ and is patched together so that it is continuously differentiable in Ω (and hence has integrable second derivatives in Ω). The appropriate degree of the polynomials to be used is actually an interesting question. Clearly linear polynomials $a + bx + cy$ are unacceptable—the only continuously differentiable functions $v^h(x, y)$ that are linear on triangles are the constant functions in Ω. Similar problems exist for quadratics and cubics, and the most natural space consists of functions $v^h(x, y)$ that reduce to a quintic polynomial,

* Some engineers have used finite-element approximations with functions that are not admissible. The use of these so-called nonconforming elements is, however, by no means universally accepted and in many instances quite dangerous. We refer the reader to (Irons, 1972; Strang, 1972; Strang and Fix, 1973).

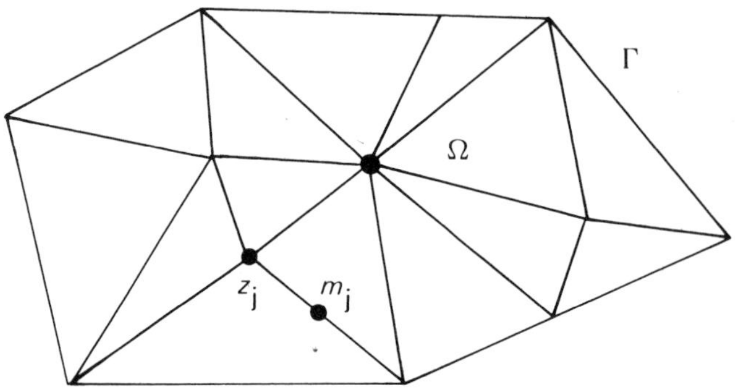

FIGURE 3 Triangular subdivision of Ω.

$$\sum_{0 \leq i+j \leq 6} a_{ij} x^i y^j \tag{11}$$

on each triangle.† The quintics are patched together by requiring that the representation (11) for v^h in each triangle give the same values of

$$\frac{\partial^{\alpha+\beta} v^h(\mathbf{z}_j)}{\partial x^\alpha \partial y^\beta}, \quad 0 \leq \alpha + \beta \leq 2 \tag{12}$$

at the nodes $\mathbf{z}_j$ of the triangles, and the same value for the normal derivative,

$$\frac{\partial v^h(\mathbf{m}_j)}{\partial n} \tag{13}$$

at the midpoints $\mathbf{m}_j$ between two vertices. Observe that for each triangle (12-13) represents 21 conditions that uniquely determine the 21 parameters, a_{ij} in the representation (11) of v^h.

To see that these conditions also imply that v^h is continuously differentiable in Ω, let $\mathbf{z}_j$ and $\mathbf{z}_k$ be two adjacent nodes. Without loss of generality, it can be assumed that the line ℓ joining $\mathbf{z}_j$ and $\mathbf{z}_k$ is horizontal (Figure 4). On this line the polynomial representations (11) of v^h in the two adjoining triangles reduce to a quintic polynomial in x on ℓ. The conditions (12) imply that these two polynomials have the same function values, first and second derivatives at the two nodes $\mathbf{z}_j$, $\mathbf{z}_k$. But these six conditions uniquely determine a quintic polynomial, and the two representations coincide on ℓ. This means that v^h is continuous across ℓ. A similar argument shows that the first derivatives are also continuous.

The space is defined as $\tilde{S}^h$, parameterized by the maximum diameter $h > 0$. Thus, each v^h in $\tilde{S}^h$ is a continuously differentiable function that reduces to a quintic polynomial

† For second-order problems, only continuity is needed and hence a much wider choice of finite elements exists. These will be discussed in the following section.

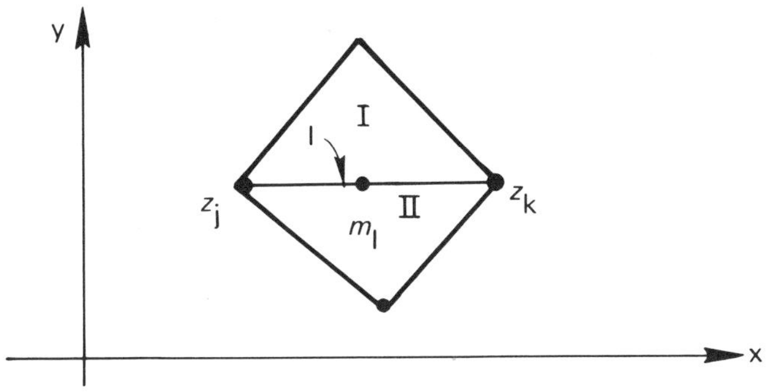

FIGURE 4 The nodes z_j and z_k.

on the triangles. The elements in $\tilde{S}^h$ are, of course, not admissible because they do not necessarily vanish on Γ; however, they can be made to do so by applying linear constraints to $\tilde{S}^h$. Let $\mathbf{z}_j$ and $\mathbf{z}_k$ be two nodes on Γ, and for simplicity assume that the line ℓ joining these nodes is horizontal. For v^h to vanish on ℓ, the argument sketched above shows that it suffices to put v^h, $\partial v^h/\partial x$, $\partial^2 v^h/\partial x^2$ equal to zero at the two nodes $\mathbf{z}_j$ and $\mathbf{z}_k$. Indeed, v^h is a quintic polynomial in x on ℓ, and its derivatives up to the second order vanish at the endpoints. This means that v^h is identically zero on ℓ. Thus, the subspace S^h of $\tilde{S}^h$, consisting of functions vanishing on Γ, is obtained from $\tilde{S}^h$ by applying appropriate linear constraints at the nodes $\mathbf{z}_j$ on Γ.

Observe that the boundary condition (3) involving the higher derivatives is not imposed on functions in S^h. Hence, it is called a natural boundary condition and appears only in terms of the boundary integral,

$$\int_\Gamma \sigma \left(\frac{\partial w}{\partial x}\right)^2, \tag{14}$$

in (10). This is undoubtedly one of the most singular advantages of the variational method—the boundary conditions involving higher derivatives that are typically the most difficult to approximate by differences are natural boundary conditions and come gratis with the variational method.

To minimize (10) over S^h, it is necessary to choose first a basis for this space. This is done by selecting a basis for $\tilde{S}^h$ and then applying the linear constraints associated with the boundary condition (2) to obtain a basis for S^h. The most convenient choice of a basis for $\tilde{S}^h$ is obtained via the interpolation conditions (12-13). In particular, let z_j be any node in $\Omega \cup \Gamma$ and let α, β $(0 \leqslant \alpha + \beta \leqslant 2)$ be two numbers. Then there is a unique function $\phi_{j,\alpha,\beta}{}^h$ in $\tilde{S}^h$ satisfying,

$$\frac{\partial^{\gamma+\delta}}{\partial x^\gamma \partial y^\delta} \phi_{j,\alpha,\beta}{}^h(\mathbf{z}_\ell) = \delta_{j\ell}\delta_{\gamma\alpha}\delta_{\delta\beta}, \quad \frac{\partial}{\partial n}\phi_{j\alpha\beta}{}^h(\mathbf{m}_\ell) = 0, \tag{15}$$

for all $0 \leqslant \gamma + \delta \leqslant 2$, nodes $\mathbf{z}_\ell$, and midpoints $\mathbf{m}_\ell$. Similarly there is a unique $\psi_j{}^h$ in $\tilde{S}^h$ satisfying

$$\frac{\partial^{\gamma+\delta}}{\partial x^\gamma \partial y^\delta} \psi_j{}^h(\mathbf{z}_\ell) = 0, \quad \frac{\partial}{\partial n}\psi_j{}^h(\mathbf{m}_\ell) = \delta_{j\ell}. \tag{16}$$

The set $\phi_{j,\alpha,\beta}{}^h$ and $\psi_\ell{}^h$ as $\mathbf{z}_j$ ranges over all nodes; $\mathbf{m}_\ell$ ranges over all midpoints; $0 \leqslant \alpha + \beta \leqslant 2$ forms a basis for $\tilde{S}^h$; and any v^h in $\tilde{S}^h$ can be written

$$v^h(x, y) = \sum_{z_j} \sum_{0 \leqslant \alpha+\beta \leqslant 2} \frac{\partial^{\alpha+\beta} v^h(z_j)}{\partial x^\alpha \partial y^\beta} \phi_{j,\alpha,\beta}{}^h(x, y) + \sum_{m_j} \frac{\partial v^h(m_j)}{\partial n} \psi_j{}^h(x, y). \tag{17}$$

A basis $\phi_1{}^h, \ldots, \phi_N{}^h$ for S^h is obtained by constraining $\phi_{j,\alpha,\beta}{}^h$ and $\psi_j{}^h$ to vanish on Γ. For example, if z_j is a node on a horizontal part of the boundary Γ, $\phi_{j,\alpha,0}$ $(\alpha = 0, 1, 2)$ can be simply omitted from the basis.

To compute the minimum of (10) over S^h, note that $\phi_1{}^h, \ldots, \phi_N{}^h$ is a basis for S^h; any v^h in S^h can be written

$$v^h(x, y) = \sum_{j=1}^{N} q_j{}^h \phi_j{}^h(x, y). \tag{18}$$

Substituting (18) into (10) gives the quadratic functional,

$$\phi(v^h) = \phi(q_1{}^h, \ldots, q_N{}^h) = (\mathbf{q}^h)^T K^h(\mathbf{q}^h) - 2(\mathbf{q}^h)^T f^h, \tag{19}$$

in terms of the vector q^h of weights $q_j{}^h$. The (j, k) entry of the matrix K^h—often called the stiffness matrix—is

$$\int_\Omega \Delta\phi_j{}^h \Delta\phi_k{}^h + \int_\Gamma \sigma \left(\frac{\partial \phi_j{}^h}{\partial n}\right)\left(\frac{\partial \phi_k{}^h}{\partial n}\right), \tag{20}$$

and the j-th entry of the vector f^h is

$$\int_\Omega f\phi_j{}^h.* \tag{21}$$

The weight $Q^h = (Q_j{}^h)$ that minimizes (19), or equivalently, the function

$$u_h(x, y) = \sum_{j=1}^{N} Q_j{}^h \phi_j{}^h(x, y) \tag{22}$$

that minimizes (10) over S^h, is obtained from

$$K^h Q^h = f^h. \tag{23}$$

The matrix K^h is symmetric and positive definite (Strang and Fix, 1973), hence (23) has a unique solution. A fact of equal importance is that K^h is sparse, i.e., like the matrix associated with the difference approximation (5-7), it has a

* These integrals are typically evaluated by quadrature. See, for example, Fix (1972a,b).

large number of zero entries. The reason for this is that the functions $\phi_{\alpha\beta j}{}^h$ and $\psi_j{}^h$ (or $\phi_j{}^h$ reordered) are nonzero only in a small region about $\mathbf{z}_j$ and $\mathbf{m}_j$; hence (20) is zero if the difference $|j-k|$ is sufficiently large. This is true for all of the finite-element spaces discussed in this paper—a locally defined basis exists for each space—and the resulting sparsity of the matrices makes the system (23) especially adaptable for direct elimination methods on a computer. As with the difference method, the nested ordering technique of George (1971) appears to be the most efficient.

The finite-element approximation u_h obtained by the above method has sixth-order accuracy, i.e., $u - u_h$, is of magnitude $O(h^6)$, provided the solution u is differentiable up to the sixth order. There are more unknowns per node in this method than with the difference approximation—approximately seven per node in the former and one per node in the latter. However, the accuracy of the finite elements is four orders of magnitude greater and hence more efficient, because cruder meshes can be used.

Numerical efficiency is not considered by most engineers to be the major advantage of finite elements. On the contrary, the method's popularity is that it has the ability to treat complicated boundaries and singularities, which is discussed below. Starting first with the curved boundaries, it is noted that the essential boundary condition (2) becomes troublesome in this setting. In fact, it is clearly impossible to satisfy this condition exactly with piecewise polynomial functions. We could approximate Γ by a polygon (Figure 5) and apply the variational method to the problem on the polygon where it is easy to satisfy the Dirichlet boundary conditions (2). However, this seriously compromises the convergence of the finite-element approximation; and, in fact, the $O(h^6)$ accuracy that is normally obtained is reduced to $O(h^{3/2})$ (Strang and Berger, 1971). In addition, because of the corners in the polygon, the largest magnitude and most irregular behavior of the error occurs near the boundary (Irons, 1966), which is usually where the values of the stress function u are most interesting physically.

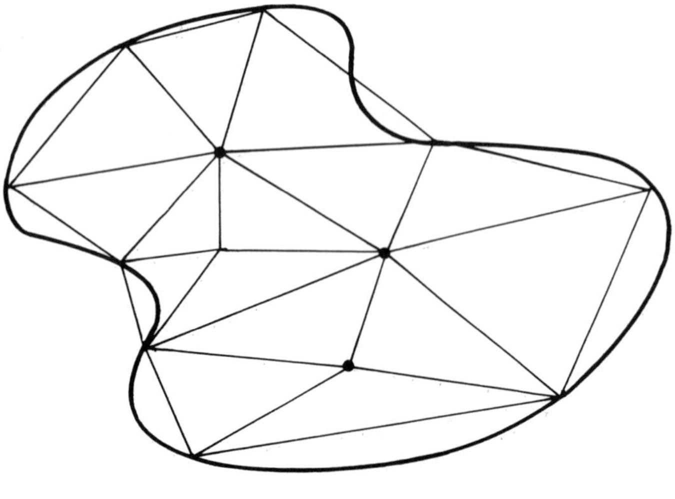

FIGURE 5 Polygonal approximation of Ω.

A more efficient technique involves the use of isoparametric elements (Irons, 1966; Zienkiewicz, 1970, 1971; Strang and Fix, 1973). Given the element near the boundary Γ (shown in Figure 6), the region E^h is bounded by the nodes $\mathbf{z}_i$ $(i = 1, 2, 3)$; and the part of the boundary Γ_1 intersecting $\mathbf{z}_2$ and $\mathbf{z}_3$ is approximately the image of the right triangle E under the quintic transformation,

$$x = \sum_{0 \leq 1+j \leq 5} a_{ij}\xi^i\eta^j, \qquad y = \sum_{0 \leq 1+j \leq 5} b_{ij}\xi^i\eta^j. \tag{24}$$

The constants a_{ij} and b_{ij} are determined by the usual interpolation conditions associated with the quintics, i.e.,

$$\frac{\partial^{\alpha+\beta}x}{\partial\xi^\alpha\partial\eta^\beta}, \qquad \frac{\partial^{\alpha+\beta}y}{\partial\xi^\alpha\partial\eta^\beta} \tag{25}$$

are specified at the nodes $\tilde{\mathbf{z}}_i$ $(i = 1, 2, 3)$. In fact, an appropriate choice of (25) permits one to approximate Γ_1 by $\Gamma_1{}^h$, the image of $\tilde{\Gamma}_1$, to order $O(h^6)$.

Our finite-element space S^h consists not of functions that are quintic polynomials in (x, y) in E^h, but rather images

$$V^h(x, y) = V[\xi(x, y), \eta(x, y)] \tag{26}$$

of function $V(\xi, \eta)$, which are quintic polynomials in $\tilde{E}$. By the technique discussed above, V can vanish on $\tilde{\Gamma}_1$, and hence v^h on $\tilde{\Gamma}_1{}^h$. This is performed for each element adjacent to the boundary (it can also be done for interior elements if desired). If the local maps $x = x(\xi, \eta)$ and $y = y(\xi, \eta)$ have the same values (25) at the nodes, then the C^1 continuity of the functions $V^h(x, y)$ is preserved.

This technique, now widely used in engineering circles, by no means exhausts all the possibilities. Other techniques include the use of Lagrange multipliers (Babuska, 1972) and least-squares methods (Nitsche, 1970; Bramble and Schatz, 1971). In both cases, a variational method is established in which all boundary conditions are natural and hence need not be imposed on S^h.

We will now address the question of singularities. As noted above, the quintic polynomials will lead to sixth-order convergence provided the solution u has six derivatives (in a mean-square sense). If the solution is less smooth, then a corresponding reduction in the accuracy is obtained. However, triangular elements permit the use of local mesh refinement (Figure 7); and, with such a choice of nodes, sixth-order accuracy can be restored (Babuska, 1970). If one knows *a priori* where the singularities are located, then more mesh points can be added in this area. If the location of the singularity is not known, then adaptative techniques can be

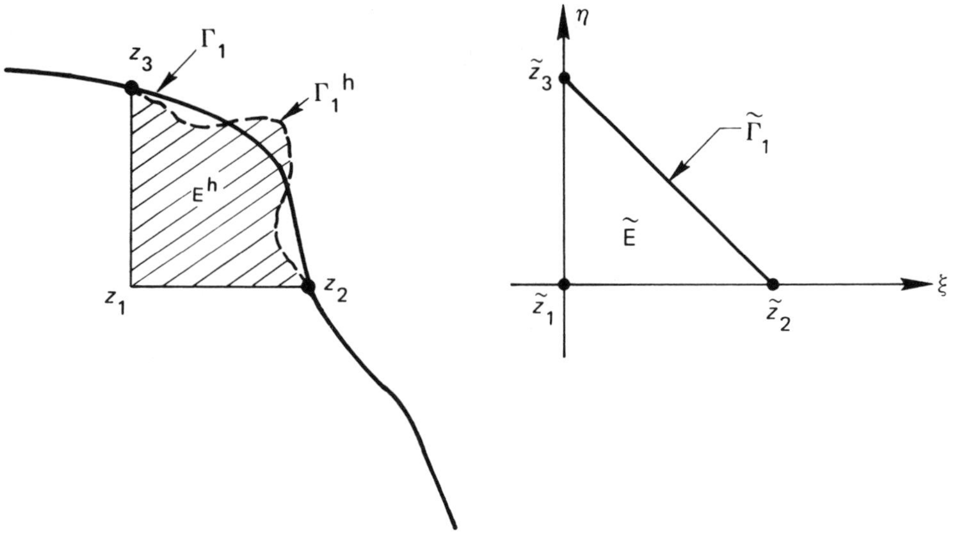

FIGURE 6 Isoparametrics.

used. First, the solution is computed on a crude mesh; and, with this information, adds more nodes where large changes are found in the solution. This is typically performed in three or more steps. The key, of course, is that the mesh refinement is purely local—one need add extra unknowns only in the regions where they are needed.

An interesting alternative exists to local mesh refinement for treating singularities in solid mechanics problems when the form of the singularity is known. For example, in the slit region (Figure 2), u behaves like $r^{3/2}\phi(\theta)$, where (r, θ) are the polar coordinates at P and ϕ is a known function of θ (Fix, 1969). Thus, such functions can be added to the finite-element space S^h, obtaining a new space $S_*{}^h$ and applying the variational method with $S_*{}^h$. This, in effect, subtracts off the singularity. There is insufficient space to discuss such a technique in detail [see (Birkhoff and Fix, 1967; Fix, 1969; Fix *et al.*, 1972) for more information].

Final examples of finite-element approximations are rectangular elements. Although such subdivisions are awkward in curved regions and local mesh refinement becomes quite complicated, their advantage is that the admissibility conditions are more easily satisfied. In fact, unlike triangular elements, it is possible to obtain C^1 continuity with cubics

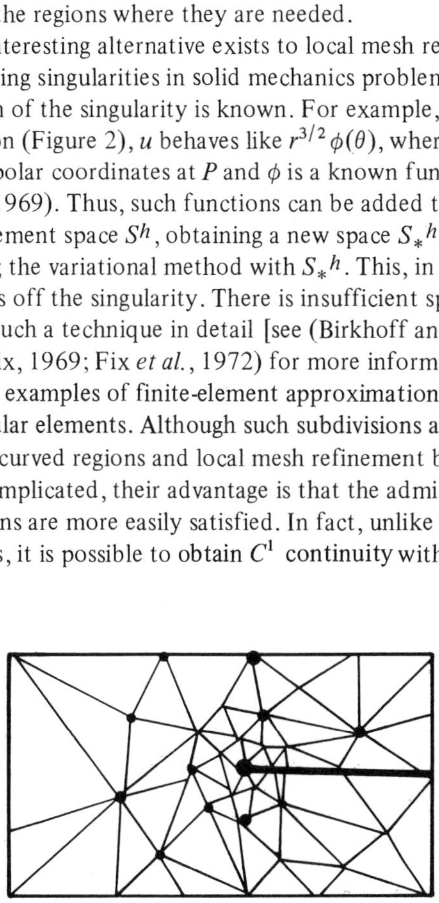

FIGURE 7 Local mesh refinement.

in rectangular subdivisions. The bicubic Hermite space (Schultz, 1972) is one of the most important examples of the latter. This consists of functions $v^h(x, y)$ that reduce to bicubic polynomials,

$$v^h(x, y) = \sum_{i=0}^{3} \sum_{j=0}^{3} a_{ij}x^iy^j, \tag{27}$$

on each rectangular subdivision. The 16 constants a_{ij} are determined by specifying the values of

$$v^h, \quad \frac{\partial v^h}{\partial x}, \quad \frac{\partial v^h}{\partial y}, \quad \frac{\partial^2 v^h}{\partial x \partial y} \tag{28}$$

at the four nodes z_i (Figure 8). A basis for this space is obtained via the interpolation conditions (28) as for the quintics.

If the boundary has straight lines, then the Dirichlet condition (2) is satisfied by requiring v^h and its tangential derivatives to be zero at the nodes. For a curved region, either Lagrange multipliers (Babuska, 1972) or isoparametrics must be used (see Figure 9). The resulting system of equations has four unknowns per node (except at the boundary) and leads to a four-order accurate approximation.*

Another finite element based on rectangular subdivisions is the bicubic spline functions. This space leads to fourth-order accuracy; yet, like the difference approximation, it has roughly only one unknown per node. Thus, theoretically it is the most efficient cubic element and is very popular in mathematical circles. Unfortunately, it is quite complicated—it cannot be characterized through local interpolation conditions like (12-13) and (28)—and is rarely used in

* In general, if polynomials of degree $k - 1$ are used, then the error is of order $O(h^k)$, provided u has k derivatives.

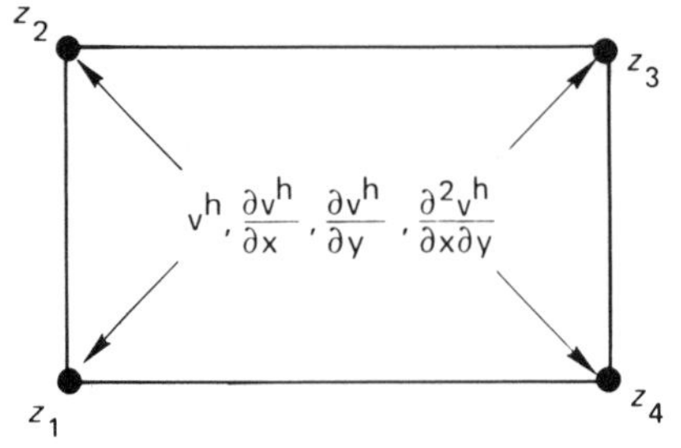

FIGURE 8 Bicubic hermite.

engineering calculations. Nevertheless, recent numerical experiments with splines (see, for example, Fix, 1969) have been quite successful and perhaps may be more widely used in the future. A large amount of literature is available on splines (see Ahlberg *et al.*, 1967; Schoenberg, 1969; Douglas and Dupont, 1970; Strang and Fix, 1973; and Rice, n.d.).

DIFFUSION PROBLEM

The finite-element ideas have also been used successfully for diffusion problems like

$$\frac{\partial u}{\partial t} - \Delta u = f(x, y) \quad \text{for } (x, y)\epsilon\Omega, \qquad t > 0, \tag{29}$$

$$u(t, x, y) = 0 \quad \text{for } (x, y)\epsilon\Gamma, \qquad t > 0, \tag{30}$$

and

$$u(0, x, y) = u_o(x, y) \quad \text{for } (x, y)\epsilon\Omega. \tag{31}$$

Although in this case, the comparison with finite differences is not nearly so one-sided, this section shall review briefly the major advantages and disadvantages of both approaches and also point out some of the more important references. As noted in the introduction, excellent references for the literature prior to 1970 are given in Forsythe and Wasow (1960) and Richtmeyer and Morton (1967).

Unfortunately, (29-31) do not admit a physically natural extremal principle from which finite-element approximations can be derived. However, stationary principles are available. To describe the most elementary of such principles, let us denote by H_A the space of functions $v(x, y)$ vanishing on Γ and having integrable first derivatives. Then the principle states that the solution u of (29-31) is the unique function in H_A satisfying

$$\iint_\Omega \left(\frac{\partial u}{\partial t} v + \nabla u \cdot \nabla v - fv\right) dx\, dy = 0 \tag{32}$$

for each $v = v(x, y)$ in H_A and each $t > 0$ (Strang and Fix, 1973). At $t = 0$, it is assumed that u is equal to u_o. Formally, (32) is derived from (29) by multiplying the latter by v, integrating over Ω, and using Green's theorem.

To derive a finite-element approximation, time is left as a continuous variable; and Eq. (32) is used to approximate spatial variables. More precisely, let S^h be a finite-element space having the basis $\phi_1{}^h, \ldots, \phi_N{}^h$. For simplification, it is assumed that each $\phi_j{}^h$ vanishes on the boundary Γ of Ω. For each fixed $t > 0$, we approximate the solution $u(t, x)$ by the function,

$$u_h(t, x, y) = \sum_{j=1}^{N} Q_j{}^h(t)\phi_j{}^h(x, y), \tag{33}$$

where the weights $Q_j{}^h(t)$ are chosen by requiring that (32) hold on the subspace S^h; i.e.,

$$\int_\Omega \left(\frac{\partial u^h}{\partial t} v^h + \nabla u^h \cdot \nabla v^h - fv^h\right) dx\, dy = 0, \qquad \text{all } v^h \text{ in } S^h. \tag{34}$$

The latter is equivalent to the system

$$m^h \frac{dQ^h}{dt} + K^h Q^h = f^h(t) \tag{35}$$

of implicit ordinary differential equations in the vector $Q^h(t) = [Q_j{}^h(t)]$ of weights. The (j, k) entry of the matrix

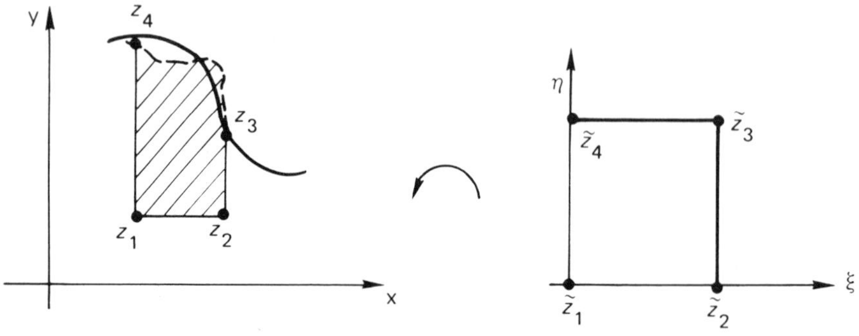

FIGURE 9 Bicubic hermite isoparametrics.

M^h—commonly called the mass matrix—is

$$\int_\Omega \phi_j{}^h(x,y)\phi_k{}^h(x,y)\,dx\,dy. \tag{36}$$

The generic entries of the stiffness matrix K^h (see the previous section) and the source term f^h are

$$\int_\Omega \nabla\phi_j{}^h(x,y)\nabla\phi_k{}^h(x,y)\,dx\,dy,$$

$$\int_\Omega f(x,y)\phi_j{}^h(x,y)\,dx\,dy. \tag{37}$$

The mass matrix M^h is invertible—it is the Grain matrix for the basis $\phi_1{}^h, \ldots, \phi_N{}^h$ of S^h—hence (35) has a unique solution $Q^h(t)$ once the initial data $Q^h(0)$ are specified. The latter is chosen by letting

$$u^h(o,x,y) = \sum_{j=1}^{N} Q_j{}^h(0)\phi_j{}^h(x,y) \tag{38}$$

be any good approximation to $u(0,x,y) = u_o(x,y)$, e.g., the interpolant of u_o (Strang and Fix, 1973).

Perhaps the most important property of the approximation $u_h(t,x,y)$ is its unconditional stability. Indeed, replacing v^h with $u^h(t,\cdot)$ for each $t > 0$ in (34), we obtain

$$\frac{1}{2}\frac{d}{dt}\int_\Omega |u_h(t,x,y)|^2\,dx\,dy + \int_\Omega |\nabla u_h(t,x,y)|^2\,dx\,dy$$

$$= \int_\Omega f(t,x,y)\,u_h(t,x,y)\,dx\,dy. \tag{39}$$

Because

$$\int_\Omega |\nabla u_h(t,x,y)|^2 \geqslant \lambda_1 \int_\Omega |u_h(t,x,y)|^2 \tag{40}$$

for each $t > 0$ by the Rayleigh principle — λ_1 is the smallest eigenvalue of $\Delta w + \lambda w = 0$ in Ω, $w = 0$ on Γ —(39) gives

$$\left[\int_\Omega |u_h(t,x,y)|^2\right]^{1/2}$$

$$\leqslant \exp(-\lambda t)\left[\int_\Omega |u_h(0,x,y)|^2\,dx\,dy\right]^{1/2}$$

$$+\int_o^t \exp\left[-\lambda_1(t-\sigma)\right]$$

$$\left[\int_\Omega |f(\sigma,x,y)|^2\,dx\,dy\right]^{1/2} d\sigma. \tag{41}$$

That is, $u_h(t,x,y)$ at any time $t > 0$ is bounded by the initial conditions and data for $0 \leqslant \sigma \leqslant t$, which of course is a statement of unconditional numerical stability. In a sense, this property comes at a rather high price; for (35) is implicit and hence some care must be used in its solution. Some examples involving specific finite-element spaces will be discussed.

Greater latitude is possible in choosing a finite-element space than was possible for the fourth-order problem in the previous section. The latter involved second derivatives, and, hence, for a piecewise polynomial function to be admissible, it was necessary for it to have continuous first derivatives. In the present setting, only continuity is required; because (32) involves only first derivatives. This greater flexibility means that lower-degree polynomials can be used; and the most elementary case is the space S^h of continuous piecewise linear functions. To describe this space, Ω is subdivided into triangles as in Figure 10. S^h consists of continuous functions $v^h(x,y)$ that reduce to a linear polynomial,

$$v^h(x,y) = a + bx + cy \tag{42}$$

on each triangle. To insure that v^h is continuous in Ω, the representation (42) on each triangle must give the same values at the nodes z_j. In fact, any v^h in S^h is uniquely determined by specifying its values at the nodes z_j; and to insure that $v^h = 0$ on the (polygonal) boundary Γ, it is sufficient to require that v^h be zero at the nodes $\mathbf{z}_j$ on Γ.

A basis $\phi_1{}^h, \ldots, \phi_N{}^h$ for S^h (where N is the number of nodes in the interior of Ω) is constructed by requiring

$$\phi_j{}^h(\mathbf{z}_\ell) = \begin{cases} 1 & \text{if } j = \ell \\ 0 & \text{if } j \neq \ell \end{cases}. \tag{43}$$

It is easy to see that $\phi_j{}^h$ is the "hill function" shown in Figure 11, and any v^h in S^h has the form

$$v^h(x,y) = \sum v^h(\mathbf{z}_j)\phi_j{}^h(x,y). \tag{44}$$

When Ω is a rectangle and the triangularization is regular with nodes at (x_j, y_k) (Figure 10b), the system reduces to

$$1/3\left[q_{jk}{}^h + (1/3)\left(q_{j+1,k}{}^{\cdot h} + q_{j-1,k}{}^{\cdot h} + q_{j,k+1}{}^{\cdot h}\right.\right.$$

$$\left.\left. + q_{j,k-1}{}^{\cdot h} + q_{j+1,k+1}{}^{\cdot h} + q_{j-1,k-1}{}^{\cdot h}\right)\right]$$

$$-(\Delta_h q^h)_{jk} = f_{jk}{}^h \tag{45}$$

in the weights

$$q_{jk}{}^h(t) = u_h(t,x_j,y_k), \qquad q_{jk}{}^{\cdot h}(t) = \frac{\partial}{\partial t}u_h(t,x_j,y_k), \tag{46}$$

where Δ_h is the difference operator (4) and $f_{jk}{}^h(t)$ is a suitable average of $f(t,x,y)$ about (x_j, y_k). In fact, if (x_j, y_k) is

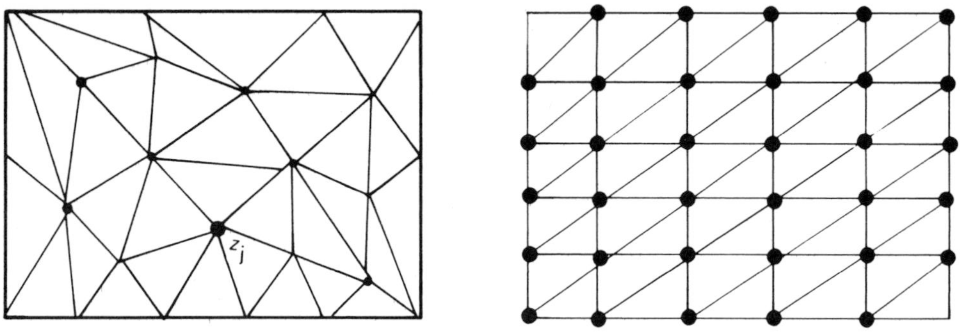

FIGURE 10 Triangularzations of Ω: (a) irregular and (b) regular.

the node z_ℓ, then

$$f_{jk}{}^h(t) = h^{-2} \int f(t,x,y)\phi_\ell(x,y)\,dx\,dy. \tag{47}$$

For a general polygon and triangularization, the system is more complicated but nevertheless of the same form.

A proposed method (Zienkiewicz, 1970) for solving (45) has been to simplify it by lumping, i.e., replacing the mass matrix M^h with the identity. This gives

$$q_{jk}{}^{\cdot h}(t) = (\Delta_h q^h)_{jk} + f_{jk}{}^h(t). \tag{48}$$

If the time derivative is replaced with a forward difference, Eq. (48) reduces to the standard explicit-difference approximation. However, this equation is no longer unconditionally stable. To obtain stability, the Courant-Fredericks-Levy condition (Richtmeyer and Morton, 1967), $\tau/h^2 \leqslant C$, on the time steps τ must be satisfied. This phenomena points out

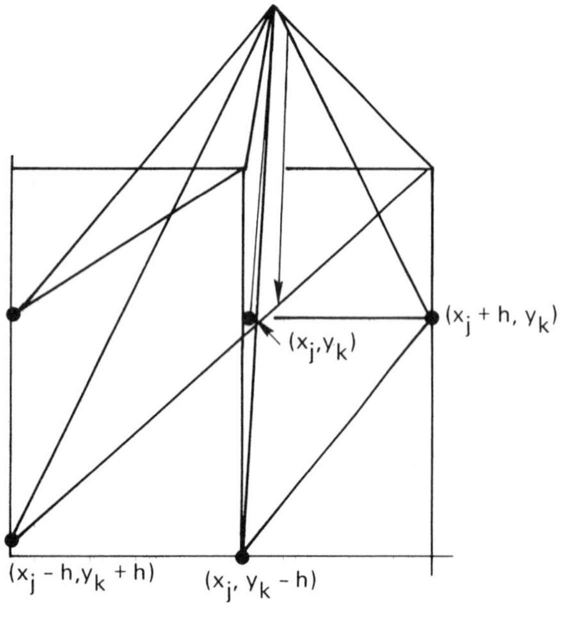

FIGURE 11 Hill function.

one of the main lessons drawn from computational experience with finite elements. Any attempt at simplification, violating the variational rules, must be performed with great care. In the present setting, the damage has not been that great, and the result is that a suitable reformation of the most elementary finite-element approximation reproduces known difference schemes. However, in the next section examples are given where more disastrous results are produced by "simplifications." In conclusion, implicitness is central to the finite-element approximation. This is one of its greatest strengths, because it means that the system is unconditionally stable. The distinct and striking advantage of finite-difference approximations is that it produces easier working systems.

An appropriate time differencing of (45) that preserves stability is the implicit Crank-Nicholson scheme,

$$M^h\,[U^{(n+1)} - U^{(n)}] + (\tau/2)K^h\,[U^{(n+1)} + U^{(n)}] = (\tau/2)\,[f^h(n\tau + \tau) + f^h(n\tau)]\,, \tag{49}$$

in the weights

$$U^{(n)} = q^h(n\tau) = [u_h(n\tau, x_j, y_k)]\,, \tag{50}$$

(see Descloux, 1970; Yanenho, 1970). Observe that (49) requires the solution of a linear equation at each time; and, as a consequence, fractional step (Douglas and Dupont, 1971) and ADI techniques (Zlámal, 1968) are typically used when applicable.

Because the finite-element approximation described above involved only linear polynomials, it gives an $O(h^2)$ approximation in the spatial variables. Therefore, this system offers little, if any, improvement over finite differences. There are, of course, the advantages of the variational approach mentioned in the previous section—the most notable in this setting being the ability to treat singularities by local mesh refinement or the use of special functions. However, the implicitness of the finite-element system demands that one use higher-degree, piecewise, polynomial functions to obtain a smaller system for given accuracy requirement.

Perhaps the most widely used higher-order elements for the heat equation is piecewise cubics. The most popular cubic element is based on a triangularization of Ω. It consists of continuous functions that are of the form

$$v^h(x, y) = \sum_{o \leqslant i+j \leqslant 3} a_{ij} x^i y^j, \tag{51}$$

on the triangles. The 10 constants a_{ij} are determined by specifying v^h, $\partial v^h/\partial x$, and $\partial v^h/\partial y$ at the nodes and v^h at the midpoints of the triangles (Figure 12). The space gives fourth-order accuracy and is quite convenient for computations (Gear, 1971). Moreover, if Γ is curved, an isoparametric element based on the above cubics can be defined analogously to quintics in the previous section. The rectangular cubics (Hermite and splines) are also used; however, if the boundary Γ does not consist of straight lines, it is necessary to use Lagrange multipliers as in the steady-state case.

The increased accuracy in the spatial approximation means that the accuracy requirement for solving the ordinary differential equation (35) is increased. As a consequence, simple time approximations such as forward differences or Crank-Nicholson schemes must be rejected, except for certain special cases where extrapolation techniques can be effectively used (Descloux, 1970). To make matters worse, Eq. (35) is a stiff system—the frequencies of its normal modes vary from $O(1)$ to $O(h^{-2})$. A great deal is known about the numerical solution of stiff systems involving large but sparse matrices—M^h, K^h (see Crane and Fox, 1969; Finlayson, 1972). The codes designed for such systems are typically adaptive, i.e., the time steps are chosen during the calculation; and limited numerical experience (some examples will be cited in the next section) indicates that they work quite well for (35) once the special properties of that system have been fully exploited in the code. Nevertheless, the final finite-element approximation in space and time so obtained is extremely complicated. It may well be used only for very difficult problems, as in three dimensions with singularities, where computational efficiency and resolving power outweigh the simplicity of difference methods.

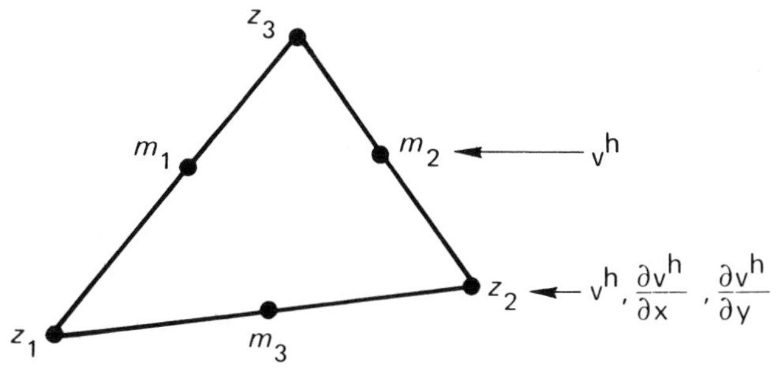

FIGURE 12 C° cubic.

HYPERBOLIC EQUATIONS

In steady-state problems, finite elements appear to be completely replacing difference methods. In parabolic problems, such as the heat equation, the attractive mathematical and computational properties are attained; yet, because of the complexity of the finite-element approximation, they will probably coexist with difference methods. With hyperbolic systems, the picture completely changes. There are cases where very serious mathematical and physical objections can be raised to the type of approximations produced by a straightforward application of the finite-element ideas. This subject is still in its infancy; however, it does appear that considerable work and revision of the finite-element techniques will be required before they are used for hyperbolic problems. This subject is also discussed in Finlayson (1972) and Strang and Fix (1973). In this section we shall briefly outline some of the more important issues. The first systematic paper in the field, by Schwartz and Wendroff (1969), is still an excellent reference and contains some interesting numerical experiments. Error estimates for linear systems are given in (Fix and Nassif, 1972).

To start with, let the linear system be

$$\frac{\partial u_\mu}{\partial t} + \sum_{\nu=1}^{M} \left(a_{\mu,\nu} \frac{\partial u_\nu}{\partial x} + b_{\mu,\nu} \frac{\partial u_\nu}{\partial y} \right) = 0, \qquad 1 \leqslant \mu \leqslant M. \tag{52}$$

or more compactly, $\partial u/\partial t + L\mathbf{u} = 0$, defined on the entire plane $-\infty < x, y < \infty$ with initial conditions $\mathbf{u}(0,x,y) = \mathbf{g}(x,y)$. Defining the inner product

$$(\mathbf{u}, \mathbf{w}) = \iint_{-\infty}^{\infty} \mathbf{v}(x, y)^* \mathbf{w}(x, y)\, dx\, dy, \tag{53}$$

the energy of the system (29) is

$$E(t) = \iint_{-\infty}^{\infty} |\mathbf{u}(t,x,y)|^2\, dx\, dy.^* \tag{54}$$

Two cases shall be discussed here. In the first, Eq. (52) is conservative in the sense that

$$\frac{d}{dt} E(t) = 0, \tag{55}$$

and is the same as

$$(L\mathbf{u}, \mathbf{u}) = 0 - \left(\frac{\partial \mathbf{u}}{\partial t}, \mathbf{u}\right) = \frac{1}{2}\frac{d}{dt} E(t) = 0. \tag{56}$$

*We are using the Euclidian inner product $\mathbf{v}^*\mathbf{w} = \sum_{\nu=1}^{M} v_\nu w_\nu$ and the Euclidian norm $|v| = (v^T v)^{1/2}$ in (53–54).

The most common example of a conservative system is the wave equation $w_{tt} = c^2 \Delta w$, which can be put into a first-order system ($M = 3$) by the change of dependent variables $u_1 = w_t, u_2 = w_x, u_3 = w_y$. Observe that $E(t)$ is the sum of the kinetic energy $\int\int w_t^2$ and the strain energy $\int\int (w_x^2 + w_y^2)$ and hence represents the total energy of the system.

The other case of interest is the dissipative case,

$$\frac{d}{dt} E(t) \leqslant 0, \tag{57}$$

or, equivalently,

$$(L\mathbf{u}, \mathbf{u}) \leqslant 0. \tag{58}$$

Examples of the latter include the diffusion equation discussed in the previous section—except that L in this case is a second-order operator in the spatial variables—and the vibrating string with friction $w_{tt} + Kw_t = c^2 \Delta w$.

To approximate (52) with finite elements, we first subdivide R^2 into triangles or rectangles and introduce a finite-element space, S^h. Let $[\phi_j{}^h(x, y)]_{j=1}{}^{\infty}$ be a locally defined basis for S^h. Then, the μth component $u_\mu(t,x,y)$ of the solution $u(t,x,y)$ is approximated by

$$u_\mu{}^h(t,x,y) = \sum_j Q_{\mu,j}{}^h(t)\phi_j{}^h(x,y).^* \tag{59}$$

The weights $Q_{\mu,j}{}^h$ are chosen by requiring

$$\int\int dx\, dy \left[\frac{\partial}{\partial t} u_\mu{}^h - \sum_{\nu=1}^{M} \left(a_{\mu\nu} \frac{\partial}{\partial x} u_\nu{}^h + b_{\mu\nu} \frac{\partial}{\partial y} u_\nu{}^h\right) v^h(x,y)\right] = 0 \tag{60}$$

for all v^h in S^h. This is equivalent to the implicit system of ordinary differential equations,

$$M\mathbf{Q}_\mu{}^{\circ h} + \sum_{\nu=1}^{M} K^{(\mu,\nu)}\mathbf{Q}_\nu{}^h = 0, \tag{61}$$

in the vector of weights $\mathbf{Q}_\mu{}^h = [Q_{\mu,j}{}^h]_{j=1}{}^N$, where M is the mass matrix (36) and

$$K_{ij}{}^{(\mu,\nu)} = \int\int \left[a_{\mu\nu} \frac{\partial \phi_j{}^h}{\partial x} + b_{\mu\nu} \frac{\partial \phi_j{}^h}{\partial y}\right] \phi^h(x,y)\, dx\, dy. \tag{62}$$

This approximation can be viewed more intuitively as "projecting" the differential equation $\mathbf{u}_t + L\mathbf{u} = 0$ onto the subspace S^h. To be more precise, the operator is defined as P^h, which takes square integrable scalar functions $w(x,y)$ into

$$(P^h w)(x,y) = \sum_{j=1}^{N} p_j{}^h \phi_j{}^h (x,y), \tag{63}$$

where the weights $\phi_j{}^h$ are determined from

$$M\mathbf{p}^h = [\int\int w(x,y)\phi_j{}^h(x,y)\, dx\, dy]_{j=1}{}^N. \tag{64}$$

In essence, $P^h w$ is the best least-squares approximation to w in S^h. A similar transformation, P^h, exists for vectors

$$\mathbf{w}(x,y) = [w_1(x,y), \ldots, w_M(x,y)], \tag{65}$$

and we put

$$\mathbf{P}^h \mathbf{w} = (P^h w_1, \ldots, P^h w_M); \tag{66}$$

thus $\mathbf{P}^h$ is a projection of $\mathbf{w}$ onto S^h x . . . x S^h (m times). It follows that (60) is exactly

$$\mathbf{P}^h \frac{\partial \mathbf{u}^h}{\partial t} + \mathbf{P}^h L \mathbf{u}^h = 0, \tag{67}$$

or, since $\mathbf{P}^h \mathbf{u}^h = \mathbf{u}^h$,

$$\frac{\partial \mathbf{u}^h}{\partial t} + \mathbf{P}^h L \mathbf{P}^h \mathbf{u}^h = 0. \tag{68}$$

In short, the finite-element method replaces L with $P^h L P^h$. From this fact, we can read off the more important properties of the finite-element approximation. For example, if L is conservative, i.e.,

$$(L\mathbf{v},\mathbf{v}) = 0 \quad \text{all } \mathbf{v}, \tag{69}$$

then so is the finite-element operator, because

$$(\mathbf{P}^h L \mathbf{P}^h \mathbf{v}^h, \mathbf{v}^h) = [L(\mathbf{P}^h \mathbf{v}^h), \quad (\mathbf{P}^h \mathbf{v}^h)] = 0 \tag{70}$$

all $\mathbf{v}^h \epsilon S^h$ x . . . x S^h. Similarly, if L is dissipative,

$$(L\mathbf{v},\mathbf{v}) \leqslant 0 \quad \text{all } \mathbf{v}, \tag{71}$$

then so is $\mathbf{P}^h L \mathbf{P}^h$:

$$(\mathbf{P}^h L \mathbf{P}^h \mathbf{v}^h, \mathbf{v}^h) = (L\mathbf{P}^h \mathbf{v}^h, \mathbf{P}^h \mathbf{v}^h) \leqslant 0. \tag{72}$$

Eq. (41) is a special case of (72). Because the finite-element approximation is obtained by projecting the differential equation onto S^h x . . . x S^h, all of the important properties of L are reflected in the approximate operator $P^h L P^h$.

The conservative property is not always desirable, par-

*Since $\phi_j{}^h$ is locally defined, (59) contains only a finite number of nonzero terms for each fixed value of (t,x,y).

ticularly in nonlinear hyperbolic equations. The solutions may develop shocks (spontaneous discontinuities); and the conservation energy $dE/dt = 0$ is lost, although in gas dynamics conservation of mass and momentum are retained. In the finite-element approximation, these shocks never appear; and the approximate equation (68) remains conservative. It follows that convergence of the approximation to the true solution cannot occur near the shock. The standard trick that is used in finite differences is to introduce artificial viscosity (Richtmeyer and Morton, 1967), and surely an analogous technique is also required for finite elements. The point is, however, that the latter must be modified before acceptable computational accuracy and efficiency are obtained.

To illustrate this point, an admittedly overworked and simple example is used,

$$\frac{\partial u}{\partial t} + u\frac{\partial u}{\partial x} = 0, \qquad -\infty < x < \infty, \qquad u(0,x) = g(x), \tag{73}$$

but one that nevertheless illustrates the basic phenomena. It is assumed that $g(x)$ is discontinuous, say

$$g(x) = \begin{cases} 1 & \text{if } x < 0 \\ 0 & \text{if } x > 0, \end{cases} \tag{74}$$

so that the solution $u(t,x)$ that satisfies the conservation of mass is

$$u(t,x) = \begin{cases} 1 & \text{if } t < x/2 \\ 0 & \text{if } t > x/2. \end{cases} \tag{75}$$

There is a shock wave given by the curve Γ in Figure 13. Piecewise linear functions,

$$u_h(t,x) = \sum_{j=1}^{N} Q_j{}^h(t)\phi_j{}^h(x),$$

will be used on a uniform mesh $x_j = jh$, so that $Q_j{}^h(t) = u_h(t,jh)$. The ordinary differential equation (60) becomes

$$(1/6)(\mathring{Q}_{j-1}{}^h + 4\mathring{Q}_j{}^h + \mathring{Q}_{j+1}{}^h) + (1/3)(Q_{j-1}{}^{h'} + Q_j{}^h + Q_{j+1}{}^h)(Q_{j+1}{}^h - Q_{j-1}{}^h)/h = 0. \tag{76}$$

Any attempt to lump and convert (76) into an explicit approximation leads to a disaster. For example, in the linear case where u is replaced with a constant h in (73), this gives

$$\frac{dQ_j{}^h}{dt} + a(Q_{j+1}{}^h - Q_{j-1}{}^h)/h = 0, \tag{77}$$

which with a forward difference in time gives the worst possible difference approximation,

$$[U_j{}^{(n+1)} - U_j{}^{(n)}]/\tau + a[U_{j+1}{}^{(n)} - U_{j-1}{}^{(n)}]/h = 0, \tag{78}$$

where $U_j{}^{(n)} = Q_j{}^h(n\tau) = u_h(n\tau, ih)$, to (73). In fact, this scheme is unstable.

It should be pointed out that the process of lumping, which physically means approximating a continuum with discrete masses, makes little sense for (73). It should be applied to the equivalent second-order equation,

$$\frac{\partial^2}{\partial t^2}u = \frac{\partial}{\partial x}u^2\frac{\partial u}{\partial x}, \tag{79}$$

where it leads to a reasonable and stable approximation. Nevertheless, in the more complicated equations of fluid dynamics, lumping should be approached with great caution, if at all.

Returning to (73), which is best solved by the standard stiff equation codes (Finlayson, 1972), a good approximation is obtained, until the shock $t = 2x$ is approached where divergence occurs. This is shown in Figure 14. In striking contrast is the classical scheme,*

$$[U_j{}^{(n+1)} - U_j{}^{(n)}]/\tau + U_j{}^{(n)}[U_j{}^{(n)} - U_{j-1}{}^{(n)}]/h = 0. \tag{80}$$

* This was taken from Peter Lax's (1971) article on nonlinear problems.

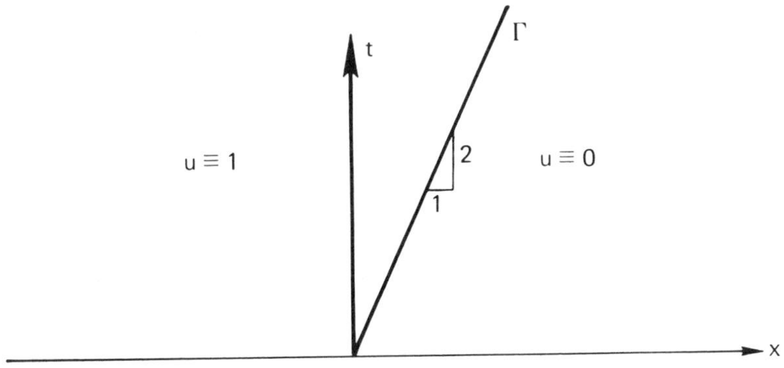

FIGURE 13 The solution u.

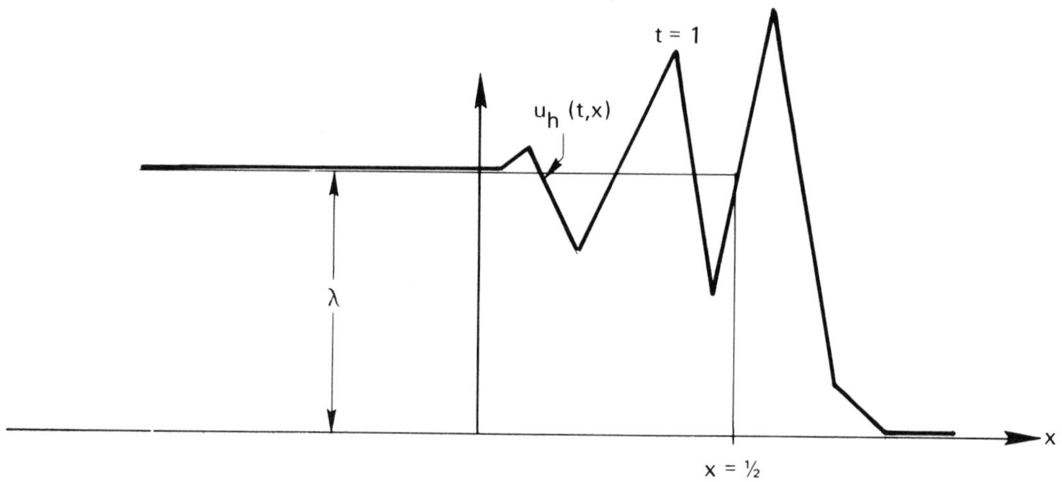

FIGURE 14 Unmodified finite-element approximation.

This scheme is only first-order accurate but nevertheless preserves the continuity of mass across the shocks. This conservation law, rather than (55), was the basis for the approximation and hence behaves quite nicely there. See Figure 15.

For the simple equation (73), it is possible to modify the finite-element approximation so that it is competitive with (80). The first step is to introduce an artificial viscosity $\lambda_h h^2$, and hence approximate

$$\frac{\partial u}{\partial t} + u\frac{\partial u}{\partial x} = h^2 \lambda_h \frac{\partial^2 u}{\partial x^2}$$

by finite elements. The parameter λ_h and the mesh spacing are chosen adaptively. That is, calculations are performed on a sequence of meshes starting with a crude uniform mesh. Regions where the solution is changing rapidly are isolated. More mesh points are added in these regions, and $\lambda_h = O(1)$ there with $\lambda_h = 0$ outside. This gives a very nice approximation, shown in Figure 16. However, this procedure is by no means a cure-all. For example, the introduction of artificial viscosity $h^2 \lambda_h$, which is of second order in h, could seriously compromise the resolving power of fourth- and higher-order elements. Thus, more substantial modifications of the basic finite-element ideas are required in these cases.

Work is still progressing on the applications of finite elements to hyperbolic systems, and whether they will retain a permanent position in such calculations is still very much in doubt. In any case, such a role will require substantial modification of the basic ideas.

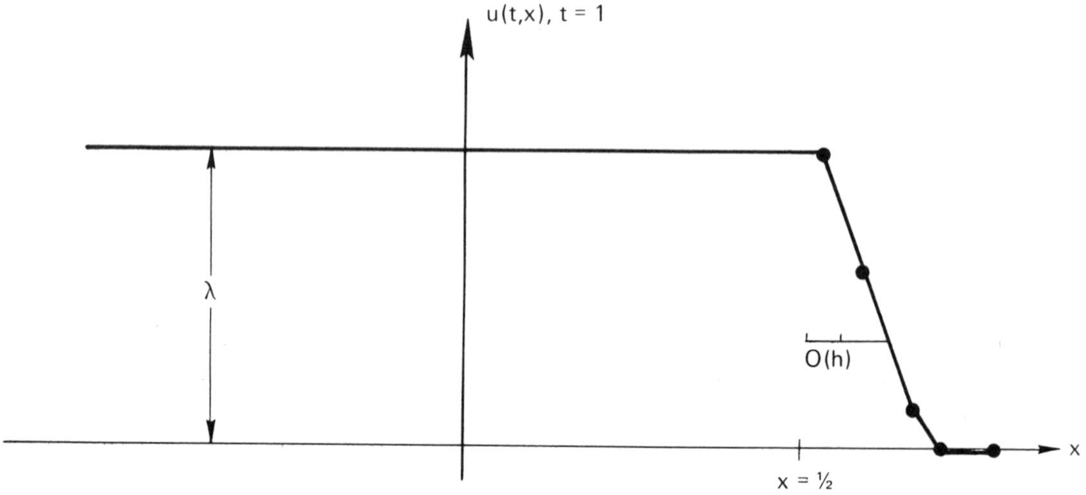

FIGURE 15 Classical difference approximation.

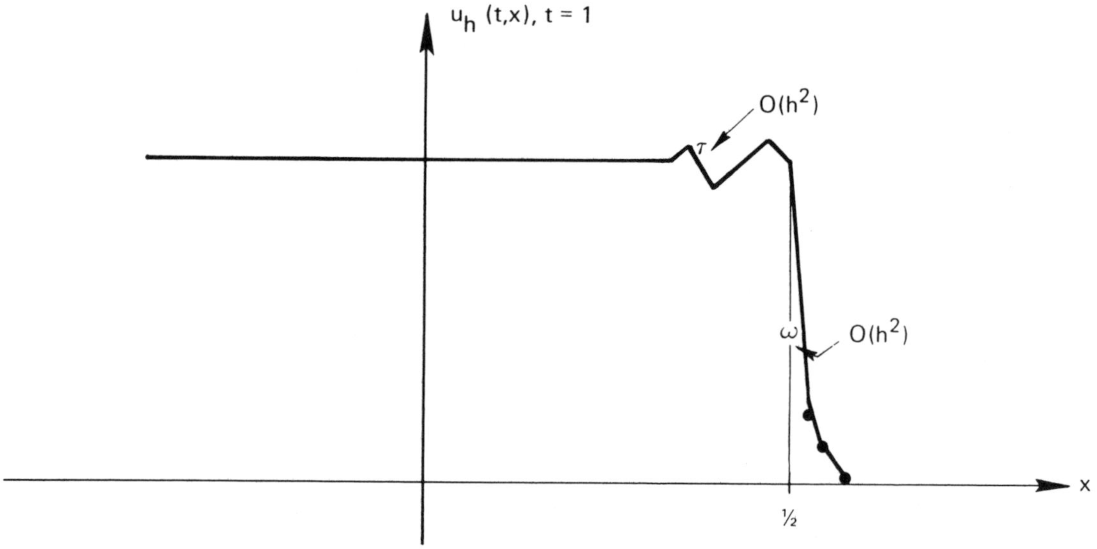

FIGURE 16 Modified finite-element approximation.

ACKNOWLEDGMENTS

This work was supported in part by the National Science Foundation under Grant No. GP 18064 and the Army Research Office–Durham under Contract No. DA ARO D 31 124 71 G133.

REVIEW: M. ISRAELI

Fix's survey paper is an interesting introduction to the finite-element method and its application to elliptic parabolic and hyperbolic partial differential equations. A qualitative comparison between the finite-element method and the finite-difference method is also presented.

The first part of the survey is devoted to a detailed description of the finite-element method as applied to equilibrium problems in elasticity and structural mechanics. (These problems give rise to linear, self-adjoint, partial differential equations with linear boundary conditions.) The following advantages of the finite-element method are indicated: (a) simple treatment of natural boundary conditions, (b) systematic derivation of high-order approximations for the equations and the essential boundary conditions, (c) straightforward approach to complicated geometrics by triangularization and isoparametric transformations, and (d) the possibility of solving problems with known singularities by enlarging the space of admissible functions and problems with unknown singularities by adaptive mesh refinement. The author's conclusion is that the finite-element method for equilibrium problems is an unqualified success.

However, the ultimate question is whether or not the finite-element method is more effective than its competitors when everything is taken into account including the above-mentioned advantages, the programming effort, and the numerical solution of the resulting systems of coupled equations. It seems to me that in connection with problems of interest in geophysical fluid dynamics, the question is still open.

Many of the basic dynamical problems are defined in (or can be easily transformed into) simple geometries. For such problems, spectral and mixed spectral-finite difference methods may give more accurate and more efficient solutions. A somewhat trivial example that is used here for illustration is Poisson's (or the biharmonic) equation with periodic boundary conditions on a rectangle; here one can get infinite-order convergence rate by using Fourier series (which involve the solution of only a diagonal matrix problem). Other boundary conditions can be handled by Fourier series without increasing the bandwidth of the matrix problem, while the order of the truncation error in the solution will depend only on the differentiability of the periodic extension of the forcing terms. The use of Chebychev series gives infinite-order convergence for the Dirichlet problem and gives rise to a periodic block tridiagonal matrix problem. The range of applicability of spectral (and pseudospectral) methods is discussed in recent papers of Orszag (more details and references can be found in Orszag, 1971, and Orszag and Israeli, pp. 284–300.

Another method, which may be computationally more

efficient than the finite-element method, is the collocation method. It may use as a basis piecewise polynomials (Douglas and Dupont, 1972; deBoor and Swartz, 1972), in which case it shares some of the advantages of the finite-element method; or it may use Chebychev expansions (Orszag, 1972), in which case it has infinite-order rate of convergence. (In this context, it is called the pseudospectral method).

The second part of the survey treats parabolic differential equations. Most of the advantages of the finite-element method carry over to these time-dependent problems; however, the resulting approximations are always of the implicit type and require the solution of large systems of coupled equations. This is not always a drawback, because implicit schemes are absolutely stable; and, therefore, the magnitude of the time step, Δt, will depend on the required accuracy and not on the stability criterion [$\Delta t = 0(h^2)$ for parabolic problems]. For nonlinear parabolic equations, the resulting systems of coupled equations will also be nonlinear.

Again, it seems that the choice of discretization method will depend on the details of the problem under consideration. Estimates of the computational effort per time step and of the size of allowable time step can be obtained and should be used.

The last part of the paper deals with hyperbolic, partial differential equations; here the author is less optimistic and indicates that comparison between the finite-element method and the finite-difference method is not simple. For hyperbolic equations, the finite-element method gives rise to sets of implicit coupled equations, as in the case of the parabolic equations; however, the stability criterion for explicit difference schemes is now $\Delta t = 0(h)$, and not $\Delta t = 0(h^2)$. Consequently, explicit difference schemes become more competitive, especially for nonlinear hyperbolic systems where the work required to solve a large system of coupled nonlinear equations for every time step should be compared with simple evaluations of algebraic (or transcendental) expressions.

Another difficulty that is common to the finite-element and to the finite-difference methods is associated with the phase error. The phase error is physically the most serious error in the simulation of advection or wave propagation; it can be linked directly to the approximation of space derivatives of the first order. On the other hand, the error is completely absent in spectral (Galerkin) or pseudospectral approximations, where the derivative is treated exactly.

The central problem for this symposium is the solution of the Navier-Stokes equations and various variants. These equations are parabolic by definition; however, when the viscous terms are relatively small, the equations have a hyperbolic character outside of viscously controlled boundary or shear layers. One would like to compare the computational effort for various numerical methods as applied to many realistic fluid-flow problems. Estimates and operation counts exist for finite-difference and spectral methods. Unfortunately, at the present time, practical experience with the finite-element method for flow problems is very limited.

REFERENCES

Ahlberg, J. H., E. N. Nilson, and J. L. Walsh. 1967. The Theory of Splines and Their Applications. Academic Press, New York.

Babuska, I. 1970. Finite element method for domains with corners. Computing 6:264-73.

Babuska, I. 1972. The finite element method with Lagrangian multipliers. University of Maryland Report BN-724.

Birkhoff, G., and G. Fix. 1967. Rayleigh-Ritz approximation by trigonometric polynomials. Ind. J. Math. 9:269-77.

Birkhoff, G., M. H. Schultz, and R. Varga. 1968. Hermite interpolation in one and more variables with applications to partial differential equations. Numer. Math 11:232-56.

Bramble, J. H., and A. H. Schatz. 1971. On the numerical solution of elliptic boundary value problems by least square approximation of the data. SYNSPADE 107-33.

Courant, R., and D. Hilbert. 1953. Methods of Mathematical Physics. Interscience.

Crane, P. C., and P. A. Fox. 1969. A comparative study of computer programs for integrating differential equations. Bell Lab. Rep.

deBoor, C., and B. Swartz. 1972. Collocation at Gaussien points. Unpublished manuscript.

Descloux, J. 1970. On the numerical integration of the heat equation. Numer. Math. 15:371-81.

Douglas, J., and T. Dupont. 1970. Galerkin methods for parabolic problems. J. SIAM Numer. Anal. 4:575-626.

Douglas, J., and T. Dupont. 1971. Alternating-direction Galerkin methods on rectangles. SYNSPADE 133-214.

Douglas, J., and T. Dupont. 1972. A finite element collocation method for nonlinear parabolic equations. Unpublished manuscript.

Finlayson, T. 1972. The Method of Weighted Residuals and Variational Principles. Academic Press, New York.

Fix, G. 1969. Higher-order Rayleigh-Ritz approximations. J. Math. Mech. 18:645-58.

Fix, G. 1972a. Effects quadrature errors for eigenvalues and parabolic problems. Proc. Symp. Math. Found. Finite Elem. Method. Academic Press, New York.

Fix, G. 1972b. Effects of quadrature errors in the finite element method. Proc. 2d Jap.-U.S. Symp. Matrix Methods Struct. Mech. McGraw-Hill.

Fix, G., and K. Larsen. 1971. On the convergence of SOR iterations for finite element approximations to elliptic boundary value problems. J. SIAM Numer. Anal. 8:536-47.

Fix, G., and N. Nassif. 1972. On finite element approximation to time dependent problems. Unpublished manuscript.

Fix, G., S. Gulati, and G. Wahoff. 1972. On the use of singular functions in the finite element method. Unpublished manuscript.

Forysythe, G., and W. Wasow. 1960. Finite difference methods for partial differential equations. Wiley.

Gear, C. 1971. Numerical Initial Value Problems in Ordinary Differential Equations. Prentice-Hall.

George, A. 1971. Block elimination of finite element systems of equations. Unpublished manuscript.

Irons, B. M. 1966. Engineering applications of numerical integration in stiffness methods. AIAA Journal 4:2035–37.

Irons, B. M. 1972. The patch test for nonconforming elements. Proc. Symp. Math. Found. Finite Elem. Methods. Academic Press, New York.

Kantorovic, L. V., and V. I. Krylov. 1952. Approximate Methods of Higher Analysis. P. Noordoff, Netherlands.

Kellogg, B. 1970. On the poisson equation with intersection interfaces. Technical Note BN-643. University of Maryland.

Kellogg, B. 1971. Singularities in interface problems. SYNSPADE. Academic Press, New York.

Kondrat'ev, V. A. 1968. Boundary problems for elliptic equations with conical or angular points. Trans. Moscow Math. Soc. 17.

Lax, P. 1971. Nonlinear partial differential equations and computing. SIAM Rev. 11:1–19.

Mikhlin, S. G. 1964. Variational Methods in Mathematical Physics. Pergamon Press, Oxford.

Nitsche, J. 1970. Über ein Variationsprinzip zur Losung von Dirichlet Problemen bei Verwendung von Teilräumen, die keinen Randbedingungen unterworfen sind. Abh. Math. Sem. Univ. Hamburg 36.

Orszag, S. 1971. Numerical simulation of incompressible flows within simple boundaries. I. Galerkin (spectral) representations. Stud. Appl. Math. 50:4.

Orszag, S. 1972. Comparison of pseudospectral and spectral approximation. 51:3.

Rice, J. Approximation of Functions. Vol. II. Addison-Wesley.

Richtmeyer, R., and K. W. Morton. 1967. Difference Methods for Initial-Value Problems. Interscience, New York.

Schoenberg, I. J., ed. 1969. Approximations with Special Emphasis on Spline Functions. Academic Press, New York.

Schultz, M. H. 1972. Spline Analysis. Prentice-Hall.

Strang, G. 1972. Variational crimes in the finite element method. Proc. Symp. Math. Found. Finite Elem. Method. Academic Press, New York.

Strang, G., and A. Berger. 1971. The change in solution due to change in domain. Proc. AMS Symp. Partial Differ. Equations. Berkeley.

Strang, G., and G. Fix. 1973. An Analysis of the Finite Element Method. Unpublished manuscript.

Swartz, B., and B. Wendroff. 1969. Generalized finite difference schemes. Math. Comp. 23:37–50.

Thomée, V. 1969. Stability theory for partial difference operators. SIAM Rev. 11(2):152–95.

Timoshenho, S., and J. N. Goodier. 1951. Theory of Electricity. 2d ed. McGraw-Hill, New York.

Varga, R. S. 1962. Matrix Iterative Analysis. Prentice-Hall.

Yanenho, N. N. 1970. The Method of Fractional Steps. Springer-Verlag.

Young, D. 1972. Iterative Methods for the Solution of Large Linear Equations. Academic Press, New York.

Zienkiewicz, O. C. 1970. The finite element method: From intuition to generality. Appl. Mech. Rev. 23:249–56.

Zienkiewicz, O. C. 1971. The Finite Element Method in Engineering Science. 2d ed. McGraw-Hill, New York.

Zlámal, M. 1968. On the finite element method. Numer. Math. 12:394–409.

NUMERICAL FLOW SIMULATION BY SPECTRAL METHODS

S. A. ORSZAG and M. ISRAELI

INTRODUCTION

Spectral methods for the solution of geophysical and meteorological flow problems have a long and colorful history. It is a standard mathematical technique to seek a solution to a dynamic equation as a series (or integral) of known functions, in the hope that each of the spectral components in the decomposition of the solution is more easily determined than the complete solution itself. Most of this work has been concerned with obtaining analytical solutions.

The use of spectral decompositions for the primary purpose of numerical simulation of the solutions of dynamic equations has not had such a glorious past. It has only been in the last few years that spectral methods have been developed that may turn out to have more than academic interest as viable methods for numerical simulations. The subject is very much in a state of development now. A variety of applications of spectral methods to flows of geophysical and meteorological interest are currently under way or contemplated—some of these applications will be reviewed later.

The present paper is intended as a short review of the status of spectral simulation. In addition to reviewing the subject as it now exists, we will illustrate a new kind of spectral method for spherical flow problems by considering the linearized motion of homogeneous fluid in a rotating spherical annulus. Results are reported concerning resonant trapped modes of motion in the spherical annulus.

REVIEW OF SPECTRAL METHODS

The first published work on numerical integration of planetary scale flows by spectral methods appears to be that of Silberman (1954). Silberman considered the solution of the barotropic vorticity equation on a sphere by expansion of the flow field in series of surface harmonics. Further work on essentially the same problem was performed in the important papers of Platzman (1960), Baer and Platzman (1961), Ellsaesser (1966), and Robert (1966), among others. A two-dimensional flow simulation on a sphere using these methods requires order $N^{2.5}$ arithmetic operations per time step if order N surface harmonics are retained in the spectral representations. Because finite-difference simulation with N grid points over the sphere require only order N arithmetic operations per time step, these spectral methods can hardly be competitive with the finite-difference methods for large N. Nevertheless, some impressive results with moderate resolution spectral models ($N = 333$) were obtained (Ellsaesser, 1966).

Other uses of spectral methods include the application of Fourier series to the numerical solution of flow problems in rectangular geometries. Bray (1966), as reported by Batchelor (1969), considered the decay of two-dimensional turbulence using a Fourier series representation of the flow field. Veronis (1966) studied thermal convection, also using a Fourier series representation of the flow field. Even more common are mixed spectral and finite-difference calculations in which the dependence on some spatial variables is spectrally decomposed (usually in Fourier series) and the remaining spatial directions are handled by finite differences. Recent examples are the works of George and Hellums (1972) on transition in plane Poiseuille flow and Meyer (1969) on Couette flow. All the works cited here are restricted to moderate resolution spectral components, because they require order N^2 arithmetic operations per time step if order N spectral components are retained. In contrast, finite-difference methods require only order N operations per time step with N grid points, so that spectral methods apparently are not competitive with finite-difference calculations if N is large.

Several recent developments make spectral methods considerably more promising than earlier research indicated. The new developments include methods to improve the computational efficiency of spectral methods and methods to extend the type of problems to which spectral methods can profitably be applied. The principal tool to improve efficiency is transform methods for evaluation of the spectral form of nonlinear and variable coefficient terms. The simplest transform method, and the first to be discovered (Orszag, 1969), applies to Fourier series representations of flow within rectangular boundaries with periodic boundary conditions. Using the fast Fourier transform, this method requires only order $N \log_2 N$ operations per time step when order N modes are retained, in contrast to order N^2 operations per time step required when the transform method is not used. Various improvements and extensions of the transform method are given by Orszag (1971a). An important improvement that permits efficiency gains of about a factor four in three dimensions over the original transform method is especially well suited to isotropic turbulence studies (Orszag, 1971a; Patterson and Orszag, 1971). Some computer times provide perspective. Two-dimensional turbulence simulations using 128 × 128 modes now require about 0.8 s per time step (including buffered data operations) on the CDC 7600 (Fox and Orszag, 1973), a time that is quite competitive with finite-difference simulations using 128 × 128 grid points. These spectral methods have been applied to the first numerical simulations of three-dimensional, homogeneous, isotropic turbulence at wind-tunnel-like Reynolds numbers (Orszag and Patterson, 1972).

Whenever a spectral code can be made as efficient as a finite-difference code with the same number of independent degrees of freedom, there results an important increase of efficiency by using the spectral code. It has been shown (Orszag, 1971b) that finite-difference simulations require at least twice the resolution in each space direction to achieve the same (say, order 5 percent) accuracy as spectral simulations. In addition, spectral simulations give infinite-order accurate results in the sense that errors decrease more rapidly than any finite power of $1/N$ as the resolution N goes to infinity. In contrast, finite-difference simulations are only finite-order accurate, so that spectral methods are advantageous when very accurate results are desired. The infinite-order accurate character of spectral approximation carries over to the class of more general spectral approximations considered below.

Transform methods have also been developed for spherical flows represented by surface-harmonic expansions. For the spectral vorticity equation, with N-retained surface-harmonic components in two dimensions, the transform method reduces the number of operations per time step from order $N^{2.5}$ to order $N^{1.5}$ (Orszag, 1970), an important improvement when N is large. This surface-harmonic transform method has been improved and extended to the dynamical equations expressed in terms of primitive variables by Eliasen *et al.* (1970). Applications of transform methods to primitive equation models have been reported by Bourke (1972) and Machenhauer and Rasmussen (1972). Bourke reports that the transform method gives efficiency gains of a factor ten over direct evaluation even at the moderately low resolution of truncation wave number fifteen.

Nevertheless the surface-harmonic transform method still must be inefficient compared to finite-difference calculations at high resolution, since the transform method requires order $N^{1.5}$ operations per time step, while finite-difference models require only order N. The trouble with the surface-harmonic transform method is the need to perform discrete Legendre transforms (Orszag, 1970). However, a new method for spectral modeling of flows on spheres has recently been developed that requires only fast Fourier transforms and, therefore, reduces $N^{1.5}$ to $N \log_2 N$ (Orszag, 1974). The new method involves use of special Fourier series instead of surface-harmonic expansions. A simple case of the new expansions is applied to the numerical simulation of resonant trapped modes in a spherical annulus in the following two sections.

Extensions of spectral methods have recently been made to handle flows within rigid no-slip boundaries using Chebyshev expansions (Orszag, 1971c) and to flows in more complicated geometries (Orszag, 1971a). All these extensions give infinite-order accurate spectral approximations and are associated with efficient transform methods.

SPECTRAL EQUATIONS FOR HOMOGENEOUS ROTATING FLUID IN A SPHERICAL ANNULUS

We consider infinitesimal Rossby number, axisymmetric, viscous, incompressible flow of a homogeneous rotating fluid in the spherical annulus formed by the region between two concentric spheres of radii $a > b$. Spherical coordinates (r, θ, ϕ) are used, where r is the radius, θ is the co-latitude, and ϕ is the longitude; the coordinate system is assumed rotating about the pole at the constant angular velocity Ω_0. Physical variables are nondimensionalized in the usual way by choosing a and Ω_0^{-1} as representative length and time scales, respectively. If U is a typical relative velocity of motion in the rotating frame, the flow is characterized by the Rossby number $\epsilon = U/\Omega_0 a$ and the Ekman number $E = \nu/\Omega_0 a^2$, where ν is the kinematic viscosity. Here the limiting case $\epsilon \ll 1$ is considered, so that the dynamic equations may be linearized about the state of uniform rotation.

Because the flow is assumed axisymmetric and incompressible, Stokes' stream function $\psi(r,\theta)$ is introduced by

$$u_r = \frac{1}{r^2 \sin\theta} \frac{\partial\psi}{\partial\theta}, \qquad u_\theta = -\frac{1}{r \sin\theta} \frac{\partial\psi}{\partial r}, \tag{1}$$

where $\mathbf{u} = (u_r, u_\theta, u_\phi)$ is the velocity field. Furthermore,

$$\Omega(r,\theta) = r \sin\theta u_\phi, \qquad \xi(r,\theta) = -r \sin\theta (\nabla \times \mathbf{u})_\phi, \tag{2}$$

Eq. (2) is set so that Ω is the angular momentum per unit mass relative to the rotating frame and ξ is $r \sin\theta$ times the azimuthal component of vorticity. The dependence of ψ, Ω, and ξ on time is not written explicitly. It follows from Eqs. (1-2) that

$$\xi = D^2 \psi, \tag{3}$$

where the differential operator D^2 is given by

$$D^2 \psi = \frac{\partial^2 \psi}{\partial r^2} + \frac{\sin\theta}{r^2} \frac{\partial}{\partial\theta} \frac{1}{\sin\theta} \frac{\partial\psi}{\partial\theta}. \tag{4}$$

It follows that the dynamical equations linearized in the rotating frame are

$$\frac{\partial\xi}{\partial t} + \frac{2}{r} \frac{\partial(\Omega, r\sin\theta)}{\partial(r,\theta)} = ED^2 \xi, \tag{5}$$

$$\frac{\partial\Omega}{\partial t} - \frac{2}{r} \frac{\partial(\psi, r\sin\theta)}{\partial(r,\theta)} = ED^2 \Omega, \tag{6}$$

where (5) is the azimuthal vorticity equation and (6) follows from the azimuthal momentum equation. Eqs. (3-6) are to be solved with rigid boundary conditions on the boundaries of the spherical annulus.

The numerical results reported in the following section are obtained by solving (3-6) using a spectral representation for the angular dependence of the dynamical variables and finite-difference discretization for the radial and time dependence. The radial dependence is not spectrally analyzed, because the aim is to obtain a direct comparison of spectral angular representations with finite-difference angular representations; however, it would be appropriate to use Chebyshev series representations for the radial dependence.

The choice of spectral representation for the angular dependence requires some discussion. It may be shown (Orszag, 1974) that any physically realizable axisymmetric velocity field has the property that u_r, $u_\theta/\sin\theta$, and $u_\phi/\sin\theta$ are naturally expansible in Fourier cosine series for $0 \leqslant \theta \leqslant \pi$, in the sense that each is formally extensible without loss of differentiability to an even periodic function of θ of period 2π. Consequently, $\psi/\sin^2\theta$, $\xi/\sin^2\theta$, and $\Omega/\sin^2\theta$ are naturally expansible in Fourier cosine series that converge with infinite-order accuracy if ψ, ξ, and Ω are infinitely differentiable (as when $E > 0$). The usual procedure for representing this kind of angular dependence spectrally is to expand ψ, ξ, and Ω in the functions

$$p_n(\theta) = \int_{\cos\theta}^{1} P_n(t)\, dt \tag{7}$$

for $n \geqslant 1$, where $P_n(t)$ is the Legendre polynomial of degree n (cf., Dennis and Walker, 1971). When $n \geqslant 1$, $p_n(\theta)$ is of the form $\sin^2\theta$ times a truncated cosine series in θ. A set of spectral equations for (3-6), based on expansions in $p_n(\theta)$, is straightforward to work out and may be expected to give results at least as good as those reported in the following section by the method to be explained next. [An alternative expansion using Legendre polynomials is to expand ξ, ψ, and Ω in the functions $\sin^2\theta P_n(\cos\theta)$ as done by Munson and Joseph (1971) in their study of steady flows in a rotating spherical annulus.]

Instead of expanding in the functions $p_n(\theta)$, we choose to illustrate a new kind of spectral representation suitable for spherical (and spheroidal) flow problems (Orszag, 1974). The new method takes a particularly simple form for axisymmetric flow: $\psi/\sin^2\theta$, $\xi/\sin^2\theta$, and $\Omega/\sin^2\theta$ are represented by Fourier cosine series. In other words, we seek spectral approximations to ψ, ξ, and Ω as

$$\begin{Bmatrix} \psi(r,\theta) \\ \xi(r,\theta) \\ \Omega(r,\theta) \end{Bmatrix} = \sin^2\theta \sum_{n=0}^{N} \begin{Bmatrix} \psi_n(r) \\ \xi_n(r) \\ \Omega_n(r) \end{Bmatrix} \cos n\theta, \tag{8}$$

where N is a cutoff. If these series are substituted in (3-6) and the resulting terms reexpanded in series of the form (8), it follows by equating coefficients of $\sin^2\theta \cos n\theta$ $(n = 0, \ldots, N)$ that

$$\xi_n = D^2 \psi_n, \tag{9}$$

$$D^2 \psi_n = \frac{\partial^2 \psi_n}{\partial r^2} - (n+1)(n+2)\frac{\psi_n(r)}{r^2} - \frac{6}{r^2 c_n} \sum_{\substack{p = n+2 \\ p+n \text{ even}}}^{N} p\psi_p(r), \tag{10}$$

$$\frac{\partial\xi_n}{\partial t} + c_{n-1}\left(\frac{\partial\Omega_{n-1}}{\partial r} - \frac{n+1}{r}\Omega_{n-1}\right) + \frac{\partial\Omega_{n+1}}{\partial r} + \frac{n-1}{r}\Omega_{n+1} = ED^2 \xi_n, \tag{11}$$

$$\frac{\partial \Omega_n}{\partial t} - c_{n-1}\left(\frac{\partial \psi_{n-1}}{\partial r} - \frac{n+1}{r}\psi_{n-1}\right) - \frac{\partial \psi_{n+1}}{\partial r} - \frac{n-1}{r}\psi_{n+1} = ED^2\Omega_n, \quad (12)$$

corresponding to (3-6), respectively, where $c_0 = 2$, $c_n = 1 (n > 0)$, $c_n = 0 (n < 0)$. Eqs. (9-12) are closed by taking $\psi_{N+1} = \psi_{N+2} = 0$, etc. A systematic derivation of (9-12) is obtained by manipulating Chebyshev series, as explained in the appendix of Orszag (1971d).

A simple analytical test of the spectral representations (8) and Eqs. (9-12) is obtained by considering the modes of inertial oscillation in the inviscid ($E = 0$) fluid in a thin annulus of large radius. In this case, it is appropriate to drop both viscous terms (dependent on E) and terms involving proportionality factors $1/r$ in (3-6), resulting in the system

$$\xi = \frac{\partial^2 \psi}{\partial r^2}, \quad (13)$$

$$\frac{\partial \xi}{\partial t} + 2\cos\theta \frac{\partial \Omega}{\partial r} = 0, \quad (14)$$

$$\frac{\partial \Omega}{\partial t} - 2\cos\theta \frac{\partial \psi}{\partial r} = 0. \quad (15)$$

It follows that

$$\frac{\partial^2 \xi}{\partial t^2} + 4\cos^2\theta\, \xi = 0, \quad (16)$$

(where ξ can be any function of r) so that the natural modes of oscillation are singular and form a continuous spectrum with $0 \leqslant |\omega| \leqslant 2$, where the mode of frequency $\omega = \pm 2 \cos\theta$ is confined to co-latitudes θ and $\pi - \theta$.

If the viscous and curvature terms are dropped in (9-12), there results the following spectral approximation to (13-15):

$$\xi_n = \frac{\partial^2 \psi_n}{\partial r^2}, \quad (17)$$

$$\frac{\partial \xi_n}{\partial t} + c_{n-1}\frac{\partial \Omega_{n-1}}{\partial r} + \frac{\partial \Omega_{n+1}}{\partial r} = 0, \quad (18)$$

$$\frac{\partial \Omega_n}{\partial t} - c_{n-1}\frac{\partial \psi_{n-1}}{\partial r} - \frac{\partial \psi_{n+1}}{\partial r} = 0, \quad (19)$$

for $n = 0, \ldots, N$. It follows that

$$\frac{\partial^2 \xi_n}{\partial t^2} + c_{n-2}\xi_{n-2} + (c_n + c_{n-1})\xi_n + \xi_{n+2} = 0. \quad (20)$$

Only those modes with $\xi_n = 0$ for n odd and ξ_n proportional to $e^{-i\omega t}$ for n even are considered; the analysis is easily extended to cover modes with nonzero ξ_n for n odd. Substitution in (20) gives the difference equations

$$c_{n-2}\xi_{n-2} + (c_{n-1} + c_n - \omega^2)\xi_n + \xi_{n+2} = 0, \quad (21)$$

where each ξ_n is proportional to the same arbitrary function of r. For a nontrivial solution ξ_n to exist, the determinant of the coefficients in (21) must vanish, giving an eigenvalue relation for ω. In fact, if we denote by $D_N(\omega)$ the value of the determinant obtained from (21) for $n = 0, 2, \ldots, N$, it follows easily by expanding the determinant about its last row that

$$D_N(\omega) = (2 - \omega^2)D_{N-2}(\omega) - D_{n-4}(\omega). \quad (22)$$

Because $D_0(\omega) = 2 - \omega^2$ and $D_2(\omega) = (2 - \omega^2)^2 - 2$, it follows from (22) that

$$D_N(\omega) = \alpha_+^{N+2} + \alpha_-^{N+2}, \quad (23)$$

where $\alpha_\pm = \tfrac{1}{2} i[\omega \pm (\omega^2 - 4)^{1/2}]$. The dispersion relation $D_N(\omega) = 0$ has roots

$$\omega = \pm 2\cos\frac{\pi}{N+2}\left(k + \frac{1}{2}\right)\left(k = 0, 1, \ldots, \frac{N}{2}\right). \quad (24)$$

Consequently, the $N/2 + 1$ modes of (20) for $n = 0, 2, \ldots, N$ are well distributed in the interval $|\omega| \leqslant 2$ with each mode concentrated near $\theta = \pi(k + \tfrac{1}{2})/N + 2)$ or $\pi - \theta$, as may be verified by a separate calculation of the modal structure in θ. These modes of the spectral approximation (20) are remarkably similar to those of the exact system (13-15).

RESONANT TRAPPED MODES IN A ROTATING SPHERICAL ANNULUS

The spectral decomposition of the previous section results in a system of $3N + 3$ coupled partial differential equations, the independent variables being the time and the radial distance r. These equations are discretized by replacing the radial derivatives with second-order, centered, finite-difference approximations and integrated in time by means of the time-centered implicit (Crank-Nicholson) scheme. The time-centered implicit scheme is absolutely stable; and, therefore, substantial gains can be realized by its use when stability restricts the allowable time step of explicit methods. This is especially true when a singular point of the coordinates exists inside the region of integration (like the interior of a sphere) or when a nonuniform mesh is used to resolve sharp gradients in a boundary (or interior) layer. The time-centered implicit scheme is also more accurate* than second-order explicit methods; and, therefore, bigger time steps can be used even when numerical stability is not important. However, the overall efficiency of the scheme depends on the effort required to solve a system of $3MN$ coupled linear equations (M being the number of radial grid intervals). The iterative method described below requires on the average between two and three iterations for convergence.

Here, the notation $\zeta_{i,n}{}^{k,l}$ is used where ζ is a dependent variable; the index i indicates the radial position, n denotes the mode number, k is the time index, and l is the iteration index. The difference equations for the spectral components can be compressed into the following form:

$$A(\Omega_{i\ \ ,n}^{k+1,l+1}) + L(\Omega_{i\ \ ,p}^{k+1,l+1}) + B(\psi_{i\ \ ,n+1}^{k+1,l+1}, \psi_{i\ \ ,n-1}^{k+1,l}) = P_{i,n}^{k}, \qquad (25)$$

$$A(\xi_{i\ \ ,n}^{k+1,l+1}) + L(\xi_{i\ \ ,p}^{k+1,l+1}) - B(\Omega_{i\ \ ,n+1}^{k+1,l+1}, \Omega_{i\ \ ,n-1}^{k+1,l+1}) = Q_{i,n}^{k}, \qquad (26)$$

$$C(\psi_{i\ \ ,n}^{k+1,l+1}) - \xi_{i\ \ ,n}^{k+1,l+1} = L(\psi_{i\ \ ,p}^{k+1,l+1}), \qquad (27)$$

where

$$n+2 \leqslant p \leqslant N, \quad l \geqslant 0, \quad 2 \leqslant i \leqslant M, \quad 0 \leqslant n \leqslant N.$$

Here A, B, C, L are linear operators involving the variables in parentheses, as well as their two closest neighbors in the radial direction. $P_{i,n}{}^{k}$, $Q_{i,n}{}^{k}$ involve only known quantities from the k time step and are computed only once. The quantities $\psi_{i\ \ ,n}^{k+1,0}$ are obtained by a second-order extrapolation in time, the exact form of which depends on the nature of the forcing.

The iteration starts by solving (25), starting from $n = N$ and proceeding to $n = 0$. A tridiagonal system of $M - 1$ equations is solved for every n, and the sum in L is augmented by the addition of one term. Because $\Omega_{i\ \ ,n}^{k+1,l+1}$ is known, (26) and (27) can be solved in a similar manner. The above procedure is complete if two boundary conditions for each of Ω_n, ξ_n, and ψ_n separately are known on the rigid boundaries $r = a$ and $r = b$. This is not the case when a no-slip condition is required on one or both of the spherical shells. In this latter case, two conditions for ψ_n are available on the no-slip shell and none for ξ_n. An iterative method similar to the one used in Israeli (1970, 1972) is applied. The modified method, when applied successively to each spectral component, gives the exact boundary values of ζ_n in two (one) iterations when there are two (one) no-slip boundaries (a convergence check often stops the procedure after only one iteration). The details of the method are described in Israeli and Orszag (1972).

The problem of resonant modes of a homogeneous fluid in a rotating spherical shell is of interest in problems of geomagnetism (Hide and Stewartson, 1972) and in connection with the general initial value problem of rotating fluids (Greenspan, 1969; Israeli, 1970, 1971). The addition of stratification will further extend the range of relevance to meteorology and oceanography.

The question of the existence of axisymmetric modes was approached by means of an inviscid ray theory and numerical simulation by Israeli (1971, 1972). Ray theory, which in some cases predicts a discrete set of possible modes (Høiland, 1962) and in other cases indicates that no modes are possible (Greenspan, 1969), predicts in the present case the existence of a set of m nonoverlapping continuous bands of possible frequencies of resonance, where $m = [a^2/(a^2 - b^2)]$. The significance of the latter result is unclear and still requires verification.

The oscillations corresponding to the lowest band were simulated numerically by integrating equations (3), (5), and (6), where the angular velocity of the boundaries is assumed to oscillate slightly about a state of mean rotation. The integration is continued until a state of steady oscillations is obtained. The maximum amplitude is then recorded and the simulation repeated for a wide range of oscillation frequencies. The peaks in the response curve (amplitude versus frequency) are associated with the resonant frequencies of oscillations. Good agreement is found (when $a - b \leqslant a/4$) between the numerical results and the maximum frequency in the first band. It has been conjectured that the selection of the maximum frequency is related to the influence of viscosity, which in fact drives the oscillation through the viscous boundary layers, and also that a different method of forcing may shift the selected frequency inside the allowable band.

The original scheme of simulation was an alternating-direction implicit method with a fine mesh and a second-order difference scheme in the radial direction (where thin boundary layers exist) and a fourth-order, finite-difference scheme in the latitudinal direction with 20 intervals between $0°$ and $90°$ (with a reflection condition on the equator). Only 20 points were used, because both the number of operations and the storage required for the inversion of the (septa-diagonal but block tridiagonal) matrix Poisson equation (3) were proportional to the square of the number of latitudinal mesh intervals. Nevertheless, by comparison with computations using 15 angular intervals, it was estimated that the results obtained with 20 angular intervals are within 3 percent of the extrapolated values.

The method discussed in this and the previous section is now applied to the computation of the fluid response (amplitude of oscillations versus frequency) to forcing frequencies

*For a comparison of the accuracy of explicit and implicit schemes based on the truncation error in the application of no-slip conditions on rigid boundaries, see Israeli (1970).

TABLE 1 Value of the Peak of the Stream Function ψ and Maximum Values of the Most Energetic Spectral Components at Time $T = 57.5/\Omega$ and Frequency $\omega = .6614$.

N/2	maximum stream-function × 10^3	$\psi_1 \times 10^3$	$\psi_3 \times 10^3$	$\psi_5 \times 10^3$	$\psi_7 \times 10^3$	$\psi_9 \times 10^3$	$\psi_{11} \times 10^3$
6	6.908	–.490	1.604	–2.349	2.381	–1.749	.883
10	6.553	–.436	1.565	–2.280	2.200	–1.474	.517
15	6.308	–.427	1.509	–2.205	2.139	–1.456	.548
17	6.392	–.424	1.509	–2.198	2.139	–1.452	.553
22	6.364	–.425	1.509	–2.199	2.139	–1.453	.552

in the range $0.55 < \omega/\Omega < 0.75$). This range encloses the first band ($0.566 \leqslant \omega/\Omega \leqslant 0.645$) of frequencies of resonance predicted by inviscid ray theory for a shell of nondimensional thickness $(a - b)/a = 1/8$. Two methods of forcing are used; the first (which is also used in the finite-difference method) involves oscillations of the rigid boundary and drives the motion via the viscous Ekman layers; the second involves a forcing term in the zonal momentum equation. The Ekman number ($= 1/36{,}000$), the time step ($\Delta T = 0.25/\Omega$), and the radial mesh interval ($= a/240$) are all the same as in the finite-difference calculation. The accuracy of the simulations reported here was tested by varying the cutoff N from 12 to 44.

Because the trapped modes to be simulated have velocity fields symmetric with respect to the equator, only even modes for Ω_n and odd modes for ψ_n and ξ_n need be retained. With the cutoff N, this gives $N/2 + 1$ Ω_n components and $N/2$ ψ_n, ξ_n components.

Table 1 shows the values of the peak of the stream function in physical space as well as maximal values of the most energetic spectral components at time $T = 57.5/\Omega$ (when the response is maximal) and frequency $\omega = 0.6614$ (which is close to the frequency of resonance).

The simulation of the trapped modes is a severe test for the numerical method for the following reasons: (a) there is an appreciable amount of energy in high modes, (b) the amplitude depends on the frequency of resonance of a particular simulation, and (c) the amplitude depends strongly on the phase lag of the interior oscillation with respect to the forcing. Table 1 shows a fast convergence of the amplitude of the stream function. It is also evident that the modal amplitudes converge faster than their physical counterparts. The error in the maximum stream function amplitude is about 9 percent for $N/2 = 6$, 3 percent for $N/2 = 10$, 0.9 percent for $N/2 = 15$, and 0.44 percent for $N/2 = 17$.

Figures 1, 2, and 3 are contour maps of the stream function. The line K is the zero line, while the lines A to J are equally spaced between the minimum and maximum values.*

*The meanders of the K streamline ($\psi = 0$) near the pole are caused by very small changes in the weak circulation outside the trapped-mode region. It should be also mentioned that the line I in Figures 1, 2, 3, and 6, the line C in Figures 4 and 5, and the line B in Figure 7 all represent values close to $\psi = 0$.

The low cutoff $N = 12$ ($N/2 = 6$) figure shows much of the structure of the mode, which is even more pronounced in Figures 4 and 5, where the stream function corresponds to the frequency $\omega = 0.6981\Omega$. The conclusion from this experiment is that 10 spectral modes give results that are comparable to the results of a fourth-order difference scheme with 20 intervals (19 interior points), while 15 spectral modes give superior results.

Two response curves were computed with the cutoff $N = 30$, one corresponding to boundary forcing, the other to interior forcing. The first curve is similar to the one previously obtained with the difference scheme, and it has a shallow maximum at $\omega \approx 0.65\Omega$. The response curve for the interior forcing is (when suitably normalized) virtually identical to its boundary forcing counterpart, thus indicating that the observed motions are the viscous manifestation of a well-defined inviscid mode. Further evidence to support this view is available: Figures 6 and 7 show that the structure of the meridional motion is very similar, although the boundary layers have very different dynamical functions.

It can be concluded from the last experiment that the selection (Israeli, 1971, 1972) of one frequency of resonance from the continuous band of frequencies predicted by ray theory is not related to the method of excitation of the interior motion.

FUTURE PROSPECTS

The model described in the previous two sections is easily extended to include effects of stratification and nonlinearity, the latter requiring the use of transform methods for efficient implementation. The Fourier expansions (8) give spectral forms of the nonlinear terms that involve only convolution sums that require order $N \log_2 N$ operations for evaluation, where N is the cutoff in (8). However, Legendre expansions would give vector-coupled sums for the nonlinear terms that require order N^2 operations for evaluation (Orszag, 1970). The extended model can by applied to investigate stratified spin-up or time-dependent convection problems in spherical geometries. Also, stretched coordinates in the radial direction are presently being included in the code in order to better resolve the boundary layer structure at low computational cost (Israeli, 1971).

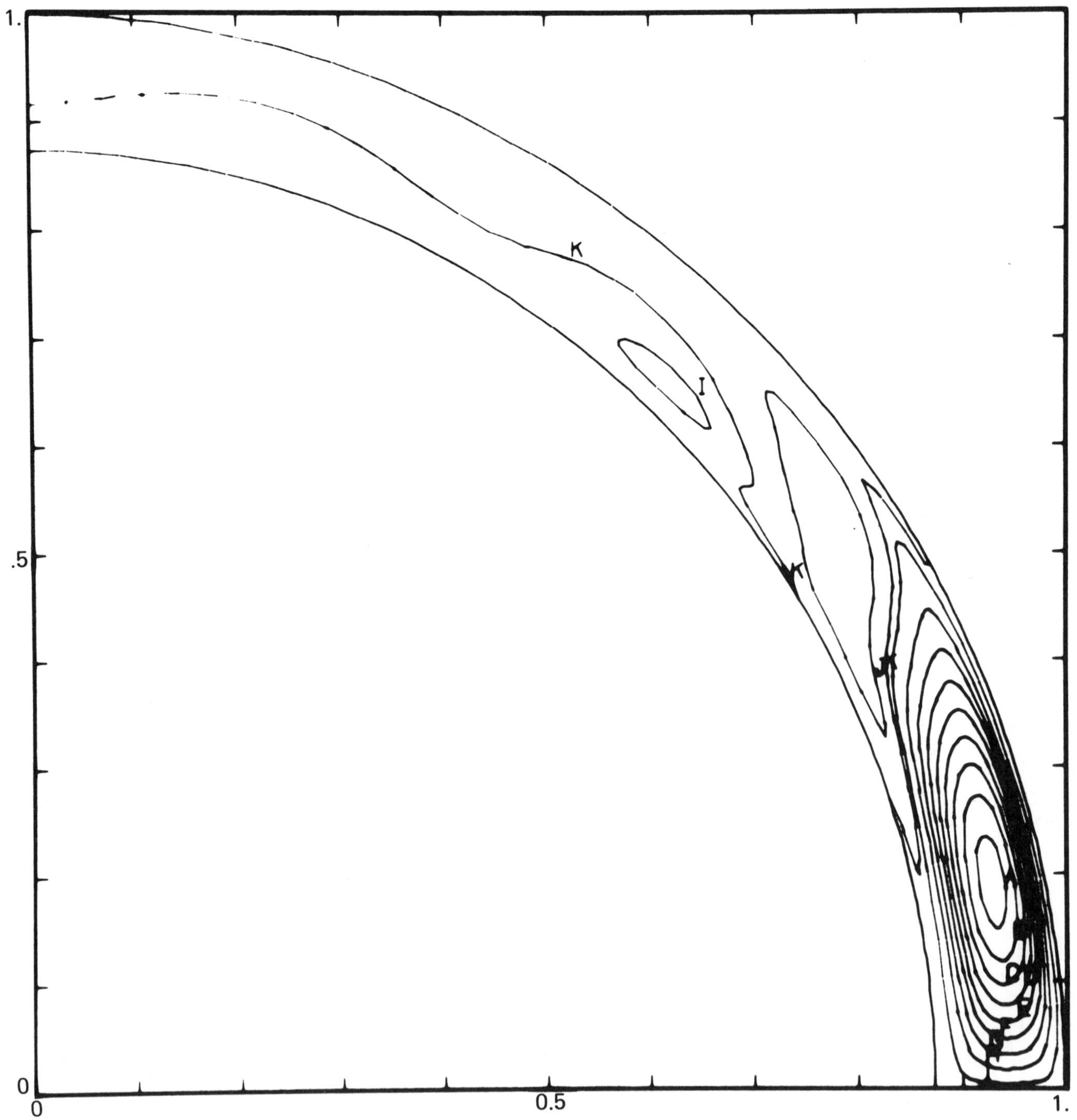

FIGURE 1 Stream function, with Ekman = 1/36,000, M = 30, N = 12, Rossby = 0.00, frequency = 0.6814, T = 57.5.

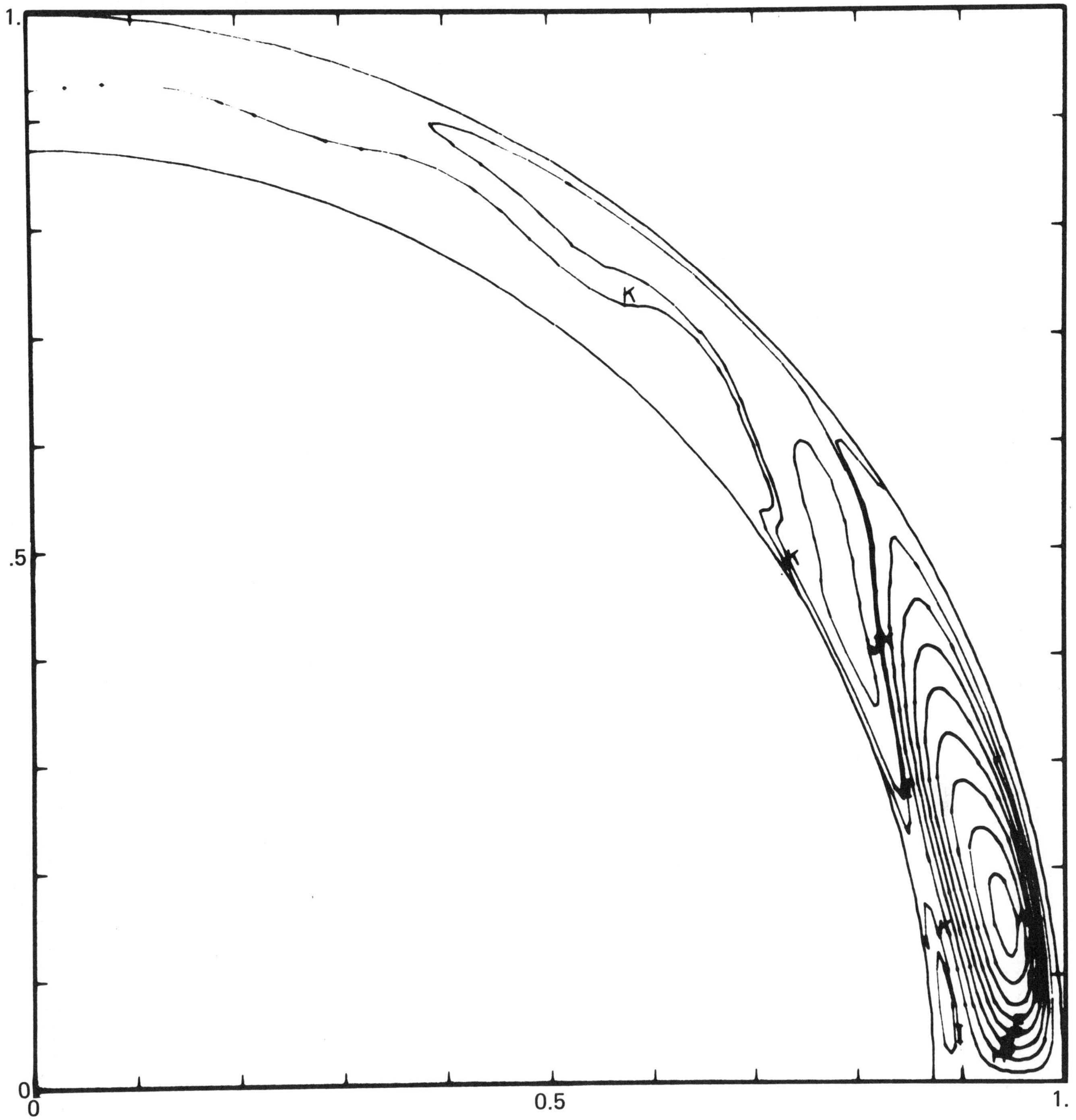

FIGURE 2 Stream function, with Ekman = 1/36,000, M = 30, N = 20, Rossby = 0.00, frequency = 0.6814, and T = 57.5.

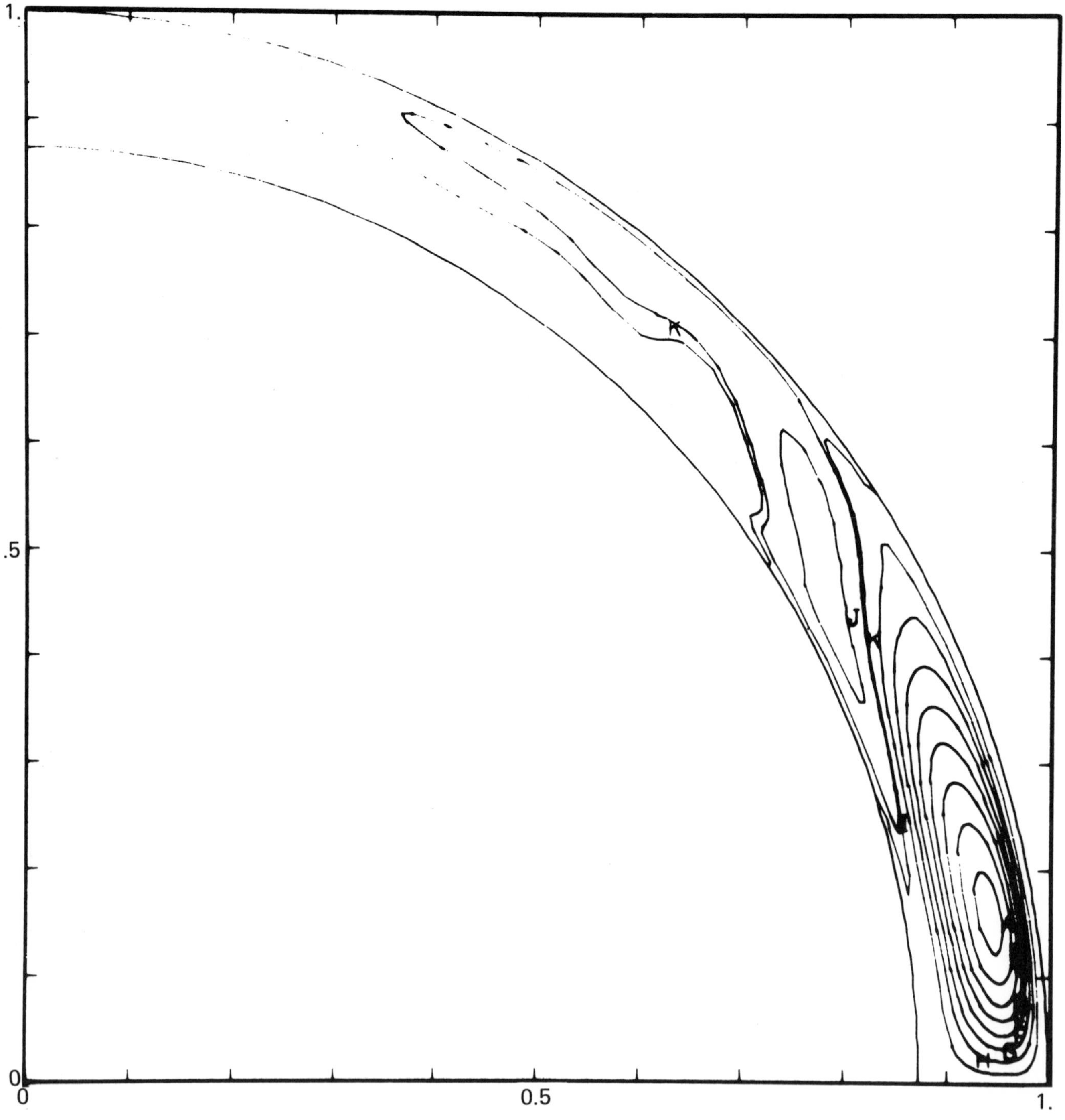

FIGURE 3 Stream function, with Ekman = 1/36,000, M = 30, N = 34, Rossby = 0.00, frequency = 0.6814, and T = 57.5.

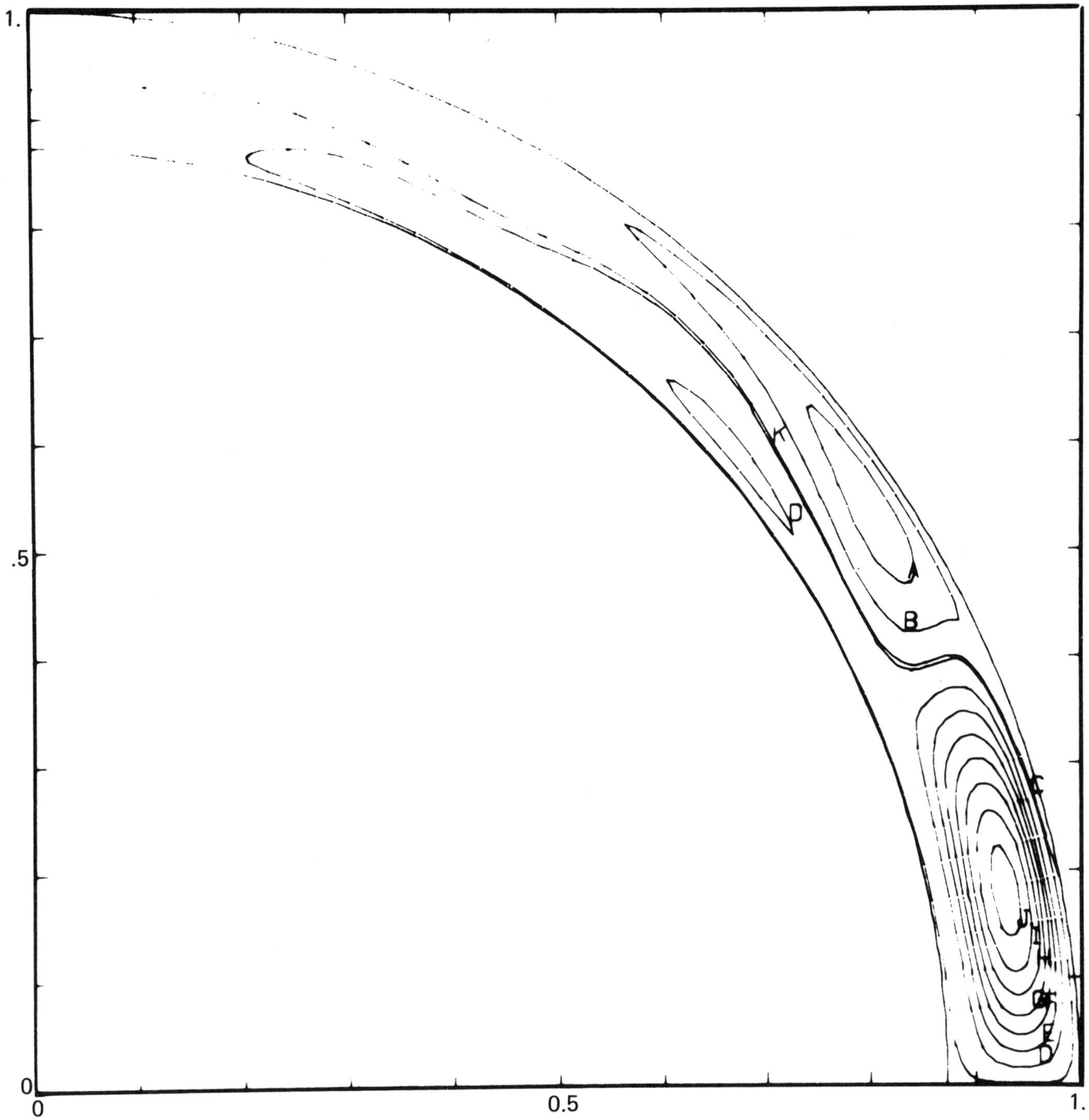

FIGURE 4 Stream function, with Ekman = 1/36,000, M = 30, N = 12, Rossby = 0.00, frequency = 0.6918, and T = 60.

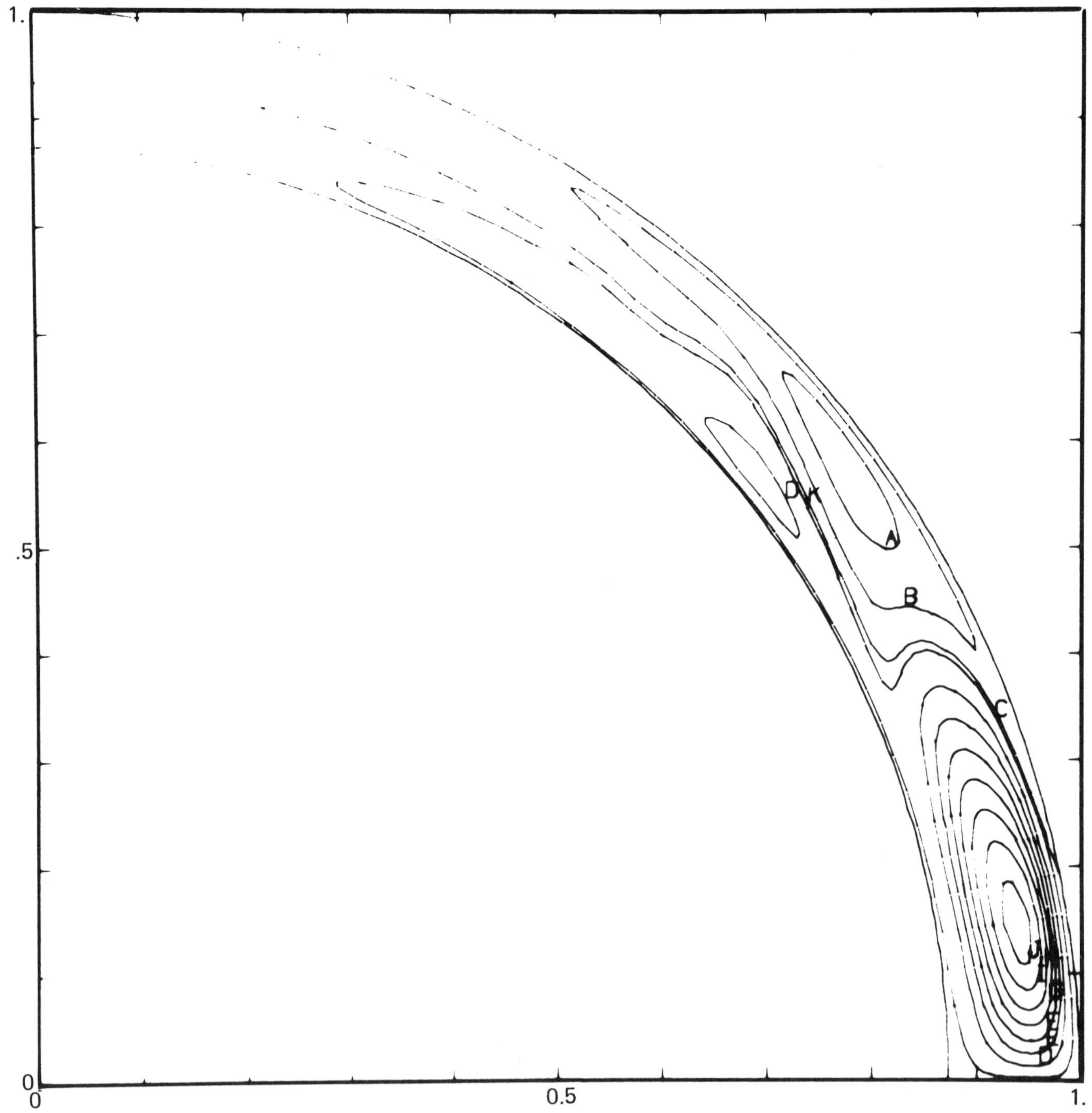

FIGURE 5 Stream function, with Ekman = 1/36,000, M = 30, N = 44, Rossby = 0.00, frequency = 0.6918, and T = 60.

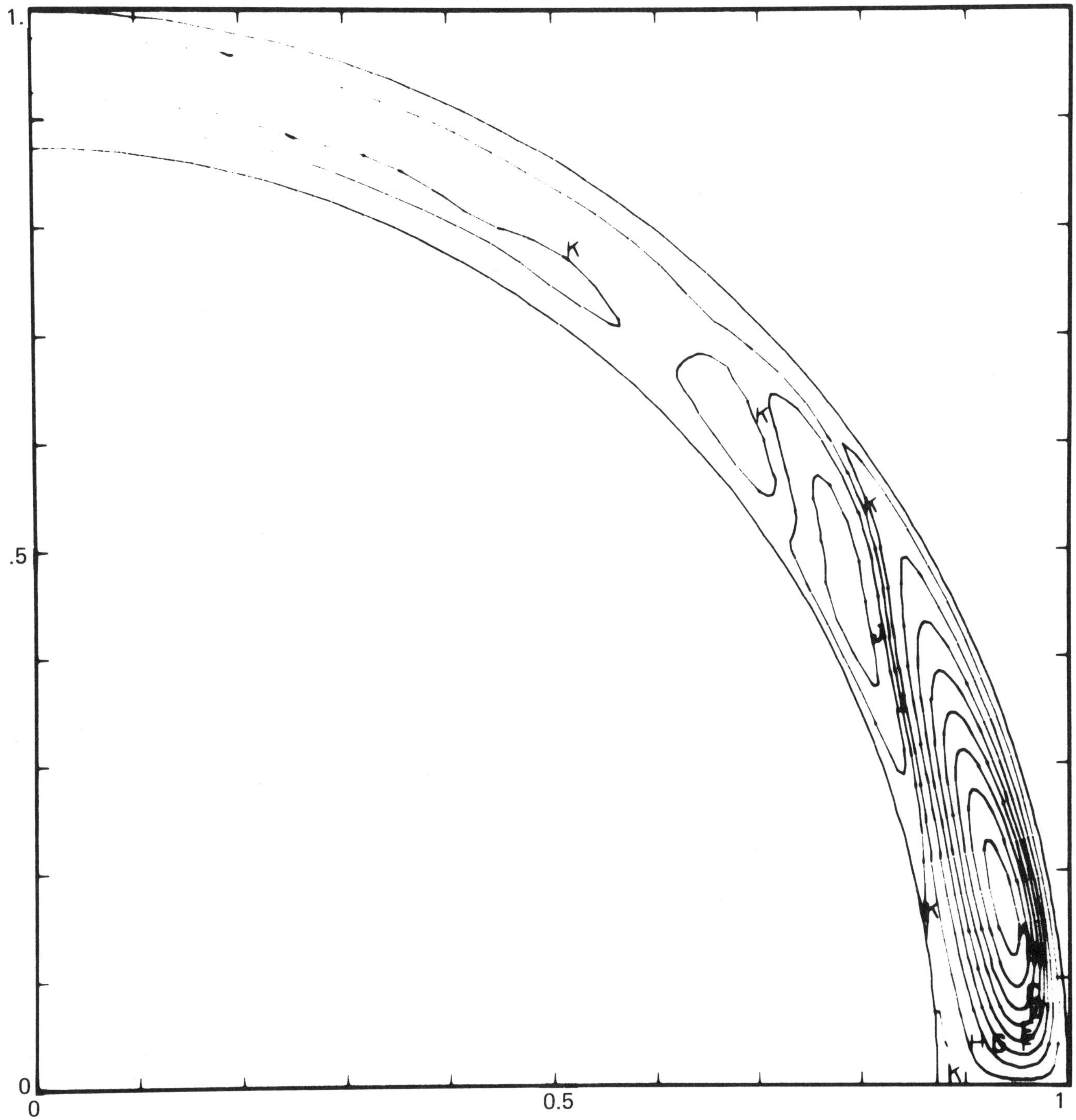

FIGURE 6 Stream function interior forcing, with Ekman = 1/36,000, M = 30, N = 30, Rossby = 0.00, frequency = 0.64, and T = 74.07.

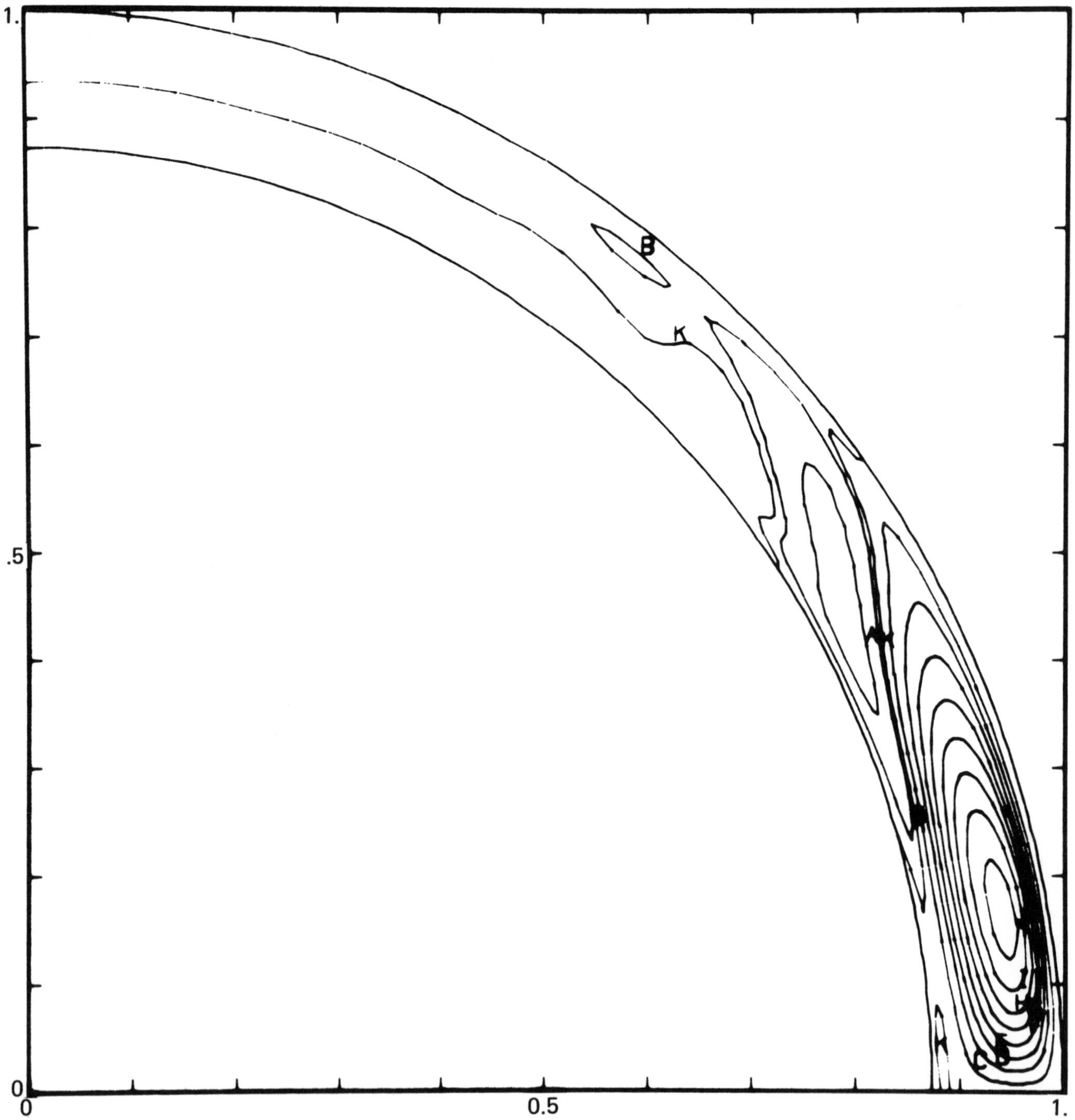

FIGURE 7 Stream function boundary forcing, with Ekman = 1/36,000, M = 30, N = 30, Rossby = 0.00, frequency = 0.64, and T = 74.07.

Stretched coordinates are especially useful for investigation of resonant modes in a sphere, where the interior geostrophic motion does not require much resolution. The results of these investigations will be published elsewhere.

The extension of the method to nonaxisymmetric flows on spheres is described elsewhere (Orszag, 1974). This new spectral method for spherical flow problems is promising for application to large-scale models of the atmospheric general circulation.

Spectral methods are especially well suited to the simple geometries of model problems now so popular for understanding geophysical fluid dynamics. Relative to finite-difference models, the spectral models offer the advantages of increased accuracy and efficiency, although suffering the disadvantage that initial coding of the problem may be much more involved (although new systematic techniques for transform methods greatly simplify the coding). A class of more complicated geometries can be handled by spectral methods using mapping techniques, although for extremely irregular boundaries finite-element methods offer many advantages over both spectral and finite-difference methods.

For some relatively simple geometries, mapping gives a very elegant formulation of spectral methods. Important examples are spherical caps and spherical annuli with limited zonal extent that are both amenable to simple Chebyshev expansion by the combination of a linear map with the map $z = \cos\theta$ (Israeli and Orszag, 1972).

The next several years will see the generation of a variety of new spectral models and methods appropriate for geophysical flow problems. However, it is not envisaged that any one of the three main numerical methods (spectral, finite-difference, or finite-element) will develop universal applicability or suitability. Rather, a sort of tripartite system of checks and balances is envisaged in which several schemes compete on a given problem to ensure that accurate and efficient simulations are achieved.

ACKNOWLEDGMENTS

Work supported in part by the Air Force Office of Scientific Research under Contract No. F 44620-67-C-0007 and by National Science Foundation Grants A38724X and GA38797.

REVIEW: E. E. SCHULMAN

With but few exceptions, all numerical models used in geophysical fluid dynamics have employed finite-difference techniques to solve the nonlinear partial differential equations of motion. Orszag, in his many papers on the subject, has contended that a more accurate and efficient method is to be found in Galerkin (spectral) approximation.

Historically, the main difficulty in employing spectral techniques is the considerable amount of arithmetic and computer storage necessary to calculate and retain the interaction coefficients for even a modest number of modes. The major problem is the efficient evaluation of these vector-coupled sums arising from the truncated harmonic representation. Without the transform methods developed by Orszag, Galerkin methods are several orders of magnitude more time- and space-consuming and quite useless for high wave number cutoff.

The method suggested by Orszag consists of expanding the flow fields in some suitably chosen basis functions—Fourier series within a box with periodic or free-slip boundaries, Chebyshev series within rigid boundaries, surface-harmonic expansions, or special Fourier series for spherical flow. Fast Fourier transforms and a finite form of the convolution theorem are used to evaluate the alias-free sums. It is much more efficient to transform, multiply, and then inversely transform than it is to compute the vector-coupled sums directly.

An alternative procedure is the use of "pseudospectral" approximations to evaluate the nonlinear forms. By pseudospectral we mean that calculations are done in either spectral or physical space, depending on whichever one is more natural. Thus, the contribution from the term uu_x is calculated by taking the product in physical space of u, with u_x evaluated by spectral methods. The latter contains no error in the phase speed, which is the principal error in finite-difference schemes.

With these new techniques, numerical simulation of many classes of flow becomes practicable. Galerkin methods are then superior to finite differences for the following reasons:

1. For the same number of independent degrees of freedom (Galerkin basis functions or space grid points), the Galerkin method, which is of infinite-order accuracy, yields more accurate results. (An approximation is said to be of infinite order if the error after N terms decreases more rapidly than any finite power of $1/N$.) If accurate simulations are required, Galerkin approximations offer the advantage of yielding infinite-order approximations to infinitely differentiable flows. When the *FFT* is employed, Galerkin procedures are at least as efficient as finite differences, involving the same number of degrees of freedom (for three-dimensional flow, Galerkin methods are an order of magnitude faster). Thus, to achieve the same accuracy, Galerkin approximations require less computer time.
2. For flows within three-dimensional simple boundaries, Galerkin methods require much less storage than finite differences for results of comparable accuracy.
3. The Galerkin equations preserve certain important

integral constraints, e.g., the total kinetic energy. A conserved quadratic integral of energy is necessary for stable long-term integration of the equations of motion by prohibiting unbounded nonlinear instabilities, which often arise with finite differences.

4. Galerkin methods allow full utilization for any symmetries and invariances of the flow to make the calculation even more efficient.

5. Boundary conditions are incorporated exactly, whereas finite differences at boundaries may lead to loss of accuracy (e.g., one-sided differences at boundaries) and perhaps instability.

6. The decomposition into modes is more convenient for certain flows (e.g., turbulence calculations).

However, even with the improved transform techniques, Galerkin techniques have several real disadvantages that render their usefulness to realistic ocean modeling questionable:

1. Transform methods restrict the applicability to simple flow geometries or regions that can be mapped to a simple geometry (slabs, cylinders, spheres). Thus modeling an oceanic circulation with variable topography and irregular continental boundaries is apparently beyond the practicable realm of these techniques.

2. Transform methods are restricted to simple forms of dynamical interactions. Thus, important features such as convective adjustment and implementation of nonlinear eddy viscosity are probably excluded.

3. Pseudospectral techniques are more promising for complicated interactions and geometries. However, they are fully aliased (i.e., wave numbers k, $k + N$, $k - N$ are all present when N is the cutoff wave number) and in general are unstable unless further care is taken (either rewriting the equations in a new form or introducing further arithmetic to reduce aliasing). Even if aliasing does not lead to instability, the errors introduced may be difficult to estimate.

4. Programing the Galerkin equations requires considerably more skill and effort. It is not always obvious how to incorporate certain of the invariances and symmetries. By contrast, finite differences lead to comparatively simpler coding, debugging, and interpretation.

Thus, the applicability of spectral methods to geophysical problems depends on appraising the above merits and deficiencies for each case. As things stand now, Galerkin methods are probably better for simple two-dimensional problems, superior for simple three-dimensional problems, and probably incapable or inferior when dealing with realistic ocean simulations.

REFERENCES

Baer, F., and G. W. Platzman. 1961. A procedure for numerical integration of the spectral vorticity equation. J. Meteorol. 18:393–401.

Batchelor, G. K. 1969. Computation of the energy spectrum in homogeneous two-dimensional turbulence. Phys. Fluid Suppl. II 12:233–39.

Bourke, W. P. 1972. An efficient one-level, primitive-equation spectral model. Mon. Weather Rev. 100:683–89.

Bray, R. W. 1966. Ph.D. Thesis. Cambridge University, England.

Dennis, S. C. R., and J. D. A. Walker. 1971. Calculation of the steady flow past a sphere at low and moderate Reynolds numbers. J. Fluid Mech. 48:771–89.

Eliasen, E., B. Machenhauer, and E. Rasmussen. 1970. On a numerical method for integration of the hydrodynamical equations with a spectral representation of the horizontal fields. Rep. No. 2, Københavns Universitet, Institut for Teoretisk Meteorologi.

Ellsaesser, H. W. 1966. Evaluation of spectral versus grid methods of hemispheric numerical weather prediction. J. Appl. Meteorol. 5:246–62.

Fox, D. G., and S. A. Orszag. 1973. Pseudospectral approximation to two-dimensional turbulence. J. Comp. Phys. 11:612–19.

George, W. D., and J. D. Hellums. 1972. Hydrodynamic stability in plane Poiseuille flow with finite-amplitude disturbances. J. Fluid Mech. 51:687–704.

Greenspan, H. P. 1969. On the inviscid theory of rotating fluids. Stud. Appl. Math. 48:19–28.

Hide, R., and K. Stewartson. 1972. Free hydromagnetic oscillation of the earth's core. Unpublished manuscript.

Høiland, E. 1962. Discussion of a hyperbolic equation relating to inertia and gravitational fluid oscillations. Geophys. Publ. 24: 211–27.

Israeli, M. 1970. A fast implicit numerical method for time dependent viscous flows. Stud. Appl. Math. 49:327–49.

Israeli, M. 1971. Time-dependent motions of confined rotating fluids. Ph.D. Thesis. MIT, Department of Mathematics, Cambridge, Mass. 182 pp.

Israeli, M. 1972. On trapped modes of rotating fluids in spherical shells. Stud. Appl. Math. 51:219–37.

Israeli, M., and S. A. Orszag. 1972. Numerical simulation of rotating fluids in spherical geometries. Unpublished manuscript.

Machenhauer, B., and E. Rasmussen. 1972. On the integration of the spectral hydrodynamical equations by a transform method. Rep. No. 3, Københavns Universitet, Institut for Teoretisk Meteorologi.

Meyer, K. A. 1969. Three-dimensional study of flow between concentric rotating cylinders. Phys. Fluids Suppl. II 12:165–70.

Munson, B. R., and D. D. Joseph. 1971. Viscous incompressible flow between concentric rotating spheres. Part I: Basic flow. J. Fluid Mech. 49:282–303.

Orszag, S. A. 1969. Numerical methods for simulation of turbulence. Phys. Fluids Suppl. II 12:250–57.

Orszag, S. A. 1970. Transform method for calculation of vector-coupled sums: Application to the spectral form of the vorticity equation. J. Atmos. Sci. 27:890–95.

Orszag, S. A. 1971a. Numerical simulation of incompressible flows within simple boundaries. I. Galerkin (spectral) representations. Stud. Appl. Math. 50:293–327.

Orszag, S. A. 1971b. Numerical simulation of incompressible flows

within simple boundaries: Accuracy. J. Fluid Mech. 49:75–112.
Orszag, S. A. 1971c. Galerkin approximations to flows within slabs, spheres and cylinders. Phys. Rev. Letters 26:1100–03.
Orszag, S. A. 1971d. Accurate solution of the Orr–Sommerfeld stability equation. J. Fluid Mech. 50:689–703.
Orszag, S. A. 1974. Fourier series on spheres. Mon. Weather Rev. 102:56–75.
Orszag, S. A., and G. S. Patterson, Jr. 1972. Numerical simulation of three-dimensional homogeneous isotropic turbulence. Phys. Rev. Letters 28:76–79.
Patterson, G. S., Jr., and S. A. Orszag. 1971. Spectral calculations of isotrophic turbulence: Efficient removal of aliasing interactions. Phys. Fluids 14:2538–41.
Platzman, G. W. 1960. The spectral form of the vorticity equation. J. Meteorol. 17:635–44.
Robert, A. 1966. The integration of a low-order spectral form of the primitive meteorological equations. J. Meteorol. Soc. Jap. 44:237–44.
Silberman, I. 1954. Planetary waves in the atmosphere. J. Meteorol. 11:27–34.
Veronis, G. 1966. Large-amplitude Benard convection. J. Fluid Mech. 26:49–68.

DISCUSSION

STEWART: I think that this Reynolds number effect is something that, if your numerical work is right, is going to work out that way. That's what happens in the physical situation, too. Observational evidence from wind-tunnel experiments and other sources indicates that, if you change the Reynolds number, the only thing that changes is the small-scale structure within the turbulent field. So, if you concoct some scheme other than viscosity for getting rid of the energy, which is, after all, all that the small scale is doing, you should end up all right.

ORSZAG: I think that involves a vote of confidence in what everybody does. The basic point I have to make is just that you have to get beyond a certain minimum resolution to reach the turbulent state. Turbulence is basically a very stable statistical state, but you have to get enough resolution to attain such a state.

BRETHERTON: There are many practical reasons why you can't go to the resolution that you really need to achieve that. Would you care to comment on the merits of using a nonlinear eddy viscosity?

ORSZAG: Okay, but not now; next year.

BRETHERTON: You are presumably doing experiments to verify this.

ORSZAG: We're doing experiments to try to decide what kind of nonlinear eddy viscosities should be used to simulate the problem. What we've done here is to prove this of molecular viscosities.

BRETHERTON: The fact that we can get the answer is a very good control on all the others. But we would like to calibrate the others.

ORSZAG: The only advantage of the nonlinear viscosity is that you can perhaps obtain this Reynolds number independence at an earlier stage.

BRETHERTON: Exactly.

VERONIS: There's a point that really puzzles me. We tend intuitively to think in terms of spectral methods. So many things are expressed in trigonometric expressions. Even in numerical analysis, when the accuracy of problems and aliasing are explored, much of our thinking is tied to spectral methods. I've used them successfully in some problems but not others—for example, successfully in a convection problem but not in an oceanic problem. They worked beautifully in the first case, because they happened to be the eigenfunctions in the linear problem. Spectral thinking seems to automatically guide much critical evaluation. Consider the simple example discussed earlier today. It was mentioned that we need 64 points to describe a wave. Assume now that one is trying to describe a sine wave, which has a sharp peak, and then a slow decay. Very many sine waves would be necessary. A finite-difference scheme is appropriate, because you probably still only need 64 points. You might need 64 Fourier components to describe the same kind of behavior for that kind of a function.

ORSZAG: Okay. First of all, Fourier series should not be used in problems of oceanic interest, except for periodic boundary conditions or free-slip boundaries. There are better representations to give a fast rate of convergence that can be efficiently implemented.

VERONIS: The case that I did was a case in which those criteria are satisfied.

ORSZAG: We have done some very careful tests of localized phenomena using spectral methods where you had something occurring in only a very small region of space. One example occurred from the movie on Tuesday night. We had a cone sitting outside the region. You see whether or not a Fourier series representation can resolve this flow. It worked rather well. We did some very careful analyses of one-dimensional problems where we have localized phenomena going on—and the spectral method works much better than the finite-difference schemes do and you still gain a factor of two or three in resolution over the best finite-difference schemes. I have not yet found an example where it does not work better.

CHARNEY: George (Veronis), you tried to model the wind-driven ocean circulation with how many Fourier components including the Gulf Stream? Come on now.

VERONIS: Well, Okay. Look, I admit, but after all, it wasn't a very good calculation. The only thing I can do is take refuge in saying I was pioneering.

ORSZAG: Let me make one more point. There's a mathematical question as to whether or not one should use eigenfunctions in general problems, and the answer is no, as far as I can see. There are very few problems where eigenfunction expressions are appropriate to get the best solution to the problem, and you were implying before that one could use functions that were more relevant. The answer is, if you can find the eigenfunctions to the exact operator, yes. Do it, of course, because it is the exact answer. But, for example, in the case of solving the Orr-Sommerfeld equation; it's been suggested to expand in terms Bessel functions. Chebyshev polynomials work many times better and give you the accurate result.

FUTURE COMPUTING MACHINE CONFIGURATIONS AND NUMERICAL MODELS

C. E. LEITH

INTRODUCTION

Most of the experience in numerical simulation of geophysical fluid flows has been with atmospheric models. Although the fundamental equations describing the circulation of the ocean are the same as for the atmosphere, there are special difficulties with ocean modeling. These arise, in part, from a wider range of important time scales, from the existence of lateral boundaries, and from a lack of adequate observations. In this paper, however, it is assumed that the evolution of oceanic models will follow the same general course as has that of atmospheric models.

After examining those common properties of models that are relevant to computer design, we shall discuss how such properties fit the characteristics of present conventional computers, as well as those of two future designs. Finally, some information on a present, large, atmospheric model may help us in extrapolating into the future.

MODEL CHARACTERISTICS

We are principally interested in the kind of calculation involved in the simulation of a geophysical fluid flow by means of a numerical model. Common examples are atmospheric and oceanic general circulation models, atmospheric boundary layer models, and models of mountain waves and clouds. Although many different numerical techniques have been used in the construction of such models, they all have certain common characteristics of importance to computer design. We shall list six of these.

1. The state of the physical system is specified at a given model time by the numerical values of a large but finite number, P, of prognostic variables. The number P is a fundamental measure of the size of a model. It is the number of values that must be specified in order to start a calculation or that must be saved if a calculation is to be interrupted and restarted. We may think of P as the dimensionality of the model phase space; the state of the model is represented at a given model time by a P-component position vector.

In certain leapfrog, time integration, numerical schemes, the prognostic model variables at a given model time correspond to physical variables defined at two consecutive real time steps. It is important to remember that P in this case is twice the number of physical variables involved.

2. The evolution of time, t, in the physical system is modeled by a sequence of calculational time cycles. A fundamental cycle is one in which each of the P prognostic variables is advanced to a value appropriate to a time later by a time step Δt. We often use numerical schemes in which the fundamental cycle is divided into subcycles in each of which a partial advancement of the P variables is carried out.

3. The execution of a fundamental cycle will require a large number, N_A, of arithmetic operations. The number N_A is a measure of the computing power required. The ratio $n_A = N_A/P$ serves as a measure of the arithmetic complexity of a model. It can be of order 10 for highly simplified models but is typically of order 100 for realistic general circulation models. The parameter n_A is important in deciding on the proper balance between the speed of execution of arithmetic operations and the speed of access to the memory holding the P prognostic variables.

4. The value of a particular prognostic variable at the

end of a fundamental cycle will depend on the values of at least some of the prognostic variables at the beginning of the cycle. Each prognostic variable thus has for a single cycle a domain of dependence consisting of a number P_D of earlier values. The domain may be the whole phase space, $P_D = P$, or in many calculations considerably less than the whole space. Of course, different variables may have different domain sizes P_D. Subcycles, too, will determine domains of dependence that are generally smaller than for the fundamental cycle.

5. In the course of a fundamental cycle, a number of diagnostic variables will be computed. These temporary variables all contribute to the efficient completion of the cycle. They may vary in effective lifetime from that of a partial result needed only until the next arithmetic operation to that of a physical quantity, such as vertical velocity, used in many different parts of the cycle. Although the total number of diagnostic variables as defined here is of order $N_A = n_A P \gg P$, the maximum number needed at any point in the fundamental cycle is usually a small fraction of P.

6. A calculational cycle may be decomposed into independent tasks with the execution of each not depending on the results of any others. The important characteristic of such a decomposition is that these independent tasks may be performed in any time sequence whatever during the calculational cycle without changing the final result. An example of such a task could be the advancing by a single time step of a prognostic variable, such as the temperature, defined at a single mesh point.

After decomposing the calculational cycle into independent tasks, we may group them together again in stages with each stage consisting of tasks that are identical in the arithmetic sequence or algorithm followed and differing only in the values of the operands involved. An example of a stage could be the advancing of a field of temperatures defined on all points of a mesh away from boundaries. Different stages in a calculation may have one, few, or many tasks. An important measure of parallelism in a model is the total number of tasks divided by the total number of stages, i.e., the average number, n, of tasks per stage.

In the numerical simulation of a particular physical system, there are many possible choices in the numerical model to be used; and these may differ considerably in the six characteristics listed. The doubling of P with leapfrog time-differencing schemes has already been mentioned. Models may differ in assigning to physical variables a prognostic or diagnostic role. Explicit or marching finite-difference schemes will involve small domains of dependence and much parallelism, whereas implicit or jury schemes will have $P_D = P$ and less obvious parallelism. Testing of variable values to decide on alternate algorithms also decreases the degree of parallelism. But these six listed characteristics decide to a large extent the effectiveness of a particular computer configuration in carrying out a numerical simulation.

CONVENTIONAL COMPUTERS

A conventional computer consists (in a highly simplified description) of three components as shown in Figure 1. The memory (M) holds values of prognostic and diagnostic variables as floating point numbers. The memory also holds the set of instructions that defines the numerical model. The arithmetic unit (AU) carries out arithmetic operations on operands supplied from the memory with results returned to the memory, a two-way flow of floating point numbers that is indicated by the solid lines in Figure 1. The control of this process is vested in the control unit (CU), which fetches instructions from the memory as indicated by the dotted line in Figure 1. The CU decodes an instruction to determine which operands are involved, fetches the proper operands from the memory to the AU, determines the operation to be performed by the AU, and stores the result back from the AU to the memory. The CU is also able to choose between alternate algorithms depending on the outcome of numerical comparisons that have been carried out in the AU.

A computer memory is designed to hold computer words, that is, units of information that may contain either a floating point number or instructions. The memory is usually divided into a hierarchy of levels of increasing word capacity and word access time but decreasing cost per word. For our purposes, the level in which the prognostic variables are stored must have a capacity of at least P words. The number of instruction words defining a model is usually much less than P, but room for them must also be found at some level. In order to complete a fundamental cycle, we need at least P fetches and P stores. If the average access time at the P-storage level is τ_M, then the total memory-accessing time in a cycle is $T_M = 2P\tau_M$.

The arithmetic unit (AU) carries out floating point operations of addition, subtraction, multiplication, and division. These generally take different execution times. We can, however, define an average arithmetic operation time τ_A

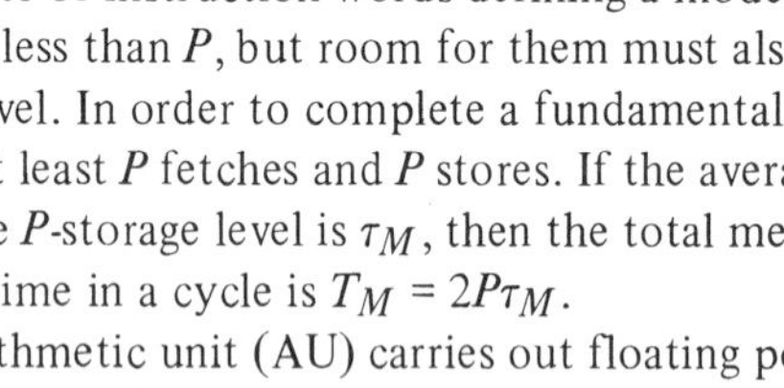

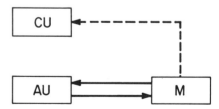

FIGURE 1 Block diagram for a conventional computer. *CU* is the control unit; *AU*, the arithmetic unit; and *M*, the memory. Solid lines indicate the flow of operands; the dashed line, the flow of instructions.

such that the total time required for arithmetic in a fundamental cycle is $T_A = N_A \tau_A = Pn_A \tau_A$. The time τ_A is usually about five hardware clock cycles.

Memory access and arithmetic operations are usually executed concurrently in present computer designs, and the total fundamental cycle time is $\Delta T = \max(T_A, T_M)$. For optimum utilization of computer hardware, we want $T_A = T_M$, thus the ratio of arithmetic and memory times should be $\tau_A/\tau_M = 2P/N_A = 2/n_A$ and depends, as mentioned earlier, on the arithmetic complexity n_A of the model.

Another parameter of interest is the ratio $\rho = \Delta t/\Delta T$ of simulated real time to computer time. A typical value of ρ for an atmospheric general circulation model is 24, so that one atmosphere day may be simulated in one hour of computation. Numerical weather prediction obviously requires models with $\rho \gg 1$; general circulation studies become tedious at values of $\rho \approx 1$.

During the past two decades, many computers have been built that more or less fit our simplified description of a conventional computer. Table 1 lists a collection of these, each of which has represented in its time one of the fastest computers available for scientific computation. The listed addition times and memory level access times give rough estimates of the times τ_A and τ_M. Both have been getting dramatically shorter, τ_A perhaps more rapidly than τ_M. But there is some possibility that this historical rate of speed increase must now slow down, since the inherent limitation on the speed of propagation of electromagnetic signals, namely, 30 cm/ns, is beginning to be felt in computers with hardware cycle times of 30 ns (1 ns = 1 nanosecond = 10^{-9} s).

A way of evading this inherent limitation imposed by the finite speed of light is to use concurrency in both memory access and arithmetic operations. This has already been done to some extent in recent conventional computers, but is being pushed much further in two new designs referred to as, respectively, parallel and pipeline computers. These designs make essential use of the parallelism found in a model; but, in so doing, they constrain the kind of model that can use them efficiently.

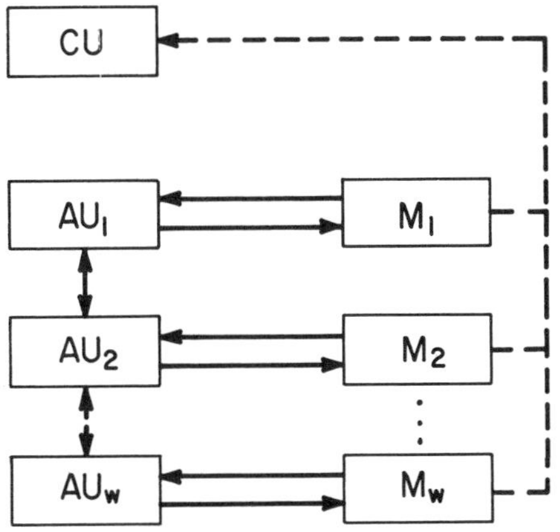

FIGURE 2 Block diagram for a parallel computer. *CU* is the control unit; AU_i, the i-th arithmetic unit; M_i, the i-th memory; and *W*, the width. Solid lines represent the flow of operands; dashed lines, the flow of instructions.

PARALLEL COMPUTERS

A parallel computer differs from a conventional computer in that the arithmetic unit (AU) and memory (M) are replicated many times, as shown in Figure 2. The number of copies, *W*, is called the width. The primary example of a parallel computer is the one-quadrant Illiac IV (Barnes *et al.*, 1968; McIntyre, 1970), which has a width $W = 64$. Each AU carries out arithmetic operations on operands supplied from its own memory, to which it then returns results. There is a single CU acting on a sequence of instructions that is

TABLE 1 Conventional Computer Characteristics

Computer	First Delivered (mo/yr)	Add Time (μs)	Memory Cycle Time (μs)	Memory Capacity (words)
Univac I	3/51	282	242	1000
IBM 704	12/55	24	12	32K
Univac LARC	5/60	4	4	30000
IBM Stretch	5/61	1.5	2.2	96K
CDC 6600	9/64	0.3	1.0	128K
IBM 360/90	2/67	0.18	0.75	512K
CDC 7600	1/69	0.0275	0.275	64K
			1.760	512K
IBM 360/195	2/71	0.054	0.054	32K
			0.810	256K
			8	16M

Note: In recent computers some concurrence has been used to decrease both add time and memory cycle time. $K = 1024 = 2^{10}$, $M = 1048576 = 2^{20}$. Data from Charles W. Adams Associates (1967) and Keydata Corporation (1971).

distributed through all the memories. After the CU fetches an instruction from a memory, it determines the local memory addresses of operands, simultaneously fetches proper operands from each memory to the corresponding AU, determines the operation to be performed simultaneously by all AU's, and simultaneously stores results from each AU back to the corresponding memory. On a given calculational step, each AU must generally carry out the same arithmetic operation that all others do. The exception is that, depending on the results of a local test, an AU may do nothing.

At times an AU may need an operand from another memory. This need is satisfied indirectly by a transfer of operands between memories using a process called routing. In a routing cycle operands are fetched to the AU's, moved to AU's that are neighboring in a one or two dimensionally cyclic sense, and stored in their new memories. In this way W operands are simultaneously shifted into neighboring memories. By one or more of such routing steps, any operand can be moved into any memory.

It is obvious that if all AU's can be kept usefully busy then a calculation can proceed W times faster than can one using the same AU in a conventional design. Keeping AU's busy requires that the fundamental calculational cycle be decomposed into stages consisting of W-independent identical tasks. In general, if we can divide a total of t tasks into s' stages, each of which contains at most W tasks, then $n' = t/s'$ is the parallelism of the calculation and n'/W is the efficiency with which it can be carried out.

A parallel computer provides a considerable saving in cost when compared to a collection of W conventional computers that together would have the same computing power and greater flexibility. Although there is no saving in the cost of AU's, there is an obvious saving in the shared CU. A less obvious saving is in the smaller individual memories. The Illiac IV individual memories have a capacity of 2,048 words. This capacity would be woefully inadequate in a conventional computer, but is sufficient for local memory and provides a total memory of $64 \times 2K = 128K$ words. (In binary computers, $K = 1{,}024 = 2^{10}$). There is also a considerable saving from sharing the peripheral equipment that accounts for a major part of the total cost of a computing system.

PIPELINE COMPUTERS

A pipeline computer, such as the CDC STAR or the TI ASC, being built by the Control Data Corporation and the Texas Instruments Corporation, respectively, achieves a speed comparable to that of a parallel computer but in a quite different way (see Graham, 1970). A pipeline computer has, as is shown in Figure 3, a single AU and a single memory. An arithmetic operation is broken down into a sequence of elementary steps, each carried out in an independent part of the AU. An operation with a new pair of operands can start in each hardware clock cycle, but it takes many such cycles for the operation to be completed and the result to be available. In order to provide a stream of operands rapidly enough to feed the AU, the memory is divided into many independent banks out of which operands are fetched and back to which results are stored sequentially.

As with a conventional computer, a separate sequence of instructions flows from the memory to the CU; but now an instruction may initiate a vector arithmetic operation in which the same operation is carried out repetitively using operands from two linear arrays and producing a linear array of results. An imaginary pipeline runs from the memory through the AU and back to the memory. The time to feed new operands into the pipeline is much shorter than the total transit time; and, if the pipeline can be kept full, the calculation can proceed many times faster than in a conventional computer.

Although the organization of a pipeline computer is quite different from that of a parallel computer, they are quite similar in their demands on program parallelism. Since a vector operation cannot use an early result in a later step, it is logically equivalent to the simultaneous execution of all steps. There is no limitation on the number, m, of operations in a vector operation. The time, τ_m, needed to complete a vector operation of length m is given by $\tau_m = (m_o + m)\tau_A$, where τ_A is the individual step time and m_o is the number of overhead steps required to start and to stop a vector operation. Consider a fundamental calculational cycle characterized by a total of t tasks divided into s stages with, therefore, a program parallelism of $n = t/s$. For such a program, the efficiency of task execution is $t/(m_o s + t) = n/(m_o + n)$. The number m_o, which seems to be about 50 for the CDC STAR and the TI ASC, serves as a measure of computer parallelism similar to the number W for parallel computers. In order to achieve an efficiency greater than ½, we must have $n > m_o$ in a pipeline computer and $n' > W/2$ in a parallel computer. It is to be hoped that some overlapping of overhead cycles with execution cycles can be achieved; but, in any case, efficiency of execution will be seriously degraded for calculations with $n \ll m_o$.

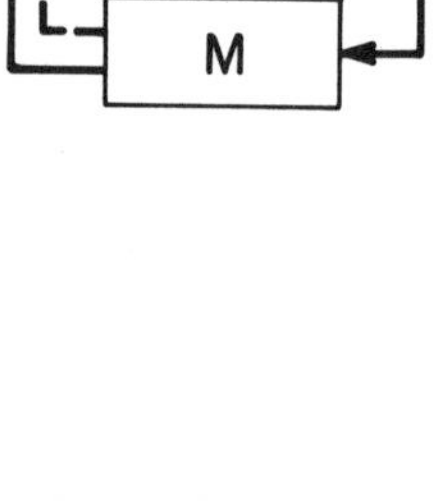

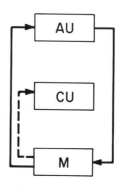

FIGURE 3 Block diagram for a pipeline computer. *CU* is the control unit; *AU*, the arithmetic unit; and *M*, the memory. Solid lines are the flow of operands and dashed lines, the flow of instructions.

Studies of present general circulation models designed for conventional computers indicate a natural degree of parallelism of about 10 to 20. Some reprograming effort will be required in order to increase this number for either parallel or pipeline computers. As mesh resolution increases, so also will program parallelism. There seems, therefore, to be little doubt of the value of these new computer designs for the present kind of geophysical fluid-flow models.

FUTURE NUMERICAL MODELS

In recent years the principal change in atmospheric models leading to larger values of P and the need for greater computing power has been the increase in resolution. Present models seem to have the proper balance of vertical and horizontal resolution. A two-fold increase in linear resolution leads, therefore, to an eight-fold increase in P, and, for usual explicit marching schemes, a two-fold decrease in Δt. This fourth-power dependence of needed computing power on resolution easily generates models that can exhaust the capacity and power of any computing machine built. But serious questions must then be asked about the value of increased resolution. The NCAR 6-level, 2½° model—with $P \approx 250{,}000$; $\Delta t = 3$ min; and a time ratio $\rho = 15$ on the CDC 7600—seems already to have sufficient resolution to describe the general circulation as defined by mean values, variances, and covariances of atmospheric variables. For detailed forecasting purposes, however, predictability studies suggest that each two-fold increase in the resolution of an observing system and numerical model adds at least a day to useful prediction times.

Of primary importance for oceanic models is the modeling of the general circulation. This task seems to be far more difficult than it is for the atmosphere, owing to the much greater range of time scales of important motions. The use of implicit schemes to deal with this time scale problem will lead to difficulties in using the new computers. The determination of adequate spatial resolution should be resolved for the ocean as for the atmosphere on the basis of the wave number distribution of kinetic energy. It is to be hoped that the basis for making such a determination will be strengthened by presently planned observations. Of course, observations that are even more detailed are needed to provide initial conditions for a forecasting model. Yet, in the possibility of an ocean circulation forecast may lie our best hope for predicting long-term changes in the climate.

REVIEW: R. T. WERT

This paper serves as an excellent introduction to the subject of parameterizing numerical model computer requirements and evaluating computer processor power. The author then uses these parameters to discuss two new types of computers that are currently under development. The paper then concludes with a brief glimpse of the future of oceanographic numerical models.

In Table 1 conventional computer characteristics are outlined for the major computers that have been used for large numerical models. I feel that some areas of this table would tend to mislead readers who are not familiar with computers. These areas are:

1. The add time shown in column three represents integer addition and not floating point arithmetic, which is the mode that is referenced many times in this paper and is normally used in numerical modeling. Consequently, these add times are shorter than those generally found in the numerical modeling process. This difference would be between a factor of two and ten, depending upon the machine in question.

2. Memory word capacity is listed in column five; however, the word size for the various machines is considerably different. In the case of the IBM 360 machines, word size is variable within the machine itself. Without some indication as to what the definition of a memory word is, the comparison of memory size is fairly meaningless. I cite, for example, the last two computers listed. In the CDC 7600, the memory word size is 60 bits in length; however, in the IBM 360/195, the memory word may refer to a unit as small as 8 bits and as many as 64 bits, depending on the mode of operation. Specifically speaking, the 32K memory, which operates in 54 ns, refers to 8 bit bytes and in the normal operation it would take 4 of these bytes to make the smallest floating point number used in the machine. Therefore, the size of this high-speed memory is really 8K, 32-bit words. IBM also states that the main memory cycle time is 756 ns, with a maximum size of about 4 million 8-bit bytes or just over 1 million 32-bit words. However, the 8 μs large-core storage unit is not available from IBM as a standard option.

3. I am unable to identify the IBM 360/90 as an existing machine. My references do not show it; however, it is quite possible that it has only been in limited production and is not listed in my source.

Although the title of the paper does not include the following subject, I feel it is one that might have been touched on—that is, the future direction of computer memory systems. Although I cannot quote any published sources, various main frame manufacturers agree that memory sizes in the future will become larger and larger with much more rapid access in the main memory. This is totally consistent with the trend in computer memories, and one would expect to see in the future main computer memories with sizes of multiple millions of words with access on the order of 100 nanoseconds. This would be a tremendous benefit to numerical modelers, since every numerical modeler I have talked to has fought the problem of limited core storage within the main frame of the computer. With these larger, faster computer memories, one would anticipate some increase in execution speed, since swapping of high-speed memory with other memories would not be necessary. It would also speed up model developments, since a considerable portion of the programing time is spent in adapting the model to fit the computer memory.

The author talks about possibly reaching a barrier in hardware speed due to the inherent limitations of the speed of propagation of electromagnetic signals. I am not about to predict that we would find some way of circumventing this limitation; however, if one looks at the increase in speed of computers over the past 8 years, one would see a change of speed on the order of a factor of 10; and I certainly would not bet that by 1980 computer speeds would not be on the order of 10 faster than current machines. I feel this is certainly true in light of the techniques of miniaturization and large-scale integration that are currently being used in computers.

REFERENCES

Barnes, G., R. Brown, M. Kato, D. Kuck, D. Slotnick, and R. Stokes. 1968. The Illiac IV Computer. IEEE Trans. Comput. C-17(8): 746–57.

Charles W. Adams Associates, Inc. 1967. Computer characteristics table. *In* Melvin Klerer and Granino Korn, eds. Digital Computer User's Handbook. McGraw–Hill, New York.

Graham, William R. 1970. The parallel and pipeline computers. Datamation 16(4):68–71.

Keydata Corporation. 1971. Characteristics of digital computers. Comp. Autom. 20(6B):24.

McIntyre, David E. 1970. An introduction to the Illiac IV computer. Datamation 16(4):60–67.

DISCUSSION

PHILLIPS: In view of the greater logical complexity, one is perhaps forced to rely even more on assembly languages. It seems both tedious and dangerous to do this programming on your own. I'm not too familiar with it, but I have the impression that there's not a great deal of satisfaction with the efficiency of FORTRAN IV at the present time. Can one count on software becoming more efficient as the machines become more efficient?

LEITH: I can tell you a little about what I think is the recent history of this. Consider the ILLIAC IV. People recognize that this is a complicated configuration, hard to use. For some years in Illinois much effort has gone into the design of new languages that permit efficient use of this parallel configuration. The effort has not been particularly successful. The last I heard the users of ILLIAC IV are in fact reverting to a more primitive language which is not counted on to solve questions of computer architecture. The scientific programer himself has to keep track of what's going on to use the computer efficiently. Until these more complicated software problems are resolved, a higher price in loss of efficiency will occur when the machine structure is ignored. The user must know that there are 64 processers there, and it must not be hidden by some higher-level language. This obviously puts more burden on the satisfactory use of the machine. The abstract solution to this problem has apparently not yet been found, and evidently it will not be easy to find it. As for the STAR, most of the programing effort that has gone into writing STAR programs so far has been essentially in assembly language rather than in a compiler language; although things look a little easier there, because it's possible to add the vector array statement fairly easily to the FORTRAN language. After all, it just looks like an inner DO loop. There are extensions of the FORTRAN language being experimented with at NCAR using the 7600, showing certain advantages in going into vector mode when possible. This will give people some experience in programing with available vector arithmetic statements.

PHILLIPS: How is GFDL preparing for the Texas Instruments machine with these pipeline operations?

BRYAN: The problem is mainly at boundaries in the ocean—we're reformulating our programs. We advance variables inside and outside of the boundaries—it turns out that it is just more efficient to do it that way in the machines.

LEITH: The recognition of that fact is built into the languages of both parallel processer and pipeline machines in that in the parallel processers you can ask the parallel processer not to do anything. The only thing it can do differently than the other processer is not do anything at all. Also, something like that is true of the pipeline machines, because one can put a bit pattern through with 1's and 0's in it, which say whether any operation should be carried out or not.

ROBINSON: How might we match these advanced techniques that we've heard about today to the new machines?

LEITH: The most obvious technique designed for parallel processers is a simple, marching, finite-difference technique. Almost any move away from that is complicating life so far as parallel processers are concerned. In addition, I know that there have been efforts to get algorithms for fast Fourier transforms working on all of these new parallel processing machines. Otherwise, it would be very hard to sell them. So certain kinds of spectral operations are going to be available. But as one gets too many of the things I've heard this morning, bearing in mind the nature of the new architecture, there are going to be a lot of programing problems associated with the parallel processers.

ISRAELI: Isn't the solution to this problem the designing of black boxes for many problems that occur, such as the Poisson equation and matrix multiplications?

LEITH: Yes, and this is presumably the direction things will take, the designing of operator boxes. This will be obviously more useful to numerical analysts who are testing numerical schemes than to physical scientists because the analysts set up simple problems for which such things work well. It will not be as useful for real geophysical flows, where one has all the awkwardness of irregular boundaries and nonlinear processes.

ORSZAG: You've already answered two of my questions, but the last one is the following. For finite-difference schemes in multidimensions, one has to have an efficient way to transpose matrices, i.e., juggling things in memory. Are there techniques for that?

LEITH: For the ILLIAC IV configuration, I know that this has been considered and probably for the others too. Recall my remark about storing in a skewed fashion. In the ILLIAC IV, everything is being done out of sequential memory locations. In the ILLIAC IV, it's possible to set things up so that you can carry out these matrix operations efficiently. There is a new problem—I don't know whether it's been resolved on the pipeline machines—if the matrix elements have been laid out in a given order in the memory of the pipeline machine and you wish to retrieve them in a different order, such as by rows rather than by columns, then you run into trouble. You have the possibility of picking up each element not sequentially but with a fixed large gap; you have no less of a problem unless you have some switching technique. I don't know the extent to which this has been resolved so far as the pipeline machines go.

WELANDER: Say you want to do a parameter study, such as running the same problem with various sets of parameters on these 64 sets of parallel processers. Can you run the same problem simultaneously with different parameter combinations?

LEITH: Yes, one of the easiest ways to get independent tasks is to have an ensemble, if you happen to be interested in ensemble parameter studies.

WELANDER: How is this different than having 64 computers?

LEITH: That's an interesting question. You would obviously be much more flexible by having 64 arithmetic units. Obviously there's a savings here. You only need one, although I think that the extra cost of adding its own control unit to each one of the arithmetic units would add. Floating-point arithmetic does cost, and decoding instructions is not that much more expensive, so it probably doubles the cost. Perhaps the biggest savings, which is not so evident, is that these memories are really quite a bit smaller than the kind of memory that people are accustomed to using, at least for a computer that's standing alone. After all, the total 64 of these represents the memory within which you have to keep the problem variables. So there is a considerable savings in cost. In the conventional machine, which only has one memory, you are really using that memory very inefficiently, because you're only using one memory location at a time and all the rest are idle. In the parallel processer, you are simultaneously using 64 memory locations, but the total memory is about the same.

NIILER: I have a practical question to which there are two parts. Actually, what machines have been ordered and, as I am from Nova University, is anyone seriously thinking of putting remote access onto these big machines, so that people from all over can call up an ocean circulation model? I'd really like that if it were possible.

LEITH: Let me first answer the question about what machines there really are and what state they're really in. The ILLIAC IV has been installed at a laboratory in California; and, as I understand, its power is on and they're trying to get it to run properly. The ILLIAC IV, which has 64 processers, is going to be terminable. In fact, it will be an important part of the ARPA net, which does make at least a number of centers available around the country. There will also be associated with the ILLIAC IV something like a trillion bits of storage, so that one can store and will only have to communicate the information necessary to initiate a calculation. That's the ILLIAC IV. The STAR computer was supposed to be delivered last summer, but the last I heard it is going to be next summer before it is delivered to the Livermore Laboratory. There will not be any external access to the computer because of the work that is done there. There is, however, a STAR that I think is being built for General Motors. I'm not quite sure what it is. If the STAR computer is used in the worst possible mode, it turns out about as fast as the 7600. If it's used in the best possible mode, it'll be 15 or 20 times faster. It turns out it doesn't cost that much more than a 7600. So they say, "Why buy a 7600? We'll just buy a STAR!" That's clever, but you figure out how to use it.

MUNK: How much more does it cost?

LEITH: I think about 50 percent more or somewhere in that range. The first one or two of the Texas Instrument machines are being built for the company itself, to be used in connection with their service bureau. One of the first to go outside the company is the one going to GFDL. I believe that's due to be installed in the middle of next summer. Isn't that right, Kirk?

BRYAN: Yes.

VII APPLICATION TO LABORATORY EXPERIMENTS

A NUMERICAL INVESTIGATION OF A LABORATORY ANALOGY OF THE WIND-DRIVEN OCEAN CIRCULATION

R. C. BEARDSLEY

INTRODUCTION

In the past two and one-half decades, since the pioneering work of Sverdrup (1947), who pointed out the interior vorticity balance between the advection of planetary vorticity and the curl of the surface wind stress, and Stommel (1948), who discovered the theoretical basis for western intensification of boundary currents, the wind-driven ocean circulation problem has been studied widely. From their work, a hierarchy of more sophisticated and realistic models have evolved, with recent interest focusing on the more complicated transient circulations generated by low-frequency, time-dependent wind stresses. A number of different laboratory models have concurrently been developed to isolate and illustrate the more important features of the wind-driven ocean circulations (see Greenspan, 1968).

We will concentrate on a single laboratory model introduced by Pedlosky and Greenspan (1967). This model, called the "sliced-cylinder" model, consists of a rapidly rotating cylindrical basin with a planar sloping bottom filled with a viscous homogeneous fluid (see Figure 1). The surface wind stress is simulated by a viscous stress caused by the slow rotation of the flat upper lid relative to the rest of the basin. Except in thin Ekman and Stewartson boundary layers on the solid surfaces of the basin, the horizontal velocity field is constrained by the rapid rotation of the basin to be independent of depth along the rotation axis (a consequence of the Taylor–Proudman theorem). The sliced-cylinder model effectively simulates planetary flows, since vortex stretching in the interior and western boundary current by flow across the sloping bottom is directly analogous to the creation of relative vorticity in large-scale oceanic flows by the northward increase in horizontal Coriolis acceleration (the β-effect).

The response of the sliced-cylinder model to a steady wind stress depends critically on the ratio of the total depth variation to the Ekman layer thickness (see Beardsley, 1969). The key external nondimensional parameters governing the flow in the laboratory model are: (a) the Ekman number, $E = \nu/\Omega L^2$, where ν is the kinematic viscosity of the fluid, Ω is the angular velocity of the basin, and L is the average depth; (b) the Rossby number, ϵ, which is the relative angular velocity of the driving lid scaled by Ω; and (c) the bottom slope, $\tan\alpha$ (see Figure 1). The aspect ratio ro/L is assumed to be unity to correspond to the laboratory experiments. When the applied stress is small ($\epsilon \lesssim E^{1/2}$) and the total depth variation less than the thickness of the Ekman layer, i.e., $\tan\alpha \ll E^{1/2} \ll 1$, the interior flow does not feel the topography and remains essentially axisymmetric. When the bottom slope slightly exceeds the scaled Ekman layer thickness, $E^{1/2} \ll \tan\alpha \ll E^{1/4}$, the interior flow exhibits a broad western boundary current in which the orographic vortex stretching is balanced by Ekman layer suction. The interior dynamics are identical in this parameter range with Stommel's (1948) model for two-dimensional, β-plane flow with bottom friction. For larger bottom slopes in the range $E^{1/4} \ll \tan\alpha \ll 1$, the stronger orographic vortex stretching in the western boundary current becomes primarily balanced by the lateral diffusion of vorticity; and thus the dynamics in the interior and western boundary layer become identical to lowest order to Munk's (1950) β-plane model with lateral friction.

A detailed experimental investigation of the sliced-cylinder model has been conducted in the Munk regime (i.e.,

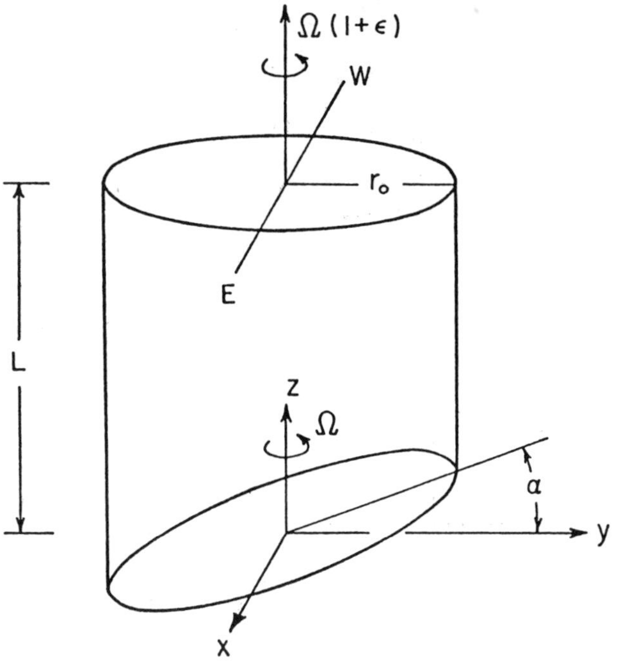

FIGURE 1 Geometry of sliced-cylinder laboratory model.

$E^{1/4} \ll \tan\alpha \ll 1$) and the results reported in Beardsley (1969). Although many features of the linear analysis were confirmed by these experiments, many questions remained concerning the nonlinear behavior of the model to large steady wind stresses. As the applied stress is increased, the flow first exhibits downstream intensification in the western boundary current because of the increased importance of inertia in the local momentum balance in the boundary layer. Separation of the western boundary current occurs at greater stresses and ultimately the observed laboratory flow becomes unstable when the Ekman layer Reynolds number exceeds a critical value. Although the key external parameters governing the onset of this low-frequency instability have been determined, the dynamical cause has not yet been explained.

A first attempt has been made (Beardsley, 1972) to study the nonlinear behavior of the sliced-cylinder laboratory model using a two-dimensional numerical model. Initially, the vorticity equation for two-dimensional flow on a β-plane, with lateral friction but no bottom friction, was considered. This vorticity equation does approximate the correct lowest-order asymptotic balances in the interior and western boundary layer of the sliced-cylinder model and has been previously studied numerically (Bryan, 1963). Bryan's numerical approach was employed with two modifications; the basin is now circular in shape, and a polar grid net with a nonuniform distribution of grid points in the radial direction has been used to increase computational speed and improve the spatial resolution of the boundary layer phenomena.

Although this numerical model did exhibit separation of the western boundary layer with increasing wind stress, the model generally failed to closely simulate the observed flow in the laboratory model. The principal reason for this failure is the omission of direct Ekman layer suction in the governing vorticity equation. Analysis shows that in the interior, where the Sverdrup balance applies, and in the high-velocity core of the western boundary layer, where the Munk-type balance holds, direct Ekman layer suction does not play an important dynamical role. On the other hand, direct Ekman layer suction is quite important in the vorticity balance in the transition regions between the interior and inner core of the western boundary layer. Omission of direct Ekman layer suction also implies that the system approaches steady state not on the Ekman layer spin-up time scale but on the much longer horizontal diffusive scale. This fact, coupled with the von Neumann stability constraint on the explicit scheme, caused the original numerical model to converge very slowly.

Recently, a second numerical model for the sliced-cylinder experiment has been developed that incorporates direct Ekman layer suction in the governing vorticity equation. Again, a polar grid net with nonuniform radial spacing is used, but a fast efficient numerical scheme has been developed using Israeli's (1970) implicit technique. This second numerical scheme has been used to study the response of the sliced-cylinder model to both steady and oscillatory forcing. Here are the results for a steady forcing. A brief derivation of the governing vorticity equation and the numerical model will be given in the next section. In the final section, a detailed comparison of the numerical and laboratory experiments will be presented.

DERIVATION OF NUMERICAL MODEL

A two-dimensional vorticity equation has recently been derived for the sliced-cylinder model in a consistent manner by Greenspan (1969). This derivation is based on a perturbation expansion with the bottom slope being the small parameter and will be given for completeness and to illustrate the scaling used in the two models.

The appropriate nondimensional momentum and continuity equations for a rotating homogeneous viscous fluid are

$$2s\frac{\delta q}{\delta t} + (\epsilon q \cdot \nabla)q + 2\hat{k}xq = -\nabla p + E\nabla^2 q, \qquad (1)$$

$$\nabla \cdot q = 0, \qquad (2)$$

where the length, time, and velocity variables have been scaled by L, $(2s\Omega)^{-1}$, and $\epsilon\Omega L$, respectively, with the bottom slope $s \equiv \tan\alpha$ assumed to be small. E and ϵ are the Ekman and external Rossby numbers for the laboratory model. We will rescale $\epsilon = sR$, and break the viscous term into horizontal and vertical components, i.e.,

$$E\nabla^2 = sE_h\nabla_h{}^2 + s^2E_v\frac{\delta^2}{\delta z^2}. \tag{3}$$

Substitution of these expressions into the momentum equation yields

$$s\left[\frac{2\delta q}{\delta t} + (Rq\cdot\nabla)q\right] + 2\hat{k}xq = -\nabla p + s(E_h\nabla_h{}^2q + sE_v\frac{\delta^2}{\delta z^2}q). \tag{4}$$

The no-slip boundary conditions are $q = 0$ at $r = a$ and $z = sy$, and $q = r\hat{k}$ at $z = 1$.

The velocity and pressure are now written as perturbation expansions in s of the form

$$q = q_o + sq_1 + \ldots, \qquad p = p_o + sp_1 + \ldots. \tag{5}$$

The substitution of these series into the basic equations and boundary conditions yields an infinite sequence of problems for the unknown functions. Greenspan has shown that a governing equation for q_o arises from the solution to the first-order problem.

The flow to lowest order in s is geostrophic,

$$2\hat{k}xq_o = -\nabla p_o, \qquad \nabla\cdot q_o = 0, \tag{6}$$

and thus satisfies the Taylor-Proudman theorem,

$$\frac{\delta q_o}{\delta z} = 0. \tag{7}$$

The flow in the sliced-cylinder laboratory model is mechanically driven by the relative rotation of the upper lid. The resulting Ekman boundary layers on the top and bottom surfaces may be analyzed separately (Greenspan, 1968); here the equivalent steady Ekman layer compatibility condition is used between the vertical velocity into the Ekman layer and the boundary and interior velocity fields, which yield

$$\hat{k}\cdot q = \frac{1}{2}E_v{}^{1/2}(+2 - \zeta_o) \quad \text{at } z = 1, \tag{8}$$

$$\hat{k}\cdot q = \hat{j}\cdot q + \frac{1}{2}E_v{}^{1/2}\zeta_o \quad \text{at } z = 0, \tag{9}$$

where $\zeta_o = \hat{k}\cdot\nabla xq_o$. Because $q_o\cdot\hat{k}$ vanishes identically, q_o must be a horizontal vector field independent of z. Thus, a stream function ψ_o exists for q_o, and the lowest-order vorticity field is given by $\zeta_o = \nabla^2\psi_o$.

The first-order problem in s is

$$\frac{2\delta q_o}{\delta t} + (Rq_o\cdot\nabla)q_o + 2\hat{k}xq_1 = -\nabla p_1 + E_h\nabla_h{}^2q_o,$$

$$\nabla\cdot q_1 = 0. \tag{10}$$

The curl of the momentum equation (10) yields

$$\frac{2\delta q_o}{\delta z} = \nabla x\left[\frac{2\delta q_o}{\delta t} + (Rq_o\cdot\nabla)q_o - E_h\nabla_h{}^2q_o\right], \tag{11}$$

which may be integrated directly to give

$$q_1 = \frac{z}{2}\nabla x\left[\frac{2\delta q_o}{\delta t} + (Rq_o\cdot\nabla)q_o - E_h\nabla_h{}^2q_o\right] + A(x,y,t). \tag{12}$$

The unknown vector function A is easily determined using the lower Ekman layer compatibility conditions (9) at $z = 0$,

$$A\cdot\hat{k} = \hat{j}\cdot q_o + \frac{1}{2}E_v{}^{1/2}\zeta_o. \tag{13}$$

Elimination of A and use of the upper Ekman layer condition (8) at $z = 1$ results in the governing vorticity equation for the lowest-order velocity field,

$$\frac{2\delta\zeta_o}{\delta t} + (Rq_o\cdot\nabla)\zeta_o + 2\hat{j}\cdot q_o = -2E_v{}^{1/2}\zeta_o + E_h\nabla^2\zeta_o - E_v{}^{1/2}2. \tag{14}$$

The interior Sverdrup balance, $j\cdot q_o = E_v{}^{1/2}$, is used to rescale the stream function and velocity fields so that the final non-dimensional vorticity equation is

$$\frac{\delta\zeta}{\delta t} + (R_o u\cdot\nabla)\zeta + \psi_x = -\delta\zeta + Ek\nabla_h{}^2\zeta - 1. \tag{15}$$

The two-dimensional velocity and vorticity fields are related through the stream function, $u = \hat{k}x\nabla\psi$ and $\zeta = \nabla^2\psi$, with the velocity satisfying the no-slip condition at the basin boundary at $r = 1$. The new Rossby number and lateral and bottom friction parameters in (15) are related to the laboratory parameters by the following expressions

$$R_o \equiv \frac{E^{1/2}\cdot R}{2S^2}, \quad Ek \equiv \frac{E}{2S}, \quad \delta \equiv \frac{E^{1/2}}{S}. \tag{16}$$

Numerical solutions to the vorticity equation (15) have been found for a number of different values of the laboratory parameters. Before the solutions are presented, a brief discussion of the numerical scheme will now be given.

Numerical solutions to (15) were obtained by using a fast implicit method recently developed by Israeli (1970) for time-dependent viscous flow problems in plane and axisymmetric geometries. Israeli first analyzed the iterative method developed by Pearson (1965) and found that a single optimum-iteration parameter exists and may be accurately estimated when the fluid is only slightly viscous, i.e., when the nondimensional parameter, $\nu\Delta t/L^2 \ll 1$, where ν is the fluid viscosity, Δt is the time step increment, and L is an interior characteristic length scale. Israeli (1971) then used this improved scheme to successfully study the flow in rotating spheres and spherical shells driven through thin Ekman layer pumping by the relative oscillation of the rotation rate of the container. Convergence occurred in one to two iterations per time step on the average, even when large time steps were used.

The application of Israeli's method to the sliced-cylinder problem considered here is straightforward. A polar grid net is used with equal azimuthal grid spacing between grid points. The governing vorticity equation (15) is first rewritten in terms of η and θ, where η is a stretched radial coordinate defined by

$$\eta(r;a,d) = (1-a)r - a + 2a\,\frac{F_o(r+1,d) - F_o(0,d)}{F_o(2,d) - F_o(0,d)}, \qquad (17)$$

where

$$F_o(z,d) = F_1\left(\frac{z}{d}\right) - F_1\left(\frac{2-z}{d}\right),$$

$$F_1(z) = \frac{1}{2}\left[\frac{3}{1+z} - \frac{1}{(1+z)^2}\right], \qquad (18)$$

and a and d are two parameters. This transformation has been examined by Israeli (1971) and satisfies the criteria $\Delta\nu d^2\eta/dr^2 \leqslant d\eta/dr$ at $r = 1$ necessary for second-order spatial accuracy. Examination of the truncation errors for a linearized one-dimensional analog to (15) suggested $a = 0.8$ and $d = 2\,Ek^{1/3}$ as optimum values for the grid parameters. The appendix to this chapter shows a plot of the transformation for several different values of a and d and a discussion of the specific criteria used to estimate the optimum a and d. The grid points are then located uniformly in η,θ space, i.e., $(\eta_i, \theta_j) = (i\Delta\eta, j\Delta\theta)$, where $\Delta\eta = 1/I$ and $\Delta\theta = 2\pi/J$.

The time integration of the finite-difference analog to (15) is performed using the Peaceman-Rachford (1955) alternating-direction implicit method. The finite-difference equations may be written in compact form using the following notation,

$$\phi^n = \phi(t + n\Delta t),$$

$$\phi^{1/k} = \frac{1}{k}\,\phi^0 + \frac{k-1}{k}\,\phi^1,$$

$$\phi_{\bar{z}} = [\phi(z_i + \Delta z) - \phi(z_i - \Delta z)]\,/\,2\Delta z,$$

$$\phi_{\bar{z}\bar{z}} = [\phi(z_i + \Delta z) + \phi(z_i - \Delta z) - 2\phi(z_i)]\,/\,\Delta z^2, \qquad (19)$$

where ϕ is any dependent variable and z is η or θ. The radial component of the Laplacian operator is in the stretched coordinate system,

$$\Delta_r\phi = \left(\frac{d\eta}{dr}\right)^2 \phi_{\bar{\eta}\bar{\eta}} + \frac{1}{r}\left(\frac{d\eta}{dr} + \frac{d^2\eta}{dr^2}\right)\phi_{\bar{\eta}}. \qquad (20)$$

The finite-difference approximation for the first half-time step is then

$$\frac{2}{\Delta t}(\zeta^{1/2} - \zeta^0) + \frac{1}{r}\frac{d\eta}{dr}\,[(R_o\zeta^0_{\bar{\eta}} + Y_{\bar{\eta}})\bar{\psi}_{\bar{\theta}}{}^{1/4} - (R_o\zeta_{\bar{\theta}}{}^{1/2}$$

$$+ Y_{\bar{\theta}})\bar{\psi}_{\bar{\eta}}{}^{1/2}] = -1 - \frac{\delta(\zeta^{1/2} + \zeta^0)}{2} + Ek\,[\Delta_r\zeta^0$$

$$+ \frac{1}{r^2}\zeta_{\bar{\theta}\bar{\theta}}{}^{1/2}), \qquad i > 0, \qquad (21)$$

and at the center of the basin,

$$\frac{2}{\Delta t}(\zeta_o{}^{1/2} - \zeta_o{}^0) + \frac{2}{Jr_1{}^2}\sum_j [(R_o\zeta^{1/2} + Y)\bar{\psi}_{\bar{\theta}}{}^{1/2}]_{i=1}$$

$$= -1 - \delta\,\frac{(\zeta_o{}^{1/2} + \zeta_o{}^0)}{2} + \frac{4Ek}{Jr_1{}^2}\sum_j (\zeta_{1_j}{}^{1/2} - \zeta_o{}^0), \qquad i = 0. \qquad (22)$$

The β-term has been written in flux with $Y \equiv r\sin\theta$. At the origin, the Jacobian is computed from the net flux of total vorticity into the polygonal-shaped area defined by the first ring of grid points ($i = 1$). The finite-difference equation for the second half-time step is

$$\frac{2}{\Delta t}(\zeta_o{}^1 - \zeta_o{}^{1/2}) + \frac{2}{Jr_1{}^2}\sum [R_o\zeta^{1/2} + Y)\bar{\psi}_{\bar{\theta}}{}^{1/2}]_{i=1}$$

$$= -1 - \delta\,\frac{(\zeta_o{}^1 + \zeta_o{}^{1/2})}{2} - \frac{4Ek}{Jr_1{}^2}\sum_j (\zeta_{1_j}{}^{1/2} - \zeta_o{}^1), \qquad i = 0, \qquad (23)$$

and off center,

$$\frac{2}{\Delta t}(\zeta^1 - \zeta^{1/2}) + \frac{1}{r}\frac{d\eta}{dr}\,[(R_o\zeta_{\overline{\eta}}^{\,1} + Y_{\overline{\eta}})\bar{\psi}_{\overline{\theta}}^{\,3/4} - (R_o\zeta_{\overline{\theta}}^{\,1/2}$$
$$+ Y_{\overline{\theta}})\bar{\psi}_{\overline{\eta}}^{\,1/2}] = -1 - \frac{\delta}{2}(\zeta^1 + \zeta^{1/2})$$
$$+ Ek\left[\Delta_r\zeta^1 + \frac{1}{r^2}\zeta_{\overline{\theta\theta}}^{\,1/2}\right], \qquad i > 0. \tag{24}$$

These expressions are of second-order accuracy in both time and space and are unconditionally stable.

The stream function ψ and vorticity ζ are related at each time step by the finite-difference approximation to Poisson's equation,

$$\Delta_r\psi + \frac{1}{r^2}\psi_{\overline{\theta\theta}} = \zeta, \qquad i > 0,$$
$$\frac{4}{Jr_1^{\,2}}\sum_j(\psi_{1j} - \psi_o) = \zeta_o, \qquad i = 0. \tag{25}$$

An exact solution for ψ given ζ may be readily found using Fourier series representation for ψ and ζ and Gaussian elimination in the radial direction (Beardsley, 1972). The Fourier decomposition and composition can be performed using fast Fourier transform techniques when J is an integer power of 2. When $J = 64$ or 128 and the coefficients used in the Gaussian elimination procedure are stored, this direct method for the solution of the Poisson problem is equivalent or slightly faster in computation speed than Buneman's scheme.

An iterative method is used to advance the alternating direction implicit equations one complete time step. The method is initiated by using extrapolation to predict the wall vorticity $\zeta_w{}^{1\phi} = \zeta^{1\phi}$ $(i = I)$ and the stream function $\psi^{1\phi}$ at the new time step (the superscript ϕ is used to denote the assumed value). Then the half-step vorticity field $\zeta^{1/2}$ is found from (21) off center using a modified form of Gaussian elimination that incorporates the periodic nature of ζ (and ψ) with respect to θ. The two prediction equations (22-23) then yield $\zeta_o{}^1$ at the origin. With $\zeta_o{}^1$ and $\zeta_w{}^1$ given, the new vorticity field ζ^1 is determined from (24) by Gaussian elimination. The new stream function ψ^{1n} is then computed from ζ^1 and compared to the initial guess $\psi^{1\phi}$. If the criteria $|\psi^{1n} - \psi^{1\phi}| \leqslant \epsilon_\psi$ is not globally satisfied, the original assumed value of ψ^1 is updated by setting $\psi^{1\phi} = \psi^{1n}$ and the calculations repeated until the above stream function convergence criterion is satisfied. This final field ψ^{1n} represents the correct solution based on the initial guess for $\zeta_w{}^{1\phi}$. This latter guess is now improved using the expression

$$\zeta_w{}^{1n} = \zeta_w{}^{1\phi} + A\left(\frac{3}{h}\frac{\delta\psi^{1n}}{\delta r}\right), \tag{26}$$

where A is the as yet unspecified iteration parameter and h is the minimum radial grid spacing adjacent to the boundary, i.e., $h = 1 - r_{I-1}$. The normal derivative of ψ at the boundary is computed using the second-order expression

$$\frac{3}{h}\frac{\delta\psi}{\delta r} = \frac{-3}{h^2}\psi_{I-1} + \zeta_w + \frac{1}{2}\zeta_{I-1}. \tag{27}$$

When $\zeta_w{}^{ln}$ and $\zeta_w{}^{1\phi}$ satisfy the wall vorticity convergence criterion $|\zeta_w{}^{ln} - \zeta_w{}^{1\phi}| \leqslant \epsilon_\zeta$, the new stream function satisfies approximately the no-slip condition at the boundary and the calculations for the full time step are complete.

Israeli (1971, 1972) has discussed methods to estimate the optimal values of the iteration parameter A. Israeli (personal communication) has more recently suggested the following direct method to compute A. (This method is exact in linear one-dimensional problems and is used by Orszag and Israeli (pp. 284-300). Suppose the initial assumption for ζ_w is incorrect, i.e., $\zeta_w{}^\phi = \zeta_w + \zeta_w{}^{\phi E}$, where ζ_w is the true value for that time step and $\zeta_w{}^{\phi E}$ is the error field. Let the numerical solution to the linearized problem be $\psi^n = \psi + \psi^{nE}$. For the error in the new estimate $\zeta_w{}^n$ to vanish and thus give convergence in one iteration, (26) and (27) are used so that

$$0 = \zeta_w{}^{\phi E} + A\left(\frac{3}{h}\frac{\delta\psi^{nE}}{\delta r}\right). \tag{28}$$

The optimum value of A is then easily computed from (28), where ψ^{nE} is the numerical solution to the homogeneous problem for an arbitrary initial wall vorticity field $\zeta_w{}^{\phi E}$. The iteration parameter A is a function of Δt and the grid parameters as well as Ek and δ, and the optimum value of A depends slightly on θ in the sliced-cylinder problem. Use of the computed optimum value of A and parabolic extrapolation gave convergence in one to two iterations on the average, even in the more nonlinear regime.

NUMERICAL SOLUTION

The fast implicit scheme outlined in the previous section has been used to generate a number of numerical solutions. The ranges of the parameters R_o, Ek, and δ that govern the numerical model have been chosen to correspond to the general parameter range explored earlier in the published sliced-cylinder laboratory experiments. Because direct Ekman layer suction is included in the governing vorticity equation, the numerical model reaches its steady state in several spin-up time periods (here δ^{-1} is called the nondimensional spin-up time scale). The total integration time for the shortest experiment was $5.9\ \delta^{-1}$; the integration time for experiments in the nonlinear regime typically exceeded $10\ \delta^{-1}$. The total kinetic energy of the system and the variability of ψ were examined to determine the steadiness of the flow. A listing of the numerical experiments and the corresponding laboratory parameters is given in Table 1. The grid parameters for all experiments were $a = 0.8$ and $d = 2\ Ek^{1/3}$. The grid consisted of an $I = 30, J = 128$ net, except in experiments N4 and N5, $I = 25, J = 64$. The convergence criteria for the vorticity and stream function iterations were $\epsilon_\zeta = 0.5$ and $\epsilon_\psi = 0.01$, except in experiments N4-N10, where $\epsilon_\psi = 0.05$. The time increment was $\Delta t = 2$ in all experiments except N11-N18, in which $\Delta t = 1$.

TABLE 1 List of Numerical Experiments and Their Corresponding Laboratory Parameter Values

Experiment #	tan α	ϵ	$10^5 \times E$
N4	.178	.0026	1.88
N5	.178	.0076	5.62
N6	.178	.0	2.03
N7	.178	.019	2.03
N8	.178	.0230	2.03
N9	.178	.0380	2.03
N10	.178	.0475	2.03
N11	.178	.0536	2.03
N12	.178	.0638	2.03
N13	.178	.0718	2.03
N14	.178	.0678	2.03
N15	.178	.125	5.0
N16	.178	.134	5.0
N17	.178	.139	5.0
N18	.178	.129	5.0
N22	.178	.0441	0.9
N23	.178	.0400	0.9
N25	.144	.0441	0.9
N26	.144	.0400	0.9
N27	.144	.0360	0.9

Linear Regime

Experiments N4 and N5 were conducted in the linear regime so that a direct comparison could be made with velocity profiles observed in the western boundary layer of the sliced-cylinder laboratory model. Figure 2 illustrates the azimuthal velocity profile measured near $\theta = \pi$ at two depths in the laboratory model and the corresponding velocity profile obtained at $\theta = \pi$ in experiment N4. The numerical model profile shows excellent agreement with the profile observed near mid-depth of the laboratory model. The velocity profile observed near the upper (driving) lid at $z = 0.83$ is 33 percent larger than the numerical profile in N4. This difference in magnitude between the observed (at $z = 0.83$) and numerical profiles has increased to 67 percent in the larger Ekman number case examined in N5. The large vertical shear observed in the western boundary layer of the laboratory model has not yet been explained.

The azimuthal dependence of the maximum azimuthal velocity V_{max} is shown in Figure 3 for N4 along with the laboratory data observed at $z = 0.83$ near the upper lid. Both sets of data have similar envelopes; the velocity maximum observed near the upper lid in the laboratory model is consistently larger than that found in the numerical model. Results from a numerical solution with $Ro = 0$ are also included in Figure 3 to illustrate the slight north-south asymmetry in the boundary layer flow in the linear regime.

The steady-state vorticity balance along the line $\theta = \pi$ through the western boundary layer is shown in Figure 4 for N4. The advection of planetary vorticity or β-term is here identical to the azimuthal velocity. The relative vorticity advection term never exceeds 5 percent of the β-term, so that the balance is essentially linear. Direct Ekman layer

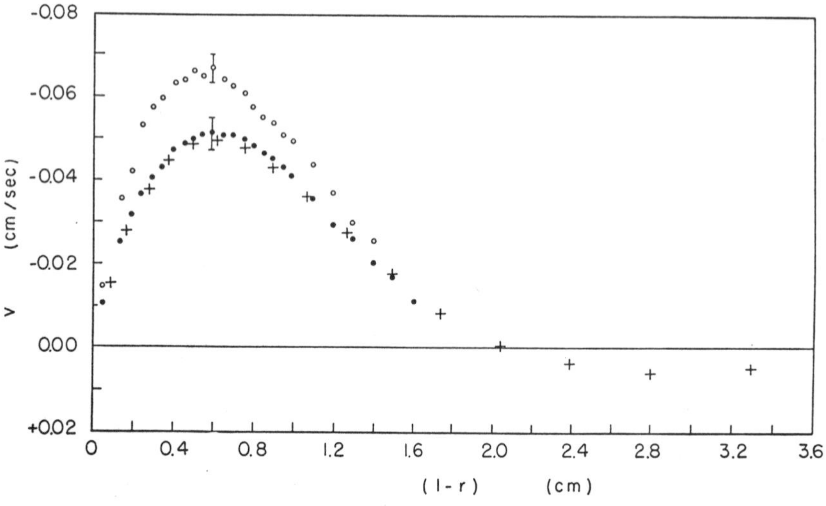

FIGURE 2 Azimuthal velocity profile measured in western boundary layer of laboratory model at depths $z = 0.83(0)$ and $z = 0.43(0)$. Numerical profile (+) from experiment N4.

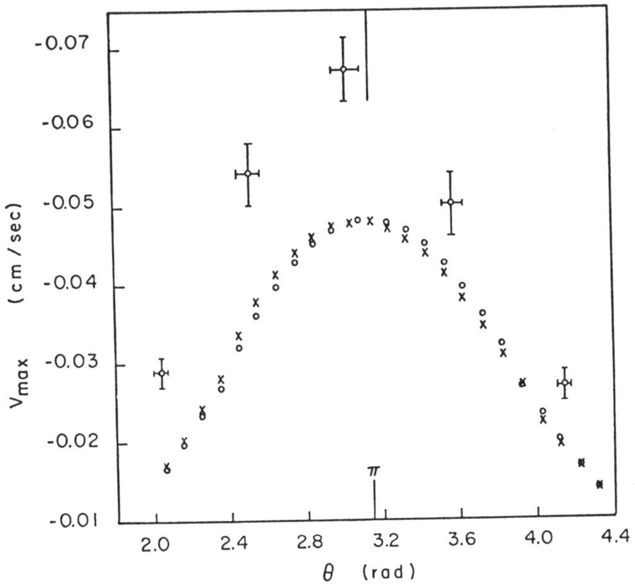

FIGURE 3 Western boundary layer azimuthal velocity maximum as function of azimuthal position θ. Laboratory data (⊢o⊣), results of N4(X), and numerical experiment N3(0) with Ro = 0.

suction clearly plays an important role in both the sublayer near the wall [$(1-r) \leqslant \cdot 3$ cm], where the tangential velocity shear and, thus, velocity reach maxima and in the transition region [$1.2 \text{ cm} \leqslant (1-r) \leqslant 3.6$ cm] between the high velocity core of the western boundary layer, where the principal balance is between the β- and lateral friction terms, and the interior region, where the Sverdrup balance applies. The change in the western boundary layer caused by the omission of direct Ekman layer suction is illustrated in Figure 5. Velocity profiles [obtained analytically from linear one-dimensional analogs to Eq. (15)] are shown together with the measured profile from N4. Inclusion of direct Ekman layer suction causes a broader but slower boundary current. While the radial separation of the azimuthal velocity maximum from the wall increases only slightly, V_{max} decreases considerably when direct Ekman layer suction is included. The net western boundary layer transports in these two cases are essentially identical due to continuity and the Sverdrup constraint on the interior flow.

Stable Nonlinear Regime

Excellent agreement is exhibited in the steady nonlinear regime between the numerical stream function and the horizontal structure of the flow field measured in the laboratory model using streak photography. As the external Rossby number $|\epsilon|$ is increased past $E^{1/2}$, the western boundary current is first intensified downstream of $\theta = \pi$; when $|\epsilon| \simeq 3E^{1/2}$, the western boundary current separates from the wall and partially closes to form a vortex that intensifies and shifts downstream as $|\epsilon|$ is further increased. For $|\epsilon| \simeq 6E^{1/2}$, the center of this vortex nears $\theta = 128°$ and moves systematically away from the side wall as the driving increases. In the transition region between the western boundary layer and the interior, stationary damped topographic Rossby waves appear, their amplitude and wavelength increasing with increasing $|\epsilon|$.

This sequence of flow dependence on $|\epsilon|/E^{1/2}$ is clearly illustrated in Figure 6. Here the steady numerical stream functions for several representative values of $|\epsilon|/E^{1/2}$ are shown superimposed on the corresponding laboratory streak photographs. The orginal streak photographs used in Figures 6a and 6c are also shown in Figure 11 (Beardsley, 1969).

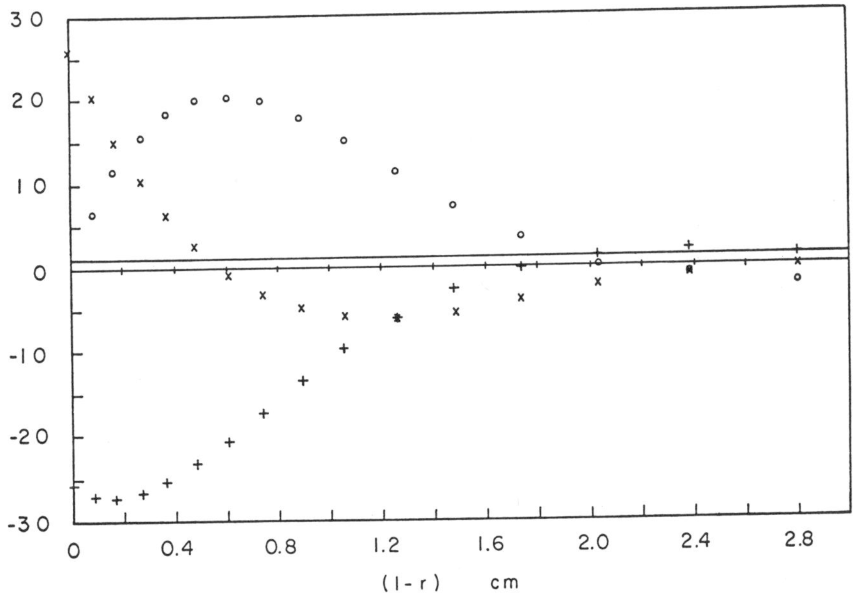

FIGURE 4 Western boundary layer vorticity balance along $\theta = \pi$ for numerical experiment N4. Notation: β-term, (0); lateral friction, (+); direct Ekman suction term, (X). Driving term represented by line at 1.

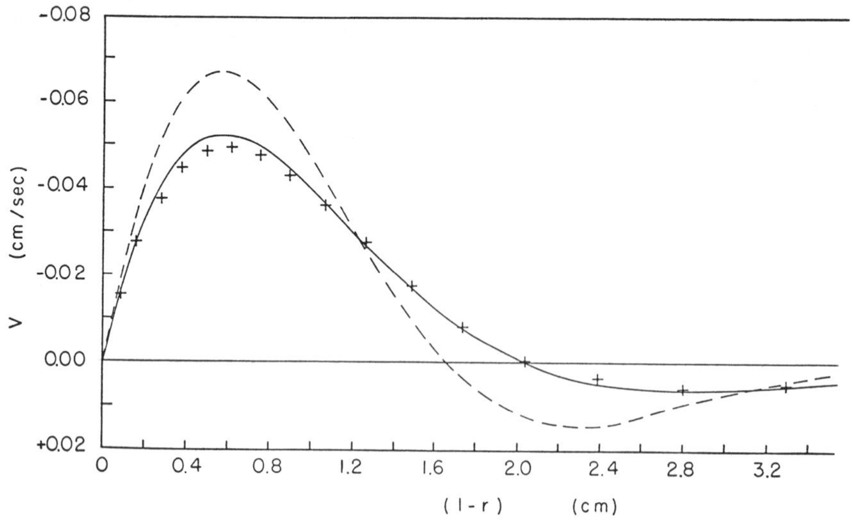

FIGURE 5 Comparison of western boundary layer azimuthal velocity profiles from analytic linear models with direct Ekman layer suction (solid line) and without (dashed line). Numerical results from N4 are (+).

The location of the western boundary layer vortex, the flow near the vortex, and the interior flow observed in both models are identical to within the basic accuracy of the laboratory measurements and photographic techniques. The principal difference between the flow patterns of the two models occurs in the transition region where the stationary topographic Rossby waves appear. The numerical model seems to correctly predict the Rossby wavelengths in Figure 6c but slightly underestimates the wave amplitudes and wave slopes. This result may be suggested by the fact that in the linear regime, the numerical model underestimates V_{max} in the western boundary current. Although the laboratory streak photographs used here were made near the mid-depth of the basin ($z = 0.62$), additional measurements at other depths indicate that the horizontal velocity structure observed in the interior and western boundary layer transition region in the laboratory model was independent of depth.

Because N11 is the most nonlinear steady numerical solution corresponding to a steady laboratory flow, a detailed examination is made. The stream function is shown superimposed on the original laboratory streak photograph in Figure 6c; good agreement appears everywhere except in the boundary layer transition region near the center of the basin.

The equilibrium numerical vorticity balance is illustrated in Figure 7 using the following notation. The fractional contributions of the various terms in the steady vorticity balance are given simply by

$$N = \frac{R_o u \cdot \nabla \zeta}{\Sigma}, \quad B = \frac{\Psi_x}{\Sigma}, \quad W = \frac{-1}{\Sigma},$$

$$BF = \frac{\delta\zeta}{\Sigma}, \quad LF = \frac{-Ek\nabla_h^2 \zeta}{\Sigma}, \tag{29}$$

when

$$\Sigma \equiv (|R_o u \cdot \nabla \zeta| + |\Psi_x| + |\delta\zeta| + |Ek\nabla_h^2 \zeta| + 1). \tag{30}$$

The linear asymptotic balances are the interior Sverdrup balance, $B + W \sim 0$ (type 1), and the western boundary layer balance, $B + BF + LF \sim 0$ (type 5). The nonlinear western boundary balance is $B + BF + LF + N \sim 0$ (type 4) where $\min(|B|, |BF + LF|) > |N|$. The nonlinear asymptotic balances include the Rossby wave regime $N + B \sim 0$ (horizontally lined areas) and the damped wave regime $N + B + BF + LF \sim 0$ (vertically lined areas) where $\min(|N|, |B|) > |BF + LF|$. All terms are important in balance type 3, while all but the nonlinear advection term are important in the type 2 balance. The advection term is clearly shown in Figure 7 to be important in most of the western boundary layer and transition zone and especially near the outer edge of the boundary layer vortex. The vorticity balance is also shown in Figure 8 as a function of arc length along the streamline $\psi = 0.7$ contained in the region $\pi/3 \leq \theta \leq 5\pi/6$. Direct Ekman layer suction provides the dominant dissipative control in the vortex region, although both Ekman layer suction and lateral friction become comparable to the driving term in the region of the damped standing Rossby waves.

The Onset in Instability

When a critical value of $|\epsilon|$ was reached, the steady flow in the numerical model became unstable. Figure 9 shows the time history of the total kinetic energy for the series of numerical experiments conducted in the more nonlinear regime at $E = 2.03 \times 10^{-5}$. The starting transients damp out more slowly as the critical value of ϵ is reached (note that

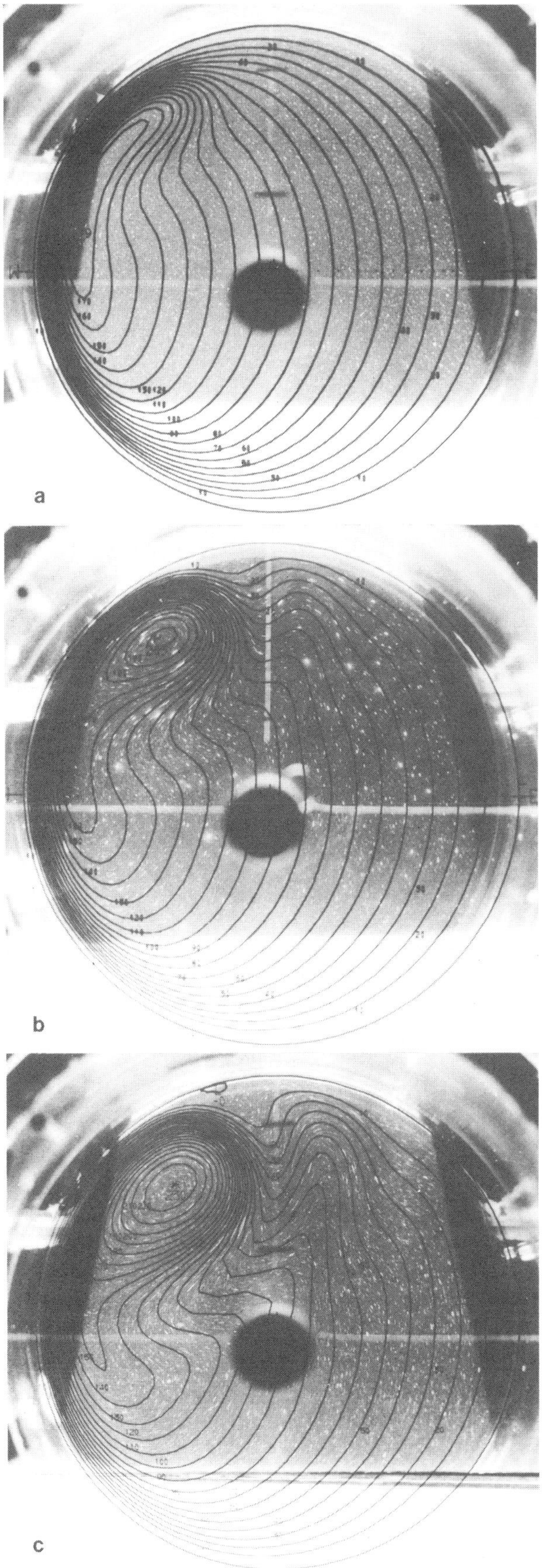

FIGURE 6 Superposition of numerical and laboratory horizontal streamlines for experiments (a) N7, (b) N9, and (c) N11.

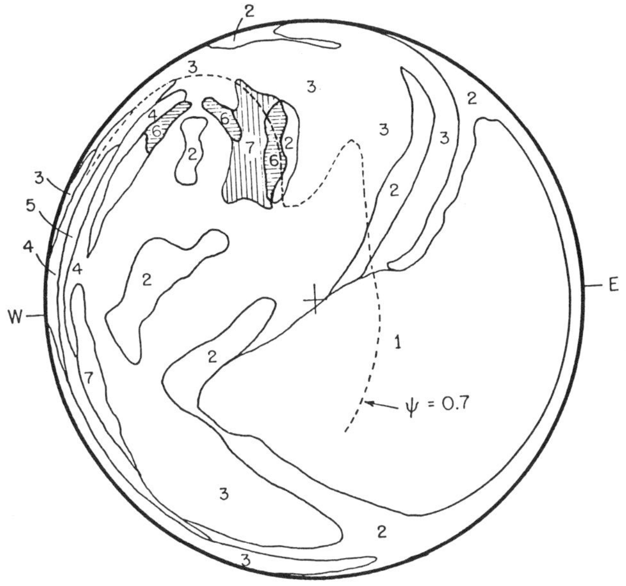

FIGURE 7 Equilibrium vorticity balance for experiment N11. See text for key to notation. The section of the ψ = 0.7 streamline contained in $5\pi/6 \leqslant \theta < \pi/3$ is also included.

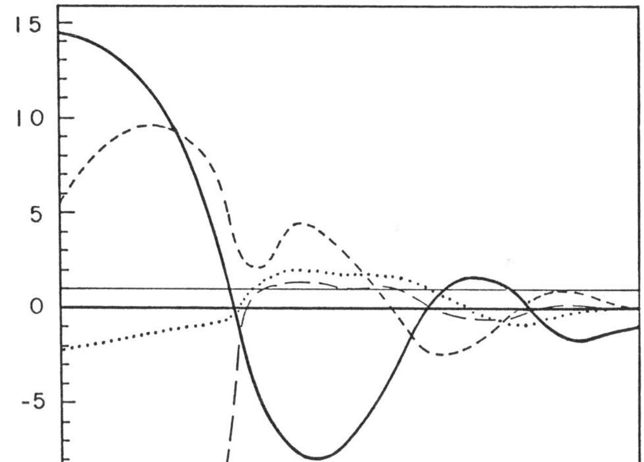

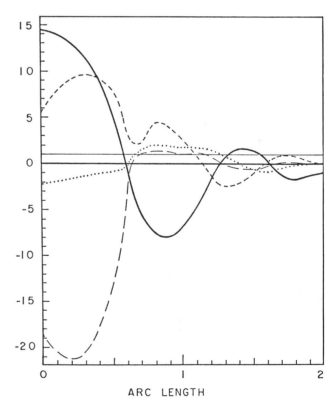

FIGURE 8 Equilibrium vorticity balance along the arc of the streamline ψ = 0.7 from $\theta = 5\pi/6$ to $\theta = \pi/3$ in experiment N11. Notation: β-term (heavy solid); lateral friction (dotted); Ekman suction term (long dash); nonlinear advection term (short dash). Driving term represented by line at 1. The abscissa is the nondimensional arc length starting from the point r = 0.946, $\theta = 5\pi/6$.

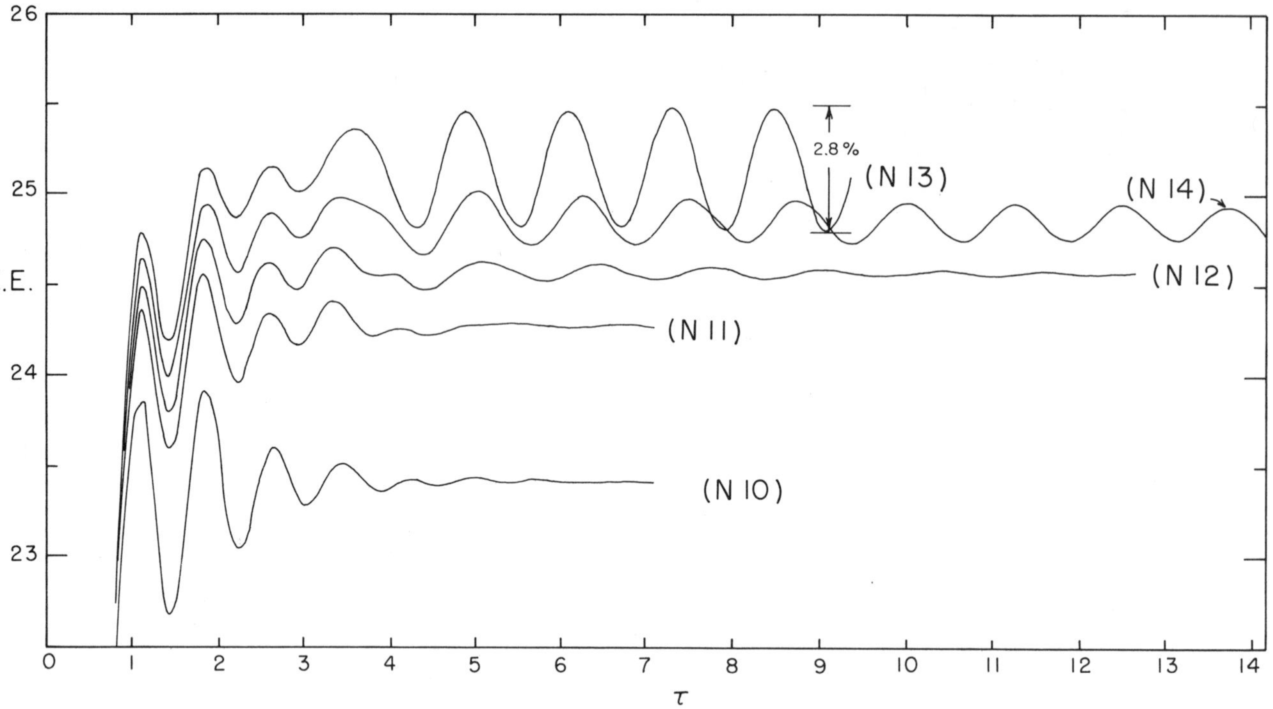

FIGURE 9 Nondimensional kinetic energy versus time in units of the spin-up time scale δ^{-1} for several different numerical experiments.

the kinetic energy for N14 is very slowly decaying); beyond this value of ϵ, the kinetic energy exhibits large oscillations, signaling the onset of a low-frequency instability.

This flow instability found in the numerical model is qualitatively identical to the slow instability observed in the laboratory model. In both models, a small secondary vortex is periodically formed in the transition region to the east of the main boundary layer vortex. This secondary vortex decays as it is swept southwestward by the primary vortex. The position of the secondary vortex is shown as a function of time in Figures 10a and 10b; the two stream function plots are separated by $\Delta\tau = 0.56\ \delta^{-1}$, which is approximately one-half of the period of the instability.

Experiments with the laboratory model indicated that the onset of the instability depends critically on ϵ and E and *not* on the bottom slope; the laboratory model stability curve is then given in terms of the critical Ekman layer Reynolds number Re_E as

$$Re_E{}^c = \frac{|\epsilon|}{E^{1/2}} = 11.3 \pm 0.2 + (1.26 \pm 0.05) \times 10^5\ E. \qquad (31)$$

The results of numerical experiments N10–18 and N22–23, conducted at three values of E for a single value of $\tan\alpha$, are shown in Figure 11. The suggested stability curve for the numerical model exhibits the observed linear dependence of $Re_E{}^c$ on E but also indicates that the numerical model requires a significantly greater driving stress than the laboratory model to become unstable.

Numerical experiments N25–27 were conducted to test the dependence of $Re_E{}^c$ on the bottom slope s for a fixed E. When the slope is decreased 19 percent from $s = 0.178$ to $s = 0.144$, the results indicate that $Re_E{}^c$ decreases approximately 4 percent. The Ekman number for these experiments was held constant at $E = 0.9 \times 10^{-5}$, whereas $E = 2.03 \times 10^{-5}$ in the corresponding laboratory test. Ignoring the slight dependence of $Re_E{}^c$ on s, as observed in the numerical model, implies that the combination of parameters governing stability in the numerical model is then $R_o\ \delta^{-2}$. The critical value $R_o\ \delta^{-2}$ depends linearly on $(Ek\ \delta^{-1})^2$. The physical interpretation of these results has not yet been given, although Godfrey (1971, personal communication) has suggested that this instability represents the breakdown of a finite-amplitude Rossby wave.

A comparison of the observed period of instability is given in Figure 12, showing good agreement between the two models. As E increases, the spin-up time decreases, resulting in a more rapid decay of the secondary vortex and a quicker repetition of the cycle.

SUMMARY

In summary, a two-dimensional numerical model, incorporating both lateral friction and direct Ekman layer suction,

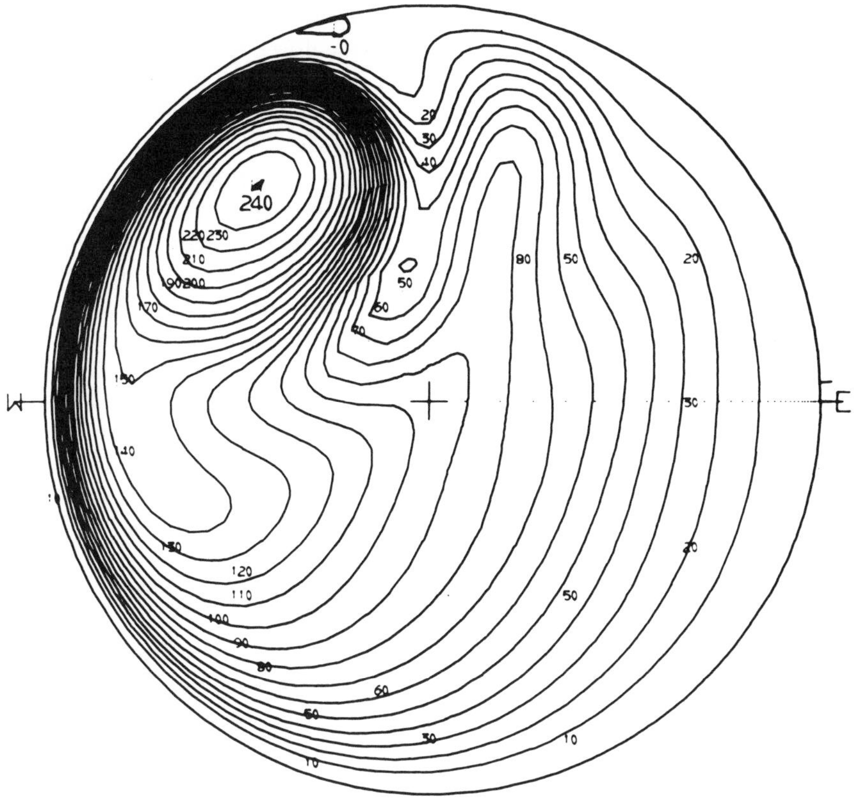

a

FIGURE 10 Stream function from N13 at (a) $t = 7.138\ \delta^{-1}$ and (b) $t = 7.695\ \delta^{-1}$.

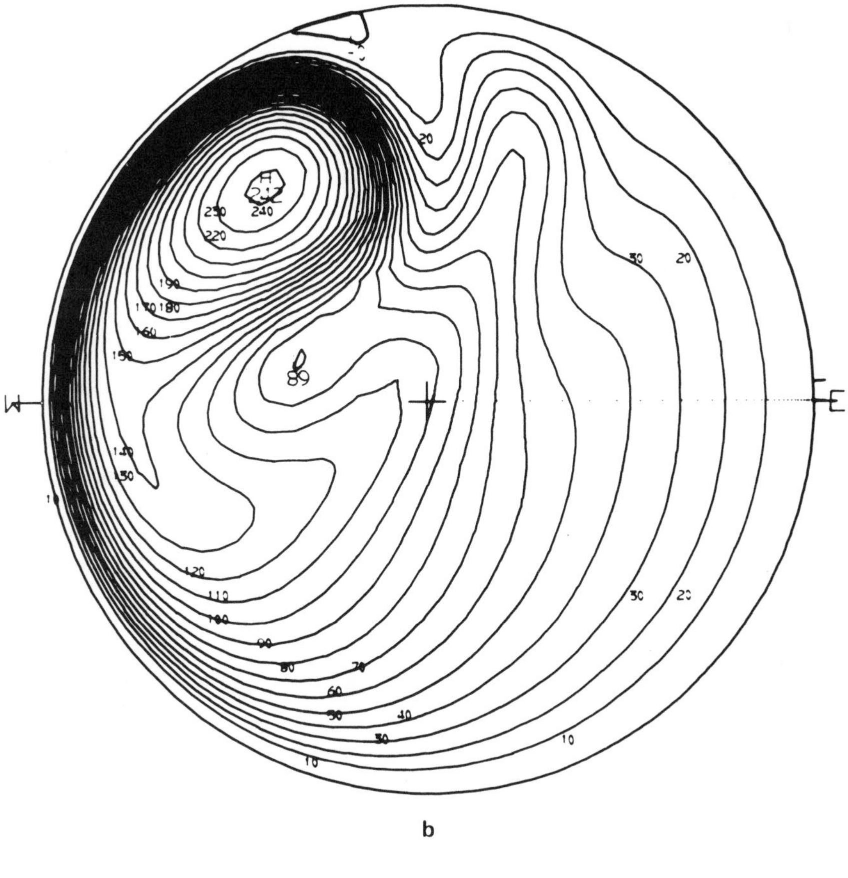

b

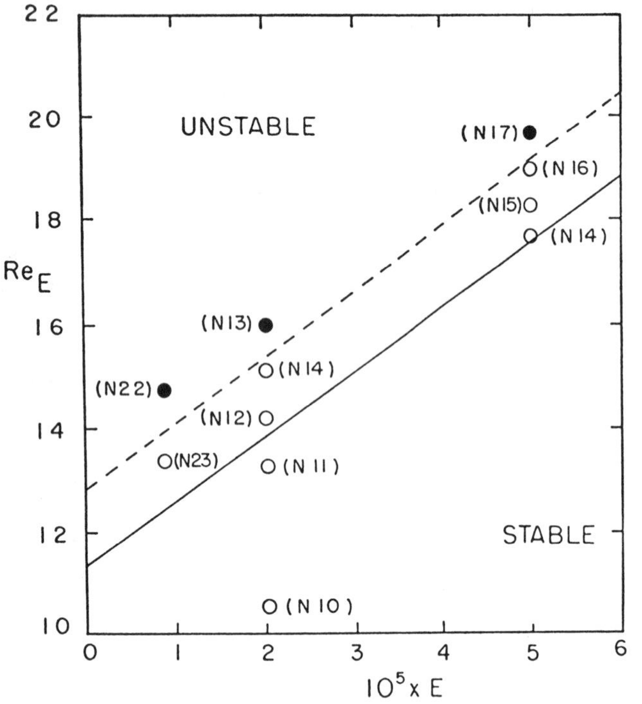

FIGURE 11 Stability diagram for numerical experiments N10–18 and N22–23. Notation: Stable (1); unstable (0); stability curve suggested by numerical results (dashed line); stability curve observed in laboratory experiments (solid line).

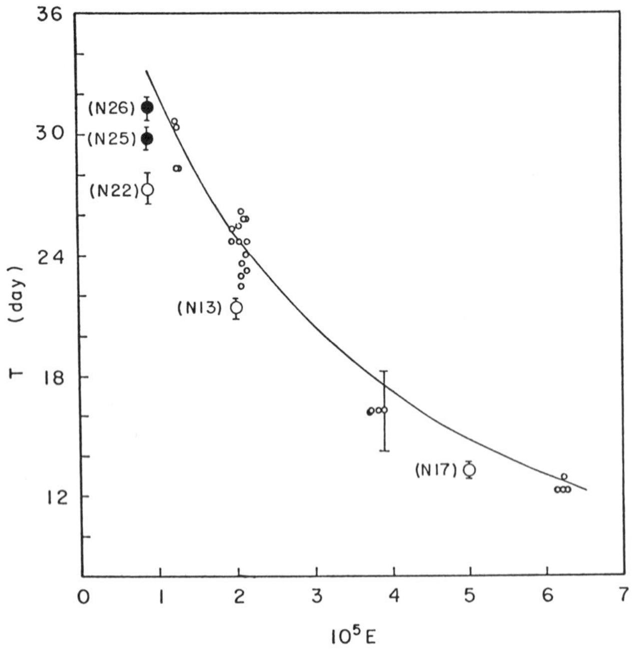

FIGURE 12 Comparison of period of instability observed in laboratory and numerical models. Notation: Laboratory data (small circles); numerical model results for tanα = 0.178 (0) and tanα = 0.144 (0). Time scale is in units of rotational days, i.e., one "day" equals $2\pi\Omega^{-1}$ in dimensional units. Solid line is empirical curve fitted to laboratory data.

reasonably simulates the flow observed in the sliced-cylinder laboratory model of the wind-driven ocean circulation. The good agreement that is shown between the two models is perhaps surprising in view of the simplicity of the governing vorticity equation, the larger values of tanα used, and the obvious approximations made to develop a two-dimensional mathematical model for a more complex three-dimensional physical situation. That the numerical model must be driven harder to produce instability seems logical, because the numerical model also underestimates the maximum azimuthal velocity in the western boundary layer in the linear regime. The numerical model exhibiting a flow instability that is qualitatively identical to the laboratory model instability strongly suggests that the mechanism causing the instability is associated with a finite-amplitude, Rossby wave breakdown and *not* with a local Ekman layer or an $E^{1/2}$ by $E^{1/2}$ corner region breakdown as speculated earlier.

APPENDIX: SELECTION OF GRID PARAMETERS

The two grid parameters a and d, which specify the radial coordinate transformation (17), were chosen in the following manner. Israeli's iterative method and the Crank–Nicholson scheme were used to obtain steady-state numeri-

TABLE 2 Truncation Errors for the Case S = 0.178 and $E = 2 \times 10^{-5}$

x	ψ_a	E_ψ	ζ_a	E_ζ	$(\psi_x)_a$	$E\psi_x$
0.0000	0.000	0.000000	1062.263	0.430	0.000	0.00000
.0070	.024	−.000043	834.110	−.464	6.653	.14445
.0143	.092	.000212	624.423	−1.014	11.943	.11852
.0220	.201	.000521	431.843	−1.383	15.987	.10927
.0302	.345	.000756	257.445	−1.592	18.810	.10787
.0392	.522	.000821	103.731	−1.687	20.403	.11108
.0490	.726	.000643	−25.934	−1.704	20.754	.11680
.0599	.948	.000160	−127.814	−1.661	19.881	.12252
.0721	1.178	−.000657	−198.407	−1.571	17.857	.12467
.0857	1.402	−.001786	−235.292	−1.431	15.846	.11839
.1013	1.604	−.003118	−238.226	−1.228	11.128	.09827
.1190	1.765	−.004425	−210.405	−.937	7.109	.06041
.1395	1.870	−.005351	−159.538	−.533	3.304	.00644
.1633	1.910	−.005476	−97.991	−.034	.251	−.05165
.1912	1.887	−.004509	−40.966	.452	−1.634	−.09016
.2240	1.819	−.002606	−1.967	.705	−2.259	−.08407
.2628	1.735	−.000585	13.373	.524	−2.955	−.03255
.3089	1.660	.000399	10.825	.023	−1.354	.02295
.3634	1.598	−.000137	3.157	−.285	−.984	.03278
.4274	1.538	−.001317	−.594	−.127	−.933	.00596
.5015	1.467	−.001840	−.515	.076	−.986	−.00760
.5860	1.382	−.001579	−.001	.038	−1.004	−.00202
.7819	1.186	−.000949	−.001	.004	−.999	−.00063
1.0000	.968	−.000049	.000	.003	−1.000	.00026

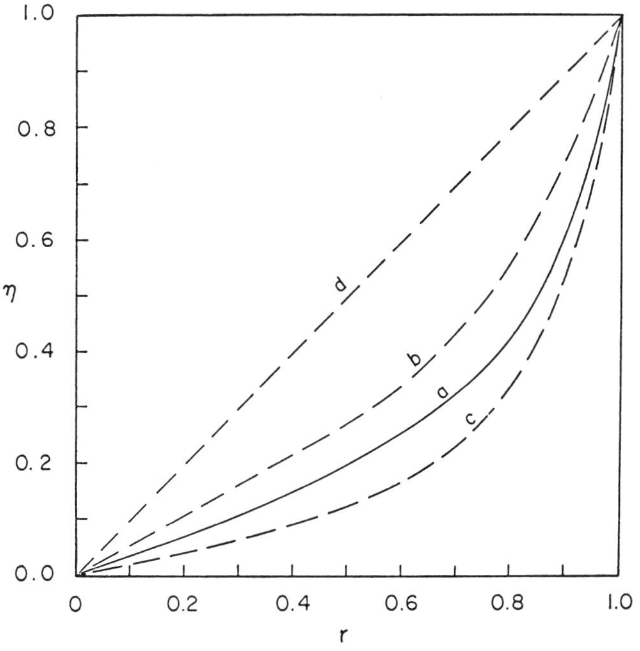

FIGURE 13 Plot of stretched radial coordinate transformation $\eta(r)$ for different values of a and d with $Ek = 5.6 \times 10^{-4}$ (or $E = 2 \times 10^{-5}$ and $\tan\alpha = 0.178$). Notation: (a) $a = 0.8$ and $d = 2\,Ek^{1/3}$; (b) $a = 0.8$ and $d = 4\,Ek^{1/3}$; (c) $a = 1.0$ and $d = 2\,Ek^{1/3}$; (d) $a = 0$.

cal solutions to the following one-dimensional linear analogy to (15),

$$\zeta_\tau + \psi_x = -\delta\zeta + Ek\zeta_{xx} - 1, \qquad \zeta = \psi_{xx}, \tag{1}$$

with the no-slip condition $\psi = \psi_x = 0$ applied at the boundaries at $x = 0,2$. The stretched coordinate η used in this one-dimensional example was defined by

$$\eta = (1 - a)x + 2a\frac{F_o(x, d) - F_o(0, d)}{F_o(2, d) - F_o(0, d)}, \tag{2}$$

where F_o and F_1 are defined as before. The analytic solution to (1) was also found and compared to the numerical solutions computed for different values of a and d. The time step $\Delta\tau$, the convergence parameters ϵ_ψ and ϵ_ζ, and the number of grid points were also varied; but for reasonable choices of these parameters, the difference between analytic and numerical solutions depended essentially on spatial truncation errors.

The final choice of $a = 0.8, d = 2(Ek)^{1/3}$ minimized the truncation errors in the prediction of ψ, ζ, the velocity ψ_x, and the total number of iterations required per spin-up time period. Table 2 illustrates the truncation errors [defined here as the difference between analytic and numerical solutions (with $E_\psi = \psi$ analytic $- \psi$ numerical, etc.)] found for the case of $S = 0.178$ and $E = 2 \times 10^{-5}$. The western boundary layer scale thickness for this example is $(Ek)^{1/3} = 0.0271$. The transformation is illustrated in Figure 13 for several different values of the grid parameters.

ACKNOWLEDGMENTS

The author acknowledges the cheerful interest and generous assistance given by Dr. Moshe Israeli. His suggestion of an exact method to compute the optimum iteration parameter substantially improved the efficiency of the numerical scheme. Mr. S. Bernbaum helped with the machine coding and Mrs. B. Wysochansky and Mr. S. Ricci assisted in the preparation of the manuscript and figures. This research was supported by the Office of Naval Research (N00014-67-A-0204-0048) and the National Science Foundation who provided access to its CDC 6600 computer at NCAR, where most of the calculations were made.

REVIEW: J. A. GALT

I am both flattered and disquieted by the opportunity to begin the review of Dr. Beardsley's paper. In front of a group with such conspicuous talent as is represented here, my aspirations are much more towards learning than enlightening. It is with some trepidation then that I introduce the following rather general comments and questions. Hopefully the process will be edifying for someone other than myself.

Physical models present a continuum in the same sense as a holograph. This means that the information content is very large and that complex processes can be simulated and visualized in great detail. This visualization is a fundamental part of physical oceanography. To put it another way, perhaps the major challenge for developing a competence in oceanography is that of augmenting ones "billiard ball mechanics"-size intuition to one that at least appreciates geophysical scales of motion and dynamics. For the development of this geophysical intuition, the visualization afforded by physical models is very useful.

On the other hand, for several reasons this visualization is never really enough. First of all, no matter how carefully the physical model is constructed and scaled, it is impossible to simultaneously satisfy all of the requirements for similarity, and thus there is at least some question as to range over which the dynamics are properly represented. Secondly, to understand the dynamics of a flow situation, a simple picture is not adequate in that a quantitative analysis of the dynamics term by term is required to ascertain the actual factors governing the flow. (For example, see Figure 7.)

This then suggests that some coupling of physical modeling and the more quantitative numerical modeling would lead to improved understanding. In fact, it would seem that all physical models might yield more information if companion numerical models could be developed.

The appropriate question to ask at this stage might be: How can these companion models be developed to give maximum information and what hazards or difficulties are likely to arise in this pursuit? The answer will be harder to come by than the question.

In some ways numerical modeling is more of a black art than a panacea. In model development, pragmatic necessity demands compromise at many levels. This, of course, results in uncertainties in the dynamics that are represented and degradation of the numerical models' reliability. Perhaps what was said a moment ago should be restated, i.e., it would seem that all numerical models might yield more information if companion physical models could be developed. Clearly a symbiotic relationship is indicated. From either point of view, the idea of companion physical and numerical models should be strongly endorsed.

I would now like to turn my attention more specifically to the model at hand. The development of the equations as a series expansion has the obvious and substantial advantage of giving a two-dimensional problem, which does not require the resolution of the thin upper and lower boundary layers. The assumption of balanced Ekman layers does introduce a smoothing with a time scale of several time steps so it is possible that some of the details of the transients are lost or misrepresented. In particular, any transients associated with time-dependent Ekman layers cannot be represented. This does not appear significant in the applications investigated in the present study but might limit future extensions of the general technique. A second potential difficulty associated with the development of the equations as a series is the unknown magnitude of the truncation error. The size of these errors relative to the ones introduced by the finite-difference approximations is of interest if an understanding of small differences between the physical and numerical models is to be obtained. The numerical model actually gives the simultaneous solution to the sum of the zero- and first-order problem, so it isn't strictly analogous to the usual asymptotic series. It is hard to get a feeling for what the errors might be.

Given the two-dimensional governing equation for the flow, the grid system used in the solution should be considered. The stretched coordinate is a valuable tool for the resolution of the lateral boundary layer, and the second-order accuracy puts a useful bound on the local expected errors. In addition, it might prove informative to investigate the spacial variations in the phase velocity errors for topographic Rossby waves. Spacial variations in phase velocity can cause shearing and focusing of waves as they propagate through the model. It is not clear whether this is significant in this model or not; but since the quasi-steady solution is clearly a topographic Rossby wave phase locked by the current, these processes should be checked. It seems possible that this sort of shearing might shift or modify the onset of instability.

Since the object of these studies is an understanding of ocean circulation, it seems worth while considering how to translate the results of the physical and numerical model back to the real ocean. For example, the direct Ekman suction in the boundary layer doesn't seem to have a real ocean analog, and the results given in Figure 5 are useful and seem to me worth extending. One might wonder how these topographic Rossby waves with some net divergence are modified by the Ekman suction compared to say free Rossby waves in a flat bottom, β-plane or spherical ocean. In some real ways this model might be more directly related to the Beaufort gyre of the Arctic than the classical picture of the Atlantic. Here the rigid rotating lid and readjustments dominated by topography Rossby wave may not be bad assumptions.

As a final point, this set of companion models seems to have come up with many useful insights. One wonders if there are any plans to try an exponential bathymetry to simulate a β-plane or perhaps even greater polar flattening to simulate a sphere with the possibility of trapped modes.

REFERENCES

Beardsley, R. C. 1969. A laboratory model of the wind-driven ocean circulation. J. Fluid Mech. 38(2):255–71.

Beardsley, R. C. 1972. A numerical model of the wind-driven ocean circulation in a circular basin. (In press)

Bryan, K. 1963. A numerical investigation of a non-linear model of a wind-driven ocean. J. Atmos. Sci. 20:596–606.

Greenspan, H. P. 1968. The Theory of Rotating Fluids. Cambridge University Press, England.

Greenspan, H. P. 1969. A note on the laboratory simulation of planetary flows. Stud. Appl. Math. 48(2):147–52.

Israeli, M. 1970. A fast implicit numerical method for time dependent viscous flows. Stud. Appl. Math. 49(4):327–49.

Israeli, M. 1971. Time dependent motions of confined rotating fluids. Ph. D. Thesis. Department of Mathematics, MIT, Cambridge, Mass.

Israeli, M. 1972. On the evaluation of iteration parameters for the boundary vorticity. Stud. Appl. Math. 51(1):67–74.

Munk, W. H. 1950. On the wind-driven ocean circulation. J. Meteorol. 7:79–93.

Peaceman, D., and Rachford, H. 1955. The numerical solution of parabolic and elliptic differential equations. J. Soc. Ind. Appl. Math. 3:28–41.

Pearson, C. E. 1965. A computational method for viscous flow problems. J. Fluid Mech. 21:611–22.

Pedlosky, J., and Greenspan, H. P. 1967. A simple laboratory model for the oceanic circulation. J. Fluid Mech. 27:291–304.

Stommel, H. 1948. The westward intensification of wind-driven ocean currents. Trans. Am. Geophys. Union 29:202–6.

Sverdrup, H. 1947. Wind-driven currents in a baroclinic ocean. Proc. Nat. Acad. Sci. 33:318.

DISCUSSION

MUNK: Can you calculate the fluxes associated with your unstable Rossby waves and interpret them in terms of some sort of horizontal eddy coefficient, and if so, how does that compare to the one you put in? And could you throw it out, now that you have a physical model for lateral fluxes?

BEARDSLEY: We haven't calculated them.

MUNK: It would be very interesting, because that probably is the physical basis of the huge coefficients that we "require."

BEARDSLEY: We mentioned this question earlier about the splitting-up of the vorticity diffusion term. We haven't cheated by using a large eddy viscosity.

NIILER: It's remarkable that none of your instabilities go to the southeast corner of the basin; or am I not seeing the whole picture?

BEARDSLEY: The phase velocity is in the southwest direction.

NIILER: So when the instabilities of those systems are formed, they propagate directly to the southwest again? One would tend to think that not all the eddy motions in the ocean are homogeneous—that there are parts of the ocean that are quite different than other parts, as George Morgan suggested years ago.

RATTRAY: This is probably a continuation of the earlier questioning, in a sense. It seems to me that it would be interesting to look at the dynamics of the energy exchange between what would be called the mean flow and the growing wave motion, which should then give an estimate of momentum transfer and energy transfer out of the mean flow to the Rossby waves, which are apparently dissipated in such a way that they don't recirculate because of high frictional effect, because they are barotropic and there is an Ekman suction on the bottom.

BEARDSLEY: It's not clear that's true. In Ed Lorenz's (J. Atmos. Sci., 1972) calculations, the fastest growing mode was the one with zero phase velocity. It just sits there and grows. In this particular case, if the basic flow had a southward component, the phase velocity was in the southern direction.

RATTRAY: Somehow you end up with a balance between dissipation and generation.

BEARDSLEY: Yes, that's right. That type of energy budget calculation was not attempted numerically. Ed Lorenz did that in his model and showed where the eddy energy came from. I think we will try to do that in our model.

RATTRAY: The life history of your instabilities requires an average balance between two processes that might have different wave number dependences controlling the resulting spectral energy distribution.

ISRAELI: Two short questions. One, did you get the details of the separation? Two, is the disagreement in your stability curve due to numerical errors or to the approximations in your original equations?

BEARDSLEY: I'm not quite sure I understood the first question.

ISRAELI: There is a separation of the boundary layer from the wall before the instability sets in. Why does it separate where it separates, and what is the balance of forces there?

BEARDSLEY: For a detailed answer to that question we have a vorticity analysis of that region. But we still don't have a simple kind of physical explanation. Your second question had to do with the numerical method. In the nonlinear regime, the interesting phenomena take place far away from the boundary layer, where the spatial resolution is the highest. There actually is a trade-off here. The higher radial resolution is near the boundary, and the lowest radial resolution is at the center of the basin. What we found experimentally is that if you adjust the Ekman number and the Rossby number in such a way that the instabilities first appear near the center, and then try to find the critical Reynolds number, you could not get basically consistent results. We had to overdrive the flow. When we keep the formation zone for the instability away from the center of the basin (by either making use of a very large Ekman number, which makes the boundary layer thick, or using a relatively small Ekman number to keep the western boundary layer thin), we get essentially the straight-line dependence that we showed in Figure 11.

PEDLOSKY: I just want to mention what is probably an obvious fact, that, when you use an analogue like this, you have to be very careful in thinking about the real ocean. In relation to the comment that was made earlier about where you might and might not see eddies in the real ocean on the basis of this kind of thing, obviously you only have a barotropic source of energy here in that high shear energy layer. For instability arising in the real ocean, for example, you have in what would be analogous to the southern part of the basin, vertical shears and additional sources of energy, and it would be really pushing the situation to ask so much from this theory.

CHARNEY: The instability of Lorenz's, I think, is basically like a Rayleigh point of inflection instability. You must have a maximum in the absolute vorticity. Although not rigorous, this is the basic mechanism. In other words, you have to have a big enough amplitude to give you the maximum required to overcome the β-effect.

PEDLOSKY: The way I always like to think about Ed's (Lorenz) instability mechanism here is that it's a version of a resonant interaction approach on Rossby waves. In fact, I think Ed's analysis is in a sense more complicated than it needs to be. Just think of it in terms of resonant interaction.

CHARNEY: Well, that's the way you like to think of it.

BRETHERTON: But it's guaranteed to be there, whatever the amplitude of the wave. If it's a frictionless case, then any amplitude wave will grow provided the north-south wavelength satisfies the appropriate constraint. The growth rate depends on the amplitude however.

CHARNEY: No, the instability depends on the amplitude of the wave, amplitude of the stationary wave being greater than some critical value.

BEARDSLEY: At least in the viscous case it definitely depends on the initial amplitude of the wave.

BRETHERTON: Oh, in the viscous case it will, but in the inviscid case it will not.

CHARNEY: I think it does.

VERONIS: I think there's a very simple explanation for this problem. You have this kind of a motion in the linear case, and there must be an incoming region. As the system becomes more nonlinear, we know that inertia will carry the intense jet up along here (points to diagram), but fluid still has to be supplied from the offshore side, north of the center line. And that has to take place via some kind of a loop up here. It forms a high pressure region here, principally to bring in fluid. As the fluid goes up along here, the thin boundary layer that is maintained by the β-effect has to get much thicker, because there's no place to go in this purely viscous system.

NUMERICAL ANALYSIS OF LABORATORY EXPERIMENTS ON TOPOGRAPHICALLY CONTROLLED FLOW

D. L. BOYER

INTRODUCTION

During the past several years, my coworkers and I have examined in some detail the effects of bottom topography on flows in rotating systems. The studies were concerned with the physical system sketched in Figure 1. Identical topographies are mounted symmetrically on two horizontal plane surfaces. The region between the bounding surfaces is filled with a homogeneous incompressible fluid and the entire system rotates with a constant angular velocity, Ω_l, about a vertical axis. Upstream of the topographies and outside of the Ekman layers on the horizontal surfaces, the fluid is in a uniform rectilinear motion. The objectives of the studies were to determine both theoretically and by laboratory experiment the characteristics of the resulting flow fields.

By choosing a symmetrical system: (a) The analysis is simplified, since it is readily shown that the vertical velocity component is odd and the horizontal components are even in the vertical coordinate. The analysis need thus be made only for the lower half of the system. (b) Since the vertical velocity in the midplane (i.e., $z = 0$) is zero, the streamlines in this plane can be observed by releasing a neutrally buoyant tracer from a fixed position in the plane. For the range of parameters considered, the flow outside the Ekman layers is geostrophic to lowest order and thus the horizontal motion is independent of the vertical coordinate. The midplane streamline pattern is thus a good approximation for the horizontal motion throughout the depth of the fluid. (c) The lower half of the system approximates the conditions for flow past a submerged topography above which there is a horizontal free surface on which there are no shearing stresses.

The problem as posed is a four parameter one; the following are chosen:

$$E = \nu/2\Omega_l L_l^2,\ Ro = U_l/2\Omega_l L_l,\ H_l/L_l,\ h_l/L_l,$$

where E is the Ekman number; Ro, the Rossby number; ν, the kinematic viscosity; U_l, the free-stream speed; and where the other terms are defined in Figure 1. For general values of the dimensionless quantities, the problem is intractable and one is thus led to making simplifying assumptions.

By making the following a priori restrictions, the problem can be reduced to one that can readily be solved numerically and, for certain very simple topographies (e.g., a long ridge), can be solved analytically:

(a) $E \ll 1$;

(b) $Ro = k_l E^{1/2}$, where k_l is of order unity;

(c) H_l/L_l is of order unity;

(d) The bottom topography is given by $z = -H_l/L_l + E^{1/2} h_{ol}(x,y)$, where $h_{ol} = E^{-1/2} h_l(x,y)/L_l$ is of order unity—i.e., the topography height-to-width ratio is small; and

(e) h_{olx}, h_{oly} are of order unity everywhere—i.e., no large slopes occur in the bottom topography.

The simplifications in the equations of motion resulting from these restrictions are given in Vaziri (1971) and Vaziri and Boyer (1971) and are not repeated here. The flow field to lowest order can be shown to consist of an interior geostrophic region and Ekman layers along the bounding surfaces. The analysis proceeds by expanding the dependent variables in a series in $E^{1/2}$ for the two regions. By matching the vertical velocity components (of order $E^{1/2}$) obtained for

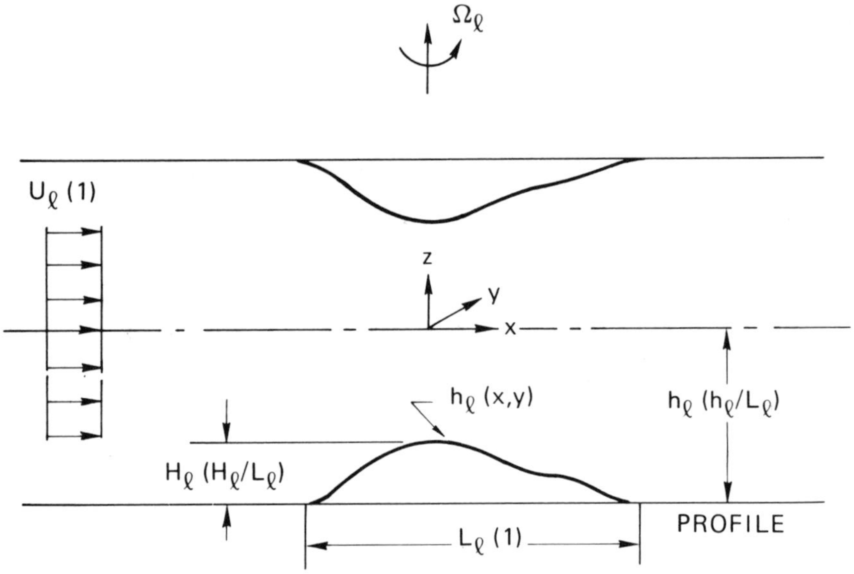

FIGURE 1 The physical system considered in the laboratory experiments. The quantities in parentheses are dimensionless.

the interior and Ekman layers along the bottom boundary, one determines the governing equations for the lowest-order interior motion as:

$$k_l(H_l/L_l)\,[\zeta_{lt} + J(\psi_l,\zeta_l)] + 2^{-1/2}\zeta_l + J(\psi_l,h_{ol}) = 0, \quad (1)$$

$$w_l = k_l z\,[\zeta_{lt} + J(\psi_l,\zeta_l)]\,E^{1/2}, \quad (2)$$

where

$$\zeta_l = \nabla^2 \psi_l \quad (3)$$

and where J is the Jacobian.

Here ζ_l is the vertical component of relative vorticity and ψ_l is the stream function. The horizontal velocity components (u_l,v_l) in the (x,y) directions are related to the stream function by $u_l = -\psi_{ly}$ and $v_l = \psi_{lx}$; w_l is the vertical velocity component.

The boundary conditions for topographies with finite extent in both the x and y directions are

$$\psi_l(x \to -\infty, y) = -y,$$

$$\psi_l(x, y \to \pm\infty) = \pm y,$$

$$\psi_{lx}(x \to \infty, y) = 0. \quad (4)$$

Solutions for ψ_l and ζ_l for (1) and (3) subject to the boundary conditions (4) can be obtained numerically using a procedure similar to that given by Charney *et al.* (1950). The solution for w_l then follows from (2).

The theoretical results obtained can be compared with experiment by utilizing the rotating water-tunnel apparatus described in Boyer (1971). Very briefly, the tunnel is a channel of rectangular cross section (115 cm long, 35 cm wide, and 3.8 cm deep). Water is pumped through the channel, and the entire system rotates counterclockwise at a constant angular velocity about a vertical axis. By properly adjusting the entrance and exit conditions, the tunnel can provide a test section flow that is uniform outside the Ekman layers on the horizontal plane surfaces.

The uniform flow is at a slight angle to the right of the channel axis as one faces downstream. This angle can be estimated by balancing the Ekman transport with the cross-channel interior flow. One obtains $\tan\theta = (\tfrac{1}{2}H_l)(\nu/\Omega_l)^{1/2}$. Within experimental error this relation is satisfied in the laboratory.

The lab experiments for the most part have been addressed at observing the geostrophic flow and, in particular, the motion in the midplane. In this regard a tracer is released from a series of equally spaced lateral positions in the midplane ($z = 0$) of the tunnel and upstream of the topographies. Since the vertical velocity in the midplane is zero, the streaklines so formed depict the streamlines in the plane (for steady flows). Since the lowest-order motion is geostrophic, these streamlines are representative of the horizontal motion throughout the depth of the fluid.

For topographies that are two-dimensional, in the sense that they are long ridges with constant cross sections, Eqs. (1) and (2) are linear, since derivatives of velocity components along the ridge are identically zero. Solutions of (1) subject to the first and third of (4) can thus be obtained (Boyer, 1971). In particular, solutions are obtained for flow over a ridge with a triangular cross section.

In a recent study (Boyer, 1972), it is shown that the restriction of infinitesimal topographic slopes [(*e*) above] can be relaxed. This study considers the special case of flow over a long step-ridge of constant cross section. In the vicinity of vertical surfaces, defined by the infinite slope portions of the topography, it is shown that vertical shear layers exist in which there is a balance between inertial, pressure, and Coriolis effects, viscous terms being negligible. These layers separate the flow field into three geostrophic regions, in each of which relations (1–3) are applicable. The shear layer analysis provides the proper matching conditions between the adjacent geostrophic regions. Solutions for both the triangular and step-ridges are in good agreement with the laboratory experiments.

For topographies of limited extent in the x–y plane, the governing equations are nonlinear; and one is thus led to seeking numerical solutions (Vaziri and Boyer, 1971). This study is restricted to topographies with infinitesimal slopes and, in particular, emphasizes the flow over conical obstacles.

One would also like to obtain solutions for bodies with large slopes and of limited extent in the x–y plane, e.g., a disc. It is a relatively easy matter to extend the shear layer analysis made for the step to that of the disc. Whereas the shear layer structure for the step depends only on the coordinate perpendicular to the step, that for the disc depends both on a radial, as well as an azimuthal, coordinate. The difficulty arises in attempting to set up the disc problem numerically. The reason is that it has not been possible to devise a numerical scheme for the jump in relative vorticity that occurs along the disc boundary. This problem remains unresolved.

It has been possible, however, to obtain satisfactory numerical solutions by utilizing the numerical analysis for a smooth topography and approximating the edge of the disc by a large but finite slope. A comparison between a numerical analysis using this approximation and a laboratory experiment is shown in Figure 2. Figure 2a is a laboratory experiment, and 2b is the corresponding numerical run. The flow is from left to right and the rotation is counterclockwise. The streamlines in the experiment are in the midplane of the tunnel.

While the derivation of (1–3) is restricted to topographies of infinitesimal amplitudes, solutions for topographies of rather large amplitudes (order unity or larger) are found to be also in good agreement with experiment. This agreement can be explained, at least in a qualitative way.

Above bottom features of large slope, the topographic term in (1) is large. Correspondingly, it must thus be balanced by either or both of the inertial and Ekman suction terms. Further, in the neighborhood of large slope features, strong streamline deflections will occur. Since the Ekman suction is a second-order derivative in the horizontal coordinates, while the inertial term is third-order, the former is negligible; and thus the balance in (1) is inertial $\sim$ topographic. This balance is an expression for conservation of potential vorticity. In regions in which topographic features

$$Ro = 4 \times 10^{-2}, \quad E = 1 \times 10^{-4}, \quad H/D = 0.375, \quad h/D = 6.25 \times 10^{-2}$$

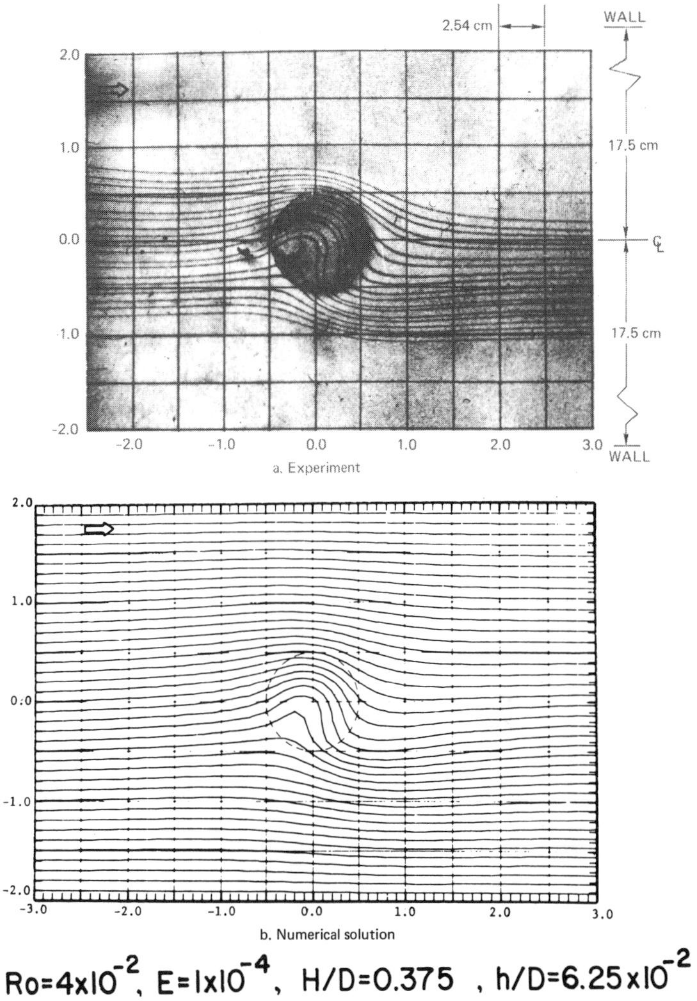

FIGURE 2 Flow over a disc. (2a) Laboratory experiment midplane streamlines. The flow is from left to right and the rotation is counterclockwise. (2b) Corresponding numerical run. Parameters: $E = 8.0(10)^{-5}$, $Ro = 6.0(10)^{-3}$, $H_I/L_I = 0.38$, $h_I/L_I = 0.03$.

are absent, (1) expresses an inertial $\sim$ Ekman suction balance. For small slopes, all terms in (1) are important. Thus (1) can be used to a good approximation for the entire flow field, even if portions contain topographic features of large slope.

Thus a laboratory capability has been developed and a theory advanced for the prediction of bottom topography effects on a class of rotating fluid motions. The objective now is to investigate the possibility of applying some of these techniques to the study of real geophysical fluid phenomena—in particular, the influence of bottom topography on the deflection of ocean currents.

Let us take the point of view of examining a limited area model of the ocean. That is, we do not consider an entire ocean basin, but rather assume that a basic current structure (e.g., Antarctic circumpolar current) is specified and then limit the modeling to a small portion of the total current.

At the outset, one must emphasize that many assumptions must be made in relating real ocean flows to the laboratory (and theoretical) system described above. These include, for example, taking the fluid to be homogeneous and incompressible, the dissipative mechanism to be defined by constant eddy viscosity coefficients, and the bottom bathymetry to be greatly simplified. Needless to say, at this stage in modeling development, one hopes, at best, to reproduce only major features of the real ocean in the model.

In considering what portions of the ocean might be reasonable for modeling, one would like to restrict to a current with a reasonably well-defined "free stream" and further a current for which the effects of stratification would be minimized. Such considerations lead one to a study of certain portions of the Antarctic circumpolar current. The particular examples discussed below are the region in the vicinity of the Macquarie Ridge and that near the Kerguelen Gaussberg Ridge.

The derivation of the governing equations for the ocean model will contain contributions from wind shear as well as β effects. We have not incorporated these into the laboratory model.

In the next section, the ocean model equations are derived. In the final section, models of the flow in the neighborhood of the Macquarie and Kerguelen Guassberg Ridges are considered.

GOVERNING EQUATIONS FOR THE OCEAN MODEL

For the sake of brevity, the derivation of the ocean model equations will be outlined; for more details, the reader is referred to Guala (1972). Let us begin with the standard set of equations of motion for a homogeneous incompressible fluid on a rotating sphere, i.e., the three equations for conservation of momentum and the equation for conservation of mass. Take the spherical coordinates as (λ,ϕ,r) with the corresponding velocity components (u,v,w), where λ is the longitude; ϕ, the latitude; and r, the radius.

We then define the new coordinates,

$$x = R\cos\phi_o\lambda,$$

$$y = R\hat{\phi},$$

$$z = r - R, \tag{5}$$

where R is the earth's radius, ϕ_o is the latitude of the approximate center of the limited ocean area under consideration, and $\hat{\phi} = \phi - \phi_o$.

Now introduce the following dimensionless quantities:

$$(x^*,y^*) = (x/L,\ y/L), \qquad z^* = z/H,$$

$$t^* = (U/L)t, \qquad p^* = p/\rho f_o UL,$$

$$(u^*,v^*) = (u/U,\ v/U), \qquad w^* = (L/H)(w/U), \tag{6}$$

where L is the characteristic horizontal dimension of the topographic feature; H, the ocean depth; U, the upstream velocity; p, the reduced pressure (i.e., obtained by subtracting out the hydrostatic contribution at the origin of the coordinate system from the total pressure); ρ, the density; $f_o = 2\Omega\sin\phi_o$, the Coriolis parameter; and Ω, the earth's rotation rate. Also introduce constant horizontal (N_H) and vertical (N_V) eddy viscosity coefficients.

Further assume that

$$H/R \ll L/R \sim O(\hat{\phi}) \ll 1, \tag{7}$$

i.e., assume that the ocean depth is much smaller than the horizontal extent of the topographic feature. By utilizing (5-7), the (λ,ϕ,r) momentum equations and the equation for conservation of mass can be written respectively as

$$R_o[u_t + uu_x + vu_y + wu_z + O(\hat{\phi})] =$$
$$-[1 + \tan\phi_o\hat{\phi} + O(\hat{\phi}^2)]\,p_x + [(v - \frac{H}{L}\cot\phi_o w)$$
$$+(v\cot\phi_o + \frac{H}{L}w)\hat{\phi} + O(\hat{\phi}^2)]$$
$$+[E_H(u_{xx} + u_{yy}) + E_V u_{zz} + O(\hat{\phi})],$$

$$R_o\left[v_t + uv_x + vv_y + wv_z + O(\hat{\phi})\right] = -p_y$$
$$-u\left[1 - \cot\phi_o\hat{\phi} + O(\hat{\phi}^2)\right]$$
$$+\left[E_H(v_{xx} + v_{yy}) + E_V v_{zz} + O(\hat{\phi})\right],$$

$$R_o[w_t + uw_x + vw_y + ww_z + O(\hat{\phi})] = -\left(\frac{L}{H}\right)^2 p_z$$
$$+\left(\frac{L}{H}\right)u[\cot\phi_o - \hat{\phi} + O(\hat{\phi}^2)]$$
$$+[E_H(w_{xx} + w_{yy}) + E_V v_{zz} + O(\hat{\phi})],$$

$$[1 + \tan\phi_o\hat{\phi} + O(\hat{\phi}^2)]\,u_x + v_y$$
$$-\frac{L}{R}[\tan\phi_o + O(\hat{\phi})]\,v + w_z + 2\left(\frac{L}{R}\right)w = 0, \tag{8}$$

where $R_o = U/f_oL$ is the Rossby number, $E_V = N_V/f_oH^2$ and $E_H = N_H/f_oL^2$ are the Ekman numbers, and where asterisks have been omitted from dimensionless quantities. Note that for each term of different character (i.e., inertia, etc.) the lowest-order neglected contribution is specified.

One other parameter enters through the boundary condition of the wind shear on the upper surface. Define S as

$$S = \tau_o/\rho(f_oN_V)^{1/2}U, \tag{9}$$

where τ_o is the maximum wind shear.

Eqs. (8) are intractable unless they are simplified by placing restrictions on the magnitude of the various parameters. Before introducing these restrictions, let us assign some more or less typical values to the pertinent quantities. Let

$\phi_o = 60°$	$H = 5$ km
$R = 6{,}400$ km	$U = 10$ cm/s
$\Omega = 7.3(10)^{-5}$ rad/s	$\tau_o = 1$ dyn/cm^2
$L = 500$ km	$\rho = 1$ gm/cm^3

It then follows that

$R_o = 1.5(10)^{-3}$	$E_V = 3.1(10)^{-8} N_V$
$H/L = 10^{-2}$	$E_H = 3.1(10)^{-12} N_H$
$L/R = 7.8(10)^{-2} \sim \hat{\phi}$	$S = 8.8(N_V)^{-1/2}$

The specification of values for N_V and N_H is much more uncertain, even as regards the correct order of magnitude. Sverdrup *et al.* (1942) give ranges for N_V and N_H of say $10 < N_V < 10^4$ cm^2/s and $10^6 < N_H < 10^8$ cm^2/s, respectively. The parameter restrictions imposed below lead to an elimination of N_H from the governing equations for the model. It will thus not be possible to satisfy the no-slip condition along lateral boundaries that one may wish to model. The condition along such boundaries (e.g., a shoreline) is thus that the flow is parallel to the boundary. The coefficient N_V is treated as a free parameter, i.e., the model behavior is investigated over a range of N_V.

Let us now make the following a priori assumptions:

(a) $E_V \ll 1$; i.e., $N_V \ll 10^7$ cm^2/s.

(b) $E_H \ll E_V^{1/2}$; i.e., $N_H \ll 10^7\, N_V^{1/2}$ cm^2/s.

(c) $R_o = kE_V^{1/2}$, where k is of order unity.

(d) $H/L = (H/L)_o E_V^{1/2}$, where $(H/L)_o$ is of order unity.

(e) $h(\lambda,\phi)/H = h_o(x,y)E_V^{1/2}$, where $(h_o(x,y)$ is of order unity.

(f) $\hat{\phi} = (L/R)y = (L/R)_o E_V^{1/2} y$, where $(L/R)_o$ is of order unity.

(g) S is of order unity.

The above restrictions lead to a flow field consisting of Ekman layers along the ocean surface and bottom and an interior geostrophic region. In each of these regions, the dependent variables can be expanded in a power series in $E_V^{1/2}$.

In the interior we let

$$u = U_o E_V^{o} + U_1 E_V^{1/2} + \cdots,$$
$$v = V_o E_V^{o} + V_1 E_V^{1/2} + \cdots,$$
$$w = W_o E_V^{o} + W_1 E_V^{1/2} + \cdots,$$
$$p = p_o E_V^{0} + p_1 E_V^{1/2} + \cdots, \qquad (10)$$

where $U_o, \ldots, p_1, \ldots$ are of order unity, the order of the leading terms is dictated by the method of nondimensionalization, and the first-order terms are obtained by the magnitude of the suction (pumping) velocity in the Ekman layers. Substituting (10) into (8), one determines the zeroth- and first-order equations as

$$0 = -p_{ox} + V_o,$$
$$0 = -p_{oy} - U_o,$$
$$0 = -p_{oz},$$
$$U_{ox} + V_{oy} + W_{oz} = 0, \qquad (11)$$

and

$$k(U_{ot} + V_o U_{ox} + V_o U_{oy}) = -p_{1x} - \tan\phi_o \left(\frac{L}{R}\right)_o y\, p_{ox} + V_1 + \cot\phi_o \left(\frac{L}{R}\right)_o y\, V_o,$$
$$k(V_{ot} + U_o V_{ox} + V_o V_{oy}) = -p_{1x} - U_1 - \cos\phi_o \left(\frac{L}{R}\right)_o y U_o,$$
$$O = \left(\frac{H}{L}\right)_o^{-1} p_{1z} + \cot\phi_o U_o,$$
$$U_{1x} + V_{1y} + W_{1z} + \tan\phi_o \left(\frac{L}{R}\right)_o y U_{ox} - \tan\phi_o \left(\frac{L}{R}\right)_o V_o = 0, \qquad (12)$$

respectively.

The zeroth-order equations (11) show that the interior flow is geostrophic; in particular, $U_o = U_o(x,y)$, $V_o = V_o(x,y)$, $W_o = 0$. Note that $W_o = 0$ from the constraint that w must vanish to this order at the sea surface and bottom and from (11) that W_o must be linear in z.

If we now cross-differentiate the first two of (12), substitute the resulting expression for $(U_{1x} + V_{1y})$ into the last of (12), introduce a stream function for the lowest-order horizontal motion defined by $U_o = -\psi_y$ and $V_o = \psi_x$, and finally integrate the resulting expression, we obtain

$$W_1 = z\left[k\left\{\nabla^2\psi_t + J(\psi_1\nabla^2\psi)\right\} + \cot\phi_o \left(\frac{L}{R}\right)_o V_o\right] + f(x,y), \qquad (13)$$

where $f(x,y)$ is to be determined.

The governing equation for ψ is then obtained by matching (13) with the Ekman layers. For the bottom layer, the analysis is similar to that given in Vaziri and Boyer (1971). Letting η_B be a stretched coordinate for the bottom Ekman layer, one obtains

$$w(\eta_B \to \infty) = \left[\frac{1}{(2)^{1/2}}\nabla^2\psi + J(\psi, h_o)\right] E_V{}^{1/2}. \tag{14}$$

For the surface Ekman layer,

$$w(\eta_S \to \infty) = \gamma \operatorname{curl}_z \bar{\tau} E_V{}^{1/2}, \tag{15}$$

where

$$\gamma = \frac{HE_V{}^{1/2}\tau_o}{\rho N_V U}, \qquad \bar{\tau} = (\tau_x \hat{i} + \tau_y \hat{j})/\tau_o. \tag{16}$$

Here (τ_x, τ_y) are the dimensional wind shear stresses in the (x,y) directions respectively.

Equating (13), evaluated at $z = -1$, with (14) and at $z = 0$, with (15), one finally obtains

$$k[\nabla^2\psi_t + J(\psi_1 \nabla^2\psi)] + \frac{1}{(2)^{1/2}}\nabla^2\psi + J(\psi, h_o) + \cot\phi_o \left(\frac{L}{R}\right)_o \psi_x = \gamma \operatorname{curl}_z \bar{\tau}. \tag{17}$$

Relation (17) is a transport equation for the relative vorticity $\zeta = \nabla^2\psi$. The first two terms represent the rate of change of relative vorticity following a fluid column. The third is the dissipation due to Ekman suction (pumping). The fourth, the topographic term, may be a source or a sink of relative vorticity. The last term is the contribution of wind shear and may be a source or sink.

In the present discussion, we ignore the β and wind shear terms in (17) and thus are able to relate this ocean model equation to the laboratory model (1). In this regard, we require

$$k_l \frac{H_l}{L_l} = k \to \frac{U_l}{(2\Omega_l \nu)^{1/2}} \frac{H_l}{L_l} = \frac{U}{(f_o N_v)^{1/2}} \frac{H}{L},$$
$$h_{ol} = h_o \to h_l \left(\frac{2\Omega_l}{\nu}\right)^{1/2} = h\left(\frac{f_o}{N_V}\right)^{1/2}. \tag{18}$$

In attempting to conduct a laboratory model experiment, we assume that $L, H, h(x,y), U$, and f_o are specified for the ocean model. We then choose values for L_l, H_l and $h_l(x,y)$ and specify a viscosity coefficient N_V. Relations (18) are then used to determine the laboratory settings Ω_l and U_l. It should be noted, however, that in practice the ranges of possible Ω_l and U_l are very limited; i.e., typically, $0.5 < \Omega_l < 2.0$ rad/s and $0.1 < U_l < 0.5$ cm/s. Consequently the range of N_V that can be considered is also limited.

SOME EXAMPLES

We now apply the above modeling scheme to two limited areas of the Antarctic circumpolar current. The first, the region in the vicinity of the Macquarie Ridge, was reported in Boyer and Guala (1972) (Region A in Figure 3). The second, the area near the Kerguelen Gaussberg Ridge, is discussed in Guala (1972) (Region B in Figure 3).

Macquarie Ridge

A generalized bathymetry of the Macquarie Ridge is given in Figure 4 (Hayes *et al.*, 1972). The area to be modeled is indicated by the dashed lines. The model topography is given in Figure 5. The ocean floor away from topographic features is taken to be horizontal and of depth H. All of the surfaces of the model topography are plane. Trenches are indicated by the dotted areas; the maximum depth of the trench is $H + h/2$ below the free surface. Elevated features are indicated by the cross-hatched areas; the peaks are $H - h$ below the free surface. The characteristic horizontal scale, L, is taken to be the width of the Macquarie Ridge. It is assumed that the current is uniform upstream of the ridge system and, furthermore, that it is bounded by "slip walls" on the north, representing the Tasman basin, and on the south by the mid-ocean ridge.

The following parameters are specified for the ocean model:

$L = 75$ km	$U = 25$ cm/s
$H = 5$ km	$\phi_o = 56°$
$h = 4$ km	

Further, for the laboratory flow we let:

$L_l = 2.54$ cm	$h_l = 1.52$ cm
$H_l = 1.90$ cm	$\nu = 0.01$ cm^2/s

By choosing $N_V = 2.5(10)^4$ cm^2/s, it is possible to examine the flow field both in the laboratory and numerically. For this choice relations (18) require $\Omega_l = 1.65$ rad/s and $U_l = 0.24$ cm/s for similarity between the laboratory and ocean models.

The boundary conditions for the numerical solution are

$$\psi(-X,y,t) = -y,$$
$$\psi_x(X,y,t) = 0,$$
$$\psi(x,-Y,t) = Y,$$
$$\psi(x,Y,t) = 0, \tag{19}$$

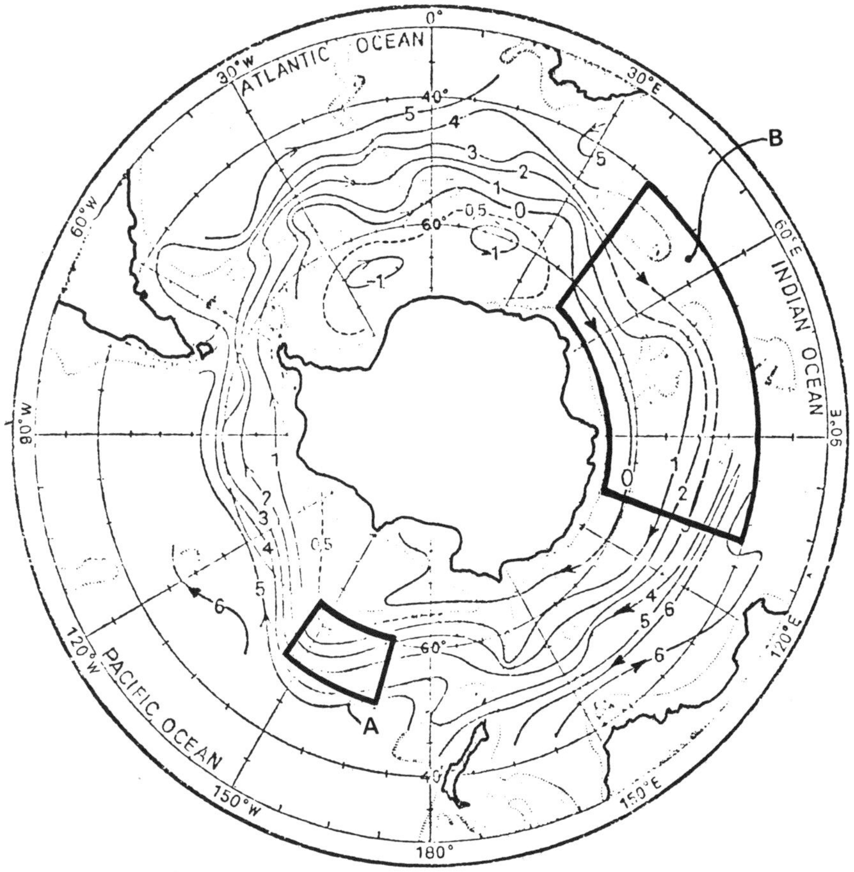

FIGURE 3 Antarctic circumpolar current. Location of limited area models considered. (A) Macquarie Ridge. (B) Kerguelen Gaussberg Ridge.

and the initial condition is taken as

$$\psi(x,y,o) = -y. \tag{20}$$

Numerical solutions are thus obtained by applying (19) and (20) to (17) (minus β and wind shear terms).

Let us now consider some oceanographic observations; in particular, those made by Gordon (1972). Gordon (1967) has shown that a well-defined relation exists between the depth of the maximum salinity core layer, S_{max} and the relative sea surface dynamic topography; the shallower the S_{max} layer, the lower the sea surface dynamic topography. This relationship allows one to determine the sea surface dynamic topography relative to a given pressure surface even in regions where that surface would be below the sea floor. In addition, using this relation, the sea surface dynamic topography can be determined from salinity data alone.

Figure 6 shows the isobaths of the depth of the S_{max} layer, which, as noted, can be related to the sea surface dynamic topography. The isobaths are streamlines of the geostrophic flow with the separation of the contours being inversely proportional to the velocity.

Since the laboratory and ocean models (numerical) are essentially the same, let us use "model" to designate both in the following. We first note that the model and oceanographic data indicate that a major portion of the flow is deflected southward on approaching the ridge system. While the model indicates a strong southward flow over the Hjort Trench, such an intense current is not evident in Figure 7. While the reason for this discrepancy is not evident, it may well be that more detailed oceanographic data would indicate the presence of such a current.

Both the model and oceanographic data show that there is an upstream (westward) current in the vicinity of the southern tip of the Macquarie Ridge before the flow passes into the Emerald basin. In addition, both model and prototype indicate a large transport through the 56° fracture zone. The oceanographic data shows a relatively large transport through the 53½° fracture zone. Such a strong current is absent in the model. The difficulty here may be that the model fracture zone has been made too small. It should also be noted that both model and prototype show that the flow skirts the Campbell Plateau.

Gordon (1972) indicates that the temperature structure in the upper few hundred meters along 159°30′ E is given qualitatively by the diagram in Figure 7; i.e., on moving north the temperature increases to about 58° N, then decreases to about 57° N, and then increases again. Gordon also

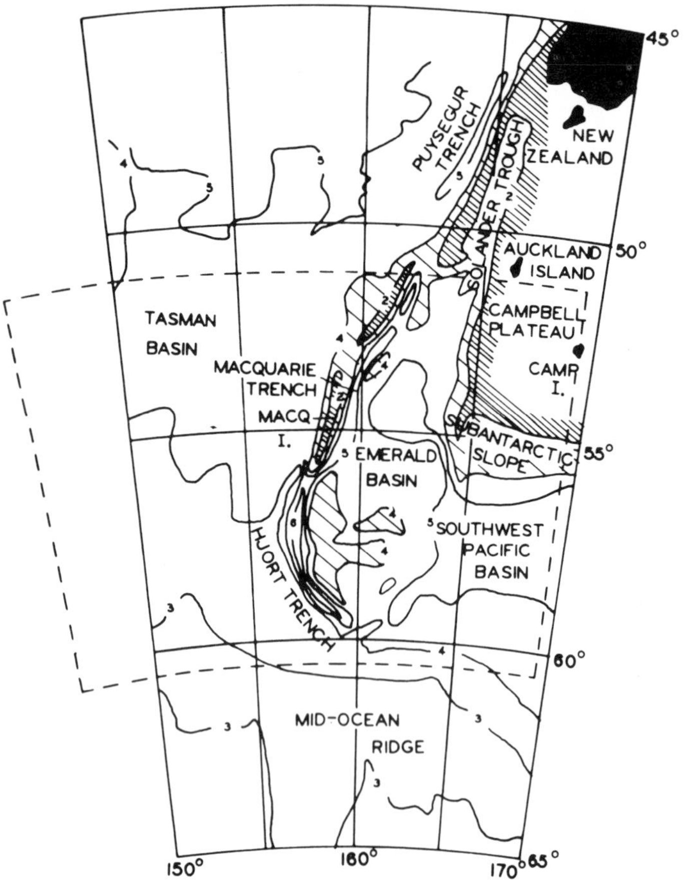

FIGURE 4 Bathymetry in the vicinity of the Macquarie Ridge. The numbers on the diagram represent the ocean depth in kilometers and the dashed line designates the region considered in the model studies.

suggests that this feature appears to be a permanent characteristic of the current in this area. If one assumes that temperature is a conservative property of fluid parcels moving through the system and, further, that west of the Macquarie Ridge the temperature increases monotonically to the north, then the model flows are in agreement with Gordon's observations.

Gordon (1971) also observed temperature profiles similar to that given in Figure 7 east of the Macquarie Ridge; he used the term double polar front zone for the profile. Gordon points out that this feature seems to be transient and that it is not observed west of the ridge. He finally suggests that the double polar front zone is created at the southern end of the Macquarie Ridge by the shedding of eddies. These eddies (in the form of observed double polar front zones) migrate across a major part of the Pacific Ocean; i.e., they are observed to 108° W.

The model studies (Figure 6) do not predict such eddies. The reason, presumably, is that the eddy viscosity coefficient used in the model is too large. A series of numerical experiments were thus conducted for smaller N_V; the capabilities of the laboratory apparatus did not allow experimentation for these values of N_V. Figure 8 shows the flow near the tip of the ridge for $N_V = 10^4/\text{cm}^2$ s. One notes quite clearly the shedding of an eddy, its movement downstream, and its being partially dissipated by Ekman suction. Thus the numerical model seems to support Gordon's suggestion. It must be emphasized, however, that the choice of N_V has been made here in a quite arbitrary fashion. Nevertheless, the model results are encouraging and are thought

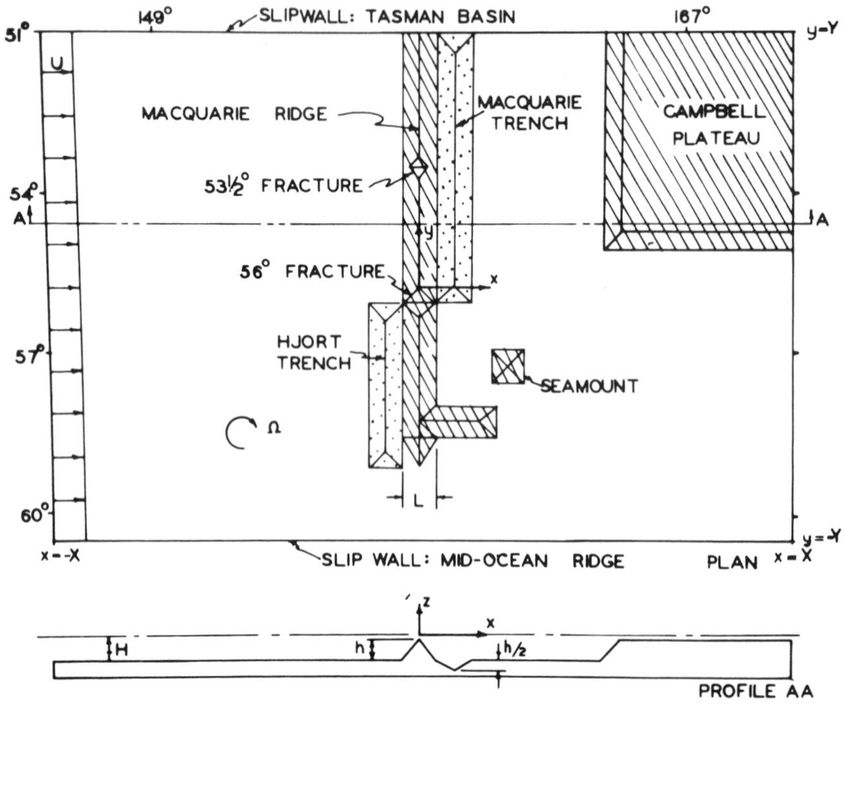

FIGURE 5 Model of the bathymetry in the vicinity of the Macquarie Ridge.

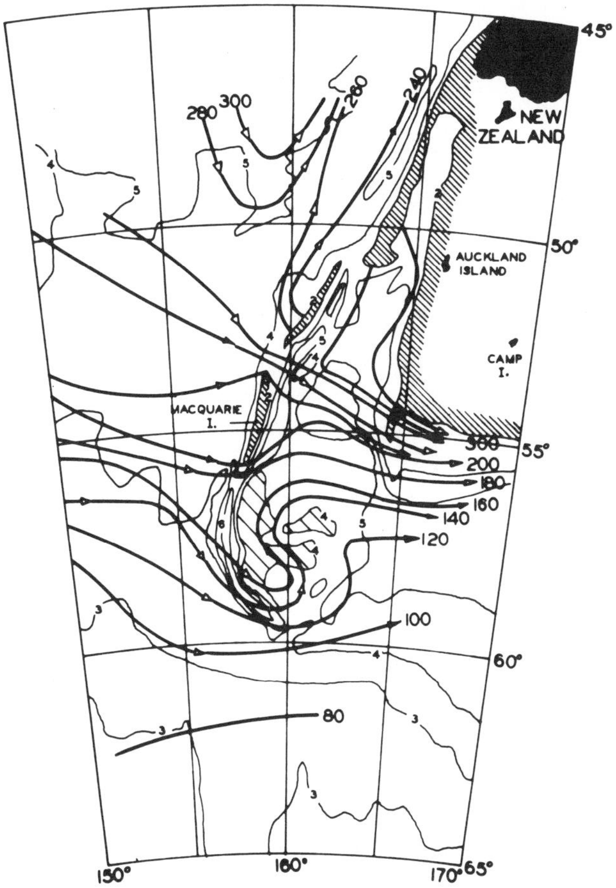

FIGURE 6 Depth of salinity maximum core layer.

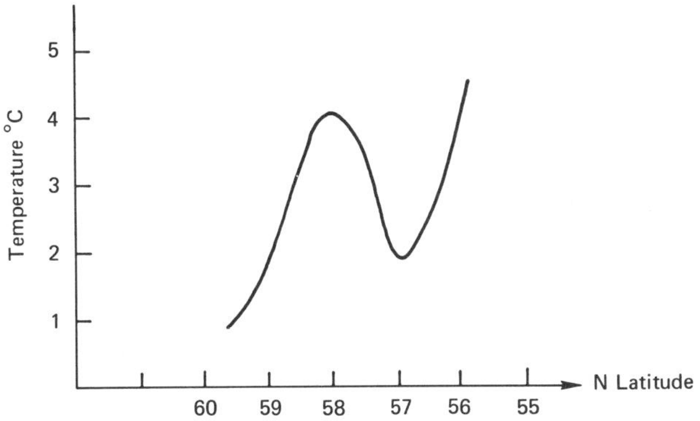

FIGURE 7 "Average" temperature distribution in upper 200 m along 159° 30′ E.

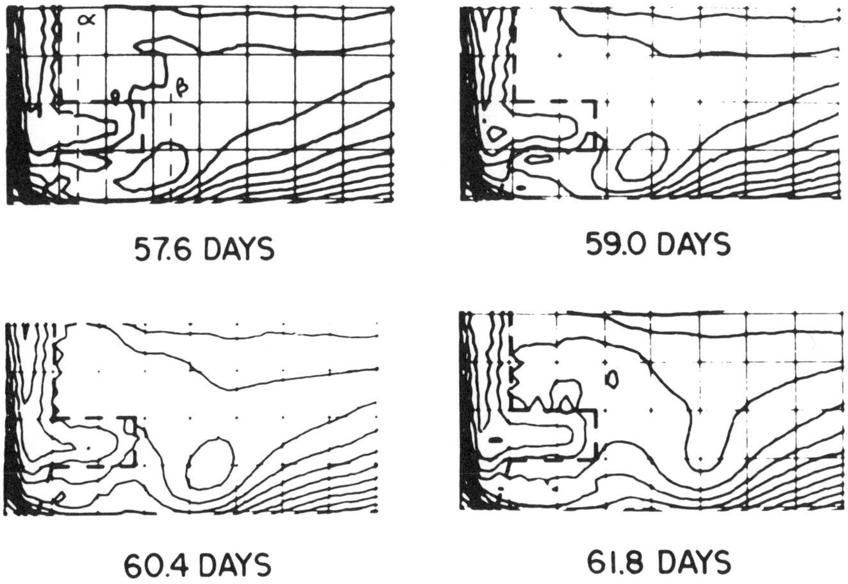

FIGURE 8 Time sequence of an eddy shedding near the southern tip of the Macquarie Ridge model. $N_V = (10)^4$ cm²/s, $E_V = 3.3(10)^{-4}$, $Ro = 2.8(10)^{-2}$.

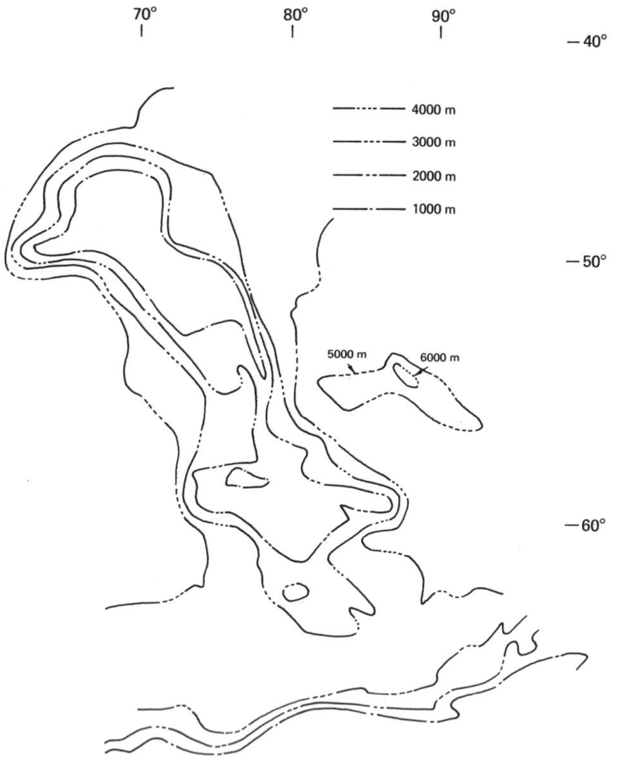

FIGURE 9 Bathymetry in the vicinity of the Kerguelen Gaussberg Ridge.

to qualitatively describe some of the major current characteristics in this region.

Kerguelen Gaussberg Ridge

A sketch of the bathymetry of the sea floor in the vicinity of the Kerguelen Gaussberg Ridge is given in Figure 9 (Heezen, 1972). In the numerical model, slip walls are assumed at 40° N and 65° N. Further, the same boundary and initial conditions as given in (19) and (20), respectively, are utilized. No laboratory experiments have been conducted for the Kerguelen Gaussberg Ridge studies.

The pertinent parameters for the numerical analysis are:

$L = 700$ km $\quad U = 25$ cm/s

$H = 4$ km $\quad \phi_o = 52.5°$

$h = 3$ km

Figure 10a is a computer plot of the model topography. The entire region away from the topographic features is taken to have a constant depth equal to unity (dimensionless). The depth contour interval in Figure 10a is 0.125. The cross-hatched area is a depression in the ocean basin. Figure 10b is a streamline plot for the geostrophic flow for $N_V = 10^4$ cm^2/s. The solution has converged and hence represents a steady-state flow. It is not possible to compare these model results with real data, since there is a lack of such data for the region in the vicinity of the Kerguelen Gaussberg Ridge. Presumably, a model feature such as the strong current between the mid-ocean ridge and the southern part of the Kerguelen Gaussberg Ridge should be observed in the real ocean.

Runs were also conducted for $N_V = 10^2$ cm^2/s and $N_V = 10^3$ cm^2/s. For both of these values the flow is unsteady with eddies being shed from the northern edge of the ridge system (Figure 11). The domain in Figure 11 is the same as the upper right quadrant of the domain in Figure 10. To the author's knowledge, no presently available oceanographic data suggest the presence of such eddies.

ACKNOWLEDGMENTS

The author would like to acknowledge the efforts of Drs. John Guala and Arsalan Vaziri in carrying out this research. The work was supported by the Office of Naval Research under contract NR 083-259. The numerical computations were made on the CDC-6600 and CDC-7600 computers at the National Center for Atmospheric Research. The Center is supported by the National Science Foundation.

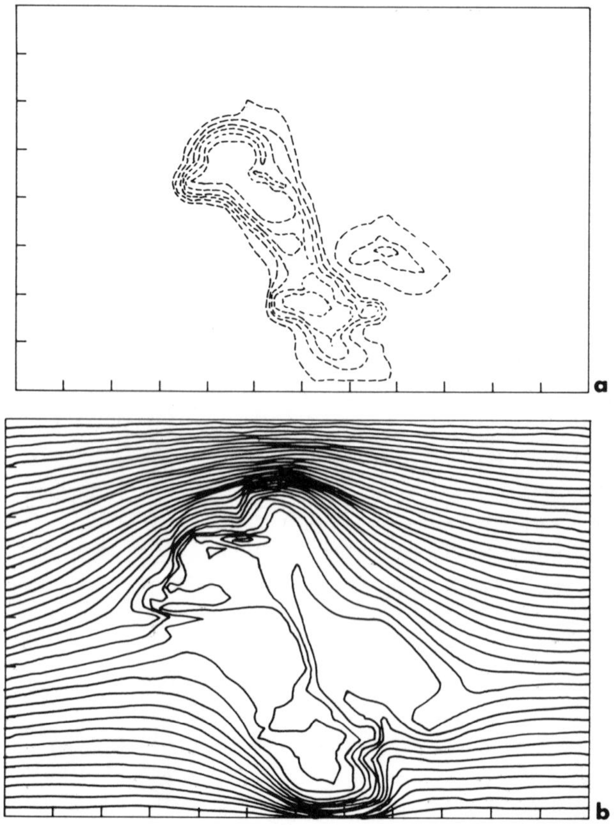

FIGURE 10 Kerguelen Gaussberg Ridge model. (a) Model topography–depth contour interval equals 0.125. (b) Geostrophic flow. $N_V = (10)^4$ cm^2/s, $E_V = 5.2(10)^{-4}$, $Ro = 3.0(10)^{-3}$.

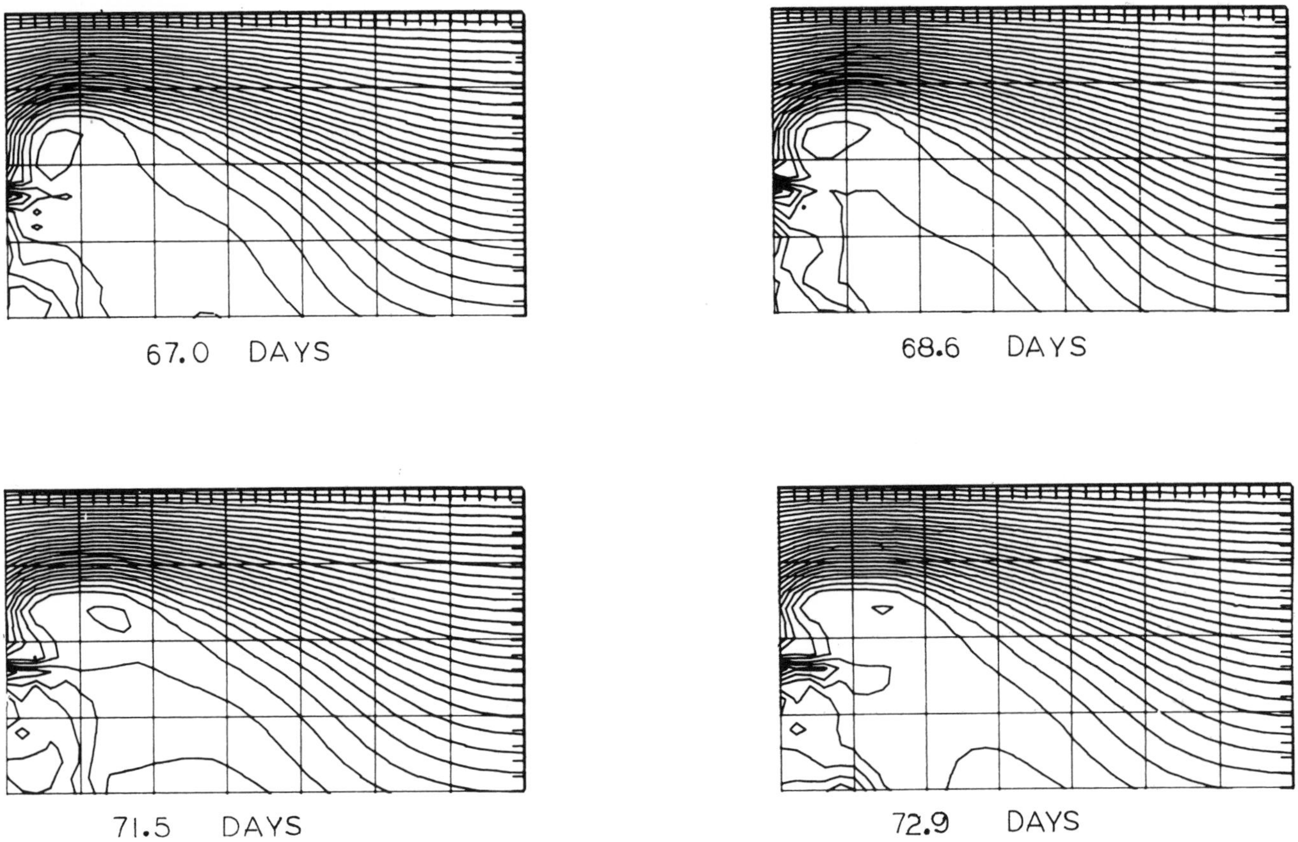

FIGURE 11 Time sequence of an eddy shedding near the northern tip of the Kerguelen Gaussberg Ridge model. $N_V = 10^3$ cm^2/s, $E_V = 5.2(10)^{-3}$, $Ro = 3.0(10)^{-3}$.

REVIEW: P. P. NIILER

In the region of the Macquarie Ridge, the broad Antarctic circumpolar current has a strong barotropic component of flow. Masinof and Vorob'yev (1962) have shown that its geostrophic attenuation between the sea surface and 3,000 m is only about 40 percent of the surface flow. In comparison with such narrow western boundary current systems as the Gulf Stream, which are attenuated 95 percent at a depth of 1,000 m (Warren, 1968), it is quite likely that a strong interaction takes place between the Antarctic circumpolar current and the underlying topographic features of the ridge. The bathymetry of the ridge near 160° E rises sharply from 5,000 m to a mean depth of 2,000 m; the width of the ridge is small (200 km) compared to the breadth of the current (600 km). It is observed that the center of the current is deflected over 1,000 km to the south as it approaches the ridge. While direct current measurements are not available in this region, it is estimated that only a small part of the flow passes through the narrow passages within the ridge.

Dr. D. L. Boyer and his colleagues have developed a hierarchy of numerical models and rapidly rotating water tank experiments to study the horizontal structure of slow barotropic flow over obstacles of small aspect ratio. This paper is a review of their contribution to the field. Their quasi-geostrophic model of the circulation outside the Ekman layers (for both oceanic and laboratory applications) is not new, for it has been used by a large number of other investigators in similar contexts (vide Schulman and Niiler, 1970; Carrier, 1965; and Gadgil, 1971). In this reviewer's view, Dr. Boyer's chief contribution is a series of calculations and laboratory experiments that can be related directly to the simplest, barotropic model of the dynamical situation of the Antarctic circumpolar current over realistic topography. The bulk of the numerical experiments cover a range of bottom topography configurations that are not readily amenable to analytical treatment. In a range of Rossby and Ekman numbers, where the laboratory experiments are steady flows, these are in qualitative agreement with the numerical solutions. An intriguing feature of the numerical solutions is a periodic eddy formation behind the ridge, the cause of which has not been adequately resolved. The unsteady condition in the tank experiment are not reproduced numerically.

One basic difficulty is apparent in making quantitative comparison of the numerical solutions and water tank experiments. The qualitative agreement can be shown to be principally a consequence of the conservation of potential vorticity, which constrains the flow to skirt the southern side of a rotating ridge. The numerical solutions are valid for the case where the depth of the ridge is no greater than the thickness of the Ekman layer, a severe restriction in any physical situation. It is surprising that the author is not aware of the work of Welander (1968), Carrier (1965) and others, which is not bounded by this restriction.* If in the vorticity equation (17), the second and third term on the left-hand side and the term on the right-hand side is divided by the nondimensional depth H, the quasi-geostrophic equations are still valid for small slopes, but finite changes in the total depth of the fluid (a condition that exists in the flow tank model and the Macquarie Ridge). It is easily seen that this modification results in only a quantitative change in the numerical solutions for the flow that passes over the ridge.

The apparent qualitative agreement of Dr. Boyer's barotropic calculations and Gordon's (1972) observations in the stratified Antarctic circumpolar current at first surprised even this reviewer. It is quite simple to show, however, that under steady conditions, the barotropic or an "equivalent" barotropic model is, indeed, an appropriate model for describing the flow of the current near the Macquarie Ridge. In the latter "equivalent" scheme, replace horizontal bottom velocities in the derivation by $v\left\{z=[H(x,y)x,y]\right\}$, where the z dependence is specified *a priori*. [The quasi-geostrophic vorticity equation is developed in Niiler (pp. 216–236)].

The test of the validity of the barotropic assumption can be formed by computing the amount of vertical shear (as distinct from the already-existing shear of the impinging flow), which is generated by flow over the ridge. Use the conservation equation for density and the thermal wind relationship, $\mathbf{u}_o \cdot \nabla \rho_1 + w_o (\partial \rho_1/\partial z) = 0$, $\rho_o f\hat{x} (\partial v_1/\partial z) = g\nabla\rho_1$, to estimate the horizontal density changes $|\nabla \rho_1|$ and the production of vertical shear $\mathbf{v}_1$, respectively. In the above, $\mathbf{u}_o$ and w_o are barotropic components (w_o is a linear function of z).

In the ocean model, $w_o \sim \mathbf{u}_o \cdot \nabla H$, whence $|\nabla\rho_1| \sim |\nabla H| (\partial\rho_o/\partial z)$, where horizontal gradients are taken along the direction of the barotropic flow. It now follows that $|\mathbf{v}_1| \sim gH/f\rho_o \cdot \partial\rho_o/\partial z |\nabla \mathbf{H}|$. In the region of the Antarctic circumpolar current, $(H/\rho_o)(\partial\rho_o/\partial z) \sim 1/2\sigma_t$, $f \sim 1.2 \times 10^{-4}\ s^{-1}$, $|\nabla \mathbf{H}| \sim 2{,}000$ m/1,000 km $\sim 2 \times 10^{-3}$, whereby $|\mathbf{v}_1| \sim 8$ to 10 cm/s. Since it is estimated that the barotropic component is $\sim$25 cm/s, the barotropic assumption for the description of the flow over the Macquarie Ridge is qualitatively valid. Of course, baroclinic vortex generation is comparable to bottom Ekman dissipation, β-effect, and vorticity input by the wind. The primary mechanism in steering the flow past the ridge quite clearly is that of conservation of potential vorticity in the water column; and, in this reviewer's opinion, Dr. Boyer's work is a welcome contribution to the field.

*For greater detail of the derivation and the unresolved problem see Boyer and Guala (1972). This review does not permit a detailed derivation of the relation, which is readily available in the cited literature.

REFERENCES

Boyer, D. L. 1971. Rotating flow over long shallow ridges. J. Geophys. Fluid Dyn. 2:165.

Boyer, D. L. 1972. Rotating flow over a step. J. Fluid Mech. 50: 675.

Boyer, D. L., and J. Guala. 1972. A model of the Antarctic circumpolar current in the vicinity of the Macquarie Ridge. Antarct. Oceanol. 2. In press.

Carrier, G. 1965. J. Fluid Mech. 23:145–72.

Charney, J. G., R. Fjörtoft, and J. von Neumann. 1950. Numerical integration of the barotropic vorticity equation. Tellus 2:237.

Gadgil, S. 1971. J. Fluid Mech. 47:417–36.

Gordon, A. L. 1967. Structure of Antarctic waters between 20° W and 170° W. *In* V. Bushnell, ed. Antarctic Map Folio Series No. 6. American Geographic Society, New York.

Gordon, A. L. 1971. Antarctic polar front zone, p. 205. *In* J. L. Reid, ed. Antarctic Oceanology I. Am. Geophys. Union Antarct. Res. Ser. 15. Washington, D.C.

Gordon, A. L. 1972. On the interaction of the Antarctic circumpolar current and the Macquarie Ridge, pp. 71–78. *In* Antarctic Oceanology II. Am. Geophys. Union Antarct. Res. Ser. Washington, D.C.

Guala, J. 1972. Bottom topography effects on ocean currents. Ph.D. Dissertation. University of Delaware, Wilmington.

Hayes, D. C., M. Talwani, and D. Christoffel. 1972. Geophysical survey of the Macquarie Ridge. *In* Antarctic Oceanology II. Am. Geophys. Union Antarct. Res. Ser. Washington, D.C.

Heezen, B. C. 1972. Antarctic Map Folio Series. American Geographic Society, New York.

Masinof, I. V., and V. N. Vorob'yev. 1962. Sov. Antarct. Exped. Inf. Bull. 4:17–19.

Schulman, E., and P. P. Niiler. 1970. Geophys. Fluid Dyn. 1:439–62.

Shapiro, R. 1970. Smoothing, filtering and boundary effects. Rev. Geophys. Space Phys. 8(2).

Sverdrup, H. U., M. W. Johnson, and R. H. Fleming. 1942. *In* The Oceans. Prentice-Hall, New York.

Vaziri, A. 1971. Rotating flow over shallow topographies. Ph.D. Dissertation. University of Delaware, Wilmington.

Vaziri, A., and D. L. Boyer. 1971. Rotating flow over shallow topographies. J. Fluid Mech. 50:79.

Warren, B. A., and G. H. Volkman. 1968. J. Mar. Res. 26(2):110–26.

Welander, P. 1968. Tellus 20:1–15.

DISCUSSION

STEWART: I wonder why you thought that 10^4 is too big an eddy viscosity in the vertical when you have already assumed an essentially barotropic state. If it's barotropic, 10^4 is not that much; it could actually be a good deal more than that if the thing is really homogeneous. The smaller coefficient is necessarily associated with baroclinicity; and, if it's baroclinic, then other things happen.

PHILLIPS: If I recall correctly, the ratio of the height of the ridge to the total depth is of about the same order as a Rossby number.

BOYER: That's correct in the theory and in some of the experiments.

PHILLIPS: If I recall correctly, that's the kind of handwaving amplitude that separates blocking from the ability to go over the obstacle. If the amplitude is larger than that, you expect a very strong Taylor column and no flow over the obstacle. Have you tried looking at this?

BOYER: Strictly speaking we never obtain Taylor columns in our experiment. We've investigated almost every imaginable topography, and we've never observed a full Taylor column over the entire obstacle. The experiments are generally limited to Rossby numers of the order of $E^{1/2}$. There's almost no way of getting around that. One might imagine building a table that rotates many times faster, but it's just not very practical. We did some numerical experiments with conical topographies in which we allowed the Ekman number to decrease (increased rotation rate) and in which we did obtain some Taylor columns over a portion of the cone. As I recall, the velocities over the lower portion of the cone (flow left to right) were much larger than those in the free stream. Small bound eddies were present on the top of the cone.

THE FINITE-ELEMENT METHOD APPLIED TO OCEAN CIRCULATION PROBLEMS

J. E. HIRSH

INTRODUCTION

The object of this paper is the development of efficient numerical techniques for the solution of ocean circulation problems. Finite-difference methods currently used have not allowed solution of problems over full ranges of parameters because of the lack of resolution of the smaller-scale phenomena. Application of higher-order techniques will allow resolution of mesoscale phenomena with a high degree of confidence using the current computer power.

The finite-element Galerkin technique using cubic splines is the method chosen for application to ocean circulation problems. It has the advantage over second-order finite differences in that the error estimates are fourth order in the mesh size. In addition, because it is a Galerkin technique, it can be applied in a simple "cookbook" fashion, whereas higher-order difference schemes require special treatment near the boundaries. This method has been successfully applied to large classes of problems (Greville, 1969).

An algorithm will be developed for the solution of the primitive Navier–Stokes equations for an incompressible fluid that can be applied to two- and three-dimensional models. This model was chosen over the usual hydrostatic models (e.g., Bryan and Cox, 1968) with the idea of solving the equation of motion for the laboratory β-plane of Baker and Robinson (1969). To test the method, a solution was computed to a two-dimensional problem that has previously been solved by Bryan (1963), who used second-order finite differences applied to a vorticity equation. Some results were also obtained on a frictionally dominated, wind-driven, three-dimensional model.

THE FINITE-ELEMENT GALERKIN METHOD

For a given partial differential equation, $Lu^* = f$, in a domain Ω, where L is a differential operator, $u^*(x)$ is the solution and f is a given function of the independent variable x, the Galerkin method will be interpreted as follows. The approximation to the solution $u(x)$ will be expanded as a linear combination of a suitable set of n basis functions that define a function space, S,

$$u(x) = \sum_{i=1}^{n} \hat{u}_i \, \phi_i(x), \tag{1}$$

where $\hat{u}_i$ is the set of coefficients to be determined. The conditions for determining $\hat{u}_i$ are that the residual, defined as $Lu - f$, be orthogonal to all functions in the space S,

$$(\phi_k, Lu - f) = 0, \qquad k = 1, 2, \ldots, n, \tag{2}$$

where the inner product $[r(x), s(x)]$ is defined to be the integral $\int r(x)\, s(x)\, dx$ over the domain Ω. With these definitions, the set of equations to be solved is

$$(\phi_k, L \sum_j \hat{u}_j \phi_j) = (\phi_k, f), \qquad k = 1, 2, \ldots, n, \tag{3}$$

or, if L is linear,

$$\sum_{j=1}^{n} A_{kj}\, \hat{u}_j = \tilde{f}_k, \qquad k = 1, 2, \ldots, n, \tag{4}$$

where the matrix element A_{kj} is defined as $(\phi_k, L\phi_j)$ and the vector $\tilde{f}_k$ is equal to (ϕ_k, f). The boundary conditions are included in the space S.

The space of functions S will be a space of cubic splines. For one-dimensional problems, a spline function is defined as follows. Given a strictly increasing set of grid points $x_0 < x_1 < \ldots < x_n$, a spline function $Sp(x)$ has the following two properties: (a) in each interval (x_i, x_{i+1}), $Sp(x)$ is given by some polynomial of degree m or less, and (b) $Sp(x)$ and its derivatives of orders $1, 2, \ldots, m-1$ are continuous everywhere. Splines have the property that given a grid of uniform spacing h, a function $u^*(x)$ of sufficient smoothness can be approximated by a spline function of degree m such that

$$\max_{\Omega} |u - u^*| = O(h^{m+1})$$

(de Boor and Fix, in press). For large classes of differential operators L, solutions can be computed with the error estimated stated above (Greville, 1969, pp. 103-55).

The basis functions chosen to span the function space $S_h{}^m$, where h refers to the grid size and m the degree of the polynomials, are commonly known as B-splines. These basis functions, $\alpha_{m,i}(x)$ have minimal support, i.e., they are functions that span the space $S_h{}^m$ whose domain of nonzero definition is a minimum. The basis function $\alpha_{m,i}(x)$ is zero when x is outside the region (x_i, x_{i+m+1}).

To illustrate the B-spline basis functions, consider the case of linear splines $m = 1$. The function $\alpha_{1,i}(x)$ are "hat" functions of the form:

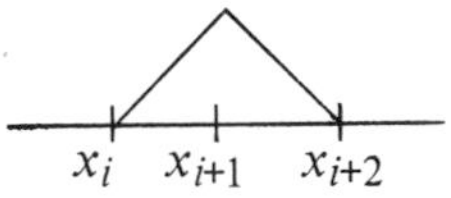

$$\alpha_{1,i}(x) = \begin{cases} \dfrac{x - x_i}{x_{i+1} - x_i}, & x_i < x \leqslant x_{i+1} \\[2ex] \dfrac{x_{i+2} - x}{x_{i+2} - x_{i+1}}, & x_{i+1} < x \leqslant x_{i+2} \\[2ex] 0, & \text{otherwise} \end{cases}$$

From the definition above and Eq. (1), it is clear that if $u(x)$ is a linear spline function, $u(x_{i+1})$ is simply the coefficient $\hat{u}_i$. Because of the finite span of $\alpha_{1,i}(x)$, application of Galerkin's method with these basis functions and a linear operator L will yield a matrix $A_{i,j} = (\alpha_{1,i}, L\alpha_{1,j})$ such that $A_{i,j} = 0$ for $|i - j| > 1$ or a tridiagonal matrix. For second-order differential equations, the use of Galerkin's method with linear splines is very close to the finite-difference method using standard second-order difference schemes. In fact, for the simple differential operator d^2/dx^2, the matrix of coefficient $A_{ij} = (\alpha_{1,i}, \alpha''_{1,j})$ is exactly the same as the matrix obtained from finite differences.

Cubic splines were chosen for the present study because they represent a compromise between ease of application and order of accuracy. The cubic B-spline basis functions with a uniform grid of size h takes the form:

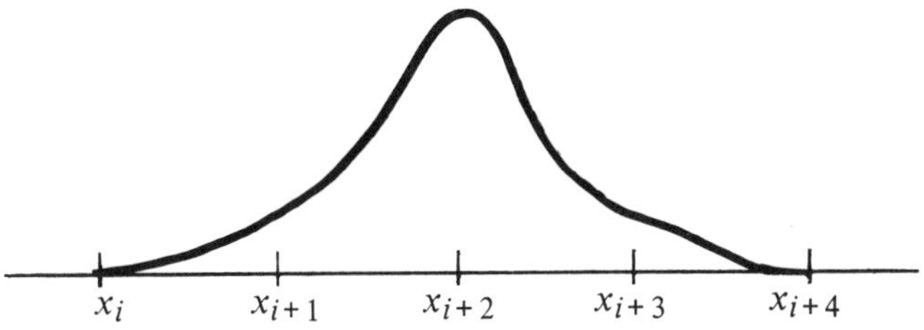

$$\alpha_{3,i}(x) = \frac{1}{6} \begin{cases} \left(\dfrac{x - x_i}{h}\right)^3, & x_i \leqslant x < x_{i+1} \\[2ex] 1 + 3\left(\dfrac{x - x_{i+1}}{h}\right) + 3\left(\dfrac{x - x_{i+1}}{h}\right)^2 \\[2ex] \quad - 3\left(\dfrac{x - x_{i+1}}{h}\right)^3, & x_{i+1} \leqslant x < x_{i+2} \\[2ex] 1 + 3\left(\dfrac{x_{i+3} - x}{h}\right) + 3\left(\dfrac{x_{i+3} - x}{h}\right)^2 \\[2ex] \quad - 3\left(\dfrac{x_{i+3} - x}{h}\right)^3, & x_{i+2} \leqslant x < x_{i+3} \\[2ex] \left(\dfrac{x_{i+4} - x}{h}\right)^3, & x_{i+3} \leqslant x < x_{i+4} \\[2ex] 0, & \text{otherwise} \end{cases}$$

An interval divided into N grid spaces requires $N + 3$ independent B-spline basis functions. If the bandwidth of a matrix, $2\mu + 1$, is defined such that the element $A_{ij} = 0$ for $|i - j| > \mu$, then matrices resulting from the application of Galerkin's method with cubic splines have a bandwidth of seven, as opposed to a bandwidth of three for the usual finite-difference techniques when applied to second-order differential equations. Boundary conditions are imposed by locally modifying basis functions that are nonzero at the boundaries.

To apply the Galerkin method to multiple dimensions, a tensor product basis will be employed. If $[\alpha_i(x)]$ and $[\beta_j(y)]$ are B-spline basis functions, each defined on a given x and y grid of N grid spaces in each direction, then a function $u(x,y)$ in this bicubic spline space has the representation

$$u(x,y) = \sum_{i=1}^{N+3} \sum_{j=1}^{N+3} \hat{u}_{i,j}\alpha_i(x)\beta_j(y), \qquad (5)$$

where $\hat{u}_{i,j}$ is the set of $(N + 3)^2$ coefficients to be determined. (The subscript m, referring to the degree of the polynomials, will be dropped.)

NAVIER-STOKES EQUATIONS IN RECTANGLES

In this section an algorithm will be developed for the solution of the time-dependent Navier-Stokes equations in a rectangular domain. The algorithm will be described for a two-dimensional domain; however, extension to three dimensions is quite straightforward. The equations of motion are

$$\frac{\partial \mathbf{v}}{\partial t} = \nu \nabla^2 \mathbf{v} - \nabla p + f(\mathbf{v}), \qquad (6)$$

$$\nabla \cdot \mathbf{v} = 0, \qquad (7)$$

where $f(\mathbf{v})$ includes inertial terms plus any other forcing f functions. The vector $\mathbf{v}$ has components u and v,p is the pressure, and ν is the kinematic viscosity. The vector function $f(\mathbf{v})$ has components f^x and f^y.

Notation

All unknown functions will be represented by a linear combination of bicubic B-splines as in Eq. (5), where the vector of coefficients will have the same symbol as the function except that it will have a hat ($\hat{}$), i.e., the vector of coefficients corresponding to the function $u(x,y)$ is $\hat{u}$ with elements $\hat{u}_{ij}$. A tilda ($\tilde{}$) symbol will mean the projection of a function into the bicubic spline space, i.e., the vector of coefficients $\tilde{f}^x$ has elements $\tilde{f}_{ij}{}^x$, where $\tilde{f}_{ij}{}^x = [\alpha_i(x)\beta_j(y), f^x]$.

If the domain is the rectangble $(0, a) \times (0, b)$, consider the following definitions of inner products:

$$[r_1(x), s_1(x)]^x = \int_0^a r_1(x)s_1(x)\,dx,$$

$$[r_2(y), s_2(y)]^y = \int_0^b r_2(y)s_2(y)\,dy,$$

$$[r(x,y), s(x,y)] = \int_0^b \int_0^a r(x,y)\,s(x,y)\,dx\,dy,$$

and

$$[r(x,y), s(x,y)] = [r_1(x), s_1(x)]^x\,[r_2(x), s_2(y)]^y,$$

if

$$r(x,y) = r_1(x)r_2(y)$$

and

$$s(x,y) = s_1(x)s_2(y).$$

With this notation, the following inner product matrices will be defined:

$$C_{ki}{}^x = (\alpha_k, \alpha_i)^x,$$

$$D_{ki}{}^x = (\alpha_k, \alpha_i{}')^x,$$

$$A_{ki}{}^x = (\alpha_k, \alpha_i{}'')^x,$$

where the primes represent differentiation with respect to x. The corresponding operators are also defined in the y direction. The notation $C^x \otimes C^y\,\hat{u}$ is taken to be the matrix operation,

$$\sum_i \sum_j C_{ki}{}^x\, C_{lj}{}^y\, \hat{u}_{ij}, \qquad \forall k,l.$$

With this notation, the operator L is defined as $A^x \otimes C^y + C^x \otimes A^y$ and is the Laplacian operator in Galerkin form.

With these definitions, the finite-element equations corresponding to (6-7) are

$$C^x \otimes C^y \frac{d\hat{u}}{dt} = \nu L\hat{u} - D^x \otimes C^y\,\hat{p} + \tilde{f}^x, \qquad (8)$$

$$C^x \otimes C^y \frac{d\hat{v}}{dt} = \nu L\hat{v} - C^x \otimes D^y\,\hat{p} + \tilde{f}^y, \qquad (9)$$

$$D^x \otimes C^y\,\hat{u} + C^x \otimes D^y\,\hat{v} = 0, \qquad (10)$$

where the coefficient vectors $\hat{u}$, $\hat{v}$, and $\hat{p}$ are functions of t, the time.

The time-stepping algorithm

The algorithm used to solve the system defined by Eqs. (8-10) uses ideas derived from Douglas and Dupont (1970) and Chorin (1968).

A modified leap-frog scheme (Douglas and Dupont, 1970) is used to approximate the time derivative in the momentum equation (8-9). This scheme takes the form

$$C^x \otimes C^y \left(\frac{\hat{u}^{n+1} - \hat{u}^{n-1}}{2\Delta t}\right) = \nu L\hat{u}^n + \tilde{g}^n + \lambda L(\hat{u}^{n+1} - 2u^n + u^{n-1}), \qquad (11)$$

when applied to the simple heat equation $\partial u/\partial t = \nu\nabla^2 u + g$. The superscript refers to the time $t_n = n\Delta t$, where Δt is the time step. The scheme is unconditionally stable for the heat equation if $\lambda > \nu/4$. Note that the last term in (11) is $O(\Delta t)^2$, which is the same order in Δt as the truncation error obtained when approximating the time derivative by the centered difference. To solve (11) at each time step, Douglas and Dupont (1970) make use of alternating-direction methods by adding the term $(\lambda\Delta t)^2\, A^x \otimes A^y\,(u^{n+1} - u^{n-1})$ to yield

$$G^x \otimes G^y (\hat{u}^{n+1} - \hat{u}^{n-1}) = 2\Delta t L [\nu \hat{u}^n + 2\lambda(\hat{u}^n - \hat{u}^{n-1})] + 2\Delta t \tilde{g}^n, \quad (12)$$

where

$$G^x = C^x - 2\lambda\Delta t A^x, \quad G^y = C^y - 2\lambda\Delta t A^y. \quad (13)$$

Equation (12) can be solved for u^{n+1} in $0(N^2)$ operations, while solution of (11) would require $0(N^3)$ operations (see Douglas and Dupont, 1970, for details). The introduction of the alternating-direction method to the solution of the parabolic problem does not affect the stability condition on λ. This leap-frog scheme will be applied to the Navier–Stokes equations.

The only remaining problems are finding a solution for the pressure and satisfying the mass continuity equation (10). This is accomplished by an iterative approach similar to that used by Chorin (1968) on a finite-difference model. The iteration is used to find the pressure such that when its gradient is added into the momentum equation, the velocity will be divergence-free for all time. In terms of the finite-element equations, the iteration takes the form:

$$G^x \otimes G^y \, \hat{u}^{n+1,m+1} = \tilde{b}^x - D^x \otimes C^y \, \hat{p}^{n,m},$$

$$H^x \otimes H^y (\hat{p}^{n,m+1/2} - \hat{p}^{n,m}) = -(D^x \otimes C^y \hat{u}^{n+1,m+1} + C^x \otimes D^y \hat{v}^{n+1,m}),$$

$$G^x \otimes G^y \hat{v}^{n+1,m+1} = \tilde{b}^y - C^x \otimes D^y \hat{p}^{n,m+1/2},$$

$$H^x \otimes H^y (\hat{p}^{n,m+1} - \hat{p}^{n,m+1/2}) = -(D^x \otimes C^y \hat{u}^{n+1,m+1} + C^x \otimes D^y \hat{v}^{n+1,m+1}), \quad (14)$$

where m is the iteration number,

$$\tilde{b}^x = G^x \otimes G^y \hat{u}^{n-1} + 2\Delta t \left\{ L [\nu \hat{u}^n + 2\lambda(\hat{u}^n - \hat{u}^{n-1})] + \tilde{f}^{x,n} \right\},$$

$$\tilde{b}^y = G^x \otimes G^y \hat{v}^{n-1} + 2\Delta t \left\{ L [\nu \hat{v}^n + 2\lambda (\hat{v}^n - \hat{v}^{n-1})] + \tilde{f}^{y,n} \right\},$$

and the iteration matrices H^x, H^y are

$$H^x = (\mu C^x - A^x)/(2\mu)^{1/2}; \quad H^y = (\mu C^y - A^y)/(2\mu)^{1/2}.$$

The scalar μ is chosen to give the most rapid convergence of the iteration (14). The iteration is said to have converged when

$$\max_{k,l} \left| \left(D^x \otimes C^x \hat{u}^{n+1,m+1} + C^x \otimes D^y \hat{v}^{n+1,m+1} \right)_{k,l} \right|$$

is less than a previously specified constant. The motivation for the choice of the iteration matrices H^x, H^y comes from an alternating-direction scheme proposed by Douglas and Dupont for the solution of elliptic boundary value problems (see Douglas and Dupont, 1970, for details).

THE TWO-DIMENSIONAL NONLINEAR WIND-DRIVEN OCEAN

The model chosen to test the finite-element method with the algorithm (14) is a two-dimensional, side-frictional model that has previously been solved by Bryan (1963) using the vorticity-stream function approach. The equations of motion in nondimensional form are

$$\frac{\partial u}{\partial t} + \epsilon(uu_x + vu_y) - fv + p_x = \frac{\epsilon}{Re} \nabla^2 u + \tau^x,$$

$$\frac{\partial v}{\partial t} + \epsilon(uv_x + vv_y) + fu + p_y = \frac{\epsilon}{Re} \nabla^2 v,$$

$$u_x + v_y = 0, \quad (15)$$

in the rectangular domain $0 < x < 1, 0 < y < 2$. The wind stress τ^x is $-2/\pi \cos \pi/2(y)$, ϵ is a Rossby number, Re is a Reynolds number, and f is nondimensional Coriolis parameter and is equal to $y + c$. The constant c is set to zero for simplicity since it would drop out upon forming a vorticity equation and thus does not affect the solutions for u and v. The details of the nondimensionalization can be found in Bryan (1963). The boundary conditions are $x = 0, 1$; $u = v = 0$; $y = 0, 2$; $u_y = v = 0$. The initial condition is $u = v = 0$.

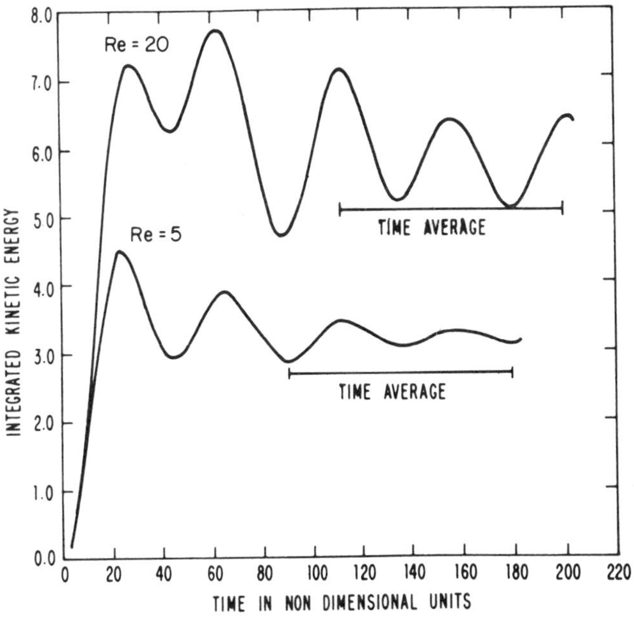

FIGURE 1 **Integrated kinetic energy vs. time, with a Rossby number of $\epsilon = 1.28 \times 10^{-3}$ for *Re* = 5 and 20.**

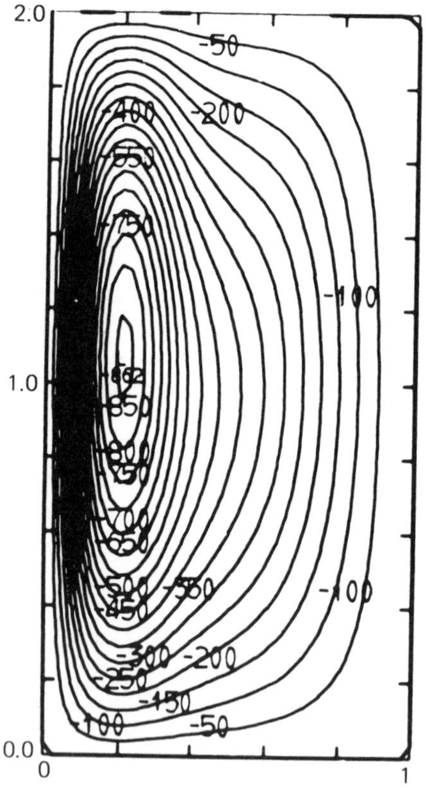

FIGURE 2 Contour plot of the stream function for the solution averaged over the interval indicated in Figure 1. $\epsilon = 1.28 \times 10^{-3}$, $Re = 5$, $\Delta t = 1.4$, $\lambda = 1.2 \times 10^{-3}$.

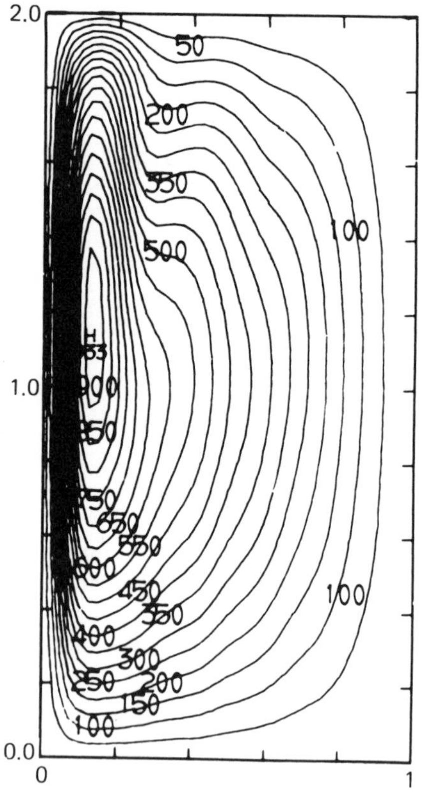

FIGURE 3 Contour plot of the stream function for the solution averaged over the interval indicated in Figure 1. $\epsilon = 1.28 \times 10^{-3}$, $Re = 20$, $\Delta t = 0.75$, $\lambda = 1.0 \times 10^{-3}$.

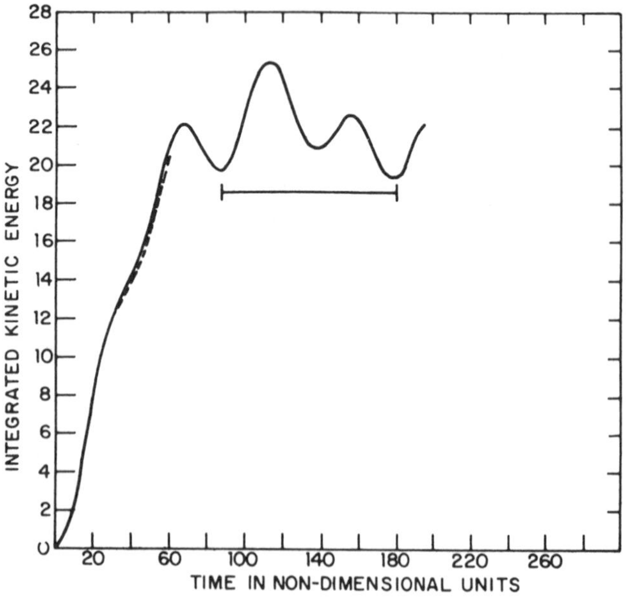

FIGURE 4 Integrated kinetic energy vs. time, with a Rossby number of $\epsilon = 3.2 \times 10^{-4}$ and a Reynolds number of $Re = 100$.

Results

The first cases were Bryan's simplest, which had the least narrow boundary layers. The Rossby number was set to 1.28×10^{-3} and Re was set at 5 and 20. Curves of the non-dimensional integrated kinetic energy vs. time is shown in Figure 1. In order to compare the results with Bryan's streamline contours, a stream function, ψ, was computed by integrating the equation $\psi_y = u$ with $\psi(x,y = 0) = 0, 0 < x < 1$. Contour plots of the stream function averaged over two periods of the Rossby wave (see Figure 1) are shown in Figures 2 and 3. The dots to the right and above the contour plots indicate the grid points.

The $Re = 5$ case used a uniform 9×9 grid with a time step of $\Delta t = 1.4$. The $Re = 20$ case used a uniform 12×12 grid with $t = 0.75$. Bryan used a uniform 20×40 ($h = 1/20$ in both x and y directions) grid for both cases.

The next case computed was Bryan's most extreme (smallest Ekman number ϵ/Re) case, where $\epsilon = 3.2 \times 10^{-4}$ and $Re = 100$. Figures 4 and 5 show the kinetic energy curve and the time-averaged stream function. The grid used was a nonuniform 10×10 grid with the spacings as shown in

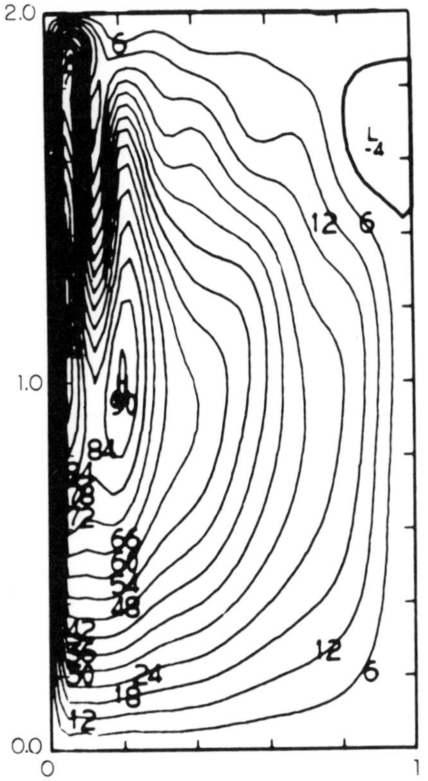

FIGURE 5 Contour plot of the stream function for the solution averaged over the interval indicated in Figure 4. $\epsilon = 3.2 \times 10^{-4}$, $Re = 100$, $t = 0.4$, $\lambda = 1.0 \times 10^{-3}$. Grid points are indicated by the dots above and to the right of the plot.

Figure 5. The time step was $\Delta t = 0.4$. Figure 4 also shows a kinetic energy curve for a similarly spaced nonuniform 12×12 grid, which was run in order to obtain an estimate of the accuracy of the solution.

An attempt was made to compute solutions in a range of parameters into which Bryan was unable to go, due to the lack of resolution of his finite-difference method. Denser and more nonuniform grids were employed. However, difficulties arose with the convergence of the pressure iteration (14). The convergence of this iteration is extremely sensitive to the number of grid points, the nonuniformity of the grid, and the parameter $\lambda\Delta t$ that appears in the matrices G^x, G^y. Further work on this model was not attempted until a better understanding of the convergence properties of the iteration is obtained.

A three-dimensional model of a frictionally controlled homogeneous ocean was also run using a uniform $6 \times 6 \times 6$ grid. The algorithm was an exact three-dimensional analog of the two-dimensional algorithm given in Equation (14). Some results were obtained. However, convergence of the pressure iteration was troublesome, and it was decided not to pursue the three-dimensional problem until a thorough understanding of the two-dimensional problem is obtained.

SUMMARY

The above results show that the finite-element method in conjunction with cubic splines can successfully be applied to the solution of Navier–Stokes equations, using far fewer grid points than the finite-difference methods currently used. Direct comparison with Bryan's (1963) method for efficiency was not possible because Bryan solved a single vorticity equation, while we used the momentum equations. However, rough estimates of operation counts indicate that the amount of work required for each model was of the same order of magnitude, although the storage requirements for the finite-element method is considerably smaller.

It has been demonstrated (Greville, 1969) that the finite-element method with cubic splines is far more efficient for solving large classes of elliptic, parabolic, and hyperbolic problems. Therefore, future work on this method must be directed towards defining more efficient algorithms for solving the finite-element equations to take full advantage of the higher resolving power that the method yields.

ACKNOWLEDGMENTS

I would like to thank Professors A. R. Robinson, George Fix, and D. G. M. Anderson for the many fruitful discussions on the problem. This research was supported by the Office of Naval Research through Contract No. N00014-67-A-0298-0011 (under Project NR 083-201) to Harvard University. Acknowledgment also is made to the National Center for Atmospheric Research, which is sponsored by the National Science Foundation, for computer time used in this research.

REFERENCES

Baker, D. J., Jr., and A. R. Robinson. 1969. A laboratory model for the general ocean circulation. Philos. Trans. R. Soc. Lond. 265: 253–366.

Bryan, K. 1963. A numerical investigation of a nonlinear model of a wind-driven ocean. J. Atmos. Sci. 20:594–606.

Bryan, K., and M. C. Cox. 1968. A nonlinear model of an ocean driven by wind and differential heating. J. Atmos. Sci. 25:945–67.

Chorin, A. J. 1968. Numerical solution of the Navier–Stokes equations. Math. Comp. 22:745–62.

de Boor, C., and G. Fix. Spline approximation by quasi-interpolants. J. Approx. Theory. In press.

Douglas, J., Jr., and T. Dupont. 1970. Alternating direction methods on rectangles. Proc. Symp. Numer. Solution Partial Differ. Equations. II. SIAM, Philadelphia.

Greville, T. N. E., ed. 1969. Theory and Application of Spline Functions. Academic Press, New York.

DISCUSSION

ROBINSON: Joel began development of his program for comparison with laboratory experiments, as the title of his talk indicates, although the material that he actually presented was different.

CHARNEY: I was going to ask that question—what happened?

ROBINSON: He reduced down to a simpler problem but kept the algorithm. If he had initially decided to compare with Bryan's vorticity calculation (indeed, a wiser first problem) rather than trying both to get a program to use for our laboratory comparisons and to innovate the use of splines, the algorithm problem would not be involved.

VIII CONCLUSIONS

WHERE DO WE GO FROM HERE?

A. W. MUNK

I'm elected to be the first of the sages, and my outstanding asset is that I know less about numerical modeling of ocean circulation than anyone else in this room. Norman Phillips assigned me to say something about high ω and high κ, and I gather this is to say something about small-scale processes. All right, an obvious calculation: if you consider that the heat flux into the bottom of the sea is a microcalorie per square centimeter per second and you work out the necessary numbers, then the entire ocean would be heated to 20 °C in 400,000 years. Why isn't it? Well, because there are sources of cold water that keep the bottom ventilated. And if you now speak only of these sources of cold water, you will come to the conclusion that if nothing else happened eventually the entire ocean would be cold, 1° water. Again, it isn't. So the model that people have in mind (and have had in mind for a long time) is that you have some sort of a balance of the upwelling cold water and a diffusive downward flux of heat from above. If the observed distribution of variables is to be accounted for in terms of this vertical advection-vertical diffusion model, you come out with the magic figures that the order of magnitude of vertical upwelling is a centimeter per day (which by the way gives you the appropriate 1,000-year time constant of overturn) and the appropriate eddy viscosity is 1 cgs—everything is nice and 1, you see. And the geochemists have made rather much of this simple-minded model. Now, of course, this kind of thing tells you nothing about what the processes really are like. They give you some numbers that people might be tempted to use in modeling, but they give you no physics.

Professor Walsh was just talking about the biological problems. I once amused myself by asking what the diffusivity would be due to diurnal migration of the biomass (10^{-8} g per g of water) eating at the surface at night and defecating at depths in the daytime. The result is 10^{-4} cgs, falling far short of that magic figure of 1 cgs.

One trouble is that the upwelling-vertical eddy diffusion model may be completely wrong. To anticipate Bob Stewart's reaction, a much more likely way of effective downward diffusion is to have good mixing in special places, like against the coasts and against islands, and then communicate the local mixing into the interior by advective processes along isodensity lines. Yesterday, Wally Broecker discussed some very interesting results of the geochemical work, indicating long, thin, horizontal, coherent anomalies that do speak for this kind of philosophy rather than for seeking some sort of a vertical diffusive process all over the ocean.

One new development in oceanography is the so-called microstructure—the fact that when you plot a temperature depth-curve (previously considered smooth) you get a wiggly curve that some people have called layers or sheets (it looks more like a random process), but it is a highly wiggly curve. The degree of wiggliness can be represented by the dimensionless ratio between the mean square gradient and the mean gradient squared, a ratio that would be 1 if it were smooth and that can be as large as 1,000. This wiggliness tells you that there are some kind of random processes going on. There is a thermodynamics argument by Charles Cox and Tom Osborne that implies that the eddy transport coefficients have a ratio to the molecular coefficients of just this ratio of the mean square gradient to the mean gradient square. With a molecular heat conductivity of 10^{-3} cm^2 s^{-1} multiplied by 1,000, you come out with that magic number 1, thus indicating that there are places in the oceans where the equivalent eddy coefficient would be of order 1; but this line of evidence tells us even more strongly that different places differ by one or two orders magnitude, and that these processes are less effective at depths than near the surface. The constant eddy coefficient model is, I'm afraid, seriously wrong.

The general belief is that microstructure is related to instabilities associated with breaking internal waves. Meteorologists, using scatterometry of radar waves, have mapped out times when internal waves in the atmosphere broke, followed by patches of turbulence. This is connected to the so-called "CAT" (clear air turbulence) problem. I have been intrigued by the asymmetry between meteorology and oceanography in the sense that the meteorologists have learned everything they know about this problem from scatterometry, and virtually nothing from direct sounding; the oceanographers know everything that is known from direct sounding, and nothing from scatterometry.

A completely different high ω,κ process, certainly important locally, is the process of double diffusion. This was invented as a curiosity by Stommel, Blanchard, and Stearns some years ago and has now turned into a quite respectable subject with its special slogans and strong proponents like Stewart Turner and Herbert Huppert. Consider a densitometric gradient diagram, with $\beta\partial_z S$ and $\alpha\partial_z T$ for x- and y-axes where $\rho = -\alpha T + \beta S$ designates the equation of state. The angle θ is drawn counterclockwise from the positive x-axis. Conditions are unstable from $\theta = 45°$ to $225°$, and absolutely stable from $\theta = 270°$ to $360°$. Between $225°$ and $270°$ double diffusion can occur by *fingering,* and between 0 and $45°$ there is the so-called *diffusive* regime. The two regimes are distinctively different, though both are associated with fine scales. Some observed fingering regimes off Gibraltar and Bermuda, when interpreted in terms of Turner's laboratory results, yield eddy diffusivities of 5 $cm^2\ s^{-1}$. So again this magic order of 1 emerges, indicating that in certain cases double diffusion is a significant oceanographic process.

It then appears as if widely different small-scale processes, such as internal wave breaking, double diffusion, breaking against shores with horizontal intrusions, all give rise to significant fluxes. How can one expect to solve a problem where these mixing processes are important without getting the physics solved first? It is not fair to expect the numerical analyists, no matter how good they are, to come out with a realistic model until some of these processes are sorted out, and that's our job to do.

DISCUSSION

VERONIS: Walter, the point that you make here I think perhaps you make a bit too strongly, because although your point about fingering when you consider things on a small scale is correct, I think that some of the ideas that have come out of it are that as fingering develops and you get these streamers, and they do a tremendous amount of vertical mixing of salt. If you think about the vertical convection of salt as a smaller-scale process, you simply stand back a little bit and consider it as a quasi-molecular process, I mean somewhat more macroscopic than molecular, but still a process that transports salt. Effectively what happens is that the salt is transported so rapidly that it becomes a more diffusive process than the heat. Then you flip over into that region, and then you get layering as a result, or what you would call diffusive, but not on a molecular scale, on a somewhat larger scale so that you can start out with a fingering and end up with layering simply because you stand back and let the scale medium that you focus on increase above the molecular level. It seems as if that might be an important process in the somewhat larger picture than the molecular–that is, if instead of focusing on a scale in centimeters, one focuses on a scale of meters and the things flip over, in a sense they are connected, I think perhaps a set ratio.

MUNK: George, my 5 $cm^2\ s^{-1}$ figure is gotten as follows. If you take the observed layering off Bermuda or in the Mediterranean outflow, and then use Turner's results, you obtain both the driving and the driven fluxes. In this case, the driving fluxes are salt and the driven fluxes are heat. In this way you interpret the observed field measurements in the Atlantic in terms of fluxes. If you then divide by the mean gradients (ignoring the microstructure), you get what one would call, by definition, an eddy coefficient. It does come out to be of the order as mentioned.

D. KIRWAN: Walter, I just can't accept right off the top of my head the idea that the North Pacific is a normal ocean. It's immaterial to me living in the middle of the country.

STOMMEL: Walter, I think it's been pretty difficult to get any direct observational evidence of any saltmaking process in the ocean. A few people have been looking for it. Tuesday there was a talk at Woods Hole by Sandy Williams, who had just come back from the first sea trials of his device to try to photograph salt-finger processes by using one of the University of New Hampshire water-prone devices, to slowly search through the water column. He was between Bermuda and Puerto Rico. He claims to have gotten some very clear pictures of salt-finger processes and near/sharp interfaces, about 30 cm high and about 1 cm in length. But I don't think we have statistics on how many of those there are in the ocean or things like that as yet. He may have more information than I'm aware of. They may not be a predominant process, but the fact that there are any at all is kind of . . .

MUNK: The key word is then intermittency. It may not occur all over, but it does occur in certain spots.

STOMMEL: Well, I think the nice thing is that now there is a technique to distinguish it very clearly. It will be possible to find out how long they are, how thick they are, what their sizes are, how much volume of the ocean at one time is filled with them. And presumably also find out how much they are actually transported. Those quantitative answers look a little more accessible, just like the pictures of Woods encourages people to go ahead and think about billows and breaking and things like that. I think pictures of the ocean are very encouraging.

MUNK: I am sorry that I didn't mention Woods and Swift (the two oceanographers) who had found these inversions much before Cox and Gregg did, and I'm aware of that.

SCHULMAN: What is the current thinking about these homogeneous layers? Are they a consequence of salt-fingering, or are they a cause of salt-fingering?

STOMMEL: In some of the general experiments, they've been demonstrated to be a consequence of salt-fingering.

MUNK: But they also occur in regions that are called normal.

STOMMEL: Yes, they occur in other cases, too, so we don't really know. Walter doesn't know it, but he's entitled to bring the original stimulus of the salt-finger physics. He doesn't know it, but he was the original stimulus.

POND: I'd like to comment about this homogeneous business—it's a bit dangerous, I think. It isn't really a sheet-and-layer system, because of the gradient itself. If you are trying to play this game, you find that the gradients across the layers and the net temperature change is bigger than the jump through the so-called sheet.

POND: Not always, but very often, so that only in very special circumstances do you get the homogeneous layers—they are not common, and the conditions that may produce them are not common—you have to look very hard to find them.

MUNK: More often than not the $T(z)$ and $S(z)$ records look more like stochastic processes than like layers and sheets.

POND: Well, some of the photographs really do look like this, but it may be associated with the shear rather than with the density.

MUNK: The message that I was trying to convey is that the flux processes, which apparently on the average are essential to numerical modeling, are really quite complicated and surprising. There are surely other processes that have not yet been discovered.

BRETHERTON: I would just like to inject a note of caution into the Cox-Osborne calculation of the vertical diffusivity, because although within their assumptions their calculations are perfectly correct, I think you can state the basis of their argument simply saying that turbulent processes in the ocean are generating perturbations of temperature, because you've got turbulence in a temperature gradient, and you balance the rate of production of $\overline{0.2}$ (theta prime squared bar) against its rate of diffusion and its rate of dissipation due to molecular processes. Now what they're fundamentally doing is measuring that rate of dissipation due to molecular processes, assuming balance, and inferring the rate of production. Now that rate of production can arise in two different ways: It can arise due to vertical mixing in the vertical temperature gradient, vertical eddy diffusivity—it can also arise due to horizontal mixing, in a horizontal temperature gradient. We don't in fact know what the relative magnitude of those two terms are. And it is still conceivable that their measurements can be related to a process that is fundamentally one of horizontal mixing in a horizontal temperature gradient. Now with that remark I'd like to throw in another area that I think has not perhaps received the attention it might. If you take a reasonably accurate STD tracer—there's a problem as to what a reasonably accurate STD tracer is—and you do smooth it in the vertical over 10 meters or 20 meters or so, it does come out smooth. And you take another one a few kilometers away, or a few tens or hundreds of kilometers away, it is not the same. There are horizontal variations in the *Ts* relationship. I've used the word horizontal here, and I must now qualify it—I'm referring to mixing in a surface of constant potential density as horizontal mixing. If you do that, the *Ts* curve at a given potential density is a dynamically neutral tracer, which can be used to estimate the magnitudes of horizontal mixing. Now it's virtually unexplored as to what these horizontal variations in *Ts* mean, but let me just throw in another remark. If they're on the sorts of scales of 50 kilometers down to 1 kilometer, we've got quasi-geostrophic 2½ to that dimensional turbulence out of Charney, with a k^{-3} spectrum in both horizontal and vertical. That's k^{-3} in the velocities. If you think of a cascade of $\overline{0.2}$ (theta prime squared bar) stuff down to smaller and smaller scales, it's k^{-1} in that. In other words, there should be a large amount of small-scale horizontal and vertical variability of the *Ts* relationship, due simply to the tight end of the spectrum of the two-dimensional turbulence working on the large-scale horizontal variations in *Ts*. The particular point that I wanted to indicate, which I think is of some interest, is that we could at this point in time get a good deal more information about the shape of the spectrum of horizontal variation, and it had a lot of important information in it.

STEWART: There is in fact a fair amount of data on this, some of the best of which has been obtained by the University of Washington applied physics lab people, who've got this little trained torpedo. They've obtained conclusions which I find absolutely bewildering over very large scales—solid −5/3 spectra in the temperature. I can't think of any theoretical reason why this should be the case, but that is in fact what they get, running horizontally. Now it has to be admitted that running horizontally is not quite the same as running on a constant density line. They're running on a constant pressure surface, not on a constant density surface. And only constant pressure within limit, because of course their device is not capable of completely constant pressure.

MUNK: May I say something about these observations? Chris Garrett and I looked at them last year. They don't differ significantly from −2, but that isn't important. What is interesting is that there were other observations. Charnock towed a thermal cable in the Atlantic, and LaFond has towed a similar cable in the Pacific; and with a little bit of pushing you could fit those three observations to a single −2 slope of horizontal temperature spectra.

BRETHERTON: There is a critical difference here between the spectrum of variations in *Ts* and the spectrum of variations in temperature. Far bigger are the variations in density due to the internal waves and those sorts of things which cause essentially vertical displacement. That is not the point. We're looking at a given potential density surface, and we're looking at a dynamically passive process, and there you have to go to the *Ts* relation. And that's where the information is.

Where do you expect to get the −1 from?

MUNK: Well, he multiplies by k^2 to make the gradient, so that's where you go from a −3 to −1.

BRETHERTON: No. If you take, for example, the Geerer theory of turbulence and you pile some source of $\overline{0.2}$ to the large scale, and you have it cascade down to the smaller scales, and you use similarity theory as to what the spectrum has to be from that cascade, for the temperature variation it turns out to be a −5/3 as well. Through identical arguments for two-dimensional turbulence, where it's the rate of dissipation of entropy, not energy, that's controlling the shape, and you don't get a k^{-3}, you get a k^{-1}. Now we can visualize this: the turbulence in two-dimensional turbulence, or small wavelengths, is, relatively speaking, weaker than the three-dimensional turbulence. There's less activity on a small scale, let's say spectrally speaking. Now if the turbulence is weaker to get the given flux through the cascade of $\overline{0.2}$* (theta prime squared bar star) down to the molecular scale where it can be dissipated, it has to pile up to greater levels, and that's why you get a k^{-1} spectrum in this.

CHARNEY: Well, it behaves like vorticity, which is also k^{-1}, another conservative matter. Bud, I wanted to ask you—it would be very gratifying if this quasi-geostrophic turbulence idea—I'd be very curious to find it in the oceans, because this has to be a fairly high energy region, that is the particle velocities have to be larger than the Rossby phase velocities. Otherwise, you get this Rhines dispersive effect.

BRETHERTON: That's why I carefully measured my scales of 50 km to 1 km, which is for low Rossby waves deformation of a region that we know is nonlinear, where I believe that toxifies the region and is satisfied. When you get down to 1 km, another effect comes in; mainly that you get inertial oscillations and that sort of thing gives you shears and horizontal displacement, as you know. Now 50 km to 1 km is not a wide range to start spectral estimates off. But the point that I'm trying to get at is that we do in fact have a continuous cascade down; the magnitude of the spectral there should be directly relatable to the sort of things that Cox has been getting at.

CHARNEY: But if it is k^{-2}, isn't that what you would have if you had a lot of fronts or blobs? In other words, if you take a spectrum of a bunch of density discontinuity, you get k^{-2}.

H. STOMMEL

I think that what emerges very clearly from the sessions in this meeting is that there are certain kinds of problems, such as upwelling and mesoscale eddy, in which there are pretty good day-to-day relations between theoreticians, numerical modelers, and observers, who are trying to make some experiments related to those models. And so, it would be really very impertinent for me to make any suggestions or comments upon what the observational programs might be or could be in programs like CUE and MODE, where this kind of interaction is very clearly operating. On the other hand, we've also seen a class of large-scale models, seasonal fluctuations of currents, etc., where there's a much looser connection between the theoretical and the numerical modeling people and the people who are conducting field experiments. There must be many reasons for that discrepancy. I think one of the things that we should not overlook is that these larger-scale models represent much bigger efforts observationally, probably, and are devoted to problems in bigger areas and over longer periods. So, whereas theoreticians and observers can get together in an informal kind of way—a loose association of individual investigators to raise the neighbor's barn, so to speak—if you think about joining up to do one of these longer-term, big-scale things, you're really sort of becoming an employee of a construction company. And that's not very attractive to many of us. We're a little bit scared of the long-term commitments that might be involved in programs like this. I think the observational people are scared of this, because they know it's not just a question of four months, or a summertime, or a cruise, or an experiment they can carry out even themselves. They realize that when it comes to observational programs that are going to be maintained for decades—they certainly must be in many of these cases—they realize that those are not the proper kinds of programs for research people to be associated with. But those longer programs should possibly be the kind of work that a government agency would undertake. After all, that's what NOAA is all about, I suppose. There must be something equivalent to a weather bureau for the ocean. So those are examples of other reasons for this very big discrepancy between the social structure of these different efforts—the CUE and the MODE effort on the one side, and efforts toward understanding the long-period, large-scale fluctuations of ocean climate, which I think we have to agree are very important things and are becoming more and more visible to everyone as desirable kinds of programs. I think they're just different. It's pretty obvious to anyone anyway.

I wanted to direct my remarks toward trying to estimate or get your judgment about possible observational-type programs that are related to these large-scale, long-period modeling and theoretical efforts. Within those problems are a number of subproblems that clearly are the proper kind of things for individual, uncoordinated investigators to work on. We certainly do want to know more about the physics of the upper ocean. There are individual investigators who are seriously working on this, as you all know, and they probably would prefer not to be hooked into some large project. They like to work undisturbed on these programs. And I'm sure that they will. There are many questions, moreover, that I think lie intermediate between the development of the physical knowledge of the detailed mixing processes that determine mixed-layer depth and heat storage in the ocean that still could be worked on by individual groups.

I'm thinking, for example, of the problem of actually measuring the change of the heat storage in the mixed layer in the ocean over reasonably short periods. There is some talk about experiments in the Arabian Sea during the first global GARP experiment in 1977. This immediately brings up the question of getting measurements in a big area, such as the changes of heat storage on a week-by-week or other basis of the mixed layer in the Arabian Sea when the winds are blowing very strongly. Some of you have tried to make measurements of simpler things, such as the development of the diurnal thermocline, and to trace in detail how much heat is stored each day—some days are clear and calm and others are windy and cloudy. Can you really use these parametric heat flux equations and measurements of the radiation to compute the observed heat storage on a day-to-day basis. Well, you know that one of the major difficulties is that, even with nice STD's and so forth, in the stratified upper layer there are lots of internal waves and horizontal heterogeneities in which the ship drifts in an uncontrollable fashion and that there is a pooling of upper water. When the sunlight comes in, it doesn't spray uniformly over the whole surface. So you have a hard time measuring total heat content. It doesn't seem to me outside the realm of possibility that some kind of measuring scheme for heat storage in the upper layers of the ocean could be directed primarily at getting around this horizontal sampling.

There are other kinds of problems. Not only do we need to know about the heat storage on a day-to-day basis and think about ways of observing it, but we have other kinds of ideas. Peter Niiler mentioned a manuscript investigation by himself and Gill in which they have made some efforts to look at the seasonal heat storage in the oceans from the theoretical point of view, and looking at the equations, to scale them and isolate certain simple balances that they think hold in the period of a year on a large scale, in the interior of the ocean away from the coasts. And from these very simple balances, without elaborate computing machines at all, they can compute the annual heat storage, the annual change in sea level, and the annual change in pressure on the bottom. These simple ideas could be tested and explored by comparison with more complete numerical models, but they also ought to be able to be checked by certain kinds of field programs. And actually some of the statements they make—that the seasonal heat storage is a purely local phenomenon and that horizontal advection is not important—are very challenging and different.

The reason I'm talking this way is because in the background I have this kind of nightmare of groups going out and putting buoys all over the ocean, and it seems to me that there are somewhat more realistic field programs that they could concentrate on. I think Dr. Huang, who's been associated with the early stages of the NORPAC experiment has been thinking along these lines, and I believe he has done some calculations from some of the buoys that Scripps had in the ocean in 1969. Maybe he would like to say something about how he would envisage a Scripps effort to help resolve the model. The model is not really of isolated interest, because all of those scaling ideas for the year might also apply to the periods in the continuum around those frequencies; and three months to three years is not an uninteresting period for finding the fluctuations.

Betty Schroeder and I have tried to look at the heat storage from the Panulirus stations off Bermuda. I'm sure more serious work has been done on this since then. We were able to compare the instantaneous steric levels that we got from the stations to the actual levels taken at the tide gauge. And it looks to us, from just a few hundred stations, that there really were significant differences of heat storage at the Panulirus site from year to year. In September of one year you might have twice the height of steric level that you might have another year. It kind of looked to us like this might be true. But we had no idea, of course, about the cause of this. We tried to get some graduate students interested in looking at the meteorological data and seeing if they could find some evidence of these variabilities, but I think the results were rather inconclusive.

And so I think another thing that observers who are interested in these as yet unexplored, long-period, large-scale aspects of the ocean might consider addressing themselves to is to embark upon some spatial coherence studies for these kinds of things. But that's going to take a long time. If one embarks upon those spatial coherent studies, and that means you're going to delay a big program, if there is ever a bigger program, by 5 or 8 years. The MODE field program is a 4-month program. But it's been preceded by about maybe 16 months of preliminary arrays and experiments leading to the design of the MODE-I experiment. I think CUE is operating in something of the same kind of spirit. If the NORPAX experiment is going to be 10 years long, they have to spend something like 40 years getting ready for it. And that's why programs like this are so scary and slightly unattractive, because they last your lifetime.

Now the next thing is that there are some other aspects of these numerical models, like Cox's model of the fluctuating currents in the Indian Ocean. As you know, in the 1977 FGGE (First Global GARP Experiment), there's going to be very good meteorological coverage over the whole world. This is going to be very interesting to oceanographers who are interested in transience, because it's going to be an excellent time. Under the benign influence of GARP, I think a hundred flowers are going to bloom; and I can foresee Niiler, for example, stepping up the transport calculations in the Florida Straits. I can see Baker's polar group really trying to aim at that period to observe the variability of the Antarctic circumpolar current.

I think that things like that are going to happen and the people who are going to try to make observational programs are going to want very much to work with large-scale numerical models, even if the numerical models don't incorporate the correct physics completely. It would be an exercise that probably won't come around again; it's an opportunity the observational people are not going to miss, and I don't think it hurts for the numerical people to see what their models can do, even if their models are not perfect yet. I myself am going to try to get a ship forward to study the Somali current. That immediately opens up all kinds of interesting questions, such as how are you actually going to monitor effectively at several different sections at several different places at the same time the time of onset of the Somali current with a resolution of 2 or 3 days over that coast and what techniques are you going to use.

There are other things that I think are kind of interesting, and I don't know how many groups in the country or the world are actually engaged in them. Larry Gates has a subpanel under a larger panel of Yale Mintz's that is investigating climatic fluctuations from 0.1 to 10 years, I think it is.

One of the things NORPAX is trying to do, and NCAR too, is to begin to get some idea of what the actual available data is of climatic structure over the whole world ocean and how it's distributed in time. They want also to get some idea of what the central nervous system is, as to how the data's actually coming in now. I think that there probably is a lot of information in this material that will be useful towards understanding the large-scale fluctuations. Eventually, it could all be laid out in some kind of a systematic way so we all know what data there is, at what rate it's coming in, and what areas of the oceans are covered. In developing these climate models, that would help.

Finally, of course, we have people like the GEOSEC people, and they don't need any help at all. In a way it's simpler for them—the period is so long that it's hopeless to monitor cycles, and the best they can do is to establish what it is now for these long-scale tracers. And if they establish that neatly and clearly now, those readings will probably be good for another generation. I've been trying to visualize this whole business, and I kind of see a caravan of vehicles going over unknown and sort of dangerous-looking terrain. I see some little swarms of private cars going around—maybe they're CUE and MODE people—but they're all private cars and in little groups. There's an old green station wagon in front of the MODE group, I think, that might be the staff car. Then I see some other gallant little private cars running off the road from place to place, but they keep going; somehow, I think I see Rattray and Veronis in there, I'm not quite sure. I see some big, heavy trucks with maybe half-tracks that look a little bit like they're carrying computing machines, and I don't know what's going to happen to them if they run into any soft ground. I see the motorcycle gang, too—the Niilers and the Gills and the Welanders of this world. They're all on their own, but I don't know how long they're going to last. Then there's one crowded bus that isn't paying any attention to anybody, and that's the GEOSEC bus. Then there are some very big buses, with not very many people in them, and they seem to have UNESCO diplomatic plates, and everybody's scared they're going to use up all the gas. Then I see one lonely individual, Arthur D. Little, who's been hired by the National Data Buoy Project, who's handing out questionnaires like, "Do you like your speedometer to be calibrated in miles per hour or kilometers per hour?"

A. S. SARKISYAN

About hydrological observational data. I think that last year oceanographers tried to make more and more observations on current velocity, which is very expensive. But the temperature and salinity observations, which are cheaper and I think not less interesting, are not being made so much. As we can see from theoretical computations, diagnostic or prognostic, the temperature field as well as salinity has very interesting information on current velocity. So I think it would be very interesting in the future to try to make many simultaneous observations on temperature and salinity fields and hydrological observations for enough large territory. It is not possible to do this with current velocity, because current meters are more expensive. One can make current velocity observations only in some points but temperature observations over large territories.

I think that, in the future, such an observation, if it is done, will give us very interesting information; and one can make a diagnostical calculation on the basis of such observation. But the temperature field is necessary not only for diagnostical calculation. We can also see now that baroclinicity is a very, very interesting problem, so any theoretical model cannot predict the temperature field. So, if in any theoretical model, one cannot describe the temperature field, he also cannot describe the current velocities. That's why I think temperature observations are of particular interest.

I have made some predictive calculations, and I am going to make other new calculations. Dr. Veronis said that it isn't enough. He said that it is not only necessary to make predictive calculations, but to understand what we are doing, a much more difficult task! Meteorologists are predicting every day, but I am not so sure about their understanding. I quite agree with Allan Robinson's ideas on numerical methods—I mean, not only numerical method, but numerical dynamical method. We have heard some reports about exact numerical method, but if such a mathematical problem is solved only for equations, du/dt is equal to du/dx, it will not make too many interesting results for modeling of dynamical ocean calculation. I hope that in future symposiums on numerical modeling there will be such a report, not for simple equations, but for equations we have to solve. For instance, mesoscale eddies are very difficult for theoretical description.

It would be very nice for theorists to solve the problem of general circulation. We cannot even do this one. I think that we will, in the near future, have a picture of whole ocean general circulation. It's well known that the worst atlases of temperature and salinity are much better than the finest theoretical results of temperature and salinity distribution. But I think that one can have a crude picture of whole ocean circulation and temperature and salinity distribution without mesoscale eddies. Mesoscale eddies will be the next, more difficult, task. I am quite sure that these eddies interact very closely with large-scale circulation, but it is much more difficult for today's theoretical investigations.

Our knowledge, observational data, theoretical results, and hydrological data are very poor on abyssal circulation. That's why the total transport function is a very crude one. The JEBAR present isn't such a happy thing. It shows us that we don't know the deep-layer circulation, even in a crude form. Stommel's prediction, for instance, is in a very crude form. Such a form isn't enough. If by predictive models or observational data we have more accurate information on the deep-layer temperature field, then we'll have enough in any accuracy model. A less accurate form will have information on total transport function, which is much different on the deep-layer temperature field. There enters a question about jet-like currents in the ocean. You know that in the last year it was found that there are many jet-like currents in the ocean. Every time a ship goes to sea, it returns with findings of new jet-like currents and countercurrents. So, in the future, the most surprising result will be if the ship returns without countercurrents. Such a jet-like circulation shows us that it is important to observe the fine structure of the baroclinicity, not only for the local problem, but for the general ocean circulation problem. We are now trying to create a crude picture of the general ocean circulation. But it will be very crude until we can take into account the interaction between such a jet-like current and the whole ocean circulation.

A. R. ROBINSON

Computers are big, complicated machines; and the ocean is a big, complicated system; and this has been a long, complicated meeting. So I will try to make a few simple remarks. They are motivated by one axiom—that it is desirable to exploit the capabilities of big computing machines in getting at a deeper understanding of the general circulation of the ocean.

This is a particularly appropriate moment at which to assess the role of numerical models in understanding the general ocean circulation. During the last decade or two, much hard, important, and very commendable pioneering work has been done. These computations, by Bryan, Sarkisyan, and others, firmly establish the importance of numerical modeling and provide a substantial basis for our assessment. But now it is time to examine what we have learned from this work and to evaluate alternative avenues for future progress.

When one says simply numerical model, one is leaving out something of importance in the middle. I want to address myself particularly to a discussion of numerical dynamical models. Part of the complexity in the oceanic system is due to the complex geometry; part is due to the driving forces. But there is another source of complexity. This lies in the myriad of physical processes that are simultaneously occurring in the sea over decades of scales in time and space. For example, the preceding remarks of Walter Munk stimulated a debate about the details of various small-scale vertical transfer mechanisms.

Now and in the forseeable future, it is within the realm of possibility to construct numerical models that are direct dynamic analogs in that they contain the myriad of physical processes occurring in the real ocean. In such a primitive model, the myriad of processes would occur in the Navier–Stokes equations. However, what one can and does construct are numerical dynamical models that contain certain physical processes; and what such models can do is to show how the analogous physical system behaves over the range of internal parameters that is numerically investigated and analyzed. In these circumstances it is, of course, important to state clearly in the formulation of the models the hypotheses that define the physical processes that are allowed to occur both explicitly and parametrically.

There is a big gap between observations and primitive equations, which must be bridged by the development of pertinent dynamical models. Existence, description, and geography of phenomena are defined by the observations; basic physical principles provide the primitive equations. In other words, we know something about what kind of processes we have to model correctly dynamically definitive. Because of their generality and the consequent wealth of fluid phenomena they describe, the primitive equations themselves do not elucidate directly the underlying dynamical processes associated with observed oceanic phenomena, which must be incorporated into numerical models. Thus we are at something of an impasse, because we want to make a numerical model that has the right dynamics and physics in it, yet we don't know what that dynamics and physics are. But what we can do is to construct numerical models and perform numerical experiments that are purposefully directed towards revealing what the underlying physics and dynamics are of these phenomena, which have been geographically defined by the data. This can be a most important use of computing machines today in advancing our understanding of the ocean circulation.

I want now to address my discussion to general mesoscale processes and the problem of including them dynamically correctly in computer models. By mesoscale, in general, I mean scales that are smaller than that of the main gyres but large enough to be in some sense geostrophic to zeroth order and that are associated with features that individually or in aggregate are kinematically or dynamically important parts of the larger-scale general circulation. Consider a geometrically simplified ocean model that nonetheless encompasses a variety of complicated physics, e.g., a model ocean basin bounded by the equator, a northern latitude, and two longitudes. In addition to the overall mean circulation, the model circulation has a western boundary current (Gulf Stream), which leaves the coast and meanders, and it has eddy shedding by the meandering current. It has upwelling at an eastern boundary region, an equatorial undercurrent, and a field of mesoscale eddies in mid-ocean. All of these phenomena are mesoscale features of the circulation. Most of them we know very little about dynamically; about some of them, virtually nothing. I think that computer models provide the possibility of and are particularly suitable for an attack on the resolution of underlying physical processes of these mesoscale phenomena via direct, numerical experimentation.

A strong but local current may or may not be of dynamic significance to the general circulation, depending upon whether or not it has dynamic feedback to the oceanic interior or to another general circulation feature. If the current is passive, i.e., simply driven by the general circulation (e.g., by prescribed mass flux determined by extraneous physical factors), then it doesn't matter for the overall circulation whether the dynamics of the current is correct or not. If this is not the case, however, modeling correctly the local current dynamics may be of crucial importance. Numerical experiments on local currents, which can be intimately linked to observational programs, may provide a means of unambiguously determining the local dynamics of the current and its consequent role in the general circulation. The dynamics of the Gulf Stream, its meandering and vortex production, have been attacked in this spirit by a number of workers, as summarized in Niiler's paper. The question of whether the dynamics of the equatorial undercurrent affect the extra-equatorial circulation arose following Adrian Gill's paper. Charney and Spiegel have developed a numerical model in an attempt to resolve some of the dynamics of the undercurrent. What does their detailed local model imply about the necessity of the bigger gyre and global-scale models, in which equatorial phenomena do occur, to include such currents with oceanically correct dynamics? A striking example of a dynamically important coupling was mentioned by George Veronis, who pointed out that whether upwelling or downwelling occurred over a model ocean interior was controlled by the dynamics of the western boundary current. In that case the overall qualitative pattern of circulation in the main gyre was controlled by the value of the frictional parameter in the western boundary region.

In general, regional features that turn out to be of importance to the general circulation rather than only of local importance must be included correctly in large-scale numerical circulation models. How can this be done? They may be either directly resolved in the big model or included by the interfacing of a local numerical model to the circulation-scale model, or successfully parameterized in some way that describes the overall physical effect of the local feature on the circulation, i.e., a parameterization of the feedback mechanism rather than an inclusion of detail. Such a parameterization requires understanding of process. The generation of statistics in real time may require many years of activity and an extensive field program. Long before real data is available, numerical experiments can provide simulated statistical data upon which to base initial parameterizations.

A big general circulation model has many dynamical components. One kind of modeling, which is presently undertaken, is to construct, under the constraints of available computing machines and understanding, a model representing the dynamics of each piece as well as we can at the moment. If the big model is to be an ocean analog, all the pieces (on required time and space scales) must be dynamically correct. What I am suggesting is that some investigators might fruitfully devote their full effort and exploit the full capabilities of computing machines on the investigation of the isolatable pieces. The construction and study of a hierarchy of numerical models, containing one or several dynamically correct pieces, affords a logical method for the evolution of a general ocean circulation numerical dynamical model, which is the ultimate goal.

A most important piece of the general circulation is the dynamics of the open ocean itself. We now know, as pointed out in Bretherton's lecture, that low-frequency fluctuations of the intermediate scale swamp the mean flow in mid-ocean, energetically by as much as several orders of magnitude. Thus my suggestion that an investigation of mesoscale quasi-geostrophic eddy processes in mid-ocean is of pressing importance is obvious. We know from the experience of the meteorologists that one must get the associated processes of transport correct. At the present time, dynamically correct ocean circulation models on longer time scales and slower space scales are obtainable only by averaging over models explicitly resolving the eddy scales.

In the open ocean, as well as in regions of strong current, mesoscale processes may provide effectively negative eddy viscosities, an important fact that I don't believe has been explicitly stated previously in this meeting. We've talked about parameter ranges of vertical and horizontal transfer coefficients and about the fact that one must construct the anisotropic eddy viscosity terms in a way that is logically correct in spherical coordinates, etc. These may be absolutely irrelevant questions, because of the negativeness of the eddy viscosity itself and the consequent unsuitability of the concept. Is there any approach intermediate between a direct attack on the relevant mesoscale dynamics followed by a reparameterization and the present approach via eddy viscosities?

I should like to conclude my discussion by making a few isolated remarks. The first concerns the treatment of computer output from numerical models. When one defines a numerical dynamical model and generates data, one truly has done a numerical experiment. The analysis of the simulated data presents the same sort of problem as the analysis of field data. The data available should be fully exploited for its ability to yield physical insights about the model system. Unlike the field experimentalists, the numerical experimentalists have no data collection problems. The energetic study described by Holland is an example of the kind of posterior understanding of model mechanism that is obtainable by numerical experimentation.

Next I should like to emphasize the desirability of even better feedback between analytical theory and numerical experimentation. To some extent there presently exists a communication gap between the two areas. Many analytical theorists claim that not a single solution of the thermocline problem exists in a closed basin—notably, Welander. Yet we see the idealized solutions of thermal ocean circulations discussed by Bryan as a means of calibrating numerical models. The communication problem here, of course, has to do with parameter range. It is the job of theorists to explain phenomena discovered numerically, as well as to provide a basis for rational design of model experiments. In particular, as a practical matter, numerical analysis cannot adequately define dependence of phenomena on parameters; the combination of a few solutions combined with analytical arguments can be more fully exploited in the future. The present generation of computer models is based, to a large extent, on the wind-driven ocean circulation and thermocline theories developed from the late forties through the early sixties. Not only, however, have numerical solutions revealed flow patterns under complex forcing and in realistic geometries, but they have also revealed physical processes of unexpected importance. For example, it behooves analytical theorists to explore fully the significance of the important physical process—the joint effect of baroclinicity and topographic relief—that has been discovered in the experiments of Sarkisyan and Holland. Analytical theorists have a responsibility to help design the second generation of computer models. Sample questions are: What is the role of baroclinic instability in the general ocean circulation, what is the minimum horizontal scale desirable to be explicitly resolved, and what are the actual micromechanisms responsible for vertical heat and momentum transfer?

The use of laboratory dynamical modeling as a tool to help solve the general ocean circulation problem is just beginning. Used in conjunction with analytical theory and numerical modeling, it represents a powerful method of attack on accessible processes, as demonstrated by Beardsley in his study of meanders and eddies, which developed in his sliced-cylinder model.

I should draw attention here also to the questions that were brought up yesterday in the technical discussions that we had on modern computing techniques. Are we going to progress more by exploiting modern techniques and sophisticated schemes, or are we going to progress more by exploiting in a relatively simple way new and bigger machines? If the former, is it necessary to expect a full order of magnitude in efficiency from the application of new techniques before it is really worth the time and trouble to use them?

We are at a very early stage in the development of a complete, dynamically correct ocean circulation model. But we are at an exciting point in time, one at which it is apparent that accelerated progress in the future is possible. The dynamics of the general circulation is a problem ultimately tractable to our science. The selective and perceptive use of numerical experimentation can help to cut down the time necessary for the construction of a dynamically correct ocean model, which can be connected to an atmospheric circulation model for the study of the dynamics of global climate. The dynamically correct, coupled, planetary circulation model is the essential element for man's understanding and control of his global environment. Global and regional climatological and predictive models, interfaced with geochemical, biological, and fisheries models, will be of profound human benefit.

DISCUSSION

PHILLIPS: Could I take one of your points, I think it was the second one, and put forth the philosophy that no results of numerical model experiments should be published unless either the model has been run over several parameter ranges or the results are accompanied by a theoretical analysis. Some computations have been made over ranges of parameters, e.g., various Rossby number regimes, various wind stresses, but I think there haven't been enough explorations. There have been perhaps only one or two comparisons. Instead, what one is tempted to do in oceanography is to obtain for a fixed model the most "accurate" computation compatible with whatever computer is available. I can understand this being done in the case of the atmosphere, because in the atmosphere the problem is a forecast problem. Then there is something to compare with the results of numerical computation—what the weather is going to be—and there is social pressure to live up to implied claims. But I agree with your point that there is a lot of virtue, in the oceanic case, in emphasizing a slower approach, one in which the "kitchen sink" is not thrown into the model. In this slower approach, from the very beginning certain realistic aspects of the model are sacrificed purposely as a trade-off for the investigation of other effects in more detail. I would even go so far as to say that perhaps the larger computations should be reserved for the fitting-in of local models into a global model and that one should concentrate most on exploring specific phenomena that do not in themselves explain everything about the ocean. I gather, for example, that Bill Holland has made a computation of the equatorial undercurrent. I have not seen the results, but presumably this does not purport to explain the entire ocean. This is the kind of thing that I think is the most fruitful way to proceed at this time.

ROBINSON: I agree, but with one qualification on your first remark. I think that a good criterion would be that nothing should be published without a clear statement of what the physics of the model is, what the parameter range is, and what the parameter range implies about implicit physical processes, plus an analysis of the data similar to the kind of analysis that an observationalist would be expected to provide with his data.

VERONIS: I think I would like to support what Norman Phillips said by simply mentioning that the meterologists, after all, have a predictive model; and they can measure their success on the basis of whether they predict well or not. And they don't have to understand what they're doing, as long as they predict well. I think it's an important difference from what we have to do in oceanography. We don't really have a prediction problem, so we can't defend our calculations for that purpose. I think basically it has to be a question of understanding. Understanding doesn't necessarily mean that you get a gross pattern; because we know that, in most situations, if you heat at the equator and cool at the poles, you're going to end up with a temperature difference that on the average goes in the right direction. That's obviously simplistic—you do more than that. But, nonetheless, there is a tendency to settle for gross patterns that are fairly obvious on much simpler grounds as a result of some very large computations. The burden is much more on us to try to get an understanding of these numerical computations, and it is something that we don't always do.

WELANDER: I would like to give an example of a problem where help from "numerical people" would be useful. A main problem of theoretical interest in the determination of the circulation and temperature field in a rectangular box on the β-plane, driven by prescribed steady wind stresses and heat fluxes at the top. The complete problem involves turbulence, but as a first approximation one may use an equivalent-laminar model, with exchange coefficient large enough to prevent instability. This problem involved only two major parameters, giving the strength of the mechanical and thermodynamical driving in nondimensional form. There are other parameters, such as vertical and horizontal Ekman numbers that determine the thickness of boundary layers. However, the main features are not expected to depend critically on these parameters, excluding such phenomena as separation, etc. It is feasible to make the effective friction so large that the side boundary layers take up a quarter or a third of the basin and still retain the interesting features. This allows a simple numerical approach, using a horizontally uniform grid.

The problem is difficult analytically, since there is a basic nonlinearity in the temperature advection. It has been neglected numerically. Basic numerical work on the homogeneous model is going on, and probably it will soon be extended to the two-layer case. With regard to continuously stratified models, present work goes in the direction of further complications. Topography, feedback to the atmosphere, etc., is being included in present and planned models. However, it may be more important that a simple, continuous model of the type described here is explored at this time.

WALSH: On the basic biological arguments, I'd like to speak a little bit in favor of building larger models. I'm not so sure we can say we don't have to predict; and, therefore, I might disagree with Dr. Veronis, because an easy dodge of the applied scientist is, "I can't predict anything." But on the biological side, people at EPA are asking, "What happens if I dump DDT in? What happens if I build a dam here? What happens if you put in that thermal reactor?" So in the long run, you are going to have to make some predictions, or at least the biologists are. And we can only make them on the basis of the circulation models you build. There's a controversy between the molecular biologists and the ecologists. The molecular biologists would say, "The hell with the environment! I do everything from the molecule!" Except they never get around to doing the organism. On the other side, we have the ecologists versus the population biologists. The population biologists say, "I'm only going to work with the population, and I'll eventually build, too." A good example is Buss Holling at UBC, who has a delightful praying mantis model, and it asks how long it has been fed and where does it pray? That's for one praying mantis. And, if you apply that to a population, you'll find that there isn't a computer in the world that can handle the required computation.

ROBINSON: Yes, we should predict those things that are useful to predict. We ought to make some predictions on the mesoscale, because that's one way of knowing we've got the dynamics right. And we should build big models and interface them with biology and meteorology, as required for understanding. But we should interface those big models only after the ocean model is dynamically correct.

WALSH: Models aren't just correct or incorrect; it's not a matter of black and white.

ROBINSON: They are correct or incorrect in the following way. If a biologist wants to interface with a big numerical model, he wants to do it for a reason—there is a process or a phenomenon that is coupled, possibly with feedback. So that process is either correct or not correct in the big model. The process that he is interested in interfacing has to be correct.

WALSH: However, if we don't start interfacing now, we may never do it.

ROBINSON: It's a lot of hard work—it's a distribution of effort. We can't do everything at once.

UNIDENTIFIED: Well, there is another point, which is that on the mesoscale it's possible to verify the dynamical models so that one is being honest in trying to make a prediction.

RATTRAY: Not all the problems are mesoscale; a lot of the biological problems are large-scale.

PEDLOSKY: I'd like to make a simple point about the mesoscale problem, going along with what Allan said, and talk about off-gradient transports. From the lessons one learns in meteorology, I think we can make a big advance in understanding, really take a big step forward, without achieving a mesoscale model that is so realistic that it can describe in a very detailed way mesoscale circulations. That would be nice, but I think one can still go a tremendous distance with more simplified models, ones that give you a relationship between eddy transport structures and the mean field, giving you the right directions of transport and the right orders of magnitude for the eddy and the mean flow interactions without getting down to the last detail about current paths and precise structures. That would be nice, too, but I think one can make a tremendous advance on the immediate level beyond what we have now.

CHARNEY: Allan didn't mention one of the most important functions of model building, and that is as a guide to observation. And I think MODE-I modeling is a very beautiful example of the kind of model-building that is very useful in guiding observations and bringing about such interplay, which will, of course, in turn lead to corrections to the models. It is such productive interplay that really leads to the major advances. Because in science, historically, you always need a lot of solved problems on the basis of the physics you know in order to crack the physics you don't know.

My other remark is about negative viscosity. I would like to mention a kind of negative viscosity that is implied by some of the calculations Francis Bretherton did. Namely, we know from meteorology and in general that any time you have baroclinic instability that means that you're deriving the energy from the thermal field; and, if you have a stable fluid, the process of releasing the potential energy means that the cold fluid has to sink and the warm fluid has to rise. Thus, you have a $w'T'$ correlation, which gives you a negative conductivity. Heat will flow toward where it's warm, and cold will flow toward where it's cold. If these baroclinic eddies are really important, here is your negative viscosity. I realize that your immediate goal is to understand this process, but I can't help speculating about what is going to be their function. They work opposite to the direction of the usual kind of thermal diffusion; and, if they are important at all in the circulation, you now have another heat flow that you're going to have to counteract.

ROBINSON: I think that many people are aware of this phenomenon. Let me answer you by broadening the base of discussion. A major difficulty is, of course, with respect to the mesoscale eddies—that there are a number of possible eddy energy sources, of which baroclinic instability is one of the strongest contending processes. There are others, though, such as transfer from higher frequencies, baroclinic instabilities of major currents, rather than the open ocean, with subsequent open ocean decaying eddies that may have a local transfer, which is different from the transfer that occurs in the region of production. One of the major goals in studying the eddies is to understand them well enough to be able to get their effect back on the general circulation.

CHARNEY: It's not clear about momentum, but it's very clear about heat, it seems to me. I think the most clearly documented laboratory example involving momentum was the one that Beardsley described yesterday. It would be interesting to try and carry out an analysis of those unstable eddies to see what effects they have on the total integrated transport. For example, if one uses Malkus' plots of number as a function of Rossby number at the point where you begin to get this unstable effect.

NIILER: I'd like to mention the largest eddy size in the ocean, that of the seasonal variability. We have data now from large regions of the oceans with a high signal-to-noise ratio, which demonstrates seasonal variability, both in the atmospheric driving force and in the ocean response. Because of the good data, which has been and is being made available, there is a lot to be learned from numerical models of the seasonal variability, a completely unexplored problem in numerical modeling.

BRYAN: What you really come down to is the kind of data you have available that a man should model with. We've been talking a lot about various processes, but I think if we look at the whole history of science, some rather unlikely models have proven to be very successful when related to a very precise kind of data. In physics, for example, one can calculate in agreement with data within 1/10 of 1 percent with a rather "screwball" model; that is, one that may have seemed to have left out some essential process, but there exists the data to show that the model works. What we need now if we want to concentrate on smaller parts of the ocean is that kind of data for a smaller part of the ocean. The kind of data that we've had so far that I felt was the only data to try to match against was the very large-scale temperature and salinity structure. That is a tremendous body of data, and it has taken a great deal of effort to collect such an amount. If you want to work with a local part of the ocean and set up a boundary value problem, you're faced with the fact that the solution in the interior area is going to be largely determined by what is coming in and out of the boundaries. To handle a thing like that, you really want to solve for the interior of it. Such a measurement around the edges of a part of the ocean would have to be done for quite a long period of time. It would be desirable to pick some part of the ocean that can be partly closed by land. Make repeated measurements with also some measurements in the interior that could be used to verify the results of the model, which would be calculated using these boundary conditions.

ROBINSON: These boundary conditions, of course, represent, when you have a limited region model, a parameterization of external processes. Such connection parameters replace other parameters in a larger model. There is a trade-off; if one works only on the larger scale, in the usual manner, one is paying the price of having to parameterize the unresolved mesoscale. Probably, it's useful also to begin to explore some of these other kinds of parameters that are involved in connecting isolated regions to the rest of the ocean. I agree with Bryan entirely about the necessity of relating such modeling to real data.

WENDROFF: I'd like to make some perhaps naive comments. It seems to me that there are four levels involved in this question of theory and models: There is the ocean itself, which exists; there are physical theories as to why and how the ocean exists; from those physical theories you then deduce the mathematical model, or the differential equations; then you provide a numerical model of those differential equations. Now it's not quite right to take the numbers from the numerical model and compare them directly with physical experiments. You first have to be sure that the numbers that are provided are an accurate picture of the mathematical model. Then you can with confidence test the mathematical model against the experiment. At the present time it still requires a considerable amount of work by numerical analysts and mathematicians to provide a confidence level in those numbers relative to the mathematical model.

SUMMARY, CONCLUSIONS, AND RECOMMENDATIONS

R. O. REID, A. R. ROBINSON, and K. BRYAN

The review papers and original contributions to this symposium indicate the wide range of possible objectives for numerical models of the ocean circulation. Numerical methods have a role in (a) the investigation of relatively simple theoretical models under conditions of realistic and/or complex forcing and geometry, (b) the exploration of theoretical models, which for reasons such as nonlinearity or the coupling of processes, cannot be efficiently developed analytically even in simplified circumstances, (c) the performance of numerical experiments designed to establish dynamical processes associated with observed phenomena, and (d) the generation and statistical analysis of simulated (numerical) data via long-time integration of specified dynamical models.

Contributions to this symposium on the abyssal circulation of the world ocean, the western boundary current regions, and the equatorial undercurrent illustrate the need for a combined attack by a combination of observational experimentation, theorizing, and numerical modeling with a strong interaction and feedbacks among the three activities. The relationship between theory and numerical modeling should now be strengthened. Theorists can profitably invest a greater effort in the interpretation of numerical results, such as the recently discovered baroclinic–topographic effect, and in the design of future models and experiments. Numerical models should be modified and developed in order to exploit the interpretation and enhance the significance of new techniques of oceanographic measurement. The papers of O'Brien and Bretherton presented in this conference are examples of numerical modeling studies that have had an important impact on the planning of major field studies. The larger programs sponsored by the International Decade of Ocean Exploration require extensive and detailed planning, in which numerical models can play an important role.

The complexity of ocean circulation problems is characterized by a large range of space and time scales, spanning many orders of magnitude. For this reason the Navier–Stokes equations cannot be applied directly. Reynolds-averaging must be applied as a low-pass filter to the general equations. In the averaged equations, the turbulent fluxes of salinity, heat, and momentum appear as important new variables. Ocean circulation models need additional relationships to specify these fluxes. This requirement is the familiar closure problem of turbulence theory. In the formulation of an ocean circulation model, the dividing line between those large scales that are treated explicitly and the smaller scales that are parameterized by the closure scheme should be clarified in each case for different purposes. A clear statement of the hypotheses and assumptions defining a model is required, including (a) which scales of the motions and physical processes are explicitly resolved in the model, (b) which scales and processes are included implicitly by parameterization, and (c) which scales are excluded entirely by filtering or by lack of resolvability. Three areas in which parameterization is presently critical for the development of dynamically correct ocean circulation and planetary climatological models were emphasized in the summary discussion: small-scale vertical flux processes; mesoscale and eddy processes for horizontal transfer of momentum; heat and salinity; and the exchange processes at the air–sea interface, including their variability.

The vertical heat flux required over the oceans has been estimated and the layered microstructure is being probed observationally, but a realistic parameterization depends upon the physical processes involved, e.g., breaking internal waves or (intermittent) double diffusion. The possibility of a vertical mixing process localized near coasts or islands with streamered interior intrusion along isodensity surfaces has also been mentioned. Such macroscopic aspects of the mixing would require very skillful parameterization.

The oceanic mesoscale requires numerical models with horizontal grid resolution on the order of tens of kilometers over regions of the open ocean containing energetic eddies, as well as in regions of intense and variable currents. Numerical experimentation devoted to the establishment of the dynamics of these processes is now fundamental and must involve a considerable concentration of effort on the development of local and regional models. Such models will either be linked into a general circulation model or else provide the understanding of process requisite for a successful parameterization of the mesoscale. Past parameterization of horizontal eddy processes by the use of horizontal eddy viscosities, which may indeed be negative, is generally inadequate.

A great deal of what is presently known about the ocean circulation comes from geochemistry, and active cooperation between numerical models and geochemists has already begun. In a review paper presented during the second day of the conference, G. Veronis described his own numerical model developed in collaboration with Kuo for the prediction of radiocarbon and oxygen fields in abyssal waters. A significant pioneering contribution to this field has also been made by W. D. Holland, using a more complete three-dimensional model of the ocean circulation. The rapid accumulation of new, very precise geochemical data calls for greatly expanded efforts along these lines.

The surface layers of the ocean exchanges heat, energy, and momentum with the atmosphere; and the construction of realistic models is a necessary part of an investigation into the important scales and processes of air-sea interaction and feedback. The degree and variety of related numerical modeling should be increased, including models of local heat storage, seasonal variability, and large-scale sea surface temperature anomalies. Rapid advancement in realistic modeling will be possible only for those scales on which the surface layer processes are determined to be essentially superficial, i.e., on which an intimate dynamical coupling to the deeper ocean circulation is not fundamental.

On the longer oceanic time scales, the commitment of resources, manpower, and money required for rational progress is formidable; it is essential to support experimental/observational programs with numerical/experimental models. Present modeling developments may be guided by the exploitation of already existing, routinely acquired data. The acquisition of such additional data from, e.g., ships and planes of opportunity should be encouraged. Accurate input flux data surrounding a local oceanic region is difficult to obtain experimentally, and alternative input data for regional models should be explored in order to best match numerical and field programs. The data base in physical oceanography is increasing in quality, diversity, and quantity. The deployment of new instruments, moored and free-floating, both at depth and at the surface and carried aloft by aircraft and satellite, implies a new diversity of modeling opportunities. The value of numerical experimentation depends ultimately upon the parameter range explored with the model and the extent of interpretation of numerical data, e.g., in terms of internal energy conversions. New techniques of numerical data analysis should be encouraged.

The numerical ocean model, which is programmed into the computer, is separated from the real ocean via intermediary physical and analytical mathematical models. The state of the art of numerical modeling in fluid dynamics in general is such that care must be exercised in assuring that the numerical mathematical model be a discrete analog of the analytical mathematical model. It is timely to consider the application of new numerical techniques, e.g., spectral and finite elements, to the circulation problem and to encourage a closer dialogue between ocean modelers and numerical analysts. A small working symposium between these specialists would be profitable. Compatibility is required among the model problem, numerical technique, and available computers. The "fifth-generation" machines are almost here. Since many aspects of the circulation problem, such as baroclinic adjustments, are machine limited, we must be prepared with programs that knowledgeably exploit their capabilities. Theoretical/numerical oceanographers must assess the present availability and future needs of their field in the area of computing facilities. Is it possible and expeditious to share facilities with atmospheric colleagues and other geophysical fluid dynamicists? This question involves the accessibility of big machines to university and other scientific talent not resident at a big machine-operating institution and includes consideration of the availability of software.

PARTICIPANTS

ALLEN, JOHN S., The Pennsylvania State University
BEARDSLEY, ROBERT C., Massachusetts Institute of Technology
BOYER, DON L., National Science Foundation
BRETHERTON, FRANCIS P., The Johns Hopkins University
BROECKER, WALLACE, Lamont-Doherty Geological Observatory
BRYAN, KIRK, NOAA, Princeton
CHARNEY, JULE G., Massachusetts Institute of Technology
COX, MICHAEL D., NOAA, Princeton
FIADEIRO, MANUEL, University of California, San Diego
FISCHER, HUGO B., University of California, Berkeley
FIX, GEORGE, University of Maryland
FRIEDRICH, HANS, New York University
GALT, J. A., Naval Postgraduate School
GATES, W. LAWRENCE, The Rand Corporation
GILL, ADRIAN, University of Cambridge
GORDON, ARNOLD L., Lamont-Doherty Geological Observatory
HENDERSHOTT, MYRL C., University of California, San Diego
HIRSCH, JOEL, Harvard University
HOLLAND, WILLIAM R., NOAA, Princeton
HUANG, JOSEPH C. K., University of California, San Diego
ISRAELI, MOSHE, Massachusetts Institute of Technology
KAMENKOVICH, VLADIMIR, USSR Academy of Sciences
KATSOUROS, MARY HOPE M., Ocean Affairs Board
KIRWAN, A. D., Ocean Sciences and Technology
KREISS, H.-O., University of Uppsala
LARSON, LARRY, National Science Foundation
LEITH, CECIL, Massachusetts Institute of Technology
MINTZ, YALE, Hebrew University
MOORE, DENNIS, Massachusetts Institute of Technology
MUNK, WALTER, University of California, San Diego
NIILER, PEARN P., NOVA
O'BRIEN, JAMES, Oregon State University

ORSZAG, STEVEN A., Massachusetts Institute of Technology
PEDLOSKY, JOSEPH, University of Chicago
PHILLIPS, NORMAN, Massachusetts Institute of Technology
PHILLIPS, OWEN, The Johns Hopkins University
PLATZMAN, GEORGE W., University of Chicago
POND, STEVEN, University of British Columbia
RATTRAY, MAURICE, University of Washington
REID, ROBERT O., Texas A&M University
ROBINSON, ALLAN R., Harvard University
SARKISYAN, ARTEM, USSR Academy of Sciences
SCHULMAN, ELLIOTT E., National Center for Atmospheric Research
SMAGORINSKY, JOSEPH, NOAA, Princeton
STEWART, R. W., Marine Sciences Directorate Pacific Region
STOMMEL, HENRY M., Massachusetts Institute of Technology
TAKANO, KENZO, Institute of Physical and Chemical Research
VERONIS, GEORGE, Stockholm 19, Sweden
VESTANO, A. C., Texas A&M University
WARREN, BRUCE, Woods Hole Oceanographic Institute
WELANDER, PIERRE, University of Göteborg
WENDROFF, BURTON, University of Denver
WILSON, STANLEY, Office of Naval Research
VETTER, RICHARD C., Ocean Affairs Board